HARDPRESS.NET
HOME OF HARD-TO-FIND BOOKS

Atlantic Monthly
by Unknown

Address:
HardPress
8345 NW 66TH ST #2561
MIAMI FL 33166-2626
USA
Email: info@hardpress.net

Per. 254° (9 1862

THE

ATLANTIC MONTHLY.

A MAGAZINE OF

Literature, Science, Art, and Politics.

VOLUME XVIII.

18
1866

BOSTON:
TICKNOR AND FIELDS,
124 TREMONT STREET.
1866.

UNIVERSITY PRESS : WELCH, BIGELOW, & CO.,
CAMBRIDGE.

CONTENTS.

Contents.

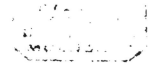

THE

ATLANTIC MONTHLY.

A Magazine of Literature, Science, Art, and Politics.

VOL. XVIII. — JULY, 1866. — NO. CV.

THE CASE OF GEORGE DEDLOW.

THE following notes of my own case have been declined on various pretexts by every medical journal to which I have offered them. There was, perhaps, some reason in this, because many of the medical facts which they record are not altogether new, and because the psychical deductions to which they have led me are not in themselves of medical interest. I ought to add, that a good deal of what is here related is not of any scientific value whatsoever ; but as one or two people on whose judgment I rely have advised me to print my narrative with all the personal details, rather than in the dry shape in which, as a psychological statement, I shall publish it elsewhere, I have yielded to their views. I suspect, however, that the very character of my record will, in the eyes of some of my readers, tend to lessen the value of the metaphysical discoveries which it sets forth.

I am the son of a physician, still in large practice, in the village of Abington, Scofield County, Indiana. Expecting to act as his future partner, I studied medicine in his office, and in 1859 and 1860 attended lectures at the Jefferson Medical College in Philadelphia. My second course should have been in the following year, but the outbreak of the Rebellion so crippled my father's means that I was forced to abandon my intention. The demand for army surgeons at this time became very great ; and although not a graduate, I found no difficulty in getting the place of Assistant-Surgeon to the Tenth Indiana Volunteers. In the subsequent Western campaigns this organization suffered so severely, that, before the term of its service was over, it was merged in the Twenty-First Indiana Volunteers ; and I, as an extra surgeon, ranked by the medical officers of the latter regiment, was transferred to the Fifteenth Indiana Cavalry. Like many physicians, I had contracted a strong taste for army life, and, disliking cavalry service, sought and obtained the position of First-Lieutenant in the Seventy-Ninth Indiana Volunteers, — an infantry regiment of excellent character.

On the day after I assumed command of my company, which had no captain, we were sent to garrison a part

Entered according to Act of Congress, in the year 1866, by Ticknor and Fields, in the Clerk's Office of the District Court of the District of Massachusetts.

VOL. XVIII. — NO. 105.   I

of a line of block-houses stretching along the Cumberland River below Nashville, then occupied by a portion of the command of General Rosecrans.

The life we led while on this duty was tedious, and at the same time dangerous in the extreme. Food was scarce and bad, the water horrible, and we had no cavalry to forage for us. If, as infantry, we attempted to levy supplies upon the scattered farms around us, the population seemed suddenly to double, and in the shape of guerillas "potted" us industriously from behind distant trees, rocks, or hasty earthworks. Under these various and unpleasant influences, combined with a fair infusion of malaria, our men rapidly lost health and spirits. Unfortunately, no proper medical supplies had been forwarded with our small force (two companies), and, as the fall advanced, the want of quinine and stimulants became a serious annoyance. Moreover, our rations were running low; we had been three weeks without a new supply; and our commanding officer, Major Terrill, began to be uneasy as to the safety of his men. About this time it was supposed that a train with rations would be due from the post twenty miles to the north of us; yet it was quite possible that it would bring us food, but no medicines, which were what we most needed. The command was too small to detach any part of it, and the Major therefore resolved to send an officer alone to the post above us, where the rest of the Seventy-Ninth lay, and whence they could easily forward quinine and stimulants by the train, if it had not left, or, if it had, by a small cavalry escort.

It so happened, to my cost, as it turned out, that I was the only officer fit to make the journey, and I was accordingly ordered to proceed to Block House No. 3, and make the required arrangements. I started alone just after dusk the next night, and during the darkness succeeded in getting within three miles of my destination. At this time I found that I had lost my way, and, although aware of the danger of my act, was forced to turn aside and ask at a log-cabin for directions. The house contained a dried-up old woman, and four white-headed, half-naked children. The woman was either stone-deaf, or pretended to be so; but at all events she gave me no satisfaction, and I remounted and rode away. On coming to the end of a lane, into which I had turned to seek the cabin, I found to my surprise that the bars had been put up during my brief parley. They were too high to leap, and I therefore dismounted to pull them down. As I touched the top rail, I heard a rifle, and at the same instant felt a blow on both arms, which fell helpless. I staggered to my horse and tried to mount; but, as I could use neither arm, the effort was vain, and I therefore stood still, awaiting my fate. I am only conscious that I saw about me several Graybacks, for I must have fallen fainting almost immediately.

When I awoke, I was lying in the cabin near by, upon a pile of rubbish. Ten or twelve guerillas were gathered about the fire, apparently drawing lots for my watch, boots, hat, etc. I now made an effort to find out how far I was hurt. I discovered that I could use the left forearm and hand pretty well, and with this hand I felt the right limb all over until I touched the wound. The ball had passed from left to right through the left biceps, and directly through the right arm just below the shoulder, emerging behind. The right hand and forearm were cold and perfectly insensible. I pinched them as well as I could, to test the amount of sensation remaining; but the hand might as well have been that of a dead man. I began to understand that the nerves had been wounded, and that the part was utterly powerless. By this time my friends had pretty well divided the spoils, and, rising together, went out. The old woman then came to me and said, "Reckon you'd best git up. Theyuns is agoin' to take you away." To this I only answered, "Water, water." I had a grim sense of amusement on finding that the old woman was not deaf, for she went out, and presently came back with a gourdful, which I eagerly drank. An hour later the Graybacks returned, and, finding that I was too weak to walk, carried me out, and laid me on the bottom of a common cart, with which they set off on a trot. The jolting was horrible, but within an hour I began to have in my dead right hand a strange burning, which was rather a relief to me. It increased as the sun rose and the day grew warm, until I felt as if the hand was caught and pinched in a red-hot vice. Then in my agony I begged my guard for water to wet it with, but for some reason they desired silence, and at every noise threatened me with a revolver. At length the pain became absolutely unendurable, and I grew what it is the fashion to call demoralized. I screamed, cried, and yelled in my torture, until, as I suppose, my captors became alarmed, and, stopping, gave me a handkerchief, — my own, I fancy, — and a canteen of water, with which I wetted the hand, to my unspeakable relief.

It is unnecessary to detail the events by which, finally, I found myself in one of the Rebel hospitals near Atlanta. Here, for the first time, my wounds were properly cleansed and dressed by a Dr. Oliver Wilson, who treated me throughout with great kindness. I told him I had been a doctor ; which, perhaps, may have been in part the cause of the unusual tenderness with which I was managed. The left arm was now quite easy ; although, as will be seen, it never entirely healed. The right arm was worse than ever, — the humerus broken, the nerves wounded, and the hand only alive to pain. I use this phrase because it is connected in my mind with a visit from a local visitor, — I am not sure he was a preacher, — who used to go daily through the wards, and talk to us, or write our letters. One morning he stopped at my bed, when this little talk occurred.

" How are you, Lieutenant ? "

" O," said I, " as usual. All right, but this hand, which is dead except to pain."

" Ah," said he, " such and thus will the wicked be, — such will you be if

you die in your sins : you will go where only pain can be felt. For all eternity, all of you will be as that hand, — knowing pain only."

I suppose I was very weak, but somehow I felt a sudden and chilling horror of possible universal pain, and suddenly fainted. When I awoke, the hand was worse, if that could be. It was red, shining, aching, burning, and, as it seemed to me, perpetually rasped with hot files. When the doctor came, I begged for morphia. He said gravely : " We have none. You know you don't allow it to pass the lines."

I turned to the wall, and wetted the hand again, my sole relief. In about an hour, Dr. Wilson came back with two aids, and explained to me that the bone was so broken as to make it hopeless to save it, and that, besides, amputation offered some chance of arresting the pain. I had thought of this before, but the anguish I felt — I cannot say endured — was so awful, that I made no more of losing the limb than of parting with a tooth on account of toothache. Accordingly, brief preparations were made, which I watched with a sort of eagerness such as must forever be inexplicable to any one who has not passed six weeks of torture like that which I had suffered.

I had but one pang before the operation. As I arranged myself on the left side, so as to make it convenient for the operator to use the knife, I asked : " Who is to give me the ether ? " " We have none," said the person questioned. I set my teeth, and said no more.

I need not describe the operation. The pain felt was severe ; but it was insignificant as compared to that of any other minute of the past six weeks. The limb was removed very near to the shoulder-joint. As the second incision was made, I felt a strange lightning of pain play through the limb, defining every minutest fibril of nerve. This was followed by instant, unspeakable relief, and before the flaps were brought together I was sound asleep. I have only a recollection that I said, pointing to the arm which lay on the floor: "There is the pain, and here am I. How queer!" Then I slept, — slept the sleep of the just, or, better, of the painless. From this time forward, I was free from neuralgia; but at a subsequent period I saw a number of cases similar to mine in a hospital in Philadelphia.

It is no part of my plan to detail my weary months of monotonous prison life in the South. In the early part of August, 1863, I was exchanged, and, after the usual thirty days' furlough, returned to my regiment a captain.

On the 19th of September, 1863, occurred the battle of Chickamauga, in which my regiment took a conspicuous part. The close of our own share in this contest is, as it were, burnt into my memory with every least detail. It was about six P. M., when we found ourselves in line, under cover of a long, thin row of scrubby trees, beyond which lay a gentle slope, from which, again, rose a hill rather more abrupt, and crowned with an earthwork. We received orders to cross this space, and take the fort in front, while a brigade on our right was to make a like movement on its flank.

Just before we emerged into the open ground, we noticed what, I think, was common in many fights, — that the enemy had begun to bowl round-shot at us, probably from failure of shell. We passed across the valley in good order, although the men fell rapidly all along the line. As we climbed the hill, our pace slackened, and the fire grew heavier. At this moment a battery opened on our left, — the shots crossing our heads obliquely. It is this moment which is so printed on my recollection. I can see now, as if through a window, the gray smoke, lit with red flashes, — the long, wavering line, — the sky blue above, — the trodden furrows, blotted with blue blouses. Then it was as if the window closed, and I knew and saw no more. No other scene in my life is thus scarred, if I may say so, into my memory. I have a fancy that the horrible shock which suddenly fell upon me must have had something to do

with thus intensifying the momentary image then before my eyes.

When I awakened, I was lying under a tree somewhere at the rear. The ground was covered with wounded, and the doctors were busy at an operating-table, improvised from two barrels and a plank. At length two of them who were examining the wounded about me came up to where I lay. A hospital steward raised my head, and poured down some brandy and water, while another cut loose my pantaloons. The doctors exchanged looks, and walked away. I asked the steward where I was hit.

"Both thighs," said he; "the Doc's won't do nothing."

"No use?" said I.

"Not much," said he.

"Not much means none at all," I answered.

When he had gone, I set myself to thinking about a good many things which I had better have thought of before, but which in no way concern the history of my case. A half-hour went by. I had no pain, and did not get weaker. At last, I cannot explain why, I began to look about me. At first, things appeared a little hazy; but I remember one which thrilled me a little, even then.

A tall, blond-bearded major walked up to a doctor near me, saying, "When you 've a little leisure, just take a look at my side."

"Do it now," said the doctor.

The officer exposed his left hip. "Ball went in here, and out here."

The Doctor looked up at him with a curious air, — half pity, half amazement. "If you 've got any message, you 'd best send it by me."

"Why, you don't say its serious?" was the reply.

"Serious! Why, you 're shot through the stomach. You won't live over the day."

Then the man did what struck me as a very odd thing. "Anybody got a pipe?" Some one gave him a pipe. He filled it deliberately, struck a light with a flint, and sat down against a tree near to me. Presently the doctor came over to him, and asked what he could do for him.

"Send me a drink of Bourbon."

"Anything else?"

"No."

As the doctor left him, he called him back. "It 's a little rough, Doc, is n't it?"

No more passed, and I saw this man no longer, for another set of doctors were handling my legs, for, the first time causing pain. A moment after, a steward put a towel over my mouth, and I smelt the familiar odor of chloroform, which I was glad enough to breathe. In a moment the trees began to move around from left to right, — then faster and faster; then a universal grayness came before me, and I recall nothing further until I awoke to consciousness in a hospital-tent. I got hold of my own identity in a moment or two, and was suddenly aware of a sharp cramp in my left leg. I tried to get at it to rub it with my single arm, but, finding myself too weak, hailed an attendant. "Just rub my left calf," said I, "if you please."

"Calf?" said he, "you ain't none, pardner. It 's took off."

"I know better," said I. "I have pain in both legs."

"Wall, I never!" said he. "You ain't got nary leg."

As I did not believe him, he threw off the covers, and, to my horror, showed me that I had suffered amputation of both thighs, very high up.

"That will do," said I, faintly.

A month later, to the amazement of every one, I was so well as to be moved from the crowded hospital at Chattanooga to Nashville, where I filled one of the ten thousand beds of that vast metropolis of hospitals. Of the sufferings which then began I shall presently speak. It will be best just now to detail the final misfortune which here fell upon me. Hospital No. 2, in which I lay, was inconveniently crowded with severely wounded officers. After my third week, an epidemic of hospital gangrene broke out in my ward. In three days it attacked twenty persons. Then an inspector came out, and we were transferred at once to the open air, and placed in tents. Strangely enough, the wound in my remaining arm, which still suppurated, was seized with gangrene. The usual remedy, bromine, was used locally, but the main artery opened, was tied, bled again and again, and at last, as a final resort, the remaining arm was amputated at the shoulder-joint. Against all chances I recovered, to find myself a useless torso, more like some strange larval creature than anything of human shape. Of my anguish and horror of myself I dare not speak. I have dictated these pages, not to shock my readers, but to possess them with facts in regard to the relation of the mind to the body; and I hasten, therefore, to such portions of my case as best illustrate these views.

In January, 1864, I was forwarded to Philadelphia, in order to enter what was then known as the Stump Hospital, South Street. This favor was obtained through the influence of my father's friend, the late Governor Anderson, who has always manifested an interest in my case, for which I am deeply grateful. It was thought, at the time, that Mr. Palmer, the legmaker, might be able to adapt some form of arm to my left shoulder, as on that side there remained five inches of the arm bone, which I could move to a moderate extent. The hope proved illusory, as the stump was always too tender to bear any pressure. The hospital referred to was in charge of several surgeons while I was an inmate, and was at all times a clean and pleasant home. It was filled with men who had lost one arm or leg, or one of each, as happened now and then. I saw one man who had lost both legs, and one who had parted with both arms; but none, like myself, stripped of every limb. There were collected in this place hundreds of these cases; which gave to it, with reason enough, the not very pleasing title of Stump-Hospital.

I spent here three and a half months, before my transfer to the United States Army Hospital for nervous diseases. Every morning I was carried out in an arm-chair, and placed in the library, where some one was always ready to write or read for me, or to fill my pipe. The doctors lent me medical books ; the ladies brought me luxuries, and fed me ; and, save that I was helpless to a degree which was humiliating, I was as comfortable as kindness could make me.

I amused myself, at this time, by noting in my mind all that I could learn from other limbless folk, and from myself, as to the peculiar feelings which were noticed in regard to lost members. I found that the great mass of men who had undergone amputations, for many months felt the usual consciousness that they still had the lost limb. It itched or pained, or was cramped, but never felt hot or cold. If they had painful sensations referred to it, the conviction of its existence continued unaltered for long periods ; but where no pain was felt in it, then, by degrees, the sense of having that limb faded away entirely. I think we may to some extent explain this. The knowledge we possess of any part is made up of the numberless impressions from without which affect its sensitive surfaces, and which are transmitted through its nerves to the spinal nerve-cells, and through them, again, to the brain. We are thus kept endlessly informed as to the existence of parts, because the impressions which reach the brain are, by a law of our being, referred by us to the part from which they came. Now, when the part is cut off, the nerve-trunks which led to it and from it, remaining capable of being impressed by irritations, are made to convey to the brain from the stump impressions which are as usual referred by the brain to the lost parts, to which these nerve - threads belonged. In other words, the nerve is like a bell-wire. You may pull it at any part of its course, and thus ring the bell as well as if you pulled at the end of the wire ; but, in any case, the intelligent servant will refer the pull to the front door, and obey it accordingly. The impressions made on the cut ends of the nerve, or on its sides, are due often to the changes in the stump during healing, and consequently cease as it heals, so that finally, in a very healthy stump, no such impressions arise ; the brain ceases to correspond with the lost leg, and, as *les absents ont toujours tort*, it is no longer remembered or recognized. But in some cases, such as mine proved at last to my sorrow, the ends of the nerves undergo a curious alteration, and get to be enlarged and altered. This change, as I have seen in my practice of medicine, passes up the nerves towards the centres, and occasions a more or less constant irritation of the nerve-fibres, producing neuralgia, which is usually referred to that part of the lost limb to which the affected nerve belongs. This pain keeps the brain ever mindful of the missing part, and, imperfectly at least, preserves to the man a consciousness of possessing that which he has not.

Where the pains come and go, as they do in certain cases, the subjective sensations thus occasioned are very curious, since in such cases the man loses and gains, and loses and regains, the consciousness of the presence of lost parts, so that he will tell you, " Now I feel my thumb, — now I feel my little finger." I should also add, that nearly every person who has lost an arm above the elbow feels as though the lost member were bent at the elbow, and at times is vividly impressed with the notion that his fingers are strongly flexed.

Another set of cases present a peculiarity which I am at a loss to account for. Where the leg, for instance, has been lost, they feel as if the foot was present, but as though the leg were shortened. If the thigh has been taken off, there seems to them to be a foot at the knee ; if the arm, a hand seems to be at the elbow, or attached to the stump itself.

As I have said, I was next sent to

the United States Army Hospital for Injuries and Diseases of the Nervous System. Before leaving Nashville, I had begun to suffer the most acute pain in my left hand, especially the little finger ; and so perfect was the idea which was thus kept up of the real presence of these missing parts, that I found it hard at times to believe them absent. Often, at night, I would try with one lost hand to grope for the other. As, however, I had no pain in the right arm, the sense of the existence of that limb gradually disappeared, as did that of my legs also.

Everything was done for my neuralgia which the doctors could think of; and at length, at my suggestion, I was removed to the above-named hospital. It was a pleasant, suburban, old-fashioned country - seat, its gardens surrounded by a circle of wooden, one-story wards, shaded by fine trees. There were some three hundred cases of epilepsy, paralysis, St. Vitus's dance, and wounds of nerves. On one side of me lay a poor fellow, a Dane, who had the same burning neuralgia with which I once suffered, and which I now learned was only too common. This man had become hysterical from pain. He carried a sponge in his pocket, and a bottle of water in one hand, with which he constantly wetted the burning hand. Every sound increased his torture, and he even poured water into his boots to keep himself from feeling too sensibly the rough friction of his soles when walking. Like him, I was greatly eased by having small doses of morphia injected under the skin of my shoulder, with a hollow needle, fitted to a syringe.

As I improved under the morphia treatment, I began to be disturbed by the horrible variety of suffering about me. One man walked sideways ; there was one who could not smell ; another was dumb from an explosion. In fact, every one had his own grotesquely painful peculiarity. Near me was a strange case of palsy of the muscles called rhomboids, whose office it is to hold down the shoulder-blades flat on the back during the motions of the arms, which, in

themselves, were strong enough. When, however, he lifted these members, the shoulder - blades stood out from the back like wings, and got him the soubriquet of the Angel. In my ward were also the cases of fits, which very much annoyed me, as upon any great change in the weather it was common to have a dozen convulsions in view at once. Dr. Neek, one of our physicians, told me that on one occasion a hundred and fifty fits took place within thirty-six hours. On my complaining of these sights, whence I alone could not fly, I was placed in the paralytic and wound ward, which I found much more pleasant.

A month of skilful treatment eased me entirely of my aches, and I then began to experience certain curious feelings, upon which, having nothing to do and nothing to do anything with, I reflected a good deal. It was a good while before I could correctly explain to my own satisfaction the phenomena which at this time I was called upon to observe. By the various operations already described, I had lost about four fifths of my weight. As a consequence of this, I ate much less than usual, and could scarcely have consumed the ration of a soldier. I slept also but little ; for, as sleep is the repose of the brain, made necessary by the waste of its tissues during thought and voluntary movement, and as this latter did not exist in my case, I needed only that rest which was necessary to repair such exhaustion of the nerve-centres as was induced by thinking and the automatic movements of the viscera.

I observed at this time also, that my heart, in place of beating as it once did seventy-eight in the minute, pulsated only forty-five times in this interval, — a fact to be easily explained by the perfect quiescence to which I was reduced, and the consequent absence of that healthy and constant stimulus to the muscles of the heart which exercise occasions.

Notwithstanding these drawbacks, my physical health was good, which I confess surprised me, for this among other reasons. It is said that a burn of two thirds of the surface destroys life, because then all the excretory matters which this portion of the glands of the skin evolved are thrown upon the blood, and poison the man, just as happens in an animal whose skin the physiologist has varnished, so as in this way to destroy its function. Yet here was I, having lost at least a third of my skin, and apparently none the worse for it.

Still more remarkable, however, were the physical changes which I now began to perceive. I found to my horror that at times I was less conscious of myself, of my own existence, than used to be the case. This sensation was so novel, that at first it quite bewildered me. I felt like asking some one constantly if I were really George Dedlow or not ; but, well aware how absurd I should seem after such a question, I refrained from speaking of my case, and strove more keenly to analyze my feelings. At times the conviction of my want of being myself was overwhelming, and most painful. It was, as well as I can describe it, a deficiency in the egoistic sentiment of individuality. About one half of the sensitive surface of my skin was gone, and thus much of relation to the outer world destroyed. As a consequence, a large part of the receptive central organs must be out of employ, and, like other idle things, degenerating rapidly. Moreover, all the great central ganglia, which give rise to movements in the limbs, were also eternally at rest. Thus one half of me was absent or functionally dead. This set me to thinking how much a man might lose and yet live. If I were unhappy enough to survive, I might part with my spleen at least, as many a dog has done, and grown fat afterwards. The other organs, with which we breathe and circulate the blood, would be essential ; so also would the liver ; but at least half of the intestines might be dispensed with, and of course all of the limbs. And as to the nervous system, the only parts really necessary to life

are a few small ganglia. Were the rest absent or inactive, we should have a man reduced, as it were, to the lowest terms, and leading an almost vegetative existence. Would such a being, I asked myself, possess the sense of individuality in its usual completeness, — even if his organs of sensation remained, and he were capable of consciousness ? Of course, without them, he could not have it any more than a dahlia, or a tulip. But with it — how then ? I concluded that it would be at a minimum, and that, if utter loss of relation to the outer world were capable of destroying a man's consciousness of himself, the destruction of half of his sensitive surfaces might well occasion, in a less degree, a like result, and so diminish his sense of individual existence.

I thus reached the conclusion that a man is not his brain, or any one part of it, but all of his economy, and that to lose any part must lessen this sense of his own existence. I found but one person who properly appreciated this great truth. She was a New England lady, from Hartford, — an agent, I think, for some commission, perhaps the Sanitary. After I had told her my views and feelings, she said : " Yes, I comprehend. The fractional entities of vitality are embraced in the oneness of the unitary Ego. Life," she added, " is the garnered condensation of objective impressions ; and, as the objective is the remote father of the subjective, so must individuality, which is but focused subjectivity, suffer and fade when the sensation lenses, by which the rays of impression are condensed, become destroyed." I am not quite clear that I fully understood her, but I think she appreciated my ideas, and I felt grateful for her kindly interest.

The strange want I have spoken of now haunted and perplexed me so constantly, that I became moody and wretched. While in this state, a man from a neighboring ward fell one morning into conversation with the chaplain, within ear-shot of my chair. Some of their words arrested my attention, and

I turned my head to see and listen. The speaker, who wore a sergeant's chevron and carried one arm in a sling, was a tall, loosely made person, with a pale face, light eyes of a washed-out blue tint, and very sparse yellow whiskers. His mouth was weak, both lips being almost alike, so that the organ might have been turned upside down without affecting its expression. His forehead, however, was high and thinly covered with sandy hair. I should have said, as a phrenologist, Will feeble, — emotional, but not passionate, — likely to be enthusiast, or weakly bigot.

I caught enough of what passed to make me call to the sergeant when the chaplain left him.

"Good morning," said he. "How do you get on?"

"Not at all," I replied. "Where were you hit?"

"O, at Chancellorsville. I was shot in the shoulder. I have what the doctors call paralysis of the median nerve, but I guess Dr. Neek and the lightnin' battery will fix it in time. When my time's out I'll go back to Kearsage and try on the school-teaching again. I was a fool to leave it."

"Well," said I, "you're better off than I."

"Yes," he answered, "in more ways than one. I belong to the New Church. It's a great comfort for a plain man like me, when he's weary and sick, to be able to turn away from earthly things, and hold converse daily with the great and good who have left the world. We have a circle in Coates Street. If it wa'n't for the comfort I get there, I should have wished myself dead many a time. I ain't got kith or kin on earth; but this matters little, when one can talk to them daily, and know that they are in the spheres above us."

"It must be a great comfort," I replied, "if only one could believe it."

"Believe!" he repeated, "how can you help it? Do you suppose anything dies?"

"No," I said. "The soul does not,

I am sure; and as to matter, it merely changes form."

"But why then," said he, "should not the dead soul talk to the living. In space, no doubt, exist all forms of matter, merely in finer, more ethereal being. You can't suppose a naked soul moving about without a bodily garment. No creed teaches that, and if its new clothing be of like substance to ours, only of ethereal fineness, — a more delicate recrystallization about the eternal spiritual nucleus, — must not it then possess powers as much more delicate and refined as is the new material in which it is reclad?"

"Not very clear," I answered; "but after all, the thing should be susceptible of some form of proof to our present senses."

"And so it is," said he. "Come to-morrow with me, and you shall see and hear for yourself."

"I will," said I, "if the doctor will lend me the ambulance."

It was so arranged, as the surgeon in charge was kind enough, as usual, to oblige me with the loan of his wagon, and two orderlies to lift my useless trunk.

On the day following, I found myself, with my new comrade, in a house in Coates Street, where a "circle" was in the daily habit of meeting. So soon as I had been comfortably deposited in an arm-chair, beside a large pine-table, the rest of those assembled seated themselves, and for some time preserved an unbroken silence. During this pause I scrutinized the persons present. Next to me, on my right, sat a flabby man, with ill-marked, baggy features, and injected eyes. He was, as I learned afterwards, an eclectic doctor, who had tried his hand at medicine and several of its quackish variations, finally settling down on eclecticism, which I believe professes to be to scientific medicine what vegetarianism is to common sense, every-day dietetics. Next to him sat a female, — authoress, I think, of two somewhat feeble novels, and much pleasanter to look at than her books. She was, I thought, a good deal excited at the prospect of spiritual revelations. Her neighbor was a pallid, care-worn girl, with very red lips, and large brown eyes of great beauty. She was, as I learned afterwards, a magnetic patient of the doctor, and had deserted her husband, a master mechanic, to follow this new light. The others were, like myself, strangers brought hither by mere curiosity. One of them was a lady in deep black, closely veiled. Beyond her, and opposite to me, sat the sergeant, and next to him, the medium, a man named Blake. He was well dressed, and wore a good deal of jewelry, and had large, black sidewhiskers, — a shrewd - visaged, large-nosed, full-lipped man, formed by nature to appreciate the pleasant things of sensual existence.

Before I had ended my survey, he turned to the lady in black, and asked if she wished to see any one in the spirit-world.

She said, "Yes," rather feebly.

"Is the spirit present?" he asked. Upon which two knocks were heard in affirmation.

"Ah!" said the medium, "the name is — it is the name of a child. It is a male child. It is Albert, — no, Alfred!"

"Great Heaven!" said the lady. "My child! my boy!"

On this the medium arose, and became strangely convulsed. "I see," he said, "I see — a fair-haired boy. I see blue eyes, — I see above you, beyond you — " at the same time pointing fixedly over her head.

She turned with a wild start. "Where, — whereabouts?"

"A blue-eyed boy," he continued, "over your head. He cries, — he says, Mamma, mamma!"

The effect of this on the woman was unpleasant. She stared about her for a moment, and, exclaiming, "I come, — I am coming, Alfy!" fell in hysterics on the floor.

Two or three persons raised her, and aided her into an adjoining room; but the rest remained at the table, as though well accustomed to like scenes.

After this, several of the strangers were called upon to write the names of the dead with whom they wished to communicate. The names were spelled out by the agency of affirmative knocks when the correct letters were touched by the applicant, who was furnished with an alphabet card upon which he tapped the letters in turn, the medium, meanwhile, scanning his face very keenly. With some, the names were readily made out. With one, a stolid personage of disbelieving type, every attempt failed, until at last the spirits signified by knocks that he was a disturbing agency, and that while he remained all our efforts would fail. Upon this some of the company proposed that he should leave, of which invitation he took advantage with a sceptical sneer at the whole performance.

As he left us, the sergeant leaned over and whispered to the medium, who next addressed himself to me. "Sister Euphemia," he said, indicating the lady with large eyes, "will act as your medium. I am unable to do more. These things exhaust my nervous system."

"Sister Euphemia," said the doctor, "will aid us. Think, if you please, sir, of a spirit, and she will endeavor to summon it to our circle."

Upon this, a wild idea came into my head. I answered, "I am thinking as you directed me to do."

The medium sat with her arms folded, looking steadily at the centre of the table. For a few moments there was silence. Then a series of irregular knocks began. "Are you present?" said the medium.

The affirmative raps were twice given.

"I should think," said the doctor, "that there were two spirits present."

His words sent a thrill through my heart.

"Are there two?" he questioned.

A double rap.

"Yes, two," said the medium. "Will it please the spirits to make us conscious of their names in this world?"

A single knock. "No."

"Will it please them to say how they are called in the world of spirits?"

Again came the irregular raps, — 3, 4, 8, 6; then a pause, and 3, 4, 8, 7.

"I think," said the authoress, "they must be numbers. Will the spirits," she said, "be good enough to aid us? Shall we use the alphabet?"

"Yes," was rapped very quickly.

"Are these numbers?"

"Yes," again.

"I will write them," she added, and, doing so, took up the card and tapped the letters. The spelling was pretty rapid, and ran thus as she tapped in turn, first the letters, and last the numbers she had already set down : —

"UNITED STATES ARMY MEDICAL MUSEUM, NOS. 3486, 3487."

The medium looked up with a puzzled expression.

"Good gracious!" said I, "they are *my legs! my legs!*"

What followed, I ask no one to believe except those who, like myself, have communed with the beings of another sphere. Suddenly I felt a strange return of my self-consciousness. I was reindividualized, so to speak. A strange wonder filled me, and, to the amazement of every one, I arose, and, staggering a little, walked across the room on limbs invisible to them or me. It was no wonder I staggered, for, as I briefly reflected, my legs had been nine months in the strongest alcohol. At this instant all my new friends crowded around me in astonishment. Presently, however, I felt myself sinking slowly. My legs were going, and in a moment I was resting feebly on my two stumps upon the floor. It was too much. All that was left of me fainted and rolled over senseless.

I have little to add. I am now at home in the West, surrounded by every form of kindness, and every possible comfort; but, alas! I have so little surety of being myself, that I doubt my own honesty in drawing my pension, and feel absolved from gratitude to those who are kind to a being who is uncertain of being enough himself to be conscientiously responsible. It is needless to add, that I am not a happy fraction of a man; and that I am eager for the day when I shall rejoin the lost members of my corporeal family in another and a happier world.

ON TRANSLATING THE DIVINA COMMEDIA.

SECOND SONNET.

I ENTER, and see thee in the gloom
    Of the long aisles, O poet saturnine!
    And strive to make my steps keep pace with thine.
    The air is filled with some unknown perfume;
The congregation of the dead make room
    For thee to pass; the votive tapers shine;
    Like rooks that haunt Ravenna's groves of pine
    The hovering echoes fly from tomb to tomb.
From the confessionals I hear arise
    Rehearsals of forgotten tragedies,
    And lamentations from the crypts below;
And then a voice celestial that begins
    With the pathetic words, "Although your sins
    As scarlet be," and ends with "as the snow."

THE GREAT DOCTOR.

A STORY IN TWO PARTS.

PART I.

"HELLO! hello! which way now, Mrs. Walker? It 'll rain afore you git there, if you 've got fur to go. Had n't you better stop an' come in till this thunder-shower passes over?"

"Well, no, I reckon not, Mr. Bowen. I 'm in a good deal of a hurry. I 've been sent for over to John's." And rubbing one finger up and down the horn of her saddle, for she was on horseback, Mrs. Walker added, "Johnny 's sick, Mr. Bowen, an' purty bad, I 'm afeard." Then she tucked up her skirts, and, gathering up the rein, that had dropped on the neck of her horse, she inquired in a more cheerful tone, "How 's all the folks, — Miss Bowen, an' Jinney, an' all?"

By this time the thunder began to growl, and the wind to whirl clouds of dust along the road.

"You 'd better hitch your critter under the wood-shed, an' come in a bit. My woman 'll be glad to see you, an' Jinney too, — there she is now, at the winder. I 'll warrant nobody goes along the big road without her seein' 'em." Mr. Bowen had left the broad kitchen-porch from which he had hallooed to the old woman, and was now walking down the gravelled path, that, between its borders of four-o'clocks and other common flowers, led from the front door to the front gate. "We 're all purty well, I 'm obleeged to you," he said, as, reaching the gate, he leaned over it, and turned his cold gray eyes upon the neat legs of the horse, rather than the anxious face of the rider.

"I 'm glad to hear you 're well," Mrs. Walker said; "it a'most seems to me that, if I had Johnny the way he was last week, I would n't complain about anything. We think too much of our li..le hardships, Mr. Bowen, — a good deal too much!" And Mrs. Walker looked at the clouds, perhaps in the hope that their blackness would frighten the tears away from her eyes. John was her own boy, — forty years old, to be sure, but still a boy to her, — and he was very sick.

"Well, I don't know," Mr. Bowen said, opening the mouth of the horse and looking in it; "we all have our troubles, an' if it ain't one thing it 's another. Now if John was n't sick, I s'pose you 'd be frettin' about somethin' else; you must n't think you 're particularly sot apart in your afflictions, any how. This rain that 's getherin' is goin' to spile a couple of acres of grass for me, don't you see?"

Mrs. Walker was hurt. Her neighbor had not given her the sympathy she expected; he had not said anything about John one way nor another; had not inquired whether there was anything he could do, nor what the doctor said, nor asked any of those questions that express a kindly solicitude.

"I am sorry about your hay," she answered, "but I must be going."

"Don't want to hurry you; but if you will go, the sooner the better. That thunder-cloud is certain to bust in a few minutes." And Mr. Bowen turned toward the house.

"Wait a minute, Mrs. Walker," called a young voice, full of kindness; "here 's my umberell. It 'll save your bonnet, any how; and it 's a real purty one. But did n't I hear you say somebody was sick over to your son's house?"

"Yes, darlin'," answered the old woman as she took the umbrella; "it 's Johnny himself; he 's right bad, they say. I just got word about an hour ago, and left everything, and started off. They think he 's got the small-pox."

Jenny Bowen, the young girl who

had brought the umbrella, looked terribly frightened. "*They* won't let me go over, you know," she said, nodding her head toward the house, "not if it 's really small-pox!" And then, with the hope at which the young are so quick to catch, she added, "May be it is n't small-pox. I have n't heard of a case anywhere about. I don't believe it is." And then she told Mrs. Walker not to fret about home. "I will go," she said, "and milk the cow, and look after things. Don't think one thought about it." And then she asked if the rest of them at John Walker's were well.

"If it 's Hobert you want to know about," the grandmother said, smiling faintly, "he 's well; but, darlin', you 'd better not think about him : they 'll be ag'in it, in there!" and she nodded toward the house as Jenny had done before her.

The face of the young girl flushed, — not with confusion, but with self-asserting and defiant brightness that seemed to say, "Let them do their worst." The thunder rattled sharper and nearer, bursting right upon the flash of the lightning, and then came the rain. But it proved not one of those bright, brief dashes that leave the world sparkling, but settled toward sunset into a slow, dull drizzle.

Jenny had her milking, and all the other evening chores, done betimes, and with an alertness and cheerfulness in excess of her usual manner, that might have indicated an unusual favor to be asked. She had made her evening toilet ; that is, she had combed her hair, tied on a pair of calf-skin shoes, and a blue checked apron, newly washed and ironed ; when she said, looking toward a faint light in the west, and as though the thought had just occurred to her, "It 's going to break away, I see. Don't you think, mother, I had better just run over to Mrs. Walker's, and milk her cow for her?"

"Go to Miss Walker's!" repeated the mother, as though she were as much outraged as astonished. She was seated in the door, patching, by the waning light, an old pair of mud-spat-

tered trousers, her own dress being very old-fashioned, coarse, and scanty, — so scant, in fact, as to reveal the angles of her form with ungraceful definiteness, especially the knees, that were almost suggestive of a skeleton, and now, as she put herself in position, as it were, stood up with inordinate prominence. Her hands were big in the joints, ragged in the nails, and marred all over with the cuts, burns, and scratches of indiscriminate and incessant toil. But her face was, perhaps, the most sadly divested of all womanly charm. It had, in the first place, the deep yellow, lifeless appearance of an old bruise, and was expressive of pain, irritation, and fanatical anxiety.

"Go to Miss Walker's!" she said again, seeing that Jenny was taking down from its peg in the kitchen-wall a woollen cloak that had been hers since she was a little girl, and her mother's before her.

"Yes, mother. You know John Walker is very sick, and Mrs. Walker has been sent for over there. She 's very down-hearted about him. He 's dangerous, they think ; and I thought may be I 'd come round that way as I come home, and ask how he was. Don't you think I 'd better?"

"I think you had better stay at home and tend to your own business. You 'll spile your clothes, and do no good that I can see by traipsin' out in such a storm."

"Why, you would think it was bad for one of our cows to go without milking," Jenny said, "and I suppose Mrs. Walker's cow is a good deal like ours, and she is giving a pailful of milk now."

"How do you know so much about Miss Walker's cow? If you paid more attention to things at home, and less to other folks, you 'd be more dutiful."

"That 's true, mother, but would I be any better?"

"Not in your own eyes, child ; but your 're so much wiser than your father and me, that words are throwed away on you."

"I promised Mrs. Walker that I would milk for her to-night," Jenny said, hesitating, and dropping her eyes.

"O yes, you've always got some excuse! What did you make a promise for, that you knowed your father would n't approve of? Take your things right off now, and peel the potaters, and sift the meal for mush in the morning; an' if Miss Walker's cow must be milked, what's to hender that Hobe, the great lazy strapper, should n't go and milk her?"

"You forget how much he has to do at home now; and one pair of hands can't do everything, even if they are Hobert Walker's!"

Jenny had spoken with much spirit and some bitterness; and the bright defiant flush, before noticed, came into her face, as she untied the cloak and proceeded to sift the meal and peel the potatoes for breakfast. She did her work quietly, but with a determination in every movement that indicated a will not easily overruled.

It was nearly dark, and the rain still persistently falling, when she turned the potato-peelings into the pig-trough that stood only a few yards from the door, and, returning, put the cloak about her shoulders, tied it deliberately, turned the hood over her head, and, without another word, walked straight out into the rain.

"Well, I must say! Well, I *must* say!" cried the mother, in exasperated astonishment. "What on airth is that girl a-comin' to?" And, resting her elbows on her knees, she leaned her yellow face in her hands, and gathered out of her hard, embittered heart such consolation as she could.

Jenny, meantime, tucked up her petticoats, and, having left a field or two between her and the homestead, tripped lightly along, debating with herself whether or not she should carry out her will to the full, and return by the way of Mr. John Walker's,—a question she need hardly have raised, if unexpected events had not interfered with her predeterminations. At Mrs. Walker's gate she stopped and pulled half a dozen roses from the bush that was almost lying

on the ground with its burden,—they seemed, somehow, brighter than the roses at home,—and, with them swinging in her hand, had wellnigh gained the door, before she perceived that it was standing open. She hesitated an instant,—perhaps some crazy wanderer or drunken person might have entered the house,—when brisk steps, coming up the path that led from the milking-yard, arrested her attention, and, looking that way, she recognized through the darkness young Hobert Walker, with the full pail in his hand.

"O Jenny," he said, setting down the pail, "we are in such trouble at home! The doctor says father is better, but I don't think so, and I ain't satisfied with what is being done for him. Besides, I had such a strange dream,—I thought I met you, Jenny, alone, in the night, and you had six red roses in your hand,—let me see how many have you." He had come close to her, and he now took the roses and counted them. There were six, sure enough. "Humph!" he said, and went on. "Six red roses, I thought; and while I looked at them they turned white as snow; and then it seemed to me it was a shroud you had in your hand, and not roses at all; and you, seeing how I was frightened, said to me, 'What if it should turn out to be my wedding-dress?' And while we talked, your father came between us, and led you away by a great chain that he put round your neck. But you think all this foolish, I see." And, as if he feared the apprehension he had confessed involved some surrender of manhood, he cast down his eyes, and awaited her reply in confusion. She had too much tact to have noticed this at any time; but in view of the serious circumstances in which he then stood, she could not for the life of her have turned any feeling of his into a jest, however unwarranted she might have felt it to be.

"My grandmother was a great believer in dreams," she said, sympathetically; "but she always thought they went by contraries; and, if she was right, why, yours bodes ever so much good. But come, Hobert, let us go into the house: it 's raining harder."

"How stupid of me, Jenny, not to remember that you were being drowned, almost! You must try to excuse me: I am really hardly myself to-night."

"Excuse you, Hobert! As if you could ever do anything I should not think was just right!" And she laughed the little musical laugh that had been ringing in his ears so long, and skipped before him into the house.

He followed her with better heart; and, as she strained and put away the milk, and swept the hearth, and set the house in order, he pleased himself with fancies of a home of which she would be always the charming mistress.

And who, that saw the sweet domestic cheer she diffused through the house with her harmless little gossip about this and that, and the artfully artless kindnesses to him she mingled with all, could have blamed him? He was given to melancholy and to musing; his cheek was sometimes pale, and his step languid; and he saw, all too often, troublesome phantoms coming to meet him. This disposition in another would have incited the keenest ridicule in the mind of Jenny Bowen, but in Hobert it was well enough; nay, more, it was actually fascinating, and she would not have had him otherwise. These characteristics — for her sake we will not say weaknesses — constantly suggested to her how much she could be to him, — she who was so strong in all ways, — in health, in hope, and in enthusiasm. And for him it was joy enough to look upon her full bright cheek, to see her compact little figure before him; but to touch her dimpled shoulder, to feel one tress of her hair against his face, was ecstasy; and her voice,— the tenderest trill of the wood-dove was not half so delicious! But who shall define the mystery of love? They were lovers; and when we have said that, is there anything more to be said? Their love had not, however, up to the time of which we write, found utterance in words. Hobert was

the son of a poor man, and Jenny was prospectively rich, and the faces of her parents were set as flints against the poor young man. But Jenny had said in her heart more than once that she would marry him; and if the old folks had known this, they might as well have held their peace. Hobert did not dream that she had talked thus to her heart, and, with his constitutional timidity, he feared she would never say anything of the kind. Then, too, his conscientiousness stood in his way. Should he presume to take her to his poor house, even if she would come? No, no, he must not think of it; he must work and wait, and defer hope. This hour so opportune was also most inopportune, — such sorrow at home! He would not speak to-night, — O no, not to-night! And yet he could bear up against everything else, if she only cared for him! Such were his resolves, as she passed to and fro before him, trifling away the time with pretence of adjusting this thing and that; but at last expedients failed, and reaching for her cloak, which hung almost above him as he sat against the wall, she said it was time to go. As frostwork disappears in the sunshine, so his brave resolutions vanished when her arm reached across his shoulder, and the ribbon that tied her beads fluttered against his cheek. With a motion quite involuntary, he snatched her hand. "No, Jenny, not yet, — not quite yet!" he said.

"And why not?" demanded Jenny; for could any woman, however innocent, or rustic, be without her little coquetries? And she added, in a tone that contradicted her words, "I am sure I should not have come if I had known you were coming!"

"I dare say not," replied Hobert, in a voice so sad and so tender withal, as to set the roses Jenny wore in her bosom trembling. "I dare say not, indeed. I would not presume to hope you would go a step out of your way to give me pleasure; only I was feeling so lonesome to-night, I thought may be — no, I did n't think anything; I certainly did n't hope anything. Well, no matter, I am ready to go." And he let go the hand he had been holding, and stood up.

It was Jenny's privilege to pout a little now, and to walk sullenly and silently home, — so torturing herself and her honest-hearted lover; but she was much too generous, much too noble, to do this. She would not for the world have grieved poor Hobert, — not then, — not when his heart was so sick and so weighed down with shadows; and she told him this with a simple earnestness that admitted of no doubt, concluding with, " I only wish, Hobert, I could say or do something to comfort you."

" Then you will stay? Just a moment, Jenny!" And the hand was in his again.

" Dear Jenny, — dear, dear Jenny!" She was sitting on his knee now; and the rain, with its pattering against the window, drowned their heart-beats; and the summer darkness threw over them its sacred veil.

"Shall I tell you, darling, of another dream I have had to-night — since I have been sitting here?" The fair cheek bent itself close to his to listen, and he went on. " I have been dreaming, Jenny, a very sweet dream; and this is what it was. You and I were living here, in this house, with grandmother; and she was your grandmother as well as mine; and I was farmer of the land, and you were mistress of the dairy; and the little room with windows toward the sunrise, and the pretty bureau, and bed with snow-white coverlet and pillows of down, — that was " — perhaps he meant to say " *ours*," but his courage failed him, and, with a charming awkwardness, he said, " yours, Jenny," and hurried on to speak of the door-yard flowers, and the garden with its beds of thyme and mint, its berry-bushes and hop-vines and bee-hives, — all of which were brighter and sweeter than were ever hives and bushes in any other garden; and when he had run through the catalogue of rustic delights, he said: "And now,

Jenny, I want you to tell me the meaning of my dream; and yet I am afraid you will interpret it as your grandmother used to hers."

Jenny laughed gayly. " That is just what I will do, dear Hobert," she said; " for she used to say that only bad dreams went by contraries, and yours was the prettiest dream I ever heard."

The reply to this sweet interpretation was after the manner of all lovers since the world began. And so, forgetting the stern old folks at home, — forgetting everything but each other, — they sat for an hour at the very gate of heaven. How often Hobert called her his sweetheart, and his rosebud, and other fond names, we need not stop to enumerate: how often he said that for her sake he could brave the winter storm and the summer heat, that she should never know rough work nor sad days, but that she should be as tenderly protected, as daintily cared for, as any lady of them all, — how often he said all these things, we need not enumerate; nor need we say with what unquestioning trust, and deafness to all the suggestions of probability, Jenny believed. Does not love, in fact, always believe what it hopes? Who would do away with the blessed insanity that clothes the marriage day with such enchantment? Who would dare to do it?

No royal mantle could have been adjusted with tenderer and more reverent solicitude than was that night the coarse cloak about the shoulders of Jenny. The walk homeward was all too short; and whether the rain fell, or whether the moon were at her best, perhaps neither of them could have told until they were come within earshot of the Bowen homestead; then both suddenly stood still. Was it the arm of Jenny that trembled so? No, no! we must own the truth, — it was the arm through which hers was drawn. At her chamber window, peering out curiously and anxiously, was the yellow-white face of Mrs. Bowen; and, leaning over the gate, gazing up and down the road, the rain falling on his bent shoulders and gray head, was the father of Jenny, — angry and impatient, past doubt.

"Don't stand looking any longer, for mercy's sake!" called the querulous voice from the house. "You 'll get your death of cold, and then what 'll become of us all? Saddle your horse this minute, and ride over to John Walker's, — for there 's where you 'll find Jinny, the gad-about, — and bring her home at the tail of your critter. I 'll see who is going to be mistress here!"

"She 's had her own head too long a'ready, I 'm afeard," replied the old man, turning from the gate, with intent, probably, to execute his wife's order.

Seeing this, and hearing this, Hobert, as we said, stood still and trembled, and could only ask, by a little pressure of the hand he held, what was to be said or done.

Jenny did not hesitate a moment. "I expected this or something worse," she said. "Don't mind, Hobert; so they don't see you, I don't care for the rest. You must not go one step farther: the lightning will betray us, you see. I will say I waited for the rain to slack, and the two storms will clear off about the same time, I dare say. There, good night!" — and she turned her cheek to him; for she was not one of those impossible maidens we read of in books, who don't know they are in love, until after the consent of parents is obtained, and blush themselves to ashes at the thought of a kiss. To love Hobert was to her the most natural and proper thing in the world, and she did not dream there was anything to blush for. It is probable, too, that his constitutional bashfulness and distrust of himself brought out her greater confidence and buoyancy.

"And how and where am I ever to see you again?" he asked, as he detained her, against her better judgment, if not against her will.

"Trust that to me," — and she hurried away in time to meet and prevent her father from riding forth in search of her.

Of course there were fault-finding and quarrelling, accusations and prot-

estations, hard demands and sullen pouting, — so that the home, at no time so attractive as we like to imagine the home of a young girl who has father and mother to provide for her and protect her, became to her like a prison-house. At the close of the first and second days after her meeting with Hobert, when the work was all faithfully done, she ventured to ask leave to go over to John Walker's and inquire how the sick man was; but so cold a refusal met her, that, on the evening of the third day, she sat down on the porch-side to while away the hour between working and sleeping, without having renewed her request.

The sun was down, and the first star began to show faintly above a strip of gray cloud in the west, when a voice, low and tender, called to her, "Come here, my child!" and looking up she saw Grandmother Walker sitting on her horse at the gate. She had in the saddle before her her youngest granddaughter, and on the bare back of the horse, behind her, a little grandson, both their young faces expressive of the sorrow at home. Jenny arose on the instant, betraying in every motion the interest and sympathy she felt, and was just stepping lightly from the porch to the ground, when a strong hand grasped her shoulder and turned her back. It was her father who had overtaken her. "Go into the house!" he said. "If the old woman has got any arrant at all, it 's likely it 's to your mother and me."

Nor was his heart melted in the least when he learned that his friend and neighbor was no more. He evinced surprise, and made some blunt and coarse inquiries, but that was the amount. "The widder is left purty destitute, I reckon," he said; and then he added, the Lord helped them that helped themselves, and we must n't fly in the face of Providence. She had her son, strong and able-bodied; and of course he had no thoughts of encumbering himself with a family of his own, — young and poverty-struck as he was.

Mrs. Walker understood the insinuation; but her heart could not hold resentment just then. She must relieve her burdened soul by talking of "poor Johnny," even though it were to deaf ears. She must tell what a good boy he had been,—how kind to her and considerate of her, how manly, how generous, how self-forgetful. And then she must tell how hard he had worked, and how saving he had been in order to give his children a better chance in the world than he had had; and how, if he had lived another year, he would have paid off the mortgage, and been able to hold up his head amongst men.

After all the ploughing and sowing, —after all the preparation for the gathering in of the harvest,—it seemed very hard, she said, that Johnny must be called away, just as the shining ears began to appear. The circumstances of his death, too, seemed to her peculiarly afflictive. "We had all the doctors in the neighborhood," she said, "but none of them understood his case. At first they thought he had small-pox, and doctored him for that; and then they thought it was liver-complaint, and doctored him for that; and then it was bilious fever, and then it was typhus fever; and so it went on, and I really can't believe any of them understood anything about it. Their way seemed to be to do just what he did n't want done. In the first place, he was bled; and then he was blistered; and then he was bled again and blistered again, the fever all the time getting higher and higher; and when he wanted water, they said it would kill him, and gave him hot drinks till it seemed to me they would drive him mad; and sure enough, they did! The last word he ever said, to know what he was saying, was to ask me for a cup of cold water. I only wish I had given it to him; all the doctors in the world would n't prevent me now, if I only had him back. The fever seemed to be just devouring him: his tongue was as dry as sand, and his head as hot as fire. 'O mother!' says he, and there was such a look of beseeching in his eyes as I can never forget, 'may be I

shall never want you to do anything more for me. Cold water! give me some cold water! If I don't have it, my senses will surely fly out of my head!' 'Yes, Johnny,' says I,—and I went and brought a tin bucketful, right out of the well, and set it on the table in his sight; for I thought it would do him good to see even more than he could drink; and then I brought a cup and dipped it up full. It was all dripping over, and he had raised himself on one elbow, and was leaning toward me, when the young doctor came in, and, stepping between us, took the cup out of my hand. All his strength seemed to go from poor Johnny at that, and he fell back on his pillow and never lifted his head any more. Still he kept begging in a feeble voice for the water. 'Just two or three drops,—just one drop!' he said. I could n't bear it, and the doctor said I had better go out of the room, and so I did,—and the good Lord forgive me; for when I went back, after half an hour, he was clean crazy. He did n't know me, and he never knowed me any more."

"It 's purty hard, Miss Walker," answered Mr. Bowen, "to accuse the doctors with the murder of your son. A purty hard charge, that, I call it! So John 's dead! Well, I hope he is better off. Where are you goin' to bury him?"

And then Mrs. Walker said she did n't charge anybody with the murder of poor Johnny,—nobody meant to do him any harm, she knew that; but, after all, she wished she could only have had her own way with him from the first. And so she rode away,—her little bare-legged grandson, behind her, aggravating her distress by telling her that, when he got to be a man, he meant to do nothing all the days of his life but dig wells, and give water to whoever wanted it.

It is not worth while to dwell at length on the humiliations and privations to which Jenny was subjected,—the mention of one or two will indicate the nature of all. In the first place, the white heifer she had always called hers was sold, and the money tied up in a tow bag. Jenny would not want a cow for years to come. The piece of land that had always been known as "Jenny's Corner" was not thus denominated any more, and she was given to understand that it was only to be hers *conditionally*. There were obstacles put in the way of her going to meeting of a Sunday, — first one thing, then another; and, finally, the bureau was locked, and the best dress and brightest ribbon inside the drawers. The new side-saddle she had been promised was refused to her, unless she in turn would make a promise; and the long day's work was made to drag on into the night, lest she might find time to visit some neighbor, and lest that neighbor might be the Widow Walker. But what device of the enemy ever proved successful when matched against the simple sincerity of true love? It came about, in spite of all restraint and prohibition, that Jenny and Hobert met in their own times and ways; and so a year went by.

One night, late in the summer, when the katydids began to sing, Jenny waited longer than usual under the vine-covered beech that drooped its boughs low to the ground all round her, — now listening for the expected footstep, and now singing, very low, some little song to her heart, such as many a loving and trusting maiden had sung before her. What could keep Hobert? She knew it was not his will that kept him; and though her heart began to be heavy, she harbored therein no thought of reproach. By the movement of the shadow on the grass, she guessed that an hour beyond the one of appointment must have passed, when the far-away footfall set her so lately hushed pulses fluttering with delight. He was coming, — he was coming! And, no matter what had been wrong, all would be right now. She was holding wide the curtaining boughs long before he came near; and when they dropped, and her arms closed, it is not improbable that he was within them. It was the delight of meeting her that kept him still

so long, Jenny thought; and she prattled lightly and gayly of this and of that, and, seeing that she won no answer, fell to tenderer tones, and imparted the little vexing secrets of her daily life, and the sweet hopes of her nightly dreams.

They were seated on a grassy knoll, the moonlight creeping tenderly about their feet, and the leaves of the drooping vines touching their heads like hands of pity, or of blessing. The water running over the pebbly bottom of the brook just made the silence sweet, and the evening dews shining on the red globes of the clover made the darkness lovely; but with all these enchantments of sight and sound about him, — nay, more, with the hand of Jenny, his own true-love, Jenny, folded in his, — Hobert was not happy.

"And so you think you love me!" he said at last, speaking so sadly, and clasping the hand he held with so faint a pressure, that Jenny would have been offended if she had not been the dear, trustful little creature she was.

There was, indeed, a slight reproach in her accent as she answered, "*Think* I love you, Hobert? No, I don't think anything about it, — I *know*."

"And I know I love you, Jenny," he replied. "I love you so well that I am going to leave you without asking you to marry me!"

For one moment Jenny was silent, — for one moment the world seemed unsteady beneath her, — then she stood up, and, taking the hand of her lover between her palms, gazed into his face with one long, earnest, steadfast gaze. "You have asked me already, Hobert," she said, "a thousand times, and I have consented as often. You may go away, but you will not leave me; for 'Whither thou goest I will go, where thou diest will I die, and there will I be buried.'"

He drew her close to his bosom now, and kissed her with most passionate, but still saddest tenderness. "You know not, my darling," he said, "what you would sacrifice." Then he laid before her all her present advantages, all her bright prospects for the future,

— her high chamber with its broad eastern windows, to be given up for the low dingy walls of a settler's cabin, her free girlhood for the hard struggles of a settler's wife! Sickness, perhaps, — certainly the lonesome nights and days of a home remote from neighbors, and the dreariness and hardship inseparable from the working out of better fortunes. But all these things, even though they should all come, were light in comparison with losing him!

Perhaps Hobert had desired and expected to hear her say this. At any rate, he did not insist on a reversal of her decision, as, with his arms about her, he proceeded to explain why he had come to her that night with so heavy a heart. The substance of all he related may be recapitulated in a few words. The land could not be paid for, and the homestead must be sold. He would not be selfish and forsake his mother, and his young brothers and sisters in their time of need. By careful management of the little that could be saved, he might buy in the West a better farm than that which was now to be given up; and there to build a cabin and plant a garden would be easy, — O, so easy! — with the smile of Jenny to light him home when the day's work was done.

In fact, the prospective hardships vanished away at the thought of her for his little housekeeper. It was such easy work for fancy to convert the work-days into holidays, and the thick wilderness into the shining village, where the schoolhouse stood open all the week, and the sweet bells called them to church of a Sunday; easy work for that deceitful elf to make the chimney-corner snug and warm, and to embellish it with his mother in her easy-chair. When they parted that night, each young heart was trembling with the sweetest secret it had ever

held; and it was perhaps a fortnight thereafter that the same secret took wing, and flew wildly over the neighborhood.

John Walker's little farm was gone for good and all. The few sheep, and the cows, and the pig, and the fowls, together with the greater part of the household furniture, were scattered over the neighborhood; the smoke was gone from the chimney, and the windows were curtainless; and the grave of John, with a modest but decent headstone, and a rose-bush newly planted beside it, was left to the care of strangers. The last visits had been paid, and the last good-byes and good wishes exchanged; and the widow and her younger children were far on their journey, — Hobert remaining for a day or two to dispose of his smart young horse, as it was understood, and then follow on.

At this juncture, Mr. Bowen one morning opened the stair-door, as was his custom, soon after daybreak, and called harshly out, "Jinny! Jinny! its high time you was up!"

Five minutes having elapsed, and the young girl not having yet appeared, the call was repeated more harshly than before. "Come, Jinny, come! or I'll know what 's the reason!"

She did not come; and five minutes more having passed, he mounted the stairs with a quick, resolute step, to know what was the reason. He came down faster, if possible, than he went up. "Mother, mother!" he cried, rushing toward Mrs. Bowen, who stood at the table sifting meal, his gray hair streaming wildly back, and his cheek blanched with amazement, "Jinny's run away! — run away, as sure as you 're a livin' woman. Her piller has n't been touched last night, and her chamber 's desarted!"

And this was the secret that took wing and flew over the neighborhood.

THE RETREAT FROM LENOIR'S AND THE SIEGE OF KNOXVILLE.

LATE in October, 1863, the Ninth Army Corps went into camp at Lenoir's Station, twenty - five miles southwest of Knoxville, East Tennessee. Since April, the corps had campaigned in Kentucky, had participated in the siege of Vicksburg, had accompanied Sherman into the interior of Mississippi in his pursuit of Johnston, had returned to Kentucky, and then, in conjunction with the Twenty-third Army Corps, marching over the mountains into East Tennessee, in a brief but brilliant campaign under its old leader and favorite, Burnside, had delivered the loyal people of that region from the miseries of Rebel rule, and had placed them once more under the protection of the old flag. But all this had not been done without loss. Many of our brave comrades, who, through a storm of leaden hail, had crossed the bridge at Antietam, and had faced death in a hundred forms on the heights of Fredericksburg, had fallen on these widely separated battle-fields in the valley of the Mississippi. Many, overborne by fatigue and exposure, had laid down their wasted bodies by the roadside and in hospitals, and had gently breathed their young lives away. Many more, from time to time, had been rendered unfit for active service ; and the corps, now a mere skeleton, numbered less than three thousand men present for duty. Never did men need rest more than they ; and never was an order more welcome than that which now declared the campaign ended, and authorized the construction of winter quarters.

The Thirty-sixth Massachusetts Volunteers — then in the First Brigade, First Division, Ninth Corps — was under the command of Major Draper, — Lieutenant-Colonel Goodell having been severely wounded at the battle of Blue Springs, October 10. The place selected for the winter quarters of the regiment was a young oak grove, nearly a quarter of a mile east of the village. The camp was laid out with unusual care. In order to secure uniformity throughout the regiment, the size of the log-houses — they were to be ten feet by six — was announced in orders from regimental head-quarters. The work of construction was at once commenced. Unfortunately, we were so far from our base of supplies — Camp Nelson, Kentucky — that nearly all our transportation was required by the Commissary Department for the conveyance of its stores. Consequently, the Quartermaster's Department was poorly supplied ; and the only axes which could be obtained were those which our pioneers and company cooks had brought with them for their own use. These, however, were pressed into the service ; and their merry ringing, as the men cheerfully engaged in the work, could be heard from early morning till evening. Small oaks, four and five inches in diameter, were chiefly used in building these houses. The logs were laid one above another, to the height of four feet, intersecting at the corners of the houses like the rails of a Virginia fence. The interstices were filled with mud. Shelter-tents, buttoned together to the size required, formed the roof, and afforded ample protection from the weather, except in very heavy rains. Each house had its fireplace, table, and bunk. On the 13th of November the houses were nearly completed ; and as we sat by our cheerful fires that evening, and looked forward to the leisure and quiet of the winter before us, we thought ourselves the happiest of soldiers. Writing home at that time, I said that, unless something unforeseen should happen, we expected to remain at Lenoir's during the winter.

That something unforeseen was at hand ; and our pleasant dreams were destined to fade away like an unsubstantial pageant, leaving not a rack behind. At four o'clock on the morning of the 14th I was roused from sleep by loud knocks on the new-made door. In the order which followed, " Be ready to march at daybreak," I recognized the familiar, but unwelcome voice of the Sergeant-Major. Throwing aside my blankets, and leaving the Captain dreamily wondering what could be the occasion of so unexpected an order, I hurried to the quarters of the men of Company D, and repeated to the Orderly Sergeant the instructions just received. The camp was soon astir. Lights flashed here and there through the trees. " Pack up ! pack up !" passed from lip to lip. " Shall we take everything ? " Yes, everything. The shelter-tents were stripped from the houses, knapsacks and trunks were packed. The wagon for the officers' baggage came, was hurriedly loaded, and driven away. A hasty breakfast followed. Then, forming our line, we stacked arms, and awaited further orders.

The mystery was soon solved. Longstreet, having cut loose from Bragg's army, which still remained in the vicinity of Chattanooga, had, by a forced march, struck the Tennessee River at Hough's Ferry, a few miles below Loudon. Already he had thrown a pontoon across the river, and was crossing with his entire command, except the cavalry under Wheeler, which he had sent by way of Marysville, with orders to seize the heights on the south bank of the Holston, opposite Knoxville. The whole movement was the commencement of a series of blunders on the part of the Rebel commanders in this department, which resulted at length in the utter overthrow of the Rebel army of the Tennessee. General Grant saw at once the mistake which the enemy had made, and ordered General Burnside to fall back to Knoxville and intrench, promising reinforcements speedily. Knoxville was Longstreet's objective. It was the key of East Tennessee. Should it again fall into the enemy's hands, we would be obliged to retire to Cumberland Gap. Lenoir's did not lie in Longstreet's path. If we re-

mained there, he would push his columns past our right, and get between us and Knoxville. It was evident that the place must be abandoned ; and there was need of haste. The mills and factories in the village were accordingly destroyed, and the wagon-train started north.

The morning had opened heavily with clouds, and, as the day advanced, the rain came down in torrents. A little before noon, our division, then under the command of General Ferrero, moved out of the woods ; but, instead of taking the road to Knoxville, as we had anticipated, the column marched down the Loudon road. We were to watch the enemy, and, by holding him in check, secure the safety of our trains and material, then on the way to Knoxville.

A few miles from Lenoir's, while we were halting for rest, General Burnside passed us on his way to the front. Under his slouched hat there was a sterner face than there was wont to be. There is trouble ahead, said the men ; but the cheers which rose from regiment after regiment, as with his staff and battleflag he swept past us, told the confidence which all felt in " Old Burnie."

Chapin's brigade of White's command (Twenty-third Army Corps) was in the advance ; and about four o'clock his skirmishers met those of the enemy, and drove them back a mile and a half. We followed through mud and rain. The country became hilly as we advanced, and our artillery was moved with difficulty. At dark we were in front of the enemy's position, having marched nearly fourteen miles. The rain had now ceased. Halting, we formed our lines in thick woods, and stacked our arms, — weary and wet, and not in the happiest of moods.

During the evening a circular was received, notifying us of an intended attack on the enemy's lines at nine o'clock, P. M., by the troops of White's command ; but, with the exception of an occasional shot, the night was a quiet one.

The next morning, the usual reveille was omitted ; and, at daybreak, noiselessly our lines were formed, and we marched out of the woods into the road. But it was not an advance. During the night General Ferrero had received orders to fall back to Lenoir's. Such, however, was the state of the roads, that it was almost impossible to move our artillery. At one time our whole regiment was detailed to assist Roemer's battery. Near Loudon we passed the Second Division of our corps, which during the night had moved down from Lenoir's, in order to be within supporting distance. But the enemy did not seem disposed to press us. We reached Lenoir's about noon. Sigfried, with the Second Division, followed later in the day. Our brigade (Morrison's) was now drawn up in line of battle on the Kingston road, as it was thought that the enemy, by not pressing our rear, intended a movement from that direction. And such was the fact. The enemy advanced against our position on this road, about four o'clock, and drove in our pickets. The Eighth Michigan was at once deployed as skirmishers. The Thirty-sixth Massachusetts and Forty-fifth Pennsylvania at the same time moved forward to support the skirmishers, and formed their line of battle in the woods, on the left of the road. Just at dusk, the enemy made a dash, and pressed our skirmishers back nearly to our line, but did not seem inclined to advance any further.

A portion of the Ninth Corps, under Colonel Hartranft, and a body of mounted infantry, were now sent towards Knoxville, with orders to seize and hold the junction of the road from Lenoir's with the Knoxville and Kingston road, near the village of Campbell's Station. The distance was only eight miles, but the progress of the column was much retarded. Such was still the condition of the roads that the artillery could be moved only with the greatest difficulty. Colonel Biddle dismounted some of his men, and hitched their horses to the guns. In order to lighten the caissons, some of the ammunition was removed from the boxes and destroyed; but as

little as possible, for who could say it would not be needed on the morrow? Throughout the long night, officers and men faltered not in their efforts to help forward the batteries. In the light of subsequent events, it will be seen that they could not have performed any more important service. Colonel Hartranft that night displayed the same spirit and energy which he infused into his gallant Pennsylvanians at Fort Steadman, in the last agonies of the Rebellion, when, rolling back the fiercest assaults of the enemy, he gained the first real success in the trenches at Petersburg, and won for himself the double star of a Major-General.

Meanwhile, Morrison's brigade remained on the Kingston road in front of Lenoir's. The enemy, anticipating an evacuation of the place, made an attack on our lines about ten o'clock, P. M.; but a few shots on our part were sufficient to satisfy him that we still held the ground. Additional pickets, however, were sent out to extend the line held by the Eighth Michigan. The Thirty-sixth Massachusetts and Forty-fifth Pennsylvania still remained in line of battle in the woods. Neither officers nor men slept that night. It was bitter cold, and the usual fires were denied us, lest they should betray our weakness to the enemy. The men were ordered to put their canteens and tin cups in their haversacks, and remain quietly in their places, ready for any movement at a moment's notice. It was a long, tedious, fearful night; what would the morrow bring? It was Sunday night. The day had brought us no rest, — only weariness and anxiety. No one could speak to his fellow; and in the thick darkness, through the long, long night, we lay on our arms, waiting for the morning. Ah, how many hearts there were among us, which, overleaping the boundaries of States, found their way to Pennsylvanian and New England homes, — how many, which, on the morrow, among the hills of East Tennessee, were to pour out their young blood even unto death!

At length the morning came. It was cloudy as the day before. White's division of the Twenty-third Corps was now on the road to Knoxville; and, besides our own brigade, only Humphrey's brigade of our division remained at Lenoir's. About daybreak, as silently as possible, we withdrew from our position on the Kingston road, and, falling back through the village of Lenoir's, moved towards Knoxville, Humphrey's brigade covering the retreat. Everything which we could not take with us was destroyed. Even our baggage and books, which, for the want of transportation, had not been removed, were committed to the flames. The enemy at once discovered our retreat, but did not press us till within a mile or two of the village of Campbell's Station. Humphrey, however, held him in check, and we moved on to the point where the road from Lenoir's unites with the road from Kingston to Knoxville. It was evidently Longstreet's intention to cut off our retreat at this place. For this reason he had not pressed us at Lenoir's, the afternoon previous, but had moved the main body of his army to our right. But the mounted infantry, which had been sent to this point during the night, were able to hold him in check, on the Kingston road, till Hartranft came up.

On reaching the junction of the roads, we advanced into an open field on our left, and at once formed our line of battle in rear of a rail fence, our right resting near the Kingston road. The Eighth Michigan was on our left. The Forty-fifth Pennsylvania was deployed as skirmishers. The rest of our troops were now withdrawing to a new position back of the village of Campbell's Station; and we were left to cover the movement. Unfurling our colors, we awaited the advance of the enemy. There was an occasional shot fired in our front, and to our right; but it was soon evident that the Rebels were moving to our left, in order to gain the cover of the woods. Moving off by the left flank, therefore, we took a second position in an adjoining field. Finding

now the enemy moving rapidly through the woods, and threatening our rear, we executed a left half-wheel; and, advancing on the double-quick to the rail fence which ran along the edge of the woods, we opened a heavy fire. From this position the enemy endeavored to force us. His fire was well directed, but the fence afforded us a slight protection. Lieutenant Fairbank and a few of the men were here wounded. For a while, we held the enemy in check, but at length the skirmishers of the Forty-fifth Pennsylvania, who were watching our right, discovered a body of Rebel infantry pushing towards our rear from the Kingston road. Colonel Morrison, our brigade commander, at once ordered the Thirty-sixth Massachusetts and Eighth Michigan to face about, and establish a new line, in rear of the rail fence on the opposite side of the field. We advanced on the double-quick; and, reaching the fence, our men with a shout poured a volley into the Rebel line of battle, which not only checked its advance, but drove it back in confusion. Meanwhile, the enemy in our rear moved up to the edge of the woods, which we had just left, and now opened a brisk fire. We at once crossed the fence in order to place it between us and his fire, and were about to devote our attention again to him, when orders came for us to withdraw, — it being no longer necessary to hold the junction of the roads, for all our troops and wagons had now passed. The enemy, too, was closing in upon us, and his fire was the hottest. We moved off in good order; but our loss in killed and wounded was quite heavy, considering the length of time we were under fire.

Among the killed was Lieutenant P. Marion Holmes of Charlestown, Mass., of whom it might well be said,

"He died as fathers wish their sons to die."

Lieutenant Holmes had been wounded at the battle of Blue Springs a little more than a month before, and had made the march from Lenoir's that morning with great difficulty. But he would not leave his men. On his breast he wore the badge of the Bunker Hill Club, on which was engraved the familiar line from Horace, which Warren quoted just before the battle of Bunker Hill, — " Dulce et decorum est pro patriâ mori." In the death of Lieutenant Holmes, the Thirty-sixth Massachusetts offered its costliest sacrifice. Frank, courteous, manly, brave, he had won all hearts, and his sudden removal from our companionship at that moment will ever remind us of the great price with which that morning's success was bought.

The enemy now manœuvred to cut us off from the road, and pressed us so hard that we were obliged to oblique to the left. Moving on the double-quick, receiving an occasional volley, and barely escaping capture, we at length emerged from the woods on the outskirts of the little village of Campbell's Station. We were soon under cover of our artillery, which General Potter, under the direction of General Burnside, had placed in position on high ground just beyond the village. This village is situated between two low ranges of hills, which are nearly a mile apart. Across the intervening space, our infantry was drawn up in a single line of battle. Ferrero's division of the Ninth Corps held the right, White's division of the Twenty-third Corps held the centre, and Hartranft's division of the Ninth Corps held the left. Benjamin's, Buckley's, Getting's, and Van Schlein's batteries were on the right of the road. Roemer's battery was on the left. The Thirty-sixth Massachusetts supported Roemer.

The enemy, meanwhile, had disposed his forces for an attack on our position. At noon he came out of the woods, just beyond the village, in two lines of battle, with a line of skirmishers in front. The whole field was open to our view. Benjamin and Roemer opened fire at once ; and so accurate was their range, that the Rebel lines were immediately broken, and they fell back into the woods in confusion. The enemy, under cover of the woods on the slope of the ridge, now advanced against our

right. Christ's brigade, of our division, at once changed front. Buckley executed the same movement with his battery, and, by a well-directed fire, checked the enemy's progress in that direction. The enemy next manœuvred to turn our left. Falling back, however, to a stronger position in our rear, we established a new line about four o'clock in the afternoon. This was done under a heavy fire from the enemy's batteries. Ferrero was now on the right of the road. Morrison's brigade was placed in rear of a rail fence, at the foot of the ridge on which Benjamin's battery had been planted. The enemy did not seem inclined to attack us in front, but pushed along the ridge, on our left, aiming to strike Hartranft in flank and rear. He was discovered in this attempt ; and, just as he was moving over ground recently cleared, Roemer, changing front at the same time with Hartranft, opened his three-inch guns on the Rebel line, and drove it back in disorder, followed by the skirmishers. Longstreet, foiled in all these attempts to force us from our position, now withdrew beyond the range of our guns, and made no further demonstrations that day. Our troops were justly proud of their success ; for, with a force not exceeding five thousand men, they had held in check, for an entire day, three times their own number, — the flower of Lee's army. Our loss in the Ninth Corps was twenty-six killed, one hundred and sixty-six wounded, and fifty-seven missing. Of these, the Thirty-sixth Massachusetts lost one officer and three enlisted men killed, three officers and fourteen enlisted men wounded, and three enlisted men missing.

At six o'clock, P. M., Ferrero's division, followed by Hartranft's, moved to the rear, taking the road to Knoxville. White's division of the Twenty-third Corps covered the retreat. Campbell's Station is a little more than sixteen miles from Knoxville ; but the night was so dark, and the road so muddy, that our progress was much retarded, and we did not reach Knoxville till about four o'clock the next morning. We had now been without sleep forty-eight hours. Moreover, since the previous morning we had marched twenty-four miles and fought a battle. Halting just outside of the town, weary and worn, we threw ourselves on the ground, and snatched a couple of hours of sleep. Early in the day — it was the 17th of November — General Burnside assigned the batteries and regiments of his command to the positions they were to occupy in the defence of the place. Knoxville is situated on the northern bank of the Holston River. For the most part, the town is built on a table-land, which is nearly a mile square, and about one hundred and fifty feet above the river. On the northeast, the town is bounded by a small creek. Beyond this creek is an elevation known as Temperance Hill. Still farther to the east is Mayberry's Hill. On the northwest, this table-land descends to a broad valley; on the southwest, the town is bounded by a second creek. Beyond this is College Hill; and still farther to the southwest is a high ridge, running nearly parallel with the road which enters Knoxville at this point. Benjamin's and Buckley's batteries occupied the unfinished bastion-work on the ridge just mentioned. This work was afterwards known as Fort Sanders. Roemer's battery was placed in position on College Hill. These batteries were supported by Ferrero's division of the Ninth Corps, his line extending from the Holston River on the left to the point where the East Tennessee and Georgia Railroad crosses the creek mentioned above as Second Creek. Hartranft connected with Ferrero's right, supporting Getting's and the Fifteenth Indiana Batteries. His lines extended as far as First Creek. The divisions of White and Hascall, of the Twenty-third Corps, occupied the ground between this point and the Holston River, on the northeast side of the town, with their artillery in position on Temperance and Mayberry's Hills. Knoxville at this time was by no means in a defensible condition. The bastion-work, occupied by Benjamin's

and Buckley's batteries, was not only not finished, but was little more than begun. It required two hundred negroes four hours to clear places for the guns. There was also a fort in process of construction on Temperance Hill. Nothing more had been done. But the work was now carried forward in earnest. As fast as the troops were placed in position, they commenced the construction of rifle-pits. Though wearied by three days of constant marching and fighting, they gave themselves to the work with all the energy of fresh men. Citizens and contrabands also were pressed into the service. Many of the former were loyal men, and devoted themselves to their tasks with a zeal which evinced the interest they felt in making good the defence of the town; but some of them were bitter Rebels, and, as Captain Poe, Chief-Engineer of the Army of the Ohio, well remarked, "worked with a very poor grace, which blistered hands did not tend to improve." The contrabands engaged in the work with that heartiness which, during the war, characterized their labors in our service.

At noon, the enemy's advance was only a mile or two distant; and four companies of the Thirty-sixth Massachusetts — A, B, D, G — were thrown out as skirmishers, — the line extending from the Holston River to the Kingston road. But the enemy was held in check at some little distance from the town by Sanders's division of cavalry. The hours thus gained for our work in the trenches were precious hours, indeed. There was a lack of intrenching tools, and much remained to be done; but all day and all night the men continued their labors undisturbed; and, on the morning of the 18th, our line of works around the town presented a formidable appearance.

Throughout the forenoon of that day there was heavy skirmishing on the Kingston road; but our men — dismounted cavalry — still maintained their position. Later in the day, however, the enemy brought up a battery, which, opening a heavy fire, soon compelled our men to fall back. The Rebels, now pressing forward, gained the ridge for which they had been contending, and established their lines within rifle range of our works.

It was while endeavoring to check this advance that General Sanders was mortally wounded. He was at once borne from the field, and carried into Knoxville. While a surgeon was examining the wound, he asked, "Tell me, Doctor, is my wound mortal?"

Tenderly the surgeon replied, "Sanders, it is a fearful wound, and mortal. I am sorry to say it, my dear fellow, but the odds are against you."

Calmly the General continued, "Well, I am not afraid to die. I have made up my mind upon that subject. I have done my duty, and have served my country as well as I could."

The next day he called the attention of the surgeon to certain symptoms which he had observed, and asked him what they meant.

The surgeon replied, "General, you are dying."

"If that be so," he said, "I would like to see a clergyman."

Rev. Mr. Hayden, chaplain of the post, was summoned. On his arrival, the dying soldier expressed a desire that the ordinance of baptism should be administered. This was done, and then the minister in prayer commended the believing soul to God, — General Burnside and his staff, who were present, kneeling around the bed. When the prayer was ended, General Sanders took General Burnside by the hand. Tears — the language of that heartfelt sympathy and tender love belonging to all noble souls — dropped down the bronzed cheeks of the chief as he listened to the last words which followed. The sacrament was now about to be administered, but suddenly the strength of the dying soldier failed, and like a child he gently fell asleep. "Greater love hath no man than this, that a man lay down his life for his friends."

The enemy did not seem inclined to attack our position at once, but proceeded to invest the town on the north bank of the Holston. He then commenced the construction of a line of works. The four companies of the Thirty-sixth Massachusetts which had been detailed for picket duty on the morning of the 17th, remained on post till the morning of the 19th. Thenceforward, throughout the siege, both officers and men were on picket duty every third day. During this twenty-four hours of duty no one slept. The rest of the time we were on duty in the trenches, where, during the siege, one third, and sometimes one fourth, of the men were kept awake. The utmost vigilance was enjoined upon all.

Meanwhile, day by day, and night by night, with unflagging zeal, the troops gave themselves to the labor of strengthening the works. Immediately in front of the rifle-pits, a *chevaux-de-frise* was constructed. This was formed of pointed stakes, thickly and firmly set in the ground, and inclining outwards at an angle of forty-five degrees. The stakes were bound together with wire, so that they could not easily be torn apart by an assaulting party. They were nearly five feet in height. In front of Colonel Haskins's position, on the north side of the town, the *chevaux-de-frise* was constructed with the two thousand pikes which were captured at Cumberland Gap early in the fall. A few rods in front of the *chevaux-de-frise* was the abatis, formed of thick branches of trees, which likewise were firmly set in the ground. Still farther to the front, were wire entanglements stretched a few inches above the ground, and fastened here and there to stakes and stumps. In front of a portion of our lines another obstacle was formed by constructing dams across First and Second Creeks, so called, and throwing back the water. The whole constituted a series of obstacles which could not be passed, in face of a heavy fire, without great difficulty and fearful loss.

Just in rear of the rifle-pits occupied by the Thirty-sixth Massachusetts was an elegant brick mansion, of recent construction, known as the Powell

House. When the siege commenced, fresco-painters were at work ornamenting its parlors and halls. Throwing open its doors, Mr. Powell, a true Union man, invited Colonel Morrison and Major Draper to make it their head-quarters. He also designated a chamber for the sick of our regiment. Early during the siege, the southwestern and northwestern fronts were loopholed by order of General Burnside, and instructions were given to post in the house, in case of an attack, two companies of the Thirty - sixth Massachusetts. When the order was announced to Mr. Powell, he nobly said, " Lay this house level with the ground, if it is necessary." A few feet from the southwestern front of the house, a small earthwork was thrown up by our men, in which was placed a section of Buckley's battery. This work was afterwards known as Battery Noble.

Morrison's brigade now held the line of defences from the Holston River — the extreme left of our line — to Fort Sanders. The following was the position of the several regiments of the brigade. The Forty-fifth Pennsylvania was on the left, its left on the river. On its right lay the Thirty-sixth Massachusetts. Then came the Eighth Michigan. The Seventy-ninth New York (Highlanders) formed the garrison of Fort Sanders. Between the Eighth Michigan and Fort Sanders was the One Hundredth Pennsylvania (Roundheads).

On the evening of the 20th, the Seventeenth Michigan made a sortie, and drove the Rebels from the Armstrong House. This stood on the Kingston road, and only a short distance from Fort Sanders. It was a brick house, and afforded a near and safe position for the enemy's sharpshooters, which of late had become somewhat annoying to the working parties at the fort. Our men destroyed the house, and then withdrew. The loss on our part was slight.

For a few days during the siege, four companies of the Thirty - sixth Massachusetts were detached to support Roemer's battery on College Hill. While on this duty the officers and men were quartered in the buildings of East Tennessee College. Prior to our occupation of East Tennessee, these buildings had been used by the Rebels as a hospital ; but, after a vigorous use of the ordinary means of purification, they afforded us pleasant and comfortable quarters.

The siege had now continued several days. The Rebels had constructed works offensive and defensive in our front ; but the greater part of their force seemed to have moved to the right. On the 22d of November, however, they returned, not having found evidently the weak place in our lines which they had sought. It was now thought they might attack our front that night ; and orders were given to the men on duty in the outer works to exercise the utmost vigilance. But the night passed quietly.

With each day our confidence in the strength of our position increased ; and we soon felt able to repel an assault from any quarter. But the question of supplies was a serious one. When the siege commenced, there was in the Commissary Department at Knoxville little more than a day's ration for the whole army. Should the enemy gain possession of the south bank of the Holston, our only means of subsistence would be cut off. Thus far his attempts in this direction had failed ; and the whole country, from the French Broad to the Holston, was open to our foraging parties. In this way a considerable quantity of corn and wheat was soon collected in Knoxville. Bread, made from a mixture of meal and flour, was issued to the men, but only in half and quarter rations. Occasionally a small quantity of fresh pork was also issued. Neither sugar nor coffee was issued after the first days of the siege.

The enemy, foiled in his attempts to seize the south bank of the Holston, now commenced the construction of a raft at Boyd's Ferry. Floating this down the swift current of the stream, he hoped to carry away our pontoon, and thus cut off our communication with the country beyond. To thwart this plan, an iron cable, one thousand feet in length, was stretched across the river above the bridge. This was done under the direction of Captain Poe. Afterwards, a boom of logs, fastened end to end by chains, was constructed still farther up the river. The boom was fifteen hundred feet in length.

On the evening of the 23d the Rebels made an attack on our pickets in front of the left of the Second Division, Ninth Corps. In falling back, our men fired the buildings on the ground abandoned, lest they should become a shelter for the enemy's sharpshooters. Among the buildings thus destroyed were the arsenal and machine-shops near the depot. The light of the blazing buildings illuminated the whole town. The next day the Twenty-first Massachusetts and another picked regiment, the whole under the command of Lieutenant-Colonel Hawkes of the Twenty-first, drove back the Rebels at this point, and reoccupied our old position.

The same day an attack was made by the Second Michigan on the advanced parallel, which the enemy had so constructed as to envelop the northwest bastion of Fort Sanders. The works were gallantly carried; but before the supporting columns could come up, our men were repulsed by fresh troops which the enemy had at hand.

On the 25th of November the enemy, having on the day previous crossed the Holston at a point below us, made another unsuccessful attempt to occupy the heights opposite Knoxville. He succeeded, however, in planting a battery on a knob about one hundred and fifty feet above the river, and twenty-five hundred yards south of Fort Sanders. This position commanded Fort Sanders, so that it now became necessary to defilade the fort.

November 26th was our national Thanksgiving day, and General Burnside issued an order, in which he expressed the hope that the day would be observed by all, as far as military operations would allow. He knew the rations were short, and that the day would be unlike the joyous festival we were wont to celebrate in our distant homes; and so he reminded us of the circumstances of trial under which our fathers first observed the day. He also reminded us of the debt of gratitude which we owed to Him who during the year had not only prospered our arms, but had kindly preserved our lives. Accordingly, we ate our corn bread with thanksgiving; and, forgetting our own privations, thought only of the loved ones at home, who, uncertain of our fate, would that day find little cheer at the table and by the fireside.

Allusion has already been made to the bastion-work known as Fort Sanders. A more particular description is now needed. The main line, held by our troops, made almost a right angle at the fort, the northwest bastion being the salient of the angle. The ground in front of the fort, from which the wood had been cleared, sloped gradually for a distance of eighty yards, and then abruptly descended to a wide ravine. Under the direction of Lieutenant Benjamin, Second United States Artillery, and Chief of Artillery of the Army of the Ohio, the fort had now been made as strong as the means at his disposal and the rules of military art admitted. Eighty and thirty yards in front of the fort, rifle-pits were constructed. These were to be used in case our men were driven in from the outer line. Between these pits and the Fort were wire entanglements, running from stump to stump, and also an abatis. Sand-bags and barrels were arranged so as to cover the embrasures. Traverses, also, were built for the protection of the men at the guns, and in passing from one position to another. In the fort were four twenty-pounder Parrotts (Benjamin's battery), four light twelve-pounders (of Buckley's battery), and two three-inch guns.

Early in the evening of the 27th there was much cheering along the Rebel lines. Their bands, too, were unusually lavish of the Rebel airs they were wont occasionally to waft across the debatable ground which separated our lines. Had the enemy received reinforcements, or had Grant met with a reverse? While on picket that night, in making my rounds, I could distinctly hear the Rebels chopping on the knob which they had so recently occupied on the opposite bank of the river. They were clearing away the trees in front of the earthwork which they had constructed the day before. Would they attack at daybreak? So we thought, connecting this fact with the cheers and music of the earlier part of the night; but the morning opened as quietly as its predecessors. Late in the afternoon the enemy seemed to be placing his troops in position in our front, and our men stood in the trenches, awaiting an attack; yet the day wore away without further demonstrations.

A little after eleven o'clock, P. M., November 28th, I was aroused by heavy musketry. I hurried to the trenches. It was a cloudy, dark night, and at a distance of only a few feet it was impossible to distinguish any object. The men were already at their posts. With the exception of an occasional shot on the picket-line, the firing soon ceased. An attack had evidently been made on our pickets; but at what point, or with what success, was as yet unknown. Reports soon came in. The enemy had first driven in the pickets in front of Fort Sanders, and had then attacked *our* line, which was also obliged to fall back. The Rebels in our front, however, did not advance beyond the pits which our men had just vacated, and a new line was at once established by Captain Buffum, our brigade officer of the day.

It was now evident that the enemy intended an attack. But where would it be made? All that long, cold night — our men were without overcoats — we stood in the trenches pondering that question. Might not this demonstration in our front be only a feint to draw our attention from other parts of the line, where the chief blow was to be struck? So some thought. Gradually the night wore away.

A little after six o'clock the next morning, the enemy suddenly opened a furious cannonade. This was mostly directed against Fort Sanders; but several shots struck the Powell House, in rear of Battery Noble. Roemer immediately responded from College Hill. In about twenty minutes the enemy's fire slackened, and in its stead rose the well-known Rebel yell, in the direction of the fort. Then followed the rattle of musketry, the roar of cannon, and the bursting of shells. The yells died away, and then rose again. Now the roar of musketry and artillery was redoubled. It was a moment of the deepest anxiety. Our straining eyes were fixed on the fort. The Rebels had reached the ditch and were now endeavoring to scale the parapet. Whose will be the victory, — O, whose? The yells again died away, and then followed three loud Union cheers, — "Hurrah, hurrah, hurrah!" How those cheers thrilled our hearts, as we stood almost breathless at our posts in the trenches! They told us that the enemy had been repulsed, and that the victory was ours. Peering through the rising fog towards the fort, not a hundred yards away, — O glorious sight! — we dimly saw that our flag was still there.

Let us now go back a little. Under cover of the ridge on which Fort Sanders was built, Longstreet had formed his columns for the assault. The men were picked men, — the flower of his army. One brigade was to make the assault, two brigades were to support it,[*] and two other brigades were to

---

[*] This statement is confirmed by the following extract from Pollard's (Rebel) "Third Year of the War." Speaking of this charge on Fort Sanders, he says: "The force which was to attempt an enterprise which ranks with the most famous charges in military history should be mentioned in detail. It consisted of three brigades of McLaw's division: — that of General Wolford, the Sixteenth, Eighteenth, and Twenty-fourth Georgia Regiments, and Cobb's and Phillip's Georgia Legions; that of General Humphrey, the Thirteenth, Seventeenth, Twenty-first, Twenty-second, and Twenty-third Mississippi Regiments; and a brigade composed of General Anderson's and Bryant's brigades, embracing, among others, the Palmetto State Guard, the Fif-

watch our lines and keep up a constant fire. Five regiments formed the brigade selected for the assaulting column. These were placed in position not more than eighty yards from the fort. They were "in column by division, closed in mass." When the fire of their artillery slackened, the order for the charge was given. The salient of the northwest bastion was the point of attack. The Rebel lines were much broken in passing the abatis. But the wire entanglements proved a greater obstacle. Whole companies were prostrated. Benjamin now opened his triple-shotted guns. Nevertheless, the weight of their column carried the Rebels forward, and in two minutes from the time the charge was commenced they had filled the ditch around the fort, and were endeavoring to scale the parapet. The guns, which had been trained to sweep the ditch, now opened a most destructive fire. Lieutenant Benjamin also took shells in his hand, and, lighting the fuse, tossed them over the parapet into the crowded ditch. One of the Rebel brigades in reserve now came up in support, and planted several of its flags on the parapet of the fort. Those, however, who endeavored to scale the parapet were swept away by the fire of our musketry. The men in the ditch, satisfied of the hopelessness of the task they had undertaken, now surrendered. They represented eleven regiments. The prisoners numbered nearly three hundred. Among them were seventeen commissioned officers. Over two hundred dead and wounded, including three colonels, lay in the ditch alone. The ground in front of the fort was also strewn with the bodies of the dead and wounded. Over one thousand stands of arms fell into our hands, and the battle-flags of the Thirteenth and Seventeenth Mississippi and Sixteenth Georgia. Our loss was eight men killed and five wounded. Never was a victory more complete ; and never were brighter laurels worn than were that

teenth South Carolina Regiment, and the Fifty-first, Fifty-third, and Fifty-ninth Georgia Regiments." — pp. 161, 162.

morning laid on the brow of the hero of Fort Sanders, — Lieutenant Benjamin, Second United States Artillery.

Longstreet had promised his men that they should dine that day in Knoxville. But, in order that he might bury his dead, General Burnside now tendered him an armistice till five o'clock, P. M. It was accepted by the Rebel general ; and our ambulances were furnished him to assist in removing the bodies to his lines. At five o'clock, two additional hours were asked, as the work was not yet completed. At seven o'clock, a gun was fired from Fort Sanders, the Rebels responded from an earthwork opposite, and the truce was at an end.

The next day, through a courier who had succeeded in reaching our lines, General Burnside received official notice of the defeat of Bragg. At noon, a single gun — we were short of ammunition — was fired from Battery Noble in our rear, and the men of the brigade, standing in the trenches, gave three cheers for Grant's victory at Chattanooga. We now looked for reinforcements daily, for Sherman was already on the road. The enemy knew this as well as we, and, during the night of the 4th of December, withdrew his forces, and started north. The retreat was discovered by the pickets of the Thirty-sixth Massachusetts, under Captain Ames, who had the honor of first declaring the siege of Knoxville raised.

It would be interesting to recount the facts connected with the retreat of the Rebel army, and then to follow our men to their winter quarters, among the mountains of East Tennessee, where, throughout the icy season, they remained, without shoes, without overcoats, without new clothing of any description, living on quarter rations of corn meal, with occasionally a handful of flour, and never grumbling ; and where, at the expiration of their three years of service, standing forth under the open skies, amid all these discomforts, and raising loyal hands towards heaven, they swore to serve their country yet three years longer. But I must pause. I have already illustrated their fortitude and heroic endurance.

The noble bearing of General Burnside throughout the siege won the admiration of all. In a speech at Cincinnati, a few days after the siege was raised, with that modesty which characterizes the true soldier, he said that the honors bestowed on him belonged to his under officers and the men in the ranks. These kindly words his officers and men will ever cherish; and in all their added years, as they recall the widely separated battle-fields, made forever sacred by the blood of their fallen comrades, and forever glorious by the victories there won, it will be their pride to say, "We fought with Burnside at Campbell's Station and in the trenches at Knoxville."

RELEASED.

A LITTLE low-ceiled room. Four walls
    Whose blank shut out all else of life,
And crowded close within their bound
    A world of pain, and toil, and strife.

Her world. Scarce furthermore she knew
    Of God's great globe, that wondrously
Outrolls a glory of green earth,
    And frames it with the restless sea.

Four closer walls of common pine:
    And therein lieth, cold and still,
The weary flesh that long hath borne
    Its patient mystery of ill.

Regardless now of work to do;
    No queen more careless in her state;
Hands crossed in their unbroken calm;
    For other hands the work may wait.

Put by her implements of toil;
    Put by each coarse, intrusive sign;
She made a Sabbath when she died,
    And round her breathes a Rest Divine.

Put by, at last, beneath the lid,
    The exempted hands, the tranquil face;
Uplift her in her dreamless sleep,
    And bear her gently from the place.

Oft she hath gazed, with wistful eyes,
    Out from that threshold on the night;
The narrow bourn she crosseth now;
    She standeth in the Eternal Light.

Oft she hath pressed, with aching feet,
    Those broken steps that reach the door;
Henceforth with angels she shall tread
    Heaven's golden stair forevermore!

FRIEDRICH RÜCKERT.

THE last of the grand old generation of German poets is dead.
Within ten years Eichendorff, Heine,
Uhland, have passed away; and now the
death of Friedrich Rückert, the sole sur-
vivor of the minor gods who inhabited
the higher slopes of the Weimar Olym-
pus, closes the list of their names. Yet,
although with these poets in time, Rückert was not of them in the structure of
his mind or the character of his poetical
development. No author ever stood so
lonely among his contemporaries. Looking over the long catalogue, not only
of German, but of European poets, we
find no one with whom he can be compared. His birthplace is supposed to
be Schweinfurt, but it is to be sought,
in reality, somewhere on the banks of
the Euphrates. His true contemporaries were Saadi and Hariri of Bosrah.

Rückert's biography may be given in
a few words, his life having been singularly devoid of incident. He seems even
to have been spared the usual alterna-
tions of fortune in a material, as well as
a literary sense. With the exception of
a somewhat acridly hostile criticism,
which the *Jahrbücher* of Halle dealt out
to him for several years in succession,
his reputation has enjoyed a gradual and
steady growth since his first appearance
as a poet. His place is now so well
defined that death — which sometimes
changes, while it fixes, the impression
an author makes upon his generation —
cannot seriously elevate or depress it.
In life he stood so far aloof from the
fashions of the day, that all his successes were permanent achievements.

He was born on the 16th of May,
1788, in Schweinfurt, a pleasant old
town in Bavaria, near the baths of Kissingen. As a student he visited Jena,
where he distinguished himself by his
devotion to philological and literary
studies. For some years a private
tutor, in 1815 he became connected
with the *Morgenblatt*, published by
Cotta, in Stuttgart. The year 1818 he

spent in Italy. Soon after his return,
he married, and established himself in
Coburg, of which place, I believe, his
wife was a native. Here he occupied
himself ostensibly as a teacher, but in
reality with an enthusiastic and untiring study of the Oriental languages
and literature. Twice he was called
away by appointments which were the
result of his growing fame as poet and
scholar, — the first time in 1826, when
he was made Professor of the Oriental
Languages at the University of Erlangen; and again in 1840, when he
was appointed to a similar place in the
University of Berlin, with the title of
Privy Councillor. Both these posts
were uncongenial to his nature. Though
so competent to fill them, he discharged
his duties reluctantly and with a certain impatience; and probably there
were few more joyous moments of his
life than when, in 1849, he was allowed
to retire permanently to the pastoral
seclusion of his little property at Neuses, a suburb of Coburg.

One of his German critics remarks
that the poem in which he celebrates
his release embodies a nearer approach
to passion than all his Oriental songs
of love, sorrow, or wine. It is a joyous
dithyrambic, which, despite its artful
and semi-impossible metre, must have
been the swiftly-worded expression of a
genuine feeling. Let me attempt to
translate the first stanza: —

> " Out of the dust of the
>   Town o' the king,
>   Into the lust of the
>   Green of spring, —
>   Forth from the noises of
>   Streets and walls,
>   Unto the voices of
>   Waterfalls, —
>   He who presently
>   Flies is blest :
>   Fate thus pleasantly
>   Makes my nest ! " [*]

[*] The reader may be curious to see how smoothly
and naturally these dactyls (so forced in the translation) flow in the original : —

> " Aus der staubigen
>   Residenz,

The quaint old residence at Neuses thus early became, and for nearly half a century continued to be, the poet's home. No desire to visit the Orient — the native land of his brain — seems to have disturbed him. Possibly the Italian journey was in some respects disenchanting. The few poems which date from it are picturesque and descriptive, but do not indicate that his imagination was warmed by what he saw. He was never so happy as when alone with his books and manuscripts, studying or writing, according to the dominant mood. This secluded habit engendered a shyness of manner, which frequently repelled the strangers who came to see him, — especially those who failed to detect the simple, tender, genial nature of the man, under his wonderful load of learning. But there was nothing morbid or misanthropical in his composition ; his shyness was rather the result of an intense devotion to his studies. These gradually became a necessity of his daily life ; his health, his mental peace, depended upon them ; and whatever disturbed their regular recurrence took from him more than the mere time lost.

When I first visited Coburg, in October, 1852, I was very anxious to make Rückert's acquaintance. My interest in Oriental literature had been refreshed, at that time, by nearly ten months of travel in Eastern lands, and some knowledge of modern colloquial Arabic. I had read his wonderful translation of the *Makamât* of Hariri, and felt sure that he would share in my enthusiasm for the people to whose treasures of song he had given so many years of his life. I found, however, that very few families in the town were familiarly acquainted with the poet, — that many persons, even, who had been residents

In den laubigen
Frischen Lenz —
Aus dem tosenden
Gassenschwall
Zu dem kosenden
Wasserfall, —
Wer sich rettete,
Dank 's dem Glück,
Wie mich bettete
Mein Geschick ! "

of the place for years, had never seen him. He was presumed to be inaccessible to strangers.

It fortunately happened that one of my friends knew a student of the Oriental languages, then residing in Coburg. The latter, who was in the habit of consulting Rückert in regard to his Sanskrit studies, offered at once to conduct me to Neuses. A walk of twenty minutes across the meadows of the Itz, along the base of the wooded hills which terminate, just beyond, in the castled Kallenberg (the summer residence of Duke Ernest II.), brought us to the little village, which lies so snugly hidden in its own orchards that one might almost pass without discovering it. The afternoon was warm and sunny, and a hazy, idyllic atmosphere veiled and threw into remoteness the bolder features of the landscape. Near at hand, a few quaint old tile-roofed houses rose above the trees.

My guide left the highway, crossed a clear little brook on the left, and entered the bottom of a garden behind the largest of these houses. As we were making our way between the plum-trees and gooseberry-bushes, I perceived a tall figure standing in the midst of a great bed of late-blossoming roses, over which he was bending as if to inhale their fragrance. The sound of our steps startled him ; and as he straightened himself and faced us, I saw that it could be none other than Rückert. I believe his first impulse was to fly ; but we were already so near that his moment of indecision settled the matter. The student presented me to him as an American traveller, whereat I thought he seemed to experience a little relief. Nevertheless, he looked uneasily at his coat, — a sort of loose, commodious blouse, — at his hands, full of seeds, and muttered some incoherent words about flowers. Suddenly, lifting his head and looking steadily at us, he said, " Come into the house ! "

The student, who was familiar with his habits, led me to a pleasant room on the second floor. The windows looked towards the sun, and were filled with hot-house plants. We were scarcely seated before Rückert made his appearance, having laid aside his blouse, and put on a coat. After a moment of hesitation, he asked me, "Where have you been travelling?" "I come from the Orient," I answered. He looked up with a keen light in his eyes. "From the Orient!" he exclaimed. "Where? let me know where you have been, and what you have seen!" From that moment he was self-possessed, full of life, enthusiasm, fancy, and humor.

He was then in his sixty-fifth year, but still enjoyed the ripe maturity of his powers. A man of more striking personal appearance I have seldom seen. Over six feet in height, and somewhat gaunt of body, the first impression of an absence of physical grace vanished as soon as one looked upon his countenance. His face was long, and every feature strongly marked, — the brow high and massive, the nose strong and slightly aquiline, the mouth wide and firm, and the jaw broad, square, and projecting. His thick silver hair, parted in the middle of his forehead, fell in wavy masses upon his shoulders. His eyes were deep-set, bluish-gray, and burned with a deep, lustrous fire as he became animated in conversation. At times they had a mystic, rapt expression, as if the far East, of which he spoke, were actually visible to his brain. I thought of an Arab sheikh, looking towards Mecca, at the hour of prayer.

I regret that I made no notes of the conversation, in which, as may be guessed, I took but little part. It was rather a monologue on the subject of Arabic poetry, full of the clearest and richest knowledge, and sparkling with those evanescent felicities of diction which can so rarely be recalled. I was charmed out of all sense of time, and was astonished to find, when tea appeared, that more than two hours had elapsed. The student had magnanimously left me to the poet, devoting himself to the good Frau Rückert, the "Luise" of her husband's *Liebesfrühling* (Spring-time of Love). She still, although now a grand-

mother, retained some traces of the fresh, rosy beauty of her younger days; and it was pleasant to see the watchful, tender interest upon her face, whenever she turned towards the poet. Before I left, she whispered to me, "I am always very glad when my husband has an opportunity to talk about the Orient: nothing refreshes him so much."

But we must not lose sight of Rückert's poetical biography. His first volume, entitled "German Poems, by Freimund Raimar," was published at Heidelberg in the year 1814. It contained, among other things, his famous *Geharnischte Sonette* (Sonnets in Armor), which are still read and admired as masterpieces of that form of verse. Preserving the Petrarchan model, even to the feminine rhymes of the Italian tongue, he has nevertheless succeeded in concealing the extraordinary art by which the difficult task was accomplished. Thus early the German language acquired its unsuspected power of flexibility in his hands. It is very evident to me that his peculiar characteristics as a poet sprang not so much from his Oriental studies as from a rare native faculty of mind.

These "Sonnets in Armor," although they may sound but gravely beside the Tyrtæan strains of Arndt and Körner, are nevertheless full of stately and inspiring music. They remind one of Wordsworth's phrase, —

"In Milton's hand,
The thing became a trumpet," —

and must have had their share in stimulating that national sentiment which overturned the Napoleonic rule, and for three or four years flourished so greenly upon its ruins.

Shortly afterwards, Rückert published "Napoleon, a Political Comedy," which did not increase his fame. His next important contribution to general literature was the "Oriental Roses," which appeared in 1822. Three years before, Goethe had published his *Westöstlicher Divan*, and the younger poet dedicated his first venture in the same field to his venerable predecessor, in stanzas which express the most delicate, and at the same time the most generous homage. I scarcely know where to look for a more graceful dedication in verse. It is said that Goethe never acknowledged the compliment, — an omission which some German authors attribute to the latter's distaste at being surpassed on his latest and (at that time) favorite field. No one familiar with Goethe's life and works will accept this conjecture.

It is quite impossible to translate this poem literally, in the original metre: the rhymes are exclusively feminine. I am aware that I shall shock ears familiar with the original by substituting masculine rhymes in the two stanzas which I present; but there is really no alternative.

> " Would you taste
> Purest East,
> Hence depart, and seek the selfsame man
> Who our West
> Gave the best
> Wine that ever flowed from Poet's can :
> When the Western flavors ended,
> He the Orient's vintage spended, —
> Yonder dreams he on his own divan !

> " Sunset-red •
> Goethe led
> Star to be of all the sunset-land :
> Now the higher
> Morning-fire
> Makes him lord of all the morning-land !
> Where the two, together turning,
> Meet, the rounded heaven is burning
> Rosy-bright in one celestial brand ! "

I have not the original edition of the " Oriental Roses," but I believe the volume contained the greater portion of Rückert's marvellous " Ghazels." Count Platen, it is true, had preceded him by one year, but his adaptation of the Persian metre to German poetry — light and graceful and melodious as he succeeded in making it — falls far short of Rückert's infinite richness and skill. One of the latter's " Ghazels " contains twenty-six variations of the same rhyme; yet so subtly managed, so colored with the finest reflected tints of Eastern rhetoric and fancy, that the immense art implied in its construction is nowhere unpleasantly apparent. In fact, one dare not say that these poems are *all* art. In the Oriental measures the poet found the garment which best fitted his own

mind. We are not to infer that he did not move joyously, and, after a time, easily, within the limitations which, to most authors, would have been intolerable fetters.

In 1826 appeared his translation of the *Makamât* of Hariri. The old silk-merchant of Bosrah never could have anticipated such an immortality. The word *Makamât* means " sessions," (probably the Italian *conversazione* best translates it,) but is applied to a series of short narratives, or rather anecdotes, told alternately in verse and rhymed prose, with all the brilliance of rhetoric, the richness of alliteration, antithesis, and imitative sound, and the endless grammatical subtilties of which the Arabic language is capable. The work of Hariri is considered the unapproachable model of this style of narrative throughout all the East. Rückert called his translation " The Metamorphoses of Abou-Seyd of Serudj," — the name of the hero of the story. In this work he has shown the capacity of one language to reproduce the very spirit of another with which it has the least affinity. Like the original, the translation can never be surpassed: it is unique in literature.

As the acrobat who has mastered every branch of his art, from the spidery contortions of the India-rubber man to the double somersault and the flying trapeze, is to the well-developed individual of ordinary muscular habits, so is the language of Rückert in this work to the language of all other German authors. It is one perpetual gymnastic show of grammar, rhythm, and fancy. Moods, tenses, antecedents, appositions, whirl and flash around you, to the sound of some strange, barbaric music. Closer and more rapidly they link, chassez, and " cross hands," until, when you anticipate a hopeless tangle, some bold, bright word leaps unexpectedly into the throng, and resolves it to instant harmony. One's breath is taken away, and his brain made dizzy, by any half-dozen of the " Metamorphoses." In this respect the translation has become a representative work. The Arabic title, misunderstood, has given birth to a German word. Daring and difficult rhymes are now frequently termed *Makamen* in German literary society.

Rückert's studies were not confined to the Arabic and Persian languages; he also devoted many years to the Sanskrit. In 1828 appeared his translation of " Nal and Damayanti," and some years later, " Hamasa, or the oldest Arabian Poetry," and " Amrilkaïs, Poet and King." In addition to these translations, he published, between the years 1835 and 1840, the following original poems, or collections of poems, on Oriental themes, — " Legends of the Morning-Land " (2 vols.), " Rustem and Sohrab," and " Brahminical Stories." These poems are so bathed in the atmosphere of his studies, that it is very difficult to say which are his own independent conceptions, and which the suggestions of Eastern poets. Where he has borrowed images or phrases, (as sometimes from the Koran,) they are woven, without any discernible seam, into the texture of his own brain.

Some of Rückert's critics have asserted that his extraordinary mastery of all the resources of language operated to the detriment of his poetical faculty, — that the feeling to be expressed became subordinate to the skill displayed by expressing it in an unusual form. They claim, moreover, that he produced a mass of sparkling fragments, rather than any single great work. I am convinced, however, that the first charge is unfounded, basing my opinion upon my knowledge of the poet's simple, true, tender nature, which I learned to appreciate during my later visits to his home. After the death of his wife, the daughter who thereafter assumed her mother's place in the household wrote me frequent accounts of her father's grief and loneliness, enclosing manuscript copies of the poems in which he expressed his sorrow. These poems are exceedingly sweet and touching; yet they are all marked by the same flexile use of difficult rhythms and unprecedented rhymes. They have never yet been published, and I am there-

fore withheld from translating any one of them, in illustration.

Few of Goethe's minor songs are more beautiful than his serenade, *O gib' vom weichen Pfühle*, where the interlinked repetitions are a perpetual surprise and charm; yet Rückert has written a score of more artfully constructed and equally melodious songs. His collection of amatory poems entitled *Liebesfrühling* contains some of the sunniest idyls in any language. That his genius was lyrical and not epic, was not a fault; that it delighted in varied and unusual metres, was an exceptional — perhaps in his case a phenomenal — form of development; but I do not think it was any the less instinctively natural. One of his quatrains runs : —

> " Much I make as make the others ;
> Better much another man
> Makes than I ; but much, moreover,
> Make I which no other can."

His poetical comment on the translation of Hariri is given in prose : — " He who, like myself, unfortunate man ! is philologist and poet in the same person, cannot do better than to translate as I do. My Hariri has illustrated how philology and poetry are competent to stimulate and to complete each other. If thou, reader, wilt look upon this hybrid production neither too philologically nor over-poetically, it may delight and instruct thee. That which is false in philology thou wilt attribute to poetic license, and where the poetry is deficient, thou wilt give the blame to philology."

The critics who charge Rückert with never having produced " a whole," have certainly forgotten one of his works, — " The Wisdom of the Brahmin, a Didactic Poem, in Fragments." The title somewhat describes its character. The " fragments " are couplets, in iambic hexameter, each one generally complete in itself, yet grouped in sections by some connecting thought, after the manner of the stanzas of Tennyson's " In Memoriam." There are more than *six thousand* couplets, in all, divided into twenty books, — the whole forming a mass of poetic wisdom, coupled with such amazing wealth of illustration, that this one volume, if sufficiently diluted, would make several thousand " Proverbial Philosophies." It is not a book to read continuously, but one which, I should imagine, no educated German could live without possessing. I never open its pages without the certainty of refreshment. Its tone is quietistic, as might readily be conjectured, but it is the calm of serene reflection, not of indifference. No work which Rückert ever wrote so strongly illustrates the incessant activity of his mind. Half of these six thousand couplets are terse and pithy enough for proverbs, and their construction would have sufficed for the lifetime of many poets.

With the exception of " Kaiser Barbarossa," and two or three other ballads, the amatory poems of Rückert have attained the widest popularity among his countrymen. Many of the love-songs have been set to music by Mendelssohn and other composers. Their melody is of that subtle, delicate quality which excites a musician's fancy, suggesting the tones to which the words should be wedded. Precisely for this reason they are most difficult to translate. The first stanza may, in most cases, be tolerably reproduced ; but as it usually contains a refrain, which is repeated to a constantly varied rhyme, throughout the whole song or poem, the labor at first becomes desperate, and then impossible. An example (the original of which I possess, in the author's manuscript) will best illustrate this particular difficulty. Here the metre and the order of rhyme have been strictly preserved, except in the first and third lines.

> " He came to meet me
> In rain and thunder :
> My heart 'gan beating
> In timid wonder :
> Could I guess whether
> Thenceforth together
> Our paths should run, so long asunder ?

> " He came to meet me
> In rain and thunder,
> With guile to cheat me, —
> My heart to plunder.

> Was 't mine he captured ?
> Or his I raptured ?
> Half-way both met, in bliss and wonder !

> " He came to meet me
> In rain and thunder :
> Spring-blessings greet me
> Spring-blossoms under.
> What though he leave me ?
> No partings grieve me, —
> No path can lead our hearts asunder ! "

The Irish poet, James Clarence Mangan, (whose translations from the German comprise both the best and the worst specimens I have yet found,) has been successful in rendering one of Rückert's ghazels. I am specially tempted to quote it, on account of the curious general resemblance (accidental, no doubt) which Poe's " Lenore " bears to it.

> " I saw her once, a little while, and then no more :
> 'T was Eden's light on earth awhile, and then no more.
> Amid the throng she passed along the meadow-floor ;
> Spring seemed to smile on earth awhile, and then no more,
> But whence she came, which way she went, what garb she wore,
> I noted not ; I gazed awhile, and then no more.

> " I saw her once, a little while, and then no more :
> 'T was Paradise on earth awhile, and then no more.
> Ah ! what avail my vigils pale, my magic lore ?
> She shone before mine eyes awhile, and then no more.
> The shallop of my peace is wrecked on Beauty's shore ;
> Near Hope's fair isle it rode awhile, and then no more.

> " I saw her once, a little while, and then no more :
> Earth looked like Heaven a little while, and then no more.
> Her presence thrilled and lighted to its inmost core
> My desert breast a little while, and then no more.
> So may, perchance, a meteor glance at midnight o'er
> Some ruined pile a little while, and then no more.

> " I saw her once, a little while, and then no more :
> The earth was Eden-land awhile, and then no more.
> O, might I see but once again, as once before,
> Through chance or wile, that shape awhile, and then no more !
> Death soon would heal my grief : this heart, now sad and sore,
> Would beat anew, a little while, and then no more ! "

Here, nevertheless, something is sacrificed. The translation is by no means literal, and lacks the crispness and freshness of Oriental antithesis. Rückert, I fear, will never be as fortunate as Hariri of Bosrah.

When, in 1856, I again visited Germany, I received a friendly message from the old poet, with a kind invitation to visit him. Late in November I found him, apparently unchanged in body and spirit, — simple, enthusiastic, and, in spite of his seclusion, awake to all the movements of the world. One of his married sons was then visiting him, so that the household was larger and livelier than usual ; but, as he sat, during the evening, in his favorite arm-chair, with pipe and beer, he fell into the same brilliant, wise strain of talk, undisturbed by all the cheerful young voices around him.

The conversation gradually wandered away from the Orient to the modern languages of Europe. I remarked the special capacity of the German for descriptions of forest scenery, — of the feeling and sentiment of deep, dark woods, and woodland solitudes.

" May not that be," said he, " because the race lived for centuries in forests ? A language is always richest in its epithets for those things with which the people who speak it are most familiar. Look at the many terms for ' horse ' and ' sword ' in Arabic."

" But the old Britons lived also in forests," I suggested.

" I suspect," he answered, " while the English language was taking shape, the people knew quite as much of the sea as of the woods. You ought, therefore, to surpass us in describing coast and sea-scenery, winds and storms, and the motion of waves."

The idea had not occurred to me before, but I found it to be correct.

Though not speaking English, Rückert had a thorough critical knowledge of the language, and a great admiration of its qualities. He admitted that its chances for becoming the dominant tongue of the world were greater than those of any other. Much that he said upon this subject interested me greatly at the time, but the substance of it has escaped me.

When I left, that evening, I looked upon his cheerful, faithful wife for the last time. Five years elapsed before I visited Coburg again, and she died in the interval. In the summer of 1861 I had an hour's conversation with him, chiefly on American affairs, in which he expressed the keenest interest. He had read much, and had a very correct understanding of the nature of the struggle. He was buried in his studies, in a small house outside of the village, where he spent half of every day alone, and inaccessible to every one ; but his youngest daughter ventured to summon him away from his books.

Two years later (in June, 1863) I paid my last visit to Neuses. He had then passed his seventy-fifth birthday ; his frame was still unbent, but the waves of gray hair on his shoulders were thinner, and his step showed the increasing feebleness of age. The fire of his eye was softened, not dimmed, and the long and happy life that lay behind him had given his face a peaceful, serene expression, prophetic of a gentle translation into the other life that was drawing near. So I shall always remember him, — scholar and poet, strong with the best strength of a man, yet trustful and accessible to joy as a child.

Notwithstanding the great amount of Rückert's contributions to literature during his life, he has left behind him a mass of poems and philological papers (the latter said to be of great interest and value) which his accomplished son, Professor Rückert of the University of Breslau, is now preparing for publication.

PASSAGES FROM HAWTHORNE'S NOTE-BOOKS.

VII.

CONCORD, *August* 5, 1842. — A rainy day, — a rainy day. I am commanded to take pen in hand, and I am therefore banished to the little ten-foot-square apartment misnamed my study; but perhaps the dismalness of the day and the dulness of my solitude will be the prominent characteristics of what I write. And what is there to write about? Happiness has no succession of events, because it is a part of eternity; and we have been living in eternity ever since we came to this old manse. Like Enoch, we seem to have been translated to the other state of being, without having passed through death. Our spirits must have flitted away unconsciously, and we can only perceive that we have cast off our mortal part by the more real and earnest life of our souls. Externally, our Paradise has very much the aspect of a pleasant old domicile on earth. This antique house — for it looks antique, though it was created by Providence expressly for our use, and at the precise time when we wanted it — stands behind a noble avenue of balm-of-Gilead trees; and when we chance to observe a passing traveller through the sunshine and the shadow of this long avenue, his figure appears too dim and remote to disturb the sense of blissful seclusion. Few, indeed, are the mortals who venture within our sacred precincts. George Prescott, who has not yet grown earthly enough, I suppose, to be debarred from occasional visits to Paradise, comes daily to bring three pints of milk from some ambrosial cow; occasionally, also, he makes an offering of mortal flowers. Mr. Emerson comes sometimes, and has been feasted on our nectar and ambrosia. Mr. Thoreau has twice listened to the music of the spheres, which, for our private convenience, we have packed into a musical box. E—— H——, who is much more at home among spirits than among fleshly bodies, came hither a few times, merely to welcome us to the ethereal world; but latterly she has vanished into some other region of infinite space. One rash mortal, on the second Sunday after our arrival, obtruded himself upon us in a gig. There have since been three or four callers, who preposterously think that the courtesies of the lower world are to be responded to by people whose home is in Paradise. I must not forget to mention that the butcher comes twice or thrice a week; and we have so far improved upon the custom of Adam and Eve, that we generally furnish forth our feasts with portions of some delicate calf or lamb, whose unspotted innocence entitles them to the happiness of becoming our sustenance. Would that I were permitted to record the celestial dainties that kind Heaven provided for us on the first day of our arrival! Never, surely, was such food heard of on earth, — at least, not by me. Well, the above-mentioned persons are nearly all that have entered into the hallowed shade of our avenue; except, indeed, a certain sinner who came to bargain for the grass in our orchard, and another who came with a new cistern. For it is one of the drawbacks upon our Eden that it contains no water fit either to drink or to bathe in; so that the showers have become, in good truth, a godsend. I wonder why Providence does not cause a clear, cold fountain to bubble up at our doorstep; methinks it would not be unreasonable to pray for such a favor. At present we are under the ridiculous necessity of sending to the outer world for water. Only imagine Adam trudging out of Paradise with a bucket in each hand, to get water to drink, or for Eve to bathe in! Intolerable! (though our stout handmaiden really fetches our water). In other respects Providence has treated us pretty tolerably well; but here I shall expect something further to be done. Also, in the way of future favors, a kitten would be very acceptable. Animals (except, perhaps, a pig) seem never out of place, even in the most paradisiacal spheres. And, by the way, a young colt comes up our avenue, now and then, to crop the seldom-trodden herbage; and so does a company of cows, whose sweet breath well repays us for the food which they obtain. There are likewise a few hens, whose quiet cluck is heard pleasantly about the house. A black dog sometimes stands at the farther extremity of the avenue, and looks wistfully hitherward; but when I whistle to him, he puts his tail between his legs, and trots away. Foolish dog! if he had more faith, he should have bones enough.

Saturday, August 6. — Still a dull day, threatening rain, yet without energy of character enough to rain outright. However, yesterday there were showers enough to supply us well with their beneficent outpouring. As to the new cistern, it seems to be bewitched; for, while the spout pours into it like a cataract, it still remains almost empty. I wonder where Mr. Hosmer got it; perhaps from Tantalus, under the eaves of whose palace it must formerly have stood; for, like his drinking-cup in Hades, it has the property of filling itself forever, and never being full.

After breakfast, I took my fishing-rod, and went down through our orchard to the river-side; but as three or four boys were already in possession of the best spots along the shore, I did not fish. This river of ours is the most sluggish stream that I ever was acquainted with. I had spent three weeks by its side, and swam across it every day, before I could determine which way its current ran; and then I was compelled to decide the question by the testimony of others, and not by my own observation. Owing to this torpor of the stream, it has nowhere a bright, pebbly shore, nor is there

so much as a narrow strip of glistening sand in any part of its course; but it slumbers along between broad meadows, or kisses the tangled grass of mowing-fields and pastures, or bathes the overhanging boughs of elder-bushes and other water-loving plants. Flags and rushes grow along its shallow margin. The yellow water-lily spreads its broad, flat leaves upon its surface; and the fragrant white pond-lily occurs in many favored spots, — generally selecting a situation just so far from the river's brink, that it cannot be grasped except at the hazard of plunging in. But thanks be to the beautiful flower for growing at any rate. It is a marvel whence it derives its loveliness and perfume, sprouting as it does from the black mud over which the river sleeps, and from which the yellow lily likewise draws its unclean life and noisome odor. So it is with many people in this world: the same soil and circumstances may produce the good and beautiful, and the wicked and ugly. Some have the faculty of assimilating to themselves only what is evil, and so they become as noisome as the yellow water-lily. Some assimilate none but good influences, and their emblem is the fragrant and spotless pond-lily, whose very breath is a blessing to all the region round about. . . . . Among the productions of the river's margin, I must not forget the pickerel-weed, which grows just on the edge of the water, and shoots up a long stalk crowned with a blue spire, from among large green leaves. Both the flower and the leaves look well in a vase with pond-lilies, and relieve the unvaried whiteness of the latter; and, being all alike children of the waters, they are perfectly in keeping with one another. . . . .

I bathe once, and often twice, a day in our river; but one dip into the salt sea would be worth more than a whole week's soaking in such a lifeless tide. I have read of a river somewhere (whether it be in classic regions or among our Western Indians I know not) which seemed to dissolve and steal away the vigor of those who bathed in it. Perhaps our stream will be found to have this property. Its water, however, is pleasant in its immediate effect, being as soft as milk, and always warmer than the air. Its hue has a slight tinge of gold, and my limbs, when I behold them through its medium, look tawny. I am not aware that the inhabitants of Concord resemble their native river in any of their moral characteristics. Their forefathers, certainly, seem to have had the energy and impetus of a mountain torrent, rather than the torpor of this listless stream, — as it was proved by the blood with which they stained their river of Peace. It is said there are plenty of fish in it; but my most important captures hitherto have been a mud-turtle and an enormous eel. The former made his escape to his native element, — the latter we ate; and truly he had the taste of the whole river in his flesh, with a very prominent flavor of mud. On the whole, Concord River is no great favorite of mine; but I am glad to have any river at all so near at hand, it being just at the bottom of our orchard. Neither is it without a degree and kind of picturesqueness, both in its nearness and in the distance, when a blue gleam from its surface, among the green meadows and woods, seems like an open eye in Earth's countenance. Pleasant it is, too, to behold a little flat-bottomed skiff gliding over its bosom, which yields lazily to the stroke of the paddle, and allows the boat to go against its current almost as freely as with it. Pleasant, too, to watch an angler, as he strays along the brink, sometimes sheltering himself behind a tuft of bushes, and trailing his line along the water, in hopes to catch a pickerel. But, taking the river for all in all, I can find nothing more fit to compare it with, than one of the half-torpid earth-worms which I dig up for bait. The worm is sluggish, and so is the river, — the river is muddy, and so is the worm. You hardly know whether either of them is alive or dead; but still, in the course of time, they both manage to creep away. The best aspect of the Concord is when there is a northwestern breeze curling its surface, in a bright, sunshiny day. It then assumes a vivacity not its own. Moonlight, also, gives it beauty, as it does to all scenery of earth or water.

Sunday, August 7. — At sunset, last evening, I ascended the hill-top opposite our house; and, looking downward at the long extent of the river, it struck me that I had done it some injustice in my remarks. Perhaps, like other gentle and quiet characters, it will be better appreciated the longer I am acquainted with it. Certainly, as I beheld it then, it was one of the loveliest features in a scene of great rural beauty. It was visible through a course of two or three miles, sweeping in a semicircle round the hill on which I stood, and being the central line of a broad vale on either side. At a distance, it looked like a strip of sky set into the earth, which it so etherealized and idealized that it seemed akin to the upper regions. Nearer the base of the hill, I could discern the shadows of every tree and rock, imaged with a distinctness that made them even more charming than the reality; because, knowing them to be unsubstantial, they assumed the ideality which the soul always craves in the contemplation of earthly beauty. All the sky, too, and the rich clouds of sunset, were reflected in the peaceful bosom of the river; and surely, if its bosom can give back such an adequate reflection of heaven, it cannot be so gross and impure as I described it yesterday. Or if so, it shall be a symbol to me that even a human breast, which may appear least spiritual in some aspects, may still have the capability of reflecting an infinite heaven in its depths, and therefore of enjoying it. It is a comfortable thought, that the smallest and most turbid mud-puddle can contain its own picture of heaven. Let us remember this, when we feel inclined to deny all spiritual life to some people, in whom, nevertheless, our Father may perhaps see the image of his face.

This dull river has a deep religion of its own: so, let us trust, has the dullest human soul, though, perhaps, unconsciously.

The scenery of Concord, as I beheld it from the summit of the hill, has no very marked characteristics, but has a great deal of quiet beauty, in keeping with the river. There are broad and peaceful meadows, which, I think, are among the most satisfying objects in natural scenery. The heart reposes on them with a feeling that few things else can give, because almost all other objects are abrupt and clearly defined; but a meadow stretches out like a small infinity, yet with a secure homeliness which we do not find either in an expanse of water or of air. The hills which border these meadows are wide swells of land, or long and gradual ridges, some of them densely covered with wood. The white village, at a distance on the left, appears to be embosomed among wooded hills. The verdure of the country is much more perfect than is usual at this season of the year, when the autumnal hue has generally made considerable progress over trees and grass. Last evening, after the copious showers of the preceding two days, it was worthy of early June, or, indeed, of a world just created. Had I not then been alone, I should have had a far deeper sense of beauty, for I should have looked through the medium of another spirit. Along the horizon there were masses of those deep clouds in which the fancy may see images of all things that ever existed or were dreamed of. Over our old manse, of which I could catch but a glimpse among its embowering trees, appeared the immensely gigantic figure of a hound, crouching down, with head erect, as if keeping watchful guard while the master of the mansion was away. . . . . How sweet it was to draw near my own home, after having lived homeless in the world so long! . . . . With thoughts like these, I descended the hill, and clambered over the stone wall, and crossed the road, and passed up our avenue, while the quaint old house put on an aspect of welcome.

Monday, August 8. — I wish I could give a description of our house, for it really has a character of its own, which is more than can be said of most edifices in these days. It is two stories high, with a third story of attic chambers in the gable roof. When I first visited it, early in June, it looked pretty much as it did during the old clergyman's lifetime, showing all the dust and disarray that might be supposed to have gathered about him in the course of sixty years of occupancy. The rooms seemed never to have been painted; at all events, the walls and panels, as well as the huge crossbeams, had a venerable and most dismal tinge of brown. The furniture consisted of high-backed, short-legged, rheumatic chairs, small, old tables, bedsteads with lofty posts, stately chests of drawers, looking-glasses in antique black frames, all of which were probably fashionable in the days of Dr. Ripley's predecessor. It required some energy of imagination to conceive the idea of transforming this ancient edifice into a comfortable modern residence. However, it has been successfully accomplished. The old Doctor's sleeping apartment, which was the front room on the ground floor, we have converted into a parlor; and, by the aid of cheerful paint and paper, a gladsome carpet, pictures and engravings, new furniture, *bijouterie*, and a daily supply of flowers, it has become one of the prettiest and pleasantest rooms in the whole world. The shade of our departed host will never haunt it; for its aspect has been changed as completely as the scenery of a theatre. Probably the ghost gave one peep into it, uttered a groan, and vanished forever. The opposite room has been metamorphosed into a store-room. Through the house, both in the first and second story, runs a spacious hall or entry, occupying more space than is usually devoted to such a purpose in modern times. This feature contributes to give the whole house an airy, roomy, and convenient appearance; we can breathe the freer by the aid of the broad passage-way. The front door of the hall looks up the stately avenue, which I have already mentioned; and the opposite door opens into the orchard, through which a path descends to the river. In the second story we have at present fitted up three rooms, one being our own chamber, and the opposite one a guest-chamber, which contains the most presentable of the old Doctor's ante-Revolutionary furniture. After all, the moderns have invented nothing better, as chamber furniture, than these chests of drawers, which stand on four slender legs, and rear an absolute tower of mahogany to the ceiling, the whole terminating in a fantastically carved summit. Such a venerable structure adorns our guest-chamber. In the rear of the house is the little room which I call my study, and which, in its day, has witnessed the intellectual labors of better students than myself. It contains, with some additions and alterations, the furniture of my bachelor-room in Boston; but there is a happier disposal of things now. There is a little vase of flowers on one of the book-cases, and a larger bronze vase of graceful ferns that surmounts the bureau. In size the room is just what it ought to be; for I never could compress my thoughts sufficiently to write in a very spacious room. It has three windows, two of which are shaded by a large and beautiful willow-tree, which sweeps against the over-hanging eaves. On this side we have a view into the orchard, and beyond, a glimpse of the river. The other window is the one from which Mr. Emerson, the predecessor of Dr. Ripley, beheld the first fight of the Revolution, — which he might well do, as the British troops were drawn up within a hundred yards of the house; and on looking forth, just now, I could still perceive the western abutments of the old bridge, the passage of which was contested. The new monument is visible from base to summit.

Notwithstanding all we have done to modernize the old place, we seem scarcely to have disturbed its air of antiquity. It is evident that other wedded pairs have spent their honeymoons here, that children have been born here, and people have grown old and died in these rooms, although for our behoof the same apartments have consented to look cheerful once again. Then there are dark closets, and strange nooks and corners, where the ghosts of former occupants might hide themselves in the daytime, and stalk forth when night conceals all our sacrilegious improvements. We have seen no apparitions as yet; but we hear strange noises, especially in the kitchen, and last night, while sitting in the parlor, we heard a thumping and pounding as of somebody at work in my study. Nay, if I mistake not, (for I was half asleep,) there was a sound as of some person crumpling paper in his hand in our very bedchamber. This must have been old Dr. Ripley with one of his sermons. There is a whole chest of them in the garret; but he need have no apprehensions of our disturbing them. I never saw the old patriarch myself, which I regret, as I should have been glad to associate his venerable figure at ninety years of age with the house in which he dwelt.

Externally the house presents the same appearance as in the Doctor's day. It had once a coat of white paint; but the storms and sunshine of many years have almost obliterated it, and produced a sober, grayish hue, which entirely suits the antique form of the structure. To repaint its reverend face would be a real sacrilege. It would look like old Dr. Ripley in a brown wig. I hardly know why it is that our cheerful and lightsome repairs and improvements in the interior of the house seem to be in perfectly good taste, though the heavy old beams and high wainscoting of the walls speak of ages gone by. But so it is. The cheerful paper-hangings have the air of belonging to the old walls; and such modernisms as astral lamps, card-tables, gilded Cologne-bottles, silver taper-stands, and bronze and alabaster flower-vases, do not seem at all impertinent. It is thus that an aged man may keep his heart warm for new things and new friends, and often furnish himself anew with ideas; though it would not be graceful for him to attempt to suit his exterior to the passing fashions of the day.

August 9. — Our orchard in its day has been a very productive and profitable one; and we were told, that in one year it returned Dr. Ripley a hundred dollars, besides defraying the expense of repairing the house. It is now long past its prime: many of the trees are moss-grown, and have dead and rotten branches intermixed among the green and fruitful ones. And it may well be so; for I suppose some of the trees may have been set out by Mr. Emerson, who died in the first year of the Revolutionary war. Neither will the fruit, probably, bear comparison with the delicate productions of modern pomology. Most of the trees seem to have abundant burdens upon them; but they are homely russet apples, fit only for baking and cooking. (But we have yet to have practical experience of our fruit.) Justice Shallow's orchard, with its choice pippins and leather-coats, was doubtless much superior. Nevertheless, it pleases me to think of the good minister, walking in the shadows of these old, fantastically-shaped apple-trees, here plucking some of the fruit to taste, there pruning away a too luxuriant branch, and all the while computing how many barrels may be filled, and how large a sum will be added to his stipend by their sale. And the same trees offer their fruit to me as freely as they did to him, — their old branches, like withered hands and arms, holding out apples of the same flavor as they held out to Dr. Ripley in his lifetime. Thus the trees, as living existences, form a peculiar link between the dead and us. My fancy has always found something very interesting in an orchard. Apple-trees, and all fruit-trees, have a domestic character which brings them into relationship with man.

They have lost, in a great measure, the wild nature of the forest-tree, and have grown humanized by receiving the care of man, and by contributing to his wants. They have become a part of the family; and their individual characters are as well understood and appreciated as those of the human members. One tree is harsh and crabbed, another mild; one is churlish and illiberal, another exhausts itself with its free-hearted bounties. Even the shapes of apple-trees have great individuality, into such strange postures do they put themselves, and thrust their contorted branches so grotesquely in all directions. And when they have stood around a house for many years, and held converse with successive dynasties of occupants, and gladdened their hearts so often in the fruitful autumn, then it would seem almost sacrilege to cut them down.

Besides the apple-trees, there are various other kinds of fruit in close vicinity to the house. When we first arrived, there were several trees of ripe cherries, but so sour that we allowed them to wither upon the branches. Two long rows of currant-bushes supplied us abundantly for nearly four weeks. There are a good many peach-trees, but all of an old date, — their branches rotten, gummy, and mossy, — and their fruit, I fear, will be of very inferior quality. They produce most abundantly, however,—the peaches being almost as numerous as the leaves; and even the sprouts and suckers from the roots of the old trees have fruit upon them. Then there are pear-trees of various kinds, and one or two quince-trees. On the whole, these fruit-trees, and the other items and adjuncts of the place, convey a very agreeable idea of the outward comfort in which the good old Doctor must have spent his life. Everything seems to have fallen to his lot that could possibly be supposed to render the life of a country clergyman easy and prosperous. There is a barn, which probably used to be filled, annually, with his hay and other agricultural products. There are sheds, and a hen-house, and a pigeon-house, and an old stone pig-sty, the open portion of which is overgrown with tall weeds, indicating that no grunter has recently occupied it. . . . . I have serious thoughts of inducting a new incumbent in this part of the parsonage. It is our duty to support a pig, even if we have no design of feasting upon him; and, for my own part, I have a great sympathy and interest for the whole race of porkers, and should have much amusement in studying the character of a pig. Perhaps I might try to bring out his moral and intellectual nature, and cultivate his affections. A cat, too, and perhaps a dog, would be desirable additions to our household.

August 10. — The natural taste of man for the original Adam's occupation is fast developing itself in me. I find that I am a good deal interested in our garden, although, as it was planted before we came here, I do not feel the same affection for the plants that I should if the seed had been sown by my own hands. It is something like nursing and educating another person's children. Still, it was a very pleasant moment when I gathered the first string-beans, which were the earliest esculent that the garden contributed to our table. And I love to watch the successive development of each new vegetable, and mark its daily growth, which always affects me with surprise. It is as if something were being created under my own inspection, and partly by my own aid. One day, perchance, I look at my bean-vines, and see only the green leaves clambering up the poles; again, to-morrow, I give a second glance, and there are the delicate blossoms; and a third day, on a somewhat closer observation, I discover the tender young beans, hiding among the foliage. Then, each morning, I watch the swelling of the pods, and calculate how soon they will be ready to yield their treasures. All this gives a pleasure and an ideality, hitherto unthought of, to the business of providing sustenance for my family. I suppose Adam felt it in Paradise; and, of merely and exclusively earthly enjoyments, there are few purer and more harmless to be experienced. Speaking of beans, by the way, they are a classical food, and their culture must have been the occupation of many ancient sages and heroes. Summer-squashes are a very pleasant vegetable to be acquainted with. They grow in the forms of urns and vases, — some shallow, others deeper, and all with a beautifully scalloped edge. Almost any squash in our garden might be copied by a sculptor, and would look lovely in marble, or in china; and, if I could afford it, I would have exact imitations of the real vegetable as portions of my dining-service. They would be very appropriate dishes for holding garden-vegetables. Besides the summer-squashes, we have the crook-necked winter-squash, which I always delight to look at, when it turns up its big rotundity to ripen in the autumn sun. Except a pumpkin, there is no vegetable production that imparts such an idea of warmth and comfort to the beholder. Our own crop, however, does not promise to be very abundant; for the leaves formed such a superfluous shade over the young blossoms, that most of them dropped off without producing the germ of fruit. Yesterday and to-day I have cut off an immense number of leaves, and have thus given the remaining blossoms a chance to profit by the air and sunshine; but the season is too far advanced, I am afraid, for the squashes to attain any great bulk, and grow yellow in the sun. We have muskmelons and watermelons, which promise to supply us with as many as we can eat. After all, the greatest interest of these vegetables does not seem to consist in their being articles of food. It is rather that we love to see something born into the world; and when a great squash or melon is produced, it is a large and tangible existence, which the imagination can seize hold of and rejoice in. I love, also, to see my own works contributing to the life and well-being of animate nature. It is pleasant to have the bees come and suck honey out of my squash - blossoms, though, when they have laden themselves, they fly away to some unknown hive, which will give me back nothing in return for what my garden has given them. But there is much more honey in the world, and so I am content. Indian corn, in the prime and glory of its verdure, is a very beautiful vegetable, both considered in the separate plant, and in a mass in a broad field, rustling, and waving, and surging up and down in the breeze and sunshine of a summer afternoon. We have as many as fifty hills, I should think, which will give us an abundant supply. Pray Heaven that we may be able to eat it all! for it is not pleasant to think that anything which Nature has been at the pains to produce should be thrown away. But the hens will be glad of our superfluity, and so will the pigs, though we have neither hens nor pigs of our own. But hens we must certainly keep. There is something very sociable, and quiet, and soothing, too, in their soliloquies and converse among themselves; and, in an idle and half-meditative mood, it is very pleasant to watch a party of hens picking up their daily subsistence, with a gallant chanticleer in the midst of them. Milton had evidently contemplated such a picture with delight.

I find that I have not given a very complete idea of our garden, although it certainly deserves an ample record in this chronicle, since my labors in it are the only present labors of my life. Besides what I have mentioned, we have cucumber-vines, which to-day yielded us the first cucumber of the season, a bed of beets, and another of carrots, and another of parsnips and turnips, none of which promise us a very abundant harvest. In truth, the soil is worn out, and, moreover, received very little manure this season. Also, we have cabbages in superfluous abundance, inasmuch as we neither of us have the least affection for them; and it would be unreasonable to expect Sarah, the cook, to eat fifty head of cabbages. Tomatoes, too, we shall have by and by. At our first arrival, we found green peas ready for gathering, and these, instead of the string-beans, were the first offering of the garden to our board.

TO J. B.

ON SENDING ME A SEVEN-POUND TROUT.

I.

FIT for an Abbot of Theleme,
　　For the whole Cardinals' College, or
The Pope himself to see in dream
Before his lenten vision gleam,
He lies there, — the sogdologer!

2.

His precious flanks with stars besprent,
Worthy to swim in Castaly!
The friend by whom such gifts are sent, —
For him shall bumpers full be spent, —
His health! be Luck his fast ally!

To J. B.

3.

I see him trace the wayward brook
Amid the forest mysteries,
Where at themselves shy aspens look,
Or where, with many a gurgling crook,
It croons its woodland histories.

4.

I see leaf-shade and sun-fleck lend
Their tremulous, sweet vicissitude
To smooth, dark pool, to crinkling bend, —
(O, stew him, Ann, as 't were your friend,
With amorous solicitude!)

5.

I see him step with caution due,
Soft as if shod with moccasins,
Grave as in church, — and who plies you,
Sweet craft, is safe as in a pew
From all our common stock o' sins.

6.

The unerring fly I see him cast,
That as a rose-leaf falls as soft, —
A flash! a whirl! he has him fast!
We tyros, — how that struggle last
Confuses and appalls us oft!

7.

Unfluttered he; calm as the sky
Looks on our tragicomedies,
This way and that he lets him fly,
A sunbeam-shuttle, then to die
Lands him with cool *aplomb*, at ease.

8.

The friend who gave our board such gust, —
Life's care, may he o'erstep it half,
And when Death hooks him, as he must,
He 'll do it featly, as I trust,
And J. H. write his epitaph!

9.

O, born beneath the Fishes' sign,
Of constellations happiest,
May he somewhere with Walton dine,
May Horace send him Massic wine,
And Burns Scotch drink, — the nappiest!

10.

And when they come his deeds to weigh,
And how he used the talents his,
One trout-scale in the scales he 'll lay,
(If trout had scales,) and 't will outsway
The wrong side of the balances.

PHYSICAL HISTORY OF THE VALLEY OF THE AMAZONS.

I.

A YEAR or two ago I published in the Atlantic Monthly, as part of a series of geological sketches, a number of articles on the glacial phenomena of the Northern hemisphere. To-day I am led to add a new chapter to that strange history, taken from the Southern hemisphere, and even from the tropics themselves.

I am prepared to find that the statement of this new phase of the glacial period will awaken among my scientific colleagues an opposition even more violent than that by which the first announcement of my views on this subject was met. I am, however, willing to bide my time; feeling sure that, as the theory of the ancient extension of glaciers in Europe has gradually come to be accepted by geologists, so will the existence of like phenomena, both in North and South America, during the same epoch, be recognized sooner or later as part of a great series of physical events extending over the whole globe. Indeed, when the ice period is fully understood, it will be seen that the absurdity lies in supposing that climatic conditions so intense could be limited to a small portion of the world's surface. If the geological winter existed at all, it must have been cosmic; and it is quite as rational to look for its traces in the Western as in the Eastern hemisphere, to the south of the equator as to the north of it. Impressed by this wider view of the subject, confirmed by a number of unpublished investigations which I have made during the last three or four years in the United States, I came to South America, expecting to find in the tropical regions new evidences of a by-gone glacial period, though, of course, under different aspects. Such a result seemed to me the logical sequence of what I had already observed in Europe and in North America.

On my arrival in Rio de Janeiro,— the port at which I first landed in Brazil,— my attention was immediately attracted by a very peculiar formation, consisting of an ochraceous, highly ferruginous sandy clay. During a stay of three months in Rio, whence I made many excursions into the neighboring country, I had opportunities of studying this deposit, both in the province of Rio de Janeiro and in the adjoining province of Minas Geraes. I found that it rested everywhere upon the undulating surfaces of the solid rocks in place, was almost entirely destitute of stratification, and contained a variety of pebbles and boulders. The pebbles were chiefly quartz, sometimes scattered indiscriminately throughout the deposit, sometimes lying in a seam between it and the rock below; while the boulders were either sunk in its mass or resting loose on the surface. At Tijuca, a few miles out of the city of Rio, among the picturesque hills lying to the southwest of it, these phenomena may be seen in great perfection. Near Bennett's Hotel — a favorite resort, not only with the citizens of Rio, but with all sojourners there who care to leave the town occasionally for its beautiful environs — may be seen a great number of erratic boulders, having no connection whatever with the rock in place, and also a bluff of this superficial deposit studded with boulders, resting above the partially stratified metamorphic rock. Other excellent opportunities for observing this formation, also within easy reach from the city, are afforded along the whole line of the Railroad of Dom Pedro Segundo, where the cuts expose admirable sections, showing the red, unstratified, homogeneous mass of sandy clay resting above the solid rock, and often divided from it by a thin bed of pebbles. There can be no doubt, in the mind of any one familiar with similar facts observed in other parts of the world, that this is one of the many forms of drift connected with glacial action. I was, however, far from anticipating, when I first met it in the neighborhood of Rio, that I should afterwards find it spreading over the surface of the country, from north to south and from east to west, with a continuity which gives legible connection to the whole geological history of the continent.

It is true that the extensive decomposition of the underlying rock, penetrating sometimes to a considerable depth, makes it often difficult to distinguish between it and the drift ; and the problem is made still more puzzling by the fact that the surface of the drift, when baked by exposure to the hot sun, often assumes the appearance of decomposed rock, so that great care is required for a correct interpretation of the facts. A little practice, however, trains the eye to read these appearances aright, and I may say that I have learned to recognize everywhere the limit between the two formations. There is indeed one safe guide, namely, the undulating line, reminding one of *roches moutonnées,** and marking the irregular surface of the rock on which the drift was accumulated ; whatever modifications the one or the other may have undergone, this line seems never to disappear. Another deceptive feature, arising from the frequent disintegration of the rocks and from the brittle character of some of them, is the presence of loose fragments, which simulate erratic boulders, but are in fact only detached masses of the rock in place. A careful examination of their structure, however, will at once show the geologist whether they belong where they are found, or have been brought from a distance to their present resting-place.

But while the features to which I have

* The name consecrated by De Saussure to designate certain rocks in Switzerland, which have had their surfaces rounded under the action of the glaciers. Their gently swelling outlines are thought to resemble sheep resting on the ground, and for this reason the people in the Alps call them *roches moutonnées.*

alluded are unquestionably drift phenomena, they present in their wider extension, and especially in the northern part of Brazil, as will hereafter be seen, some phases of glacial action hitherto unobserved. Just as the investigation of the ice period in the United States has shown us that ice-fields may move over open level plains, as well as along the slopes of mountain valleys, so does a study of the same class of facts in South America reveal new and unlooked-for features in the history of the ice period. Some will say, that the fact of the advance of ice-fields over an open country is by no means established, inasmuch as many geologists believe all the so-called glacial traces, viz. striæ, furrows, polish, etc., found in the United States, to have been made by floating icebergs at a time when the continent was submerged. To this I can only answer, that in the State of Maine I have followed, compass in hand, the same set of furrows, running from north to south in one unvarying line, over a surface of one hundred and thirty miles from the Katahdin Iron Range to the sea-shore. These furrows follow all the inequalities of the country, ascending ranges of hills varying from twelve to fifteen hundred feet in height, and descending into the intervening valleys only two or three hundred feet above the sea, or sometimes even on a level with it. I take it to be impossible that a floating mass of ice should travel onward in one rectilinear direction, turning neither to the right nor to the left, for such a distance. Equally impossible would it be for a detached mass of ice, swimming on the surface of the water, or even with its base sunk considerably below it, to furrow in a straight line the summits and sides of the hills, and the beds of the valleys. It would be carried over the depressions without touching bottom. Instead of ascending the mountains, it would remain stranded against any elevation which rose greatly above its own basis, and, if caught between two parallel ridges, would float up and down between them. Moreover, the action of solid, unbroken ice, moving over the ground in immediate contact with it, is so different from that of floating ice-rafts or icebergs, that, though the latter have unquestionably dropped erratic boulders, and made furrows and striæ on the surface where they happened to be grounded, these phenomena will easily be distinguished from the more connected traces of glaciers, or extensive sheets of ice, resting directly upon the face of the country and advancing over it.

There seems thus far to be an inextricable confusion, in the ideas of many geologists, as to the respective action of currents, icebergs, and glaciers. It is time they should learn to distinguish between classes of facts so different from each other, and so easily recognized after the discrimination has once been made. As to the southward movement of an immense field of ice, extending over the whole north, it seems inevitable, the moment we admit that snow may accumulate around the pole in such quantities as to initiate a pressure radiating in every direction. Snow, alternately thawing and freezing, must, like water, find its level at last. A sheet of snow ten or fifteen thousand feet in thickness, extending all over the northern and southern portions of the globe, must necessarily lead, in the end, to the formation of a northern and southern cap of ice, moving toward the equator.

I have spoken of Tijuca and the Dom Pedro Railroad as favorable localities for studying the peculiar southern drift; but one meets it in every direction. A sheet of drift, consisting of the same homogeneous, unstratified paste, and containing loose materials of all sorts and sizes, covers the country. It is of very uneven thickness, — sometimes thrown into relief, as it were, by the surrounding denudations, and rising into hills, — sometimes reduced to a thin layer, — sometimes, as, for instance, on steep slopes, washed entirely away, leaving the bare face of the rock exposed. It has, however, remained comparatively undisturbed on some very abrupt ascents; as, for instance, on the Corcovado, along the path leading up the mountain, are some very fine banks of drift, — the more striking from the contrast of their deep red color with the surrounding vegetation. I have myself followed this sheet of drift from Rio de Janeiro to the top of the Serra do Mar, where, just outside the pretty town of Petropolis, the river Piabanha may be seen flowing between banks of drift, in which it has excavated its bed; thence I have traced it along the beautiful macadamized road leading to Juiz de Fora in the province of Minas Geraes, and beyond this to the farther side of the Serra da Babylonia. Throughout this whole tract of country, in the greater part of which travelling is easy and delightful, — an admirable line of diligences, over one of the finest roads in the world, being established as far as Juiz de Fora, — the drift may be seen along the roadside, in immediate contact with the native crystalline rock. The fertility of the land, also, is a guide to the presence of drift. Wherever it lies thickest over the surface, there are the most flourishing coffee-plantations; and I believe that a more systematic regard to this fact would have a most beneficial influence upon the agricultural interests of the country. No doubt the fertility arises from the great variety of chemical elements contained in the drift, and the kneading process it has undergone beneath the gigantic ice-plough, — a process which makes glacial drift everywhere the most fertile soil. Since my return from the Amazons, my impression as to the general distribution of these phenomena has been confirmed by the reports of some of my assistants, who have been travelling in other parts of the country. Mr. Frederick C. Hartt, accompanied by Mr. Copeland, one of the volunteer aids of the expedition, has been making collections and geological observations in the province of Spiritu Santo, in the valley of the Rio Doce, and afterwards in the valley of the Mucury. He informs me that he has found everywhere the same sheet of red, unstratified clay, with pebbles and occasional boulders, overlying the rock in place. Mr. Orestes St. John, who, taking the road through the interior, has visited, with the same objects in view, the valleys of the Rio San Francisco and the Rio das Velhas, and also the valley of Piauhy, gives the same account, with the exception that he found no erratic boulders in these more northern regions. The rarity of erratic boulders, not only in the deposits of the Amazons proper, but in those of the whole region which may be considered as the Amazonian basin, is accounted for, as we shall see hereafter, by the mode of their formation. The observations of Mr. Hartt and Mr. St. John are the more valuable, because I had employed them both, on our first arrival in Rio, in making geological surveys of different sections on the Dom Pedro Railroad, so that they had a great familiarity with those formations before starting on their separate journeys. Recently, Mr. St. John and myself having met at Pará on returning from our respective journeys, I have had an opportunity of comparing on the spot his geological sections from the valley of the Piauhy with the Amazonian deposits. There can be no doubt of the absolute identity of the formations in these valleys.

Having arranged the work of my assistants, and sent several of them to collect and make geological examinations in other directions, I myself, with the rest of my companions, proceeded up the coast to Pará. I was surprised to find at every step of my progress the same geological phenomena which had met me at Rio. As the steamer stops for a number of hours, or sometimes for a day or two, at Bahia, Maceio, Pernambuco, Parahiba, Natal, Ceara, and Maranham, I had many opportunities for observation. It was my friend Major Coutinho, already an experienced Amazonian traveller, who first told me that this formation continued through the whole valley of the Amazons, and was also to be found on all of its affluents which he had vis-

ited, although he had never thought of referring it to so recent a period. And here let me interrupt the course of my remarks to say, that the facts recorded in this article are by no means exclusively the result of my own investigations. They are in great part due to this able and intelligent young Brazilian, a member of the government corps of engineers, who, by the kindness of the Emperor, was associated with me in my Amazonian expedition. I can truly say that he has been my good genius throughout the whole journey, saving me, by his previous knowledge of the ground, from the futile and misdirected expenditure of means and time often inevitable in a new country, where one is imperfectly acquainted both with the people and their language. We have worked together in this investigation; my only advantage over him being my greater familiarity with like phenomena in Europe and North America, and consequent readiness in the practical handling of the facts, and in perceiving their connection. Major Coutinho's assertion, that on the banks of the Amazons I should find the same red, unstratified clay as in Rio and along the southern coast, seemed to me at first almost incredible, impressed as I was with the generally received notions as to the ancient character of the Amazonian deposits, referred by Humboldt to the Devonian, and by Martius to the Triassic period, and considered by all travellers to be at least as old as the Tertiaries. The result, however, confirmed his report, at least so far as the component materials of the formation are concerned; but, as will be seen hereafter, the mode of their deposition, and the time at which it took place, have not been the same at the north and south; and this difference of circumstances has modified the aspect of a formation essentially the same throughout. At first sight, it would indeed appear that this formation, as it exists in the valley of the Amazons, is identical with that of Rio; but it differs from it in the rarity of its boulders, and in showing occasional signs of stratification. It is also everywhere underlaid by coarse, well-stratified deposits, resembling somewhat the recife of Bahia and Pernambuco; whereas the unstratified drift of the south rests immediately upon the undulating surface of whatever rock happens to make the foundation of the country, whether stratified or crystalline. The peculiar sandstone on which the Amazonian clay rests exists nowhere else. Before proceeding, however, to describe the Amazonian deposits in detail, I ought to say something of the nature and origin of the valley itself.

The Valley of the Amazons was first sketched out by the elevation of two tracts of land; namely, the plateau of Guiana on the north, and the central plateau of Brazil on the south. It is probable that, at the time these two table-lands were lifted above the sea-level, the Andes did not exist, and the ocean flowed between them through an open strait. It would seem (and this is a curious result of modern geological investigations) that the portions of the earth's surface earliest raised above the ocean have trended from east to west. The first tract of land lifted above the waters in North America was also a long continental island, running from Newfoundland almost to the present base of the Rocky Mountains. This tendency may be attributed to various causes, — to the rotation of the earth, the consequent depression of its poles, and the breaking of its crust along the lines of greatest tension thus produced. At a later period, the upheaval of the Andes took place, closing the western side of this strait, and thus transforming it into a gulf, open only toward the east. Little or nothing is known of the earlier stratified deposits resting against the crystalline masses first uplifted in the Amazonian Valley. There is here no sequence, as in North America, of Azoic, Silurian, Devonian, and Carboniferous formations, shored up against each other by the gradual upheaval of the continent, although unquestionably older palæozoic and secondary beds underlie, here and there, the later formations. Indeed,

Major Coutinho has found palæozoic deposits, with characteristic shells, in the valley of the Rio Tapajos, at the first cascade, and carboniferous deposits have been noticed along the Rio Guapore and the Rio Mamore. But the first chapter in the valley's geological history about which we have connected and trustworthy data is that of the cretaceous period. It seems certain, that, at the close of the secondary age, the whole Amazonian basin became lined with a cretaceous deposit, the margins of which crop out at various localities on its borders. They have been observed along its southern limits, on its western outskirts along the Andes, in Venezuela along the shore-line of mountains, and also in certain localities near its eastern edge. I well remember that one of the first things which awakened my interest in the geology of the Amazonian Valley was the sight of some cretaceous fossil fishes from the province of Ceara. These fossil fishes were collected by Mr. George Gardner, to whom science is indebted for the most extensive information yet obtained respecting the geology of that part of Brazil. In this connection, let me say that here and elsewhere I shall speak of the provinces of Ceara, Piauhy, and Maranham as belonging geologically to the Valley of the Amazons, though their shore is bathed by the ocean, and their rivers empty directly into the Atlantic. But I entertain no doubt, and I hope I may hereafter be able to show, that, at an earlier period, the northeastern coast of Brazil stretched much farther seaward than in our day; so far, indeed, that in those times the rivers of all these provinces must have been tributaries of the Amazon in its eastward course. The evidence for this conclusion is substantially derived from the identity of the deposits in the valleys belonging to these provinces with those of the valleys through which the actual tributaries of the Amazons flow; as, for instance, the Tocantins, the Xingu, the Tapajos, the Madura, etc. Besides the fossils above alluded to from the eastern borders of this ancient basin, I have had recently another evidence of its cretaceous character from its southern region. Mr. William Chandless, on his return from a late journey on the Rio Purus, presented me with a series of fossil remains of the highest interest, and undoubtedly belonging to the cretaceous period. They were collected by himself on the Rio Aquiry, an affluent of the Rio Purus. Most of them were found in place between the tenth and eleventh degrees of south latitude, and the sixty-seventh and sixty-ninth degrees of west longitude from Greenwich, in localities varying from 430 to 650 feet above the sea-level. There are among them remains of Mososaurus, and of fishes closely allied to those already represented by Faujas in his description of Maestricht, and characteristic, as is well known to geological students, of the most recent cretaceous period.

Thus in its main features the Valley of the Amazons, like that of the Mississippi, is a cretaceous basin. This resemblance suggests a further comparison between the twin continents of North and South America. Not only is their general form the same, but their framework as we may call it, that is, the lay of their great mountain-chains and of their table-lands, with the extensive intervening depressions, presents a striking similarity. Indeed, a zoölogist, accustomed to trace a like structure under variously modified animal forms, cannot but have his homological studies recalled to his mind by the coincidence between certain physical features in the northern and southern parts of the Western hemisphere. And yet here, as throughout all nature, these correspondences are combined with a distinctness of individualization, which leaves its respective character not only to each continent as a whole, but also to the different regions circumscribed within its borders. In both, however, the highest mountain-chains, the Rocky Mountains and Coast Range with their wide intervening table-land in North America, and the chain of the Andes with its lesser plateaus in

South America, run along the western coast ; both have a great eastern promontory, — Newfoundland in the northern continent, and Cape St. Roque in the southern ;—and though the resemblance between the inland elevations is perhaps less striking, yet the Canadian range, the White Mountains, and the Alleghanies may very fairly be compared to the table-lands of Guiana and Brazil, and the Serra do Mar. Similar correspondences may be traced among the river systems. The Amazons and the St. Lawrence, though so different in dimensions, remind us of each other by their trend and geographical position ; and while the one is fed by the largest river system in the world, the other drains the most extensive lake surfaces known to exist in immediate contiguity. The Orinoco, with its bay, recalls Hudson's Bay and its many tributaries, and the Rio Magdalena may be said to be the South American Mackenzie ; while the Rio de la Plata represents geographically our Mississippi, and the Paraguay recalls the Missouri. The Parana may be compared to the Ohio ; the Pilcomayo, Vermejo, and Salado rivers, to the River Platte, the Arkansas, and the Red River in the United States ; while the rivers farther south, emptying into the Gulf of Mexico, represent the rivers of Patagonia and the southern parts of the Argentine Republic. Not only is there this general correspondence between the mountain elevations and the river systems, but as the larger river basins of North America — those of the St. Lawrence, the Mississippi, and the Mackenzie — meet in the low tracts extending along the foot of the Rocky Mountains, so do the basins of the Amazons, the Rio de la Plata, and the Orinoco join each other along the eastern slope of the Andes.

But while in geographical homology the Amazons compare with the St. Lawrence, and the Mississippi with the Rio de la Plata, the Mississippi and the Amazons, as has been said, resemble each other in their local geological character. They have both received a substratum of cretaceous beds, above which are accumulated their more recent deposits, so that, in their most prominent geological features, both may be considered as cretaceous basins, containing extensive deposits of a very recent age. Of the history of the Amazonian Valley during the periods immediately following the Cretaceous, we know little or nothing. Whether the Tertiary deposits are hidden under the more modern ones, or whether they are wholly wanting, the basin having, perhaps, been raised above the sea-level before that time, or whether they have been swept away by the tremendous inundations in the valley, which have certainly destroyed a great part of the cretaceous deposit, they have never been observed in any part of the Amazonian basin. Whatever tertiary deposits are represented in geological maps of this region are so marked in consequence of an incorrect identification of strata belonging, in fact, to a much more recent period.

A minute and extensive survey of the Valley of the Amazons is by no means an easy task, and its difficulty is greatly increased by the fact that the lower formations are only accessible on the river margins during the *vasante*, as it is called, or dry season, when the waters shrink in their beds, leaving a great part of their banks exposed. It happened that the first three or four months of my journey, August, September, October, and November, were those when the waters are lowest, — reaching their minimum in September and October, and beginning to rise again in November, — so that I had an excellent opportunity in ascending the river to observe its geological structure. Throughout its whole length, three distinct geological formations may be traced, the two lower of which have followed in immediate succession, and are conformable with one another, while the third rests unconformably upon them, following all the inequalities of the greatly denudated surface presented by the second formation. Notwithstanding this seeming interruption in the sequence of these deposits,

the third, as we shall presently see, belongs to the same series, and was accumulated in the same basin. The lowest set of beds of the whole series is rarely visible, but it seems everywhere to consist of sandstone, or even of loose sands well stratified, the coarser materials lying invariably below, and the finer above. Upon this lower set of beds rests everywhere an extensive deposit of fine laminated clays, varying in thickness, but frequently dividing into layers as thin as a sheet of paper. In some localities they exhibit in patches an extraordinary variety of beautiful colors, — pink, orange, crimson, yellow, gray, blue, and also black and white. The Indians are very skilful in preparing paints from these colored clays, with which they ornament their pottery, and the bowls of various shapes and sizes made from the fruit of the Cuieira-tree. These clay deposits assume occasionally a peculiar appearance, and one which might mislead the observer as to their true nature. When their surface has been long exposed to the action of the atmosphere and to the heat of the burning sun, they look so much like clay slates of the oldest geological epochs, that, at first sight, I took them for primary slates, my attention being attracted to them by a regular cleavage as distinct as that of the most ancient clay slates. And yet at Tonantins, on the banks of the Solimoens, in a locality where their exposed surfaces had this primordial appearance, I found in these very beds a considerable amount of well-preserved leaves, the character of which proves their recent origin. These leaves do not even indicate as ancient a period as the Tertiaries, but resemble so closely the vegetation of to-day, that I have no doubt, when examined by competent authority, they will be identified with living plants. The presence of such an extensive clay formation, stretching over a surface of more than three thousand miles in length and about seven hundred in breadth, is not easily explained under any ordinary circumstances. The fact that it is so thoroughly laminated shows that, in the basin in which it was formed, the waters must have been unusually quiet, containing identical materials throughout, and that these materials must have been deposited over the whole bottom in the same way. It is usually separated from the superincumbent beds by a glazed crust of hard, compact sandstone, almost resembling a ferruginous quartzite.

Upon this follow beds of sand and sandstone, varying in the regularity of their strata, reddish in color, often highly ferruginous, and more or less nodulous or porous. They present frequent traces of cross-stratification, alternating with regularly stratified horizontal beds, with here and there an intervening layer of clay. It would seem as if the character of the water basin had now changed, and as if the waters under which this second formation was deposited had vibrated between storm and calm, — had sometimes flowed more gently, and again had been tossed to and fro, — giving to some of the beds the aspect of true torrential deposits. Indeed, these sandstone formations present a great variety of aspects. Sometimes they are very regularly laminated, or assume even the appearance of the hardest quartzite. This is usually the case with the uppermost beds. In other localities, and more especially in the lowermost beds, the whole mass is honeycombed, as if drilled by worms or boring shells, the hard parts enclosing softer sands or clays. Occasionally the ferruginous materials prevail to such an extent, that some of these beds might be mistaken for bog ore, while others contain a large amount of clay, more regularly stratified, and alternating with strata of sandstone, thus recalling the most characteristic forms of the Old Red or Triassic formations. This resemblance has, no doubt, led to the identification of the Amazonian deposits with the more ancient formations of Europe. At Monte Alegre, of which I shall presently speak more in detail, such a clay bed divides the lower from the upper sandstone. The thickness of these sandstones is extremely variable. In the basin of the Amazons proper, they hardly rise anywhere above the level of high water during the rainy season, while at low water, in the summer months, they may be seen everywhere along the riverbanks. It will be seen, however, that the limit between high and low water gives no true measure of the original thickness of the whole series.

In the neighborhood of Almeirim, at a short distance from the northern bank of the river, and nearly parallel with its course, there rises a line of low hills, interrupted here and there, but extending in evident connection from Almeirim through the region of Monte Alegre to the heights of Obidos. These hills have attracted the attention of travellers, not only from their height, which appears greater than it is, because they rise abruptly from an extensive plain, but also on account of their curious form, many of them being perfectly level on top, like smooth tables, and very abruptly divided from each other by low, intervening spaces.* Nothing has hitherto been known of the geological structure of these hills, but they have been usually represented as the southernmost spurs of the table-land of Guiana. On ascending the river, I felt the greatest curiosity to examine them; but at the time I was deeply engrossed in studying the distribution of fishes in the Amazonian waters, and in making large ichthyological collections, for which it was very important not to miss the season of low water, when the fishes are most easily obtained. I was, therefore, obliged to leave this most interesting geological problem, and content myself with examining the structure of the valley so far as it could be seen on the riverbanks and in the neighborhood of my different collecting stations. On my return, however, when my collections were completed, I was free to pursue

* The atlas in Martins's "Journey to Brazil," or the sketch accompanying Bates's description of these hills in his "Naturalist on the Amazons," will give an idea of their aspect.

this investigation, in which Major Coutinho was as much interested as myself. We determined to select Monte Alegre as the centre of our exploration, the serra in that region being higher than elsewhere. As I was detained by indisposition at Manaos, for some days, at the time we had appointed for the excursion, Major Coutinho preceded me, and had already made one trip to the serra, with some very interesting results, when I joined him, and we made a second journey together.

Monte Alegre lies on a side arm of the Amazons, a little off from its main course. This side arm, called the Rio Gurupatuba, is simply a channel running parallel with the Amazons, and cutting through from a higher to a lower point. Its dimensions are, however, greatly exaggerated in all the maps thus far published, where it is usually made to appear as a considerable northern tributary of the Amazons. The town stands on an elevated terrace, separated from the main stream by the Rio Gurupatuba, and by an extensive flat, consisting of numerous lakes divided from each other by low alluvial land, and mostly connected by narrow channels. To the west of the town, this terrace sinks abruptly to a wide sandy plain called the Campos, covered with a low forest growth, and bordered on its farther limit by the picturesque serra of Erreré. The form of this mountain is so abrupt, its rise from the plain so bold and sudden, that it seems more than twice its real height. Judging by the eye, and comparing it with the mountains I had last seen, — the Corcovado, the Gavia and Tijuca range in the neighborhood of Rio, — I had supposed it to be three or four thousand feet high, and was greatly astonished when our barometric observations showed it to be somewhat less than nine hundred feet in its most elevated point. This, however, agrees with Martins's measurement of the Almeirim hills, which he says are eight hundred feet in height.

Major Coutinho and I reached the serra by different roads; he crossing the Campos on horseback with Captain Faria, the commander of our steamer, and one or two other friends from Monte Alegre, who joined our party, while I went by canoe. The canoe journey is somewhat longer. A two hours' ride across the Campos brings you to the foot of the mountain, whereas the trip by boat takes more than twice that time. But I preferred going by water, as it gave me an opportunity of seeing the vast variety of animals haunting the river-banks and lakes. As this was almost the only occasion in all my journey when I passed a day in the pure enjoyment of nature, without the labor of collecting, — which in this hot climate, where specimens require such immediate and constant attention, is very great, — I am tempted to interrupt our geology for a moment, to give an account of it. I learned how rich a single day may be in this wonderful tropical world, if one's eyes are only open to the wealth of animal and vegetable life. Indeed, a few hours so spent in the field, in simply watching animals and plants, teaches more of the distribution of life than a month of closet study; for under such circumstances all things are seen in their true relations. Unhappily, it is not easy to present the picture as a whole, for all our written descriptions are more or less dependent on nomenclature, and the local names are hardly known out of the districts where they belong, while systematic names are familiar to few.

I started before daylight; but, as the dawn began to redden the sky, large flocks of ducks, and of the small Amazonian geese, might be seen flying towards the lakes. Here and there a cormorant sat alone on the branch of a dead tree, or a kingfisher poised himself over the water, watching for his prey. Numerous gulls were gathered in large companies on the trees along the river-shore; alligators lay on its surface, diving with a sudden plash at the approach of our canoe; and occasionally a porpoise emerged from the water, showing himself for a moment and then disappearing again. Sometimes we startled a herd of capivara, resting on the water's edge; and once we saw a sloth, sitting upon the branch of an Imbauba (Cecropia) tree, rolled up in its peculiar attitude, the very picture of indolence, with its head sunk between its arms. Much of the river-shore consisted of low alluvial land, and was covered with that peculiar and beautiful grass known as Capim; this grass makes an excellent pasturage for cattle, and the abundance of it in this region renders the district of Monte Alegre very favorable for agricultural purposes. Here and there, where the red clay soil rose above the level of the water, a palm-thatched cabin stood on the low bluff, with a few trees about it. Such a house was usually the centre of a cattle farm, and large herds might be seen grazing in the adjoining fields. Along the river-banks, where the country is chiefly open, with extensive low marshy grounds, the only palm to be seen is the Maraja. After keeping along the Rio Gurupatuba for some distance, we turned to the right into a narrow stream, which has the character of an Igarapé in its lower course, though higher up it drains the country between the serra of Ereré and that of Tajury, and assumes the appearance of a small river. It is named after the serra, and is known as the Rio Ereré. This stream, narrow and picturesque, and often so overgrown with capim that the canoe pursued its course with difficulty, passed through a magnificent forest of the beautiful fan-palm, called here the Miriti (*Mauritia flexuosa*). This forest stretched for miles, overshadowing, as a kind of underbrush, many smaller trees and innumerable shrubs, some of which bore bright, conspicuous flowers. It seemed to me a strange spectacle, —a forest of monocotyledonous trees with a dicotyledonous undergrowth; the inferior plants thus towering above and sheltering the superior ones. Among the lower trees were many Leguminosæ, —one of the most striking, called Fava, having a colossal pod. The whole mass of vegetation was woven together

by innumerable lianas and creeping vines, in the midst of which the flowers of the Bignonia, with its open, trumpet-shaped corolla, were conspicuous. The capim was bright with the blossoms of the mallow growing in its midst, and was often edged with the broad-leaved Aninga, a large aquatic Arum. Through such a forest, where the animal life was no less rich and varied than the vegetation, our boat glided slowly for hours. The number and variety of birds struck me with astonishment. The coarse sedgy grasses on either side were full of water birds, one of the most common of which was a small chestnut-brown wading bird, the Jaçana (Parra), whose toes are immensely long in proportion to its size, enabling it to run upon the surface of the aquatic vegetation, as if it were solid ground. It was in the month of January, their breeding season, and at every turn of the boat we started them up in pairs. Their flat, open nests generally contained five flesh-colored eggs, streaked in zigzag with dark brown lines. The other waders were a snow-white heron, another ash-colored, smaller species, and a large white stork. The ash-colored herons were always in pairs, the white one always single, standing quiet and alone on the edge of the water, or half hidden in the green capim. The trees and bushes were full of small warbler-like birds, which it would be difficult to characterize separately. To the ordinary observer they might seem like the small birds of our woods; but there was one species among them which attracted my attention by its numbers, and also because it builds the most extraordinary nest, considering the size of the bird itself, that I have ever seen. It is known among the country people by two names, as the Pedreiro or the Forneiro, both names referring, as will be seen, to the nature of its habitation. This singular nest is built of clay, and is as hard as stone (*pedra*), while it has the form of the round mandioca oven (*forno*) in which the country people prepare their farinha, or flour, made from the mandioca root. It is about a foot in diameter, and stands edgewise upon a branch, or in the crotch of a tree. Among the smaller birds, I noticed bright Tanagers, and also a species resembling the Canary. Besides these, there were the wagtails, the black and white widow finches, the hang-nests, or Japé, as they are called here, with their pendent bag-like dwellings, and the familiar "Bem ti vi." Humming-birds, which we are always apt to associate with tropical vegetation, were very scarce. I saw but a few specimens. Thrushes and doves were more frequent, and I noticed also three or four kinds of woodpeckers. Of these latter there were countless numbers along our canoe path, flying overhead in dense crowds, and, at times, drowning every other sound in their high, noisy chatter.

These made a deep impression upon me. Indeed, in all regions, however far away from his own home, in the midst of a fauna and flora entirely new to him, the traveller is startled occasionally by the song of a bird or the sight of a flower so familiar that it transports him at once to woods where every tree is like a friend to him. It seems as if something akin to what in our own mental experience we call reminiscence or association existed in the workings of nature; for though the organic combinations are so distinct in different climates and countries, they never wholly exclude each other. Every zoölogical and botanical province retains some link which binds it to all the rest, and makes it part of the general harmony. The Arctic lichen is found growing under the shadow of the palm on the rocks of the tropical serra, and the song of the thrush and the tap of the woodpecker mingle with the sharp discordant cries of the parrot and paroquet.

Birds of prey, also, were not wanting. Among them was one about the size of our kite, and called the Red Hawk, which was so tame that, even when our canoe passed immediately under the low branch on which he was sitting, he did not fly away. But of all the groups of birds, the most striking as compared with corresponding groups in the temperate zone, and the one which reminded me the most directly of the fact that every region has its peculiar animal world, was that of the gallinaceous birds. The most frequent is the Cigana, to be seen in groups of fifteen or twenty, perched upon trees overhanging the water, and feeding upon berries. At night they roost in pairs, but in the daytime are always in larger companies. In their appearance they have something of the character of both the pheasant and peacock, and yet do not closely resemble either. It is a curious fact, that, with the exception of some small partridge-like gallinaceous birds, all the representatives of this family in Brazil, and especially in the Valley of the Amazons, belong to types which do not exist in other parts of the world. Here we find neither pheasants, nor cocks of the woods, nor grouse; but in their place abound the Mutun, the Jaçu, the Jacami, and the Unicorn (Crax, Penelope, Psophia, and Palamedea), all of which are so remote from the gallinaceous types found farther north, that they remind one quite as much of the bustard, and other ostrich-like birds, as of the hen and pheasant. They differ also from Northern gallinaceous birds in the greater uniformity of the sexes, none of them exhibiting those striking differences between the males and females which we see in the pheasants, the cocks of the woods, and in our barn-yard fowls. While birds abounded in such numbers, insects were rather scarce. I saw but few and small butterflies, and beetles were still more rare. The most numerous insects were the dragon-flies, — some with crimson bodies, black heads, and burnished wings, — others with large green bodies, crossed by blue bands. Of land shells I saw but one creeping along the reeds; and of water shells I gathered only a few small Ampullariæ.

Having ascended the river to a point nearly on a line with the serra, I landed, and struck across the Campos on foot. Here I entered upon an entirely different region,—a dry, open plain, with scanty vegetation. The most prominent plants were clusters of cactus and curua palms, a kind of stemless, low palm, with broad, elegant leaves springing vase-like from the ground. In these dry, sandy fields, rising gradually toward the serra, I observed in the deeper gullies formed by the heavy rains the laminated clays which are everywhere the foundation of the Amazonian strata. They here presented again so much the character of ordinary clay slates, that I thought I had at last come upon some old geological formation. Instead of this I only obtained fresh evidence that, by baking them, the burning sun of the tropics may produce upon laminated clays of recent origin the same effect as plutonic agents have produced upon the ancient clays, that is, it may change them into metamorphic slates. As I approached the serra, I was again reminded how, under the most dissimilar circumstances, similar features recur everywhere in nature. I came suddenly upon a little creek, bordered with the usual vegetation of such shallow watercourses, and on its brink stood a sandpiper, which flew away at my approach, uttering its peculiar cry, so like what one hears at home that, had I not seen him, I should have recognized him by his voice.

After an hour's walk under the scorching sun, I was glad to find myself at the hamlet of Erreré, near the foot of the serra, where I rejoined my companions. It was already noon, and they had arrived some time before. They had, however, waited breakfast for me, to which we all brought a good appetite. Breakfast over, we slung our hammocks under the trees, and during the heat of the day enjoyed the rest which we had so richly earned.

A BUNDLE OF BONES.

AND a very large bundle it was, as it lay, in *disjecta membra*, before the astonished eyes of the first learned palæontologist who gazed, in wondering delight, on its strange proportions. As it rears its ungainly form some eighteen feet above us, Madam, you may gather some idea of what it was in its native forests, I don't know how many hundreds of thousands of years ago. You need not snuggle up to me so, Tommy. The creature is not alive, unless it is enjoying Sydney Smith's idea of comfort, and, having taken off its flesh, is airing itself in its bones. Megatherium was a very proper name for it, if not a very common one ; for *large animal* it was, beyond any dispute, and could scarcely have been much of a pet with the human beings of old, unless "there were giants in those days," and enormous ones at that. How Owen must have gloated over that treasure-trove ! Captain Kyd's buried booty would have been worse trash to him than Iago's stolen purse, beside this unearthed deposit of an antediluvian age. Its missing caudal vertebræ would outweigh now, in his anatomical scales, all the hidden gains of the whole race of pirates, past, present, and to come. Think of those bones with all the original muscle upon them ! Why, they would outweigh all the worthy members of the Boston Society of Natural History together, unless they are uncommonly obese. Where could Noah have stowed a pair of such enormous beasts, supposing that they existed as late as when the ark was launched ? Sloth, indeed ! I am inclined to think the five or six tons of flesh these bones must have carried round might reasonably permit the bearer to rank, on *a priori* reasons, among the most confirmed of sluggards, even if Owen and Agassiz and Wyman had not so decided on strictly scientific, anatomical grounds.

My dear Madam, does it ever occur to you, when you wonderingly gaze on the strange relics around this hall,—these stony skeletons, these silent remnants of extinct races, that you are face to face with rock-buried creatures, who lived and sported and mated, who basked in the sunlight and breathed in the air of this world, hundreds of thousands of years before you were thought of? who rested in the shade of the trees which made the coal that warms you to-day? who trod the soft mud which now builds in solid strength the dwellings which shelter you? who darted through the deep waters that foamed over a bed now raised into snow-capped mountains? who frolicked on a shore now piled with miles of massive rock? whose bones were petrifactions untold ages before the race was born which built the Pyramids? Do you really understand how far back into antiquity these grim fossils bear you? Can you really conceive of Nature, our dear, kind, gentle mother, in those early throes of her maternity which brought forth Megatheria and Ichthyosauri,—when the "firm and rock-built earth" was tilted into mountain ranges, wrinkled by earthquakes, and ploughed by mighty hills of moving ice? And yet in those distant days, which have left their ripple-marks and rain-drops in the weighty stone, there was life, warm, breathing, sentient life, which, dying, traced its own epitaph on its massive tomb. Shakespeare, Cæsar, Brahma, Noah, Adam, lived but yesterday compared with these creatures, whose stone-bound bones were buried in the sands that drifted on the shores of this world centuries before the first man drew into his nostrils the breath of life. Does the thought ever occur to you, that, ages hence, some enthusiastic student of nature may puzzle his brains over the bones of some such humble individuals as you and I,

and wonder to what manner of creature they belonged? Or that, perched upon the shelves of some museum in the year 500000, they may be treasures of an unknown past to the Owens and Wymans of that day?

You wish I would not talk so?—Well, Madam, let us leave this mausoleum of the past, and come forth into the life of 1866; and let us see whether all the *disjecta membra* of extinct being are ranged around the walls of this classic hall, or whether we may not find something akin near our own snug and comfortable homes. I think I know some hardened hearts which have ossified around the soft emotions which in earlier years played therein. And, bless you, Madam, I meet every day, in my down-town walks, some strange animated fossils, more repellent than any I ever beheld in the Natural History cabinet. These bear the unfamiliar look which belongs to a fabulous age, and rest, silent and unobtrusive, in their halfopened cerements. The others wear a very familiar form, which belongs to our day, yet they are the exponents of a dead life which animated the buried bones of barbarism. The innocent Megatheria and Ichthyosauri crawled and paddled and died in their day; but these living fossils have the vital forms of the life above ground, while they bear within the psychical peculiarities of extinct beings. They creep about on the shores of time with the outward shapes of their fellows, and, when buried in its rising waves, will leave undistinguishable remains in their common tomb; and future explorers will never trace therein the evanescent peculiarities in which the two were so unlike.

Bones! Why, the whole earth is a big bundle of them. They are not only in graveyards, where "mossy marbles rest"; they are strewn, "unknelled, uncoffined, and unknown," over the whole surface of the globe, and lie embosomed in the gulfs of the great, restless ocean. Who knows what untamed savage rests beneath us here? Don't start, my dear Madam. I have no doubt that, when Tommy plays bo-peep round the big tree on the Common, he is tripping over the crania of some Indian sachems. Goldsmith's seat, "for whispering lovers made," very likely rested on some venerable, departed Roman; and many a Maypole has gone plump through the thorax of some defunct Gaul. If the old story be true, that, when we shudder, somebody is walking over our grave, what a shaking race of beings our remote ancestors must have been!

My dear Madam, down in the green fields, the flowery meadows, the deep woods, the damp swamps of the balmy South, are there not spread, to-day, in grievous numbers, the bones of the noble, true-hearted heroes who went forth in their strength and manhood to meet a patriot's fate? Will not the future tread of those they ransomed be light and buoyant in the long days of freedom yet to come? What will they know of the hallowed remains over which they bound with glowing, happy hearts? Some little Peterkin may find a bleached remnant of their heroism, and the Caspar of that day will surely say, "It was a famous victory." Madam, you and I would be content to have the children of the future gambol above us, if we could know their blithesome hearts were emancipated from thraldom by such deposit of our poor bones under the verdant sod. The stateliest mausoleum of crowned kings, the Pyramids that mark the resting-place of Egypt's ancient rulers, are not so proud a monument as the rich, green herbage that springs from the remains of a fallen hero, and hides the little feet that trip over him, freed by his fall. Let us rejoice, then, Madam, that we belong to that nobler race, which no curious explorer of the far future will rank with Megatheria and Ichthyosauri, or any of the soulless creatures of past geologic ages.

Backbone is a most important article, Tommy. Professor Wyman will tell you that backbone is the distinctive characteristic of the highest order of animals on this earth. When your father used to pry into all sorts of books, years ago, he found out that he belonged to the Vertebrata, which, Anglicized, meant backboned creatures. And yet do you know that there are crowds of men and women whose framework would puzzle the good Professor, with all his learning, — people who are utterly destitute of that same essential article? Carry him the first old bone you may find, and, I warrant you, he will tell, in a jiffy, to what manner of creature it belonged. But would n't he look bewildered upon a cranium and a pelvis which perambulated the earth without any osseous connection? Backbone is the grand fulcrum on which human life moves its inertia. But would n't Professor Rogers, *facile princeps* in physics, rub his nose, and look in wonder, to see peripatetic motion induced without a sign of a fulcrum for the lever of life to rest upon? And yet these anomalies are plentiful. They are everywhere, — in houses, in churches, in stores, in town, in country, on land, at sea, in public, in private, — extensive sub-orders of mammalian Invertebrata. They crouch and crawl through the world with pliant length. They wriggle through the knot-holes of fear and policy, when their stouter-boned brethren oppose them. They creep into corners and cracks when the giant, Progress, strides before them, and quake at the thunder of his tread. They cling, trembling, to the old mouldering scaffolding of the past, and look bewildered on the broad, rising arches of the new temple of thought. They stand quivering in the blast of opinion. And when Mrs. Grundy passes by, they back, like hermit-crabs, into the first time-worn old shell of precedent they can find, and hide there, shaking with dread.

My boy, strengthen well your backbone, that it may bear you upright and onward in your career. Walk erect in this world with the stature and aspect of a man. Tread forth alone with fearlessness and conscious power. Bear up your God-given intelligence with unbending pride, that it may look afar over the broad expanse of nature, and gaze with even eye upon the mountain-heights of eternal truth. I am using words too big for you? Well, one of these days you will understand them all, when your little backbone has gathered more lime.

Bone has done some remarkable things in this world. There was that little feat of Samson, in which he flourished the grinding apparatus of a defunct donkey. It has always seemed to me, Madam, that that same jaw-bone must have been either prodigiously strong and tough, or else the Philistine crania must have been of very chartaceous texture. There are the bones of the eleven thousand virgins, — the remains of ancient virtue, and loveliness, and faith. Though, if all the stories of travelled anatomists be true, there must have been some virgin heifers among them; for many of them are certainly of bovine, and not human, origin.

And then, Madam, do not the poor bones which have been strewn, for ages, over the rolling earth, play sometimes a nobler part in their decay than in their prime? The incrusted fragments, carefully treasured up in halls of science, reveal to the broadening intelligence of man the story of earth in its young days of mighty struggle, and tell of the sandy shores, the rolling waters, the waving woods of a primeval time. Turning back the stony tablets time has firmly bound, he views upon their wrinkled sides its nature-printed figures, — relics that have there remained, locked in the rocky sepulchre, built of crumbling mountains, washed and worn by tides that ebbed and flowed a million years ago. Now, opened to the eye of human thought, their crumbling forms bring tidings of a distant, wondrous past, when they were all in all of sentient life on earth. The thought

they could not know, their dead remains have wakened in the minds of a far nobler race, which was not born when they lay down and died.

When travellers over far-reaching deserts are lost in the great waste that shows no friendly, guiding sign, they sometimes find, half buried in the shifting sands, the bleaching bones of some poor creature which has fainted and fallen, left to its fate by the companions of its journey. Then, taking heart, they cheerier move along, secure in the forgotten path these silent relics show. Thus over life's drear desert do we move, seeking the path that leads us on direct, and often guided in our wandering way by the chance sight of lost and fallen ones, whose sad remains our errant footsteps cross. Not always clad in soft, warm, beating life do our bones perform their noblest purpose. Beauty may lure to ruin, but, the witching charm removed, decay may waken sober thought and high resolve. Poor Yorick might have set King Hamlet's table in a roar and been forgot, if, from his unknown grave, the sexton had not brought him forth, to teach an unborn age philosophy.

My dear Madam, I am really getting too serious, philosophic, and melancholic. I had no idea, when I asked you down to the Natural History Society rooms to see the great Megatherium, that I was either to bury or resuscitate you in imagination. But I must have my moral, if I draw it from such a lean text as crumbling bones. Let us hope that what we leave behind us, when our journey over the drear expanse of mortal life shall cease, may serve to guide some future wanderer in the devious way, and lead him to the bright oasis of eternal life and rest.

AN ENGLISHMAN IN NORMANDY.

A TOUR in Normandy is a very
commonplace thing; and mine
was not even a tour in Normandy. In
the six weeks which I spent there, I
did not see as many sights as an ordinary English tourist sees in ten
days, or an American, perhaps, in five.
Going abroad in need of rest, I ram-
bled slowly about, sojourning at each
place as long as I found it agreeable,
then moving on to another, avoiding
the railroads, the tyranny of the time-
table, the flurry of packing up every
morning. My time was divided between some seven or eight places;
and I stayed longest where there was
least, according to the guide-books, to
be seen.

Travelling in this way, you at all
events see something of the people;
that is, if you will live among them and
fall in with their ways.

Normandy — at least the sequestered
part of it in which most of my time was
passed — is a good country for a traveller minded as I was. The scenery is
not grand. It does not exact the highest admiration; but it is, perhaps, not
on that account the less suitable for the
purpose of those who seek repose. The
country is very like the most rich and
beautiful parts of England. Its lanes
and hedge-rows are indeed so thoroughly English, as to suggest that it
was laid out under influences similar
to those which determined the aspect
of the country in England, and unlike
those which determined it in other
parts of France. It is well wooded;
and as the trees stand not in masses,
but in lines along the hedge-rows, you
see distinctly the form of each tree.
This is one of its characteristic features. The number of poplars interspersed with the trees of rounder outline is another, and very grateful to the
eye The general greenness rivals that
of England. The valleys are wide, and
the views from the hill-tops very extensive. I am speaking chiefly of the

western part of Normandy: the parts
about Caen approach more nearly to
the flatness, monotony, and dreary tree-
lessness of ordinary French and German scenery. The air is pure and
bracing, — especially in the little towns
built on old castled heights. Why do
we not always build our towns, when
we can, on heights, in what Shakespeare calls nimble and sweet air?

The Norman towns are full of grand
old churches, old castles, historic memories, shadows of the past. In these,
where I spent most of my holiday, there
are no garrisons, no Zouaves, no *fan-
fares*, no signs of the presence of the
empire, except occasionally the abode
of a *sous-préfet*. The province retains
a good deal of its old character. In the
great towns, such as Rouen and Caen,
the people are French; but in the country they are Normans still. The French
are sensible of the difference, and do
the Normans the honor (as, if I were a
Norman, I should think it) of acknowledging it by habitual flouts and sneers
at the "heavy" race who inhabit "the
land of cider."

If you do not mind outward appearances, — if you have the resolution to
penetrate beyond a very dirty entrance,
perhaps through the kitchen, into the
rooms within. — you may make yourself extremely comfortable in a little
Norman inn. You have only to behave to your landlord and landlady as
a guest, not as a customer, and you
will find yourself treated with the utmost civility and kindness. You will
get a large, airy room, not so tidy as an
English room, but with a better bed,
and excellent fare, beginning with a
delicious cup of *café au lait* in the early morning, — that is, if you choose to
breakfast and dine at the *table d'hôte;*
for, if, like many English travellers, you
insist on living in English privacy, and
taking your meals at English hours,
all the resources of the little establishment being expended on the public

meals, you will probably pay the penalty of your patriotic and stoical adherence to the customs of your country.

In my passage from Weymouth to Normandy, I landed at Jersey. The little, secluded bays of that island are the most perfect poetry of the sea. They are types of the spot in which Horace, in his poetic mood of imaginary misanthropy, wished to end his days.

> " Oblitusque meorum obliviscendus et illis
> Neptunum procul e terra spectare furentem."

I was told that the scenery of Guernsey was even more beautiful ; but the rough passage between the two islands is rather a heavy price to pay for the enjoyment. The islands are curious from their old Norman character, laws, and customs ; their Norman *patois;* their system of small proprietors, whose little holdings, divided from each other by high hedges, cut the island into a multitude of paddocks ; and the miniature republicanism and universal suffrage which the inhabitants enjoy, though under the paternal eye of an English governor, who, if the insects grew too angry, would no doubt sprinkle a little dust. But all that is native and original is fast being overlaid by the influx of English residents, — unhappy victims of genteel pauperism flying from the heavy taxes of England, which the Channel Islands escape ; or, in not a few cases, persons whose reputation has suffered some damage in their own country. There are also a few exiles of a more honorable kind, — French liberals, who have taken refuge from imperial tyranny under the shield of English law, — the most illustrious of whom is Victor Hugo. The Emperor would fain get hold of these men, and he is now trying to force upon us a modification of the extradition treaty for that purpose. But the sanctity of our asylum is a tradition dear to the English people, and one which they will not be induced to betray. An attempt to change the English law for the purposes of the French police was fatal to Palmerston, at the height of his popularity and power.

The French government employs agents to decoy the refugees into conspiracies, in order that it may obtain a pretext for criminal proceedings against them. The fact has fallen under my personal observation. To estimate the character of these practices, and of the present attempt to tamper with the extradition treaty, we must remember that Louis Napoleon himself long enjoyed, as a political refugee, the shelter of the asylum which he is now endeavoring to subvert.

Jersey is studded with fortifications. England and France frown at each other in arms from the neighboring coasts. I thought of poor Cobden, and of the day when his policy shall finally prevail, as it begins to prevail already, over these national divisions and jealousies ; and when there shall be at once a better and a cheaper security for the peace of nations than fortresses bristling with the instruments of mutual destruction. The Norman islands are of no use to England, while they involve us in a large military expenditure. In a maritime war, we should find it very difficult to defend dependencies so far from our coast and so close to that of the enemy. But the people are loyal to England, and very unwilling to be annexed to France.

Granville, where I landed in Normandy, is a hideous seaport ; but its hideousness was almost turned to beauty, on that golden afternoon, by the bright French atmosphere, which can do for bad scenery what French cookery does for bad meat. The royal and imperial roads of France are as despotically straight as those of the Roman Empire. But it was a pleasant evening drive to Avranches, through the rich champaign, — the active little Norman horses trotting the sixteen miles merrily to the jingling of their bells. The figure of the *gendarme,* in his cocked hat and imposing uniform, setting out upon his rounds, tells me that I am in France.

Avranches stands on the steep and towering extremity of a line of hills, commanding a most magnificent and varied view of land and sea, with Mont

St. Michel in the distance. Its cathedral must have occupied a site as striking as the temple of Poseidon, on the headland of Sunium. But of that cathedral nothing is now left but a heap of fragments, and a stone, on which, fabling tradition says, Henry II. was reconciled to the Church after the murder of Becket. It was pulled down in consequence of the injuries it received at the time of the Revolution ; and the bare area where it stood is typical of that devastating tornado which swept feudal and Catholic France out of existence. Where once the learned Huetius lived and wrote, the house of the *sous-préfet* now stands. The building of churches, however, is going on actively in Avranches, and attests the reviving influence of the priests. And one should be glad to see the revival of any form of religion, however different from one's own, in France, if it were not that this Church is so intensely political, and that it presents Christianity as the ally of atheist and sensualist despotism, and the enemy of morality, liberty, justice, and the hopes of man. The French Cæsars, Napoleon I. and Napoleon III., though themselves absolutely devoid of any faith but the self-idolatry which they call faith in their " star, ' find it politic, like the Roman Cæsars, to have their official creed and their augurs.

I went to the distribution of prizes at the school of the Christian Brothers. I had greatly admired the schools of the brotherhood in Ireland, and felt an interest in their system, notwithstanding their main object, like that of the famous Jesuit teachers of the sixteenth century, was rather to proselytize than to educate. The ceremony was thoroughly French, each boy being crowned with a tinsel wreath, and kissed by one of the company when he was presented with his prize. Everything, however, was arranged with the greatest taste and skill ; and the recitations and dialogues, by which the endless distribution of prizes was relieved, were very cleverly and gracefully performed. Some of them were comic. The one which made us laugh most was a dialogue

between a barber and a young gentleman who had come into his shop to be shaved. The barber pausing with the razor in his hand, the young gentleman asked him, angrily, why he did not begin. " I am waiting," replied the barber, " for your beard to grow." Specimens of writing were handed round, which were good ; drawings, which, strange to say, were detestable. I praised the recitations and dialogues to the gentleman who sat next me. " Ah ! oui," was his reply, " tout cela vient de Paris." So complete is the centralization of French intellect, even in such little matters as these ! While I was in France, some leading politicians were attempting to set on foot a movement in favor of political decentralization. They must begin deeper, if they would hope to succeed.

In Ireland, the Christian Brothers maintain the most purely spiritual character, and the most complete independence of the state. But here, alas ! a different tendency peeped out. The alliance of a Jesuit Church with the Empire, and the subserviency of education to their common objects, were typified by the presence of the *sous-préfet* and the *maire* in their gold-laced coats of office, who arrived escorted by a guard of soldiers with fixed bayonets. The harangue of the reverend head of the establishment was highly political, and amply merited by its recommendations of the duty of obedience to authority the eulogy of the *sous-préfet* on " the good direction " which the brotherhood were giving to the studies of youth. There is no garrison at Avranches. But all the soldiers in the place seemed to have been collected to give a military character to the scene. Other incentives of military aspiration were not wanting ; and the boy who delivered the allocution told us, amidst loud applause, that he and his companions were being brought up to be, " not only good Christians, but, in case of need, good soldiers."

In France under the Empire a military character is studiously given to every act of public, and almost of social life. There you see everywhere the pomp of war in the midst of peace, as in America you saw everywhere peace in the midst of civil war. The images of war and conquest are constantly kept before the eyes of a people naturally full of military vanity, and now, by the decay alike of religious and political faith, almost entirely bereft of all other aspirations. There is at the same time a vast standing army, which is not occupied, as the army of the Roman Empire was, in defending the frontiers, nor, as the Austrian army is, in holding down disaffected provinces, and which is full of the memory of the Napoleonic conquests, and longs again to overrun and pillage Europe in the name of "glory." There is no restraining influence either of morality or of religion to keep the war spirit in check. The French priesthood are as ready as any priests of Jupiter or Baal to bless national aggression, if by so doing they can gain political power. In what can all this end? In what but a European war? The children in the schools of the Christian Brothers are no doubt faithfully taught the precepts of a religion of peace; but there is a teaching of a different kind before their eyes, which, it is to be feared, they more easily imbibe and less easily forget.

It was amusing, on this and other occasions, to see the state which surrounds the subordinate officials of the Empire. I had found the head of the American Republic and all its armaments without any insignia of dignity, without a guard or attendants, in a common office room. And here was a *sous-préfet* parading the streets in solemn state, in a gilded coat, and with a line of bayonets glittering on either hand.

From Avranches it is a pleasant walk (by the country road) to the village of Ducie, where there is good fishing, a nice little village inn, and a deserted chateau in the Louis Quatorze style, and of sumptuous dimensions, which, if it was ever completely finished, is now in a state of great dilapidation. No doubt it shared the fate of its fellows, when the Revolution proclaimed "peace to the cottage, war to the castle." The peasantry almost everywhere rose, like galley-slaves whose chains had been suddenly struck off, and gutted the chateaux, the strongholds of feudal extortion and injustice. How violent and sweeping have been the revolutions of this people compared with those of the stronger and more self-controlled race! In England, the Tudor mansions, and not unfrequently even the feudal castles, are still tenanted by the heirs, or by those who have peacefully purchased from the heirs, of their ancient lords; and the insensible gradations by which the feudal guard-room has softened down into the modern drawing-room, and the feudal moat into the flower-garden, are emblematic of the continuous and comparatively tranquil progress of English history. In France, how different! Scarcely eighty years have passed since the Chateau de Montgomeri was proud and gay; since the village idlers gathered here to see its lord, and his little provincial court, assemble along those mouldering balustrades, and ride through the now deserted gates. But to the grandchildren of those villagers the chateau is a strange, mysterious relic of the times before the flood. A group of peasants tried in vain, when I asked them, to recollect the name of its former proprietors. One of them said that it had been inhabited by a great lord, who shod his horses with shoes of gold, — much the sort of tale that an Irish peasant tells you about the primeval monuments of his country. The mansions of France before the Revolution belong as completely to the past as the tombs of the Pharaohs. The old aristocracy and the old dynasty are no longer hated or regretted. Their names excite no emotion whatever in the French peasant's heart. They are wiped out of the memory of the nation, and their place knows them no more. In the midst of their shows and their pleasures and their shallow philosophies, they could not read the handwriting on the wall, and therefore they are blotted out of existence. They went on marrying and giving in marriage; this chateau, perhaps, was still being enlarged and embellished, when the flood came upon them and destroyed them all. The science of politics is the science of regulating progress and avoiding revolutions.

The hostess of the Lion d'Or is about to transfer her establishment to an inn of greater pretensions, to which, aware that the old chateau is an object of interest to visitors, she means to give the name of the Hotel de Montgomeri. On the wall of her *café* is a coarse medallion bust taken from a room in the chateau. She did not know whom it represented ; and I dare say it was only my fancy that made me think I recognized a rude effigy of the once adored features of Marie Antoinette.

The plates at the Lion d'Or were adorned with humorous devices. On one was a satire on the hypocritical rapacity of perfidious Albion. Two English soldiers were standing with their swords hidden behind their backs, and trying to coax back to them some Indians who were running away in the distance. "Come to us, dear little Indians ; you know we are your best friends ! " Suppose " Arabs " or " Mexicans " had been substituted for " Indians." To a Frenchman, our conquests in India are rapine ; his own conquests in Algeria or Mexico are the extension of civilization by the "holy bayonets " (I forget whether the phrase is Michelet's or Quinet's) of the chosen people. Justice gives the same name (no matter which) to both.

At Ducie a handsome new church had just been built,— mainly, I was told, by the munificence of two maiden ladies. The congregation at vespers was large and apparently devout ; and here the number of the men was in fair proportion to that of the women. In the churches of the cities. though the power of the clergy has everywhere increased of late, you see scarcely one man to a hundred women.

On the road, a shower drove me for refuge into the house of a peasant, who received me with the usual kindliness of the French peasantry, and,

when the shower was over, walked two or three miles with me on my way. The condition of these present proprietors is a subject of great interest to English economists, especially as we are evidently on the eve of a great controversy — perhaps a great struggle — respecting the law of succession to landed property in our own country. Not that any English economist would go so far as to advocate the French system of compulsory subdivision, which owes its existence in great measure to the policy of the first Napoleon, — who took care, with the instinct of a true despot, to secure the solitary power of the throne against the growth of an independent class of wealthy proprietors. All'that English economists contemplate is the abolition of primogeniture and entail. I must not found any conclusion on observations so partial and cursory as those which I was able to make ; but I suspect that the French peasant is better off than the English laborer. He is not better housed, clothed, or fed ; perhaps not so well housed, clothed, or fed. He eats black bread, which the English peasant would reject, and clumps about in wooden shoes, which the English laborer would regard with horror ; but this, according to statements which I have heard, and' am inclined to trust, arises, generally speaking, not so much from indigence as from self-denying frugality, pushed to an extreme. The French peasant is the possessor of property, and has a passion, almost a mania, for acquisition. He saves money and subscribes to government loans, which are judiciously brought out in very small shares, so as to draw forth his little hoard, and thus bind him as a creditor to the interest of the Empire. The cottage of the peasant which I entered on my way to Ducie was very mean and comfortless, and the food which his hospitality offered me was of the coarsest kind. But he had a valuable mare and foal ; his yard was full of poultry ; and his orchard showed, for a bad season, a fair crop of apples. There are some large estates, the result frequently of great fortunes made in trade. Not far from the place where the high-born lords of the Chateau de Montgomeri once reigned, a chocolate-merchant had bought broad lands, and built himself a princely mansion. I should have thought that the great proprietors would have crushed the small; but I was assured that the two systems went on very well side by side. But this is a matter for exact inquiry, not for casual remark. The population in France is stationary, or nearly so, while that of England increases rapidly; and this is an important element in the question, and itself raises questions of a difficult, perhaps of a disagreeable kind.

The cares of proprietorship must necessarily interfere with the lightness of heart once proverbially characteristic of the French peasant. Still, he appears to a stranger cheerful, ready to chat, and at least as inquisitive as to the stranger's history and objects as Americans are commonly believed to be. It would be a happy thing if the Irish peasant's lightness of heart, pleasant as it often is, could be interfered with in the same way. There is a certain gayety which springs from mere recklessness, and is sister to despair.

They are hard economical problems that we have to solve in this Old World, and terribly complicated by social and political entanglements; and there is no boundless West, with bread for all who want it, to assist us in the solution.

From Avranches you visit Mont St. Michel, — not without difficulty, for you have to drive along over sands which are never dry, and over which the tide — its advance can be seen even from the distant height of Avranches — rushes in with the speed of a race-horse. But you are well repaid. Mont St. Michel is one of the most astonishing and beautiful monuments of the Catholic and feudal age. Its fortifications, and the halls, church, and cloisters of the chivalrous and monastic fraternities of which it was the seat, rise like an efflorescence from the solitary cone of granite, surrounded at low tide by the vast flat of sand, at high tide by the sea. Gothic architecture, to which we are apt to attach the notion of a sort of infantine unconsciousness, here seems consciously to revel and disport itself in its power, and to exult in investing the sea-girt rock with the playful elegance of a Cellini vase. It is a real *jeu d'esprit* of mediæval art. The cloisters are a model of airy grace, enhanced by contrast with the massiveness of the fortress and the wildness of the scene. A strange life the monks must have led in their narrow boundaries. But they had the visits of the knights to relieve their dulness; and probably they were rude natures, not liable to the unhappiness which such seclusion would produce in men of cultivated sensibilities and active minds. Both monks and knights are gone long ago. But there are still six priests on the rock. I asked what they did. "Ils prient le bon Dieu."

In feudal times this sea-girt fortress was almost impregnable. Two ancient cannon lying at its gate show that the conqueror of Agincourt thundered against it in vain. Its weak point was want of water: it had none but the rain-water collected in a great cistern. In these days it could not hold out an hour against a single gun-boat.

It is a pleasant drive from Avranches to Vire; and Vire itself is a pleasant place, — a quiet little town, placed high, in bracing air, and with beautiful walks round it. The comfortable, though unpretending, little Hôtel de St. Pierre stands outside the town, and commands a fine view. While I was at Vire, the *fête* day of the Emperor was celebrated — with profound apathy. Not a dozen houses responded to the *préfet's* invitation to illuminate. There being no troops in the town, and a military show being indispensable, there was a review of the firemen in military uniforms; a single brass cannon pestered us with its noise all the morning; the "veterans" of the Napoleonic army (every surviving drummer-boy of the army of 1815 goes by that name) were dismally paraded about, and the firemen practised with their muskets, very awkwardly, at a mark which was so placed among the trees that they could hardly see it.

Why has not the government the sense to let these people alone? After all their revolutions and convulsions, they have sunk into perfect political indifference, and literally care not a straw whether they are governed by Napoleon. Nero, or Nebuchadnezzar. To be always appealing to them with Bonapartist demonstrations and manifestoes, is to awaken political sentiments, in them, and so to create a danger which does not exist.

If Louis Napoleon is in any peril, it is not from the republican or constitutional party, but from his own lavish expenditure, which begins to irritate the people. They are careless of their rights as freemen, but they are fond, and growing daily fonder, of money; and they do not like to be heavily taxed, and to hear at the same time that the Emperor is wasting on his personal expenses and those of his relatives and courtiers some six millions of dollars a year. Regard for economy is the only profession which distinguishes the addresses of the so-called opposition candidates from those of their competitors. I asked a good many people what they thought of the Mexican expedition. Not one of them objected to its injustice, but they all objected to its cost. "Cela mangera beaucoup d'argent," was the invariable reply. And in this point of view the government has committed what it would think much worse than any crime, — a very damaging blunder.

It does not appear that the Orleans family have any hold on the mind of the French people. When I mentioned their name, it seemed to produce no emotion, one way or the other. But if the marshals and grandees, who have hold of the wires of administration at the point where they are centralized, chose to make Napoleon III abdicate, (as they made Napoleon I. abdicate at Fontainebleau,) and to set up a king of the House of Orleans in his place,

they could probably do it; and they might choose to do it, if, by such blunders as the Mexican expedition, he seemed to be placing their personal interests in jeopardy.

Stopping to breakfast at Condé, on the way from Vire to Falaise, I fell in with the only Frenchman, with a single exception, who showed any interest in the affairs of America. Generally speaking, I was told, and found by experience, that profound apathy prevailed upon the subject. This gentleman, on learning that I had recently been in America, entered eagerly into conversation on the subject. But his inquiries were only about the prospects of cotton; and all I could tell him on that point was, that, if the growth of cotton was profitable, the Yankee would certainly make it grow.

The castle of Falaise is the reputed birthplace of the Conqueror. They even pretend to show you the room in which he was born. The existing castle, however, is of considerably later date. It is even doubtful, according to the best antiquaries, whether there were any stone castles at the date of his birth, or only earthworks with palisades. There is, however, one genuine monument of that time. You look down from the castle on the tanneries in the glen below, and see the women washing their clothes in the stream, as in the days when Robert the Devil wooed the tanner's daughter. Robert, however, must have had diabolically good eyes to choose a mistress at such a distance.

Annexed to the castle is Talbot's Tower, — a beautiful piece of feudal architecture, and a monument of a later episode in that long train of miserable wars between England and France, of which the Conqueror's cruel rapacity may be regarded as the spring; for the English conquests were an inverted copy and counterpart of his. But the Conqueror's crimes, like those of Napoleon I., were on the grandiose scale, and therefore they impose, like those of Napoleon, on the slavishness of mankind; while the petty bandit, though endowed perhaps with the same powers of destruction and only lacking the ampler sphere, is buried under the gallows. The equestrian statue of William in the public place at Falaise prances, it has been remarked, close to the spot where rest the ashes of Walter and Biona, Count and Countess of Pontoise, poisoned, if contemporary accounts are true, by the same ambition which launched havoc and misery on a whole nation. They and the Conqueror were rival claimants to the sovereignty of Maine. They supped with the Conqueror one evening at Falaise, and next morning William was the sole claimant. The Norman, like the Corsican, was an assassin as well as a conqueror.

I must leave it to architects to describe the architectural glories of Caen. But I had no idea that the Norman style, in England grand only from its massiveness, could soar to such a height of beauty as it has attained in the Church of St. Stephen and the Abbaye aux Dames. I afterwards did homage again to its powers when standing before the august ruin of Jumièges. There is something peculiarly delightful in the freshness of early art, whether Greek or mediæval, and whether in architecture or in poetry, — when you see the mind first beginning to feel its power over the material, and to make it the vehicle of thought. There is something, too, in all human works, which makes the early hope more charming than the fulfilment.

St. Stephen is the church of the Conqueror, as the Abbaye aux Dames is that of his Queen. There he lies buried. Every one knows the story of Ascelin demanding the price of the ground in which William was going to be buried, and which the tyrant had taken from him by force ; and how, at last, the corpse of the Conqueror was thrust, amidst a scene of horror and loathing, into its grave. But *Rex Invictissimus* is the inscription on his tomb.

The spire of St. Pierre is very graceful ; the body of the church, in the latest and most debased style of Gothic architecture, stands signally contrasted with St. Stephen, — St. Stephen the simple vigor of the prime, St. Pierre the florid weakness of the decay.

Caen is a large city, and, of course, full of soldiers, who are as completely the dominant caste in France now, as the old *noblesse* were before the Revolution. To this the French have come after their long train of sanguinary revolutions, — after all their visions of a perfect social state, — after all their promises of a new era of happiness to mankind. "A light and cruel people," Coleridge calls them. And how lightly they turned from regenerating to pillaging and oppressing the world ! They have great intellectual gifts, and still greater social graces ; but, in the political sphere, they have no real regard for freedom, and will gladly lay their liberties at the feet of any master who will enable them to domineer over other nations. Napoleon I. is more than their hero : he is their God. Many of them, the soldiery especially, have no other object of worship. I saw in a shop-window a print of Napoleon I., Napoleon II., and the Prince Imperial, all in military uniform and surrounded by the emblems of war. It was entitled, "The Past, the Present, and the Future of France." Military ambition has been the Past of France, is her Present, and seems too likely to be her Future. In some directions, she has promoted civilization ; but, politically speaking, she has done, and probably will long continue to do, more harm than good to mankind.

I may say with truth, that, having seen America, and brought away an assured faith in human liberty and progress, I looked with far more serenity than I should otherwise have done on the Zouaves, swaggering, in the insolence of triumphant force, over the neglected ashes of Turgot and Mirabeau. I felt as though, strong as the yoke of these janizaries and their master looked, I had the death-warrant of imperialism in my pocket. There is a Power which made the world for other ends than these, and which will not suffer its ends to give way even to those of the Bonapartes! But to all appearances there will be a terrible struggle in Europe, — a struggle to which the old "wars of the mercenaries" were a trifling affair, — before the nations can be redeemed from subjection to these armed hordes and the masters whom they obey.

From Caen I visited Bayeux, — a sleepy, ecclesiastical town with a glorious cathedral, which, however, shows by a huge crack in the tower that even such edifices know decay. Gems of the Norman style are scattered all round Caen and Bayeux; and one of the finest is the little church of St. Loup, in the environs of Bayeux.

I found that the old French office-book had been completely banished from the French churches by the Jesuit and Ultramontane party, and the Roman (though much inferior, Roman Catholics tell me, as a composition) everywhere thrust into its place. The people in some places recalcitrated violently; but the Jesuits and Ultramontanes triumphed. The old Gallican spirit of independence is extinct in the French Church, and its extinction is not greatly to be deplored; for it tended not to a real independence, but to the substitution of a royal for an ecclesiastical Pope. Louis XIV. was quite as great a spiritual tyrant as any Hildebrand or Innocent, and his tyranny was, if anything, more degrading to the soul. In fact, the Ultramontane French Church, resting for support on Rome, may be regarded by the friends of liberty, with a qualified complacency, as a check, though a miserable one, on the absolute dominion of physical force embodied in the Emperor.

The Bayeux tapestry, representing the expedition of William the Conqueror, is curious and valuable as an historical monument, though it cannot be proved to be contemporary. As a work of art it is singularly spiritless, and devoid of merit of any kind. One of the fancy figures on the border reveals the indelicacy of the ladies (a queen, perhaps, and her handmaidens) who wrought it in a way which would be startling to any one who had taken the manners and morals of the age of chivalry on trust.

The heat drove me from Caen before I had "done" all the antiquities and curiosities prescribed by the guide-book. Migrating to Lisieux, I found myself in such pleasant quarters that I was tempted to settle there for some days. The town is almost an unbroken assemblage of the quaintest and most picturesque old houses. There are whole streets without any taint of modern architecture to disturb the perfect image of the past. Two magnificent churches, one of them formerly a cathedral, rise over the whole; and there is a very pretty public garden, with its terraces, pastures, and green alleys. A public garden is the invariable appendage of a city in France, as it ought to be everywhere. We do not do half enough in England for the innocent amusement of the people.

At Lisieux we had a public *fête*. It is evidently a part of the business of the *sous-préfets* to get up these things as antidotes to political aspiration. *Panem et circenses* is the policy of the French, as it was of the Roman Cæsars. For two or three days beforehand, the people were engaged in planting little fir-trees in the street before their doors, and decorating them and the houses with little tricolor flags. Larger flags (of which this little quiet town produced a truly formidable number) were hung out from all the houses. As the weather was very dry, the population was at work keeping the fir-trees alive with squirts. The *fête* consisted of a horse and cattle show, in which the Norman horses made a very good display; the inevitable military review, which, Lisieux being as happily free from soldiery as Vire, was here, too, performed by the firemen; the band of a regiment of the line, which had been announced as a magnificent addition to the festivities, by a special proclamation of the *sous-préfet;* balloons not of the common shape, but in the shape of dogs, pigs, and grotesque human figures, a gentleman and lady waltzing, etc., which must have rather puzzled any scientific observer whose telescope was at that moment directed to the sky; and, to crown all, fireworks (the noise of which, a French gentleman remarked to me, the people loved, as reminding them of musketry) and an illumination. The illumination — all the little trees before the houses, as well as the houses themselves and the green arches thrown across the streets, being covered with lamps — was an extremely pretty sight. The outline of the old houses, and the windings and declivities of the old streets, wonderfully favored the effect. But the French are peerless in these things. The childish delight of the people was pleasant to see. Why cannot they be satisfied with their *fêtes*, and with the undisputed empire of cookery and dress, instead of making themselves a scourge to the world, and keeping all Europe in disquietude and under arms?

The Emperor is trying to inoculate his subjects with a taste for English sports, but with rather doubtful success. He tries to make them play at cricket, but they do not much like the swift bowling. There was a caricature in the Charivari of a Frenchman standing up to his wicket with an implement which the artist intended for a bat, but which was more like a pavior's rammer, in his hand. A friend was asking him whether he had a wife, children, any tie to life. "None." "Then you may begin." In a window at Lisieux there was a print of a foxhunt, with the master of the hounds dismounting to despatch the fox with a gun! At Vire there was a print of a horse-race, with the horses in a cantering attitude, and a large dog running and barking by their side. I have seen something equally funny of the same kind in America, but I need not say what or where. I never witnessed a French horse-race, but I am told that they enjoy it *moult tristement*, as they say we English enjoy all our amusements.

Close to Lisieux is the fashionable watering-place of Trouville, a place without any charms that I could see, puffed into celebrity by Alexander Dumas. The Duke de Morny invested in building there a good deal of the money which he made by the *coup d'état*. Life at a French watering-place seems to be as close an imitation of life at Paris as French ingenuity can produce under the adverse circumstances of the case. Nothing but the religion of fashion can compel these people periodically to leave the capital for the sea. The mode of bathing is rather singular. I found that the Americans did not, as is commonly believed in England, put trousers on the legs of their pianos, but I believe you are more particular than we are; and therefore, perhaps, you would be still more surprised than we are at seeing a gentleman wrapped in a sheet stalk before the eyes of all the promenaders over the sands to the sea, and there throw off the sheet, and at his leisure get into the water. At the risk of exposing my English prudishness, I ventured to remark to a French acquaintance that the fashion was *un peu libre*. I found, rather to my astonishment, that he thought so too.

At Val Richer, near Lisieux, is the pleasant country-house of M. Guizot. There, surrounded by his children and his grandchildren, a pretty patriarchal picture, the veteran statesman and historian reposes after the prodigious labors and tragic vicissitudes of his life. I say he reposes; but his pen is as active as ever, only that he has turned from politics and history to the more enduring and consoling topic of religion. He has just given us a volume on Christianity; he is about to give us one on the state of religion in France. It will be deeply interesting. In the revival of religion lies the only hope of regeneration for the French nation. And whence is that revival to come? From the official priesthood, and the jesuitical influences depicted in *Le Maudit?* Or from the Protestant Church of France, itself full of dissensions and turmoils, in which M. Guizot himself has been recently involved?

Or from the school of Natural Theologians represented by Jules Simon? We shall see, when M. Guizot's work appears. It is from his religious character as well as from his attachment to constitutional liberty, I imagine, that M. Guizot has, unlike the mass of his countrymen, watched the American struggle with ardent interest, and cordially rejoiced in the triumph of the Union and of freedom.

There are of course very different opinions as to this eminent man's career; and there are parts of his conduct of which no Liberal can approve. But I have always thought that a tranquil and happy old age is a proof, as well as a reward, of a good life; and if this be the case, M. Guizot's life, though not free from faults, must on the whole have been good.

His resistance to reform is commonly regarded as having led to the fall of the constitutional monarchy. I should attribute that catastrophe much more to the prevalence of the military spirit, which the peaceful policy of Louis Philippe disappointed, and to which even the conquest of Algeria failed (as its authors deserved) to give a sufficient vent. The reign of Louis Philippe was essentially an attempt to found a civil in place of a military government in France, which was foiled by the passions excited by the presence of a large standing army and the recent memory of the Napoleonic wars. The translation of the body of Napoleon from St. Helena to Paris was the greatest mistake committed by the king and his advisers. It was the self-humiliation of the government of peace before the Genius of War.

At Lisieux, as at Caen, and afterwards at Rouen, I saw on the Sunday a great church full of women, with scarcely a score of men. And what wonder? Close to where I sat was the altar of Our Lady of La Salette, offering to the adoration of the people the most coarse and revolting of impostures. And in the course of the service, an image of the Virgin, from which the taste of a Greek Pagan would have recoiled, was borne round the aisles in procession, manifestly the favorite object of worship in a church nominally devoted to the worship of God. An educated man in France, even one of the best character and naturally religious, would almost as soon think of entering a temple of Jupiter as a church. Religion in Roman Catholic countries being thus left, so far as the educated classes are concerned, to the priests and women, its recent developments have been inspired exclusively by priestly ambition and female imagination. The infallibility of the Pope and the worship of the Virgin have made, and are still making, tremendous strides. The Romanizing party in the Episcopal Church of England are left panting behind, in their vain efforts to keep up with the superstitions of Rome.

From Lisieux my road lay by Pont-Audemer in its beautiful valley to Caudebec on the Seine; then along the Seine, — here most pleasant, — by the towers of Jumièges, the masterpiece, even in its ruins, of the grand Norman style, and the great Norman Church of St. George de Boscherville, to Rouen.

Everybody knows Rouen and its sights, — the Cathedral, the Church of St. Ouen, the magnificent view of the city from St. Catherine's Hill, — magnificent still, though much marred by the tall chimneys and their smoke. St. Ouen is undoubtedly the perfection of Gothic art. Unlike most of the cathedrals, it is built all in the same style and on one plan, complete in every part, admirable in all its proportions, and faultless in its details. But there is something disappointing in perfection. The less perfect cathedrals suggest more to the imagination than is realized in St. Ouen.

In the Museum is a portion of the heart of Richard Cœur-de-Lion. The Crusader king loved the Normans, and bequeathed his heart to them. He did not bequeath it to Imperial France. With all his faults, he was an illustrious soldier of Christendom; and he deserves to rest, not within the pale of this sensualist and atheist Empire, but in some land where the spirit of religious enterprise is not yet dead.

In the outskirts is St. Gervais, the church of the monastery to which William the Conqueror was carried, out of the noise and the feverish air of the great city, to die, and which witnessed the strange struggle, in his last moments, between his rapacious passions and his late-awakened remorse. So insecure was the state of society, that, when he whose iron hand had preserved order among his feudal nobles had expired, those about him fled to their strongholds in expectation of a general anarchy. Government was still only personal: law had not yet been enthroned in the minds of men. Even the personal attendants of the Conqueror abandoned his corpse,—a singular illustration of the theory, cherished by lovers of the past, that the relations of master and servant were more affectionate, and of a higher kind, in the days of chivalry than they are in ours.

Among the workingmen of Rouen, there probably lurks a good deal of republicanism, akin to that which exists among the workingmen of Paris. Unfortunately it is of a kind which, though capable of spasmodic attempts to revolutionize society by force, is little capable of sustained constitutional effect, and which alarms and arrays against it, not only despots, but moderate friends of liberty and progress. The outward appearances, however, at Rouen are all in favor of the Zouave and the Priest; and of the dominion of these two powers in France, if they can abstain from quarrelling with each other, it is difficult to foresee the end.

I have spoken bitterly of the French Empire. It has not only crushed the liberties of France, but it is the keystone and the focus of the system of military despotism in Europe. Bismarck, O'Donnell, and all the rest who rule by sabre-sway, are its pupils. It is intensely propagandist, — feeling, like slavery, that it cannot endure the contagious neighborhood of freedom. It has to a terrible extent corrupted even English politics, and inspired our oligarchical party with ideas of violence quite foreign to the temper of English Tories in former days. It is killing not only all moral aspirations, but almost all moral culture in France, and leaving nothing but the passion for military glory, the thirst of money, and the love of pleasure. It is reducing all education to a centralized machine, the wires of which are moved by a bureau at Paris; and we shall see the effects of this on French intellect in the next generation. " Ils ont tué la jeunesse," were the bitter words of an eminent and chivalrous Frenchman to the author of this article. Commerce is no doubt flourishing, and money is being made by the commercial classes, at present, under the Empire; but the highest industry is intimately connected with the moral and intellectual energies of a nation; and if these perish, it will in time perish too.

I have no means of knowing whether the morality of the court and the upper classes at Paris is what it is commonly reported to be; though, assuredly, if the performances of Thérèse are truly described to us, strange things must go on in the highest circles. Historical experience would be at fault, if a military despotism, with a political religion, did not produce moral effects in Paris somewhat analogous to those which it produced in Rome. The fashionable literature of the Empire, which can scarcely fail to reflect pretty accurately the moral state of the fashionable world, is not merely loose in principle, (as literature might possibly be in a period of transition between a narrower and an ampler moral code,) but utterly vile and loathsome; it seeks the materials of sensation novels from the charnel-house as well as from the brothel.

At Dieppe, my last point, I visited that very picturesque as well as memorable ruin, the Chateau d'Arques. It is a monument of the great victory gained near it by the Huguenots under Henri IV. over the League. This and the other Huguenot victories, alas! proved bootless; and it is melancholy to visit the fields where they were won.

By a series of calamities, the party was in the end erased from history; and scarcely a trace of its existence remains in the religious or political condition of Roman Catholic and Imperial France. It has left some noble names, and the memory of some noble deeds, which no doubt work upon national character to a certain extent; but this is all.

There was nothing in the fashionable watering-place of Dieppe to tempt my stay; and I turned from the Chateau d'Arques to embark for the land where, in spite of our political reaction and the efforts of the priest-party in our Church, the principles for which the field of Arques was fought and won have still a home.

AUNT JUDY.

A SOFT white bosom, kissed by lips and fondled by fingers pure as itself! ·

Back through the tender twilight of my one dim dream of a sinless childhood I catch that accusing glimpse of my mother — and myself. And as I stand here on this shapeless cairn of remorses, which, after forty years, I have piled upon my butchered and buried promise, that child turns from "the cup of his life and couch of his rest," to look upon me wondering, pitying.

My mother died when I was scarce five years old; and save the blurred beauty of that reproachful phantom, — caught and lost, caught and lost, by the unfaithful eyes of a graceless spirit, — she is as though she never had been. But in her place she left me a vicarious mother, — old, foolish, doting, black, — the youngest, loveliest, wisest, fairest lady I have ever known, — young with the youth of the immortal heart, lovely with the loveliness of the gleaning Ruth, wise with the wisdom of the most blessed among mothers when she "pondered all those things in her heart," and fair with the fairness of her who goeth her way forth by the footsteps of the flock, and feedeth her kids beside the shepherds' tents, — black, but comely.

"Aunt Judy," — Judith was her company name, — as the oldest of my uncles and aunts, and other boys' grandfathers and grandmothers, and all the rest of us children, delighted to call her,

— was pure negro; not grafted, scandalous mulatto, nor muddled, niggerish "gingerbread," but downright, unmixed, old-fashioned blackamoor. Her father and mother were genuine importations from the coast of Africa, snatched from some cannibal's calaboose, — where else they might have been butchered to make a Dahomeyan holiday, — and set up in a country gentleman's kitchen in Maryland, where they and their Christian progeny helped to make many a happy Christmas.

Of this antique Ethiopian couple I remember nothing, — they died long before I was born, — nor have I gathered any notable *ana* concerning them. Only of the father, I learned from my darling old nurse that he was one hundred and four years old when the Almighty Emancipator set him free; and from my father, and the brothers and sisters of my mother, that he possessed in a remarkable degree those simple, childlike virtues, characteristic of the original domesticated African, which his daughters Judith and Rachel so richly inherited.

Aunt Judy was one of many slaves set free by my grandfather's will, partly in reward of faithful service, partly from an impulse of conscientiousness; for our fine old Maryland gentleman was that social and political phenomenon, a slaveholder with a practical scruple. Not that he doubted the moral wholesomeness of the "institution," which, in his theory, was patriarchal and protective, and in his practice eminently beneficent; — if he were living this day, I doubt not he would be found among its most earnest and confident champions; — but he did not believe in holding human beings in bondage "on principle," as it were, and for the mere sake of bondage. The patriarchal element was, he thought, an essential in the moral right of the system, and *that* no longer necessary, the system became wrong. Therefore, so soon as it became clear to him that he (so peculiarly had God blessed him) could protect, advise, relieve his servants as effectually, they being free, as if their persons and their poor little goods, their labor and almost their lives, were at his disposal, he set them at liberty without asking the advice, or caring for the opinion, of any man; and by the same instrument which gave them the right to work, think, live, and die for themselves, he imposed upon his children a solemn responsibility for their well-being, in the future as in the past, — the honorable care of seeing to it that their wants were judiciously provided for, their training virtuous, their instruction useful, their employers just, their families united, and their homes happy. Those who were already of age went forth free at once; the minors received their "papers „ on their twenty-first birthday. And thus it was that, when I was born, Aunt Judy was as much freer than her "boy" is now, as simple, natural wants are freer than impatient, artificial appetites.

But that was the beginning and the end of Aunt Judy's freedom. For all the change it wrought in her feelings and her ways toward us, or in ours toward her, she might as well have remained the slave and the baby she was born; the old relations, so natural and gentle, of affection and faithful service on her side, of affection and grateful care on ours, no mere legal forms could alter: no papers could disturb their peacefulness, no privileges impair their confidence. Indeed, that same freedom — or at least her personal interest in it — was matter

of magnificent contempt to both nurse and child; she understood it too well to pet it, I understood it too little to be jealous of it. It was only by asking her that you could discover that Aunt Judy was free; it was only by being asked that she could recollect it. For her, freedom meant the right to "go where she pleased"; but her love knew no *where* but my father's roof and her darling's crib, nor anything so wrong as that right. For us, her freedom meant our freedom, the right to send her away when we chose; but our love knew no such *when* in all the shameful possibilities of time, nor anything in all the cruel conspiracies of ingratitude so wrong as that right. Could we entreat her to leave us, or to return from following after us, when each of our hearts had spoken and said, "The Lord do so to me, and more also, if aught but death part thee and me"? So she and I have gone on together ever since, and shall go on, until we come to the Bethlehem of love at rest. What though she had been there before we started, and were there now? To the saints and their eternal spaceless spirits there are nor days, nor miles, nor starting-points, nor resting-places, nor journey's ends.

From my earliest remembered observation, when I first began to "take notice," as nurses say of vague babies, with pinafore comparison and judgment, Aunt Judy was an old woman; I knew that, because she had explained to me why I had not wrinkles like hers, and why she could not read her precious Bible without spectacles, as I could, and why my back was not bent too, and how if I lived I would grow so. From such instructions I derived a blurred, bewildering notion that from me to her, suffering an Aunt-Judy change, was a long, slow, wearisome process of puckering and dimming and stiffening. But when she told me how she had carried my mother in her arms, as she had carried me, and had made the proud discovery of her first tooth, as, piously exploring among my tender gums with her little finger, she had found mine, I stared at the Pacific of her possible nursings, in a wild surmise, silent upon a peak of wonder. "Well, then, Auntie," I asked, "do you think you 're much more than a thousand ? "

She was not noticeably little as a woman, but wonderfully little as a bundle, to contain so many great virtues,— rather below the medium stature, slender, and bent with age, rather than with burdens ; for she had had no heartless master to lay heavy packs upon her. Her face, far from unpleasing in its lines, was lovely in its blended expression of intelligence, modesty, the sweetest guilelessness, an almost heroic truthfulness, devoted fidelity, a dove - like tranquillity of mind, and that abiding, reposeful trust in God which is equal to all trials, and can never be taken by surprise. Her voice was soft and soothing, her motions singularly free from clumsiness or fretfulness, her manners so beautifully blended of unaffected humility, patience, and self-respect as to command, in cheerful reciprocity, the deference they tendered ; in which respect she was a severe ordeal to the sham gentlemen and ladies who had the honor to be presented to her, — the slightest trace of snobbery betraying itself at once to the sensitive test-paper of Aunt Judy's true politeness. Her ways were ways of pleasantness, and all her paths were peace. Faith, hope, and charity were met in her dusky, shrunken bosom, — more at home there, perhaps, than in a finer dwelling.

A sneering philosophy was never yet challenged to contemplate a piety more complete than that which made this venerable " nigger " a lady on earth, and a saint in heaven ; but on her knees she found it, and on her knees she held it fast, — watching, praying, trembling.

> " When she sat, her head was, prayer-like, bending :
>   When she rose, it rose not any more.
>   Faster seemed her true heart grave-ward tending
>   Than her tired feet, weak and travel-sore."

She was, indeed, a living prayer, a lying-down and rising-up, a going-out and coming-in prayer, — a loving, longing, working, waiting prayer, — a black and wrinkled, bent and tottering incense and aspiration. With her to labor was literally to worship ; she washed dishes with confession, ironed shirts with supplication, and dusted furniture with thanksgiving, — morning. evening, noon, and night, praising God. From resting-place to resting-place, over tedious stretches of task, she prayed her way,

> " And ever, at each period,
>   She stopped and sang, ' Praise God ! ' "

like Browning's Theocrite. And, as if answering Blaise, the listening monk, when he said,

> " Well done !
> I doubt not thou art heard, my son :
> As well as if thy voice to-day
> Were praising God the Pope's great way,"

her longing was,

> " Would God that I
> Might praise him *some* great way and die."

Many a time have I, bursting boisterously into my little bedroom in quest of top or ball, checked myself, with a feeling more akin to superstition than to reverence, on finding Aunt Judy on her knees beside the pretty cot she had just made up so snugly and tenderly for me, pouring her ever-brimming heart out in clear, refreshing springs of prayer. Led by these still waters, she rested there from the heat and burden of life, as the camel by wells in the desert. On such occasions I always knew that my dear old nurse had just finished making a bed or sweeping a room, and had sunk down to rest in a prayer, as a fagged drudge on a stool. If you ever gloried — and what gentleman has not ? — in Gregg's brave old hymn, beginning

> " Jesus, and shall it ever be,
>   A mortal man ashamed of thee ? "

you would ask for no more intrepid illustration of its loyal spirit than the figure of Aunt Judy on her knees at the foot of my father's bed, where he often found her in the act, — turning her face for an instant, but without offering to rise, from her Divine Master to the mild fellow-servant in whom she affectionately recognized an earthly master, and asking, with a manner far less embarrassed than his own, " Was you lookin' for your gloves, sir ? They 's on de

bureau, — and your umbrell's behind
de door' ; — and then placidly turning
back again to that Master whom most of
us white slaves of the Devil think we
have honored enough when we have
printed His title with a capital M.

"My Master, shall I speak?   O that to Thee
My Servant were a little so
As flesh may be!
That these two words might creep and grow
To some degree of spiciness to Thee!"

But the hour of my Aunt-Judyness
most sacred and inspiring to me, weird-
ly filling my imagination with solemn
reaches beyond my childish ken, was
at the close of the day, when — I having been undressed, with many a cradle
lecture and many a blessing, many an
admonition and endearment, line upon
line and precept upon precept, here a
text and there a pious rhyme, between
the buttons and the strings, and having
said my awful " Now I lay me," lest
" I should die before I wake," and been
tucked in with careful fondling fingers,
the party of the first part honorably
contracting to "shut his eyes and go
straight to sleep," provided the party of
the second part would remain at the bedside till the last heavy-lingering wink
was winked, — that image of her Maker
carved in ebony took up her part in
creation's pausing chorus, and poured
her little human praise into the echoing
ear of God in such a burst of triumphant humility, of exulting hope and
trust, and all-embracing charity and
love, — wherein master and mistress
and fellow-servant, friend and stranger,
the kind and the cruel, the just and the
unjust, the believer and the scoffer, had
each his welcome place and was called
by his name, — as only Ruth could
have said or Isaiah sung.   As for me,
I only lay there with closed eyes, very
still, lest I should offend the angels,
for I knew the room was full of them,
— as for me, I only write here with
a faltering heart, lest I should offend
those prayers, for I know heaven is
full of them, and I know that for every
time my name arose to the throne of
God on that beatified handmaid's hopes
and cries, I have been forgiven seventy
times seven.

And so Aunt Judy prayed and praised,
sitting upon the landing to rest herself,
as she descended from the garret side-
wise, the same foot always advanced,
as is the way of weak old folks in coming down stairs ; and so she prayed
and praised between the splitting spells
of her forty years' asthmatic cough,
rocking backward and forward, with her
hands upon her knees.   And sometimes she preached to me, the ironing-
table being her pulpit ; for oh ! she was
an excellent divine, that had the Bible
at her fingers' ends, and many a moving sermon did she deliver, "how God
doth make his enemies his friends."
And sometimes she baptized me, the
bath-tub being her Jordan, in the name
of duty, love, and patience.   In truth,
Aunt Judy took as much prophylactic
pains with my soul as if it had been
tainted with a congenital sulphuric di-
athesis ; and if I had sunk under a com-
plication of profane disorders, no post-
mortem statement of my spiritual pa-
thology would have been complete and
exact which failed to take note of her
stringent preventive measures.

Now be it known, that Aunt Judy's
piety was in no respect of the niggerish kind ; when I say "colored," I
mean one thing, respectfully ; and when
I say "niggerish," I mean another, dis-
gustedly.   I am not responsible for
the distinction : it is a true "cullud"
nomenclature, and very significant ;
our fellow-citizens of African descent
themselves employ it, nicely and wisely ; and when they call each other
"nigger," the familiar term of opprobrium is applied with all the malice of a
sting, and resented with all the sensitiveness of a raw.   So when I say that
my Auntie's piety was not of the niggerish kind, even Zoe, "The Octo-
roon," or any other woman or man in
whose veins courses the blood of Ham
four times diluted, knows that I mean
it was not that glory-hallelujah variety
of cunning or delusion, compounded of
laziness and catalepsy, which is popular among the shouting, shirt-tearing
sects of plantation darkies, who "git
relijin" and fits twelve times a year.

To all such she used to say, " 'T ain't de real grace, honey, — 't ain't de sure glory, — you hollers too loud. When you gits de Dove in your heart, and de Lamb on your bosom, you 'll feel as ef you was in dat stable at Bethlehem and de Blessed Virgin had lent you de sleepin' Baby to hold." She would not have shrunk from lifting up her voice and crying aloud in the market-place, if thereby she might turn one smart butcher from the error of his *weighs;* but for steady talking to the Lord, she preferred my bedside or the back-stairs

But in those days the kitchen was my paradise, by her transmuted. As a child, and not less now than then, I had a consuming longing for snuggery ; my one fair, clear idea of the consummate golden fruit of the spirit's sweet content was a cosey place to get away to. In my longing I purred with the cat rolled up in her furry ball on the rug by the fire, making a high-post bedstead of a chair ; in my longing I stole with furtive rats to their mysterious cave-nests in the wall. So do I now, — the more for that I lost, so long ago, my dear kitchen, my Aunt-Judy-ness, — my home.

> " I behold it everywhere,
> On the earth, and in the air,
> But it never comes again."

At this moment I feel the dresser in the corner, gleaming with the cook's refulgent pride of polished tins ; I am sensible of that pulpit ironing-table — alas ! the flat-iron on its ring is as cold as the hand that erst so deftly guided it. I bask before the old-fashioned hospitable fireplace, capacious and embracing, and jolly with its old-fashioned hickory blaze, and the fat old-fashioned kettle hung upon the old-fashioned crane, swinging and singing of old-fashioned abundance and good cheer. I behold the Madras turban, the white neckerchief crossed over the bosom, the clumsy steel-bowed spectacles, the check apron, and the old-fashioned love that is forever new. But they never come again.

That kitchen was my hospital and my school, — as much better than the whole round of select academies and classical institutes that my father tried, and that tried me, as check aprons and love are more inculcating than canes and quarterly bills ; and however it may be with my head, my heart never has forgotten the lessons I learned there. Thither, on the nipping nights of winter, brought I my small fingers and toes, numbed and aching with snow-balling and skating, to be tenderly rubbed before the fire, or fondly folded in the motherly apron. Thither brought I an extensive and various assortment of splinters and fresh cuts ; thither my impervious nose, to be lubricated with goose-grease, or my swollen angry tonsils (" waxen kernels," Aunt Judy called them), to be mollified with volatile liniment.

It was here that my own free mind, uncompelled by pedagogues and unallured by prizes, first achieved a whole chapter in the Bible. Cook and laundress and chambermaid were out for the evening ; the table had been cleared and covered with the fresh white cloth ; and I, perched on Aunt Judy's lap at the end next the fireplace, glided featly over the short words, plunged pluckily through the long, (braced, as it were, against the superior education and the spectacles behind me,) of the first chapter of the Gospel according to St. John, from the Word that was in the beginning, to the Hereafter of the glorified Son of man. After which so large performance for so small a boy, we re-refreshed ourselves with that cheerful hymn, in which Dr. Watts lyrically disposes of the questions,

> " And must this body die,
> This mortal frame decay ?
> And must these active limbs of mine
> Lie mouldering in the clay ? "

For so infantile a heart, my darling old mammy had a wonderful lack of active imagination, even in her religion ; for there all was real and actual to her. Her pleasures of memory and her pleasures of hope were alike founded upon fact. Christ was as personal to her as her own rheumatic frame, and heaven as positive as her kitchen.

" Blessed are they that have not seen, and yet have believed " ; — but for her, to believe and to see were one. So whatever imagination she may by nature have possessed seemed to have dwindled for lack of exercise : it was long since she had had any use for it. She had no folk-lore, no faculty of story-telling, — only a veracious legend or two of our family, which she invariably related with an affidavit-like scrupulousness of circumstance. I cannot recollect that she ever once beguiled me with a mere nurse's tale. So when at that kitchen-table we read " The Pilgrim's Progress " together, we presented a curious entertainment for the student of intellectual processes, — nurse and child arriving by diverse arguments of imagination at the same result of reality ; — she knowing that Sin was a burden, because she had borne it ; I, because I had seen it in the picture strapped to Christian's back ; — she, that Despair was a giant, because he had often appalled her soul within her ; I, because in a dream he had made me scream last night ;—she, that Death was a river, because so many of her dear ones had gone over, and because on her clear days she could see the other shore ; I, because, as I lay with my young cheek against her old heart, I could hear the beating of its waves.

Blessed indeed is the mother who is admitted to the sanctuary of her darling's secrets with the freedom with which Aunt Judy penetrated (was invited rather, with parted lips and sparkling eyes) to mine, — into whose sympathetic ear are poured, in all the dream-borne melody of the first songs of the heart, in all " the tender thought, the speechless pain " of its first violets, his earliest confessions, aspirations, loves, wrongs, troubles, triumphs. Well do I remember that day when, trembling, ghastly, faint, I fell in tears upon her neck, and poured into her bosom and basin the spasmodic story of My First Cigar ! Well do I remember that night, when, bursting from the evening party in the parlor, and the thick red married lady in the thin blue

tarletan, and all my raptures and my anguish, I flung myself into Aunt Judy's arms and acknowledged the soft corn of My First Love, raving at the fatal sandy-whiskered gulf that yawned between me and Mine thick blue Own One in the thin red tarletan !

Well do I remember — though I was only seven times one — the panting exultation with which I flung into her lap the cheap colored print of the Tower of Babel (showing the hurly-burly of French bricklayers and Irish hod-carriers, and the grand row generally) that I had just won at school by correctly committing to memory, and publicly reciting, the whole of

" Almighty God, thy piercing eye
   Strikes through the shades of night," etc.

My first prize ! The Tower of Babel fell untimely into the wash-tub, but she dried it on her warm bosom ; and I have never forgotten that All our secret actions lie All open to His sight ; though I have never seen the verses (they were in Comly's Spelling-Book) from that day to this.

In those days we had a youth of talent in the family, — a sort of sophomorical boil, that the soap and sugar of indiscriminate adulation had drawn to a head of conceit. This youth bestowed a great deal of attention on a certain young woman of a classical turn of mind, who once had a longing to attend a fancy-ball as a sibyl. About the same time Sophomore missed the first volume of his Potter's " Antiquities of Greece " ; and, having searched for it in vain, made up his mind that I had presented it as a keepsake, together with a lock of my hair and a cent's worth of pea-nut taffy, to the head girl of the infant class at my Sunday school. So Sophomore, being in morals a pedant and in intellect a bully, accused me of appropriating the book, and offered me a dollar if I would restore it to him. With swelling heart and quivering lip I carried the wanton insult — my first great wrong — straight to Aunt Judy, who, in her mild way, resented it as a personal outrage to her own feelings, and tried to soothe and console me by assuring me that "it would all rub out when it got dry." Three years later, as I was passing the sibyl's house one morning, her mother met me at the door and handed me an odd volume of Potter's "Antiquities of Greece," which she had just discovered in some out-of-the-way corner, where it had been mislaid, and which she desired me to hand to Sophomore with the sibyl's compliments, thanks, regrets, and several other delicacies of the season. But I handed it first to Aunt Judy, who gloried boisterously in my first triumph. Sophomore patronized me magnificently with apologies ; but if the wrong never gets any drier than Aunt Judy's joyful eyes were then, it never will rub out.

So heartily disgusted was I with this classical episode that I conceived the original and desperate project of running away and going to sea. At that time I enjoyed the proud privilege of a personal acquaintance with the Siamese Twins, and was the envied holder of a season ticket to the Museum, where they exhibited their attractive duplicity. It was an essential part of my preparations to procure from the amiable Chang-Eng a letter of introduction to their ingenious mother, who, I was told, was in the duck-fishing line at Bangkok. Of course, I confided my plan to Aunt Judy ; and, although she opposed it with extra prayers of peculiar length and strength, and finally succeeded in dissuading me from it, I am by no means certain that she would not have connived at my flight, rather than betray my confidence or consent to my punishment.

Those were the days of the *Morus multicaulis* mania, and I embarked with spirit in the silk-worm business. The original capital upon which I erected the enterprise was furnished from the surplus of Aunt Judy's wages. It was in the first silk dress that should come of all those moths and eggs and wriggling spinners and cocoons that she invested with such sanguine cheerfulness ; and although she never got her money back in that form,—owing to the unfortunate exhaustion of my mulberry-leaves

and the refusal of my worms to spin silk from tea, which, they being of pure Chinese stock, I thought very unreasonable, — she conceived that she reaped abundant returns in her share of my happy enthusiasm, while it lasted ; and when I wept over the famine-stricken forms of my operatives, she said, "Never mind, honey ; dey was an awful litter anyhow, and I spec' dey was only de or'nary caterpillar poor trash, after all, else dey 'd a-kep' goin' on dat tea ; fur 't was de rale high-price Chany kind, sure 's ye 'r born."

It was a striking oddness in the dear old soul, that, whilst in her hours of familiar ease she indulged in the homely lingo of her tribe, in her " company talk " she displayed a graver propriety of language, and in her prayers was always fluent, forcible, and correct.

The watchful tenderness with which I loved my gentle, childlike father was the most interesting of the many secrets that my heart shared only with Aunt Judy's. When I was twelve years old, he fell into a touching despondency, caused by certain reverses in his business and the unremitting anxieties consequent upon them. So intense and sensitive was my magnetic sympathy with him, that I contracted the same sadness, in a form so aggravated and morbid that the despondency, in me, became despair, and the anxiety horror. The cruel fancy took possession of my mind, installed there by my treacherously imaginative temperament, that some awful calamity was about to befall my dear father ; that he, patient, submissive Christian that he was, even meditated suicide ; and that shape of fear so shook my soul with terror in the daytime, so filled my dreams with horror in the night, that, as if it were not myself, I turn back to pity the poor child now, and wonder that he did not go mad.

Does he know the truth now up in Heaven, the beloved old man ? Surely ; for the beloved old woman, who alone knew it on earth, is she not there ? He knows now how his selfish, wilful, school-hating scamp, of whom only he and Aunt Judy ever boded any good, stole away from his playmates and his games, every afternoon when school was dismissed, and with that baleful phantom before him, and that doleful cry in his ears, flew through the bustle and clatter of the wharves to where his father's warehouse was, two miles away; and, dodging like a thief among crates and boxes, bales and casks, and choking down the appeal of his lonely, shame-faced terror, watched that door with all the eager, tenacious, panting fidelity of a dog, until the merchant came forth on his way homeward for the night.   And how the scamp followed, dodging, watching, trembling, unconsciously moaning, unconsciously sobbing, seeing no form but his, hearing no sound but his footfall, keeping cunningly between that form and the dock, lest it should suddenly dart through the drays and the moored vessels and plunge into the river, as the scamp had seen it do in his dreams.   And how, at the end of that walk through the Valley of the Shadow of Death, when we reached our own door, and the simple-hearted, good old man passed in, as ignorant of my following as he was innocent of the monstrous purpose I imputed to him, I lingered some minutes at the gate to ease with a sluice of tears my pent-up fears and pains; and then burst into the yard, whistling, whooping, prancing, swinging my satchel, without feeling or manners, — a shameless, heartless brat and nuisance.   And how, when the day, with all its secret sighs and sobs, was over, and he and I retired to the same bed, I prayed to our Father in heaven (muffling my very thoughts in the bedclothes lest he should hear them) to keep my earthly father safe for me from all the formless dangers of the darkness; and how, when at the first gray streak of dawn the spectre shook me, and I awoke, I held my heart and my breathing still, to listen for his breathing, and thanked God when he groaned in his sleep; and how, when his shaving-water was brought and he stood before the glass, baring his throat, I crept close behind him, still watching, gasping, — now pretending to hum a tune, now pressing my hand upon my mouth lest I should shriek in my helpless suspense; and how, when he drew the razor from its sheath —   Well! I am forty years old now, and I have been pursued since then by so many and such torturing shapes of desperation and dismay as should refresh the heart of my stupidest enemy with an emotion of relenting; but I would consent to weep, groan, rave them all over again, beginning where that haunted child left off, rather than begin where he began, though my spectres should forever vanish with his.

Aunt Judy trembled and watched with me, and, accepting my phantom as if it were a reasonable fear, hid away her share of the sacred secret in her heart, and helped me to cover up mine with a disguise of carelessness, lest any foolish or brutal mockery should find it out.

My darling had but few superstitions: her spiritually informed intelligence rose superior to vulgar signs and dreams, and saw through the little warnings and wonders of darker and less pure minds with a science of its own, which she called Gospel light.   Still, there was here a sign and there a legend that she clung to for old acquaintance' sake, rather than by reason of any credulity in her strong enough to take the place of faith.   But these constituted the peculiar poetry of her personality, the fireside balladry and folk-lore of her Aunt-Judyness; and I could no more mock them than I could mock the good fairy in her, that changed all my floggings to feathers, — no sooner tear away their comfortable homeliness to jeer at their honored absurdity, than I could snatch off her dear familiar turban to mock the silver reverence of her " wool." Ah! I wish you could have heard her tell me that I must pass through fourteen years of trouble, — seven on account of the big old mirror in the parlor that I, lying on the sofa beneath it, kicked clear off its hook and into the middle of the floor, — and seven for that very looking-glass which my father used to shave by, and which I, sparring at my image in it, to amuse my little brother, knocked into smithareens with my fractious fist. Why, man, it was not only awful, it all came true.

Aunt Judy, like most of those antiques, the old-fashioned house-servants of the South,—coachmen and waiters, nurses and lady's maids,—was a towering aristocrat: she believed in blood, and was a connoisseur in pedigrees. Her family pride was lofty, vast, and imposing, and embraced in the scope of its sympathy whoever could boast of a family Bible containing a well-filled record of births, marriages, and deaths, —a dear dead-and-gone inheritance of family portraits, lace, trinkets, and silver spoons,—a family vault in an Orthodox burial-ground,—and above all, one or two venerable family servants, just to show "dese mushroom folks, wid der high-minded notions, how diff'-ent things was in ole missus's time!" Measured by this standard, if you had the misfortune to be a nobody, Aunt Judy, as a lady, might patronize you, as a Christian, would cheerfully advise and assist you; but to the exclusive privilege of what she superbly styled family-arities, you must in vain aspire. *Our* family, in the broadest sense of that word, was a large one,—by blood and marriage a numerous connection; and when Aunt Judy said, "So-and-so b'longs to our family," she included every man, woman, and child who could produce the genuine patent of our nobility, and especially all who had ever worn our livery, from my great-grandfather's tremendous coachman to the slipshod young gal that "nussed" our last new cousin's last new baby. Sometimes one of these cousins — quite telescopic, so distant was the relationship — would come to dine with us. Then Aunt Judy, in gorgeous turban, immaculate neckerchief, and lively satisfaction, would be served up in state, our *pièce de résistance.* The guest would compliment her with sympathetic inquiries about the state of her health, which was always "only tol'able," or "ra-a-ther poorly," or it "did 'pear as

ef she could shuffle round a leetle yit, praise de Master! But she was a-gettin' older and shacklier every day; her cough was awful tryin' sometimes, and it 'peared as ef she war n't of much account, nohow. But de Lord's will be done; when He wanted her, she reckined He 'd call. And how does you find yourself, Miss? And how does your ma git along wid de servants now? You know she always was a great hand to be pertickler, Miss; we had n't sich another young lady in our family, to be pertickler, as your ma, Miss, — 'specially 'bout de pleetin' and clare-starchin'."

I have to accuse myself of habitually shocking her aristocratic sensibilities by profanely ignoring, in favor of the society of dirty little plebeians, the relations to whom the sacred charm of a common ancestry should have drawn me. "Make haste, honey," she used to say; "wash yer face and hands, and pull up yer stockin's, and tie yer shoes, and bresh de sand out of yer hair, and blow yer nose, and go into de parlor, and shake hands wid yer Cousin Jorjana." But I would not. "O bother, Auntie! who 's my Cousin Georgiana?" "Why, honey, don't you know? Miss Arabella Jane — dat 's your dear dead-an'-gone grandma's second cousin — had seven chiidern by her first husband, — he was a Patterson, — and nine by her second, — *he* was a McKim, — and five — but 'tain't no use, honey; you don't 'pear to take no int'res' in yer own kith and kin, no more dan or'nary white trash. I 'spec' you don't know de diff'-ence, dis minnit, 'twixt yer poor old Aunt Judy and any no-account poorhouse nigger." And so my Cousin Georgiana, of whom I had never heard before, remains a myth to me, one of Aunt Judy's Mrs. Harrises, to this day. It was wonderful what an exact descriptive list of them she could call at a moment's notice; and for keeping the run of their names and numbers, she was as good as an enrolling officer or a directory man. "Our family" could boast of many Pharisees, as well as blush for many prodigals; but her sympathies were wholly with the latter; and for these she was eternally killing fatted calves, in spite of angry elder brothers and the whole sect of whited sepulchres, who forgive exactly four hundred and ninety times by the multiplication-table, and compass sea and land to make one hypocrite. If she had had a fold of her own, all her sheep would have been black.

One day in January, 1849, I called to see Aunt Judy for the last time. Superannuated, and rapidly failing, she had been installed by my father in a comfortable room in the house of a sort of cousin of hers, a worthy and "well-to-do" woman of color, where she might be cheered by the visits of the more respectable people of her own class, — darkies of substantial character and of the first families, among whom she was esteemed as a mother in Israel. Thither either my father or one or two of his children came every day, to watch her declining health, to administer to her comfort, and to wait upon her with those offices of respect to which she had earned her right by three quarters of a century of humble, patient love and faithful service. My chest was packed, and on the morrow I must sail for the ends of the earth; but she knew nothing of that. All that afternoon we talked together as we had never talked before; and many an injury that my indignant tears had kept fresh and sticky was "dried" in the warmth of her earnest, anxious peace-making, and

"rubbed out" then and there. No page of my inditing could be pure enough to record it all; but is it not written in the Book of Life, among the regrets and the forgivenesses, the confessions and the consolations and the hopes?

The last word I ever uttered to Aunt Judy was a careful, loving, pious lie. She said, "Won't you come ag'in to-morrow, son, and see de poor ole woman?" And I replied, "O yes, Auntie!" — though I well knew that, even as I spoke, I was looking into the wise truth of those patient, tender eyes for the last time in this world. The sun was going down as we parted, — that sun has never risen again for me.

In June, 1850, on board a steamboat in the Sacramento River, I received the very Bible I had first learned to read in, sitting on her lap by the kitchen fire, — in the beginning was the Word. She was dead; and, dying, she had sent it me, with her blessing, — at the end was the Word.

In August, 1852, that Bible was tossed ashore from a wreck in an Indian river, and by angels delivered at a mission school in the jungle, where other heathens beside myself have doubtless learned from it the Word that was, and is, and ever shall be. On the inside of the cover, sitting on her lap by the kitchen fire, I had written, with appropriate "pot-hooks and hangers," AUNT JUDY.

Such her quiet consummation and renown!

THE CHIMNEY-CORNER FOR 1866.

VII.

BODILY RELIGION: A SERMON ON GOOD HEALTH.

ONE of our recent writers has said, that "good health is physical religion"; and it is a saying worthy to be printed in golden letters. But good health being physical religion, it fully shares that indifference with which the human race regards things confessedly the most important. The neglect of the soul is the trite theme of all religious teachers; and, next to their souls, there is nothing that people neglect so much as their bodies. Every person ought to be perfectly healthy, just as everybody ought to be perfectly religious; but, in point of fact, the greater part of mankind are so far from perfect moral or physical religion that they cannot even form a conception of the blessing beyond them.

The mass of good, well-meaning Christians are not yet advanced enough to guess at the change which a perfect fidelity to Christ's spirit and precepts would produce in them. And the majority of people who call themselves well, because they are not, at present, upon any particular doctor's list, are not within sight of what perfect health would be. That fulness of life, that vigorous tone, and that elastic cheerfulness, which make the mere fact of existence a luxury, that suppleness which carries one like a well-built boat over every wave of unfavorable chance, — these are attributes of the perfect health seldom enjoyed. We see them in young children, in animals, and now and then, but rarely, in some adult human being, who has preserved intact the religion of the body through all opposing influences. Perfect health supposes not a state of mere quiescence, but of positive enjoyment in living. See that little fellow, as his nurse turns him out in the morning, fresh from his bath, his hair newly curled, and his cheeks polished like apples. Every step is a spring or a dance; he runs, he laughs, he shouts, his face breaks into a thousand dimpling smiles at a word. His breakfast of plain bread and milk is swallowed with an eager and incredible delight, — it is *so good*, that he stops to laugh or thump the table now and then in expression of his ecstasy. All day long he runs and frisks and plays; and when at night the little head seeks the pillow, down go the eye-curtains, and sleep comes without a dream. In the morning his first note is a laugh and a crow, as he sits up in his crib and tries to pull papa's eyes open with his fat fingers. He is an embodied joy, — he is sunshine and music and

laughter for all the house. With what a magnificent generosity does the Author of life endow a little mortal pilgrim in giving him at the outset of his career such a body as this! How miserable it is to look forward twenty years, when the same child, now grown a man, wakes in the morning with a dull, heavy head, the consequence of smoking and studying till twelve or one the night before; when he rises languidly to a late breakfast, and turns from this, and tries that, — wants a devilled bone, or a cutlet with Worcestershire sauce, to make eating possible; and then, with slow and plodding step, finds his way to his office and his books. Verily the shades of the prison-house gather round the growing boy; for, surely, no one will deny that life often begins with health little less perfect than that of the angels.

But the man who habitually wakes sodden, headachy, and a little stupid, and who needs a cup of strong coffee and various stimulating condiments to coax his bodily system into something like fair working order, does not suppose he is out of health. He says, "Very well, I thank you," to your inquiries, — merely because he has entirely forgotten what good health is. He is well, not because of any particular pleasure in physical existence, but well simply because he is not a subject for prescriptions. Yet there is no store of vitality, no buoyancy, no superabundant vigor, to resist the strain and pressure to which life puts him. A checked perspiration, a draught of air ill-timed, a crisis of perplexing business or care, and he is down with a bilious attack, or an influenza, and subject to doctors' orders for an indefinite period. And if the case be so with men, how is it with women? How many women have at maturity the keen appetite, the joyous love of life and motion, the elasticity and sense of physical delight in existence, that little children have? How many have any superabundance of vitality with which to meet the wear and strain of life? And yet they call themselves well.

But is it possible, in maturity, to have

the joyful fulness of the life of childhood? Experience has shown that the delicious freshness of this dawning hour may be preserved even to midday, and may be brought back and restored after it has been for years a stranger. Nature, though a severe disciplinarian, is still, in many respects, most patient and easy to be entreated, and meets any repentant movement of her prodigal children with wonderful condescension. Take Bulwer's account of the first few weeks of his sojourn at Malvern, and you will read, in very elegant English, the story of an experience of pleasure which has surprised and delighted many a patient at a water-cure. The return to the great primitive elements of health — water, air, and simple food, with a regular system of exercise — has brought to many a jaded, weary, worn-down human being the elastic spirits, the simple, eager appetite, the sound sleep, of a little child. Hence, the rude huts and châlets of the peasant Priessnitz were crowded with battered dukes and princesses, and notables of every degree, who came from the hot, enervating luxury which had drained them of existence to find a keener pleasure in peasants' bread under peasants' roofs than in soft raiment and palaces. No arts of French cookery can possibly make anything taste so well to a feeble and palled appetite as plain brown bread and milk taste to a hungry water-cure patient, fresh from bath and exercise.

If the water-cure had done nothing more than establish the fact that the glow and joyousness of early life are things which may be restored after having been once wasted, it would have done a good work. For if Nature is so forgiving to those who have once lost or have squandered her treasures, what may not be hoped for us if we can learn the art of never losing the first health of childhood? And though with us, who have passed to maturity, it may be too late for the blessing, cannot something be done for the children who are yet to come after us?

Why is the first health of childhood lost? Is it not the answer, that childhood is the only period of life in which bodily health is made a prominent object? Take our pretty boy, with cheeks like apples, who started in life with a hop, skip, and dance, — to whom laughter was like breathing, and who was enraptured with plain bread and milk, — how did he grow into the man who wakes so languid and dull, who wants strong coffee and Worcestershire sauce to make his breakfast go down? When and where did he drop the invaluable talisman that once made everything look brighter and taste better to him, however rude and simple, than now do the most elaborate combinations? What is the boy's history? Why, for the first seven years of his life his body is made of some account. It is watched, cared for, dieted, disciplined, fed with fresh air, and left to grow and develop like a thrifty plant. But from the time school education begins, the body is steadily ignored, and left to take care of itself.

The boy is made to sit six hours a day in a close, hot room, breathing impure air, putting the brain and the nervous system upon a constant strain, while the muscular system is repressed to an unnatural quiet. During the six hours, perhaps twenty minutes are allowed for all that play of the muscles which, up to this time, has been the constant habit of his life. After this he is sent home with books, slate, and lessons to occupy an hour or two more in preparing for the next day. In the whole of this time there is no kind of effort to train the physical system by appropriate exercise. Something of the sort was attempted years ago in the infant schools, but soon given up; and now, from the time study first begins, the muscles are ignored in all primary schools. One of the first results is the loss of that animal vigor which formerly made the boy love motion for its own sake. Even in his leisure hours he no longer leaps and runs as he used to; he learns to sit still, and by and by sitting and lounging come to be the habit, and vigorous motion the exception, for most of the hours of the day. The education thus begun goes on from primary to high school, from high school to college, from college through professional studies of law, medicine, or theology, with this steady contempt for the body, with no provision for its culture, training, or development, but rather a direct and evident provision for its deterioration and decay.

The want of suitable ventilation in school-rooms, recitation-rooms, lecture-rooms, offices, court-rooms, conference-rooms, and vestries, where young students of law, medicine, and theology acquire their earlier practice, is something simply appalling. Of itself it would answer for men the question, why so many thousand glad, active children come to a middle life without joy, — a life whose best estate is a sort of slow, plodding endurance. The despite and hatred which most men seem to feel for God's gift of fresh air, and their resolution to breathe as little of it as possible, could only come from a long course of education, in which they have been accustomed to live without it. Let any one notice the conduct of our American people travelling in railroad cars. We will suppose that about half of them are what might be called well-educated people, who have learned in books, or otherwise, that the air breathed from the lungs is laden with impurities, — that it is noxious and poisonous ; and yet, travel with these people half a day, and you would suppose from their actions that they considered the external air as a poison created expressly to injure them, and that the only course of safety lay in keeping the cars hermetically sealed, and breathing over and over the vapor from each others' lungs. If a person in despair at the intolerable foulness raises a window, what frowns from all the neighboring seats, especially from great rough-coated men, who always seem the first to be apprehensive ! The request to "put down that window" is almost sure to follow a moment or two of fresh air. In vain have rows of ventilators been put in the tops

of some of the cars, for conductors and passengers are both of one mind, that these ventilators are inlets of danger, and must be kept carefully closed.

Railroad travelling in America is systematically, and one would think carefully, arranged so as to violate every possible law of health. The old rule to keep the head cool and the feet warm is precisely reversed. A red-hot stove heats the upper stratum of air to oppression, while a stream of cold air is constantly circulating about the lower extremities. The most indigestible and unhealthy substances conceivable are generally sold in the cars or at way-stations for the confusion and distress of the stomach. Rarely can a traveller obtain so innocent a thing as a plain good sandwich of bread and meat, while pie, cake, doughnuts, and all other culinary atrocities, are almost forced upon him at every stopping-place. In France, England, and Germany the railroad cars are perfectly ventilated ; the feet are kept warm by flat cases filled with hot water and covered with carpet, and answering the double purpose of warming the feet and diffusing an agreeable temperature through the car, without burning away the vitality of the air ; while the arrangements at the refreshment-rooms provide for the passenger as wholesome and well-served a meal of healthy, nutritious food as could be obtained in any home circle.

What are we to infer concerning the home habits of a nation of men who so resignedly allow their bodies to be poisoned and maltreated in travelling over such an extent of territory as is covered by our railroad lines ? Does it not show that foul air and improper food are too much matters of course to excite attention ? As a writer in "The Nation" has lately remarked, it is simply and only because the American nation like to have unventilated cars, and to be fed on pie and coffee at stopping-places, that nothing better is known to our travellers ; if there were any marked dislike of such a state of things on the part of the people, it would not exist. We have wealth enough, and enterprise enough, and ingenuity enough, in our American nation, to compass with wonderful rapidity any end that really seems to us desirable. An army was improvised when an army was wanted, — and an army more perfectly equipped, more bountifully fed, than so great a body of men ever was before. Hospitals, Sanitary Commissions, and Christian Commissions all arose out of the simple conviction of the American people that they must arise. If the American people were equally convinced that foul air was a poison, — that to have cold feet and hot heads was to invite an attack of illness, — that maple-sugar, pop-corn, peppermint candy, pie, doughnuts, and peanuts are not diet for reasonable beings, — they would have railroad accommodations very different from those now in existence.

We have spoken of the foul air of court-rooms. What better illustration could be given of the utter contempt with which the laws of bodily health are treated, than the condition of these places? Our lawyers are our highly educated men. They have been through high-school and college training, they have learned the properties of oxygen, nitrogen, and carbonic-acid gas, and have seen a mouse die under an exhausted receiver, and of course they know that foul, unventilated rooms are bad for the health; and yet generation after generation of men so taught and trained will spend the greater part of their lives in rooms notorious for their close and impure air, without so much as an attempt to remedy the evil. A well-ventilated court-room is a four-leaved clover among court-rooms. Young men are constantly losing their health at the bar : lung diseases, dyspepsia, follow them up, gradually sapping their vitality. Some of the brightest ornaments of the profession have actually fallen dead as they stood pleading, — victims of the fearful pressure of poisonous and heated air upon the excited brain. The deaths of Salmon P. Chase of Portland, uncle of our present Chief Justice, and of Ezekiel Webster, the brother of our great statesman, are memorable examples of the calamitous effects of the errors dwelt upon ; and yet, strange to say, nothing efficient is done to mend these errors, and give the body an equal chance with the mind in the pressure of the world's affairs.

But churches, lecture - rooms, and vestries, and all buildings devoted especially to the good of the soul, are equally witness of the mind's disdain of the body's needs, and the body's consequent revenge upon the soul. In how many of these places has the question of a thorough provision of fresh air been even considered ? People would never think of bringing a thousand persons into a desert place, and keeping them there, without making preparations to feed them. Bread and butter, potatoes and meat, must plainly be found for them ; but a thousand human beings are put into a building to remain a given number of hours, and no one asks the question whether means exist for giving each one the quantum of fresh air needed for his circulation, and these thousand victims will consent to be slowly poisoned, gasping, sweating, getting red in the face, with confused and sleepy brains, while a minister with a yet redder face and a more oppressed brain struggles and wrestles, through the hot, seething vapors, to make clear to them the mysteries of faith. How many churches are there that for six or eight months in the year are never ventilated at all, except by the accidental opening of doors ? The foul air generated by one congregation is locked up by the sexton for the use of the next assembly ; and so gathers and gathers from week to week, and month to month, while devout persons upbraid themselves, and are ready to tear their hair, because they always feel stupid and sleepy in church. The proper ventilation of their churches and vestries would remove that spiritual deadness of which their prayers and hymns complain. A man hoeing his corn out on a breezy hillside is bright and alert, his mind works clearly, and he feels interested in religion, and thinks of many a thing that might be said at the prayer-meeting at night. But at night, when he sits down in a little room where the air reeks with the vapor of his neighbor's breath and the smoke of kerosene lamps, he finds himself suddenly dull and drowsy, — without emotion, without thought, without feeling, — and he rises and reproaches himself for this state of things. He calls upon his soul and all that is within him to bless the Lord ; but his indignant body, abused, insulted, ignored, takes the soul by the throat, and says, " If you won't let *me* have a good time, neither shall you." Revivals of religion, with ministers and with those people whose moral organization leads them to take most interest in them, often end in periods of bodily ill-health and depression. But is there any need of this ? Suppose that a revival of religion required, as a formula, that all the members of a given congregation should daily take a minute dose of arsenic in concert, — we should not be surprised after a while to hear of various ill effects therefrom ; and, as vestries and lecture-rooms are now arranged, a daily prayer-meeting is often nothing more nor less than a number of persons spending half an hour a day breathing poison from each other's lungs. There is not only no need of this, but, on the contrary, a good supply of pure air would make the daily prayer-meeting far more enjoyable. The body, if allowed the slightest degree of fair play, so far from being a contumacious infidel and opposer, becomes a very fair Christian helper, and, instead of throttling the soul, gives it wings to rise to celestial regions.

This branch of our subject we will quit with one significant anecdote. A certain rural church was somewhat famous for its picturesque Gothic architecture, and equally famous for its sleepy atmosphere, the rules of Gothic symmetry requiring very small windows, which could be only partially opened. Everybody was affected alike in this church : minister and people complained that it was like the enchanted ground in the Pilgrim's Progress. Do what they would, sleep was ever at their elbows ; the blue, red, and green of the painted windows melted into a rainbow dimness of hazy confusion ; and ere they were aware, they were off on a cloud to the land of dreams.

An energetic sister in the church suggested the inquiry, whether it was ever ventilated, and discovered that it was regularly locked up at the close of service, and remained so till opened for the next week. She suggested the inquiry, whether giving the church a thorough airing on Saturday would not improve the Sunday services ; but nobody acted on her suggestion. Finally, she borrowed the sexton's key one Saturday night, and went into the church and opened all the windows herself, and let them remain so for the night. The next day everybody remarked the improved comfort of the church, and wondered what had produced the change. Nevertheless, when it was discovered, it was not deemed a matter of enough importance to call for an order on the sexton to perpetuate the improvement.

The ventilation of private dwellings in this country is such as might be expected from that entire indifference to the laws of health manifested in public establishments. Let a person travel in private conveyance up through the valley of the Connecticut, and stop for a night at the taverns which he will usually find at the end of each day's stage. The bed-chamber into which he will be ushered will be the concentration of all forms of bad air. The house is redolent of the vegetables in the cellar, — cabbages, turnips, and potatoes ; and this fragrance is confined and retained by the custom of closing the window-blinds and dropping the inside curtains, so that neither air nor sunshine enters in to purify. Add to this the strong odor of a new feather-bed and pillows, and you have a combination of perfumes most appalling to a delicate sense. Yet travellers take possession of these rooms, sleep in them all night without raising the window or opening the blinds, and leave them to be shut up for other travellers.

The spare chamber of many dwellings seems to be an hermetically closed box, opened only twice a year, for spring and fall cleaning; but for the rest of the time closed to the sun and the air of heaven. Thrifty country housekeepers often adopt the custom of making their beds on the instant after they are left, without airing the sheets and mattresses; and a bed so made gradually becomes permeated with the insensible emanations of the human body, so as to be a steady corrupter of the atmosphere.

In the winter, the windows are calked and listed, the throat of the chimney built up with a tight brick wall, and a close stove is introduced to help burn out the vitality of the air. In a sitting-room like this, from five to ten persons will spend about eight months of the year, with no other ventilation than that gained by the casual opening and shutting of doors. Is it any wonder that consumption every year sweeps away its thousands? — that people are suffering constant chronic ailments,—neuralgia, nervous dyspepsia, and all the host of indefinite bad feelings that rob life of sweetness and flower and bloom?

A recent writer raises the inquiry, whether the community would not gain in health by the demolition of all dwelling-houses. That is, he suggests the question, whether the evils from foul air are not so great and so constant, that they countervail the advantages of shelter. Consumptive patients far gone have been known to be cured by long journeys, which have required them to be day and night in the open air. Sleep under the open heaven, even though the person be exposed to the various accidents of weather, has often proved a miraculous restorer after everything else had failed. But surely, if simple fresh air is so healing and preserving a thing, some means might be found to keep the air in a house just as pure and vigorous as it is outside.

An article in the May number of "Harpers' Magazine" presents drawings of a very simple arrangement by which any house can be made thoroughly self-ventilating. Ventilation, as this article shows, consists in two things, — a perfect and certain expulsion from the dwelling of all foul air breathed from the lungs or arising from any other cause, and the constant supply of pure air.

One source of foul air cannot be too much guarded against, — we mean imperfect gas-pipes. A want of thoroughness in execution is the sin of our American artisans, and very few gas-fixtures are so thoroughly made that more or less gas does not escape and mingle with the air of the dwelling. There are parlors where plants cannot be made to live, because the gas kills them; and yet their occupants do not seem to reflect that an air in which a plant cannot live must be dangerous for a human being. The very clemency and long-suffering of Nature to those who persistently violate her laws is one great cause why men are, physically speaking, such sinners as they are. If foul air poisoned at once and completely, we should have well-ventilated houses, whatever else we failed to have. But because people can go on for weeks, months, and years, breathing poisons, and slowly and imperceptibly lowering the tone of their vital powers, and yet be what they call "pretty well, I thank you," sermons on ventilation and fresh air go by them as an idle song. "I don't see but we are well enough, and we never took much pains about these things. There 's air enough gets into houses, of course. What with doors opening and windows occasionally lifted, the air of houses is generally good enough"; — and so the matter is dismissed.

One of Heaven's great hygienic teachers is now abroad in the world, giving lessons on health to the children of men. The cholera is like the angel whom God threatened to send as leader to the rebellious Israelites. "Beware of him, obey his voice, and provoke him not; for he will not pardon your transgressions." The advent of this fearful messenger seems really to be made necessary by the contempt with which men treat the physical laws of their being. What else could have purified the dark places of New York? What a wiping-up and reforming and cleansing is going before him through the country! At last we find that Nature is in earnest, and that her laws cannot be always ignored with impunity. Poisoned air is recognized at last as an evil, — even although the poison cannot be weighed, measured, or tasted; and if all the precautions that men are now willing to take could be made perpetual, the alarm would be a blessing to the world.

Like the principles of spiritual religion, the principles of physical religion are few and easy to be understood. An old medical apothegm personifies the hygienic forces as the Doctors Air, Diet, Exercise, and Quiet; and these four will be found, on reflection, to cover the whole ground of what is required to preserve human health. A human being whose lungs have always been nourished by pure air, whose stomach has been fed only by appropriate food, whose muscles have been systematically trained by appropriate exercises, and whose mind is kept tranquil by faith in God and a good conscience, has *perfect physical religion*. There is a line where physical religion must necessarily overlap spiritual religion and rest upon it. No human being can be assured of perfect health, through all the strain and wear and tear of such cares and such perplexities as life brings, without the rest of *faith in God*. An unsubmissive, unconfiding, unresigned soul will make vain the best hygienic treatment; and, on the contrary, the most saintly religious resolution and purpose may be defeated and vitiated by an habitual ignorance and disregard of the laws of the physical system.

Perfect spiritual religion cannot exist without perfect physical religion. Every flaw and defect in the bodily system is just so much taken from the spiritual vitality: we are commanded to glorify God, not simply in our spirits, but in our *bodies* and spirits. The only example of perfect manhood the world ever saw impresses us more than anything else by an atmosphere of perfect healthiness. There is a calmness, a steadiness, in the character of Jesus, a naturalness in his evolution of the sublimest truths under the strain of the most absorbing and intense excitement, that could come only from the *one* perfectly trained and developed body, bearing as a pure and sacred shrine the One Perfect Spirit. Jesus of Nazareth, journeying on foot from city to city, always calm yet always fervent, always steady yet glowing with a white heat of sacred enthusiasm, able to walk and teach all day and afterwards to continue in prayer all night, with unshaken nerves, sedately patient, serenely reticent, perfectly self-controlled, walked the earth, the only man that perfectly glorified God in his body no less than in his spirit. It is worthy of remark, that in choosing his disciples he chose plain men from the laboring classes, who had lived the most obediently to the simple, unperverted laws of nature. He chose men of good and pure bodies, — simple, natural, childlike, healthy men, — and baptized their souls with the inspiration of the Holy Spirit.

The hygienic bearings of the New Testament have never been sufficiently understood. The basis of them lies in the solemn declaration, that our bodies are to be temples of the Holy Spirit, and that all abuse of them is of the nature of sacrilege. Reverence for the physical system, as the outward shrine and temple of the spiritual, is the peculiarity of the Christian religion. The doctrine of the resurrection of the body, and its physical immortality, sets the last crown of honor upon it. That bodily system which God declared worthy to be gathered back from the dust of the grave, and re-created, as the soul's immortal companion, must necessarily be dear and precious in the eyes of its Creator. The one passage in the New Testament in which it is spoken of disparagingly is where Paul contrasts it with the brighter glory of what is to come, — "He shall change our *vile* bodies, that they may be fashioned like his glorious body." From this passage has come abundance of reviling of the physical system. Memoirs of good men are full of abuse of it, as the clog, the load, the burden, the chain. It is spoken of as pollution, as corruption, — in short, one would think that the Creator had imitated the cruelty of some Oriental despots who have been known to chain a festering corpse to a living body. Accordingly, the memoirs of these pious men are also mournful records of slow suicide, wrought by the persistent neglect of the most necessary and important laws of the bodily system ; and the body, outraged and down-trodden, has turned traitor to the soul, and played the adversary with fearful power. Who can tell the countless temptations to evil which flow in from a neglected, disordered, deranged nervous system, — temptations to anger, to irritability, to selfishness, to every kind of sin of appetite and passion ? No wonder that the poor soul longs for the hour of release from such a companion.

But that human body which God declares expressly was made to be the temple of the Holy Spirit, which he considers worthy to be perpetuated by a resurrection and an immortal existence, cannot be intended to be a clog and a hindrance to spiritual advancement. A perfect body, working in perfect tune and time, would open glimpses of happiness to the soul approaching the joys we hope for in heaven. It is only through the images of things which our *bodily* senses have taught us, that we can form any conception of that future bliss ; and the more perfect these senses, the more perfect our conceptions must be.

The conclusion of the whole matter, and the practical application of this sermon, is : — First, that all men set themselves to form the idea of what perfect health is, and resolve to realize it for themselves and their children. Second, that with a view to this they study the religion of the body, in such simple and popular treatises as those of George Combe, Dr. Dio Lewis, and others, and with simple and honest hearts practise what they there learn. Third, that the training of the bodily system should form a regular part of our common-school education, — every common school being provided with a well-instructed teacher of gymnastics ; and the growth and development of each pupil's body being as much noticed and marked as is now the growth of his mind. The same course should be continued and enlarged in colleges and female seminaries, which should have professors of hygiene appointed to give thorough instruction concerning the laws of health.

And when this is all done, we may hope that crooked spines, pimpled faces, sallow complexions, stooping shoulders, and all other signs indicating an undeveloped physical vitality, will, in the course of a few generations, disappear from the earth, and men will have bodies which will glorify God, their great Architect.

The soul of man has got as far as it can without the body. Religion herself stops and looks back, waiting for the body to overtake her. The soul's great enemy and hindrance can be made her best friend and most powerful help ; and it is high time that this era were begun. We old sinners, who have lived carelessly, and almost spent our day of grace, may not gain much of its good ; but the children, — shall there not be a more perfect day for them ? Shall there not come a day when the little child, whom Christ set forth to his disciples as the type of the greatest in the kingdom of heaven, shall be the type no less of our physical than our spiritual advancement, — when men and women shall arise, keeping through long and happy lives the simple, unperverted appetites, the joyous freshness of spirit, the keen delight in mere existence, the dreamless sleep and happy waking of early childhood ?

GRIFFITH GAUNT; OR, JEALOUSY.

CHAPTER XXVIII.

THE bill was paid; the black horse saddled and brought round to the door. Mr. and Mrs. Vint stood bareheaded to honor the parting guest; and the latter offered him the stirrup-cup.

Griffith looked round for Mercy. She was nowhere to be seen.

Then he said, piteously, to Mrs. Vint, "What, not even bid me good by?"

Mrs. Vint replied, in a very low voice, that there was no disrespect intended. "The truth is, sir, she could not trust herself to see you go; but she bade me give you a message. Says she, 'Mother, tell him I pray God to bless him, go where he will.'"

Something rose in Griffith's throat. "O Dame!" said he, "if she only knew the truth, she would think better of me than she does. God bless her!"

And he rode sorrowfully away, alone in the world once more.

At the first turn in the road, he wheeled his horse, and took a last lingering look.

There was nothing vulgar, nor inn-like, in the "Packhorse." It stood fifty yards from the road, on a little rural green, and was picturesque itself. The front was entirely clad with large-leaved ivy. Shutters there were none: the windows, with their diamond panes, were lustrous squares, set like great eyes in the green ivy. It looked a pretty, peaceful retreat, and in it Griffith had found peace and a dove-like friend.

He sighed, and rode away from the sight; not raging and convulsed, as when he rode from Hernshaw Castle, but somewhat sick at heart, and very heavy.

He paced so slowly that it took him a quarter of an hour to reach the "Woodman," — a wayside inn, not two miles distant. As he went by, a farmer hailed him from the porch, and insisted on drinking with him; for he was very popular in the neighborhood. Whilst they were thus employed, who should come out but Paul Carrick, booted and spurred, and flushed in the face, and rather the worse for liquor imbibed on the spot.

"So you are going, are ye?" said he. "A good job, too." Then, turning to the other, "Master Gutteridge, never you save a man's life, if you can anyways help it. I saved this one's; and what does he do but turn round and poison my sweetheart against me?"

"How can you say so?" remonstrated Griffith. "I never belied you. Your name scarce ever passed my lips."

"Don't tell me," said Carrick. "However, she has come to her senses, and given your worship the sack. Ride you into Cumberland, and I to the 'Packhorse,' and take my own again."

With this, he unhooked his nag from the wall, and clattered off to the "Packhorse."

Griffith sat a moment stupefied, and then his face was convulsed by his ruling passion. He wheeled his horse, gave him the spur, and galloped after Carrick.

He soon came up with him, and yelled in his ear, "I'll teach you to spit your wormwood in my cup of sorrow."

Carrick shook his fist defiantly, and spurred his horse in turn.

It was an exciting race, and a novel one, but soon decided. The great black hunter went ahead, and still improved his advantage. Carrick, purple with rage, was full a quarter of a mile behind, when Griffith dashed furiously into the stable of the "Packhorse," and, leaving Black Dick panting and covered with foam, ran in search of Mercy.

The girl told him she was in the dairy. He looked in at the window, and there she was with her mother. With instinctive sense and fortitude she had fled to work. She was trying to churn; but it would not do: she had laid her shapely arm on the churn, and her head on it, and was crying.

Mrs. Vint was praising Carrick, and offering homely consolation.

"Ah, mother," sighed Mercy, "I could have made him happy. He does not know that; and he has turned his back on content. What will become of him?"

Griffith heard no more. He went round to the front door, and rushed in.

"Take your own way, Dame," said he, in great agitation. "Put up the banns when you like. Sweetheart, wilt wed with me? I'll make thee the best husband I can."

Mercy screamed faintly, and lifted up her hands; then she blushed and trembled to her very finger ends; but it ended in smiles of joy and her brow upon his shoulder.

In which attitude, with Mrs. Vint patting him approvingly on the back, they were surprised by Paul Carrick. He came to the door, and there stood aghast.

The young man stared ruefully at the picture, and then said, very dryly, "I'm too late, methinks."

"That you be, Paul," said Mrs. Vint, cheerfully. "She is meat for your master."

"Don't — you — never — come to me — to save your life — no more," blubbered Paul, breaking down all of a sudden.

He then retired, little heeded, and came no more to the "Packhorse" for several days.

CHAPTER XXIX.

IT is desirable that improper marriages should never be solemnized; and the Christian Church saw this, many hundred years ago, and ordained that, before a marriage, the banns should be cried in a church three Sundays, and any person there present might forbid the union of the parties, and allege the just impediment.

This precaution was feeble, but not wholly inadequate—in the Middle Ages; for we know by good evidence that the priest was often interrupted and the banns forbidden.

But in modern days the banns are never forbidden; in other words, the precautionary measure that has come down to us from the thirteenth century is out of date and useless. It rests, indeed, on an estimate of publicity that has become childish, and almost asinine. If persons about to marry were compelled to inscribe their names and descriptions in a Matrimonial Weekly Gazette, and a copy of this were placed on a desk in ten thousand churches, perhaps we might stop one lady per annum from marrying her husband's brother, and one gentleman from wedding his neighbor's wife. But the crying of banns in a single parish church is a waste of the people's time and the parson's breath.

And so it proved in Griffith Gaunt's case. The Rev. William Wentworth published, in the usual recitative, the banns of marriage between Thomas Leicester, of the parish of Marylebone in London, and Mercy Vint, spinster, of *this* parish; and creation, present *ex hypothesi mediævale*, but absent in fact, assented, by silence, to the union.

So Thomas Leicester wedded Mercy Vint, and took her home to the "Packhorse."

It would be well if those who stifle their consciences, and commit crimes, would set up a sort of medico-moral diary, and record their symptoms minutely day by day. Such records might help to clear away some vague conventional notions.

To tell the truth, our hero, and now malefactor, (the combination is of high antiquity,) enjoyed, for several months, the peace of mind that belongs of right to innocence; and his days passed in a state of smooth complacency. Mercy was a good, wise, and tender wife; she naturally looked up to him after marriage more than she did before; she studied his happiness, as she had never studied her own ; she mastered his character, admired his good qualities, discerned his weaknesses, but did not view them as defects ; only as little traits to be watched, lest she should give pain to "her master," as she called him.

Affection, in her, took a more obsequious form than it could ever assume in Kate Peyton. And yet she had great influence, and softly governed "her master" for his good. She would come into the room and take away the bottle, if he was committing excess ; but she had a way of doing it, so like a good, but resolute mother, and so unlike a termagant, that he never resisted. Upon the whole, she nursed his mind, as in earlier days she had nursed his body.

And then she made him so comfortable : she observed him minutely to that end. As is the eye of a maid to the hand of her mistress, so Mercy Leicester's dove-like eye was ever watching "her master's" face, to learn the minutest features of his mind.

One evening he came in tired, and there was a black fire in the parlor. His countenance fell the sixteenth of an inch. You and I, sir, should never have noticed it. But Mercy did, and, ever after, there was a clear fire when he came in.

She noted, too, that he loved to play the *viol da gambo,* but disliked the trouble of tuning it. So then she tuned it for him.

When he came home at night, early or late, he was sure to find a dry pair of shoes on the rug, his six-stringed viol tuned to a hair, a bright fire, and a brighter wife, smiling and radiant at his coming, and always neat ; for, said she, " Shall I don my bravery for strangers, and not for my Thomas, that is the best of company ? "

They used to go to church, and come back together, hand in hand like lovers ; for the arm was rarely given in those days. And Griffith said to himself every Sunday, " What a comfort to have a Protestant wife ! "

But one day he was off his guard, and called her " Kate, my dear."

" Who is Kate ? " said she softly, but with a degree of trouble and intelligence that made him tremble.

" No matter," said he, all in a flutter. Then, solemnly, " Whoever she was, she is dead, — dead."

" Ah ! " said Mercy, very tenderly and solemnly, and under her breath. " You loved her ; yet she must die." She paused ; then, in a tone so exquisite I can only call it an angel's whisper, " Poor Kate ! "

Griffith groaned aloud. " For God's sake, never mention that name to me again. Let me forget she ever lived. She was not the true friend to me that you have been."

Mercy replied, softly, " Say not so, Thomas. You loved her well. Her death had all but cost me thine. Ah, well ! we cannot all be the first. I am not very jealous, for my part ; and I thank God for 't. Thou art a dear good husband to me, and that is enow."

Paul Carrick, unable to break off his habits, came to the " Packhorse " now and then ; but Mercy protected her husband's heart from pain. She was kind, and even pitiful ; but so discreet and resolute, and contrived to draw the line so clearly between her husband and her old sweetheart, that Griffith's foible could not burn him, for want of fuel.

And so passed several months, and the man's heart was at peace. He could not love Mercy passionately as he had loved Kate ; but he was full of real regard and esteem for her. It was one of those gentle, clinging attachments that outlast grand passions, and survive till death ; a tender, pure affection, though built upon a crime.

They had been married, and lived in sweet content, about three quarters of a year — when trouble came ; but in a vulgar form. A murrain carried off several of Harry Vint's cattle ; and it then came out that he had purchased six of them on credit, and had been induced to set his hand to bills of exchange for them. His rent was also behind, and, in fact, his affairs were in a desperate condition.

He hid it as long as he could from them all; but at last, being served with a process for debt, and threatened with a distress and an execution, he called a family council and exposed the real state of things.

Mrs. Vint rated him soundly for keeping all this secret so long.

He whom they called Thomas Leicester remonstrated with him. "Had you told me in time," said he, "I had not paid forfeit for 'The Vine,' but settled there, and given you a home."

Mercy said never a word but "Poor father!"

As the peril drew nearer, the conversations became more animated and agitated, and soon the old people took to complaining of Thomas Leicester to his wife.

"Thou hast married a gentleman; and he hath not the heart to lift a hand to save thy folk from ruin."

"Say not so," pleaded Mercy: "to be sure he hath the heart, but not the means. 'T was but yestreen he bade me sell his jewels for you. But, mother, I think they belonged to some one he loved,—and she died. So, poor thing, how could I? Then, if you love me, blame me, and not him."

"Jewels, quotha! will they stop such a gap as ours?" was the contemptuous reply.

From complaining of him behind his back, the old people soon came to launching innuendoes obliquely at him. Here is one specimen out of a dozen.

"Wife, if our Mercy had wedded one of her own sort, mayhap he'd have helped us a bit."

"Ay, poor soul; and she so near her time: if the bailiffs come down on us next month, 't is my belief we shall lose her, as well as house and home."

The false Thomas Leicester let them run on, in dogged silence; but every word was a stab.

And one day, when he had been

baited sore with hints, he turned round on them fiercely, and said: "Did I get you into this mess? It's all your own doing. Learn to see your own faults, and not be so hard on one that has been the best servant you ever had, gentleman or not."

Men can resist the remonstrances that wound them, and so irritate them, better than they can those gentle appeals that rouse no anger, but soften the whole heart. The old people stung him; but Mercy, without design, took a surer way. She never said a word; but sometimes, when the discussions were at their height, she turned her dove-like eyes on him, with a look so loving, so humbly inquiring, so timidly imploring, that his heart melted within him.

Ah, that is a true touch of nature and genuine observation of the sexes, in the old song,—

> "My feyther urged me sair;
> My mither didna speak;
> But she looked me in the face,
> Till my hairt was like to break."

These silent, womanly, imploring looks of patient Mercy were mightier than argument or invective.

The man knew all along where to get money, and how to get it. He had only to go to Hernshaw Castle. But his very soul shuddered at the idea. However, for Mercy's sake, he took the first step; he compelled himself to look the thing in the face, and discuss it with himself. A few months ago he could not have done even this, — he loved his lawful wife too much; hated her too much. But now, Mercy and Time had blunted both those passions; and he could ask himself whether he could not encounter Kate and her priest without any very violent emotion.

When they first set up house together, he had spent his whole fortune, a sum of two thousand pounds, on repairing and embellishing Hernshaw Castle and grounds. Since she had driven him out of the house, he had a clear right to have back the money; and he now resolved he would have it;

but what he wanted was to get it without going to the place in person.

And now Mercy's figure, as well as her imploring looks, moved him greatly. She was in that condition which appeals to a man's humanity and masculine pity, as well as to his affection. To use the homely words of Scripture, she was great with child, and in that condition moved slowly about him, filling his pipe, and laying his slippers, and ministering to all his little comforts; she would make no difference: and when he saw the poor dove move about him so heavily, and rather languidly, yet so zealously and tenderly, the man's very bowels yearned over her, and he felt as if he could die to do her a service.

So, one day, when she was standing by him, bending over his little round table, and filling his pipe with her neat hand, he took her by the other hand and drew her gently on his knee, her burden and all. "Child!" said he, "do not thou fret. I know how to get money; and I'll do 't, for thy sake."

"I know that," said she, softly; "can I not read thy face by this time?" and so laid her cheek to his. "But, Thomas, for my sake, get it honestly,—or not at all," said she, still filling his pipe, with her cheek to his.

"I'll but take back my own," said he; "fear naught."

But, after thus positively pledging himself to Mercy, he became thoughtful and rather fretful; for he was still most averse to go to Hernshaw, and yet could hit upon no other way; since to employ an agent would be to let out that he had committed bigamy, and so risk his own neck, and break Mercy's heart.

After all his scale was turned by his foible.

Mrs. Vint had been weak enough to confide her trouble to a friend: it was all over the parish in three days.

Well, one day, in the kitchen of the inn, Paul Carrick, having drunk two pints of good ale, said to Vint, "Landlord, you ought to have married her to me. I've got two hundred pounds laid by. I'd have pulled you out of the mire, and welcome."

"Would you, though, Paul?" said Harry Vint; "then, by G——, I wish I had."

Now Carrick bawled that out, and Griffith, who was at the door, heard it.

He walked into the kitchen, ghastly pale, and spoke to Harry Vint first.

"I take your inn, your farm, and your debts on me," said he; "not one without t' other."

"Spoke like a man!" cried the landlord, joyfully; "and so be it — before these witnesses."

Griffith turned on Carrick: "This house is mine. Get out on 't, ye *jealous*, mischief-making cur." And he took him by the collar and dragged him furiously out of the place, and sent him whirling into the middle of the road; then ran back for his hat and flung it out after him.

This done, he sat down boiling, and his eyes roved fiercely round the room in search of some other antagonist. But his strength was so great, and his face so altered with this sudden spasm of reviving jealousy, that nobody cared to provoke him further.

After a while, however, Harry Vint muttered dryly, "There goes one good customer."

Griffith took him up sternly: "If your debts are to be mine, your trade shall be mine too, that you had not the head to conduct."

"So be it, son-in-law," said the old man; "only you go so fast: you do take possession afore you pays the fee."

Griffith winced. "That shall be the last of your taunts, old man." He turned to the ostler: "Bill, give Black Dick his oats at sunrise; and in ten days at furthest I'll pay every shilling this house and farm do owe. Now, Master White, you'll put in hand a new sign-board for this inn; a fresh 'Packhorse,' and paint him jet black, with one white hoof (instead of chocolate), in honor of my nag Dick; and in place of Harry Vint you'll put in Thomas Leicester. See that is done against I come back, or come *you* here no more."

Soon after this scene he retired to tell Mercy; and, on his departure, the suppressed tongues went like mill-clacks.

Dick came round saddled at peep of day; but Mercy had been up more than an hour, and prepared her man's breakfast. She clung to him at parting, and cried a little; and whispered something in his ear, for nobody else to hear: it was an entreaty that he would not be long gone, lest he should be far from her in the hour of her peril.

Thereupon he promised her, and kissed her tenderly, and bade her be of good heart; and so rode away northwards with dogged resolution.

As soon as he was gone, Mercy's tears flowed without restraint.

Her father set himself to console her. "Thy good man," he said, "is but gone back to the high road for a night or two, to follow his trade of 'stand and deliver.' Fear naught, child; his pistols are well primed: I saw to that myself; and his horse is the fleetest in the county. You'll have him back in three days, and money in both pockets. I warrant you his is a better trade than mine; and he is a fool to change it."

Griffith was two days upon the road, and all that time he was turning over and discussing in his mind how he should conduct the disagreeable but necessary business he had undertaken.

He determined, at last, to make the visit one of business only: no heat, no reproaches. That lovely, hateful woman might continue to dishonor his name, for he had himself abandoned it. He would not deign to receive any money that was hers; but his own two thousand pounds he would have; and two or three hundred on the spot by way of instalment. And, with these hard views, he drew near to Hernshaw; but the nearer he got, the slower he went; for what at a distance had seemed tolerably easy began to get more and more difficult and repulsive.

Moreover, his heart, which he thought he had steeled, began now to flutter a little, and somehow to shudder at the approaching interview.

CHAPTER XXX.

CAROLINE RYDER went to the gate of the Grove, and stayed there two hours; but, of course, no Griffith came.

She returned the next night, and the next; and then she gave it up, and awaited an explanation. None came, and she was bitterly disappointed, and indignant.

She began to hate Griffith, and to conceive a certain respect, and even a tepid friendship, for the other woman he had insulted.

Another clew to this change of feeling is to be found in a word she let drop in talking to another servant. "My mistress," said she, "bears it *like a man.*"

In fact, Mrs. Gaunt's conduct at this period was truly noble.

She suffered months of torture, months of grief; but the high-spirited creature hid it from the world, and maintained a sad but high composure.

She wore her black, for she said, "How do I know he is alive?" She retrenched her establishment, reduced her expenses two thirds, and busied herself in works of charity and religion.

Her desolate condition attracted a gentleman who had once loved her, and now esteemed and pitied her profoundly, — Sir George Neville.

He was still unmarried, and she was the cause; so far at least as this: she had put him out of conceit with the other ladies at that period when he had serious thoughts of marriage: and the inclination to marry at all had not since returned.

If the Gaunts had settled at Boulton, Sir George would have been their near neighbor; but Neville's Court was nine miles from Hernshaw Castle: and when they met, which was not very often, Mrs. Gaunt was on her guard to give Griffith no shadow of uneasiness.

She was therefore rather more dignified, and distant with Sir George than her own inclination and his merits would have prompted; for he was a superior and very agreeable man.

When it became quite certain that her husband had left her, Sir George rode up to Hernshaw Castle, and called upon her.

She begged to be excused from seeing him.

Now Sir George was universally courted, and this rather nettled him; however, he soon learned that she received nobody except a few religious friends of her own sex.

Sir George then wrote her a letter that did him credit: it was full of worthy sentiment and good sense. For instance, he said he desired to intrude his friendly offices and his sympathy upon her, but nothing more. Time had cured him of those warmer feelings which had once ruffled his peace; but Time could not efface his tender esteem for the lady he had loved in his youth, nor his profound respect for her character.

Mrs. Gaunt wept over his gentle letter, and was on the verge of asking herself why she had chosen Griffith instead of this chevalier. She sent him a sweet, yet prudent reply; she did not encourage him to visit her; but said, that, if ever she should bring herself to receive visits from the gentlemen of the county during her husband's absence, he should be the first to know it. She signed herself his unhappy, but deeply grateful, servant and friend.

One day, as she came out of a poor woman's cottage, with a little basket on her arm, which she had emptied in the cottage, she met Sir George Neville full.

He took his hat off, and made her a profound bow. He was then about to ride on, but altered his mind, and dismounted to speak to her.

The interview was constrained at first; but erelong he ventured to tell her she really ought to consult with some old friend and practical man like himself. He would undertake to scour the country, and find her husband, if he was above ground.

"Me go a-hunting the man," cried she, turning red; "not if he was my king as well as my husband. He knows where to find *me;* and that is enough."

"Well, but madam, would you not like to learn where he is, and what he is doing?"

"Why, yes, my good, kind friend, I *should* like to know that." And, having pronounced these words with apparent calmness, she burst out crying, and almost ran away from him.

Sir George looked sadly after her, and formed a worthy resolution. He saw there was but one road to her regard. He resolved to hunt her husband for her, without intruding on her, or giving her a voice in the matter. Sir George was a magistrate, and accustomed to organize inquiries; spite of the length of time that had elapsed, he traced Griffith for a considerable distance. Pending further inquiries, he sent Mrs. Gaunt word that the truant had not made for the sea, but had gone due south.

Mrs. Gaunt returned him her warm thanks for this scrap of information. So long as Griffith remained in the island there was always a hope he might return to her. The money he had taken would soon be exhausted; and poverty might drive him to her; and she was so far humbled by grief, that she could welcome him even on those terms.

Affliction tempers the proud. Mrs. Gaunt was deeply injured as well as insulted; but, for all that, in her many days and weeks of solitude and sorrow, she took herself to task, and saw her fault. She became more gentle, more considerate of her servants' feelings, more womanly.

For many months she could not enter "the Grove." The spirited woman's very flesh revolted at the sight of the place where she had been insulted and abandoned. But, as she went deeper in religion, she forced herself to go to the gate and look in, and say out loud, "I gave the first offence," and then she would go in-doors again, quivering with the internal conflict.

Finally, being a Catholic, and therefore attaching more value to self-torture than we do, the poor soul made this very grove her place of penance. Once a week she had the fortitude to drag herself to the very spot where Griffith had denounced her; and there she would kneel and pray for him and for herself. And certainly, if humility and self-abasement were qualities of the body, here was to be seen their picture; for her way was to set her crucifix up at the foot of a tree; then to bow herself all down, between kneeling and lying, and put her lips meekly to the foot of the crucifix, and so pray long and earnestly.

Now, one day, while she was thus crouching in prayer, a gentleman, booted and spurred and splashed, drew near, with hesitating steps. She was so absorbed, she did not hear those steps at all till they were very near; but then she trembled all over; for her delicate ear recognized a manly tread she had not heard for many a day. She dared not move nor look, for she thought it was a mere sound, sent to her by Heaven to comfort her.

But the next moment a well-known mellow voice came like a thunder-clap, it shook her so.

"Forgive me, my good dame, but I desire to know —"

The question went no further, for Kate Gaunt sprang to her feet, with a loud scream, and stood glaring at Griffith Gaunt, and he at her.

And thus husband and wife met again, — met, by some strange caprice of Destiny, on the very spot where they had parted so horribly.

CHAPTER XXXI.

THE gaze these two persons bent on one another may be half imagined: it can never be described.

Griffith spoke first. "In black!" said he, in a whisper.

His voice was low; his face, though pale and grim, had not the terrible aspect he wore at parting.

So she thought he had come back in an amicable spirit; and she flew to him, with a cry of love, and threw her arm round his neck, and panted on his shoulder.

At this reception, and the tremulous contact of one he had loved so dearly, a strange shudder ran through his frame, — a shudder that marked his present repugnance, yet indicated her latent power.

He himself felt he had betrayed some weakness; and it was all the worse for her. He caught her wrist and put her from him, not roughly, but with a look of horror. "The day is gone by for that, madam," he gasped. Then, sternly: "Think you I came here to play the credulous husband?"

Mrs. Gaunt drew back in her turn, and faltered out, "What! come back here, and not sorry for what you have done? not the least sorry? O my heart! you have almost broken it."

"Prithee, no more of this," said Griffith, sternly. "You and I are naught to one another now, and forever. But there, you are but a woman, and I did not come to quarrel with you." And he fixed his eyes on the ground.

"Thank God for that," faltered Mrs. Gaunt. "O sir, the sight of you — the thought of what you were to me once — till jealousy blinded you. Lend me your arm, if you are a man; my limbs do fail me."

The shock had been too much; a pallor overspread her lovely features, her knees knocked together, and she was tottering like some tender tree cut down, when Griffith, who, with all his faults, was a man, put out his strong arm, and she clung to it, quivering all over, and weeping hysterically.

That little hand, with its little feminine clutch, trembling on his arm, raised a certain male compassion for her piteous condition; and he bestowed a few cold, sad words of encouragement on her. "Come, come," said he, gently; "I shall not trouble you long. I'm cured of my jealousy. 'T is gone, along with my love. You and your saintly sinner are safe from me. I am come hither for my own, my two thousand pounds, and for nothing more."

" Ah ! you are come back for money, not for me ? " she murmured, with forced calmness.

" For money, and not for you, of course," said he, coldly.

The words were hardly out of his mouth, when the proud lady flung his arm from her. " Then money shall you have, and not me ; nor aught of me but my contempt."

But she could not carry it off as heretofore. She turned her back haughtily on him ; but, at the first step, she burst out crying, " Come, and I 'll give you what you are come for," she sobbed. " Ungrateful ! heartless ! O, how little I knew this man ! "

She crept away before him, drooping her head, and crying bitterly ; and he followed her, hanging his head, and ill at ease ; for there was such true passion in her voice, her streaming eyes, and indeed in her whole body, that he was moved, and the part he was playing revolted him. He felt confused and troubled, and asked himself how on earth it was that she, the guilty one, contrived to - appear the injured one, and made him, the wronged one, feel almost remorseful.

Mrs. Gaunt took no more notice of him now than if he had been a dog following at her heels. She went into the drawing-room, and sank helplessly on the nearest couch, threw her head wearily back, and shut her eyes. Yet the tears trickled through the closed lids.

Griffith caught up a hand-bell, and rang it vigorously.

Quick, light steps were soon heard pattering ; and in darted Caroline Ryder, with an anxious face ; for of late she had conceived a certain sober regard for her mistress, who had ceased to be her successful rival, and who bore her grief *like a man.*

At sight of Griffith, Ryder screamed aloud, and stood panting.

Mrs. Gaunt opened her eyes. " Ay, child, he has come home," said she, bitterly ; " his body, but not his heart."

She stretched her hand out feebly, and pointed to a bottle of salts that stood on the table. Ryder ran and put them to her nostrils. Mrs. Gaunt whispered in her ear, " Send a swift horse for Father Francis ; tell him. life or death ! "

Ryder gave her a very intelligent look, and presently slipped out, and ran into the stable-yard.

At the gate she caught sight of Griffith's horse. What does this quick-witted creature do but send the groom off on that horse, and not on Mrs. Gaunt's.

" Now, Dame," said Griffith, doggedly, " are you better ? "

" Ay, I thank you."

" Then listen to me. When you and I set up house together, I had two thousand pounds. I spent it on this house. The house is yours. You told me so, one day, you know."

" Ah, you can remember my faults."

" I remember all, Kate."

" Thank you, at least, for calling me Kate. Well, Griffith, since you abandoned us, I thought, and thought, and thought, of all that might befall you ; and I said, ' What will he do for money ? ' My jewels, that you did me the honor to take, would not last you long, I feared. So I reduced my expenses three fourths at least, and I put by some money for your need."

Griffith looked amazed. " For my need ? " said he.

" For whose else ? I 'll send for it, and place it in your hands — to-morrow."

" To-morrow ? Why not to-day ? "

" I have a favor to ask of you first."

" What is that ? "

" Justice. If you are fond of money, I too have something I prize : my honor. You have belied and insulted me, sir ; but I know you were under a delusion. I mean to remove that delusion, and make you see how little I am to blame ; for, alas ! I own I was imprudent. But, O Griffith, as I hope to be saved, it was the imprudence of innocence and over-confidence."

"Mistress," said Griffith, in a stern, yet agitated voice, "be advised, and leave all this : rouse not a man's sleeping wrath. Let bygones be bygones."

Mrs. Gaunt rose, and said, faintly, "So be it. I must go, sir, and give some orders for your entertainment."

"O, don't put yourself about for me," said Griffith : "I am not the master of this house."

Mrs. Gaunt's lip trembled, but she was a match for him. "Then are you my guest," said she ; "and my credit is concerned in your comfort."

She made him a courtesy, as if he were a stranger, and marched to the door, concealing, with great pride and art, a certain trembling of her knees.

At the door she found Ryder, and bade her follow, much to that lady's disappointment ; for she desired a *tête-à-tête* with Griffith, and an explanation.

As soon as the two women were out of Griffith's hearing, the mistress laid her hand on the servant's arm, and, giving way to her feelings, said, all in a flutter : "Child, if I have been a good mistress to thee, show it now. Help me keep him in the house till Father Francis comes."

"I undertake to do so much," said Ryder, firmly. "Leave it to me, mistress."

Mrs. Gaunt threw her arms round Ryder's neck and kissed her.

It was done so ardently, and by a woman hitherto so dignified and proud, that Ryder was taken by surprise, and almost affected.

As for the service Mrs. Gaunt had asked of her, it suited her own designs.

"Mistress," said she, "be ruled by me ; keep out of his way a bit, while I get Miss Rose ready. You understand."

"Ah ! I have one true friend in the house," said poor Mrs. Gaunt. She then confided in Ryder, and went away to give her own orders for Griffith's reception.

Ryder found little Rose, dressed her

to perfection, and told her her dear papa was come home. She then worked upon the child's mind in that subtle way known to women, so that Rose went down stairs loaded and primed, though no distinct instructions had been given her.

As for Griffith, he walked up and down, uneasy ; and wished he had stayed at the "Packhorse." He had not bargained for all these emotions ; the peace of mind he had enjoyed for some months seemed trickling away.

"Mercy, my dear," said he to himself, "'t will be a dear penny to me, I doubt."

Then he went to the window, and looked at the lawn, and sighed. Then he sat down, and thought of the past.

Whilst he sat thus moody, the door opened very softly, and a little cherubic face, with blue eyes and golden hair, peeped in. Griffith started. "Ah !" cried Rose, with a joyful scream ; and out flew her little arms, and away she came, half running, half dancing, and was on his knee in a moment, with her arms round his neck.

"Papa ! papa !" she cried. "O my dear, dear, dear, darling papa !" And she kissed and patted his cheek again and again.

Her innocent endearments moved him to tears. "My pretty angel !" he sighed : "my lamb !"

"How your heart beats ! Don't cry, dear papa. Nobody is dead : only we thought you were. I 'm so glad you are come home alive. Now we can take off this nasty black : I hate it."

"What, 't is for me you wear it, pretty one ? "

"Ay. Mamma made us. Poor mamma has been so unhappy. And that reminds me : you are a wicked man, papa. But I love you all one for that. It *tis* so dull when everybody is good like mamma ; and she makes me dreadfully good too ; but now you are come back, there will be a little, little wickedness again, it is to be hoped. Are n't you glad you are not dead, and are come home instead ? I am."

"I am glad I have seen thee. Come,

take my hand, and let us go look at the old place."

"Ay. But you must wait till I get on my new hat and feather."

"Nay, nay; art pretty enough bareheaded."

"O papa! but I must, for decency. You are company now; you know."

"Dull company, sweetheart, thou 'lt find me."

"I don't mean that: I mean, when you were here always, you were only papa; but now you come once in an age, you 're COMPANY. I won't budge without 'em; so there, now."

"Well, little one, I do submit to thy hat and feather; only be quick, or I shall go forth without thee."

"If you dare," said Rose impetuously; "for I won't be half a moment."

She ran and extorted from Ryder the new hat and feather, which by rights she was not to have worn until next month.

Griffith and his little girl went all over the well-known premises, he sad and moody, she excited and chattering, and nodding her head down, and cocking her eye up every now and then, to get a glimpse of her feather.

"And don't you go away again, dear papa. It *tis* so dull without you. Nobody comes here. Mamma won't let 'em."

"Nobody except Father Leonard," said Griffith, bitterly.

"Father Leonard? Why, he never comes here. Leonard! That is the beautiful priest that used to pat me on the head, and bid me love and honor my parents. And so I do. Only mamma is always crying, and you keep away; so how can I love and honor you, when I never see you, and they keep telling me you are good for nothing, and dead."

"My young mistress, when did you see Father Leonard last?" said Griffith, gnawing his lip.

"How can I tell? Why, it was miles ago; when I was a mere girl. You know he went away before you did."

"I know nothing of the kind. Tell me the truth now. He has visited here since I went away."

"Nay, papa."

"That is strange. She visits him, then?"

"What, mamma? She seldom stirs out; and never beyond the village. We keep no carriage now. Mamma is turned such a miser. She is afraid you will be poor; so she puts it all by for you. But now you are come, we shall have carriages and things again. O, by the by, Father Leonard! I heard them say he had left England, so I did."

"When was that?"

"Well, I think that was a little bit after you went away."

"That is strange," said Griffith, thoughtfully.

He led his little girl by the hand, but scarcely listened to her prattle; he was so surprised and puzzled by the information he had elicited from her.

Upon the whole, however, he concluded that his wife and the priest had perhaps been smitten with remorse, and had parted — when it was too late.

This, and the peace of mind he had found elsewhere, somewhat softened his feelings towards them. "So," thought he, "they were not hardened creatures after all. Poor Kate!"

As these milder feelings gained on him, Rose suddenly uttered a joyful cry; and, looking up, he saw Mrs. Gaunt coming towards him, and Ryder behind her. Both were in gay colors, which, in fact, was what had so delighted Rose.

They came up, and Mrs. Gaunt seemed a changed woman. She looked young and beautiful, and bent a look of angelic affection on her daughter; and said to Griffith, "Is she not grown? Is she not lovely? Sure you will never desert her again."

"'T was not her I deserted, but her mother; and she had played me false with her d—d priest," was Griffith's reply.

Mrs. Gaunt drew back with horror. "This, before my girl?" she cried. "GRIFFITH GAUNT, YOU LIE!"

And this time it was the woman who menaced the man. She rose to six feet high, and advanced on him with her great gray eyes flashing flames at him. "O that I were a man!" she cried: "this insult should be the last. I 'd lay you dead at her feet and mine."

Griffith actually drew back a step; for the wrath of such a woman was terrible, — more terrible perhaps to a brave man than to a coward.

Then he put his hands in his pockets with a dogged air, and said, grinding his teeth, "But — as you are not a man, and I 'm not a woman, we can't settle it that way. So I give you the last word, and good day. I 'm sore in want of money; but I find I can't pay the price it is like to cost me. Farewell."

"Begone!" said Mrs. Gaunt: "and, this time, forever. Ruffian, and fool, I loathe the sight of you."

Rose ran weeping to her. "O mamma, don't quarrel with papa": then back to Griffith, "O papa, don't quarrel with mamma, — for my sake."

Griffith hung his head, and said, in a broken voice: "No, my lamb, we twain must not quarrel before thee. We will part in silence, as becomes those that once were dear, and have thee to show for 't. Madam, I wish you all health and happiness. Adieu."

He turned on his heel; and Mrs. Gaunt took Rose to her knees, and bent and wept over her. Niobe over her last was not more graceful, nor more sad.

As for Ryder, she stole quietly after her retiring master. She found him peering about, and asked him demurely what he was looking for.

"My good black horse, girl, to take me from this cursed place. Did I not tie him to yon gate?"

"The black horse? Why I sent him for Father Francis. Nay, listen to me, master; you know I was always your friend, and hard upon *her.* Well, since you went, things have come to pass that make me doubt. I do begin to fear you were too hasty."

"Do you tell me this now, woman?" cried Griffith, furiously.

"How could I tell you before? Why

did you break your tryst with me? If you had come according to your letter, I 'd have told you months ago what I tell you now; but, as I was saying, the priest never came near her after you left; and she never stirred abroad to meet him. More than that, he has left England."

"Remorse! Too late."

"Perhaps it may, sir. I could n't say; but there is one coming that knows the very truth."

"Who is that?"

"Father Francis. The moment you came, sir, I took it on me to send for him. You know the man: he won't tell a lie to please our dame. And he knows all; for Leonard has confessed to him. I listened, and heard him say as much. Then, master, be advised, and get the truth from Father Francis."

Griffith trembled. "Francis is an honest man," said he; "I 'll wait till he comes. But O, my lass, I find money may be bought too dear."

"Your chamber is ready, sir, and your clothes put out. Supper is ordered. Let me show you your room. We are all so happy now."

"Well," said he, listlessly, "since my horse is gone, and Francis coming, and I 'm wearied and sick of the world, do what you will with me for this one day."

He followed her mechanically to a bedroom, where was a bright fire, and a fine shirt, and his silver-laced suit of clothes airing.

A sense of luxurious comfort struck him at the sight.

"Ay," said he, "I 'll dress, and so to supper; I 'm main hungry. It seems a man must eat, let his heart be ever so sore."

Before she left him, Ryder asked him coldly why he had broken his appointment with her.

"That is too long a story to tell you now," said he, coolly.

"Another time then," said she; and went out smiling, but bitter at heart.

Griffith had a good wash, and enjoyed

certain little conveniences which he had not at the "Packhorse." He doffed his riding suit, and donned the magnificent dress Ryder had selected for him ; and with his fine clothes he somehow put on more ceremonious manners.

He came down to the dining-room. To his surprise he found it illuminated with wax candles, and the table and sideboard gorgeous with plate.

Supper soon smoked upon the board ; but, though it was set for three, nobody else appeared.

Griffith inquired of Ryder whether he was to sup alone.

She replied : " My mistress desires you not to wait for her. She has no stomach."

" Well, then, I have," said Griffith, and fell to with a will.

Ryder, who waited on this occasion, stood and eyed him with curiosity : his conduct was so unlike a woman's.

Just as he concluded, the door opened, and a burly form entered. Griffith rose, and embraced him with his arms and lips, after the fashion of the day. "Welcome, thou one honest priest!" said he.

"Welcome, thrice welcome, my long-lost son!" said the cordial Francis.

"Sit down, man, and eat with me. I 'll begin again, for you."

" Presently, Squire ; I 've work to do first. Go thou and bid thy mistress come hither to me."

Ryder, to whom this was addressed, went out, and left the gentlemen together.

Father Francis drew out of his pocket two packets, carefully tied and sealed. He took a knife from the table and cut the strings, and broke the seals. Griffith eyed him with curiosity.

Father Francis looked at him. "These," said he, very gravely, "are the letters that Brother Leonard hath written, at sundry times, to Catharine Gaunt, and these are the letters Catharine Gaunt hath written to Brother Leonard."

Griffith trembled, and his face was convulsed.

"Let me read them at once," said he : and stretched out his hand, with eyes like a dog's in the dark.

Francis withdrew them, quietly. "Not till she is also present," said he.

At that Griffith's good-nature, multiplied by a good supper, took the alarm. "Come, come, sir," said he, "have a little mercy. I know you are a just man, and, though a boon companion, most severe in all matters of morality. But, I tell you plainly, if you are going to drag this poor woman in the dirt, I shall go out of the room. What is the use tormenting her ? I 've told her my mind before her own child : and now I wish I had not. When I caught them in the grove I lifted my hand to strike her, and she never winced ; I had better have left that alone too, methinks. D—n the women : you are always in the wrong if you treat 'em like men. They are not wicked : they are weak. And this one hath lain in my bosom, and borne me two children, and one he lieth in the churchyard, and t' other hath her hair and my very eyes : and the truth is, I can't bear any man on earth to miscall her, but myself. God help me ; I doubt I love her still too well to sit by and see her tortured. She was all in black for her fault, poor penitent wretch. Give me the letters ; but let her be."

Francis was moved by this appeal, but shook his head solemnly ; and, ere Griffith could renew his argument, the door was flung open by Ryder, and a stately figure sailed in, that took both the gentlemen by surprise.

It was Mrs. Gaunt, in full dress. Rich brocade that swept the ground ; magnificent bust, like Parian marble varnished ; and on her brow a diadem of emeralds and diamonds that gave her beauty an imperial stamp.

She swept into the room as only fine women can sweep, made Griffith a haughty courtesy, and suddenly lowered her head, and received Father Francis's blessing : then seated herself, and quietly awaited events.

"The brazen jade!" thought Griffith. "But how divinely beautiful!" And he became as agitated as she was calm — in appearance. For need I say her calmness was put on? Defensive armor made for her by her pride and her sex.

The voice of Father Francis now rose, solid, grave, and too impressive to be interrupted.

"My daughter, and you who are her husband and my friend, I am here to do justice between you both, with God's help; and to show you both your faults. Catharine Gaunt, you began the mischief, by encouraging another man to interfere between you and your husband in things secular."

"But, father, he was my director, my priest."

"My daughter, do you believe, with the Protestants, that marriage is a mere civil contract; or do, you hold, with us, that it is one of the holy sacraments?"

"Can you ask me?" murmured Kate, reproachfully.

"Well, then, those whom God and the whole Church have in holy sacrament united, what right hath a single priest to disunite in heart, and make the wife false to any part whatever of that most holy vow? I hear, and not from you, that Leonard did set you against your husband's friends, withdrew you from society, and sent him abroad alone. In one word, he robbed your husband of his companion and his friend. The sin was Leonard's; but the fault was yours. You were five years older than Leonard, and a woman of sense and experience; he but a boy by comparison. What right had you to surrender your understanding, in a matter of this kind, to a poor silly priest, fresh from his seminary, and as manifestly without a grain of common sense as he was full of piety?"

This remonstrance produced rather a striking effect on both those who heard it. Mrs. Gaunt seemed much struck with it. She leaned back in her chair, and put her hand to her brow with a sort of despairing gesture that Griffith could not very well understand, it seemed to him so disproportionate.

It softened him, however, and he faltered out, "Ay, father, that is how it all began. Would to heaven it had stopped there."

Francis resumed. "This false step led to consequences you never dreamed of; for one of your romantic notions is, that a priest is an angel. I have known you, in former times, try to take me for an angel: then would I throw cold water on your folly by calling lustily for chines of beef and mugs of ale. But I suppose Leonard thought himself an angel too; and the upshot was, he fell in love with his neighbor's wife."

"And she with him," groaned Griffith.

"Not so," said Francis; "but perhaps she was nearer it than she thinks."

"Prove that," said Mrs. Gaunt, "and I'll fall on my knees to him before you."

Francis smiled, and proceeded. "To be sure, from the moment you discovered Leonard was in love with you, you drew back, and conducted yourself with prudence and propriety. Read these letters, sir, and tell me what you think of them."

He handed them to Griffith. Griffith's hand trembled visibly as he took them.

"Stay," said Father Francis; "your better way will be to read the whole correspondence according to the dates. Begin with this of Mrs. Gaunt's."

Griffith read the letter in an audible whisper.

Mrs. Gaunt listened with all her ears.

"DEAR FATHER AND FRIEND, — The words you spoke to me to-day admit but one meaning; you are jealous of my husband.

"Then you must be — how can I write it? — almost in love with me.

"So then my poor husband was wiser than I. He saw a rival in you: and he has one.

"I am deeply, deeply shocked. I ought to be very angry too ; but, thinking of your solitary condition, and all the good you have done to my soul, my heart has no place for aught but pity. Only, as I am in my senses, and you are not, you must now obey me, as heretofore I have obeyed you. You must seek another sphere of duty, without delay.

"These seem harsh words from me to you. You will live to see they are kind ones.

"Write me one line, and no more, to say you will be ruled by me in this.

"God and the saints have you in their holy keeping. So prays your affectionate and

"Sorrowful daughter and true friend,
"CATHARINE GAUNT."

"Poor soul ! " said Griffith. "Said I not that women are not wicked, but weak ? Who would think that after this he could get the better of her good resolves, — the villain ! "

"Now read his reply," said Father Francis.

"Ay," said Griffith. "So this is his one word of reply, is it ? three pages closely writ, — the villain, O the villain ! "

"Read the villain's letter," said Francis, calmly.

The letter was very humble and pathetic, — the reply of a good, though erring man, who owned that in a moment of weakness he had been betrayed into a feeling inconsistent with his holy profession. He begged his correspondent, however, not to judge him quite so hardly. He reminded her of his solitary life, his natural melancholy, and assured her that all men in his condition had moments when they envied those whose bosoms had partners. "Such a cry of anguish," said he, "was once wrung from a maiden queen, maugre all her pride. The Queen of Scots hath a son ; and I am but a barren stock." He went on to say that prayer and vigilance united do much. "Do not despair so soon of me. Flight is not cure : let me rather

stay, and, with God's help and the saints', overcome this unhappy weakness. If I fail, it will indeed be time for me to go, and never again see the angelic face of my daughter and my benefactress."

Griffith laid down the letter. He was somewhat softened by it, and said, gently, "I cannot understand it. This is not the letter of a thorough bad man neither."

"No," said Father Francis, coldly, "'t is the letter of a self-deceiver ; and there is no more dangerous man to himself and others than your self-deceiver. But now let us see whether he can throw dust in her eyes, as well as his own." And he handed him Kate's reply.

The first word of it was, "You deceive yourself." The writer then insisted, quietly, that he owed it to himself, to her, and to her husband, whose happiness he was destroying, to leave the place at her request.

"Either you must go, or I," said she : "and pray let it be you. Also, this place is unworthy of your high gifts : and I love you, in my way, the way I mean to love you when we meet again — in heaven ; and I labor your advancement to a sphere more worthy of you."

I wish space permitted me to lay the whole correspondence before the reader ; but I must confine myself to its general purport.

It proceeded in this way : the priest, humble, eloquent, pathetic ; but gently, yet pertinaciously, clinging to the place : the lady, gentle, wise, and firm, detaching with her soft fingers, first one hand, then another, of the poor priest's, till at last he was driven to the sorry excuse that he had no money to travel with, nor place to go to.

"I can't understand it," said Griffith. "Are these letters all forged, or are there two Kate Gaunts ? the one that wrote these prudent letters, and the one I caught upon this very priest's arm. Perdition ! "

Mrs. Gaunt started to her feet.

"Methinks 't is time for me to leave the room," said she, scarlet.

"Gently, my good friends; one thing at a time," said Francis. "Sit thou down, impetuous. The letters, sir, —what think you of them?"

"I see no harm in them," said Griffith.

"No harm! Is that all? But I say these are very remarkable letters, sir: and they show us that a woman may be innocent and unsuspicious, and so seem foolish, yet may be wise for all that. In her early communication with Leonard,

'At Wisdom's gate Suspicion slept;
And thought no ill where no ill seemed.'

But, you see, suspicion being once aroused, wisdom was not to be lulled nor blinded. But that is not all: these letters breathe a spirit of Christian charity; of true, and rare, and exalted piety. Tender are they, without passion; wise, yet not cold; full of conjugal love, and of filial pity for an erring father, whom she leads, for his good, with firm yet dutiful hand. Trust to my great experience: doubt the chastity of snow rather than hers who could write these pure and exquisite lines. My good friend, you heard me rebuke and sneer at this poor lady for being too innocent and unsuspicious of man's frailty: now hear me own to you that I could no more have written these angelic letters than a barn-door fowl could soar to the mansions of the saints in heaven."

This unexpected tribute took Mrs. Gaunt's heart by storm; she threw her arms round Father Francis's neck, and wept upon his shoulder.

"Ah!" she sobbed, "you are the only one left that loves me."

She could not understand justice praising her: it must be love.

"Ay," said Griffith, in a broken voice, "she writes like an angel: she speaks like an angel: she looks like an angel. My heart says she is an angel. But my eyes have shown me she is naught. I left her, unable to walk, by her way of it; I came back and found

her on that priest's arm, springing along like a greyhound." He buried his head in his hands, and groaned aloud.

Francis turned to Mrs. Gaunt, and said, a little severely, "How do you account for that?"

"I 'll tell *you*, Father," said Kate, "because you love me. I do not speak to *you*, sir: for you never loved me."

"I could give thee the lie," said Griffith, in a trembling voice; "but 't is not worth while. Know, sir, that within twenty-four hours after I caught her with that villain, I lay a-dying for her sake; and lost my wits; and, when I came to, they were a-making my shroud in the very room where I lay. No matter; no matter; I never loved her."

"Alas! poor soul!" sighed Kate. "Would I had died ere I brought thee to that!" And, with this, they both began to cry at the same moment.

"Ay, poor fools," said Father Francis, softly; "neither of ye loved t' other; that is plain. So now sit you there, and let us have your explanation; for you must own appearances are strong against you."

Mrs. Gaunt drew her stool to Francis's knee; and addressing herself to him alone, explained as follows:—

"I saw Father Leonard was giving way, and only wanted one good push, after a manner. Well, you know I had got him, by my friends, a good place in Ireland: and I had money by me for his journey; so, when my husband talked of going to the fair, I thought, 'O, if I could but get this settled to his mind before he comes back!' So I wrote a line to Leonard. You can read it if you like. 'T is dated the 30th of September, I suppose."

"I will," said Francis, and read this out:—

"DEAR FATHER AND FRIEND,— You have fought the good fight, and conquered. Now, therefore, I *will* see you once more, and thank you for my husband (he is so unhappy), and put the money for your journey into your hand myself, — your journey to Ireland. You are the Duke of Leinster's chaplain ; for I have accepted that place for you. Let me see you to-morrow in the Grove, for a few minutes, at high noon. God bless you.

           " CATHARINE GAUNT."

"Well, father," said Mrs. Gaunt, "'t is true that I could only walk two or three times across the room. But, alack, you know what women are : excitement gives us strength. With thinking that our unhappiness was at an end, — that, when he should come back from the fair, I should fling my arm round his neck, and tell him I had removed the cause of his misery, and so of mine, — I seemed to have wings ; and I did walk with Leonard, and talked with rapture of the good he was to do in Ireland, and how he was to be a mitred abbot one day (for he is a great man), and poor little me be proud of him ; and how we were all to be happy together in heaven, where is no marrying nor giving in marriage. This was our discourse ; and I was just putting the purse into his hands, and bidding him God-speed, when he — for whom I fought against my woman's nature, and took this trying task upon me — broke in upon us, with the face of a fiend ; trampled on the poor, good priest, that deserved veneration and consolation from him, of all men ; and raised his hand to me ; and was not man enough to kill me after all ; but called me — ask him what he called me — see if he dares to say it again before you ; and then ran away, like a coward as he is, from the lady he had defiled with his rude tongue, and the heart he had broken. Forgive him ? that I never will, — never, — never."

"Who asked you to forgive him ? " said the shrewd priest. "Your own heart. Come, look at him."

"Not I," said she, irresolutely. Then, still more feebly : "He is naught to me." And so stole a look at him.

Griffith, pale as ashes, had his hand on his brow, and his eyes were fixed with horror and remorse.

"Something tells me she has spoken the truth," he said, in a quavering voice. Then, with concentrated horror, "But if so — O God, what have I done ? — What shall I do ? "

Mrs. Gaunt extended her arms towards him across the priest.

"Why, fall at thy wife's knees and ask her to forgive thee."

Griffith obeyed : he fell on his knees, and Mrs. Gaunt leaned her head on Francis's shoulder, and gave her hand across him to her remorse-stricken husband.

Neither spoke, nor desired to speak ; and even Father Francis sat silent, and enjoyed that sweet glow which sometimes blesses the peacemaker, even in this world of wrangles and jars.

But the good soul had ridden hard, and the neglected meats emitted savory odors ; and by and by he said dryly, "I wonder whether that fat pullet tastes as well as it smells : can you tell me, Squire ? "

" O, inhospitable wretch that I am ! " said Mrs. Gaunt : "I thought but of my own heart."

"And forgot the stomach of your unspiritual father. But, my dear, you are pale, you tremble."

" 'T is nothing, sir : I shall soon be better. Sit you down and sup : I will return anon."

She retired, not to make a fuss ; but her heart palpitated violently, and she had to sit down on the stairs.

Ryder, who was prowling about, found her there, and fetched her hartshorn.

Mrs. Gaunt got better ; but felt so languid, and also hysterical, that she retired to her own room for the night, attended by the faithful Ryder, to whom she confided that a reconciliation had taken place, and, to celebrate it, gave her a dress she had only worn a year. This does not sound queenly to you ladies ; but know that a week's wear tells far more on the flimsy trash you wear now-a-days, than a year did on the glorious silks of Lyons Mrs. Gaunt put on; thick as broadcloth, and embroidered so cunningly by the loom, that it would pass for rarest needle-work. Besides, in those days, silk was silk.

As Ryder left her, she asked, "Where is master to lie to-night?"

Mrs. Gaunt was not pleased at this question being put to her. She would have preferred to leave that to Griffith. And, as she was a singular mixture of frankness and finesse, I believe she had retired to her own room partly to test Griffith's heart. If he was as sincere as she was, he would not be content with a public reconciliation.

But the question being put to her plump, and by one of her own sex, she colored faintly, and said, "Why, is there not a bed in his room?"

"O yes, madam."

"Then see it be well aired. Put down all the things before the fire; and then tell me: I'll come and see. The feather-bed, mind, as well as the sheets and blankets."

Ryder executed all this with zeal. She did more; though Griffith and Francis sat up very late, she sat up too; and, on the gentlemen leaving the supper-room, she met them both, with bed-candles, in a delightful cap, and undertook, with cordial smiles, to show them both their chambers.

"Tread softly on the landing, an if it please you, gentlemen. My mistress hath been unwell; but she is in a fine sleep now, by the blessing, and I would not have her disturbed."

Good, faithful, single-hearted Ryder!

Father Francis went to bed thoughtful. There was something about Griffith he did not like: the man every now and then broke out into boisterous raptures, and presently relapsed into moody thoughtfulness. Francis almost feared that his cure was only temporary.

In the morning, before he left, he drew Mrs. Gaunt aside, and told her his misgivings. She replied that she thought she knew what was amiss, and would soon set that right.

Griffith tossed and turned in his bed, and spent a stormy night. His mind was in a confused whirl, and his heart distracted. The wife he had loved so tenderly proved to be the very reverse of all he had lately thought her! She was pure as snow, and had always loved him; loved him now, and only wanted a good excuse to take him to her arms again. But Mercy Vint!—his wife, his benefactress! a woman as chaste as Kate, as strict in life and morals,—what was to become of her? How could he tell her she was not his wife? how reveal to her her own calamity, and his treason? And, on the other hand, desert her without a word! and leave her hoping, fearing, pining, all her life! Affection, humanity, gratitude, alike forbade it.

He came down in the morning, pale for him, and worn with the inward struggle.

Naturally there was a restraint between him and Mrs. Gaunt; and only short sentences passed between them.

He saw the peacemaker off, and then wandered all over the premises, and the past came nearer, and the present seemed to retire into the background.

He wandered about like one in a dream; and was so self-absorbed, that he did not see Mrs. Gaunt coming towards him, with observant eyes.

She met him full; he started like a guilty thing.

"Are you afraid of me?" said she, sweetly.

"No, my dear, not exactly; and yet I am: afraid, or ashamed, or both."

"You need not. I said I forgive you; and you know I am not one that does things by halves."

"You are an angel!" said he, warmly; "but" (suddenly relapsing into despondency) "we shall never be happy together again."

She sighed. "Say not so. Time and sweet recollections may heal even this wound by degrees."

"God grant it," said he, despairingly.

"And, though we can't be lovers

again all at once, we may be friends. To begin, tell me, what have you on your mind? Come, make a friend of me."

He looked at her in alarm.

She smiled. "Shall I guess?" said she.

"You will never guess," said he; "and I shall never have the heart to tell you."

"Let me try. Well, I think you have run in debt, and are afraid to ask me for the money."

Griffith was greatly relieved by this conjecture; he drew a long breath; and, after a pause, said cunningly, "What made you think that?"

"Because you came here for money, and not for happiness. You told me so in the Grove."

"That is true. What a sordid wretch you must think me!"

"No, because you were under a delusion. But I do believe you are just the man to turn reckless, when you thought me false, and go drinking and dicing." She added eagerly, "I do not suspect you of anything worse."

He assured her that was not the way of it.

"Then tell me the way of it. You must not think, because I pester you not with questions, I have no curiosity. O, how often I have longed to be a bird, and watch you day and night unseen! How would you have liked that? I wish you had been one, to watch me. Ah, you don't answer. Could you have borne so close an inspection, sir?"

Griffith shuddered at the idea; and his eyes fell before the full gray orbs of his wife. .

"Well, never mind," said she. "Tell me your story."

"Well, then, when I left you, I was raving mad."

"That is true, I 'll be sworn."

"I let my horse go; and he took me near a hundred miles from here, and stopped at — at — a farm-house. The good people took me in."

"God bless them for it. I 'll ride and thank them."

"Nay, nay; 't is too far. There I

fell sick of a fever, a brain-fever: the doctor blooded me."

"Alas! would he had taken mine instead."

"And I lost my wits for several days; and when I came back, I was weak as water, and given up by the doctor; and the first thing I saw was an old hag set a-making of my shroud."

Here the narrative was interrupted a moment by Mrs. Gaunt seizing him convulsively; and then holding him tenderly, as if he was even now about to be taken from her.

"The good people nursed me, and so did their daughter, and I came back from the grave. I took an inn; but I gave up that, and had to pay forfeit; and so my money all went; but they kept me on. To be sure I helped on the farm: they kept a hostelry as well. By and by came that murrain among the cattle. Did you have it in these parts, too?"

"I know not; nor care. Prithee, leave cattle, and talk of thyself."

"Well, in a word, they were ruined, and going to be sold up. I could not bear that: I became bondsman for the old man. It was the least I could do. Kate, they had saved thy husband's life."

"Not a word more, Griffith. How much stand you pledged for?"

"A large sum." ·

"Would five hundred pounds be of any avail?"

"Five hundred pounds! Ay, that it would, and to spare; but where can I get so much money? And the time so short."

"Give me thy hand, and come with me," said Mrs. Gaunt, ardently.

She took his hand, and made a swift rush across the lawn. It was not exactly running, nor walking, but some grand motion she had when excited. She put him to his stride to keep up with her at all; and in two minutes she had him into her boudoir. She unlocked a bureau, all in a hurry, and took out a bag of gold. "There!" she cried, thrusting it into his hand, and blooming all over with joy and eagerness: "I thought you would want money ; so I saved it up. You shall not be in debt a day longer. Now mount thy horse, and carry it to those good souls ; only, for my sake, take the gardener with thee, — I have no groom now but he, — and both well armed."

"What! go this very day ?"

"Ay, this very hour. I can bear thy absence for a day or two more,— I have borne it so long ; but I cannot bear thy plighted word to stand in doubt a day, no, not an hour. I am your wife, sir, your true and loving wife : your honor is mine, and is as dear to me now as it was when you saw me with Father Leonard in the Grove, and read me all

awry. Don't wait a moment. Begone at once."

" Nay, nay, if I go to-morrow, I shall be in time."

"Ay, but," said Mrs. Gaunt, very softly, " I am afraid if I keep you another hour I shall not have the heart to let you go at all ; and the sooner gone, the sooner back for good, please God. There, give me one kiss, to live on, and begone this instant."

He covered her hands with kisses and tears. " I 'm not worthy to kiss any higher than thy hand," he said, and so ran sobbing from her.

He went straight to the stable, and saddled Black Dick.

INDIAN MEDICINE.

EVERY one who has fed his boyish fancy with the stories of pioneers and hunters has heard of the character known among Indians as the "medicine-man." But it may very likely be the case that few of those familiar with the term really know the import of the word. A somewhat protracted residence among the Blackfoot tribe of Indians, and an extensive observation of men and manners as they appear in the wilder parts of the Rocky Mountains and British America, have enabled the writer to give some facts which may not prove wholly uninteresting.

By the term "medicine" much more is implied than mere curative drugs, or a system of curative practice. Among all the tribes of American Indians, the word is used with a double signification, — a literal and narrow meaning, and a general and rather undefined application. It signifies not only physical remedies and the art of using them, but second-sight, prophecy, and preternatural power. As an adjective, it embraces the idea of supernatural as well as remedial.

As an example of the use of the word in its mystic signification, the following may be given. The *horse*, as is well known, was to the Indian, on its first importation, a strange and terrible beast. Having no native word by which to designate this hitherto unknown creature, the Indians contrived a name by combining the name of some familiar animal, most nearly resembling the horse, with the "medicine" term denoting astonishment or awe. Consequently the Blackfeet, adding to the word "Elk" (*Pounika*) the adjective "medicine" (*tòs*), called the horse *Pounika-ma-ta*, i. e. Medicine Elk. This word is still their designation for a horse.

With this idea of medicine, and recollecting that the word is used to express two classes of thoughts very different, and separated by civilization, though confounded by the savage, it will not surprise one to find that the medicine-men are conjurers as well as doctors, and that their conjurations partake as much of medical quackery as does their medical practice of affected incantation. As physicians, the medicine-men are below contempt, and, but for the savage cruelty of their ignorance, undeserving of notice. The writer has known a man to have his uvula and palate torn out by a medicine-man. In that case the disease was a hacking cough caused by an elongation of the uvula; and the remedy adopted (after preparatory singing, dancing, burning buffalo hair, and other conjurations) was to seize the uvula with a pair of bullet-moulds, and tear from the poor wretch every tissue that would give way. Death of course ensued in a short time. The unfortunate man had, however, died in "able hands," and according to the "highest principles of [Indian] medical art."

Were I to tell how barbarously I have seen men mutilated, simply to extract an arrow-head from a wound, the story would scarce be credited. Common sense has no place in the system of Indian medicine-men, nor do they appear to have gained an idea, beyond the rudest, from experience.

In their quality of seers, however, they are more important, and frequently more successful persons, attaining, of course, various degrees of proficiency and reputation. An accomplished dreamer has a sure competency in that gift. He is reverently consulted, handsomely paid, and, in general, strictly obeyed. His influence, when once established, is more potent even than that of a war chief. The dignity and profit of the position are baits sufficient to command the attention and ambition of the ablest men; yet it is not unfrequently the case that persons otherwise undistinguished are noted for clear and strong powers of "medicine."

Of the three most distinguished medicine-men known to the writer, but one was a man of powerful intellect. Even this person preferred a somewhat sedentary, and what might be called a strictly professional life, to the usual active habits of the hunting and warring tribes. He dwelt almost alone on a far northern branch of the Saskatchewan River, revered for his gifts, feared for his power, and always approached with something

of reluctance by the Indians, who firmly believed the spirit of the gods to dwell within him. He was an austere and taciturn man, difficult of access, and as vain and ambitious as he was haughty and contemptuous. Those who professed to have witnessed the scene told of a trial of power between this man —the Black Snake, as he was called —and a renowned medicine-man of a neighboring tribe. The contest, from what the Indians said, must have occurred about 1855.

The rival medicine-men, each furnished with his medicine-bag, his amulets, and other professional paraphernalia, arrayed in full dress, and covered with war-paint, met in the presence of a great concourse. Both had prepared for the encounter by long fasting and conjurations. After the pipe, which precedes all important councils, the medicine-men sat down opposite to each other, a few feet apart. The trial of power seems to have been conducted on principles of animal magnetism, and lasted a long while without decided advantage on either side; until the Black Snake, concentrating all his power, or "gathering his medicine," in a loud voice commanded his opponent to die. The unfortunate conjurer succumbed, and in a few minutes "his spirit," as my informant said, "went beyond the Sand Buttes." The only charm or amulet ever used by the Black Snake is said to have been a small bean-shaped pebble suspended round his neck by a cord of moose sinew. He had his books, it is true, but they were rarely exhibited.*

The death of his rival, by means so purely non-mechanical or physical, gave the Black Snake a pre-eminence in "medicine" which he has ever since maintained. It was useless to suggest

---

* The Mountain Assinaboins, of which tribe the Black Snake is (if living) a distinguished ornament, were visited more than a hundred years since by an English clergyman named Wolsey, who devised an alphabet for their use. The alphabet is still used by them, and they keep their memoranda on dressed skins. With the exception of the Cherokees, they are, perhaps, the only tribe possessing a written language. They have no other civilization.

poison, deception, or collusion, to explain the occurrence. The firm belief was that the spiritual power of the Black Snake had alone secured his triumph.

I mentioned this story to a highly educated and deeply religious man of my acquaintance. He was a priest of the Jesuit order, a European by birth, formerly a professor in a Continental university of high repute, and beyond doubt a guileless and pious man. His acquaintance with Indian life extended over more than twenty years of missionary labor in the wildest parts of the west slope of the Rocky Mountains. To my surprise, (for I was then a novice in the country,) I found him neither astonished, nor shocked, nor amused, by what seemed to me so gross a superstition.

"I have seen," said he, "many exhibitions of power which my philosophy cannot explain. I have known predictions of events far in the future to be literally fulfilled, and have seen medicine tested in the most conclusive ways. I once saw a Kootenai Indian (known generally as Skookum-tamaherewos, from his extraordinary power) command a mountain sheep to fall dead, and the animal, then leaping among the rocks of the mountain-side, fell instantly lifeless. This I saw with my own eyes, and I ate of the animal afterwards. It was unwounded, healthy, and perfectly wild. Ah!" continued he, crossing himself and looking upwards, "Mary protect us! the medicine-men have power from Sathanas." *

This statement, made by so responsible a person, attracted my attention to what before seemed but a clumsy

species of juggling. During many months of intimate knowledge of Indian life, — as an adopted member of a tribe, as a resident in their camps, and their companion on hunts and war-parties, — I lost no opportunity of gathering information concerning their religious belief and traditions, and the system of *medicine*, as it prevails in its purity. It would be foreign to the design of this desultory paper to enter at large upon the history of creation as preserved by the Indians in their traditions, the conflicts of the Beneficent Spirit with the Adversary, and the Indian idea of a future state. With all these, the present sketch has no further concern than a mere statement that "medicine" is based upon the idea of an overruling and all-powerful Providence, who acts at His good pleasure, through human instruments. Those among Christians who entertain the doctrine of Special Providences may find in the untutored Indian a faith as firm as theirs, — not sharply defined, or understood by the Indian himself, but inborn and ineradicable.

The Indian, being thoroughly ignorant of all things not connected with war or the chase, is necessarily superstitious. His imagination is active, — generally more so than are his reasoning powers, — and fits him for a ready belief in the powers of any able mediciner. On one occasion, Meldram, a white man in the employ of the American Fur Company, found himself suddenly elevated to high rank as a seer by a foolish or petulant remark. He was engaged in making a rude press for baling furs, and had got a heavy lever in position. A large party of Crow Indians who were near at hand, considering his press a marvel of mechanical ingenuity, were very inquisitive as to its uses. Meldram, with an assumption of severity, told them the machine was "snow medicine," and that it would make snow to fall until it reached the end of a cord that dangled from the lever and reached within a yard of the ground. The fame of so potent a medicine spread rapidly through the Crow

---

* I do not feel at liberty to give the name of this excellent man, now perhaps no more. In 1861, he lived and labored, with a gentleness and zeal worthy of the cause he heralded, as a missionary among the Kalispelm Indians, on the west slope of the Rocky Mountains. Such devotion to missionary labor as was his may well challenge admiration even from those who think him in fatal error. His memory will long be cherished by those who knew the purity of his character, his generous catholicity of spirit, and the native and acquired graces of mind which made him a companion at once charming and instructive.

nation. The machine was visited by hundreds, and the fall of snow anxiously looked for by the entire tribe. To the awe of every Indian, and the astonishment of the few trappers then at the mouth of the Yellowstone, the snow actually reached the end of the rope, and did not during the winter attain any greater depth. Meldram found greatness thrust upon him. He has lived for more than forty years among the Crows, and when I knew him was much consulted as a medicine-man. His chief charms, or amulets, were a large bull's-eye silver watch, and a copy of "Ayer's Family Almanac," in which was displayed the human body encircled by the signs of the zodiac.

The position and ease attendant upon a reputation for medicine power cause many unsuccessful pretenders to embrace the profession; and it would seem strange that their failures should not have brought medicine into disrepute. In looking closely into this, a well-marked distinction will always be found between *medicine* and the *medicine-man,* — quite as broad as is made with us between religion and the preacher. I have seen would-be medicine-men laughed at through the camp, — men of reputation as warriors, and respected in council, but whose *forte* was not the reading of dreams or the prediction of events. On the other hand, I have seen persons of inferior intellect, without courage on the war-path or wisdom in the council, revered as the channels through which, in some unexplained manner, the Great Spirit warned or advised his creatures.

Of course it is no purpose of this paper to uphold or attack these peculiar ideas. A meagre presentation of a few facts not generally known is all that is aimed at. Whether the system of Indian medicine be a variety of Mesmerism, Magnetism, Spiritualism, or what not, others may inquire and determine. One bred a Calvinist, as was the writer, may be supposed to have viewed with suspicion the exhibitions of medicine power that almost daily presented themselves. And while, in very

numerous instances, they proved to be but the impudent pretensions of charlatans, it must be conceded, if credible witnesses are to be believed, that sometimes there is a power of second-sight, or something of a kindred nature, which defies investigation. Instances of this kind are of frequent occurrence, and easily recalled, I venture to say, by every one familiar with the Indian in his native state. The higher powers claimed for medicine are, in general, doubtfully spoken of by the Indians. Not that they deny the possibility of the power, but they question the probability of so signal a mark of favor being bestowed on a mere mortal. Powers and medicine privileges of a lower degree are more readily acknowledged. An aged Indian of the Assinaboin tribe is very generally admitted, by his own and neighboring tribes, to have been shown the happy hunting-grounds, and conducted through them and returned safely to the camp of his tribe, by special favor of the Great Spirit. He once drew a map of the Indian paradise for me, and described its pleasant prairies and crystal rivers, its countless herds of fat buffalo and horses, its perennial and luxuriant grass, and other charms dear to an Indian's heart, in a rhapsody that was almost poetry. Another, an obscure man of the Cathead Sioux, is believed to have seen the hole through which issue the herds of buffalo which the Great Spirit calls forth from the centre of the earth to feed his children.

Medicine of this degree is not unfavorably regarded by the masses; but instances of the highest grades are extremely rare, and the claimants of such powers few in number. The Black Snake and the Kootenai, before referred to, are, if still alive, the only instances with which I am acquainted of admitted and well-authenticated powers so great and incredible. The common use of medicine is in affairs of war and the chase. Here the medicine-man will be found, in many cases, to exhibit a prescience truly astounding. Without attempting a theory to account for this, a suggestion may be ventured. The Indian passes a life that knows no repose. His vigilance is ever on the alert. No hour of day or night is to him an hour of assured safety. In the course of years, his perceptions and apprehensions become so acute, in the presence of constant danger, as to render him keenly and delicately sensitive to impressions that a civilized man could scarce recognize. The Indian, in other words, has a development almost like the instinct of the fox or beaver. Upon this delicate barometer, whose basis is physical fear, impressions (moral or physical, who shall say?) act with surprising power. How this occurs, no Indian will attempt to explain. Certain conjurations will, they maintain, aid the medicine-man to receive impressions; but how or wherefore, no one pretends to know. This view of *minor medicine* is the one which will account for many of its manifestations. Whether sound or defective, we will not contend.

The medicine-man whom I knew best was Ma-què-a-pos (the Wolf's Word), an ignorant and unintellectual person. I knew him perfectly well. His nature was simple, innocent, and harmless, devoid of cunning, and wanting in those fierce traits that make up the Indian character. His predictions were sometimes absolutely astounding. He has, beyond question, accurately described the persons, horses, arms, and destination of a party three hundred miles distant, not one of whom he had ever seen, and of whose very existence neither he, nor any one in his camp, was before apprised.

On one occasion, a party of ten voyageurs set out from Fort Benton, the remotest post of the American Fur Company, for the purpose of finding the Kaimè, or Blood Band of the Northern Blackfeet. Their route lay almost due north, crossing the British line near the Chief Mountain (Nee-na-stà-ko) and the great Lake O-màx-een (two of the grandest features of Rocky Mountain scenery, but scarce ever seen by whites), and extending indefinitely beyond the Saskatchewan and towards the tributaries of the Coppermine and Mackenzie Rivers. The expedition was perilous from its commencement, and the danger increased with each day's journey. The war-paths, war-party fires, and similar indications of the vicinity of hostile bands, were each day found in greater abundance.

It should be borne in mind that an experienced trapper can, at a glance, pronounce what tribe made a war-trail or a camp-fire. Indications which would convey no meaning to the inexperienced are conclusive proofs to the keen-eyed mountaineer. The track of a foot, by a greater or less turning out of the toes, demonstrates from which side of the mountains a party has come. The print of a moccasin in soft earth indicates the tribe of the wearer. An arrow-head or a feather from a war-bonnet, a scrap of dressed deer-skin, or even a chance fragment of jerked buffalo-meat, furnishes data from which unerring conclusions are deduced with marvellous facility.

The party of adventurers soon found that they were in the thickest of the Cree war-party operations, and so full of danger was every day's travel that a council was called, and seven of the ten turned back. The remaining three, more through foolhardiness than for any good reason, continued their journey, until their resolution failed them, and they too determined that, after another day's travel northward, they would hasten back to their comrades.

On the afternoon of the last day, four young Indians were seen, who, after a cautious approach, made the sign of peace, laid down their arms, and came forward, announcing themselves to be Blackfeet of the Blood Band. They were sent out, they said, by Ma-què-a-pos, to find three whites mounted on horses of a peculiar color, dressed in garments accurately described to them, and armed with weapons which they, without seeing them, minutely described. The whole history of the expedition had been detailed to them by Ma-què-a-pos. The purpose of the journey, the *personnel* of the party, the exact locality at which to find the three who persevered, had been detailed by him with as much fidelity as could have been done by one of the whites themselves. And so convinced were the Indians of the truth of the old man's medicine, that the four young men were sent to appoint a rendezvous, for four days later, at a spot a hundred miles distant. On arriving there, accompanied by the young Indians, the whites found the entire camp of " Rising Head," a noted war-chief, awaiting them. The objects of the expedition were speedily accomplished ; and the whites, after a few days' rest, returned to safer haunts. The writer of this paper was at the head of the party of whites, and himself met the Indian messengers.

Upon questioning the chief men of the Indian camp, many of whom afterwards became my warm personal friends, and one of them my adopted brother, no suspicion of the facts, as narrated, could be sustained. Ma-què-a-pos could give no explanation beyond the general one, — that he "saw us coming, and heard us talk on our journey." He had not, during that time, been absent from the Indian camp.

A subsequent intimate acquaintance with Ma-què-a-pos disclosed a remarkable medicine faculty as accurate as it was inexplicable. He was tested in every way, and almost always stood the ordeal successfully. Yet he never claimed that the gift entitled him to any peculiar regard, except as the instrument of a power whose operations he did not pretend to understand. He had an imperfect knowledge of the Catholic worship, distorted and intermixed with the wild theogony of the red man. He would talk with passionate devotion of the Mother of God, and in the same breath tell how the Great Spirit restrains the Rain Spirits from drowning the world, by tying them with the rainbow. I have often seen him make the sign of the cross, while he recounted, in all the soberness of implicit belief, how the Old Man (the God of the Black-

feet) formed the human race from the mud of the Missouri, — how he experimented before he adopted the human frame, as we now have it, — how he placed his creatures in an isolated park far to the north, and there taught them the rude arts of Indian life, — how he staked the Indians on a desperate game of chance with the Spirit of Evil, — and how the whites are now his peculiar care. Ma-què-a-pos's faith could hardly stand the test of any religious creed. Yet it must be said for him, that his simplicity and innocence of life might be a model for many, better instructed than he.

The wilder tribes are accustomed to certain observances which are generally termed the tribe-medicine. Their leading men inculcate them with great care, — perhaps to perpetuate unity of tradition and purpose. In the arrangement of tribe-medicine, trivial observances are frequently intermixed with very serious doctrines. Thus, the grand war-council of the Dakotah confederacy, comprising thirteen tribes of Sioux, and more than seventeen thousand warriors, many years since promulgated a national medicine, prescribing a red stone pipe with an ashen stem for all council purposes, and (herein was the true point) an eternal hostility to the whites. The prediction may be safely ventured, that every Sioux will preserve this medicine until the nation shall cease to exist. To it may be traced the recent Indian war that devastated Minnesota ; and there cannot, in the nature of things, and of the American Indian especially, be a peace kept in good faith until the confederacy of the Dakotah is in effect destroyed.

The Crows, or Upsàraukas, will not smoke in council, unless the pipe is lighted with a coal of buffalo chip, and the bowl rested on a fragment of the same substance. Their chief men have for a great while endeavored to engraft teetotalism upon their national medicine, and have succeeded better than the Indian character would have seemed to promise.

Among the Flat-Heads female chastity is a national medicine. With the Mandans, friendship for the whites is supposed to be the source of national and individual advantage.

Besides the varieties of medicine already alluded to, there are in use charms of almost every kind. When game is scarce, medicine is made to call back the buffalo. The Man in the Sun is invoked for fair weather, for success in war or chase, and for a cure of wounds. The spirits of the dead are appeased by medicine songs and offerings. The curiosity of some may be attracted by the following rude and literal translation of the song of a Blackfoot woman to the spirit of her son, who was killed on his first war-party. The words were written down at the time, and are not in any respect changed or smoothed.

" O my son, farewell !
    You have gone beyond the great river,
    Your spirit is on the other side of the Sand Buttes ;
    I will not see you for a hundred winters ;
    You will scalp the enemy in the green prairie,
    Beyond the great river.
    When the warriors of the Blackfeet meet,
    When they smoke the medicine-pipe and dance the
        war-dance,
    They will ask, ' Where is Isthumaka ? —
    Where is the bravest of the Mannikappi ? '
    He fell on the war-path.
            Mai-ram-bo, mai-ram-bo.

" Many scalps will be taken for your death :
    The Crows will lose many horses :
    Their women will weep for their braves,
    They will curse the spirit of Isthumaka.
    O my son ! I will come to you
    And make moccasins for the war-path,
    As I did when you struck the lodge
    Of the ' Horse-Guard ' with the tomahawk.
    Farewell, my son ! I will see you
    Beyond the broad river.
            Mai-ram-bo, mai-ram-bo," etc., etc.

Sung in a plaintive minor key, and in a wild, irregular rhythm, the dirge was far more impressive than the words would indicate.

It cannot be denied that the whites, who consort much with the ruder tribes of Indians imbibe, to a considerable degree, their veneration for medicine. The old trappers and voyageurs are, almost without exception, observers of omens and dreamers of dreams. They claim that medicine is a faculty which can in some degree be cultivated, and aspire to its possession as eagerly as does the Indian. Sometimes they acquire a reputation that is in many ways beneficial to them.

As before said, it is no object of this paper to defend or combat the Indian notion of medicine. Such a system exists as a fact ; and whoever writes upon American Demonology will find many fruitful topics of investigation in the daily life of the uncontaminated Indian. There may be nothing of truth in the supposed prediction by Tecumseh, that Tuckabatchee would be destroyed by an earthquake on a day which he named ; the gifts of the " Prophet " may be overstated in the traditions that yet linger in Kentucky and Indiana ; the descent of the Mandans from Prince Madoc and his adventurous Welchmen, and the consideration accorded them on that account, may very possibly be altogether fanciful ; but whoever will take the trouble to investigate will find in the *real* Indian a faith, and occasionally a power, that quite equal the faculties claimed by our civilized clairvoyants, and will approach an untrodden path of curious, if not altogether useful research.

THE DEATH OF SLAVERY.

O THOU great Wrong, that, through the slow-paced years,
    Didst hold thy millions fettered, and didst wield
The scourge that drove the laborer to the field,
And look with stony eye on human tears,
      Thy cruel reign is o'er;
      Thy bondmen crouch no more
In terror at the menace of thine eye;
    For He who marks the bounds of guilty power,
Long-suffering, hath heard the captive's cry,
    And touched his shackles at the appointed hour,
And lo! they fall, and he whose limbs they galled
Stands in his native manhood, disenthralled.

A shout of joy from the redeemed is sent;
    Ten thousand hamlets swell the hymn of thanks;
    Our rivers roll exulting, and their banks
Send up hosannas to the firmament.
      Fields, where the bondman's toil
      No more shall trench the soil,
Seem now to bask in a serener day;
    The meadow-birds sing sweeter, and the airs
Of heaven with more caressing softness play,
    Welcoming man to liberty like theirs.
A glory clothes the land from sea to sea,
For the great land and all its coasts are free.

Within that land wert thou enthroned of late,
    And they by whom the nation's laws were made,
    And they who filled its judgment-seats, obeyed
Thy mandate, rigid as the will of fate.
      Fierce men at thy right hand,
      With gesture of command,
Gave forth the word that none might dare gainsay;
    And grave and reverend ones, who loved thee not,
Shrank from thy presence, and, in blank dismay,
    Choked down, unuttered, the rebellious thought;
While meaner cowards, mingling with thy train,
Proved, from the book of God, thy right to reign.

Great as thou wert, and feared from shore to shore,
    The wrath of God o'ertook thee in thy pride;
    Thou sitt'st a ghastly shadow; by thy side
Thy once strong arms hang nerveless evermore.
      And they who quailed but now
      Before thy lowering brow

Devote thy memory to scorn and shame,
  And scoff at the pale, powerless thing thou art.
And they who ruled in thine imperial name,
  Subdued, and standing sullenly apart,
Scowl at the hands that overthrew thy reign,
And shattered at a blow the prisoner's chain.

Well was thy doom deserved ; thou didst not spare
  Life's tenderest ties, but cruelly didst part
  Husband and wife, and from the mother's heart
Didst wrest her children, deaf to shriek and prayer ;
    Thy inner lair became
    The haunt of guilty shame ;
Thy lash dropped blood ; the murderer, at thy side,
  Showed his red hands, nor feared the vengeance due.
Thou didst sow earth with crimes, and, far and wide,
  A harvest of uncounted miseries grew,
Until the measure of thy sins at last
Was full, and then the avenging bolt was cast.

Go then, accursed of God, and take thy place
  With baleful memories of the elder time,
  With many a wasting pest, and nameless crime,
And bloody war that thinned the human race ;
    With the Black Death, whose way
    Through wailing cities lay,
Worship of Moloch, tyrannies that built
  The Pyramids, and cruel creeds that taught
To avenge a fancied guilt by deeper guilt, —
  Death at the stake to those that held them not.
Lo, the foul phantoms, silent in the gloom
Of the flown ages, part to yield thee room.

I see the better years that hasten by
  Carry thee back into that shadowy past,
  Where, in the dusty spaces, void and vast,
The graves of those whom thou hast murdered lie.
    The slave-pen, through whose door
    Thy victims pass no more,
Is there, and there shall the grim block remain
  At which the slave was sold ; while at thy feet
Scourges and engines of restraint and pain
  Moulder and rust by thine eternal seat.
There, 'mid the symbols that proclaim thy crimes,
Dwell thou, a warning to the coming times.

REVIEWS AND LITERARY NOTICES.

Ecce Homo : a Survey of the Life and Work of Jesus Christ. Boston : Roberts Brothers.

THE merits of this book are popular and obvious, consisting in a strain of liberal, enlightened sentiment, an ingenious and original cast of thought, and a painstaking lucidity of style which leaves the writer's meaning even prosaically plain. There is a good deal of absurd and even puerile exegesis in its pages, which makes you wonder how so much sentimentality can coexist with so much ability ; but the book is vitiated for all purposes beyond mere literary entertainment by one grand defect, which is the guarded theologic obscurity the writer keeps up, or the attempt he makes to estimate Christianity apart from all question of the truth or falsity of Christ's personal pretensions towards God. The author may have reached in his own mind the most definite theologic convictions, but he sedulously withholds them from his reader ; and the consequence is, that the book awakens and satisfies no intellectual interest in the latter, but remains at best a curious literary speculation. For what men have always been moved by in Christianity is not so much the superiority of its moral inculcations to those of other faiths, as its uncompromising pretension to be a final or absolute religion. If Christ be only the eminently good and wise and philanthropic man the author describes him to be, deliberating, legislating, for the improvement of man's morals, he may be very admirable, but nothing can be inferred from that circumstance to the deeper inquiry. If he claim no essentially different significance to our regard, on God's part, than that claimed by Zoroaster, Confucius, Mahomet, Hildebrand, Luther, Wesley, he is to be sure still entitled to all the respect inherent in such an office ; but then there is no *a priori* reason why his teaching and influence should not be superseded in process of time by that of any at present unmentionable Anne Lee, Joanna Southcote, or Joe Smith. And what the human mind craves, above all things else, is repose towards God, — is not to remain a helpless sport to every fanatic sot that comes up from the abyss of human vanity, and claims to hold it captive by the assumption of a new Divine mission.

The objection to the *mythic* view of Christ's significance, which is that maintained by Strauss, is, that it violates men's faith in the integrity of history as a veracious outcome of the providential love and wisdom which are extant and operative in human affairs. And the objection to what has been called the *Troubadour* view of the same subject, which is that represented by M. Renan, is, that it outrages men's faith in human character, regarded, if not as habitually, still as occasionally capable of heroic or consistent veracity. We may safely argue, then, that neither Strauss nor Renan will possess any long vitality to human thought. They are both fascinating reading ; — the one for his profound sincerity, or his conviction of a worth in Christianity so broadly human and impersonal as to exempt it from the obligations of a literal historic doctrine ; the other for his profound insincerity, so to speak, or an egotism so subtile, so capacious and frank, as permits him to take up the grandest character in history into the hollow of his hand, and turn him about there for critical inspection and definite adjustment to the race, with absolutely no more reverence nor reticence than a buyer of grain shows to a handful of wheat, as he pours it dexterously from hand to hand, and blows the chaff in the seller's face.* But both writers alike are left behind us in the library, and are not subsequently brought to mind by anything we encounter in the fields or the streets.

The author of *Ecce Homo* does no dishonor to the Christian history as history, however foolishly he. expatiates at times upon its incidents and implications ; much less to the simple and perfect integrity of Christ as a man, but no more than Strauss or Renan does he meet the supreme want of the popular understanding, which is to know wherein Christianity has the right it claims to be regarded as a final or complete revelation of the Divine name upon the earth. We think, moreover, that the reason of the omission is the same in every case, being the sheer and contented indifference which each of the writers feels

---

* Of course we have no disposition to deny M. Renan's right to reduce Christ and every other historic figure to the standard of the most modern critical art. We merely mean to say that this is all M. Renan does, and that the all is not much.

to the question of a revelation in the abstract or general, regarded as a *sine qua non* of any sympathetic or rational intercourse which may be considered as possible between God and man. We should not be so presumptuous as to invite our readers' attention to the discussion of so grave a philosophic topic as the one here referred to, in the limited space at our command ; but surely it may be said, without any danger of misunderstanding from the most cursory reader, that if creation were the absolute or unconditioned verity which thoughtless people deem it, there could be no *ratio* between Creator and creature, hence no intercourse or intimacy, inasmuch as the one is being itself, and the other does not even exist or *seem* to be but by him. In order that creation should be a rational product of Divine power, in order that the creature should be a being of reason, endowed with the responsibility of his own actions, it is imperative that the Creator disown his essential infinitude and diminish himself to the creature's dimensions ; that he hide or obscure his own perfection in the creature's imperfection, to the extent even of rendering it fairly problematic whether or not an infinite being really exist, so putting man, as it were, upon the spontaneous search and demand for such a being, and in that measure developing his rational possibilities. And if this be so, — if creation philosophically involve a descending movement on the Creator's part proportionate to the ascending one contemplated on the creature's part, — then it follows that creation is not a simple, but a complex process, involving equally a Divine action and a human reaction, or the due adjustment of means and ends ; and that no writer, consequently, can long satisfy the intellect in the sphere of religious thought, who either jauntily or ignorantly overlooks this philosophic necessity. This, however, is what Messrs. Strauss and Renan and the author of *Ecce Homo* agree to do ; and this is what makes their several books, whatever subjective differences characterize them to a literary regard, alike objectively unprofitable as instruments of intellectual progress.

The Masquerade and Other Poems. By JOHN GODFREY SAXE. Boston : Ticknor and Fields.

IT was remarked lately by an ingenious writer, that " it never seems to occur to some people, who deliver upon the books they read very unhesitating judgments, that they may be wanting, either by congenital defect, or defect of experience, or defect of reproductive memory, in the qualifications which are necessary for judging fairly of any particular book." To poetry this remark applies with especial force.

By poetry we do not understand mere verse, but any form of literary composition which reproduces in the mind certain emotions which, in the absence of an epithet less vague, we shall call *poetical*. These emotions may be a compound of the sensuous and the purely intellectual, or they may partake much more of the one than of the other. (The rigorous metaphysician will please not begin to carp at our definition.) These emotions may be excited by an odor, the state of the atmosphere, a strain of music, a form of words, or by a single word ; and, as they result largely from association, it is obvious that what may be poetry to some minds may not be poetry to others, — may not be poetry to the same mind at different periods of life or in different moods. The most sympathetic, most catholic, most receptive mind will always be the best qualified to detect and appreciate poetry under all its various forms, and would as soon think of denying the devotional faculty to a man of differing creed, as of denying the poetical to one whose theory or habit of expression may chance to differ from its own. Goethe was so apt to discover something good in poems which others dismissed as wholly worthless, that it was said of him, " his commendation is a brevet of mediocrity." Perhaps it was his " many-sidedness " that made him so accurate a " detective " in criticism.

According to Wordsworth, " poetry is the spontaneous overflow of powerful feelings ; it takes its origin from emotion recollected in tranquillity." A good definition so far as it goes. But Wordsworth could see only one side of the shield. He was notoriously so deficient in the faculty of humor, that even Sydney Smith was unintelligible to him. Few specimens of what can be called wit can be found in his writings. He could not see that there is a poetry of wit as well as of sentiment, — of the intellect as well as of the emotions. No wonder he could not enjoy Pope, and had little relish for Horace. And yet how grand is Wordsworth in his own peculiar sphere !

Those narrow views of the province of poetry, which roused the indignation of Byron, and which would exclude such writers as Goldsmith, Pope, Campbell, Scott, Praed, Moore, and Saxe from the rank of poets, are not unfrequently reproduced in our own day. We do not perceive that they spring from a liberal or philosophical consideration of the subject. Poetry, ποίησις, or " making," creation, or re-creation, does not address itself to any single group of those faculties of our complex nature, the gratification of which brings a sense of the agreeable, the exhilarating, or the elevating. As well might we deny to didactic verse the name of poetry, as to those *vers de société* in which a profound truth may be found in a comic mask, or the foibles which scolding could not reach may be reflected in the mirror held up in gayety of heart. As well might we deny that a waltz is music, and claim the name of music only for a funeral march or a nocturne, as deny that Shakespeare's description of Queen Mab is as much poetry as the stately words in which Prospero compares the vanishing of his insubstantial pageant to that of

" The cloud-capped towers, the gorgeous palaces,
  The solemn temples, the great globe itself."

The new volume of poems by Mr. Saxe is, in many respects, an improvement on all that he has given us hitherto. There is more versatility in the style, a freer and firmer touch in the handling. Like our best humorists, he shows that the founts of tears and of laughter lie close together ; for his power of pathos is almost as marked as that of fun. As good specimens of what he has accomplished in the minor key, we may instance " The Expected Ship," " The Story of Life," and " Pan Immortal." But it is in his faculty of turning upon us the whimsical and humorous side of a fact or a character that Saxe especially excels. The lines entitled " The Superfluous Man " are an illustration of what we mean. In some learned treatise the author stumbles on the following somewhat startling reflection : " It is ascertained by inspection of the registers of many countries, that the uniform proportion of male to female births is as 21 to 20 : accordingly, in respect to marriage, every 21st man is naturally superfluous." Here is hint enough to set Saxe's bright vein of humor flowing. The Superfluous Man becomes a concrete embodiment, and sings his discovery of the cause of his forlorn single lot and his hopeless predicament. It flashes upon him that he is that 21st man alluded to by the profound statistician. He is un-

der a natural ban, — for he 's a superfluous man. There 's no use fighting 'gainst nature 's inflexible plan. There 's never a woman for him, — for he 's a superfluous man. The whole conception and execution of the poem afford a fine example of the manner in which a genuine artist may inform a subtile and an extravagant whim with life, humor, and consistency.

" The Mourner à la Mode " contains some good instances of the neatness and felicity with which the author floods a whole stanza with humor by a single epithet.

"What tears of *vicarious* woe,
    That else might have sullied her face,
  Were kindly permitted to flow
    In ripples of ebony lace !
  While even her fan, in its play,
    Had quite a lugubrious scope,
  And seemed to be waving away
    The ghost of the angel of Hope !"

The sentiments of a young lover on finding that the object of his adoration had an excellent appetite, and was always punctual at lunch and dinner, are expressed with a Sheridan-like sparkle in the concluding stanza of " The Beauty of Ballston."

"Ah me ! of so much loveliness
    It had been sweet to be the winner ;
  I know she loved me only less —
    The merest fraction — than her dinner ;
  'T was hard to lose so fair a prize,
    But then (I thought) 't were vastly harder
  To have before my jealous eyes
    A constant rival in my larder !"

There is one practical consideration in regard to the poetry of Saxe, which may excite the distrust of those critics who, with Horace, hate the profane multitude. Fortunately or unfortunately for his reputation, Saxe's poems are *popular*, and — not to put too fine a point of it — *sell*. His books have a regular market value, and this value increases rather than diminishes with years. This is, we confess, rather a suspicious circumstance. Did Milton sell ? Did Wordsworth sell ? Must not the fame that is instantaneous prove hollow and ephemeral ? Are we not acquainted with a certain volume of poems that shall be nameless, the whole edition of which lies untouched and unclaimed on the publisher's shelves ? And are we not perfectly well aware that those poems — well, we can wait. If Mr. Saxe would only put forth a volume that should prove, in a mercantile sense, a failure, we think he would be surprised to find how happily he would hit certain critics who can now see little in his writings to justify their success. Let him once join the fraternity of unappreciated geniuses, and he will find compensation, — though not, perhaps, in the form of what some vulgar fellow has called "solid pudding."

The Giant Cities of Bashan; and Syria's Holy Places. By the Rev. J. L. PORTER, A. M., Author of "Murray's Hand-Book for Syria and Palestine," etc., etc. New York : T. Nelson and Sons.

TRAVELLERS who have merely visited the classic scenes of Greece and Italy, or at the best have "browsed about" the ruinous sites of Tyre and Carthage, must have a mortifying sense of the newness of such recent settlements, in reading of Mr. Porter's journey through Bashan, and sojourn in Bozrah, Salcah, Edrei, and the other cities of the Rephaim. As Chicago is to Athens, so is Athens to these mighty and wonderful cities of doom and eld, which are marvellous, not alone for their antiquity, (so remote that one looks into it dizzily and doubtfully, as a depth into which it is not wholly safe to peer,) but also for the perfection in which they stand and have stood amid the desolation of unnumbered ages. A Cockney clergyman travelling through Eastern Syria, with his Ezekiel in his hand, arrives at nightfall before the gates of a town which was a flourishing metropolis in the days of Moses, and takes up his lodging in a house built by some newly-married giant, say five or six thousand years ago. It is in perfect repair, "the walls are sound, the roofs unbroken, the doors and even window-shutters" — being of solid basalt monoliths, incapable of decay or destruction — "are in their places." In the town whose dumb streets no foot but the Bedouin's has trodden for centuries and centuries, there are hundreds of such houses as this ; and in a province not larger than Rhode Island there are a hundred such towns. According to Mr. Porter, the language of Scripture, which the strongest powers of deglutition have sometimes rejected as that of Eastern hyperbole, is literally verified at every step in the land of Bashan. The facts, he says, would not stand the arithmetic of Bishop Colenso for an instant ; yet from the summit of the castle of Salcah (capital of his late gigantic Majesty, King Og) he counted thirty utterly deserted and perfectly habitable towns ; so that he finds no difficulty in

believing the bulletin of Jair in which the Israelite general declares he took in the province of Argob sixty great cities "fenced with high walls, gates, and bars, besides unwalled towns a great many." Nor is the fulfilment of prophecy in regard to this kingdom, populous and prosperous beyond any other known to history, less literal or less startling.

"Thus saith the Lord God of Israel : They shall eat their bread with carefulness, and drink their water with astonishment, that her land may be desolate from all that is therein, because of the violence of all that dwell therein. And the cities that are inhabited shall be laid waste, and the land shall be desolate."

Everywhere Mr. Porter witnessed the end predicted by Ezekiel : a nation might dwell in these enchanted cities, but they are all empty and silent as the desert. Their architecture, however, is eloquent in witness of the successive changes through which they have passed in reaching the state of final desolation foretold of the prophet. The dwellings, so ponderous and so simple, are the work of the original Rephaim, or giants, from whom the Israelites conquered the land, and the masonry is of these first conquerors. The Greeks have left the proof of their presence in the temples and inscriptions, and the Romans in the structure of the roads ; while the Saracens have added mosques, and the Turks solitude and danger, — for the whole land is infested with robbers. But while Jewish masonry has crumbled to dust, while Roman roads are weed-grown, and the temples of the gods and the mosques of Mahomet mingle their ruins, the dwellings of the Rephaim stand intact and everlasting, as if the earth had loved her mighty first-born too well to suffer the memory of their greatness to perish from her face.

It must be acknowledged that Mr. Porter has not done the best that could be done for the country through which he travels. With a style extremely graphic at times, he seems wanting in those arts of composition by which he could convey to his readers an impression of things at once vivid and comprehensive. He visits the cities of Bashan, one after another, and tells us repeatedly that they are desolate, and in perfect repair, and quotes the proper text of Scripture in which their desolation is foretold, and their number and strength not exaggerated. Yet he fails, with all this, to describe any one place completely, and is of opinion that he should weary his reader in recounting, at Bozrah, for example, " the wonders of art and architecture, and the curiosities of votive tablet, and dedicatory inscription on altar, tomb, church, and temple " ; whereas we must confess that nothing would have pleased us better than to hear about all these things, with ever so much minuteness, and that we should have been willing to take two passages of prophecy instead of twenty, if we might have had the omitted description in the place of them. But Mr. Porter being made as he is, we are glad to get out of him what we can, and have to thank him for a full account of at least one of the houses of the Rephaim, in which he passed a night.

" The walls were perfect, nearly five feet thick, built of large blocks of hewn stones, without lime or cement of any kind. The roof was formed of large slabs of the same black basalt, lying as regularly, and jointed as closely as if the workmen had only just completed them. They measured twelve feet in length, eighteen inches in breadth, and six inches in thickness. The ends rested on a plain stone cornice, projecting about a foot from each side wall. The chamber was twenty feet long, twelve wide, and ten high. The outer door was a slab of stone, four and a half feet high, four wide, and eight inches thick. It hung upon pivots formed of projecting parts of the slab, working in sockets in the lintel and threshold ; and though so massive, I was able to open and shut it with ease. At one end of the room was a small window with a stone shutter. An inner door, also of stone, but of finer workmanship, and not quite so heavy as the other, admitted to a chamber of the same size and appearance. From it a much larger door communicated with a third chamber, to which there was a descent by a flight of stone steps. This was a spacious hall, equal in width to the two rooms, and about twenty-five feet long by twenty high. A semicircular arch was thrown across it, supporting the stone roof ; and a gate, so large that camels could pass in and out, opened on the street. The gate was of stone, and in its place ; but some rubbish had accumulated on the threshold, and it appeared to have been open for ages. Here our horses were comfortably installed. Such were the internal arrangements of this strange old mansion. It had only one story ; and its simple, massive style of architecture gave evidence of a very remote antiquity."

Mr. Porter does not tell us whether all the dwellings of the Rephaim are constructed after one plan, as, for instance, the houses of Pompeii were, or whether there was variety in the architecture, and on many other points of inquiry he is equally unsatisfactory. His strength is in his one great fact, — that these cities are older than any known to profane history, and that they yet exist undecayed and undecaying. The charm of such a fact is so great, that we recur again and again to his pages, with a forever unappeased famine for more knowledge, which we hope some garrulous and gossipal traveller will soon arise to satisfy.

Of him — the beneficent future tourist — we shall willingly accept any number of fables, if only he will add something more filling than Mr. Porter has given us. It is true that this tourist will not have a mere pleasure excursion, but will undergo much to merit the gratitude of his readers. The land of Bashan is nomadically inhabited by a race of men much fiercer than its ancient bulls ; and Bedouins beset the movements of the traveller, to pillage and slay wherever they are strong enough to overcome his escort of Druses. Mr. Porter tells much of the perils he incurred, and even of actual attacks made upon him by fanatical Mussulmans while he sketched the wonders of the world's youth among which they dwelt. For the present his book has a value unique and very great : the scenes through which he passes have been heretofore unvisited by travel, and the interest attaching to them is intense and universal. The literal verification of many passages of Scripture supposed more or less allegorical, must have its weight with all liberal thinkers ; and, as a contribution to the means of religious inquiry, this work will be earnestly received.

Life of Benjamin Silliman, M.D., LL.D., late Professor of Chemistry, Mineralogy, and Geology in Yale College. Chiefly from his Manuscript Reminiscences, Diaries, and Correspondence. By GEORGE P. FISHER, Professor in Yale College. In Two Volumes. New York : Charles Scribner & Co.

PROFESSOR FISHER, in allowing the subject of this biography to tell the story of his life, restricts himself very self-denyingly to here and there a line of introduction or comment. We have ample passages from Professor Silliman's journal, and from an autobiographical memoir written during his last years, as well as extracts from his letters and the letters addressed to him. It is an easy and pleasant way of writing personal history, and it would be an easy and pleasant way of reading it, if life were as long as art. But we fear that the popular usefulness of this work — and the biography of the eminent man who did so much to popularize science should be in the hands of all — must be impaired by its magnitude ; and we are disposed to regret that Professor Fisher did not think fit to reject that part of the correspondence which contributes nothing to the movement of the narrative or the development of character, and condense much of that material which has only a value reflected from the interest already felt in Professor Silliman. These are faults in a work from which we have risen with a clear sense of the beauty and goodness, as well as the greatness, of the eminent scientist. It is admirable to see how his career, begun in another century and another phase of civilization, ended in what was best and most enlightened and liberal in our own time. A man could hardly have started from better things, or been subject at important points of his progress to better influences. Benjamin Silliman was of Revolutionary stock, which had its roots in the soil of the Reformation. The Connecticut Puritan came of Tuscan Puritans, who fled their city of Lucca, and finally passed from Switzerland through Holland to our shores. Brain and heart in him were thus imbued with an unfaltering love of freedom, chastised by religious fervor ; and when he became a man, he married with a race of kindred origin in faith, sentiment, and principles. He advanced with his times in a patriotic devotion to democracy and equality, but he seems to have always kept, together with great simplicity of character, the impression of early teaching and associations, and something of old-time stateliness and formality. His youth, like his age, was very sober, modest, and discreet. The ties which united him to his family were strong ; and he loved his mother, who long survived his father, with the reverent affection of the past generation. He inherited certain theological principles from his parents, and never swerved from them for a moment. Some friendships came down to him from his father which he always honored ; and the institution of learning with which he maintained a life-long connection was in his early days the object of a regard mixed with awe, and always of pride and devotion. He used to think President Styles the greatest of human beings ; and one reads with a kind of dismay, that he was once fined sixpence for kicking a football into the President's door-yard.

There was in this grave youth the making of many kinds of greatness. He who became so eminent in science could have been a great jurist, for he had the tranquillity and perseverance necessary to legal success ; he could have been a great statesman, for his political views were clear and just and far-reaching ; he wrote some of the most popular books of travels in his day, and he could have shone in literature ; while he appears to have been conscious of the direction in which a sole weakness lay, and with early wisdom forsook the muse of poetry. He tells us that it was no instinctive preference which led him to the study and pursuit of the natural sciences, but the persuasion of Dr. Dwight, who was President of Yale in Silliman's twenty-third year, and who opened this career to him by offering him the Professorship of Chemistry, then about to be established. At that time Silliman was studying law ; but, once convinced that he can be of greater use to himself and others in the way proposed, he enters it and never looks back ; goes to Philadelphia to hear the learnedest professors of that day ; goes to Europe for the culture unattainable in this country ; overcomes poverty in himself and in Yale ; will not be tempted from New Haven by the offer of the Presidency of the University of South Carolina, but devotes himself to a generous study of science, to the diffusion of scientific knowledge, and the promotion of the greatness of the institution to which he belongs. His devotion is not blind, however : he finds time to write attractive accounts of his voyages to Europe, to concern himself in religious affairs, to sympathize and co-operate with whatever is noble and good in political movements. He lives long enough to enjoy his fame, to see Yale prosperous and great, and his country about to triumph forever over the evil of slavery, which he had hated and combated. It was a noble life, — simple, pure, and illustrious, — and its history is full of instruction and encouragement.

Fifteen Days. An Extract from EDWARD COLVIL'S Journal. Boston : Ticknor and Fields.

THIS is a work of fiction, in which the passion of love, so far from being the prime motive, as in other fictions, does not enter at all. The author seeks to reach, without other incident, one tragic event, and endeavors to make up for a want of adventure by the subtile analysis of character and the study of a civil problem. The novelty and courage of the attempt will attract the thoughtful reader, and will probably tempt him so far into the pages of the book, that he will find himself too deeply interested in its persons to part from them voluntarily. The national sin with which the author so pitilessly deals has been expiated by the whole nation, and is now no more ; but its effects upon the guilty and guiltless victims, here alike so leniently treated, remain, and the question of slavery must always command attention till the question of reconstruction is settled.

In " Fifteen Days " the political influences of slavery are only very remotely considered, while the personal and social results of the system are examined with incisive acuteness united to a warmth of feeling which at last breaks forth into pathetic lament. Is not the tragedy, of which we discern the proportions only in looking back, indeed a fateful one ? A young New-Englander, rich, handsome, generous, and thoroughly taught by books and by ample experience of the Old World and the New to honor men and freedom, passes a few days in a Slave State, in the midst of that cruel system which could progress only from bad to worse ; to which reform was death, and which with the instinct of self-preservation punished all open attempts to ameliorate the relations of oppressor and oppressed, and permitted no kindness to exist but in the guise of severity or the tenderness of a good man for his beast ; which boasted itself an aristocracy, and was an oligarchy of plebeian ignorance and meanness ; which either dulled men's brains or chilled their hearts. In the presence of this system, Harry Dudley lingers long enough to rescue a slave and to die by the furious hand of the master, — a man in whose soul the best impulse was the love he bore his victim, and in whom the evil destiny of the drama triumphs.

From the conversation of Harry and the botanist, his friend, the author retrospectively develops in its full beauty a character illustrated in only one phase by the episode which the passages from Edward Colvil's journal cover, while she sketches with other touches, slight, but skilful, the people of a whole neighborhood, and the events of years. Doctor Borrow, the botanist, is made to pass, by insensible changes, from a learned indifference concerning slavery to eloquent and ardent argument against it, and thus to present the history of the process by which even science, the coldest element of our civilization, found itself at last unconsciously arrayed against a system long abhorrent to feeling. In the Doctor's talk with Westlake, we have a close and clear comparison of the origin and result of the civilizations of New England and the South, the high equality of the North and the mean aristocracy of the Slave States, and the Doctor's first perfect consciousness of loving the one and hating the other. The supposititious Mandingo's observations of the state of Europe at the time of opening the African slave-trade form a humorous protest against judgment of Africa by travellers' stories, and suggest more than a doubt whether the first men-stealers were better than their victims, and whether they conferred the boon of a higher civilization upon negroes by enslaving them. But the humor of the book, like its learning, is subordinated to the story, which is imbued with a sentiment not wanting in warmth because so noble and lofty. The friendship of Colvil and Dudley is less like the friendship between two men, than the affectionate tenderness of two women for each other ; and the character of Dudley in its purity and elevation is sometimes elusive. The personality of Colvil is also rather shadowy ; but the Doctor is human and tangible, and the other persons, however slightly indicated, are all real, and bear palpable witness, in their lives, to the influences of that system which, though cruel to the oppressed, wrought a ruin yet more terrible in the oppressor.

THE

ATLANTIC MONTHLY.

A Magazine of Literature, Science, Art, and Politics.

VOL. XVIII. — AUGUST, 1866. — NO. CVI.

HOW MY NEW ACQUAINTANCES SPIN.

THE strictly professional man may have overcome his natural aversion to some of the most interesting objects of his study, such as snakes, and toads, and spiders, and vermin of all kinds; but people in general have always required that any attempt to force such abominations upon their notice should be preceded by a more or less elaborate and humble acknowledgment of their hideous aspect, their ferocious disposition, their dark and bloody deeds, and the utter impossibility of their conducing in any way to human comfort and convenience.

But, while admitting the truth of much that has been thus urged against spiders as a class, I must decline, or at least defer, conforming to custom in speaking of the particular variety which we are about to consider, and I believe that it will need only a glance at the insect and its silk, and a brief notice of its habits, to justify my indisposition to follow the usual routine.

Without apology, then, I shall endeavor to show that in the structure, the habits, the mode of growth, and, above all, in the productions of this spider are to be found subjects worthy the attention of every class of minds; for to the naturalist is exhibited a species which, though not absolutely new to science, was never seen nor heard of by Professor Agassiz till the spring of 1865, and which is so narrowly circumscribed in its geographical distribution that, so far as I can ascertain, it was never observed by Hentz, — a Southern entomologist, who devoted himself particularly to spiders, — and is met with only upon a few low, marshy islands on the coast of South Carolina, and perhaps of other Southern States. Its habits, too, are so interesting, and so different in many respects from those recorded of other species, that the observer of living creatures has here an abundant opportunity, not only for increasing his own knowledge, but for enlarging the domain of science. And this more especially in America; for while, in England, Blackwall and others have been laboring for more than thirty years, spiders seem to have received little attention on this side of the Atlantic.

We have now, moreover, in our observation of these insects, an incentive of sovereign effect, namely, the hope of increasing our national wealth ; for to the practical man, to the manufacturer and the mechanic, is offered a new silken material which far surpasses in beauty and elegance that of the silkworm, and which, however small in quantity at present, demands some attention in view of the alarming decrease in the silk crops of Europe. This material is obtained in a manner entirely new, — not, as with the worm, by unwinding the cocoons, nor yet, as might be suggested for the spider, by unravelling the web, but by *drawing* or *winding* or *reeling directly from the body of the living insect*, even as you would milk a cow, or, more aptly, as wire is pulled through a wire-drawing machine.

To the admirer of the beautiful and perfect in nature is presented a fibre of absolute smoothness, roundness, and finish, the colors of which resemble, and in the sunlight even excel in brilliancy those of the two precious metals, silver and gold ; while the moralist who loves to illustrate the workings of God's providence in bringing forth good out of evil, by comparing the disgusting silk-worm with its beautiful and useful product, may now enforce the lesson by the still more striking contrast between this silk and the loathed and hated spider.

The statesman who, after a four years' war, sees few indications of a better spirit on the part of the South, and is almost ready to exclaim, " Can any good thing come out of Nazareth ? " may now perhaps discern a spot, small indeed, but brilliant, on the very edge of the dark Carolina cloud ; and it may not be too much to hope that, in course of time, the cords of our spider's golden and silver silk may prove potent bonds of union with the first of the rebellious States.

As to the mathematician who believes in the inborn tendency of mankind to variation and imperfection, and holds up to us, as shining examples of mathematical accuracy, the work of certain insects, and who—since Professor Wyman has shown that the hexagonal form of the bee's cell is not of original design, but rather the necessary result of difficulties met and overcome in the most economical manner, though by no means always with perfect exactness and uniformity—has fallen back upon the ancient and still prevalent belief in the precise construction of the spider's web, (which, as will be seen, really displays it no more than does the bee's cell,)—to this disappointed man of geometry and figures is now offered the alternative of either finding a new and truer illustration, or of abandoning his position entirely.

Let us, then, wait till we have seen this spider and heard his story. *His* story ! That reminds me of another class which may possibly be represented among my readers, and whose members, in the contemplation of the domestic economy of these insects, will, I fear, discover many and weighty arguments in favor of the various opinions entertained by the advocates of Woman's Rights ; for here is a community in which the females not only far exceed the males in number, but present so great a contrast to them in size and importance, that, but for absolute proof, they never would be regarded as belonging to the same species.

Here, then, is a life-size picture of our spider and of— I was about to say, *his* partner ; but in truth it is *she* who is *the* spider, and *he* is only *her* partner. Such is the real physical, and, so to speak, mental superiority of the female, that, even if we insist upon the legal equality at least of the masculine element, we can do so only in name, and will find it hard to avoid speaking of him as the male of the *Nephila plumipes*, thus tacitly admitting her as the truer representative of the species. Their relative size and appearance are shown by the figures ; but it may be added that she is very handsome ; the fore part of her body, which, being composed of the head and chest soldered together, is termed *cephalothorax*, is glossy-black and covered, except in

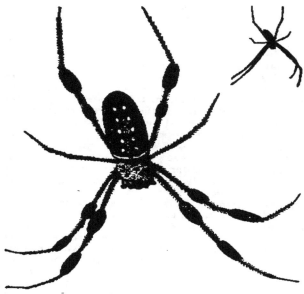

Fig. 1.   Male and Female *Nephila plumipes.*

answer these questions, we must go back three years, to the 19th of August, 1863, and to the camp of the Fifty-fifth Regiment of Massachusetts Volunteers, on a desolate island a little south from the harbor of Charleston, South Carolina, and in sight of the fortress which Gillmore had just begun to strengthen by the addition of tons of Union shot and shell, till, from tolerably strong masonry, its walls became solid earthworks which nothing could pierce or greatly injure. There, at the north end of Folly Island, — scarce wider than our camp at that point, and narrower than the magnificent beach which, at low tide, afforded ample space for the battalion drill, — I found in a tree a very large and handsome spider, whose web was at least three feet in diameter.

Glad enough to meet with anything new, and bearing in mind the interest with which, when a boy, I had watched and recorded the operations of our common house and hunting spiders, I entangled him — I did n't then know it was *her*, so let it pass — in the web, and carried it to my tent. The insect was very quiet, and did not attempt to escape; but presently, after crawling slowly along my sleeve, she let herself down to the floor, taking first the precaution, after the prudent fashion of most spiders, to attach to the point she left a silken line, which, as she descended, came from her body. Rather than seize the insect itself, I caught the thread and pulled. The spider was not moved, but the line readily drew out, and, being wound upon my hands, seemed so strong that I attached the end to a little quill, and, having placed the spider upon the side of the tent, lay down on my couch and turned the quill between my fingers at such a rate that in one minute six feet of silk were wound upon it. At the end of an hour and a half I estimated, with due allowance for stop-

spots, with white hairs; she has also upon six of her legs one or two brushes of black hairs; — while he is an insignificant-looking insect of a dull-brown color and half-starved look, with only a few scattered bristles upon his slender limbs.   He does nothing for himself, leaving her to make the web and provide the food, and even to carry him on her back when removal is necessary; but she makes up for the imposition by keeping him on short allowance and at a respectful distance, excepting when the impregnation of her eggs is necessary; and even then she is mistress of the situation, and, *etiam in amoribus sæva,* may afterward eat him up.   But of this contrast between the two sexes, of their functions and their relations to each other, more hereafter.   It is sufficient to observe that, when this spider is mentioned, and the sex is not specified, the *female* is always referred to.

When, where, and how was this spider discovered? and why is it that we have never heard of it before?   To

pages, that I had four hundred and fifty feet, or *one hundred and fifty yards*, of the most brilliant and beautiful golden silk I had ever seen.

During all this operation the spider had remained perfectly quiet, but finally put an end to my proceedings by grasping the line with the tip of one of her hind legs so that it snapped. I was tired, however, and contented myself with the quantity already obtained, which now formed a raised band of gold upon the quill. This specimen is now in my possession, but has been removed from the quill to ascertain its weight, which is one third of a grain.

It is worthy of notice, perhaps, that in all this was involved no new *fact*, but only a happy deduction from one known ages ago; namely, that a spider, when dropping, leaves her line attached, and so allows it to be drawn from her body. Nothing was more natural than to simply reverse the position of the fixed point, and, instead of letting the spider go away from the end of her line, to take the end of her line away from her. So natural, indeed, did it seem, that my gratification at having been (as was then supposed) the first to do it was, on reflection, mixed with surprise that no one had ever thought of it before, and I am very glad to find that at least *four* individuals have, within the last century, pulled silk out of a spider, though of these only one, whose researches I hope to make known, regarded the matter as anything more than a curious experiment.

I had never before seen such a spider, nor even paid attention to any geometrical species; though one large black and yellow variety is, or used to be, common enough in our fields at the North. Neither had I ever heard of such a method of obtaining silk. But though my first specimen was not preserved, and a second was never seen on Folly Island, yet I was so impressed with its size and brilliant colors, and especially with the curious brushes of black hairs on its legs, that when, during the following summer, another officer described

to me a great spider which was very common on Long Island, where he was stationed, I knew it was the same, and told him what I had done the year before, adding that I was sure something would come of it in time.

With leisure and many spiders at his command, this officer improved upon my suggestion, by substituting for my quill turned in the fingers a wooden cylinder worked by a crank, and by securing, at a proper distance, (between pins, I think,) one or more spiders, whose threads were guided between pins upon the cylinder. He thus produced more of the silk, winding it upon rings of hard rubber so as to make very pretty ornaments. With this simple machine I wound the silk in two grooves cut on a ring of hard rubber and parallel except at one point, where they crossed so as to form a kind of signet. Another officer now suggested and put in operation still another improvement, in the shape of the "gear-drill-stock" of our armorer's chest. This, being a machine for drilling iron, was rough in its construction and uneven in its action, but, having cog-wheels, a rapid and nearly steady motion could be given to its shaft. To this shaft he attached a little cross of rubber, and covered it with silk, which was of a silver-white color instead of golden-yellow, as in other cases. The difference in color was then supposed to depend upon individual peculiarities, but the true explanation will be given farther on. With this gear-drill-stock, upon a larger ring, one inch in diameter and three eighths of an inch in width, in a groove upon its periphery one fourth of an inch in width, and across the sides of the ring in two directions, I wound *three thousand four hundred and eighty-four yards*, or *nearly two miles, of silk*. The length was estimated by accurately determining the different dimensions of the ring where wound upon, and multiplying by this the number of revolutions of the cylinder per minute (170), and this product again by the number of minutes of actual winding (285), deducting from the gross time of winding (about nine hours) each moment of stoppage for any cause.

This was late in the fall of 1864, and, our specimens being sent home, further experiments, and even thoughts upon the subject, were prevented by the expedition against the Charleston and Savannah Railroad, and the many changes of station that followed the disastrous battle of Honey Hill. But, when I was at the North in February, 1865, a friend expressed to me his confident belief that this new silken product could be made of practical utility, and advised me to make inquiries on the subject. So, before presenting it to the scientific societies, I tested the strength of the silk by attaching to a fixed point one end of a thread *one four-thousandth* of an inch in diameter, and tying the other end upon the arm of an accurate balance : weights were then dropped in to the amount of *fifty-four grains* before the line was broken. By a calculation from this, a solid bar of spider's silk, one inch in diameter, would sustain a weight of more than *seventy tons;* while a similar bar of steel will sustain only fifty-six, and one of iron twenty-eight tons. The specimens were then exhibited to Professors Wyman, Agassiz, and Cooke, of Harvard University, to all of whom the species of spider was unknown, though Professor Wyman has since found a single specimen among some insects collected at the South ; while to them as well as to the silk-manufacturers the idea of reeling silk directly from a living insect was entirely new. The latter, of course, wished to see a quantity of it before pronouncing upon its usefulness. So most of my furlough was spent in making arrangements for securing a number of the spiders, and reeling their silk during the coming summer. These comprised six light wooden boxes with sliding fronts, each eighteen inches wide and high and one foot deep, and containing six tin trays one above another, each of which, again, held twenty-four square paper boxes two and a half inches in diameter, and with lids closed by an elastic. Into these the spiders

were to be put for transportation. Then I had made a costly machine for reeling the silk, which, however, proved of no practical value.

In March, with these and other real or fancied adjuvants, (some of which proved even less useful and trustworthy than the machine,) but, above all, with a determination to put this matter to the test of actual experiment, I rejoined the regiment at Charleston, which had just fallen into our hands. It was not until April, however, that we were so situated that I could make any attempt to get spiders. Of course it was not expected that the full-grown ones should be found at that season, but the eggs or young should be abundant where the spiders had been in the summer.

Before recounting my adventures in pursuit of my spinster friends, it may be well to say a few words of the locality which they inhabited.

Charleston stands upon the extremity of a narrow peninsula, between the Cooper and the Ashley Rivers. Charleston Harbor, supplied by these and some smaller streams, lies between Mt. Pleasant and Sullivan's Island on the northeast, and James and Morris Islands on the southwest. One cannot but be struck with the resemblance, so great as to be almost symmetrical, between the two sides of the harbor. Mt. Pleasant and James Island are quite high land, — high at least for the coast of South Carolina,—and are sep-

Fig. 2. Map of Charleston and Vicinity.

arated from the mainland, the one by the Wando River, the other by Wappoo Creek; while Sullivan's Island, where stand Fort Moultrie and other Rebel batteries, corresponds almost precisely to Morris Island, both being low and sandy, and being, as it were, bent inland from the sea, with sharp points looking toward the city, their convex shores forming a rounded entrance to the harbor. Extending southward from Morris Island, and separated from it by Lighthouse Inlet, is Folly Island; and in exact correspondence to the latter, north of Sullivan's Island, and separated from it by Breach Inlet, is a similar sand-ridge called Long Island. But now occurs a difference; for while between Long and Sullivan's Islands and Christ's Church Parish is an immense salt marsh intersected by creeks, but presenting an unbroken surface, in the midst of the corresponding marsh between Morris and Folly Islands and James Island is a group of low wooded islands, the largest of which lies opposite the upper or north end of Folly Island. To this no name is given on the maps, nor is it even distinguished from the marsh. It is, however, completely surrounded by water; and, though this is in the form of creeks neither wide nor deep, yet the peculiar softness of the mud, and the absence of any landing-place except upon the side toward Folly Island, render it almost inaccessible.

To this narrow strip of land, not three miles in length, was given the name of Long Island, — perhaps by our own troops, who knew nothing of an island of the same name *north* of the harbor; and in case it is found that no other name belongs to it, we may properly avoid a confusion, and christen it *Spider* Island, in honor of the remarkable insects for whose especial benefit it seems to have been made, and which, with the exception of the mosquitoes, are its sole inhabitants.

As was said, the first spider was found on Folly Island on the 19th of August, 1863: it was also the last there seen. During the summer of 1864, many were found on Long Island (so called); and when, in the spring of 1865, our regiment was encamped on James Island near Wappoo Creek, it was toward Long Island that all my attention, so far as concerned spiders, was directed.

But first, as a bit of collateral history, and to show how easily and how far one may go astray when one of the links in the chain of argument is only an *inference*, let me relate that, while riding over James Island, I observed upon trees and bushes numbers of small brown bags, from half an inch to an inch and a half in diameter, pear-shaped, and suspended by strong silken cords. The bags themselves were made of a finer silk so closely woven as to resemble brown paper, and, when opened, were found to contain a mass of loose silk filled with young spiders to the number of five hundred or more. In certain localities, especially in a swampy field just outside the first line of Rebel works, they were quite abundant. I had soon collected about four hundred of them, which, by a moderate estimate, contained *two hundred thousand little spiders*, — quite enough, I thought, with which to commence operations. But one hot day in June I placed them all on a tray in the sun. I was called away, and on my return found my one fifth of a million young spiders dead, — baked to death.

Prior to this catastrophe, however, I had become convinced that these were not the spiders I sought. Indeed, my only reasons for thinking they might be were, first, the abundance of these cocoons in a locality so near Long Island; and, second, my own great desire that they should prove the spiders I wanted. The young spiders, it is true, did not at all resemble their supposed progenitors, as to either shape, or color, or markings; yet all of these evidently changed during growth, and would not of themselves disprove the relationship.

One day in April, however, a cocoon was found in a tree on James Island, of a very different appearance from the others. It was of loose texture, and, instead of being pear-shaped, was hemispherical in form, and attached by its flat surface to the lower side of a leaf. This also contained young spiders, a little larger and a little brighter in color than the others, but really bearing no resemblance to the full-grown spiders of Long Island. This single cocoon formed the entering wedge of doubt, and soon it was clear that the only means of proof lay on Long Island itself.

But how was this to be reached? Easily enough while we were upon Folly Island and could row through the creeks to a wharf on the east side of Long Island. But now the case was altered; for between James and Long Islands was the immense marsh already mentioned, intersected by creeks, and composed of mud practically without bottom, and ranging from eighteen to twenty-three feet in depth by actual measurement. Around or over or through this marsh it was necessary to go, in order to reach Long Island, the home of the spiders.

I could easily occupy the rest of my allotted space in recounting my various attempts to reach this El Dorado, which my fancy, excited by every delay, stocked with innumerable cocoons of the kind already found so abundantly on James Island. These I expected would furnish thousands of spiders, the care of which, with the reeling of their silk, would give employment to all the freed people in South Carolina, — for even then the poor creatures were finding their way to the coast. And perhaps, I thought, some day, the Sea-Island silk may be as famous as the choice Sea-Island cotton. This hope I still cherish, together with the belief that, under certain conditions, the spiders may also be reared at the North.

After riding miles and miles in all directions in search of the readiest point of attack; after having once engaged a row-boat to go around through Stono River and meet me at the nearest point of land, — on which occasion I dismounted to give my horse a better

chance of getting over a bad place in the road, and the ungrateful beast left me in the lurch and went home much faster than he came, while I, being now half-way, walked on through the marsh, and had the pleasure of sitting on a log in a pouring rain for an hour, with Long Island just on the other side of a creek over which no boat came to carry me, — after this and other disappointments, I at last made sure by going in the boat myself, and so finally reached the island. But now, to my discomfiture, after a most careful search, I saw only two or three cocoons of the kind I looked for, while the others, of loose texture, were quite abundant, and doubtless would have been found in still greater numbers but for their always being under leaves, and often at a considerable height. It was probable now that these latter cocoons contained *the* spiders, and that the former were a different species.

The regiment now removed to the interior of the State, and while there occurred the *coup de soleil* above mentioned. We remained at Orangeburg until the middle of August, and then, being stationed at Mt. Pleasant, I again made raids for spiders. Upon James Island, in the localities where during the spring the cocoons were abundant, I found many large geometrical spiders, all of one kind, but not of the kind I sought. They were bad-tempered, and their legs were so short and strong that it was not easy to handle them, while their silk was of a light, and not brilliant, yellow.

My first attempt upon Long Island was made by leaving Charleston in a boat, which, after touching at Sumter, landed me at Fort Johnson. Here I was joined by a sergeant and corporal of the Fifty-fourth Massachusetts, and we walked across to a little settlement of freed people not far from Secessionville, where a boat and crew were engaged. It would be tedious to relate how, after sticking on invisible oyster-beds and mud-flats, and losing our way among the creeks, at two o'clock we found ourselves about one hundred yards from the north end of the island ; and how, since it was too late to try to reach the wharf on the east side, even had we been sure of the way, the two Fifty-fourth boys and myself got out of the boat and essayed to cross upon the marsh. Such a marsh ! We have marshes at the North, but they are as dry land in comparison. I had seen them at the South, had stepped upon and into them, but never one like this. It was clear mud, as soft as mud could be and not run like the water that covered it at high tide. Even the tall rushes wore an unsteady look ; and the few oysters upon its surface evidently required all their balancing powers to lie upon their flat sides and avoid sinking edgewise into the oozy depths. In we sank, over ankles, at the first step, and deeper and deeper till we took a second ; for our only safety lay in pushing down the rushes with the inside of one foot and treading upon them, till the other could be withdrawn from its yielding bed, and a spot selected for the next step forward. I say *selected*, for even this mud was more firm than a hole in it filled with water and treacherously concealed by a few rushes. A misstep into one of these pitfalls brought me to my knees, and well-nigh compelled me to call for help ; but a sudden and determined spring, and a friendly bunch of rushes beyond, spared me that mortification. When two thirds of the way across, and while thinking we should soon reach dry land, we came upon the edge of a creek, not wide, it is true, but with soft, slimy, sloping sides, (for *banks* they could not properly be called,) and no one knew how many feet of mud beneath its sluggish stream. Under ordinary circumstances I might have sounded a retreat ; but, remembering that there was twice as much mud behind as before us, and feeling ourselves sinking slowly but surely in our tracks, we slid down the sides into the water. This received our bodies to the waist, the mud our legs to the knees ; but we struggled through, and, after another terrible thirty yards of mud, reached

Long Island. Leaving my faithful companions to rest, I struck off down the east side of the island, and soon found spiders in plenty. Stopping at the wharf, and returning upon the west side, I counted one hundred spiders in less than an hour. This was only a voyage of discovery, but I could not resist the temptation to capture one big fellow and put it in my hat, which, with the edges brought together, I was forced to carry in my teeth, for one hand was required to break down the webs stretched across my path, and the other to do battle in vain with the thousands of mosquitoes, of huge size and bloody intent, besetting me on every side. What with the extreme heat and my previous fatigue, and the dread lest my captive should escape and revenge herself upon my face while I was avoiding the nets of her friends, and the relentless attacks of their smaller but more venomous associates, it was the most uncomfortable walk imaginable. To complete my misery, the path led me out upon the marsh where I could see nothing of the boat or my companions, and whence, to reach them, I had to walk across the head of the island. Excepting the dreaded recrossing of the mud, I hardly remember how we made our way back ; but by one means and another I finally reached Charleston at nine o'clock, about as disreputable-looking a medical man as ever was seen.

However, all this was soon forgotten, and, being now assured of the presence of the spiders in their former haunts, on the 30th of August, 1865, I organized a new expedition, which was to proceed entirely by water, and which consisted of a sail-boat and crew of picked volunteers. Leaving Mt. Pleasant in the morning, we crossed the harbor, and were soon lost in the meanderings of the creeks behind Morris Island. *Lost* is appropriate, for, once in these creeks, you know nothing, you see and hear nothing, and, if you change your course, must do so by mere guess. But the most annoying thing is, after an apparent advance of a quarter of a mile, to find yourself not twenty yards from your starting-point, so tortuous are the windings of the creeks.

By dint of hard rowing (in the wrong direction, as we soon found), then by walking across Morris Island to Light-House Inlet, and still harder rowing from there to the wharf of Long Island, we succeeded in securing sixty spiders; but now arose a furious storm of wind and rain, which not only compelled our retreat, but drenched us to the skin, blew us back faster than we could row, and threatened to overturn our boat if we hoisted the sail; so slow was our progress, that it was eleven o'clock at night before we reached Mt. Pleasant. Thus ended my last and only successful raid upon Long Island.

It may seem that I have dwelt longer than was necessary upon the circumstances attending the discovery of this spider and its silk. If so, it is not merely because at that time both were new to myself and all to whom I showed them, and everything concerning them was likely to be impressed upon my mind, but also because I then hoped that the idea of obtaining silk directly from a living insect might be found of practical importance, as I still hope it may. The incidents illustrate, too, the nature of the obstacles daily encountered and overcome by our troops; for no one who has never seen or stepped into a Sea-Island marsh can realize how difficult it was for our forces to obtain a foothold in the vicinity of Charleston. This was appreciated by the old freedman whom we left in the boat while crossing the mud. "No wonder," he said, "the Yankees whipped the Rebels, if they will do such things for to catch *spiders*."

The sixty spiders so obtained were kept for several weeks in the little boxes in which they had been deposited when caught. Every day each box was opened, the occupant examined, and its condition, if altered, noted on the cover. They generally spun a few irregular lines on which to hang, and so remained quiet except when the boxes were opened: then, of course, they tried to escape.

Half a dozen of the larger ones were placed on the window-seats and in corners of the room, where they speedily constructed webs. By preference these were stretched across the windows, illustrating one of the three principal instincts of this spider, which are, first, to *seek the light;* second, to *ascend;* and third, to take a position with the *head downward.*

It was now a question how they were to be fed; not so much while there, where flies were abundant, but after their arrival at the North. So, remembering that the young ones had seemed to relish blood, I took the tender liver of a chicken, cut it into little pieces, and dipped them in water, not, I am sorry to say, with any view to supply them with that fluid for the want of which they afterward perished, but in order that the bits of liver should be more easily pulled from the pins by the spiders. To my delight they greedily accepted the new food, and now I felt assured of keeping them during the winter.

Deferring, however, a more particular account of what was observed at Mt. Pleasant, until their habits and mode of life are taken up in order, it should be understood that, during our short stay, my attention was chiefly directed to getting from the spiders as much silk as possible; for it was evident that practical men would not credit the usefulness of spiders' silk until an appreciable quantity could be shown to them. The first trial of the machine with a live spider proved it an utter failure; for though quite ingenious and complicated, it had been devised with reference only to *dead* spiders. In regard to the arrangement (wherein lay its chief, if not sole, peculiarity) by which a thin slip of brass was sprung against a rubber band by the latter's elasticity, with a view to secure the spider's legs between them, it was found that, as the spider was alive, and, literally, kicking, and two of its legs were smaller than the rest, these were at once extricated, and the others soon followed; while, if the spring was made forcible enough to hold the smaller legs, the larger were in danger of being crushed, and the spider, fearing this, often disjointed them, according to the convenient, though loose habit of most Arachnida, crabs, and other articulates. It was also proposed to secure several spiders in the above manner upon the periphery of a wheel, the revolution of which would give a twist to their conjoined threads, carried through a common eyelet upon the spindle; but this can be accomplished without the inconvenience of whirling the spiders out of sight, by modifications of the apparatus which has always been used for twisting ordinary silk. It will probably be inferred from the above, that, in securing the spider, two points are to be considered; first, to prevent its escape, and second, so to confine the legs that it cannot reach with their tips either the *silk* or the *spinners*. Now the machine accomplished this by putting all the legs together in a vice, as it were, entailing upon the captive much discomfort and perhaps the loss of some of its legs, which, though eight in number, are each appropriated to a special use by their possessor.

So, abandoning the machine, I fell back upon a simple reel, and a modification of my little contrivance of the previous year; which was, to grasp the spider by all the legs, holding them behind her back, and to let her body down into a deep notch or slot cut in a thin card, the edges of which reached the constriction between the two regions of the body, the *cephalothorax* and *abdomen;* so that, when a second piece of card was let down upon it, the *cephalothorax*, with the *legs* of the spider, was upon one side of a partition, while on the other was the *abdomen*, bearing upon its posterior extremity the spinning organs. The head and horns of a cow to be milked are secured in a similar manner. By placing in a row, or one behind another, several spiders thus secured, a compound thread was simultaneously obtained from them, and wound upon a spindle of hard rubber.

By this means were produced several very handsome bands of bright yellow silk; but the time was so short, and the means of constructing and improving my apparatus so deficient, that I could procure no more than these few specimens, which were very beautiful, and shone in the sun like polished and almost translucent gold; but which, being wound upon a cylinder only an inch in diameter, and from several spiders at different times, could not be unwound, and so made of any further use.

I tried now to ascertain how much silk could be obtained from a single spider at once. It will be remembered that the first specimen, wound on Folly Island, was one hundred and fifty yards in length, and weighed one third of a grain. I now exhausted the supply of a spider for three days, using the same spindle, one inch in diameter, and turning this at the rate of one hundred and sixty times per minute. On the first day I reeled for twenty minutes, which gave two hundred and sixty-six and two thirds yards; on the third day, the second being Sunday, for twenty-five minutes, giving three hundred and thirty-three and one third yards; and on the fourth day, for eighteen minutes, giving two hundred and thirty-three and one third yards, — amounting in all to eight hundred and thirty-three and one third yards in three or four days. This was all that could be got, and the spider herself seemed unable to evolve any more; but on killing her and opening her abdomen, plenty of the gum was found in the little silk bags into which it is secreted. As this has always been the case, I have concluded that the evolution of the silk is almost entirely a mechanical process, which is but little controlled by the spinners themselves, and that the gum requires some degree of preparation after it is secreted before it is fit for use as silk; for it must be remembered that with the spider, as with the silk-worm, the silk is formed and contained in little bags or glands in the abdomen, not as *threads*, but as a very viscid gum. This passes in little tubes or ducts to the spinners, through minute openings, in which it is drawn out into filaments, uniting and drying instantly in the air, and so forming the single fibre from each spinner.

The silk obtained the first day was of a deep yellow; to my great astonishment, the second reeling from the same spider gave silk of a brilliant silver-white color; while on the third occasion, as if by magic, the color had changed again, and I got only *yellow* silk. The hypothesis of individual peculiarity, adopted the previous year to explain why some spiders gave yellow, and others white silk, was now untenable; and, remembering that, beside these two positive colors there was also (and indeed more commonly) a *light yellow*, as if a combination of the other two, I saw that the real solution of the mystery must lie in the spinners themselves. Examining carefully the thread as it came from the body, it was seen to be composed of two distinct portions, differing materially in their size, their color, their elasticity, and their relative position; for one of them was *white* and *inelastic*, crinkling and flying up when relaxed, and seemed to proceed from the *posterior* of the two principal pairs of spinners, while the other was *larger*, *yellow*, so *elastic* that when relaxed it kept its direction, and seemed to come from the *anterior* pair of spinners, and so, in the inverted position of the spider, was *above* the other. By putting a spider under the influence of chloroform, and then carrying the first thread under a pin stuck in a cork to one part of a spindle, and the second or yellow line over another pin to a different part of the spindle, I reeled off from the same spider, at the same time, two distinct bands of silk, of which one was a deep golden-yellow, the other a bright silver-white; while, if both threads ran together, there was formed a band of *light yellow* from the union of the two. Thinking such a difference must subserve some use in the economy of the insect, I made a more careful examination of its webs. At first sight these resembled those of most geometrical spiders, in being broad, rounded, nearly vertical nets; but they were unusually large, and in their native woods often stretched between trees and across the paths, so as to be two, three, and even more, feet in diameter, and in my room at Mt. Pleasant hung like curtains before the windows. They were of a bright yellow color and very viscid; but now I noticed that neither the color nor the viscidity pertained to the entire net, for although the concentric circles constituting the principal part of the web were *yellow*, and very *elastic*, and studded with little beads of *gum*, (Fig 3,) yet the diverging

Fig. 3.   Silk threads, viscid and dry.

lines or *radii* of the wheel-shaped structure, with all the guys and stays by which it was suspended and braced, were *dry* and *inelastic*, and of a *white* or lighter yellow color.

Now, however, a new mystery presented itself. We will admit that the spider had the power, not only to vary the *size* of her lines according to the number of spinners, or of the minute holes in each spinner, which were applied to the surface whence the line was to proceed, but also to make use of either golden or silver silk at will. But how was it that this yellow silk — which was quite dry and firm, though elastic, as reeled from the spider, or as spun by her in the formation of her cocoons — was nevertheless, when used for the concentric circles of the web, so viscid as to follow the point of a pin, stretching in so doing many times its length? A satisfactory explanation of this has never yet been offered, nor can be until the minute anatomy of the spinning organs is better understood, and the evolution of the silk more carefully observed at every stage, and under all conditions. I will merely state very briefly the few facts already established, with some of the possible explanations.

The spinning *mammulæ* are placed in pairs at the lower part of the abdomen, near its hinder end, and number four, six, or eight in different species. They are little conical or cylindrical papillæ, closely resembling the prolegs of caterpillars, and are composed of two or three joints, the terminal one of which is pierced with a greater or less number of minute holes, the sides of these, in some, if not all, cases, being prolonged into tubes. Through these holes or tubes issue the fine filaments, which, uniting as they dry in the air, constitute the line from each spinner.

Fig. 4. Spinners.

Now the *Nephila plumipes* possesses at least three pairs of spinners. Of these, two are much larger than the third, which indeed does not appear till they are separated. From the *posterior* of the two largest pairs *seems* to proceed the *white*, and from the *anterior* the *yellow* silk, while from the small intermediate pair seem to proceed very fine filaments of a pale-blue color, the use of which is to envelop the prey after it has been seized and killed, being drawn out by the bristles near the tips of the spider's hinder legs. Beside these six papillæ there is, just in front of the anterior pair, a single small papilla on the middle line, the nature and use of which I have not ascertained, though I feel quite sure that no silk comes from it. The large median papilla, just *behind* the posterior pair, surrounds the termination of the intestines, and through it the excrement is voided, the insect for this purpose turning back the abdomen as she hangs

head downward, so that neither the web nor the spinners shall be contaminated. Now it has recently been ascertained that the minute globules with which the circles are studded, and the number of which on a web of average size is estimated at *one hundred thousand*, do not exist in that form when the viscid lines are first spun by the spider, but as a uniform coating of gum upon a thread ; this gum, of itself and according to physical laws, soon exhibits little undulations, and then separates into the globules which have long been observed and supposed to be formed by the spider. The fact of spiders selecting the night for the construction of their webs, the difficulty of making any close observations upon them while so engaged without disturbing them, and the near approximation of the two larger pairs of spinners while the viscid line is slowly drawn out by the hind leg, have hitherto prevented my determining its exact source and manner of formation. If it comes from the anterior pair only, then one and the same organ has the power of evolving a central axis and covering it with viscid gum ; and it seems less improbable that the axis is white and formed by the posterior pair, the yellow gum being spread upon it by the anterior pair, which also would then have the power to evolve this same gum at other times as an equally dry, though more elastic thread. But in either case we have only *three* pairs of spinners and *four* kinds of silk, the *pale-blue fasciculi*, the *dry white*, the *dry yellow*, and the *viscid* and very *elastic* silk which is employed only in the circles of the web, and which often does not become yellow till after exposure to the light. Apparently the surest method of investigation will be carefully to destroy one pair of spinners at a time without injuring the others, and then note the effect upon the spinning.

Let us go back now to the sixty spiders left at Mt. Pleasant. A few of these died on the way North, but the majority reached Boston in safety about the 20th of September, 1865 ;

for some time I had observed that they all were becoming more or less emaciated, and relished their food less than at first. Occasionally one died from no apparent cause. The mortality increasing toward the end of the month, and all of them losing both flesh and vigor, I was persuaded to try them with water, — a thing I had thus far declined to do, never having heard of a spider's drinking water, and knowing that our common house species can hardly get it at all. The result was most gratifying : a drop of water upon the tip of a camel's-hair pencil, not only was not avoided, but greedily seized and slowly swallowed, being held between the jaws and the palpi. All of the spiders took it, and some even five or six drops in succession. You will exclaim, " Poor things ! what tortures they must have suffered ! " I admit that it could not have been pleasant for them to go so long without that which they crave every day, but I cannot believe that creatures whose legs drop off on very slight provocation, and which never show any sign whatever of real pain, suffered very acute pangs even when subjected to what occasions such distress to ourselves.

The few survivors straightway improved in health and spirits ; but being now convinced that a moist atmosphere was almost as needful as water to drink, I turned them loose in the north wing of the hot-house in Dr. Gray's Botanical Garden at Cambridge. They all mysteriously disappeared, excepting one, which made a nice web at one end just under the ridge-pole, and for several weeks lived and grew fat upon the flies ; but a thorough fumigation of the house with tobacco so shocked her not yet civilized organization that she died. Her untimely death, however, afforded opportunity for a closer examination of the web itself. The first one she had made was not *vertical ;* and, following the prevalent ideas as to the precise construction of the spider's web, I had felt somewhat ashamed of my pet, but supposed the next she made would be an improvement. But

no, the rebellious insect constantly made them all (for, it should have been said before, this spider seldom uses the same web more than forty-eight hours) after the same manner, and finally I laid it to a depraved idiocrasy, incident to captivity and poor health. But now another and most unexpected feature developed itself ; for, on attempting to remove the last web by placing against it a large wire ring, and cutting the guy-lines, I found that this most degenerate spider had not only failed to make her house *perpendicular*, but had so far departed from the traditions of our ancestors as to have the centre thereof decidedly eccentric, and four times as near the upper as the lower border of the web, so that its upper portion was only a confused array of irregular lines, which it was impossible to secure to the frame. For any accurate observation my web was of no value. But perhaps this was best ; for had I then learned what I have since, that our spider utterly ignores every precedent, not only in the *position* and *shape* of her web, but also in its *minute arrangement*, I might have been so affected by her evident bad character and radical proclivities, as to have feared paying her any further attentions, — much more, presenting her to the world.

But in order to understand how these further discoveries were made, we must again go back to the original sixty spiders in my room at Mt. Pleasant, South Carolina.

At the time of their capture, I had observed upon a few of the webs little brown spiders, which I then imagined might be the half-grown young. Six of these were found among the sixty larger spiders, and a moment's examination of their palpi or feelers (Fig. 5) showed that they were males, though even then I could not believe they had reached their maturity ; for their bodies were only about one fourth of an inch in length, and weighed only one thirty-second part of a grain, while the females were from an inch to an inch and a quarter in length, and weighed from three to four grains. It was as absurd

Fig. 5.   Palpi, or Feelers.

as if a man weighing one hundred and fifty pounds were joined to a bigger half of *eighteen thousand pounds' weight,* and I was not fully convinced that these small spiders were really the males of the *Nephila plumipes* till I had witnessed the impregnation of the eggs of the females by them.

One morning, in the cell of a large female, I found a cocoon of beautiful yellow silk containing a rounded mass of eggs. Soon the same occurred with other females, and there were fifteen cocoons, which would give about *seven thousand spiders.* Early in October, just one month after they were laid, the eggs of the first cocoon were broken and disclosed little spiders with rounded yellow bodies and short legs, looking about as little like their parents as could be imagined. The eggs in the other cocoons followed in their order, and now each contained four or five hundred little spiders closely packed.

For some time they seemed to eat nothing at all; but within a few days all had shed their skins, and now the abdomen was smaller, while the *cephalothorax* and legs were larger and darker : but they showed no desire to leave their cocoons. Still they grew perceptibly; and coincident with this was a less pleasing fact: their numbers were decreasing in the same proportion, and occasionally one was seen eating another. It was some time before I could reconcile the good temper and quiet behavior of the parents with this instinctive and habitual fratricide on the part of their children. But look at

it in this way : here were several hundred active little creatures in a space just large enough to contain them; presently they were hungry, and as no two could be of exactly the same size, the smaller and weaker naturally fell a prey to their larger brethren, or rather sisters, for either very few males are hatched, or else they are particularly good eating, and a very small proportion survive the perils of infancy. It is evidently an established and well-understood thing among them : all seem to be aware of their destiny, to *eat* or *be eaten.* What else can they do ? Human beings would do the same under the same circumstances; and I have never seen the least sign of personal spite or malignity in the spider. There is no pursuit, for there is no escape; and we can only conclude that, as the new-born fish's first nourishment is the contents of the yolk-sac, partly outside, though still a portion of its body, so the first food of the young spiders is, if not themselves, the next best thing, — each other. Thus it is provided that the smaller and less vigorous shall furnish food for the larger until the latter are strong enough to venture forth in search of other means of support.

In consequence of this mutual destruction, aided materially by the depredations of birds and of other insects, and by exposure to the weather, only about one per cent of those hatched reach maturity. If properly protected, however, a far larger proportion may be saved ; and as their multiplication is so rapid, no fear need be entertained of a limit to the supply.

By keeping these little spiders in glass jars, inverted, and with a wet sponge at the bottom, they were easily watched and cared for. At first only about one twentieth of an inch long and nearly as wide, they increased in length as they grew, but for many weeks lived in common on an irregular web, feeding together on the crushed flies or bugs thrown to them. But when one fourth of an inch in length, they showed a disposition to separate, and to spin each for herself a regular web, out of which all intruders were kept. And now it was found that all these webs were *inclined* at nearly the same angle, and were *never exactly vertical;* that, like the spider in the first web she made in the Botanical Garden, the insect took a position much nearer the upper than the lower border; and also that, instead of a web of *perfect circles* laid upon *regular radii,* as used to be described and is still figured in our books, or even one of a *spiral line,* as is now more correctly described of ordinary geometrical spiders (Fig. 6),

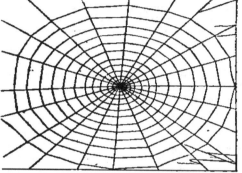

Fig. 6. Web of common Garden Spider.

these never made a circle, nor even a spiral, but a *series of concentric loops* or arcs of circles, the lines turning back upon themselves before reaching a point over the spider, and leaving the larger portion of the web below her;

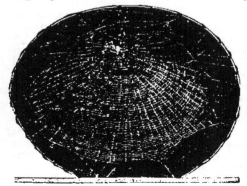

Fig. 7. Web of *Nephila plumipes.*

and more than this, that the lines, though quite regular, were by no means perfectly so, as may be seen in Fig. 7, copied from a photograph.

As usual, the *radii,* or *spokes,* of the wheel-shaped structure are first made; then the spider begins a little way from the centre, and, passing from one radius to another, spins a series of loops at considerable distances from each other till she reaches the circumference. These first loops, like the radii, are of *white, dry,* and *inelastic* silk, and may be recognized by the little notches at their junction with the radii. The notches are made by the spider's drawing her body a little inward toward the centre of the web at the time of attaching them to the radii, and so they always point in the direction in which the spider is moving at that time, and in opposite directions on any two successive lines (Fig. 8). Having reached

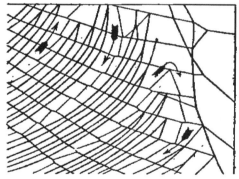

Fig. 8. Section of Web.

what is to be the border of her web, and thus constructed a firm framework or scaffolding, she begins to retrace her steps, moving more slowly and spinning now in the *intervals* of the dry loops two or three similar loops, but much nearer together and made of the *elastic* and *viscid* silk, till she has again reached her starting-point near the middle of the web, where, on its under side, she takes a position, head downward, hanging by her claws, and thus keeping her body from direct contact with the web.

Here she will remain quiet for hours as if asleep; but no sooner does a fly or other insect strike the web, than she darts in the direction whence the vibrations proceed, and usually seizes her prey; but, strangely enough, if the insect have ceased its struggles before she reaches it, she stops, and if she cannot renew them by shaking the web with her claws, will slowly and disconsolately return to the centre of the web, there to await fresh vibrations. These and many other facts, even more conclusive, have satisfied me that, although this spider has eight eyes (Fig. 9), it is as blind as a man

Fig. 9. Face and Jaws, magnified (eyes dimly seen).

with his eyelids shut, and can only distinguish light from darkness, nothing more. This seems to be the case with other geometrical species, but not at all with the field and hunting spiders, some of which will boldly turn upon you and look right in your eyes; they alone, of all insects, seeming to recognize the *face* of man as different from his body. The hearing and touch of this spider are very acute. The latter is exercised by the palpi and the tips of the legs, especially the first pair, but no ear has yet been discovered; neither is anything known of the organs of taste and smell, or even whether the insect possesses these senses at all.

I ought before this to have anticipated and answered a question which nine out of ten, perhaps, of my readers have already asked themselves, " Do not spiders bite? and is not their bite poisonous, nay, at times, deadly even to man?" The answer is, in brief, Yes, spiders do bite, probably all of them, if provoked and so confined that they cannot escape; though only a few tropical species can be said to seek of their own accord an opportunity for attacking man, or any creature larger than

the insects that form their natural prey. Even the *Nephila plumipes*, which, it has been intimated, is " Christian in its disposition, and well-behaved beyond most of its kind," will readily bite, if it is held in the fingers and anything is put to its jaws. But that is nothing. So would you, most gentle reader, if a great giant pinched you between his thumb and finger, and held your hands and feet and head; and if, too, like our spider, you could not see enough to distinguish friends from foes. Spiders, then, will bite. But to the second part of the inquiry our answer must be less positive. They have a very bad name; but much of this is due to their grim and forbidding aspect, and their bloody trade of trapping and eating poor little insects. It is to be remembered that there are very few, if any, medical reports of injuries from the bites of spiders, and that the accounts of such cases occurring in the newspapers consist in great measure of inference, and either make no mention of the offender at all, or merely speak of a little black or gray spider being found in the vicinity. A number of experiments have been made in England to ascertain the effect of the bite of the larger geometrical spiders upon the experimenter himself, upon other spiders, and upon common insects; and the conclusion was, that it produces no greater effect than the prick of a pin, or any other injury of equal extent and severity; while the speedy death of its victim is ascribed to the spider's sucking its juices, rather than to any poison instilled into the wound. But these experiments, though somewhat reassuring, are not conclusive; for they were tried only on one person, and people vary much in their susceptibility to poison of all kinds; moreover, the spiders employed were of the *geometrical* kinds, which have never been so much feared as the larger *field* and *hunting* spiders. Indeed, it may be found that among spiders there is as great a difference in respect to venom as among serpents, and that those which depend upon their jaws for taking and holding their prey, such as the field and hunting spiders, are poisonous, while the web-builders which ensnare their victims are not so. In regard to our spiders, I have caused a large one to bite, so as to draw blood, a kitten three days old, and the kitten has not appeared to suffer in the least on that account.

They are very quiet insects, and never appear disturbed at what goes on about them ; neither do they run away and hide in holes and corners, like our common spiders ; but if their webs are injured, or they are startled by a noise, they will shake themselves from side to side in their webs, so as to be wholly invisible. Their natural food is insects of all kinds ; but they soon learn to eat soft flesh, such as the liver of chickens, for which, as well as for water, they will sometimes stretch themselves and turn in their webs so as to take it from the point of a pin or camel's-hair pencil. Besides water to drink, they require an atmosphere saturated with moisture, like that of their native island, the relative humidity being about *seventy* on the Hygrodeik scale. If stroked upon the back, they often raise their bodies as a cat does, and sometimes put back a leg to push away your finger. They may be allowed to run over one's person with perfect safety, but, if suddenly seized, will hold on with tooth as well as nail.

They are quite economical, and every few days, when the web has become too dry and dusty for use, will gather it up in a mass, which they stuff into their jaws and masticate for hours, swallowing the gum, but throwing out the rest, with the little particles of dust, in the form of a hard black pellet, — an instance rare, if not indeed unique, of an animal eating a substance already excreted from its body.

Here I must close, though much against my will. It would please me to describe, as it has almost fascinated me to observe, the doings of my spiders, as they grew older and made their webs in the Wardian cases to which they were removed when too many and too large for the jars ; how

the young are gregarious, and move from place to place in a close column, protected on all sides by skirmishers, which continually report to the main body ; how some of these young, whose parents were caught on Long Island, South Carolina, a year ago, and which were hatched from the egg in October last, have grown up during a Northern winter, have themselves become parents and laid eggs ; how they periodically cast off their skins, even to that of the eyes, the jaws, and the breathing tubes, and how, from too great impatience, sad accidents sometimes befall them on these occasions ; how, also, I have reeled silk from several of these spiders, and made a thread which has been woven in a power-loom as a woof or filling upon a warp of common black silk, so as to make a bit of ribbon two inches wide, thereby proving that it is real silk and can be treated as such.

Much, too, could be said of the only other attempts to utilize spiders' silk, a knowledge of which would have materially aided me. In France, one hundred and fifty years ago, M. Bon made gloves and stockings of silk got by carding spiders' cocoons, and seventy years later, as I have but recently ascertained, Termeyer, a Spaniard, not only used the cocoons, but also, by an observation similar to my own, was led to reel the silk from the living insect. He, however, had poorer spiders or too little perseverance, or friends and a government influenced by a most short-sighted economy and prudence, else the highly interesting and instructive account of his experiments would have been familiar to some one in this country, and would not have waited these many years to be found by accident last spring in an obscure corner of the Astor Library.

I will add, finally, that I believe some other geometrical spiders, especially of the genus *Nephila*, may be found as docile, and as productive of beautiful silk, as the species I have described. At any rate, you cannot find a more interesting inmate of your Wardian case than some large geometrical spider.

WHAT DID SHE SEE WITH?

I COULD not have been more than seven or eight years old, when it happened; but it might have been yesterday. Among all other childish memories, it stands alone. To this very day it brings with it the old, utter sinking of the heart, and the old, dull sense of mystery.

To read the story, you should have known my mother. To understand it, you should understand her. But that is quite impossible now, for there is a quiet spot over the hill, and past the church, and beside the little brook where the crimsoned mosses grow thick and wet and cool, from which I cannot call her. It is all I have left of her now. But after all, it is not of her that you will chiefly care to hear. The object of my story is simply to acquaint you with a few facts, which, though interwoven with the events of her life, are quite independent of it as objects of interest. It is, I know, only my own heart that makes these pages a memorial, — but, you see, I cannot help it.

Yet, I confess, no glamour of any earthly love has ever utterly dazzled me, — not even hers. Of imperfections, of mistakes, of sins, I knew she was guilty. I know it now, — even with the sanctity of those crimsoned mosses, and the hush of the rest beneath, so close to my heart, I cannot forget them. Yet somehow — I do not know how — the imperfections, the mistakes, the very sins, bring her nearer to me as the years slip by, and make her dearer.

The key to her life is the key to my story. That given, as I can give it, I will try to compress. It lies in the fact that my mother was what we call an aristocrat. I do not like the term, as the term is used. I am sure she does not now; but I have no other word. She was a royal-looking woman, and she had the blood of princes in her veins. Generations back — how we children used to reckon the thing over!

— she was cradled in a throne. A miserable race, to be sure, they were, — the Stuarts; and the most devout genealogist might deem it dubious honor to own them for great-grandfathers by innumerable degrees removed. So she used to tell us, over and over, as a damper on our childish vanity, looking such a very queen as she spoke, in every play of feature, and every motion of her hand, that it was the old story of preachers who did not practise. The very baby was proud of her. The beauty of a face, and the elegant repose of a manner, are by no means influences more unfelt at three years than at thirty.

As insanity will hide itself away, and lie sleeping, and die out, — while old men are gathered to their fathers scathless, and young men follow in their footsteps safe and free, — and start into life, and claim its own when children's children have forgotten it; as a single trait of a single scholar in a race of clods will bury itself in day-laborers and criminals, unto the third and fourth generation, and spring then, like a creation from a chaos, into statesmen and poets and sculptors; — so, I have sometimes fancied, the better and truer nature of voluptuaries and tyrants was sifted down through the years, and purified in our little New England home, and the essential autocracy of monarchical blood refined and ennobled in my mother into royalty.

A broad and liberal culture had moulded her; she knew its worth, in every fibre of her heart; scholarly parents had blessed her with their legacies of scholarly mind and name. With the soul of an artist, she quivered under every grace and every defect; and the blessing of a beauty as rare as rich had been given to her. With every instinct of her nature recoiling from the very shadow of crimes the world winks at, as from a loathsome reptile, the family record had been stainless for a generation. God had indeed blessed her; but the very blessing was a temptation.

I knew, before she left me, what she might have been, but for the merciful and tender watch of Him who was despised and rejected of men. I know, for she told me, one still night when we were alone together, how she sometimes shuddered at herself, and what those daily and hourly struggles between her nature and her Christianity *meant*.

I think we were as near to one another as mother and daughter can be; but yet as utterly different. Since I have been talking in such lordly style of those miserable Jameses and Charleses, I will take the opportunity to confess that I have inherited my father's thorough-going democracy,—double measure, pressed down and running over. She not only pardoned it, but I think she loved it in me, for his sake.

It was about a year and a half, I think, after he died, that she sent for Aunt Alice to come to Creston. "Your aunt loves me," she said, when she told us in her quiet way, "and I am so lonely now."

They had been the only children, and they loved each other,—how much, I afterwards knew. And how much they love each other *now*, I like to think,—quite freely and fully, and without shadow or doubt between them, I dare to hope.

A picture of Aunt Alice always hung in mother's room. It was taken down years ago. I never asked her where she put it. I remember it, though, quite well; for mother's sake I am glad I do. For it was a pleasant face to look upon, and a young, pure, happy face,—beautiful too, though with none of the regal beauty crowned by my mother's massive hair, and pencilled brows. It was a timid, girlish face, with reverent eyes, and ripe, tremulous lips,—weak lips, as I remember them. From babyhood, I felt a want in the face. I had, of course, no capacity to define it; it was represented to me

only by the fact that it differed from my mother's.

She was teaching school out West when mother sent for her. I saw the letter. It was just like my mother:— "Alice, I need you. You and I ought to have but one home now. Will you come?"

I saw, too, a bit of a postscript to the answer,—"I'm not fit that you should love me so, Marie."

And how mother laughed at it!

When it was all settled, and the waiting weeks became at last a single day, I hardly knew my mother. She was in her early married years; she was a girl; she was a child; she was every young thing, and merry thing, that she could have ever been. So full of fitful moods, and little fantastic jokes! such a flush on her cheeks too, as she ran to the window every five minutes, like a child! I remember how we went all over the house together, she and I, to see that everything looked neat, and bright, and welcome. And how we lingered in the guest-room, to put the little finishing touches to its stillness, and coolness, and coseyness. The best spread on the bed, and the white folds smoothed as only mother's fingers could smooth them; the curtain freshly washed, and looped with its crimson cord; the blinds drawn, cool and green; the late afternoon sunlight slanting through, in flecks upon the floor. Flowers, too, upon the table. I remember they were all white, —lilies of the valley, I think; and the vase of Parian marble, itself a solitary lily, unfolding stainless leaves. Over the mantle she had hung the finest picture in the house,—an "Ecce Homo," and an exquisite engraving. It used to hang in grandmother's room in the old house. We children wondered a little that she took it up stairs.

"I want your aunt to feel at home, and see home things," she said. "I wish I could think of something more to make it pleasant in here."

Just as we left the room she turned and looked into it. "Pleasant, is n't it? I am so glad, Sarah," her eyes dimming a little. "She 's a very dear sister to me."

She stepped in again to raise a stem of the lilies that had fallen from the vase, and lay like wax upon the table, then she shut the door and came away.

That door was shut just so for years; the lonely bars of sunlight flecked the solitude of the room, and the lilies faded on the table. We children passed it with hushed footfall, and shrank from it at twilight, as from a room that held the dead. But into it we never went.

Mother was tired out that afternoon; for she had been on her feet all day, busied in her loving cares to make our simple home as pleasant and as welcome as home could be. But yet she stopped to dress us in our Sunday clothes, — and no sinecure was it to dress three persistently undressable children; Winthrop was a host in himself. "Auntie must see us look our prettiest," she said.

She was a picture herself when she came down. She had taken off her widow's cap and coiled her heavy hair low in her neck, and she always looked like a queen in that lustreless black silk. I do not know why these little things should have made such an impression on me then. They are priceless to me now. I remember how she looked, framed there in the doorway, while we were watching for the coach, — the late light ebbing in golden tides over the grass at her feet, and touching her face now and then through the branches of trees, her head bent a little, with eager, parted lips, and the girlish color on her cheeks, her hand shading her eyes as they strained for a sight of the lumbering coach. She must have been a magnificent woman when she was young, — not unlike, I have heard it said, to that far-off ancestress whose name she bore, and whose sorrowful story has made her sorrowful beauty immortal. Somewhere abroad there is a reclining statue of Queen Mary, to which, when my mother stood beside it, her resemblance was so strong that the by-standers clustered about her,

whispering curiously. "Ah, mon Dieu!" said a little Frenchman, aloud, "c'est une résurrection."

We must have tried her that afternoon, Clara and Winthrop and I; for the spirit of her own excitement had made us completely wild. Winthrop's scream of delight when, stationed on the gate-post, he caught the first sight of the old yellow coach, might have been heard a quarter of a mile.

"Coming?" said mother, nervously, and stepped out to the gate, full in the sunlight that crowned her like royal gold.

The coach lumbered on, and rattled up, and passed.

"Why, she has n't come!" All the eager color died out of her face. "I am so disappointed!" speaking like a troubled child, and turning slowly into the house.

Then, after a while, she drew me aside from the others, — I was the oldest, and she was used to make a sort of confidence between us, instinctively, as it seemed, and often quite forgetting how very few my years were. "Sarah, I don't understand. You think she might have lost the train? But Alice is so punctual. Alice never lost a train. And she said she would come." And then, a while after, "I *don't* understand."

It was not like my mother to worry. The next day the coach lumbered up and rattled past, and did not stop, — and the next, and the next.

"We shall have a letter," mother said, her eyes saddening every afternoon. But we had no letter. And another day went by, and another.

"She is sick," we said; and mother wrote to her, and watched for the lumbering coach, and grew silent day by day. But to the letter there was no answer.

Ten days passed. Mother came to me one afternoon to ask for her pen, which I had borrowed. Something in her face troubled me vaguely.

"What are you going to do, mother?"

"Write to your aunt's boarding-place. I can't bear this any longer," sharply. She had already grown unlike herself.

She wrote, and asked for an answer by return of mail.

It was on a Wednesday, I remember, that we looked for it. I remember everything that happened that day. I came home early from school. Mother was sewing at the parlor window, her eyes wandering from her work, up the road. It was an ugly day. It had rained drearily from eight o'clock till two, and closed in suffocating mist, creeping and dense and chill. It gave me a childish fancy of long-closed tombs and lowland graveyards, as I walked home in it.

I tried to keep the younger children quiet when we went in, mother was so nervous. As the early, uncanny twilight fell, we grouped around her timidly. A dull sense of awe and mystery clung to the night, and clung to her watching face, and clung even then to that closed room up stairs where the lilies were fading.

Mother sat leaning her head upon her hand, the outline of her face dim in the dusk against the falling curtain. She was sitting so when we heard the first rumble of the distant coach-wheels. At the sound, she folded her hands in her lap and stirred a little, rose slowly from her chair, and sat down again.

"Sarah."

I crept up to her. At the near sight of her face, I was so frightened I could have cried.

"Sarah, you may go out and get the letter. I — I can't."

I went slowly out at the door and down the walk. At the gate I looked back. The outline of her face was there against the window-pane, white in the gathering gloom.

It seems to me that my older and less sensitive years have never known such a night. The world was stifling in a deluge of gray, cold mists, unstirred by a breath of air. A robin with feathers all ruffled, and head hidden, sat on the gate-post, and chirped a little mournful chirp, like a creature dying in a vacuum. The very daisy that nodded and drooped in the grass at my feet seemed to be gasping for breath. The neighbor's house, not forty paces across the street, was invisible. I remember the sensation it gave me, as I struggled to find its outlines, of a world washed out, like the figures I washed out on my slate. As I trudged, half-frightened, into the road, and the fog closed about me, it seemed to my childish superstition like a horde of long-imprisoned ghosts let loose and angry. The distant sound of the coach, which I could not see, added to the fancy.

The coach turned the corner presently. On a clear day I could see the brass buttons on the driver's coat at that distance. There was nothing visible now of the whole dark structure but the two lamps in front, like the eyes of some evil thing, glaring and defiant, borne with swift motion down upon me by a power utterly unseen,—it had a curious effect. Even at this time, I confess I do not like to see a lighted carriage driven through a fog.

I summoned all my little courage, and piped out the driver's name, standing there in the road.

He reined up his horses with a shout, — he had nearly driven over me. After some searching, he discovered the small object cowering down in the mist, handed me a letter, with a muttered oath at being intercepted on such a night, and lumbered on and out of sight in three rods.

I went slowly into the house. Mother had lighted a lamp, and stood at the parlor door. She did not come into the hall to meet me.

She took the letter and went to the light, holding it with the seal unbroken. She might have stood so two minutes.

"Why don't you read, mamma?" spoke up Winthrop. I hushed him.

She opened it then, read it, laid it down upon the table, and went out of the room without a word. I had not seen her face. We heard her go up stairs and shut the door.

She had left the letter open there before us. After a little awed silence, Clara broke out into sobs. I went up and read the few and simple lines.

Aunt Alice had left for Creston on the appointed day.

Mother spent that night in the closed room where the lilies had drooped and died. Clara and I heard her pacing the floor till we cried ourselves to sleep. When we woke in the morning, she was pacing it still.

Well, weeks wore into months, and the months became many years. More than that we never knew. Some inquiry revealed the fact, after a while, that a slight accident had occurred upon the Erie Railroad to the train which she should have taken. There was some disabling, but no deaths, the conductor had supposed. The car had fallen into the water. She might not have been missed when the half-drowned passengers were all drawn out.

So mother added a little crape to her widow's weeds, the key of the closed room lay henceforth in her drawer, and all things went on as before. To her children my mother was never gloomy, — it was not her way. No shadow of household affliction was placed like a skeleton confronting our uncomprehending joy. Of what those weeks and months and years were to her, — a widow, and quite uncomforted in their dark places by any human love, — she gave no sign. We thought her a shade paler, perhaps. We found her often alone with her little Bible. Sometimes, on the Sabbath, we missed her, and knew that she had gone into that closed room. But she was just as tender with us in our little faults and sorrows, as merry with us in our plays, as eager in our gayest plans, as she had always been. As she had always been, — our mother.

And so the years slipped by, to her and to us. Winthrop went into business in Boston; he never took to his books, and mother was too wise to *push* him through college; but I think she was disappointed. He was her only boy, and she would have chosen

for him the profession of his father and grandfather. Clara and I graduated in our white dresses and blue ribbons, like other girls, and came home to mother, crochet-work, and Tennyson. And then something happened, as the veriest little things — which, unnoticed and uncomprehended, hold the destinies of lives in their control — will happen.

I mean that our old and long-tried cook, Bathsheba, who had been an heirloom in the family, suddenly fell in love with the older sexton, who had rung the passing-bell for every soul who died in the village for forty years, and took it into her head to marry him, and desert our kitchen for his little brown house under the hill.

So it came about that we hunted the township for a handmaiden; and it also came about that our inquiring steps led us to the poor-house. A stout, not over-brilliant-looking girl, about twelve years of age, was to be had for her board and clothes, and such schooling as we could give her, — in country fashion, to be "bound out" till she should be eighteen. The economy of the arrangement decided in her favor; for, in spite of our grand descent and grander notions, we were poor enough, after father died, and the education of three children had made no small gap in our little principal, and she came.

Her name was a singular one, — Selphar. It always savored too nearly of brimstone to please me. I used to call her Sel, "for short." She was a good, sensible, uninteresting-looking girl, with broad face, large features, and limp, tow-colored curls. I doubt if I ever see curls like them now without a little shudder. They used to hang straight down about her eyes, and were never otherwise than perfectly smooth. She proved to be of good temper, which is worth quite as much as brains in a servant, as honest as the daylight, dull enough at her books, but a good, plodding worker, if you marked out every step of the way for her beforehand. I do not think she would ever have discovered the laws of gravitation; but she might have jumped off a precipice to prove them, if she had been bidden.

Until she was seventeen, she was precisely like any other rather stupid girl; never given to novel-reading or fancies; never frightened by the dark or ghost-stories; proving herself warmly attached to us, after a while, and rousing in us, in return, the kindly interest naturally felt for a faithful servant; but she was not in any respect *un*common, — quite far from it, — except in the circumstance that she never told a falsehood.

At seventeen she had a violent attack of diphtheria, and her life hung by a thread. Mother's aristocracy had nothing of that false pride which is afraid of contamination from kindly association with its inferiors. She was too thoroughly a lady. She was as tender and unwearying in her care of Selphar as the girl's own mother might have been. She was somehow touched by the child's orphaned life, — suffering always, in all places, appealed to her so strongly, — every sorrow found so warm a place in her heart.

From that time, I believe Sel was immovable in her faith in my mother's divinity. Under such nursing as she had, she slowly recovered, but her old, stolid strength never came back to her. Severe headaches became of frequent occurrence. Her stout, muscular arms grew weak. As weeks went on, it became evident in many ways that, though the diphtheria itself was quite out of her system, it had left her thoroughly diseased. Strange fits of silence came over her: her volubility had been the greatest objection we had to her hitherto. Her face began to wear a troubled look. She was often found in places where she had stolen away to be alone.

One morning she slept late in her little garret-chamber, and we did not call her. The girl had gone up stairs the night before crying with the pain in her temples, and mother, who was always thoughtful of her servants, said it was a pity to wake her, and, as there were only three of us, we might get our own breakfast for once. While we were at work together in the kitchen, Clara heard her kitten mewing out in the snow, and went to the door to let her in. The creature, possessed by some sudden frolic, darted away behind the well-curb. Clara was always a bit of a romp, and, with never a thought of her daintily-slippered feet, she flung her trailing dress over one arm and was off over the three-inch snow. The cat led her a brisk chase, and she came in flushed, and panting, and pretty, her little feet drenched, and the tip of a Maltese tail just visible above a great bundle she had made of her apron.

"Why!" said mother, "you have lost your ear-ring."

Clara dropped the kitten with unceremonious haste on the floor, felt of her little pink ear, shook her apron, and the corners of her mouth went down into her dimpled chin.

"They 're the ones Winthrop sent, of all things in the world!"

"You 'd better put on your rubbers, and have a hunt out-doors," said mother.

We hunted out-doors, — on the steps, on the well-boards, in the wood-shed, in the snow; Clara looked down the well till her nose and fingers were blue, but the ear-ring was not to be found. We hunted in-doors, under the stove, and the chairs, and the table, in every possible and impossible nook, cranny, and crevice, but gave up the search in despair. It was a pretty trinket, — a leaf of delicately wrought gold, with a pearl dew-drop on it, — very becoming to Clara, and the first present Winthrop had sent her from his earnings. If she had been a little younger she would have cried. She came very near it as it was, I suspect, for when she went after the plates she stayed in the cupboard long enough to set two tables.

When we were half through breakfast, Selphar came down, blushing, and frightened half out of her wits, her apologies tumbling over each other with such skill as to render each one unintelligible, — and evidently undecided in her own mind whether she was to be hung or burnt at the stake.

"It's no matter at all," said mother, kindly; "I knew you felt sick last night. I should have called you if I had needed you."

Having set the girl at her ease, as only she could do, she went on with her breakfast, and we forgot all about her. She stayed, however, in the room to wait on the table. It was afterwards remembered that she had not been out of our sight since she came down the garret-stairs. Also, that her room looked out upon the opposite side of the house from that on which the well-curb stood.

"Why, look at Sel!" said Clara, suddenly, "she has her eyes shut."

The girl was just passing the toast. Mother spoke to her. "Selphar, what is the matter?"

"I don't know."

"Why don't you open your eyes?"

"I can't."

"Hand the salt to Miss Sarah."

She took it up and brought it around the table to me, with perfect precision.

"Sel, how you act!" said Clara, petulantly. "Of course you saw."

"Yes 'm, I saw," said the girl in a puzzled way, "but my eyes are shut, Miss Clara."

"Tight?"

"Tight."

Whatever this freak meant, we thought best to take no notice of it. My mother told her, somewhat gravely, that she might sit down until she was wanted, and we returned to our conversation about the ear-ring.

"Why!" said Sel, with a little jump, "I see your ear-ring, Miss Clara, — the one with a white drop on the leaf. It's out by the well."

The girl was sitting with her back to the window, her eyes, to all appearance, tightly closed.

"It's on the right-hand side, under the snow, between the well and the wood-pile. Why, don't you see?"

Clara began to look frightened, mother displeased.

"Selphar," she said, "this is non-sense. It is impossible for you to see through the walls of two rooms and a wood-shed."

"May I go and get it?" said the girl, quietly.

"Sel," said Clara, "on your word and honor, are your eyes shut *perfectly* tight?"

"If they ain't, Miss Clara, then they never was."

Sel never told a lie. We looked at each other, and let her go. I followed her out, and kept my eyes on her closed lids. She did not once raise them; nor did they tremble, as lids will tremble, if only partially closed.

She walked without the slightest hesitation directly to the well-curb, to the spot which she had mentioned, stooped down, and brushed away the three-inch fall of snow. The ear-ring lay there, where it had sunk in falling. She picked it up, carried it in, and gave it to Clara.

That Clara had the thing on when she started after her kitten, there could be no doubt. She and I both remembered it. That Sel, asleep on the opposite side of the house, could not have seen it drop, was also settled. That she, with her eyes closed and her back to the window, had seen through three walls, and through three inches of snow, at a distance of fifty feet, was an inference.

"I don't believe it!" said my mother, "it's some nonsensical mistake." Clara looked a little pale, and I laughed.

We watched her carefully through the day. Her eyes remained tightly closed. She understood all that was said to her, answered correctly, but did not seem inclined to talk. She went about her work as usual, and performed it without a mistake. It could not be seen that she groped at all with her hands to feel her way, as is the case with the blind. On the contrary, she touched everything with her usual decision. It was impossible to believe, without seeing them, that her eyes were closed.

We tied a handkerchief tightly over them; see through it or below it she could not, if she had tried. We then sent her into the parlor, with orders to bring from the book-case two Bibles which had been given as prizes to Clara and me at school, when we were children. The books were of precisely the same size, color, and texture. Our names in gilt letters were printed upon the binding. We followed her in, and watched her narrowly. She went directly to the book-case, laid her hands upon the books at once, and brought them to my mother. Mother changed them from hand to hand several times, and turned them with the gilt lettering downwards upon her lap.

"Now, Selphar, which is Miss Sarah's?"

The girl quietly took mine up. The experiment was repeated and varied again and again. In every case the result was the same. She made no mistake. It was no guess-work. All this was done with the bandage tightly drawn about her eyes. *She did not see those letters with them.*

That evening we were sitting quietly in the dining-room. Selphar sat a little apart with her sewing, her eyes still closed. We kept her with us, and kept her in sight. The parlor, which was a long room, was between us and the front of the house. The distance was so great that we had often thought, if prowlers were to come around at night, how impossible it would be to hear them. The curtains and shutters were closely drawn. Sel was sitting by the fire. Suddenly she turned pale, dropped her sewing, and sprang from her chair.

"Robbers, robbers!" she cried. "Don't you see? they're getting in the east parlor window! There's three of 'em, and a lantern. They've just opened the window, — hurry, hurry!"

"I believe the girl is insane," said mother, decidedly. Nevertheless, she put out the light, opened the parlor door noiselessly, and went in.

The east window was open. There was a quick vision of three men and a dark lantern. Then Clara screamed, and it disappeared. We went to the window, and saw the men running down the street. The snow the next morning was found trodden down under the window, and their footprints were traced out to the road.

When we went back to the other room, Selphar was standing in the middle of it, a puzzled, frightened look on her face, her eyes wide open.

"Selphar," said my mother, a little suspiciously, "how did you know the robbers were there?"

"Robbers!" said the girl, aghast.

She knew nothing of the robbers. She knew nothing of the ear-ring. She remembered nothing that had happened since she went up the garret-stairs to bed, the night before. And, as I said, the girl was as honest as the sunlight. When we told her what had happened, she burst into terrified tears.

For some time after this there was no return of the "tantrums," as Selphar had called the condition, whatever it was. I began to get up vague theories of a trance state. But mother said, "Nonsense!" and Clara was too much frightened to reason at all about the matter.

One Sunday morning Sel complained of a headache. There was an evening service that night, and we all went to church. Mother let Sel take the empty seat in the carryall beside her.

It was very dark when we started to come home. But Creston was a safe old Orthodox town, the roads were filled with returning church-goers like ourselves, and mother drove like a man. A darker night I think I have never seen. Literally, we could not see a hand before our eyes. We met a carriage on a narrow road, and the horses' heads touched, before either driver had seen the other.

Selphar had been quite silent during the drive. I leaned forward, looked closely into her face, and could dimly see through the darkness that her eyes were closed.

"Why!" she said at last, "see those gloves!"

"Where?"

"Down in the ditch; we passed

them before I spoke. I see them on a blackberry-bush; they 've got little brass buttons on the wrist."

Three rods past now, and we could not see our horse's head.

"Selphar," said my mother, quickly, "what *is* the matter with you?"

"If you please, ma'am, I don't know," replied the girl, hanging her head. "May I get out and bring 'em to you?"

Prince was reined up, and Sel got out. She went so far back, that, though we strained our eyes to do it, we could not see her. In about two minutes she came up, a pair of gentleman's gloves in her hand. They were rolled together, were of cloth so black that on a bright night it would never have been seen, and had small brass buttons at the wrist.

Mother took them without a word.

The story leaked out somehow, and spread all over town. It raised a great hue and cry. Four or five antediluvian ladies declared at once that we were nothing more nor less than a family of "them spirituous mediums," and seriously proposed to expel mother from the prayer-meeting. Masculine Creston did worse. It smiled a pitying smile, and pronounced the whole thing the fancy of "scared women-folks." I could endure with calmness any slander upon earth but that. I sent by the next mail for Winthrop, and stated the case to him in a condition of suppressed fury. He very politely bit back an incredulous smile, and said he should be *very* happy to see her perform. The answer was somewhat dubious. I accepted it in silent suspicion.

He came on Saturday noon. That afternoon we attended *en masse* one of those refined inquisitions commonly known as picnics, and Winthrop lost his pocket-knife. Selphar, of course, kept house at home.

When we returned, Winthrop made some careless reference to his loss in her presence, and thought no more of it. About half an hour after, we observed that she was washing the dishes with her eyes shut. The condition had not been upon her five minutes before she dropped the spoon suddenly into the water, and asked permission to go out to walk. She "saw Mr. Winthrop's knife somewhere under a stone, and wanted to get it." It was fully two miles to the picnic grounds, and nearly dark. Winthrop followed the girl, unknown to her, and kept her in sight. She went rapidly, and without the slightest hesitation or search, to an out-of-the-way gully down by the pond, where Winthrop afterwards remembered having gone to cut some willow-twigs for the girls, parted a thick cluster of bushes, lifted a large, loose stone under which the knife had rolled, and picked it up. She returned it to Winthrop, quietly, and hurried away about her work to avoid being thanked.

I observed that, after this incident, masculine Creston became more respectful.

Of several peculiarities in this development of the girl I made at the time careful memoranda, and the exactness of these can be relied upon.

1. She herself, so far from attempting to bring on these trance states, or taking any pride therein, was intensely troubled and mortified by them, — would run out of the room, if she felt them coming on in the presence of visitors.

2. They were apt to be preceded by severe headaches, but came often without any warning.

3. She never, in any instance, recalled anything that happened during the trance, after it was passed.

4. She was powerfully and unpleasantly affected by electricity from a battery, or acting in milder forms. She was also unable at any time to put her hands and arms into hot water; the effect was to paralyze them at once.

5. Space proved to be no impediment to her vision. She has been known to follow the acts, words, and expressions of countenance of members of the family hundreds of miles away, with accuracy; as was afterwards proved by comparing notes as to time.

6. The girl's eyes, after her trances became habitual, assumed, and always retained, the most singular expression I ever saw on any face. They were oblong and narrow, and set back in her head like the eyes of a snake. They were not — smile if you will, O practical and incredulous reader! — but they were not *human* eyes. The eyes of Elsie Venner are the only eyes I can think of as at all like them. The most horrible circumstance about them — a circumstance that always made me shudder, familiar as I was with it — was, that, though turned fully on you, *they never looked at you*. Something behind them or out of them did the seeing, not they.

7. She not only saw substance, but soul. She has repeatedly told me my thoughts when they were upon subjects to which she could not by any possibility have had the slightest clew.

8. We were never able to detect a shadow of deceit about her.

9. The clairvoyance never failed in any instance to be correct, so far as we were able to trace it.

As will be readily imagined, the girl became a useful member of the family. The lost valuables restored and the warnings against mischances given by her quite balanced her incapacity for peculiar kinds of work. This incapacity, however, rather increased than diminished, and, together with her fickle health, which also grew more unsettled, caused us a great deal of care. The Creston physician — who was a keen man in his way, for a country doctor — pronounced the case altogether undreamt of before in Horatio's philosophy, and kept constant notes of it. Some of these have, I believe, found their way into the medical journals.

After a while there came, like a thief in the night, that which I suppose was poor Selphar's one unconscious, golden mission in this world. It came on a quiet summer night, that ended a long trance of a week's continuance. Mother had gone out into the kitchen to give an order for breakfast. I heard a few eager words in Selphar's voice, and then the door shut quickly, and it was an hour before it was opened.

Then my mother came to me without a particle of color in lips or cheek, and drew me away alone, and told the secret to me.

Selphar had seen Aunt Alice.

We sat down and looked at one another. There was a singular pinched look about my mother's mouth.

"Sarah."

"Yes."

"She says" — and then she told me what she said. She had seen Alice Stuart in a Western town, seven hundred miles away. Among the living, she desired to be counted of the dead. And that was all.

My mother paced the room three times back and forth, her hands locked.

"Sarah." There was a chill in her voice — it had been such a gentle voice! — that froze me. "Sarah, the girl is an impostor."

"Mother!"

She paced the room, once more, three times, back and forth. "At any rate, she is a poor, self-deluded creature. How *can* she see, seven hundred miles away, a dead woman who has been an angel all these years? Think! an *angel*, Sarah! So much better than I, and I — I loved — "

Before or since, I never heard my mother speak like that. She broke off sharply, and froze back into her chilling voice.

"We will say nothing about this, if you please. I do not believe a word of it."

We said nothing about it, but Selphar did. The delusion, if delusion it were, clung to her, haunted her, pursued her, week after week. To rid her of it, or to silence her, was impossible. She added no new facts to her first statement, but insisted that the long-lost dead was yet alive, with a quiet pertinacity that it was simply impossible to ridicule, frighten, threaten, or cross-question out of her. Clara was so thoroughly alarmed that she would not have slept alone for any mortal — perhaps not for any immortal — considerations. Winthrop and I talked the matter over often and gravely when we were alone and in quiet places. Mother's lips were sealed. From the day when Sel made the first disclosure, she was never heard once to refer to the matter. A perceptible haughtiness crept into her manner towards the girl. She even talked of dismissing her; but repented it, and melted into momentary gentleness. I could have cried over her that night. I was beginning to understand what a pitiful struggle her life had become, and how utterly alone she must be in it. She *would* not believe — she knew not what. She could not doubt the girl. And with the conflict even her children could not intermeddle.

To understand the crisis into which she was brought, the reader must bear in mind our long habit of belief, not only in Selphar's personal honesty, but in the infallibility of her mysterious power. Indeed, it had almost ceased to be mysterious to us, from daily familiarity. We had come to regard it as the curious working of physical disease, had taken its results as a matter of course, and had ceased, in common with converted Creston, to doubt the girl's capacity for seeing anything that she chose to, at any place.

Thus a year wore on. My mother grew sleepless and pallid. She laughed often, in a nervous, shallow way, as unlike her as a butterfly is unlike a sunset; and her face settled into an habitual sharpness and hardness unutterably painful to me.

Once only I ventured to break into the silence of the haunting thought that she knew, and we knew, was never escaped by either. "Mother, it would do no harm for Winthrop to go out West, and — "

She interrupted me sternly: "Sarah, I had not thought you capable of such childish superstition. I wish that girl and her nonsense had never come into this house!" — turning sharply away, and out of the room.

Just what that year was to my mother, I suppose only God and she have ever known, or will know.

But it ended. It ended at last, as I had prayed every night and morning of it that it should end. Mother came into my room one night, locked the door behind her, and, walking over to the window, stood with her face turned from me.

"Sarah."

"Yes."

"Sarah."

But that was all for a little while. Then, — "Sick and in suffering, Sarah, — the girl — she may be right, God Almighty knows ! *Sick and in suffering*, you see. I am going. I think, I — "

The voice broke and melted utterly. I stole away and left her alone.

Creston put on its spectacles and looked wise on learning, the next day, that Mrs. Dugald had taken the earliest morning train for the West, on sudden and important business. It was precisely what Creston expected, and just like the Dugalds for all the world, — gone to hunt up material for that genealogical book, or map, or tree, or something, that they thought nobody knew they were going to publish. O yes, Creston understood it perfectly.

Space forbids me to relate in detail the clews which Selphar had given as to the whereabouts of the wanderer. Her trances, just at this time, were somewhat scarce and fragmentary, and the information she had professed to give had come in snatches and very imperfectly, — the trance being apt to end suddenly at the moment when some important question was pending, and then, of course, all memory of what she had said, or was about to say, was gone. The names and appearance of persons and places necessary to the search had, however, been given with sufficient distinctness to serve as a guide in my mother's rather chimerical undertaking. I suppose ninety-nine persons out of a hundred would have thought her a candidate for the State Lunatic Asylum. Exactly what she herself expected, hoped, or feared, I think it doubtful if she knew. I confess to a condition of simple bewilderment, when she was fairly gone, and Clara and I were left alone with Selphar's ghostly eyes forever on us. One night I had to lock the poor thing into her garret-room before I could sleep.

Just three weeks from the day mother started for the West, the coach rattled up to the door, and two women, arm in arm, came slowly up the walk. The one, erect, royal, with her great stead-fast eyes alight; the other, bent and worn, gray-haired and sallow and dumb, crawling feebly through the golden afternoon sunshine, as the ghost of a glorious life might crawl back to its grave.

Mother threw open the door, and stood there like a queen. "Children, your aunt has come home. She is too tired to talk just now By and by she will be glad to see you."

We took her gently up stairs, into the room where the lilies were mouldering to dust, and laid her down upon the bed. She closed her eyes wearily, turned her face over to the wall, and said no word.

What was the story of those tired eyes I never asked, and I never knew. Once, as I passed the room, a quick picture showed through the open door. The two women lying with their arms about each other's neck, as they used to do when they were children together; and above them, still and watchful, the wounded Face that had waited there so many years for this.

One was speaking with weak sobs, and very low. It was Aunt Alice. I caught but two words, — "My husband."

But what that husband was remains unknown till the day when the grave shall give up its dead, and the secrets of hearts oppressed and sinned against and sorrowful shall be revealed.

She lingered weakly there, within the restful room, for seven days, and then one morning we found her with her eyes upon the thorn-crowned face, her own quite still and smiling.

A little funeral train wound away one night behind the church, and left her down among those red-cup mosses that opened in so few months again to cradle the sister who had loved her. Two words only, by mother's orders, marked the simple headstone, —

"ALICE BROWNING."

I have given you facts. Explain them as you will. I do not attempt it, for the simple reason that I cannot.

A word must be said as to the fate of poor Sel, which was mournful enough. Her trances grew gradually more frequent and erratic, till she became so thoroughly diseased in mind and body as to be entirely unfitted for household work, and, in short, nothing but an encumbrance. We kept her, however, for the sake of charity, and should have done so, till her poor, tormented life wore itself out ; but after the advent of a new servant, and my mother's death, she conceived the idea that she was a burden, cried over it a few weeks, and at last one bitter winter's night she disappeared. We did not give up all search for her for years, but nothing was ever heard from her. He, I hope, who permitted life to be such a terrible mystery to her, has cared for her somehow, and kindly, and well.

THE MINER.

DOWN 'mid the tangled roots of things
  That coil about the central fire,
I seek for that which giveth wings,
To stoop, not soar, to my desire.

Sometimes I hear, as 't were a sigh,
The sea's deep yearning far above.
" Thou hast the secret not," I cry,
" In deeper deeps is hid my Love."

They think I burrow from the sun,
In darkness, all alone and weak ;
Such loss were gain if He were won.
For 't is the sun's own Sun I seek.

The earth, they murmur, is the tomb
That vainly sought his life to prison;
Why grovel longer in its gloom ?
He is not here ; He hath arisen.

More life for me where He hath lain
Hidden, while ye believed him dead,
Than in cathedrals cold and vain,
Built on loose sands of " It is said."

My search is for the living gold,
Him I desire who dwells recluse,
And not his image, worn and old,
Day-servant of our sordid use.

If Him I find not, yet I find
The ancient joy of cell and church,
The glimpse, the surety undefined,
The unquenched ardor of the search.

Happier to chase a flying goal,
Than to sit counting laurelled gains,
To guess the Soul within the soul,
Than to be lord of what remains.

PHYSICAL HISTORY OF THE VALLEY OF THE AMAZONS.

II.

MAJOR COUTINHO and myself passed three days in the investigation of the Serra of Erreré. We found it to consist wholly of the sandstone deposits described in my previous article, and to have exactly the same geological constitution. In short, the Serra of Monte Alegre, and of course all those connected with it on the northern side of the river, lie in the prolongation of the lower beds forming the banks of the river, their greater height being due simply to the fact that they have not been worn to the same low level. The opposite range of Santarem, which has the same general outline and character, shares, no doubt, the same geological structure. In one word, all these hills were formerly part of a continuous formation, and owe their present outline and their isolated position to a colossal denudation. The surface of the once unbroken strata, which in their original condition must have formed an immense plain covered by water, has been cut into ravines or carried away over large tracts, to a greater or less depth, leaving only such portions standing as from their hardness could resist the floods which swept over it. The longitudinal trend of these hills is to be ascribed to the direction of the current which caused the denudation, while their level summits are due to the regularity of the stratification. They are not all table-topped, however; among them are many of smaller size, in which the sides have been gradually worn down, producing a gently rounded surface. Of course, under the heavy tropical rains this denudation is still going on, though in a greatly modified form.

I cannot leave this Serra without alluding to the great beauty and extraordinary extent of the view to be obtained from it. Indeed, it was here that for the first time the geography of the country presented itself to my mind as a living reality, in all its completeness. Insignificant as is its actual height, the Serra of Erreré commands a wider prospect than is to be had from many a more imposing mountain; for the surrounding plain, covered with forests, and ploughed by countless rivers, stretches away for hundreds of leagues in every direction, without any object to obstruct the view. Standing on the brow of the Serra, with the numerous lakes intersecting the low lands at its base, you look across the Valley of the Amazons, as far as the eye can reach, and through its midst you follow for miles on either side the broad flood of the great river, carrying its yellow waters to the sea. As I stood there, panoramas from the Swiss mountains came up to my memory, and I fancied myself standing on the Alps, looking across the plain of Switzerland, instead of the bed of the Amazons, the distant line of the Santarem hills on the southern bank of the river, and lower than the northern chain, representing the Jura range. As if to complete the comparison, I found Alpine lichens growing among cactus and palms, and a crust of Arctic cryptogamous growth covered rocks, between which sprang tropical flowers. On the northern flank of this Serra I found the only genuine erratic boulders I have seen in the whole length of the Amazonian Valley, from Pará to the frontier of Peru, though there are many detached masses of rock, as, for instance, at Pedreira, near the junction of the Rio Negro and Rio Branco, which might be mistaken for them, but are due to the decomposition of the rocks in place. The boulders of Erreré are entirely distinct from the rock of the Serra, and consist of masses of compact hornblende.

It would seem that these two ranges

skirting a part of the northern and southern banks of the Lower Amazons are not the only remnants of this arenaceous formation in its primitive altitude. On the banks of the Japura, in the Serra of Cupati, Major Coutinho has found the same beds rising to the same height. It thus appears, by positive evidence, that over an extent of a thousand miles these deposits had a very considerable thickness in the present direction of the valley. How far they extended in width has not been ascertained by direct observation, for we have not seen how they sink away to the northward, and towards the south the denudation has been so complete that, except in the very low range of hills in the neighborhood of Santarem, they do not rise above the plain. But the fact that this formation once had a thickness of more than eight hundred feet within the limits where we have had an opportunity of observing it, leaves no doubt that it must have extended to the edge of the basin, filling it to the same height throughout its whole extent. The thickness of the deposits gives a measure for the colossal scale of the denudations by which this immense accumulation was reduced to its present level. Here then is a system of high hills, having the prominence of mountains in the landscape, produced by causes to whose agency inequalities on the earth's surface of this magnitude have never yet been ascribed. We may fairly call them denudation mountains.

At this stage of the inquiry we have to account for two remarkable phenomena. First, the filling of the Amazonian bottom with coarse arenaceous materials and finely laminated clays, immediately followed by sandstones rising to a height of more than eight hundred feet above the sea ; the basin meanwhile having no rocky barrier towards the ocean on its eastern side. Second, the wearing away and reduction of these formations to their present level, by a denudation, more extensive than any thus far recorded in the annals of geology, which has

given rise to all the most prominent hills and mountain chains along the northern bank of the river. Before seeking an explanation of these facts, let us look at the third and uppermost deposit.

This deposit, essentially the same as the Rio drift, has been minutely described in my former article ; but in the north, it presents itself under a somewhat different aspect. As in Rio, it is a clayey deposit, containing more or less sand, and reddish in color, though varying from deep ochre to a brownish tint. It is not so absolutely destitute of stratification here as in its more southern range, though the traces of stratification are rare, and, when they do occur, are faint and indistinct. The materials are also more completely comminuted, and, as I have said above, contain hardly any large masses, though quartz pebbles are sometimes scattered throughout the deposit, and occasionally a thin seam of pebbles, exactly as in the Rio drift, is seen resting between it and the underlying sandstone. In some places this bed of pebbles even intersects the mass of the clay, giving it in such instances an unquestionably stratified character. There can be no question that this more recent formation rests unconformably upon the sandstone beds beneath it ; for it fills all the inequalities of their denuded surfaces, whether they be more or less limited furrows, or wide, undulating depressions. It may be seen everywhere along the banks of the river, above the stratified sandstone, sometimes with the river mud accumulated against it ; at the season of the *enchente*, or high water, it is the only formation left exposed above the water level. Its thickness is not great ; it varies from twenty or thirty to fifty feet, and may occasionally rise nearly to a hundred feet in height, though this is rarely the case. It is evident that this formation also was once continuous, stretching over the whole basin at one level. Though it is now worn down in many places, and has wholly disappeared in others, its connection may be readily traced ; since it is everywhere visible, not only on opposite banks of the Amazons, but also on those of all its tributaries, as far as their shores have been examined. I have said that it rests always above the sandstone beds. This is true, with one exception. Wherever the sandstone deposits retain their original thickness, as in the hills of Monte Alegre and Almeyrim, the red clay is not found on their summits, but occurs only in their ravines and hollows, or resting against their sides. This shows that it is not only posterior to the sandstone, but was accumulated in a shallower basin, and consequently never reached so high a level. The boulders of Erreré do not rest on the stratified sandstone of the Serra, but are sunk in the unstratified mass of the clay. This should be remembered, as it will presently be seen that their position associates them with a later period than that of the mountain itself. The unconformability of the ochraceous clay and the underlying sandstones might lead to the idea that the two formations belong to distinct geological periods, and are not due to the same agency, acting at successive times. One feature, however, shows their close connection. The ochraceous clay exhibits a remarkable identity of configuration with the underlying sandstones. An extensive survey of the two, in their mutual relations, shows clearly that they were both deposited by the same water-system within the same basin, but at different levels. Here and there the clay formation has so pale and grayish a tint, that it may be confounded with the mud deposits of the river. These latter, however, never rise so high as the ochraceous clay, but are everywhere confined within the limits of high and low water. The islands also in the main course of the Amazons consist invariably of river-mud, while those arising from the intersection and cutting off of portions of the land by diverging branches of the main stream always consist of the well-known sandstones, capped by the ochre-colored clay.

It may truly be said that there does not exist on the surface of the earth a formation known to geologists resembling that of the Amazons. Its extent is stupendous ; it stretches from the Atlantic shore, through the whole width of Brazil, into Peru, to the very foot of the Andes. Humboldt speaks of it "in the vast plains of the Amazons, in the eastern boundary of Jaen de Bracamoros," and says, "This prodigious extension of red sandstone in the low grounds stretching along the east of the Andes is one of the most striking phenomena I observed during my examination of rocks in the equinoctial regions." [*] When the great natural philosopher wrote these lines, he had no idea how much these deposits extended beyond the field of his observations. Indeed, they are not limited to the main bed of the Amazons ; they have been followed along the banks of its tributaries to the south and north as far as these have been ascended. They occur on the margins of the Huallaga and the Ucayall, on those of the Iça, the Jutahy, the Jurua, the Japura, and the Purus. On the banks of the Japura, where Major Coutinho has traced them, they are found as far as the Cataract of Cupati. I have followed them along the Rio Negro to its junction with the Rio Branco ; and Humboldt not only describes them from a higher point on this same river, but also from the valley of the Orinoco. Finally, they may be tracked along the banks of the Madeira, the Tapajos, the Xingu, and the Tocantins, as well as on the shores of the Guatuma, the Trombetas, and other northern affluents of the Amazons. The observations of Martius, those of Gardner, and the recent survey above

[*] Bohn's edition of Humboldt's Personal Narrative, p. 134. Humboldt alludes to these formations repeatedly ; it is true that he refers them to the ancient conglomerates of the Devonian age, but his description agrees so perfectly with what I have observed along the banks of the Amazons, that there can be no doubt he speaks of the same thing. He wrote at a time when many of the results of modern geology were unknown, and his explanation of the phenomena was then perfectly natural. The passage from which the few lines in the text are taken shows that these deposits extend even to the Llanos.

alluded to, made by my assistant, Mr. St. John, of the valley of the Rio Guruguea and that of the Rio Paranahyba, show that the great basin of Piauhy is also identical in its geological structure with the lateral valleys of the Amazons. The same is true of the large island of Marajo, lying at the mouth of the Amazons. And yet I believe that even this does not cover the whole ground, and that some future writer may say of my estimate, as I have said of Humboldt's, that it falls short of the truth ; for, if my generalizations are correct, the same formation will be found extending over the whole basin of the Paraguay and the Rio de la Plata, and along their tributaries, to the very heart of the Andes.

Such are the facts. The question now arises, How were these vast deposits formed ? The easiest answer, and the one which most readily suggests itself, is that of a submersion of the continent at successive periods to allow the accumulation of these materials, and its subsequent elevation. I reject this explanation for the simple reason that the deposits show no sign whatever of a marine origin. No sea-shells nor remains of any marine animal have as yet been found throughout their whole extent, over a region several thousand miles in length and from five to seven hundred miles in width. It is contrary to all our knowledge of geological deposits to suppose that an ocean basin of this size, which must have been submerged during an immensely long period in order to accumulate formations of such a thickness, should not contain numerous remains of the animals formerly inhabiting it.* The only fossil remains of any kind truly belonging to it, which I have found in the formation, are the leaves men-

tioned above, taken from the lower clays on the banks of the Solimoens at Tonantins ; and these show a vegetation similar in general character to that which prevails there to-day. Evidently, then, this basin was a fresh-water basin ; these deposits are fresh-water deposits. But as the Valley of the Amazons exists to-day, it is widely open to the ocean on the east, with a gentle slope from the Andes to the Atlantic, determining a powerful seaward current. When these vast accumulations took place, the basin must have been closed ; otherwise the loose materials would constantly have been carried down to the ocean.

It is my belief that all these deposits belong to the ice period in its earlier or later phases, and to this cosmic winter, which, judging from all the phenomena connected with it, may have lasted for thousands of centuries, we must look for the key to the geological history of the Amazonian Valley. I am aware that this suggestion will appear extravagant. But is it, after all, so improbable that, when Central Europe was covered with ice thousands of feet thick; when the glaciers of Great Britain ploughed into the sea, and when those of the Swiss mountains had ten times their present altitude ; when every lake in Northern Italy was filled with ice, and these frozen masses extended even into Northern Africa ; when a sheet of ice, reaching nearly to the summit of Mount Washington in the White Mountains (that is, having a thickness of nearly six thousand feet), moved over the continent of North America, — is it so improbable that, in this epoch of universal cold, the Valley of the Amazons also had its glacier poured down into it from the accumulations of snow in the Cordille-

---

* I am aware that Bates mentions having heard, that at Obydos calcareous layers, thickly studded with marine shells, had been found interstratified with the clay, but he did not himself examine the strata. The Obydos shells are not marine, but are fresh-water Unios, greatly resembling Aviculas, Solens, and Arcas. Such would-be marine fossils have been brought to me from the shore opposite to Obydos, near Santarem, and I have readily recognized them for what they truly are, fresh-water shells of the family of Naiades. I have myself collected specimens of

these shells in the clay beds along the banks of the Solimoens, near Teffe, and might have mistaken them for fossils of that formation had I not known how Naiades burrow in the mud. Their resemblance to the marine genera mentioned above is very remarkable, and the mistake as to their true zoological character is as natural as that by which earlier ichthyologists, and even travellers of very recent date, have confounded some fresh-water fishes from the Upper Amazons of the genus Pterophyllum (Heckel) with the marine genus Platax.

ras, and swollen laterally by the tributary glaciers descending from the tablelands of Guiana and Brazil? The movement of this immense glacier would be eastward, and determined as well by the vast reservoirs of snow in the Andes as by the direction of the valley itself. It must have ploughed the valley bottom over and over again, grinding all the materials beneath it into a fine powder or reducing them to small pebbles, and it must have accumulated at its lower end a moraine of proportions as gigantic as its own; thus building a colossal sea-wall across the mouth of the valley. I shall be asked at once whether I have found here also the glacial inscriptions, — the furrows, striæ, and polished surfaces so characteristic of the ground over which glaciers have travelled. I answer, not a trace of them; for the simple reason that there is not a natural rock surface to be found throughout the whole Amazonian Valley. The rocks themselves are of so friable a nature, and the decomposition caused by the warm torrential rains and by exposure to the burning sun of the tropics so great and unceasing, that it is hopeless to look for marks which in colder climates and on harder substances are preserved through ages unchanged. With the exception of the rounded surfaces so well known in Switzerland as the *roches moutonnées* heretofore alluded to, which may be seen in many localities, and the boulders of Erreré, the direct traces of glaciers as seen in other countries are wanting here. I am, indeed, quite willing to admit that, from the nature of the circumstances, I have not here the positive evidence which has guided me in my previous glacial investigations. My conviction in this instance is founded, first, on the materials in the Amazonian Valley, which correspond exactly in their character to materials accumulated in glacier bottoms; secondly, on the resemblance of the upper or third Amazonian formation to the Rio drift,* of the glacial

origin of which there cannot, in my opinion, be any doubt; thirdly, on the fact that this fresh-water basin must have been closed against the sea by some powerful barrier, the removal of which would naturally give an outlet to the waters, and cause the extraordinary denudations, the evidences of which meet us everywhere throughout the valley.

On a smaller scale, phenomena of this kind have long been familiar to us. In the present lakes of Northern Italy, in those of Switzerland, Norway, and Sweden, as well as in those of New England, especially in the State of Maine, the waters are held back in their basins by moraines. In the ice period these depressions were filled with glaciers, which, in the course of time, accumulated at their lower end a wall of loose materials. These walls still remain, and serve as dams to prevent the escape of the waters. But for their moraines, all these lakes would be open valleys. In the Roads of Glen Roy, in Scotland, we have an instance of a fresh-water lake, which has now wholly disappeared, formed in the same manner, and reduced successively to lower and lower levels by the breaking down or wearing away of the moraines which originally prevented its waters from flowing out. Assuming then, that, under the low temperature of the ice period, the climatic conditions necessary for the formation of land-ice existed in the Valley of the Amazons, and that it was actually filled with an immense glacier, it follows that, when these fields of ice yielded to a gradual change of climate, and slowly melted away, the whole basin, then closed

* As I have stated in the beginning, I am satisfied that the unstratified clay deposit of Rio and its vicinity is genuine glacial drift, resulting from the grinding of the loose materials interposed between the glacier and the solid rock in place, and retaining to this day the position in which it was left by the ice. Like all such accumulations, it is totally free from stratification. If this be so, it is evident, on comparing the two formations, that the ochraceous sandy clay of the Valley of the Amazons has been deposited under different circumstances; that, while it owes its resemblance to the Rio drift to the fact that its materials were originally ground by glaciers in the upper part of the valley, these materials have subsequently been spread throughout the whole basin and actually deposited under the agency of water.

against the sea by a huge wall of *débris*, was transformed into a vast fresh-water lake. The first effect of the thawing process must have been to separate the glacier from its foundation, raising it from immediate contact with the valley bottom, and thus giving room for the accumulation of a certain amount of water beneath it ; while the valley as a whole would still be occupied by the glacier. In this shallow sheet of water under the ice, and protected by it from any violent disturbance, those finer triturated materials always found at a glacier bottom, and ground sometimes to powder by its action, would be deposited, and gradually transformed from an unstratified paste containing the finest sand and mud, together with coarse pebbles and gravel, into a regularly stratified formation. In this formation the coarse materials would of course fall to the bottom, while the most minute would settle above them. It is at this time and under such circumstances that I believe the first formation of the Amazonian Valley, with the coarse, pebbly sand beneath, and the finely laminated clays above, to have been accumulated.

I shall perhaps be reminded here of my fossil leaves, and asked how any vegetation would be possible under such circumstances. But it must be remembered, that, in considering all these periods, we must allow for immense lapses of time and for very gradual changes ; that the close of this first period would be very different from its beginning ; and that a rich vegetation springs on the very borders of the snow and ice fields in Switzerland. The fact that these were accumulated in a glacial basin would, indeed, at once account for the traces of vegetable life, and for the absence, or at least the great scarcity, of animal remains in these deposits. For while fruits may ripen and flowers bloom on the very edge of the glaciers, it is also well known that the fresh-water lakes formed by the melting of the ice are singularly deficient in life.

There are indeed hardly any animals to be found in glacial lakes.

The second formation belongs to a later period, when, the whole body of ice being more or less disintegrated, the basin contained a larger quantity of water. Beside that arising from the melting of the ice, this immense valley bottom must have received, then as now, all which was condensed from the atmosphere above, and poured into it in the form of rain or dew. Thus an amount of water equal to that now flowing in from all the tributaries of the main stream must have been rushing towards the axis of the valley, seeking its natural level, but spreading over a more extensive surface than now, until, finally gathered up as separate rivers, it flowed in distinct beds. In its general movement toward the central and lower part of the valley, the broad stream would carry along all the materials small enough to be so transported, as well as those so minute as to remain suspended in the waters. It would gradually deposit them in the valley bottom in horizontal beds, more or less regular, or here and there, wherever eddies gave rise to more rapid and irregular currents, characterized by torrential stratification. Thus has been consolidated in the course of ages that continuous sand formation spreading over the whole Amazonian basin, and attaining a thickness of eight hundred feet.

While these accumulations were taking place within this basin, it must not be forgotten that the sea was beating against its outer walls, — against that gigantic moraine which I suppose to have closed it at its eastern end. It would seem that, either from this cause, or perhaps in consequence of some turbulent action from within, a break was made in this defence, and the waters rushed violently out. It is very possible that the waters, gradually swollen at the close of this period by the further melting of the ice, by the additions poured in from lateral tributaries, by the rains, and also by the filling of the basin with loose materials, would overflow, and thus contribute to destroy the moraine. However this may be, it follows from my premises that, in the end, these waters obtained a sudden release, and poured seaward with a violence which cut and denuded the deposits already formed, wearing them down to a much lower level, and leaving only a few remnants standing out in their original thickness, where the strata were solid enough to resist the action of the currents. Such are the hills of Monte Alegre, of Obydos, Almeyrim, and Cupati, as well as the lower ridges of Santarem. This escape of the waters did not, however, entirely empty the whole basin; for the period of denudation was again followed by one of quiet accumulation, during which was deposited the ochraceous sandy clay resting upon the denudated surfaces of the underlying sandstone. To this period I refer the boulders of Erreré, sunk as they are in the clay of this final deposit. I suppose them to have been brought to their present position by floating ice at the close of the glacial period, when nothing remained of the ice-fields except such isolated masses, — ice-rafts as it were; or perhaps by icebergs dropped into the basin from glaciers still remaining in the Andes and on the edges of the plateaus of Guiana and Brazil. From the general absence of stratification in this clay formation, it would seem that the comparatively shallow sheet of water in which it was deposited was very tranquil. Indeed, after the waters had sunk much below the level which they held during the deposition of the sandstone, and the currents which gave rise to the denudation of the latter had ceased, the whole sheet of water would naturally become much more placid. But the time came when the water broke through its boundaries again, perhaps owing to the further encroachment of the sea and consequent destruction of the moraine. In this second drainage, however, the waters, carrying away a considerable part of the new deposit, furrowing it to its very foundation, and even cutting through it into the underlying sand-

stone, were, in the end, reduced to something like their present level, and confined within their present beds. This is shown by the fact that in this ochre-colored clay, and penetrating to a greater or less depth the sandstone below, are dug, not only the great longitudinal channel of the Amazons itself, but also the lateral furrows through which its tributaries reach the main stream, and the network of anastomosing branches flowing between them; the whole forming the most extraordinary river system in the world.

My assumption that the sea has produced very extensive changes in the coast of Brazil — changes more than sufficient to account for the disappearance of the glacial wall which I suppose to have closed the Amazonian Valley in the ice period — is by no means hypothetical. This action is still going on to a remarkable degree, and is even now rapidly modifying the outline of the shore. When I first arrived at Pará, I was struck with the fact that the Amazons, the largest river in the world, has no delta. All the other rivers which we call great, though some of them are insignificant as compared with the Amazons, — the Mississippi, the Nile, the Ganges, and the Danube, — deposit extensive deltas, and the smaller rivers also, with few exceptions, are constantly building up the land at their mouths by the materials they bring along with them. Even the little river Kander, emptying into the Lake of Thun, is not without its delta. Since my return from the Upper Amazons to Pará, I have made an examination of some of the harbor islands, and also of parts of the coast, and have satisfied myself that, with the exception of a few small, low islands, never rising above the sea-level, and composed of alluvial deposit, they are portions of the mainland detached from it, partly by the action of the river itself, and partly by the encroachment of the ocean. In fact the sea is eating away the land much faster than the river can build it up. The great island of Marajo was originally a continuation of the

Valley of the Amazons, and is identical with it in every detail of its geological structure. My investigation of the island itself, in connection with the coast and the river, leads me to suppose that, having been at one time an integral part of the deposits described above, at a later period it became an island in the bed of the Amazons, which, dividing in two arms, encircled it completely, and then, joining again to form a single stream, flowed onward to the sea-shore, which in those days lay much farther to the eastward than it now does. I suppose the position of the island of Marajo at that time to have corresponded very nearly to the present position of the island of Tupinambaranas, just at the junction of the Madeira with the Amazons. It is a question among geographers whether the Tocantins is a branch of the Amazons, or should be considered as forming an independent river system. It will be seen that, if my view is correct, it must formerly have borne the same relation to the Amazons that the Madeira River now does, joining it just where Marajo divided the main stream, as the Madeira now joins it at the head of the island of Tupinambaranas. If in countless centuries to come the ocean should continue to eat its way into the Valley of the Amazons, once more transforming the lower part of the basin into a gulf, as it was during the cretaceous period, the time might arrive when geographers, finding the Madeira emptying almost immediately into the sea, would ask themselves whether it had ever been indeed a branch of the Amazons, just as they now question whether the Tocantins is a tributary of the main stream or an independent river. But to return to Marajo, and to the facts actually in our possession.

The island is intersected, in its southeastern end, by a considerable river called the Igarapé Grande. The cut made through the land by this stream seems intended to serve as a geological section, so perfectly does it display the three characteristic Amazonian forma-

tions above described. At its mouth, near the town of Souré, and at Salvaterra, on the opposite bank, may be seen, lowest, the well-stratified sandstone, with the finely laminated clays resting upon it, overtopped by a crust; then the cross-stratified, highly ferruginous sandstone, with quartz pebbles here and there; and, above all, the well-known ochraceous, unstratified sandy clay, spreading over the undulating surface of the denudated sandstone, following all its inequalities, and filling all its depressions and furrows. But while the Igarapé Grande has dug its channel down to the sea, cutting these formations, as I ascertained, to a depth of twenty-five fathoms, it has thus opened the way for the encroachments of the tides, and the ocean is now, in its turn, gaining upon the land. Were there no other evidence of the action of the tides in this locality, the steep cut of the Igarapé Grande, contrasting with the gentle slope of the banks near its mouth, wherever they have been modified by the invasion of the sea, would enable us to distinguish the work of the river from that of the ocean, and to prove that the denudation now going on is due in part to both. But besides this, I was so fortunate as to discover here unmistakable and perfectly convincing evidence of the onward movement of the sea. At the mouth of the Igarapé Grande, both at Souré and at Salvaterra, on the southern side of the Igarapé, is a submerged forest. Evidently this forest grew in one of those marshy lands constantly inundated, for between the stumps is accumulated the loose, felt-like peat characteristic of such grounds, and containing about as much mud as vegetable matter. Such a marshy forest, with the stumps of the trees still standing erect in the peat, has been laid bare on both sides of the Igarapé Grande by the encroachments of the ocean. That this is the work of the sea is undeniable, for all the little depressions and indentations of the peat are filled with sea-sand, and a ridge of tidal sand divides it from the forest still standing behind. Nor is this all. At Vigia, immediately opposite to Souré, on the continental side of the Pará River, just where it meets the sea, we have the counterpart of this submerged forest. Another peat-bog, with the stumps of innumerable trees standing in it, and encroached upon in the same way by tidal sand, is exposed here also. No doubt these forests were once all continuous, and stretched across the whole basin of what is now called the Pará River.

Since I have been pursuing this inquiry, I have gathered much information to the same effect from persons living on the coast. It is well remembered that, twenty years ago, there existed an island, more than a mile in width, to the northeast of the entrance of the Bay of Vigia, which has now entirely disappeared. Farther eastward, the Bay of Braganza has doubled its width in the last twenty years, and on the shore, within the bay, the sea has gained upon the land for a distance of two hundred yards during a period of only ten years. The latter fact is ascertained by the position of some houses, which were two hundred yards farther from the sea ten years ago than they now are. From these and the like reports, from my own observations on this part of the Brazilian coast, from some investigations made by Major Coutinho at the mouth of the Amazons, on its northern continental shore, near Macapa, and from the reports of Mr. St. John respecting the formations in the valley of the Paranahyba, it is my belief that the changes I have been describing are but a small part of the destruction wrought by the sea on the northeastern shore of this continent. I think it will be found, when the coast has been fully surveyed, that a strip of land not less than a hundred leagues in width, stretching from Cape St. Roque to the northern extremity of South America, has been eaten away by the ocean. If this be so, the Paranahyba and the rivers to the northwest of it, in the province of Maranham, were formerly tributaries of the Amazons ; and all that we know thus far of their geological character goes to prove that this was actually the case. Such an extensive oceanic denudation must have carried away not only the gigantic glacial moraine here assumed to have closed the mouth of the Amazonian basin, but the very ground on which it stood.

During the last four or five years I have been engaged in a series of investigations, in the United States, upon the subject of the denudations connected with the close of the glacial period there, and the encroachments of the ocean upon the drift deposits along the Atlantic coast. Had these investigations been published in detail, with the necessary maps, it would have been far easier for me to explain the facts I have lately observed in the Amazonian Valley, to connect them with facts of a like character on the continent of North America, and to show how remarkably they correspond with facts accomplished during the same period in other parts of the world. While the glacial epoch itself has been very extensively studied in the last half-century, little attention has been paid to the results connected with the breaking up of the geological winter and the final disappearance of the ice. I believe that the true explanation of the presence of a large part of the superficial deposits lately ascribed to the agency of the sea, during temporary subsidences of the land, will be found in the melting of the ice-fields. To this cause I would refer all those deposits which I have designated in former publications as remodelled drift. When the sheet of ice, extending from the Arctic regions over a great part of North America and coming down to the sea, slowly melted away, the waters were not distributed over the face of the country as they now are. They rested upon the bottom deposits of the ice-fields, upon the glacial paste, consisting of clay, sand, pebbles, boulders, etc., underlying the ice. This bottom deposit did not, of course, present an even surface, but must have had extensive undulations and depressions. After the waters had been drained off from the more elevated ridges, these depressions would still remain full. In the lakes and pools thus formed, stratified deposits would be accumulated, consisting of the most minutely comminuted clay, deposited in thin laminated layers, or sometimes in considerable masses, without any sign of stratification; such differences in the formation being determined by the state of the water, whether perfectly stagnant or more or less agitated. Of such pool deposits overlying the drift there are many instances in the Northern United States. By the overflowing of some of these lakes, and by the emptying of the higher ones into those on a lower level, channels would gradually be formed between the depressions. So began to be marked out our independent river-systems, — the waters always seeking their natural level, gradually widening and deepening the channels in which they flowed, as they worked their way down to the sea. When they reached the shore, there followed that antagonism between the rush of the rivers and the action of the tides, — between continental outflows and oceanic encroachments, — which still goes on, and has led to the formation of our eastern rivers, with their wide, open estuaries, such as the James, the Potomac, and the Delaware. All these estuaries are embanked by drift, as are also, in their lower course, the rivers connected with them. Where the country was low and flat, and the drift extended far into the ocean, the encroachment of the sea gave rise, not only to our large estuaries, but also to the sounds and deep bays forming the most prominent indentations of the continental coast. such as the Bay of Fundy, Massachusetts Bay, Long Island Sound, and others. The unmistakable traces of glacial action upon all the islands along the coast of New England, sometimes lying at a very considerable distance from the mainland, give an approximate, though a minimum, measure of the former extent of the glacial drift seaward, and the subse-

quent advance of the ocean upon the land. Like those of the harbor of Pará, all these islands have the same geological structure as the continent, and were evidently continuous with it at some former period. All the rocky islands along the coast of Maine and Massachusetts exhibit the glacial traces wherever their surfaces are exposed by the washing away of the drift; and where the drift remains, its character shows that it was once continuous from one island to another, and from all the islands to the mainland.

It is difficult to determine with precision the ancient limit of the glacial drift, but I think it can be shown that it connected the shoals of Newfoundland with the continent; that Nantucket, Martha's Vineyard, and Long Island made part of the mainland; that, in like manner, Nova Scotia, including Sable Island, was united to the southern shore of New Brunswick and Maine, and that the same sheet of drift extended thence to Cape Cod, and stretched southward as far as Cape Hatteras; — in short, that the line of shallow soundings along the whole coast of the United States marks the former extent of glacial drift. The ocean has gradually eaten its way into this deposit, and given its present outlines to the continent. These denudations of the sea no doubt began as soon as the breaking up of the ice exposed the drift to its invasion; in other words, at a time when colossal glaciers still poured forth their load of ice into the Atlantic, and fleets of icebergs, far larger and more numerous than those now floated off from the Arctic seas, were launched from the northeastern shore of the United States. Many such masses must have stranded along the shore, and have left various signs of their presence. In fact, the glacial phenomena of the United States and elsewhere are due to two distinct periods: the first of these was the glacial epoch proper, when the ice was a solid sheet; while to the second belongs the breaking up of this epoch, with the gradual disintegration and dispersion of the ice. We talk of the theory of glaciers and the theory of icebergs in reference to these phenomena, as if they were exclusively due to one or the other, and whoever accepted the former must reject the latter, and *vice versa.* When geologists have combined these now discordant elements, and consider these two periods as consecutive, — part of the phenomena being due to the glaciers, part to the icebergs and to freshets consequent on their breaking up, — they will find they have covered the whole ground, and that the two theories are perfectly consistent with each other. I think the present disputes upon this subject will end somewhat like those which divided the Neptunic and Plutonic schools of geologists in the early part of this century; the former of whom would have it that all the rocks were due to the action of water, the latter that they were wholly due to the action of fire. The problem was solved, and harmony restored, when it was found that both elements had been equally at work in forming the solid crust of the globe. To the stranded icebergs alluded to above, I have no doubt, is to be referred the origin of the many lakes without outlet existing all over the sandy tract along our coast of which Cape Cod forms a part. Not only the formation of these lakes, but also that of our salt marshes and cranberry-fields, I believe to be connected with the waning of the ice period.

I hope at some future time to publish in detail, with the appropriate maps and illustrations, my observations on our coast changes, and upon other phenomena connected with the close of the glacial epoch in the United States. It is reversing the natural order of things to give results without the investigations which have led to them; and I should not have introduced the subject here except to show that the fresh-water denudations and the oceanic encroachments which have formed the Amazonian Valley, with its river system, are not isolated facts, but that the process has been the same in both continents. The extraordinary continuity and uniformity of the Amazonian deposits are due to the immense size of the basin enclosed, and the identity of the materials contained in it.

A glance at any geological map of the world will show the reader that the Valley of the Amazons, so far as any attempt is made to explain its structure, is represented as containing isolated tracts of Devonian, Triassic, Jurassic, cretaceous, tertiary, and alluvial deposits. As is shown by the above sketch, this is wholly inaccurate; and whatever may be thought of my interpretation of the actual phenomena, I trust that, in presenting for the first time the formations of the Amazonian basin in their natural connection and sequence, as consisting of three uniform sets of comparatively recent deposits, extending throughout the whole valley, the investigations here recorded have contributed something to the results of modern geology.

A MANIAC'S CONFESSION.

I AM a maniac. I have for some years been the victim of a peculiar insanity, which has greatly distressed several of my friends and relatives. They generally soften it in their talk by the name *mono*mania; but they do not hesitate to aver, when speaking their minds, that it has in truth infected my whole soul, and made me incapable of doing or thinking anything useful or rational. This sad delusion, which they endeavor to remove by serious advice, by playful banter, or by seeming to take an interest in my folly for a moment, is encountered with great acrimony by less gentle friends. They who are not bound to me by blood or intimacy — and some who are — deride, insult, and revile me in every way for my subjection to a mental aberration which is rapidly consuming a pretty property, more than average talents, and unrivalled opportunities.

Of course, like all madmen, I think just the reverse. When the fit is on me, I assert that this fever — this madness — far from being the bane of my life, is a blessing to it; that I am habitually devoting money, time, and wits to an object at once beautiful and elevating; that I have found consolation in its visions for many sufferings, which all the amusements offered me by my revilers are utterly inadequate to touch. I declare that I have found a better investment for my money than all the West Virginia coal companies that ever sunk oil-wells, and am making more useful acquaintances than if I danced every German during the season. I have not been shut up yet, for my friends know that, if they attempt any such thing, the Finance Committee on the Harvard Memorial and Alumni Hall are in possession of a bond conveying all my money to them; so I am still at large, scolded by my brother Henry, laughed at by my sister Bathsheba, the aversion of Beacon Street, and the scorn of Winthrop Square.

The other day, I took a little journey to Europe, with the view of feeding my madness on that whereby it grows. My friends did not choose to stop me, for they thought the charms of foreign travel might win me from my waywardness. To be sure, when they found, on my return, that I had never left England, they were convinced, if never before, that I was hopelessly insane; for what American, they very sanely said, "would stay in that dull, dingy island, among those stupid, cowardly bullies, when he might live in that lovely Paris, the most interesting and amusing city in the world, unless he were incomprehensibly mad." And, in truth, I begin to think I must be mad, when I find myself, like the man shut up with eleven obstinate jurymen, alone in thinking England a gay, beautiful, happy country, teeming with every gratification of art or nature, and inhabited by a manly, generous, and intelligent race; and that life in Paris, as Americans live it, is a senseless rush after excitement, where comfort is abandoned for unreal luxury, and society for vicious boon-companionship. Still I am very willing to admit that my special mania can be very capitally gratified in Paris, and I am meditating a little trip there for the purpose.

On my return from England, I was observed to be in great distress about a certain box that I missed at Liverpool, looked for at Halifax, and all but lost at East Boston; and when it was found and opened, it only contained two suits of clothes, when, as Henry said, "I might have brought forty, the only thing they did have decent in England," and all the rest — mad, mad! I beg the readers of the Atlantic to listen to my humble confession of madness, as it culminated in this box.

It is this. The most valuable property a man can possibly have is books; if he has a hundred or a thousand dollars to spare, he had better at once put it into books than into any "paying investments," or any horses, clothes, pictures, or opera-tickets. A life passed among books, thinking, talking, living only for books, is the most amusing and improving life ; and to make this possible, the acquisition of a library should be the first object of any one who makes any claim to the possession of luxuries. (My madness only allows me to make one exception, — I do acknowledge the solemn duty of laying in a stock of old Madeira.) But so far I have many fellow-maniacs. The special reason why I ought always to stop the Lowell cars at Somerville is, that I consider the reading of books only half the battle. I must have them in choice bindings, in rare imprints, in original editions, and in the most select forms. I must have several copies of a book I have read forty times, as long as there is anything about each copy that makes it peculiar, *sui generis*. I must own the first edition of Paradise Lost, because it is the first, and in ten books ; the second, because it is the first in twelve ; then Newton's, then Todd's, then Mitford's, and so on, till my catalogue of Miltons gets to equal Jeames de la Pluche's portraits of the "Dook." "And when," as Henry indignantly says, "he could read Milton all he wanted to, more than I should ever want to, notes and all, in Little and Brown's edition that father gave him, he must go spending money on a parcel of old truck printed a thousand years ago." Mad, quite mad.

Now, to finish the melancholy picture, I am classic mad. I prefer the ancient authors, decidedly, to the moderns. I love them as I never can the moderns ; they are my most intimate friends, my heart's own darlings. And how I love to lavish money on them, to see them adorned in every way ! How I love to heap them up, Aldines, and Elzevirs, and Baskervilles, and Biponts, in all their grace and majesty. This was what filled that London box. This was all I had to show for twenty-five or thirty guineas of good money ; a parcel of trumpery old Greek and

Latin books I had by dozens already ! Mad, mad.

Will you come in and see them, ladies and gentlemen ? Here they are, all ranged out on my table, large and small, clean and dirty. What have we first ?

A goodly fat quarto in white vellum, " Plinii Panegyricus, cum notis Schwarzii, Norimbergæ, 1733." A fine, clean, fresh copy, — one of those brave old Teutonic classics of the last century, less exquisitely printed than the Elzevirs, less learnedly critical than the later Germans, but perfectly trustworthy and satisfactory, and attracting every one's eye on a library shelf, by the rich sturdiness of their creamy binding, that smacks of the true Dutch and German burgher wealth. The model of them all is Oudendorp's Cæsar. But there is nothing very great about Pliny's Panegyric, and a man must be a very queer bibliomaniac who would buy up all the vellum classics of the last century he saw. Look inside the cover ; read under the book-plate the engraved name, " Edward Gibbon, Esq." What will you, my sanest friend, not give for a book that belonged to the author of the " Decline and Fall " ?

The next is also a large quarto, but of a very different character. It is the Baskerville impression of the elegiac poets, — Catullus, Tibullus, and Propertius : Birmingham, 1772. No books are more delightful to sight and touch than the Baskerville classics. This Catullus of mine is printed on the softest and glossiest post paper, with a mighty margin of two inches and a half at the side, and rich broad letters, — the standard n is a tenth of an inch wide, — of a glorious blackness in spite of their ninety-two years of age. The classics of all languages have never been more fitly printed than by Baskerville ; and the present book may serve as an admirable lesson to those who think a large-paper book means an ordinary octavo page printed in the middle of a quarto leaf, — for instance, Irving's Washington. My Catullus is bound in glossy calf, with a richly gilt back, and bears within the inscription, "From H. S. C. | to her valued friend | Doctor Southey | Feby ye 24th, 1813," in a true English lady's hand. This cannot be the poet Southey, who was not made LL. D. till 1821; but it may be his brother, Henry Herbert Southey, M. D.

Next comes a very neat and compact little Seneca, in four 18mo volumes, bound in rich old Russia, and bearing the esteemed imprint, "Amstelodami apud Ludovicum et Danielem Elzevirios, M.D.CLVIII." As the Baskerville classics are the noblest for the library table, so the Elzevirs are the neatest and prettiest for the pocket or the lecture-room. And to their great beauty of mechanical execution is generally added a scrupulous textual accuracy, which the great Birmingham printer did not boast. This edition of Seneca, for instance, is that of Gronovius. His dedicatory epistle, and the title-pages of Vols. II., III. and IV., are all dated 1658, but the general title-page in Vol. I. is 1659, as if, like White's Shakespeare, the first volume was the last published. Contrasting a *bijou* edition with a magnificent one, it may be noted that in the Elzevir the four words and two stops, "Moriar : die ergo verum," occupy just an inch, exactly the space of the one word "compositis " in the Baskerville ; but the printing of each is in its way exquisite.

Just about a century after the Elzevirs, and contemporary with Baskerville, an English publisher of the name of Sandby, who appears to have been, as we should say, the University printer and bookseller at Cambridge, projected a series of classics, which are highly prized on large paper and not despised on small. I possess two of the latter, a Terence and a Juvenal ; the second, curiously enough, lettered "Juvenal*u*s," a regular binder's blunder. They are called pocket editions, but are much larger than the Elzevirs, and, though very pretty, just miss that peculiar beauty and finish which have made the former the delight of all scholars. There is a

carelessness somewhere — it is hard to say where — about the printing, which prevents their being perfect; but a "Sandby" is a very nice thing.

My next "wanity" is a Virgil, — Justice's Virgil ; a most elaborate and elegant edition, in five octavo volumes, published in the middle of the last century. It is noted, first, for the great richness and beauty of its engravings from ancient gems, coins, and drawings, which form an unrivalled body of illustration to the text. But, secondly, it will be seen, on inspection, that the whole book is one vast engraving, every line, word, and letter being cut on a metallic plate. Consequently, only every other page is printed on. The same idea was still more perfectly carried out by Pine, a few years later, who executed all Horace in this way, but only lived to complete one volume of Virgil, choicer even than Justice's. It is well bound, in perfect order, and ranks with the choicest of ornamental classics.

Side by side with this Virgil is another, the rare Elzevir Virgil, and a gem, if ever there was one. It is the corrected text of Heinsius, and thus has a fair claim to rank as the earliest of the modern critical editions of Maro. The elegance of this little book in size and shape, the clearness and beauty of the type, and the truly classical taste and finish of the whole design, can never be surpassed in Virgilian bibliography, unless by Didot's matchless little copies. Elzevir Virgils are common enough ; but mine is, as I have said, the rare Elzevir, known by the pages introductory to the Eclogues and Æneid being printed in rubric, while the ordinary Elzevirs have them in black. It dates 1637, — the year when John Harvard left his money to the College at Newtowne, and the first printing-press in the United States was set up hard by.

The books, then, that I have described so far all date within the two hundred and thirty years of our collegiate history. But I have behind three of an earlier — a much earlier date ; books which John Cotton and Charles

Chauncy might have gazed upon as old in Emmanuel College Library.

First, I show you a pair of Aldines, and, what is better, a pair *editionum principum*, — the first Sophocles and the first Thucydides. Both have the proper attestation at the end that they come from the Aldi in Venice in the year 1502, — the Thucydides in May, and the Sophocles in August; hence the former has not the Aldine anchor at the extreme end. Both are in exquisitely clean condition; but the Sophocles, though taller than other known copies of the same edition, has suffered from the knife of a modern binder, who otherwise has done his work with the greatest elegance and judgment. The Thucydides has a grand page, over twelve inches by eight; the Sophocles is about seven by four. The type of both is small, and, though distinct, especially the Thucydides, not at all what we should call elegant. In fact, elegant Greek type is a very late invention. There is, I believe, no claim to textual criticism in these early Aldines; the publishers printed from such manuscripts as they could get. The Thucydides has a long dedicatory address by Aldus to a Roman patrician; the Sophocles has no such introduction. But it is, at any rate, most curious to consider that these two writers, who stand at the very head of Greek, or at least Attic, prose and verse, both for matter and style, should not have found a printer till the fifteenth century was long past, and then in a style which, for the Sophocles, can only be called neat. The Thucydides is handsome, but far inferior to the glory of the *princeps* Homer. And to own them — for a maniac — O, it is glorious!

Last comes my special treasure, — my fifteener, — my book as old as America, — my darling copy of my darling author. Here, at the culmination of my madness, my friends, especially my brother Henry, are all ready to say at once what author I mean. For it has been my special mania for twenty years — thereby causing the deepest distress to nearly all my friends, even those who

have been thought fellow-lunatics, except one,[*] who is for me about the only sane man alive — to prefer, VIRGIL to all authors, living or dead, and to seek to accumulate as many different editions and copies of him as possible. I have in these pages chronicled two. My library holds twelve more, besides two translations, and I consider myself very short; for to my mind no breadth of paper, no weight of binding, no brilliancy of print, no delicacy of engraving, no elaboration of learning, can ever do honor enough to the last and best of the ancients, who was all but the first of the Christians, — who would have been, if his frame had not broken down under a genius too mighty and a soul too sweet for earth. (Mad, you see, beyond all question. Virgil is allowed to be a servile copyist, far inferior to Lucretius. Compare Lucr. V. 750 with Georg. II. 478, and Heyne's note.) This Virgil of mine bears the imprint of Antony Koburger, Nuremberg, 1492. It is in the original binding of very solid boards overlaid with stamped vellum, and is still clasped with the original skin and metal. It is a small folio, on very coarse paper, and the only one of my rare classics not in the cleanest condition. Its stains appear to be caused by its use in a school; for it is covered with notes, in German current hand, very antiquated, and very elementary in their scholarship. It has all the poetry ascribed to Virgil, and the Commentaries of Servius and Landini, which are so voluminous that the page looks like a ha'p'orth of sack to an intolerable deal of very dry bread. It is very rare, being unknown to the great Dibdin, and was snapped up by me for three guineas out of a London bookseller's catalogue. A Virgil printed by Koburger in the year America was discovered, original binding and clasps, not in Dibdin, for three guineas! Hurrah! It excites my madness so that I must rush straight to Piper's and buy right and left. Kind friends, come and take me away ere I am reduced to beggary.

[*] F. W. H. M., you know I mean you.

THE GREAT DOCTOR.

A STORY IN TWO PARTS.

II.

FIVE or six years of the life of our hero we must now pass over in silence, saying of them, simply, that Fancy had not cheated much in her promises concerning them. The first rude cabin had given place to a white-washed cottage ; the chimney-corner was bright and warm ; the easy-chair was in it, and the Widow Walker often sat there with her grandson on her knee, getting much comfort from the reflection that he looked just as her own Johnny did when he was a baby !

The garden smiled at the doorside, and the village had sprung up just as Fancy promised ; and Hobert and Jenny walked to church of a Sunday, and after service shook hands with their neighbors, — for everybody delighted to take their strong, willing hands, and look into their honest, cheerful faces, — they were amongst the first settlers of the place, and held an honored position in society. Jenny was grown a little more stout, and her cheek a little more ruddy, than it used to be ; but the new country seemed not so well suited to Hobert, and the well-wishing neighbor often said when he met him, " You must n't be too ambitious, and overdo ! Your shoulders ain't so straight as they was when you come here ! Be careful in time ; nothing like that, Walker, nothing like that." And Hobert laughed at these suggestions, saying he was as strong as the rest of them ; and that, though his cheek was pale, and his chest hollow, he was a better man than he seemed.

The summer had been one of the wildest luxuriance ever known in the valley of the Wabash ; for it was in that beautiful valley that our friend Hobert had settled. The woods cast their leaves early, and the drifts lay rotting knee-deep in places. Then came the long, hot, soaking rains, with hotter sunshine between. Chills and fever prevailed, and half the people of the neighborhood were shivering and burning at once. It was a healthy region, everybody said, but the weather had been unusually trying ; as soon as the frost came, the ague would vanish ; the water was the best in the world, to be sure, and the air the purest.

Hobert was ploughing a piece of low ground for wheat, cutting a black snake in two now and then, and his furrow behind him fast filling with water that looked almost as black as the soil. Often he stopped to frighten from the quivering flank of the brown mare before him the voracious horse-flies, colored like the scum of the stagnant pools, and clinging and sucking like leeches. She was his favorite, the pride of his farm, — for had she not, years before, brought Jenny on her faithful shoulder to the new, happy home ? Many a fond caress her neck had had from his arm ; and the fine bridle with the silver bit, hanging on the wall at home, would not have been afforded for any other creature in the world. Hobert often said he would never sell her as long as he lived ; and in the seasons of hard work he favored her more than he did himself. She had been named Fleetfoot, in honor of her successful achievement when her master had intrusted to her carrying the treasure of his life ; but that name proving too formal, she was usually called Fleety. She would put down her fore-head to the white hands of little Jenny, four years old and upward now, and tread so slow and so carefully when she had her on her back ! Even the white dress of Johnny Hobert had swept down her silken side more than once, while his dimpled hands clutched her mane, and his rosy feet paddled against her. He was going to be her master after a while, and take care of her in her old age, when the time of her rest was come ; he knew her name as well as he knew his own, and went wild with delight when he saw her taking clover from the tiny hand of his sister or drinking water from the bucket at the well.

"She grows handsomer every year," Hobert often said ; "and with a little training I would not be afraid to match her against the speediest racer they can bring." And this remark was always intended as in some sort a compliment to Jenny, and was always so received by her.

On this special day he had stopped oftener in the furrow than common ; and as often as he stopped Fleety twisted round her neck, bent her soft eyes upon him, and twitched her little ears as though she would say, "Is not all right, my master ? " And then he would walk round to her head, and pass his hand along her throat and through her foretop, calling her by her pet name, and pulling for her handfuls of fresh grass, and while she ate it resting himself against her, and feeling in her nearness almost a sense of human protection. His feet seemed to drag under him, and there was a dull aching in all his limbs ; the world appeared to be receding from him, and at times he could hardly tell whether he stood upon solid ground. Then he accused himself of being lazy and good for nothing, and with fictitious energy took up the reins and started the plough.

He looked at the sun again and again. He was not used to leaving off work while the sun shone, and the clear waters of the Wabash held as yet no faintest evening flush. There were yet two good hours of working time before him, when the quick shooting of a pain, like the running of a knife through his heart, caused him to stagger in the furrow. Fleety stopped of her own accord, and looked pityingly back. He sat down beside the plough

to gather up his courage a little. A strange sensation that he could not explain had taken possession of him, a feeling as if the hope of his life was cut off. The pain was gone, but the feeling of helpless surrender remained. He opened his shirt and passed his hand along his breast. He could feel nothing, — could see nothing ; but he had, for all that, a clearly defined consciousness as of some deadly thing hold of him that he would fain be rid of.

He had chanced to stop his plough under an elm-tree, and, looking up, he perceived that from the fork upward one half of it was dead ; mistletoe had sucked the life out of it, and lower and lower to the main body, deeper and deeper to the vital heart of it, the sap was being drawn away. An irresistible impulse impelled him to take the jack-knife from his pocket, and as far as he could reach cut away this alien and deadly growth. The sympathy into which he was come with the dying tree was positively painful to him, and yet he was withheld from moving on by a sort of fascination, — *he* was that tree, and the mistletoe was rooted in his bosom !

The last yellow leaves fluttered down and lodged on his head and shoulders and in his bosom, — he did not lift his hand to brush them away ; the blue lizard slid across his bare ankle and silently vanished out of sight, but he did not move a muscle. The brown mare bent her side round like a bow, and stretched her slender neck out more and more, and at last her nose touched his cheek, and then he roused himself and shook the dead leaves from his head and shoulders, and stood up. "Come, Fleety," he said, "we won't leave the plough in the middle of the furrow." She did not move. "Come, come ! " he repeated, "it seems like a bad sign to stop here " ;— and then he put his hand suddenly to his heart, and an involuntary shudder passed over him. Fleety had not unbent her side, and her dumb, beseeching eyes were still upon him. He looked at the sun, low, but still shining out bright, and almost as hot as ever; he looked at his shadow stretching so far over the rough, weedy ground, and it appeared to him strange and fantastic. Then he loosed the traces, and, winding up the long rein, hung it over the harness; the plough dropped aslant, and Fleety turned herself about and walked slowly homeward, — her master following, his head down and his hands locked together behind him.

The chimney was sending up its hospitable smoke, and Jenny was at the well with the teakettle in her hand when he came into the dooryard.

"What in the world is going to happen?" she exclaimed, cheerfully. "I never knew you to leave work before while the sun shone. I am glad you have, for once. But what is the matter?"

He had come nearer now, and she saw that something of light and hope had gone out of his face. And then Hobert made twenty excuses, — there was n't anything the matter, he said, but the plough was dull, and the ground wet and heavy, and full of green roots; besides, the flies were bad, and the mare tired.

"But you look so worn out, I am afraid you are sick, yourself!" interposed the good wife; and she went close to him, and pushed the hair, growing thinner now, away from his forehead, and looked anxiously in his face, — so anxiously, so tenderly, that he felt constrained to relieve her fears, even at some expense of the truth.

"Not to look well in your eyes is bad enough," he answered, with forced cheerfulness, "but I feel all right; never better, never better, Jenny!" And stooping to his little daughter, who was holding his knees, he caught her up, and tossed her high in the air, but put her down at once, seeming almost to let her fall out of his hands, and, catching for breath, leaned against the well-curb.

"What is it, Hobert? what is it?" and Jenny had her arm about him, and was drawing him toward the house.

"Nothing, nothing, — a touch of rheumatism, I guess, — no, no! I

must take care of the mare first." And as she drank the water from the full bucket he held poised on the curb for her, he thought of the elm-tree in the field he had left, of the mistletoe sucking the life out of it, and of the unfinished furrow. "Never mind, Fleety," he said, as he led her away to the stable, "we 'll be up betimes to-morrow, and make amends, won't we?"

"I believe, mother, I 'll put on the new teacups!" Jenny said, as she set a chair before the cupboard, and climbed on it so as to reach the upper shelf. She had already spread the best table-cloth.

"Why, what for?" asked the provident mother, looking up from the sock she was knitting.

"O, I don't know; I want to make things look nice, that 's all."

But she did know, though the feeling was only half defined. It seemed to her as if Hobert were some visitor coming, — not her husband. A shadowy feeling of insecurity had touched her; the commonness of custom was gone, and she looked from the window often, as the preparation for supper went on, with all the sweetness of solicitude with which she used to watch for his coming from under the grape-vines. Little Jenny was ready with the towel when he came with his face dripping, and the easy-chair was set by the door that looked out on the garden. "I don't want it," the good grandmother said, as he hesitated; "I have been sitting in it all day, and am tired of it!"

And as he sat there with his boy on his knee, and his little girl, who had climbed up behind him, combing his hair with her slender white fingers, — his own fields before him, and his busy wife making music about the house with her cheerful, hopeful talk, — he looked like a man to be envied; and so just then he was.

The next morning he did not fulfil his promise to himself by rising early; he had been restless and feverish all night, and now was chilly. If he lay till breakfast was ready, he would feel better, Jenny said ; she could milk, to be sure, and do all the rest of the work, and so he was persuaded. But when the breakfast was ready the chilliness had become a downright chill, so that the blankets that were over him shook like leaves in a strong wind.

Jenny had a little money of her own hidden away in the bottom of the new cream-pitcher. She had saved it, unknown to Hobert, from the sale of eggs and other trifles, and had meant to surprise him by appearing in a new dress some morning when the church-bell rang ; but now she turned the silver into her hand and counted it, thinking what nice warm flannel it would buy to make shirts for Hobert. Of course he had them, and Jenny had not made any sacrifice that she knew of, — indeed, that is a word of which love knows not the meaning.

"We will have him up in a day or two," the women said, one to the other, as they busied themselves about the house, or sat at the bedside, doing those things that only the blessed hands of women can do, making those plans that only the loving hearts of women can make. But the day or two went by, and they did n't have Hobert up. Then they said to one another, "We must set to work in earnest ; we have really done nothing for him as yet." And they plied their skill of nursing with new hope and new energy. Every morning he told them he was better, but in the afternoon it happened that he did n't feel quite like stirring about ; he was still better, but he had a little headache, and was afraid of bringing on a chill.

"To be sure ! you need 'rest and quiet ; you have been working too hard, and it 's only a wonder you did n't give out sooner !" So the two women said to him ; and then they told him he looked better than he did yesterday, and, with much tender little caressing of neck and arms and hands, assured him that his flesh felt as healthy and nice as could be. Nevertheless, his eyes settled deeper and deeper, and gathered more and more of

a leaden color about them ; his skin grew yellow, and fell into wrinkles that were almost rigid, and that beseeching, yearning expression, made up of confidence in you, and terror of some nameless thing, — that look, as of a soul calling and crying to you, which follows you when you go farther than common from a sick-pillow, — all that terrible appealing was in his face ; and often Jenny paused with her eyes away from him, when she saw that look, — paused, and steadied up her heart, before she could turn back and meet him with a smile.

And friendly neighbors came in of an evening, and told of the sick wife or boy at home ; of the mildewed crop, and the lamed horse ; of the brackish well, and of the clock bought from the pedler that would n't go, and would n't strike when it did go ; — dwelling, in short, on all the darker incidents and accidents of life, and thus establishing a nearness and equality of relation to the sick man, that somehow soothed and cheered him. At these times he would be propped up in bed, and listen with sad satisfaction, sometimes himself entering with a sort of melancholy animation into the subject.

He would not as yet accept any offers of assistance. The wood-pile was getting low, certainly, and the plough still lying slantwise in the furrow ; the corn-crop was to be gathered, and the potatoes to be got out of the ground, — but there was time enough yet ! He did n't mean to indulge his laziness much longer, — not he !

And then the neighbor who had offered to serve him would laugh, and answer that he had not been altogether disinterested : he had only proposed to *lend* a helping hand, expecting to need the like himself some day. "Trouble comes to us all, Mr. Walker, and we don't know whose turn it will be next. I want to take out a little insurance, — that 's all !"

"Well, another day, if I don't get better !"

And the long hot rains were over at last ; the clouds drew themselves off, and the sharp frosts, of a morning, were glistening far and near ; the pumpkin-vines lay black along the ground, and the ungathered ears of corn hung black on the stalk.

Hobert was no better. But still the two women told each other they did n't think he was any worse. His disease was only an ague, common to the time of year and to the new country. It had come on so late it was not likely now that he would get the better of it before spring ; making some little sacrifices for the present, they must all be patient and wait ; and the nursing went on, till every device of nursing was exhausted, and one remedy after another was tried, and one after another utterly failed, and the fond hearts almost gave out. But there was the winter coming on, cold and long, and there was little Hobert, only beginning to stand alone, and prattling Jenny, with the toes coming through her shoes, and her shoulder showing flat and thin above her summer dress. Ah ! there could be no giving out ; the mother's petticoat must be turned into aprons for the pinched shoulders, and the knit-wool stockings must make amends for the worn-out shoes. So they worked, and work was their greatest blessing. A good many things were done without consulting Hobert at all, and he was led to believe that all went easily and comfortably ; the neighbors, from time to time, lent the helping hand, without so much as asking leave ; and by these means there were a few potatoes in the cellar, a little corn in the barn, and a load of wood under the snow at the door.

The table was not spread in the sick-room any more, as it had been for a while. They had thought it would amuse Hobert to see the little household ceremonies going on ; but now they said it was better to avoid all unnecessary stir. Perhaps they thought it better that he should not see their scantier fare. Still they came into his presence very cheerfully, never hinting of hardship, never breathing the apprehension that began to trouble their hearts.

It was during these long winter evenings, when the neighbors sat by the fire and did what they could to cheer the sick man and the sad women, that the wonderful merits of the great Doctor Kill-many began to be frequently discussed. Marvellous stories were told of his almost superhuman skill. He had brought back from the very gate of death scores of men and women who had been given up to die by their physicians, — so it was said ; and special instances of cures were related that were certainly calculated to inspire hope and confidence. None of these good people could of their own knowledge attest these wonderful cures ; but there were many circumstances that added weight to the force of the general rumor.

Dr. Killmany lived a great way off, and he charged a great price. He would not look at a man for less than a hundred dollars, so report said, and that was much in his favor. He had a very short way with patients, — asked no questions, and never listened to explanations, — but could tie down a man and take off his leg or arm, as the case might be, in an incredibly short space of time, paying as little heed to the cries and groans as to the buzzing of the flies. If anything further had been needed to establish his fame, it would have been found in the fact that he was very rich, wearing diamonds in his shirt-bosom, driving fine horses, and being, in fact, surrounded with all the luxuries that money can procure. Of course, he was a great doctor. How could it be otherwise ? And it was enough to know that a Mr. A had seen a Mr. B who knew a Mr. C whose wife's mother was cured by him !

At first these things were talked of in hearing of the sick man ; then there began to be whispers about the fire as to the possibility of persuading him to sell all that he had and go to the great Doctor ; for it was now pretty generally felt that the ague was only the accompaniment of a more terrible disease.

Then at last it was suggested, as a wild pleasantry, by some daring visitor,

"Suppose, Hobert, we should send you off one of these days, and have you back after a few weeks, sound and vigorous as a young colt! What should you say to that, my boy?"

To the surprise of everybody, Hobert replied that he only wished it were possible.

"Possible! Why, of course it 's possible! Where there 's a will, you know!" And then it began to be talked of less as an insane dream.

One morning, as Jenny came into the sick man's room, she found him sitting up in bed with his shirt open and his hand on his breast.

"What is it, Hobert?" she said; for there was a look in his eyes that made her tremble.

"I don't know, Jenny; but whatever it is, it will be my death," he answered, and, falling upon her shoulder, — for she had come close to him and had her arm about his neck, — he sobbed like a child.

The little hand was slipped under his, but Jenny said she could feel nothing; and I think she will be forgiven for that falsehood. He was sick, she said, worn out, and it was no wonder that strange fancies should take possession of him. She had neglected him too much; but now, though everything should go to pieces, he should have her first care, and her last care, and all her care; he should not be left alone any more to conjure up horrors; and when he said he was weak and foolish and ashamed of his tears, she pacified him with petting and with praises. He was everything that was right, everything that was strong and manly. A little more patience, and then it would be spring, and the sunshine would make him well. She put the hair away from his forehead, and told him how fair in the face he was grown; and then she shoved his sleeve to his elbow, and told him that his arms were almost as plump as they ever were; and so he was comforted, cheered even, and they talked over the plans and prospects of years to come. At last he fell asleep with a bright smile of hope in his face,

and Jenny stooped softly and kissed him, and, stealing away on tiptoe, hid herself from her good old mother and from the eyes of her children, and wept long and bitterly.

And the spring came, and Hobert crept out into the sunshine; but his cheek was pale, and his chest hollow, and there was more than the old listlessness upon him. As a tree that is dying will sometimes put forth sickly leaves and blossoms, and still be dying all the while, so it was with him. His hand was often on his breast, and his look often said, "This will be the death of me." The bees hummed in the flowers about his feet, the birds built their nests in the boughs above his head, and his children played about his knees; but his thoughts were otherwhere, — away beyond the dark river, away in that beautiful country where the inhabitants never say, "I am sick."

It was about midsummer that one Mrs. Brown, well known to Mrs. Walker's family, and to all the people of the neighborhood, as having suffered for many years with some strange malady which none of the doctors understood, sold the remnant of her property, having previously wasted nearly all she had upon physicians, and betook herself to the great Dr. Killmany. What her condition had actually been is not material to my story, nor is it necessary to say anything about the treatment she received at the hands of the great doctor. It is enough to say that it cost her her last dollar, — that she worked her slow way home as best she could, arriving there at last with shoes nearly off her feet and gown torn and faded, but with health considerably improved. That she had sold her last cow, and her feather-bed, and her tea-kettle, and her sheep-shears, and her grandfather's musket, all added wonderfully to the great doctor's reputation.

"You can't go to him if you don't go full-handed," said one to another; and he that heard it, and he that said it, laughed as though it were a good joke.

Some said he could see right through

a man: there was no need of words with him! And others, that he could take the brains out of the skull, or the bones out of the ankles, and leave the patient all the better for it. In short, there was nothing too extravagant to be said of him; and as for Mrs. Brown, the person who had seen her became semi-distinguished. She was invited all over the neighborhood, and her conversation was the most delightful of entertainments. Amongst the rest, she visited Mr. Walker; and through her instrumentality, his strong desire to see the great Dr. Killmany was shaped into purpose.

Two of the cows were sold, most of the farming implements, and such articles of household furniture as could be spared; and with all this the money realized was but a hundred and fifty dollars. Then Jenny proposed to sell her side-saddle; and when that was gone, she said Fleety might as well go with it. "If you only come home well, Hobert," she said, "we will soon be able to buy her back again; and if you don't — but you will!"

So Fleetfoot went with the rest; and when for the last time she was led up before the door, and ate grass from the lap of little Jenny, and put her neck down to the caressing hands of young Hobert, it was a sore trial to them all. She seemed half conscious herself, indeed, and exhibited none of her accustomed playfulness with the children, but stood in a drooping attitude, with her eye intent upon her master; and when they would have taken her away, she hung back, and, stretching her neck till it reached his knees, licked his hands with a tenderness that was pitiful to see.

"Don't, Hobert, don't take on about it," Jenny said, putting back the heart that was in her mouth; "we will have her back again, you know!"—and she gave Fleetfoot a little box on the ear that was half approval and half reproach, and so led Hobert back into the house.

And that day was the saddest they had yet seen. And that night, when the sick man was asleep, the two women talked together and cried together, and in the end got such comfort as women get out of great sacrifices and bitter tears.

They counted their little hoard. They had gathered three hundred dollars now, and there required to be yet as much more; and then they made plans as to what yet remained to be done. "We must mortgage the land," Jenny said, "that is all, — don't mind, mother. I don't mind anything, so that we only have Hobert well again." And then they talked of what they would do another year when they should be all together once more, and all well. "Think what Dr. Killmany has done for Mrs. Brown!" they said.

And now came busy days; and in the earnestness of the preparation the sorrow of the coming parting was in some sort dissipated. Hobert's wearing-apparel was all brought out, and turned and overturned, and the most and the best made of everything. The wedding coat and the wedding shirt were almost as good as ever, Jenny said; and when the one had been brushed and pressed, and the other done up, she held them up before them all, and commented upon them with pride and admiration. The fashions had changed a little, to be sure, but what of that? The new fashions were not so nice as the old ones, to her thinking. Hobert would look smart in the old garments, at any rate, and perhaps nobody would notice. She was only desirous that he should make a good impression on the Doctor. And all that could be done to that end was done, many friends contributing, by way of little presents, to the comfort and respectability of the invalid. "Here is a leather pouch," said one, "that I bought of a pedler the other day. I don't want it; but as you are going to travel, may be you can make use of it, Walker; take it, any how."

"I have got a new pair of saddle-bags," said the circuit-rider, "but I believe I like the old ones best. So, Brother Walker, you will oblige me by taking these off my hands. I find extra things more trouble to take care of than they are worth."

It was not proposed that Hobert should travel with a trunk, so the saddle-bags were just what was required.

"Here is a pair of shoes," said another. "Try them on, Walker, and see if you can wear them : they are too small for my clumsy feet !" They had been made by the village shoemaker to Mr. Walker's measure. Of course they fitted him, and of course he had them.

"I 'll bet you a new hat," said another, "that I come to see you ag'in, day after to-morrer, fur off as I live."

The day after the morrow he did not come : he was "onaccountably hendered," he said ; but when he did come he brought the new hat. He thought he would be as good as his word in one thing if not in another, and redeem his bet at any rate.

"I 'll bring my team : I want to go to town anyhow ; and we 'll all see you off together !" This was the offer of the farmer whose land adjoined Mr. Walker's ; and the day of departure was fixed, and the morning of the day saw everything in readiness.

"Hobert looks a'most like a storekeeper or a schoolmaster, don't he, mother ?" Jenny said, looking upon him proudly, when he was arrayed in the new hat and the wedding coat.

"Why, you are as spry as a boy !" exclaimed the farmer who was to drive them to town, seeing that Hobert managed to climb into the wagon without assistance. "I don't believe there is any need of Dr. Killmany, after all !" And the neighbors, as one after another they leaned over the sideboard of the wagon, and shook hands with Mr. Walker, made some cheerful and lighthearted remark, calculated to convey the impression that the leave-taking was a mere matter of form, and only for a day.

As Jenny looked back at the homestead, and thought of the possibilities, the tears would come ; but the owner of the team, determined to carry it bravely through, immediately gathered up the slack reins, and, with a lively crack of his whip, started the horses upon a brisk trot.

"Don't spare the money," Jenny entreated, as she put the pocket-book in Hobert's hand ; but she thought in her heart that Dr. Killmany would be touched when he saw her husband, and knew how far he had travelled to see him, and what sacrifices he had made to do so. "He must be good, if he is so great as they say," she argued ; "and perhaps Hobert may even bring home enough to buy back Fleety." This was a wild dream. And the last parting words were said, the last promises exacted and given ; the silent tears and the lingering looks all were past, and the farmer's wagon, with an empty chair by the side of Jenny's, rattled home again.

It was perhaps a month after this that a pale, sickly-looking man, with a pair of saddle-bags over his arm, went ashore from the steamboat Arrow of Light, just landed at New Orleans, and made his slow way along the wharf, crowded with barrels, boxes, and cotton-bales, and thence to the open streets. The sun was oppressively hot, and the new fur hat became almost intolerable, so that the sick man stopped more than once in the shade of some friendly tree, and, placing the saddlebags on the ground, wiped the sweat from his forehead, and looked wistfully at the strange faces that passed him by.

"Can you tell me, my friend," he said at last, addressing a slave-woman who was passing by with a great bundle on her head, — "Can you tell me where to find Doctor Killmany, who lives somewhere here ?"

The woman put her bundle on the ground, and, resting her hands on her hips, looked pitifully upon the stranger. "No, masser, cante say, not for sure," she answered. "I knows dar 's sich a doctor somewhars 'bout, but just whars I cante say, an' he 's a poor doctor fur the likes o' you, — don't have noffen to do with him, nohow."

"A poor doctor !" exclaimed the stranger. "Why, I understood he was the greatest doctor in the world ; and

I 've come all the way from the Wabash country to see him."

" Warbash ! whar 's dat ? Norf, reckon ; well you jes be gwine back Norf de fus boat, an dat 's de bery bes' advice dis yere nigger can guv."

" But what do you know about Dr. Killmany."

" I knows dis yere, masser : he mos'ly sends dem ar' as ar' doctored by him to dar homes in a box ! "

Mr. Walker shuddered. " I don't want your advice," he said directly ; " I only want to know where Dr. Killmany lives."

" Cante say, masser, not percisely, as to dat ar' ; kind o' seems to me he 's done gone from hur, clar an' all ; but jes over thar 's a mighty good doctor ; you can see his name afore the door if you 'll step this yere way a bit. He doctors all de pour, an' dem dat ar' halt, and dem dat ar' struck with paralasy, jes for de love ob de ark and de covenant ; an' he 's jes de purtiest man to look at dat you ever sot eyes onto. Go in dar whar ye sees de white bline at de winder an' ax for Dr. Shepard, an' when you 's once seen him, I reckon you won't want to find de udder man ; but if you does, why he can pint de way. An' de Lord bless you and hab mercy on your soul."

The sick man felt a good deal discouraged by what the old slave had said, and her last words impressed him with feelings of especial discomfort. He knew not which way to turn ; and, in fact, found himself growing dizzy and blind, and was only able, with great effort, to stand at all. He must ask his way somewhere, however, and it might as well be there as another place.

Dr. Shepard, who happened to be in his office, answered the inquiry promptly. Dr. Killmany was in quite another part of the city. " You don't look able to walk there, my good friend," he said ; "but if you will sit here and wait for an hour, I shall be driving that way, and will take you with pleasure."

Mr. Walker gratefully accepted the proffered chair, as indeed he was almost obliged to do ; for within a few minutes the partial blindness had become total darkness, and the whole world seemed, as it were, slipping away from him.

When he came to himself he was lying on a sofa in an inner room, and Dr. Shepard, who had just administered some cordial, was bending over him in the most kindly and sympathetic manner. It seemed not so much what he said, not so much what he did, but as though he carried about him an atmosphere of sweetness and healing that comforted and assured without words and without medicine. He made no pretence and no noise, but his smile was sunshine to the heart, and the touch of his hand imparted strength and courage to the despairing soul. It was as if good spirits went with him, and his very silence was pleasant company. Mr. Walker was in no haste to be gone. All his anxious cares seemed to fall away, and a peaceful sense of comfort and security came over him ; his eyes followed Dr. Shepard as he moved about, and when a door interposed between them he felt lost and homesick. " If this were the man I had come to see, I should be happy." That was his thought all the while. Perhaps — who shall say not ? — it was the blessings of the poor, to whom he most generously ministered, which gave to his manner that graciousness and charm which no words can convey, and to his touch that magnetism which is at once life-giving and love-inspiring.

How it was Mr. Walker could not tell, and indeed wiser men than he could not have told, but he presently found himself opening his heart to this new doctor, as he had never opened it to anybody in all his life, — how he had married Jenny, how they had gone to the new country, the birth of the boy and the girl, the slow coming on of disease, the selling of Fleety, and the mortgaging of the farm. Doctor Shepard knew it all, and, more than this, he knew how much money had been accumulated, and how much of it was still left. He had examined the tumor in the breast, and knew that it could end in but one way. He had told Mr. Walker that he could be made more comfortable, and might live for years, perhaps, but that he must not hope to be cured, and that to get home to his family with all possible speed was the best advice he could give him. His words carried with them the weight of conviction, and the sick man was almost persuaded; but the thought of what would be said at home if he should come back without having seen the great Dr. Killmany urged him to try one last experiment.

"What do you suppose he will charge me to look at this?" he inquired of Dr. Shepard, laying his hand on his breast.

"Half you have, my friend."

"And if he cuts it out?"

"The other half."

"O, dear me!"—and the sick man fell back upon the sofa, and for a good while thought to himself. Then came one of those wild suggestions of a vain hope. "Perhaps this man is the impostor, and not the other!" it said. "And what do I owe you for all you have done for me to-day?" he inquired.

"Why, nothing, my good friend. I have done nothing for you; and my advice has certainly been disinterested. I don't want pay for that."

"And suppose you should operate?"

And then the doctor told him that he could not do that on any terms,—that no surgeon under the sun could perform a successful operation,—that all his hope was in quiet and care. "I will keep you here a few days," he said, "and build you up all I can, and when the Arrow of Light goes back again, I will see you aboard, and bespeak the kind attentions of the captain for you on the journey." That was not much like an impostor, and in his heart the sick man knew it was the right course to take,—the only course; and then he thought of Mrs. Brown and her wonderful cure, and of the great hopes they were entertaining

at home, and he became silent, and again thought to himself.

Three days he remained with Dr. Shepard, undecided, and resting and improving a little all the while. On the morning of the fourth day he said, placing his hand on his breast, "If I were only rid of this, I believe I should get quite well again." He could not give up the great Dr. Killmany. "I do not intend to put myself in his hands,—indeed, I am almost resolved that I will not do so," he said to Dr. Shepard; "but I will just call at his office, so that I can tell my folks I have seen him."

"I must not say more to discourage you," replied Dr. Shepard; "perhaps I have already said too much,—certainly I have said much more than it is my habit to say, more than in any ordinary circumstances I would permit myself to say; but in your case I have felt constrained to acquit myself to my conscience";—and he turned away with a shadow of the tenderest and saddest gloom upon his face.

"Are you, sir, going to Dr. Killmany?" asked an old man, who had been sitting by, eying Mr. Walker with deep concern; and on receiving an affirmative nod, he went on with zeal, if not with discretion: "Then, sir, you might as well knock your own brains out! I regard him, sir, as worse than a highway robber,—a good deal worse! The robber will sometimes spare your life, if he can as well as not, but Dr. Killmany has no more regard for human life than you have for that of a fly. He has a skilful hand to be sure, but his heart is as hard as flint. In short, sir, he is utterly without conscience, without humanity, without principle. Gain is his first object, his last object, his sole object; and if he ever did any good, it was simply incidental. Don't put yourself in his hands, whatever you do,—certainly not without first making your will!" And the old man, with a flushed and angry countenance, went away.

Presently the sick man, relapsing

into silent thought, drowsed into sleep, and a strange dream came to him. He seemed at home, sitting under the tree with the mistletoe in its boughs; he was tired and hungry, and there came to him a raven with food in its mouth, and the shadow of its wings was pleasant. He thought, at first, the food was for him; but the bird, perching on his shoulder, devoured the food, and afterward pecked at his breast until it opened a way to his heart, and with that in its claws flew away; and when it was gone, he knew it was not a bird, but that it was Dr. Killmany who had thus taken out his heart. "I will go home," he thought, "and tell Jenny"; and when he arose and put his hand on the neck of Fleety, who had been standing in the furrow close by, she became a shadow, and instantly vanished out of sight. He then strove to walk, and, lo! the strength was gone out of his limbs, and, as he sank down, the roots of the mistletoe struck in his bosom, ran through and through him, and fastened themselves in the earth beneath, and he became as one dead, only with the consciousness of being dead.

When he awoke, he related the dream, having given it, as it appeared, a melancholy interpretation, for he expressed himself determined to return home immediately. "I will take passage on the Arrow," he said to Dr. Shepard; and then he counted up the number of days that must go by before he could have his own green fields beneath his eyes, and his little ones climbing about his knees.

"I wish I had never left my home," he said; "I wish I had never heard of Dr. Killmany!" and then he returned to his dream and repeated portions of it; and then he said, seeming to be thinking aloud, "My good old mother! my dear, poor Jenny!"

"The sick man's brain is liable to strange fancies," says Dr. Shepard; "you must not think too seriously of it, but your resolve is very wise." He then said he would see the captain of the Arrow, as he had promised, and

went away with a smile on his face, and a great weight lifted off his heart.

A few minutes after this, Hobert Walker was again in the street, the heavy fur hat on his head, and the well-filled saddle-bags across his arm.

Perhaps sickness is in some sort insanity. At any rate, he no sooner found himself alone than the desire to see the great Dr. Killmany came upon him with all the force of insanity; his intention probably being to go and return within an hour, and keep his little secret to himself. Perhaps, too, he wished to have it to say at home that he had seen the great man for himself, and decided against him of his own knowledge.

Dr. Killmany was found without much difficulty; but his rooms were crowded with patients, and there was no possibility of access to him for hours.

"It cannot be that so many are deceived," thought Hobert. "I will wait with the rest." Then came the encouraging hope, "What if I should go home cured, after all!" He felt almost as if Dr. Shepard had defrauded him out of two or three days, and talked eagerly with one and another, as patient after patient came forth from consultation with Dr. Killmany, all aglow with hope and animation. It was near sunset when his turn came. He had waited five hours, but it was come at last; and with his heart in his mouth, and his knees shaking under him, he stood face to face with the arbitrator of his destiny. There was no smile on the face of the man, no sweetness in his voice as he said, looking at Hobert from under scowling brows, "What brings *you*, sir? Tell it, and be brief: time with me is money."

Then Hobert, catching at a chair to sustain himself, for he was not asked to sit, explained his condition as well as fright and awkwardness would permit him to do; going back to the commencement of his disease, and entering unnecessarily into many particulars, as well as making superfluous mention of wife and mother. "It is n't with your wife and mother that I have to deal," interposed Dr. Killmany;—"dear to you, I dare say, but nothing to me, sir, — nothing at all. I have no time to devote to your relatives. Open your shirt, sir! there, that 'll do! A mere trifle, sir, but it is well you have come in time."

"Do you mean to say you can cure me?" inquired Hobert, all his heart a-flutter with the excitement of hope.

"Exactly so. I can remove that difficulty of yours in five minutes, and have you on your feet again, — operation neglected, death certain within a year, perhaps sooner. Done with you sir. You now have your choice, make way!"

Hobert went staggering out of the room, feeling as if the raven of his dream already had its beak in his heart, when a pert official reached out his hand with the demand, "Consultation fee, if you please, sir."

"How much?" asked Hobert, leaning against the wall, and searching for his pocket-book?

"Fifty dollars, sir," — and the official spoke as though that were a trifle scarcely worth mentioning. The hands of the sick man trembled, and his eyes grew blind as he sought to count up the sum; and as his entire treasure was formed out of the smallest notes, the process was a slow one, and before it was accomplished it seemed to him that not only Fleety was turning to a shadow, but the whole world as well.

Somehow, he hardly knew how, he found himself in the fresh air, and the official still at his elbow. "You are not going to leave us this way?" he said. "You will only have thrown your money away." And he pocketed the sum Hobert had just put in his hand.

"Better that than more," Hobert answered, and was turning sadly away.

"Allow me to detain you, sir, one moment, only just one moment!" And the official, or rather decoy, whispered in his ear tales of such wonderful cures as almost dissuaded him from his purpose.

"But I am resolved to go home on the Arrow," he said, making a last stand, "and I must have something to leave my poor Jenny."

And then the official told him that he could go home aboard the Arrow, if he chose, and go a well man, or the same as a well man; and what could he bring to his wife so acceptable as himself, safe and sound! And then he told other tales of sick men who had been carried to Dr. Killmany on their beds, and within a few hours walked away on their feet, blessing his name, and publishing his fame far and wide.

Hobert began to waver, nor is it strange; for what will not a man give for his life? The world had not loosened its hold upon him much as yet; the grass under his feet and the sunshine over his head were pleasant things to him, and his love for his good little wife was still invested with all the old romance; and to die and go he knew not where, there was a terror about that which his faith was not strong enough to dissipate. The decoy watched and waited. He contrasted the husband returning home with haggard cheek and listless step and the shadow of dark doom all about him, having a few hundred dollars in his pocket, with a husband empty-handed, but with bright cheeks, and cheerful spirits, and with strong legs under him! Then Hobert repeated the story he had told to Dr. Shepard, — all about the little treasure with which he had set out, how hardly it had been gathered together, what had been already fruitlessly expended, and just how much remained, — he told it all as he had told it in the first instance, but with what different effect!

Dr. Killmany never touched any case for a sum like that! Indeed, his services were in such requisition, it was almost impossible to obtain them on any terms; but he, the decoy, for reasons which he did not state, would exert to the utmost his own personal influence in Hobert's favor. "I cannot promise you a favorable answer," he said; "there is just a possibility, and that is all. A man like Dr. Killmany, sir, can't be haggling about dollars and cents!" And then he intimated that such things might be well enough for Dr. Shepard and his sort of practice.

There was some further talk, and the time ran by, and it was night. Against his will almost, Hobert had been persuaded. He was to sleep in the Doctor's office that night, and his case was to be the first attended to in the morning. "You can rest very well on the floor, I suppose," the decoy had said, "taking your saddle-bags for a pillow. The whole thing will be over in half an hour, and I myself will see you aboard the Arrow before ten o'clock, and so you need take no more thought for yourself."

That night, when at last Hobert made a pillow of his saddle-bags and coiled himself together, he felt as if a circle of fire were narrowing around him, and yet utter inability to escape.

"You need take no more thought for yourself." These words kept ringing in his ears like a knell, and the mistletoe striking through his bosom, and the beak of the raven in his heart, — these were the sensations with which, long after midnight, he drowsed into sleep.

When he awoke, there was a rough hand on his shoulder and a harsh voice in his ear. The room was light with the light of morning, but dark with the shadow of coming doom. There came upon him a strange and great calmness when he found himself in the operating-room. There were all the frightful preparations, — the water, the sponges, the cloths and bandages, the Doctor with his case of instruments before him, and looking more like a murderer than a surgeon. Almost his heart misgave him as he looked around, and remembered Jenny and the little ones at home; but the carriage that was to take him aboard the Arrow already waited at the door, and the sight of it reassured him.

"You will hardly know where you are till you find yourself safe in your berth," said Dr. Killmany; "and to avoid any delay after the operation, from which you will necessarily be somewhat weak, you had perhaps bet-

ter pay me now." And these were the most civil words he had yet spoken.

So Hobert paid into his hand the last dollar he had.

"Now, sir," he said; and Hobert laid himself down on the table. A minute, and of what befell him after that he was quite unconscious. It was as the doctor had told him; he knew not where he was until he found himself in his berth aboard the Arrow. "Where am I?" was his first inquiry, feeling a sense of strangeness, — feeling, indeed, as though he were a stranger to himself.

"You are going home, my poor friend, — going home a little sooner than you expected, — that is all."

Then the sick man opened his eyes; for he had recognized the tender voice, and saw Dr. Shepard bending over him, and he knew where he was, and what had happened; for he was shivering from head to foot. The sleeve of his right arm was red and wet, and there was a dull, slow aching in his bosom. "Ay, Doctor," he answered, pressing faintly the hand that held his, "I am going home, — home to a better country. 'T is all like a shadow about me now, and I am cold, — so cold!" He never came out of that chill, and these were the last words he ever spoke.

"That man has been just the same as murdered, I take it!" exclaimed the captain of the Arrow, meeting Dr. Shepard as he turned away from the bedside.

"I must not say that," replied the Doctor; "but if I had performed the operation, under the circumstances, I should think myself his murderer."

"And if you had taken his money, you would perhaps think yourself a thief, too! At any rate, I should think you one," was the answer of the captain. And he then related to Dr. Shepard how the man, in an almost dying condition, had been brought aboard the Arrow by one of Dr. Killmany's menials, hustled into bed, and so left to his fate; and he concluded by saying, "And what are we to do now, Doctor?"

What the Doctor's reply was need not

be reported at length. Suffice it to say, that the departure of the Arrow was deferred for an hour, and when she sailed the state-room in which Hobert had breathed his last was occupied by a lively little lady and two gayly-dressed children, and on the wall from which the fur hat and the saddle-bags had been removed fluttered a variety of rainbow-hued scarfs and ribbons, and in the window where the shadow had been a golden-winged bird was singing in the sunshine.

Some two or three weeks went by, and the farmer who had driven to town when Hobert was about to set out on his long journey, starting so smartly, and making so light of the farewells, drove thither again, and this time his wagon-bed was empty, except for the deep cushion of straw. He drove slowly and with downcast looks ; and as he returned, a dozen men met him at the entrance of the village, and at sober pace followed to the meeting-house, the door of which stood wide.

A little low talk as they all gathered round, and then four of them lifted from the wagon the long box it contained, and bore it on their shoulders reverently and tenderly within the open gate, through the wide door, along the solemn aisle and close beneath the pulpit, where they placed it very softly, and then stood back with uncovered heads, while a troop of little girls, who waited, with aprons full of flowers, drew near and emptied them on the ground, so that nothing was to be seen but a great heap of flowers ; and beneath them was the body of HOBERT WALKER

MY FARM: A FABLE.

WITHIN a green and pleasant land
    I own a favorite plantation,
Whose woods and meads, if rudely planned,
    Are still, at least, my own creation.
      Some genial sun or kindly shower
      Has here and there wooed forth a flower,
And touched the fields with expectation.

I know what feeds the soil I till,
    What harvest-growth it best produces.
My forests shape themselves at will,
    My grapes mature their proper juices.
      I know the brambles and the weeds,
      But know the fruits and wholesome seeds, —
Of those the hurt, of these the uses.

And working early, working late,
    Directing crude and random Nature,
'T is joy to see my small estate
    Grow fairer in the slightest feature.
      If but a single wild-rose blow,
      Or fruit-tree bend with April snow,
That day am I the happiest creature!

But round the borders of the land
  Dwell many neighbors, fond of roving;
With curious eye and prying hand
  About my fields I see them moving.
    Some tread my choicest herbage down,
    And some of weeds would weave a crown,
And bid me wear it, unreproving.

"What trees!" says one; "who ever saw
  A grove, like this, of *my* possessing?
This vale offends my upland's law;
  This sheltered garden needs suppressing.
    My rocks this grass would never yield,
    And how absurd the level field!
What here will grow is past my guessing."

"Behold the slope!" another cries:
  "No sign of bog or meadow near it!
A varied surface I despise:
  There's not a stagnant pool to cheer it!"
    "Why plough at all?" remarked a third.
    "Heaven help the man!" a fourth I heard, —
"His farm's a jungle: let him clear it!"

No friendly counsel I disdain:
  My fields are free to every comer;
Yet that, which one to praise is fain,
  But makes another's visage glummer.
    I bow them out, and welcome in,
    But while I seek some truth to win
Goes by, unused, the golden summer!

Ah! vain the hope to find in each
  The wisdom each denies the other;
These mazes of conflicting speech
  All theories of culture smother.
    I'll raise and reap, with honest hand,
    The native harvest of my land;
Do thou the same, my wiser brother!

PASSAGES FROM HAWTHORNE'S NOTE-BOOKS.

VIII.

CONCORD, *Saturday, August* 13, 1842. — My life, at this time, is more like that of a boy, externally, than it has been since I was really a boy. It is usually supposed that the cares of life come with matrimony; but I seem to have cast off all care, and live on with as much easy trust in Providence as Adam could possibly have felt before he had learned that there was a world beyond Paradise. My chief anxiety consists in watching the prosperity of my vegetables, in observing how they are affected by the rain or sunshine, in lamenting the blight of one squash and rejoicing at the luxurious growth of another. It is as if the original relation between man and Nature were restored in my case, and that I were to look exclusively to her for the support of my Eve and myself, — to trust to her for food and clothing, and all things needful, with the full assurance that she would not fail me. The fight with the world, — the struggle of a man among men, — the agony of the universal effort to wrench the means of living from a host of greedy competitors, — all this seems like a dream to me. My business is merely to live and to enjoy; and whatever is essential to life and enjoyment will come as naturally as the dew from heaven. This is, practically at least, my faith. And so I awake in the morning with a boyish thoughtlessness as to how the outgoings of the day are to be provided for, and its incomings rendered certain. After breakfast, I go forth into my garden, and gather whatever the bountiful Mother has made fit for our present sustenance; and of late days she generally gives me two squashes and a cucumber, and promises me green corn and shell-beans very soon. Then I pass down through our orchard to the river-side, and ramble along its margin in search of flowers.

Usually I discern a fragrant white lily, here and there along the shore, growing, with sweet prudishness, beyond the grasp of mortal arm. But it does not escape me so. I know what is its fitting destiny better than the silly flower knows for itself; so I wade in, heedless of wet trousers, and seize the shy lily by its slender stem. Thus I make prize of five or six, which are as many as usually blossom within my reach in a single morning; — some of them partially worm-eaten or blighted, like virgins with an eating sorrow at the heart; others as fair and perfect as Nature's own idea was, when she first imagined this lovely flower. A perfect pond-lily is the most satisfactory of flowers. Besides these, I gather whatever else of beautiful chances to be growing in the moist soil by the river-side, — an amphibious tribe, yet with more richness and grace than the wild-flowers of the deep and dry woodlands and hedge-rows, — sometimes the white arrow-head, always the blue spires and broad green leaves of the pickerel-flower, which contrast and harmonize so well with the white lilies. For the last two or three days, I have found scattered stalks of the cardinal-flower, the gorgeous scarlet of which it is a joy even to remember. The world is made brighter and sunnier by flowers of such a hue. Even perfume, which otherwise is the soul and spirit of a flower, may be spared when it arrays itself in this scarlet glory. It is a flower of thought and feeling, too; it seems to have its roots deep down in the hearts of those who gaze at it. Other bright flowers sometimes impress me as wanting sentiment; but it is not so with this.

Well, having made up my bunch of flowers, I return home with them. . . . . Then I ascend to my study, and generally read, or perchance scribble in this journal, and otherwise suffer Time to loiter onward at his own pleasure, till the dinner-hour. In pleasant days, the chief event of the afternoon, and the happiest one of the day, is our walk. . . . . So comes the night ; and I look back upon a day spent in what the world would call idleness, and for which I myself can suggest no more appropriate epithet, but which, nevertheless, I cannot feel to have been spent amiss. True, it might be a sin and shame, in such a world as ours, to spend a lifetime in this manner ; but for a few summer weeks it is good to live as if this world were heaven. And so it is, and so it shall be, although, in a little while, a flitting shadow of earthly care and toil will mingle itself with our realities.

Monday, August 15th. — George Hillard and his wife arrived from Boston in the dusk of Saturday evening, to spend Sunday with us. It was a pleasant sensation, when the coach rumbled up our avenue, and wheeled round at the door ; for I felt that I was regarded as a man with a household, — a man having a tangible existence and locality in the world, — when friends came to avail themselves of our hospitality. It was a sort of acknowledgment and reception of us into the corps of married people, — a sanction by no means essential to our peace and well-being, but yet agreeable enough to receive. So we welcomed them cordially at the door, and ushered them into our parlor, and soon into the supper-room. . . . . The night flitted over us all, and passed away, and up rose a gray and sullen morning, ... and we had a splendid breakfast of flapjacks, or slapjacks, and whortleberries, which I gathered on a neighboring hill, and perch, bream, and pout, which I hooked out of the river the evening before. About nine o'clock, Hillard and I set out for a walk to Walden Pond, calling by the way at Mr. Emerson's, to obtain his guidance or directions, and he accompanied us in his own illustrious person. We turned aside a little from

our way, to visit Mr. ——, a yeoman, of whose homely and self-acquired wisdom Mr. Emerson has a very high opinion. We found him walking in his fields, a short and stalwart and sturdy personage of middle age, with a face of shrewd and kind expression, and manners of natural courtesy. He had a very free flow of talk, and not much diffidence about his own opinions ; for, with a little induction from Mr. Emerson, he began to discourse about the state of the nation, agriculture, and business in general, uttering thoughts that had come to him at the plough, and which had a sort of flavor of the fresh earth about them. I was not impressed with any remarkable originality in his views ; but they were sensible and characteristic, and had grown in the soil where we found them ; . . . . and he is certainly a man of intellectual and moral substance, a sturdy fact, a reality, something to be felt and touched, whose ideas seem to be dug out of his mind as he digs potatoes, beets, carrots, and turnips out of the ground.

After leaving Mr. ——, we proceeded through wood paths to Walden Pond, picking blackberries of enormous size along the way. The pond itself was beautiful and refreshing to my soul, after such long and exclusive familiarity with our tawny and sluggish river. It lies embosomed among wooded hills, — it is not very extensive, but large enough for waves to dance upon its surface, and to look like a piece of blue firmament, earth-encircled. The shore has a narrow, pebbly strand, which it was worth a day's journey to look at, for the sake of the contrast between it and the weedy, oozy margin of the river. Farther within its depths, you perceive a bottom of pure white sand, sparkling through the transparent water, which, methought, was the very purest liquid in the world. After Mr. Emerson left us, Hillard and I bathed in the pond, and it does really seem as if my spirit, as well as corporeal person, were refreshed by that bath. A good deal of mud and river slime had accumulated on my soul ;

but these bright waters washed it all away.

We returned home in due season for dinner. . . . . To my misfortune, however, a box of Mediterranean wine proved to have undergone the acetous fermentation ; so that the splendor of the festival suffered some diminution. Nevertheless, we ate our dinner with a good appetite, and afterwards went universally to take our several siestas. Meantime there came a shower, which so besprinkled the grass and shrubbery as to make it rather wet for our after-tea ramble. The chief result of the walk was the bringing home of an immense burden of the trailing clematis-vine, now just in blossom, and with which all our flower-stands and vases are this morning decorated. On our return we found Mr. and Mrs. S——, and E. H——, who shortly took their leave, and we sat up late, telling ghost-stories. This morning, at seven, our friends left us. We were both pleased with the visit, and so I think were our guests.

Monday, August 22d. — I took a walk through the woods yesterday afternoon, to Mr. Emerson's, with a book which Margaret Fuller had left, after a call on Saturday eve. I missed the nearest way, and wandered into a very secluded portion of the forest ; for forest it might justly be called, so dense and sombre was the shade of oaks and pines. Once I wandered into a tract so overgrown with bushes and underbrush that I could scarcely force a passage through. Nothing is more annoying than a walk of this kind, where one is tormented by an innumerable host of petty impediments. It incenses and depresses me at the same time. Always when I flounder into the midst of bushes, which cross and intertwine themselves about my legs, and brush my face, and seize hold of my clothes, with their multitudinous grip, — always, in such a difficulty, I feel as if it were almost as well to lie down and die in rage and despair as to go one step farther. It is laughable, after I have got out of the moil, to think how miserably it affected me for the moment ; but I had better learn patience betimes, for there are many such bushy tracts in this vicinity, on the margins of meadows, and my walks will often lead me into them. Escaping from the bushes, I soon came to an open space among the woods, — a very lovely spot, with the tall old trees standing around as quietly as if no one had intruded there throughout the whole summer. A company of crows were holding their Sabbath on their summits. Apparently they felt themselves injured or insulted by my presence ; for, with one consent, they began to Caw! caw! caw! and, launching themselves sullenly on the air, took flight to some securer solitude. Mine, probably, was the first human shape that they had seen all day long, — at least, if they had been stationary in that spot ; but perhaps they had winged their way over miles and miles of country, had breakfasted on the summit of Greylock, and dined at the base of Wachusett, and were merely come to sup and sleep among the quiet woods of Concord. But it was my impression at the time, that they had sat still and silent on the tops of the trees all through the Sabbath day, and I felt like one who should unawares disturb an assembly of worshippers. A crow, however, has no real pretensions to religion, in spite of his gravity of mien and black attire. Crows are certainly thieves, and probably infidels. Nevertheless, their voices yesterday were in admirable accordance with the influences of the quiet, sunny, warm, yet autumnal afternoon. They were so far above my head that their loud clamor added to the quiet of the scene, instead of disturbing it. There was no other sound, except the song of the cricket, which is but an audible stillness ; for, though it be very loud and heard afar, yet the mind does not take note of it as a sound, so entirely does it mingle and lose its individuality among the other characteristics of coming autumn. Alas for the summer! The grass is still verdant on the hills and in the valleys ;

the foliage of the trees is as dense as ever, and as green ; the flowers are abundant along the margin of the river, and in the hedge-rows, and deep among the woods ; the days, too, are as fervid as they were a month ago ; and yet in every breath of wind and in every beam of sunshine there is an autumnal influence. I know not how to describe it. Methinks there is a sort of coolness amid all the heat, and a mildness in the brightest of the sunshine. A breeze cannot stir, without thrilling me with the breath of autumn, and I behold its pensive glory in the far, golden gleams among the long shadows of the trees. The flowers, even the brightest of them, — the golden-rod and the gorgeous cardinals, — the most glorious flowers of the year, — have this gentle sadness amid their pomp. Pensive autumn is expressed in the glow of every one of them. I have felt this influence earlier in some years than in others. Sometimes autumn may be perceived even in the early days of July. There is no other feeling like that caused by this faint, doubtful, yet real perception, or rather prophecy, of the year's decay, so deliciously sweet and sad at the same time.

After leaving the book at Mr. Emerson's I returned through the woods, and, entering Sleepy Hollow, I perceived a lady reclining near the path which bends along its verge. It was Margaret herself. She had been there the whole afternoon, meditating or reading ; for she had a book in her hand, with some strange title, which I did not understand, and have forgotten. She said that nobody had broken her solitude, and was just giving utterance to a theory that no inhabitant of Concord ever visited Sleepy Hollow, when we saw a group of people entering the sacred precincts. Most of them followed a path which led them away from us ; but an old man passed near us, and smiled to see Margaret reclining on the ground, and me sitting by her side. He made some remark about the beauty of the afternoon, and withdrew himself into the shadow of the wood.

Then we talked about autumn, and about the pleasures of being lost in the woods, and about the crows, whose voices Margaret had heard ; and about the experiences of early childhood, whose influence remains upon the character after the recollection of them has passed away ; and about the sight of mountains from a distance, and the view from their summits ; and about other matters of high and low philosophy. In the midst of our talk, we heard footsteps above us, on the high bank ; and while the person was still hidden among the trees, he called to Margaret, of whom he had gotten a glimpse. Then he emerged from the green shade, and, behold ! it was Mr. Emerson. He appeared to have had a pleasant time ; for he said that there were Muses in the woods to-day, and whispers to be heard in the breezes. It being now nearly six o'clock, we separated, — Margaret and Mr. Emerson towards his home, and I towards mine. . . . .

Last evening there was the most beautiful moonlight that ever hallowed this earthly world ; and when I went to bathe in the river, which was as calm as death, it seemed like plunging down into the sky. But I had rather be on earth than even in the seventh heaven, just now.

Wednesday, August 24th. — I left home at five o'clock this morning to catch some fish for breakfast. I shook our summer apple-tree, and ate the golden apple which fell from it. Methinks these early apples, which come as a golden promise before the treasures of autumnal fruit, are almost more delicious than anything that comes afterwards. We have but one such tree in our orchard ; but it supplies us with a daily abundance, and probably will do so for at least a week to come. Meantime other trees begin to cast their ripening windfalls upon the grass ; and when I taste them, and perceive their mellowed flavor and blackening seeds, I feel somewhat overwhelmed with the impending bounties of Providence. I suppose Adam, in Paradise, did not like to see his fruits decaying on the ground, after he had watched them through the sunny days of the world's first summer. However, insects, at the worst, will hold a festival upon them, so that they will not be thrown away, in the great scheme of Nature. Moreover, I have one advantage over the primeval Adam, inasmuch as there is a chance of disposing of my superfluous fruits among people who inhabit no Paradise of their own.

Passing a little way down along the river-side, I threw in my line, and soon drew out one of the smallest possible of fishes. It seemed to be a pretty good morning for the angler, — an autumnal coolness in the air, a clear sky, but with a fog across the lowlands and on the surface of the river, which a gentle breeze sometimes condensed into wreaths. At first I could barely discern the opposite shore of the river; but, as the sun arose, the vapors gradually dispersed, till only a warm, smoky tint was left along the water's surface. The farm-houses across the river made their appearance out of the dusky cloud; the voices of boys were heard, shouting to the cattle as they drove them to the pastures; a man whetted his scythe, and set to work in a neighboring meadow. Meantime, I continued to stand on the oozy margin of the stream, beguiling the little fish; and though the scaly inhabitants of our river partake somewhat of the character of their native element, and are but sluggish biters, still I contrived to pull out not far from two dozen. They were all bream, a broad, flat, almost circular fish, shaped a good deal like a flounder, but swimming on their edges, instead of on their sides. As far as mere pleasure is concerned, it is hardly worth while to fish in our river, it is so much like angling in a mud-puddle; and one does not attach the idea of freshness and purity to the fishes, as we do to those which inhabit swift, transparent streams, or haunt the shores of the great briny deep. Standing on the weedy margin, and throwing the line

over the elder-bushes that dip into the water, it seems as if we could catch nothing but frogs and mud-turtles, or reptiles akin to them. And even when a fish of reputable aspect is drawn out, one feels a shyness about touching him. As to our river, its character was admirably expressed last night by some one who said "it was too lazy to keep itself clean." I might write pages and pages, and only obscure the impression which this brief sentence conveys. Nevertheless, we made bold to eat some of my fish for breakfast, and found them very savory; and the rest shall meet with due entertainment at dinner, together with some shell-beans, green corn, and cucumbers from our garden; so this day's food comes directly and entirely from beneficent Nature, without the intervention of any third person between her and us.

Saturday, August 27th. — A peach-tree, which grows beside our house and brushes against the window, is so burdened with fruit that I have had to prop it up. I never saw more splendid peaches in appearance, — great, round, crimson-cheeked beauties, clustering all over the tree. A pear-tree, likewise, is maturing a generous burden of small, sweet fruit, which will require to be eaten at about the same time as the peaches. There is something pleasantly annoying in this superfluous abundance; it is like standing under a tree of ripe apples, and giving it a shake, with the intention of bringing down a single one, when, behold, a dozen come thumping about our ears. But the idea of the infinite generosity and exhaustless bounty of our Mother Nature is well worth attaining; and I never had it so vividly as now, when I find myself, with the few mouths which I am to feed, the sole inheritor of the old clergyman's wealth of fruits. His children, his friends in the village, and the clerical guests who came to preach in his pulpit, were all wont to eat and be filled from these trees. Now, all these hearty old people have passed away, and in their stead is a solitary pair, whose appetites are more than satisfied with the windfalls which the trees throw down at their feet. Howbeit, we shall have now and then a guest to keep our peaches and pears from decaying.

G—— B——, my old fellow-laborer at the community at Brook Farm, called on me last evening, and dined here to-day. He has been cultivating vegetables at Plymouth this summer, and selling them in the market. What a singular mode of life for a man of education and refinement, — to spend his days in hard and earnest bodily toil, and then to convey the products of his labor, in a wheelbarrow, to the public market, and there retail them out, — a peck of peas or beans, a bunch of turnips, a squash, a dozen ears of green corn! Few men, without some eccentricity of character, would have the moral strength to do this; and it is very striking to find such strength combined with the utmost gentleness, and an uncommon regularity of nature. Occasionally he returns for a day or two to resume his place among scholars and idle people, as, for instance, the present week, when he has thrown aside his spade and hoe to attend the Commencement at Cambridge. He is a rare man, — a perfect original, yet without any one salient point; a character to be felt and understood, but almost impossible to describe : for, should you seize upon any characteristic, it would inevitably be altered and distorted in the process of writing it down.

Our few remaining days of summer have been latterly grievously darkened with clouds. To-day there has been an hour or two of hot sunshine ; but the sun rose amid cloud and mist, and before he could dry up the moisture of last night's shower upon the trees and grass, the clouds have gathered between him and us again. This afternoon the thunder rumbles in the distance, and I believe a few drops of rain have fallen ; but the weight of the shower has burst elsewhere, leaving us nothing but its sullen gloom. There is a muggy warmth in the atmosphere, which takes all the spring and vivacity out of the mind and body.

Sunday, August 28th. — Still another rainy day, — the heaviest rain, I believe, that has fallen since we came to Concord (not two months ago). There never was a more sombre aspect of all external nature. I gaze from the open window of my study, somewhat disconsolately, and observe the great willow-tree which shades the house, and which has caught and retained a whole cataract of rain among its leaves and boughs ; and all the fruit-trees, too, are dripping continually, even in the brief intervals when the clouds give us a respite. If shaken to bring down the fruit, they will discharge a shower upon the head of him who stands beneath. The rain is warm, coming from some southern region ; but the willow attests that it is an autumnal spell of weather, by scattering down no infrequent multitude of yellow leaves, which rest upon the sloping roof of the house, and strew the gravel-path and the grass. The other trees do not yet shed their leaves, though in some of them a lighter tint of verdure, tending towards yellow, is perceptible. All day long we hear the water drip, drip, dripping, splash, splash, splashing, from the eaves, and babbling and foaming into the tubs which have been set out to receive it. The old unpainted shingles and boards of the mansion and out-houses are black with the moisture which they have imbibed. Looking at the river, we perceive that its usually smooth and mirrored surface is blurred by the infinity of rain-drops ; the whole landscape — grass, trees, and houses — has a completely water-soaked aspect, as if the earth were wet through. The wooded hill, about a mile distant, whither we went to gather whortleberries, has a mist upon its summit, as if the demon of the rain were enthroned there ; and if we look to the sky, it seems as if all the water that had been poured down upon us were as nothing to what is to come. Once in a while, indeed, there is a gleam of sky along the horizon, or a half-cheerful, half-sullen lighting up of the atmosphere ; the raindrops cease to patter down, except when the trees shake off a gentle shower; but soon we hear the broad, quiet, slow, and sure recommencement of the rain. The river, if I mistake not, has risen considerably during the day, and its current will acquire some degree of energy.

In this sombre weather, when some mortals almost forget that there ever was any golden sunshine, or ever will be any hereafter, others seem absolutely to radiate it from their own hearts and minds. The gloom cannot pervade them; they conquer it, and drive it quite out of their sphere, and create a moral rainbow of hope upon the blackest cloud. As for myself, I am little other than a cloud at such seasons, but such persons contrive to make me a sunny one, shining all through me. And thus, even without the support of a stated occupation, I survive these sullen days and am happy.

This morning we read the Sermon on the Mount. In the course of the forenoon, the rain abated for a season, and I went out and gathered some corn and summer-squashes, and picked up the windfalls of apples and pears and peaches. Wet, wet, wet, — everything was wet; the blades of the corn-stalks moistened me; the wet grass soaked my boots quite through; the trees threw their reserved showers upon my head; and soon the remorseless rain began anew, and drove me into the house. When shall we be able to walk again to the far hills, and plunge into the deep woods, and gather more cardinals along the river's margin? The track along which we trod is probably under water now. How inhospitable Nature is during a rain! In the fervid heat of sunny days, she still retains some degree of mercy for us; she has shady spots, whither the sun cannot come; but she provides no shelter against her storms. It makes one shiver to think how dripping with wet are those deep, umbrageous nooks, those overshadowed banks, where we find such enjoyment during sultry afternoons. And what becomes of the birds in such a soaking rain as this? Is hope and an instinctive faith so mixed up with their nature, that they can be cheered by the thought that the sunshine will return? or do they think, as I almost do, that there is to be no sunshine any more? Very disconsolate must they be among the dripping leaves; and when a single summer makes so important a portion of their lives, it seems hard that so much of it should be dissolved in rain. I, likewise, am greedy of the summer-days for my own sake: the life of man does not contain so many of them that one can be spared without regret.

Tuesday, August 30th.—I was promised, in the midst of Sunday's rain, that Monday should be fair, and, behold! the sun came back to us, and brought one of the most perfect days ever made since Adam was driven out of Paradise. By the by, was there ever any rain in Paradise? If so, how comfortless must Eve's bower have been! It makes me shiver to think of it. Well, it seemed as if the world was newly created yesterday morning, and I beheld its birth; for I had risen before the sun was over the hill, and had gone forth to fish. How instantaneously did all dreariness and heaviness of the earth's spirit flit away before one smile of the beneficent sun! This proves that all gloom is but a dream and a shadow, and that cheerfulness is the real truth. It requires many clouds, long brooding over us, to make us sad, but one gleam of sunshine always suffices to cheer up the landscape. The banks of the river actually laughed when the sunshine fell upon them; and the river itself was alive and cheerful, and, by way of fun and amusement, it had swept away many wreaths of meadow-hay, and old, rotten branches of trees, and all such trumpery. These matters came floating downwards, whirling round and round in the eddies, or hastening onward in the main current; and many of them, before this time, have probably been carried into the Merrimack, and will be borne onward to the sea. The spots where I stood to fish, on my preceding excursion, were now under water ; and the tops of many of the bushes, along the river's margin, barely emerged from the stream. Large spaces of meadow are overflowed.

There was a northwest wind throughout the day ; and as many clouds, the remnants of departed gloom, were scattered about the sky, the breeze was continually blowing them across the sun. For the most part, they were gone again in a moment ; but sometimes the shadow remained long enough to make me dread a return of sulky weather. Then would come the burst of sunshine, making me feel as if a rainy day were henceforth an impossibility. . . . .

In the afternoon Mr. Emerson called, bringing Mr. ——. He is a good sort of humdrum parson enough, and well fitted to increase the stock of manuscript sermons, of which there must be a fearful quantity already in the world. Mr. ——, however, is probably one of the best and most useful of his class, because no suspicion of the necessity of his profession, constituted as it now is, to mankind, and of his own usefulness and success in it, has hitherto disturbed him ; and therefore he labors with faith and confidence, as ministers did a hundred years ago.

After the visitors were gone, I sat at the gallery window, looking down the avenue, and soon there appeared an elderly woman, — a homely, decent old matron, dressed in a dark gown, and with what seemed a manuscript book under her arm. The wind sported with her gown, and blew her veil across her face, and seemed to make game of her, though on a nearer view she looked like a sad old creature, with a pale, thin countenance, and somewhat of a wild and wandering expression. She had a singular gait, reeling, as it were, and yet not quite reeling, from one side of the path to the other ; going onward as if it were not much matter whether she went straight or crooked. Such were my observations as she approached through the scattered sunshine and shade of our long avenue, until, reaching the door, she gave a knock, and inquired for the lady of the house. Her manuscript contained a certificate, stating that the old woman was a widow from a foreign land, who had recently lost her son, and was now utterly destitute of friends and kindred, and without means of support. Appended to the certificate there was a list of names of people who had bestowed charity on her, with the amounts of their several donations, — none, as I recollect, higher than twenty-five cents. Here is a strange life, and a character fit for romance and poetry. All the early part of her life, I suppose, and much of her widowhood were spent in the quiet of a home, with kinsfolk around her, and children, and the life - long gossiping acquaintances that some women always create about them. But in her decline she has wandered away from all these, and from her native country itself, and is a vagrant, yet with something of the homeliness and decency of aspect belonging to one who has been a wife and mother, and has had a roof of her own above her head, — and, with all this, a wildness proper to her present life. I have a liking for vagrants of all sorts, and never, that I know of, refused my mite to a wandering beggar, when I had anything in my own pocket. There is so much wretchedness in the world, that we may safely take the word of any mortal professing to need our assistance ; and even should we be deceived, still the good to ourselves resulting from a kind act is worth more than the trifle by which we purchase it. It is desirable, I think, that such persons should be permitted to roam through our land of plenty, scattering the seeds of tenderness and charity, as birds of passage bear the seeds of precious plants from land to land, without even dreaming of the office which they perform.

THE CHIMNEY–CORNER FOR 1866.

VIII.

HOW SHALL WE ENTERTAIN OUR COMPANY?

"THE fact is," said Marianne, "we must have a party. Bob don't like to hear of it, but it must come. We are in debt to everybody: we have been invited everywhere, and never had anything like a party since we were married, and it won't do."

"For my part, I hate parties," said Bob. "They put your house all out of order, give all the women a sick-head-ache, and all the men an indigestion; you never see anybody to any purpose; the girls look bewitched, and the women answer you at cross-purposes, and call you by the name of your next-door neighbor, in their agitation of mind. We stay out beyond our usual bedtime, come home and find some baby crying, or child who has been sitting up till nobody knows when; and the next morning, when I must be at my office by eight, and wife must attend to her children, we are sleepy and headachy. I protest against making overtures to entrap some hundred of my respectable married friends into this snare which has so often entangled me. If I had my way, I would never go to another party; and as to giving one — I suppose, since my empress has declared her intentions, that I shall be brought into doing it; but it shall be under protest."

"But, you see, we must keep up society," said Marianne.

"But I insist on it," said Bob, "it is n't keeping up society. What earthly thing do you learn about people by meeting them in a general crush, where all are coming, going, laughing, talking, and looking at each other? No person of common sense ever puts forth any idea he cares twopence about, under such circumstances; all that is exchanged is a certain set of commonplaces and platitudes which people keep for parties, just as they do their kid gloves and finery. Now there are our neighbors, the Browns. When they drop in of an evening, she knitting, and he with the last article in the paper, she really comes out with a great deal of fresh, lively, earnest, original talk. We have a good time, and I like her so much that it quite verges on loving; but see her in a party, when she manifests herself over five or six flounces of pink silk and a perfect egg-froth of tulle, her head adorned with a thicket of craped hair and roses, and it is plain at first view·that *talking* with her is quite out of the question. What has been done to her head on the outside has evidently had some effect within, for she is no longer the Mrs. Brown you knew in her every-day dress, but Mrs. Brown in a party state of mind, and too distracted to think of anything in particular. She has a few words that she answers to everything you say, as, for example, 'O, very!' 'Certainly!' 'How extraordinary!' 'So happy to,' &c. The fact is, that she has come into a state in which any real communication with her mind and character must be suspended till the party is over and she is rested. Now I like society, which is the reason why I hate parties."

"But you see," said Marianne, "what are we to do? Everybody can't drop in to spend an evening with you. If it were not for these parties, there are quantities of your acquaintances whom you would never meet."

"And of what use is it to meet them? Do you really know them any better for meeting them got up in unusual dresses, and sitting down together when the only thing exchanged is the remark that it is hot or cold, or it rains, or it is dry, or any other patent surface-fact that answers the purpose of making believe you are talking when neither of you is saying a word?"

"Well, now, for my part," said Marianne, "I confess I *like* parties : they amuse me. I come home feeling kinder and better to people, just for the little I see of them when they are all dressed up and in good humor with themselves. To be sure we don't say anything very profound, — I don't think the most of us have anything very profound to say ; but I ask Mrs. Brown where she buys her lace, and she tells me how she washes it, and somebody else tells me about her baby, and promises me a new sack-pattern. Then I like to see the pretty, nice young girls flirting with the nice young men ; and I like to be dressed up a little myself, even if my finery is all old and many times made over. It does me good to be rubbed up and brightened."

"Like old silver," said Bob.

"Yes, like old silver, precisely ; and even if I do come home tired, it does my mind good to have that change of scene and faces. You men do not know what it is to be tied to house and nursery all day, and what a perfect weariness and lassitude it often brings on us women. For my part, I think parties are a beneficial institution of society, and that it is worth a good deal of fatigue and trouble to get one up."

"Then there 's the expense," said Bob. "What earthly need is there of a grand regale of oysters, chicken-salad, ice-creams, coffee, and champagne, between eleven and twelve o'clock at night, when no one of us would ever think of wanting or taking any such articles upon our stomachs in our own homes ? If we were all of us in the habit of having a regular repast at that hour, it might be well enough to enjoy one with our neighbor ; but the party fare is generally just so much in addition to the honest three meals which we have eaten during the day. Now, to spend from fifty to one, two, or three hundred dollars in giving all our friends an indigestion from a midnight meal, seems to me a very poor investment. Yet if we once begin to give the party, we must have

everything that is given at the other parties, or wherefore do we live ? And caterers and waiters rack their brains to devise new forms of expense and extravagance ; and when the bill comes in, one is sure to feel that one is paying a great deal of money for a great deal of nonsense. It is, in fact, worse than nonsense, because our dear friends are in half the cases, not only no better, but a great deal worse, for what they have eaten."

"But there is this advantage to society," said Rudolph, — "it helps us young physicians. What would the physicians do if parties were abolished ? Take all the colds that are caught by our fair friends with low necks and short sleeves, all the troubles from dancing in tight dresses and inhaling bad air, and all the headaches and indigestions from the *mélange* of lobster-salad, two or three kinds of ice-cream, cake, and coffee on delicate stomachs, and our profession gets a degree of encouragement that is worthy to be thought of."

"But the question arises," said my wife, "whether there are not ways of promoting social feeling less expensive, more simple and natural and rational. I am inclined to think that there are."

"Yes," said Theophilus Thoro ; "for large parties are not, as a general thing, given with any wish or intention of really improving our acquaintance with our neighbors. In many cases they are openly and avowedly a general tribute paid at intervals to society, for and in consideration of which you are to sit with closed blinds and doors and be let alone for the rest of the year. Mrs. Bogus, for instance, lives to keep her house in order, her closets locked, her silver counted and in the safe, and her china-closet in undisturbed order. Her 'best things' are put away with such admirable precision, in so many wrappings and foldings, and secured with so many a twist and twine, that to get them out is one of the seven labors of Hercules, not to be lightly or unadvisedly taken in hand, but reverently, discreetly, and once for all, in an annual or biennial party. Then says Mrs. Bogus, 'For Heaven's sake, let's have every creature we can think of, and have 'em all over with at once. For pity's sake, let's have no driblets left that we shall have to be inviting to dinner or to tea. No matter whether they can come or not, — only send them the invitation, and our part is done; and, thank Heaven! we shall be free for a year.'"

"Yes," said my wife; "a great stand-up party bears just the same relation towards the offer of real hospitality and good-will as Miss Sally Brass's offer of meat to the little hungry Marchioness, when, with a bit uplifted on the end of a fork, she addressed her, 'Will you have this piece of meat? No? Well, then, remember and don't say you have n't had meat *offered* to you!' You are invited to a general jam, at the risk of your life and health; and if you refuse, don't say you have n't had hospitality offered to you. All our debts are wiped out and our slate clean; now we will have our own closed doors, no company and no trouble, and our best china shall repose undisturbed on its shelves. Mrs. Bogus says she never could exist in the way that Mrs. Easygo does, with a constant drip of company, — two or three to breakfast one day, half a dozen to dinner the next, and little evening gatherings once or twice a week. It must keep her house in confusion all the time; yet, for real social feeling, real exchange of thought and opinion, there is more of it in one half-hour at Mrs. Easygo's than in a dozen of Mrs. Bogus's great parties.

"The fact is, that Mrs. Easygo really does like the society of human beings. She is genuinely and heartily social; and, in consequence, though she has very limited means, and no money to spend in giving great entertainments, her domestic establishment is a sort of social exchange, where more friendships are formed, more real acquaintance made, and more agreeable hours spent, than in any other place that can be named. She never has large parties, — great general pay-days of social debts, — but small, well-chosen circles of people, selected so thoughtfully, with a view to the pleasure which congenial persons give each other, as to make the invitation an act of real personal kindness. She always manages to have something for the entertainment of her friends, so that they are not reduced to the simple alternatives of gaping at each other's dresses and eating lobster-salad and ice-cream. There is either some choice music, or a reading of fine poetry, or a well-acted charade, or a portfolio of photographs and pictures, to enliven the hour and start conversation; and as the people are skilfully chosen with reference to each other, as there is no hurry or heat or confusion, conversation, in its best sense, can bubble up, fresh, genuine, clear, and sparkling as a woodland spring, and one goes away really rested and refreshed. The slight entertainment provided is just enough to enable you to eat salt together in Arab fashion, — not enough to form the leading feature of the evening. A cup of tea and a basket of cake, or a salver of ices, silently passed at quiet intervals, do not interrupt conversation or overload the stomach."

"The fact is," said I, "that the art of society among us Anglo-Saxons is yet in its ruder stages. We are not, as a race, social and confiding, like the French and Italians and Germans. We have a word for home, and our home is often a moated grange, an island, a castle with its drawbridge up, cutting us off from all but our own home-circle. In France and Germany and Italy there are the boulevards and public gardens, where people do their family living in common. Mr. A is breakfasting under one tree, with wife and children around, and Mr. B is breakfasting under another tree, hard by; and messages, nods, and smiles pass backward and forward. Families see each other daily in these public resorts, and exchange mutual offices of good-will. Perhaps from these customs of society come that naïve simplicity and *abandon* which one remarks in the Continental, in opposition to the Anglo-Saxon, habits of conversation. A Frenchman or an Italian will talk to you of his feelings and plans and prospects with an unreserve that is perfectly unaccountable to you, who have always felt that such things must be kept for the very innermost circle of home privacy. But the Frenchman or Italian has from a child been brought up to pass his family life in places of public resort, in constant contact and intercommunion with other families; and the social and conversational instinct has thus been daily strengthened. Hence the reunions of these people have been characterized by a sprightliness and vigor and spirit that the Anglo-Saxon has in vain attempted to seize and reproduce. English and American *conversazioni* have very generally proved a failure, from the rooted, frozen habit of reticence and reserve which grows with our growth and strengthens with our strength. The fact is, that the Anglo-Saxon race as a race does not enjoy talking, and, except in rare instances, does not talk well. A daily convocation of people, without refreshments or any extraneous object but the simple pleasure of seeing and talking with each other, is a thing that can scarcely be understood in English or American society. Social entertainment presupposes in the Anglo-Saxon mind *something to eat,* and not only something, but a great deal. Enormous dinners or great suppers constitute the entertainment. Nobody seems to have formed the idea that the talking — the simple exchange of the social feelings — *is*, of itself, the entertainment, and that *being together* is the pleasure.

"Madame Recamier for years had a circle of friends who met every afternoon in her *salon,* from four to six o'clock, for the simple and sole pleasure of talking with each other. The very first wits and men of letters and statesmen and *savans* were enrolled in it, and each brought to the entertainment some choice *morceau* which he had laid aside from his own particular field to add to the feast. The daily intimacy gave each one such perfect insight into all the others' habits of thought, tastes, and preferences, that the conversation was like the celebrated music of the *Conservatoire* in Paris, a concert of perfectly chorded instruments taught by long habit of harmonious intercourse to keep exact time and tune together.

"*Real* conversation presupposes intimate acquaintance. People must see each other often enough to wear off the rough bark and outside rind of commonplaces and conventionalities in which their real ideas are enwrapped, and give forth without reserve their innermost and best feelings. Now what is called a large party is the first and rudest form of social intercourse. The most we can say of it is, that it is better than nothing. Men and women are crowded together like cattle in a pen. They look at each other, they jostle each other, exchange a few common bleatings, and eat together; and so the performance terminates. One may be crushed evening after evening against men or women, and learn very little about them. You may decide that a lady is good-tempered, when any amount of trampling on the skirt of her new silk dress brings no cloud to her brow. But *is* it good temper, or only wanton carelessness, which cares nothing for waste? You can see that a man is not a gentleman who squares his back to ladies at the supper-table, and devours boned turkey and *paté de fois gras,* while they vainly reach over and around him for something, and that another is a gentleman so far as to prefer the care of his weaker neighbors to the immediate indulgence of his own appetites; but further than this you learn little. Sometimes, it is true, in some secluded corner, two people of fine nervous system, undisturbed by the general confusion, may have a sociable half-hour, and really part feeling that they like each other better, and know more of each other than before. Yet these general gatherings have, after all, their value. They are not so good as something better would be, but they cannot be wholly dispensed with. It is far better that Mrs. Bogus should give an annual party, when she takes down all her bedsteads and throws open her whole house, than that she should never see her friends and neighbors inside her doors at all. She may feel that she has neither the taste nor the talent for constant small reunions. Such things, she may feel, require a social tact which she has not. She would be utterly at a loss how to conduct them. Each one would cost her as much anxiety and thought as her annual gathering, and prove a failure after all; whereas the annual demonstration can be put wholly into the hands of the caterer, who comes in force, with flowers, silver, china, servants, and, taking the house into his own hands, gives her entertainment for her, leaving to her no responsibility but the payment of the bills; and if Mr. Bogus does not quarrel with them, we know no reason why any one else should; and I think Mrs. Bogus merits well of the republic, for doing what she can do towards the hospitalities of the season. I'm sure I never cursed her in my heart, even when her strong coffee has held mine eyes open till morning, and her superlative lobster-salads have given me the very darkest views of human life that ever dyspepsia and east wind could engender. Mrs. Bogus is the Eve who offers the apple; but, after all, I am the foolish Adam who take and eat what I know is going to hurt me, and I am too gallant to visit my sins on the head of my too obliging tempter. In country places in particular, where little is going on and life is apt to stagnate, a good, large, generous party, which brings the whole neighborhood into one house to have a jolly time, to eat, drink, and be merry, is really quite a work of love and mercy. People see one another in their best clothes, and that is something; the elders exchange all manner of simple pleasantries and civilities, and talk over their domestic affairs, while the young people flirt, in that wholesome manner which is one of the safest of youthful follies. A coun-

try party, in fact, may be set down as a work of benevolence, and the money expended thereon fairly charged to the account of the great cause of peace and good-will on earth."

"But don't you think," said my wife, "that, if the charge of providing the entertainment were less laborious, these gatherings could be more frequent? You see, if a woman feels that she must have five kinds of cake, and six kinds of preserves, and even ice-cream and jellies in a region where no confectioner comes in to abbreviate her labors, she will sit with closed doors, and do nothing towards the general exchange of life, because she cannot do as much as Mrs. Smith or Mrs. Parsons. If the idea of meeting together had some other focal point than eating, I think there would be more social feeling. It might be a musical reunion, where the various young people of a circle agreed to furnish each a song or an instrumental performance. It might be an impromptu charade party, bringing out something of that taste in arrangement of costume, and capacity for dramatic effect, of which there is more latent in society than we think. It might be the reading of articles in prose and poetry furnished to a common paper or portfolio, which would awaken an abundance of interest and speculation on the authorship, or it might be dramatic readings and recitations. Any or all of these pastimes might make an evening so entertaining that a simple cup of tea and a plate of cake or biscuit would be all the refreshment needed."

"We may with advantage steal a leaf now and then from some foreign book," said I. "In France and Italy, families have their peculiar days set apart for the reception of friends at their own houses. The whole house is put upon a footing of hospitality and invitation, and the whole mind is given to receiving the various friends. In the evening the *salon* is filled. The guests, coming from week to week, for years, become in time friends; the resort has the charm of a home circle; there are certain faces that you are always sure to meet there. A lady once said to me of a certain gentleman and lady whom she missed from her circle, 'They have been at our house every Wednesday evening for twenty years.' It seems to me that this frequency of meeting is the great secret of agreeable society. One sees, in our American life, abundance of people who are everything that is charming and cultivated, but one never sees enough of them. One meets them at some quiet reunion, passes a delightful hour, thinks how charming they are, and wishes one could see more of them. But the pleasant meeting is like the encounter of two ships in mid-ocean : away we sail, each on his respective course, to see each other no more till the pleasant remembrance has died away. Yet were there some quiet, home-like resort where we might turn in to renew from time to time the pleasant intercourse, to continue the last conversation, and to compare anew our readings and our experiences, the pleasant hour of liking would ripen into a warm friendship.

"But in order that this may be made possible and practicable, the utmost simplicity of entertainment must prevail. In a French *salon*, all is, to the last degree, informal. The *bouilloire*, the French tea-kettle, is often tended by one of the gentlemen, who aids his fair neighbors in the mysteries of tea-making. One nymph is always to be found at the table dispensing tea and talk ; and a basket of simple biscuit and cakes, offered by another, is all the further repast. The teacups and cake-basket are a real addition to the scene, because they cause a little lively social bustle, a little chatter and motion, — always of advantage in breaking up stiffness, and giving occasion for those graceful, airy nothings that answer so good a purpose in facilitating acquaintance.

"Nothing can be more charming than the description which Edmond About gives, in his novel of 'Tolla,' of the reception evenings of an old noble Roman family, — the spirit of repose and quietude through all the apartments, — the ease of coming and go-ing, — the perfect homelike spirit in which the guests settle themselves to any employment of the hour that best suits them, — some to lively chat, some to dreamy, silent lounging, some to a game, others, in a distant apartment, to music, and others still to a promenade along the terraces.

"One is often in a state of mind and nerves which indisposes for the effort of active conversation ; one wishes to rest, to observe, to be amused without an effort ; and a mansion which opens wide its hospitable arms, and offers itself to you as a sort of home, where you may rest, and do just as the humor suits you, is a perfect godsend at such times. You are at home there, your ways are understood, you can do as you please, — come early or late, be brilliant or dull, — you are always welcome. If you can do nothing for the social whole to-night, it matters not. There are many more nights to come in the future, and you are entertained on trust, without a challenge.

"I have one friend, — a man of genius, subject to the ebbs and flows of animal spirits which attend that organization. Of general society he has a nervous horror. A regular dinner or evening party is to him a terror, an impossibility ; but there is a quiet parlor where stands a much-worn old sofa, and it is his delight to enter without knocking, and be found lying with half-shut eyes on this friendly couch, while the family life goes on around him without a question. Nobody is to mind him, to tease him with inquiries or salutations. If he will, he breaks into the stream of conversation, and sometimes, rousing up from one of these dreamy trances, finds himself, ere he or they know how, in the mood for free and friendly talk. People often wonder, 'How do you catch So-and-so? He is so shy ! I have invited and invited, and he never comes.' We never invite, and he comes. We take no note of his coming or his going ; we do not startle his entrance with acclamation, nor clog his departure with expostulation ; it is fully understood that with us he shall do just as he chooses; and so he chooses to do much that we like.

"The sum of this whole doctrine of society is, that we are to try the value of all modes and forms of social entertainment by their effect in producing real acquaintance and real friendship and good-will. The first and rudest form of seeking this is by a great promiscuous party, which simply effects this, — that people at least see each other on the outside, and eat together. Next come all those various forms of reunion in which the entertainment consists of something higher than staring and eating, — some exercise of the faculties of the guests in music, acting, recitation, reading, etc.; and these are a great advance, because they show people what is in them, and thus lay a foundation for a more intelligent appreciation and acquaintance. These are the best substitute for the expense, show, and trouble of large parties. They are in their nature more refining and intellectual. It is astonishing, when people really put together, in some one club or association, all the different talents for pleasing possessed by different persons, how clever a circle may be gathered — in the least promising neighborhood. A club of ladies in one of our cities has had quite a brilliant success. It is held every fortnight at the house of the members, according to alphabetical sequence. The lady who receives has charge of arranging what the entertainment shall be, — whether charade, tableau, reading, recitation, or music; and the interest is much increased by the individual taste shown in the choice of the diversion and the variety which thence follows.

"In the summer time, in the country, open-air reunions are charming forms of social entertainment. Croquet parties, which bring young people together by daylight for a healthy exercise, and end with a moderate share of the evening, are a very desirable amusement. What are called 'lawn teas' are finding great favor in England and some parts of our country. They are simply an early tea enjoyed in a sort of picnic style in the grounds about the house. Such an entertainment enables one to receive a great many at a time, without crowding, and, being in its very idea rustic and informal, can be arranged with very little expense or trouble. With the addition of lanterns in the trees and a little music, this entertainment may be carried on far into the evening with a very pretty effect.

"As to dancing, I have this much to say of it. Either our houses must be all built over and made larger, or female crinolines must be made smaller, or dancing must continue as it now is, the most absurd and ungraceful of all attempts at amusement. The effort to execute round dances in the limits of modern houses, in the prevailing style of dress, can only lead to developments more startling than agreeable. Dancing in the open air, on the shaven green of lawns, is a pretty and graceful exercise, and there only can full sweep be allowed for the present feminine toilet.

"The English breakfast is an institution growing in favor here, and rightfully, too; for a party of fresh, good-natured, well-dressed people, assembled at breakfast on a summer morning, is as nearly perfect a form of reunion as can be devised. All are in full strength from their night's rest; the hour is fresh and lovely, and they are in condition to give each other the very cream of their thoughts, the first keen sparkle of the uncorked nervous system. The only drawback is, that, in our busy American life, the most desirable gentlemen often cannot spare their morning hours. Breakfast parties presuppose a condition of leisure; but when they can be compassed, they are perhaps the most perfectly enjoyable of entertainments."

"Well," said Marianne, "I begin to waver about my party. I don't know, after all, but the desire of paying off social debts prompted the idea; perhaps we might try some of the agreeable things suggested. But, dear me! there's the baby. We'll finish the talk some other time."

GRIFFITH GAUNT; OR, JEALOUSY.

CHAPTER XXXII.

HE went straight to the stable, and saddled Black Dick.

But, in the very act, his nature revolted. What, turn his back on her the moment he had got hold of her money, to take to the other. He could not do it.

He went back to her room, and came so suddenly that he caught her crying. He asked her what was the matter.

"Nothing," said she, with a sigh: "only a woman's foolish misgivings. I was afraid perhaps you would not come back. Forgive me."

"No fear of that," said he. "However, I have taken a resolve not to go to-day. If I go to-morrow, I shall be just in time; and Dick wants a good day's rest."

Mrs. Gaunt said nothing; but her expressive face was triumphant.

Griffith and she took a walk together; and he, who used to be the more genial of the two, was dull, and she full of animation.

This whole day she laid herself out to bewitch her husband, and put him in high spirits.

It was up-hill work; but when such a woman sets herself in earnest to delight a man, she reads our sex a lesson in the art, that shows us we are all babies at it.

However, it was at supper she finally conquered.

Here the lights, her beauty set off with art, her deepening eyes, her satin skin, her happy excitement, her wit and tenderness, and joyous sprightliness, enveloped Griffith in an atmosphere of delight, and drove everything out of his head but herself; and with this, if the truth must be told, the sparkling wines co-operated.

Griffith plied the bottle a little too freely. But Mrs. Gaunt, on this one occasion, had not the heart to check

him. The more he toasted her, the more uxorious he became, and she could not deny herself even this joy; but, besides, she had less of the prudent wife in her just then than of the weak, indulgent mother. Anything rather than check his love: she was greedy of it.

At last, however, she said to him, "Sweetheart, I shall go to bed; for, I see, if I stay longer, I shall lead thee into a debauch. Be good now; drink no more when I am gone. Else I'll say thou lovest thy bottle more than thy wife."

He promised faithfully. But, when she was gone, modified his pledge by drinking just one bumper to her health, which bumper let in another; and, when at last he retired to rest, he was in that state of mental confusion wherein the limbs appear to have a memory independent of the mind.

In this condition do some men's hands wind up their watches, the mind taking no appreciable part in the ceremony.

By some such act of what physicians call "organic memory," Griffith's feet carried him to the chamber he had slept in a thousand times, and not into the one Mrs. Rider had taken him to the night before.

The next morning he came down rather late for him, and found himself treated with a great access of respect by the servants.

His position was no longer doubtful; he was the master of the house.

Mrs. Gaunt followed in due course, and sat at breakfast with him, looking young and blooming as Hebe, and her eye never off him long.

She had lived temperately, and had not yet passed the age when happiness can restore a woman's beauty and brightness in a single day.

As for him, he was like a man in a heavenly dream: he floated in the past and the present: the recent and the future seemed obscure and distant, and comparatively in a mist.

But that same afternoon, after a most affectionate farewell, and many promises to return as soon as ever he had discharged his obligations, Griffith Gaunt started for the " Packhorse," to carry to Mercy Leicester, alias Vint, the money Catharine Gaunt had saved by self-denial and economy.

And he went south a worse man than he came.

When he left Mercy Leicester, he was a bigamist in law, but not at heart. Kate was dead to him : he had given her up forever, and was constant and true to his new wife.

But now he was false to Mercy, yet not true to Kate ; and, curiously enough, it was a day or two passed with his lawful wife that had demoralized him. His unlawful wife had hitherto done nothing but improve his character.

A great fault once committed is often the first link in a chain of acts that look like crimes, but are, strictly speaking, consequences.

This man, blinded at first by his own foible, and after that the sport of circumstances, was single-hearted by nature ; and his conscience was not hardened. He desired earnestly to free himself and both his wives from the cruel situation ; but to do this, one of them, he saw, must be abandoned entirely ; and his heart bled for her.

A villain or a fool would have relished the situation ; many men would have dallied with it ; but, to do this erring man justice, he writhed and sorrowed under it, and sincerely desired to end it.

And this was why he prized Kate's money so. It enabled him to render a great service to her he had injured worse than he had the other, to her he saw he must abandon.

But this was feeble comfort, after all. He rode along a miserable man ; none the less wretched and remorseful, that, ere he got into Lancashire, he saw his way clear. This was his resolve: to pay old Vint's debts with Kate's money ; take the " Packhorse," get it made over to Mercy, give her the odd two hundred pounds and his jewels, and fly. He would never see her again ; but would return home, and get the rest of the two thousand pounds from Kate, and send it Mercy by a friend, who should tell her he was dead, and had left word with his relations to send her all his substance.

At last the " Packhorse " came in sight. He drew rein, and had half a mind to turn back ; but, instead of that, he crawled on, and very sick and cold he felt.

Many a man has marched to the scaffold with a less quaking heart than he to the " Packhorse."

His dejection contrasted strangely with the warm reception he met from everybody there. And the house was full of women ; and they seemed, somehow, all cock-a-hoop, and filled with admiration of *him.*

" Where is she ? " said he, faintly.

" Hark to the poor soul ! " said a gossip. " Dame Vint, where 's thy daughter ? gone out a-walking belike ? "

At this, the other women present chuckled and clucked.

" I 'll bring you to her," said Mrs. Vint ; " but prithee be quiet and reasonable ; for to be sure she is none too strong."

There was some little preparation, and then Griffith was ushered into Mercy's room, and found her in bed, looking a little pale, but sweeter and comelier than ever. She had the bedclothes up to her chin.

" You look wan, my poor lass," said he ; " what ails ye ? "

" Naught ails me now thou art come," said she, lovingly.

Griffith put the bag on the table. " There," said he, " there 's five hundred pounds in gold. I come not to thee empty-handed."

" Nor I to thee," said Mercy, with a heavenly smile. " See ! "

And she drew down the bedclothes a little, and showed the face of a babe scarcely three days old, — a little boy.

She turned in the bed, and tried to hold him up to his father, and said, "Here 's *my* treasure for thee!" And the effort, the flush on her cheek, and the deep light in her dove-like eyes, told plainly that the poor soul thought she had contributed to their domestic wealth something far richer than Griffith had with his bag of gold.

The father uttered an ejaculation, and came to her side, and, for a moment, Nature overpowered everything else. He kissed the child; he kissed Mercy again and again.

"Now God be praised for both," said he, passionately; "but most for thee, the best wife, the truest friend —" Here, thinking of her virtues, and the blow he had come to strike her, he broke down, and was almost choked with emotion; whereupon Mrs. Vint exerted female authority, and bundled him out of the room. "Is that the way to carry on at such an a time?" said she. "'T was enow to upset her altogether. O, but you men have little sense in women's matters. I looked to you to give her courage, not to set her off into hysterics after a manner. Nay, keep up her heart, or keep your distance, say I, that am her mother."

Griffith took this hint, and ever after took pity on Mercy's weak condition; and, suspending the fatal blow, did all he could to restore her to health and spirits.

Of course, to do that, he must deceive her; and so his life became a lie.

For, hitherto, she had never looked forward much; but now her eyes were always diving into futurity; and she lay smiling and discussing the prospects of her boy; and Griffith had to sit by her side, and see her gnaw the boy's hand, and kiss his feet, and anticipate his brilliant career. He had to look and listen with an aching heart, and assent with feigned warmth, and an inward chill of horror and remorse.

One Drummond, a travelling artist,

called; and Mercy, who had often refused to sit to him, consented now; "for," she said, "when he grows up, he shall know how his parents looked in their youth, the very year their darling was born." So Griffith had to sit with her, and excellent likenesses the man produced; but a horrible one of the child. And Griffith thought, "Poor soul! a little while and this picture will be all that shall be left to thee of me."

For all this time he was actually transacting the preliminaries of separation. He got a man of law to make all sure. The farm, the stock, the furniture and good-will of the "Packhorse," all these he got assigned to Mercy Leicester for her own use, in consideration of three hundred and fifty pounds, whereof three hundred were devoted to clearing the concern of its debts, the odd fifty was to sweeten the pill to Harry Vint.

When the deed came to be executed, Mercy was surprised, and uttered a gentle remonstrance. "What have I to do with it?" said she. "'T is thy money, not mine."

"No matter," said Griffith; "I choose to have it so."

"Your will is my law," said Mercy.

"Besides," said Griffith, "the old folk will not feel so sore, nor be afraid of being turned out, if it is in thy name."

"And that is true," said Mercy. "Now who had thought of that, but my good man?" And she threw her arms lovingly round his neck, and gazed on him adoringly.

But his lion-like eyes avoided her dove-like eyes; and an involuntary shudder ran through him.

The habit of deceiving Mercy led to a consequence he had not anticipated. It tightened the chain that held him. She opened his eyes more and more to her deep affection, and he began to fear she would die if he abandoned her.

And then her present situation was so touching. She had borne him a lovely boy; that must be abandoned too, if he left her; and somehow the birth of this child had embellished the mother; a delicious pink had taken the place of her rustic bloom; and her beauty was more refined and delicate. So pure, so loving, so fair, so maternal, to wound her heart now, it seemed like stabbing an angel.

One day succeeded to another, and still Griffith had not the heart to carry out his resolve. He temporized; he wrote to Kate that he was detained by the business; and he stayed on and on, strengthening his gratitude and his affection, and weakening his love for the absent, and his resolution; till, at last, he became so distracted and divided in heart, and so demoralized, that he began to give up the idea of abandoning Mercy, and babbled to himself about fate and destiny, and decided that the most merciful course would be to deceive both women. Mercy was patient. Mercy was unsuspicious. She would content herself with occasional visits, if he could only feign some plausible tale to account for long absences.

Before he got into this mess, he was a singularly truthful person; but now a lie was nothing to him. But, for that matter, many a man has been first made a liar by his connection with two women; and by degrees has carried his mendacity into other things.

However, though now blessed with mendacity, he was cursed with a lack of invention; and sorely puzzled how to live at Hernshaw, yet visit the "Packhorse."

The best thing he could hit upon was to pretend to turn bagman; and so Mercy would believe he was travelling all over England, when all the time he was quietly living at Hernshaw.

And perhaps these long separations might prepare her heart for a final parting, and so let in his original plan a few years hence.

He prepared this manœuvre with some art: he told her, one day, he had been to Lancaster, and there fallen in with a friend, who had as good as promised him the place of a commercial traveller for a mercantile house there.

"A traveller!" said Mercy. "Heaven forbid! If you knew how I wearied for you when you went to Cumberland!"

"To Cumberland! How know you I went thither?"

"O, I but guessed that; but now I know it, by your face. But go where thou wilt, the house is dull directly. Thou art our sunshine. Is n't he, my poppet?"

"Well, well; if it kept me too long from thee, I could give it up. But, child, we must think of young master. You could manage the inn, and your mother the farm, without me; and I should be earning money on my side. I want to make a gentleman of him."

"Anything for *him*," said Mercy: "anything in the world." But the tears stood in her eyes.

In furtherance of this deceit, Griffith did one day actually ride to Lancaster, and slept there. He wrote to Kate from that town, to say he was detained by a slight illness, but hoped to be home in a week: and the next day brought Mercy home some ribbons, and told her he had seen the merchant, and his brother, and they had made him a very fair offer. "But I've a week to think of it," said he; "so there's no hurry."

Mercy fixed her eyes on him in a very peculiar way, and made no reply. You must know that something very curious had happened whilst Griffith was gone to Lancaster.

A travelling pedler, passing by, was struck with the name on the sign-board. "Hallo!" said he, "why here's a namesake of mine; I'll have a glass of his ale any way."

So he came into the public room, and called for a glass; taking care to open his pack, and display his inviting wares. Harry Vint served him. "Here's your health," said the pedler. "You must drink with me, you must."

"And welcome," said the old man.

"Well," said the pedler, "I do travel five counties; but for all that, you are the first namesake I have found. I am Thomas Leicester, too, as sure as you are a living sinner."

The old man laughed, and said,

"Then no namesake of mine are you; for they call me Harry Vint. Thomas Leicester, he that keeps this inn now, is my son-in-law: he is gone to Lancaster this morning."

The pedler said that was a pity, he should have liked to see his namesake, and drink a glass with him.

"Come again to-morrow," said Harry Vint, ironically. "Dame," he cried, "come hither. Here's another Thomas Leicester for ye, wants to see our one."

Mrs. Vint turned her head, and inspected the pedler from afar, as if he was some natural curiosity.

"Where do you come from, young man?" said she.

"Well, I came from Kendal last; but I am Cumberland born."

"Why, that is where t'other comes from," suggested Paul Carrick, who was once more a frequenter of the house.

"Like enow," said Mrs. Vint.

With that she dropped the matter as one of no consequence, and retired. But she went straight to Mercy, in the parlor, and told her there was a man in the kitchen that called himself Thomas Leicester.

"Well, mother?" said Mercy, with high indifference, for she was trying new socks on King Baby.

"He comes from Cumberland."

"Well, to be sure, names do run in counties."

"That is true; but, seems to me, he favors your man: much of a height, and — There, do just step into the kitchen a moment."

"La, mother," said Mercy, "I don't desire to see any more Thomas Leicesters than my own: 't is the man, not the name. Is n't it, my lamb?"

Mrs. Vint went back to the kitchen discomfited; but, with quiet pertinacity, she brought Thomas Leicester into the parlor, pack and all.

"There, Mercy," said she, "lay out a penny with thy husband's namesake."

Mercy did not reply, for at that moment Thomas Leicester caught sight of Griffith's portrait, and gave a sudden start, and a most extraordinary look besides.

Both the women's eyes happened to be upon him, and they saw at once that he knew the original.

"You know my husband?" said Mercy Vint, after a while.

"Not I," said Leicester, looking askant at the picture.

"Don't tell no lies," said Mrs. Vint. "You do know him well." And she pointed her assertion by looking at the portrait.

"O, I know him whose picture hangs there, of course," said Leicester.

"Well, and that *is* her husband."

"O, that is her husband, is it?" And he was unaffectedly puzzled.

Mercy turned pale. "Yes, he is my husband," said she, "and this is our child. Can you tell me anything about him? for he came a stranger to these parts. Belike you are a kinsman of his?"

"So they say."

This reply puzzled both women.

"Any way," said the pedler, "you see we are marked alike." And he showed a long black mole on his forehead.

Mercy was now as curious as she had been indifferent. "Tell me all about him," said she: "how comes it that he is a gentleman and thou a pedler?"

"Well, because my mother was a gypsy, and his a gentlewoman."

"What brought him to these parts?"

"Trouble, they say."

"What trouble?"

"Nay, I know not." This after a slight but visible hesitation.

"But you have heard say."

"Well, I am always on the foot, and don't bide long enough in one place to learn all the gossip. But I do remember hearing he was gone to sea: and that was a lie, for he had settled here, and married you. I'fackins, he might have done worse. He has got a bonny buxom wife, and a rare fine boy, to be sure."

And now the pedler was on his guard, and determined he would not be the one to break up the household he saw before him, and afflict the dove-eyed wife and mother. He was a good-natured fellow, and averse to make mischief with his own hands. Besides, he took for granted Griffith loved his new wife better than the old one; and, above all, the punishment of bigamy was severe, and was it for him to get the Squire indicted, and branded in the hand for a felon?

So the women could get nothing more out of him; he lied, evaded, shuffled, and feigned utter ignorance; pleading, adroitly enough, his vagrant life.

All this, however, aroused vague suspicions in Mrs. Vint's mind, and she went and whispered them to her favorite, Paul Carrick. "And, Paul," said she, "call for what you like, and score it to me; only treat this pedler till he leaks out summut: to be sure he'll tell a man more than he will us."

Paul entered with zeal into this commission: treated the pedler to a chop, and plied him well with the best ale.

All this failed to loose the pedler's tongue at the time, but it muddled his judgment: on resuming his journey, he gave his entertainer a wink. Carrick rose and followed him out.

"You seem a decent lad," said the pedler, "and a good-hearted one. Wilt do me a favor?"

Carrick said he would, if it lay in his power.

"O, it is easy enow," said the pedler. "'T is just to give young Thomas Leicester, into his own hand, this here trifle as soon as ever he comes home." And he handed Carrick a hard substance wrapped up in paper. Carrick promised.

"Ay, ay, lad," said the pedler, "but see you play fair, and give it him unbeknown. Now don't you be so simple as show it to any of the womenfolk. D' ye understand?"

"All right," said Carrick, knowingly. And so the boon companions for a day shook hands and parted.

And Carrick took the little parcel straight to Mrs. Vint, and told her every word the pedler had said.

And Mrs. Vint took the little parcel straight to Mercy, and told her what Carrick said the pedler had said.

And the pedler went off flushed with beer and self-complacency; for he thought he had drawn the line precisely; had faithfully discharged his promise to his lady and benefactress, but not so as to make mischief in another household.

Such was the power of Ale — in the last century.

Mercy undid the paper and found the bullet, on which was engraved

"I LOVE KATE."

As she read these words a knife seemed to enter her heart, the pang was so keen.

But she soon took herself to task. "Thou naughty woman," said she. "What! jealous of the dead?"

She wrapped the bullet up; put it carefully away; had a good cry; and was herself again.

But all this set her watching Griffith, and reading his face. She had subtle, vague misgivings, and forbade her mother to mention the pedler's visit to Griffith yet awhile. Woman-like she preferred to worm out the truth.

On the evening of his return from Lancaster, as he was smoking his pipe, she quietly tested him. She fixed her eyes on him, and said, "One was here to-day that knows thee, and brought thee this." She then handed him the bullet, and watched his face.

Griffith undid the paper carelessly enough; but, at sight of the bullet, uttered a loud cry, and his eyes seemed ready to start out of his head.

He turned as pale as ashes, and stammered piteously, "What? what? What d' ye mean? In Heaven's name, what is this? How? Who?"

Mercy was surprised, but also much concerned at his distress; and tried to soothe him. She also asked him piteously, whether she had done wrong to give it him. "God knows," said she, "'t is no business of mine to go and remind thee of her thou hast loved better mayhap than thou lovest me. But to keep it from thee, and she in her grave, — O, I had not the heart."

But Griffith's agitation increased instead of diminishing; and, even while she was trying to soothe him, he rushed wildly out of the room, and into the open air.

Mercy went, in perplexity and distress, and told her mother.

Mrs. Vint, not being blinded by affection, thought the whole thing had a very ugly look, and said as much. She gave it as her opinion that this Kate was alive, and had sent the token herself, to make mischief between man and wife."

"That shall she never," said Mercy, stoutly; but now her suspicions were thoroughly excited, and her happiness disturbed.

The next day, Griffith found her in tears. He asked her what was the matter. She would not tell him.

"You have your secrets," said she; "and so now I have mine."

Griffith became very uneasy.

For now Mercy was often in tears, and Mrs. Vint looked daggers at him.

All this was mysterious and unintelligible, and, to a guilty man, very alarming.

At last he implored Mercy to speak out. He wanted to know the worst.

Then Mercy did speak out. "You have deceived me," said she. "Kate is alive. This very morning, between sleeping and waking, you whispered her name; ay, false man, whispered it like a lover. You told me she was dead. But she is alive, and has sent you a reminder, and the bare sight of it hath turned your heart her way again. What shall I do? Why did you marry me, if you could not forget her? I did not want you to desert any woman for me. The desire of my heart was always for your happiness. But O Thomas, deceit and falsehood will not bring you happiness, no more than they will me. What shall I do? what shall I do?"

Her tears flowed freely, and Griffith sat down, and groaned with horror and remorse, beside her.

He had not the courage to tell her the horrible truth, — that Kate was his wife, and she was not.

"Do not thou afflict thyself," he muttered. "Of course, with you putting that bullet in my hand so sudden, it set my fancy a wandering back to other days."

"Ah!" said Mercy, "if it be no worse than that, there's little harm. But why did thy namesake start so at sight of thy picture?"

"My namesake!" cried Griffith, all aghast.

"Ay, he that brought thee that love-token, — Thomas Leicester. Nay, for very shame, feign not ignorance of him. Why, he hath thy very mole on his temple, and knew thy picture in a moment. He is thy half-brother, is he not?"

"I am a ruined man," cried Griffith, and sank into a chair without power of motion.

"God help me, what is all this?" cried Mercy. "O Thomas, Thomas, I could forgive thee aught but deceit: for both our sakes speak out, and tell me the worst. No harm shall come near thee while I live."

"How can I tell thee? I am an unfortunate man. The world will call me a villain; yet I am not a villain at heart. But who will believe me? I have broken the law. Thee I could trust, but not thy folk; they never loved me. Mercy, for pity's sake, when was that Thomas Leicester here?"

"Four days ago."

"Which way went he?"

"I hear he told Paul he was going to Cumberland."

"If he gets there before me, I shall rot in gaol."

"Now God forbid! O Thomas, then mount and ride after him."

"I will, and this very moment."

He saddled Black Dick, and loaded his pistols for the journey; but, ere he went, a pale face looked out into the yard, and a finger beckoned. It was Mercy. She bade him follow her. She took him to her room, where their child was sleeping; and then she closed and even locked the door.

"No soul can hear us," said she; "now look me in the face, and tell me God's truth. Who and what are you?"

Griffith shuddered at this exordium; he made no reply.

Mercy went to a box and took out an old shirt of his,—the one he wore when he first came to the "Packhorse." She brought it to him and showed him "G. G." embroidered on it with a woman's hair. (Ryder's.)

"Here are your initials," said she; "now leave useless falsehoods; be a man, and ·tell me your real name."

"My name is Griffith Gaunt."

Mercy, sick at heart, turned her head away; but she had the resolution to urge him on. "Go on," said she, in an agonized whisper: "if you believe in God and a judgment to come, deceive me no more. The truth, I say! the truth!"

"So be it," said Griffith, desperately: "when I have told thee what a villain I am, I can die at thy feet, and then thou wilt forgive me.

"Who is Kate?" was all she replied.

"Kate is my wife."

"I thought her false; who could think any other? appearances were so strong against her: others thought so beside me. I raised my hand to kill her; but she never winced. I trampled on him I believed her paramour: I fled, and soon I lay a-dying in this house for her sake. I told thee she was dead. Alas! I thought her dead to me. I went back to our house (it is her house) sore against the grain, to get money for thee and thine. Then she cleared herself, bright as the sun, and pure as snow. She was all in black for me; she had put by money, against I should come to my senses and need it. I told her I owed a debt in Lancashire, a debt of gratitude as well as money: and so I did. How have I repaid it? The poor soul forced five hundred pounds on me. I had

much ado to keep her from bringing it hither with her own hands. O, villain! villain! Then I thought to leave thee, and send thee word I was dead, and heap money on thee. Money! But how could I? thou wast my benefactress, my more than wife. All the riches of the world can make no return to thee. What, what shall I do? Shall I fly with thee and thy child across the seas? Shall I go back to her? No; the best thing I can do is to take this good pistol, and let the life out of my dishonorable carcass, and free two honest women from me by one resolute act."

In his despair he cocked the pistol; and, at a word from Mercy, this tale had ended.

But the poor woman, pale and trembling, tottered across the room, and took it out of his hand. "I would not harm thy body, nor thy soul," she gasped. "Let me draw my breath and think."

She rocked herself to and fro in silence.

Griffith stood trembling like a criminal before his judge.

It was long ere she could speak, for anguish. Yet when she did speak, it was with a sort of deadly calm.

"Go tell the truth to *her*, as you have done to me; and, if she can forgive you, all the better for you. I can never forgive you, nor yet can harm you. My child! my child! Thy father is our ruin. O, begone, man, or the sight of you will kill us both."

Then he fell at her knees; kissed, and wept over her cold hand; and, in his pity and despair, offered to cross the seas with her and her child, and so repair the wrong he had done her.

"Tempt me not," she sobbed. "Go, leave me! None here shall ever know thy crime, but she whose heart thou hast broken, and ruined her good name."

He took her in his arms, in spite of her resistance, and kissed her passionately; but, for the first time, she shuddered at his embrace; and that gave him the power to leave her.

He rushed from her, all but distracted, and rode away to Cumberland; but not to tell the truth to Kate, if he could possibly help it.

CHAPTER XXXIII.

At this particular time, no man's presence was more desired in that county than Griffith Gaunt's.

And this I need not now be telling the reader, if I had related this story on the plan of a miscellaneous chronicle. But the affairs of the heart are so absorbing, that, even in a narrative, they thrust aside important circumstances of a less moving kind.

I must therefore go back a step, before I advance further. You must know that forty years before our Griffith Gaunt saw the light, another Griffith Gaunt was born in Cumberland: a younger son, and the family estate entailed; but a shrewd lad, who chose rather to hunt fortune elsewhere than to live in miserable dependence on his elder brother. His godfather, a city merchant, encouraged him, and he left Cumberland. He went into commerce, and in twenty years became a wealthy man, — so wealthy that he lived to look down on his brother's estate, which he had once thought opulence. His life was all prosperity, with a single exception; but that a bitter one. He laid out some of his funds in a fashionable and beautiful wife. He loved her before marriage; and, as she was always cold to him, he loved her more and more.

In the second year of their marriage she ran away from him; and no beggar in the streets of London was so miserable as the wealthy merchant.

It blighted the man, and left him a sore heart all his days. He never married again; and railed on all womankind for this one. He led a solitary life in London till he was sixty-nine; and then, all of a sudden, Nature, or accident, or both, changed his whole habits. Word came to him that the family estate, already deeply mortgaged, was for sale, and a farmer who had

rented a principal farm on it, and held a heavy mortgage, had made the highest offer.

Old Griffith sent down Mr. Atkins, his solicitor, post haste, and snapped the estate out of that purchaser's hands.

When the lands and house had been duly conveyed to him, he came down, and his heart seemed to bud again, in the scenes of his childhood.

Finding the house small, and built in a valley instead of on rising ground, he got an army of bricklayers, and began to build a mansion with a rapidity unheard of in those parts; and he looked about for some one to inherit it.

The name of Gaunt had dwindled down to three, since he left Cumberland; but a rich man never lacks relations. Featherstonhaughs, and Underhills, and even Smiths, poured in, with parish registers in their laps, and proved themselves Gauntesses, and flattered and carneyed the new head of the family.

Then the perverse old gentleman felt inclined to look elsewhere. He knew he had a namesake at the other side of the county, but this namesake did not come near him.

This independent Gaunt excited his curiosity and interest. He made inquiries, and heard that young Griffith had just quarrelled with his wife, and gone away in despair.

Griffith senior took for granted that the fault lay with Mrs. Gaunt, and wasted some good sympathy on Griffith junior.

On further inquiry he learned that the truant was dependent on his wife. Then, argued the moneyed man, he would not run away from her but that his wound was deep.

The consequence of all this was, that he made a will very favorable to his absent and injured (?) namesake. He left numerous bequests; but made Griffith his residuary legatee; and, having settled this matter, urged on, and superintended his workmen.

Alas! just as the roof was going on, a narrower house claimed him, and he made good the saying of the wise bard, —

> " Tu secanda marmora
> Locas sub ipsum funus et sepulchri
> Immemor struis domos."

The heir of his own choosing could not be found to attend his funeral; and Mr. Atkins, his solicitor, a very worthy man, was really hurt at this. With the quiet bitterness of a displeased attorney, he merely sent Mrs. Gaunt word her husband inherited something under the will, and she would do well to produce him, or else furnish him (Atkins) with proof of his decease.

Mrs. Gaunt was offended by this cavalier note, and replied very like a woman, and very unlike Business.

"I do not know where he is," said she, "nor whether he is alive or dead. Nor do I feel disposed to raise the hue and cry after him. But favor me with your address, and I shall let you know should I hear anything about him."

Mr. Atkins was half annoyed, half amused, at this piece of indifference. It never occurred to him that it might be all put on.

He wrote back to say that the estate was large, and, owing to the terms of the will, could not be administered without Mr. Griffith Gaunt; and, in the interest of the said Griffith Gaunt, and also of the other legatees, he really must advertise for him.

La Gaunt replied, that he was very welcome to advertise for whomsoever he pleased.

Mr. Atkins was a very worthy man; but human. To tell the truth, he was himself one of the other legatees. He inherited (and, to be just, had well deserved) four thousand guineas, under the will, and could not legally touch it without Griffith Gaunt. This little circumstance spurred his professional zeal.

Mr. Atkins advertised for Griffith Gaunt, in the London and Cumberland papers, and in the usual enticing form. He was to apply to Mr. Atkins, Solicitor, of Gray's Inn, and he would hear of something greatly to his advantage.

These advertisements had not been out a fortnight, when Griffith Gaunt came home, as I have related.

But Mr. Atkins had punished Mrs. Gaunt for her *insouciance*, by not informing her of the extent of her good fortune; so she merely told Griffith, casually, that old Griffith Gaunt had left him some money, and the solicitor, Mr. Atkins, could not get on without him. Even this information she did not vouchsafe until she had given him her £500, for she grudged Atkins the pleasure of supplying her husband with money.

However, as soon as Griffith left her, she wrote to Mr. Atkins to say that her husband had come home in perfect health, thank God; had only stayed two days, but was to return in a week.

When ten days had elapsed, Atkins wrote to inquire.

She replied he had not yet returned; and this went on till Mr. Atkins showed considerable impatience.

As for Mrs. Gaunt, she made light of the matter to Mr. Atkins; but, in truth, this new mystery irritated her and pained her deeply.

In one respect she was more unhappy than she had been before he came back at all. Then she was alone; her door was closed to commentators. But now, on the strength of so happy a reconciliation, she had re-entered the world, and received visits from Sir George Neville, and others; and, above all, had announced that Griffith would be back for good in a few days. So now his continued absence exposed her to sly questions from her own sex, to the interchange of glances between female visitors, as well as to the internal torture of doubt and suspense.

But what distracted her most was the view Mrs. Ryder took of the matter.

That experienced lady had begun to suspect some other woman was at the bottom of Griffith's conduct; and her own love for Griffith was now soured. Repeated disappointments and affronts, *spretæque injuria formæ*, had not quite extinguished it, but had mixed so much spite with it that she was equally ready to kiss or to stab him.

So she took every opportunity to instil into her mistress, whose confidence she had won at last, that Griffith was false to her.

"That is the way with these men that are so ready to suspect others. Take my word for it, Dame, he has carried your money to his leman. 'T is still the honest woman that must bleed for some nasty trollop or other."

She enforced this theory by examples drawn from her own observations in families, and gave the very names ; and drove Mrs. Gaunt almost mad with fear, anger, jealousy, and cruel suspense. She could not sleep, she could not eat ; she was in a constant fever.

Yet before the world she battled it out bravely, and indeed none but Ryder knew the anguish of her spirit, and her passionate wrath.

At last there came a most eventful day.

Mrs. Gaunt had summoned all her pride and fortitude, and invited certain ladies and gentlemen to dine and sup.

She was one of the true Spartan breed, and played the hostess as well as if her heart had been at ease. It was an age in which the host struggled fiercely to entertain the guests ; and Mrs. Gaunt was taxing all her powers of pleasing in the dining-room, when an unexpected guest strolled into the kitchen : the pedler, Thomas Leicester.

Jane welcomed him cordially, and he was soon seated at a table eating his share of the feast.

Presently Mrs. Ryder came down, dressed in her best, and looking handsomer than ever.

At sight of her, Tom Leicester's affection revived ; and he soon took occasion to whisper an inquiry whether she was still single.

"Ay," said she, " and like to be."

" Waiting for the master still ? Mayhap I could cure you of that complaint. But least said is soonest mended."

This mysterious hint showed Ryder he had a secret burning his bosom. The sly hussy said nothing just then, but plied him with ale and flattery ; and, when he whispered a request for a private meeting out of doors, she cast her eyes down, and assented.

And in that meeting she carried herself so adroitly, that he renewed his offer of marriage, and told her not to waste her fancy on a man who cared neither for her nor any other she in Cumberland.

" Prove that to me," said Ryder, cunningly, " and may be I 'll take you at your word."

The bribe was not to be resisted. Tom revealed to her, under a solemn promise of secrecy, that the Squire had got a wife and child in Lancashire ; and had a farm and an inn, which latter he kept under the name of— Thomas Leicester.

In short, he told her, in his way, all the particulars I have told in mine.

Which told it the best will never be known in this world.

She led him on with a voice of very velvet. He did not see how her cheek paled and her eyes flashed jealous fury.

When she had sucked him dry, she suddenly turned on him, with a cold voice, and said, " I can't stay any longer with you just now. She will want me."

" You will meet me here again, lass ? " said Tom, ruefully.

" Yes, for a minute, after supper."

She then left him, and went to Mrs. Gaunt's room, and sat crouching before the fire, all hate and bitterness.

What ? he had left the wife he loved, and yet had not turned to her !

She sat there, waiting for Mrs. Gaunt, and nursing her vindictive fury, two mortal hours.

At last, just before supper, Mrs. Gaunt came up to her room, to cool her fevered hands and brow, and found this creature crouched by her fire, all in a heap, with pale cheek, and black eyes that glittered like basilisk's.

" What is the matter, child ? " said Mrs. Gaunt. " Good heavens ! what hath happened ? "

"Dame!" said Ryder, sternly, "I have got news of him."

"News of *him?*" faltered Mrs. Gaunt. "Bad news?"

"I don't know whether to tell you or not," said Ryder, sulkily, but with a touch of human feeling.

"What cannot I bear? What have I not borne? Tell me the truth."

The words were stout, but she trembled all over in uttering them.

"Well, it is as I said, only worse. Dame, he has got a wife and child in another county; and no doubt been deceiving her, as he has *us.*"

"A wife!" gasped Mrs. Gaunt, and one white hand clutched her bosom, and the other the mantel-piece.

"Ay, Thomas Leicester, that is in the kitchen now, saw her, and saw his picture hanging aside hers on the wall. And he goes by the name of Thomas Leicester. That was what made Tom go into the inn, seeing his own name on the signboard. Nay, Dame, never give way like that. Lean on me, — so. He is a villain, — a false, jealous, double-faced villain."

Mrs. Gaunt's head fell back on Ryder's shoulder, and she said no word; but only moaned and moaned, and her white teeth clicked convulsively together.

Ryder wept over her sad state : the tears were half impulse, half crocodile.

She applied hartshorn to the sufferer's nostrils, and tried to rouse her mind by exciting her anger. But all was in vain. There hung the betrayed wife, pale, crushed, and quivering under the cruel blow.

Ryder asked her if she should go down and excuse her to her guests.

She nodded a feeble assent.

Ryder then laid her down on the bed with her head low, and was just about to leave her on that errand, when hurried steps were heard outside the door; and one of the female servants knocked ; and, not waiting to be invited, put her head in, and cried, "O, Dame, the Master is come home. He is in the kitchen."

CHAPTER XXXIV.

MRS. RYDER made an agitated motion with her hand, and gave the girl such a look withal, that she retired precipitately.

But Mrs. Gaunt had caught the words, and they literally transformed her. She sprang off the bed, and stood erect, and looked a Saxon Pythoness : golden hair streaming down her back, and gray eyes gleaming with fury.

She caught up a little ivory-handled knife, and held it above her head.

"I'll drive this into his heart before them all," she cried, "and tell them the reason *afterwards.*"

Ryder looked at her for a moment in utter terror. She saw a woman with grander passions than herself; a woman that looked quite capable of executing her sanguinary threat. Ryder made no more ado, but slipped out directly to prevent a meeting that might be attended with terrible consequences.

She found her master in the kitchen, splashed with mud, drinking a horn of ale after his ride, and looking rather troubled and anxious ; and, by the keen eye of her sex, she saw that the female servants were also in considerable anxiety. The fact is, they had just extemporized a lie.

Tom Leicester, being near the kitchen window, had seen Griffith ride into the court-yard.

At sight of that well-known figure, he drew back, and his heart quaked at his own imprudence, in confiding Griffith's secret to Caroline Ryder.

"Lasses," said he, hastily, "do me a kindness for old acquaintance. Here's the Squire. For Heaven's sake, don't let him know I am in the house, or there will be bloodshed between us. He is a hasty man, and I'm another. I'll tell ye more by and by."

The next moment Griffith's tread was heard approaching the very door, and Leicester darted into the housekeeper's room, and hid in a cupboard there.

Griffith opened the kitchen door, and stood upon the threshold.

The women courtesied to him, and were loud in welcome.

He returned their civilities briefly; and then his first word was, "Hath Thomas Leicester been here?"

You know how servants stick together against their master! The girls looked him in the face, like candid doves, and told him Leicester had not been that way for six months or more.

"Why, I have tracked him to within two miles," said Griffith, doubtfully.

"Then he is sure to come here," said Jane, adroitly. "He wouldn't ever think to go by us."

"The moment he enters the house, you let me know. He is a mischief-making loon."

He then asked for a horn of ale; and, as he finished it, Ryder came in, and he turned to her, and asked her after her mistress.

"She was well, just now," said Ryder; "but she has been took with a spasm: and it would be well, sir, if you could dress, and entertain the company in her place awhile. For I must tell you, your being so long away hath set their tongues going, and almost broken my lady's heart."

Griffith sighed, and said he could not help it, and now he was here, he would do all in his power to please her. "I'll go to her at once," said he.

"No, sir!" said Ryder, firmly. "Come with me. I want to speak to you."

She took him to his bachelor's room, and stayed a few minutes to talk to him.

"Master," said she, solemnly, "things are very serious here. Why did you stay so long away? Our dame says some woman is at the bottom of it, and she'll put a knife into you if you come a-nigh her."

This threat did not appall Griffith, as Ryder expected. Indeed, he seemed rather flattered.

"Poor Kate!" said he; "she is just the woman to do it. But I am afraid she does not love me enough for that. But indeed how should she?"

"Well, sir," replied Ryder, "oblige me by keeping clear of her for a little while. I have got orders to make your bed here. Now, dress, like a good soul, and then go down and show respect to the company that is in your house; for they know you are here."

"Why, that is the least I can do," said Griffith. "Put you out what I am to wear, and then run and say I'll be with them anon."

Griffith walked into the dining-room, and, somewhat to his surprise, after what Ryder had said, found Mrs. Gaunt seated at the head of her own table, and presiding like a radiant queen over a brilliant assembly.

He walked in, and made a low bow to his guests first: then he approached to greet his wife more freely; but she drew back decidedly, and made him a courtesy, the dignity and distance of which struck the whole company.

Sir George Neville, who was at the bottom of the table, proposed, with his usual courtesy, to resign his place to Griffith. But Mrs. Gaunt forbade the arrangement.

"No, Sir George," said she; "this is but an occasional visitor; you are my constant friend."

If this had been said pleasantly, well and good; but the guests looked in vain into their hostess's face for the smile that ought to have accompanied so strange a speech and disarmed it.

"Rarities are the more welcome," said a lady, coming to the rescue; and edged aside to make room for him.

"Madam," said Griffith, "I am in your debt for that explanation; but I hope you will be no rarity here, for all that."

Supper proceeded; but the mirth languished. Somehow or other, the chill fact that there was a grave quarrel between two at the table, and those two man and wife, insinuated itself into the spirits of the guests. There began to be lulls, — fatal lulls. And in one of these, some unlucky voice was heard to murmur, "Such a meeting of man and wife I never saw."

The hearers felt miserable at this personality, that fell upon the ear of silence like a thunderbolt.

Griffith was ill-advised enough to notice the remark, though clearly not intended for his ears. For one thing, his jealousy had actually revived at the cool preference Kate had shown his old rival, Neville.

"Oh!" said he, bitterly, "a man is not always his wife's favorite."

"He does not always deserve to be," said Mrs. Gaunt, sternly.

When matters had gone that length, one idea seemed to occur pretty simultaneously to all the well-bred guests ; and that idea was, *Sauve qui peut.*

Mrs. Gaunt took leave of them, one by one, and husband and wife were left alone.

Mrs. Gaunt by this time was alarmed at the violence of her own passions, and wished to avoid Griffith for that night at all events. So she cast one terribly stern look upon him, and was about to retire in grim silence. But he, indignant at the public affront she had put on him, and not aware of the true cause, unfortunately detained her. He said, sulkily, "What sort of a reception was that you gave me ?"

This was too much. She turned on him furiously. "Too good for thee, thou heartless creature ! Thomas Leicester is here, and I know thee for a villain."

"You know nothing," cried Griffith. "Would you believe that mischief-making knave ? What has he told you ?"

"Go back to *her !*" cried Mrs. Gaunt furiously. "Me you can deceive and pillage no more. So, this was your jealousy ! False and forsworn yourself, you dared to suspect and insult me. Ah ! and you think I am the woman to endure this ? I 'll have your life for it ! I 'll have your life."

Griffith endeavored to soften her, — protested that, notwithstanding appearances, he had never loved but her.

"I 'll soon be rid of you, and your love," said the raging woman. "The constables shall come for you to-morrow. You have seen how I can love, you shall know how I can hate."

She then, in her fury, poured out a torrent of reproaches and threats that made his blood run cold. He could not answer her : he *had* suspected her wrongfully, and been false to her himself. He *had* abused her generosity, and taken her money for Mercy Vint.

After one or two vain efforts to check the torrent, he sank into a chair, and hid his face in his hands.

But this did not disarm her, at the time. Her raging voice and raging words were heard by the very servants, long after he had ceased to defend himself.

At last she came out, pale with fury, and, finding Ryder near the door, shrieked out, "Take that reptile to his den, if he is mean enough to lie in this house," — then, lowering her voice, "and bring Thomas Leicester to me."

Ryder went to Leicester, and told him. But he objected to come. "You have betrayed me," said he. "Curse my weak heart and my loose tongue. I have done the poor Squire an ill turn. I can never look him in the face again. But 't is all thy fault, double-face. I hate the sight of thee."

At this Ryder shed some crocodile tears ; and very soon, by her blandishments, obtained forgiveness.

And Leicester, since the mischief was done, was persuaded to see the dame, who was his recent benefactor, you know. He bargained, however, that the Squire should be got to bed first ; for he had a great dread of meeting him. "He 'll break every bone in my skin," said Tom ; "or else I shall do *him* a mischief in my defence."

Ryder herself saw the wisdom of this. She bade him stay quiet, and she went to look after Griffith.

She found him in the drawing-room, with his head on the table, in deep dejection.

She assumed authority, and said he must go to bed.

He rose humbly, and followed her like a submissive dog.

She took him to his room. There was no fire.

"That is where you are to sleep," said she, spitefully.

"It is better than I deserve," said he, humbly.

The absurd rule about not hitting a man when he is down has never obtained a place in the great female soul; so Ryder lashed him without mercy.

"Well, sir," said she, "methinks you have gained little by breaking faith with me. Y' had better have set up your inn with me, than gone and sinned against the law."

"Much better: would to Heaven I had!"

"What d' ye mean to do now? You know the saying. Between two stools — "

"Child," said Griffith, faintly, "methinks I shall trouble neither long. I am not so ill a man as I seem; but who will believe that? I shall not live long. And I shall leave an ill name behind me. *She* told me so just now. And oh! her eye was so cruel; I saw my death in it."

"Come, come," said Ryder, relenting a little; "you must n't believe every word an angry woman says. There, take my advice; go to bed; and in the morning don't speak to her. Keep out of her way a day or two."

And with this piece of friendly advice she left him; and waited about till she thought he was in bed and asleep.

Then she brought Thomas Leicester up to her mistress.

But Griffith was not in bed; and he heard Leicester's heavy tread cross the landing. He waited and waited behind his door for more than half an hour, and then he heard the same heavy tread go away again.

By this time nearly all the inmates of the house were asleep.

About twenty-five minutes after Leicester left Mrs. Gaunt, Caroline Ryder stole quietly up stairs from the kitchen, and sat down to think it all over.

She then proceeded to undress; but had only taken off her gown, when she started and listened; for a cry of distress reached her from outside the house.

She darted to the window and threw it open.

Then she heard a cry more distinct, "Help! help!"

It was a clear starlight night, but no moon.

The mere shone before her, and the cries were on the bank.

Now came something more alarming still. A flash, — a pistol shot, — and an agonized voice cried loudly, "Murder! Help! Murder!"

That voice she knew directly. It was Griffith Gaunt's.

CHAPTER XXXV.

RYDER ran screaming, and alarmed the other servants.

All the windows that looked on the mere were flung open.

But no more sounds were heard. A terrible silence brooded now over those clear waters.

The female servants huddled together, and quaked; for who could doubt that a bloody deed had been done?

It was some time before they mustered the presence of mind to go and tell Mrs. Gaunt. At last they opened her door. She was not in her room. Ryder ran to Griffith's. It was locked. She called to him. He made no reply.

They burst the door open. He was not there; and the window was open.

While their tongues were all going, in consternation, Mrs. Gaunt was suddenly among them, very pale.

They turned, and looked at her aghast.

"What means all this?" said she. "Did not I hear cries outside?"

"Ay," said Ryder. "Murder! and a pistol fired. O, my poor master!"

Mrs. Gaunt was white as death; but self-possessed. "Light torches this moment, and search the place," said she.

There was only one man in the house; and he declined to go out alone. So Ryder and Mrs. Gaunt went with him, all three bearing lighted links.

They searched the place where Ryder had heard the cries. They went up and down the whole bank of the mere, and cast their torches' red light over the placid waters themselves. But there was nothing to be seen, alive or dead, — no trace either of calamity or crime.

They roused the neighbors, and came back to the house with their clothes all draggled and dirty.

Mrs. Gaunt took Ryder apart, and asked her if she could guess at what time of the night Griffith had made his escape. "He is a villain," said she, "yet I would not have him come to harm, God knows. There are thieves abroad. But I hope he ran away as soon as your back was turned, and so fell not in with them."

"Humph!" said Ryder. Then, looking Mrs. Gaunt in the face, she said, quietly, "Where were you when you heard the cries?"

"I was on the other side of the house."

"What, out o' doors, at that time of night!"

"Ay; I was in the grove, — praying."

"Did you hear any voice you knew?"

"No: all was too indistinct. I heard a pistol, but no words. Did you?"

"I heard no more than you, madam," said Ryder, trembling.

No one went to bed any more that night in Hernshaw Castle.

CHAPTER XXXVI.

THIS mysterious circumstance made a great talk in the village and in the kitchen of Hernshaw Castle; but not in the drawing-room; for Mrs. Gaunt instantly closed her door to visitors, and let it be known that it was her intention to retire to a convent; and, in the mean time, she desired not to be disturbed.

Ryder made one or two attempts to draw her out upon the subject, but was sternly checked.

Pale, gloomy, and silent, the mistress of Hernshaw Castle moved about the place, like the ghost of her former self. She never mentioned Griffith; forbade his name to be uttered in her hearing; and, strange to say, gave Ryder strict orders not to tell any one what she had heard from Thomas Leicester.

"This last insult is known but to you and me. If it ever gets abroad, you leave my service that very hour."

This injunction set Ryder thinking. However, she obeyed it to the letter. Her place was getting better and better; and she was a woman accustomed to keep secrets.

A pressing letter came from Mr. Atkins.

Mrs. Gaunt replied that her husband had come to Hernshaw, but had left again; and the period of his ultimate return was now more uncertain than ever.

On this Mr. Atkins came down to Hernshaw Castle. But Mrs. Gaunt would not see him. He retired very angry, and renewed his advertisements, but in a more explicit form. He now published that Griffith Gaunt, of Hernshaw and Bolton, was executor and residuary legatee to the late Griffith Gaunt of Coggleswade; and requested him to apply directly to James Atkins, Solicitor, of Gray's Inn, London.

In due course this advertisement was read by the servants at Hernshaw, and shown by Ryder to Mrs. Gaunt.

She made no comment whatever; and contrived to render her pale face impenetrable.

Ryder became as silent and thoughtful as herself, and often sat bending her black judicial brows.

By and by dark mysterious words began to be thrown out in Hernshaw village.

"He will never come back at all."

"He will never come into that fortune."

"'T is no use advertising for a man that is past reading."

These, and the like equivocal sayings, were followed by a vague buzz, which was traceable to no individual author, but seemed to rise on all sides, like a dark mist, and envelop that unhappy house.

And that dark mist of Rumor soon condensed itself into a palpable and terrible whisper, — "Griffith Gaunt hath met with foul play."

No one of the servants told Mrs. Gaunt this horrid rumor.

But the women used to look at her, and after her, with strange eyes.

She noticed this, and felt, somehow, that her people were falling away from her. It added one drop to her bitter cup. She began to droop into a sort of calm, despondent lethargy.

Then came fresh trouble to rouse her.

Two of the county magistrates called on her in their official capacity, and, with perfect politeness, but a very grave air, requested her to inform them of all the circumstances attending her husband's disappearance.

She replied, coldly and curtly, that she knew very little about it. Her husband had left in the middle of the night.

" He came to stay ? "

" I believe so."

" Came on horseback ? "

" Yes."

" Did he go away on horseback ? "

" No ; for the horse is now in my stable."

"Is it true there was a quarrel between you and him that evening ? "

"Gentlemen," said Mrs. Gaunt, drawing herself back, haughtily, "did you come here to gratify your curiosity ? "

"No, madam," said the elder of the two ; "but to discharge a very serious and painful duty, in which I earnestly request you, and even advise. you, to aid us. Was there a quarrel ? "

"There was — a mortal quarrel."

The gentlemen exchanged glances, and the elder made a note.

"May we ask the subject of that quarrel ? "

Mrs. Gaunt declined, positively, to enter into a matter so delicate.

A note was taken of this refusal.

" Are you aware, madam, that your husband's voice was heard calling for help, and that a pistol-shot was fired ? "

Mrs. Gaunt trembled visibly.

" I heard the pistol-shot," said she ; " but not the voice distinctly. O, I hope it was not his voice Ryder heard ! "

" Ryder, who is he ? "

" Ryder is my lady's maid : her bedroom is on that side the house."

" Can we see Mrs. Ryder ? "

" Certainly," said Mrs. Gaunt, and rose and rang the bell.

Mrs. Ryder answered the bell, in person, very promptly ; for she was listening at the door.

Being questioned, she told the magistrates what she had heard down by "the mere " ; and said she was sure it was her master's voice that cried " Help ! " and " Murder ! " And with this she began to cry.

Mrs. Gaunt trembled and turned pale.

The magistrates confined their questions to Ryder.

They elicited, however, very little more from her. She saw the drift of their questions, and had an impulse to defend her mistress there present. Behind her back it would have been otherwise.

That resolution once taken, two children might as well have tried to extract evidence from her as two justices of the peace.

And then Mrs. Gaunt's pale face and noble features touched them. The case was mysterious, but no more ; and they departed little the wiser, and with some apologies for the trouble they had given her.

The next week down came Mr. Atkins, out of all patience, and determined to find Griffith Gaunt, or else obtain some proof of his decease.

He obtained two interviews with Ryder, and bribed her to tell him all she knew. He prosecuted other inquiries with more method than had hitherto been used, and elicited an important fact, namely, that Griffith Gaunt had been seen walking in a certain direction at one o'clock in the morning, followed at a short distance by a tall man with a knapsack, or the like, on his back.

The person who gave this tardy information was the wife of a certain farmer's man, who wired hares upon the sly. The man himself, being assured that, in a case so serious as this, no particular inquiries should be made how he came to be out so late, confirmed what his wife had let out, and added, that both men had taken the way that would lead them to the bridge, meaning the bridge over the mere. More than that he could not say, for he had met them, and was full half a mile from the mere before those men could have reached it.

Following up this clew, Mr. Atkins learned so many ugly things, that he went to the Bench on justicing day, and demanded a full and searching inquiry on the premises.

Sir George Neville, after in vain opposing this, rode off straight from the Bench to Hernshaw, and in feeling terms conveyed the bad news to Mrs. Gaunt; and then, with the utmost delicacy, let her know that some suspicion rested upon herself, which she would do well to meet with the bold front of innocence.

"What suspicion, pray?" said Mrs. Gaunt, haughtily.

Sir George shrugged his shoulders, and replied, "That you have done Gaunt the honor to put him out of the way."

Mrs. Gaunt took this very differently from what Sir George expected.

"What!" she cried, "are they so sure he is dead, — murdered?"

And with this she went into a passion of grief and remorse.

Even Sir George was puzzled, as well as affected, by her convulsive agitation.

CHAPTER XXXVII.

THOUGH it was known the proposed inquiry might result in the committal of Mrs. Gaunt on a charge of murder, yet the respect in which she had hith-

erto been held, and the influence of Sir George Neville, who, having been her lover, stoutly maintained her innocence, prevailed so far that even this inquiry was private, and at her own house. Only she was present in the character of a suspected person, and the witnesses were examined before her.

First, the poacher gave his evidence.

Then Jane, the cook, proved that a pedler called Thomas Leicester had been in the kitchen, and secreted about the premises till a late hour; and this Thomas Leicester corresponded exactly to the description given by the poacher.

This threw suspicion on Thomas Leicester, but did not connect Mrs. Gaunt with the deed in any way.

But Ryder's evidence filled this gap. She revealed three serious facts: —

First, that, by her mistress's orders, she had introduced this very Leicester into her mistress's room about midnight, where he had remained nearly half an hour, and had then left the house.

Secondly, that Mrs. Gaunt herself had been out of doors after midnight.

And, thirdly, that she had listened at the door, and heard her threaten Griffith Gaunt's life.

This is a mere *précis* of the evidence, and altogether it looked so suspicious, that the magistrates, after telling Mrs. Gaunt she could ask the witnesses any question she chose, a suggestion she treated with marked contempt, put their heads together a moment and whispered. Then the eldest of them, Mr. Underhill, who lived at a considerable distance, told her gravely he must commit her to take her trial at the next assizes.

"Do what you conceive to be your duty, gentlemen," said Mrs. Gaunt, with marvellous dignity. "If I do not assert my innocence, it is because I disdain the accusation too much."

"I shall take no part in the committal of this innocent lady," said Sir George Neville, and was about to leave the room.

But Mrs. Gaunt begged him to stay. "To be guilty is one thing," said she, "to be accused is another. I shall go to prison as easy as to my dinner; and to the gallows as to my bed."

The presiding magistrate was staggered a moment by these words; and it was not without considerable hesitation he took the warrant and prepared to fill it up.

Then Mr. Houseman, who had watched the proceedings very keenly, put in his word. "I am here for the accused person, sir, and, with your good leave, object to her committal — on grounds of law."

"What may they be, Mr. Houseman?" said the magistrate, civilly; and laid his pen down to hear them.

"Briefly, sir, these. Where a murder is proven, you can commit a subject of this realm upon suspicion. But you cannot suspect the murder as well as the culprit, and so commit. The murder must be proved to the senses. Now in this case, the death of Mr. Gaunt by violence is not proved. Indeed, his very death rests but upon suspicion. I admit that the law of England in this respect has once or twice been tampered with, and persons have even been executed where no *corpus delicti* was found; but what was the consequence? In each case the murdered man turned out to be alive, and justice was the only murderer. After Harrison's case, and ——'s, no Cumberland jury will ever commit for murder, unless the *corpus delicti* has been found, and with signs of violence upon it. Come, come, Mr. Atkins, you are too good a lawyer, and too humane a man, to send my client to prison on the suspicion of a suspicion, which you know the very breath of the judge will blow away, even if the grand jury let it go into court. I offer bail, ten thousand pounds in two sureties; Sir George Neville here present, and myself."

The magistrate looked to Mr. Atkins.

"I am not employed by the crown," said that gentleman, "but acting on mere civil grounds, and have no right nor wish to be severe. Bail by all means: but is the lady so sure of her innocence as to lend me her assistance to find the *corpus delicti?*"

The question was so shrewdly put, that any hesitation would have ruined Mrs. Gaunt.

Houseman, therefore, replied eagerly and promptly, "I answer for her, she will."

Mrs. Gaunt bowed her head in assent.

"Then," said Atkins, "I ask leave to drag, and, if need be, to drain that piece of water there, called 'the mere.'"

"Drag it or drain it, which you will," said Houseman.

Said Atkins, very impressively, "And, mark my words, at the bottom of that very sheet of water there, I shall find the remains of the late Griffith Gaunt."

At these solemn words, coming as they did, not from a loose unprofessional speaker, but from a lawyer, a man who measured all his words, a very keen observer might have seen a sort of tremor run all through Mr. Houseman's frame. The more admirable, I think, was the perfect coolness and seeming indifference with which he replied, "Find him, and I'll admit suicide; find him, with signs of violence, and I'll admit homicide — by some person or persons unknown."

All further remarks were interrupted by bustle and confusion.

Mrs. Gaunt had fainted dead away.

CHAPTER XXXVIII.

OF course pity was the first feeling; but, by the time Mrs. Gaunt revived, her fainting, so soon after Mr. Atkins's proposal, had produced a sinister effect on the minds of all present; and every face showed it, except the wary Houseman's.

On her retiring, it broke out first in murmurs, then in plain words.

As for Mr. Atkins, he now showed the moderation of an able man who feels he has a strong cause.

He merely said, "I think there should be constables about, in case of an escape being attempted; but I agree with

Mr. Houseman that your worships will be quite justified in taking bail, provided the *corpus delicti* should not be found. Gentlemen, you were most of you neighbors and friends of the deceased, and are, I am sure, lovers of justice; I do entreat you to aid me in searching that piece of water, by the side of which the deceased gentleman was heard to cry for help; and, much I fear, he cried in vain."

The persons thus appealed to entered into the matter with all the ardor of just men, whose curiosity as well as justice is inflamed.

A set of old, rusty drags was found on the premises; and men went punting up and down the mere, and dragged it.

Rude hooks were made by the village blacksmith, and fitted to cart-ropes; another boat was brought to Hernshaw in a wagon; and all that afternoon the bottom of the mere was raked, and some curious things fished up. But no dead man.

The next day a score of amateur dragsmen were out; some throwing their drags from the bridge; some circulating in boats, and even in large tubs.

And, meantime, Mr. Atkins and his crew went steadily up and down, dragging every foot of those placid waters.

They worked till dinner-time, and brought up a good copper pot with two handles, a horse's head, and several decayed trunks of trees, which had become saturated, and sunk to the bottom.

At about three in the afternoon, two boys, who, for want of a boat, were dragging from the bridge, found something heavy but elastic at the end of their drag: they pulled up eagerly, and a thing like a huge turnip, half gnawed, came up, with a great bob, and blasted their sight.

They let go, drags and all, and stood shrieking, and shrieking.

Those who were nearest them called out, and asked what was the matter; but the boys did not reply, and their faces showed so white, that a woman, who saw them, hailed Mr. Atkins, and said she was sure those boys had seen something out of the common.

Mr. Atkins came up, and found the boys blubbering. He encouraged them, and they told him a fearful thing had come up; it was like a man's head and shoulders all scooped out and gnawed by the fishes, and had torn the drags out of their hands.

Mr. Atkins made them tell him the exact place; and he was soon upon it with his boat.

The water here was very deep; and though the boys kept pointing to the very spot, the drags found nothing for some time.

But at last they showed, by their resistance, that they had clawed hold of something.

"Draw slowly," said Mr. Atkins: "and, *if it is*, be men, and hold fast."

The men drew slowly, slowly, and presently there rose to the surface a Thing to strike terror and loathing into the stoutest heart.

The mutilated remains of a human face and body.

The greedy pike had cleared, not the features only, but the entire flesh off the face; but had left the hair, and the tight skin of the forehead, though their teeth had raked this last. The remnants they had left made what they had mutilated doubly horrible; since now it was not a skull, not a skeleton; but a face and a man gnawed down to the bones and hair and feet. These last were in stout shoes, that resisted even those voracious teeth; and a leathern stock had offered some little protection to the throat.

The men groaned, and hid their faces with one hand, and pulled softly to the shore with the other; and then, with half-averted faces, they drew the ghastly remains and fluttering rags gently and reverently to land.

Mr. Atkins yielded to nature, and was violently sick at the sight he had searched for so eagerly.

As soon as he recovered his powers, he bade the constables guard the body (it was a body, in law), and see that no one laid so much as a finger on it until some magistrate had taken a deposition. He also sent a messenger to Mr. Houseman, telling him the *corpus delicti* was found. He did this, partly to show that gentleman he was right in his judgment, and partly out of common humanity ; since, after this discovery, Mr. Houseman's client was sure to be tried for her life.

A magistrate soon came, and viewed the remains, and took careful notes of the state in which they were found.

Houseman came, and was much affected both by the sight of his dead friend, so mutilated, and by the probable consequences to Mrs. Gaunt. However, as lawyers fight very hard, he recovered himself enough to remark that there were no marks of violence before death, and insisted on this being inserted in the magistrate's notes.

An inquest was ordered next day, and, meantime, Mrs. Gaunt was told she could not quit the upper apartments of her own house. Two constables were placed on the ground-floor night and day.

Next day the remains were removed to the little inn where Griffith had spent so many jovial hours ; laid on a table, and covered with a white sheet.

The coroner's jury sat in the same room, and the evidence I have already noticed was gone into, and the finding of the body deposed to. The jury, without hesitation, returned a verdict of wilful murder.

Mrs. Gaunt was then brought in. She came, white as a ghost, leaning upon Houseman's shoulder.

Upon her entering, a juryman, by a humane impulse, drew the sheet over the remains again.

The coroner, according to the custom of the day, put a question to Mrs. Gaunt, with the view of eliciting her guilt. If I remember right, he asked her how she came to be out of doors so late on the night of the murder. Mrs. Gaunt, however, was in no condition to answer queries. I doubt if she even heard this one. Her lovely eyes, dilated with horror, were fixed on that terrible sheet, with a stony glance. " Show me," she gasped, " and let me die too."

The jurymen looked, with doubtful faces, at the coroner. He bowed a grave assent.

The nearest juryman withdrew the sheet. The belief was not yet extinct that the dead body shows some signs of its murderer's approach. So every eye glanced on her and on It by turns ; as she, with dilated, horror-stricken eyes, looked on that awful Thing.

LONDON FORTY YEARS AGO.

FROM THE MEMORANDA OF A TRAVELLER.

THE COURT OF CHANCERY. — Feeling a desire to see for myself the highest embodiment of English law where it lurked — a huge and bloated personification of all that was monstrous and discouraging to suitors — in the secret place of thunder, just behind the altar of sacrifice, forever spinning the web that for hundreds of years hath enmeshed and overspread the mightiest empire upon earth with entanglement, perplexity, and procrastination, till estates have disappeared and families have died out, sometimes, while waiting for a decision, — I dropped into the Court of Chancery.

The first thing I saw was the Lord Chancellor himself, — Lord Eldon, — the mildest, wisest, slowest, and most benignant of men, — milder than Byron's Ali Pacha, wiser than Lord Bacon himself ; and, if not altogether worthy of being called "the greatest, wisest, meanest of mankind," like his prototype, yet great enough as a lawyer to set people wondering what he would say next. He was quite capable of arguing a question on both sides, and then of deciding against himself; and so patient, withal, that he had just then finished a sitting of three whole days to Sir Thomas Lawrence, for a portrait of his hand, — a beautiful hand, it must be acknowledged, though undecided and womanish, as if he had never quite made up his mind whether to keep it open or shut.

And the next thing I took notice of, after a hurried glance at the carved ceiling and painted windows, and over the array of bewigged and powdered solicitors and masters, — a magnificent bed of cauliflowers, in appearance, with some of the finest heads I ever saw in my life — out of a cabbage-garden, — was a large, dark, heavy picture of Paul before Felix, by Hogarth, representing these great personages at the moment when Felix, that earliest of Lord Chancellors, having heard Paul through, says: "Go thy way for this time; when I have a convenient season, I will call for thee." Lord Eldon was larger than I supposed from the portrait above mentioned. And this is the more extraordinary, because the heads of Lawrence, like those of ancient statuary, are always smaller than life, to give them an aristocratic, high-bred air, and the bodies are larger. The expression of countenance, too, was benignity itself, — just such as Titian would have been delighted with, — calm, clear, passionless, without a prevailing characteristic of any strength. "Felix trembled," they say. Whatever Felix may have done, I do not believe that Lord Eldon would have trembled till he had put on his night-cap and weighed the whole question by himself at his chambers.

Kean. — Wishing to see how this grotesque but wonderful actor — a mountebank sometimes and sometimes a living truth — would play at home after driving us all mad in America, I

went to see him in Sir Giles Overreach. He played with more spirit, more of settled purpose, than with us, being more in earnest, I think, and better supported. There is one absurdity in the play, which was made particularly offensive by Oxberry's exaggeration. The dinner is kept waiting, and the whole business of the play suspended, for the Justice to make speeches. But the last scene was capital, — prodigious, — full of that dark, dismal, despairing energy you would look for in a dethroned spirit, baffled, like Mephistopheles, at the very moment his arm is outstretched, and his long, lean fingers are clutching at the shoulder of his victim. Being about to cross blades with his adversary, in a paroxysm of rage he plucks at the hilt of his sword, and stops suddenly, as if struck with paralysis, pale, and gasping for breath, and says, — in that far-off, moaning voice we all remember in his famous farewell to the "big wars that make ambition virtue," — "The widow sits upon my arm, and the wronged orphan's tear glues it to the scabbard, — it will *not* be drawn," etc., etc., — or something of the sort. It was not so much a thrilling as a curdling you felt.

Young, in Sir Pertinax. — Very good, though full of stage trick, or what they call, when they get bothered, or would like to bother you, stage *business;* — as where he throws his pocket-handkerchief before him on leaving the stage, somewhat after the style of Macready in Hamlet, which Forrest called *le pas à mouchoir,* and took the liberty of hissing. Good Scotch, generally, with a few wretched blunders, though his "booin', and booin', and booin'," and his vehement snuff-taking, and the declaration that "he could never stand oopright in the presence of a great mon in a' his life," were evidently copied from, or suggested by, George Frederick Cooke, who borrowed both from Macklin, if we may trust surviving contemporaries.

Robert Owen. — Breakfasted with Rob—

ert Owen, after having attended a conference of the brotherhood, where they talked a world of nonsense, and argued for a whole hour, without coming to a conclusion, about whether we are governed by circumstances or circumstances are governed by us. You would swear Owen was a Yankee, born and bred. He has the shrewd, inquisitive look, the spare frame, the sharp features, of a Connecticut farmer, and constantly reminds me of Henry Clay when he moves about. He is evidently sincere; but such a visionary! and so thoroughly satisfied that the world is coming to an end just as he would have it, that he allows no misgivings to trouble him, and never loses his temper, nor "bates one jot of heart or hope," happen what may. The last time we met — only three days ago — his great project was coming up before Parliament, and he told me, in confidence, that he was sure of a favorable result, — that he had counted noses, and had the most comfortable assurances from all the great leaders of the day, — and in short, between ourselves, that grass would be growing on the London Exchange within two years. The petition came up on the day appointed, and was allowed to drop out of the tail end of the cart, almost without a remark. But so far was he from being disheartened, that he lost no time in preparing for a trip across the Atlantic, which he had long had in contemplation, but was hindered from taking by the hopes he had been persuaded to entertain from his friends in Parliament, and by the business at Lanark, — a manufacturing place which he had built up of himself in Scotland, with eminent success, and most undoubted practical wisdom.

Wishing to leave a record with me for future ages, he wrote as follows in my album, with a cheerfulness, an imperturbability, a serene self-confidence, past all my conceptions of a visionary or enthusiast.

"I leave this country with a deep impression that my visit to America will be productive of permanent benefit to the Indian tribes, to the negro race, and to the whole population of the Western Continent, North and South, and to Europe.

"ROBERT OWEN.

"LONDON, 4th September, 1824."

What a magnificent scheme! How comprehensive and how vast! But nothing came of it, beyond the translation of his son, Robert Dale Owen, to this country, — a very clever, well-educated, and earnest, though rather awkward and sluggish young man, who has achieved a large reputation here, and will be yet more distinguished if he lives, being well grounded and rooted in the foundation principles of government, and both conscientious and fearless.

Old Bailey. — This and other like places, of which we have all read so much that we feel acquainted with them, not as pictures or descriptions, at second hand, but as decided and positive realities, I lost no time in seeing.

I found the court-room small, much smaller than the average with us, badly arranged, and worse lighted. A prisoner was up for burglary. He was a sullen, turbulent-looking fellow; and his counsel, an Old Bailey lawyer, was inquiring, with a pertinacity that astonished while it amused me, about the dirt in a comb. His object was to ascertain "whether it had been used or *not*"; and, as there were two sides to it, which side had become dirty from being carried in the pocket, and which from legitimate use. Before the prisoner was a toilet-glass, in which he could not help seeing his own pale, haggard, frightened face whenever he looked up, — a refinement of barbarism I was not prepared for in a British court of justice. I occupied a seat in the gallery, surrounded by professional pickpockets, burglars, and highwaymen, I dare say; for they talked freely of the poor fellow's chances, and like experts.

Joanna Baillie. — "Here," said Lady Bentham, wife of General Sir Samuel

Bentham, the originator of that Panopticon, which was the germ of all our prison discipline as well as of all penitentiary improvements, the world over, — " Here is an autograph you will think worth having, I am sure, after what I have heard you say of the writer, and of her tragedies, and I want you to see her " ; — handing me, as she spoke, the following brief note, written upon a bit of coarse paper about six inches by four.

" If you are perfectly disengaged this evening, Agnes and I will have the pleasure of taking tea with you, if you give us leave.

"J. BAILLIE."

Now, if there was a woman in the world I wanted to see, or one that I most heartily reverenced, it was Joanna Baillie. Her " De Montfort " I had always looked upon as one of the greatest tragedies ever written, — equal to anything of Shakespeare's for strength of delineation, simplicity, and effect, however inferior it might be in the superfluities of genius, in the overcharging of character and passion, of which we find so much in Shakespeare ; and, on the whole, not unlike that wonderful Danish drama, " Dyveke," or a part of " Wallenstein."

My great desire was now to be satisfied. We met, and I passed one of the pleasantest evenings of my life with *Mrs.* Baillie, as they called her, Lady Bentham, her most intimate if not her oldest friend, and " sister Agnes."

I found Mrs. Baillie wholly unlike the misrepresentations I had seen of her. She was rather small, — though far from being diminutive, like her sister Agnes, — with a charming countenance, full of placid serenity, almost Quakerish, beautiful eyes, and gray hair, nearly white indeed, combed smoothly away from her forehead. We talked freely together, avoiding the shop, and the impression she left on my mind was that of a modest, unpretending gentlewoman, full of quiet strength and shrewd pleasantry, with a Scottish flavor, but altogether above being brilliant or showy, even in conversation with a stranger and an author. She questioned me closely about my country and about the people, and appeared to take much interest in our doings and prospects. Her sister Agnes never opened her mouth, to the best of my recollection and belief, though she listened with her eyes and ears to the conversation, and appeared to enjoy it exceedingly ; and as for Lady Bentham, though a clever woman of large experience and great resources, such was her self-denial and her generous admiration of the " queenly stranger," as I had called her friend in sport, — remembering how it was applied to the magnificent Siddons, when she represented Jane de Montfort, — that she did nothing more and said nothing more than what was calculated to bring out her friend to advantage. There was nothing said, however, from which a person unacquainted with the writings of Joanna Baillie would have inferred her true character, — no flashing lights, no surprises, no thunder-bursts. The conversation was, at the best, but sociable and free, as if we were all of the same neighborhood or household ; but knowing her by her great work on the Passions, I was profoundly impressed, nevertheless, and left her well satisfied with her revelations of character.

Catalani. — What a magnificent creature! How majestic and easy and graceful! And then what a voice! One would swear she had a nest of nightingales and a trumpet obligato in her throat. No wonder she sets the great glass chandeliers of the Argyle rooms ringing and rattling when she charges in a bravura.

That she is, in some passages, a little — not vulgar — but almost vulgar, with a dash of the contadina, is undeniable ; and she certainly has not a delicate ear, and often sings false ; yet, when that tempestuous warbling in her throat breaks forth, and the flush of her heart's blood hurries over her face and empurples her neck, why then " bow the high banners, roll the answering drums," and shut up, if you would n't be torn to pieces by a London mob.

Say what you will, you must acknowledge — you *must* — that you never heard such a voice before, if there ever was one like it on earth, — so full and so impassioned, so rich and sympathetic. More educated, more brilliant organs there may be, like those of Pasta or Velluti, poor fellow! — more satisfying to the ear, — but none, I believe, so satisfying to the heart; none that so surely lifts you off your feet, and blinds and deafens you to all defects, and sets you wandering far away through the empyrean of musical sounds, till you are lost in a labyrinth of triumphant harmonies. The sad, mournful intonations of Velluti may bring tears into your eyes, but you are never transported beyond yourself by his piteous wailing.

And yet, if you will believe me, this woman has just been called out of bed to a London audience, who, instead of paying a guinea or half a guinea to hear her in opera, are paying only 2*s.* 6*d.* a head to hear her let off " God s*h*ave the King! " like a roll of musical thunder. She appears " in *dish-abille* " as they call it here, and in *tears*. And why is she summoned ? Because the *sufferin'* people, having understood that she shares the house, insist on having their half-crowns and sixpences returned. It has been quite impossible to hear a word, ever since they were informed that she had been taken suddenly ill, and was not allowed to appear by her medical attendants. But what of that ? Dead or alive, a British audience must have her out. And so a great banner was lifted on which was inscribed " Catalani sent for ! " and then, after a while, as the uproar continued, and the outcries grew more violent, and the white handkerchiefs more and more stormy and threatening, another inscription appeared, " Catalani coming ! " And lo! she comes ! and comes weeping. But the people refuse to be comforted. And why ? Because of their disappointment? Because of their passion for music ? No indeed ; but because they are told that she is to go snacks with the manager ; and, her parsimony being proverbial, they are determined to rebuke it in a liberal spirit. Pshaw !

These people pretend to love music, and to love it with such a devouring passion that nothing less than the very best will satisfy them, cost what it may. Yet the opera-house, with the patronage of the royal family, the nobility, and the gentry, and open only twice a week, is never full even at the representation of the finest works of genius ; and when such an artist as Catalani is engaged at one of the theatres, and the people are admitted for theatre prices, the first thing they do, after crowding the house to suffocation, is to call for " God save the King," or, if Braham is out, for " Kelvin Grove." Enthusiasts indeed, — carried away, and justly, by " Black-eyed Susan," or " Cherry Ripe," which they do understand, feel, and enjoy, — they are all ready to swear, and expect you to believe, that their passion is for opera music, — Italian or German, the Barber of Seville, or *Der Freischütz.* And therefore I say again, Pshaw !

John Dunn Hunter. — This luckiest and boldest of humbugs, whose book, by the merest accident, has obtained for him the favor of the Duke of Sussex, and, through the Duke, access to the highest nobility, has just been presented at Court, and is not a little mortified that his Majesty, on receiving a copy of the book, Hunter's " Captivity among the Indians," did not inquire after his health or make him a speech. He does not so much mind paying five guineas for the loan of a court suit, consisting of a single-breasted claret coat with steel buttons, a powdered tie, small-clothes, white-silk stockings, and a dress sword, — with instructions on which side it is to be worn, and how it is to be managed in backing out so as not to get between his legs and trip him up, — nor the having to pay for being mentioned in the Court Journal by a fellow who is called the King's Reporter ; but then he will have the worth of his money, and so takes it out in grumbling and sulking. Not long ago he sent a note through the penny-post, sealed with a wafer, directed to the Marchioness of Conyngham, the king's mistress, in reply to an invitation from her ladyship, which he accepted, to meet the king! At least, such was the interpretation he put upon it. And now, after all this, to be fobbed off with a bow by "Gentleman George," the "fat friend" of poor Brummell, was indeed a little too bad.

Nothing he can say or do, however, will undeceive these people. Though he cannot shout decently, cannot bear fatigue or pain, is so far from being swift of foot that he is not even a good walker, talks little or no Indian, and is continually outraging all the customs of society after getting well acquainted with them, and doing all this by calculation, as in the case of the note referred to above, they persist in believing his story. I shall have to expose him. — P. S. I have exposed him.

While speaking just now of his acquaintance with the Duke of Sussex, who was very kind to him, and a believer to the last, I said that it was obtained for him by accident. It was in this way. At the house where he lodged a Mr. Norgate of Norfolk — not far from Holkham, the seat of Mr. Coke afterward Earl of Leicester — was also a lodger. Mr. Norgate invited Hunter down to his father's, and they went over to Holkham together. And there they met the Duke of Sussex, a great friend of Mr. Coke, both being Liberals and Oppositionists. His Royal Highness took a great fancy to Hunter, got him to sit to Chester Harding for his picture, gave him a gold watch and lots of agricultural tools to subdue the Indians with, and stuck to him through thick and thin, till I found it necessary to tear off the fellow's mask.

On separating from me, before I had got possession of the facts which soon after appeared in the "London Magazine," he wrote in my album the following sententious and pithy apothegm, which, of course, only went to show the marvellous power of adaptation to circumstances which would naturally characterize the man, if his story were true. It was in this way his dupes reasoned. If he sealed a letter with a wafer, and sent it through the penny-post to a woman of rank, that proved his neglected education or a natural disregard of polite usage, and of course that he had been carried off in childhood by the Indians, and knew not where to look for father or mother, sister or brother, — while, on the contrary, if he used wax, and set the seal upon it which had been given to him by the Duke of Sussex, that showed, of course, the sagacity and readiness of adaptation which ought to characterize the hero of Hunter's narrative. In short, he was another Princess Caraboo, or young Chatterton, or Cagliostro, or Count Eliorich, all of whom were made great impostors by the help of others, the over-credulous and the over-confident in themselves.

"He who would do great actions," writes our enormous bug-a-boo, "must learn to *empoly* his powers to the least possible loss. The possession of brilliant and extraordinary talents" (this was probably meant for me, as he had been trying to prevail upon my "brilliant and extraordinary talents" to return to America with him, and go among the savages about the neighborhood of the Rocky Mountains, and there establish a confederacy of our own) "is not always the most valuable to its possessor. Moderate talents, properly directed, will enable one to do a great deal; and the most distinguished gifts of nature may be thrown away by an unskilful application of them.

"J. D. HUNTER.

"LONDON, 15th May, 1824."

Kean at a Public Dinner. — A terrible outcry just now, in consequence of certain exposures and a published correspondence. At a public dinner, he says he is going to America. The Duke of York, who presides, cries out, "No, no!" Shouts follow and the rattling of glasses, and men leap on the chairs and almost on the tables, repeating the Duke's "No, no!" till at last

Kean promises to make an apology from the stage,— a perilous experiment, he will find, after which he cannot stay here. The object of Price, who has engaged him, is to kill off Cooper. The best actors now get fifty guineas a week, or twenty-five pounds a night for so many nights, play or pay, with a benefit.

Architecture. — I have seen no greater barbarisms anywhere than I find here. The screen of Carleton House, — a long row of double columns, with a heavy entablature supporting the arms of Great Britain, — "that and nothing more"; the doings of Inigo Jones in his water-gates and arches, with two or three orders intermixed; and the late achievements of Mr. Nash along Regent Street, — with the church spire, which has the attractiveness and symmetry of an exaggerated marlin-spike, for a vanishing point, — are of themselves enough to show that the people here have no taste, and no feeling for this department of the Fine Arts, however much they may brag and bluster.

But I have just returned from a visit to one of Sir Christopher Wren's masterpieces, which has greatly disturbed my equanimity, and obliges me to modify my opinion. It is a church back of the Mansion House; and is the original of Godefroy's Unitarian church at Baltimore, beyond all question: the dome rests on arches, and springs into the air, as if buoyed up and aspiring of itself. Bad for the music, however. Here I find West's picture of the Martyrdom of St. Stephen, with a figure which he has repeated in "Christ Healing the Sick," and a woman, — or young man, you do not feel certain which, — weeping upon the hand of the martyr, precisely as in a painting in Baltimore Cathedral by Renou, who must have borrowed or stolen it from West, if West did not borrow or steal it from him.

Drawings. — I have just returned from visiting a collection of drawings by the old masters, — Raphael, Michael Angelo, Rembrandt, Titian, &c., &c. Wonderful, to be sure! There is a pen-and-ink drawing by Munro, of uncommon merit; another from a capital old engraving by Tiffen, hardly to be distinguished from an elaborate line engraving, full of good faces and straight lines, with nothing picturesque. A moonlight and cottage by Gainsborough, very fine. Jackson's and Robinson's miniatures, and sketches in water-colors, — charming. Leslie's designs, with Stothard's on the same subject, are delightfully contrasted: Leslie's, neatly finished and full of individuality; Stothard's, a beautiful, free generalization, without finish. (But the engraver understands him, and finishes for him, adding the hands and feet in his own way.) It is a representation of Jeanie Deans's interview with the Queen. Leslie's figure is standing; Stothard's, kneeling: yet both are expressive and helpful to our conceptions. Here, too, I saw Rembrandt's celebrated "Battle of Death," with a skeleton blowing a horn, and helmeted and plumed, and having a thigh-bone for a battle-axe, — shadows on the shoulders of horsemen, and skeleton feet; — on the whole, a monstrous nightmare, such as you might expect from Fuseli after a supper on raw beef, but never from such a painter as Rembrandt.

Phrenology. — There must be something in this new science, — for they persist in calling it a science, — though I cannot say how much. Just returned from a visit to De Ville, in the Strand, in company with Chester Harding, Robert M. Sully, the painter, and Humphries, the engraver, — each differing from the others in character and purpose; yet, after manipulating our crania, this man says of each what all the rest acknowledge to be true, and what, said of any but the particular person described, would be preposterous. Why are the busts of Socrates and Solon what they should be, according to this theory of Gall and Spurzheim? Were they modelled from life, or from characters resembling them? Compared the head of a Greek boy with that of a young Hottentot. One was largely developed in the intellectual region, the other in the animal region, and the latter cries whenever his home or his mother is mentioned. Both are at school here. Thurtell's head is a great confirmation, which anybody can judge of. I must find time for a thorough investigation.

P. S. — I have kept my promise, and am thoroughly satisfied. Phrenology deserves to be called a science, and one of the greatest and best of sciences, notwithstanding all the quackery and self-delusion that I find among the professors. I have now studied it and experimented upon it for more than thirty years, and have no longer any misgivings upon the subject, so far as the great leading principles are involved.

Manners. — If we do not record our first impressions they soon disappear; and the greatest novelties are overlooked or forgotten. Already I begin to see women with heavily-laden wheelbarrows, without surprise. I have now learned, I hope, that a postman's rap is *one*, *two*, and no more; a servant's, *one*; while a footman gives from four to twenty, as hard as he can bang, so as to startle the whole neighborhood and make everybody run to the windows. Eating fish with a knife said to be fatal. Great personages give you a finger to shake. I did not know this when I took the forefinger of a cast-off mistress, the original of Washington Irving's Lady Sillicraft, a painted and withered old vixen, who meant to signify her liking for me, as I had reason to believe. Moles are reckoned such a positive beauty here that my attention has been called to them, as to fine eyes or a queenly bearing. A *fine* woman here means a large woman, tall, dignified, and showy, like a fine horse or a fine bullock.

Never shall I forget the looks and tones of a bashful friend, in describing his embarrassment. He was at Holkham, the seat of Mr. Coke, our Revolutionary champion, who, being in Parliament at the time, moved, session after session, the acknowledgment of our independence, — am I right here? — and actually gave the health of George Washington at a large dinner-party while the Revolutionary fires were raging. There was a large company at dinner, but for his life my friend did not know what to do with the ladies nor with his hands. Goes through room after room to get his dinner; is called upon to serve a dish he has never seen before, and knows not how to manage. Asked to take wine, and wants to ask somebody else, but cannot recall the name of a single person within reach, and whispers to the servant for relief, while his eye travels up and down both sides of the long table; is reminded of the guest who said to himself, loud enough to be overheard by the waiter behind his chair, "I wish I had some bread," to which the waiter replied without moving, "I wish you had." Durst not offer his arm to a lady, lest he should violate some of the multitudinous every-day usages of society, and so, instead of enjoying his dinner, just nibbled and choked and watched how others ate of the dishes he had never seen before. Yet this man was no fool, he was not even a blockhead; but he was frightened out of all propriety nevertheless. Poor fellow! Soon after this he went to Paris, and, having picked up a few French sentences, undertook to pass off one upon a servant who took his cloak as he entered the hotel of a French celebrity in a violent rainstorm. He flung the phrase off with an air, saying, "Mauvais temps," whereupon the word was passed up from mouth to mouth, and, to his unutterable horror, he was introduced to the company as M. Mauvais Temps.

Painting. — I have just been to see Mulready's famous "Lion and Lamb." He is a Royal Academician; and, spite of the cleverness we see in every touch, we are reminded of Pison's reply to the Academician, who asked what he was, — " I ? O, I am nobody; not even an Academician." The picture is about eighteen by twenty-two inches, and belongs to his Majesty, George the Fourth. It represents two boys, a little child, a woman, and a dog. One boy has broken the strap of his trousers, and, bracing himself up for a clinch, is evidently encroaching on the other with his foot. He stands with his legs on the straddle, both fists made up for mischief, and head turned away in profile, with hat and books flung down upon the turf; while the other — the lamb — keeps his satchel in his hand, with one arm raised to parry the blow he is expecting. He has a meek, boyish face, and we have it in full. The back of the child is towards you, the mother terribly frightened; parts very fine, but as a whole the picture is not worthy of its reputation, to say nothing of the extravagant price paid for it, — some hundreds of guineas, they say.

Greenwich Fair. — Having read so much in story-books and novels, from my earliest childhood, — at one time in the gilt-covered publication of E. Newbury, St. Paul's Church Yard, and after that in larger books, — of the rioting at Greenwich Fair (another Donnybrook in its way), I determined to see for myself, and went down for the purpose, April 19th, 1824. Universal decorum characterized the whole proceedings till the day was over, after which there was a large amount of dancing and frolicking and sight-seeing and beer-drinking, but no drunkenness and no quarrelling. The people were saucy, but good-natured, like the Italian rabble, with their plaster confectionery, at a carnival. Women and girls would run down the long green slope together, which it is said the cockneys believe to be the highest land in the world, after Richmond Hill; and many of them stumble and slip and roll to the bottom, screaming and laughing as they go. This I understand to be a favorite pastime with people who are big enough to know better; for a part of the fun, and that which all seem to enjoy most, is in tripping one another up. Plenty of giants and dwarfs to be seen for a penny, with white Circassians, silver-haired, and actors of all sorts and sizes. "Walk in, ladies and gentlemen ! walk in ! Here 's the rope-dancing and juggling, with lots of gilt gingerbread, — and all for sixpence ! Here is the great Numidian lion !" — leading forth a creature not larger than a moderate-sized English mastiff, — "with a throat like a turnpike gate, and teeth like mile-stones, and every hair on his mane as big as a broomstick !" It was worth sixpence to see the fellow's face when he said this ; but most of the people round me seemed to believe what they heard rather than what they saw. Actors and actresses turn out and dance and strut before the curtain.

Went into the Hospital, of which we have all heard so much, and into the Chapel. Here is the best picture West ever painted, I think. It is the shipwreck of St. Paul, with the viper and the fire : rocks rather crowded and confused ; on the right are two figures, frequently, I had almost said always, to be found in his pictures, and always together. Old man on the right, capital ! — Roof of the Hospital highly ornamented, though chaste, with painted pilasters, fluted ; ceiling done by Sir James Thornhill, and is really a grand affair, not only for coloring and drawing, but for composition and general treatment. Architecture of the building, once a palace, worthy of the highest commendation, though it needs a back part to correspond with the two wings. Cupolas made to correspond, but seem rather out of place, — not wanted.

Had quite an adventure before I got away. I saw a young girl running down hill by herself. She fell, and stained her white frock all over one hip of a grass-green. She seemed to be much hurt and near fainting. I found her young, pretty, and modest, as you may readily infer from what follows, — usually if you hear of a woman being run over in the street, you may be sure she is neither young nor pretty,—and so seeing her greatly distressed about the figure she cut, and companionless, I took pity on her, and going with her found, after some search, an old woman in a garret with a husband, child, and grandchild, all huddled and starving in one room together. The husband was a waterman. He had "stove" his boat some years before, and was never able to get another; had two sons at sea; paid two shillings a week for the room, which they said was one shilling too dear, being only large enough to allow of two or three chairs, a table, and a turn-up bed. Poor Sarah took off her frock and washed it before me, without a sign of distress or embarrassment; and then we went off together and had a bit of a dance,—a rough-and-tumble fore-and-after,—at the nearest booth. With her bonnet off, and neat cap, her beautiful complexion and dark hair and eyes, how happened it that she was really modest and well-behaved? And how came she there? After some resolute questioning, I determined to see her home, at least so far as to set her down in safety in the neighborhood where she lived. The coach was crowded with strangers. It was late, and they were silent, and I thought sulky. Just as we were passing a lamp, after we had entered a wide thoroughfare, I saw a man's face under a woman's bonnet. Though not absolutely frightened, I was rather startled, and more and more unwilling to leave the poor girl to the mercy of strangers; for I saw, or thought I saw, signs of intelligence between two of the party; and in short, I never left her till the danger was over.

There were mountebanks and fortune-tellers and gypsies at every turn. The prettiest I met with told my fortune. "You are liked better by the women," said she, "than by the men." Very true. "You are loved by a widow named Mary." My landlady was a widow, and her name was Mary. "Which do you like best, Mary or Bessie?" In addition to Mary, there was another pleasant friend, supposed to be a natural daughter of George IV., named Bessie. But how the plague did the little gypsy know this? I found out, I believe, long after the whole affair was forgotten. There was present, without my knowledge, a man who was always full of such tricks, who knew me well, and who threw the gypsy in my way and put her up to all she knew. This was Humphries the engraver.

There was a great ball too,—a magnificent ball,—one shilling entrance. More than fifty couples stood up for a contra-dance, and tore down the middle and up outside, and cast off, as if they were all just out of a lunatic hospital. And yet, as I have said before, I believe, there was no drunkenness and no quarrelling.

Shooting the Bridge.—Wanting to go to the Tower, I took a boat above London Bridge at the wrong time of the tide, in spite of all remonstrances, and came near being swamped. Not being a good swimmer, and aware that people were often drowned there, I cannot understand what possessed me; but as the watermen were not afraid, and asked no questions, why should I be troubled? For aught they knew, I might be made of cork, or have a swimming-jacket underneath my coat, or a pocket life-preserver ready to be blown up at a moment's notice; and they were sure of the fee. At the mouth of the St. John's River, New Brunswick, they have a fall both ways, at a certain time of tide, through which and up and down which boats and rafts plunge headlong so as to take away your breath, while you are watching them from the bridge; but really, this little pitch of not more than three or four feet under London Bridge I should think more dangerous, and the people seem to think so too, for they are always on the watch after the tide turns, and swarm along the parapets, and rush from one side to the other, as the wherry shoots through the main arch, with a feeling akin to that of the man who followed Van Amburgh month after month to see him "chawed up" by the lion or tiger.

Major Cartwright. — Another fast friend of our country and the institutions of our country, and always ready to take up the quarter-staff in our defence. A great reformer, and honest as the day is long. Wrote much in favor of American independence in 1774, and, with Sir Francis Burdett and others, who chose to meddle with the British Constitution wherever they found a fragment large enough to talk about, has been visited by the government, and tried and imprisoned. His book on the British Constitution is, though somewhat visionary, both original and ingenious. He is six feet high, with a very broad chest ; wears a fur cap and blue cotton-velvet dressing-gown in the sultriest weather ; is a great admirer of Jeremy Bentham, Mrs. Wheeler, and Fanny Wright, by the way.

Woolwich. — After spending a day here under special advantages, I have succeeded in seeing whatever was worth seeing for my purpose, and in getting a fine sketch of a Woolwich Pensioner by Sully, — Robert M. Sully, nephew of Thomas Sully, and a capital draughtsman,—to serve as a companion piece for the Greenwich Pensioner by the same artist. The man had served against us in the Revolutionary War, and participated in the "affair" of Bunker Hill. The shovel hats, the long chins and retreating mouths of these aged men at Greenwich, are wonderfully hit off by Cruikshank, with a mere flourish of the pen. I have a scene in a watch-house, with half a score of heads, thoroughly Irish, drunk or sleepy, and as many more of these shovel hats, which the clever artist amused himself with scratching off, — as we sat talking together at a table, — on a little bit of waste paper, which fluttered away in the draft from a window, and fell upon the floor.

Saw a prodigious quantity of guns to be "let loose" in the dock-yard, to which I was admitted as a great privilege. When Alexander of Russia and the king of Prussia were admitted after the war, they were greatly disappoint-

ed and mortified, I was told, at seeing such a vast accumulation of warlike material. They supposed England to be exhausted.

The English artillery is far superior in details to the French, though not half so abundant. Where the French bring eighty pieces at once into the field, the English never have more than twenty pieces. The English lost only two guns in the whole Peninsular war ; the French lost nearly eleven hundred, Waterloo included.

At Woolwich there are two or three hundred acres full of machinery, with saw - mills, planing - mills, &c. Saw, among other inventions and improvements, anchor shanks made largest about one third of the distance from the crown, where they always bend or break ; an original screw-cutter of uncommon merit ; and a perpetual capstan for drawing in wood for the mill.

Illuminations. — His Majesty's birthday. By one odd arrangement of colored lamps, which was intended for George IV., it reads thus, *Giver*, being G. IV. R. The populace break windows which are not lighted up. The king's tradesmen are most astonishing in their manifestations of loyalty ; and, among others, I see an establishment with this inscription : "Bug Destroyer to his Majesty."

Chimney-Sweeps. — May 1. The little monsters appear in cocked hats and gilt paper, with their faces painted, and with dancing and music, and a very pretty girl pirouetting in a hogshead of cut paper, with large boys about her, like trees dancing. Of course, we are constantly reminded of Edward Wortley Montagu, and of his delightful experience with the chimney-sweeps.

John Randolph. — This madman is full of his vagaries here ; says the most offensive things, but in such a high-bred, supercilious, if not gentlemanly way, that people cannot make up their minds about him, nor whether to cut him dead or acknowledge him for a genius and a humorist. Sir Robert Inglis says, publicly, that Mr. Randolph " on these boards " claimed for Virginia the first attempt at abolition. "And I am disposed to believe the gentleman correct," adds Sir Robert, " because of his opportunities for knowledge." Whatever related to the United States was received better than anything else in the proceedings of to-day at the Freemasons' Tavern. Very comfortable and gratifying.

Marquis of Stafford's Gallery. — Here I find about three hundred fine pictures, most of them by the old masters, and a large part worthy of enthusiastic admiration. Thirty-eight in the National Gallery cost sixty thousand pounds. What, then, are these worth as a collection ?

Cary, the Translator of Dante. — Met him at Mr. Griffith's, — Sylvanus Urban's, — another great friend of our country, who insisted on my occupying the seat which Dr. Franklin used to sit in, and after him Lord Byron. Mr. Cary has a good, sensible face, is about five feet seven in height, and forty-six years old, very moderate of speech, and talks with a low voice. Among the guests were Captain Brace, who was with Lord Exmouth when he put through the Dey of Algiers after the fashion of our Preble. He seemed about sixty, with gray hair, and a youthful countenance.

Horticultural Exhibition. — Great show and surprising. No sales made. Pears better than ours ; peaches nearly as good, and sell from a shilling to one and sixpence apiece. They resemble not our New Jersey or Maryland peaches, but such as grow about Boston. Grapes fine, nectarines capital ; gooseberries, plums, mulberries, currants, all better than ours ; apples wretched, "not fit to give the pigs," liked all the better for being hard, or ligneous.

I have just understood here, on the best authority, that Mr. Coke, of Norfolk, did move for an abandonment of the war, session after session, and finally gave the casting vote as mover. He did also give Washington's health at his own table once, with a large company of leading men about him, in the hottest part of the struggle. He looks like one of Trumbull's generals or statesmen, of the old Revolutionary type, and not unlike Washington himself, or General Knox.

Duke of Sussex. — Prodigious ; even Chester Harding, who is a large man, over six feet, appears under-sized alongside of his Royal Highness. Went to a meeting for the encouragement of the arts. The Duke presided, and, being popular and willing so to continue, he made a speech. "Ladies and gentlemen," said he, "it affords me gratification to see, to recognize, so many persons assembled for the encouragement of what I may say is one of the best institutions of the country. Good deal of business coming up. I shall therefore reserve myself for the conclusion, and now call upon the Secretary to read the proceedings." Effect of the show seems to be very good. Some persons, girls and women, received three prizes.

Theatre. — Munden's farewell. Dosey and Sir Robert Bramble ; among the finest pieces of acting I ever saw, — rich, warm, and full of unadulterated strength. Terrible crush at the entrance, the corners being neither stuffed nor rounded. Great screaming and screeching. "Take care o' that corner !" "Mind there !" "Oh ! oh ! you 'll kill me !" "There now, lady's killed !" And it was indeed about as much as a woman's life was worth to venture into such a brutal mob. No consideration for women, as usual. They are pushed, crowded, overthrown sometimes, and sometimes trampled on without remorse or shame, as at the Duke of York's funeral.

Washington Irving. — Met him for the second time, and had more reason than ever for believing that, with all his daintiness and fastidiousness, he is altogether a man, hearty and generous, and his books, with all their shifting shadows, but a transcript of himself and of his unacknowledged visions and meditations. His pleasantry, too, is delightful; and, as you cannot question his truthfulness, he gains upon you continually, even while you pity his girlish sensitiveness. I do not see any picture of him that satisfies me, or does him justice. Newton cannot paint a portrait, nor indeed can Leslie; and the result is, that what we have foisted off upon us for portraits are only misunderstandings.

A YEAR IN MONTANA.

WHERE the Wind River Chain of the Rocky Mountains stretches far away to the east, and the Bitter Root Range far away to the northwest, like giant arms holding in their embrace the fertile valleys whence the myriad springs which form the two great rivers of the continent take their rise, — on the northern border of the United States, and accessible only through leagues of desert, — lie the gold fields of Montana. Four years ago all this region was *terra incognita*. In 1805, Lewis and Clarke passed through it; but beyond a liberal gift of geographical inaccuracies, they have left only a few venerable half-breeds as relics of their journey. Among the Indians, what they did and said has passed into tradition; and the tribes of which they speak, the Keheet-sas, Minnetarees, Hohilpoes, and Tus-he-pahs, are as extinct as the dodo. Later explorers have added little to the scanty stock of information, save interesting descriptions of rich valleys and rough mountain scenery and severe hardships in the winters. For the most part, it was a country unexplored and unknown, and held by the various Indian tribes in the Northwest as a common hunting-ground.

One bright morning in August, 1864, after a brief rest at Salt Lake, we left Brigham's seraglios for this new El Dorado. We had taken the long trip of twelve hundred miles on the overland stage, which Mr. Bowles describes in his admirable book "Across the Continent." But his was the gala-day excursion of Speaker Colfax and his party, so full of studied and constant attention as to lead Governor Bross to tell the good people of Salt Lake, a little extravagantly, that the height of human happiness was to live in one of Holladay's stages. This life loses its rose-color when nine inside passengers, to fortune and to fame unknown, are viewed as so much freight, and transported accordingly.

It is four hundred miles due north from Salt Lake City to Montana. The low canvas-covered Concord hack, in which we travel, is constructed with an eye rather to safety than comfort, and, like a city omnibus, is never full. Still, our passengers look upon even their discomforts as a joke. They are most of them old miners, hard-featured but genial and kindly, and easily distinguished from men reared in the easy life of cities. Mr. Bowles describes them as characterized by a broader grasp and more intense vitality. I could not but notice, particularly, their freedom from all the quarrels and disagreements sometimes known among travellers in the States. The heavy revolver at every man's belt, and the miner's proverbial love of fair play, keep in every one's mind a clear perception of the bounds of *meum* and *tuum*.

I must hurry over our four days'

journey and its many objects of interest. All the first day we ride through brisk Mormon villages, prosperous in their waving cornfields and their heavy trade with the mines. At a distance is the Great Salt Lake, — properly an inland sea, like the Caspian and Sea of Aral, — having a large tributary, the Bear River, and no outlet. Crossing Bear River, and the low mountains beyond, we follow down the Portneuf Cañon to Snake River, or Lewis's Fork of the Columbia, along which and its affluents lies the rest of our journey.

Hurrying past the solitary station-houses, and over here and there a little creek, our fourth night brings us to a low hill, which we need to be told is a pass of the Rocky Mountains. We cross this during the night, and morning dawns upon us in a level prairie among the network of brooks which form the extreme sources of the Missouri. Here, more than sixty years ago, Lewis and Clarke followed the river up to the " tiny bright beck," so narrow that "one of the party in a fit of enthusiasm, with a foot on each side, thanked God that he had lived to bestride the Missouri." It is called Horse Prairie, from the circumstance that they here bartered for horses with the Shoshonee Indians. They had often seen the men, mounted on fleet steeds, watching them like timid antelopes at a distance, but never allowing this distance to lessen. No signs or proffered presents could induce a near approach. One lucky day, however, Captain Lewis surprised a chattering bevy of their squaws and made prisoner a belle of the tribe. Finding all effort to escape hopeless, the woman held down her head as if ready for death. There was among them the same effeminate fear of capture and the same heroic fortitude when death seemed inevitable, that Clive and Hastings found in the Bengalee. But the Captain gallantly painted her tawny cheeks with vermilion, and dismissed her loaded with presents. It is hardly necessary to add, that captures of Shoshonee Sabines were not long matters of difficult accomplishment. Very soon

all the chiefs followed, with a rather exuberant cordiality towards the party, and with forced smiles the explorers "received the caresses and no small share of the grease and paint of their new friends."

Lewis and Clarke called Horse Prairie by the prettier name of Shoshonee Cove. But the names they gave have passed into as deep oblivion as the forgotten great man, Rush, whose pills they publish to the world as a sovereign specific in bilious fevers. Of all the names on their map only those of the three forks of the Missouri, from President Jefferson and his Secretaries Madison and Gallatin, remain. The unpoetical miner has invented a ruder nomenclature; and on the rivers which they called Wisdom, Philosophy, and Philanthropy, he bestows the barbarous names of Big Hole, Willow Creek, and Stinking Water.

A few hours' ride brings us to Grasshopper Creek, another affluent of the Missouri, and, like them all, a crooked little stream of clear cold water, fringed with alders and willows, and with a firm pebbly bed, along which the water tinkles a merry tune. What a pity that these pure mountain children should develop to such a maturity as the muddy Missouri! Parallel with this little stream, where it winds into a narrow chasm between abrupt mountain walls, winds a crooked street, with a straggling row of log-cabins on either side, and looking from the mountain-tops very much like the vertebræ of a huge serpent. This is Bannack, so called from the Indian tribe whose homes were in the vicinity. These were the bravest, the proudest, and the noblest looking Indians of the mountains till the white man came. Yet seldom has there been a stronger illustration of the inexorable law, that when a superior and inferior race come in contact the lower is annihilated. Every step of the white man's progress has been a step of the red man's decay. And now this tribe, once so warlike, is a nation of spiritless beggars, crouching near the white settlements for protection from their old foes, over whom in times past they were easy victors.

At Bannack, in the summer of 1862, a party of Colorado miners, lost on their way to Gold Creek in the Deer Lodge Valley, discovered the first rich placer diggings of Montana. A mining town grew up straightway; and ere winter a nondescript crowd of two thousand people — miners from the exhausted gulches of Colorado, desperadoes banished from Idaho, bankrupt speculators from Nevada, guerilla refugees from Missouri, with a very little leaven of good and true men — were gathered in. Few of them speak with pleasant memories of that winter. The mines were not extensive, and they were difficult to work. Scanty supplies were brought in from Denver and Salt Lake, and held at fabulous prices. An organized band of ruffians, styled Road Agents, ruled the town. Street murders were daily committed with impunity, and travellers upon the road were everywhere plundered. Care was not even taken to conceal the bodies of the victims, which were left as food for the wolves by the roadside.

Next year, the discovery of richer mines at Virginia left Bannack a deserted village of hardly two hundred people. It is a dull town for the visitor; but the inhabitants have all Micawber's enthusiastic trust in the future, and live in expectation of the wealth which is to turn up in the development of the quartz lodes. We visited the most famous of these lodes, — the Dacotah, — almost every specimen from which is brilliant with little shining stars of gold. And deep down in the shaft of this lode has been found a spacious cave full of stones of a metallic lustre, sending out all the tints of the rainbow, and many-colored translucent crystallizations, varying from the large stalactites to the fragile glass-work that crumbles at the touch.

Leaving Bannack, the road ascends a very lofty range of mountains, and passes by much wild and picturesque scenery. Mountaineers call these ranges, where they separate two streams, by the name of "divides." They have a scanty but nutritious herbage, and are for many months in the year covered with snow. On many of them a stunted growth of hybrid pines and cedars flourishes in great abundance. These, with the quaking ash and cottonwood along the streams, are the only woods of Montana. None of the harder woods, such as oak or maple, are found. It is inconceivably grand from the top of this range to look out upon the endless succession of vast peaks rolling away on every side, like waves in the purple distance. High above them all towers Bald Mountain, — the old Indian landmark of this section, — like Saul among his brethren. I have crossed this range in the gray of a February morning, with the thermometer at thirty-five below zero, and I never felt such a sense of loneliness as in gazing out from our sleigh — little atom of life as it seemed — upon this boundless ocean of snow, whose winters had been unbroken solitude through all the centuries.

Over this divide we pass among a low range of hills seamed with veins of silver, having already a more than local reputation. The hills embosom a clear little creek called after the yellow rattlesnake, which is almost as plentiful a luxury in these wilds as the grasshopper. It is, however, less venomous than its Eastern brethren, for not even the oldest inhabitant can instance a death from its bite. Nervous people avoid it studiously, but it has many friends among the other animals. The prairie-dog, the owl, and the rattlesnake live a happy family in one burrow, and the serpent has another fast friend in the turtle-dove. These doves are called the rattlesnake's brothers-in-law, and there runs a pretty legend, that when an Indian kills one of them, or mocks their plaintive cry, they tell the rattlesnake, who lies in wait and avenges the wrong by a deadly sting. And when one of the snakes is killed, the turtle-doves watch long over his dead body and chant mournful dirges at his funeral.

The road to Virginia passes through

the basin in which lie the tributaries of Jefferson Fork. It is a barren waste. Being in the rich mineral section of the country, its agricultural resources are proportionally deficient. Providence does not sprinkle the gold among the grain lands, but, by the wise law of compensation, apportions it to remote and volcanic regions which boast of little else. Along the water-courses is a narrow belt of cottonwood, and then rise the low table-lands, too high for irrigation, and with a parched, alkaline soil which produces only the wild sage and cactus. Miners curse this sprawling cactus most heartily, and their horses avoid its poisonous porcupine thorns with great care. All through these brown wastes one sees no shelter for the herds, no harvests of grain or hay, and wonders not a little how animal life — as well the flocks of antelope, elk, and deer in the mountains, as the cattle and horses of the rancheros — is preserved through the deep snows of the Northern winter. But even when the mountains are impassable, there is seldom snow in the valleys; and along the sides of the hills grow stunted tufts of bunch-grass, full of sweetness and nutriment. Horses always hunt for it in preference to the greener growth at the water's edge. And it is not an annual, but a perennial, preserving its juices during the winters, and drawing up sap and greenness into the old blades in the first suns of spring. This bunch-grass grows in great abundance, and it is only in winters of extreme severity that animals suffer from a lack of nourishing food.

Specks of gold may be found in a pan of dirt from any of these streams, followed back to the mountain chasm of its source. Upon one of them, in June, 1863, a party of gold-hunters stopped to camp on their return to Bannack, after an unsuccessful trip to the Yellowstone. While dinner was being cooked, one of them washed out a pan of dirt and obtained more than a dollar. Further washings showed even greater richness; and, hurrying to Bannack, they returned at once with supplies and

friends, and formed a mining district. In the absence of law, the miners frame their own law; and so long as its provisions are equal and impartial, it is everywhere recognized. The general principle of such laws is to grant a number of linear feet up and down the gulch or ravine to the first squatter, upon compliance with certain conditions necessary for mutual benefit. In deliberations upon these laws, technicalities and ornament are of little weight, and only the plainest common-sense prevails. Prominent among their conditions was a provision — for the exorcism of drones — that every claim must be worked a fixed number of days in each week, or else, in the miners' expressive vocabulary, it should be considered "jumpable." Compliance with law was never more rigidly exacted by Lord Eldon than by the miners' judges and courts, and in the first days of this legislation a hundred revolvers, voiceless before any principle of justice, yet too ready before any technicality, fixed the construction of every provision beyond all cavil.

This was the beginning of Virginia Gulch, from which twenty-five millions of dollars in gold have been taken, and which has to-day a population of ten thousand souls. The placer proved to be singularly regular, almost every claim for fifteen miles being found profitable. From the mouth of the cañon to its very end, among snows almost perpetual, are the one-storied log-cabins, gathered now and then into clusters, which are called cities, and named by the miner from his old homes in Colorado and Nevada. In travelling up the crazy road, with frowning mountains at our left, and yawning pit-holes at our right, we pass seven of these cities, — Junction, Nevada, Central, Virginia, Highland, Pine Grove, and Summit.

Virginia, the chief of the hamlets, has since developed into an organized city, and the capital of the Territory. Its site was certainly not chosen for its natural beauty. Along the main gulch are the mines, — huge piles of earth turned up in unsightly heaps. At one side of the mines, and up a ravine which crosses the gulch at right angles, lies the city. In shape it was originally like the letter T, but its later growth has forced new streets and houses far up the hillsides. Not so much regard was paid, in laying the foundations of the new city, to its future greatness, as Penn gave when he planned Philadelphia. The miner only wanted a temporary shelter, and every new-comer placed a log-cabin of his own style of architecture next the one last built. Where convenience required a street, lo! a street appeared. There were no gardens, for beyond the narrow centre of the ravine only sage-brush and cactus would grow. But the mines thrived, and also grew and thrived the little city and its vices.

Gradually a better class of buildings appeared. What were called hotels began to flourish; but it was long before the monotony of bacon, bread, and dried apples was varied by a potato. And for sleeping accommodations, a limited space was allotted upon the floor, the guest furnishing his own blankets. A theatre soon sprang up. And either because of the refined taste of some of the auditors, or the advanced talent of the performers, the playing was not the broad farce which might have been entertaining, but was confined to Shakespeare and heavy tragedy, which was simply disgusting. This style of acting culminated in the *début* of a local celebrity, possessed of a sonorous voice and seized with a sudden longing for Thespian laurels. He chose the part of Othello, and all Virginia assembled to applaud. The part was not well committed, and sentences were commenced with Shakespearian loftiness and ended with the actor's own emendations, which were certainly questionable improvements. Anything but a tragic effect was produced by seeing the swarthy Moor turn to the prompter at frequent intervals, and inquire, "What?" in a hoarse whisper. A running colloquy took place between Othello and his audience, in which he made good his assertion that he was

rude in speech. Since then, Shakespeare has not been attempted on the Virginia boards. "Othello's occupation's gone"; and all tragic efforts are confined to the legitimate Rocky Mountain drama. "Nick of the Woods" has frequently been produced with great applause, though the illusion is somewhat marred by the audible creaking of the wheels of the boat in which the Jibbenainosay sails triumphantly over the cataract.

Sunday is distinguished from other days in being the great day of business. The mines are not worked and it is the miners' holiday. All is bustle and confusion. A dozen rival auctioneers vend their wares, and gallop fast horses up and down the street. The drinking and gambling saloons and dance-houses are in full blast, all with bands of music to allure the passing miner, who comes into town on Sunday to spend his earnings. The discoverer of Virginia is the miner *par excellence*, — a good-natured Hercules clad in buckskin, or a lion in repose. All the week he toils hard in some hole in the earth for this Sunday folly. The programme for the day is prepared on a scale of grandeur in direct ratio to the length of his purse. The necessity of spending the entire week's earnings is obvious, and to assist him in doing so seems to be the only visible means of support of half the people of the town. The dance-house and the gambling-saloon, flaunting their gaudy attractions, own him for the hour their king. His Midas touch is all-powerful. I must confess, with all my admiration for his character, that his tastes are low. I know that the civilization of the East would bore him immeasurably, and that he considers Colt, with his revolvers, a broader philanthropist than Raikes with his Sunday schools. But he is frank and open, generous and confiding, honorable and honest, scorning anything mean and cowardly. Mention to him, in his prodigal waste of money, that a poor woman or child is in want of the necessaries of life, and the purse-strings open with a tear. Tell him that corruption and wrong have worked an injury to a comrade or a stranger, and his pistol flashes only too quickly, to right it. Circumstances have made him coarse and brutal, but below all this surface beats a heart full of true instincts and honest impulses. I am certain the recording angel will blot out many of his sins, as he did those of Uncle Toby. His means exhausted, he abdicates his ephemeral kingdom, and, uncomplaining, takes his pick and shovel, his frying-pan, bacon, and flour, and starts over the mountains for new diggings. Yet he gains no wisdom by experience. The same bacchanalian orgies follow the next full purse.

The Road Agents came to the new city from Bannack increased in strength and boldness. Long impunity had made them scarcely anxious to conceal their connection with the band. Life and property were nowhere secure. Spies in Virginia announced to confederates on the road every ounce of treasure that left the city, and sometimes reports came back of robberies of the coaches, sometimes of murder of the travellers, and still more frequently the poor victim was never heard of after his departure. There were no laws or courts, except the miners' courts, and these were powerless. Self-protection demanded vigorous measures, and a few good men of Bannack and Virginia met together and formed a Vigilance Committee, similar in all respects to that which has had such a beneficent influence in the growth of California. It was, of course, secret, and composed of a mere handful. It must be secret, for the Road Agents had so overawed the people that few dared acknowledge themselves as champions of law and order. They had threatened, and they had the power to crush such an organization at its inception, by taking the lives of its members. But moving stealthily and unknown, the little organization grew. Whenever a good man and true was found, he became a link of the chain. At last it tried its power over a notorious desperado named Ives, by calling a public trial

of the miners. It was a citizens' trial, but the Vigilantes were the leading spirits. Ives confronted his accusers boldly, relying on the promised aid of his confederates. They lay in wait to offer it, but the criminal was too infamous for just men to hesitate which side to take, and the cowards, as always in such cases, though probably a numerical majority, dared not meet the issue. Ives was hanged without any attempt at rescue.

The proceedings thus vigorously commenced were as vigorously continued. The Road Agents still trusted their power, and the contest was not settled. The Vigilantes settled it soon and forever. One morning their pickets barred every point of egress from Virginia. A secret trial had been held and six well-known robbers sentenced to death. Five of them were one by one found in the city. The quickness of their captors had foiled their attempts at escape or resistance, and their impotent rage at seeing every point guarded sternly by armed Vigilantes knew no bounds. They were all executed together at noon. It was a sickening scene, — five men, with the most revolting crimes to answer for, summoned with hardly an hour's preparation into eternity. Yet they are frequently spoken of with respect because they "died game." All of them, drinking heavily to keep up their courage, died with the most impious gibes and curses on their lips. Boone Helm, a hoary reprobate, actually said, as the block was being removed from him, " Good by, boys ! I will meet you in hell in five minutes." Harsh measures were these, but their effect was magical. One of the leaders had been hanged at Bannack, and the others as fast as found were promptly executed, — perhaps thirty in all. A few fled, and are heard of now and then among the robbers of Portneuf Cañon ; but under the sway of the Vigilantes life and property in Virginia became safer than to-day in Boston. For minor offences they banished the guilty, and for grave offences they took life. As their history is now recounted by the people, there is no man who does not praise their work and agree that their acts were just and for the public good. The first courts were held in December, 1864, and the Vigilantes were the earliest to support their authority. They are still in existence, but as a support and ally of the courts, and only appearing when the public safety demands the most rigorous dealing.

Virginia can never be a pretty city, but in many respects it is a model one. The earlier log-houses are now giving way to substantial stores of granite; and the number of gambling and tippling shops is steadily decreasing, the buildings being taken up by the wholesale traders. An organized city government preserves strict police regulations. Two thriving churches have grown up, and very recently the principal merchants have agreed to close their houses on the Sabbath. The old residents are bringing in their wives and children, and society constantly gains in tone. Erelong, it will compare favorably with the steadiest town in the land of steady habits.

Eight miles above Virginia is Summit. Its name sufficiently designates its location, which is at the head of the gulch and among the highest mountains. The sun is not seen there till a late hour in the winter, and the few who make it their home burrow closely as rabbits from the bitter cold and deep snows. The placer diggings are at their greatest depth here, but exceedingly rich. Here also are the richest gold lodes of the Territory. All the quartz seems impregnated with gold, sometimes in little pockets of nuggets, sometimes spattered by the intense heat of old into all forms of wires and spangles.

Quartz mining is yet in its rudest form. The gold is buried in solid rock, and requires heavy crushing-mills and cumbrous machinery, which must be built and transported at immense expense by capitalists. It is a question with such capitalists how certain is the promise of returns. The uncertainty of mining, as shown by the results of ventures in Colorado, has naturally deterred them. Under the old process of crushing the quartz to powder by stamps, and then separating the gold by amalgamation with quicksilver, but twenty-five per cent of the gold is saved. After the amalgamation a practical chemist could take the "tailings" of the Dacotah ore, and produce almost the full assay of the original rock. Very much depends in the mountain territories upon the success of experiments, now in operation, with the various new desulphurizing processes. This success established, the wealth of the territories is incalculable.

All the mining of Montana is now confined to the placer or gulch diggings. There are many of these, but probably none to compare in all respects with those at Virginia. At Bannack is found purer gold, at Biven's are larger nuggets, and many diggings at McClellan's yield larger amounts per day. But these are lotteries, — some claims paying largely to-day and nothing to-morrow, or one yielding enormously, while the next, after all the labor and expense of opening, gives nothing. They are called "spotted," while nearly every claim at Virginia has yielded with great regularity. How the gold came into these gulches is of little consequence to the miner. It suffices him to know that it is there, and his practical experience enables him to point out its location with great accuracy, though without any scientific knowledge of its origin. Most probably, far away in the Preadamite periods, when these mountains were much loftier than to-day, they were cloven and pierced by volcanic fires, and then into their innumerable vents and fissures infiltrated the molten quartz and the base and precious metals. Afterwards followed the period of the glaciers, and all the working of the seasons and chemical decompositions. Traces of the glaciers and the rotten burnt quartz of the volcanic periods exist everywhere. Thus washing and crumbling away in the waters and suns of untold springs and summers, the gold has come down the mountain gorges into the valleys below. The manner of gathering it is rude and incomplete enough. In all the gulches, at depths varying from six to fifty feet, is a *bed-rock* of the same general conformation as the surface. Usually this is granite; but sometimes before reaching the primitive rock two or three strata of pipe-clay — the later beds of the stream, upon which frequently lies a deposit of gold — are passed. Upon the bed-rock is a deposit, from three to four feet in depth, of gravel and boulders, in which the gold is hidden. This is called by the miners "pay-dirt," and to remove it to the surface and wash it is the end of mining. It is an expensive and laborious process indeed. The water has first to be controlled; and in mines of not too great depth this is done by a drain ditch along the bed-rock, commenced many claims below. In this all the claimholders are interested, and all contribute their quota of the labor and expense of digging it. The district laws permit every person to run such a drain through all the claims below his own, and force every man to contribute alike towards its construction, on pain of not being allowed to use the water, even though it flows through his own land. The water controlled, the rest is mere physical labor, which only bones and sinews of iron can endure. In the shallow diggings the superincumbent earth above the pay-dirt is removed, and the process is called "stripping." In deep diggings a shaft is sunk to the bed-rock, and tunnels are run in every direction, — and this is called "drifting." The roof is supported by strong piles, but these supports too frequently give way, and hurry the poor miners to untimely deaths. The pay-dirt, in whichever way obtained, is then shovelled into the sluice-boxes, — a series of long troughs, set at the proper angle to prevent the gold from washing past, or the dirt from settling to the bottom. Managed with the skill which experience has taught, the constant stream of water carries over the sand, while the gold, being seven times heavier, sinks to the bottom, and is caught by cross-bars called "*riffles*," placed there for the purpose.

In the lower boxes is frequently placed quicksilver, with which the lighter particles amalgamate. During the washings the larger stones and boulders are removed by a fork. These boxes, after a successful day's work, are a pleasant sight to see, all brilliant with gold and black sand and magnetic iron. All is gold that glitters. The heavy sand and iron are separated by a more careful washing by hand and by the magnet. Of course, all this system is very rude and imperfect, — so much so, that it has been found profitable in California to wash over the same earth nine times.

The gold-dust thus obtained is the only circulating medium in the Territory, and is the standard of trade. Treasury notes and coin are articles of merchandise. Everybody who has gold has also his little buckskin pouch to hold it. Every store has its scales, and in these is weighed out the fixed amount for all purchases according to Troy weight. An ounce is valued at eighteen dollars, a pennyweight at ninety cents, and so on. It is amusing to notice how the friction of the scales is made by some men — particularly the Jews, whose name is legion — to work them no loss. In *weighing in*, the scale-beam bows most deferentially to the gold side; but in *weighing out*, it makes profound obeisance to the weights. The same cupidity has given rise to two new terms in the miners' glossary, — *trade dust* and *bankable dust*. Bankable dust means simply gold, pure and undefiled. Trade dust is gold with a plentiful sprinkling of black sand, and is of three grades, described very clearly by the terms *good*, *fair*, and *dirty*. The trader, in receiving our money, complains if it does not approximate what is bankable, but in paying us his money pours out a combination in which black sand is a predominating ingredient. Many merchants even keep a saucer of black sand in readiness to dilute their bankable gold to the utmost thinness it will bear.

As might be expected, the courts were hardly opened before grave questions arose as to the construction of contracts based on this anomalous currency. Notes were usually made to pay a given number of "dollars, in good, bankable dust." But the laws recognized no such commodity as a dollar in dust. The decision of the court protecting a trickster in paying treasury-notes worth but fifty cents for the gold loaned by a friend, savored to the plain miner of rank injustice. To avoid even this opportunity for a legal tender, sometimes notes promised to pay a certain number of ounces and pennyweights, with interest at a fixed rate. The question was immediately sprung as to whether such an agreement was to be construed as a promissory note, or was to be sued for as a contract to do a specified act, by setting out a breach and claiming damages for the non-performance. The miners listened to the long discussions on these points impatiently, and compared the courts unfavorably with the miners' courts, which unloosed all such Gordian knots with Alexander's directness.

In the month of September, 1864, reports came to Virginia of mines on the Yellowstone. The reports were founded on some strange tales of old trappers, and were clothed with a vagueness and mystery as uncertain as dreams. Yet on such unsubstantial bases every miner built a pet theory, and a large "stampede" took place in consequence. I started with a party for the new mines, early in October. A day's ride brought us to the Madison Fork, a broad, shallow stream, difficult of fording on account of its large boulders, and flowing through a narrow strip of arable land. Very different is the Gallatin, beyond. It is cut up into narrow streams of a very rapid current, and waters a valley of surprising fertility. The Snakes called it Swift River. This valley is forty miles long and from ten to fifteen wide, and rising at its sides into low plateaus plenteously covered with rich bunch-grass. It is already pre-empted by farmers, and by easy irrigation are produced all the hardier vegetables and cereals, in quantity, size, and closeness of fibre not equalled on the Iowa prai-

ries. The valley gradually widens as you descend the stream, until, at the junction of the Three Forks, it stretches into a broad prairie, sufficient alone to supply all the mines with grain and vegetables. A few enterprising speculators once laid out a town here, with all the pomp and circumstance of Martin Chuzzlewit's Eden. Pictures of it were made, with steamers lying at the wharves and a university in the suburbs. Liberal donations of lots were made to the first woman married, to the first newspaper, to the first church, to the first child born. But there were no mines near, and the city never had an inhabitant. The half-dozen buildings put up by the proprietors are left for the nightly carnivals of bats and owls.

On our road we passed a half-dozen huts, dignified with the name of Bozeman City. Here lives a Cincinnatus in retirement, one of the great pioneers of mountain civilization, named Bozeman. To him belongs the credit of having laid out the Bozeman Cut-off, on the road from Fort Laramie to Virginia, and he is looked up to among emigrants much as Chief-Justice Marshall is among lawyers. I saw the great man, with one foot moccasoned and the other as Nature made it, giving Bunsby opinions to a crowd of miners as to the location of the mythical mines.

Parting from him, we crossed a high range of mountains, and from their tops looked down upon the spiral line of the Yellowstone, marked by the rich tints of its willows and cottonwoods, red, yellow, and green, in the crisp frosts of October. The air on these mountain-tops is much rarefied, and so very clear and pure that objects at a great distance seem within the reach of an easy walk. The Yellowstone flows in the eastern portion of Montana through an uninhabitable desert called the Mauvaises Terres, or Bad Lands, which, mingling their soil with its waters, give it the yellow color from which it is named. These lands are vast wastes, covered with what appears to be pine ashes. No signs of vegetation are found, but they are abundant in strange petrifactions.

I have seen from them petrified reptiles and portions of the human body, having a pearly lustre and inlaid with veins, and looking like the finest work in *papier-maché*.

The valley of the Upper Yellowstone has a thin, rocky soil, almost worthless for farming land. But what a paradise it would be for Izaak Walton and Daniel Boone! Quaint old Izaak would have realized a dream of Utopia in watching in the crystal stream its millions of speckled trout. It almost seems as if the New England trout had learned their proverbial wariness from long experience. There is none of it in these Yellowstone fish. They leap at the bare hook with the most guileless innocence. Trout are rarely found in the waters of the Missouri, but they fill all the brooks west of the mountains. They bite ravenously; one veracious traveller going so far as to assert that they followed him from the water far into the woods, and bit at the spurs on his boots. But mountaineers, even of the most scrupulous veracity, are occasionally given to hyperbole. Daniel Boone, too, would have found his paradise of a solitude undisturbed by white men, and full of wild game. Every night our camp was entertained with the hungry cry of wolves, the melancholy hooting of owls, and the growls of bears crackling the underbrush. The grizzly bear is not found in Montana; only the small black and cinnamon bears are seen. When wounded, these exhibit the most extreme ferocity; but persons who choose to avoid them will find them always willing to preserve the most distant relations. The most interesting of all the wild animals is the antelope. Every hour we passed flocks of these little fellows. They are timid as school-girls, but as inquisitive as village gossips; and while frightened and trembling at our presence, they could not resist keeping long in our view, and stopping every few moments to watch us, with most childish curiosity. Though fleet as the wind, I have seen many of the meek-eyed little fellows watch too long, and pay for their curiosity with their lives.

The most eastern settlement of Montana is at the mouth of a cañon near the Yellowstone, one hundred and thirty miles from Virginia. A party of Iowa emigrants found fair prospects here, and made it their home, calling their mines Emigrant Gulch, and their half-dozen log-huts Yellowstone City. Their gulch is rich in gold, but the huge boulders, many tons in weight, make it impossible to obtain the treasure by the present rude methods. The few profitable claims are high up in the mountains, and are free from ice only in the hottest days of summer. Even the donkeys, so much in use in transporting supplies to the mountain miners, cannot travel here, and every pound of flour is carried on men's backs over giddy paths almost impassable for the chamois. Still the emigrants went to work with a will, and full of confidence. They built themselves log-cabins, not so convenient as those at Virginia, — for they had not the miner's knack of reaping large results from such limited resources, — but still substantial and comfortable. They enacted written laws, as ample as the Code Napoleon. Almost every day during our visit they met to revise this code and enact new provisions. Its most prominent feature was the ample protection it afforded to women in the distribution of lots in their prospective city, and the terrible punishment with which it visited any man who dared offer one of them an insult. They certainly founded their republic on principles of adamant, but in spite of high hopes and wise laws the boulders refused to move. Even Iowa enterprise at last gave way under constant disaster, and the people of the little city are one by one forsaking it for the older mines.

The swift Yellowstone and the Colorado rise in lakes in the enchanted Wind River Mountains. Mr. Stuart mentions the weird tales, told by trappers and hunters, of places — avoided, if possible, by man and beast — in these mountains where trees and game and even Indians are petrified, and yet look natural as in life. These trappers are accustomed to exaggerate. I remember hearing a very serious account from one of them of a vast mountain of quartz so transparent that he could see mules feeding on the other side. There is also a story of a trapper who was lost in the fastnesses of the mountains years ago, and wandered for many days among streams whose bottoms were pebbled with gold. It is the miner's romance to repeat these fables of the Wind River Mountains, and to look forward to the day when the Indians shall be forced to yield them to his enterprise.

We arrived at Virginia at the end of October, and the commencement of the long mountain winter. The snows were soon blown in deep drifts over the hills, and the roads became almost impassable. A few hardy prospecters braved them in the search for quartz lodes, but many perished, and others were brought back to the city with frozen limbs. The mines lay idle, and the business of the city, dependent upon them for support, was completely stagnant. It was humanity living a squirrel life among its little garners of roots and nuts. But as usual, the reason of humanity fell far behind the instinct of the squirrel. Before spring came, the supply of flour at Virginia failed, and the most hideous of all calamities was threatened, — a famine. The range on the Salt Lake road lay utterly impassable under more than fifteen feet of snow. No mails had arrived for three months. The fear of famine soon became a panic, and flour speedily rose from twenty dollars per sack of one hundred pounds to one hundred and ten dollars in gold. A mob was organized by the drones, who would rather steal than work; and the miners were wrought upon by statements that a few speculators held an abundance of flour, and were extorting money from the necessities of the people. The Robespierres of the new reform drew the miners into passing a resolution to place all the flour in Virginia in the hands of a committee, with authority to distribute it among the most needy, at a fair and reasonable compensation, payable to the owner. A riot followed, and the flour-merchants quietly awaited the mob behind barricades of their own flour. The County Sheriff stood at the front of these with cocked revolver, and threatened to kill the first who advanced. The thieves knew that he did not threaten idly, and, though a hundred were ready to follow, not one was bold enough to lead. The riot failed for want of a courageous leader, and towards night slowly dwindled away. Another mob followed in a few days; but the merchants had sold their flour at sacrifices, and the booty was only a few sacks. The want of this staff of life caused great suffering. All other vegetable food was rapidly consumed, and for six weeks the poorer classes were forced to live on beef alone. The effect was in all cases an inability to labor, and in some cases serious sickness.

While thus cut off from all communication with the outer world, and buried in the dull town, there was little for us to do save to study each other's characters and talk the miners' language. In all new and thinly settled countries, many ideas are expressed by figures drawn from the pursuits of the people. Among the Indians, more than half of every sentence is expressed by signs. And miners illustrate their conversation by the various terms used in mining. I have always noticed how clearly these terms conveyed the idea sought. Awkwardness in comprehending this dialect easily reveals that the hearer bears the disgrace of being a "pilgrim," or a "tender-foot," as they style the new emigrant. To master it is an object of prime necessity to him who would win the miner's respect. Thus the term "adobe," the sun-dried brick, as applied to a man, signifies vealiness and verdancy. A "corral" is an enclosure into which the herds are gathered; hence a person who has everything arranged to his satisfaction announces that he has everything "corralled." A man fortunate in any business has "struck the pay-dirt"; unfortunate, has "reached the bed-rock." Everything viewed in the aggregate, as a train, a family, or a town, is an "outfit." I was much at a loss, on my first arrival, to comprehend the exact purport of a miner's criticism upon a windy lawyer of Virginia, — "When you come to pan him out, you don't find color." But this vocabulary is not extensive, and the pilgrim soon learns to perceive and use its beauties.

Helena, the second point of importance in the Territory, is one hundred and twenty-five miles north from Virginia. We travel to it over a fine, hard road, through the low valleys of the Missouri. The beauty and richness of these valleys increase as we leave Virginia, and everywhere the green spots are becoming the homes of thrifty farmers. On the divide near Boulder Creek are wonderful proofs of the gradual levelling of the mountains, in the huge blocks of rock piled up in the most grotesque shapes. Many of these are colossal pillars, surmounted by boulders weighing many tons. The softer rock and gravel have washed down the ravines, leaving these as monuments of the primal ages. The ravines penetrate the mountain on every side, and little by little wear the monster away. The beavers choose the prettiest nooks in them for their villages, and the miner, finding the water cut off, often learns that in a single night these busy architects have built a tight and closely interwoven dam up the stream, which it takes him many hours to demolish. Is it strange that, in speaking of the beaver dam, he should sometimes transpose the words?

We ride down the pleasantest of the ravines, till it develops into the Prickly Pear River, and past embryo cities, — at present noticeable for nothing except their rivalry of each other, — and hurry on to Last Chance Gulch and the city of Helena. A few emigrants from Minnesota had been here for many months. They made no excitement, no parade, but steadily worked on amid their majestic mountain scenery, and asked no heralding of their wealth. On either side of their

cabins grew tall pines straight as arrows, and in front spread a vast fertile valley watered by clear rivulets, marked here and there with the low cottages of the rancheros, and dotted everywhere with innumerable herds of cattle. Beyond the Missouri rose abruptly chains of snow-capped mountains, glistening in the sunlight and veined with gold and silver. Reports of these men came at times to Virginia, — reports always of a quiet and unostentatious prosperity. In the winter of 1864 their secret became known, and half the nomadic population of Virginia hurried to the new mines, and puzzled the slow-moving Minnesotians by their bustle and activity. Claims advanced rapidly in price, and the discoverers reaped fortunes. A city rose like an exhalation. Yet I never saw better order than in the earliest days of Helena, though I am afraid that Hangman's Tree could tell some stories of too much haste and injustice in taking the lives of criminals.

The hundred ravines near Helena showed gold, and every one of them was soon claimed from mouth to source. Every night I heard the clattering hoofs of the stampeders for some new gulch, starting in the utmost secrecy to gain the first right for themselves and friends. A trifling hint induces these stampedes. A wink from one old miner to another, and hundreds mounted their horses to seek some inaccessible mountain fissure. The more remote the diggings, so much the greater the excitement. Half the people of Helena lately hurried, in the depth of winter, to diggings on Sun River, (where many and many a brave fellow perished in the snows,) to learn that far richer mines had lain unclaimed for months within a stone's throw of their homes. The excitement over quartz lodes rapidly followed; and every spot on the mountains which showed any slight indications of auriferous quartz was claimed by the prospecters. Hardly a third of these can ever prove rich, but here and there is one of great value.

Helena, supported by the trade of

the surrounding mines, already rivals Virginia. Perhaps in years to come it may have a larger population and a more reckless enterprise. One hundred and fifty miles north from Helena is Fort Benton, an old fortified post of the American Fur Company, and the head of navigation on the Missouri. Steamers have arrived here in the spring, but the uncertainty of the water will fix the terminus of travel at some point farther down. A town charter for such a terminus was granted to a party of Virginia speculators at the mouth of Maria's River. They called it Ophir, which a friend of mine says is a very appropriate name and of poetic origin, being derived from Cowper's line,

" O for a lodge in some vast wilderness ! "

On the first visit of the proprietors to their new site, every one of them was murdered and scalped by the Indians. These regions are held by the Blackfeet, who, with their offshoots, the Bloods, Gros Ventres, and Piegans, are the most formidable Indians of Montana. They are polygamists, being in that respect exceptional among the Indians. But Catlin rather unsentimentally apologizes for this, on the ground that the chiefs are required to give expensive entertainments, in getting up which the labor of a hundred wives is no trifling assistance. Attempts have long been made to civilize and Christianize these savages by the Catholic missions under Father de Smet, and the government has furthered these attempts by establishing a fine farm on Sun River. The chiefs would sometimes be induced to stolidly witness the grain-planting ; but Captain Mullan quietly describes all this waste of philanthropy in the words : " I can only regret that the results as yet obtained would not seem commensurate with the endeavors so manfully put forth."

The noble Indians of history and poetry do not exist among the Indians of to-day. You seek in vain for Logan or Pocahontas, for Uncas or Minne-haha. The real Indians are cruel and treacherous, lazy and filthy, crafty and ungrateful. Many of them live upon ants and grasshoppers, and at the best only know enough to preserve in the rudest manner a few of the commonest roots and berries.

These tribes have no history and no growth. They live a mere animal life. Even their few traditions are rude and disgusting enough. I am indebted to Mr. Stuart for a fair example of the Bannack superstitions, from which not even Longfellow could glean any poetry or beauty. Among the caves in the rocks dwells a race of fairy imps, who, with arrow and quiver, kill game upon the mountains, and sing boisterous songs on the cliffs in summer evenings. Whenever an Indian mother leaves her infant, one of these pleasant cannibals devours it straightway, and takes its place, crying piteously. When the poor woman returns and seeks to pacify her child, the little usurper falls ravenously upon her. Fire-arms, knives, and stones are all powerless ; and when the screams of the woman bring the men to her help, the destroyer runs away and leaves her in a dying condition. She always dies before morning. When little children play at a distance from camp, these fairies seek to sport among them. Lucky is it for those timid few who, frightened at the long tail, scamper away from the intruder ; for, when allowed to mingle in the sport, he suddenly seizes the fairest child, and hurries away to make a dainty meal off him with his little wives in elfin-land. To the Indian men the fairies profess a real friendship ; and when they meet one near their dwellings they invite him in and feast him, and press him to stay all night. He invariably declines the polite invitation with his thanks, and his regrets that he has killed an elk and must take it home before the wolves can eat it.

Beyond the main chain of the Rocky Mountains are the Deer Lodge and Bitter Root Valleys, celebrated for their great grazing capabilities. I rode through these valleys in June, passing up the Pipestone Creek, whose waters flow into the Missouri, and down the Silver Bow, whose waters flow into the Columbia. At the highest point we could almost see the springs of either river, flowing on one hand to the Atlantic, on the other to the Pacific. How widely are these children of the same mother separated! Summer sprinkles all the ravines with innumerable wild-flowers, which make a rich carpet even up close to the white line of the snow. I found among them wild varieties of the harebell, larkspur, and sunflower, and many pansies. Upon the Silver Bow Creek is a city of the same name, built in the winter, when it was hoped that spring would prove the richness of its mines. From a distance it looked like a large town; but upon riding in, we found only here and there a straggling inhabitant. Other mines proved richer, and any purchaser can buy its best house for less than the cost of drawing the logs to build it. At Deer Lodge in this valley, — almost equal in extent and fertility to that of the Gallatin, — old Johnny Grant lived for many years a life of patriarchal serenity among his wives and concubines, his flocks and herds. By constant presents of beads and whiskey, and many a warm meal when on the war-path, he had raised himself high in the esteem of the savages, and had a favorite squaw from almost every tribe among his wives. When the Flatheads passed by, no woman appeared at his hearth but a Flathead; when the Blackfeet came, the sole wife of his bosom was a Blackfoot. Thus for many years, almost the only white man in these solitudes, he lived at peace with the natives, a sharer in all their spoils and arbiter in all their quarrels. And when the patriarch was gathered to his fathers, he left cattle on a thousand hills to his son. Young Johnny is a mere repetition of his father. He cannot read or write, and in conversation his nominatives are not always true to his verbs; but he has all the slyness and craftiness of the Indian. I heard that he was immensely disgusted at the white immigration. He acknowledges that his beeves are of greater value, and he has no small admiration for dollars and cents; but he fears that his moral and intellectual standing will suffer.

Passing down the Deer Lodge River, —

> "In the continuous woods
> Where rolls the Oregon, and hears no sound
> Save his own dashings," —

we come to a pass through the mountains, called Hell-Gate by the Flatheads, because through it rode the scalping parties of the Eastern tribes. Beyond is the sunny valley of the Bitter Root. It has long been settled by hardy trappers and hunters, and by comfortable farmers with well-stored barns and granaries and fenced fields. There is a charm about this isolated life, and a freshness and exhilaration about these Daniel Boones, that one meets nowhere else. Many of them are old army officers, men of education, who left the exploring parties to which they were attached to make their homes among the wild allurements of this fascinating valley. It is pleasant to hear their stories of life among the Indians, and their accounts of the strange features of the mountains, their animal life, their flora and minerals. Most of them have squaw wives, and are rearing large families of ugly pappooses, and many have amassed wealth by their long trade with the fur companies. The great Hudson's Bay Company has for many years had a station in this valley, and drawn from it large quantities of costly furs and skins. Here and farther west is spoken the famous Chinnook jargon, invented by the Company to facilitate its trade with the Indians. It borrows words from the English, from the French, from all the Indian tongues, and works them all into an incongruous combination. It has an entire lack of system or rule, but is quickly learned, and is designed to express only the simplest ideas. The powerful influence of the Company introduced it everywhere, and it was found of indispensable utility. Ardent Oregonians are said to woo their coy maidens in its unpronounceable gutturals. The white man is called "Boston" in this tongue, because the first whites whom the Oregon Indians met came in a Boston ship.

The best Indians of the mountains dwell in this valley, — the Flatheads and Pend' d'Oreilles. Many of them are devoted Catholics, but liable at times to lapse into intoxication. The Jesuits have a thriving mission among them, with a neat church, whose clear ringing bell sounds strangely enough in the mountain recesses. The strict asceticism of the fathers, their careful nursing of the sick and wounded, and their cordial co-operation in all objects of philanthropy, have enabled them to wield an immense influence among the Indians. The white miners also, who have often lain sick or frost-bitten in their hospitals, except these zealous priests in their too common sneers at religion. Captain Mullan quite reflects the universal sentiment when he

says : "The only good that I have ever seen effected among these people [the Indians] has been due to the exertions of these Catholic missionaries."

I have hurried over the points of interest in the early days of Montana. But any picture of its shifting life can only be a view of one of the combinations of the kaleidoscope. The discovery of new mines, and the abandonment of old ones, the fresh advent of gold-seekers and the exodus of the winners of fortunes, the increase of facilities for travel and of all the comforts of life, are daily and perceptibly working out new combinations. But while welcoming all changes tending towards refinement and a higher civilization, the careful observer of the life of these remote people can point to some qualities among them which he would have unchangeable as their grand old mountains, — their frankness and honesty of purpose, their love of justice, and their sturdy democracy.

REVIEWS AND LITERARY NOTICES.

The Poems of THOMAS BAILEY ALDRICH. Boston : Ticknor and Fields.

THE things which please in these poems are so obvious, that we feel it all but idle to point them out ; for who loves not graceful form, bright color, and delicate perfume ? Of our younger singers, Mr. Aldrich is one of the best known and the best liked, for he has been wise as well as poetical in his generation. The simple theme, the easy measure, have been his choice ; while he is a very Porphyro in the profusion with which he heaps his board with delicates : —

> "Candied apple, quince and plum and gourd ;
> With jellies soother than the creamy curd,
> And lucent syrops tinct with cinnamon ;
> Manna and dates, in argosy transferred
> From Fez ; and spiced dainties, every one,
> From silken Samarcand to cedared Lebanon."

And the feast is well lighted, and the guest

has not to thrid his way through knotty sentences, past perilous punctuation-points, to reach the table, nor to grope in the dark for the dainties when he has found it. We imagine that it is this charm of perfect clearness and accessibility which attracts popular liking to Mr. Aldrich's poetry : afterwards, its other qualities easily hold the favor won. He is endowed with a singular richness of fancy, and he has well chosen most of his themes from among those which allow the exercise of his best gifts. He has seldom, therefore, attempted to poetize any feature or incident of our national life ; for this might have demanded a realistic treatment foreign to his genius. But it is poetry, the result, which we want, and we do not care from what material it is produced. The honey is the same, whether the bee stores it from the meadow-clover and the wildflower of our own fields, or, loitering over city wharves, gathers it from ships laden with tropic oranges and orient dates.

If Mr. Aldrich needed any defence for the poems in which he gives rein to his love for the East and the South, he would have it in the fact that they are very beautiful, and distinctively his own, while they breathe full east in their sumptuousness of diction, and are genuinely southern in their summer-warmth of feeling. We doubt if any poet of Persia could have told more exquisitely than he what takes place

"WHEN THE SULTAN GOES TO IS-PAHAN.

" *When the Sultan Shah-Zaman*
Goes to the city Ispahan,
Even before he gets so far
As the place where the clustered palm-trees are,
At the last of the thirty palace-gates,
The pet of the harem, Rose-in-Bloom,
Orders a feast in his favorite room, —
Glittering squares of colored ice,
Sweetened with syrop, tinctured with spice,
Creams, and cordials, and sugared dates,
Syrian apples, Othmanee quinces,
Limes, and citrons, and apricots,
And wines that are known to Eastern princes :
And Nubian slaves, with smoking pots
Of spiced meats and costliest fish,
And all that the curious palate could wish,
Pass in and out of the cedarn doors :
Scattered over mosaic floors
Are anemones, myrtles, and violets,
And a musical fountain throws its jets
Of a hundred colors into the air.
The dusk Sultana loosens her hair,
And stains with the henna-plant the tips
Of her pearly nails, and bites her lips
Till they bloom again, — but, alas! *that* rose
Not for the Sultan buds and blows :
Not for the Sultan Shah-Zaman,
When he goes to the city Ispahan.

" Then, at a wave of her sunny hand,
The dancing girls of Samarcand
Float in like mists from Fairy-land !
And to the low voluptuous swoons
Of music rise and fall the moons
Of their full, brown bosoms. Orient blood
Runs in their veins, shines in their eyes :
And there, in this Eastern Paradise,
Filled with the fumes of sandal-wood,
And Khoten musk, and aloes and myrrh,
Sits Rose-in-Bloom on a silk divan,
Sipping the wines of Astrakhan ;
And her Arab lover sits with her.
That 's when the Sultan Shah-Zaman
Goes to the city Ispahan.

" Now, when I see an extra light,
Flaming, flickering on the night
From my neighbor's casement opposite,
I know as well as I know to pray,
I know as well as a tongue can say,
That the innocent Sultan Shah-Zaman
Has gone to the city Ispahan."

As subtilely beautiful as this, and even richer in color and flavor than this, is the complete little poem which Mr. Aldrich calls a fragment : —

" DRESSING THE BRIDE.

" So, after bath, the slave-girls brought
The broidered raiment for her wear,
The misty izar from Mosul,
The pearls and opals for her hair,
The slippers for her supple feet,
(Two radiant crescent moons they were,)
And lavender, and spikenard sweet,
And attars, nedd, and richest musk.
When they had finished dressing her,
(The eye of morn, the heart's desire !)
Like one pale star against the dusk,
A single diamond on her brow
Trembled with its imprisoned fire !"

Too long for quotation here, but by no means too long to be read many times over, is " Pampinea," an idyl in which the poet's fancy plays lightly and gracefully with the romance of life in Boccaccio's Florentine garden, and returns again to the beauty which inspired his dream of Italy, as he lay musing beside our northern sea. The thread of thought running through the poem is slight as the plot of dreams, — breaks, perhaps, if you take it up too abruptly ; but how beautiful are the hues and the artificing of the jewels strung upon it !

" And knowing how in other times
Her lips were ripe with Tuscan rhymes
Of love and wine and dance, I spread
My mantle by an almond-tree,
'And here, beneath the rose,' I said,
'I 'll hear thy Tuscan melody.'
I heard a tale that was not told
In those ten dreamy days of old,
When Heaven, for some divine offence,
Smote Florence with the pestilence :
And in that garden's odorous shade,
The dames of the Decameron,
With each a loyal lover, strayed,
To laugh and sing, at sorest need,
To lie in the lilies in the sun
With glint of plume and silver brede !
And while she whispered in my ear,
The pleasant Arno murmured near,
The dewy, slim chameleons run
Through twenty colors in the sun :
The breezes broke the fountain's glass,
And woke æolian melodies,
And shook from out the scented trees
The lemon-blossoms on the grass.
The tale ? I have forgot the tale, —
A Lady all for love forlorn,
A rose-bud, and a nightingale
That bruised his bosom on the thorn :
A pot of rubies buried deep,
A glen, a corpse, a child asleep,
A Monk, that was no monk at all,
In the moonlight by a castle wall.

As to " Babie Bell," that ballad has

passed too deeply into the popular heart to be affected for good or ill by criticism, — and we have only to express our love of it. Simple, pathetic, and real, it early made the poet a reputation and friends in every home visited by the newspapers, in which it has been printed over and over again. It is but one of various poems by Mr. Aldrich which enjoy a sort of perennial fame, and for which we have come to look in the papers, as we do for certain flowers in the fields, at their proper season. In the middle of June, when the beauty of earth and sky drives one to despair, we know that it is time to find the delicately sensuous and pensive little poem "Nameless Pain" in all our exchanges ; and later, when the summer is subject to sudden thunderstorms, we look out for "Before the Rain," and "After the Rain." It is very high praise of these charming lyrics, that they have thus associated themselves with a common feeling for certain aspects of nature, and we confess that we recur to them with greater pleasure than we find in some of our poet's more ambitious efforts. Indeed, we think Mr. Aldrich's fame destined to gain very little from his recent poems, "Judith," "Garnaut Hall," and "Pythagoras"; for when it comes to be decided what is his and what is his period's, these poems cannot be justly awarded to him. To borrow a figure from the polygamic usages of our Mormon brethren, they are sealed to Mr. Aldrich for time and to Mr. Tennyson for eternity. They contain many fine and original passages : the "Judith" contains some very grand ones, but they must bear the penalty of the error common to all our younger poets, — the error of an imitation more or less unconscious. It is to the example of the dangerous poet named that Mr. Aldrich evidently owes, among other minor blemishes, a mouse which does some mischief in his verses. It is a wainscot mouse, and a blood-relation, we believe, to the very mouse that shrieked behind the mouldering wainscot in the lonely moated grange. This mouse of Mr. Aldrich's appears twice in a brief lyric called "December"; in "Garnaut Hall," she makes

> "A lodging for her glossy young
> In dead Sir Egbert's empty coat of mail,"

and immediately afterwards drags the poet over the precipice of anti-climax : —

> "T was a haunted spot.
> A legend killed it for a kindly home, —

> A grim estate, which every heir in turn
> Left to the orgies of the wind and rain,
> The newt, the toad, the spider, and the mouse."

A little of Costar's well-known exterminator would rid Mr. Aldrich of this rascal rodent. Perhaps, when the mouse is disposed of, the poet will use some other word than *torso* to describe a headless, but not limbless body, and will relieve Agnes Vail of either her shield or her buckler, since she can hardly need both.

We have always thought Mr. Aldrich's "Palabras Cariñosas" among the most delicious and winning that he has spoken, and nearly all of his earlier poems please us ; but on the whole it seems to us that his finest is his latest poem, "Friar Jerome's Beautiful Book"; for it is original in conception and expression, and noble and elevated in feeling, with all our poet's wonted artistic grace and felicity of diction. We think it also a visible growth from what was strong and individual in his style, before he allowed himself to be so deeply influenced by study of one whose flower indeed becomes a weed in the garden of another.

The United States during the War. By AUGUST LAUGEL. New York: Baillière Brothers. Paris : Germer Baillière.
The Civil War in America. An Address read at the last Meeting of the Manchester Union and Emancipation Society. By GOLDWIN SMITH. London : Simpkin, Marshall, & Co. Manchester : A. Ireland & Co.

As a people, we are so used to policeman-like severity or snobbish ridicule from European criticism, that we hardly know what to make of the attentions of a Frenchman who is not an Inspector Javert, or of an Englishman who is not a Commercial Traveller. M. Laugel eulogizes us without the least patronage in his manner ; Mr. Goldwin Smith praises us with those reserves which enhance the value of applause. We are ourselves accustomed to deal generously and approvingly with the facts of our civilization, but our pride in them falls short of M. Laugel's ; and our most sanguine faith in the national future is not more cordial than Mr. Goldwin Smith's.

The diverse methods in which these writers discuss the same aspects and events of our history are characteristic and interesting, and the difference in spirit is even greater than that of form, — greater than the difference between a book, which, made from articles in the *Revue de Deux Mondes*, recounts the political, military, and financial occurrences of the last four years, sketches popular scenes and characters, and deals with the wonders of our statistics, and a slender pamphlet address, in which the author concerns himself rather with the results than the events of our recent war. This is always Mr. Smith's manner of dealing with the past; but in considering a period known in all its particulars to his audience, he has been able to philosophize history more purely and thoroughly than usual. He arrives directly and clearly at the moral of the Ilias Americana, and sees that Christianity is the life of our political system, and that this principle, without which democracy is a passing dream, and equality an idle fallacy, triumphed forever in the downfall of slavery. He has been the first of our commentators to discern that the heroism displayed in the war could only come from that principle which made our social life decent and orderly, built the school-house and the church, and filled city and country with prosperous and religious homes. He has seen this principle at work under changing names and passing creeds, and has recognized that here, for the first time in the history of the world, a whole nation strives to govern itself according to the Example and the Word that govern good men everywhere.

In the Introduction to his book, M. Laugel declares as the reasons for his admiration of the United States, that they " have shown that men can found a government on reason, where equality does not stifle liberty, and democracy does not yield to despotism; they have shown that a people can be religious when the State neither pays the Church nor regulates belief; they have given to woman the place that is her due in a Christian and civilized society." It is this Introduction, indeed, that will most interest the American reader, for here also the author presents the result of his study of our national character in a sketch that the nation may well glass itself in when low-spirited. The truth is, that we looked our very best to the friendly eyes of M. Laugel, and we cannot but be gratified with the portrait he has made of us. An American would hardly have ventured to draw so flattering a picture, but he cannot help exulting that an alien should see us

poetic in our realism, curious of truth and wisdom as well as of the stranger's personal history, cordial in our friendships, and not ignoble even in our pursuit of wealth, but having the Republic's greatness at heart as well as our own gain.

In the chapters which succeed this Introduction, M. Laugel discusses, in a spirit of generous admiration, the facts of our civilization as they present themselves in nearly all the States of the North and West; and while he does not pretend to see polished society everywhere, but very often an elemental ferment, he finds also that the material of national goodness and greatness is sound and of unquestionable strength. He falls into marvellously few errors, and even his figures have not that bad habit of lying to which the figures of travellers so often fall victims.

The books of M. Laugel and Mr. Goldwin Smith come to us, as we hinted, after infinite stupid and dishonest censure from their countrymen; but the intelligent friendship of such writers is not the less welcome to us because we have ceased to care for the misrepresentations of the French and English tourists.

Hospital Life in the Army of the Potomac. By WILLIAM HOWELL REED. Boston: William V. Spencer.

THE advice of friends, so often mistaken, and so productive of mischief in goading reluctant authorship to the publication of unwise, immature, or feeble literature, prevailed upon Mr. Reed to give the world the present book; and we have a real pleasure in saying that for once this affectionate counsel has done the world a favor and a service. We have read the volume through with great interest, and with a lively impression of the author's good sense and modesty. In great part it is a personal narrative; but Mr. Reed, in recounting the story of the unwearied vigilance and tenderness and dauntless courage with which the corps of the Sanitary Commission discharged their high duties, contrives to present his individual acts as representative of those of the whole body, and to withdraw himself from the reader's notice. With the same spirit, in describing scenes of misery and suffering, he has more directly celebrated the patience and heroism of the soldiers who bore the pain than the indefatigable goodness that ministered to them, though he does full justice to this also. The book is a record of every variety of wretchedness; yet one comes from its perusal strengthened and elevated rather than depressed, and with new feelings of honor for the humanity that could do and endure so much. Mr. Reed does not fail to draw from the scenes and experiences of hospital life their religious lesson, and throughout his work are scattered pictures of anguish heroically borne, and of Christian resignation to death, which are all the more touching because the example of courage through simple and perfect faith is enforced without cant or sentimentality.

The history of the great Christian aspect of our war cannot be too minutely written nor too often read. There is some danger, now the occasion of mercy is past, that we may forget how wonderfully complete the organization of the Sanitary Commission was, and how unfailingly it gave to the wounded and disabled of our hosts all the succor that human foresight could afford,— how, beginning with the establishment of depots convenient for the requisitions of the surgeons, it came to send out its own corps of nurses and watchers, until its lines of mercy were stretched everywhere almost in sight of the lines of battle, and its healing began almost at the hour the hurt was given. Mr. Reed devotes a chapter to this history, in which he briefly and clearly describes the practical operation of the system of national charity, accrediting to Mr. Frank B. Fay the organization of the auxiliary corps, and speaking with just praise of its members who perished in the service, or clung to it, till, overtaken by contagion or malaria, they returned home to die. The subject is dealt with very frankly; and Mr. Reed, while striving to keep in view the consoling and self-recompensing character of their work, does not conceal that, though they were rewarded by patience and thankfulness in far the greater number of cases, their charities were sometimes met by disheartening selfishness and ingratitude. But they bore up under all, and gave the world such an illustration of practical Christianity as it had never seen before.

Mr. Reed's little book is so earnestly and unambitiously written, that its graphic power may escape notice. Yet it is full of picturesque touches; and in the line of rapidly succeeding anecdote there is nothing of repetition.

A History of the Gypsies: with Specimens of the Gypsy Language. By WALTER SIMPSON. Edited, with Preface, Introduction, and Notes, and a Disquisition on the Past, Present, and Future of Gypsydom, by JAMES SIMPSON. New York: M. Doolady.

THE history of the Gypsies, according to the editor of the present work, is best presented in a series of desultory anecdotes which relate chiefly to the Egyptian usages of murder, pocket-picking, and horse-stealing, and the behavior of the rogues when they come to be hanged for their crimes. Incidentally, a good deal of interesting character is developed, and both author and editor show a very intimate acquaintance with the life and customs and speech of an inexplicable people. But here the value of their book ends; and we imagine that the earlier Simpson, who contributed the greater part of it in articles to Blackwood's Magazine, scarcely supposed himself to be writing anything more than sketches of the Scotch Gypsies whom he found in the different shires, and of the Continental and English Gypsies of whom he had read. The later Simpson thought it, as we have seen, a history of the Gypsies, and he has furnished it with an Introduction and a Disquisition of amusingly pompous and inconsequent nature. His subject has been too much for him, and his mental vision, disordered by too ardent contemplation of Gypsies, reproduces them wherever he turns his thought. If he values any one of his illusions above the rest, — for they all seem equally pleasant to him, — it is his persuasion that John Bunyan was a Gypsy. "He was a tinker," says our editor. "And who were the tinkers?" "Why, Gypsies, without a doubt," answers the reader, and makes no struggle to escape the conclusion thus skilfully sprung upon him. Will it be credited that the inventor of this theory was denied admittance to the columns of the religious newspapers in this country, on the flimsy pretext that the editors could not afford the space for a disquisition on John Bunyan's Gypsy origin?

The comparison of the Gypsy language in this book with a dialect of the Hindostanee is interesting and useful, and the accounts of Gypsy habits and usages are novel and curious; and otherwise the work is a mass of rather entertaining rubbish.

Eros. A Series of connected Poems. By
LORENZO SOMERVILLE. London: Trüb-
ner & Co.
Patriotic Poems. By FRANCIS DE HAES
JANVIER. Philadelphia: J. B. Lippin-
cott & Co.
The Contest: a Poem. By G. P. CARR.
Chicago: P. L. Hanscom.
Poems. By ANNIE E. CLARK. Philadel-
phia: J. B. Lippincott & Co.

ALL these little books are very prettily
printed and very pleasingly bound. Each
has its little index and its little dedication,
and each its hundred pages of rhymes, and
so each flutters forth into the world.

  "Dove vai, povera foglia frale?"

To oblivion, by the briefest route, we think;
and we find a pensive satisfaction in speculating upon the incidents of the journey.
Shall any one challenge the wanderers in
their flight, and seek to stay them? Shall
they all reach an utter forgetfulness, and
be resolved again into elemental milk and
water, or shall one of them lodge in a
dusty library, here and there, and, having
ceased to be literature, lead the idle life of
a curiosity? We imagine another as finding a moment's pause upon the centre-
table of a country parlor. Perhaps a third,
hastily bought at a railway station as the
train started, and abandoned by the purchaser, may at this hour have entered upon
a series of railway journeys in company
with the brakeman's lamps and oil-bottles,
with a fair prospect of surviving many
generations of short-lived railway travellers. We figure to ourselves the heart-
breaking desolation of a village-tavern,
where, on the bureau under the mirror,
to which the public comb and brush
are chained, a fourth might linger for a
while.

But in all the world shall anybody read
one of these books? We fancy not even a
critic; for the race so vigilantly malign in
other days has lost its bitterness, or has
been broken of its courage by the myriad
numbers of the versifiers once so exulting-
ly destroyed. Indeed, that cruel slaughter
was but a combat with Nature, —

  "So careful of the type she seems,
    So careless of the single life";

and from the exanimate dust of one crushed
poetaster she bade a thousand rhymesters
rise. Yet one cannot help thinking with
a shudder of the hideous spectacle of

"Eros" in the jaws of Blackwood or the
mortal Quarterly, thirty years ago; or of
how ruthlessly our own Raven would have
plucked the poor trembling life from the
"Patriotic Poems," or "The Contest," or
the "Poems."

The world grows wiser and better-na-
tured every day, and the tender statistician
has long since stayed the hand of the critic.
"Why strike," says the gentle sage, "when
figures will do your work so much more
effectually, and leave you the repose of a
compassionate soul? Do you not know
that but one book in a thousand survives
the year of its publication?" etc., etc., etc.
"And then as to the infinite reproduc-
tion of the species," adds Science, "*is*
Nature,

  "'So careful of the single type?' But no,
    From scarped cliff and quarried stone
    She cries, 'A thousand types are gone.'"

Patience! the glyptodon and the dodo
have been dead for ages. Perhaps in a
million years the poetaster also shall pass.

Thirty Years of Army Life on the Border.
By COLONEL R. B. MARCY, U. S. A.
With Numerous Illustrations. New
York: Harper and Brothers.

THERE is not much variety in frontier life,
it must be confessed, though there is abundant adventure. A family likeness runs
through nearly all histories of bear-fights,
and one Indian-fight might readily be mistaken for another. So also bear-fighters
and Indian-fighters are akin in character,
and the pioneers who appear in literature
leave a sense of sameness upon the reader's
mind. Nevertheless, one continues to read
of them with considerable patience, and
likes the stories because he liked their ancestral legends when a boy.

Colonel Marcy's book offers something
more than the usual attractions of the class
to which it belongs; for it contains the history of his own famous passage of the
Rocky Mountains in mid-winter, and notices of many frontiersmen of original and
striking character (like the immortal Captain Scott), as well as much shrewd observation of Indian nature and other wild-
beast nature. All topics are treated with
perfect common-sense; if our soldierly author sometimes philosophizes rather narrowly, he never sentimentalizes, though he
is not without poetry; and he is thoroughly

imbued with the importance of his theme. One, therefore, suffers a great deal from him, in the way of unnecessary detail, without a murmur, and now and then willingly accepts an old story from him, charmed by the simplicity and good faith with which he attempts to pass it off as new.

The style of the book is clear and direct, except in those parts where light and humorous narration is required. There it is bad, and seems to have been formed upon the style of the sporting newspapers and the local reporters, with now and then a hint from the witty passages of the circus, as in this colloquy : —

" ' Mought you be the boss hossifer of that thar army ? '

" ' I am the commanding officer of that detachment, sir.'

" ' Wall, Mr. Hossifer, be them sure 'nuff sogers, or is they only make-believe chaps, like I see down to Orleans ? '

" ' They have passed through the Mexican war, and I trust have proved themselves not only worthy of the appellation of real, genuine soldiers, but of veterans, sir.' "

And so forth. We like Colonel Mercy when he talks of himself better than when he talks for himself. In the latter case he is often what we see him above, and in the former he is always modest, discreet, and entertaining.

Memoirs of a Good-for-Nothing. From the German of JOSEPH VON EICHENDORFF, by CHARLES GODFREY LELAND. With Vignettes by E. B. Bensell. New York : Leypoldt and Holt.

WHEN, as Heine says, Napoleon, who was Classic like Cæsar and Alexander, fell to the ground, and Herren August Wilhelm and Friedrich Schlegel, who were Romantic like Puss in Boots, arose as victors, Baron von Eichendorff was one of those who shared the triumph. He wrote plays and poems and novels to the tunes set by the masters of his school, but for himself practically he was a wise man, — held comfortable offices all his life long, and, in spite of vast literary yearning, sentiment, and misanthropy, was a Philister of the Philisters. The tale which Mr. Leland translates so gracefully is an extravaganza, in marked contrast to all the other romances of Eichendorff, in so far as it is purposely farcical, and they are serious ; but we imagine it does not differ from them greatly in its leading qualities of fanciful incoherency and unbridled feebleness. An idle boy, who is driven from home by his father, the miller, and is found with his violin on the road to nowhere by two great ladies and carried to their castle near Vienna, — who falls in love with one of these lovely countesses, and runs away for love of her to Italy, and, after passing through many confused adventures there, with no relation to anything that went before or comes after, returns to the castle, and finds that his lovely countess is not a countess, but a poor orphan adopted by the great folk, — and so happily marries her, — this is the Good-for-Nothing and his story. A young student of the German language, struggling through the dusty paths of the dictionary to a comprehension of the tale, would perhaps think it a wonderful romance, when once he had achieved its meaning ; but being translated into our pitiless English, its poverty of wit and feeling and imagination is apparent ; and one is soon weary of its mere fantasticality.

THE

ATLANTIC MONTHLY.

A Magazine of Literature, Science, Art, and Politics.

VOL. XVIII. — SEPTEMBER, 1866. — NO. CVII.

THE SURGEON'S ASSISTANT.

I.

THE sickness of the nation not being unto death, we now begin to number its advantages. They will not all be numbered by this generation; and as for story-tellers, essayists, letter-writers, historians, and philosophers, if their "genius" flags in half a century with such material as hearts, homes, and battle-fields beyond counting afford them, they deserve to be drummed out of their respective regiments, and banished into the dominion of silence and darkness, forever to sit on the borders of unfathomable ink-pools, minus pen and paper, with fool's-caps on their heads.

I know of a place which you may call Dalton, if it must have a name. At the beginning of our war, — for which some true spirits thank Almighty God, — a family as wretched as Satan wandering up and down the earth could wish to find lived there, close beside the borders of a lake which the Indians once called — but why should not your fancy build the lowly cottage on whatsoever green and sloping bank it will?

Fair as you please the outside world may be, — waters pure as those of Lake St. Sacrament, with islands on their bosom like those of Horicon, and shores beautifully wooded as those of Lake George, — but what delight will you find in all the heavenly mansions, if love be not there?

"I 'll enlist," said the master of this mansion of misery in the midst of the garden of delight, one day.

"I would," replied his wife.

They spoke with equal vigor, but neither believed in the other. The instant the man dropped the book he had been reading, he was like Samson with his hair shorn, for his wife could n't tell one letter from another; and when she saw him sit down on the stone wall which surrounded their potato-field, overgrown with weeds, she marched out boldly to the corner of the wood-shed, where never any wood was, and attacked him thus : —

"S'pose you show fight awhile in that potato-patch afore you go to fight Ribils. Gov'ment don't need you any more than I do. May be it 'll find out getting ain't gaining !"

She had no answer. The man was thinking, when she interrupted him, as she was always doing, that, if he could secure the State and town bounty, that would be some provision for the woman and child. As for himself, he was indifferent as to where he was sent, or how soon. But if he went away, they might look for him to come again. Gabriel's trumpet, he thought, would be a more welcome sound than his wife's voice.

He enlisted. The bounties paid him were left in the hands of a trusty neighbor, and were to be appropriated to the supply of his family's needs; and he went away along with a boat-load of recruits, — his own man no longer. Even his wife noticed the change in him, from the morning when he put on his uniform and began to obey orders, for she had time to notice. Several days elapsed after enlistment before the company's ranks were complete, and the captain would not report at head-quarters, he said, until his own townsfolk had supplied the number requisite.

Even his wife noticed the change, I said; for, contrary to what is usual and expected, she was not the first to perceive that the slow and heavy step had now a spring in it, and that there was a light in his clouded eyes. She supposed the new clothes made the difference.

Nearly a year had passed away, and this woman was leaning over the rail fence which surrounded a barren field, and listening, while she leaned, to the story of Ezra Cramer, just home from the war. She listened well, even eagerly, to what he had to tell, and seemed moved by the account in ways various as pride and indignation.

"I wish I had him here!" she said, when he had come to the end of his story, — the story of her husband's promotion.

Ezra looked at her, and thought of the pretty girl she used to be, and wondered how it happened that such a one could grow into a woman like this. The vindictiveness of her voice accorded well with her person, — expressed it.

Where were her red cheeks? What had become of her brown hair? She was once a free one at joking with, and rallying the young men about; but now how like a virago she looked! and her tongue was sharp as a two-edged sword.

Ezra was sorry that he had taken the trouble to ascertain in the village where Nancy Elkins lived. Poor fellow! While enduring the hardships of the past year, his imagination had transformed all the Dalton women into angels, and the circuit of that small hamlet had become to his loving thought as the circuit of Paradise.

Some degree of comprehension seemed to break upon him while he stood gazing upon her, and he said: "O well, Miss Nancy, he 's got his hands full, and besides he did n't know I was coming home so quick. I did n't know it myself till the last minute. He would 'a' sent some message, — course he would!"

"I guess there ain't anything to hender his *writing* home to his folks," she answered, unappeased and unconvinced. "Other people hear from the war. There 's Mynders always a-writing and sending money to the old folks, and that 's the difference."

"We 've been slow to get our pay down where we was," said Ezra. "It 's been a trouble to me all the while, having nothing to show for the time I was taking from father."

The woman looked at the young fellow who had spoken so seriously, and her eyes and her voice softened.

"Nobody would mind about your not sending money hum, Ezra. They 'd know *you* was all right. Such a hardworking set as you belong to! You 're looking as if you wondered what I was doing here 'n this lot. I 'm living in that shanty! Like as not I 'll have its pictur' taken, and sent to my man. Old Uncle Torry said we might have it for the summer; and I expect the town was glad enough to turn me and my girl out anywhere. They won't do a thing towards fixing the old hut up. Say 't ain't worth it. We can't stay there in cold weather. Roof leaks like a sieve. If he don't send me some money pretty quick, I 'll list myself, and serve long enough to find *him* out, see 'f I don't."

At this threat, the soldier, who knew something about WAR, straightened himself, and with a cheery laugh limped off towards the road. "I 'll see ye ag'in, Miss Nancy, afore you start," said he, looking back and nodding gayly at her. Things were n't so bad as they seemed about her, he guessed. He was going home, and his heart was soft. Happiness is very kind ; but let it do its best it cannot come very near to misery.

Nancy stood and watched the young man as he went, commenting thus : "Well, *he* 's made a good deal out of 'listing, any way." His pale face and his hurt did not make him sacred in her sight.

She was speaking to herself, and not to her little daughter, who, when she saw her mother talking to a soldier, ran up to hear the conversation. A change that was wonderful to see had passed over the child's face, when she heard that her father had been promoted from the ranks. The bald fact, unilluminated by a single particular, seemed to satisfy her. She had n't a question to ask. Her first thought was to run down to the village and tell Miss Ellen Holmes, who told *her*, not long ago, so proud and wonderful a story about her brother's promotion.

If it were not for this Jenny, my story would be short. Is it not for the future we live ? For the children the world goes on.

Does this little girl — she might be styled a beauty by a true catholic taste, but oh! I fear that the Boston Convention "ORTHODOX," lately convened to settle all great questions concerning the past, present, and future, would never recognize her, on any showing, as a babe of grace ! — does she, as she runs down the hill and along the crooked street of Dalton, look anything like a messenger of Heaven to your eyes ? Must the angels show their wings before they shall have recognition ?

Going past the blacksmith's shop she was hailed by the blacksmith's self, with the blacksmith's own authority. "See here, Jenny ! " At the call, she stood at bay like a fair little fawn in the woods.

"I 'm writing a letter to my boy," he continued. "Step in here. Did you know Ezra Cramer had come back ? "

"I saw him just now," she answered. "He told us about father." She said it with a pride that made her young face shine.

"So ! what about him, I wonder ? " asked the blacksmith.

And that he really did wonder, Jenny could not doubt. She heard more in his words than she liked to hear, and answered with a tremulous voice, in spite of pride, "O, he 's been promoted."

"The deuse ! what 's *he* permoted to ? "

"I don't know," she said, and for the first time she wondered.

"Where is he, though ? " asked the blacksmith.

"I don't know, — in the war."

"That 's 'cute. Well, see here, sis, we 'll find that out, — you and me will." The angry voice of the blacksmith became tender. "You sit down there and write him a letter. My son, he 'll find out if your pa is alive. As for Ezra, he don't know any more 'n he did when he went away ; but, poor fellow, he 's been mostually in the hospertal, instead of fighting Ribils, so p'r'aps he ain't to blame. You write to yer pa, and I 'll wage you get an answer back, and he 'll tell you all about his permotion quick enough."

Jenny stood looking at the blacksmith for a moment, with mouth and eyes wide open, so much astonished by the proposition as not to know what answer should be made to it. She had never written a line in her life, except in her old copy-book. If her hand could be made to express what she was thinking of, it would be the greatest work and wonder in the world. But then, it never could !

That decisive *never* seemed to settle the point. She turned forthwith to the blacksmith, smiling very seriously. At the same time she took three decided steps, which led her into his dingy shop, as awed as though she were about to have some wonderful exhibition there. But she must be her own astrologer.

The blacksmith, elated by his own success that morning in the very difficult business of letter - writing, was mightily pleased to have under direction this little disciple in the work of love, and forthwith laid his strong hands on the bench and brought it out into the light, setting it down with a force that said something for the earnestness of his purpose in regard to Miss Jenny.

When he wrote his own letter, he did it in retirement and solitude, having sought out the darkest corner of his shop for the purpose. A mighty man in the shoeing of horses and the handling of hammers, he shrank from exposing his incompetence in the management of a miserable pen, even to the daylight and himself.

His big account-book placed against his forge, with a small sheet of paper spread thereon, his pen in Jenny's hands, and the inkstand near by, there was nothing for him to do but to go away and let her do her work.

"Give him a tall letter!" said he. "And you must be spry-about it. He 'll be glad to hear from his little girl, I reckon. See, the stage 'll be along by four o'clock, and now it 's —" — he stepped to the door and looked out on the tall pine-tree across the road, — that was his sun-dial, — "it 's just two o'clock now, Jenny. Work away!" So saying, he went off as tired, after the exertion he had made, as if he had shod all the Dalton horses since daybreak.

She had just two hours for doing the greatest piece of work she had done in her short life. And consciously it was the greatest work. Every stroke of that pen, every straight line and curve and capital, seemed to require as much deliberation as the building of a house ; and how her brain worked! Fly to and fro, O swallows, from your homes beneath the eaves of the blacksmith's old stone shop in the shade of the far-spreading walnut, — stretch forth your importunate necks and lift aloft your greedy voices, O young ones in the nests ! — the little girl who has so often stood to watch you is sitting in the shadow within there, blind and deaf to you, and unaware of everything in the great world except the promotion of her father "in the war," and the letter he will be sure to get, because the blacksmith is going to send it along with *his* letter to his son.

She was doing her work well. Any one who had ever seen the girl before must have asked with wonder what had happened to her, — it was so evident that something had happened which stirred heart and soul to the depths.

So, even so, unconsciously, love sometimes works out the work of a lifetime, touches the key - note of an anthem of everlasting praise, — does it with as little ostentation as the son of science draws yellow gold from the quartz rock which tells no tale on the face of it concerning its "hid treasure." So, wisely and without ostentation, work the true agents, the apostles of liberty in this world.

"O dear papa! my dear papa!" she wrote, "Ezra has come home, and he says you are promoted! But he could n't tell for what it was, or where you were, or anything. And O, it seems as if I could n't wait a minute, I want to hear so all about it." When she had written thus far the spirit of the mother seemed to stir in the child. She sat and mused for a moment. Her eyes flashed. Her right hand moved nervously. Strange that her father had not sent some word by Ezra ; but then he did n't know, of course, that Ezra was coming. Ay! that was a lucky thought. What she had written seemed to imply some blame. So, with many a blot and erasure, her loving belief that all was right must make itself evident.

At the end of the two hours she found herself at the bottom of the page the blacksmith had spread before her. Twice he had come into the shop and assured himself that the work was going on, and smiled to see the progress she was making. The third time he came he was under considerable excitement.

"Ready!" he shouted. "The stage 'll be along now in ten minutes."

She did not answer, she was so busy, and so *hard* at work, signing her name to the sheet that was covered with what looked like hieroglyphics.

When she had made the last emphatic pen-stroke, she turned towards him, flushed and smiling. "There!" she said.

He looked over her shoulder.

"Good!" said he. "But you have n't writ his name out. Give me the pen here, quick!" Then he took the quill and wrote her father's name up in one blank corner, and dried the ink with a little sand, and put the note into the envelope containing his own, and the great work was done.

Do you know how great a work, you dingy old Dalton blacksmith?

Do *you* know, fair child, — who must fight till the day of your death with alien, opposite forces, because the blood-vessels of Nancy Elkins, as they sail through the grand canals of the city of your life, so often hang out piratical banners, and bear down on better craft as they near the dangerous places, or put out, like wreckers after a storm, seeking for treasure the owners somehow lost the power to hold?

In a few minutes after the letter was inscribed and sealed, the stage came rattling along, and Jenny stood by and saw the blacksmith give it to the driver, and heard him say: "Now be kerful about that ere letter. It's got two inside. One 's my boy's, as ye 'll see by the facing on it; t' other 's this little girl's. She 's been writin' to her pa. So be kerful."

They stood together watching the stage till it was out of sight, then the blacksmith nodded at Jenny as if they had done a good day's work, and proceeded to light his pipe. That was not her way of celebrating the event. She remembered now that she had promised a little girl, Miss Ellen Holmes indeed, that she would some time show her where the red-caps and fairy-cups grew, and there was yet time, before sunset, for a long walk in the woods.

The little town-bred lady happened to come along just then, while Jenny stood hesitating whether to go home first and tell her mother of this great thing she had done. The question was therefore settled; and now let them go seeking red-caps. Good luck attend the children! Jenny will be sure to say something about promotions before they separate. She will say that something with a genuine human pride; and the end of the hunt for red-caps may be, conspicuously, success in finding them; but still more to the purpose, it will be the child's establishment on a better basis — a securer basis of equality — than she has occupied before. She forgets about Dalton and poverty. She thinks about camps and honor. She has something to claim of all the world. She is the citizen of a great nation. She bears the name of one who is fighting for the Union, who *has* fought, and fought so well that those in authority have beckoned him up higher. Why, it is as though a crown were placed on her dear father's head.

II.

GOING out of quiet and beautiful green Dalton, and into the hospital of Frere's Landing, 't is a wonderful change we make.

The silence of one place is as remarkable as the silence of the other, perhaps. That of the hospital does not resemble that of the hamlet, however. At times it grows oppressive and appalling, being the silence of anguish or of death. A stranger reaching Dalton in the night might wonder in the morning if there were in reality any passage out of it, for there the lake, on one of whose western slopes is the "neighborhood," seems locked in completely by the hills, and an ascent towards heaven is apparently the only way of egress. Yet there 's another way; for I am not writing this true story among celestial altitudes for you. I returned from Dalton by a mundane road.

Out of Frere's Hospital, however, *its* silence and seclusion, many a stranger never found his way except by the high mountains of transfiguration, in the chariots of fire, driven by the horsemen of Heaven, covered with whose glory they departed.

Through the wards of this well-ordered hospital a lady passed one night, and, entering a small apartment separated from the others, advanced with noiseless step to a bedside, and there sat down. You may guess if her heart was beating fast, and whether it was with difficulty that she kept her gray eyes clear of tears. There were about her traces of long and hurried journeying.

Under no limitations of caution had she passed so noiselessly through the wards. Involuntary was that noiselessness, — involuntary also the surprise with which one and another of the more wakeful patients turned to follow her, with hopeless, weary eyes, as she passed on. Now and then some feeble effort was made to attract her attention and arrest her progress, but she went, absorbed beyond observation by the errand that constrained her steps and thoughts.

When she reached the door of the apartment to which the surgeon had directed her, she seemed for an instant to hesitate; then she pushed the door open and passed into the room. The next instant she sank into a chair by the bedside of a man who was lying there asleep. It seemed as if the silent room had a profounder stillness added to it since she entered.

It was Colonel Ames whom she saw lying on the cot before her with a bandage round his forehead, so evidently asleep. He was smiling in a dream. He was not going to give up the ghost, it seemed, though he had given up so much — how much ! — with that passion of giving which possessed this nation, North and South, during four awful,

glorious years. *He* had given up the splendor and the beauty of this world. All its radiance was blotted out in that moment of fury and of death when the shot struck him, and left him blind upon the field.

Never on earth would it be said to him, "Receive thy sight." The lady knew this who sat down by his bedside to wait for his awaking. The surgeon had told her this, when at last, after having searched for her brother long among the dead, she came to Frere's Hospital and found him alive.

She sat so close beside him it seemed that he could not remain a moment unconscious of her immediate presence after waking. Her hand lay just where his hand, moving when he wakened, must touch it. She had rightly calculated the chances; he did touch it, and started and said: "Who 's here? Doctor !" Then with a firmer grasp he seized the unresisting fingers, and exclaimed, "My God, am I dreaming? it ought to be Lizzie's hand."

"The doctor told me I should find you here, and might come," she answered; and, disguised as the voice was by the feeling that tore her heart, the Colonel, poor young fellow, listening as if for life, knew it, and said, "O Lizzie, my child, I don't know about this, — why could n't you wait ?"

"I waited and waited forever," she answered. "You 're not sorry that I 've found you out after such a hunt? Of course you 'll make believe, but then — you need n't; I 'm here, any way !"

Just then the surgeon came in. The Colonel knew his step, and said, "Doctor, look here; is this Lizzie ?"

"I believe you 're right," said the doctor. "She said she had a hero for a brother, and I have no doubt about that myself."

"O Dan, we had given you up ! Though I knew all the time we should n't. I could not believe — "

"Must come to that Lizzie, — do it over again; for what you have here is n't your old Dan."

"My old Dan !" she exclaimed, and

then there was a little break in the conversation the two heroes were endeavoring to maintain.

Meanwhile the surgeon had seated himself on the edge of the bed waiting the moment when there should be a positive need of him. He saw when it arrived.

"Colonel," said he, in his hearty, cheery voice, which alone had lifted many a poor fellow from the slough of misery, and put new heart and soul in him, since his ministrations began in the hospital, — "Colonel, your aids are in waiting."

The soldier smiled; his face flushed. "My aids can wait," said he.

"That is a fine thing to say. Here he has been bothering me, madam, not to say browbeating me, and I've been moving heaven and earth for my part, and at last have secured the aids, and now hear him dismiss them!"

"Bring them round here," said the patient suddenly.

The surgeon quietly lifted from the floor a pair of crutches, and placed them in his patient's hands.

"How many years must I rely on my aids?" he asked quietly.

"Perhaps three months. By that time you will be as good as ever."

A change passed over the young man's face at this. Whatever the emotion so expressed, it had otherwise no demonstration. He turned now abruptly toward his sister, and said: "They can wait. I've got another kind of aid now. Come, Lizzie, say something."

A sudden radiance flashed across his face when he ceased to speak, and waited for that voice.

"I shall be round again in an hour,' said the surgeon.

He could well be spared. The brother and sister had now neither eye nor thought except for each other.

The surgeon's face changed as he closed the door. Every one of their faces changed. As for the gentleman whose duty took him now from ward to ward, from one sick-bed to another, it was only by an effort that he gave his cheerful words and courageous looks to the men who had found day after day a tonic in his presence.

The brother and sister clasped each other's hands. Few were the words they spoke. He was looking forward to the years before him, endeavoring to steady himself, in a moment of weakness, by the remembrance of past months of active service.

She was thinking of the days when she walked with her hero out of delightsomeness and ease into danger and anxiety, all for the nation's succor, in the nation's time of need. Some had deemed it a needless sacrifice. Of old, when sacrifice was to be offered, it was not the worthless and the worst men dared or cared to bring. The spotless, the pure, the beautiful, these were no vain oblations. These two said in solemn conference, "We will make an offering of our all." And their all they offered. See how much had been accepted!

Having offered, having sacrificed, it was not in either of these to repent the doing, or despise the honor that was put upon them. No going back for them! No looking back! No secret repining! The Colonel had done his work. As for the Colonel's sister, there was no place on earth where she would not find work to do.

And here in this hospital, in her brother's room, she found a sphere. Going and coming through the various wards, singing hymns of heavenly love and purest patriotism, scattering comforts with ministering hands, which found brothers on all those beds of languishing, how many learned to look for her appearing, and to bless her when she came! But concerning her work there, and that of other women, some of whom will go crippled to the grave from their service, — soldiers and veterans of the army of the Union, — enough has everywhere been said.

Among all these patients there was one, a sick man, to whom her coming and her going, her speech and her silence, became most notable events. Living within the influence of such manner and degree of social life as her presence in the hospital established, he was like a returned exile, who, yet under ban, felt all the awkwardness, constraint, and danger of his position. This man, who discovered in himself merely helplessness, was not accounted helpless, but the helper of many. He was, in short, the surgeon of the hospital.

One day the Colonel said to him, "You don't like to have my sister here. Are the hired nurses making a row?"

The surgeon's face betrayed so much interest in this subject, and so much embarrassment, it seemed probable he would come out with an absolute "Yes"; but his speech contradicted him, for he said with indifference, "Where did you get that pretty notion?"

"Out of you, and nowhere else. What puzzles me, though, is, she seems to think she is doing some good here. And did n't you say you 'd no objection to her visiting the wards?"

"I should think it a positive loss if she were called or sent away from the hospital," said the surgeon, speaking now seriously enough. "She is of the greatest service, out of this room as well as in it."

"Why do I feel then as if something had happened, — something disagreeable? We don't have such good times as we used to have when you sat here and told stories, and let me run on like a school-boy."

"You have better company, that 's all. I 'm not such a fool that I can't see it. You have better times, lad, — if I don't."

"Then all you did for me before she came was for pity's sake! Who 's in the ditch now, getting all the favor you used to show to me?"

The voice and manner with which these words were spoken produced an effect not readily yielded to, though the surgeon was perfectly aware that his emotion was unperceived and unguessed by the man on the bed there, who was investigating a difficulty which had puzzled him.

So we have come to *this* point. Away down at Frere's Landing, amid scenes of anguish, tribulation, and death, where elect souls did minister, there was found ministration by these elect souls in their own behalf.

They had gained a "Landing-Place" that was sacred ground, and if Philosophy and Science would also stand there they must put their shoes from off their feet, for the ground was holy. Priests whose right it was to stand within the veil were servants there; and day by day, as they discerned each other's work, it was not required of them always to dwell upon the nature of sacrifice.

Each, in such work as now was occupying the doctor and Miss Ames, had need of the other's strengthening sympathy, day by day, and of all the consolations of friendship, such as royal souls are permitted to bestow on one another.

With the surgeon, not a young man in anything except happiness, it was as if there were broad openings, not *rents*, in the heavy leaden skies. Pure, bright lights shone along the horizon, warmth overspread the cold.

With her, perpetual and sufficient are the compensations of love. To him who plants of this it is returned out of earth, and out of heaven, in good measure, pressed down, and running over. Nay, let us not argue.

The sick man lying on his cot, the convalescent guided by her to balcony or garden, the crippled and the dying, had all to give her of their hearts' best bloom. And if it proved that there was one among these who, to her apprehension, walked in white, like an angel, of whom she asked no thanks, no praise, only aid and sympathy, what mortal should look surprise? The constant, the pure, the alive through all generations, the Alive Forever, will not. And the rest may apologize for overhearing a story not intended for their ears.

It happened one evening that the surgeon and Miss Ames met outside the hospital doors, near the old sea-wall. They were walking in no haste, watching, it seemed, the flight of the brave little sea-birds, as they made their way now above and now among the breakers. After the heart-trying labors of the day, an hour like this was full of balm to those who were now entered on its rest. But it was not secure from invasion. Even now a voice was shouting to the surgeon, and he heard it, though he walked on as if he were determined not to hear. He had taken to himself this hour; he had earned it, he needed it; surely the world could go on for one hour without him!

But the importunity of the call was not to be resisted. So, because the irresistible must be met, the surgeon stood still and looked around. A poor little fellow was making toward him with all speed.

"Mail for you, sir," he said, as he came nearer, and he gave a package of newspapers, and one little letter, into the surgeon's hands.

So Miss Ames and he sat down on the stone wall to scan those newspapers, and the surgeon opened his note.

Obviously a scrawl from some poor fellow who had obtained a discharge on account of sickness, and gone home. It was not rare for the surgeon to receive such missives from the men who had been under his charge. Wonderful was the influence he gained over the majority of his patients. Wonderful? No. The man of meanest talents, who gives himself body and spirit to a noble work, can no more fail of his great reward, than the seasons of their glory. Never man on this Landing thought meanly of the hospital surgeon's skill, or questioned his right to rank among the ablest of his tribe, — no man, and certainly not the woman who was making a hero out of him, to her heart's great content.

While Miss Ames looked at the papers, he proceeded, without much interest in the business, to open and read his note.

One glance down the blurred and blotted page served to arrest his attention, in a way that letters could not always do. Here was not a cup of cold water to sip and put aside. He glanced at Miss Ames. She was absorbed in a report of "the situation," getting items of renown out of one column and another, which should ease many an aching body, smooth many a sick man's pillow, ere the night-lamps were lighted in the wards.

If she had chanced to look up at him just then, while he, with scared, astonished eyes, was glancing at her, it is impossible to say what words might have escaped him, or what might have forever been prevented utterance. But she was not looking. What heavenly angel turned her eyes away?

And now, before him whose prerogative was Victory, what vision did arise? An apocalyptic vision: blackness of darkness forever, and side by side with chaos, fair fields of living green, through which a young girl walked towards a womanhood as fair as hers who sat beside him. Unconscious of wrong that child, and yet how deeply, how variously wronged! If he had meditated a great robbery, he could not have quailed in the light of the discovered enormity as he did now before the vision of his Janet.

Years upon years of struggle and of conquest could hardly give to the surgeon of Frere's a more notable victory, one which could fill his soul with a serener sense of triumph, than this hour gave, when he sat on the old stone wall that guarded shore from sea, with the child's letter in his hands, which had not miscarried, but had moved straight, straight — do not Divine providences always? — as an arrow to its mark.

Out of the secret place of strength he came, and he held that letter open towards Miss Ames.

"Here 's something to be thought of," said he, endeavoring to speak in a natural and easy tone of voice. "I don't know that I could ask for better counsel than yours. My little girl has written me a letter. I didn't know that she could write. See what work she has made of it. But what sort of parents can she have, do you think, twelve years old, and writing a thing like that?"

Miss Ames laid aside, or rather, to speak correctly, she *dropped* the newspapers. There was nothing in all their printed columns to compare with this item of intelligence, — that the surgeon had a living wife and a living daughter. She took the letter he was holding towards her, and said, "Indeed, Doctor," quite as naturally as he had spoken. But she did not look at him. She read the letter, — every misspelled word of it, — then she said: "Perhaps it does n't say much for the parents. But something — I should think a great deal — for the child. Strange you did n't tell me about her before. But I like to have her introduce herself."

"You do!"

"Promotion, eh!" she was looking the scrawl over again.

The word, as she pronounced it, was not an interrogation. Miss Ames seemed to be musing, yet with no activity of curiosity, on the one idea which had evidently possessed the child's mind in writing.

There was silence for a moment after this ejaculation; then the surgeon spoke.

"I enlisted as a private," said he, speaking with a difficulty that might not have been manifest to any ordinary hearer. "My daughter did not know that I had a profession; but my diploma satisfied the Department when my promotion was spoken of. When I became a live man in the service, I wished to serve where I could bring the most to pass, and it was not in camp, or on the field, — except as a healer." He looked at his watch as he uttered these last words, and arose as if his hour of rest had expired; but then, instead of taking one step forward, he turned and looked at Miss Ames, and she seemed to hear him saying, "Is this a time for flight?"

He answered that question, for he had asked it of himself, by sitting down again.

"I *ought* to take a few minutes to myself," he said, with grave deliberation, "I shall have no time like this to speak of my child, — for her, I mean"; and if, while he spoke thus, he lacked perfect composure, the hour was his, and he knew it. "More than a dozen years ago," he continued, "I went to Dalton. I was sick and dying, as I thought. Janet's mother nursed me through a fever, and was the means of saving my life. I married her. I was grateful for the care she had taken of me; and while regaining my strength, during that September and October, I fell into the mistake of thinking that it was she who made the world seem beautiful to me again, and life worth keeping. But you have seen enough since you have been in this hospital to understand that this war has been salvation to a good many men, as it will prove to the nation. I enlisted as much as anything to get away from — where I was. The Devil himself could n't hold me there any longer. He had managed things long enough. The child is capable of love, you see. Can you help us? I don't know, but I think you were sent from above to do it, somehow. I see — I must live for Janet. When I think that she might live in the same world where you do, that I have no right to surround her with any other conditions — does God take me for a robber? No! for he managed to get this letter to me when — " He stopped speaking, — it seemed as if he were about to look at his watch again; but instead of that, he said "Good evening" to Miss Ames, and bowed, and walked back towards the hospital.

His assistant gathered up the newspapers, and then sat down again and looked out towards the sea. The tide was coming in. She sat awhile and watched the great waves lift aloft the graceful branches of green and purple sea-weed, and saw the stormy petrels going to and fro, and listened to the ocean's roar. She was sounding deeper depths than those awful caverns which were hidden by the green and shining water from her eyes.

If Janet Saunders, child of Nancy Elkins, at that moment felt a thrill of joy, and broke forth into singing, would you deem the fact inconsequent, not to be classed among the wonders of telegraphic achievement?

I think her little cold, pinched, meagre life — nay, *lot* — was brightened consciously on that great day of being, — that the sun felt warmer, and the skies looked fairer than they ever had before. The destiny which had seemed to be in the hands or charge of no one on earth was in the hands of two as capable as any in this world for services of love.

But now what was to be done by Dr. Saunders? Every man and woman sees the "situation." For the present, of course, he was sufficiently occupied; he was in the service of his country. But when these urgent demands on his time, patience, and humanity, which were now incessant, should no longer be made, because the country had need of him no longer, — what then? Men mustered out of service generally went home; family and neighborhood claimed them. What family, what neighborhood, claimed him? His very soul abhorred the thought of Dalton, where he had died to life; where he had buried his manhood. The very thought that the neighbors would not be able to recognize him was a thought which made him say to himself they never *should* recognize him. He would *not* be identified as the poor creature who went out of Dalton with one hope, and only one, — that the first day's engagement might see him lying among the unnamed and unknown dead. But if the neighbors and his wife exposed to him relations which he swore he would not degrade himself so far as to resume, what was to become of his daughter? That was more easily managed. He could send

her away from home to school, if he could find a lady in the land who would compassionate that neglected little girl, and teach her, and train her, and be a mother to her.

Miss Ames knew such a one. Let the little girl be sent to Charlestown to Miss Hall, Miss Ames's dear friend, and no better training than she would have in her school could be found for her throughout the land. Miss Ames gave this advice the day she went away from Frere's, for she had decided, for her brother, that he never would recover his strength until he was removed to a cooler climate. So they were going on a government transport, which would sail for Charlestown direct. This little business in regard to Janet Saunders could be managed by her immediately on arrival home. And so the surgeon wrote a letter, which he sent by his assistant, to Miss Hall, and another to the minister of Dalton, and another still to Janet and her mother. And all these concerned little Jenny; and all this grew out of the letter written in the blacksmith's shop, and the doctor's recovered integrity.

But the question yet remained, What could be done for Nancy? If education in that direction were possible, — to what purpose? That she might become his equal when the strength of his hope that he had done with her was lying merely in this, that they were unequal? But hope, — what had he to do with hope, especially with such a hope as this? What had he to do with hope, who had come forth from Dalton as from a pit of despair? There were no foes like those of his own household; he was hoping that for all time he had rid himself of them. That would have been desertion, in point of fact. Well; but all that a man hath will he give for his life. He was safely distant from that place of disaster and death; but he must recognize his home duties, at least by the maintenance of his family. Yes, that he would do. He began to consider how much was due to him for services rendered to the government, — for the first time to consider.

So, long before winter came, Nancy Saunders found herself on intimate terms with the minister and his wife, — for the minister had received his letters from the surgeon, and promptly accepted his commission, securing comfortable winter quarters for Nancy, and escorting Janet to Charlestown, after his wife had aided the doctor's wife in preparing the child for boarding-school. All these changes and transactions excited talk in Dalton. Every kind of rumor went abroad that you can imagine; and it was currently believed at last that the doctor had made a fortune by some army contract. So well persuaded of this fact was his wife, that, as time wore on, she began to think, and to say, that, if such was the case, she didn't know why she should be kept on short allowance, and to inquire among the neighbors the easiest and the shortest route from Dalton to Frere's Landing. Nobody seemed able to answer the question so well as Ezra Cramer; and he assured her that she would lose her head before she got half through the army lines which stretched between her and the hospital. But then Ezra was a born know-nothing, said Nancy, — that everybody knew.

Walking up and down the sea-wall, night after night, during the hour of rest he appropriated to himself, — knowing that these things were accomplished, for in due time letters came informing him of the fulfilment of his wishes, — the surgeon had ample leisure for considering and reconsidering this case. It was one that would not stay disposed of. What adjournments were made! what exceptions were taken! and what appeals to higher courts were constantly being made!

As often as a scrawl came from Colonel Ames reporting progress, and the plans he and his sister were making, the deeds they were doing, the grand-jury was sworn and the surgeon arraigned before it; the chief justice came into court, and all the witnesses, and the accusation was read. Then the counsel for the defendant and the counsel for the plaintiff appeared. But, with every new trial of the case, new charges and new specifications were brought forward and made, and it was equal to being in chancery. If the war lasted through a generation, it was likely that the surgeon's suit would last as long.

This was as notable a divorce case as ever was made public.

On the plaintiff's behalf the argument ran thus: Here was a man, a gentleman by birth, education, and profession, legally united to a woman low-born, low-bred, and so ignorant that she could neither read nor write. He had come to the neighborhood where she lived, to the door of the very house she occupied, sick in body and in mind. Disappointments and ill-health had reduced him to the shadow of himself in person, and his mind, of course, shared his body's disaffection.

A sick person, as all experience in practice has proved over and over again, is hardly to be called a responsible being. Invalids love and hate without reason, — which is contrary, he said, as he stood in the presence of the court, — contrary to what is done among persons in sound health.

Under the shelter of her uncle's roof he had lain for weeks, sick of a fever. He was saved alive, but so as by fire. This girl waited on him through that time as a servant. He was thrown chiefly on her hands, — no other person could be spared to wait on the poor stranger. She comforted him. Her ways were not refined and gentle as if she had been taught refinement and tenderness by precept or example. She had strong good-sense. So far as she understood his orders, she obeyed them. When he could not give any, she made use of her own judgment, and sought first of all his comfort. She was kind. In her rough honesty and unwearied attention he found cause for gratitude.

Rising for the first time from his bed of sickness, he would have fallen if she had not lifted him and laid him back upon his bed. When he became strong enough to stand, but not without support, she gave him that support. She assisted him from the little room, and the little house when the walls became intolerable to him, and it happened to be in the early morning of a day so magnificent that it seemed another could never be made like it. He could not forget how the world looked that morning ; how the waters shone ; how the islands stood about ; how the surrounding hills were arrayed in purple glory ; how the birds sang. This land to which he was a stranger, which he had seen before only on that night when he came in the dark to her uncle's door, looked like Paradise to him ; he gazed and gazed, and silent tears ran down his pale face through the furrows of his wasted cheeks. She saw them shining in his beard, and said something to soothe him in a comforting way, as any woman would have spoken who saw any creature in weakness and pain. The manner or the word, whatever it was, expressed a superiority of health, if of no other kind, and he was in no condition to investigate either its quality or its degree.

When, with voice feeble and broken as a sick child's ; he thanked her for all she had done, and she answered that it was nothing but a pleasure, and he need not thank her, he did not forthwith forget that she had watched day and night over him for nearly two months ; that many a time weariness so overpowered her that she sat and slept in the broad daylight, and looked paler than when he lay like a dead weight on her hands.

He remembered in court, and could not deny it, that when, believing that this was destiny as it was also pleasure, he asked the girl to marry him, she answered, " No," — as if she did not trust what he said, that she was necessary to his happiness. She told him that he did not belong in Dalton, and that he would not be happy there with her and her people. He answered that all he desired to know was whether she loved him. By and by he was able to gather from the answers she gave, as well as failed to

give, all he desired to know, and they were married.

And, since he was beginning life anew, it was shown in court, nothing of the old life should enter into this of Dalton. He buried his profession in the past, and undertook other labors, — labors like those of Uncle Elkins ; he would abide on that level where he found himself on his recovery, and make no effort to lift his wife to that he had renounced. She was a child of Nature. He would learn life anew of her ; but he failed of success in all his undertakings. Shall a man attempt to extenuate his failures ? It seemed new to him ; he acknowledged it in open court, that from the day of his entrance into Dalton to the day he left it, he was under some enchantment there. And if an insane man is not to be held responsible in law for his offences, he had the amplest title to a quitclaim deed from that which had grown out of the Dalton experience.

So the lower courts disposed of the case. He was free. But after a time the suit was carried up before superior powers, and thus the advocate for the defendant showed cause on the new trial.

She was living among the people of whom she had been born. In person she was attractive as any girl to be found on all the lake or hillside ; a rosy-cheeked, fair-faced, fair-haired blue-eyed girl, with a frank voice and easy address. She had a " Hail fellow ! well met ! " for every man, woman, and child of the vicinity. She had lovers, all the way up from her childhood, rustic admirers, and one who looked at her from a not far distance, who dressed himself in his best and went to her uncle's house on Sundays and other holidays, and who was courting Nancy after his fashion, with all plans for their future marked out fully in his mind, — and these would have fulfilment if his suit were only successful ; and in regard to that he had no fears or doubts.

Until this stranger came to Uncle Elkins's house ! During his long sickness the young lover was helpful in many ways to Nancy. But he began to be suspicious by and by of the results of this much waiting. At last, before he was himself ready to do it, he asked Nancy to be his wife; but he was too late. She had "given her word" to the poor fellow whom she had lured back from Death's door.

The court was admonished to take cognizance of this fact, that, if Nancy had married the man in whom her heart had been interested up to the time when the stranger came, she would have married in her own sphere, a man of her own rank, and would have loved him as he did her, with an equal love; they would have lived out their lives, animating them with skirmishes and small warfare, and winning victories over each other, which would have proved disastrous as defeats to neither.

It would have been no high crime to such a man that Nancy was ignorant up and down through the range of knowledge; he would not have turned away in disgust from his endeavors to teach her, if she took it into her head to learn, though she dropped and regained the ambition through every winter of her life. He would have plodded on in his accustomed ways, would have protected his wife and child from starvation and cold, without imagining that a husband and father could retire from his position as such, or abrogate his duties. No vague expectations in regard to herself, no bitter disappointment in regard to him, would have attended her. The very changes in her character, which had made her not to be endured, — how far was he whose name she bore responsible for them? She had been accustomed to thrift and labor, she saw in him idleness and waste of power and life. She had exhausted the resources readiest to her hand in vain, and had only then given up her expectation.

It was not be denied that it was humiliation and wrath to live with her; but her husband had sought her,— she had not sought him! If he could plead for himself the force and constraint of circumstances, should not the same defence

be set up for her? And what might not patience, and better management, and gentler and more noble demeanor towards her, have done for her? Was *he* the same man he was when he went away from Dalton? Was he the same man in Dalton that he had been in his youth? Was it not out of the pit that he himself had been digged? It became evident that the arguments for the defendant were producing a result in court. The judge on his throne, as well as the grand-jury, listened to the argument in favor of the woman. And at last the case was decided; for the judge charged the jury, that, if it could be shown that there was mere incompatibility, it was the business of the superior mind to make straight a highway for the Lord across those lives. Let every valley be exalted, every hill be brought low.

Dr. Saunders *acquiesced* in this verdict, and wrote a letter to his wife. He knew she could not read it, but he knew also that she could procure it to be read to her. He filled it with accounts of his situation, occupation, expectation; and he sent her money. He said that, if he could get a furlough, he might run up North for a few days, as other men went home who could get leave of absence, to see that those whom he had left behind him were doing well; and they would both perhaps be able to go and see their daughter Jenny, or else they might have her home for a holiday. He wrote a letter saying these things and others, and any wife might have been proud to receive such from her husband, "in the war."

And when he had sent it, he looked for no answer. This was a kind of giving which must look for no return. And yet an answer was sent him. He did not receive it, however, it was sent at so late a date; he was then on his way to Dalton.

When the whistle of the miniature boat which plied the lake sent a warning along the hillside that a passenger was on board who wished to land, or that mail was to be sent ashore, a small boat was rowed from the Point by a lad who was lingering about, waiting to know if any such signal were to come, and one passenger stood at the head of the ladder, waiting for him to come alongside. This was Dr. Saunders, who, having been rowed ashore, walked three miles down the road, and up along the mountain, to the Dalton neighborhood.

The first man whom he met as he walked on was the blacksmith, who had been instrumental in getting Jenny's letter written. He was sitting in front of his shop, alone. There was nothing about this man who was walking into Dalton to excite a suspicion in the mind of the shrewdest old inhabitant who should meet him that his personality was familiar to Dalton eyes. He might safely ask what questions he would, and pursue his way if he chose to do it. Nobody would recognize him.

The doctor lingered as he went past the shop; but the blacksmith did not speak, and he walked on; and he passed others, his old neighbors, as he went. This was hardly pleasant, though it might be the thing he desired.

He walked on until he came to the red farm-gate of Farmer Elkins, Nancy's uncle. There he stopped. Under the chestnut-trees, before the door, the farmer sat. The doctor walked in, and towards him like a man at home, and said, " Good evening, Uncle."

The wrinkled old farmer looked up from his drowse. He had hardly heard the words spoken; but the voice that spoke had in it a tone that was familiar, were it not for the cheeriness of it; and — but no ! one glance at the figure before him assured him of anything rather than Saunders ! Yet the old man, either because of his vague expectation or because of the confusion of his half-awake condition, said something audibly, of which the name of Nancy, and her name alone, was intelligible.

" Well, where *is* Nancy," said the other, laying his hand on the farmer's shoulder in a manner calculated to dissipate his dream.

The old man looked at the doctor with serious, suspicious eyes, scanned him from head to foot, and there was a dash of anger, of unbelief, of awe, and of deference in the spirit with which he said, " If you 're Saunders, I 'm glad you 've come, but you might 'a' come sooner."

" You 're right, and you 're wrong, Uncle. I 'm Saunders, true enough. But I could n't come before, — this is my first furlough."

" Did you get the letter ? "

" No, what letter ? Who wrote to me ? "

The judge and the jury looked down from the awful circle, in the midst of which stood Saunders, and surveyed the little hard-faced, yellow-haired farmer, with eyes which seemed intent on searching him through all his shadowy ambiguity. If only he would make such answer as any other man in all the land might expect, —thought the prisoner, — " Why, your wife, of course." The doctor was prepared to believe in a miracle. Since he went away his wife might have been spurred on by the ambition to rival her daughter, who was being educated. She perhaps had learned to write, and in her pride had written to her husband !

The answer Elkins gave was the only one of which the doctor's mind had taken no thought.

" Nancy died a month ago." There the old man paused. But as the doctor made no answer, merely stood looking at him, he went on. " She got your letter first, though, Nancy did. I think, if anything could a-hindered her dying, that would. She came out here to read your letter," (he did not say to hear it read, and Saunders noticed that,) " and my folks, she found, was busy, and nobody was round to talk it over with her, so nothing could stop her, but she put right in and worked till night, and on top o' that she would go back to the village, and it was raining, and so dark you could scurce see the road ; but she 'd made up her mind to go South and find you, and so we could n't persuade her to stop over night. But the next day, when she come back to tell us when she was going to start, for Dixie, she was took down right here, that suddin. There's been a good deal of that sickness round here sense, and fatalish, most always. But I tell 'em it took the smartest of the lot off first, when it took Nancy."

The doctor stood there when the teller of this story had stopped speaking. He was not looking at *him*, — of that the old man was certain. He seemed to be looking nowhere, and to see nothing that was near or visible.

"Come into the house and take something," said Uncle Elkins, for he began to be alarmed.

"Was Janet here?" asked the doctor, as if he had not heard the invitation.

"We had to send for her. Nancy was calling for her all the time," said Farmer Elkins, as if he doubted how far this story ought to be continued, for he did not understand the man before him. He only knew that once he had fallen down on his door-step, and lain helpless beneath his roof hard on to two months; and he watched him now as if he anticipated some renewal of that old attack, — and there was no Nancy now to nurse, and watch, and slave herself to death for him; for that was the way folk in the house were talking about Nancy and her husband in these days.

"Did she get here in time? Who went after her?"

"The minister went. We had 'em here a fortnight, — well on to 't."

"What, the minister, too?"

"No, I mean the young woman who come from Charlestown with Jenny. Her name was—" He paused long, endeavoring to recall that name. It trembled on the doctor's lips, but he did not utter it. At last said Farmer Elkins, "There! it was Miss Amey, — Amey? Yes. She took the little girl back hum with her. It was right in there, in the room where you had that spell of fever of yourn. She got you well through that! Ef anything could 'a' brought her through that turn, your letter would.

It came across my mind once that, as she 'd saved *your* life, may be you was going to save hern by that are letter! And she was so determined to get to your hospital!"

"Thank God she got the letter, any way!" exclaimed the doctor.

At that the old man walked into the house to set its best cheer before Nancy's husband, who looked so much like a mourner as he stood there under the trees, with the bitter recollections of the past overwhelming every other thought and feeling of the present.

Because it seemed to him that he could not sleep under old Elkins's roof that night, he remained there and slept there, — in the room where his fever ran its course, — in the room where Nancy died.

Because this story of the last months of her life was as gall and wormwood to him, he refused it not, but went over it with his wife's relations, and helped them spread a decent pall, according to the custom of mourners, over what had been.

Was he endeavoring to deceive himself and others into the belief that he was a mourning man? He was but accepting the varied humiliations of death; for they do not all pertain to the surrendering life. He was not thinking at all of his loss through her, nor of his gain by her. He was thinking, as he stood above the grave of fifteen years, how high Disgrace and Misery had heaped the mound. So bitterly he was thinking of the past, it was without desire that he at last arose and faced the future.

When he went to Charlestown — for a man on furlough had no time to lose — and saw his Janet in the Colonel's house, — Miss Ames took Janet home with her after that death and funeral, — when he saw how fair and beautiful a promise of girlhood was budding on the poor neglected branch, he said to his assistant, "Will you keep this child with you until the war is over? I am afraid to touch her, or interfere with her destiny. It has been so easy for me to mar, so hard to mend."

Miss Ames kept the child; the war ended. The surgeon then, like other men, returned home; his regiments were disbanded, and now, one duty, to mankind and the ages, well discharged, another, less conspicuous, but as urgent, claimed him. There was Janet, and Janet's mother, — she who had risen, not from the grave indeed, but from the midst of dangers, sacredly to guard and guide the child.

On his way to them he asked himself this question, "How many times must a man be born before he is fit to live?"

He did not answer that question; neither can I.

He informed his assistant of the court's decision in reference to the plea of "incompatibility," and she said that the justice of the sentence was not to be controverted with success by any counsellor on earth; but the reader may smile, and say that it was not difficult to come to this decision under the circumstances.

We will not argue that point. I had only the story to tell, and have told it.

ON TRANSLATING THE DIVINA COMMEDIA.

THIRD SONNET.

I LIFT mine eyes, and all the windows blaze
     With forms of Saints and holy men who died,
     Here martyred and hereafter glorified;
     And the great Rose upon its leaves displays
Christ's Triumph, and the angelic roundelays,
     With splendor upon splendor multiplied;
     And Beatrice, again at Dante's side,
     No more rebukes, but smiles her words of praise.
And then the organ sounds, and unseen choirs
     Sing the old Latin hymns of peace and love
     And benedictions of the Holy Ghost;
And the melodious bells among the spires
     O'er all the house-tops and through heaven above
     Proclaim the elevation of the Host!

WOMAN'S WORK IN THE MIDDLE AGES.

"King Arthur's sword, Excalibur,
Wrought by the lonely maiden of the Lake.
Nine years she wrought it, sitting in the deeps
Upon the hidden bases of the hills."

SIR BEDIVERE'S heart misgave him twice ere he could obey the dying commands of King Arthur, and fling away so precious a relic. The lonely maiden's industry has been equalled by many of her mortal sisters, sitting, not indeed "upon the hidden bases of the hills," but in all the varied human habitations built above them since the days of King Arthur.

The richness, beauty, and skill displayed in the needle-work of the Middle Ages demonstrate the perfection that art had attained ; while church inventories, wills, and costumes represented in the miniatures of illuminated manuscripts and elsewhere, amaze us by the quantity as well as the quality of this department of woman's work. Though regal robes and heavy church vestments were sometimes wrought by monks, yet to woman's taste and skill the greater share of the result must be attributed, the professional hands being those of nuns and their pupils in convents. The life of woman in those days was extremely monotonous. For the mass of the people, there hardly existed any means of locomotion, the swampy state of the land in England and on the Continent allowing few roads to be made, except such as were traversed by pack-horses. Ladies of rank who wished to journey were borne on litters carried upon men's shoulders, and, until the fourteenth and fifteenth centuries, few representations of carriages appear. Such a conveyance is depicted in an illustration of the Romance of the Rose, where Venus, attired in the fashionable costume of the fifteenth century, is seated in a *chare*, by courtesy a chariot, but in fact a clumsy covered wagon without springs. Six doves are perched upon the shafts, and

fastened by mediæval harness. The goddess of course possessed superhuman powers for guiding this extraordinary equipage, but to mere mortals it must have been a slow coach, and a horribly uncomfortable conveyance even when horses were substituted for doves. An ordinance of Philip le Bel, in 1294, forbids any wheel carriages to be used by the wives of citizens, as too great a luxury. As the date of the coach which Venus guides is two hundred years later, it is difficult to imagine what style of equipage belonged to those ladies over whom Philip le Bel tyrannized.

With so little means of going about, our sisters of the Middle Ages were perforce domestic ; no wonder they excelled in needle-work. To women of any culture it was almost the only tangible form of creative art they could command, and the love of the beautiful implanted in their souls must find some expression. The great pattern-book of nature, filled with graceful forms, in ever-varied arrangement, and illuminated by delicate tints or gorgeous hues, suggested the beauty they endeavored to represent. Whether religious devotion, human affection, or a taste for dress prompted them, the needle was the instrument to effect their purpose. The monogram of the blessed Mary's name, intertwined with pure white lilies on the deep blue ground, was designed and embroidered with holy reverence, and laid on the altar of the Lady-chapel by the trembling hand of one whose sorrows had there found solace, or by another in token of gratitude for joys which were heightened by a conviction of celestial sympathy. The pennon of the knight — a silken streamer affixed to the top of the lance — bore his crest, or an emblematic allusion to some event in his career, embroidered, it was supposed, by the hand of his lady-love. A yet more sacred gift was the scarf worn across the shoulder, an indispensable appendage to a knight fully equipped. The emotions of the human soul send an electric current through the ages, and women who during four years of war toiled to aid our soldiers in the great struggle of the nineteenth century felt their hearts beat in unison with hers who gave, with tears and prayers, pennon and scarf to the knightly and beloved hero seven hundred years ago.

Not only were the appointments of the warriors adorned by needle-work, but the ladies must have found ample scope for industry and taste in their own toilets. The Anglo-Saxon women as far back as the eighth century excelled in needle-work, although, judging from the representations which have come down to us, their dress was much less ornamented than that of the gentlemen. During the eighth, ninth, and tenth centuries there were few changes in fashion. A purple gown or robe, with long yellow sleeves, and coverchief wrapt round the head and neck, frequently appears, the edges of the long gown and sleeves being slightly ornamented by the needle. How the ladies dressed their hair in those days is more difficult to decide, as the coverchief conceals it. Crisping-needles to curl and plat the hair, and golden haircauls, are mentioned in Saxon writings, and give us reason to suppose that the locks of the fair damsels were not neglected. In the eleventh century the embroidery upon the long gowns becomes more elaborate, and other changes of the mode appear.

From the report of an ancient Spanish ballad, the art of needle-work and taste in dress must have attained great perfection in that country while our Anglo-Saxon sisters were wearing their plain long gowns. The fair Sybilla is described as changing her dress seven times in one evening, on the arrival of that successful and victorious knight, Prince Baldwin. First,

she dazzles him in blue and silver, with a rich turban; then appears in purple satin, fringed and looped with gold, with white feathers in her hair; next, in green silk and emeralds; anon, in pale straw-color, with a tuft of flowers; next, in pink and silver, with varied plumes, white, carnation, and blue; then, in brown, with a splendid crescent. As the fortunate Prince beholds each transformation, he is bewildered (as well he may be) to choose which array becomes her best; but when

> " Lastly in white she comes, and loosely
>   Down in ringlets floats her hair,
> 'O,' exclaimed the Prince, 'what beauty!
>   Ne'er was princess half so fair.' "

Simplicity and natural grace carried the day after all, as they generally do with men of true taste. "Woman is fine for her own satisfaction alone," says that nice observer of human nature, Jane Austen. "Man only knows man's insensibility to a new gown." We hope, however, that the dressmakers and tirewomen of the fair Sybilla, who had expended so much time and invention, were handsomely rewarded by the Prince, since they must have been most accomplished needle-women and handmaids to have got up their young lady in so many costumes and in such rapid succession.

A very odd fashion appears in the thirteenth and fourteenth centuries, of embroidering heraldic devices on the long gowns of the ladies of rank. In one of the illuminations of a famous psalter, executed for Sir Geoffery Loutterell, who died in 1345, that nobleman is represented armed at all points, receiving from the ladies of his family his tilting helmet, shield, and *pavon*. His coat of arms is repeated on every part of his own dress, and is embroidered on that of his wife, who wears also the crest of her own family.

Marie de Hainault, wife of the first Duke of Bourbon, 1354, appears in a corsage and train of ermine, with a very fierce-looking lion rampant embroidered twice on her long gown. Her jewels are magnificent. Anne,

Dauphine d'Auvergne, wife of Louis, second Duke of Bourbon, married in 1371, displays an heraldic dolphin of very sinister aspect upon one side of her corsage, and on the skirt of her long gown, — which, divided in the centre, seems to be composed of two different stuffs, that opposite to the dolphin being powdered with *fleurs de lis.* Her circlet of jewels is very elegant, and is worn just above her brow, while the hair is braided close to the face. An attendant lady wears neither train nor jewels, but her dress is likewise formed of different material, divided like that of the Dauphine. Six little parrots are emblazoned on the right side, one on her sleeve, two on her corsage, and three on her skirt. The fashion of embroidering armorial bearings on ladies' dresses must have given needle-women a vast deal of work. It died out in the fifteenth century.

It was the custom in feudal times for knightly families to send their daughters to the castles of their suzerain lords, to be trained to weave and embroider. The young ladies on their return home instructed the more intelligent of their female servants in these arts. Ladies of rank in all countries prided themselves upon the number of these attendants, and were in the habit of passing the morning surrounded by their workwomen, singing the *chansons à toile,* as ballads composed for these hours were called.

Estienne Jodelle, a French poet, 1573, addressed a fair lady whose cunning fingers plied the needle in words thus translated : —

"I saw thee weave a web with care,
  Where at thy touch fresh roses grew,
  And marvelled they were formed so fair,
  And that thy heart such nature knew.
  Alas ! how idle my surprise,
  Since naught so plain can be :
  Thy cheek their richest hue supplies,
  And in thy breath their perfume lies :
  Their grace and beauty all are drawn from thee.

If needle-work had its poetry, it had also its reckonings. Old account-books bear many entries of heavy payments for working materials used by industrious queens and indefatigable ladies of rank. Good authorities state that, before the sixth century, all silk materials were brought to Europe by the Seres, ancestors of the ancient Bokharians, whence it derived its name of Serica. In 551, silk-worms were introduced by two monks into Constantinople, but the Greeks monopolized the manufacture until 1130, when Roger, king of Sicily, returning from a crusade, collected some Greek manufacturers, and established them at Palermo, whence the trade was disseminated over Italy.

In the thirteenth century, Bruges was the great mart for silk. The stuffs then known were velvet, satin (called samite), and taffeta, — all of which were stitched with gold or silver thread. The expense of working materials was therefore very great, and royal ladies condescended to superintend sewing-schools.

Editha, consort of Edward the Confessor, was a highly accomplished lady, who sometimes intercepted the master of Westminster School and his scholars in their walks, questioning them in Latin. She was also skilled in all feminine works, embroidering the robes of her royal husband with her own hands.

Of all the fair ones, however, who have wrought for the service of a king, since the manufacture of Excalibur, let the name of Matilda of Flanders, wife of William the Conqueror, stand at the head of the record, in spite of historians' doubts. Matilda, born about the year 1031, was carefully educated. She had beauty, learning, industry ; and the Bayeux tapestry connected with her name still exists, a monument of her achievements in the art of needle-work. It is, as everybody knows, a pictured chronicle of the conquest of England, — a wife's tribute to the glory of her husband.

As a specimen of ancient stitchery and feminine industry, this work is extremely curious. The tapestry is two hundred and twenty-two feet in length and twenty in width. It is worked in different-colored worsteds on white cloth, now brown with age. The attempts to represent the human figure are very rude, and it is merely given in outline. Matilda evidently had very few colors at her disposal, as the horses are depicted of any hue,—blue, green, or yellow; the arabesque patterns introduced are rich and varied.

During the French Revolution, this tapestry was demanded by the insurgents to cover their guns; but a priest succeeded in concealing it until the storm had passed. Bonaparte knew its value. He caused it to be brought to Paris and displayed, after which he restored the precious relic to Bayeux.

We have many records of royal ladies who practised and patronized needle-work. Anne of Brittany, first wife of Louis XII. of France, caused three hundred girls, daughters of the nobility, to be instructed in that art under her personal supervision. Her daughter Claude pursued the same laudable plan. Jeanne d'Albret, queen of Navarre, and mother of Henry IV. of France, a woman of vigorous mind, was skilled also in the handicraft of the needle, and wrought a set of hangings called "The Prison Opened," meaning that she had broken the bonds of the Pope.

The practice of teaching needle-work continued long at the French court, and it was there that Mary of Scotland learned the art in which she so much excelled. When cast into prison, she beguiled the time, and soothed the repentant anxieties of her mind, with the companionship of her needle. The specimens of her work yet existing are principally bed-trimmings, hangings, and coverlets, composed of dark satin, upon which flowers, separately embroidered, are transferred.

The romances and lays of chivalry contain many descriptions of the ornamental needle-work of those early days. In one of the ancient ballads, a knight, after describing a fair damsel whom he had rescued and carried to his castle, adds that she " knewe how to sewe and marke all manner of silken worke," and no doubt he made her repair many of his mantles and scarfs frayed and torn by time and tourney.

The beautiful Elaine covered the shield of Sir Launcelot with a case of silk, upon which devices were braided by her fair hands, and added, from her own design,

" A border fantasy of branch and flower,
And yellow-throated nestling in the nest."

When he went to the tourney she gave him a red sleeve "broidered with great pearls," which he bound upon his helmet. It is recorded that, in a tournament at the court of Burgundy in 1445, one of the knights received from his lady a sleeve of delicate dove-color, which he fastened on his left arm. These sleeves were made of a different material from the dress, and generally of a richer fabric elaborately ornamented; so they were considered valuable enough to form a separate legacy in wills of those centuries. Maddalena Doni, in her portrait, painted by Raphael, which hangs in the Pitti Palace at Florence, wears a pair of these rich, heavy sleeves, fastened slightly at the shoulder, and worn over a shorter sleeve belonging to her dress. Thus we see how it was that a lady could disengage her sleeve at the right moment, and give it to the fortunate knight.

The art of adorning linen was practised from the earliest times. Threads were drawn and fashioned with the needle, or the ends of the cloth unravelled and plaited into geometrical patterns. St. Cuthbert's curious graveclothes, as described by an eyewitness to his disinterment in the twelfth century, were ornamented with cut-work, which was used principally for ecclesiastical purposes, and was looked upon in England till the dissolution of the monasteries as a church secret. The open-work embroidery, which went under the general name of cut-work, is the origin of lace.

The history of lace by Mrs. Bury Palliser, recently published in London, is worthy of the exquisite fabric of which it treats. The author has woven valuable facts, historical associations, and curious anecdotes into the web of her narrative, with an industry and skill rivalling the work of her mediæval sisters. The illustrations of this beautiful volume are taken from rare specimens of ancient and modern lace, so perfectly executed as quite to deceive the eye, and almost the touch.

. Italy and Flanders dispute the invention of point or needle-made lace. The Italians probably derived the art of needle-work from the Greeks who took refuge in Italy during the troubles of the Lower Empire. Its origin was undoubtedly Byzantine, as the places which were in constant intercourse with the Greek Empire were the cities where point-lace was earliest made. The traditions of the Low Countries also ascribe it to an Eastern origin, assigning the introduction of lace-making to the Crusaders on their return from the Holy Land. A modern writer, Francis North, asserts that the Italians learned embroidery from the Saracens, as Spaniards learned the same art from the Moors, and, in proof of his theory, states that the word *embroider* is derived from the Arabic, and does not belong to any European language. In the opinion of some authorities, the English word *lace* comes from the Latin word *licina*, signifying the hem or fringe of a garment ; others suppose it derived from the word *laces*, which appears in Anglo-Norman statutes, meaning braids which were used to unite different parts of the dress. In England the earliest lace was called *passament*, from the fact that the threads were passed over each other in its formation ; and it is not until the reign of Richard III. that the word *lace* appears in royal accounts. The French term *dentelle* is also of modern date, and was not used until fashion caused *passament* to be made with a toothed edge, when the designation *passament dentelé* appears.

But whatever the origin of the name, lace-making and embroidery have employed many fingers, and worn out many eyes, and even created revolutions. In England, until the time of Henry VIII., shirts, handkerchiefs, sheets, and pillow-cases were embroi-

dered in silks of different colors, until the fashion gave way to cut-work and lace. Italy produced lace fabrics early in the fifteenth century ; and the Florentine poet, Firenzuola, who flourished about 1520, composed an elegy upon a collar of raised point lace made by the hand of his mistress. Portraits of Venetian ladies dated as early as 1500 reveal white lace trimmings ; but at that period lace was, professedly, only made by nuns for the service of the Church, and the term *nuns' work* has been the designation of lace in many places to a very modern date. Venice was famed for point, Genoa for pillow laces. English Parliamentary records have statutes on the subject of Venice laces ; at the coronation of Richard III., fringes of Venice and mantle laces of gold and white silk appear.

"To know the age and pedigrees
    Of points of Flanders and Venise,"

depends much upon the ancient pattern-books yet in existence. Parchment patterns, drawn and pricked for pillow lace, bearing the date of 1577, were lately found covering old law-books, in Albisola, a town near Savona, which was a place celebrated for its laces, as we infer from the fact that it was long the custom of the daughters of the nobles to select these laces for their wedding shawls and veils. There is a pretty tradition at Venice, handed down among the inhabitants of the Lagoons, which says that a sailor brought home to his betrothed a branch of the delicate coralline known as "mermaids' lace." The girl, a worker in points, attracted by the grace of the coral, imitated it with her needle, and after much toil produced the exquisite fabric which, as Venice point, soon became the mode in all Europe. Lace-making in Italy formed the occupation of many women of the higher classes, who wished to add to their incomes. Each lady had a number of workers, to whom she supplied patterns, pricked by herself, paying her workwomen at the end of every week, each day being notched on a tally.

In the convent of Gesù Bambino, at

Rome, curious specimens of old Spanish conventual work — parchment patterns with lace in progress — have been found. They belonged to Spanish nuns, who long ago taught the art of lace-making to novices. Like all point lace, this appears to be executed in separate pieces, given out by the nuns, and then joined together by a skilful hand. We see the pattern traced, the work partly finished, and the very thread left, as when "Sister Felice Vittoria" laid down her work, centuries ago. Mrs. Palliser received from Rome photographs of these valuable relics, engravings from which she has inserted in her history of lace. Aloe-thread was then used for lace-making, as it is now in Florence for sewing straw-plait. Spanish point has been as celebrated as that of Flanders or Italy. Some traditions aver that Spain taught the art to Flanders. Spain had no cause to import laces: they were extensively made at home, and were less known than the manufacture of other countries, because very little was exported. The numberless images of the Madonna and patron saints dressed and undressed daily, together with the albs of the priests and decorations of the altars, caused an immense consumption for ecclesiastical uses. Thread lace was manufactured in Spain in 1492, and in the Cathedral of Granada is a lace alb presented to the church by Ferdinand and Isabella, — one of the few relics of ecclesiastical grandeur preserved in the country. Cardinal Wiseman, in a letter to Mrs. Palliser, states that he had himself officiated in this vestment, which was valued at ten thousand crowns. The fine church lace of Spain was little known in Europe until the revolution of 1830, when splendid specimens were suddenly thrown into the market, — not merely the heavy lace known as Spanish point, but pieces of the most exquisite description, which could only have been made, says Mrs. Palliser, by those whose time was not money.

Among the Saxon Hartz Mountains is the old town of Annaburg, and beneath a lime-tree in its ancient burial-ground stands a simple monument with this inscription:

"Here lies Barbara Uttman, died on the 14th of January, 1576, whose invention of lace in the year 1561 made her the benefactress of the Hartz Mountains.

'An active mind, a skilful hand,
Bring blessings down on Fatherland.'"

Barbara was born in 1514. Her parents, burghers of Nuremberg, removed to the Hartz Mountains for the purpose of working a mine in that neighborhood. It is said that Barbara learned the art of lace-making from a native of Brabant, a Protestant, whom the cruelties of the Duke of Alva had driven from her country. Barbara, observing the mountain girls making nets for the miners to wear over their hair, took great interest in the improvement of their work, and succeeded in teaching them a fine knitted *tricot*, and afterwards a lace ground. In 1561, having procured aid from Flanders, she set up a workshop in Annaburg for lace-making. This branch of industry spread beyond Bavaria, giving employment to thirty thousand persons, and producing a revenue of one million thalers.

Italy and Flanders dispute the invention of lace, but it was probably introduced into both countries about the same time. The Emperor Charles V. commanded lace-making to be taught in schools and convents. A specimen of the manufacture of his day may be seen in his cap, now preserved in the museum at Hôtel Cluny, Paris. It is of fine linen, with the Emperor's arms embroidered in relief, with designs in lace, of exquisite workmanship. The old Flemish laces are of great beauty and world-wide fame.

Many passages in the history of lace show how severely the manufacture of this beautiful fabric has strained the nerves of eye and brain. The fishermen's wives on the Scottish coast apostrophize the fish they sell, after their husbands' perilous voyages, and sing,

"Call them lives o' men."

Not more fatal to life are the blasts

from ocean winds than the tasks of laborious lace-makers ; and this thought cannot but mingle with our admiration for the skill displayed in this branch of woman's endless toil and endeavor to supply her own wants and aid those who are dear to her, in the present as well as in the past centuries.

In the British Museum there is a curious manuscript of the fourteenth century, afterwards translated "into our maternall englisshe by me William Caxton, and emprynted at Westminstre the last day of Januer, the first yere of the regne of King Richard the thyrd," called "the booke which the Knight of the Towere made for the enseygnement and teching of his doughtres."

The Knight of the Tower was Geoffory Landry, surnamed De la Tour, of a noble family of Anjou. In the month of April, 1371, he was one day reflecting beneath the shade of some trees on various passages in his life, and upon the memory of his wife, whose early death had caused him sorrow, when his three daughters walked into the garden. The sight of these motherless girls naturally turned his thoughts to the condition of woman in society, and he resolved to write a treatise, enforced by examples of both good and evil, for their instruction. The state of society which the "evil" examples portray might well cause a father's heart to tremble.

The education of young ladies, as we have before stated, was in that age usually assigned to convents or to families of higher rank. It consisted of instruction in needle-work, confectionery, surgery, and the rudiments of church music. Men were strongly opposed to any high degree of mental culture for women ; and although the Knight of the Tower thinks it good for women to be taught to read their Bibles, yet the pen is too dangerous an instrument to trust to their hands. The art of writing he disapproves, — "Better women can naught of it." Religious observances he strictly recommends ; but we shudder at some of the stories which even this well-meaning father

relates as illustrations of the efficacy of religious austerities. Extravagance in dress prevailed at that time among men and women to such a degree that Parliament was appealed to on the subject in 1363. From the Knight's exhortations on the subject, this mania seems to have affected the women alarmingly, and the examples given of the passion for dress appear to surpass what is acknowledged in our day. Yet the vast increase of materials, as well as the extended interests and objects opened to woman now, renders the extravagance of dress in the Middle Ages far less reprehensible.

The record of woman's work in the Middle Ages includes far more than the account of what her needle accomplished. The position of the mistress of a family in those centuries was no sinecure. When we look up at castles perched on rocks, or walk through the echoing apartments of baronial halls, we know that woman must have worked there with brain and fingers. The household and its dependencies, in such mansions, consisted of more than a score of persons, and provisions must be laid in during the autumn for many months. As we glance at the enormous fireplaces and ovens in the kitchens of those castles and halls, and remember the weight of the armor men wore, we can readily imagine that no trifling supply of brawn and beef was needed for their meals ; and the sight of a husband frowning out of one of those old helmets because the dinner was scanty, must have been a fearful trial to feminine nerves. The title of "Lady" means the "Giver of bread" in Saxon, and the lady of the castle dispensed food to many beyond her own household.

The task of preparing the raiment of the family devolved upon the women ; for there were no travelling dealers except for the richest and most expensive articles. Wool, the produce of the flock, was carded and spun ; flax was grown, and woven into coarse linen ; and both materials were prepared and fashioned into garments at home. Glimpses of domestic life come down to us through early legends and records, some of which modern genius has melodized. Authentic history and romantic story often show us that women of all ranks were little better, in fact, than household drudges to these splendid knights and courtly old barons. The fair Enid sang a charming song as she turned her wheel; but when Geraint arrived, she not only assisted her mother to receive him, but, by her father's order, led the knight's charger to the stall, and gave him corn. If she also relieved the noble animal of his heavy saddle and horse-furniture, gave him water as well as corn, and shook down the dry furze for his bed, she must have had the courage and skill of a feminine Rarey; and we fear her dress of faded silk came out of the stable in a very dilapidated condition. After the horse was cared for, Enid put her wits and hands to work to prepare the evening meal, and spread it before her father and his guest. The knight, indeed, condescended to think her "sweet and serviceable"!

The women of those days are often described only as they appeared at festivals and tournaments, — Ladies of Beauty, to whom knights lowered their lances, and of whom troubadours sang. They had their amusements and their triumphs, doubtless; but they also had their work, domestic, industrial, and sanitary. They knew how to bind up wounds and care for the sick, and we read many records of their knowledge in this department. Elaine, when she found Sir Launcelot terribly wounded in the cave, so skilfully aided him that, when the old hermit came who was learned in all the simples and science of the times, he told the knight that "her fine care had saved his life," — a pleasing assurance that there were medical men in those days, as well as in our own, who expressed no unwillingness to allow a woman credit for success in their own profession.

Illuminated books sometimes show us pictures of women of the humbler ranks of life at their work. On the

border of a fine manuscript of the time of Edward IV. there is the figure of a woman employed with her distaff, her head and neck enveloped in a coverchief. The figure rises out of a flower. In a manuscript of 1316, a countrywoman is engaged in churning, dressed in a comfortable gown and apron, the gown tidily pinned up, and her head and neck in a coverchief. The churn is of considerable height, and of very clumsy construction. A blind beggar approaches her, led by his dog, who holds apparently a cup in his mouth to receive donations. In another part of the same volume is a beautiful damsel with her hair spread over her shoulders, while her maid arranges her tresses with a comb of ivory set in gold. The young lady holds a small mirror, probably of polished steel, in her hand. Specimens of these curious combs and mirrors yet exist in collections. A century later we see a pretty laundress, holding in her hands a number of delicately woven napkins, which look as if they might have come out of the elaborately carved napkin press of the same period in the collection of Sir Samuel Myrick at Goodrich Court.

Although the Knight of the Tower disapproved of young ladies being taught to write, there were women whose employment writing seems to have been; but these were nuns safely shut up from the risk of *billets-doux.* In Dr. Maitland's Essays on the Dark Ages, he quotes from the biography of Diemudis, a devout nun of the eleventh century, a list of the volumes which she prepared with her own hand, written in beautiful and legible characters, to the praise of God, and of the holy Apostles Peter and Paul, the patrons of the monastery, which was that of Wessobrunn in Bavaria. The list comprises thirty-one works, many of them in three or four volumes; and although Diemudis is not supposed to have been an authoress, she is certainly worthy of having her name handed down through eight centuries in witness of woman's indefatigable work in the scriptorium. One missal prepared by Diemudis was given to the Bishop of Treves, another to the Bishop of Augsburg, and one Bible in two volumes is mentioned, which was exchanged by the monastery for an estate.

We can picture to ourselves Diemudis in her conventual dress, seated in the scriptorium, with her materials for chirography. The sun, as it streams through the window, throws a golden light over the vellum page, suggesting the rich hue of the gilded nimbus, while in the convent garden she sees the white lily or the modest violet, which, typical of the Madonna, she transfers to her illuminated borders. Thus has God ever interwoven truth and love with their correspondences of beauty and development in the natural world, which were open to the eyes of Diemudis eight hundred years ago, perhaps as clearly as to our own in these latter days. That women of even an earlier century than that of Diemudis were permitted to read, if not to write, is proved by the description of a private library, given in the letters of C. S. Sidonius Apollinaris, and quoted in Edwards's "History of Libraries." This book-collection was the property of a gentleman of the fifth century, residing at his castle of Prusiana. It was divided into three departments, the first of which was expressly intended for the ladies of the family, and contained books of piety and devotion. The second department was for men, and is rather ungallantly stated to have been of a higher order; yet, as the third department was intended for the whole family, and contained such works as Augustine, Origen, Varro, Prudentius, and Horace, the literary tastes of the ladies should have been satisfied. We are also told that it was the custom at the castle of Prusiana to discuss at dinner the books read in the morning, — which would tend to a belief that conversation at the dinner-tables of the fifth century might be quite as edifying as at those of the nineteenth.

A few feminine names connected with the literature of the Middle Ages

have come down to us. The lays of Marie de France are among the manuscripts in the British Museum. Marie's personal history, as well as the period when she flourished, is uncertain. Her style is extremely obscure; but in her Preface she seems aware of this defect, yet defends it by the example of the ancients. She considers it the duty of all persons to employ their talents; and as her gifts were intellectual, she cast her thoughts in various directions ere she determined upon her peculiar mission. She had intended translating from the Latin a good history, but some one else unluckily anticipated her; and she finally settled herself down to poetry, and to the translation of numerous lays she had treasured in her memory, as these would be new to many of her readers. Like other literary ladies, she complains of envy and persecution, but she perseveres through all difficulties, and dedicates her book "to the King."

Marie was born in France. Some authorities suppose she wrote in England during the reign of Henry III., and that the patron she names was William Langue-espée, who died in 1226; others, that this *plus vaillant* patron was William, Count of Flanders, who accompanied St. Louis on his first crusade in 1248, and was killed at a tournament in 1251. A later surmise is that the book was dedicated to Stephen, French being his native language. Among the manuscripts of the Bibliothèque Royale at Paris, is Marie's translation of the fables which Henry Beauclerc translated from Latin into English, and which Marie renders into French. A proof that Marie's poems are extremely ancient is deduced from the names in one of these fables applied to the wolf and the fox. She uses other names than those of Ysengrin and Renard, which were introduced as early as the reign of Cœur de Lion, and it would seem that she could not have failed to notice these remarkable names, had they existed in her time. A complete collection of the works of Marie de France was published in

Paris in 1820, by M. de Roquefort, who speaks of her in the following terms : "She possessed that penetration which distinguishes at first sight the different passions of mankind, which seizes upon the different forms they assume, and, remarking the objects of their notice, discovers at the same time the means by which they are attained." If this be a true statement, the acuteness of feminine observation has gained but little in the progress of the centuries, and her literary sisters of the present era can hardly hope to eclipse the penetration of Marie de France.

The Countesses de Die, supposed to be mother and daughter, were both poetesses. The elder lady was beloved by Rabaud d'Orange, who died in 1173, and the younger is celebrated by William Adhémar, a distinguished troubadour. He was visited on his death-bed by both these ladies, who afterwards erected a monument to his memory. The younger countess retired to a convent, and died soon after Adhémar.

In the Harleian Collection is a fine manuscript containing the writings of Christine de Pisan, a distinguished woman of the fourteenth century. Her father, Thomas de Pisan, a celebrated *savant* of Bologna, had married a daughter of a member of the Grand Council of Venice. So renowned was Thomas de Pisan that the kings of Hungary and France determined to win him away from Bologna. Charles V. of France, surnamed the Wise, was successful, and Thomas de Pisan went to Paris in 1368 ; his transfer to the French court making a great sensation among learned and scientific circles of that day. Charles loaded him with wealth and honors, and chose him Astrologer Royal. According to the history, as told by Louisa Stuart Costello, in her "Specimens of the Early Poetry of France," Christine was but five years old when she accompanied her parents to Paris, where she received every advantage of education, and, inheriting her father's literary tastes, early became learned in languages and sci-

ence. Her personal charms, together with her father's high favor at court, attracted many admirers. She married Stephen Castel, a young gentleman of Picardy, to whom she was tenderly attached, and whose character she has drawn in most favorable colors. A few years passed happily, but, alas ! changes came. The king died, the pension and offices bestowed upon Thomas de Pisan were suspended, and the Astrologer Royal soon followed his patron beyond the stars. Castel was also deprived of his preferments ; and though he maintained his wife and family for a time, he was cut off by death at thirty-four years of age.

Christine had need of all her energies to meet such a succession of calamities, following close on so brilliant a career. Devoting herself anew to study, she determined to improve her talents for composition, and to make her literary attainments a means of support for her children. The illustrations in the manuscript volume of her works picture to us several scenes in Christine's life. In one, the artist has sliced off the side of a house to allow us to see Christine in her study, giving us also the exterior, roof, and dormer-windows, with points finished by gilt balls. The room is very small, with a crimson and white tapestry hanging. Christine wears what may be called the regulation color for literary ladies, — blue, with the extraordinary two-peaked head-dress of the period, put on in a decidedly strong-minded manner. At her feet sits a white dog, small, but wise-looking, with a collar of gold bells round his neck. Before Christine stands a plain table, covered with green cloth ; her book, bound in crimson and gold, in which she is writing, lies before her.

Christine's style of holding the implements, — one in each hand, — and the case of materials for her work which lies beside her, are according to representations of the *miniatori caligrafi* at their labors ; and, as the art of caligraphy was well known at Bologna, so learned a man as Thomas de Pisan must have been acquainted with it, and would have caused his talented daughter to be instructed in so rare an accomplishment. It is not therefore unreasonable to believe that, in the beautiful volume now in the British Museum, the work of Christine's hand, as well as the result of her genius, is preserved. The next picture shows us Christine presenting her book to Charles VII. of France, who is dressed in a black robe edged with ermine; he wears a golden belt, order, and crown. The king is seated beneath a canopy, blue, powdered with *fleurs de lis.* Four courtiers stand beside him, dressed in robes of different colors, — one in pink, and wearing a large white hat of Quaker-like fashion. Christine has put on a white robe over her blue dress, perhaps as a sign of mourning, — she being then a widow. A white veil depends from the peaks of her head-dress. She kneels before the king, and presents her book.

Another and more elaborate picture represents the repetition of the same ceremony before Isabelle of Bavaria, queen of Charles VI. We are here admitted into the private royal apartments of the fourteenth century. The hangings of the apartment consist of strips, upon which are alternately emblazoned the armorial devices of France and Bavaria. A couch or bed, with a square canopy covered with red and blue, having the royal arms embroidered in the centre, stands on one side of the room. The queen is seated upon a lounge of modern shape, covered to correspond with the couch. She is dressed in a splendid robe of purple and gold, with long sleeves sweeping the ground, lined with ermine; upon her head arises a structure of stuffed rolls, heavy in material and covered with jewels, which shoots up into two high peaks above her forehead. Six ladies are in waiting, two in black and gold, with the same enormous head-gears. They sit on the edge of her Majesty's sofa, while four ladies of inferior rank and plainer garments are

contented with low benches. Christine reappears in her blue dress, and white-veiled, peaked cap. She kneels before the queen, on a square carpet with a geometrical-patterned border, and presents her book. A white Italian hound lies at the foot of the couch, while beside Isabelle sits a small white dog, resembling the one we saw in Christine's study. As we can hardly suppose Christine would bring her pet on so solemn an occasion, — far less allow him to jump up beside the queen, — and as this little animal wears no gold bells, we are led to suppose that little white dogs were in fashion in the fourteenth century.

We cannot say that the portrait of Isabelle gives us any idea of her splendid beauty; but "handsome is that handsome does," and as Isabelle's work was a very bad one in the Middle Ages, we will say no more about her.

Christine was but twenty-five years of age when she became a widow, and her personal charms captivated the heart of no less a personage than the Earl of Salisbury, who came ambassador from England to demand the hand of the very youthful princess, Isabelle, for his master.

They exchanged verses; and although Salisbury spoke by no means mysteriously, the sage Christine affected to view his declarations only in the light of complimentary speeches from a gallant knight. The Earl considered himself as rejected, bade adieu to love, and renounced marriage. To Christine he made a very singular proposal for a rejected lover, — that of taking with him to England her eldest son, promising to devote himself to his education and preferment. The offer was too valuable to be declined by a poor widow, whose pen was her only means of supporting her family. That such a proof of devotion argued a tenderer feeling than that of knightly gallantry must have been apparent to Christine; but for reasons best understood by herself, — and shall we not believe with a heart yet true to her husband's memory? — she merely acknowledged the kindness shown to her son; and the Earl and his adopted boy left France together. When Richard II. was deposed, Henry Bolingbroke struck off the head of the Earl of Salisbury. Among the papers of the murdered man the lays of Christine were found by King Henry, who was so much struck with their purity and beauty, that he wrote to the fair authoress of her son's safety, under his protection, and invited her to his court.

This invitation was at once a compliment and an insult, for the hand that sent it was stained with the blood of her friend. Christine, however, had worldly wisdom enough to send a respectful, though firm refusal, to a crowned head, a successful soldier, and one, moreover, who held her son in his power. Feminine tact must have guided her pen, for Henry was not offended, and twice despatched a herald to renew the invitation to his court. She steadily declined to leave France, but managed the affair so admirably that she at last obtained the return of her son from England.

Like her father, Thomas de Pisan, Christine seems to have been sought as an ornament of their courts by several rulers. Henry Bolingbroke could not gain her for England, and the Duke of Milan in vain urged her to reside in that city. Seldom has a literary lady in any age received such tempting invitations; yet Christine refused to leave France, although her own fortunes were anything but certain. The Duke of Burgundy took her son under his protection, and urged Christine to write the history of her patron, Charles V. of France. This was a work grateful to her feelings, and she had commenced the memoir when the death of the Duke deprived her of his patronage, and threw her son again upon her care, involving her in many anxieties. But Christine bore herself through all her trials with firmness and prudence, and her latter days were more tranquil. She took a deep interest in the affairs of her adopted country, and welcomed in her writings the appearance of the Maid of Orleans. We believe, however, that she was spared the pain of witnessing the last act in that drama of history, where an innocent victim was given up by French perfidy to English cruelty.

The deeds of Joan of Arc need no recital here. A daughter of France in the nineteenth century had a soul pure enough to reflect the image of the Maid of Orleans, and with a skilful hand she embodied the vision in marble. The statue of Joan of Arc, modelled by the Princess Marie, adorns — or rather sanctifies — the halls of Versailles.

Of woman's work as an artist in the early centuries we have a curious illustration in a manuscript belonging to the Bibliothèque Royale at Paris, which exhibits a female figure painting the statue of the Madonna. The artist holds in her left hand a palette, which is the earliest notice of the use of that implement with which antiquarians are acquainted. The fashion of painting figures cut in wood was once much practised, and we see here the representation of a female artist of very ancient date. Painting, music, and dancing come under the designation of accomplishments; yet to obtain distinction in any of these branches implies a vast amount of work. An illustration of Lygate's Pilgrim shows us a young lady playing upon a species of organ with one hand; in the other she holds to her lips a mellow horn, through which she pours her breath, if not her soul; lying beside her is a stringed instrument called a sawtry. Such varied musical acquirements certainly argue both industry and devotion to art. Charlemagne's daughters were distinguished for their skill in dancing; and we read of many instances in the Middle Ages of women excelling in these fine arts.

The period of time generally denominated the Middle Ages commences with the fifth century, and ends with the fifteenth. We have in several instances ventured to extend the limits as far as a part of the sixteenth century, and therefore include among female artists the name of Sofonisba Anguisciola, who was born about 1540. She was a noble lady of Cremona, whose fame spread early throughout Italy. In 1559, Philip II. of Spain invited her to his court at Madrid, where on her arrival she was treated with great distinction. Her chief study was portraiture, and her pictures became objects of great value to kings and popes.

Her royal patrons of Spain married their artist to a noble Sicilian, giving her a dowry of twelve thousand ducats and a pension of one thousand ducats, beside rich presents in tapestries and jewels. She went with her husband to Palermo, where they resided several years. On the death of her husband the king and queen of Spain urged her to return to their court; but she excused herself on account of her wish to visit Cremona. Embarking on board a galley for this purpose, bound to Genoa, she was entertained with such gallantry by the captain, Orazio Lomellini, one of the merchant princes of that city, that the heart of the distinguished artist was won, and she gave him her hand on their arrival at Genoa.

History does not tell us whether she ever revisited Cremona, but she dwelt in Genoa during the remainder of her long life, pursuing her art with great success. On her second marriage, her faithful friends in the royal family of Spain added four hundred crowns to her pension. The Empress of Germany visited Sofonisba on the way to Spain, and accepted from her hand a little picture. Sofonisba became blind in her old age, but lost no other faculty. Vandyck was her guest when at Genoa, and said that he had learned more of his art from one blind old woman than from any other teacher. A medal was struck in her honor at Bologna. The Academy of Fine Arts at Edinburgh contains a noble picture by Vandyck, painted in his Italian manner. It represents individuals of the Lomellini family, and was probably in progress when he visited this illustrious woman, who had become a member of that house.

Stirling in his "Artists of Spain" states that few of Sofonisba's pictures are now known to exist, and that the beautiful portrait of herself, probably the one mentioned by Vasari in the wardrobe of the Cardinal di Monte at Rome, or that noticed by Soprani in the palace of Giovanni Lomellini at Genoa, is now in the possession of Earl Spencer at Althorp. The engraving from this picture, in Dibdin's *Ædes Althorpianæ*, lies before us. We think the better of kings and queens who prized a woman with eyes so clear, and an expression of such honesty and truth. The original is said to be masterly in its drawing and execution. Sofonisba is represented in a simple black dress, and wears no jewels. She touches the keys of a harpsichord with her beautiful hands; a duenna-like figure of an old woman stands behind the instrument, apparently listening to the melody.

Whatever of skill or fame women have acquired through the ages in other departments, the nursery has ever been an undisputed sphere for woman's work. Nor have we reason to think that, in the centuries we have been considering, she was not faithful to this her especial province. The cradle of Henry V., yet in existence, is one of the best specimens of nursery furniture in the fourteenth century which have come down to us. Beautifully carved foliage fills the space between the uprights and stays and stand of the cradle, which is not upon rockers, but apparently swings like the modern crib. On each of these uprights is perched a dove, carefully carved, whose quiet influences had not much effect on the infant dreams of Prince Hal.

Henry was born at Monmouth, 1388, and sent to Courtfield, about seven miles distant, where the air was considered more salubrious. There he was nursed under the superintendence of Lady Montacute, and in that place this cradle was preserved for many years. It was sold by a steward of the Montacute property, and, after passing through several hands, was in the possession of a gentleman near Bristol when engraved for Shaw's "Ancient Furniture," in 1836.

In the Douce Collection of the Bodleian Library, Oxford, there is figured in a manuscript of the fifteenth century a cradle, with the baby very nicely tucked up in it. The cradle resembles those of modern date, and is upon rockers. Another illustration of the same period shows us a cradle of similar form, the "cradle, baby, and all" carried on the head of the nursery-maid, — a caryatid style of baby-tending which we cannot suppose to have been universal. The inventories of household furniture belonging to Reginald de la Pole, after enumerating some bed-hangings of costly stuff, describe: "Item, a pane" (piece of cloth which we now call counterpane) "and head-shete for y⁰ cradell, of same sute, bothe furred with mynever,"—giving us a comfortable idea of the nursery establishment in the De la Pole family. The recent discovery in England of that which tradition avers to be the tomb of Canute's little daughter, speaks of another phase in nursery experience. The relics, both of the cradle and the grave, bear their own record of the joys, cares, and sorrows of the nursery in vanished years, and bring near to every mother's heart the baby that was rocked in the one, and the grief which came when that little form was given to the solemn keeping of the other.

A miniature in an early manuscript, called "The Birth of St. Edmund," gives us a picture of a bedroom and baby in the fifteenth century. St. Edmund himself was born five hundred years previous to that date; but as saints and sinners look very much alike when they are an hour old, we can imagine that, as far as the baby is concerned, it may be considered a portrait. A pretty young woman, in a long white gown, whose cap looks like magnified butterflies' wings turned upside down, sits on a low seat before the blazing wood-fire burning on great andirons in a wide fireplace, which, instead of a mantelpiece, has three niches for ornamental vases. She holds the baby very nicely, and, having warmed his feet, has wrapt him in a long white garment, so that we see only his little head in a plain night-cap, surrounded indeed by the gilded nimbus of his saintship, which we hope was not of tangible substance, as it would have been an appendage very inconvenient to all parties concerned. The mother reposes in a bed with high posts and long curtains. She must have been a woman of strong nerves to have borne the sight of such stupendous head-gears as those in which her attendants are nid-nodding over herself and baby, or to have supported the weight of that which she wears by way of night-cap. One nurse raises the lady, while another, who, from her showy dress, appears to be the head of the department, offers a tall, elegant, but very inconveniently-shaped goblet, which contains, we presume, mediæval gruel. The room has a very comfortable aspect, from which we judge that some babies in those times were carefully attended.

Many centuries ago, a young woman sat one day among the boys to whom she had come, as their father's bride, from a foreign land, to take the name and place of their mother. She showed to them a beautiful volume of Saxon poems, one of her wedding-gifts, — perhaps offered by the artists of the court of Charles le Chauve, of whose skill such magnificent specimens yet exist. As the attention of the boys was arrested by the brilliant external decorations, Judith, with that quick instinct for the extension of knowledge which showed her a true descendant of Charlemagne, promised that the book should be given to him who first learned to read it. Young Alfred won the prize, and became Alfred the Great.

We are brought near to the presence of a woman of the Middle Ages when we stand beside the monument of Eleanor of Castile, queen of Edward I., in Westminster Abbey. The figure is lifelike and beautiful, with flowing drapery folded simply around it. The countenance, with its delicate features, wears a look of sweetness and dignity as fresh to-day as when sculptured seven hundred years ago. The hair, confined by a coronet, falls on each side of her face in ringlets ; one hand lies by her side, and once held a sceptre ; the other is brought gracefully upward ; the slender fingers, with trusting touch, are laid upon a cross suspended from her neck.

Historians have done their best, or their worst, to throw doubt upon the story of Eleanor's sucking the poison with her lips from the arm of her husband when a dastardly assassin of those days struck at the life of Edward. But such a tradition, whether actually a fact or not, is a tribute to the affection and strength of Eleanor's character ; and all historians agree that she instilled no poison into the life of king or country. As a wife, a mother, and a queen, Eleanor of Castile stands high on the record of the women of the Middle Ages.

Coming from Westminster Abbey, in the spring of 1856, we stood one day at a window in the Strand, and watched a multitude which no man could number, pulsing through that great artery of the mighty heart of London. It was the day of the great Peace celebration, and a holiday. Hour after hour the mighty host swept on, in undiminished numbers. The place where we stood was Charing Cross, and our thoughts went back seven hundred years, when Edward, following the mortal remains of his beloved Eleanor, erected on this spot, then a country suburb of London, the last of that line of crosses which marked those places where the mournful procession paused on its way from Herdeby to Westminster. It was the cross of the dear queen, *la chère reine*, which time and changes of language have since corrupted into Charing Cross. Through this pathway crowds have trodden for many centuries, and few remember that its name is linked with the queenly dead or with a kingly sorrow. Thus it is, as we hasten on through the busy thoroughfares of life from age to age, even as one of our own poets hath said, —

"We pass, and heed each other not."

In these pages we have made some record of woman's work in past centuries, and also caught glimpses of duties, loves, hopes, fears, and sorrows not unlike our own. A wider sphere is now accorded, and a deeper responsibility devolves upon woman to fill it wisely and well. We should never forget that, as far as they were faithful to the duties appointed to them, they elevated their sex to a higher and nobler position, and therein performed the best work of the women of the Middle Ages.

PASSAGES FROM HAWTHORNE'S NOTE-BOOKS.

IX.

CONCORD, *Thursday, Sept.* 1, 1842. — Mr. Thoreau dined with us yesterday. . . . . He is a keen and delicate observer of nature, — a genuine observer, — which, I suspect, is almost as rare a character as even an original poet ; and Nature, in return for his love, seems to adopt him as her especial child, and shows him secrets which few others are allowed to witness. He is familiar with beast, fish, fowl, and reptile, and has strange stories to tell of adventures and friendly passages with these lower brethren of mortality. Herb and flower, likewise, wherever they grow, whether in garden or wild wood, are his familiar friends. He is also on intimate terms with the clouds, and can tell the portents of storms. It is a characteristic trait, that he has a great regard for the memory of the Indian tribes, whose wild life would have suited him so well; and, strange to say, he seldom walks over a ploughed field without picking up an arrow-point, spear-head, or other relic of the red man, as if their spirits willed him to be the inheritor of their simple wealth.

With all this he has more than a tincture of literature, — a deep and true taste for poetry, especially for the elder poets, and he is a good writer, — at least he has written a good article, a rambling disquisition on Natural History, in the last Dial, which, he says, was chiefly made up from journals of his own observations. Methinks this article gives a very fair image of his mind and character, — so true, innate, and literal in observation, yet giving the spirit as well as letter of what he sees, even as a lake reflects its wooded banks, showing every leaf, yet giving the wild beauty of the whole scene. Then there are in the article passages of cloudy and dreamy metaphysics, and also passages where his thoughts seem to measure and attune themselves into spontaneous verse, as they rightfully may, since there is real poetry in them. There is a basis of good sense and of moral truth, too, throughout the article, which also is a reflection of his character; for he is not unwise to think and feel, and I find him a healthy and wholesome man to know.

After dinner, (at which we cut the first watermelon and muskmelon that our garden has grown,) Mr. Thoreau and I walked up the bank of the river, and at a certain point he shouted for his boat. Forthwith a young man paddled it across, and Mr. Thoreau and I voyaged farther up the stream, which soon became more beautiful than any picture, with its dark and quiet sheet of water, half shaded, half sunny, between high and wooded banks. The late rains have swollen the stream so much that many trees are standing up

to their knees, as it were, in the water, and boughs, which lately swung high in air, now dip and drink deep of the passing wave. As to the poor cardinals which glowed upon the bank a few days since, I could see only a few of their scarlet hats, peeping above the tide. Mr. Thoreau managed the boat so perfectly, either with two paddles or with one, that it seemed instinct with his own will, and to require no physical effort to guide it. He said that, when some Indians visited Concord a few years ago, he found that he had acquired, without a teacher, their precise method of propelling and steering a canoe. Nevertheless he was desirous of selling the boat of which he was so fit a pilot, and which was built by his own hands; so I agreed to take it, and accordingly became possessor of the Musketaquid. I wish I could acquire the aquatic skill of the original owner.

Sept. 2. — Yesterday afternoon Mr. Thoreau arrived with the boat. The adjacent meadow being overflowed by the rise of the stream, he had rowed directly to the foot of the orchard, and landed at the bars, after floating over forty or fifty yards of water where people were lately making hay. I entered the boat with him, in order to have the benefit of a lesson in rowing and paddling. . . . . I managed, indeed, to propel the boat by rowing with two oars, but the use of the single paddle is quite beyond my present skill. Mr. Thoreau had assured me that it was only necessary to will the boat to go in any particular direction, and she would immediately take that course, as if imbued with the spirit of the steersman. It may be so with him, but it is certainly not so with me. The boat seemed to be bewitched, and turned its head to every point of the compass except the right one. He then took the paddle himself, and though I could observe nothing peculiar in his management of it, the Musketaquid immediately became as docile as a trained steed. I suspect that she has not yet transferred her affections from her old master to her new one. By and by, when we are better acquainted, she will grow more tractable. . . . . We propose to change her name from Musketaquid (the Indian name of the Concord River, meaning the river of meadows) to the Pond-Lily, which will be very beautiful and appropriate, as, during the summer season, she will bring home many a cargo of pond-lilies from along the river's weedy shore. It is not very likely that I shall make such long voyages in her as Mr. Thoreau has made. He once followed our river down to the Merrimack, and thence, I believe, to Newburyport, in this little craft.

In the evening, ——— ——— called to see us, wishing to talk with me about a Boston periodical, of which he had heard that I was to be editor, and to which he desired to contribute. He is an odd and clever young man, with nothing very peculiar about him, — some originality and self-inspiration in his character, but none, or very little, in his intellect. Nevertheless, the lad himself seems to feel as if he were a genius. I like him well enough, however; but, after all, these originals in a small way, after one has seen a few of them, become more dull and commonplace than even those who keep the ordinary pathway of life. They have a rule and a routine, which they follow with as little variety as other people do their rule and routine, and when once we have fathomed their mystery, nothing can be more wearisome. An innate perception and reflection of truth give the only sort of originality that does not finally grow intolerable.

Sept. 4. — I made a voyage in the Pond - Lily all by myself yesterday morning, and was much encouraged by my success in causing the boat to go whither I would. I have always liked to be afloat, but I think I have never adequately conceived of the enjoyment till now, when I begin to feel a power over that which supports me. I suppose I must have felt something like this sense of triumph when I first learned to swim; but I have forgotten

it. O that I could run wild! — that is, that I could put myself into a true relation with Nature, and be on friendly terms with all congenial elements.

We had a thunder-storm last evening; and to-day has been a cool, breezy autumnal day, such as my soul and body love.

Sept. 18. — How the summer - time flits away, even while it seems to be loitering onward, arm in arm with autumn! Of late I have walked but little over the hills and through the woods, my leisure being chiefly occupied with my boat, which I have now learned to manage with tolerable skill. Yesterday afternoon I made a voyage alone up the North Branch of Concord River. There was a strong west wind blowing dead against me, which, together with the current, increased by the height of the water, made the first part of the passage pretty toilsome. The black river was all dimpled over with little eddies and whirlpools; and the breeze, moreover, caused the billows to beat against the bow of the boat, with a sound like the flapping of a bird's wing. The water-weeds, where they were discernible through the tawny water, were straight outstretched by the force of the current, looking as if they were forced to hold on to their roots with all their might. If for a moment I desisted from paddling, the head of the boat was swept round by the combined might of wind and tide. However, I toiled onward stoutly, and, entering the North Branch, soon found myself floating quietly along a tranquil stream, sheltered from the breeze by the woods and a lofty hill. The current, likewise, lingered along so gently that it was merely a pleasure to propel the boat against it. I never could have conceived that there was so beautiful a river-scene in Concord as this of the North Branch. The stream flows through the midmost privacy and deepest heart of a wood, which, as if but half satisfied with its presence, calm, gentle, and unobtrusive as it is, seems to crowd upon it, and barely to allow it passage; for the trees are rooted on the very verge of the water, and dip their pendent branches into it. On one side there is a high bank, forming the side of a hill, the Indian name of which I have forgotten, though Mr. Thoreau told it to me; and here, in some instances, the trees stand leaning over the river, stretching out their arms as if about to plunge in headlong. On the other side, the bank is almost on a level with the water; and there the quiet congregation of trees stood with feet in the flood, and fringed with foliage down to its very surface. Vines here and there twine themselves about bushes or aspens or alder-trees, and hang their clusters (though scanty and infrequent this season) so that I can reach them from my boat. I scarcely remember a scene of more complete and lovely seclusion than the passage of the river through this wood. Even an Indian canoe, in olden times, could not have floated onward in deeper solitude than my boat. I have never elsewhere had such an opportunity to observe how much more beautiful reflection is than what we call reality. The sky, and the clustering foliage on either hand, and the effect of sunlight as it found its way through the shade, giving lightsome hues in contrast with the quiet depth of the prevailing tints, — all these seemed unsurpassably beautiful when beheld in upper air. But on gazing downward, there they were, the same even to the minutest particular, yet arrayed in ideal beauty, which satisfied the spirit incomparably more than the actual scene. I am half convinced that the reflection is indeed the reality, the real thing which Nature imperfectly images to our grosser sense. At any rate, the disembodied shadow is nearest to the soul.

There were many tokens of autumn in this beautiful picture. Two or three of the trees were actually dressed in their coats of many colors, — the real scarlet and gold which they wear before they put on mourning. These stood on low, marshy spots, where a frost has probably touched them already. Others were of a light, fresh green, resembling the hues of spring, though this, likewise, is a token of decay. The great mass of the foliage, however, appears unchanged; but ever and anon down came a yellow leaf, half flitting upon the air, half falling through it, and finally settling upon the water. A multitude of these were floating here and there along the river, many of them curling upward, so as to form little boats, fit for fairies to voyage in. They looked strangely pretty, with yet a melancholy prettiness, as they floated along. The general aspect of the river, however, differed but little from that of summer, — at least the difference defies expression. It is more in the character of the rich yellow sunlight than in aught else. The water of the stream has now a thrill of autumnal coolness; yet whenever a broad gleam fell across it, through an interstice of the foliage, multitudes of insects were darting to and fro upon its surface. The sunshine, thus falling across the dark river, has a most beautiful effect. It burnishes it, as it were, and yet leaves it as dark as ever.

On my return, I suffered the boat to float almost of its own will down the stream, and caught fish enough for this morning's breakfast. But, partly from a qualm of conscience, I finally put them all into the water again, and saw them swim away as if nothing had happened.

Monday, October 10, 1842. — A long while, indeed, since my last date. But the weather has been generally sunny and pleasant, though often very cold; and I cannot endure to waste anything so precious as autumnal sunshine by staying in the house. So I have spent almost all the daylight hours in the open air. My chief amusement has been boating up and down the river. A week or two ago (September 27 and 28) I went on a pedestrian excursion with Mr. Emerson, and was gone two days and one night, it being the first and only night that I have spent away from home. We were that night at the village of Harvard, and the next morning walked three miles farther, to the Shaker village, where we breakfasted. Mr. Emerson had a theological discussion with two of the Shaker brethren; but the particulars of it have faded from my memory; and all the other adventures of the tour have now so lost their freshness that I cannot adequately recall them. Wherefore let them rest untold. I recollect nothing so well as the aspect of some fringed gentians, which we saw growing by the roadside, and which were so beautiful that I longed to turn back and pluck them. After an arduous journey, we arrived safe home in the afternoon of the second day, — the first time that I ever came home in my life; for I never had a home before. On Saturday of the same week, my friend D. R—— came to see us, and stayed till Tuesday morning. On Wednesday there was a cattle-show in the village, of which I would give a description, if it had possessed any picturesque points. The foregoing are the chief outward events of our life.

In the mean time autumn has been advancing, and is said to be a month earlier than usual. We had frosts, sufficient to kill the bean and squash vines, more than a fortnight ago; but there has since been some of the most delicious Indian-summer weather that I ever experienced, — mild, sweet, perfect days, in which the warm sunshine seemed to embrace the earth and all earth's children with love and tenderness. Generally, however, the bright days have been vexed with winds from the northwest, somewhat too keen and high for comfort. These winds have strewn our avenue with withered leaves, although the trees still retain some density of foliage, which is now embrowned or otherwise variegated by autumn. Our apples, too, have been falling, falling, falling; and we have picked the fairest of them from the dewy grass, and put them in our store-room and elsewhere. On Thursday, John Flint began to gather those which remained

on the trees; and I suppose they will amount to nearly twenty barrels, or perhaps more. As usual when I have anything to sell, apples are very low indeed in price, and will not fetch me more than a dollar a barrel. I have sold my share of the potato-field for twenty dollars and ten bushels of potatoes for my own use. This may suffice for the economical history of our recent life.

12 o'clock, A. M. — Just now I heard a sharp tapping at the window of my study, and, looking up from my book (a volume of Rabelais), behold! the head of a little bird, who seemed to demand admittance! He was probably attempting to get a fly, which was on the pane of glass against which he rapped; and on my first motion the feathered visitor took wing. This incident had a curious effect on me. It impressed me as if the bird had been a spiritual visitant, so strange was it that this little wild thing should seem to ask our hospitality.

November 8. — I am sorry that our journal has fallen so into neglect; but I see no chance of amendment. All my scribbling propensities will be far more than gratified in writing nonsense for the press; so that any gratuitous labor of the pen becomes peculiarly distasteful. Since the last date, we have paid a visit of nine days to Boston and Salem, whence we returned a week ago yesterday. Thus we lost above a week of delicious autumnal weather, which should have been spent in the woods or upon the river. Ever since our return, however, until to-day, there has been a succession of genuine Indian-summer days, with gentle winds or none at all, and a misty atmosphere, which idealizes all nature, and a mild, beneficent sunshine, inviting one to lie down in a nook and forget all earthly care. To-day the sky is dark and lowering, and occasionally lets fall a few sullen tears. I suppose we must bid farewell to Indian summer now, and expect no more love and tenderness from Mother Nature till next spring be well advanced. She has already made herself as unlovely in outward aspect as can well be. We took a walk to Sleepy Hollow yesterday, and beheld scarcely a green thing, except the everlasting verdure of the family of pines, which, indeed, are trees to thank God for at this season. A range of young birches had retained a pretty liberal coloring of yellow or tawny leaves, which became very cheerful in the sunshine. There were one or two oaktrees whose foliage still retained a deep, dusky red, which looked rich and warm; but most of the oaks had reached the last stage of autumnal decay, — the dusky brown hue. Millions of their leaves strew the woods, and rustle underneath the foot; but enough remain upon the boughs to make a melancholy harping when the wind sweeps over them. We found some fringed gentians in the meadow, most of them blighted and withered; but a few were quite perfect. The other day, since our return from Salem, I found a violet; yet it was so cold that day, that a large pool of water, under the shadow of some trees, had remained frozen from morning till afternoon. The ice was so thick as not to be broken by some sticks and small stones which I threw upon it. But ice and snow too will soon be no extraordinary matters with us.

During the last week we have had three stoves put up, and henceforth no light of a cheerful fire will gladden us at eventide. Stoves are detestable in every respect, except that they keep us perfectly comfortable.

Thursday, November 24. — This is Thanksgiving Day, a good old festival, and we have kept it with our hearts, and, besides, have made good cheer upon our turkey and pudding, and pies and custards, although none sat at our board but our two selves. There was a new and livelier sense, I think, that we have at last found a home, and that a new family has been gathered since the last Thanksgiving Day. There have been many bright, cold days latterly, so cold that it has required a pretty rapid pace to keep one's self warm a-walking. Day before yesterday I saw a party of boys skating on a pond of water that has overflowed a neighboring meadow. Running water has not yet frozen. Vegetation has quite come to a stand, except in a few sheltered spots. In a deep ditch we found a tall plant of the freshest and healthiest green, which looked as if it must have grown within the last few weeks. We wander among the wood-paths, which are very pleasant in the sunshine of the afternoons, the trees looking rich and warm, — such of them, I mean, as have retained their russet leaves; and where the leaves are strewn along the paths, or heaped plentifully in some hollow of the hills, the effect is not without a charm. To-day the morning rose with rain, which has since changed to snow and sleet; and now the landscape is as dreary as can well be imagined, — white, with the brownness of the soil and withered grass everywhere peeping out. The swollen river, of a leaden hue, drags itself sullenly along; and this may be termed the first winter's day.

Friday, March 31, 1843. — The first month of spring is already gone; and still the snow lies deep on hill and valley, and the river is still frozen from bank to bank, although a late rain has caused pools of water to stand on the surface of the ice, and the meadows are overflowed into broad lakes. Such a protracted winter has not been known for twenty years, at least. I have almost forgotten the wood-paths and shady places which I used to know so well last summer; and my views are so much confined to the interior of our mansion, that sometimes, looking out of the window, I am surprised to catch a glimpse of houses at no great distance which had quite passed out of my recollection. From present appearances, another month may scarcely suffice to wash away all the snow from the open country; and in the woods and hollows it may linger yet longer. The winter will not have been a day less than five months long; and it would not be unfair to call it seven. A great space, indeed, to miss the smile of Nature, in a single year of human life. Even out of the midst of happiness I have sometimes sighed and groaned; for I love the sunshine and the green woods, and the sparkling blue water; and it seems as if the picture of our inward bliss should be set in a beautiful frame of outward nature. . . . . As to the daily course of our life, I have written with pretty commendable diligence, averaging from two to four hours a day; and the result is seen in various magazines. I might have written more, if it had seemed worth while; but I was content to earn only so much gold as might suffice for our immediate wants, having prospect of official station and emolument which would do away with the necessity of writing for bread. Those prospects have not yet had their fulfilment; and we are well content to wait, because an office would inevitably remove us from our present happy home, — at least from an outward home; for there is an inner one that will accompany us wherever we go. Meantime, the magazine people do not pay their debts; so that we taste some of the inconveniences of poverty. It is an annoyance, not a trouble.

Every day, I trudge through snow and slosh to the village, look into the post-office, and spend an hour at the reading-room; and then return home, generally without having spoken a word to a human being. . . . . In the way of exercise I saw and split wood, and, physically, I never was in a better condition than now. This is chiefly owing, doubtless, to a satisfied heart, in aid of which comes the exercise above mentioned, and about a fair proportion of intellectual labor.

On the 9th of this month, we left home again on a visit to Boston and Salem. I alone went to Salem, where I resumed all my bachelor habits for nearly a fortnight, leading the same life in which ten years of my youth flitted away like a dream. But how much changed was I! At last I had caught hold of a reality which never could be taken from me. It was good thus to get apart from my happiness, for the sake of contemplating it. On the 21st, I returned to Boston, and went out to Cambridge to dine with Longfellow, whom I had not seen since his return from Europe. The next day we came back to our old house, which had been deserted all this time; for our servant had gone with us to Boston.

Friday, April 7. — My wife has gone to Boston to see her sister M——, who is to be married in two or three weeks, and then immediately to visit Europe for six months. . . . . I betook myself to sawing and splitting wood; there being an inward unquietness which demanded active exercise, and I sawed, I think, more briskly than ever before. When I re-entered the house, it was with somewhat of a desolate feeling; yet not without an intermingled pleasure, as being the more conscious that all separation was temporary, and scarcely real, even for the little time that it may last. After my solitary dinner, I lay down, with the Dial in my hand, and attempted to sleep; but sleep would not come. . . . . So I arose, and began this record in the journal, almost at the commencement of which I was interrupted by a visit from Mr. Thoreau, who came to return a book, and to announce his purpose of going to reside at Staten Island, as private tutor in the family of Mr. Emerson's brother. We had some conversation upon this subject, and upon the spiritual advantages of change of place, and upon the Dial, and upon Mr. Alcott, and other kindred or concatenated subjects. I am glad, on Mr. Thoreau's own account, that he is going away, as he is out of health and may be benefited by his removal; but, on my account, I should like to have him remain here, he being one of the few persons, I think, with whom to hold intercourse is like hearing the wind among the boughs of a forest-tree; and with all this wild freedom, there is high and classic cultivation in him too. . . . .

I had a purpose, if circumstances would permit, of passing the whole term of my wife's absence without speaking a word to any human being; but now my Pythagorean vow has been broken, within three or four hours after her departure.

Saturday, April 8. — After journalizing yesterday afternoon, I went out and sawed and split wood till tea-time, then studied German, (translating Lenore,) with an occasional glance at a beautiful sunset, which I could not enjoy sufficiently by myself to induce me to lay aside the book. After lamplight, finished Lenore, and drowsed over Voltaire's Candide, occasionally refreshing myself with a tune from Mr. Thoreau's musical box, which he had left in my keeping. The evening was but a dull one.

I retired soon after nine, and felt some apprehension that the old Doctor's ghost would take this opportunity to visit me; but I rather think his former visitations have not been intended for me, and that I am not sufficiently spiritual for ghostly communication. At all events, I met with no disturbance of the kind, and slept soundly enough till six o'clock or thereabouts. The forenoon was spent with the pen in my hand, and sometimes I had the glimmering of an idea, and endeavored to materialize it in words; but on the whole my mind was idly vagrant, and refused to work to any systematic purpose. Between eleven and twelve I went to the post-office, but found no letter; then spent above an hour reading at the Athenæum. On my way home, I encountered Mr. Flint, for the first time these many weeks, although he is our next neighbor in one direction. I inquired if he could sell us some potatoes, and he promised to send half a bushel for trial. Also, he encouraged me to hope that he might buy a barrel of our apples. After my encounter with Mr. Flint, I returned to our lonely old abbey, opened the door

without the usual heart-spring, ascended to my study, and began to read a tale of Tieck. Slow work, and dull work too! Anon, Molly, the cook, rang the bell for dinner, — a sumptuous banquet of stewed veal and macaroni, to which I sat down in solitary state. My appetite served me sufficiently to eat with, but not for enjoyment. Nothing has a zest in my present widowed state. [Thus far I had written, when Mr. Emerson called.] After dinner, I lay down on the couch, with the Dial in my hand as a soporific, and had a short nap; then began to journalize.

Mr. Emerson came, with a sunbeam in his face; and we had as good a talk as I ever remember to have had with him. He spoke of Margaret Fuller, who, he says, has risen perceptibly into a higher state since their last meeting. [There rings the tea-bell.] Then we discoursed of Ellery Channing, a volume of whose poems is to be immediately published, with revisions by Mr. Emerson himself and Mr. Sam G. Ward. . . . . He calls them "poetry for poets." Next Mr. Thoreau was discussed, and his approaching departure; in respect to which we agreed pretty well. . . . . We talked of Brook Farm, and the singular moral aspects which it presents, and the great desirability that its progress and developments should be observed and its history written; also of C. N——, who, it appears, is passing through a new moral phasis. He is silent, inexpressive, talks little or none, and listens without response, except a sardonic laugh; and some of his friends think that he is passing into permanent eclipse. Various other matters were considered or glanced at, and finally, between five and six o'clock, Mr. Emerson took his leave. I then went out to chop wood, my allotted space for which had been very much abridged by his visit; but I was not sorry. I went on with the journal for a few minutes before tea, and have finished the present record in the setting sunshine and gathering dusk. . . . .

UNIVERSITY REFORM.

AN ADDRESS TO THE ALUMNI OF HARVARD, AT THEIR TRIENNIAL FESTIVAL, JULY 19, 1866.

WE meet to-day under auspices how different from those which attended our last triennial assembling ! We were then in the midst of a civil war, without sight of the end, though not without hope of final success to the cause of national integrity. The three days' agony at Gettysburg had issued in the triumph of the loyal arms, repelling the threatened invasion of the North. The surrender of Vicksburg had just reopened the trade of the Mississippi. The capture of Port Hudson was yet fresh in our ears, when suddenly tidings of armed resistance to conscription in the city of New York gave ominous note of danger lurking at the very heart of the Union. In the shadow of that omen, we celebrated our academic festival of 1863.

The shadow passed. With varying fortunes, but unvarying purpose, the loyal States pursued the contest. And when, in the autumn of 1864, by a solemn act of self-interrogation, they had certified their will and their power to maintain that contest to the end of disunion, and when a popular election expressing that intent had overcome the land like a summer-cloud without a bolt in its bosom, the victory was sown with the ballot which Grant and Sherman reaped with the sword.

Secession collapsed. Its last and most illustrious victim, borne to his rest through territories draped in mourning, through sobbing commonwealths, through populations of uncovered heads, revealed to all time the spirit that was in it and the spirit that subdued it. And to-day, as we meet our Reverend Mother in this scene of old affections, the stupendous struggle has already receded into the shadowland of History. The war is a thing of the past. If hatred still rankles, open hostilities have ceased. If rumblings of the recent tempest still mutter along the track of its former desolation, the storm is over. The conflict is ended. No more conscription of husbands, sons, and brothers for the weary work of destruction ; no more the forced march by day, the bivouac at night, and to-morrow the delirium of carnage. No more anxious waiting in distant homes for tidings from the front, and breathless conning of the death-list to know if the loved ones are among the slain. No more the fresh grief-agony over the unreturning brave. All that is past, —

" For the terrible work is done,
And the good fight is won
For God and for Fatherland."

The sword has returned to its sheath. The symbol-flags that shed their starry pomp on the field of death hang idly drooping in the halls of state. And before new armies in hostile encounter on American soil shall unfurl new banners to the breeze, may every thread and thrum of their texture ravel and rot and resolve itself into dust !

Another and nearer interest distinguishes this occasion and suggests its appropriate theme, — our Alma Mater.

The General Court of Massachusetts, which has hitherto elected the Board of Overseers of Harvard College, after so many years of fitful and experimental legislation, has finally enacted, that " the places of the successive classes in the Board of Overseers of Harvard College, and the vacancies in such classes, shall hereafter be annually supplied by ballot of such persons as have received from the College a degree of Bachelor of Arts, or Master of Arts, or any honorary degree, voting on Commencement-day in the city of

Cambridge; such election to be first held in the year 1866."

This act initiates a radical change in the organization of this University. It establishes for one of its legislative Houses a new electorate. The State hereby discharges itself of all active participation in the conduct of the College; and devolves on the body of the Alumni responsibilities assumed in former enactments extending through a period of more than two hundred years. The wisdom or justice of this measure I am not inclined to discuss. Certainly there is nothing in the history of past relations between the Commonwealth and the University that should make us regret the change. That history has not been one of mere benefactions on one side, and pure indebtedness on the other. Whatever the University may owe to the State, the balance of obligation falls heavily on the other side. In the days of Provincial rule the Colony of Massachusetts Bay appears to have exhausted its zeal for collegiate education in the much-lauded promissory act by which the General Court, in 1636, "agree to give four hundred pounds towards a school or college, whereof two hundred pounds shall be paid next year." The promise was not fulfilled, and the record of those years leaves it doubtful whether legislative action alone would during that or the next generation have accomplished the work, had not a graduate of Emanuel College in English Cambridge, who seems providentially enough to have dropped on these shores, where he lived but a year, for that express purpose, supplied the requisite funds.

The College once started and got under way, the fathers of the Province assumed a vigilant oversight of its orthodoxy, but discharged with a lax and grudging service the responsibility of its maintenance. They ejected the first President, the protomartyr of American learning, the man who sacrificed more to the College than any one individual in the whole course of its history, on account of certain scruples

about infant baptism, of which, in the language of the time, "it was not hard to discover that they came from the Evil One," and for which poor Dunster was indicted by the grand-jury, sentenced to a public admonition, and laid under bonds for good behavior.

They starved the second President for eighteen years on a salary payable in Indian corn; and in answer to his earnest prayer for relief, alleging instant necessity, the sacrifice of personal property, and the custom of English universities, a committee of the General Court reported that "they conceive the country to have done honorably toward the petitioner, and that his parity with English colleges is not pertinent."

The third President, by their connivance and co-operation, was sacrificed to the machinations of the students, egged on, it is thought, by members of the Corporation, and died, "as was said, with a broken heart."

Meanwhile, through neglect of the Province to provide for its support, the material fortunes of the College, in the course of thirty years, had fallen into such decay that extinction was inevitable, had not the people of another Colony come to the rescue. The town of Portsmouth, in New Hampshire, hearing, says their address, "the loud groans of the sinking College, ... and hoping that their example might provoke . . . . the General Court vigorously to act for the diverting of the omen of calamity which its destruction would be to New England," pledged themselves to an annual contribution of sixty pounds for seven years. This act of chivalrous generosity fairly shamed our lagging Commonwealth into measures for the resuscitation of an institution especially committed to its care.

The most remarkable feature of this business is that the Province all this while was drawing, not only moral support, but pecuniary aid, from the College. "It is manifest," says Quincy,[*]

---

[*] *The History of Harvard University*, by Josiah Quincy, LL.D., Vol. I. pp. 42, 43. All the facts relating to the history of the College are taken from this work.

"that the treasury of the Colony, having been the recipient of many of the early donations to the College, was not a little aided by the convenience which these available funds afforded to its pecuniary necessities. Some of these funds, although received in 1647, were not paid over to the treasury of the College until 1713; then, indeed, the College received an allowance of simple interest for the delay. With regard, therefore, to the annual allowance of £100, whereby," during the first seventy years, "they enabled the President of the College simply to exist, it is proper to observe, that there was not probably one year in the whole seventy in which, by moneys collected from friends of the institution in foreign countries, by donations of its friends in this country, by moneys brought by students from other Colonies, and above all by furnishing the means of education at home, and thus preventing the outgoing of domestic wealth for education abroad, the College did not remunerate the Colony for that poor annual stipend five hundred fold."

The patronage extended to the College after the Revolution was not more cordial and not more adequate than the meagre succors of Colonial legislation. The first Governor of independent Massachusetts, from the height of his impregnable popularity, for more than twelve years defied the repeated attempts of the Corporation, backed by the Overseers, to obtain the balance of his account as former Treasurer of the College, and died its debtor in a sum exceeding a thousand pounds. The debt was finally paid by his heirs, but not without a loss of some hundreds of dollars to the College.

At the commencement of hostilities between the Colonies and the mother country, the Revolutionary authorities had taken possession of these grounds. Reversing the old order, "Cedant arma togæ," they drove out the *togæ* and brought in the arms. The books went one way, the boys another,—the books to Andover, the boys to Concord. The dawn of American liberty was not an "Aurora musis amica." The Muse of History alone remained with Brigadier Putnam and General Ward. The College was turned into a camp,—a measure abundantly justified by public necessity, but causing much damage to the buildings occupied as barracks by the Continentals. This damage was nominally allowed by the General Court, but was reckoned in the currency of that day, whereby the College received but a quarter of the cost.

In 1786, the State saw fit to discontinue the small pittance which till then had been annually granted toward the support of the President; and from that time to this, with the exception of the proceeds of a bank-tax, granted for ten years in 1814, and the recent large appropriation from the School Fund for the use of the Museum of Natural History, the College has received no substantial aid from the State. The State has, during the last ten years, expended two millions of dollars in a vain attempt to bore a hole through one of her hills: in the whole two hundred and thirty years of our academic history she has not expended a quarter of that sum in filling up this hole in her educational system.

I intend no disrespect to the noble Commonwealth of which no native can be insensible to the glory of his birthright. No State has done more for popular education than the State of Massachusetts. But for reasons satisfactory, no doubt, to themselves, her successive legislators have not seen fit to extend to her colleges the fostering care bestowed on her schools. And certainly, if one or the other must be neglected, we shall all agree in saying, Let the schools be cherished, and let the colleges take care of themselves. Let due provision be made for popular instruction in the rudiments of knowledge, which are also rudiments of good citizenship; let every citizen be taxed for that prime exigency, and let literature and science find patrons where they can. Literature and science will find patrons, and here in Massachusetts have always found them. If the legislators of the State have been sparing of their benefactions, the wealthy sons of the State have been prodigal of theirs. In no country has the private patronage of science been more liberal and prompt than in Massachusetts. Seldom, in the history of science, has there been a nobler instance of that patronage than this University is now experiencing, in the mission of one of her professors on an enterprise of scientific exploration, started and maintained by a private citizen of Boston. When our Agassiz shall return to us reinforced with the lore of the Andes, and replenished with the spoils of the Amazon, — *tot millia squamigeræ gentis,* — the discoveries he shall add to science, and the treasures he shall add to his Museum, whilst they splendidly illustrate his own qualifications for such a mission, will forever attest the liberality of a son of Massachusetts.

The rich men of the State have not been wanting to literature and science. They have not been wanting to this University. Let their names be held in everlasting remembrance. When the Memorial Hall, which your committee have in charge, shall stand complete, let its mural records present, together with the names of those who have deserved well of the country by their patriotism, the names of those who have deserved well of the College by their benefactions. Let these fautors of science, the heroes of peace, have their place side by side with the heroes of war.

Individuals have done their part, but slow is the growth of institutions which depend on individual charity for their support. As an illustration of what may be done by public patronage, when States are in earnest with their universities, and as strangely contrasting the sluggish fortunes of our own *Alma,* look at the State University of Michigan. Here is an institution but twenty-five years old, already numbering thirty-two professors and over twelve hundred students, having public buildings equal in extent to those which two centuries have given to

Cambridge, and all the apparatus of a well-constituted, thoroughly furnished university. All this within twenty-five years! The State itself which has generated this wonderful growth had no place in the Union until after Harvard had celebrated her two hundredth birthday. In twenty-five years, in a country five hundred miles from the seaboard, — a country which fifty years ago was known only to the fur trade, — a University has sprung up, to which students flock from all parts of the land, and which offers to thousands, free of expense, the best education this continent affords. Such is the difference between public and private patronage, between individual effort and the action of a State.

A proof of the broad intent and œcumenical consciousness of this infant College appears in the fact that its Medical Department, which alone numbers ten professors and five hundred students, allows the option of one of four languages in the thesis required for the medical degree. It is the only seminary in the country whose liberal scope and cosmopolitan outlook satisfy the idea of a great university. Compared with this, our other colleges are all provincial ; and unless the State of Massachusetts shall see fit to adopt us, and to foster our interest with something of the zeal and liberality which the State of Michigan bestows on her academic masterpiece, Harvard cannot hope to compete with this precocious child of the West.

Meanwhile, Alumni, the State has devolved upon us, as electors of the Board of Overseers, an important trust. This trust conveys no right of immediate jurisdiction, but it may become the channel of an influence which shall make itself felt in the conduct of this University. It invites us to take counsel concerning her wants and her weal. I therefore pursue the theme which this crisis in our history suggests.

Of existing universities the greater part are the product of an age whose intellectual fashion differed as widely from the present as it did from that of

Greek and Roman antiquity. Our own must be reckoned with that majority, dating, as it does, from a period antecedent, not only to all other American colleges, but to some of the most eminent of other lands. Half of the better known and most influential of German universities are of later origin than ours. The University of Göttingen, once the most flourishing in Germany, is younger than Harvard by a hundred years. Halle is younger, and Erlangen, and Munich with its vast library, and Bonn, and Berlin, by nearly two hundred years.

When this College was founded, two of the main forces of the intellectual world of our time had scarcely come into play, — modern literature and modern science. Science knew nothing as yet of chemistry, nothing of electricity, of geology, scarce anything of botany. In astronomy, the Copernican system was just struggling into notice, and far from being universally received. Lord Bacon, I think, was the latest author of note in the library bequeathed by John Harvard ; and Lord Bacon rejected the Copernican system. English literature had had its great Elizabethan age ; but little of the genius of that literature had penetrated the Puritan mind. It is doubtful if a copy of Shakespeare had found its way to these shores in 1636. Milton's star was just climbing its native horizon, invisible as yet to the Western world.

The College was founded for the special and avowed purpose of training young men for the service of the Church. All its studies were arranged with reference to that object : endless expositions of Scripture, catechetical divinity, "commonplacing" of sermons, — already, one fancies, sufficiently commonplace, — Chaldee, Syriac, Hebrew without points, and other Semitic exasperations. Latin, as the language of theology, was indispensable, and within certain limits was practically better understood, perhaps, in Cambridge of the seventeenth century, than in Cambridge of the nineteenth. It was the language of official intercourse. In-

deed, the use of the English was forbidden to the students within the College walls. *Scholares vernacula lingua intra Collegii limites nullo praetextu utuntor,* was the law, — a law which Cotton Mather complains was so neglected in his day "as to render our scholars · very unfit for a conversation with strangers." But the purpose for which chiefly the study of Latin is now pursued — acquaintance with the Roman classics — was no recognized object of Puritan learning. Cicero appears to have been for a long time the only classic of whom the students were supposed to have any knowledge. The reading of Virgil was a daring innovation of the eighteenth century. The only Greek required was that of the New Testament and the Greek Catechism. The whole rich domain of ancient Greek literature, from Homer to Theokritos, was as much an unexplored territory as the Baghavad - Gita or ·the Mahabharata. Logic and metaphysic and scholastic disputations occupied a prominent place. As late as 1726, the books most conspicuous in Tutor Flynt's official report of the College exercises, next to Cicero and Virgil, are such as convey to the modern scholar no idea but that of intense obsoleteness, — Ramus's Definitions, Burgersdicius's Logic, Heereboord's Meletemata ; and for Seniors, on Saturday, Ames's Medulla. This is such a curriculum as Mephistopheles, in his character of Magister, might have recommended in irony to the student who sought his counsel.

With the multiplication of religious sects, with the progress of secular culture, with the mental emancipation which followed the great convulsions of the eighteenth century, the maintenance of the ecclesiastical type originally impressed on the College ceased to be practicable, — ceased to be desirable. The preparation of young men for the service of the Church is still a recognized part of the general scheme of University education, but is only one in the multiplicity of objects which that scheme embraces, and can never again have the prominence once assigned to it. This secularization, however it might seem to compromise the design of the founders of the College, was inevitable, — a wise and needful concession to the exigencies of the altered time. Nor is there, in a larger view, any real contravention here of the purpose of the founders. The secularization of the College is no violation of its motto, "*Christo et Ecclesiæ.*" For, as I interpret those sacred ideas, the cause of Christ and the Church is advanced by whatever liberalizes and enriches and enlarges the mind. All study, scientifically pursued, is at bottom a study of theology ; for all scientific study is the study of Law ; and "of Law nothing less can be acknowledged than that her seat is in the bosom of God."

But something more than secularization of the course of study is required to satisfy the idea of a university. What is a university? Dr. Newman answers this question with the ancient designation of a *Studium Generale*, — a school of universal learning. "Such a university," he says, "is in its essence a place for the communication and circulation of thought by means of personal intercourse over a wide tract of country." * Accepting this definition, can we say that Harvard College, as at present constituted, is a University? Must we not rather describe it as a place where boys are made to recite lessons from text-books, and to write compulsory exercises, and are marked according to their proficiency and fidelity in these performances, with a view to a somewhat protracted exhibition of themselves at the close of their college course, which, according to a pleasant academic fiction, is termed their "Commencement"? This description applies only, it is true, to what is called the Undergraduate Department. But that department stands for the College, constitutes the College, in the public estimation. The professional schools which have gathered about it are

* The Office and Work of Universities, by John Henry Newman.

scarcely regarded as a part of the College. They are incidental appendages, of which, indeed, one has its seat in another city. The College proper is simply a more advanced school for boys, not differing essentially in principle and theory from the public schools in all our towns. In this, as in those, the principle is coercion. Hold your subject fast with one hand, and pour knowledge into him with the other. The professors are task-masters and police-officers, the President the chief of the College police.

Now, considering the great advance of our higher town schools, which carry their pupils as far as the College carried them fifty years ago, and which might, if necessary, have classes still more advanced of such as are destined for the university, I venture to suggest that the time has come when this whole system of coercion might, with safety and profit, be done away. Abolish, I would say, your whole system of marks, and college rank, and compulsory tasks. I anticipate an objection drawn from the real or supposed danger of abandoning to their own devices and optional employment boys of the average age of college students. In answer, I say, advance that average by fixing a limit of admissible age. Advance the qualifications for admission ; make them equal to the studies of the Freshman year, and reduce the college career from four years to three ; or else make the Freshman year a year of probation, and its closing examination the condition of full matriculation. Only give the young men, when once a sufficient foundation has been laid, and the rudiments acquired, the freedom of a true University, — freedom to select their own studies and their own teachers from such material, and such *personnel*, as the place supplies. It is to be expected that a portion will abuse this liberty, and waste their years. They do it at their peril. At the peril, among other disadvantages, of losing their degree, which should be conditioned on satisfactory proof that the student has not wholly misspent his time.

An indispensable condition of intellectual growth is liberty. That liberty the present system denies. More and more it is straitened by imposed tasks. And this I conceive to be the reason why, with increased requirements, the College turns out a decreasing proportion of first-class men. If the theory of college rank were correct, the highest marks should indicate the men who are to be hereafter most conspicuous, and leaders in the various walks of life. This is not the case, — not so much so now as in former years. Of the present chief lights of American literature and science, how many, if graduates of Harvard, took the first honors of the University here ? Or, to put the question in another form, Of those who took the first honors at Harvard, within the last thirty years, how many are now conspicuous among the great lights of American literature and science ?

Carlyle, in his recent talk to the students at Edinburgh, remarks that, " since the time of Bentley, you cannot name anybody that has gained a great name for scholarship among the English, or constituted a point of revolution in the pursuits of men, in that way." The reason perhaps is, that the system of the English universities, though allowing greater liberty than ours, is still a struggle for college honors, in which renown, not learning for the sake of learning, is the aim. The seeming proficiency achieved through the influence of such motives — knowledge acquired for the nonce, not assimilated — is often delusive, and is apt to vanish when the stimulus is withdrawn. The students themselves have recorded their judgment of the value of this sort of learning in the word " cramming," a phrase which originated in one of the English universities.

The rudiments of knowledge may be instilled by compulsory tasks ; but to form the scholar, to really educate the man, there should intervene between the years of compulsory study and the active duties of life a season of comparative leisure. By leisure I mean, not cessation of activity, but self-deter-

mined activity, — command of one's time for voluntary study.

There are two things which unless a university can give, it fails of its legitimate end. One is opportunity, the other inspiration. But opportunity is marred, not made, and inspiration quenched, not kindled, by coercion. Few, I suspect, in recent years, have had the love of knowledge awakened by their college life at Harvard, — more often quenched by the rivalries and penalties with which learning here is associated. Give the student, first of all, opportunity ; place before him the best apparatus of instruction ; tempt him with the best of teachers and books ; lead him to the fountains of intellectual life. His use of those fountains must depend on himself. There is a homely proverb touching the impossibility of compelling a horse to drink, which applies to human animals and intellectual draughts as well. The student has been defined by a German pedagogue as an animal that cannot be forced, but must be persuaded. If, beside opportunity, the college can furnish also the inspiration which shall make opportunity precious and fruitful, its work is accomplished. The college that fulfils these two conditions — opportunity and inspiration — will be a success, will draw to itself the frequency of youth, the patronage of wealth, the consensus of all the good. Such a university, and no other, will be a power in the land.

Nothing so fatal to inspiration as excessive legislation. It creates two parties, the governors and the governed, with efforts and interests mutually opposed ; the governors seeking to establish an artificial order, the governed bent on maintaining their natural liberty. I need not ask you, Alumni, if these two parties exist at Cambridge. They have always existed within the memory of " the oldest graduate."

Professors should not be responsible for the manners of students, beyond the legitimate operation of their personal influence. Academic jurisdiction should have no criminal code, should inflict no penalty but that of expulsion, and that only in the way of self-defence against positively noxious and dangerous members. Let the civil law take care of civil offences. The American citizen should early learn to govern himself, and to re-enact the civil law by free consent. Let easy and familiar relations be established between teachers and taught, and personal influence will do more for the maintenance of order than the most elaborate code. Experience has shown that great reliance may be placed on the sense of honor in young men, when properly appealed to and fairly brought into play. Raumer, in his "History of German Universities," testifies that the Burschenschaften abolished there the last vestige of that system of hazing practised on new-comers, which seems to be an indigenous weed of the college soil. It infested the ancient universities of Athens, Berytus, Carthage,* as well as the mediæval and the modern. Our ancestors provided a natural outlet for it when they ordained that the Freshmen should be subject to the Seniors, should take off their hats in their presence, and run of their errands. This system, under the name of "Pennalism," had developed, in the German universities, in the seventeenth and eighteenth centuries, a degree of oppression and tyrannous abuse of the new-comer unknown to American colleges, and altogether incredible were it not sufficiently vouched by contemporary writers, and by the acts of the various governments which labored to suppress it. A certain German worthy writes to his son, who is about to enter the university: "You think, perhaps, that in the universities they sup pure wisdom by spoonfuls, ... but when you are arrived there, you will find that you must be made a fool of for the first year. .... Consent to be a fool for this one year; let yourself be plagued and abused; and when an old veteran steps up to you and tweaks your nose, let it

not appear singular; endure it, harden yourself to it. *Olim meminisse juvabit.*"* The universities legislated against this barbarism; all the governments of Germany conspired to crush it; but in spite of all their efforts, which were only partially successful, traces of it still lingered in the early years of this century. It was not completely abolished until, in 1818, there was formed at Jena by delegates from fourteen universities a voluntary association of students on a moral basis, known as "The General German Burschenschaft," the first principle in whose constitution was, "Unity, freedom, and equality of all students among themselves, — equality of all rights and duties,"—and whose second principle was "Christian German education of every mental and bodily faculty for the service of the Fatherland." This, according to Raumer, was the end of Pennalism in Germany. What the governments, with their stringent enactments and formidable penalties, failed to accomplish, was accomplished at last by a voluntary association of students, organizing that sense of honor which, in youth and societies of youth, if rightly touched, is never appealed to in vain.

The question has been newly agitated in these days, whether knowledge of Greek and Latin is a necessary part of polite education, and whether it should constitute one of the requirements of the academic course. It has seemed to me that those who take the affirmative in this discussion give undue weight to the literary argument, and not enough to the glossological. The literary argument fails to establish the supreme importance of a knowledge of these languages as a part of polite education. The place which the Greek and Latin authors have come to occupy in the estimation of European scholars is due, not entirely to their intrinsic merits, great as those merits unquestionably are, but in part to traditional prepossessions. When after a millen-

---

* St. Augustine records his connection, when a student at Carthage, with the "Eversores" (Destructives), an association which flourished at that university.

* Raumer's "History of German Universities." Translated by Frederic B. Perkins.

nial occultation the classics, and especially, with the fall of the Palæologi, the Greek classics burst upon Western Europe, there was no literature with which to compare them. The Jewish Scriptures were not regarded as literature by readers of the Vulgate. Dante, it is true, had given to the world his immortal vision, and Boccaccio, its first expounder, had shown the capabilities of Italian prose. But the light of Florentine culture was even for Italy a partial illumination. On the whole, we may say that modern literature did not exist, and the Oriental had not yet come to light. What wonder that the classics were received with boundless enthusiasm! It was through the influence of that enthusiasm that the study of Greek was introduced into schools and universities with the close of the fifteenth century. It was through that influence that Latin, still a living language in the clerical world, was perpetuated, instead of becoming an obsolete ecclesiasticism. The language of Livy and Ovid derived fresh impulse from the reappearing stars of secular Rome.

It is in vain to deny that those literatures have lost something of the relative value they once possessed, and which made it a literary necessity to study Greek and Latin for their sakes. The literary necessity is in a measure superseded by translations, which, though they may fail to communicate the aroma and the verbal felicities of the original, reproduce its form and substance. It is furthermore superseded by the rise of new literatures, and by introduction to those of other and elder lands. The Greeks were masters of literary form, but other nations have surpassed them in some particulars. There is but one Iliad, and but one Odyssee; but also there is but one Job, but one Sakoontalâ, but one Hafiz-Nameh, but one Gulistan, but one Divina Commedia, but one Don Quixote, but one Faust. If the argument for the study of Greek and Latin is grounded on the value of the literary treasures contained in those

tongues, the same argument applies to the Hebrew, to the Sanscrit, to the Persian, to say nothing of the modern languages, to which the College assigns a subordinate place.

But, above all, the literary importance of Greek and Latin for the British and American scholar is greatly qualified by the richness and superiority of the English literature which has come into being since the Græcomania of the time of the Tudors, when court ladies of a morning, by way of amusement, read Plato's Dialogues in the original. If literary edification is the object intended in the study of those languages, that end is more easily and more effectually accomplished by a thorough acquaintance with English literature, than by the very imperfect knowledge which college exercises give of the classics. Tugging at the Chained Prometheus, with the aid of grammar and lexicon, may be good intellectual discipline, but how many of the subjects of that discipline ever divine the secret of Æschylus's wonderful creation, or receive any other impression from it than the feeling perhaps that the worthy Titan's sense of constraint could hardly have been more galling than their own.

Give them Shakespeare's Tempest to read, and with no other pony than their own good will, though they may not penetrate the deeper meaning of that composition, they will gain more ideas, more nourishment from it, than they will from compulsory study of the whole trio of Greek tragedians. And if this be their first introduction to the great magician, they will say, with Miranda,

> "O, wonder!
> How many goodly creatures are there here!
> . . . . O brave new world,
> That has such people in it!"

The literary argument for enforced study of Greek and Latin in our day has not much weight. What I call the glossological argument has more. Every well-educated person should have a thorough understanding of his own language, and no one can thoroughly understand the English without some knowledge of languages which touch it so nearly as the Latin and the Greek. Some knowledge of those languages should constitute, I think, a condition of matriculation. But the further prosecution of them should not be obligatory on the student once matriculated, though every encouragement be given and every facility afforded to those whose genius leans in that direction. The College should make ample provision for the study of ancient languages, and also for the study of the mathematics, but should not enforce those studies on minds that have no vocation for such pursuits. There is now and then a born philologer, one who studies language for its own sake, — studies it perhaps in the spirit of "the scholar who regretted that he had not concentrated his life on the dative case." There are also exceptional natures that delight in mathematics, minds whose young affections run to angles and logarithms, and with whom the computation of values is itself the chief value in life. The College should accommodate either bias, to the top of its bent, but should not enforce either with compulsory twist. It should not insist on making every alumnus a linguist or a mathematician. If mastery of dead languages is not an indispensable part of polite education, mathematical learning is still less so. Excessive requirements in that department have not even the excuse of intellectual discipline. More important than mathematics to the general scholar is the knowledge of history, in which American scholars are so commonly deficient. More important is the knowledge of modern languages and of English literature. More important the knowledge of Nature and Art. May the science of sciences never want representatives as able as the learned gentlemen who now preside over that department in the mathematical and presidential chairs. Happy will it be for the University if they can inspire a love for the science in the pupils committed to their charge. But where inspiration fails, coercion can never supply its place. If the mathematics shall continue to reign at Harvard, may their empire become a law of liberty.

I have ventured, fellow-graduates, to throw out these hints of University Reform, well aware of the opposition such views must encounter in deep-rooted prejudice and fixed routine; aware also of the rashness of attempting, within the limits of such an occasion, to grapple with such a theme; but strong in my conviction of the pressing need of a more emancipated scheme of instruction and discipline, based on the facts of the present and the real wants of American life. It is time that the oldest college in the land should lay off the *prætexta* of its long minority, and take its place among the universities, properly so called, of modern time.

One thing more I have to say while standing in this presence. The College has a duty beyond its literary and scientific functions, — a duty to the nation, — a patriotic, I do not scruple to say a political duty.

Time was when universities were joint estates of the realms they enlightened. The University of Paris was, in its best days, an association possessing authority second only to that of the Church. The faithful ally of the sovereigns of France against the ambition of the nobles and against the usurpations of Papal Rome, she bore the proud title of "The eldest Daughter of the King," — *La Fille aînée du Roi.* She upheld the Oriflamme against the feudal gonfalons, and was largely instrumental in establishing the central power of the crown.[*] In the terrible struggle of Philip the Fair with Boniface VIII., she furnished the legal weapons of the contest. She furnished, in her Chancellor Gerson, the leading spirit of the Council of Constance. In the Council of Bâle she

[*] "C'est ainsi que peu à peu ils [that is, "les lettres"] parvinrent à sapper les fondements du pouvoir féodal et à élever l'étendard royal là où flottait la bannière du baron." — *Histoire de l'Université*, par M. Eugène Dubarle, Vol. I. p. 135.

obtained for France the "Pragmatic Sanction." Her voice was consulted on the question of the Salic Law; unhappily, also in the trial of Jeanne d'Arc; and when Louis XI. concluded a treaty of peace with Maximilian of Austria, the University of Paris was the guaranty on the part of France.

Universities are no longer political bodies, but they may be still political powers, — centres and sources of political influence. Our own College in the time of the Revolution was a manifest power on the side of liberty, the political as well as academic mother of Otis and the Adamses. In 1768, "when the patronage of American manufactures was the test of patriotism," the Senior Class voted unanimously to take their degrees apparelled in the coarse cloths of American manufacture. In 1776, the Overseers required of the professors a satisfactory account of their political faith. So much was then thought of the influence on young minds of the right or wrong views of political questions entertained by their instructors. The fathers were right. When the life of the nation is concerned, — in the struggle with foreign or domestic foes, — there is a right and a wrong in politics which casuistry may seek to confuse, but which sound moral sentiment cannot mistake, and which those who have schools of learning in charge should be held to respect. Better the College should be disbanded than be a nursery of treason. Better these halls even now should be levelled with the ground, than that any influence should prevail in them unfriendly to American nationality. No amount of intellectual acquirements can atone for defective patriotism. Intellectual supremacy alone will not avert the downfall of states. The subtlest intellect of Greece, the sage who could plan an ideal republic of austere virtue and perfect proportions, could not preserve his own; but the love of country inspired by Lycurgus kept the descendants of the Dorians free two thousand years after the disgrace of Chæronea had sealed the fate of the rest of Greece.

In my college days it was the fashion with some to think lightly of our American birthright, to talk disparagingly of republics, and to sigh for the dispositions and pomps of royalty.

> " Sad fancies did we then affect
> In luxury of disrespect
> To our own prodigal excess
> Of too familiar happiness."

All such nonsense, if it had not already yielded to riper reason, would ere this have been washed out of us by the blood of a hundred thousand martyrs. The events of recent years have enkindled, let us hope, quite other sentiments in the youth of this generation. May those sentiments find ample nutriment within these precincts evermore.

Soon after the conquest of American independence, Governor Hancock, in his speech at the inauguration of President Willard, eulogized the College as having "been in some sense the parent and nurse of the late happy Revolution in this Commonwealth." Parent and nurse of American nationality, — such was the praise accorded to Harvard by one of the foremost patriots of the Revolution! Never may she cease to deserve that praise! Never may the Mother refuse to acknowledge the seed herself has propagated! Never may her seed be repelled by the Mother's altered mind!

> " Mutatam ignorent subito ne semina matrem."

When Protagoras came to Athens to teach in the university as self-appointed professor, or sophist, according to the fashion of that time, it was not to instruct Athenian youth in music or geometry or astronomy, but to teach them the art of being good citizens, — Τὴν πολιτικὴν τεχνήν, καὶ ποιεῖν ἄνδρας ἀγαθοὺς πολίτας. That was his profession. With which, as we read, Hippocrates was so well pleased, that he called up Socrates in the middle of the night to inform him of the happy arrival. We have no professorship at Cambridge founded for the express purpose of making good citizens. In the absence of such, may all the professorships work together for that end. The youth intrusted to their tutelage are soon to take part, if not as legislators, at least as freemen, in the government of our common land. May the dignity and duty and exceeding privilege of an American citizen be impressed upon their minds by all the influences that rule this place! Trust me, Alumni, the country will thank the University more for the loyalty her influences shall foster, than for all the knowledge her schools may impart. Learning is the costly ornament of states, but patriotism is the life of a nation.

THE VOICE.

A SAINTLY Voice fell on my ear,
   Out of the dewy atmosphere : —
"O hush, dear Bird of Night, be mute, —
Be still, O throbbing heart and lute !"
The Night-Bird shook the sparkling dew
Upon me as he ruffed and flew:
My heart was still, almost as soon,
My lute as silent as the moon :
I hushed my heart, and held my breath,
And would have died the death of death,
To hear — but just once more — to hear
That Voice within the atmosphere.

Again The Voice fell on my ear,
Out of the dewy atmosphere ! —
The same words, but half heard at first, —
I listened with a quenchless thirst ;
And drank as of that heavenly balm,
The Silence that succeeds a psalm :
My soul to ecstasy was stirred : —
It was a Voice that I had heard
A thousand blissful times before ;
But deemed that I should hear no more
Till I should have a spirit's ear,
And breathe another atmosphere !

Then there was Silence in my ear,
And Silence in the atmosphere,
And silent moonshine on the mart,
And Peace and Silence in my heart :
But suddenly a dark Doubt said,
"The fancy of a fevered head !"
A wild, quick whirlwind of desire
Then wrapt me as in folds of fire.
I ran the strange words o'er and o'er,
And listened breathlessly once more :
And lo, the third time I did hear
The same words in the atmosphere !

They fell and died upon my ear,
As dew dies on the atmosphere;
And then an intense yearning thrilled
My Soul, that all might be fulfilled:
"Where art thou, Blessed Spirit, where? —
Whose Voice is dew upon the air!"
I looked, around me, and above,
And cried aloud: "Where art thou, Love?
O let me see thy living eye,
And clasp thy living hand, or die!" —
Again upon the atmosphere
The self-same words fell: "*I Am Here.*"

"Here? Thou art here, Love!" — "*I Am Here.*"
The echo died upon my ear!
I looked around me — everywhere, —
But ah! there was no mortal there!
The moonlight was upon the mart,
And awe and wonder in my heart.
I saw no form! — I only felt
Heaven's Peace upon me as I knelt,
And knew a Soul Beatified
Was at that moment by my side: —
And there was Silence in my ear,
And Silence in the atmosphere!

LIFE ASSURANCE.

ONE of the subjects which for some time has commanded the public attention is that of Life Assurance: the means by which a man may, through a moderate annual expenditure, make provision for his family when death shall have deprived them of his protection.

The number of companies organized for this purpose, their annual increase, the assiduity with which their agents press their respective claims, the books, pamphlets, and circulars which are disseminated, and the large space occupied by their announcements in the issues of the press, all unite in creating a spirit of inquiry on this interesting subject. We propose in this article to submit a few statements, the collection of which has been greatly furthered by recourse to the treatises of Babbage, Park, Duer, Ellis, Angell, Bunyon, Blayney, and other writers on insurance.

In the early history of insurance, objection was continually made that it was of the nature of a wager, and consequently not only unlawful, but *contra bonos mores;* yet the courts of law in England from the first drew a distinction between a wager and a contract founded on the principle of indemnity, which principle runs through and underlies the whole subject of insurance. Lord Mansfield denominated insurance "a contract upon speculation," and it has universally been considered as a contract of indemnity against loss or damage arising from some uncertain and future events.

Insurance may be defined generally as "a contract by which one of the parties binds himself to the other to pay him a sum of money, or otherwise indemnify him, in the case of the happening of a fortuitous event provided for in a general or special manner in the contract, in consideration of the sum of money which the latter party pays or binds himself to pay"; or, in the words of an eminent English judge, "It is a contract to protect men against uncertain events which in any wise may be a disadvantage to them."

The contract securing this indemnity is called a policy, from the Italian *polizza d' assicurazione*, or *di sicurtà*, which signifies a memorandum in writing, or bill of security. The sum paid for the indemnity is called a premium, or price; the party taking upon himself the risk being termed the underwriter, because his name is written at the bottom of the policy, while the person protected by the instrument is called the assured. Says one, "The premium paid by the latter and the peril assumed by the former are two correlatives inseparable from each other, and the union constitutes the essence of the contract."

Some writers, Mr. Babbage among others, use the words "assurance" and "insurance" as having distinct meanings; but with all underwriters at this day they are considered synonymous.

Insurance in the first instance was exclusively maritime, and great efforts have been made to prove its antiquity. Some have endeavored, by appeals to Livy, Suetonius, Ulpian, and Cicero, to show that insurance was in use in ancient Rome, and that it was invented at Rhodes a thousand years before the Christian era; while others' claim that it existed at Tyre, Carthage, Corinth, Athens, and Alexandria.

There is little doubt, however, that it was first practised by the Lombards, and was introduced into England by a Lombard colony, which in the thirteenth century settled in London, and controlled entirely the foreign trade of the kingdom. After the great fire in London, in 1666, the protection hitherto afforded by insurance to ships only was extended to goods and houses; and insurance as a contract of indemnity was subsequently extended to human life.

It is a singular fact that the subject of effecting insurance on lives was largely and excitingly discussed on the continent of Europe before it had attracted the slightest attention in England; yet at this day it prevails throughout Great Britain, while upon the Continent it is comparatively unknown; its operations there being chiefly confined to France, the Netherlands, Germany, and Denmark.

In Holland, as early as 1681, Van Hadden and De Witt produced elaborate works upon the subject, while no publication appeared in England until twenty years after. These writers were followed by Struyck, in 1740, and by Kirseboon, in 1743; while Parcieux, father and son, St. Cyran, and Duvillard, in France, with Euler, Suchmilch, and Wargentin, in Germany, were with great ability pressing the subject upon the notice of their countrymen. But these efforts led to no practical results, and it was reserved for England at a later day to illustrate the principles of life assurance, and enable the public to enjoy extensively its privileges.

Policies of life assurance were issued in England before any companies were organized to prosecute the business. Like marine policies, they were subscribed by one or more individuals; and the first case we find is that of a ship captain, in 1641, whose life had been insured by two persons who had become his bail. The policy was subscribed by individual underwriters, and an able author observes that the case singularly illustrates the connection which probably once existed between life and maritime insurance, and shows how naturally the latter may have sprung from the former.

No business, with the exception, perhaps, of the express system and of photography, has grown in the United States so rapidly as that of life assurance. There is scarcely a State that has not one or more companies organized for the prosecution of this business. There are six chartered under the laws of Massachusetts, and twenty-six of those organized in other States are doing business in this Commonwealth. These companies had in force, November 1, 1865, 211,537 policies, assuring the sum of $ 563,396,862.30. In 1830 the New York Life and Trust Company was the only life assurance company in New York. At the close of the year 1865 there were eighteen companies chartered under the laws of that State. They had 101,780 policies in force, assuring the sum of $ 289,846,316.50, while their gross combined assets reach the sum of $ 32,296,832.03.

An insurance upon life is defined as "a contract by which the underwriter, for a certain sum proportioned to the age, health, profession, and other circumstances of the person whose life is the object of insurance, engages that that person shall not die within the time limited in the policy; or if he do, that he will pay a sum of money to him in whose favor the policy was granted."

A person desiring to effect an insurance on his life usually procures from the office in which he proposes to insure a blank form, containing a series of interrogatories, all of which must be answered in writing by the applicant. To these answers must be appended the certificate of his usual medical attendant as to his present and general state of health, with a like certificate from an intimate personal friend. The party is then subjected to an examination by the medical examiner of the company, and, if the application is in all respects satisfactory, a policy is issued.

On the death of the party assured, and due proof being made thereof, the company must pay the full sum insured. The time fixed for this payment varies with different companies. Some agree to pay at thirty, some at sixty, and some at ninety days after the proofs of death have been received and duly approved.

The peculiarity of life assurance companies is, that they are required to pay the entire sum assured on the happening of a single event, making the loss a total one; but in fire and marine policies there is a distinction made between total and partial loss.

A clause is usually inserted declaring the policy void in case the assured should fall in a duel, die by the hands of justice, or by his own hand, or while engaged in the violation of any public law. An interesting case in point is reported in the English books. On the 25th of November, 1824, Henry Fauntleroy, a celebrated banker in London, was executed for forgery. The Amicable Society of London, the first company established in England, had written a policy on his life, upon which all the premiums had been paid. The rules of the company declared that in such cases the policy was vitiated, but the clause was not inserted in the instrument. The company resisted payment, but a decision was given sustaining the validity of the contract, which was, however, reversed, on an appeal being made to the House of Lords.

This clause, declaring a policy void in case the assured commits suicide, has given rise to much litigation. Some companies use the word "suicide," while others insert the words "shall die by his own hand"; but the courts of law in various adjudications have considered the expressions as amounting to the same thing. The word "suicide" is not to be found in any English author anterior to the reign of Charles II. Lexicographers trace it to the Latin word *suicidum*, though that word does not appear in the older Latin dictionaries. It is really derived from two Latin words, *se* and *cædere*, — to slay one's self. The great commentator on English law, Sir William Blackstone, defines suicide to be "the act of designedly destroying one's own life. To constitute suicide, the person must be of years of discretion and of sound mind."

In a case submitted to the Supreme Court of the State of New York, Chief-Justice Nelson settled the whole question. A life company resisted payment of the amount specified in their policy, on the ground that the assured had committed suicide by drowning himself in the Hudson River. To this it was replied, that, when he so drowned himself, he was of unsound mind, and wholly unconscious of the act.

Judge Nelson, after stating the question to be whether the act of self-destruction by a man in a fit of insanity can be deemed a death by his own hand within the meaning of the policy, decided that it could not be so considered. That the terms "commit suicide," and "die by his own hand," as used indiscriminately by different companies, express the same idea, and are so understood by writers in this branch of law. That self-destruction by a man bereft of reason can with no more propriety be ascribed to the act of his own hand, than to the deadly instrument that may have been used for the purpose. That the drowning was no more the act of the assured, in the sense of the law, than if he had been impelled by irresistible physical power; and that the company could be no more exempt from payment, than if his death had been occasioned by any uncontrollable means. That suicide involved the deliberate termination of one's existence while in the full possession of the mental faculties. That self-slaughter by an insane man or a lunatic was not suicide within the meaning of the law.

This opinion of Judge Nelson was subsequently affirmed by the Court of Appeals.

The whole current of legal decisions, the suggestions thrown out by learned judges, and the growing opinion that no sane man would be guilty of self-slaughter, have induced several new companies to exclude this proviso from their policies, while many older ones have revised their policies and eliminated the obnoxious clause. It is not that any man contemplates the commission of suicide; but every one feels that, if there should be laid upon him that most fearful of all afflictions, insanity, or if, when suffering from disease, he should, in the frenzy of delirium, put an end to his existence, every principle of equity demands that the faithful payments of years should not be lost to his family.

Another important principle, which has involved much discussion, is, that "the party insuring upon a life must have an interest in the life insured." Great latitude has been given in the construction of the law as to this point; the declaration of a real, subsisting interest being all that is required by the underwriters. In fact, the offices are constantly taking insurances where the interest is upon a contingency which may very shortly be determined, and if the parties choose to continue the policy, *bona fide*, after the interest ceases, they never meet with any difficulty in recovering. So also offices frequently grant policies upon interests so slender that, although it may be difficult to deny some kind of interest, it is such as a court of law would scarcely recognize. This practice of paying upon policies without raising the question of interest is so general, that it has even been allowed in courts of law.

The great advantages derived from life assurance are proved by its rapid progress, both in Great Britain and the United States, after its principles had once been fully explained. As already stated, the first society for the general assurance of life was the Amicable, founded in 1706; but, most unreasonably, its rates of premium were made uniform for all ages assured; nor was any fixed amount guaranteed in case of death. Hence very little was done; and it was not until 1780 that the business of life assurance may be said to have fairly begun. Since then, companies have been formed from time to time, so that at present there are in Great Britain some two hundred in active operation, and the amount assured upon life is estimated at more than £200,000,000.

In America, the first life-assurance company open to all was the Pennsylvania, established in 1812. And though many others, devoted in whole or in part to this object, were formed in the interim, so little pains was taken to inform the public upon the system, that in 1842 the amount assured probably did not exceed $ 5,000,000. But, in a Christian country, all material enterprises go swiftly forward, and of late years the progress of life assurance has equalled that of railroads and telegraphs ; so that there are in the United States at least fifty companies, which are disbursing in claims, chiefly to widows and orphans, about five millions of dollars annually.

With this large extension of business, the fundamental principles of life assurance are now universally agreed on ; but, in carrying them out, there are differences deserving attention.

Life-assurance companies may be divided into three classes, — the stock, the mutual, and the mixed. In the stock company, the management is in the hands of the stockholders, or their agents, with whom the applicant for insurance contracts to pay so much while living, in consideration of a certain sum to be paid to his representatives at his death, and here his connection with it ceases ; the profits of the business being divided among the stockholders. In the mutual company the assured themselves receive all the surplus premium or profit. The law of the State of New York passed in 1849 requires that all life-insurance companies organized in the State shall have a capital of at least one hundred thousand dollars. Mutual life-insurance companies organized in that State since 1849 pay only seven per cent on their capital, which their stock by investment may produce. In the mixed companies there are various combinations of the principles peculiar to the other two. They differ from the mutual companies only in the fact that, besides paying the stockholders legal interest, they receive a portion of the profits of the business, which in some cases in this country has caused the capital stock to appreciate in value over three hundred per cent, and in England over five hundred per cent.

To decide which of these is most advantageous to the assured, we must consider the subject of premiums, and understand whence companies derive their surplus, or, as it is sometimes called, the profits. This is easily explained. As the liability to death increases with age, the proper annual premium for assurance would increase with each year of life. But as it is important not to burden age too heavily, and as it is simpler to pay a uniform sum every year, a mean rate is taken, — one too little for old age, but greater than is absolutely necessary to cover the risk in the first years of the assurance. Hence the company receives at first more than it has to pay, and thus accumulates funds to provide for the time when its payments will naturally be in excess of its receipts. Now these funds may be invested so as of themselves to produce an income, and the increase thence derived may, by the magical power of compound interest, reaching through a long series of years, become very large. In forming rates of premium, regard is had to this ; but, to gain security in a contract which may extend far into the future, it is prudent to base the calculations on so low a rate of interest that there can be a certainty of obtaining it. The rate adopted is usually three per cent in England, and four or five per cent in this country. But, in point of fact, the American companies now obtain on secure investments six or seven per cent.

Again, in order to cover expenses and provide against possible contingencies, it is common to add to the rates obtained by calculation from correct tables of mortality a certain percentage, called *loading*, which is usually found more than is necessary, and forms a second source of profit.

Again, most tables of mortality are derived from the experience of whole communities, while all companies now subject applicants to a medical examination, and reject those found diseased ; it being possible to discover, through the progress of medical science, even incipient signs of disease. Hence one would expect that among these selected lives the rates of mortality would be less than by ordinary statistics; and this is confirmed by the published experience of many companies. Here we find a third source of profit.

In these three ways, and others incidental to the business, it happens that all corporations managed with ordinary prudence accumulate a much larger capital than is needed for future losses. The advocates of the stock plan contend that, by a low rate of premium, they furnish their assured with a full equivalent for that division of profits which is the special boast of other companies. In a corporation purely mutual, the whole surplus is periodically applied to the benefit of the assured, either by a dividend in cash, or by equitable additions to the amount assured without increase of premium, or by deducting from future premiums, while the amount assured remains the same. The advantages of the latter system must be evident to every one.

It is of course important in all companies, whether mutual or not, that the officers should be men of integrity, sagacity, and financial experience, as well as that due precautions should be taken in the care and investment of the company's fund; and it is now proved by experience in this country, that, when a company is thus managed, so regular are the rates of mortality, so efficient the safeguards derived from the selection of lives, the assumption of low rates of interest, and the loading of premiums, that no company, when once well established, has ever met with disaster. On the other hand, there has been a rapid accretion of funds, in some instances to the amount of many millions of dollars. The characteristics of a good company are security and assurance at cost. It should sell, not policies merely, but assurance; and it should not make a profit for the capitalist out of the widow and orphan.

The policies issued by life companies vary in their form and nature. The ordinary one is called the life policy, by which the company contracts to pay, on the death of the assured, the sum named in the policy, to the person in whose behalf the assurance is made.

In mutual (cash) companies, when the premium has been paid in full for about sixteen years, judging from past experience, the policy-holder may expect that his annual dividend on policy and additions will exceed the annual premium, thus obviating the necessity of further payments to the company, while his policy annually increases in amount for the remainder of life. But, on the contrary, when the dividends have been anticipated, as in the note system, by giving a note for part of the premium, the policy-holder insuring in this way, although he may at first receive a larger policy than he has the ability to pay for in cash, may lose the chief benefit of life insurance. For should he become unable, either by age, disease, or loss of property, to continue the payment of his premiums, his policy must lapse, because there is no accumulation of profits to his credit on which it can be continued.

In other forms of life policies, called "Non-forfeitable," premiums are made payable in "one," "five," or "ten" annual payments. In all cash companies, and in some of the note companies, after the specified number of premiums have been paid, the policy-holder draws an annual dividend in cash.

A further advantage arising from this plan is, that the policy-holder, at any time after two annual payments have been made, is always entitled to a "paid-up" policy for as many "fifths" or "tenths" of the sum assured as he shall have paid annual premiums. For example: a "five-annual-payment policy" for $10,000, on which three premiums had been paid, would entitle the holder to a "paid-up policy" for $6,000; a "ten-annual-payment policy" for $10,000, on which three payments had been made, would entitle the holder to $3,000; and so on for any number of payments and for any amount, in accordance with the face of the policy.

Another form is denominated the Endowment Policy, in which the amount assured is payable when the party attains a certain age, or at death, should he die before reaching that age. This policy is rapidly gaining favor, as it provides for the man himself in old age, or for his family in case of his death. It is also fast becoming a favorite form of investment. We can show instances where the policy-holders have received a *surplus* above all they have paid to the company, with compound interest at six per cent, and no charge whatever for expenses or cost of insurance meanwhile.

The Term Policy, as its name implies, is issued for a term of one or more years.

Policies are also issued on joint lives, payable at the death of the first of two or more parties named in the policy; and on survivorship, payable to a party named in case he survives another.

Some companies require all premiums to be paid in cash, while others take the note of the assured in part payment. These are denominated cash and note companies, and much difference of opinion exists as to their comparative merits.

The latter is at first sight an attractive system, and its advocates present many specious arguments in its favor. The friends of cash payments, however, contend that the note system is detrimental and delusive, from the fact that these notes are liable to assessment, and, in case of death, to be deducted from the amount assured; also that the notes accumulate as the years roll on, the interest growing annually larger, and the total cash payment consequently heavier, while the actual amount of assurance, that is, the difference between its nominal amount and the sum of the notes, steadily lessens; and thus a provision for one's family gradually changes into a burden upon one's self.

But whatever differences of opinion may exist as to the comparative value of various systems, few will deny the advantages which life assurance has conferred upon the public, especially in America, whose middle classes, ambitiously living up to their income, are rich mostly in their labor and their homesteads, — in their earnings rather than their savings; and whose wealthy classes are rich chiefly through the giddy uncertainties of speculation, — magnificent to-day, in ruins to-morrow. In a country like this, no one can estimate the amount of comfort secured by investment in life assurance. It is the one measure of thrift which remains to atone for our extravagance in living and recklessness in trade.

Henry Ward Beecher spoke wisely when he advised all men to seek life assurance. He says: —

"It is every man's duty to provide for his family. That provision must include its future contingent condition. That provision, in so far as it is material, men ordinarily seek to secure by their own accumulations and investments. But all these are uncertain. The man that is rich to-day, by causes beyond his reach is poor to-morrow. A war in China, a revolution in Europe, a rebellion in America, overrule ten thousand fortunes in every commercial community.

"But *in life assurance there are no risks or contingencies.* Other investments may fail. A house may burn down. Banks may break and their stock be worthless. Bonds and mortgages may be seized for debt, and all property or evidences of property may fall into the bottomless gulf of bankruptcy. But money secured to your family by life assurance will go to them without fail or interruption, provided you have used due discretion in the selection of a sound and honorable assurance company. Of two courses, one of which *may* leave your family destitute, and the other of which *assures* them a comfortable support at your decease, can there be a doubt which is to be chosen? Can there be a doubt about duty?"

A DISTINGUISHED CHARACTER.

IN order to prevent conjectures which might not be entirely pleasant to one or two persons whom I have in my mind, I prefer to state, at once and frankly, that I, Dionysius Green, am the author of this article. It requires some courage to make this avowal, I am well aware ; and I am prepared to experience a rapid diminution of my present rather extensive popularity. One result I certainly foresee, namely, a great falling-off in the number of applications for autographs ("accompanied with a sentiment "), which I daily receive ; possibly, also, fewer invitations to lecture before literary societies next winter. Fortunately, my recent marriage enables me to dispense with a large portion of my popularity, without great inconvenience ; or, rather, I am relieved from the very laborious necessity of maintaining it in the face of so many aggressive rivalries.

The day may arrive, therefore, when I shall cease to be a Distinguished Character. Since I have admitted this much, I may as well confess that my reputation — enviable as it may be considered by the public — is of that kind which seems to be meant to run for a certain length of time, at the expiration whereof it must be wound up again. I was fortunate enough to discover this secret betimes, and I have since then known several amiable and worthy persons to slip out of sight, from the lack of it. There was Mr. ———, for example, whose comic articles shook the fat sides of the nation for one summer, and whose pseudonyme was in everybody's mouth. Alas ! what he took for perpetual motion was but an eight-day clock, and I need not call your attention to the present dead and leaden stillness of its pendulum.

Although my earliest notoriety was achieved in very much the same way,— that is, by a series of comic sketches,

as many of my admirers no doubt remember, — I soon perceived the unstable character of my reputation. I was at the mercy of the next man who should succeed in inventing a new slang, or a funnier way of spelling. These things, in literature, are like "fancy drinks" among the profane. They tickle the palates of the multitude for a while, but they don't wear like the plain old beverages. I saw very plainly, that much more was to be gained, in the long run, by planting myself — not with a sudden and startling jump, but by a graceful, cautious pirouette — upon a basis of the Moral and the Didactic. I should thus reach a class of slow, but very tough stomachs, which would require ample time to assimilate the food I intended to offer. If this were somewhat crude, that would be no objection whatever : they always mistake their mental gripings for the process of digestion. Why, bless your souls ! I have known Tupper's " Proverbial Philosophy " to fill one of them to repletion, for the space of ten years !

I owe this resolution to my natural acuteness of perception, but my success in carrying it into execution was partly the result of luck. The field, now occupied by such a crowd, (I name no names,) was at that time nearly clear ; and I managed to shift my costume before the public fairly knew what I was about. I found, indeed, that a combination of the two styles enabled me to retain much of my old audience while acquiring the new. It was like singing a hymn of serious admonition to a lively, rattling tune. One is diverted : there is a present sense of fun, while a gentle feeling of the grave truths inculcated lingers in one's mind afterwards. The pious can find no fault with the matter, nor the profane with the manner. Instead of approaching the moral consciousness of one's readers with stern, lugubrious countenance, and ponderous or lamentable voice, you make your appearance with a smile and a joke, punch the reader playfully in the ribs, and say, as it were, " Ha ! ha ! I 've a good thing to tell you ! " Although I have many imitators, some of whom have attained an excellence in the art which may be considered classic, yet I may fairly claim to have originated this branch of literature, and, while it retains its present unbounded · popularity, my name cannot wholly perish.

Nevertheless, greatness has its drawbacks. I appeal to all distinguished authors, from Tupper to Weenie Willows, to confirm the truth of this assertion. I have sometimes, especially of late, doubted seriously whether it is a good thing to be distinguished. Alas ! my dear young gentleman and lady, whose albums would be so dismally incomplete without my autograph (" accompanied with a sentiment "), would that you could taste the bitter with the sweet, — the honey and aloes of an American author's life ! At first, it is exceedingly pleasant. You are like a newly-hatched chicken, or a pup at the end of his nine-days' blindness. You are petted, and stroked, and called sweet names, and fed with dainties, and carried in the arms of the gentlemen, and cuddled in the laps of the ladies. But when you get to be a big dog or a full-grown game-cock, take care ! If people would but fancy that you still wore your down or silken skin, they might continue to be delighted with every gambol of your fancy. But they suspect pin-feathers and bristles, whether the latter grow or not ; and, after doing their best to spoil you, they suddenly demand the utmost propriety of behavior. However, let me not anticipate. I can still call myself, without the charge of self-flattery, a Distinguished Character ; at least I am told so, every day, each person who makes the remark supposing that it is an entirely original and most acceptable compliment. · While this distinction lasts, (for I find that I lose it in proportion as

I gain in sound knowledge and independent common-sense,) I should like to describe, for the contemplation of future ages, some of the penalties attached to popularity at present.

I was weak enough, I admit, to be immensely delighted with the first which I experienced, — not foreseeing whitherward they led. The timid, enthusiastic notes of girls of fifteen, with the words " sweet " and "exquisite," duly underscored, the letters of aspiring boys, enclosing specimens of their composition, and the touching pleas of individuals of both sexes, in reduced circumstances, were so many evidences of success, which I hugged to my bosom. Reducing the matter to statistics, I have since ascertained that about one in ten of these letters is dictated either by honest sympathy, the warm, uncritical recognition of youth (which I don't suppose any author would diminish, if he could), or the craving for encouragement, under unpropitious circumstances of growth. But how was I, in the beginning, to guess at the motives of the writers ? They offered sugar-plums, which I swallowed without a suspicion of the drastic ingredients so many of them contained. Good Mrs. Sigourney kept a journal of her experiences in this line. I wish I had done the same.

The young lady correspondent, I find, in most cases replies to your reply, proposing a permanent correspondence. The young gentleman, who desires, above all things, your "*candid opinion* of the poems enclosed, — be sure and point out the *faults*, and how they can be *improved*," — is highly indignant when you take him at his word, and do so. You receive a letter of defence and explanation, showing that what you consider to be faults are not such. Moreover, his friends have assured him that the poem which you advise him to omit is one of ·his finest things ! The distressed aspirant for literary fame, who only requests that you shall read and correct his or her manuscript, procure a publisher, and prefix a commendatory notice, signed with your name, to the work, writes that he or she is at last undeceived in regard to the character of authors. " I thank you, Mr. Green, for the *lesson!* The remembrance of *your* former struggles is *happily* effaced in your present success. It is hard for a heart throbbing with warmth to be chilled, and a guileless confidence in human brotherhood to be crushed forever! I will strive to bury my disappointed hopes in my own darkened bosom; and that you may be saved from the experience which you have prepared for another, is the wish of, *Sir*, yours, ———."

For a day or two I went about with a horrible feeling of dread and remorse. I opened the morning paper with trembling hands, and only breathed freely when I found no item headed "Suicide" in the columns. A year afterwards, chance threw me in the way of my broken-hearted victim. I declare to you I never saw a better specimen of gross animal health. She —no, he (on second thoughts, I won't say which) — was at an evening party, laughing boisterously, with a plate of chicken-salad in one hand and a glass of champagne in the other.

One of my first admirers was a gentleman of sixty, who called upon me with a large roll of manuscript. He had retired from business two years before, so he informed me, and, having always been a great lover of poetry, he determined to fill up the tedium of his life of ease by writing some for himself. Now everybody knows that I am not a poet, — the few patriotic verses which I wrote during the war having simply been the result of excitement, — and why should he apply to me? O, there was a great deal of poetry in my prose, he said. My didactic paper called "Wait for the Wagon!" showed such a knowledge of metaphor! I looked over the innumerable leaves, here and there venturing the remark that "rain" and "shame" were not good rhymes, and that my friend's blank verse had now and then lines of four and six feet. "Poetic license, sir!" was the reply.

"I thought you were aware that poets are bound to no rules!"

What could I do with such a man? What, indeed, but to return him the manuscript with that combined gentleness and grace which I have endeavored to cultivate in my demeanor, and to suggest, in the tenderest way, that he should be content to write, and not publish?. He got up, stiffened his backbone, placed his conventional hat hard upon his head, gave a look of mingled mortification and wrath, and hurried away without saying a word. That man, I assure you, will be my secret enemy to the day of his death. He is no doubt a literary authority in a small circle of equal calibre. When my name is mentioned, he will sneer down my rising fame, and his sneer will control the sale of half a dozen copies of my last volume.

This is a business view of the subject, I grant; but then *I* have always followed literature with an eye to business. The position of a popular writer is much more independent than that of a teacher or a clergyman, for which reason I prefer it. The same amount of intellect, made available in a different way, will produce material results just as satisfactory. Compensation, however, is the law of the world; hence I must pay for my independence; and this adventure with the old gentleman is one of the many forms in which the payment is made.

When the applications for autographs first began to pour in upon me, I gladly took a sheet of Delarue's creamiest note-paper and wrote thereon an oracular sentence from one of my most popular papers. After a while my replies degenerated to "Sincerely, Your Friend, Dionysius Green," and finally, (daily blessings come at last to be disregarded,) no application was favored, which did not enclose a postage-stamp. When some school-boy requested an autograph, "accompanied with a sentiment," and forwarded slips of paper on behalf of "two other boys," I sometimes lost my patience, and left the letters unanswered for a month at a time. There was a man in Tennessee, just before the war, who had a printed circular, with a blank for the author's name; and I know of one author who replied to him with a printed note, and a printed address on the envelope, not a word of manuscript about it!

Next in frequency are the applications for private literary contributions, — such as epithalamia, obituaries, addresses for lovers, and the like. One mourning father wished me to write an article about the death of his little girl, aged four months, assuring me that "her intellect was the astonishment of all who knew her." A young lady wished for something that would "overwhelm with remorse the heart of a gentleman who had broken off an engagement without any cause." A young gentleman, about to graduate, offered five dollars for an oration on "The Past and Probable Future History of the Human Race," long enough to occupy twenty minutes in speaking, and "to be made very fine and flowery." (I had a mind to punish this youth by complying with his request, to the very letter!) It is difficult to say what people won't write about, when they write to a Distinguished Character.

There is a third class of correspondents, whose requests used to astonish me profoundly, until I surmised that their object was to procure an autograph in a roundabout way. One wants to know who is the publisher of your book; one, whether you can give the post-office address of Gordon Cumming or Thomas Carlyle; one, which is the best Latin Grammar; one, whether you know the author of that exquisite poem, "The Isle of Tears"; and one, perhaps, whether Fanny Forrester was the grandmother of Fanny Fern. And when you consider that what letters I get are not a tithe of what older and more widely known authors receive, you may form some idea of the immense number of persons engaged in this sort of correspondence.

But I have not yet come to the worst. So long as you live at home, whether it's in the city or country,

(the city would be preferable, if you could keep your name out of the Directory,) the number of applicants in person is limited; and as for the letters, we know that the post-office department is very badly managed, and a great many epistles never reach their destination. Besides, it's astonishing how soon and how easily an author acquires the reputation of being unapproachable. If he don't pour out his heart, in unlimited torrents and cascades of feeling, to a curious stranger, the latter goes away with the report that the author, personally, is "icy, reserved, uncommunicative; in the man, one sees nothing of his works; it is difficult to believe that that cold, forbidding brow conceived, those rigid, unsmiling lips uttered, and that dry, bloodless hand wrote, the fervid passion of" — such or such a book. When I read a description of myself, written in that style, I was furious; but I afterwards noticed that the number of my visitors fell off very rapidly.

Most of us American authors, however, now go to the people, instead of waiting for them to come to us. And this is what I mean by coming to the worst. Four or five years ago, I determined to talk as well as write. Everybody was doing it, and well paid; nothing seemed to be requisite except a little distinction, which I had already acquired by my comic and didactic writings. There was Mr. E—— declaiming philosophy; Drs. B—— and C—— occupying secular pulpits; Mr. C—— inculcating loftier politics; Mr. T—— talking about all sorts of countries and people; Mr. W—— reading his essays in public; and a great many more, whom you all know. Why should I not also "pursue the triumph and partake the gale"? I found that the lecture was in most cases an essay, written in short, pointed sentences, and pleasantly delivered. The audience must laugh occasionally, and yet receive an impression strong enough to last until next morning. The style which, as I said before, I claim to have invented, was the very thing! I noticed, further, that there was a great deal in the title of the lecture. It must be alliterative, antithetical, or, still better, paradoxical. There was profound skill in Artemus Ward's "Babes in the Wood." Such titles as "Doubts and Duties," "Mystery and Muffins," "Here, There, and Nowhere," "The Elegance of Evil," "Sunshine and Shrapnel," "The Coming Cloud," "The Averted Agony," and "Peeps at Peccadillos," will explain my meaning. The latter, in fact, was the actual title of my first lecture, which I gave with such signal success, — eighty-five times in one winter.

The crowds that everywhere thronged to hear me gave me a new and delicious experience of popularity. How grand it was to be escorted by the president of the society down the central aisle, amid the rustling sound of turning heads, and audible whispers of "There he is! there he is!" And always, when the name of Dionysius Green was announced, the applause which followed! Then the hush of expectation, the faint smile and murmur coming with my first unexpected flash of humor (*unexpectedness* is one of my strong points), the broad laugh breaking out just where I intended it, and finally the solemn peroration, which showed that I possessed depth and earnestness as well as brilliancy! Well, I must say that the applauses and the fees were honestly earned. I did my best, and the audiences must have been satisfied, or the societies would n't have invited me over and over again to the same place.

If my literary style was so admirably adapted to this new vocation, it was, on the other hand, a source of great annoyance. Only a small class was sufficiently enlightened to comprehend my true aim in inculcating moral lessons under a partly humorous guise. All the rest, unfortunately, took me to be either one thing or the other. While some invited me to family prayer-meetings, as the most cheering and welcome relief after the fatigue of speaking, the rougher characters of the place would claim me (on the

strength of my earlier writings) as one of themselves, would slap me on the back, call me familiarly "Dionysius," and insist on my drinking with them. Others, again, occupied a middle or doubtful ground ; they did not consider that my personal views were strictly defined, and wanted to be enlightened on this or that point of faith. They gave me a deal of trouble. Singularly enough, all these classes began their attacks with the same phrase, "O, we have a right to ask it of you : you 're a Distinguished Character, you know !"

It is hardly necessary to say that I am of rather a frail constitution : so many persons have seen me, that the public is generally aware of the fact. A lecture of an hour and a quarter quite exhausts my nervous energy. Moreover, it gives me a vigorous appetite, and my two overpowering desires, after speaking, are, first to eat, and then to sleep. But it frequently happens that I am carried, perforce, to the house of some good but ascetic gentleman, who gives me a glass of cold water, talks until midnight, and then delivers me, more dead than alive, to my bed. I am so sensitive in regard to the relation of guest and host that I can do naught but submit. Astræa, I am told, always asks for what she wants, and does what she feels inclined to do, — indeed, why should n't she ? — but I am cast in a more timid mould.

There are some small country places which I visit where I have other sufferings to undergo. Being a Distinguished Character, it would be a neglect and a slight if I were left alone for two minutes. And the people seem to think that the most delightful topic of conversation which they can select is — myself. How weary of myself I become ! I have wished, a thousand times, that my popular work, "The Tin Trumpet," had never been written. I cannot blame the people, because there are —— and ——, who like nothing better than to be talked about to their faces, and to take the principal part in the conversation. Of course the people think, in regard to lecturers, *ex uno disce omnes.*

In travelling by rail, the same thing happens over and over. When I leave a town in the morning, some one is sure to enter the car and greet me in a loud voice: " How are you, Mr. Green? What a fine lecture you gave us last night!" Then the other travellers turn and look at me, listen to catch my words, and tell the new-comers at every station, until I 'm afraid to take a nap for fear of snoring, afraid to read lest somebody should be scandalized at my novel, or to lunch lest I should be reported as a drunkard for taking a sip of sherry (the physician prescribes it) from a pocket-flask. At such times I envy the fellow in homespun on the seat in front of me, who loafs, yawns, eats, and drinks as he pleases, and nobody gives him a second glance.

When I am not recognized, I sometimes meet with another experience, which was a little annoying until I became accustomed to it. I am the subject of very unembarrassed conversation, and hear things said of me that sometimes flatter and sometimes sting. It is true that I have learned many curious and unsuspected facts concerning my birth, parentage, history, and opinions; but, on the other hand, I am humiliated by the knowledge of what texture a great deal of my reputation is made. Sometimes I am even confounded with Graves, whom, as an author, I detest; my " Tin Trumpet" being ascribed to him, and his " Drippings from the Living Rock" being admired as mine! At such times, it is very difficult to preserve my incognito. I have wondered that nobody ever reads the truth in my indignant face.

As a consequence of all these trials, I sometimes become impatient, inaccessible to compliment, and — since the truth must be told — a little ill-tempered. My temperament, as my family and friends know, is of an unusually genial and amiable quality, and I never snub an innocent but indiscreet admirer without afterwards repenting of my rudeness. I have often, indeed, a double motive for repentance; for those snubs carry their operation far beyond their recipients, and come back to me

sometimes, after months or even years, in " Book Notices," or other newspaper articles. Thus the serene path of literature, which the aspiring youth imagines to be so fair and sunny, overspread with the mellowest ideal tints, becomes rough and cloudy. No doubt I am to blame: possibly I am rightly treated: I "belong to the public," I am told with endless congratulatory iteration, and therefore I ought not to feel the difference between the public's original humoring of my moods, and my present enforced humoring of its moods. But I *do* feel it, somehow. I have of late entertained the suspicion, that I am not wholly the creation of popular favor. "The public," I am sure, never furnished me with my comic or my lively-serious vein of writing. If either of those veins had not been found good, they would not have encouraged me to work them. I declare, boldly, that I give an ample return for what I get, and when I satisfy curiosity or yield to unreasonable demands upon my patience and good-humor, it is "to boot."

Nevertheless, it is a generous public, on the whole, and gives trouble only through thoughtlessness, not malice. It delights in its favorites, because imagining that they so intensely enjoy its favor. And don't we, after all? (I say *we* purposely, and my publisher will tell you why.) Now that I have written away my vexation, I recognize very clearly that my object in writing this article is apology rather than complaint. All whom I have ever rudely treated will now comprehend the unfortunate circumstances under which the act occurred. If some one should visit me to-morrow, I have no doubt he will write: " Mr. Dionysius Green is all, and more than all, one would anticipate from reading his charming works. Benevolence beams from his brow, fancy sparkles from his eyes, and genial sympathy with all mankind sits enthroned upon his lips. It was a rare pleasure to me to listen to his conversation, and I could but wish that the many thousands of his admirers might enjoy the privilege of an interview with so Distinguished a Character!"

THE BOBOLINKS.

WHEN Nature had made all her birds,
  And had no cares to think on,
She gave a rippling laugh — and out
  There flew a Bobolinkon.

She laughed again, — out flew a mate.
  A breeze of Eden bore them
Across the fields of Paradise,
  The sunrise reddening o'er them.

Incarnate sport and holiday,
  They flew and sang forever;
Their souls through June were all in tune,
  Their wings were weary never.

The blithest song of breezy farms,
  Quaintest of field-note flavors,
Exhaustless fount of trembling trills
  And demisemiquavers.

Their tribe, still drunk with air and light
  And perfume of the meadow,
Go reeling up and down the sky,
  In sunshine and in shadow.

One springs from out the dew-wet grass,
  Another follows after;
The morn is thrilling with their songs
  And peals of fairy laughter.

From out the marshes and the brook,
  They set the tall reeds swinging,
And meet and frolic in the air,
  Half prattling and half singing.

When morning winds sweep meadow lands
  In green and russet billows,
And toss the lonely elm-tree's boughs,
  And silver all the willows,

I see you buffeting the breeze,
  Or with its motion swaying,
Your notes half drowned against the wind,
  Or down the current playing.

When far away o'er grassy flats,
  Where the thick wood commences,
The white-sleeved mowers look like specks
  Beyond the zigzag fences,

The Bobolinks.

And noon is hot, and barn-roofs gleam
  White in the pale-blue distance,
I hear the saucy minstrels still
  In chattering persistence.

When Eve her domes of opal fire
  Piles round the blue horizon,
Or thunder rolls from hill to hill
  A Kyrie Eleison, —

Still, merriest of the merry birds,
  Your sparkle is unfading, —
Pied harlequins of June, no end
  Of song and masquerading.

What cadences of bubbling mirth
  Too quick for bar or rhythm !
What ecstasies, too full to keep
  Coherent measure with them !

O could I share, without champagne
  Or muscadel, your frolic,
The glad delirium of your joy,
  Your fun un-apostolic,

Your drunken jargon through the fields,
  Your bobolinkish gabble,
Your fine anacreontic glee,
  Your tipsy reveller's babble !

Nay, — let me not profane such joy
  With similes of folly, —
No wine of earth could waken songs
  So delicately jolly !

O boundless self-contentment, voiced
  In flying air-born bubbles !
O joy that mocks our sad unrest,
  And drowns our earth-born troubles !

Hope springs with you : I dread no more
  Despondency and dullness ;
For Good Supreme can never fail
  That gives such perfect fullness.

The Life that floods the happy fields
  With song and light and color
Will shape our lives to richer states,
  And heap our measures fuller.

GRIFFITH GAUNT; OR, JEALOUSY.

CHAPTER XXXIX.

SHE recoiled with a violent shudder at first; and hid her face with one hand. Then she gradually stole a horror-stricken side-glance.

She had not looked at it a moment, when she uttered a loud cry, and pointed at its feet with quivering hand.

"THE SHOES! THE SHOES!—IT IS NOT MY GRIFFITH."

With this she fell into violent hysterics, and was carried out of the room at Houseman's earnest entreaty.

As soon as she was gone, Mr. Houseman, being freed from his fear that his client would commit herself irretrievably, recovered a show of composure, and his wits went keenly to work.

"On behalf of the accused," said he, "I admit the suicide of some person unknown, wearing heavy hobnailed shoes; probably one of the lower order of people."

This adroit remark produced some little effect, notwithstanding the strong feeling against the accused.

The coroner inquired if there were any bodily marks by which the remains could be identified.

"My master had a long black mole on his forehead," suggested Caroline Ryder.

"'T is here!" cried a juryman, bending over the remains.

And now they all gathered in great excitement round the *corpus delicti;* and there, sure enough, was a long black mole.

Then was there a buzz of pity for Griffith Gaunt, followed by a stern murmur of execration.

"Gentlemen," said the coroner solemnly, "behold in this the finger of Heaven. The poor gentleman may well have put off his boots, since, it seems, he left his horse; but he could not take from his forehead his natal sign; and that, by God's will, hath strangely escaped mutilation, and revealed a most

foul deed. We must now do our duty, gentlemen, without respect of persons."

A warrant was then issued for the apprehension of Thomas Leicester. And, that same night, Mrs. Gaunt left Hernshaw in her own chariot between two constables, and escorted by armed yeomen.

Her proud head was bowed almost to her knees, and her streaming eyes hidden in her lovely hands. For why? A mob accompanied her for miles, shouting, "Murderess!—Bloody Papist!—Hast done to death the kindliest gentleman in Cumberland. We'll all come to see thee hanged.—Fair face but foul heart!"—and groaning, hissing, and cursing, and indeed only kept from violence by the escort.

And so they took that poor proud lady and lodged her in Carlisle jail.

She was *enceinte* into the bargain. By the man she was to be hanged for murdering.

CHAPTER XL.

THE county was against her, with some few exceptions. Sir George Neville and Mr. Houseman stood stoutly by her.

Sir George's influence and money obtained her certain comforts in jail; and, in that day, the law of England was so far respected in a jail that untried prisoners were not thrown into cells, nor impeded, as they now are, in preparing their defence.

Her two stanch friends visited her every day, and tried to keep her heart up.

But they could not do it. She was in a state of dejection bordering upon lethargy.

"If he is dead," said she, "what matters it? If, by God's mercy, he is alive still, he will not let me die for want of a word from him. Impatience hath been my bane. Now, I say,

God's will be done. I am weary of the world."

Houseman tried every argument to rouse her out of this desperate frame of mind; but in vain.

It ran its course, and then, behold, it passed away like a cloud, and there came a keen desire to live and defeat her accusers.

She made Houseman write out all the evidence against her; and she studied it by day, and thought of it by night, and often surprised both her friends by the acuteness of her remarks.

Mr. Atkins discontinued his advertisements. It was Houseman, who now filled every paper with notices informing Griffith Gaunt of his accession to fortune, and entreating him for that, and other weighty reasons, to communicate in confidence with his old friend, John Houseman, attorney at law.

Houseman was too wary to invite him to appear and save his wife; for, in that case, he feared the Crown would use his advertisements as evidence at the trial, should Griffith not appear.

The fact is, Houseman relied more upon certain *lacunæ* in the evidence, and the absence of all marks of violence, than upon any hope that Griffith might be alive.

The assizes drew near, and no fresh light broke in upon this mysterious case.

Mrs. Gaunt lay in her bed at night, and thought and thought.

Now the female understanding has sometimes remarkable power under such circumstances. By degrees Truth flashes across it, like lightning in the dark.

After many such nightly meditations, Mrs. Gaunt sent one day for Sir George Neville and Mr. Houseman, and addressed them as follows:—"I believe he is alive, and that I can guess where he is at this moment."

Both the gentlemen started, and looked amazed.

"Yes, sirs; so sure as we sit here,

he is now at a little inn in Lancashire, called the 'Packhorse,' with a woman he calls his wife." And, with this, her face was scarlet, and her eyes flashed their old fire.

She exacted a solemn promise of secrecy from them, and then she told them all she had learned from Thomas Leicester.

"And so now," said she, "I believe you can save my life, if you think it is worth saving." And with this, she began to cry bitterly.

But Houseman, the practical, had no patience with the pangs of love betrayed, and jealousy, and such small deer, in a client whose life was at stake. "Great Heaven! madam," said he, roughly: "why did you not tell me this before?"

"Because I am not a man—to go and tell everything, all at once," sobbed Mrs. Gaunt. Besides, I wanted to shield his good name, whose dear life they pretend I have taken."

As soon as she recovered her composure, she begged Sir George Neville to ride to the "Packhorse" for her. Sir George assented eagerly, but asked how he was to find it. "I have thought of that, too," said she. "His black horse has been to and fro. Ride that horse into Lancashire, and give him his head: ten to one but he takes you to the place, or where you may hear of it. If not, go to Lancaster, and ask about the 'Packhorse.' He wrote to me from Lancaster: see." And she showed him the letter.

Sir George embraced with ardor this opportunity of serving her. "I'll be at Hernshaw in one hour," said he, "and ride the black horse south at once."

"Excuse me," said Houseman; "but would it not be better for me to go? As a lawyer, I may be more able to cope with her."

"Nay," said Mrs. Gaunt, "Sir George is young and handsome. If he manages well, she will tell him more than she will you. All I beg of him is to drop the chevalier for this once, and see women with a woman's eyes and not a man's,— see them as they are. Do not go telling a creature of this kind that she has had my money, as well as my husband, and ought to pity me lying here in prison. Keep me out of her sight as much as you can. Whether Griffith hath deceived her or not, you will never raise in her any feeling but love for him, and hatred for his lawful wife. Dress like a yeoman ; go quietly, and lodge in the house a day or two ; begin by flattering her ; and then get from her when she saw him last, or heard from him. But indeed I fear you will surprise him with her."

"Fear ? " exclaimed Sir George.

"Well, hope, then," said the lady ; and a tear trickled down her face in a moment. "But if you do, promise me, on your honor as a gentleman, not to affront him. For I know you think him a villain."

"A d—d villain, saving your presence."

"Well, sir, you have said it to me. Now promise me to say naught to *him,* but just this : ' Rose Gaunt's mother, she lies in Carlisle jail, to be tried for her life for murdering you. She begs of you not to let her die publicly upon the scaffold ; but quietly at home, of her broken heart.' "

"Write it," said Sir George, with the tears in his eyes, " that I may just put it in his hand ; for I can never utter your sweet words to such a monster as he is."

Armed with this appeal, and several minute instructions, which it is needless to particularize here, that stanch friend rode into Lancashire.

And next day the black horse justified his mistress's sagacity, and his own.

He seemed all along to know where he was going, and late in the afternoon he turned off the road on to a piece of green : and Sir George, with beating heart, saw right before him the sign of the " Packhorse," and, on coming nearer, the words

THOMAS LEICESTER.

He dismounted at the door, and asked if he could have a bed.

Mrs. Vint said yes ; and supper into the bargain, if he liked.

He ordered a substantial supper directly.

Mrs. Vint saw at once it was a good customer, and showed him into the parlor.

He sat down by the fire. But the moment she retired, he got up and made a circuit of the house, looking quietly into every window, to see if he could catch a glance of Griffith Gaunt.

There were no signs of him ; and Sir George returned to his parlor heavy-hearted. One hope, the greatest of all, had been defeated directly. Still, it was just possible that Griffith might be away on temporary business.

In this faint hope Sir George strolled about till his supper was ready for him.

When he had eaten his supper, he rang the bell, and, taking advantage of a common custom, insisted on the landlord, Thomas Leicester, taking a glass with him.

"Thomas Leicester ! " said the girl. " He is not at home. But I 'll send Master Vint."

Old Vint came in, and readily accepted an invitation to drink his guest's health.

Sir George found him loquacious, and soon extracted from him that his daughter Mercy was Leicester's wife, that Leicester was gone on a journey, and that Mercy was in care for him. " Leastways," said he, " she is very dull, and cries at times when her mother speaks of him ; but she is too close to say much."

All this puzzled Sir George Neville sorely.

But greater surprises were in store.

The next morning, after breakfast, the servant came and told him Dame Leicester desired to see him.

He started at that, but put on nonchalance, and said he was at her service.

He was ushered into another parlor, and there he found a grave, comely young woman, seated working, with a child on the floor beside her. She rose quietly ; he bowed low and respectfully ; she blushed faintly ; but, with every appearance of self-possession, courtesied to him; then eyed him point-blank a single moment, and requested him to be seated.

"I hear, sir," said she, "you did ask my father many questions last night. May I ask you one?"

Sir George colored, but bowed assent.

"From whom had you the black horse you ride?"

Now, if Sir George had not been a veracious man, he would have been caught directly. But, although he saw at once the oversight he had committed, he replied, "I had him of a lady in Cumberland, one Mistress Gaunt."

Mercy Vint trembled. "No doubt," said she, softly. "Excuse my question: you shall understand that the horse is well known here."

"Madam," said Sir George, "if you admire the horse, he is at your service for twenty pounds, though indeed he is worth more."

"I thank you, sir," said Mercy; "I have no desire for the horse whatever. And be pleased to excuse my curiosity: you must think me impertinent."

"Nay, madam," said Sir George, "I consider nothing impertinent that hath procured me the pleasure of an interview with you."

He then, as directed by Mrs. Gaunt, proceeded to flatter the mother and the child, and exerted those powers of pleasing which had made him irresistible in society.

Here, however, he found they went a very little way. Mercy did not even smile. She cast out of her dove-like eyes a gentle, humble, reproachful glance, as much as to say, "What! do I seem so vain a creature as to believe all this?"

Sir George himself had tact and sensibility; and by and by became discontented with the part he was playing, under those meek, honest eyes.

There was a pause; and, as her sex have a wonderful art of reading the face, Mercy looked at him steadily, and said, "Yes, sir, 'tis best to be straightforward, especially with women-folk."

Before he could recover this little

facer, she said, quietly, "What is your name?"

"George Neville."

"Well, George Neville," said Mercy, very slowly and softly, "when you have a mind to tell me what you came here for, and who sent you, you will find me in this little room. I seldom leave it now. I beg you to speak your errand to none but me." And she sighed deeply.

Sir George bowed low, and retired to collect his wits. He had come here strongly prepossessed against Mercy. But, instead of a vulgar, shallow woman, whom he was to surprise into confession, he encountered a soft-eyed Puritan, all unpretending dignity, grace, propriety, and sagacity.

"Flatter her!" said he, to himself. "I might as well flatter an iceberg. Outwit her! I feel like a child beside her."

He strolled about in a brown study, not knowing what to do.

She had given him a fair opening. She had invited him to tell the truth. But he was afraid to take her at her word; and yet what was the use to persist in what his own eyes told him was the wrong course?

Whilst he hesitated, and debated within himself, a trifling incident turned the scale.

A poor woman came begging, with her child, and was received rather roughly by Harry Vint. "Pass on, good woman," said he, "we want no tramps here."

Then a window was opened on the ground floor, and Mercy beckoned the woman. Sir George flattened himself against the wall, and listened to the two talking.

Mercy examined the woman gently, but shrewdly, and elicited a tale of genuine distress. Sir George then saw her hand out to the woman some warm flannel for herself, a piece of stuff for the child, a large piece of bread, and a sixpence.

He also caught sight of Mercy's dove-like eyes as she bestowed her alms, and they were lit with an inward lustre.

"She cannot be an ill woman," said Sir George. "I'll e'en go by my own eyes and judgment. After all, Mrs. Gaunt has never seen her, and I have."

He went and knocked at Mercy's door.

"Come in," said a mild voice.

Neville entered, and said, abruptly, and with great emotion, "Madam, I see you can feel for the unhappy; so I take my own way now, and appeal to your pity. I *have* come to speak to you on the saddest business."

"You come from *him*," said Mercy, closing her lips tight; but her bosom heaved. Her heart and her judgment grappled like wrestlers that moment.

"Nay, madam," said Sir George, "I come from *her*."

Mercy knew in a moment who "her" must be.

She looked scared, and drew back with manifest signs of repulsion.

The movement did not escape Sir George: it alarmed him. He remembered what Mrs. Gaunt had said, — that this woman would be sure to hate Gaunt's lawful wife. But it was too late to go back. He did the next best thing, he rushed on.

He threw himself on his knees before Mercy Vint.

"O madam," he cried, piteously, "do not set your heart against the most unhappy lady in England. If you did but know her, her nobleness, her misery ! Before you steel yourself against me, her friend, let me ask you one question. Do you know where Mrs. Gaunt is at this moment?"

Mercy answered coldly, "How should I know where she is?"

"Well, then, she lies in Carlisle jail."

"She — lies — in Carlisle jail?" repeated Mercy, looking all confused.

"They accuse her of murdering her husband."

Mercy uttered a scream, and, catching her child up off the floor, began to rock herself and moan over it.

"No, no, no," cried Sir George, "she is innocent, she is innocent."

"What is that to *me?*" cried Mercy, wildly. "He is murdered, he is dead, and my child an orphan." And so she went on moaning and rocking herself.

"But I tell you he is not dead at all," cried Sir George. "'T is all a mistake. When did you see him last?"

"More than six weeks ago."

"I mean, when did you hear from him last?"

"Never, since that day."

Sir George groaned aloud at this intelligence.

And Mercy, who heard him groan, was heart-broken. She accused herself of Griffith's death. "'T was I who drove him from me," she said. "'T was I who bade him go back to his lawful wife; and the wretch hated him. I sent him to his death." Her grief was wild, and deep. She could not hear Sir George's arguments.

But presently she said, sternly, "What does that woman say for herself?"

"Madam," said Sir George, dejectedly, "Heaven knows you are in no condition to fathom a mystery that hath puzzled wiser heads than yours or mine ; and I am little able to lay the tale before you fairly; for your grief, it moves me deeply, and I could curse myself for putting the matter to you so bluntly and so uncouthly. Permit me to retire a while and compose my own spirits for the task I have undertaken too rashly."

"Nay, George Neville," said Mercy, "stay you there. Only give me a moment to draw my breath."

She struggled hard for a little composure, and, after a shower of tears, she hung her head over the chair like a crushed thing, but made him a sign of attention.

Sir George told the story as fairly as he could ; only of course his bias was in favor of Mrs. Gaunt; but as Mercy's bias was against her, this brought the thing nearly square.

When he came to the finding of the body, Mercy was seized with a deadly faintness ; and though she did not become insensible, yet she was in no condition to judge, or even to comprehend.

Sir George was moved with pity, and would have called for help; but she shook her head. So then he sprinkled water on her face, and slapped her hand; and a beautifully moulded hand it was.

When she got a little better she sobbed faintly, and sobbing thanked him, and begged him to go on.

"My mind is stronger than my heart," she said. "I'll hear it all, though it kill me where I sit."

Sir George went on, and, to avoid repetition, I must ask the reader to understand that he left out nothing whatever which has been hitherto related in these pages; and, in fact, told her one or two little things that I have omitted.

When he had done, she sat quite still a minute or two, pale as a statue.

Then she turned to Neville, and said, solemnly, "You wish to know the truth in this dark matter: for dark it is in very sooth."

Neville was much impressed by her manner, and answered, respectfully, Yes, he desired to know, — by all means.

"Then take my hand," said Mercy, "and kneel down with me."

Sir George looked surprised, but obeyed, and kneeled down beside her, with his hand in hers.

There was a long pause, and then took place a transformation.

The dove-like eyes were lifted to heaven and gleamed like opals with an inward and celestial light; the comely face shone with a higher beauty, and the rich voice rose in ardent supplication.

"Thou God, to whom all hearts be known, and no secrets hid from thine eye, look down now on thy servant in sore trouble, that putteth her trust in thee. Give wisdom to the simple this day, and understanding to the lowly. Thou that didst reveal to babes and sucklings the great things that were hidden from the wise, O show us the truth in this dark matter: enlighten us by thy spirit, for His dear sake who suffered more sorrows than I suffer now. Amen. Amen."

Then she looked at Neville; and he said "Amen," with all his heart, and the tears in his eyes.

He had never heard real live prayer before. Here the little hand gripped his hard, as she wrestled; and the heart seemed to rise out of the bosom and fly to Heaven on the sublime and thrilling voice.

They rose, and she sat down; but it seemed as if her eyes once raised to Heaven in prayer could not come down again: they remained fixed and angelic, and her lips still moved in supplication.

Sir George Neville, though a loose liver, was no scoffer. He was smitten with reverence for this inspired countenance, and retired, bowing low and obsequiously.

He took a long walk, and thought it all over. One thing was clear, and consoling. He felt sure he had done wisely to disobey Mrs. Gaunt's instructions, and make a friend of Mercy, instead of trying to set his wits against hers. Ere he returned to the "Packhorse" he had determined to take another step in the right direction. He did not like to agitate her with another interview, so soon. But he wrote her a little letter.

"MADAM, — When I came here, I did not know you; and therefore I feared to trust you too far. But, now I do know you for the best woman in England, I take the open way with you.

"Know that Mrs. Gaunt said the man would be here with you; and she charged me with a few written lines to him. She would be angry if she knew that I had shown them to any other. Yet I take on me to show them to you; for I believe you are wiser than any of us, if the truth were known. I do therefore entreat you to read these lines, and tell me whether you think the hand that wrote them can have shed the blood of him to whom they are writ.

"I am, madam, with profound respect,
"Your grateful and very humble
servant,
"GEORGE NEVILLE."

He very soon received a line in reply, written in a clear and beautiful hand-writing.

"Mercy Vint sends you her duty; and she will speak to you at nine of the clock to-morrow morning. Pray for light."

At the appointed time, Sir George found her working with her needle. His letter lay on a table before her.

She rose and courtesied to him, and called the servant to take away the child for a while. She went with her to the door and kissed the bairn several times at parting, as if he was going away for good. "I'm loath to let him go," said she to Neville; "but it weakens a mother's mind to have her babe in the room, — takes her attention off each moment. Pray you be seated. Well, sir, I have read these lines of Mistress Gaunt, and wept over them. Methinks I had not done so, were they cunningly devised. Also I lay all night, and thought."

"That is just what she does."

"No doubt, sir; and the upshot is, I don't *feel* as if he was dead. Thank God."

"That is something," said Neville. But he could not help thinking it was very little; especially to produce in a court of justice.

"And now," said she, thoughtfully, "you say that the real Thomas Leicester was seen thereabouts as well as my Thomas Leicester. Then answer me one little question. What had the real Thomas Leicester on his feet that night?"

"Nay, I know not," was the half-careless reply.

"Bethink you. 'T is a question that must have been often put in your hearing."

"Begging your pardon, it was never put at all; nor do I see —"

"What, not at the inquest?"

"No."

"That is very strange. What, so many wise heads have bent over this riddle, and not one to ask how was yon pedler shod!"

"Madam," said Sir George, "our minds were fixed upon the fate of Gaunt. Many did ask how was the pedler armed, but none how was he shod."

"Hath he been seen since?"

"Not he; and that hath an ugly look; for the constables are out after him with hue and cry; but he is not to be found."

"Then," said Mercy, "I must e'en answer my own question. I do know how that pedler was shod. WITH HOB-NAILED SHOES."

Sir George bounded from his chair. One great ray of daylight broke in upon him.

"Ay," said Mercy, "she was right. Women do see clearer in some things than men. The pair went from my house to hers. He you call Griffith Gaunt had on a new pair of boots; and by the same token 't was I did pay for them, and there is the receipt in that cupboard: he you call Thomas Leicester went hence in hobnailed shoes. I think the body they found was the body of Thomas Leicester, the pedler. May God have mercy on his poor unprepared soul."

Sir George uttered a joyful exclamation. But the next moment he had a doubt. "Ay, but," said he, "you forget the mole! 'T was on that they built."

"I forget naught," said Mercy, calmly. "The pedler had a black mole over his left temple. He showed it me in this very room. You have found the body of Thomas Leicester, and Griffith Gaunt is hiding from the law that he hath broken. He is afeared of her and her friends, if he shows his face in Cumberland; he is afeared of my folk, if he be seen in Lancashire. Ah, Thomas, as if I would let them harm thee."

Sir George Neville walked to and fro in grand excitement. "O blessed day that I came hither! Madam, you are an angel. You will save an innocent, broken-hearted lady from death and dishonor. Your good heart and rare wit have read in a moment the dark riddle that hath puzzled a county."

"George," said Mercy, gravely, "you have gotten the wrong end of the stick.

The wise in their own conceit are blinded. In Cumberland, where all this befell, they went not to God for light, as you and I did, George."

In saying this, she gave him her hand to celebrate their success.

He kissed it devoutly, and owned afterward that it was the proudest moment of his life, when that sweet Puritan gave him her neat hand so cordially, with a pressure so gentle yet frank.

And now came the question how they were to make a Cumberland jury see this matter as they saw it.

He asked her would she come to the trial as a witness?

At that she drew back with manifest repugnance.

"My shame would be public. I must tell who I am; and what. A ruined woman."

"Say rather an injured saint. You have nothing to be ashamed of. All good men would feel for you."

Mercy shook her head. "Ay, but the women. Shame is shame with us. Right or wrong goes for little. Nay, I hope to do better for you than that. I must find *him*, and send him to deliver her. 'T is his only chance of happiness."

She then asked him if he would draw up an advertisement of quite a different kind from those he had described to her.

He assented, and between them they concocted the following : —

"If Thomas Leicester, who went from the 'Packhorse' two months ago, will come thither at once, Mercy will be much beholden to him, and tell him strange things that have befallen."

Sir George then, at her request, rode over to Lancaster, and inserted the above in the county paper, and also in a small sheet that was issued in the city three times a week. He had also handbills to the same effect printed, and sent into Cumberland and Westmoreland. Finally, he sent a copy to his man of business in London, with orders to insert it in all the journals.

Then he returned to the "Packhorse," and told Mercy what he had done.

The next day he bade her farewell, and away for Carlisle. It was a two days' journey. He reached Carlisle in the evening, and went all glowing to Mrs. Gaunt. "Madam," said he, " be of good cheer. I bless the day I went to see her ; she is an angel of wit and goodness."

He then related to her, in glowing terms, most that had passed between Mercy and him. But, to his surprise, Mrs. Gaunt wore a cold, forbidding air.

"This is all very well," said she. "But 't will avail me little unless *he* comes before the judge and clears me ; and she will never let him do that."

"Ay, that she will, — if she can find him."

"If she can find him ? How simple you are !"

"Nay, madam, not so simple but I can tell a good woman from a bad one, and a true from a false."

"What ! when you are in love with her ? Not if you were the wisest of your sex."

"In love with her ?" cried Sir George ; and colored high.

"Ay," said the lady. "Think you I cannot tell ? Don't deceive yourself. You have gone and fallen in love with her. At your years ! Not that 't is any business of mine."

"Well, madam," said Sir George, stiffly, "say what you please on that score ; but at least welcome my good news."

Mrs. Gaunt begged him to excuse her petulance, and thanked him kindly for all he had just done. But the next moment she rose from her chair in great agitation, and burst out, " I 'd as lief die as owe anything to that woman."

Sir George remonstrated. " Why hate her ? She does not hate you."

"O, yes, she does. 'T is not in nature she should do any other."

"Her acts prove the contrary."

"Her acts ! She has *done* nothing, but make fair promises ; and that has blinded you. Women of this sort are very cunning, and never show their real characters to a man. No more; prithee mention not her name to me. It makes me ill. I know he is with her at this moment. Ah, let me die, and be forgotten, since I am no more beloved."

The voice was sad and weary now, and the tears ran fast.

Poor Sir George was moved and melted, and set himself to flatter and console this impracticable lady, who hated her best friend in this sore strait, for being what she was herself, a woman; and was much less annoyed at being hanged than at not being loved.

When she was a little calmer, he left her, and rode off to Houseman. That worthy was delighted.

"Get her to swear to those hobnailed shoes," said he, "and we shall shake them." He then let Sir George know that he had obtained private information which he would use in cross-examining a principal witness for the crown. "However," he added, "do not deceive yourself, nothing can make the prisoner really safe but the appearance of Griffith Gaunt. He has such strong motives for coming to light. He is heir to a fortune, and his wife is accused of murdering him. The jury will never believe he is alive till they see him. That man's prolonged disappearance is hideous. It turns my blood cold when I think of it."

"Do not despair on that score," said Neville. "I believe our good angel will produce him."

Three days only before the assizes, came the long-expected letter from Mercy Vint. Sir George tore it open, but bitter was his disappointment. The letter merely said that Griffith had not appeared in answer to her advertisements, and she was sore grieved and perplexed.

There were two postscripts, each on a little piece of paper.

First postscript, in a tremulous hand, "Pray."

Second postscript, in a firm hand, "Drain the water."

Houseman shrugged his shoulders impatiently. "Drain the water? Let the crown do that. We should but fish up more trouble. And prayers quo' she! 'T is not prayers we want, but evidence."

He sent his clerk off to travel post night and day, and subpœna Mercy, and bring her back with him to the trial. She was to have every comfort on the road, and be treated like a duchess.

The evening before the assizes, Mrs. Gaunt's apartments were Mr. Houseman's head-quarters, and messages were coming and going all day, on matters connected with the defence.

Just at sunset, up rattled a post-chaise, and the clerk got out and came haggard and bloodshot before his employer. "The witness has disappeared, sir. Left home last Tuesday, with her child, and has never been seen nor heard of since."

Here was a terrible blow. They all paled under it: it seriously diminished the chances of an acquittal.

But Mrs. Gaunt bore it nobly. She seemed to rise under it.

She turned to Sir George Neville, with a sweet smile. "The noble heart sees base things noble. No wonder then an artful woman deluded *you.* He has left England with her, and condemned me to the gallows, in cold blood. So be it. I shall defend myself."

She then sat down with Mr. Houseman, and went through the written case he had prepared for her, and showed him notes she had taken of full a hundred criminal trials great and small.

While they were putting their heads together, Sir George sat in a brown study, and uttered not a word. Presently he got up a little brusquely, and said, "I 'm going to Hernshaw."

"What, at this time of night? What to do?"

"To obey my orders. To drain the mere."

"And who could have ordered you to drain my mere?"

"Mercy Vint."

Sir George uttered this in a very

curious way, half ashamed, half resolute, and retired before Mrs. Gaunt
could vent in speech the surprise and
indignation that fired her eye.

Houseman implored her not to heed
Sir George and his vagaries, but to
bend her whole mind on those approved modes of defence with which
he had supplied her.

Being now alone with her, he no
longer concealed his great anxiety.

"We have lost an invaluable witness
in that woman," said he. "I was mad
to think she would come."

Mrs. Gaunt shivered with repugnance. "I would not have her come,
for all the world," said she. "For
Heaven's sake never mention her
name to me. I want help from none
but friends. Send Mrs. Houseman to
me in the morning ; and do not distress yourself so. I shall defend myself
far better than you think. I have not
studied a hundred trials for naught."

Thus the prisoner cheered up her
attorney, and soon after insisted on
his going home to bed ; for she saw
he was worn out by his exertions.

And now she was alone.

All was silent.

A few short hours, and she was to be
tried for her life : tried, not by the All-
wise Judge, but by fallible men, and
under a system most unfavorable to
the accused.

Worse than all this, she was a Papist ; and, as ill-luck would have it,
since her imprisonment an alarm had
been raised that the Pretender meditated another invasion. This report
had set jurists very much against all
the Romanists in the country, and had
already perverted justice in one or two
cases, especially in the North.

Mrs. Gaunt knew all this, and trembled at the peril to come.

She spent the early part of the night
in studying her defence. Then she
laid it quite aside, and prayed long
and fervently. Towards morning she
fell asleep from exhaustion.

When she awoke, Mrs. Houseman
was sitting by her bedside, looking at
her, and crying.

They were soon clasped in each other's arms, condoling.

But presently Houseman came, and
took his wife away rather angrily.

Mrs. Gaunt was prevailed on to eat
a little toast and drink a glass of wine,
and then she sat waiting her dreadful
summons.

She waited and waited, until she became impatient to face her danger.

But there were two petty larcenies on
before her. She had to wait.

At last, about noon, came a message
to say that the grand jury had found a
true bill against her.

"Then may God forgive them !" said
she.

Soon afterwards she was informed
her time drew very near.

She made her toilet carefully, and
passed with her attendant into a small
room under the court.

Here she had to endure another chilling wait, and in a sombre room.

Presently she heard a voice above
her cry out, "The King *versus* Catharine Gaunt."

Then she was beckoned to.

She mounted some steps, badly lighted, and found herself in the glare of day,
and greedy eyes, in the felon's dock.

In a matter entirely strange, we seldom know beforehand what we can do,
and how we shall carry ourselves. Mrs.
Gaunt no sooner set her foot in that
dock, and saw the awful front of Justice face to face, than her tremors
abated, and all her powers awoke, and
she thrilled with love of life, and bris-
tled with all those fine arts of defence
that Nature lends to superior women.

She entered on that defence before
she spoke a word ; for she attacked the
prejudices of the court, by deportment.

She courtesied reverently to the
Judge, and contrived to make her reverence seem a willing homage, unmixed
with fear.

She cast her eyes round and saw the
court thronged with ladies and gentlemen she knew. In a moment she read
in their eyes that only two or three
were on her side. She bowed to
those only ; and they returned her

courtesy. This gave an impression (a false one) that the gentry sympathised with her.

After a little murmur of functionaries, the Clerk of Arraigns turned to the prisoner, and said, in a loud voice, "Catharine Gaunt, hold up thy hand."

She held up her hand, and he recited the indictment, which charged that, not having the fear of God before her eyes, but being moved by the instigation of the Devil, she had on the fifteenth of October, in the tenth year of the reign of his present Majesty, aided and abetted one Thomas Leicester in an assault upon one Griffith Gaunt, Esq., and him, the said Griffith Gaunt, did with force and arms assassinate and do to death, against the peace of our said Lord the King, his crown and dignity.

After reading the indictment, the Clerk of Arraigns turned to the prisoner: "How sayest thou, Catharine Gaunt; art thou guilty of the felony and murder whereof thou standest indicted, — or not guilty?"

"I am not guilty."

"Culprit, how wilt thou be tried?"

"Culprit I am none, but only accused. I will be tried by God and my country."

"God send thee a good deliverance."

Mr. Whitworth, the junior counsel for the crown, then rose to open the case; but the prisoner, with a pale face, but most courteous demeanor, begged his leave to make a previous motion to the court. . Mr. Whitworth bowed, and sat down. "My Lord," said she, "I have first a favor to ask; and that favor, methinks, you will grant, since it is but justice, impartial justice. My accuser, I hear, has two counsel; both learned and able. I am but a woman, and no match for their skill. Therefore I beg your Lordship to allow me counsel on my defence, to matter of fact as well as of law. I know this is not usual; but it is just, and I am informed it has sometimes been granted in trials of life and death, and that your Lordship hath the *power*, if you have the *will*, to do me so much justice."

The Judge looked towards Mr. Serjeant Wiltshire, who was the leader on the other side. He rose instantly and replied to this purpose: "The prisoner is misinformed. The truth is, that from time immemorial, and down to the other day, a person indicted for a capital offence was never allowed counsel at all, except to matters of law, and these must be started by himself. By recent practice the rule hath been so far relaxed that counsel have sometimes been permitted to examine and cross-examine witnesses for a prisoner; but never to make observations on the evidence, nor to draw inferences from it to the point in issue."

Mrs. Gaunt. So, then, if I be sued for a small sum of money, I may have skilled orators to defend me against their like. But if I be sued for my life and honor, I may not oppose skill to skill, but must stand here a child against you that are masters. 'T is a monstrous iniquity, and you yourself, sir, will not deny it.

Serjeant Wiltshire. Madam, permit me. Whether it be a hardship to deny full counsel to prisoners in criminal cases, I shall not pretend to say; but if it be, 't is a hardship of the law's making, and not of mine nor of my lord's; and none have suffered by it (at least in our day) but those who had broken the law.

The Serjeant then stopped a minute, and whispered with his junior. After which he turned to the Judge. "My Lord, we that are of counsel for the crown desire to do nothing that is hard where a person's life is at stake. We yield to the prisoner any indulgence for which your Lordship can find a precedent in your reading; but no more: and so we leave the matter to you."

The Clerk of Arraigns. Crier, proclaim silence.

The Crier. Oyez! Oyez! Oyez! His Majesty's Justices do strictly charge all manner of persons to keep silence, on pain of imprisonment.

The Judge. Prisoner, what my Brother Wiltshire says, the law is clear in. There is no precedent for what you ask, and the contrary practice stares us in the face for centuries. What seems to you a partial practice, and, to be frank, some learned persons are of your mind, must be set against this, — that in capital cases the burden of proof lies on the crown, and not on the accused. Also it is my duty to give you all the assistance I can, and that I shall do. Thus then it is : you can be allowed counsel to examine your own witnesses, and cross-examine the witnesses for the crown, and speak to points of law, to be started by yourself, — but no further.

He then asked her what gentleman there present he should assign to her for counsel.

Her reply to this inquiry took the whole court by surprise, and made her solicitor, Houseman, very miserable. " None, my Lord," said she. " Half-justice is injustice ; and I will lend it no color. I will not set able men to fight for me with their hands tied, against men as able whose hands be free. Counsel, on terms so partial, I will have none. My counsel shall be three, and no more, — Yourself, my Lord, my Innocence, and the Lord God Omniscient."

These words, grandly uttered, caused a dead silence in the court, but only for a few moments. It was broken by the loud mechanical voice of the crier, who proclaimed silence, and then called the names of the jury that were to try this cause.

Mrs. Gaunt listened keenly to the names, — familiar and bourgeois names, that now seemed regal ; for they who owned them held her life in their hands.

Each juryman was sworn in the grand old form, now slightly curtailed.

" Joseph King, look upon the prisoner. — You shall well and truly try, and true deliverance make, between our Sovereign Lord the King and the prisoner at the bar, whom you shall have in charge, and a true verdict give, according to the evidence. So help you God."

Mr. Whitworth, for the crown, then opened the case, but did little more than translate the indictment into more rational language.

He sat down, and Serjeant Wiltshire addressed the court somewhat after this fashion : —

" May it please your Lordship, and you, gentlemen of the jury, this is a case of great expectation and importance. The prisoner at the bar, a gentlewoman by birth and education, and, as you must have already perceived, by breeding also, stands indicted for no less a crime than murder.

" I need not paint to you the heinousness of this crime : you have but to consult your own breasts. Who ever saw the ghastly corpse of the victim weltering in its blood, and did not feel his own blood run cold through his veins ? Has the murderer fled ? With what eagerness do we pursue ! with what zeal apprehend ! with what joy do we bring him to justice ! Even the dreadful sentence of death does not shock us, when pronounced upon him. We hear it with solemn satisfaction ; and acknowledge the justice of the Divine sentence, ' Whoso sheddeth man's blood, by man shall his blood be shed.'

" But if this be the case in every common murder, what shall be thought of her who has murdered her husband, — the man in whose arms she has lain, and whom she has sworn at God's altar to love and cherish ? Such a murderer is a robber as well as an assassin ; for she robs her own children of their father, that tender parent, who can never be replaced in this world.

" Gentlemen, it will, I fear, be proved that the prisoner at the bar hath been guilty of murder in this high degree ; and, though I will endeavor rather to extenuate than to aggravate, yet I trust [*sic*] I have such a history to open as will shock the ears of all who hear me.

" Mr. Griffith Gaunt, the unfortunate deceased, was a man of descent and worship. As to his character, it was inoffensive. He was known as a worthy, kindly gentleman, deeply attached to her who now stands accused of his murder. They lived happily together for some years; but, unfortunately, there was a thorn in the rose of their wedded life: he was of the Church of England; she was, and is, a Roman Catholic. This led to disputes; and no wonder, since this same unhappy difference hath more than once embroiled a nation, let alone a single family.

"Well, gentlemen, about a year ago there was a more violent quarrel than usual between the deceased and the prisoner at the bar; and the deceased left his home for several months.

"He returned upon a certain day in this year, and a reconciliation, real or apparent, took place. He left home again soon afterwards, but only for a short period. On the 15th of last October he suddenly returned for good, as he intended; and here begins the tragedy, to which what I have hitherto related was but the prologue.

"Scarce an hour before he came, one Thomas Leicester entered the house. Now this Thomas Leicester was a creature of the prisoner's. He had been her gamekeeper, and was now a pedler. It was the prisoner who set him up as a pedler, and purchased the wares to start him in his trade.

"Gentlemen, this pedler, as I shall prove, was concealed in the house when the deceased arrived. One Caroline Ryder, who is the prisoner's gentlewoman, was the person who first informed her of Leicester's arrival, and it seems she was much moved: Mrs. Ryder will tell you she fell into hysterics. But, soon after, her husband's arrival was announced, and then the passion was of a very different kind. So violent was her rage against this unhappy man that, for once, she forgot all prudence, and threatened his life before a witness. Yes, gentlemen, we shall prove that this gentlewoman, who in appearance and manners might grace a court, was so transported out of her usual self that she held up a knife, — a knife, gentlemen, — and vowed to put it into her husband's heart. And this was no mere temporary ebullition of wrath. We

shall see presently that, long after she had had time to cool, she repeated this menace to the unfortunate man's face. The first threat, however, was uttered in her own bedroom, before her confidential servant, Caroline Ryder aforesaid. But now the scene shifts. She has, to all appearance, recovered herself, and sits smiling at the head of her table; for, you must know, she entertained company that night, — persons of the highest standing in the county.

"Presently her husband, all unconscious of the terrible sentiments she entertained towards him, and the fearful purpose she had announced, enters the room, makes obeisance to his guests, and goes to take his wife's hand.

"What does she? She draws back with so strange a look, and such forbidding words, that the company were disconcerted. Consternation fell on all present; and erelong they made their excuses, and left the house. Thus the prisoner was left alone with her husband; but, meantime, curiosity had been excited by her strange conduct, and some of the servants, with foreboding hearts, listened at the door of the dining-room. What did they hear, gentlemen? A furious quarrel, in which, however, the deceased was comparatively passive, and the prisoner again threatened his life, with vehemence. Her passion, it is clear, had not cooled.

"Now it may fairly be alleged, on behalf of the prisoner, that the witnesses for the crown were on one side of the door, the prisoner and the deceased on the other, and that such evidence should be received with caution. I grant this — where it is not sustained by other circumstances, or by direct proofs. Let us then give the prisoner the benefit of this doubt, and let us inquire how the deceased himself understood her, — he, who not only heard the words, and the accents, but saw the looks, whatever they were, that accompanied them.

"Gentlemen, he was a man of known courage and resolution; yet he was found, after this terrible interview, much cowed and dejected. He spoke to Mrs. Ryder of his death as an event not far distant, and so went to his bedroom in a melancholy and foreboding state. And where was that bedroom? He was thrust, by his wife's orders, into a small chamber, and not allowed to enter hers, — he, the master of the house, her husband, and her lord.

"But his interpretation of the prisoner's words did not end there. He left us a further comment by his actions next ensuing. He dared not — (I beg pardon, this is my inference: receive it as such) — he *did* not, remain in that house a single night. He at all events bolted his chamber door inside; and in the very dead of night, notwithstanding the fatigues of the day's journey, (for he had ridden some distance,) he let himself out by the window, and reached the ground safely, though it was a height of fourteen feet, — a leap, gentlemen, that few of us would venture to take. But what will not men risk when destruction is at their heels? He did not wait even to saddle his horse, but fled on foot. Unhappy man, he fled from danger, and met his death.

"From the hour when he went up to bed, none of the inmates of the house ever saw Griffith Gaunt alive; but one Thomas Hayes, a laborer, saw him walking in a certain direction at one o'clock that morning; and behind him, gentlemen, there walked another man.

"Who was that other man?

"When I have told you (and this is an essential feature of the case) how the prisoner was employed during the time that her husband lay quaking in his little room, waiting an opportunity to escape, — when I have told you this, I fear you will divine who it was that followed the deceased, and for what purpose.

"Gentlemen, when the prisoner had threatened her husband in person, as I have described, she retired to her own room, but not to sleep. She ordered her maid, Mrs. Ryder, to bring Thomas Leicester to her chamber. Yes, gentlemen, she received this pedler, at midnight, in her bedchamber.

"Now, an act so strange as this admits, I think, but of two interpretations. Either she had a guilty amour with this fellow, or she had some extraordinary need of his services. Her whole character, by consent of the witnesses, renders it very improbable that she would descend to a low amour. Moreover, she acted too publicly in the matter. The man, as we know, was her tool, her creature: she had bought his wares for him, and set him up as a pedler. She openly summoned him to her presence, and kept him there about half an hour.

"He went from her, and very soon after is seen, by Thomas Hayes, following Griffith Gaunt, at one o'clock in the morning, — that Griffith Gaunt who after that hour was never seen alive.

"Gentlemen, up to this point, the evidence is clear, connected, and cogent; but it rarely happens in cases of murder that any human eye sees the very blow struck. The penalty is too severe for such an act to be done in the presence of an eyewitness; and not one murderer in ten could be convicted without the help of circumstantial evidence.

"The next link, however, is taken up by an ear-witness; and, in some cases, the ear is even better evidence than the eye, — for instance, as to the discharge of firearms, — for, by the eye alone, we could not positively tell whether a pistol had gone off or had but flashed in the pan. Well, then, gentlemen, a few minutes after Mr. Gaunt was last seen alive, — which was by Thomas Hayes, — Mrs. Ryder, who had retired to her bedroom, heard the said Gaunt distinctly cry for help; she also heard a pistol-shot discharged. This took place by the side of a lake or large pond near the house, called the mere. Mrs. Ryder alarmed the house, and she and the other servants proceeded to her master's room. They found it bolted from the inside. They broke it open. Mr. Gaunt had escaped by the window, as I have already told you.

"Presently in comes the prisoner from out of doors. This was at one o'clock in the morning. Now she appears to have seen at once that she must explain her being abroad at that time, so she told Mrs. Ryder she had been out — praying."

(Here some people laughed harshly, but were threatened severely, and silenced.)

"Is that credible? Do people go out of doors at one o'clock in the morning, to pray? Nay, but I fear it was to do an act that years of prayer and penitence cannot efface.

"From that moment Mr. Gaunt was seen no more among living men. And what made his disappearance the more mysterious was that he had actually at this time just inherited largely from his namesake, Mr. Gaunt of Biggleswade; and his own interest, and that of the other legatees, required his immediate presence. Mr. Atkins, the testator's solicitor, advertised for this unfortunate gentleman; but he did not appear to claim his fortune. Then plain men began to put this and that together, and cried out, 'Foul play!'

"Justice was set in motion at last, but was embarrassed by the circumstance that the body of the deceased could not be found.

"At last, Mr. Atkins, the solicitor, being unable to get the estate I have mentioned administered, for want of proof of Griffith Gaunt's decease, entered heartily in this affair, on mere civil grounds. He asked the prisoner, before several witnesses, if she would permit him to drag that piece of water by the side of which Mr. Gaunt was heard to cry for help and, after that seen no more.

"The prisoner did not reply, but Mr. Houseman, her solicitor, a very worthy man, who has, I believe, or had, up to that moment, a sincere conviction of her innocence, answered for her, and told Mr. Atkins he was welcome to drag it or drain it. Then the prisoner said nothing. She fainted away.

"After this, you may imagine with what expectation the water was dragged.

Gentlemen, after hours of fruitless labor, a body was found.

"But here an unforeseen circumstance befriended the prisoner. It seems that piece of water swarms with enormous pike and other ravenous fish. These had so horribly mutilated the deceased, that neither form nor feature remained to swear by; and, as the law wisely and humanely demands that in these cases a body shall be identified beyond doubt, justice bade fair to be baffled again. But lo! as often happens in cases of murder, Providence interposed and pointed with unerring finger to a slight, but infallible mark. The deceased gentleman was known to have a large mole over his left temple. It had been noticed by his servants and his neighbors. Well, gentlemen, the greedy fish had spared this mole, — spared it, perhaps, by His command, who bade the whale swallow Jonah, yet not destroy him. There it was, clear and infallible. It was examined by several witnesses, it was recognized. It completed that chain of evidence, some of it direct, some of it circumstantial, which I have laid before you very briefly, and every part of which I shall now support by credible witnesses."

He called thirteen witnesses, including Mr. Atkins, Thomas Hayes, Jane Banister, Caroline Ryder, and others; and their evidence in chief bore out every positive statement the counsel had made.

In cross-examining these witnesses, Mrs. Gaunt took a line that agreeably surprised the court. It was not for nothing she had studied a hundred trials, with a woman's observation and patient docility. She had found out how badly people plead their own causes, and had noticed the reasons: one of which is that they say too much, and stray from the point. The line she took, with one exception, was keen brevity.

She cross-examined Thomas Hayes as follows.

THE CHIMNEY–CORNER FOR 1866.

IX.

HOW SHALL WE BE AMUSED?

"ONE, two, three, four, — this makes the fifth accident on the Fourth of July, in the two papers I have just read," said Jenny.

"A very moderate allowance," said Theophilus Thoro, "if you consider the Fourth as a great national saturnalia, in which every boy in the land has the privilege of doing whatever is right in his own eyes."

"The poor boys!" said Mrs. Crowfield. "All the troubles of the world are laid at their door."

"Well," said Jenny, "they did burn the city of Portland, it appears. The fire arose from fire-crackers, thrown by boys among the shavings of a carpenter's shop, — so says the paper."

"And," said Rudolph, "we surgeons expect a harvest of business from the Fourth, as surely as from a battle. Certain to be woundings, fractures, possibly amputations, following the proceedings of our glorious festival."

"Why cannot we Americans learn to amuse ourselves peaceably, like other nations?" said Bob Stephens. "In France and Italy, the greatest national festivals pass off without fatal accident, or danger to any one. The fact is, in our country we have not learned *how to be amused.* Amusement has been made of so small account in our philosophy of life, that we are raw and unpractised in being amused. Our diversions, compared with those of the politer nations of Europe, are coarse and savage, — and consist mainly in making disagreeable noises and disturbing the peace of the community by rude uproar. The only idea an American boy associates with the Fourth of July is that of gunpowder in some form, and a wild liberty to fire off pistols in all miscellaneous directions, and to throw fire-crack-

ers under the heels of horses, and into crowds of women and children, for the fun of seeing the stir and commotion thus produced. Now take a young Parisian boy and give him a fête, and he conducts himself with greater gentleness and good breeding, because he is part of a community in which the art of amusement has been refined and perfected, so that he has a thousand resources beyond the very obvious one of making a great banging and disturbance.

"Yes," continued Bob Stephens, "the fact is, that our grim old Puritan fathers set their feet down resolutely on all forms of amusement; they would have stopped the lambs from wagging their tails, and shot the birds for singing, if they could have had their way; and in consequence of it, what a barren, cold, flowerless life is our New England existence! Life is all, as Mantalini said, one 'demd horrid grind.' 'Nothing here but working and going to church,' said the German emigrants, — and they were about right. A French traveller, in the year 1837, says that attending the Thursday-evening lectures and church prayer-meetings was the only recreation of the young people of Boston; and we can remember the time when this really was no exaggeration. Think of that, with all the seriousness of our Boston east winds to give it force, and fancy the provision for amusement in our society! The consequence is, that boys who have the longing for amusement strongest within them, and plenty of combativeness to back it, are the standing terror of good society, and our Fourth of July is a day of fear to all invalids and persons of delicate nervous organization, and of real, appreciable danger of life and limb to every one."

"Well, Robert," said my wife, "though I agree with you as to the actual state of society in this respect, I must enter my protest against your slur on the memory of our Pilgrim fathers."

"Yes," said Theophilus Thoro, "the New-Englanders are the only people, I believe, who take delight in vilifying their ancestry. Every young hopeful in our day makes a target of his grandfather's gravestone, and fires away, with great self-applause. People in general seem to like to show that they are well-born, and come of good stock; but the young New-Englanders, many of them, appear to take pleasure in insisting that they came of a race of narrow-minded, persecuting bigots.

"It is true, that our Puritan fathers saw not everything. They made a state where there were no amusements, but where people could go to bed and leave their house doors wide open all night, without a shadow of fear or danger, as was for years the custom in all our country villages. The fact is, that the simple early New England life, before we began to import foreigners, realized a state of society in whose possibility Europe would scarcely believe. If our fathers had few amusements, they needed few. Life was too really and solidly comfortable and happy to need much amusement.

"Look over the countries where people are most sedulously amused by their rulers and governors. Are they not the countries where the people are most oppressed, most unhappy in their circumstances, and therefore in greatest need of amusement? It is the slave who dances and sings, and why? Because he owns nothing, and *can* own nothing, and may as well dance and forget the fact. But give the slave a farm of his own, a wife of his own, and children of his own, with a schoolhouse and a vote, and ten to one he dances no more. He needs no *amusement*, because he is *happy*.

"The legislators of Europe wished nothing more than to bring up a people who would be content with amusements, and not ask after their rights or think too closely how they were governed. 'Gild the dome of the Invalides,' was Napoleon's scornful prescription, when he heard the Parisian population were discontented. They gilded it, and the people forgot to talk about anything else. They were a childish race, educated from the cradle on spectacle and show, and by the sight of their eyes could they be governed. The people of Boston, in 1776, could not have been managed in this way, chiefly because they were brought up in the strict schools of the fathers."

"But don't you think," said Jenny, "that something might be added and amended in the state of society our fathers established here in New England? Without becoming frivolous, there might be more attention paid to rational amusement."

"Certainly," said my wife, "the State and the Church both might take a lesson from the providence of foreign governments, and make liberty, to say the least, as attractive as despotism. It is a very unwise mother that does not provide her children with playthings."

"And yet," said Bob, "the only thing that the Church has yet done is to forbid and to frown. We have abundance of tracts against dancing, whist-playing, ninepins, billiards, operas, theatres, — in short, anything that young people would be apt to like. The General Assembly of the Presbyterian Church refused to testify against slavery, because of political diffidence, but made up for it by ordering a more stringent crusade against dancing. The theatre and opera grow up and exist among us like plants on the windy side of a hill, blown all awry by a constant blast of conscientious rebuke. There is really no amusement young people are fond of, which they do not pursue, in a sort of defiance of the frown of the peculiarly religious world. With all the telling of what the young shall *not* do, there has been very little telling what they shall do.

"The whole department of amusements — certainly one of the most important in education — has been by the Church made a sort of outlaws' ground, to be taken possession of and held by all sorts of spiritual ragamuffins ; and then the faults and short-comings resulting from this arrangement have been held up and insisted on as reasons why no Christian should ever venture into it.

"If the Church would set herself to amuse her young folks, instead of discussing doctrines and metaphysical hair-splitting, she would prove herself a true mother, and not a hard-visaged step-dame. Let her keep this department, so powerful and so difficult to manage, in what are morally the strongest hands, instead of giving it up to the weakest.

"I think, if the different churches of a city, for example, would rent a building where there should be a billiard-table, one or two ninepin-alleys, a reading-room, a garden and grounds for ball-playing or innocent lounging, that they would do more to keep their young people from the ways of sin than a Sunday school could. Nay, more : I would go further. I would have a portion of the building fitted up with scenery and a stage, for the getting up of tableaux or dramatic performances, and thus give scope for the exercise of that histrionic talent of which there is so much lying unemployed in society.

"Young people do not like amusements any better for the wickedness connected with them. The spectacle of a sweet little child singing hymns, and repeating prayers, of a pious old Uncle Tom dying for his religion, has filled theatres night after night, and proved that there really is no need of indecent or improper plays to draw full houses.

"The things that draw young people to places of amusement are not at first gross things. Take the most notorious public place in Paris, — the Jardin Mabillé, for instance, — and the things which give it its first charm are all innocent and artistic. Exquisite beds of lilies, roses, gillyflowers, lighted with jets of gas so artfully as to make every flower translucent as a gem ; fountains where the gas-light streams out from behind misty wreaths of falling water and calla-blossoms ; sofas of velvet turf, canopied with fragrant honeysuckle ; dim bowers overarched with lilacs and roses ; a dancing ground under trees whose branches bend with a fruitage of many-colored lamps ; enchanting music and graceful motion ; in all these there is not only no sin, but they are really beautiful and desirable ; and if they were only used on the side and in the service of virtue and religion, if they were contrived and kept up by the guardians and instructors of youth, instead of by those whose interest it is to demoralize and destroy, young people would have no temptation to stray into the haunts of vice.

"In Prussia, under the reign of Frederick William II., when one good, hard-handed man governed the whole country like a strict schoolmaster, the public amusements for the people were made such as to present a model for all states. The theatres were strictly supervised, and actors obliged to conform to the rules of decorum and morality. The plays and performances were under the immediate supervision of men of grave morals, who allowed nothing corrupting to appear ; and the effect of this administration and restraint is to be seen in Berlin even to this day. The public gardens are full of charming little resorts, where, every afternoon, for a very moderate sum, one can have either a concert of good music, or a very fair dramatic or operatic performance. Here whole families may be seen enjoying together a wholesome and refreshing entertainment, — the mother and aunts with their knitting, the baby, the children of all ages, and the father, — their faces radiant with that mild German light of contentment and good-will which one feels to be characteristic of the nation. When I saw these things, and thought of our own outcast, unprovided boys and young men, haunting the streets and alleys of cities, in places far from the companionship of mothers and sisters, I felt as if it would be better for a nation to be brought up by a good strict schoolmaster king than to try to be a republic."

"Yes," said I, "but the difficulty is to *get* the good schoolmaster king. For one good shepherd, there are twenty who use the sheep only for their flesh and their wool. Republics can do all that kings can, — witness our late army and Sanitary Commission. Once fix the idea thoroughly in the public mind that there ought to be as regular and careful provision for public amusement as there is for going to church and Sunday school, and it will be done. Central Park in New York is a beginning in the right direction, and Brooklyn is following the example of her sister city. There is, moreover, an indication of the proper spirit in the increased efforts that are made to beautify Sunday-school rooms, and make them interesting, and to have Sunday-school fêtes and picnics, — the most harmless and commendable way of celebrating the Fourth of July. Why should saloons and bar-rooms be made attractive by fine paintings, choice music, flowers, and fountains, and Sunday-school rooms be four bare walls? There are churches whose broad aisles represent ten and twenty millions of dollars, and whose sons and daughters are daily drawn to circuses, operas, theatres, because they have tastes and feelings, in themselves perfectly laudable and innocent, for the gratification of which no provision is made in any other place."

"I know one church," said Rudolph, "whose Sunday-school room is as beautifully adorned as any haunt of sin. There is a fountain in the centre, which plays into a basin surrounded with shells and flowers; it has a small organ to lead the children's voices, and the walls are hung with oil-paintings and engravings from the best masters. The festivals of the Sabbath school, which are from time to time held in this place, educate the taste of

the children, as well as amuse them; and, above all, they have through life the advantage of associating with their early religious education all those ideas of taste, elegance, and artistic culture which too often come through polluted channels.

"When the *amusement* of the young shall become the care of the experienced and the wise, and the floods of wealth that are now rolling over and over, in silent investments, shall be put into the form of innocent and refined pleasures for the children and youth of the state, our national festivals may become days to be desired, and not dreaded.

"On the Fourth of July, our city fathers do in a certain dim wise perceive that the public owes some attempt at amusement to its children, and they vote large sums, principally expended in bell-ringing, cannons, and fireworks. The sidewalks are witness to the number who fall victims to the temptations held out by grog-shops and saloons; and the papers, for weeks after, are crowded with accounts of accidents. Now, a yearly sum expended to keep up, and keep pure, places of amusement which hold out no temptation to vice, but which excel all vicious places in real beauty and attractiveness, would greatly lessen the sum needed to be expended on any one particular day, and would refine and prepare our people to keep holidays and festivals appropriately."

"For my part," said Mrs. Crowfield, "I am grieved at the opprobrium which falls on the race of *boys*. Why should the most critical era in the life of those who are to be men, and to *govern* society, be passed in a sort of outlawry, — a rude warfare with all existing institutions? The years between ten and twenty are full of the nervous excitability which marks the growth and maturing of the manly nature. The boy feels wild impulses, which ought to be vented in legitimate and healthful exercise. He wants to run, shout, wrestle, ride, row, skate; and all these together are often not sufficient to relieve the need he feels of throwing off the excitability that burns within.

"For the wants of this period what safe provision is made by the Church, or by the State, or any of the boy's lawful educators? In all the Prussian schools amusements are as much a part of the regular school-system as grammar or geography. The teacher is with the boys on the play-ground, and plays as heartily as any of them. The boy has his physical wants anticipated. He is not left to fight his way, blindly stumbling, against society, but goes forward in a safe path, which his elders and betters have marked out for him.

"In our country, the boy's career is often a series of skirmishes with society. He wants to skate, and contrives ingeniously to dam the course of a brook, and flood a meadow which makes a splendid skating-ground. Great is the joy for a season, and great the skating. But the water floods the neighboring cellars. The boys are cursed through all the moods and tenses,— boys are such a plague! The dam is torn down with emphasis and execration. The boys, however, lie in wait some cold night, between twelve and one, and build it up again; and thus goes on the battle. The boys care not whose cellar they flood, because nobody cares for their amusement. They understand themselves to be outlaws, and take an outlaw's advantage.

"Again, the boys have their sleds; and sliding down hill is splendid fun. But they trip up some grave citizen, who sprains his shoulder. What is the result? Not the provision of a safe, good place, where boys *may* slide down hill without danger to any one, but an edict forbidding all sliding, under penalty of fine.

"Boys want to swim: it is best they should swim; and if city fathers, foreseeing and caring for this want, should think it worth while to mark off some good place, and have it under such police surveillance as to enforce decency of language and demeanor, they would prevent a great deal that now is

disagreeable in the unguided efforts of boys to enjoy this luxury.

"It would be *cheaper* in the end, even if one had to build sliding-piles, as they do in Russia, or to build skating-rinks, as they do in Montreal,—it would be cheaper for every city, town, and village to provide legitimate amusement for boys, under proper superintendence, than to leave them, as they are now left, to fight their way against society.

"In the boys' academies of our country, what provision is made for amusement? There are stringent rules, and any number of them, to prevent boys making any noise that may disturb the neighbors; and generally the teacher thinks that, if he keeps the boys *still*, and sees that they get their lessons, his duty is done. But a hundred boys ought not to be kept still. There ought to be noise and motion among them, in order that they may healthily survive the great changes which Nature is working within them. If they become silent, averse to movement, fond of indoor lounging and warm rooms, they are going in far worse ways than any amount of outward lawlessness could bring them to.

"Smoking and yellow-covered novels are worse than any amount of hullabaloo; and the quietest boy is often a poor, ignorant victim, whose life is being drained out of him before it is well begun. If mothers could only see the *series of books* that are sold behind counters to boarding-school boys, whom nobody warns and nobody cares for,— if they could see the poison, going from pillow to pillow, in books pretending to make clear the great, sacred mystéries of our nature, but trailing them over with the filth of utter corruption! These horrible works are the inward and secret channel of hell, into which a boy is thrust by the pressure of strict outward rules, forbidding that physical and out-of-door exercise and motion to which he ought rather to be encouraged, and even driven.

"It is melancholy to see that, while parents, teachers, and churches make no provision for boys in the way of amusement, the world, the flesh, and the Devil are incessantly busy and active in giving it. to them. There are ninepin-alleys, with cigars and a bar. There are billiard-saloons, with a bar, and, alas ! with the occasional company of girls who are still beautiful, but who have lost the innocence of womanhood, while yet retaining many of its charms. There are theatres, with a bar, and with the society of lost women. The boy comes to one and all of these places, seeking only what is natural and proper he should have, — what should be. given him under the eye and by the care of the Church, the school. He comes for exercise and amusement, — he gets these, and a ticket to destruction besides, — and whose fault is it ? "

"These are the aspects of public life," said I, "which make me feel that we never shall have a perfect state till women vote and bear rule equally with men. State housekeeping has been, hitherto, like what any housekeeping would be, conducted by the voice and knowledge of man alone.

"If women had an equal voice in the management of our public money, I have faith to believe that thousands which are now wasted in mere political charlatanism would go to provide for the rearing of the children of the state, male and female. My wife has spoken for the boys ; I speak for the girls also. What is provided for their physical development and amusement ? Hot, gas-lighted theatric and operatic performances, beginning at eight, and ending at midnight ; hot, crowded parties and balls ; dancing with dresses tightly laced over the laboring lungs, — these are almost the whole story. I bless the advent of croquet and skating. And yet the latter exercise, pursued as it generally is, is a most terrible exposure. There is no kindly parental provision for the poor, thoughtless, delicate young creature, — not even the shelter of a dressing-room with a fire, at which she may warm her numb fingers

and put on her skates when she arrives on the ground, and to which she may retreat in intervals of fatigue ; so she catches cold, and perhaps sows the seed which with air-tight stoves and other appliances of hot-house culture may ripen into consumption.

"What provision is there for the amusement of all the shop girls, seamstresses, factory girls, that crowd our cities ? What for the thousands of young clerks and operatives ? Not long since, in a respectable old town in New England, the body of a beautiful girl was drawn from the river in which she had drowned herself, — a young girl only fifteen, who came to the city, far from home and parents, and fell a victim to the temptation which brought her to shame and desperation. Many thus fall every year who are never counted. They fall into the ranks of those whom the world abandons as irreclaimable.

"Let those who have homes and every appliance to make life pass agreeably, and who yet yawn over an unoccupied evening, fancy a lively young girl all day cooped up at sewing in a close, ill-ventilated room. Evening comes, and she has three times the desire for amusement and three times the need of it that her fashionable sister has. And where can she go ? To the theatre, perhaps, with some young man as thoughtless as herself, and more depraved ; then to the bar for a glass of wine, and another ; and then, with a head swimming and turning, who shall say where else she may be led ? Past midnight and no one to look after her, — and one night ruins her utterly and for life, and she as yet only a child !

"John Newton had a very wise saying : ' Here is a man trying to fill a busbel with chaff. Now if I fill it with wheat first, it is better than to fight him.' This apothegm contains in it the whole of what I would say on the subject of amusements."

AN ITALIAN RAIN—STORM.

THE coast-road between Nice and Genoa,—known throughout the world for its unrivalled beauty of scenery, the altitudes to which it climbs, and the depths to which it dives,—now on the olive-clad heights, now close down upon the shore shaded by palm or carob-trees, now stretching inland amid orange-grounds and vineyards, now rounding some precipitous point that hangs hundreds of feet over the Mediterranean,—is generally seen with all the advantage of an unclouded sky above, and a sea as blue beneath.

It was the fortune of a certain party of four to behold it under the unusual aspect of bad weather. They set out in the diligence one winter evening, expecting to arrive at Genoa by the same time next day, according to ordinary course. But no one unaccustomed to the effect of rain, continuous rain, in mountainous districts, can conceive the wonders worked by a long succession of wet days. The arrival was retarded six hours, and the four found themselves in *Genova la superba* somewhere about midnight. However, this was only the commencement of the pouring visitation; and the roads had been rendered merely so "heavy" as to make the horses contumacious when dragging the ponderous vehicle up hill, which contumacy had occasioned the delay in question. Despite the hopes entertained that the weather would clear, the rain set in; and during no interval did it hold up, with the exception of a short period, which permitted one gentleman of the party of four to visit on business two bachelor brothers, manufacturers in Genoa. The residence of these brothers being in rather an out-of-the-way quarter of the city, and being very peculiar in itself, the gentleman advised the rest of his party to accompany him on this visit.

The four, only too glad to find themselves able to get out of doors, set forth on foot through the steep and narrow streets of Genoa, which make driving in a carriage a fatigue, and walking a feat of great excitement, especially when mud prevails. Trucks, ponderously laden with bales of goods, and pushed along at a reckless rate of speed by mahogany-complexioned men; dashing coaches, impelled by drivers hallooing when close upon you with distracting loudness and abruptness; mules coming onward with the blundering obtuseness peculiar to their tribe, or with their heads fastened to doorways, and their flanks extending across the street, affording just space enough for the passenger to slide behind their heels; a busy, jostling crowd of people hurrying to and fro, with no definite current, but streaming over any portion of the undistinguishable carriage-way and foot-way,—all combine to make Genoese pedestrianism a work only less onerous than driving.

Choosing the minor trouble, our party trusted to their own legs; and, after picking their way through sludge and mire, along murky alleys that branched off into wharves and quays, and up slippery by-ways that looked like paved staircases without regular steps, the four emerged upon an open space in front of a noble church. Leaving this on their left hand, they turned short into a place that wore something the appearance of a stable-yard,—with this difference, that there were neither steeds nor stabling to be seen; but instead there were blank walls, enclosing a kind of court adjoining a huge old mansion, and beyond there was a steep descent leading down to the sea-side.

On ringing a bell that hung beside a gate in the wall enclosure, the door opened apparently of itself, and a dismal scream ensued. The scream proceeded from a sea-gull, peering out of a kind of pen formed by a wooden paling in one corner of a grass-grown patch, half cabbage-garden, half excavated earth and rock; and the mysterious opening of the door was explained by a connecting cord pulled by some unseen hand within a smaller house that stood near to the huge old mansion. From the house appeared, advancing towards us, the two bachelor brothers, who welcomed our friend and his three companions with grave Italian courtesy. Understanding the curiosity the four felt to see their premises, they did the honors of their place, with a minuteness as politely considerate towards the strangers as it was gratifying to the interest felt by them.

First the visitors were led by the bachelor brothers to see the huge old mansion, which they called the *Palazzo*. Let no one who has seen an ordinary Genoese palace, magnificent with gilding, enriched by priceless pictures, supplied with choice books, and adorned with gorgeous furniture, figure to himself any such combination in the *palazzo* in question. This was a vast pile of building, that would make five moderate-sized dwelling-houses, one in the roof, and the other four in the habitable portion of the edifice. A general air of ramshackledness pervaded the exterior, while the interior presented an effect of interminable ranges of white-washed walls, divided off into numberless apartments of various sizes, from a saloon on the *piano nobile*, or principal floor, measuring more than forty feet long, to small square attic rooms that were little more than cupboards. But this attic story was not all composed of chambers thus dimensioned. Among its apartments were rooms that might have accommodated a banqueting assemblage, had diners been so inclined; while among the accommodations comprised in this garret range was a kitchen, with spacious dressers, stoves, closets, and a well of water some hundred and odd feet deep. It was impossible for the imagination to refrain from picturing the troops of

ghosts which doubtless occupied these upper chambers of the old *palazzo*, and held nightly vigil, undisturbed, amid the silence and solitude of their neglected spaces. Through one of the dwarf windows that pierced at intervals all sides of the mansion, just beneath the lofty roof, and which gave light to the attic story, we were directed to look by the emphatic words of the elder bachelor brother, — "Ma, veda che vista c' è!"

The view thence was indeed well worthy his praise; and he himself formed an appropriate companion-picture to the scene. Bluish-gray eyes, a fairer complexion than usually belongs to men of his clime and country, a look of penetration, combined with an expression of quiet content, were surmounted by a steeple-crowned hat that might have become a Dutch burgomaster, or one of Teniers's land-proprietors, rather than a denizen of a southern city. Yet the association which his face, figure, and costume had with some of George Cruikshank's illustrations of German tales afforded pictorial harmony with the range of ghostly rooms we were viewing. He "marshalled us the way that we should go," by leading us down a steep flight of steps, which landed us on the *piano nobile*. This, for the present, was tenanted by a set of weavers, to whom the principal floor of the *palazzo* had been let for a short term. They had proved but turbulent occupants, being in a constant state of refractoriness against their landlords, the bachelor brothers, who seemed to be somewhat in awe of them. On the present occasion, for instance, the brothers apologized for being unable to show us the grand saloon, as the weavers (whom we could hear, while he spoke, singing in a loud, uproarious, insurgent kind of way, that might well have drawn three souls out of one of their own craft, and evidently made the souls of their two landlords quail) did not like to be disturbed.

Their contumacious voices, mingled with the clamor of their looms, died off in the distance, while we proceeded down the back staircase to the ground-floor. We at first fancied that this apparently surreptitious proceeding was perhaps traceable to the awe entertained by the bachelor brothers for their unruly tenants ; but we were relieved from the sense of acting in a style bordering on poltroonery, by finding that the principal staircase had been boarded up to preserve its marble steps and sides from injury. On arriving at the foot we found ourselves in a spacious hall, opposite the approach to the grand staircase, which looked like an archway built for giants, toweringly defined above the scaffold-planks by which it was barricaded. Many doors opened from this hall, to each of which, in turn, one of the bachelor brothers applied successive keys from a ponderous bunch that he held in his hand. These doors led to vast suites of apartments, all unfurnished, like the upper rooms, with the exception of one suite, which the brothers had lent to a friend of theirs, and which was sparely supplied with some old Italian furniture, of so antique a fashion that each article might have been a family heirloom ever since the times of that famous Genoese gentleman, Christopher Columbus. One peculiarity the four remarked, which spoke volumes for the geniality of the climate : in all this huge rambling edifice they saw only one room which could boast of a fireplace. The sun's warmth evidently supplied all the heat necessary, and — as might be conjectured from its other peculiarities as well as this — anything like what the English call "the joys and comforts of the domestic hearth" seemed an impossible attainment in this dreary old *palazzo.* The social amenities must wither in its desolate atmosphere, and dwindle to chill shadows, like the ghosts that haunt the attic story.

To complete the air of saddening vacancy that clung like a damp to the really arid white walls, when the brothers led us down a wide staircase to the vaulted space beneath the basement, we came upon some hundreds of small bird-cages, containing each a miserable linnet, titmouse, or finch,

condemned to chirp out its wretched existence in this airless underground region. In reply to our pitying exclamation, we were told that the bachelors' friend who occupied the corner apartment on the ground-floor was a great sportsman, and devotedly fond of *la caccia;* that these unhappy little prisoners were employed by him in the season as decoy-birds ; that they were kept in these dungeons during the other months of the year ; and that they were BLINDED to make them sing better and be more serviceable at the period when he needed them. As we looked shudderingly at these forlorn little creatures, and expressed our commiseration at their fate, the younger brother stepped forward, and, examining one of the cages, in which sat hunched up in one corner a stiff lump of feathers, coolly announced that "this goldfinch" was dead.

It was with a feeling of relief that we left the death-released bird, and the vaults beneath the old *palazzo,* to return once more to the fresh air and the breathing-space of the broad earth and sky. Our next visit was to the bachelor brothers' factory, which was for the fabrication of wax candles. Adjoining this was a terrace-plot of ground, dotted over with what looked like Liliputian tombstones. We were beginning to wonder whether this were a cemetery for the dead birds, — speculating on the probability that these might be the monumental tributes placed over their graves by the sportsman friend of the two brothers, — when the elder informed us that this was the place they used for bleaching the wax, and that the square stones we saw were the supports on which rested the large flat stands whereon it was laid to whiten in the sun. From this terrace-plot of ground, — which projected in a narrowish green ledge, skirted by a low ivy-grown wall, over the sea, — we beheld a prospect of almost matchless beauty. Before us stretched a wide expanse of Mediterranean waters ; to the extreme left was just visible the bold rocky point of Porto Fino; to the right extended westward a grand line of picturesque coast, including the headlands of Capo di Noli and Capo delle Mele; and near at hand lay the harbor of Genoa, with its shipping, its amphitheatre of palaces, surmounted by the high ground above, and crowned by the fortressed summits beyond.

We were roused from the absorbing admiration which this majestic sea and land view had excited, by one of the four asking whether there were any access to the *palazzo* from this terrace. Whereupon the brothers showed us a winding turret staircase, which led by a subterranean passage into one of the lower vaulted rooms. Nothing more like a place in a wonderful story-book ever met us in real life; and while we were lost in a dream of romantic imaginings, one of the brothers was engaged in giving a prosaic relation of how the old *palazzo* had come into their family by a lawsuit, which terminated in their favor, and left them possessors of this unexpected property. During the narrative a brood of adolescent chickens had come near to where we stood listening on the green plot, and eyed us with expectant looks, as if accustomed to be fed or noticed. The elder brother indulged the foremost among the poultry group — a white bantam cock of courageous character — by giving him his foot to assault. Valiantly the little fellow flew at, and spurred, and pecked the boot and trousers; again and again he returned to the charge, while the blue-gray eyes beamed smilingly down from beneath the steeple-crowned hat, as the old man humored the bird's pugnacious spirit.

Presently a shy little girl of some ten or twelve years came peering out at the strangers from beneath a row of evergreen oaks that ornamented the back of the dwelling-house overlooking the terrace. There she stood at the foot of the ilexes, shading her eyes with one hand, (for the sun coyly gleamed through the rain-clouds at that moment,) while the other was employed in restraining the lumbering fondness of two large bull-dogs, that gambolled heavily round her. She was introduced to us as the daughter of the younger of the two brothers; who proved after all to be no bachelor, but a widower. One ponderous brindled brute poked his black muzzle against the child with such a weight of affection that we expected to see her overturned on the sward; but she seemed to have complete control over her canine favorites, and to live with them and a large macaw she had up stairs in her own room (we afterwards found it perched there, when taken to see the upper floor of the bachelor residence), as her familiars and sole associates, — like some enchanted princess in a fairy-tale.

On entering the house from the terrace, we found ourselves in its kitchen, which strongly resembled a cavern made habitable. It was hewn out of the rock on which the dwelling stood; and it only required the presence of the black man and the old woman who figure in Gil Blas's story to give, to the life, the cooking-department of the robbers' cave there. As we ascended a rude stone staircase that led from it, we heard the lowing of cows; and, turning, we saw two of these animals comfortably stalled in a side recess, not far from the rocky ledge on which the culinary apparatus for dressing the food of the establishment was deposited. Mounting into the parlor, we discovered a good-sized apartment, its windows looking out through the foliage of the ilexes over the sea, skirted by the extensive coast view. Behind was the dining-room; on each side were the brothers' bedrooms; and leading from a small entrance-hall at the back was a large billiard-room. This opened on a small garden nook, in which were orange-trees and camellias, full of bud and blossom, — from which some of the flowers were gathered for us by the Italian brethren, on our taking leave and thanking them for the unusual treat we had had in going over their curious abode.

The transient gleam of sunshine that

had shone forth while we were there was the only intermission vouchsafed by the rain, which afterwards poured down with a steady vehemence and pertinacity seldom seen on the Ligurian Riviera. The effects of this rare continuance of wet weather were soon made impressively perceptible to the four as they emerged upon the open road, after passing the Lighthouse of Genoa and the long straggling suburbs of San Pier d' Arena, Pegli, and Voltri. The horses splashed through channels of water which filled the spongy ruts, smoking, and toiling, and plunging on ; while the whoops and yells of the postilion urging them forward, together with the loud smacks of his whip, made a savage din. This was farther increased as we crashed along a ledge road, cut in a cliff overhanging the sea ; — the waves tearing up from beneath with a whelming roar ; the rocks jutting forth in points, every one of which was a streaming water-spout ; the rain pelting, the wind rushing, the side-currents pouring and dashing. These latter, ordinarily but small rills, carrying off the drainage of the land by gentle course, were now swollen to rough cataracts, leaping with furious rapidity from crag to crag in deluges of turbid water, discolored to a dingy yellow-brown by the heaps of earth and stone which they dislodged and brought down with them, and hurled hither and thither over the precipitous projections, and occasionally flung athwart the highway. At one spot, where a heap of such stones — large, flat slabs — had been tossed upon the road, and a few of their companions were in the very act of plunging down after them, our postilion drew up to guide his cattle among those already fallen ; and, raising his voice above the thunder of the sea-waves, rain, wind, and waters, shouted out in broad Genoese to the falling ones, "Halloo, you there, up above ! Stop a bit, will you ? Wait a moment, you up there !" Then, driving on carefully till he had steered by the largest of the fragments that lay prostrate, he turned back his head, shook his whip

at it, and apostrophised it with, "Ah, you big pig ! I 've passed you, for this time !"

The first change of horses took place at a village close down on the sea-shore, where some fishermen were busily employed hauling up the last of a row of boats that lay upon the beach. Every available hand, not occupied in aiding the conductor and postilion to unharness the diligence horses and put to the fresh team, was enlisted in the service of the boat-hauling. Young gentlemen out for an evening's amusement, attired in sacks or tarpaulins thrown over their shoulders, while their nether garments were rolled up tightly into a neat twist that encircled the top of each thigh, were frisking about a line of men with weather-beaten countenances and blown hair, who tugged bare-legged at the sides of the fishing-boat, half in the water and half out. Occasionally one of these young gentry, feeling perhaps that he had aided sufficiently in the general work, betook himself to a doorway near, dripping and shaking himself, and looking out through the sheeted rain at his companions, who were still in the excitement of whisking round the heaving and tugging fishermen, while the waves rose high, the spray dashed up in mist over their grizzled heads and beards, and the wind whistled sharply amid the deeper tumult of the sea and torrent waters. To heighten the grim wildness of the scene, the shades of evening were closing round, and by the time the four travellers were off again and proceeding on their way, darkness was fast setting in.

Nightfall found them toiling up a steep ascent that diverges inland for a few miles, winding round the estate of some inflexible proprietor, upon whom nothing can prevail to permit the high-road to take its passage through his land, there bordering the sea-side. Up the ascent we labored, and down the descent we lunged, the wheels lodging in deep mire at every moment, and threatening to abide in the deeper holes and furrows which the water-courses (forced from their due channels by overflowing and by obstructive fallen masses) had cut and dug into the road as they strayed swiftly over it.

By the time the next stage was reached, the conductor consulted the four on the advisability of stopping to sleep, instead of proceeding on such a tempestuous night, the like of which, for perilous effects, he said he had but once before encountered during the whole of the sixteen years he had been in office on this road. The three *coupé* passengers, consisting of two ladies — sisters — and a ruddy-faced, cheerful gentleman in a velvet travelling-cap, who made it a principle, like Falstaff, to take things easily, and "not to sweat extraordinarily," warmly approved the conductor's proposal as a sensible one ; and even the alert gentleman in the *banquette* agreed that it would be more prudent to remain at the first good inn the diligence came to. This, the conductor replied, was at Savona, one stage farther, as the place they now were at was a mere boat-building hamlet, that scarcely boasted an inn at all, — certainly not "good beds." A group of eager, bronzed faces were visible by lamp-light, assembled round the conductor, listening to him as he held this conference with his coach-passengers ; and at its close the bronze-faced crowd broke into a rapid outburst of Genoese dialect, which was interrupted by our conductor's making his way through them all, and disappearing round the corner of the small *piazza* wherein the diligence stood to have its horses changed. After some moments' pause, — not in the rain, or wind, or sea-waves, for they kept pouring and rushing and roaring on, — but in the hurly-burly of rapid talk, which ceased, owing to the talkers' hurrying off in pursuit of the vanished conductor, he returned, saying, "Andiamo a Savona." It soon proved that he had been to ascertain the feasibility of what the group of bronze-faced men had proposed, namely, that they would undertake to convey

the diligence (without its horses, its "outsides," and its "insides") bodily over a high, steep, slippery mule-bridge, which crossed a torrent near at hand, now swollen to an unfordable depth and swiftness. The four beheld this impassable stream, boiling and surging and sweeping on to mingle itself with the madly leaping sea-waves out there in the dim night-gloom to the left, as they descended from the diligence and prepared to go on foot across something that looked like a rudely-constructed imitation of the Rialto Bridge at Venice, seen through a haze of darkness, slanting rain, faintly-beaming coach-lamps, pushing and heaving men, panting led horses, passengers muffled up and umbrellaed, conductor leading and directing. Then came the reharnessing of the horses, the reassembling of the passengers, the remounting of the "insides," the reclambering to his seat of the alert *banquette* "outside" (after a hearty interchange of those few brief, smiling words with his *coupé* companions which, between English friends, say so much in so little utterance at periods of mutual anxiety and interest), the payment of the agreed-for sum by the conductor to the bronze-faced pushers and heavers, amid a violent renewal of the storm of Genoese jargon, terminated by an authoritative word from the payer as he swung himself up into his place by a leathern strap dangling from the coach-side, a smart crack of the postilion's whip, a forward plunge of the struggling horses, an onward jerk of the diligence, and the final procedure into the wet and dark and roar of the wild night.

The gas and stir of Savona came as welcome tokens of repose to the toilsome journey ; and the four alighted at one of the hotels there with an inexpressible sense of relief. His fellow-travellers were warned, however, by the alert gentleman, that they must hold themselves in readiness to start before dawn next morning, as the conductor wished to avail himself of the first peep of daylight in passing several torrents on the road which lay beyond Savona. Velvet-cap assented with a grunt; one of the sisters — all briskness at night, but fit for nothing of a morning — proposed not to go to bed at all; while the other — quite used up at night, but "up to everything" of a morning — undertook to call the whole party in time for departure.

This she did, — ordering coffee, seeing that some was swallowed by the sister who had been unwillingly roused from the sleep she had willingly offered to forego overnight, collecting cloaks, baskets, and travelling-rugs, and altogether looking so wakeful and ready that she wellnigh drove her drowsy sister to desperation.

The preannounced torrents proved as swollen as were expected; so that the passengers had to unpack themselves from the heaps of wrappings stowed snugly round their feet and knees, and issue forth into the keen morning air, armed with difficultly-put-up umbrellas, to traverse certain wooden foot-bridges, in the midst of which they could not help halting to watch the lightened diligence dragged splashingly through the deep and rapid streams, expecting, at every lunge it made into the water-dug gullies, to see it turn helplessly over on its side in the very midst of them. Nevertheless, no such accident occurred; and the four jogged on, along soaking, soppy, drenched roads, that seemed never to have known dust or drought. At one saturated village, they saw a dripping procession of people under crimson umbrellas, shouldering two rude coffins of deal boards, which were borne to the door of a church that stood by the wayside, — where the train waited in a kind of moist dejection to be admitted, and to look dispiritedly after the passing diligence. The alert gentleman heard from what the conductor gathered from an old woman wrapped in a many-colored gaudy-patterned scarf of chintz, which, wet through, covered her head and shoulders clingingly, that this was the funeral of a poor peasant-man and his wife, who had both died suddenly and both on the same day. The old woman held up her brown, shrivelled hands, and gesticulated pityingly with them in the pouring rain, as she mumbled her hurried tale of sorrow; while the postilion involuntarily slackened pace, that her words might be heard where he and the conductor sat.

The horses were suffered to creep on at their own snail pace, while the influence of the funeral scene lasted; but soon the long lash was plied vivaciously again, and we came to another torrent, more deep, more rapid, more swollen than any previous one. Fortunately for us, a day or two before there had been a postilion nearly drowned in attempting to drive through this impassable ford; and still more fortunately for us, this postilion chanced to have a relation who was a servant in the household of Count Cavour, then prime-minister to King Victor Emanuel. "Papa Camillo's" servant's kinsman's life being endangered, an order had come from Turin only a few hours before our diligence arrived at the bank of the dangerous stream, — now swollen into a swift, broad river, — decreeing that the new road and bridge, lately in course of construction on this spot, should be opened immediately for passage to and fro. The road was more like a stone-quarry than a carriageable public highway, so encumbered was it with granite fragments, heaped ready for top-dressing and finishing; and the bridge led on to a raised embankment, coming to a sudden fissure, where the old coach-road crossed it. Still, our conductor, finding that some few carts and one diligence had actually passed over the ground, set himself to the work of getting ours also across. First, the insides and outsides were abstracted from the coach, — which they had by this time come to regard as quite an extraneous part of their travelling, not so much a "conveyance" as something to be conveyed, — and the four took their way over the stones, amused at this new and most unexpected obstacle to their progress. Hastening across the fissure, they went and placed themselves (always under umbrellas) beside a troop of little vagabond boys, — who had come to see the fun, and had secured good front places on the opposite bank, — to view the diligence brought down the sharp declivity of the embankment to the old road below. The spectators beheld the jolting vehicle come slowly and gratingly along, like a sturdy recusant, holding back, until the straining horses had tugged it by main force to the brink of the fissure. Here the animals stopped, snorted, eyed the sheer descent with twitching ears and quivering skins, as though they said in equine language, "We 're surely not required to drag it down *this !*" They were soon relieved from their doubt, by being taken out of the traces, patted, and gently led down the embankment, leaving their burdensome charge behind. There it stuck, helplessly alone, — even more thoroughly belying its own name than diligences usually do, — perched on the edge of a declivity of the height of a tall house, stock still, top-heavy with piled luggage, deserted by its passengers, abandoned of its friend in the velvet cap, a motionless and apparently objectless coach. How it was to be dislodged and conveyed down the "vast abrupt" became matter of conjecture to the four, when presently some men came to the spot with a large coil of cable-cord, which they proceeded to pass through the two hindmost side-windows of the diligence, threading it like a bead on a string ; and then they gradually lowered the lumbering coach down the side of the descent, amid the *evvivas* of the vagabond boys, led by an enthusiastic "*Bravissimo !*" from Velvet-cap.

This incident occupied much time ; and though the travellers made some progress during the afternoon, the gray shades of twilight were gathering over and deepening the gloom of the already gray sky and gray landscape, — deadened to that color from their naturally brilliant hues by the prevailing wet, — as the travellers stopped to change horses again at the entrance of

the town of Oneglia. Here, while the conductor ran into a house to make purchase of a loaf about half a yard in length and a corpulent bottle of wine, the four saw another funeral train approaching. This time it was still more dreary, being attended by a show of processional pomp, inexpressibly forlorn and squalid. The coffin was palled with a square of rusty black velvet, whence all the pile had long been worn, and which the soaking rain now helped age to embrown and make flabby ; a standard cross was borne by an ecclesiastical official, who had on a quadrangular cap surmounted by a centre tuft ; two priests followed, sheltered by umbrellas, their sacerdotal garments dabbled and draggled with mud, and showing thick-shod feet beneath the dingy serge and lawn that flapped above them, as they came along at a smart pace, suggestive of anything but solemnity. As little of that effect was there in the burial-hymn which they bawled, rather than chanted, in a careless, off-hand style, until they reached the end of the street and of the town, when the bawlers suddenly ceased, took an abrupt leave of the coffin and its bearers, fairly turned on their heels, accompanied by the official holy standard-bearer, and went back at a brisk trot, having, it seems, fulfilled the functions required of them. Obsequies more heartless in their manner of performance, it was never the fate of the four to behold. The impression left by this sight assorted well with the deep and settled murkiness that dwelt like a thick veil on all around. Even the cheery tones of Velvet-cap's voice lost their elasticity, and the sprightliness of the sister's spirits, that invariably rose with the coming on of night, failed under the depressing influence of that rain-hastened funeral and that "set-in" rainy evening. As for the sister whose spirits fell with the fall of day, she was fast lapsing into a melancholy condition of silence and utter "giving-up."

Rattling over the pavement of the long, straggling town, — plashing along a few miles of level road, — struggling up hill, — rattling through another pavemented town, — striking into the country again, — we came to another long ascent. As we toiled to the top, a postilion, having the care of five return horses, joined company with ours, the two men walking up hill together, while their beasts paced slowly on, with drooping heads and smoking sides. Now and then, when the road was less steep, and levelled into trotting-ground, the postilions climbed to their seats, — ours on his rightful box-seat, the other on an impromptu one, which he made for himself upon a sack of corn slung beneath the front windows of the *coupé*, — and while our horses fell into an easy jog, we could see the return ones go on before at a swagging run, with their loosened harness tossing and hanging from them as they took their own course, now on one side of the way, now on the other, according to the promptings of their unreined fancy.

Suddenly, at a turn of the road, we came upon an undistinguishable something, which, when our eyes could pierce through and beyond the immediate light afforded by our diligence-lamp, we discovered to be another diligence leaning heavily over a ditch, while its conductor and postilion were at their horses' heads, endeavoring to make them extricate it from its awkward position. This, however, was a feat beyond the poor beasts' strength; and our conductor, after a few "Sacramentos" at this new delay, got down and ran to see what could be done to help them out of the scrape. It had been occasioned partly by the carelessness of the conductor, who, unlike ours, (for the latter was a man of good sense and judgment, self-possessed, and perfectly attentive to the duties of his office,) had neglected to light the diligence-lamp, and partly by the obstinacy of a drunken postilion, who insisted on keeping too close to the ditch side of the road, while he instinctively avoided the precipice side. Nearly two mortal hours was our diligence detained, during which time our cattle were taken

from their traces and harnessed to those of the half-overturned coach, in various attempts to dislodge it. The first resulted in a further locking of the wheel against a projecting point of rock, and an additional bundling sideways of the leaning diligence; the second was made by attaching the horses to the back of it, while the men set their strength to the wheels, endeavoring to push them round by main force in aid of the straining team. The weight of the heavily-loaded coach resisted their efforts to move it; and then the passengers were requested to descend. Out into the rain and mud and darkness they came, warned by our conductor, in his prompt, thoughtful way, to beware of stumbling over the precipitous cliff, which dropped straight from the roadside there, hundreds of feet down, into the sea. We could hear the dash of the waves far below, as our conductor's voice sounded out clear and peremptory, uttering the timely reminder; we could hear the words of two French *commis-voyageurs*, coming from the ditch-sunk diligence, making some facetious remark, one to the other, about their present adventure being very much like some of Alexandre Dumas's *Impressions de Voyage;* we could hear the cries and calls of the men refastening the horses, and preparing to push anew at the wheels; we could distinguish a domestic party dismounting from the back portion of the other diligence, consisting of a father and mother with their baby and the *bonne;* we could see the little white cap covered up carefully with a handkerchief by the young mother, while the father held an umbrella over their heads, and conducted them to the counterpart portion of our diligence, where the family took refuge during the fresh attempts to drag theirs forth.

Then there came a tap against our *coup'* window, and an unmistakably British accent was heard to say : "Anglais ? Anglais ?" Tap — tap — tap. "Any English here ?"

Velvet-cap let the window down, and answered in his cheerfullest tone, "Yes."

This reply seemed to rejoice the heart of the inquirer, who immediately rejoined, "Oh! — Well, I really wished to know if there were any one here who could understand me. These fellows don't comprehend · one word that I say; and I can't speak one word of their jabber. Just listen to them! What a confounded row they keep up! Parcel of stupid brutes! If I could only have made myself understood, I could have told them how to get it out in a minute. Confounded thing this, ain't it? Kept last night, too, by something of the same kind of accident; and I could n't get those stupid fellows to make out what I meant, and give me my carpet-bag."

Polite condolences from Velvet-cap.

"I say, are these your Italian skies? Is Nice no better than this? By George, I did n't come here for this, though!"

Assurances of the unusually bad weather this season from Velvet-cap.

"No, but just hark! what a confounded row and jabber those fellows keep up."

A simultaneous "Ee - ye - ho! ee - yuch - yuch!" came from the striving men at this moment, and our British acquaintance, with a hasty "Good night!" hurried off to see the result. It was this time a successful one; the leaning diligence was plucked out, restored to an upright position, and its passengers were reassembled. Once more on its way, our conductor returned to his own coach; and, with the help of our postilion, reharnessed our horses. But the difficulty now was to start them. Tired with their unexpected task of having to tug at another and a stuck-fast diligence, — made startlish with having to stand in the rain and chill night air, in the open road, while the debates were going on as to the best method of attaching them to the sunken vehicle, — when once put back into their own traces, they took to rearing and kicking instead of proceeding. It is by no means amusing to sit in a diligence behind five plunging horses, on a cliff-road, — one edge of

which overhangs the sea, and the other consists of a deep ditch or water-way, beneath a sheer upright rock, — "when rain and wind beat dark December"; and even after whip and whoop had succeeded in prevailing on the rearers and kickers to "take the road" again, that road proved so unprecedentedly bad as almost to render futile the struggles of the poor beasts. They did their best; they strained their haunches, they bent their heads forward, they actually made leaps of motion, in trying to lug the clogged wheels on through the sludge and clammy soil; but this was a *mauvais pas*, where the *cantonniers'* good offices in road-mending had been lately neglected, and it seemed almost an impossibility to get through with our tired cattle. However, the thing was achieved, and the town of San Remo at length reached.

Here, with a change of horses, it was now our turn to have a drunken postilion; whom our conductor, after seizing him by the collar with both hands, permitted to mount to his high seat and gather up the reins, there being no other driver to be had. Smacking his long whip with an energy that made the night-echoes resound far and wide, galloping his horses up hill at a rate that swayed the coach to and fro and threatened speedy upsetting, screaming and raving like a wild Indian uttering his battle-cry, our charioteer pursued his headlong course, until brought to a stop by something that suddenly obstructed his career.

A voice before us shouted out, "We must all go back to San Remo!"

A silence ensued; and then our conductor got down, running forward to see what was the matter. The three in the *coupé* saw their alert friend of the *banquette* descend; which caused Velvet-cap to bestir himself, and let down the window. Not obtaining any satisfactory information by looking out into the darkness and confusion, he opened the door also, and called to some one to help him forth. Whereupon he found himself in the arms of the maudlin postilion; who, taking him doubtless for some foreign lady passenger in great alarm, hugged him affectionately, stuttering out, " N' ayez pas peur ! Point de danger ! point de danger ! "

" Get off with you, will you ? " was the ejaculation from Velvet-cap, as he pushed away the man, and went in search of his alert friend.

The latter soon came running back to the coach-side, bidding the sisters get out quickly and come and look at what was well worth seeing.

It was indeed ! There lay a gigantic mass of earth, stones, and trees, among which were several large blocks of solid rock, hurled across the road, showing a jagged outline against the night-sky, like an interposing mountain-barrier but just recently dropped in their path. The whole had fallen not an hour ago; and it was matter of congratulation to the four, that it had not done so at the very moment their diligence passed beneath.

There was nothing to be done but what the voice (which proved to be that of the conductor belonging to the other diligence) had proposed, namely, to go back to San Remo.

Here the travellers of both diligences soon arrived ; the four, as they passed to their rooms, hearing the British accent on the landing, in disconsolate appeal to a waiter : " Oh ! — look here, — sack, you know, sack, sack ! "

" Oui, monsieur ; votre sac de nuit. Il est en bas, — en bas, sur la diligence. On le montera bientôt."

The lady whose spirits rose at night was flitting about, brisk as a bee, getting morsels of bread and dipping them into wine to revive her sister ; who, worn out with fatigue and exhaustion, sat in a collapsed and speechless state on a sofa.

Next morning, however, she was herself again, and able to note the owner of the British accent, who had certainly obtained his desired carpet-bag, since there he was, at the *coupé* window, brushed and beaming, addressing Velvet-cap with, " Excuse me, as

an Englishman ; but, could you oblige me with change for a napoleon ? I want it to pay my bill with. They could get some from the next shop, if these jabbering fellows would but understand, and go and try."

The morning-animated sister was now also able to observe upon the more promising aspect of the weather, which was evidently clearing up ; for it not only did not rain, but showed streaks of brightness over the sea, in lines between the hitherto unbroken gray clouds. She adverted to the pleasant look of the cap-lifting *cantonniers*, as they stood drawn up and nodding encouragement at the diligence, near the mass of earth which had fallen overnight ; and which they, by dint of several hours' hard work from long before dawn, had sufficiently dug away to admit of present passage. She said how comforting the sight of their honest weather-lined faces was, bright with the touch of morning and early good-humor.

This brought a muttered rejoinder from the other sister ; who, huddled up in one corner, still half asleep, remarked that the faces of the *cantonniers* were surely far more comforting when visible by the light of the diligence-lamp, coming to bring succor amid darkness and danger.

" But it is precisely because they are never to be seen during the darkness, when danger is increased by there rarely being help at hand, that I dread and dislike night," returned Morning-lover.

" How oppressive the scent of those truffles is, the first thing after breakfast ! " exclaimed Night-favorer.

" I had not yet perceived it," replied Morning-lover. " Last evening, indeed, after a whole day's haunting with it, the smell of that hamper of truffles which the conductor took up at Finale was almost insupportable ; but now, in the fresh morning air, it is anything but disagreeable. I shall never hereafter encounter the scent of truffles without being forcibly reminded of all the incidents of this journey. That smell seems absolutely interwoven with images of torrent-crossing, cliff-falling, pouring rain, and roaring waves."

The talk fell upon associations of sense with events and places; sounds, sights, and scents, intimately connected with and vividly recalling certain occurrences of our lives. We had missed the glimpse of the baby face and little white cap from the back of the diligence that preceded us during the first portion of the day, owing to our coach having been delayed at Ventimiglia by some peculiar arrangement which required the team that had dragged us up a steep ascent to stop and bait, — merely resting instead of changing, before we went on again.

The Pont St. Louis, with the picturesque ravine it crosses, had been passed, and the pretty town of Mentone was full in view, when we caught sight of the other diligence, some way on the road before us, brought once more to a stand-still, while a crowd of persons surrounded it, and its passengers were to be seen, in the distance, descending, with the baby cap among them. At this instant, an excited French official darted out from a doorway by the side of the road near us, raising his arms distractedly, and throwing his sentences up at the conductor, who understood him to say that there was no going on; that a whole garden had come tumbling down across the road just at the entrance to Mentone, and prevented passing.

We drove on to the spot, and found it was indeed so; the grounds of a villa, skirting the highway on a terrace-ledge, had been loosened by the many days' rain, and had fallen during the forenoon, a heap of ruins, — shrubs, plants, garden-walls, flowers, borders, railings, — one mass of obstruction.

With a glance at the *coupé* passengers, another French official (the newly-appointed frontier custom-house being close at hand) stepped forward to suggest that the "insides" could be accommodated, during the interim required for the *cantonniers* to do their work, at a lately-built hotel he pointed

to; but the four agreed to spend the time in walking round by the path above the obstruction, so as to see its whole extent.

The wet, percolating and penetrating through the softer soil, gradually accumulates a weight of water behind and beneath the harder and rockier portions, which dislodges them from their places, pushes them forward, and finally topples them over headlong. This is generally prevented where terrace-walls are built up, by leaving holes here and there in the structure, which allow the wet to drain through innocuously; but if, as in the present instance, this caution be neglected, many days' successive rain is almost sure to produce the disaster in question. It had a woful look, — all those garden elegances cast there, flung out upon the high-road, like discarded rubbish; pots of selected flowers, favorite seats, well-worn paths, carefully-tended beds, trailing climbers, torn and snapped branches, all lying to be shovelled away as fast as the road-menders could ply their pickaxes and spades.

At length this task was accomplished; the diligences were hauled over the broken ground (their contents being also "hauled over" at the custom-house); the passengers (after the important ceremonial of handing their passports for inspection, and having them handed back by personages who kept their countenances wonderfully) were in again and off again.

But one more torrent to cross, — where the foremost coach had nearly been overset, and where the occupants of the hindmost one, profiting by example, got out and walked over the foot-bridge, in time to behold the owner of the British accent wave his hat triumphantly from the *coupé* with a hearty (English) "Huzza!" as the vehicle recovered, by a violent lurch to the left, from an equally violent one to the right, issuing scathless from the last flood that lay in the way, — and then both diligences began at a leisurely pace to crawl up a long ascent of road, bordered on each side by olive-grounds; — until the view opened to a fine stretch of prospect, now colored and vivified by a glance of the afternoon sun, — the diminutive peninsular kingdom of Monaco, lying down in the very sea, bright, and green, and fairy-like ; the bold barren crag of the Turbia rock frowning sternly in front, with its antique Roman tower and modern Italian church ; the rocky heights above to the right, with their foreground of olive-trees, vine-trellises, and orange-groves, interspersed with country - houses ; while through all wound the ever-climbing road, a white thread in the distance, with the telegraphic poles, dwindled to pin-like dimensions, indicating its numberless turns and bends.

As the sun sank over the far western lines of the Estrelle Mountains, and the sky faded into grayish purple, succeeded by an ever-deepening suffusion of black, unpierced by a single star, the high reach of road above Villafranca Bay was passed ; and, on our turning the corner of the last intervening upland, full in view came the many lights of Nice, with its castled rock, its minarets and cupolas, its stretch of sea, its look of sheltered repose ; — all most welcome to sight, after our sensational journey on the Cornice Road in a great rain.

INCIDENTS OF THE PORTLAND FIRE.

NEVER had Portland looked more beautiful than when the sunrise-gun boomed across the waters, announcing the ninetieth anniversary of our independence. The sun, which on another day should look down on the city's desolation, rose unclouded over the houses, that stood forth from the foliage of the embowering elms, or nestled in their shadow ; over the quaintness of the old-fashioned churches and the beauty of the more modern temples ; over the stately public edifices, and the streets everywhere decked with flags and thronged with crowds of happy, well-dressed people. Of course, the popular satisfaction expressed itself in the report of pistols, guns, and fire-crackers ; and all through the day the usual amusements went on, and in the afternoon almost everybody was on the street.

A few minutes before five o'clock, when the festivity was at its wildest, the alarm of fire rang out. Every circumstance was favorable for a conflagration, — the people scattered, the city dry and heated by a July sun, and a high southwesterly wind blowing. It needed only the exciting cause in the shape of a fire-cracker, and lo ! half the city was doomed.

My youngest brother, at the first sound of the bell, came and begged me to take him to the fire ; so I went, to please him. Poor child ! I little thought that by twelve o'clock at night there would be no place at home to lay the little head.

We found the fire near Brown's sugar-house, where there was a large crowd already assembled. But, though the smoke and masses of flame were rising only from one house, the wind was blowing a perfect gale ; and a foreboding of the calamity impending seemed to possess the spectators. There was none of the usual noise, and men appeared to look at the burning house with a feeling of awe. We did not stop there at all ; and some idea of the rapid progress of the fire may be gathered from the fact, that about four squares distant, where, on the way up, we could see one fire, on our return we saw three, — two lighted by sparks from the first. We slowly retraced our way, and met people on every side quickening their steps in the direction of the fire.

About seven o'clock, mother and I thought it would be wise to pack up our silver and valuables ; for it seemed as if we were directly in the path of the conflagration. Down Fore Street, and from Fore to Free, it was rushing on. The southwestern heavens were entirely shut from our view by the flames and smoke ; cinders, ashes, and blazing embers were falling like rain down Middle Street, and across to Congress, as far as the eye could see. The scene was terrible ; but it was soon surpassed in fearfulness, for the work of desolation was not half completed. The Irish population were the chief sufferers up to this hour. It was heart-rending to see the women rushing hither and thither, trying to save their few possessions. Here, a poor creature was dragging a mattress, followed by several little crying children, her face the picture of despair ; there, another, with her family, stood over the remnants of her scanty stock. A poor woman, who was in the habit of working for us, lived near the corner of Cross and Fore Streets. She had five children and a sick husband to care for. Almost all her energies were bent in getting them to a place of safety ; and the few little things which she succeeded in rescuing from the flames were afterwards stolen from her by some one of the many wretches who gathered the spoils that awful night.

It soon became evident that we must decide upon some plan of action, in case it should come to the worst. We had two married sisters, — one living in India Street, the other at the west end of the city. As the former had no family, and was alone, even her husband being away, and as the latter had three children, and a house full of company, we decided that, if we must move, it should be to India Street. We sent off one team, and my youngest brother with it, before the fire was anywhere near us ; and then, while my two little sisters assisted mother in getting things together, I worked with my brother and cousin, hanging wet blankets against the walls, pouring water on the roof, and taking other precautionary meas-

ures. But all was useless. On came the fire with a steady sweep. We saw that it was idle to combat it longer, and turned all our energies to saving what we could. Our home was to be ours no longer. The dear old roof-tree, under which had assembled so many loved ones, now gone forever, — where the eyes of all our home circle first saw the light of life, — where three of that number closed theirs in death, — the centre of the hopes and joys of a lifetime, — was to be abandoned to the flames. It was like tearing our heart-strings to leave it so ; but there was no time for lingering. With streaming eyes and aching hearts we started out, taking what we could in our hands. There was by this time no vehicle to be obtained in which we could ride ; and, supporting my mother, my sisters clinging to us in silent terror, we were borne along with the crowd down Middle Street to India. I cannot remember any incidents of that walk. The hurrying throng around me, the flying sparks, and the roar of the engines, seem like the confusion of a dream.

Our sister, who met us at the door, felt perfectly secure, and had done nothing towards packing. I gave her an account of our proceedings, thinking each moment of some precious thing I might have brought away. We went to the front door, and looked out on the scene before us. The fire seemed to come on the wings of the wind. Middle Street was ablaze ; Wood's marble hotel was in flames, together with the beautiful dwelling opposite. The fire leaped from house to house, and, if for a moment checked, it was but to rush on in wilder fury. Churches, one by one, were seized by the flame, and crumbled into ruin before it. No human power could arrest its fierce progress. In vain the firemen put forth a strength almost superhuman : their exertions seemed but to add to its fury. Explosion after explosion gave greater terror to the scene : buildings were successively blown up in the useless effort to bar its pathway ; the fire leaped the chasm and sped on. Fugitives of every age and condition were hurrying through the streets, laden with everything imaginable, — especially looking-glasses, which seem the one important thing to be saved during a fire. My brother and cousin had not yet made their appearance, nor had we seen anything of my brother-in-law, from the other end of the city. But we knew they must be at their places of business, which were now in the heart of the burning district. Swiftly the destruction hurried towards us ; and people were now seen bringing in their goods and seeking shelter on our premises. O what heart-broken faces surrounded us that fearful night ! Friends, and people we had never seen, alike threw themselves on our kindness ; and I must say that a spirit of humanity and good-will seemed everywhere prevalent among the citizens. We were now ourselves tortured by suspense. Could we escape, or should we again have to seek refuge from the flames ? Surely the work of destruction would stop before it reached India Street ? The hot breath of the maddening fire, and its lurid glare, were the only response. O, if the wind would only change ! But a vane, glistening like gold in the fire-light, steadfastly pointed to the southeast. For one moment it veered, and our hearts almost stood still with hope ; but it swung back, and a feeling of despair settled upon us.

Our house was full. One poor lady, with a little baby only a week old, lay on a sofa in one of the rooms ; near her, bent over in a rocking-chair, sat an old woman who had not been out of her house for five years, with a look of hopeless bewilderment on her wrinkled face. But people were now beginning to move from our house. India Street was almost blocked up. Every kind of vehicle that went upon wheels, from a barouche to a wheelbarrow, passed by laden with furniture.

At this moment my brother and brother-in-law approached, blackened almost beyond recognition. It was not until C—— spoke that I really knew him.

" We must be calm and collected, and save what we can. John is trying to get a team to carry mother up to L——'s ; the rest of us will have to go to the graveyard. But John may not be successful, so you stay here, and see if you can get any one to take mother : they may do it for you, when they would n't for a man."

I stood on the edge of the sidewalk, clinging to the horse-post, and appealed in vain to wagons going by.

" *Won't* you take a lady and children away from here ? "

" I *can't*, ma'am, not if you was to give me twenty-five dollars, — not if you was to give me five hundred. I 'm taking a load for a gentleman now."

So it was in every case. Very many were worse off than we were, — had not even a man to help. One well-known citizen was appealed to for help, in the early part of the evening, by a poor woman, — a sort of dependant of his family. He took her and her daughter, with their effects, outside the city, and returned to find India Street on fire and no means of getting through the crowd to his house, which was burned, with all that was not saved by the exertions of his wife. They had visiting them a lady whose child lay dead in the house, awaiting burial. The mother took the little corpse in her arms and carried it herself up to the other end of the city !

While I was making these vain attempts, John drove up in a light, open-topped buggy. We hurriedly got mother and E—— into it, and gave into their charge the jewelry and silver, and they drove away. I could not but tremble for their safety. The road seemed impassable, so dense was the struggling crowd. On every side the fire was raging. Looking up India Street it was one sheet of flame, and equally so before us. It looked like a world on fire, for we could see no smoke, — it was too near for that, — and the heat was terribly intense.

There was no time to be lost. Both our servants and M——'s were away spending the Fourth, so we had to depend entirely on ourselves. Our back fence was soon torn down, and we all worked as we never had before. We saved a good deal, but not one half of what we brought from our house in the first place. We had thrown things out of the window, and C—— and J—— worked hard dragging them out of the yard, until, scorched and almost suffocated, they were compelled to desist. The flames were upon us so quickly, it seemed incredible that they could have seized the house so soon after we thought we were in danger.

"Thank God, we are all safe!" cried M——, sinking upon the ground in the graveyard, where we took refuge. She tried to look cheerful; but the sight before her — her house in flames — and the thought of her husband's absence overcame her, and she burst into tears. I laid the two little girls upon the grass; and, wearied out, they soon fell asleep. It was a strange scene in that quiet old cemetery, where the dead of more than a century had lain undisturbed in their graves. Where only the reverent tread of the mourner, or of some visitor carefully threading his way among the grassy mounds, was wont to be known, crowds of frantic people were hurrying across; while here and there were family groups clustered together, watching the destruction of their property.

How long the remaining hours seemed! Would the daylight never come? The children slept on, and we four talked in low tones of the morrow.

At length, faint, rosy lights began to streak the eastern horizon, and slowly the day dawned. The sun rose unclouded above the hills, sending down his beams upon the desolation which the night had wrought, lighting up the islands and the blue waters, flecked with sail-boats.

Not less welcome to us, J—— now also appeared, — with a hay-cart, whose driver he had engaged to come and remove us. Our goods were put into it; we took our places among them, and, as soon as the tardy oxen could carry us, were safe in my sister's house, living

over again in words that fearful night, and relating to each other some of those incidents of the fire which can never all be told. A little friend of ours, when leaving her home, took in her arms her doll, nearly as large as herself; obliged to flee a second time, her mother told her it was useless to try and save the doll, and she must leave it there. With many tears she laid it on the sofa, feeling, no doubt, as if she were leaving a human being to be burnt. The next day, a friend brought to her the identical dolly, which had been found in the graveyard! The little one's joy may be imagined.

One of the women in the Irish quarter picked up her big pig in her arms and carried it to a place of safety, then returned to take care of her children and furniture. A woman went by our house in the early part of the evening bent nearly double beneath the weight of a trunk strapped upon her back. We saw women that night with loads under which almost any man would have staggered in ordinary circumstances.

Before we were supposed to be in danger, I walked out with a young friend to see what progress the fire was making. At a corner we observed a woman with a child about eight years old, talking, in great agitation, to a lady, and evidently urging her to accede to some request. My companion suggested that we should see if we could aid her in any way. As we approached, the lady had taken the child by the hand, with the words, "What is your address?" which was given. We inquired if we could be of any service. "No, thank you," was the reply. "I asked that lady to take care of my daughter. I keep store on that street over there. My husband is out of town, and I don't know what I shall do!" — and, wringing her hands, she hurried away. I have wondered since what was the fate of the little girl thus intrusted to the care of strangers; for the lady went in the direction afterwards swept by the fire.

One family, whose house the flames did not reach until near two o'clock in the morning, behaved with great coolness. The head of the household lay ill. It was their first care to provide for him. Then they went deliberately about, gathering up their valuables, taking just what they wanted. They secured a wagon to carry away their things. Their house, meanwhile, had been full of refugees from the flames. One of the young ladies, going for the last time through the deserted rooms, found, on a sofa in the parlor, a sick woman, utterly unable to move. At first, she felt almost in despair at sight of this poor creature, so near meeting a fearful fate. But quickly recovering her presence of mind, she called in men from the street, and, by their united efforts, they carried her out, and forced a passing wagon to take her to a safe place. A young lady, who lived at a little distance from this family, was spending the night at the other end of the city. They sat up till half past twelve, and she was then in the act of retiring, never dreaming that her home was in danger, when a loaded wagon stopped at the door, and out stepped her sister and child. She went back in the same vehicle, and worked till twelve the next day, getting things out of the house, collecting and guarding them till they could be removed.

There was, of course, the usual difference shown amongst people in such circumstances, — energy and coolness contrasted with imbecility and frantic excitement. A friend who moved three times, with her husband so ill that he had to be carried from place to place, never once forgot to administer his medicine at regular intervals, — with a steady hand pouring out the drops by the light of the fire.

A gentleman was carrying some of his books, preceded by an assistant, who also had his arms full. The latter walked so rapidly that his employer could not keep up with him. He called upon him to slacken his pace; but, as no attention was paid to this, the gentleman dropped his books upon the ground, and, running forward, knocked him down, determined to be obeyed, fire or no fire.

But all were not so cool. One man, seeing the flames advancing in the direction of his house, rushed thither to save his property. He worked with might and main, but, when the house was nearly emptied, became aware of the fact that it was his neighbor's. By this time his own dwelling was on fire, from which he saved scarcely anything. I know one person who passed through his hall perfectly empty-handed, while all around him were bundles and boxes, which were consumed in the fire; another walked out of his house with a package of envelopes in his hand, leaving, close by, an article worth thirty dollars.

I must mention one of many instances of unselfishness that came under my observation. A gentleman was comfortably established in a house which he had recently bought and furnished, expecting there to enjoy the pleasures of a home. One half of the house he had rented; but the husband of the woman to whom it was let was not in town. Their dwelling shared the fate of those around them, being burnt. He first set to work to save his own things; but, struck by the forlorn condition of his tenant, he did his best to save her effects, even to the detriment of his own; for when they were examined, the greater portion of them was found to be hers. Time has not exhausted the truth and beauty of the saying, that " in the night the stars shine forth," and the stars did not pale even in the terrible light of the fire that consumed half a city.

MY LITTLE BOY.

THERE were nine of us, all told, when mother died; myself, the eldest, aged twenty, a plain and serious woman, well fitted by nature and circumstance to fill the place made vacant by death.

I cannot remember when I was young. Indeed, when I hear other women recount the story of their early days, I think I had no childhood, for mine was like no other.

Mother was married so young, that at the age when most women begin to think seriously of marriage she had around her a numerous brood, of which I was less the elder sister than the younger mother. She was delicate by nature, and peevish by reason of her burdens, and I think could never have been a self-reliant character; so she fretted and sighed through life, and when death came, unawares, she seemed not sorry for the refuge.

She called me to her bed one day in a tone so cheerful that I wondered, and when I saw the calm and brightness in her face, hope made me glad. "Margaret," she said, "you have been a good daughter. I never did you justice until this illness opened my eyes. You have shamed me by your patience and your sacrifices so gently borne. You are more fit to be a mother than I ever was; and I leave the children to your care without a fear. It is not likely you will ever marry, and I die content, knowing that you will do your duty."

After this came many sad days,— the parting, the silent form which death had made majestic, the funeral hymns, the tolling bell, the clods upon the coffin-lid; and when the sun shone out and the birds sang again, it seemed to me I had dreamed it all, and that the sun could not shine nor the birds sing above a grave on which the grass had not yet had time to grow. But I had not dreamed, nor had I time for dreaming. Mother was dead, and eight children claimed from me a mother's care, — the youngest a wailing babe but seven days old, whom I came to cherish and love as my little boy.

When I had settled down, and grown accustomed to the vacuum which never could be filled for me, I thought a great deal upon mother's last words. I was proud of the trust she reposed in me, and I meant to be faithful to it. I wondered much why she had thought it likely I should never marry; for I was a woman with strong instincts, and, amid all the toil and care of my barren life, I had seen afar, through gleaming mists, the mountains of hope arise, and beyond the heat and dust and labor of duty caught glimpses of green ways made pleasant by quiet waters.

I do not think my burden seemed heavier now that mother no longer helped me to bear it; for my sense of responsibility had been increased by her complaining spirit. Her discouraging views of life held in check the reins of my eager fancy: it seemed wrong to enjoy a happiness I could not share with her. Now I no longer felt this restraint; but, knowing that somehow she had missed this happiness for which I waited, the knowledge invested her memory with a tender pity, and tempered my pleasure with a feeling akin to pain.

I was never ·idle. Behind the real work of life, my fancy wrought on, unknown and unsuspected by the world; my lamp of joy, fed by the sweet oil of hope, was ready for the lighting, and I was content to wait.

My little boy throve bravely. Every morning I awoke him with a kiss; and, perhaps because each day seemed but a continuation of the other, time stood still for him. He was for me the incarnation of all loveliness. The fair face, and blond hair, and brown, brooding eyes, were beautiful as an angel's, and goodness set its seal on his perfections.

He gave me no trouble : grief brings age, joy confirms youth, and I and my little boy grew young together. He was with me everywhere, lightening my labor with his prattling tongue, helping me with his sweet, hindering ways ; and when the kisses had been many that had waked him many morns, he stood beside me, my little boy, hardly a hand's breadth lower than myself.

The world had changed for all but him and me. My father had wandered off to foreign parts ; sisters and brothers, one by one, had gone forth to conquer kingdoms and reign in their own right, and one young sister, just on the border-land of maiden fancies, (O friends, I write this line with tears !) turned from earth and crossed the border-land of heaven.

But he and I remained alone in the old homestead, and walked together sweetly down the years.

If I came upon disappointment, I had not sought it, neither did I fall by it ; but that which was my future slid by me and became the past, so gently that I scarce remember where one ended or the other began ; and though all other lovers failed me, one true remained, to whom I ever would be true. The future did not look less fair ; nay, I deemed it more full of promise than ever. It was as though I had passed from my old stand-point of observation to a more easterly window ; and the prospect was not the less enchanting that I looked upon it over the shoulder of my little boy. We talked much of it together ; and though he had the nearer view, it was my practised vision that saw pathways of beauty not yet suspected by him.

But we were still happy in the present, and did not speculate much upon the future. The rolling years brought him completeness, and to the graces of person were added the gifts of wisdom and knowledge. The down that shaded his cheek, like the down upon a ripe peach, had darkened and strengthened to the symbol of manhood, and his words had the clear ring of purpose. For there was a cloud upon the horizon

which at first was no bigger than a man's hand, but it grew until it filled the land with darkness, and the fair prospect on which I had so loved to gaze was hidden behind the storm. My little boy and I looked into each other's faces, and he cried, " Margaret, I must go ! "

I did not say nay,—for the tears which were not in my eyes were in my voice, and to speak was to betray them, — but I turned about to make him ready.

In these days my little boy's vision was finer than my own ; and when we stood together, looking from our orient window, he saw keener and farther than I had ever done ; for my eyes now looked through a veil of tears, while his, like the eagle's, penetrated the cloud to the sunshine behind it. He was full of the dream of glory ; and his words, fraught with purpose and power, stirred me like a trumpet. I caught the inspiration that thrilled his soul ; for we had walked so long together that all paths pursued by him must find me ever at his side.

One day I was summoned to meet a visitor ; and going, a tall figure in military dress gave me a military salute. It was my little boy, who, half abashed at his presumption, drew himself up, and sought refuge from shyness in valor. It was not a sight to make me smile, though I smiled to please my warrior, who, well pleased, displayed his art, to show how fields were won. Won ! He had no thought of loss ; for youth and hope dream not of defeat, and he talked of how the war was to be fought and ended, and all should be well.

I kissed my little boy good night ; and he slept peacefully, dreaming of fields of glory, as Jacob dreamed and saw a heavenly vision.

He went ; and then it seemed as if there had been with him one fair long summer day, and this was the evening thereof ; and my heart was heavy within me.

But many letters reached me from the distant field,— long and loving letters, full of hope, portraying all the poetry and beauty of camp-life, casting the grosser part aside ; and to me at home, musing amid peaceful scenes, it seemed a great, triumphant march, which must crush, with its mere *display* of power, all wicked foes. But the sacrifice of blood was needed for the remission of sin, and these holiday troops — heroes in all save the art of war — lost the day, and, returning, brought back with their thinned ranks my little boy unharmed. Unharmed, thank God! but bronzed and bearded like the pard, and tarnished with the wear and burnished with the use of war.

How he talked and laughed, making light of danger, and, growing serious, said the fight had but begun, — the business of the nation must, for years, be war, — and that his strength and manhood, nay, his life if need be, should be given to his country. Then his words made me brave, and his looks made me proud. I blessed him with unfaltering lips ; and above the hills of promise, which my little boy and I saw looking from our orient window, rose higher yet the mountains of truth, with the straight path of duty leading to the skies. But when he was gone again, — gone, — there fell a shadow of the coming night, and the evening and the morning were the second day.

His frequent letters dissipated the sense of danger, and brought me great comfort. War is not a literary art, and letters from the "imminent deadly breach," made it seem less deadly. His self-abnegation filled me with wonder. "It is well that few should be lost, that many may be saved," he wrote. In what school had this tender youth learned heroism, I asked myself, as I read his noble words and trembled at his courage.

My dreams and my gaze turned southward. No eastern beams lured me to that lookout so long endeared ; for the eyes through which I once gazed looked through the smoke of battle, and hope and faith had fled with him, and left me but suspense.

Now came hot work. The enemy pressed sorely, and men's — ay, and women's — souls were tried. Long days of silence passed, days of sickening doubt, and then came the news of *victory*, — victory bought with precious blood and heavy loss. Over the ghastly hospital lists I hung, fearing and dreading to meet the name of my little boy, taking hope, as the list shortened, from the despair of others, *and no mention*. Thank God, who giveth *us* the victory !

And later, when details come in, I see in "official report" my little boy's name mentioned for meritorious and gallant conduct, and recommended for promotion. Ah! the groans of the dying are lost in the shouts of the victor ; and, forgetting the evil because of this good, a woman's heart cried, *Laus Deo !*

After the battle, hardly fought and dearly purchased, my hero came home on furlough. War had developed him faster than the daily kisses of love had done ; for my little boy — crowned with immortal youth for me — for all the world came from this rude embrace a man in stature and wisdom, a hero in valor and endurance, a leader beloved and revered.

But for all this I tucked him in o' nights, and shut off harmful draughts from him who oft had lain upon the sod, and for covering had but the cloudy sky.

These were blissful days, — marked in the past by white memories, — in which we talked of future plans, the future so near, yet to our vision so remote, and purposed this and that, not considering that Heaven disposes all things.

And when he must be off, I kissed him lightly ; for success brings security, and I was growing accustomed to these partings ; but he drew me to his breast, struck by some pang of coming evil, and called me *mother*. Ah! then my heart yearned over my little boy, and I would fain have stayed his going ; but, dashing the tears from his eyes, he hurried away, nor looked behind him once.

All through the winter, which for him was summer, my heart lay lightly in its place, and I waited calmly the coming of the end. The struggle was almost over; the storm-cloud had rolled back, after deluging the land in blood; in this consecrated soil slavery was forever buried; the temple of freedom was reared in the name of all men, and the dove of peace sat brooding in its eaves.

All this my little boy had said must come to pass before he sheathed his sword; and this had come to pass.

He had marched "to the sea," my conquering hero, and was "coming up," crowned with new laurels. I was waiting the fulness of time, lulled with the fulness of content. Sherman had gathered his hosts for another combat, — the last, — and then the work would be done, and well done. Thus wrote my little boy; and my heart echoed his words, "well done."

This battle-day I worked out of doors from morning until night, seeking to bring order and beauty out of confusion and decay, striving to have all things ready when he came. My sleep was sweet that night, and I awoke with these words in my mind: —

"Lord, in the morning Thou shalt hear
My voice ascending high."

The sun streamed in through the eastern window, and all the hills beyond were bathed in glory; the earth was fair to look upon, and happiness, descending from the skies, nestled in my heart.

I planted all this day, covering precious seed, thinking on their summer beauty; and, as the evening fell, I stood at the garden gate watching the way he must come for whose coming I longed with a longing that could not be uttered.

As I looked, idly speculating on his speed, a horseman dashed up in mad haste, his steed spent and flecked with foam. Men do not ride so hot with good tidings, — what need to make such haste with evil?

Still, no sense of loss, no shadow of the coming night. Peace covered my heart, and would not be scared away. Blind infatuation! that could not see.

"Was it not then a victory?" I cried; for sadness and defeat were written in his face.

"Nay, not that." The outstretched hand turned white with pity. "But this —"

Too kind to speak the words, at sight of which I fell, struck by a bolt that, riving *his* heart, through leagues of space had travelled straight to mine.

Months later, when the long night had passed away, and the dawn brought patience and resignation, one who saw him fall, gloriously, told me the story. I could bear it then; for in my soul's eclipse I had beheld him walking on the heavenly hills, and knew that there he was waiting for me.

He lies buried, at his own request, where he fell, on Southern soil.

O pilgrim to those sacred shrines, if in your wandering ye come upon a nameless grave, marked by a sunken sword, tread lightly above the slumbers of my little boy!

LAKE CHAMPLAIN.

NOT thoughtless let us enter thy domain;
  Well did the tribes of yore,
Who sought the ocean from the distant plain,
  Call thee their country's door.*

And as the portals of a saintly pile
  The wanderer's steps delay,
And, while he musing roams the lofty aisle,
  Care's phantoms melt away

In the vast realm where tender memories brood
  O'er sacred haunts of time,
That woo his spirit to a nobler mood
  And more benignant clime, —

So in the fane of thy majestic hills
  We meekly stand elate;
The baffled heart a tranquil rapture fills
  Beside thy crystal gate:

For here the incense of the cloistered pines,
  Stained windows of the sky,
The frescoed clouds and mountains' purple shrines,
  Proclaim God's temple nigh.

Through wild ravines thy wayward currents glide,
  Round bosky islands play;
Here tufted headlands meet the lucent tide,
  There gleams the spacious bay;

Untracked for ages, save when crouching flew,
  Through forest-hung defiles,
The dusky savage in his frail canoe,
  To seek the thousand isles,

Or rally to the fragrant cedar's shade
  The settler's crafty foe,
With toilsome march and midnight ambuscade
  To lay his dwelling low.

Along the far horizon's opal wall
  The dark blue summits rise,
And o'er them rifts of misty sunshine fall,
  Or golden vapor lies.

And over all tradition's gracious spell
  A fond allurement weaves;

---

* One of the aboriginal names of Lake Champlain signifies the open door of the country.

Lake Champlain.

Her low refrain the moaning tempest swells,
  And thrills the whispering leaves.

To win this virgin land, — a kingly quest, —
  Chivalric deeds were wrought ;
Long by thy marge and on thy placid breast
  The Gaul and Saxon fought.

What cheers of triumph in thy echoes sleep !
  What brave blood dyed thy wave !
A grass-grown rampart crowns each rugged steep,
  Each isle a hero's grave.

And gallant squadrons manned for border fray,
  That rival standards bore,
Sprung from thy woods and on thy bosom lay, —
  Stern warders of the shore.

How changed since he whose name thy waters bear,
  The silent hills between,
Led by his swarthy guides to conflict there.
  Entranced beheld the scene !

Fleets swiftly ply where lagged the lone batteau,
  And quarries trench the gorge ;
Where waned the council-fire, now steadfast glow
  The pharos and the forge.

On Adirondack's lake-encircled crest
  Old war-paths mark the soil,
Where idly bivouacks the summer guest,
  And peaceful miners toil.

Where lurked the wigwam, cultured households throng ;
  Where rung the panther's yell
Is heard the low of kine, a blithesome song,
  Or chime of village bell.

And when, to subjugate the peopled land,
  Invaders crossed the sea,
Rushed from thy meadow-slopes a stalwart band,
  To battle for the free.

Nor failed the pristine valor of the race
  To guard the nation's life ;
Thy hardy sons met treason face to face,
  The foremost in the strife.

When locusts bloom and wild-rose scents the air,
  When moonbeams fleck the stream,
And June's long twilights crimson shadows wear,
  Here linger, gaze, and dream !

YESTERDAY.

THERE is a gleam of ultramarine, — which, most of all tints, say the painters, possesses the quality of light in itself, — banished to the farthest horizon of the ocean, where it lies all day, a line of infinite richness, not to be drawn by Apelles, and in its compression of expanse — leagues of sloping sea and summer calm being written in that single line — suggestive of more depth than plummet or diver can ever reach. Such an enchantment of color deepens the farther and interior horizon with most men, — whether it is the atmosphere of one's own identity still warming and enriching it, or whether the orbed course of time has dropped the earthy part away, and left only the sunbeams falling there. But Leonardo da Vinci supposed that the sky owed its blue to the darkness of vast space behind the white lens of sunlit air; and perhaps where the sea presents through the extent of its depth, as it slips over into other hemispheres, tangents with the illumined atmosphere beyond, it affords a finer filter for these blue rays, and thenceforth hoards in its heart the wealth and beauty of tint found in that line of ultramarine. Thus too, perhaps, in the eyes of these fortunate men, every year of their deepening past presents only a purer strain for such sunshine as is theirs, until it becomes indeed

"The light that never was, on sea or land."

The child's conjecture of the future is one of some great, bright, busy thing beyond the hills or over the river. But the thought is not definite: having nothing to remember, he has nothing by which to model his idea.

The man looks back at the past in much the same manner, to be sure, — always with something between, — if not the river or the hills, at least a breath of mist out of which rises the vision he invokes; but the vision has a shape, precise and clear.

If it is sadness that he seeks, sadness comes, dark as the nun of the Penseroso, without a glimmer of the countless and daily trifles of fairer aspect that made her actual presence possible to suffer, — comes to flatter his memory with assurance of strength in having endured so much and yet survived, or to stab him with her phantom poniards freshly and fiercely as ever, — no diffused affair, but a positive shape of melancholy.

But if the phase to be recalled is of a cheerful sort, how completely likewise does it assert its essence, — a sunbeam falling through that past from beginning to end. All the vexatious annoyances of the period that then seemed to counterbalance pleasure are lost to view, and only the rosy face of an experience that was happiness itself smiles upon him. What matter the myriad frets that then beset him in the flesh? They were superficial substance, — burrs that fell; he was happy in spite of them; he does not remember them; he sees nothing but the complete content; he in fact possesses his experience only in the ideal.

It is the dropping out of detail that accomplishes this in one case and the other. In either, the point of view alone is fixed. The rest is variable, and depends, it may be, on the nature of that subtile and volatile ether through which each man gazes.

That the latter, the brighter vision, predominates, is as true as that sunny days outnumber rainy ones. Though Argemone, rather than remember, may have blotted out her memory; or though Viviani, after fifty years of renowned practice in his profession, may be unable to look back at it without a shudder, — then endowed with youth, health, energy, ambition, — now lacking these, the recollection of the suffering he has seen overwhelming his sensitive nature blackly and heavily as clods of burial might do; — yet they are but those points of shadow that throw the fact into prominence. It has been said that pain, remembered, is delight. This is true only of physical pain. Mental agony ever remains agony; for it is the body that perishes and the affections of the body. Still, with most men the past is an illuminated region, forever throwing the present into the shade. In the Zend Avesta, a farsang is defined to be the space within which a long-sighted man can see a camel and distinguish whether it be white or black; but the milestones of the memory are even less arbitrary than this: no matter how far the glance flies, in those distances every man's camel is white. Thus the backward view is ever of

> "Summits soft and fair,
> Clad in colors of the air,
> Which to those who journey near
> Barren, brown, and rough appear."

The maidens of to-day are not so beautiful as the maidens were when our young senses could drink in their beauty; the St. Michael pears have died out; the blight has got possession of the roses. When we married, a white one climbed up the house-side and thrust its snowy sprays in at the casement of the wedding-chamber. Find us such climbers now! A young girl once on the beach, watching her father's ship slip away on the wind, had her glance caught by a sparkle in the sand; and there lay a treasure at her feet, a heap of crimson crystals, a mine of jewels. What wealth! What possibilities! No more going to sea! No more watching ships out of sight! She gathered a double-handful of the splendid cubes as earnest, and ran back to the house with them. Such assurance having been displayed, there was no hesitation. The man-servant followed her swift guidance to the shore again, with shovel and sack and a train of the whole household, — but the tide had come in, and the place was not there. Day after day was search made for that mass of garnets, but always in vain. It was one of those deposits that Hugh Miller somewhere speaks of, as disclosed by one tide and hidden by another. But all her life long, though she wore jewels and scattered gold, no gem rivalled the blood-red lustre of that sudden sparkle in the sands; and no wealth equalled the fabulous dreams that were born of it. It was to her as precious and irreparable as to the poet the Lost Bower.

> "I affirm that since I lost it
> Never bower has seemed so fair;
> Never garden-creeper crossed it,
> With so deft and brave an air;
> Never bird sang in the summer, as I saw and heard
> them there."

This light of other days is unfailingly, by its owners, carried over to every child they meet. As if the caterpillar were in better estate than the butterfly, each boy is seeing his best days. Yet there is not a child in the world but is pursued by cares. His desk-mate's marbles oppress him more than will forcemeat-balls and turtle-soup when he becomes an alderman; there are lessons to learn, terrible threats of telling the teacher to brave, and many a smart to suffer. Childhood is beautiful in truth, but not therefore blest, — that is, for the little bodiless cherubs of the canvas. It was one of Origen's fancies that the coats of skins given to Adam and Eve on their expulsion from Paradise were their corporeal textures, and that in Eden they had neither flesh nor blood, bones nor nerves. The opening soul, that puts back petal after petal till the fructifying heart of it is bare to all the sweet influences of the universe, is something lovely for older eyes to see, — perhaps no lovelier than the lawful development of later lives to larger eyes than ours, — perhaps no lovelier than that we are to undergo. The first moment when the force of beauty strikes a child's perceptions would be an ineffable one, if he had anything to compare it with or measure it by; but as it is, even though it pierce him through and through with rapture, he is not aware of that rapture till after-years reproduce it for him and sweeten the sensation with full knowledge. The child is so dear to the parents, because it is their own beings bound together in one ; the baby is so beautiful to all, because so sacred and mysterious. Where was this life a moment since ? Whither will it fleet a moment hence ? He may be a fiend or an archangel by and by, as he and Fate together please ; but now his little skin is like a blush rose-leaf, and his little kisses are so tender and so dear ! yet it is as an object of nature that he charms, not in his identity as a sufferer of either pain or pleasure. Childhood, by these blind worshippers of yesterday, is simply so vaunted and so valued because it is seen again in the ideal : the detail is lost in distance ; the fair fact alone remains.

But yesterday has its uses, of more value than its idolatries. Though too often with its aerial distances and borrowed hues it is a mere pleasure region, instead of that great reservoir from which we might draw fountains of inexhaustible treasure, yet, if we cultivated our present from our past, homage to it might be as much to the purpose at least as the Gheber's worship of the sun. The past is an atmosphere weighing over each man's life. The skilful farmer with his subsoil-plough lets down the wealthy air of the actual atmosphere into his furrows, deeper than it ever went before ; the greedy loam sucks in the nitrogen there, and one day he finds his mould stored with ammonia, the great fertilizer, worth many a harvest. Are they numerous who thus enrich the present with the disengaged agents of the past, the chemic powers obtained from that superincumbent atmosphere ever elastically stretching over them ? Let our farmer scatter pulverized marble upon his soil forever, — crude carbonate of lime, — and it remains unassimilated ; but let him powder burnt bones there, and his crop uses it to golden advantage, — now merely the phosphate of lime, but material that has passed through the operations of animal life, of organism. With whatever manure he work his land, be it wood-ashes or guano or compost, he knows that that which has received the action of or-

ganic tissues fattens it the best ; and so a wise man may fertilize to-day better with the facts of an experience that he has once lived through, than with any vague and unorganized dreams. But the fool has never lived ; — life, said Bichat, is the totality of the functions ; — his past has endured no more organization than his future has ; he never understood it ; he can make no use of it ; so he deifies it, and burns the flying moment like a joss-stick before the wooden image in which he has caricatured all its sweet and beneficent capabilities ; — as if it were likely that one moment of his existence could be of any more weight than another.

The sentiment which a generation feels for another long antecedent to itself, is not utterly dissimilar from this. Its individuals being regarded with the veneration due to parents and due to the dead, it is forgotten that they were men, and men whose lessons were necessarily no wiser than those of the men among us ; men, too, of no surpassing humility, since they presumed to prescribe inviolable laws to ages far wiser than themselves. Yet though the philosophy of the Greek and Roman were lost, would it need more than the years of a generation to replace what scarcely can exceed the introspection of a single experience ? If their art were lost, does not the ideal of humanity remain the same so long as the nature of humanity endures ? But of the seven sciences of antiquity, two alone deserve the name, — their arithmetic and their geometry. Their music was a cumbrous and complicated machinery, and the others were exercises of wit and pleasure and superstition. It is true that the Egyptian excelled, that the Arabian delved somewhat into the secrets of nature ; but who venerates those people, and who spends all that season in study of their language that he should spend in putting oxygen into his blood and lime into his bones ? The sensuous Greek loved beauty ; he did not care to puzzle his brain when he could please it instead.. Euclid and

Apollonius, indeed, carried the positive science of mathematics to great height, but physical science is the growth of comparative to-day; with habits of thought hampered by priesthoods and systems, the efforts of antiquity were like abortive shoots,—it is within the last four centuries that the strong stem has sprung up, and the plant has flowered. Neither do our youth study the classics for their science; and yet is not the pursuit of science nobler than all other pursuits, since it leads its followers into the mysteries of the creation and into the purposes of God? Small is the profit to be found in recital of the fancies of heathen ages or the warfares of savage tribes. But so far is the mere breath of the ancients exalted above this sacred search, that a university will turn out proficients who write Greek verses by the ream, but cannot spell their own speech; who can name you the winning athletes of the first Olympiad, but are unable to state the constituents of the gas that lights their page, and never dream, as the chemist does, that these "sunbeams absorbed by vegetation in the primordial ages of the earth, and buried in its depths as vegetable fossils through immeasurable eras of time, until system upon system of slowly formed rocks has been piled above, come forth at last, at the disenchanting touch of science, and turn the night of civilized man into day." They can paint to you the blush of Rhodope or Phryne, till you see the delicious color blend and mingle on the ivory of their tablets; but until, like Agassiz, we can all of us deduce the fish from the scale, and from that blush alone deduce the human race, we are no nearer the Divine intentions in the creation of man, for all such lore as that. An author has somewhere asked, What signify our telegraphs, our anæsthetics, our railways? What signifies our knowledge of the earth's structure, of the stars' courses? Are we any the more or less men? But certainly he is the more a man, he comes nearer to God's meaning in a man, who conquers matter, circumstance, time,

and space. That one who sees the universe move round him understandingly, and fathoms in some degree the wonder and the beauty of the eternal laws, must be a pleasanter object to his Creator than any other who, merely employing pleasure, makes a fetich of his luxuries, his Aldines and Elzevirs, and, dying, goes into the unknown world no wiser concerning the ends and aims of this one than when he entered it. Rather than periods that decay and sin might bring again, should one remember the wonderful history of the natural world when the Spirit of God moved upon the face of the waters. Rather should one read the record of the rain, it seems,—the story of the weather some morning, cycles since, with the way the wind was blowing written in the slanting drip of the rain-drops caught and petrified on the old red sandstone,— marks of the Maker as he passed, one day, a million years ago,—than decipher on the scroll of any palimpsest, under the light-headed visions of an anchorite, some half-erased ode of Anacreon.

But, after all, this veneration for the ancients — who personally might be forgiven for their misfortune in having lived when the world was young, were not one so slavish before them — is only because again one looks at the ideal, — looks through that magical Claude Lorraine glass which makes even the commonest landscape picturesque. We forget the dirty days of straw-strewn floors, and see the leather hangings stamped with gold; we forget the fearful feet of sandal shoon, but see the dust of a Triumph rising in clouds of glory. We look at that past, feeling something like gods, too.

> "The gods are happy:
> They turn on all sides
> Their shining eyes,
> And see, below them,
> The earth and men."

We cannot consider those things happening remotely from us on the earth's surface, even now, without suffering them to partake somewhat of the property of by-gone days. It makes little difference whether the distance be that of meridians or of eras. When at sunrise we fancy some foreign friend beholding dawn upon the silver summits of the Alps, we are forced directly to remember that with him day is at the noon, and his sunrise has vanished with those of all the yesterdays, — so that even our friend becomes a being of the past; or when, bathed in the mellow air of an autumn afternoon, the sunshine falling on us like the light of a happy smile, and all the vaporous vistas melting in clouded sapphire, it occurs to us that possibly it is snowing on the Mackenzie River, and night has already darkened down over the wide and awful icefields, — then distance seems a paradox, and time and occasion mere phantasmagoria; there are no beings but ourselves, there is no moment but the present; all circumstance of the world becomes apparent to us only like pictures thrown into the perspective of the past. It requires the comprehensive vision of the poet to catch the light of existing scenes as they shift along the globe, and harmonize them with the instant; — whether he view

> "The Indian
> Drifting, knife in hand,
> His frail boat moored to
> A floating isle thick matted
> With large-leaved, low-creeping melon-plants,
> And the dark cucumber.
> He reaps and stows them,
> Drifting, — drifting. Round him,
> Round his green harvest-plot,
> Flow the cool lake waves:
> The mountains ring them " : —

or whether, far across the continent, he chance to see

> "The ferry
> On the broad, clay-laden
> Lone Chorasmian stream : thereon,
> With snort and strain,
> Two horses, strongly swimming, tow
> The ferry-boat, with woven ropes
> To either bow
> Firm harnessed by the mane : — a chief
> With shout and shaken spear
> Stands at the prow, and guides them : but astern,
> The cowering merchants, in long robes,
> Sit pale beside their wealth
> Of silk-bales and of balsam-drops,
> Of gold and ivory,
> Of turquoise-earth and amethyst,
> Jasper and chalcedony,
> And milk-barred onyx-stones.

> The loaded boat swings groaning
> In the yellow eddies.
> The gods behold them," —

the gods and the poets. But, except to these blest beholders, the inhabitants of the dead centuries are mere spectral shades; for it takes a poet's fancy to vitalize with warmth and breath again those things that, having apparently left no impress on their own generation, seem to have no more signification for this than the persons of the drama or the heroes of romance.

Yet, in a far inferior way, every man is a poet to himself. In the microcosm of his own small round, every one has the power to vivify old incident, every one raises bawbles of the desk and drawer, not only into life, but into life they never had. With the flower whose leaves are shed about the box, we can bring back the brilliant morning of its blossoming, desire and hope and joyous youth once more; with the letter laid away beside it rises the dear hand that rested on the sheet, and moved along the leaf with every line it penned: each trinket has its pretty past, pleasant or painful to recall as it may be. There is no trifle, however vulgar, but, looking at its previous page, it has a side in the ideal. When one at the theatre saw so many ringlets arranged as "waterfalls," he laughed and said, they undoubtedly belonged to the "dead-heads." But Belinda, who wears a waterfall, and at night puts it into a box, considers the remark a profanity, and confesses that she never adorns herself with this addition but she thinks of that girl in France who cherished her long locks, and combed them out with care until her marriage-day, when she put on a fair white cap, and sold them for her dowry. There are more poetic locks of hair, it must be said; — the keepsake of two lovers; the lock of Keats's hair, too sacred to touch, lying in its precious salvatory. But that is the ideal of the past belonging to Belinda's waterfall, a trivial, common thing enough, yet one that has a right to its ideal, nevertheless, if we accept the ecstasies of a noted writer upon its magic material. "In spinning and weaving," says he, "the ideal that we pursue is the hair of a woman. How far are the softest wools, the finest cottons, from reaching it! At what an enormous distance from this hair all our progress leaves us, and will forever leave us! We drag behind and watch with envy this supreme perfection that every day Nature realizes in her play. This hair, fine, strong, resistant, vibrant in light sonority, and, with all that, soft, warm, luminous, and electric, — it is the flower of the human flower. There are idle disputes concerning the merit of its color. What matter? The lustrous black contains and promises the flame. The blond displays it with the splendors of the Fleece of Gold. The brown, chatoyant in the sun, appropriates the sun itself, mingles it with its mirages, floats, undulates, varies ceaselessly in its brook-like reflections, by moments smiles in the light or glooms in the shade, deceives always, and, whatever you say of it, gives you the lie charmingly. — The chief effort of human industry has combined all methods in order to exalt cotton. Rare accord of capital, machinery, arts of design, and finally chemical science, has produced those beautiful results to which England herself renders homage in buying them. Alas! all that cannot disguise the original poverty of the ungrateful tissue which has been so much adorned. If woman, who clothes herself with it in vanity, and believes herself more beautiful because of it, would but let her hair fall and unroll its waves over the indigent richness of our most brilliant cloths, what must become of them! how humiliated would the vestment be! — It is necessary to confess that one thing alone sustains itself beside a woman's hair. A single fabricator can strive there. This fabricator is an insect, — the modest silkworm."

"A particular charm surrounds the works in silk," our author then goes on to say. "It ennobles all about it. In traversing our rudest districts, the valleys of the Ardèche, where all is rock, where the mulberry, the chestnut, seem to dispense with earth, to live on air and flint, where low houses of unmortared stone sadden the eyes with their gray tint, everywhere I saw at the door, under a kind of arcade, two or three charming girls, with brown skin, with white teeth, who smiled at the passer-by and spun gold. The passer-by, whirled on by the coach, said to them under his breath: 'What a pity, innocent fays, that this gold may not be for you! Instead of disguising it with a useless color, instead of disfiguring it by art, what would it not gain by remaining itself and upon these beautiful spinners! How much better than any grand dames would this royal tissue become yourselves!'"

Perhaps it was the dowry of one of these very maidens that Belinda wears; and all this would only go to show that to every meanest thing the past can lend a halo. When one person showed another the "entire costume of a Nubian woman, purchased as she wore it," — a necklace of red beads, and two brass ear-rings simply, hanging on a nail, — how it brought up the whole scene, the wondrous ruins, the Nile, the lotos, and the palm-branch, the splendid sky soaring over all, the bronze-skinned creature shining in the sun! What a past the little glass bits had at their command, and what a more magnificent past hung yet behind them! Who would value a diamond, the product of any laboratory, were such a possibility, so much as that one which, by its own unknown and inscrutable process, defying philosopher and jeweller, has imprisoned the sunshine that moss or leaf or flower sucked in, ages since, and set its crystals in the darkness of the earth, — a drop of dew eternalized? What tree of swift and sudden springing, that grows like a gourd in the night to never so stately a height, could equal in our eyes the gnarled and may be stunted trunk that has thrown the flickering shadows of its leaves over the dying pillows alike of father, child, and grandchild? The ring upon the finger is crusted thick with memories, and, looking at it, far more than in the present do you live in the past. Perhaps it is for this that we are so jealous of events: we fear to have our memories impinged upon by pain. The woman whose lover has deserted her mourns not the man she must despise, but the love that has dropped out of her past, proving hollow and worthless. But she to whom he remains faithful borrows perpetually store of old love to enrich the daily feast; she gilds and glorifies the blest to-day with the light of that love transfigured in the past. And so, in other shapes and experiences, it is with all of us indeed; since into this fairy-land all can fly for refuge, can pick again their roses and ignore their thorns, can

> "Change
> Torment with ease, and soonest recompense
> Dole with delight."

Nor is this living in the past entirely the voluntary affair of pleasure and of memory. In another and more spiritual way it masters us. Never quite losing the vitality that once it had, with an elastic springiness it constantly rebounds, and the deed of yesterday reacts upon the deed of to-day. There is something solemn in the thought that thus the blemish or the grace of a day that long ago disappeared passes on with awfully increasing undulations into the demesne of the everlasting. And though the Judge of all may not cast each deed of other days and weigh them in the balance for us or against, yet what those deeds have made us, that we shall stand before him when,

> "'Mid the dark, a gleam
> Of yet another morning breaks;
> And, like the hand which ends a dream,
> Death, with the might of his sunbeam,
> Touches the flesh, and the soul awakes!"

Yesterday, in truth, — looking though it may like a shadow and the phantom of itself, — is the only substance that we possess, the one immutable fact. To-day is but the asymptote of to-morrow, that curve perpetually drawing near, but never reaching the straight line flying into infinity. To-morrow, the great future, belongs to the heaven where it tends. Were it otherwise, seeing the indestructible elements, and the two great central forces forever at their work, we might fancy ourselves, in one form or another, continual here on the round world. For when Laplace, through the acceleration of the moon, dropping her ten seconds a hundred years towards us, discovered the change in the earth's orbit, — swinging as it does from ellipse to circle and back again to ellipse, vibrating like a mighty pendulum, the "horologe of eternity" itself, with tremendous oscillations, through the depths of space, — he taught us that the earth endures; and so that the clay with which we are clothed still makes a part of the great revolution. Yet, since the future is no possession of our own, but a dole and pittance, we know that the earth does not endure for us, but that when we shall have submitted to the conditions of eternal spirit, yesterday, to-morrow, and to-day must alike have ceased to exist, must have vanished like illusions; for eternity can be no mere duration of time, but rather some state of being past all our power of cognition.

And though we are to inherit eternity, yet have authority now only over the period that we have passed, with what wealth then are the aged furnished! Sweet must it be to sit with folded hands and dream life over once again. How rich we are, how happy! How dear is the old hand in ours! Years have added up the sum of all the felicity that we have known together, and carried it over to to-day. Those that have left our arms and gone out into other homes are still our own; but little sunny heads besides cluster round the knees as once before they did. Not only have we age and wisdom, but youth and gayety as well. On what light and jocund scenes we look! on what deep and dearer bliss!

We see the meaning of our sorrows now, and bless them that they came. With such firm feet we have walked in the lighted way that we gaze back upon, how can we fear the Valley of the Shadow? Ah! none but they, indeed, who have threescore years and ten hived away in the past, can see the high design of Heaven in their lives, and from the wrong side of the pattern picture out the right.

" So at the last shall come old age,
Decrepit, as befits that stage.
How else wouldst thou retire apart
With the hoarded memories of thy heart,
And gather all to the very least
Of the fragments of life's earlier feast,
Let fall through eagerness to find
The crowning dainties yet behind?
Ponder on the entire past,
Laid together thus at last,
When the twilight helps to fuse
The first fresh with the faded hues,
And the outline of the whole,
As round Eve's shades their framework roll,
Grandly fronts for once thy soul!"

THE JOHNSON PARTY.

THE President of the United States has so singular a combination of defects for the office of a constitutional magistrate, that he could have obtained the opportunity to misrule the nation only by a visitation of Providence. Insincere as well as stubborn, cunning as well as unreasonable, vain as well as ill-tempered, greedy of popularity as well as arbitrary in disposition, veering in his mind as well as fixed in his will, he unites in his character the seemingly opposite qualities of demagogue and autocrat, and converts the Presidential chair into a stump or a throne, according as the impulse seizes him to cajole or to command. Doubtless much of the evil developed in him is due to his misfortune in having been lifted by events to a position which he lacked the elevation and breadth of intelligence adequately to fill. He was cursed with the possession of a power and authority which no man of narrow mind, bitter prejudices, and inordinate self-estimation can exercise without depraving himself as well as injuring the nation. Egotistic to the point of mental disease, he resented the direct and manly opposition of statesmen to his opinions and moods as a personal affront, and descended to the last degree of littleness in a political leader, — that of betraying his party, in order to

gratify his spite. He of course became the prey of intriguers and sycophants,— of persons who understand the art of managing minds which are at once arbitrary and weak, by allowing them to retain unity of will amid the most palpable inconsistencies of opinion, so that inconstancy to principle shall not weaken force of purpose, nor the emphasis be at all abated with which they may bless to-day what yesterday they cursed. Thus the abhorrer of traitors has now become their tool. Thus the denouncer of Copperheads has now sunk into dependence on their support. Thus the imposer of conditions of reconstruction has now become the foremost friend of the unconditioned return of the Rebel States. Thus the furious Union Republican, whose harangues against his political opponents almost scared his political friends by their violence, has now become the shameless betrayer of the people who trusted him. And in all these changes of base he has appeared supremely conscious, in his own mind, of playing an independent, a consistent, and especially a conscientious part.

Indeed, Mr. Johnson's character would be imperfectly described if some attention were not paid to his conscience, the purity of which is a favorite subject of his own discourse, and the perversity of which is the wonder of the rest of mankind. As a public man, his real position is similar to that of a commander of an army, who should pass over to the ranks of the enemy he was commissioned to fight, and then plead his individual convictions of duty as a justification of his treachery. In truth, Mr. Johnson's conscience is, like his understanding, a mere form or expression of his will. The will of ordinary men is addressed through their understanding and conscience. Mr. Johnson's understanding and conscience can be addressed only through his will. He puts intellectual principles and the moral law in the possessive case, thinks he pays them a compliment and adds to their authority when he makes them the adjuncts of his petted pronoun "my"; and things to him are reasonable and right, not from any quality inherent in themselves, but because they are made so by his determinations. Indeed, he sees hardly anything as it is, but almost everything as colored by his own dominant egotism. Thus he is never weary of asserting that the people are on his side; yet his method of learning the wishes of the people is to scrutinize his own, and, when acting out his own passionate impulses, he ever insists that he is obeying public sentiment. Of all the wilful men who, by strange chance, have found themselves at the head of a constitutional government, he most resembles the last Stuart king of England, James II.; and the likeness is increased from the circumstance that the American James has, in his supple and plausible Secretary of State, one fully competent to play the part of Sunderland.

The party which, under the ironical designation of the National Union Party, now proposes to take the policy and character of Mr. Johnson under its charge, is composed chiefly of Democrats defeated at the polls, and Democrats defeated on the field of battle The few apostate Republicans, who have joined its ranks while seeming to lead its organization, are of small account. Its great strength is in its Southern supporters, and, if it comes into power, it must obey a Rebel direction. By the treachery of the President, it will have the executive patronage on its side, — for Mr. Johnson's "conscience" is of that peculiar kind which finds satisfaction in arraying the interest of others against their convictions; and having thus the power to purchase support, it will not fail of those means of dividing the North which come from corrupting it. The party under which the war for the Union was conducted is to be denounced and proscribed as the party of disunion, and we are to be edified by addresses on the indissoluble unity of the nation by Secessionists, who have hardly yet had time to wash from their hands the stains of Union blood. The leading proposition on which this conspiracy against the country is to be conducted is the monstrous absurdity, that the Rebel States have an inherent, "continuous," unconditioned, constitutional *right* to form a part of the Federal government, when they have once acknowledged the fact of the defeat of their inhabitants in an armed attempt to overthrow and subvert it, — a proposition which implies that victory paralyzes the powers of the victors, that ruin begins when success is assured, that the only effect of beating a Southern Rebel in the field is to exalt him into a maker of laws for his antagonist.

In the minority Report of the Congressional Joint Committee on Reconstruction, which is designed to supply the new party with constitutional law, this theory of State Rights is most elaborately presented. The ground is taken, that during the Rebellion the States in which it prevailed were as "completely competent States of the United States as they were before the Rebellion, and were bound by all the obligations which the Constitution imposed, and entitled to all its privileges"; and that the Rebellion consisted merely in a series of "illegal acts of the citizens of such States." On this theory it is difficult to find where the guilt of rebellion lies. The States are innocent because the

Rebellion was a rising of individuals; the individuals cannot be very criminal, for it is on their votes that the committee chiefly rely to build up the National Union Party. Again, we are informed that, in respect to the admission of representatives from "such States," Congress has no right or power to ask more than two questions. These are: "Have these States organized governments? Are these governments republican in form?" The committee proceed to say: "How they were formed, under what auspices they were formed, are inquiries with which Congress has no concern. The right of the people to form a government for themselves has never been questioned." On this principle, President Johnson's labors in organizing State governments were works of supererogation. At the close of active hostilities the Rebel States had organized, though disloyal, governments, as republican in form as they were before the war broke out. The only thing, therefore, they were required to do was to send their Senators and Representatives to Washington. Congress could not have rightfully refused to receive them, because all questions as to their being loyal or disloyal, and as to the changes which the war had wrought in the relations of the States they represented to the Union, were inquiries with which Congress had no concern! And here again we have the ever-recurring difficulty respecting the "individuals" who were alone guilty of the acts of rebellion. "The right of the people," we are assured, "to form a government for themselves, has never been questioned." But it happens that "the people" here indicated are the very individuals who were before pointed out as alone responsible for the Rebellion. In the exercise of their right "to form a government for themselves," they rebelled; and now, it seems, by the exercise of the same right, they can unconditionally return. There is no wrong anywhere: it is all "right." The people are first made criminals, in order to exculpate the States, and then the innocence of the States is used to exculpate the people. When we see such outrages on common sense gravely perpetrated by so eminent a lawyer as the one who drew up the committee's Report, one is almost inclined to define minds as of two kinds, the legal mind and the human mind, and to doubt if there is any possible connection in reason between the two. To the human mind it appears that the Federal government has spent thirty-five hundred millions of dollars, and sacrificed three hundred thousand lives, in a contest which the legal mind dissolves into a mere mist of unsubstantial phrases; and by skill in the trick of substituting words for things, and definitions for events, the legal mind proceeds to show that these words and definitions, though scrupulously shielded from any contact with realities, are sufficient to prevent the nation from taking ordinary precautions against the recurrence of calamities fresh in its bitter experience. The phrase "State Rights," translated from legal into human language, is found to mean, the power to commit wrongs on individuals whom States may desire to oppress, or the power to protect the inhabitants of States from the consequences of their own crimes. The minority of the committee, indeed, seem to have forgotten that there has been any real war, and bring to mind the converted Australian savage, whom the missionary could not make penitent for a murder committed the day before, because the trifling occurrence had altogether passed from his recollection.

In fact, all attempts to discriminate between Rebels and Rebel States, to the advantage of the latter, are done in defiance of notorious facts. If the Rebellion had been merely a rising of individual citizens of States, it would have been an insurrection against the States, as well as against the Federal government, and might have been easily put down. In that case, there would have been no withdrawal of Southern Senators and Representatives from Congress, and therefore no question as to their inherent right to return. In Missouri and Kentucky, for example, there was civil war, waged by inhabitants of those States against their local governments, as well as against the United States ; and nobody contends that the rights and privileges of those States were forfeited by the criminal acts of their citizens. But the real strength of the Rebellion consisted in this, that it was not a rebellion *against* States, but a rebellion *by* States. No loose assemblage of individuals, though numbering hundreds of thousands, could long have resisted the pressure of the Federal power and the power of the State governments. They would have had no means of subsistence except those derived from plunder and voluntary contributions, and they would have lacked the military organization by which mobs are transformed into formidable armies. But the Rebellion being one of States, being virtually decreed by the people of States assembled in convention, was sustained by the two tremendous governmental powers of taxation and conscription. The willing and the unwilling were thus equally placed at the disposition of a strong government. The population and wealth of the whole immense region of country in which the Rebellion prevailed were at the service of this government. So completely was it a rebellion of States, that the universal excuse of the minority of original Union men for entering heartily into the contest after it had once begun was, that they thought it their duty to abide by the decision, and share the fortunes, of their respective *States.* Nobody at the South believed at the time the war commenced, or during its progress, that his State possessed any " continuous " right to a participation in the privileges of the Federal Constitution, the obligations of which it had repudiated. When confident of success, the Southerner scornfully scouted the mere suspicion of entertaining such a degrading notion ; when assured of defeat, his only thought was to " get his State back into the Union on the best terms that could be made." The idea of " conditions

of readmission " was as firmly fixed in the Southern as in the Northern mind. If the politicians of the South now adopt the principle that the Rebel States have not, as States, ever altered their relations to the Union, they do it from policy, finding that its adoption will give them " better terms " than they ever dreamed of getting before the President of the United States taught them that it would be more politic to bully than to plead.

In the last analysis, indeed, the theory of the minority of the Reconstruction Committee reduces the Rebel States to mere abstractions. It is plain that a State, in the concrete, is constituted by that portion of the inhabitants who form its legal people ; and that, in passing back of its government and constitution, we reach a convention of the legal people as its ultimate expression. By such conventions the acts of secession were passed ; and, as far as the people of the Rebel States could do it, they destroyed their States considered as organized communities forming a part of the United States. The claim of the United States to authority over the territory and inhabitants was of course not affected by these acts ; but in what condition did they place the people ? Plainly in the condition of rebels, engaged in an attempt to overturn the Constitution and government of the United States. As the whole force of the people in each of the Rebel communities was engaged in this work, the whole of the people were rebels and public enemies. Nothing was left, in each case, but an abstract State, without any external body, and as destitute of people having a right to enjoy the privileges of the Constitution as if the territory had been swept clean of population by a pestilence. It is, then, only this abstract State which has a right to representation in Congress. But how can there be a right to representation when there is nobody to be represented ? All this may appear puerile, but the puerility is in the premises as well as in the logical deductions, and the premises are laid down as in.

disputable constitutional principles by the eminent jurists who supply ideas for the National Union Party.

The doctrine of the unconditional right of the Rebel States to representation being thus a demonstrated absurdity, the only question relates to the conditions which Congress proposes to impose. Certainly these conditions, as embodied in the constitutional amendment which has passed both houses by such overwhelming majorities, are the mildest ever exacted of defeated enemies by a victorious nation. There is not a distinctly "radical" idea in the whole amendment, — nothing that President Johnson has not himself, within a comparatively recent period, stamped with his high approbation. Does it ordain universal suffrage? No. Does it ordain impartial suffrage? No. Does it proscribe, disfranchise, or expatriate the recent armed enemies of the country, or confiscate their property? No. It simply ordains that the national debt shall be paid and the Rebel debt repudiated; that the civil rights of all persons shall be maintained; that Rebels who have added perjury to treason shall be disqualified for office; and that the Rebel States shall not have their political power in the Union increased by the presence on their soil of persons to whom they deny political rights, but that representation shall be based throughout the Republic on voters, and not on population. The pith of the whole amendment is in the last clause; and is there anything in that to which reasonable objection can be made? Would it not be a curious result of the war against Rebellion, that it should end in conferring on a Rebel voter in South Carolina a power equal, in national affairs, to that of two loyal voters in New York? Can any Democrat have the face to assert that the South should have, through its disfranchised negro freemen alone, a power in the Electoral College and in the national House of Representatives equal to that of the States of Ohio and Indiana combined?

Yet these conditions, so conciliatory, moderate, lenient, almost timid, and which, by the omission of impartial suffrage, fall very far below the requirements of the average sentiment of the loyal nation, are still denounced by the new party of "Union" as the work of furious radicals, bent on destroying the rights of the States. Thus Governor James L. Orr of South Carolina, a leading Rebel, pardoned into a Johnsonian Union man, implores the people of that region to send delegates to the Philadelphia Convention, on the ground that its purpose is to organize "conservative" men of all sections and parties, "to drive from power that radical party who are daily trampling under foot the Constitution, and fast converting a constitutional Republic into a consolidated despotism." The terms to which South Carolina is asked to submit, before she can be made the equal of Ohio or New York in the Union, are stated to be "too degrading and humiliating to be entertained by a freeman for a single instant." When we consider that this "radical party" constitutes nearly four fifths of the legal legislature of the nation, that it was the party which saved the country from dismemberment while Mr. Orr and his friends were notoriously engaged in "trampling the Constitution under foot," and that the man who denounces it owes his forfeited life to its clemency, the astounding insolence of the impeachment touches the sublime. Here is confessed treason inveighing against tried loyalty, in the name of the Constitution it has violated and the law it has broken! But why does Mr. Orr think the terms of South Carolina's restored relations to the Union "too degrading and humiliating to be entertained by a freeman for a single instant"? Is it because he wishes to have the Rebel debt paid? Is it because he desires to have the Federal debt repudiated? Is it because he thinks it intolerable that a negro should have civil rights? Is it because he resents the idea that breakers of oaths, like himself, should be disqualified from having another opportunity of forswearing themselves? Is it because he considers that a white Rebel freeman of South Carolina has a natural right to exercise double the political power of a white loyal freeman of Massachusetts? He must return an affirmative answer to all these questions in order to make it out that his State will be degraded and humiliated by ratifying the amendment; and the necessity of the measure is therefore proved by the motives known to prompt the attacks of its vilifiers.

The insolence of Mr. Orr is not merely individual, but representative. It is the result of Mr. Johnson's attempt "to produce harmony between the two sections," by betraying the section to which he owed his election. Had it not been for his treachery, there would have been little difficulty in settling the terms of peace, so as to avoid all causes for future war; but, from the time he quarrelled with Congress, he has been the great stirrer-up of disaffection at the South, and the virtual leader of the Southern reactionary party. Every man at the South who was prominent in the Rebellion, every man at the North who was prominent in aiding the Rebellion, is now openly or covertly his partisan, and by fawning on him earns the right to defame the representatives of the people by whom the Rebellion was put down. Among traitors and Copperheads the fear of punishment has been succeeded by the hope of revenge; elation is on faces which the downfall of Richmond overcast; and a return to the old times, when a united South ruled the country by means of a divided North, is confidently expected by the whole crew of political bullies and political sycophants whose profit is in the abasement of the nation. It is even said that, if the majority of the "Rump" Congress cannot be overcome by fair means, it will be by foul; and there are noisy partisans of the President who assert that he has in him a Cromwellian capacity for dealing with legislative assemblies whose notions of the public good clash with his own. In short, we are promised, on the assembling of the next Congress, a *coup d'état.*

Garret Davis, of Kentucky, was, we believe, the first to announce this executive remedy for the "radical" disease of the state, and it has since been often prescribed by Democratic politicians as a sovereign panacea. General McClernand, indeed, proposed a scheme, simpler even than that of executive recognition, by which the Southern Senators and Representatives might effect a lodgment in Congress. They should, according to him, have gone to Washington, entered the halls of legislation, and proceeded to occupy their seats, "peaceably if they could, forcibly if they must"; but the record of General McClernand, as a military man, was not such as to give to his advice on a question of carrying positions by assault a high degree of authority, and, there being some natural hesitation in following his counsel, the golden opportunity was lost. Mr. Montgomery Blair, who professes his willingness to act with any men, "Rebels or any one else," to put down the radicals, is never weary of talking to conservative conventions of "two Presidents and two Congresses." There can be no doubt that the project of a *coup d'état* has become dangerously familiar to the "conservative" mind, and that the eminent legal gentlemen of the North who are publishing opinions affirming the right of the excluded Southern representatives to their seats are playing into the hands of the desperate gang of unscrupulous politicians who are determined to have the right established by force. It is computed that the gain, in the approaching elections, of twenty-five districts now represented by Union Republicans, will give the Johnson party, in the next Congress, a majority of the House of Representatives, should the Southern delegations be counted; and it is proposed that the Johnson members legally entitled to seats should combine with the Southern pretenders to seats, organize as the House of Representatives of the United States, and apply to the President for recognition. Should the President comply, he would be impeached by an unrecognized House before an "incomplete" Senate, and, if convicted, would deny the validity of the proceeding. The result would be civil war, in which the name of the Federal government would be on the side of the revolutionists. Such is the programme which is freely discussed by partisans of the President, considered to be high in his favor; and the scheme, it is contended, is the logical result of the position he has assumed as to the rights of the excluded States to representation. It is certain that the present Congress is as much the Congress of the United States as he is the President of the United States; but it is well known that he considers himself to represent the whole country, while he thinks that Congress only represents a portion of it; and he has in his character just that combination of qualities, and is placed in just those anomalous circumstances, which lead men to the commission of great political crimes. The mere hint of the possibility of his attempting a *coup d'état* is received by some Republicans with a look of incredulous surprise; yet what has his administration been to such persons but a succession of surprises?

But whatever view may be taken of the President's designs, there can be no doubt that the safety, peace, interest, and honor of the country depend on the success of the Union Republicans in the approaching elections. The loyal nation must see to it that the Fortieth Congress shall be as competent to override executive vetoes as the Thirty-Ninth, and be equally removed from the peril of being expelled for one more in harmony with Executive ideas. The same earnestness, energy, patriotism, and intelligence which gave success to the war, must now be exerted to reap its fruits and prevent its recurrence. The only danger is, that, in some representative districts, the people may be swindled by plausibilities

and respectabilities; for when, in political contests, any great villany is contemplated, there are always found some eminently respectable men, with a fixed capital of certain eminently conservative phrases, innocently ready to furnish the wolves of politics with abundant supplies of sheep's clothing. These dignified dupes are more than usually active at the present time; and the gravity of their speech is as edifying as its emptiness. Immersed in words, and with no clear perception of things, they mistake conspiracy for conservatism. Their pet horror is the term "radical"; their ideal of heroic patriotism, the spectacle of a great nation which allows itself to be ruined with decorum, and dies rather than commit the slightest breach of constitutional etiquette. This insensibility to facts and blindness to the tendency of events, they call wisdom and moderation. Behind these political dummies are the real forces of the Johnson party, men of insolent spirit, resolute will, embittered temper, and unscrupulous purpose, who clearly know what they are after, and will hesitate at no "informality" in the attempt to obtain it. To give these persons political power will be to surrender the results of the war, by placing the government practically in the hands of those against whom the war was waged. No smooth words about "the equality of the States," "the necessity of conciliation," "the wickedness of sectional conflicts," will alter the fact, that, in refusing to support Congress, the people would set a reward on treachery and place a bounty on treason. "The South," says a Mr. Hill of Georgia, in a letter favoring the Philadelphia Convention, "sought to save the Constitution out of the Union. She failed. Let her now bring her diminished and shattered, but united and earnest counsels and energies to save the Constitution in the Union." The sort of Constitution the South sought to save by warring against the government is the Constitution which she now proposes to save by administering it! Is this the tone of pardoned and penitent treason? Is this the spirit to build up a "National Union Party"? No; but it is the tone and spirit now fashionable in the defeated Rebel States, and will not be changed until the autumn elections shall have proved that they have as little to expect from the next Congress as from the present, and that they must give securities for their future conduct before they can be relieved from the penalties incurred by their past.

REVIEWS AND LITERARY NOTICES.

Armadale. A Novel. By WILKIE COLLINS. New York: Harper and Brothers.

EXCEPT for the fact that there is nothing at all automatic in his inventions, there seems to be no good reason why Mr. Collins should not make a perpetual motion. He has a surprising mechanical faculty, and great patience and skill in passing the figures he contrives through the programme arranged for them. Having read one of his novels, you feel as if you had been amused with a puppet-show of rare merit, and you would like to have the ingenious mechanician before the curtain. So much cleverness, however, seems to be thrown away on the entertainment of a single evening, and you sigh for its application to some work of more lasting usefulness; and the perpetual motion occurs to you as the thing worthiest such powers. Let it be a perpetual literary motion, if the public please. Given a remarkable dream and a beautiful bad woman to fulfil it; you have but to amplify the vision sufficiently, and your beautiful bad woman goes on fulfilling it forever in tens of thousands of volumes. As the brother of De Quincey said, when proposing to stand on the ceiling, head downwards, and be spun there like a whip-top, thus overcoming the attraction of gravitation by the mere rapidity of revolution, "If you can keep it up for an instant, you can keep it up all day." Alas! it is just at this point that the fatal defect of Mr. Collins's mechanism appears. But for the artisan's hand, the complicated work would not start at all, and we perceive that, if he lifted it for a moment from the crank, the painfully contrived dream would drop to pieces, and the beautiful bad woman would come to a jerky stand-still in the midst of her most atrocious development. A perpetual literary motion is therefore out of the question, so far as Mr. Collins is concerned; and we can merely examine his defective machinery, with many a regret that a plan so ingenious, and devices so labored and costly, should be of no better effect.

We think, indeed, that all his stories are constructed upon a principle as false to art as it is false to life. In this world, we have first men and women, with certain well-known good and evil passions, and these passions are the causes of all the events that happen in the world. We doubt if it has occurred to any of our readers to see a set of circumstances, even of the most relentless and malignant description, grouping themselves about any human being without the agency of his own love or hate. Yet this is what happens very frequently in Mr. Collins's novels, impoverishing and enfeebling his characters in a surprising degree, and reducing them to the condition of juiceless puppets without proper will or motion. It is not that they are all wanting in verisimilitude. Even the entirely wicked Miss Gwilt is a conceivable character; but, being destined merely to fulfil Armadale's dream, she loses all freedom of action, and, we must say, takes most clumsy and long-roundabout methods of accomplishing crimes, to which one would have thought a lady of her imputed sagacity would have found much shorter cuts. It is amazing and inartistic, however, that after all her awkwardness she should fail. Given a blockhead like Armadale, and a dreamer like Midwinter, there is no reason in nature, and no reason in art, why a lady of Miss Gwilt's advantages should not marry both of them; and the author's overruling on this point is more creditable to his heart than to his head. These three people are the chief persons of the story, and their hands are tied from first to last. They are not to act out their characters : they are to act out the plot ; and the author's designs are accomplished in defiance of their several natures. Some of the minor persons are not so ruthlessly treated. The Pedgifts, father and son, are free agents, and they are admirably true to their instincts of upright, astute lawyers, who love best to employ their legal shrewdness in a good cause. Their joint triumph over Miss Gwilt is probable and natural, and would be a successful point in the book, if it were conceivable that she should expose herself to such a defeat by so much needless plotting with Mrs. Oldershaw. But to fill so large a stage, an immense deal of by-play was necessary, and great numbers of people are visibly dragged upon the scene. Some of these accomplish nothing in the drama. To what end have we so much of Mr. Brock ? Others elaborately presented only contribute to the result in the most intricate and tedious way ; and in Major Milroy's family there is no means of discovering that Miss Gwilt is an adventuress, but for Mrs. Milroy to become jealous of her and to open her letters.

It cannot, of course, be denied that Mr. Collins's stories are interesting ; for an infinite number of persons read them through. But it is the bare plot that interests, and the disposition of mankind to listen to storytelling is such that the idlest *conteur* can entertain. We must demand of literary art, however, that it shall interest in people's fortunes by first interesting in people. Can any one of all Mr. Collins's readers declare that he sympathizes with the loves of Armadale and Neelie Milroy, or actually cares a straw what becomes of either of those insipid young persons ? Neither is Midwinter one to take hold on like or dislike ; and Miss Gwilt is interesting only as the capable but helpless spider out of which the plot of the story is spun. Pathos there is not in the book, and the humor is altogether too serious to laugh at.

Four Years in the Saddle. By COLONEL HARRY GILMORE. New York : Harper and Brothers.

IT is sometimes difficult to believe, in reading this book, that it is not the production of Major Gahagan of the Ahmednuggar Irregulars, or Mr. Barry Lyndon of Castle Lyndon. Being merely a record of personal adventure, it does not suggest itself as part of the history of our late war, and, but for the recurrence of the familiar names of American persons and places, it might pass for the narrative of either of the distinguished characters mentioned.

In dealing with events creditable to his own courage and gallantry, Colonel Gilmore has the unsparing frankness of Major Gahagan, and it must be allowed that there is a remarkable likeness in all the adventures of these remarkable men. It is true that Colonel Gilmore does not fire upon a file of twenty elephants so as to cut away all their trunks by a single shot ; but he does kill eleven Yankees by the discharge of a cannon which he touches off with a live coal held between his thumb and finger. Being made prisoner, he is quite as defiant and outrageous as the Guj-puti under similar circumstances : at one time he can scarcely restrain himself from throwing into the sea the insolent captain of a Federal gunboat ; at another time, when handcuffed by order of General Sheridan, he spends an hour in cursing his captors. The red-hair of the Lord of the White Elephants waved his followers to victory ; Colonel Gilmore's "hat, with the long black plume upon it," is the signal of triumph to his marauders. Both, finally, are loved by the ladies, and are alike extravagant in their devotion to the sex. Colonel Gilmore, indeed, withholds no touch that can go to make him the hero of a dime novel ; and there is not a more picturesque and dashing character in literature outside of the adventures of Claude Duval. Everywhere we behold him waving his steel (as he calls his sword) ; he wheels before our dazzled eyes like a meteor ; he charges, and the foe fly like sheep before him. And no sooner is he come into town from killing a score or two of Yankees, than the ladies — who are all good Union women and have just taken the oath of allegiance — crowd to kiss and caress him ; or, as he puts it in his own vivid language, he receives " a kiss from more than one pair of ruby lips, and gives many a hearty hug and kiss in return." In his wild way, he takes a pleasure in evoking the tender solicitude of the ladies for his safety, — eats a dish of strawberries in a house upon which the Yankees are charging to capture him, and remains for some minutes after the strawberries are eaten, while the ladies, proffering him his arms, are " dancing about, and positively screaming with excitement." At another time, when the bullets of the enemy are hissing about his ears, he puts on a pretty girl's slipper for her. "Such," he remarks, with a pensive air, "are some of the few happy scenes that brighten a soldier's life."

Colonel Gilmore, who has the diffidence of Major Gahagan, has also the engaging artlessness which lends so great a charm to the personal narrative of Mr. Barry Lyndon. He does not reserve from the reader's knowledge such of his exploits as stealing the chaplain's whiskey, and drinking the peach-brandy of the simple old woman who supposed she was offering it to General Lee. "Place him where you may," says Colonel Gilmore, "and under no matter what adverse circumstances, you can always distinguish a gentleman." He has a great deal of fine feeling, and can scarcely restrain his tears at the burning of Chambersburg, after setting it on fire. Desiring a memento of a brother officer, he takes a small piece of the dead man's skull. It has been supposed that civilized soldiers,

however brave and resolute, scarcely exulted in the remembrance of the lives they had taken; and it is thought to be one of the merciful features of modern warfare, that in the vast majority of cases the slayer and the slain are unknown to each other. Colonel Gilmore has none of the false tenderness which shrinks from a knowledge of homicide. On the contrary, he is careful to know when he has killed a man; and he recounts, with an exactness revolting to feebler nerves, the circumstances and the methods by which he put this or that enemy to death.

We think we could hardly admire Colonel Gilmore if he had been of our side during the war, and had done to the Rebels the things he professes to have done to us. As it is, we trust he will forgive us, if we confess that we have not read his narrative with a tranquil stomach, and that we think it will impress his Northern readers as the history of a brigand who had the good luck to be also a traitor.

RECENT AMERICAN PUBLICATIONS.

The Structure of Animal Life. Six Lectures delivered at the Brooklyn Academy of Music, in January and February, 1862. By Louis Agassiz, Professor of Zoölogy and Geology in the Lawrence Scientific School. New York. C. Scribner & Co. 8vo. pp. viii., 128. $2.50.

History of the Life and Times of James Madison. By William C. Rives. Vol. II. Boston. Little, Brown, & Co. 8vo. pp. xxii., 657. $3.50.

The Physiology of Man; designed to represent the Existing State of Physiological Science, as applied to the Functions of the Human Body. By Austin Flint, Jr., M. D., Professor of Physiology and Microscopy in the Bellevue Medical College, N. Y., and in the Long Island College Hospital; Fellow of the New York Academy of Medicine, etc. Introduction; the Blood; Circulation; Respiration. New York. D. Appleton & Co. 8vo. pp. 502. $4.50.

Poems. By Annie E. Clarke. Philadelphia. J. B. Lippincott & Co. 16mo. pp. 146. $1.00.

The Living Forces of the Universe. The Temple and the Worshippers. By George W. Thompson. Philadelphia. Howard Challen. 12mo. pp. xxiv., 358. $1.75.

Jealousy. By George Sand, Author of "Consuelo," &c. With a Biographical Sketch of the Author. Philadelphia. T. B. Peterson & Bro. 12mo. pp. 304. $2.00.

Stories told to a Child. By Jean Ingelow. Boston. Roberts Brothers. 18mo. pp. vi., 424. $1.75.

Canary Birds. A Manual of Useful and Practical Information for Bird-Keepers. New York. William Wood & Co. 16mo. paper. pp. 110. 50 cents.

The Origin of the Late War, traced from the Beginning of the Constitution to the Revolt of the Southern States. By George Lunt. New York. D. Appleton & Co. 12mo. pp. xiv., 491. $3.00.

False Pride; or, Two Ways to Matrimony. A Companion to "Family Pride." Philadelphia. T. B. Peterson & Bro. 12mo. pp. 265. $2.00.

The Genius of Edmund Burke. By J. L. Batchelder. Chicago. J. L. Batchelder. 12mo. pp. 50. $1.00.

Letters of Life. By Mrs. L. H. Sigourney. New York. D. Appleton & Co. 12mo. pp. 414. $2.50.

The Church of England a Portion of Christ's one Holy Catholic Church, and a Means of restoring Visible Unity. An Eirenicon, in a Letter to the Author of "The Christian Year." By E. B. Pusey, D. D., Regius Professor of Hebrew, and Canon of Christ Church, Oxford. New York. D. Appleton & Co. 12mo. pp. 395. $2.00.

The Temporal Mission of the Holy Ghost; or, Reason and Revelation. By Henry Edward, Archbishop of Westminster. New York. D. Appleton & Co. 12mo. pp. 274. $1.75.

The Fortune Seeker. By Mrs. Emma D. E. N. Southworth. Philadelphia. T. B. Peterson & Bro. 12mo. pp. 498. $2.00.

Stonewall Jackson : a Biography. With a Portrait and Map. By John Esten Cooke, formerly of General Stuart's Staff. New York. D. Appleton & Co. 12mo. pp. 470. $3.50.

The Phenomena of Plant Life. By Leo H. Grindon, Lecturer on Botany at the Royal School of Medicine, Manchester, etc. Boston. Nichols & Noyes. 12mo. pp. 93. $1.00.

A History of New England, from the Discovery by Europeans to the Revolution of the Seventeenth Century, being an Abridgment of his "History of New England during the Stuart Dynasty." By John Gorham Palfrey. In Two Volumes. New York. Hurd & Houghton. 12mo. pp. xx., 408 ; xii., 426. $5.00.

The Story of Kennett. By Bayard Taylor. New York. Hurd & Houghton. 12mo. pp. x., 418. $2.25.

A New Translation of the Hebrew Prophets, with an Introduction and Notes. By George R. Noyes, D. D., Hancock Professor of Hebrew, etc., and Dexter Lecturer in Harvard University. Third Edition, with a New Introduction and additional Notes. In Two Volumes. Boston. American Unitarian Association. 12mo. pp. xcii., 271 ; iv., 413. $4.50.

St. Martin's Eve. By Mrs. Henry Wood. Philadelphia. T. B. Peterson & Brothers. 8vo. pp. 327. $2.00.

The Man of the World. By William North, Author of "The Usurer's Gift," etc. Philadelphia. T. B. Peterson & Bro. 12mo. pp. 437. $2.00.

Life of Emanuel Swedenborg. Together with a brief Synopsis of his Writings, both Philosophical and Theological. By William White. With an Introduction by B. F. Barrett. First American Edition. Philadelphia. J. B. Lippincott & Co. 12mo. pp. 272. $1.50.

The Reunion of Christendom. A Pastoral Letter to the Clergy, etc. By Henry Edward, Archbishop of Westminster. New York. D. Appleton & Co. 8vo. paper. pp. 66. 50 cts.

The Principles of Biology. By Herbert Spencer. Vol. I. New York. D. Appleton & Co. 12mo. pp. x., 475. $2.50.

Notes on the History of Slavery in Massachusetts. By George H. Moore, Librarian of the New York Historical Society, and Corresponding Member of the Massachusetts Historical Society. New York. D. Appleton & Co. 8vo. pp. iv., 256. $2.50.

The Miniature Fruit-Garden ; or, The Culture of Pyramidal and Bush Fruit-Trees. By Thomas Rivers. First American, from the Thirteenth English Edition. New York. Orange Judd & Co. 12mo. pp. x., 133. $1.00.

New Book of Flowers. By Joseph Breck. New York. Orange Judd & Co. 12mo. pp. 480. $1.75.

The History of Usury, from the earliest Period to the present Time. Together with a brief Statement of General Principles concerning the Conflict of the Laws of different States and Countries, and an Examination into the Policy of Laws on Usury and their Effect upon Commerce. By J. B. C. Murray. Philadelphia. J. B. Lippincott & Co. 12mo. pp. 158. $1.50.

Hidden Depths. Philadelphia. J. B. Lippincott & Co. 12mo. pp. 351. $2.00.

A Historical Inquiry concerning Henry Hudson ; his Friends, Relatives, and Early Life, his Connection with the Muscovy Company, and Discovery of Delaware Bay. By John Meredith Read, Jr. Albany. Joel Munsell. 8vo. pp. vi., 209. $5.00.

THE

ATLANTIC MONTHLY.

A Magazine of Literature, Science, Art, and Politics.

VOL. XVIII. — OCTOBER, 1866. — NO. CVIII.

CHILDHOOD: A STUDY.

THERE is a rushing southwest wind. It murmurs overhead among the willows, and the little river-waves lap and wash upon the point below; but not a breath lifts my hair, down here among the tree-trunks, close to the water. Clear water ripples at my feet; and a mile and more away, across the great bay of the wide river, the old, compact brick-red city lies silent in the sunshine. Silent, I say truly: to me, here, it is motionless and silent. But if I should walk up into State Street and say so, my truth, like many others, when uprooted from among their circumstances, would turn into a disagreeable lie. Sharp points rise above the irregular profile of the line of roofs. Some are church spires, and some are masts, — mixed at the rate of about one church and a half to a schooner. I smell the clear earthy smell of the pure gray sand, and the fresh, cool smell of the pure water. Tiny bird-tracks lie along the edge of the water, perhaps to delight the soul of some millennial ichnologist. A faint aromatic perfume rises from the stems of the willow-bushes, abraded by the ice of the winter floods. I should not perceive it, were they not tangled and matted all around so close to my head.

Just this side of the city is the monstrous arms factory; and over the level line of its great dike, the chimneys of the attendant village of boarding-houses peep up like irregular teeth. A sail-boat glides up the river. A silent brown sparrow runs along the stems of the willow thicket, and delicate slender flies now and then alight on me. They will die to-night. It is too early in the spring for them.

The air is warm and soft. Now, and here, I can write. Utter solitude, warmth, a landscape, and a comfortable seat are the requisites. The first and the last are the chiefest; if but one of the four could be had, I think that (as a writer) I should take the seat. That which, of all my writing, I wrote with the fullest and keenest sense of creative pleasure, I did while coiled up, one summer day, among the dry branches of a fallen tree, at the tip of a long, promontory-like stretch of meadow, on the quiet, lonely, level Glastenbury shore, over against the Connecticut State Prison at Wethersfield.

Well, here on the river-shore, I begin ; but I shall not tell when I stop. Doubtless there will be a jog in the composition. The blue sky and clear water will fade out of my words all at once, and a carpet and hot-air furnace, perhaps, will appear.

Nothing.

Then, a life. And so I entered this world : a being, sliding obscurely in among human beings. But whence, or whither ? Those questions belong among the gigantic, terrible ones, insoluble, silent, — the unanswering primeval sphinxes of the mind. We can sit and stare at such questions, and wonder ; but staring and wondering are not thought. They are close to idiocy : both states drop the lower jaw and open the mouth ; and assuming the idiotic _physique_ tends, if there be any sympathetic and imitative power, to bring on the idiotic state. If we stare and wonder too long at such questions, we may make ourselves idiots, — never philosophers.

I do not recollect the innocent and sunny hours of childhood. * As to innocence, the remark of a certain ancient and reverend man, though sour, was critically accurate, — that " it is the weakness of infants' limbs, and not their minds, which are innocent." It is most true. Many an impotent infantine screech or slap or scratch embodies an abandonment and ecstasy of utter uncontrolled fury scarcely expressible by the grown-up man, though he should work the bloodiest murder to express it. And what adult manifestation, except in the violent ward of an insane retreat, or perhaps among savages,— the infants of the world,— equals, in exquisite concentration and rapture of fury, that child's trick of flinging himself flat down, and, with kicks and poundings and howls, bang-

* The paragraphs here following were written in the summer of 1862, and had been meditated or memorandumed long before. Thus they were not derived from the similar disquisitions of Gail Hamilton in the Atlantic for January, 1863. There is no danger that anybody will suspect that _spirituelle_ lady of extracting her sunbeams out of my poor old cold cucumbers.

ing his head upon the ground ? Without fear or knowledge, his whole being centres in the one faculty of anger ; he hurls the whole of himself slap against the whole world, as readily as at a kitten or a playmate. He would fain scrabble down through the heart of the earth and kill it, rend it to pieces, if he could ! If human wickedness can be expressed in such a mad child, you have the whole of it, — perfectly ignorant, perfectly furious, perfectly feeble, perfectly useless.

And as to the sunny hours, I believe those delights are like the phantasmal glories of elf-land. When the glamour is taken away, the splendid feasts and draperies, and gold and silver, and gallant knights and lovely ladies, are seen to have been a squalid misery of poor roots and scraps, tatters and pebbles and bark and dirt, misshapen dwarfs and old hags. Or else, the deceitful vision vanishes all away, and was only empty, unconscious time. Or am I indeed unfortunate, and inferior to other men in innate qualities, in social faculty, in truthfulness of remembrance ?

Let me see. Let me " set it out," as an attorney would say. Let me state and judge those primeval, or preliminary, or forming years of my life.

How many were they ? More at the North, than in the hot, hurrying South. As a rule, the Northerner should be twenty-five years old before assuming to be a man. For my own part, I have always had an unpleasant consciousness, which I am only now escaping from, of non - precocity, anti - precocity, in fact, _post_cocity. I have been relatively immature. In important particulars I have been, somehow, ten years behind men — boys if you like — of my own age. The particulars I mean are those of intercourse with other people.

The first ten years of my life seem to me now to have been almost totally empty. I can conjure up, not without some effort, a scanty platoon of small, dim images from school and Sunday school and church and home ; but they are few and faint.

I remember a little dirty-faced rampant girl at an infant school in Pine

Street, who was wont to scratch us with such fell and witch-like malignity and persistence, that the teacher was fain to sew up her small fists in unbleached cotton bags, — Miss Roquil's school (I never found out that the name was Rockwell until ten years afterwards, — so phonetic is nature!) in Parade Street, where the huge, cunning Anakim of the first class used to cajole me, poor little man, always foolishly benevolent, into bestowing upon them all the ginger-bread of my lunch, which I gave, and found a dim, vague sense of incorrect-ness remaining in my childish mind. They must have been boys of fourteen or fifteen ; but I remember them as of giantly stature and vast age.

A grisly being haunted the neighbor-hood through which I had afterwards to pass to another school, — a great, hulk-ing, brutal fellow, Tom Reddiford by name, from whom I apprehended un-imaginable tortures. I crept back and forth in such dumb, nameless frights as frontier children may have felt, who, in old times of Indian war, passed through woods where the red hand of a Wy-andot might grasp them out of any bush. I have not the least idea why this wretched Reddiford used to hunt me so, as when one doth hunt a par-tridge in the mountains, unless out of pure beastly enjoyment of my childish frights. He did, once or twice, hustle me about, I believe, but never inflicted actual bodily harm. I told my parents ; but they helped me not at all. Either they thought I was not really scared, or that the experience would do me good ; but it was a mistake. My father should have searched out this young bully and effectually quieted him. Fright is a most beneficial thing for bullies, but a sadly harmful one for a little boy. How fervently I vowed to "lick" that Tom Reddiford, if I ever grew half as big as he! Very likely he has died in a brawl or a poor-house by this time. But his outrages burnt into my mind scars so deep that they are part of its struc-ture. I will pay him off yet, if I meet him.

Another awful figure haunted the same neighborhood, — "Old Britt," a street sot, — an old, filthy, unshorn hog of a man, moving in a halo of rags and effluvium, — whom I used to meet lurching along the pavement, or sometimes prone by the roadside in a nauseous rummy sleep. Him I passed by with a wide circuit of fear and dis-gust and detestation.

My local attachments must have been stunted, like the roots of plants often transplanted. They twine close and strong about no place. How could they, when in my native city alone — not to mention the six other towns where I have sojourned, four of whose names begin with the syllable "New"— I can count twenty houses where I re-member to have lived ? The Wander-ing Jew is a parable for a tenant house-keeper that "moves" every spring ; and I might be his son. Cursed be moving ! What a long list of houses ! There is the A—— house, which I dimly recol-lect, and where I think we had some beehives ; the S—— house, where we boarded, and I fell down and broke a bone ; the L—— house, where also we boarded, and there were many young girls. There I dreamed of an angel, — a person about eight feet long, flying along past the second-story side-win-dows, in the conventional horizontal attitude, so suggestive of a "crick in the neck," with great, wide wings, toot-ing through a trumpet as long as him-self ; and out of each temple, as I dis-tinctly remember, grew a thing like a knitting - needle, with a cherry on the end. There was also the Cl—— house, where was a tree of horrible, nauseating red plums ; the W—— house, quaint and many - gabled ; the C—— house, where I had my last whipping. Ah, that whipping, — those other whip-pings ! How resolutely did they each make me vow that the next ugly thing which I could safely do should surely be done? A whipping inflicted upon a child old enough to remember it is almost certainly a horrible mis-take. No one knows how often it happens that a child's sense of per-sonal insult or degradation, though incapable of expression, is every whit as quick and deep as a man's.

Other houses I remember,— in broad streets, narrow streets, — in close-built blocks, in open outskirts, — even a mile or two away among the green fields, — lived in, boarded in. I am cheated in heart by injurious superfluity of houses. One home, remembered alone, would stand embowered forever, — if not among ancestral trees and vines, then in clustering memories far more lovely and more cherished. But what dignity or beauty or quiet or distinctness can attach to the score of tenements that scurry helter-skelter through my memory? It is little better than the vision of the drunken men-at-arms in the castle of the parodist : —

"Then straight there did appear, to each gallant Gorbalier,
Forty castles dancing near, all around ! "

An unblest memory !

I believe I once stole a quantity of rather moist brown sugar, and hid it, a clumsy, sticky, brown-paper parcel, between my bed and the sacking. A chambermaid discovered the *corpus delicti*, and something was done, — I forget what. But I wish I had never done anything worse !

O dear ! I used to have to go to church twice every Sunday, and to Sunday school before forenoon service beside. I cannot express the extreme dreariness to me, poor little boy, of perching on those uncomfortable, old-fashioned, grown-up seats, too high for my little legs, too wide for my short thighs, so that I sat backless above and dangling below. What had I to do with those grown-up sermons ? Men's talk is babble to a child, as much as children's to a man. The wind that blew past my ears meant as much, and sounded better. Or what were the prayers to me, or the singing ? This perfunctory, formal early piety of mine had much influence, long afterward, by natural reaction. Nothing can better shadow forth the weariness of those weekly *jornadas del muerto* than the fact that I found now and then an oasis of delight in pious stories for children, out of the Sabbath-school library. Thus we hear of starving men chewing upon an old boot, or famished desert-travellers sucking rapturously at a hole full of mud. I remember once being so absorbed in a story during sermon-time, that, coming to a word of new and queer physiognomy, and having forgotten all circumstance, I repeated it, according to my custom, quite aloud. "Cuddy," I said, in the middle of the silence of a pause in the sermon. Everybody stared quickly at me. I might as well have uttered a round oath. The awful shame that flushed me and crushed me cannot be imagined. My parents talked kindly, but seriously, to me for such an irreverence ; yet I suspect that by themselves they laughed. This book was a story called " Erminia," with an East India voyage in it. I don't know why the name should stick so fast in my memory these thirty years.

My parents, alike inflexible in hygiene and morality, had reasons out of either realm against those stomachic reinforcements to religion which can mollify so sweetly the child's desert pathway through "meeting." Neither cooky, raisin, nor peppermint lozenge would they dispense. It would violate two important rules, — "Attend to the sermon," and " No eating between meals " ; — the latter law, otherwise of Medo-Persic stringency, having only this severe and secular exception : " My son, if you are hungry, you can eat a piece of good dry bread. You may have that."

So much the more lovely is the remembrance of that kind interceder, usually an occupant of the same pew with ourselves, who, regarding the minister the while with unmoved countenance, was wont ever and anon, with quiet hand, to insinuate within my childish grasp the beatifying lozenge, or the snow-white and aromatic sassafras or wintergreen " pipe." The sweet savor of those frequent gifts, sweeter for their half-secret, half-forbidden conferring, will never disappear out of my memory. That candy, if I had the power, should be paid for with rewards (not one whit more worth, if loving-kindness in giving be any criterion), in a place where, we are told, " congregations ne'er break up, and Sabbaths have no end," — and where, therefore, let us earnestly hope, their delights are superior to those of their earthly antetypes.

Behind us, all one year, there sat in church a platoon of imps. They were children of a red-eyed father, who must have been a drinker; they were curiously ugly in countenance; and they used at once to prove and practise their petty demonism by tormenting us who sat in the pew just before them. They slyly pulled our hair; poked us, and then, when we turned round, made frightful, malignant faces close to ours; talked loud in sermon-time; dropped crumbs down the backs of our necks; and whispered loudly in our scandalized ears that standing, supreme reproach and insult of my childish days — then confined to little boys, since adopted by the great Democratic party — of " Nigger! Nigger!"

We had not, perhaps, too many rules at home. (There were sometimes too many at school.) Some of them were well enough. We might not have both butter and molasses, or butter and sugar, on the same piece of bread. One luxury was enough. Flavors too compound coax toward the Epicurean sty; the most compound of all is doubtless that of the feast which the pig eateth. "Shut the door," — a good rule. " No reading before breakfast, nor by firelight, nor by lamp-light, nor between daylight and dark," — an indispensable rule for such book-devouring children as we were. But on the question of rules it is to be observed, that the thing to be desired is to train a child to understand or feel a principle, and to apply it, not merely to remember and obey a rule. The reason and the moral nature should be enlisted in support of the law. The theory of American mental and moral education is, Minimum, of formal law and brute

force, maximum of intelligent self-control and kindly adaptation. Mere codes of rules, whether at home or at school, set the children at work, with all their sharp, unregenerate little wits, to pick flaws, draw distinctions, and quibble on interpretations. They become abominably shrewd in a degrading, casuistical strict-constructionism. In spite of everything, the little, cunning, irresponsible, non-moral beings will be successfully appealing to the letter of the law against the spirit, and warping and drying up all their tenderness of conscience, all their capability of broad and generous applications of right and noble principle.

I disliked fat meat and fat people. I used to like to be with the hired girls in the kitchen. I was entirely untouched by the often-repeated expositions made to me of the vulgarity of such habits, and of the low esteem in which I should be held in consequence. What is vulgarity to a child? Spontaneity, unconscious existence, has no vulgarities. Vulgarity comes of restraints and distortions; and a child's life is commonly for a time untouched by the girdling and compression of forms and conventionalities. Besides, to a child of positive traits, those persuasions are utterly forceless which, instead of being addressed to the prominent faculties, are directed to those comparatively deficient. It is no matter how well such considerations are suited to the character of the persuader, to a conventional human nature, to the *a priori* child. Thus, in the matter of kitchen-haunting, the appeal was made to my regard for the opinions of others. As I was naturally disregardful of the opinions of others, the appeal did not affect me.

Besides, we used to have hired girls as superior to the Biddies of to-day as a patriarch is to a *laquais de place.* Possibly hereditary friendly relations with a few individuals may have made us more fortunate than some other families. From whatever cause, we enjoyed through most of my childhood the ministrations of two or three women of American race, of intelligence, character, and self-respect. It is scarcely possible that the vulgarity which my parents apprehended was anything worse than colloquial New England provincialism. It is possible that they may have feared lest in time the kitchen-door should introduce me to that Devil's school for boys, the city street.

These domestics were themselves competent housekeepers, and could have maintained good repute and creditable hospitality, had they possessed the means, even among the far-renowned "old-fashioned H—— housekeepers." My remembrances of them are scanty. There were Lois and Hannah, tall, thin, angular Yankee women, grave, trustworthy, and efficient. There was Emily, a dignified personage, portly and composed, an excellent and faithful woman and a good manager, unfailingly kind to us little folks, a wondrously skilful compounder of pies, cakes, and gingerbreads. She was wont to wear a white turban or similar head-dress of wreathed draperies ; and often, with serious face, she puzzled me, and silenced my childish inquiries about the nature or purpose of ingredient or process, by saying that it was " Laro for meddlers." In those days I speculated deeply as to whether there did exist any such real substance as " Laro." In this mystic and apparently underived term, the *a* is broad, as in "ah ! " It may be spelled " Lahro," for what I know.

I do remember, in particular, a tidy, laborious, parsimonious, pragmatical little Scotchwoman, Christiana. Once upon a time, in the days of allopathic rule, my mother compounded a mighty pitcher of senna mixture. This — its actual deglutition, by some blessed chance, not becoming necessary — she set up, with a housekeeper's saving instinct, on the pantry shelf, instead of pouring it into the gutter. So Christiana, thrifty soul, and still more saving, could not endure the wasting of so much virtue, and set herself stoutly to utilize the decoction by consuming it to her own sole use and behoof, which she

accomplished by way of relaxation, so to speak, in single doses, at leisure times, within a few days. Her own and her employer's respective economies were fitly rewarded by an illness, through which my mother had to take care of her.

One morning, so early that it was not quite light, I hung about the kitchen table, slyly securing little lumps of the cold hasty-pudding which was being sliced in order to be fried for breakfast. Having snapped up a very nice one, as big as a walnut, lo and behold ! when I chewed, it was lard. There was direful retching and hasty ejection. The disagreeable, cold, soft, greasy rankness of the morsel is extreme : if you don't believe it, try it. I think this affair may have been a cold-blooded scheme of the hired-girl. But it was years before I became so suspicious as to place this sad construction upon the occurrence, though I often remembered it.

Like all children, I was fond of candy, sweetmeats, and spices. Yet not of allspice or nutmeg, nor of mace, which tastes of soap. I have known of cases where parents claimed that their children were not fond of such things. Believe them not. I liked pie, but not pudding ; the rich, heavy fruit-cake of weddings, good, honest gingerbread, the brisk, crispy heat of the brittle ginger-snap, but not " plain cake,"— absurd viand ! It is of the essence of cake not to be plain. As well say, acid sweetness. Nor did I like the hereditary election-cake of my ancient State and city. Fat pork I could not swallow ; nor onions nor cabbage,— gross, indelicate vegetables ! And even now, as well present upon my table that other diabolic cabbage of the New England swamps, — in old legend said to have been conjured up out of the ground by the Indian pow-wows, to beautify and perfume the dank and gloomy resorts where Satan was wont to drill them in their hellish exercises, — as its grandchild, the big booby of the garden. For is it not deservedly, if disrespectfully, named a cabbage-head ? That is because it is the Vegetable Booby.

Naturally, I did not like that concoction so dear to the heart of good old-fashioned Connecticut folks, a biled-dish (accent on *biled*). This, O vast majority of ignoramuses, is corned beef and cabbage boiled together. As for onions, if I could not escape them in any other way, I would organize a party on the Great Wethersfield Question, and lead it, a Connecticut Cato, with the motto, "Censeo Wethersfieldiam delendam esse." Nor would I rest until that alliaceous metropolis was fairly tipped over into Connecticut River, and sent drowning down to Long Island Sound.

There is yet another cell in the cavern of memory, — a gloomy and horrid one, — the torture-chamber. It is the remembrance of sickness and its attendant pharmaceutic devils. O ye witch's oils, hell-broths red and black, pills, and electuaries ! the unsuccessful experiments — instrumentalities of death too slow for the occasion, but masterly in their kind — of the Pandemoniac host in those Miltonian, infernal chemics which resulted in gunpowder and cannon-balls ! What agonies from horrific stench and flavor, in close, dreary rooms, under hot, unwelcome blankets, do ye recall !

It is not that I complain of all those inexplicable diseases, *opprobria medicinæ*, so pusillanimously submitted to by civilized humanity and its physicians, — chicken-pox, measles, whooping-cough, mumps. I complain, indeed, of no diseases, but of their treatment. But let me not delay longer than is needful amid such distressful recollections. Three hateful decoctions were known to me by the phonetics, Lixipro, Lixaslutis, and Lixusmatic. I don't know what they were, and I don't want to know. Devil's elixirs were they all. Rubbub and magnesia, — endless imprecations rest upon that obnoxious red mixture ! And chiefest of them all — Arimanes of the whole bad crew, though Agag is the only really suitable royal name I can think of —

is that slow, greasy horror, whose superhuman excess of unutterable abomination no words can express, and even inarticulate ejaculations made on purpose cannot at all show forth, — as urk ! huk ! agh ! — chiefest among them all, castor oil !

I hurry away from the awful scene. Let me be thankful that I swallowed but little calomel. Let me be thankful that, after a time, I could not swallow castor oil. Spasmodic regurgitations, as if one had attempted to load a gun having a live coal at the far end, closed perforce that chapter of torments. And soon thereafter arose the benign genius of homœopathy, with healing in its neat little white-paper wings. Beautiful Homœopathy, the real Angel in the House, if Mr. Coventry Patmore had only known it ! Hast thou not long ago appeared, veiled in an allegory, before an unrecognizing world ? Surely, what but homœopathic medicine was that wondrous talisman with which Adonbec El Hakim cured the Melech Ric ? To be taken in a tumbler about two thirds full of water, as now ; but in those early times, and for such a very large man, at one gulp, instead of by hourly teaspoonfuls. Or perhaps the manuscripts may have been corrupted in that passage by unscrupulous mediæval physicians of the school of Salerno, or other regular institutions.

I suppose I must have played a good deal ; but there are reasons why this may not have been the case. The chief of them is, that whereas I have subsequently commonly attained a fair degree of excellence in what I have learned, I did not in the staple games of my childhood do so. In marbles, spinning top, and ball I was inferior, — indeed, scarcely at home in the technics of some of them. The games of marbles which I see now-a-days seem to centre upon the projection of the missile into a hole in the ground. In my day we used to play upon the surface of the earth ; sometimes "in the big ring," where each combatant fired at the marbles grouped in the centre, from any point upon the external orbit ;

sometimes "in the little ring," where the shot was made from the place where the projectile lodged last; sometimes "at chasings," where the players fired alternately, each at the marble of his adversary. Concerning this last game, I remember the following terms: "ebs," which, seasonably vociferated, that is, when it is the speaker's turn to play and before his adversary can say anything, serves as an incantation authorizing the speaker to deliver his fire from any point other than that where his marble lies, equally distant from the objective point; "clearings," in like manner, authorizing the preparation of a reasonably unobstructed line of fire; and "fen ebs," "fen clearings," and "fen everythings," to be pronounced before the other player speaks, and which, by virtue of the prohibitory syllable "fen" (*défendre*, Fr.), prevent respectively ebs, clearings, and everything, — that is to say, any elusion or amelioration of the existing conditions of fire.

In games of ball, to confess the truth, I was but feeble. Scarce, indeed, was I of average skill in any of them except the simplest two,— "bung-ends," and "one old cat." In the first of these, one boy throws the ball against the side of a house, or other perpendicular unelastic plane, while the other smites it with his club at the rebound. In the second, played as a trio, boy A throws the ball at boy B, standing opposite, whose duty is to smite, while boy C, behind B, catches B out in case of a miss.

I was pretty good at "tag" and "catch," games of running and dodging. In these, one boy is called "it," i. e. leader, or victim. He pursues the rest; and the games are alike, except that in "catch" he who is to be made "it" must be caught and held by him who is "it," whereas in "tag" a touch is sufficient to transfer the responsibility, and inaugurate the new choragus.

There. Such quaint scraps are all that is left me of my existence as a little child. I know men who say, that, within their own consciousness and memories, they have the witness and knowledge of a life even before that of this humanity. But, for my own part, I should never know, by anything in my own memory, that I had been a baby, — that I was or did anything before that first school where the ferocious little girl was handcuffed in unbleached-cotton bags, for scratching.

"The child is father of the man," saith the great poet of dry sentimentalizing. Therefore the man's endeavor to remember about his childhood might reasonably be expected to bring him into *limbo patrum*. But it is a dim and narrow field to grope in. It is not wandering in a darkened world, — it is feeling in a dark closet.

It was an unconscious brief advance from nothing to very little. Yes, but still there must have been some dim features of the dawning character. No doubt. The heedless, complying, unjudging benevolence, for instance, that gave away *all* my gingerbread to the young Anakim of Parade Street, was one. It was liable afterwards to invert, by reacting from such over-operation as that, into an equally unjudging disregard of the wants and needs of others.

And now, What was it? This is no foolish nor unimportant inquiry. If I could answer it sufficiently, I should at once supply the basis of whole systems of mental and moral art and science. Such whole systems indeed — for instance, the muddy distractions of the Scotch metaphysicians — have already been based upon the phantasms of wiggy old doctors who dived backward into themselves,— jumping down their own throats, as it were, in their search after knowledge, as did the seventh Arabian Brother in the Spectator (is it not?) "with seven candles in each hand, lighted at both ends,"— and said, "When I began to think, I must necessarily have thought thus and thus." This was all very scientific. But for usefulness it would have been better to inquire, not what they must have thought, but what they did think.

Indeed, hitherto the history of mental philosophy is the history of the ignorance of man about himself ; and since science must be built upon induction, and since phrenology has now established a classification — approximately correct and sufficient for working purposes — of the mental faculties, it is now quite in order to review the old inductions from the history of the individual, and to accumulate new ones. Even the mere trifles of these recollections of mine, some of them at least, must have an actual philosophical value, if only they are true and well enough stated.

Thank goodness, that, at any rate, I was not a remarkable child ! It is the average record which has most value. The remarkable child is not a magnified child, but a distorted one ; not a young giant, but a young monster.

No tract or little 24mo would have been published about me by the American Sunday-School Union, if I had died young. No brilliant repartees by me are on record. No sweet remembrance is in blossom about me of a grim, unchildish pleasure in preferring the convenience or enjoyment of others to my own. In an instance where I remember to have tried to do as the good boys do in the story-books, by giving away my one cooky, the quick reaction into common sense sent me in grief to my mother, making use of natural tears and a specious plea of what I had done to get me another cooky, or perchance two. It was a dead failure. My mother knew too well the importance of the great moral lesson to let me reap material advantage from my good deed. She relegated me to the unfailing good dry bread, explaining how I could find abundant satisfaction within my own breast for doing a kind action,— how virtue was to be its own reward. I looked for the said reward, but could not see it. It was not satisfaction within my breast that I wanted, but within my stomach and on my palate. Benevolence will not supplement alimentiveness in the small boy. If I gathered any reward at all, it was in the hard wisdom of my resolve not

to be caught in any such nonsense again.

I had not, as had a little monster of misplaced piety whose case is recorded in the good children's books, "at the early age of six made up my mind on all the great questions of the day." Yet I think I can remember yelling out " Hurra for Jackson ! " because it was a good easy shout, although my father was a strong, steady Whig. There is practical democracy in that. First choice of shouts is much toward winning the battle.

I was not remarkable for early piety, sweetness of disposition, wit, beauty (I must certainly have been, as a child, skinny), or helpful kindness (except that irrational benevolence of mine).

I have been told that I learned to read, nobody knew how, all by myself, by the time I was four years old. How that may be I don't know ; but I do know that I did not know how to read when I was twenty years old.

I was a "natural speller." It is no joke, but one of the proverbial fools' truths, which Dogberry enounces when he says that "reading and writing come by nature." They do. And so does spelling. Abundance of well-educated people never escape from occasional perturbations in orthography, just as they never learn a desirable handwriting, nor how to read silently fast and well, or well aloud. It is because they cannot ; because they have not what Nature gave Neighbor Seacoal ; because spelling and reading and writing are "gifts," — they come by nature.

What I learned at school in those first ten years I do not know. Almost nothing. I have utterly forgotten what. I might have been much better taught. I might have been instructed in thinking. I do not mean that a child of eight or nine years old can or should be made to see, judge, and conclude upon new matters with the discovering and advancing power of a philosopher. But he may be made to perform his own proper little mental operations, no matter how small they are, on the same principle, — on the principle of actual understanding, instead of mere sole memorizing.

All my instructors, whether they meant to do so or not, did in fact proceed as if they believed children's minds to be, not live fountains, but empty cisterns ; not to be capable of thought ; like an empty house, to be furnished for a tenant ; needing to be fitted up with a store of lifeless forms, which the adult life, when it came, was to breathe vitality into and turn to living uses. I learned rules. "Here, little boy," they said, "swallow these oyster-shells. They will lie naturally and easily in your stomach until you grow up, because little boys' stomachs are adapted for the storage of oyster-shells ; and when you are a man, and want oysters, put some in there." But does it stand to reason that children, who manipulate words and figures, and produce results without understanding the rules they apply,—just as a wizard's apprentice could evoke his master's demons without knowing the meaning of the awful syllables he recited, so that Southey's arcanum of Aballiboozobanganorribo might respectably serve as one of them, —does it stand to reason that these unhappy young jugglers will the better learn to do the same work intelligently afterwards ? No ; for they have to dislodge the bad habit which has preempted, before they can install the good one. As well undertake to train a new Mozart by making the bright little music-loving boy grind ten years on a barrel-organ with *La ci darem* in its bowels.

I remember a fondness for long, large, grown-up words ; doubtless, in some measure, a result of my constant practice of reading grown-up people's books. It was a mere verbal memory, the driest of all the intellectual faculties. Scarcely a faint perfume of meaning lingered about the rattling piles of husks that I could say and spell.

What I learned at Sunday school and church was to be inexpressibly weary of them. What I learned at home I can perhaps define but little better. I gained no important result from any direct instruction. I gained something of good-boy behavior and decent manners, diligently trained into me. But what was most valuable in my home education was unconscious infiltration from a good home-atmosphere. This is an influence of incalculable importance, a thousand times outweighing all the schools. It is that for which God established the family ; the one single possible real and efficient means of well bringing up the young. And whatever shades of repression, misunderstanding, ungeniality, restraint, may have sometimes troubled me, still I constantly feel and fully know that that pure, calm, quiet, bright, loving, intelligent, refined atmosphere of my home silently and unconsciously penetrated and vivified all my being. If now I should be told, " You are no very splendid exemplar of the results of such influences," I should still say, " Most true, unfortunately true ; but what should I have been without them ? "

I had brothers and sisters,—a few playmates ; but neither they, nor any other human beings, not even my parents, seem to have been during those years, to any important extent, directly operative within or upon the sphere and character of my own real conscious existence. That life figures itself in my memory much like a magic circle, within which I was alone, and did my scanty little thinkings and imaginings alone. The rest of the living were outside, unreal,—phantoms moving to and fro, around and without, but never coming within that limit,— never entering into living communion with me. This constitutional solitude of mind has a useful office, perhaps not to be easily explained, but sometimes not otherwise to be performed.

This isolation was, in part, unnecessary. To a certain extent the necessity for it still remains. But in part it was artificial,—my unconscious reaction against an ill-adapted influence,—the resisting force of a trait which, like all those other early traits, has become visible to me, like the blind paths over bogs, now that I am a long way off.

This trait I have already spoken of. It was an insensibility to a certain motive, rather prominent among those commonly proposed to me for my own government of myself. This was variously framed thus :—It is not usual to do this ; it is usual to do that ; if you proceed so and so, it will seem singular ; people will talk about it ; you will offend people's usages and habits ; you will seem singular and odd. Against such cautions I rebelled with a mute, indignant impulse, which I was not old enough to enounce or to argue. It was, however, the result of two characteristics ; — one, the natural lack of instinctive desire for the good opinion of others ; and the other, a corresponding instinct for living out my own life fully and freely, not so as to infringe upon the just rights of others, but not stinting or distorting or amputating myself, even though others set the example. It was the old fable reversed, — the fox disinclined to cut off his tail, even though all the other foxes had cut off theirs. And the fact that people older than I, and several of them, and for year after year, urged upon me the considerations I have spoken of, never availed. That key would not move the mechanism of my mind. It did not fit.

My childhood seems to me far more memorable for what it had not, was not, than for what it had and was. I do not believe this is because mine was an especially unfortunate or unhappy childhood. As I have hinted before, it was because childhood is empty, — an unconscious, imperfect life, — almost animal, — germinal, — a life in the egg, in the jelly, in the sap. The experiences of childhood are seed-leaves. They drop quickly away and utterly disappear, and even the scars where they grew cease to show on the stem. Probably I seemed to myself to enjoy life when I was a child. Children whom I see daily seem to do so. But thought is life. Mere enjoyment is dreaming It may seem to cover hours or days or years of experience, but when we awake it has been only a point of time. But this pleasure-dream is worse than a sleep-dream. Over its costly actuality of time, cut out and dropped down out of life, the hither and thither ends of the shortened thread of existence must be knotted together into a cord of diminished length, strength, and value.

In sum : This child which I was was a semi-embryonic creature, mostly unconscious, whose ten years' career, now chiefly faded into entire blankness, showed not many mental traits. The chief were quick and retentive verbal memory, quick, undiscriminating, impulsive, unreasonable kind-heartedness, and an insensibility, even an instinctive opposition, to the approvings or disapprovings of others. Or the child might be stated thus : Nervous and sensitive organization, intellect predominant ; in the intellect the perceptive faculties most active, and of these chiefly that which notices and compares exteriors ; beside the intellect, a kind-heartedness without balance, and therefore too great ; too little caution, and too little love of approbation. Around these features others have grown up, of course ; but these were, so to speak, the primary strata of the formation, underlying the other elements, determining their tendencies, and cropping out through them.

This child was all but empty, unsubstantial, imperfect ; incapable, then, of much life from within itself, little helped by thoughts or other aid from without. The efforts made by others to operate on it were faithful, kindly, well meant, but not adapted to its individuality. The fact is, that, so far as they had any supposed basis on system, it was on the Scotch empirical analysis of perception, conception, reason, will ; a Procrustean mental philosophy which absolutely ignores individuality, and assumes that all human beings are alike. It is as good as the little boys' conventional system of portraiture. A round O, two dots, a perpendicular line between them, and a horizontal one across below, displays every face. Such was Christ and such was Judas ; such was Messalina and such was Florence Nightingale. But there is a better philosophy of the mind.

HER PILGRIMAGE.

IN MEMORIAM, JANUARY 12, 1866.

THE snow-flakes floated many a star
    To earth, from pale December's skies,
When a fair spirit from afar
    Smiled through an infant's violet eyes.

And as she sweetly breathed, the hours
    Wove, like a robe of gossamer,
All grace about her, while the flowers
    Their tints and perfumes gave to her.

In after time, when violets grew,
    And pale anemones veiled the land,
She drooped her modest eyes of blue,
    And gave to Love her maiden hand.

Four times the holy angels came,
    To greet her with a dear unrest ;
And, in a mother's saintly name,
    Left a young angel on her breast.

Eight lustrums pure celestial eyes
    Beamed through her tender, loving gaze,
Commingling all the sweet surprise
    Of heavenly with the earthly rays.

At last, her gentle face grew pale
    As the anemones of spring ;
And whiter than her bridal veil
    Was that in which she took her wing.

And than that fixed despair more white,
    Softly the stars, in feathery snows,
Came, covering with serener light
    Her folded hands, her meek repose.

Pale stars, through which the Night looked down,
    Until they wept away in showers
On those dear hands, which clasped the crown,
    And closer still the cross, of flowers.

The snow-flakes melt on earth in tears ;
    The eternal stars in glory shine ;
While in the shroud of desolate years
    Dead Love awaits the immortal sign.

FARMER HILL'S DIARY.

IN looking over the papers of our deceased friend, the following diary was discovered. It being too lengthy to copy in full, we omit many of the incidents, as well as the "Account of the Ohio Prophetess," and some religious discussions, chiefly on doctrinal points. — J. S.

DIARY.

April 13, 18—. — Captain Welles was here this morning, advising daddy to buy a horse-cart. Frederic favors it; but daddy does n't approve of new-fangled contrivances. He says we can do as we always have done, viz., carry the grain to mill on horseback, or, when there 's a heavy load, take the oxen.

Captain Welles's kindness to me is wonderful, considering that I can in no way favor him, being poor, and without knowledge, and wellnigh friendless. He talked with me to-day, while I was working on the fences, about my mind and my soul, and also about getting along in the world. He counselled me to keep a diary, mentioning many advantages arising therefrom. As what I write is only for my own eye, I will put down that he warned me against being vain of a comely face.

He was a sailor in the ship that brought over Mr. Murray, the preacher of that belief which daddy says is a sin to speak of. But Captain Welles has told me of many things he said on board the vessel, which sound heavenly; also of sermons he preached to the crew, that seem in no way blasphemous, as Aunt Bethiah says the new doctrines are.

They were shipwrecked on the Jersey coast, and experienced great suffering. Shortly after they gained the shore, a man came along, who cried out, as soon as he saw the preacher: "Why, you are the very man I 've waited for so long! I have built a meeting-house on purpose for you!" This is very wonderful, when we think that Mr. Murray was never in our country before, and that the man was never out of it.

May 1. — Twenty years old to-day! Just ten years since daddy took me out of the poor-house! How kind they 've all been to me! Frederic and Elinor and mammy, and, for the most part, Aunt Bethiah, though she is very precise. If I could only forget where I came from. Captain Welles says it is false pride; but that does n't hinder its plaguing me. When a thorn pricks, it pricks, whether of a rose-bush or a bramble.

As long as I went to school the boys called me "Poor 'us," "Poor 'us," only when Frederic was by they did n't dare, for fear of his thrashing them, he was so stout and tall; and he has been growing ever since. Aunt Bethiah says it is reaching and tiptoeing up to the high shelves after company-cake, that makes him so tall. I heard her telling mammy that she fairly laid awake nights, contriving places where to hide things.

"Poor Freddy," says mammy, "he don't have no great of an appetite to eat."

"News to me," says Aunt Bethiah. She 's always on the look-out for him; but, with the whole house on her shoulders, she can't be everywhere. Last fall, while the shoemaker was here making up our winter shoes, Frederic got him to put squeaking leather into one of hers, and not into the mate of it. Then he could tell her step, for she would go "squeak," "——," "squeak," "——." Mammy knew, for her arm-chair was n't a great ways off from the shoe-bench; but then Frederic 's her idol, and all he does is right. Many 's the nice bit she has tucked away for him, when

Aunt Bethiah's back was turned; and does yet, for all he's a man grown.

He laughs at his grandmother about her plasters and medicines; but he is as full of feeling as he is of fun. Gets up the coldest nights in winter, when she's taken worse, to run for the neighbors, crying, when he thinks nobody sees. Who would think, to see him in his capers, he could ever shed a tear? Nights, when the chores are done, he sits down close to mammy, till the candles are lit. When he was little, 't would be on a cricket, with his head in her lap, and saying his verses; and she would tell him of his pious mother, who had a lovely countenance, and who died young, being willing to go; or of his father, who mourned himself into the grave, for the loss of his dear young wife.

But now he has grown up, he relates to her whatever has happened through the day, if it is only the finding of a hen's nest. This serves to take up her mind, and gives her something to look forward to. After that he reads, or does odd jobs of mending; and, two nights a week, brushes up and goes a-courting. And he's only a year older than I am! I shall never go a-courting. "Poor 'us," "Poor 'us." Who would want a "poor 'us?"

In a few weeks, Elinor will come home for good. Her father's relations have done well by her, and would be glad to keep her always. People say she has had great advantages, and hope she will not be spoiled; but that can't be. She was always good, and always will be.

May 5.—'T was just about such a day as this, ten years ago, that Aunt Bethiah came out into the porch, and found me leaning up against the meal-chest. Daddy had just brought me home. He was n't blind then, though he wore a green shade. How scared I was at Aunt Bethiah!—she looked so tall, and dark, and—hard, like Greatheart's wife, if he ever had one. It does n't seem possible that she can be mammy's own sister.

Daddy said, "Mammy, suppose we keep him?" And she made answer, that mebby I might save poor Freddy some steps. Then Aunt Bethiah said, "More men folks, more work," and that Frederic knew how to save his own steps. But I stayed, for daddy's mind was made up beforehand, and daddy always has his will, though it is in a gentle way.

Elinor was a little girl then. She sat down with me in the window-seat, and showed me her new primer, and whispered softly that Aunt Bethiah would like me, if I wiped my feet.

Poor mammy! How long she has been sick! She sits in the same chair and in the same corner that she did the night I was brought. Some women would n't think of anybody but themselves; but she has a care over the whole neighborhood. She's always steeping up herbs or spreading plasters for somebody. Should like to know how many weight of Burgundy pitch and Dr. Oliver's salve I've run to the doctor's for. I remember how I coughed that first night.

"What a dreadful cough that poor child's got!" said she. "Elinor, reach me the bellows, and hold the blade o' the knife to the fire, and warm it warm. He must have a plaster between his shoulders."

So she laid the bellows across her lap, and spread a plaster, and told me not to tear it off as soon as it began to tickle me, but to rub my back against the door. And there were doors enough, I thought, set round that big kitchen. Nine poor boys, with dreadful coughs, could have found room.

I remember how we used to climb up to the easterly room door, which had squares of glass set in the top, and look through at the best things that were kept shut up there. And how every Sunday night we used to go into the westerly room, and watch for the sun to go down, before we could step out of doors.

May 8.—Helped Frederic to-day to weed out mammy's herb-garden. He keeps it neat as a pin, but has his fun out of it all the same. It is right under the window, where she can see growing her saffron and sage, peppermint, cumfrey, and all the rest. I don't know the names of half. Frederic calls them "health-root," "lullaby-root," "doctor's defiances," "step-quickeners," or whatever comes into his head.

Besides these, which he calls the regular practics, there are all the wild herbs to be gathered in. Mullein, motherwort, thoroughwort, golden-rod, everlasting, burdock-leaves, may-weed, must all be dried and hung up in the garret. Aunt Bethiah groans, but grabs them up with her long fingers, and has them out of the way in less than no time. Daddy calls it mammy's harvest.

Poor old man! How pitiful it is to see him groping about so, with his white face and silvery hair! Yet, to look at his countenance, nobody would say he was blind; for, though his eyes are closed, he seems to see with his whole face. I don't know how to write it down; but I mean, that the look which most people have only in their eyes seems to be spread over his whole countenance, and lights it up and makes it beautiful. Sometimes I turn my eyes away, for it seems as if I were looking at his soul, — and the soul is so mysterious!

May 12. — Frederic's great-uncle Frederic has died, and left him a little bag of silver dollars. He sat down on the floor, and made me sit down on the other side, and we rolled them to each other, just like little boys. He has given us one apiece, and put one in the drawer for Elinor. Elinor and I always used to keep our money together. When it is full, the box is to be broken open, and we shall buy the best books there are. Daddy has been asking when she will come back. By the 1st of June certainly. We've heard of several poor people finding a silver dollar under their plates. Frederic never can keep anything to himself.

May 20. — Frederic has been to Boston, and bought cloth for a tail-coat, and had it cut out by a Boston tailor. It is blue, and cost ten dollars a yard. Mary Swift has been here all the week, making it up. The buttons are gilt, and cost six dollars a dozen. A good many of the neighbors have been in to see it. Those who live farther off will have a chance to-morrow, when he goes to meeting.

May 22. — Yesterday was the Sabbath, and Frederic wore his coat to meeting. Aunt Bethiah took extra pains with his ruffles, so as to have everything correspond. He had on his new boots, with tassels on the tops, and they shone like glass bottles. He frizzed his front hair himself. But I had to braid his cue, and tie on the bow. Blue becomes him, on account of his fairness and his fresh color. I was never struck before with the resemblance of brother and sister; only she is more delicate looking.

She will be very proud of him. We all are, but try not to let it be seen. Mammy is, for all she counselled him to fix his attention on the discourse, and think only such thoughts as he would like to remember at the day of judgment. As we walked out of the yard, I caught sight of her twinkling black eyes over the window-curtain. Such a piece of work too as she makes getting up out of her chair! How handsome and noble he looked, fit for an emperor! Dreadful red, though, by the time we got sat down in meeting; for our pew is a good way up, and his boots squeaked, and we'd heard that all the singers were going early, to see him come into meeting, and Lucy sits in the seats.

After sundown took a pleasant walk through the woods, over to the schoolmaster's boarding-place, to carry back the two last books he lent me, — the poems of Burns and of Henry Kirke White.

Aunt Bethiah found one of them amongst the hay, when she was hunting for her setting-hen. She declares that reading is a dreadful waste of time, and poetry-books are worse than all, and nothing but singsong.

May 26. — I wish I knew whether there was any merit in me or not. Most people can tell, by the manners of others towards them. But I had such a mean start! No matter how well people treat me, it all, in my estimation, settles down to one thing, — " Poor 'us."

It is either, " I will treat you well *because* you came out of the poor-house," or, " I will treat you well *notwithstanding* you came from the poor-house." Captain Welles tells me I can make myself just what I want to be; but Aunt Bethiah says that is dreadful wicked doctrine, and daddy rather agrees with her; but it seems to me there can't be any harm in doing my best.

I am very ignorant, and not only so, but I hardly even know what there is to learn. From the schoolmaster's books I get but scraps of knowledge. Supposing I never saw a flower, and somebody should bring me a leaf of a violet, or a clover-head. What should I know of tulips and pinks, or the smell of roses, or of all the flowers that grow in the fields and gardens? The books speak of music, of pictures, of great authors, of the wonders of the sea, of rocks, of stars. Shall I ever learn about all these?

May 30. — In a week Elinor comes. Mammy thinks she will be all run down, and is steeping up white-oak bark and cherry-tree twigs. Elinor will make up faces, I know; but mammy will make her take it. She did n't see Frederic when he dropped in the red pepper. I would n't have him know for anything that I skimmed it out.

Captain Welles has bought a chaise. There are now two in the place. His is green-bottomed. It has a most agreeable leathery smell, and a gentle creak which is very pleasant. The minister's is dark blue. They are set high, and the tops tip forward, serving to keep out both sun and rain. Poor Mrs. Scott was buried to-day.

June 7. — Elinor came yesterday, late in the afternoon. Frederic brought her from the tavern. The horse shied at an old coat thrown over a fence and came nigh throwing them both.

I expected to be very glad when Elinor got home, but I 'm feeling many things besides gladness.

The people she 's been staying with are fashionable and polite, and she has caught their ways, and I can't say but they hang prettily about her. Her aunt is a minister's wife, and akin to a judge, so she has seen the very best of company, and heard the talk of educated people.

But she was glad enough to get home, and said pretty things to us all. Aunt Bethiah says she looks very genteel. She has had her gowns altered to the new fashion, and had on her neck a handsome handkerchief which she worked at the boarding-school. She has also worked a long white veil, very rich, and has made a cape of silk-weed. Besides this, she has painted a light-stand. It is made of bird's-eye maple, and has a green silk bag hanging from underneath. They don't speak of these in daddy's hearing.

After supper, he took her up on his knee and stroked her hair, and said, " Now let us sing rock-a-by as we used to." So, with her head on his shoulder, he rocked and sang rock-a-by, while she laughed. At last she jumped up and ran off to see the bossy.

When she was gone, daddy heaved a deep sigh; but mammy cheered him up, telling how thankful they ought to be for the safe return of their child. 'T was touching to hear them talk, each telling the other how good she was, and how from a child she had followed their wishes.

And to see how tender mammy was of his feelings! Never praising her pretty face, or saying that she looked like her mother, but only speaking of what he could take comfort in too.

Nobody but we three were in the

room. At times they would keep silence. Then something long forgotten would come to mind, — some good thing she did, or said, or prayed, when a child, — and they would begin with, "And don't you remember," and so go on with the whole story. Truly pleasant were these memories of the past. Pleasant and sweet as the fragrance which was brought to us by the evening wind from far-off flowery fields.

A time of greater satisfaction I never experienced. Suddenly came in Aunt Bethiah and began to rattle the chairs, and to gather up whatever was lying about. Mammy asked me to shut down the window, for the wind seemed to have changed to the eastward. Frederic's girl came in the evening with some others, — good-looking girls enough. All flowers can't be roses.

In the night, I lay thinking, and thinking, and wishing for I knew not what, and sighing for I knew not what, and looking forwards and backwards till I was all in a whirl.

Is this, I said to myself, the little girl that used to hear me say my catechism? And then I remembered how we used to sit opposite each other on two crickets, while she put out the questions; and how her little toes peeped out, for it was the spring of the year, and she was wearing off her stockings ready to go barefooted. Her shoes were gone long before.

And I remembered, too, how, ever since we were little children, we had gone of summer mornings after wild roses for Old Becky to still; for mammy never could do without rose-water. She used to start us early, before the dew was off, for they were stronger then.

June 8. — I thought last night that we should never go after roses any more; but this morning, just as I was about to set off with the cows, I heard the house-door shut, and then a light step on the grass. I kept myself hid, and peeped through a knot-hole. She had a basket on her arm, and looked about, and took a few steps softly, this

way and that, as if looking for somebody. At last I came out, innocent as a lamb. "Good morning, Elinor," says I. "Have you forgot the roses, Walter?" says she, a little bashful. As if I could forget the roses! The hills were all scattered over with children and young people; for it was a fine morning, and the roses were in their prime.

The sun shone, the children shouted, the birds sang, and the air was cool and fresh. It is good to be with the day at its beginning. Elinor laughed, and chatted, and danced up hill and down hill, and snapped her scissors, and snapped off the roses, and stuck the prettiest in her hair and in her apron-string, till at last I told her she looked like a rose-bush all in bloom.

June 11. — To-day Elinor and Frederic walked to meeting together. He had on his new things, and she had on a white chip hat with blue inside and outside, and blue ribbons tied under her chin, and a white gown, and a white mantle. Everybody in the meeting-house was looking at them, and several times the minister's eyes appeared to be directed that way. I could hardly tell preaching from praying, and once I let the pew-seat slam down in prayer-time. 'T would be better if they could n't turn up at all, and then there would n't be such a rattling and clattering the minute the minister says, "Amen."

'T was a young preacher. I hope our minister won't exchange with him very often. He is too young to give satisfaction, — under thirty, I should judge.

August 10. — The summer is passing. It has brought me plenty of work and but little pleasure. Elinor has had much out-of-town company, — frolicking girls and sometimes their brothers. They often come out to rake hay or ride in the cart.

My diary has been neglected. I don't believe anybody writes down their unhappiest feelings, especially when they don't know justly what they are unhappy about.

Something about Elinor. And what is it about Elinor? Do I want to become to her what Frederic is to Lucy? Do I want to make her "Mrs. Poor 'us"? Do I want to drag her down and keep her plodding all her days, clad in a homespun gown, and she fit to be a lady in her silks and satins? What is it I would be at?

September 3. — Our summer company is gone, and Aunt Bethiah is glad. We are having longer evenings. When the candles are lit Frederic bids mammy good night and goes off. Sometimes she sits up and puts on her spectacles, and reads Watts's hymns loud to daddy. Aunt Bethiah pares apples and slices them, and Elinor strings them up with a darning-needle. I am tired and sit in the chimney-corner to rest.

Yesterday Mr. Colman preached again, and to-day he took supper at our house, — rainy, and out of his way too! He was unmannerly enough to address most of his remarks to a young person when her elders were present. So seldom, too, as daddy has a chance to talk with an out-of-town minister! He is not at all good-looking. His hair is yellowish and stands up stiff on his forehead, and his eyes are no color. I don't see how he can be agreeable to any young girl. But being a minister goes a good ways.

I knew mammy would ask him to stay to tea. As soon as anybody comes, no matter if it is only in the middle of the afternoon, she always says, "Now take your things right off. Come, Bethiah, clap on the tea-kettle, and we 'll have tea airly." They say she was always just so about liking to have company.

October 18. — Mr. Scott has begun to come here evenings. He owns a house and farm and wood-lot. His wife left him no children, and he lives in a lonely house all alone ; and poor enough company he must find himself.

He comes here and sits all the evening, talking with daddy and looking at Elinor. Poor hand at talking, though, — so dull and heavy both in looks and words. I wonder what countryman he is. Very dark and thick-set. That does n't seem like any country in particular. Captain Welles would know ; for his father picked him up among the wharves in London, a little ragged boy, running about.

But then who cares what he is? He need n't trouble himself about remembering the heads of the sermon to tell mammy. I always have done it, and can yet. If he 's a mind to scratch his hands getting sarsaparilla and snapwood for her off his wood-lot, he may. Have no objection, either, to his bringing Elinor boxberry plums. I never read yet of any maiden losing her heart on boxberry plums ; though, to be sure, he might bewitch them. He looks like that.

November 21. — So Winter is coming in earnest. Well, we are all ready for him. Garret and cellar, both barns and the crib, are full. Candy frolic this evening at Lucy's. Had part of the candy stolen coming home. Elinor said she had a good tell for me. What could it be? Made believe I did n't care ; but do wish I knew. She said 't was n't the first one she 'd heard, either. Ever since we were children we 've come and gone together ; but when I was old enough to offer my arm, I did n't dare. If she had n't been away so much, out of town to school, why I might have been more forward.

November 28. — Frederic seems rather dull of late. Mammy has tried to discover his ailments, so as to know what to steep up. But daddy, by questioning and guessing, has found out that both he and his girl are ready to be married, but have nowhere to live. Daddy brags now that he can find out more without eyes than we all can with, and asked mammy which of her herbs would suit his case. Mr. Scott is getting very bold in his attention, and goes about with the young people.

Last night he walked home on the other side of Elinor.

December 2. — It is all settled. Daddy knows how to manage Aunt Bethiah. Frederic and Lucy are to be published next Sabbath. They are going to housekeeping in our easterly front-room, and have a bedroom and one chamber. Another pair of andirons will be put in the kitchen fireplace, and another crane. Aunt Bethiah is in a great flurry about her dyepot, and can't tell where to put it. I remember, the night I was brought, how mammy made me sit down on it and heat my feet hot.

Lucy has a few things. Frederic 's got a little money laid by, and his folks will see that they have what is comfortable. Daddy is going to send me to buy half a dozen spoked chairs, painted blue, with flowers on the backs. Mammy has ordered me to get also a warming-pan.

Aunt Bethiah called me one side this afternoon and asked me, in a whisper, to buy for them a skillet and a pair of green belluses, with a sprig of flowers painted on them, and a brass nose. Who 'd thought of a wedding setting her topsy-turvy !

Frederic is happy as a lord. Ever since he had his new clothes he has stood up at all the weddings, because no other fellow, for miles around, had a tail-coat. Now he will have a chance to stand up at his own.

December 13. — The schoolmaster called again this evening. He and Elinor converse well together. He brought me Thomson's " Seasons." He is a kind, thoughtful man, very entertaining. Told many stories of the different places where he had kept school. Very accommodating, too ; for, our district being short for money, he has agreed to take his pay in spinning-wheels.

'T is a pleasure to listen while a man of knowledge talks, but a pain, afterwards, to feel the difference between us.

Aunt Bethiah was the first one that made me think about learning. " What ! don't know his catechise ? " said she. That was the first night I was brought here.

" Elinor can learn him that," said daddy. And Elinor was much younger than I. I hope the schoolmaster won't think anything of my telling him that I would n't put him to the trouble of bringing books to me, when I could just as well go after them.

December 14. — This afternoon, Frederic came running into the barn, and threw himself down upon the hay, laughing, and rolling over.

" What 's the matter," says I.

" O dear," says he, " I 've been overhearing Aunt Bethiah exalt Mr. Scott. She and Elinor were in the unfinished room, and the partition 's thin.

" Says she : ' Elinor, I wonder at your being so offish with Mr. Scott. Now, he 's a nice man, and well off, and why don't you like him ? '

" ' O, he don't bring me nigh boxberries enough,' says Elinor, laughing.

" ' Laugh now, and cry by and by,' says Aunt B. ' You 'll pick over a peck-measure and get a bitter apple at last. You are old enough to have more consideration. There he has got a house all finished off and furnished, English carpet in the spare room, and yellow chairs up chamber, brass andirons and fire-tongs, great wheel and little wheel, rugs braided, quilts quilted, kiverlids wove and counterpanes worked, sheets and piller-cases all made to your hand. Nothing to do, but step right into Mrs. Scott's shoes. Cow in the barn and pig in the sty, cellar all banked up, and knocker on the front door.'

" Elinor laughed so she could n't speak. I stuffed my mittens into my mouth, and waited.

" ' Besides,' she went on, ' he would n't be forever under foot, like most men, running in and out all day tracking the floor, and wanting to be waited upon. He eats his breakfast early, goes off with his men to the woods, and you won't see him from morning to night. Nothing to do but snug up, and sit down and take comfort.'

"At this, I gave a great shout and run. But," said Frederic, growing quite serious, "Scott will get her, for all she laughs at him, because he 's in earnest; and I never yet knew a man to be dead set upon having a girl, that he did n't get her."

And then he capered off, and left me to consider of his doctrine, as follows : —

"Because he is in earnest." Well, suppose two are in earnest about the same one. What then? It must depend on the kind, or degree. Captain Welles says Scott is set as the east wind. Let him be the very east wind itself, and welcome ; and I 'll be the sunshine, or a gentle breeze of May, or the sweet breath of summer. The old fable may come true again. No doubt, a man should be honest, even to his own diary. So I must put down here that these pretty words came out of one of the books the schoolmaster lent me. But the application I made myself.

Afterwards Elinor came out into the barn to find a knitting-core. I mean to make her one, like a beauty I saw Lucy have. 'T was made of light wood, painted white, with a wreath of flowers running round it, and varnished. I shall give it to her on New-Year's Day. What a mean present ! I wish I could give her something grand, something gold.

Sunday, December 17. — Mr. Colman preached to-day. I can't deny that his sermon was good. He showed himself very glad to meet Elinor. To-morrow he will be over here. He never comes into the place but what he comes a-visiting at our house.

December 22. — Frederic was married this evening. I was about as happy as he, for Elinor and I stood up. Lucy would have her for bridesmaid ; and Frederic made her choose who should be bridesman. 'T was three days ago he told me of it. I was sitting down on the cellar-door, in the

sunshine. He came up and clapped me on the shoulder, and said he :—

"Come, Walter, brush up your best clothes, for Elinor has chosen you to stand up, and fuss enough she made about it, too. First, she would n't choose any way. Decided. Then she 'd a good deal rather not ; then she begged me to pick one out myself; and at last she hung down her head and looked sheepish, and jammed the tongs into the ashes, and said, in a little faint voice, ' I guess I 'll have Walter.' Now, you know you 're a handsome chap, and I expect you 'll look your best."

'T was a great wedding. Everybody was there. Lucy is a little, pale, gentle creature. "The lily and the damask rose," I heard the Squire's wife say to the Squire. Our minister being called away to an ordination, Mr. Colman stayed and performed the ceremony. He hung about long after 't was time for the minister to leave, and let the young folks enjoy themselves.

January 1, 18 —. — To-day is New-Year's Day, and I gave Elinor the knitting-core, which I was afterwards sorry I did. She said 't was a beauty, and tucked it in her apron-string.

Mr. Scott sent her a white merino shawl, with a border of red flowers and green leaves. Aunt Bethiah thinks 't was n't bought new, but was one Mrs. Scott kept laid away, and never wore.

Towards night, the stage - driver brought a small box, very heavy, marked with Elinor's name. It contained beautiful books, with beautiful pictures. She read the note which came with them, then looked at me and blushed.

The box was from Mr. Colman. That present of mine was mean enough.

February 2. — I have been reading in the schoolmaster's books tales setting forth the sentiment of love and its manifestations, by which it appeareth that the modest maiden aimeth to conceal her love, appearing oftentimes cold and unmoved, when the contrary is the case. These are truly most delightful books, and I do esteem the reading of them a great privilege.

As I read, I say, Perhaps so doth Elinor. Just so good, and so sweet, and so fair is Elinor. And at the end I say, And with the same love, I hope will Elinor love me.

But shall I say, My dear love, take me and poverty? When she asks for bread, shall I give her a kiss? or for raiment, looks of tenderness? No. When I speak, it shall be to say, I have everything to make life comfortable; come, let us enjoy it together.

April 4. — Captain Welles talks of going to Ohio, with a few others, to take up land, and wants I should go. This seems a good way to get the money I want so much; though I should, of course, have to wait a few years for it. Daddy is anxious to have me do what is for my advantage. He will have to hire another man to work on the farm; for Frederic can't leave his trade now.

April 10. — It is decided that I shall go to Ohio.

They are all sorry to part with me. Elinor says nothing; but there is a heaviness in her countenance delightful to my soul. This morning she got a scolding from Aunt Bethiah for putting more sand on the floor, when it was on new yesterday, and only wanted to be herring-boned.

I shall leave and say nothing.

April 13. — Last night proved that I have some steadfastness.

After eating dinner at Captain Welles's I took a walk over the hills, thinking to find some Mayflowers. I had found a few, and was scratching away the dry leaves, when I heard a rustling quite near me. Then the bushes parted and showed me a lovely face, — the lovely, rosy face of Elinor, growing lovelier and rosier every minute. She had come to find Mayflowers too.

She wanted some very pink ones, and so we went wandering about, down in deep hollows, where the moss was damp, and by little sheep-paths, and through the woods, until at last I perceived the sun was setting, and we had scarcely any flowers.

Upon climbing a tree to discover whereabouts we were, I saw, a little below us, a scraggly, one-sided cedar-tree, which I knew to be a long way from home. The Beaver Brook road led directly past it.

We gained that road, walking quickly at first, but afterwards, more slowly. Daylight left us, and the stars came out. We walked on and on along the lonely road, walked slow, and scarcely spoke. For my resolution was taken. Elinor should not be bound by any promises or confessions. Only, just as we were stepping over the door-sill, I heard a little sigh, and these few words would blunder out, " When I come back from the West, I shall — want to tell — " But there I left off, and did n't go into the house, but walked about the place till nigh midnight.

Ohio, June 6, 18—. — Two years in the wilderness, and nothing gained. Gloom gathers around me. No little spot of blue sky can I discover. The hurricane has destroyed everything. I am sick, weak. O the deathly chills, the burning fever! O the lonesomeness, the heart-loneliness, of this dreary place! The lake, the sickening, fresh-water lake, I can't endure. If I could but set foot on the hillside at the old place, and look out upon the great sea, and draw one long breath! If I could but stand on White Rock, with the spray dashing over me, and the wind, from across the broad Atlantic, rushing past! All night I dream of blue, sparkling waters, where little white-sailed boats are gliding so gently, gently off from the shore, and away into the distance. If I could but lay me down in one of these, and so float on and on, no matter where!

Why do I never dream of Elinor? Are we so utterly separated that even in visions I may not behold her face? What have I done, that God refuses me all joy? I don't know of being so bad. But I suppose this not knowing is the very badness itself.

Captain Welles and the others don't show me their letters now. But have n't we more than five senses? Else how is it I know that in these letters is the neighborhood talk of her connection with Mr. Colman? She never mentions it; neither does Frederic. But that is because they have very kind hearts.

I will drag myself once more over these hills. Better wearisome motion than wearisome rest.

June 7. — Yesterday I wandered very far away among the hills, knowing well where I wanted to go, and where I should probably go; but circling round about as if to hide from myself my own intentions. I knew of people who had been there, but had never felt heart to go myself. I crossed a desolate plain, where a fire had passed. Every bush, stump, and tree was blackened. After this came green hills, with woods and grape-vines.

On the side of a hill there stood a hut, built up against a mass of rocks. This hut was what I came to find.

I walked softly up, and looked in at the open door. A dark-looking, beautiful young girl, with long hair, sat crouching in a corner. Close by her was a great shaggy dog.

I had heard of the Prophetess, but thought to find a wrinkled old woman, and this beautiful girl startled me. Startled, but not pleased me; for there was no young look in her face. Such strange eyes I never saw. 'T was as if an old person's face had been smoothed and rounded out, and the expression left there still. By her dress I saw that she was Indian.

The hut was a damp, gloomy place, extending far back into a cavern among the rocks. She arose and beckoned me to follow her farther in, — farther from the light and sunshine. There, in half darkness, half light, she stood, with her terrible eyes fixed upon mine. I longed to step back into the sunshine, for a chill had half taken hold of

me; but some power kept me standing there, — neither could I turn my eyes from hers.

Presently I became conscious of a drowsiness. Her face, her whole figure, faded from my sight. Then, in the midst of the darkness, I perceived a spot of light, which soon took unto itself the semblance of a hand, — a pale hand, which held a damask rose, seemingly just plucked, full of fragrance and wet with dew.

While I gazed upon it, I saw that it faded and drooped, till at last its head hung lifeless upon the stalk. There only remained the pale, crumpled leaves. I wept at the sight, thinking of my own damask rose so far away.

But while I wept, the rose revived. A ray of light streamed in from above. The drooping leaves expanded; their color, even their fragrance, returned; and it sat upright upon its stalk, a perfect flower, wanting nothing save the dew-drops.

The vision passed, and after a pause there came strains of mournful music. O, so mournful, so sad, so hopeless! I seemed to hear in it groans of the dying. Tears streamed from my eyes; I sobbed like a child.

But after a little the chords were swept by a more joyous hand, and gave forth a charming melody, — strains ravishing and delightful beyond description. Again I wept, but now tears of joy. A heavenly rapture pervaded my whole being.

As the last strain melted away, consciousness returned. I was standing alone in the damp, chill cavern. The girl, with that same awful look in her face, was crouching in her corner. I tottered towards the open door, towards the sunshine, and sank, shivering, upon the ground. The girl brought me something in a cup to drink, — something dark and fiery. It put new life in my veins, and strength to my limbs.

August 18. — God be thanked for a sight of the old place once more. I could hug the very trees. The grass seems too good to walk on.

God be thanked, too, for bringing me once more under the same roof with Elinor. Captain Welles was right. I could never have survived another winter at the West.

They were all glad to see me. As I went in, Elinor burst out crying. Daddy sat shelling beans.

"What are you crying for?" said he.

"Walter has come," she sobbed out.

"And what is that to be crying about?" said he.

But I saw, as he grasped my hand, that he too brushed away a tear.

Frederic and his Lucy cannot do enough for me. He tries to laugh, scold, tease, and coax me into health. Mammy is steeping up gin and mustard, which, they say, is a sure cure for the chills. Dearly beloved friends! They little know how soothingly their kindness falls upon the heart of the lonely one.

Elinor looks troubled.

They tell me of a great revival here, the like of which was never known.

I miss Aunt Bethiah. She has gone away to visit another sister of hers.

Lucy tells me that Mr. Scott has gone to England to discover his relatives, and that his going was hastened by a talk he had with Elinor. Poor fellow! No doubt his heart can ache, as well as other people's. Lucy says that Elinor was very tender of his feelings when she refused him.

August 2. — There is to be a four days' meeting here. A great many ministers are expected from abroad. Some mighty influence is sweeping over the place. The proud and haughty are bowed low before it. Little children leave their play, and persuade each other to come to Christ. They meet to pray and sing, likewise, very solemn hymns.

August 29. — This is the second day. The meeting-house was crowded full, way up into the galleries and negro seats. Four ministers in the pulpit, besides others in the front pews, and delegates back of them. It is wonderful to hear them tell of the workings of the Spirit in their own churches. The congregation was deeply moved. Many wept. I too feel my sinfulness. I too would come under this mighty influence, but cannot. My heart is like a stone within me. With life and warmth all around, I remain cold and dead.

Elinor rose for prayers. How she can be made any better is what I cannot understand.

September 2. — The meeting is over; but Mr. Colman remains to assist our minister to gather in the abundant harvest. In a few months, he goes to India as a missionary. I must say that his departure will add to my happiness, or at least take from my uneasiness.

Elinor is in great distress, calling herself a monster of iniquity. Mr. Colman labors with her incessantly. She cannot declare it to be the true feeling of her heart, that, for the glory of God, she is willing all her friends should be forever damned.

September 4. — Last night was spent, nearly the whole of it, in prayer and exhortation. I could plainly hear my dear girl sobbing and crying. Towards morning I heard a shout of joy, and immediately afterwards Elinor's voice, singing, in rapturous tones,

"I know that my Redeemer lives."

Then she broke forth into prayer. Her voice rose high and sweet. 'T was as if she was conversing with the angels around the throne of God. I trembled lest, in its ecstatic rapture, her soul should burst its fleshly bonds and soar away.

This afternoon she talked most earnestly with me. Her face was radiant with the warmth and joy of her heart.

September 21. — Mr. Colman wishes to marry Elinor, and take her with him to India.

O God, I beseech thee to spare me this great affliction! Remove not my only joy!

But will she do this? Has there not been, without words, an understanding between us two?

September 23. — I open my journal on purpose to write down, while I am calm, that I believe Mr. Colman to be a worthy, sincere man, and truly anxious for the spread of the Gospel. I wish to set this down, because I am sensible that at times my jealous feelings have caused me to misjudge him, and may do so again. He knows nothing of my hopes and fears. He is not to blame for wishing to brighten his days of exile with the sweetest face that ever smiled. It is natural, when you see a lovely flower, to wish to gather it and have it for your own. He does not know the flower is mine. I speak boldly, but it is only to myself.

September 25. — The Rev. Mr. D——, agent of the Missionary Society, preached last evening a powerful discourse. What a man he is! His soul is all on fire! And what language! There was deep silence in the congregation. They were with him among the heathen. They saw what he had seen. They heard what he had heard. They felt what he had felt. He closed with an earnest appeal for fresh laborers in the vineyard. From a high key he came suddenly down to a low, solemn tone, which suited well with the agitated state of the audience.

"Beware," said he, "of permitting earthly joys, earthly hopes, earthly loves, to come in the way of services due to Christ. Souls are perishing for want of heavenly food, and you withhold it. Thousands, millions, are on the broad road to destruction, and you refuse to extend a helping hand. And why? Because you would enjoy a few short years of earthly happiness. How mean, how worthless, how dearly bought, will appear these few short years, when, at the judgment-day, the souls of these miserable wretches shall cry out against you, — 'We might have been saved! We might have been

saved!' And still, as the endless ages of eternity roll on, the cry shall come up to you, — 'We might have been saved! We might have been saved!'"

Elinor was greatly agitated, weeping often. Sitting next her, I could not help but take her hand in mine, to show my sympathy for her distress. I fear she will consider it a sacred duty to sacrifice herself. O, if she were a little, only a little less good! May God forgive me such a sinful wish! But I love her with an earthly love, and would not have her an·angel, lest she soar away and leave me. Still, if I love her truly, ought I not to wish for her the highest holiness? For what shall I wish? For what shall I pray? My mind is perplexed.

I think I will speak to her. She may not have understood my looks, my actions. Yes, I must speak. My pride is gone. I will say: "Elinor, you are all the world to me. I am very poor. But don't leave me alone."

September 26. — This morning Frederic came up to me and clapped me on the shoulder (just in the way he did when he asked me to stand up with him), and said, in a low voice, "Walter, don't you like Elinor?"

The tears rushed to my eyes; I could not speak.

"Come," said he, "let us walk awhile together." And he took my arm in his.

It was very early. We walked miles into the woods. I told him everything. When I had finished, he said: "Walter, marry Elinor. You must. She shall not leave us. She loves you better than anybody on earth. I guessed it before you went away; and while you were gone, I knew it. No matter about means. You are the same to me as a brother. All the farm shall be yours. My trade is enough for me. I have some money, too, that you can borrow, and repay at your leisure. I should have spoken of this long ago, if I had only known. Why did you keep so close? Ever since you came back, Lucy and I have watched, and she felt so sure that I ventured to speak. You must speak before it gets fixed in her mind that it is a duty to go. For what she thinks she ought to do she will do, and always would.

"And now," he went on in a lighter tone, for Frederic can never keep serious long, "now that I have offered you my sister, I hope you won't reject her. Lucy and I take so much comfort together, just think what a houseful of happiness there will be when you and Elinor are married!"

"O Frederic," I said, as soon as I could speak, "you are too kind; but I am afraid I am not worthy. Besides being poor, I am not a Christian, and I have had but few advantages. And she — she is pure and lovely, and has a mind that is well informed, and the manners of a lady."

"Well," said he, "you want to be good, don't you? and you want to get learning?"

"Yes."

"And you love her with all your heart?"

"I do."

"Well. Now, Walter, I tell you what I think. If a man knows his ignorance and seeks for knowledge, if he feels his badness, and longs for goodness, and loves with all his heart, he is fit to marry the king's daughter, and inherit the throne."

September 27. — I went this evening into Lucy's room, and found Elinor there alone. I sat down near her.

She looked up, with a smile on her face, and said: "I have been wanting to see you, Walter, and tell you what a glorious path is opened before me. I believe myself to be a chosen instrument for carrying the Gospel to the heathen. And Mr. Colman" (this lower) "thinks me worthy to labor with him in the vineyard."

"And you will marry him?" I asked in a constrained voice.

"Yes," said she, faintly; "I have promised."

I arose and walked many times across the room. When power of speech came, I said, standing still near her: "Eli-nor, do you remember, the night before I went away, I wanted so much to tell you something? Let me tell it now. But you know. You must have known — you must have seen — I have been waiting to make myself worth offering. I am almost sure I can make you happy, and — have thought you loved me — a little. If I could only hear you say so!"

"Walter," she replied, "I must not seek for happiness. I have loved you, not a little." Here the bright color spread over her face; for while the woman spoke, the angel blushed. "I have loved you. O God, sustain me in this my trial hour!"

This little prayer dropped softly from her lips. I scarce caught the sound of it. Then she spoke in a firmer tone: "What have I to do with happiness or unhappiness? The path of duty lies straight before me. And therein I must walk, though thorns pierce my feet."

"But," I asked, "is it right to marry without — Elinor, do you love Mr. Colman?"

"With my soul I do. He was with me in the Valley of the Shadow of Death, — spiritual, not bodily death. With his help I obtained my heavenly joy. My soul is bound to his. I have loved you, Walter, more than" — and again came the bright blushes, speaking more sweetly than her lips — "more than you can ever know. But the greater the love, the greater the glory of crushing it out. The heavier the cross, the brighter will be the crown, and with the greater rapture shall I wake the music of my golden harp through the countless years of eternity. What is this life? A puff, a breath of air. In it we must prepare for the real life, which lies beyond. When the heavens are rolled up like a scroll, what will it avail me that I passed with one whom I loved with an earthly love this brief existence?"

I prayed for calmness to reason with her, but it was not given me. I sat down, and bowed my face upon my hands. Elinor knelt, and offered up a most touching prayer, — beseeching strength for us both. As she finished, Lucy entered, and I went out without speaking.

It is now past midnight. Frederic has been up to see me. Lucy had a long talk with Elinor. It is a comfort, and still it is not a comfort, to know that she spends long solitary hours in self-communion, during which she strives to crush out the love for me, which, as she tells Lucy, fills all her heart. She had loved me almost from a child. She pined for me in my absence, and wept tears of joy at my return.

What a dear comforter is Frederic! He persuades me that before the time arrives she will grow more calm, and will view all these things differently. He advises me to be constantly near her, that my hold on her affections may not be loosened. Did ever man retire to sleep upon sweeter counsel?

October 5. — How shall I write? What words will express the anguish of my heart? O, how much of misery one short week may bring! My pen moves unguided, burning tears blind my eyes. And one week ago it had not happened. One week ago that pleasant face was still among us. But I cannot write.

October 6. — Since I cannot sleep, let me spend the dragging hours in writing the sad account. Let me sit face to face with my own misery, since only misery can I know.

Just one week ago yesterday it was that a man came hurrying through the place, telling that a ship of war was off Rocky Point Village, and that the British were expected to land in the night, to burn, steal, and may be kill. Help was wanted. Every able man prepared himself to hasten to the spot. Frederic and I got our guns and ammunition ready with all speed.

Lucy put up for us great stores of provisions. She was pale as ashes, but said no discouraging word. I rejoiced in the occasion; for, at the prospect of my life being in peril, Elinor could not hide her tenderness. "O

Walter!" she whispered, as I stooped to say good by, "may God keep you safe!"

Just as we were stepping out of the house, mammy, all wrapped up in blankets, came out into the porch, — a thing she had not done before for years. Laying her hand on Frederic's arm, she said, in a trembling voice, "Now, Frederic, be sure and not go into any danger."

He laughed, as young folks do always at the fears of their elders, and then helped her back to her arm-chair.

Rocky Point Village was ten miles off. We were going by water, — that way being the shortest, — about twenty of us in a little pinky. We kept quite close to the land, and arrived there about midnight. The moon was just rising. People were collected from all the villages about. All were watching out for boats from the ship, but none came, and in the morning no ship was to be seen, even from the tall steeple. So it proved a false alarm.

After breakfast, some of the young men proposed going to Pine Island to eat up our good things, and to fill our baskets with beach-plums. This took up all the day.

We had to wait for the tide, so that, by the time we hoisted sail, it was late in the evening. The wind blew fresh, and was dead ahead; and when we had been an hour or two on our course, there was not one aboard but would have been glad to feel the solid land beneath his feet. The little pinky, her sails close reefed, tossed up and down like an egg-shell. Black clouds spread over the sky, threatening rain and tempest.

Then it was that this terrible calamity took place. I was holding by the rail, comparing in my mind things outward with things internal. The soul, too, encountered storms and darkness. All at once I perceived that the boom was swinging over, and sprang to get out of the way. As I sprang, I heard a cry, and caught sight of a man pitching headlong into the water.

"Walter! Walter!" That was the

cry, and then I knew it to be Frederic, and took a great leap into the darkness.

I strove to shout, but the water rushed into my mouth and ears, and I could make no sound. Once more I heard that cry, — "Walter! Walter!" — but fainter this time, and by it I knew I should never reach him. Still, when the next wave lifted me high, I gathered all my strength, and shouted, "Frederic, wait!"

The boat had been lowered, and that shout saved my own worthless life. But Frederic's was gone forever. O the dreadful words!

They dragged me into the boat, with scarce the breath of life left in me. The vessel lay to, and boats were kept out till morning. But our Frederic was seen no more. And he was the very best of us all.

O what a night! I was watched. They would not let me come near the rail. No doubt there was reason.

I shall never forget the morning. The wind had gone down; the sun rose bright, and burned into my brain; the waves were to me like live creatures, dancing and laughing around us. They seemed to say, "We 've had our victim, and are now at peace with mankind. Pass on. Pass on."

As we neared the shore, I made great efforts to be calm; for at home were those to whom I must say, "Here I am safe, but Frederic is drowned."

What would they want of me?

It was still early when we landed. I could only creep along the path, holding on by the fence; for my feet were like leaden weights. My form bowed itself like an old man's. The fields, the trees, were not green, but ghastly.

The sumachs prevented my being seen from the house. As I drew near, I saw Lucy standing at the back door, looking down at the vessel.

Frederic had never left home before, since their marriage. Such a happy look as there was on her face!

I crept off to a clump of willows, and from there ran down the hill and across the Little Swamp to the minister's.

They were in the midst of family prayers. All of them started to their feet, asking what had happened. I had just strength enough to gasp out, "You must tell them. I can't. Frederic is drowned," — and then fell down in a faint.

O what a desolate home is ours! Poor Lucy! Poor heart-broken young thing!

On that same night a strange thing happened here at home. Mammy could not be got off to bed. She was anxious, and would sit up. At length, (this was about midnight,) she leaned her head back, and seemed to fall into a sleep, so quiet that they could scarce hear her breath. Then a beautiful smile spread over her face. Her lips moved, and spoke, as they thought, Frederic's name. She awoke soon after, but has never since that hour been quite herself, — never seemed conscious of Frederic's loss. She speaks of him as of one gone a journey. Some talk of her exertions the night before, of her anxiety, or of a partial stroke. But I think, and shall always think, that Frederic's angel appeared to her, and, in some way, deadened her mind to the dreadful suffering his loss would occasion.

We have sent for Aunt Bethiah. We need her firmness now.

October 20. — Elinor is in a strange way. I have never seen her either weep, or smile, or work, or read, since that terrible day. I must take back part of that. She does smile, as she sits idle, playing with her fingers, — smiles and moves her lips like — But I cannot bear to write what she is like. I will never believe it. She was in a state of excitement, and this blow has staggered her. But she will recover. God will not deal with us so hardly.

Mr. Colman is away, making his preparations. He surely will not take with him this poor, helpless girl.

November 7. — O, he was so good, so lovely! — noble-looking, and in his very best days. Always was something cheering or lively dropping from his lips. And to think that the last words he uttered were those cries of agony from the dark waters, — " Walter ! Walter ! "

All night I toss among the dreadful waves, with that cry ringing in my ears ; or I strive to clutch at a man's form, as it pitches headlong ; or take again that fearful leap, and, at the shock, wake in horror.

Such a dear friend as he was to me ! I remember that last night he came to my chamber, so kind, so comforting. And what did I ever do for him ? O, if I could only think of anything I ever did for him !

December 12. — The minister talked with me soothingly to-day of the love of God for his children. I feel to-night willing to trust all to Him.

Let the worst happen that can happen, I will bow my head in submission. What matters the few years' sadness of an obscure being ? Nothing in the universe stands affected by my grief. Can I not bear what is mine own ? Still, even Jesus prayed that the cup might pass.

January 9. — Mr. Colman is in the place. I am sorry. Let me try my best, I have to hate that man — a little. In my secret thoughts I call him my enemy. Did he think, because he was a preacher, that he could pick and choose, — that nothing was too good for him ?

I must write down my bad thoughts sometimes. No doubt he is a good man, after all. But he must not meet Elinor now, not if he were a seraph.

January 10. — He came this afternoon, and I met him at the gate. He inquired for Elinor. I asked if he would like to see her, and drew him towards the window of the east room, Lucy's room (Lucy is with her mother). The shutters of this window were partly open. All the others were closed.

Elinor was at the farther end of the room. A little light came in from the window over the kitchen door, or we could hardly have seen her. She was sitting on a low stool, bending forward a little, her head drooping, her hands loosely clasped, and oh ! so thin, so white, so lifeless, so like a blighted, wilted flower ! What semblance was there of the rosy, smiling face that had so long brightened the old home ?

Once she smiled, and then her lips moved as they do often. He shuddered at the sight. " She mourns for her brother," said he. " I will go in and speak to her some words of consolation."

" No, sir," said I. " What you see is not grief, but almost insanity. Shall I tell you the cause ? "

Then I drew him from the house to a wide field near by, and as we walked talked to him mildly, but with some boldness.

I made known my love for her, and her own confession to Lucy. I made it plain to him that, in striving against nature, her mind had become unsettled, and so unable to bear that terrible shock. And, finally, I implored him not to take away so frail a being to perish among strangers.

I was surprised that he made no answer. He left me abruptly and walked towards the minister's. Was he offended ?

January 11. — This morning a boy brought a note from Mr. Colman, requesting me to come and see him. I went as soon as I could leave home.

He came down to the door and asked me up into his chamber. After handing me a chair, he seated himself at the table, where he remained for some minutes with his head bowed. When he looked up, I was startled at the pale and sorrow-stricken look of his face.

" Young man," said he, " I have passed the night in self-examination, and now I wish to confess that I have deceived myself, injured you, and destroyed the peace of one precious to us both. In gaining a laborer for Christ, I hoped also to gain comfort for my own heart. Still," he added, earnestly, " I was not wholly selfish. I really believed that, under God, she might become a mighty instrument for good. Who so fitted to teach the Gospel as the pure-hearted? I hoped to gain her love. She seemed — there was something in her manner that — but let it pass. I was walking in a dream. 'T was surely a dream, or I should have known that such happiness was not for me.

"Love met me once. It was in early youth. As fair, as lovely a being as God ever made yielded up to me her young heart, and then drooped and died. Years passed. I never thought to meet love again.

"It was while preaching here that I first saw Elinor. I was struck with the resemblance to her who once bloomed in just such loveliness. There was the same purity, the same sweetness, the same dewy freshness. Even the dress was similar, — the lovely blue and white, harmonizing so well with that fair beauty.

"My agitation was so great I could scarcely go on with the services. From that day my dead heart became alive again. Fountains of feeling, which I had deemed sealed forever, burst forth afresh. I dreamed I should walk in light, and not in darkness.

"But it is all past. False hopes shall mislead me no more. I will live solely for the glory of God, since such is His will. Was not that will made plain to me in my early youth? I have asked His forgiveness, and now," he added, extending his hand, "I ask yours. She will recover. With her your life will be blest.

"I will not even bid her farewell. But when health and strength return, when she is yours and you are hers, will you not sometimes speak together of me? Shall you be unwilling to cast for a moment a shadow across the brightness of life, by remembering a lonely man passing his days in exile, without one flower of love to cheer him?"

He was deeply agitated, and from the first had grown more and more earnest. I stood like one confounded. A minister of the Gospel was asking my forgiveness. He whom I had thought proud and haughty was shedding tears. The moment he humbled himself, I seemed to sink below him, O so far!

I told him this, and every feeling I had ever had against him. And, sitting there together, we had a long and friendly talk about Elinor and Frederic and the old people. Before I left, he handed me a letter addressed to Elinor, which he requested me, when she should recover, to give to her.

February 27. — To-day, upon going suddenly into Frederic's room, I found Elinor there, weeping. This was a welcome sight. She had found in the drawer a pair of his mittens, — gray, spotted with red; also a little box which he had given her, and a picture, with "To my sister" written on the back.

She was crouched upon the floor, with these spread out before her, weeping bitterly. I raised her up, speaking soothing words, and drew her towards the window, where the sun shone in, bright and warm.

It was long before she grew calm. I judged it best to say but little. But O the joy of knowing she is saved!

March 17. — To-day Elinor did many little things for mammy, who is now very feeble, and requires constant attention. It is long since she has risen from her bed, and she is for the greater part of the time in a sleep or stupor. Sometimes she revives a little, and seeing, perhaps, some neighbors or friends in the room, will say, "Now you must all stay to tea," or, "Is anybody sick in your neighborhood?" and then drop off again.

I watched Elinor, as she bent over the bed, with tears in my eyes, but joy in my heart. When I left the room, she followed me out, and sat down near me, and whispered, "Let us talk about *him*."

And then we spoke freely of our dear Frederic, — spoke of his noble heart, of his goodness, of all his pleasant ways. Many little incidents of his life were remembered.

"Frederic is in heaven," I whispered.

"I know he is," she answered calmly, and as if she knew with a knowledge not of earth.

April 15. — Elinor has been growing more like herself ever since the day I found her crying in Frederic's room. She busies herself about the house, talks cheerfully with her grandfather, and does much for his comfort. Good old man! He said to me, the other day: "Walter, I am very wicked. I do not mourn for Frederic. My days here are but few; and I rejoice to think that, when I pass over the river, he will welcome me to the other shore. I strive against this happy thought, but it will come. I wanted to tell somebody of my wicked feelings."

"O, don't talk to me so!" I said, "don't call yourself wicked."

I shall always love Aunt Bethiah, she is so kind to him and to us all. She loved Frederic dearly, in her way. I have noticed that she never sets on the table, at meal-times, the things he used to like best.

June 9. — All my anxiety about Elinor is gone. The color and the smiles are coming back to her face, and the light to her eye. She is almost her old self again. Only, when people have suffered a great deal, some sign of it will always remain.

June 12. — Yesterday, I brought in to her a bunch of wild-roses. She put them in a tumbler, and carried them into mammy's room. This morning she came out with her basket. "Let us be children again," she said. "Let us go for some roses."

So we went over the hills; and, as we passed along the pasture-road, we found ourselves walking hand in hand.

Every day I think I will ask her to be my wife, and every day I put it off till another time. The reason is, that

I fear to disturb this pleasant season. I don't know what she thinks about Mr. Colman. She has never mentioned his name.

There are more ways of telling things than by word of mouth. I set my love before her in a thousand ways, and she never throws it back upon me. I shall give her the letter to-morrow.

June 16. — Yesterday, after tea, we sat all together, in mammy's room, till almost dark. She was in an uneasy way, and daddy calmed her down by saying hymns to her, — the very ones she used to read to him. Elinor was making a wreath of oak-leaves for a young girl in the next house, who was going to have a party. I was picking out for her the fairest leaves, equal in size. Daddy said his verses in a sing-song way, so that mammy at last fell quietly asleep, and we spoke to each other softly, so as not to disturb her.

All at once daddy spoke out; and says he, in a slow, quiet way: "Blind folks, you know, hear very quick. I do myself, and sometimes even more than is spoken. For instance, to-night, when Walter says, 'Here is a beautiful leaf for you,' I can hear, — the very ones with all my heart.' And when Elinor says, 'And it will just match this one,' I can hear, 'You can't love me any more than I do you.' Now, children, what are you waiting for?"

Dear old man! I felt like throwing my arms right about his neck, and started up for that purpose. But Elinor came first, and so —

"Never mind me," says daddy, "I 'm blind, you know."

Whereupon, I explained that Elinor had taken what was meant for him.

And when we grew a little calm he began to plan plans.

And after that we two took a long walk; and neither of us knew whither we went, or how long we stayed. But during the walk she confessed to me her belief, that God made the heart, as well as the soul, and would never require one to be crushed for the sake of the other. She gave me Mr. Colman's letter. It was as follows : —

[Omitted.]

About one o'clock, I should think it was, that night, something happened, and, when daylight came, I hardly knew whether it had happened or not.

I had been lying awake some hours, recalling all my past life, — thinking over and over again how a poor, friendless boy had reached a great happiness ; and every time I came to the happiness, tears of joy would fill my eyes, and I could not sleep, and did not wish to.

And while I lay in this blissful state, there came floating upon the air strains of the most heavenly music. The whole room was filled with melody. And with the music came the consciousness of its being familiar to me. Where had I heard those sweet strains before ? They grew fainter. Raising my head, that no note might escape me, I awoke myself from a sort of trance into which I did not know of having fallen ; for I was sure my eyes had not once been closed.

The last, faint sounds died away. Instantly there flashed upon my mind the remembrance of that strange music in the Western wilderness.

* * * *

THE DARWINIAN THEORY.

GREAT interest has been awakened, of late, by the promulgation of a new "Theory of Creation" ; and nonscientific readers have met with numerous controversial articles in the journals, magazines, and newspapers of the day. The name of Darwin, after having been honorably known for a quarter of a century to the scientists of the world, has become familiar to us all as that of the author of this new theory. A word has been added to our vocabulary. "Darwinian" is now a distinctive epithet wherewith to individualize the new school of thought, and an appellation to designate its votaries. Notwithstanding the interest which Mr. Darwin's writings and the replies of his opponents have created, and the constant allusion to them in publications of all kinds ; in spite of the active warfare they have incited ; in spite of the sneers and sarcasms which have been launched by writers, lecturers, and preachers,— sure means of advertisement among the people, — few really and thoroughly comprehend Mr. Darwin's idea. A lecturer, alluding to it lately, says that it will be worthy of consideration when we see an ape turn into a man ; and this is about the extent, we imagine, to which the great mass of people understand a theory which has been received as revelation by many of the first scientific men of the age, — men who have given their lives to patient, profound, untiring, unimpassioned study of nature, and who rank among the foremost thinkers of the world.

Leaving the argumentative detail to those whose learning is the only armory which can supply weapons adequate to the maintenance of the struggle, let us see if we cannot explain the idea which causes it ; nor consider its verification to lie in the metamorphosis of an ape into a man.

Darwin's idea is generally conceived to be a new one. This is not strictly the case. The real foundation was laid long ago. It is the law of persistent force, acting on the universe. This is as old as Buddha, and was a dogma of Buddhism. It has been enunciated in some form or other for ages. But Darwin has infused into it a new vital strength, has given it new application, has clearly explained its workings, has been its prophet to the people. To fully understand the history and progress of the Darwinian theory, we must look back many years, and trace the influence which theology has had upon the advance of scientific knowledge.

For centuries the Bible was understood to contain a perfect, exact, undoubted account of the origin of the world. It was believed by everybody that the world was made in six days. The very imperfect acquaintance which the ancients had with geology and physics allowed them to accept this relation unchallenged. Faith was far stronger than reason; and, during the long ages in which the Church ruled supreme, this statement was accepted and implicitly believed by the whole race of Christians. But as men began to grow more enlightened,— as, one by one, the secrets of nature were revealed to the students whose desire for knowledge overbore their tacit acceptance of tradition, — doubts began to arise as to the possibility of the truth of this long-cherished idea. When the printing-press came, and enabled these ardent explorers to communicate freely the results of their studious labors, the leaven of discredit, thus disseminated, began to work in the mass, and the reason of men began to rise beneath the superincumbent theological pressure which had so long weighed upon it. The multitude of facts gathered together by these careful students became, by and by, so vast, and the conclusions to which they led so indubitable, that the theologians were forced, out of simple common-sense, to revise their expoundings of the sacred writings.

When it was found that the earth was made up of vast depositions of matter which contained the remains of long-extinct creatures, whose fragments were buried in solid rocks, once soft, oozy mud; when it was found that other rocks, hundreds of feet in thickness, were wholly composed of the imperishable remains of other extinct animals, which once lived and died and were gathered together in waters which broke over the very spot where these rocks now rise; when it was found that untold millions of years were necessary for the formation of one single group of these rocks, among many equally vast; when it was found that, in the memory of man, during the lapse of at least five thousand years, the earth had undergone no appreciable change; when it was found that the earth was the result of the action of laws existent in matter, — an upheaving, a washing away, a hardening, a disintegrating through a period of time beyond the conception of man, — the theologians were forced to substitute *periods* for *days*. When the old walls which had circumscribed man's mind became so crumbled as to allow of egress, individuals broke through them and revelled in the freedom of intelligent thought. When these walls were demolished by those who had themselves erected them, they were leaped, in all directions, by ardent explorers; and naturalists, no longer restrained by tradition, rushed upon voyages of discovery into the teeming world before them.

For a while this emancipation exhausted itself in the contemplation of the physical world, and an inquiry into brute life. Speculations and theories might riot in a past which was a practical eternity. They had unlimited space wherein to project, backward, the structure of the universe. But this long-stretching past was to be peopled only by the lower orders of animal life. The rocks were found to be filled with stony remains of animals who perished when the sandstone, which built old crumbling castles, was sea-shore mud; the chalk hills which bore them were found to be made up of myriads of little creatures. These humble representatives of life might be, must be, credited with a remote antiquity. But man was not an animal. He was a being apart. Although he was liable to heat and cold, disease and death, although his body was made of the same materials as the brute's, and was subject to the same laws of life, he was invested with an individuality which separated him from them. For a while the old influence of theological rule held even these venturous explorers to the ancient landmarks of human origin. By and by, the same impulse which had before led men to examine the proofs of physical creation induced them to consider the evidence of their own advent upon earth. Certain Scriptural statements did not appear reconcilable with each other. Cain went forth and builded a city ; and there were artificers in brass and iron. Now Cain was only one of two men when he went forth. Whence came the citizens of that early settlement, and how did they understand the production of brass, a composite metal ? How was it that man always met man wherever he went on the globe ? Five thousand years ago the varied races were known to be distinct as now, and yet man was formerly said to be but about six thousand years old. Could one thousand years have produced the changes then evident, while five thousand succeeding years have scarce altered these different races ? These and many other difficulties led thinkers to question whether man might not look much farther back into the past for his origin, and whether the same laws which had governed the birth, continuance, and distribution of other animals were not always in action to produce in him kindred results. The old belief, that all men descended from one man, began to be shaken ; and good, honest, faithful Christians expressed their doubts of the matter. It was surmised that they were created in numbers. The old idea, that animals were all created in individual pairs, was found to be incompatible with the discovery of animal remains, in profusion, in rocks which were mud ages before any Adam could have existed to give them Hebrew names. Then, breaking away from the theological bonds, there sprang into active thought men of far-reaching minds, who began a thorough reconstruction of the whole theory of creation. The handwriting on the wall

was NATURAL LAW. All creation, man included, was but the result of one undeviating, unceasing, eternal, all-pervading law, and the state of the universe at any given moment was the state of evolution which that universe exhibited. Behind this law was the great inscrutable Spirit-power.

The infinite number of varied, aggregated facts stored up by man's patient study of this universe are irrelevant here, in a sketch of the progressive advance of his knowledge of creation. Those who desire to examine the evidence which has led to this verdict must go over the records themselves, or accept, out of their own convictions, the result of the examination. To entirely comprehend the Darwinian idea, one should be, to a certain extent, familiar with the principles of science. In other words, he should know more or less of what Darwin knows. He should be familiar with the general results of man's study in the different branches of science. He need not be an astronomer, a physicist, a geologist, a zoölogist, a botanist ; but he should have a general acquaintance with the results of the labors of those who are such. He should, to a certain extent, understand the workings of Natural Law.

This is the great battle-ground on which the struggle is now taking place. The point at issue is, whether the physical changes of the material world, the introduction, continuance, and variation of organized beings, are due to the direct, special intervention of Deity, or whether they are the results of primeval laws, inherent in matter, and out of whose workings spring the phenomena of nature. The adherents to the former opinion maintain that the Deity has created all animals individually, or in individual species, by direct action, apart from natural forces, and indeed by an interference therewith. The votaries of the latter deny special creation, and maintain that all animals are, like the rest of the universe, the results of forces acting through all time, producing, by their diverse changing influences, the variations which, as they have ·widened and strengthened, have resulted in the difference exhibited among animals. The first is the old traditional idea, having its foundation in belief, and drawing its support from the Scriptures. The last is the modern conviction, having its foundation in reason, and drawing its support from the study of nature. How are these differences among animate creatures — these wide contrasts of form, size, and habits — produced, if not by God's special creation? This is the question which Mr. Darwin and his school of thinkers are seeking to answer.

Some half a century ago, M. Lamarck, a French naturalist, propounded a theory which excited the derision of the whole world. He accounted for these variations by suggesting that, as any special want was felt by an animal, the body took on that structure which was required to relieve it. To give a broad illustration : if men needed to fly for the support of life, wings would gradually grow out from their shoulders. Ridiculous as this may be, it showed that thinkers were at that time endeavoring to account, on purely natural grounds, for what they considered natural, and not supernatural phenomena.

Some twenty years ago, a book made its appearance which startled the whole reading world, and caused as much dispute as Darwin has since done. This was "Vestiges of the Natural History of Creation." It was anonymous, and the author has never acknowledged it : to this day he is unknown. This book was learned and lucid. It was received with delight by those who were still looking for some explanation of animal origin on natural grounds ; and was derided quite as much as Lamarck's work by the adherents to the old traditional belief. Scouted by the great majority of naturalists, who still clung with tenacity to the notions of their predecessors, stigmatized as atheistic and abominable by theologians, it was first read with eagerness, and then put

aside ; and though it went through many editions, it is now almost forgotten. But this book was the beginning of Darwinism. It says : —

"We have seen powerful evidence that the construction of this globe and its associates, and, inferentially, that of all the other globes in space, was the result, not of any immediate or personal exertion on the part of Deity, but of natural laws which are expressions of his will. ' What is to hinder our supposing that the organic creation is also the result of natural laws, which are in like manner an expression of his will?"

Referring to the Deity as the great motive-power of all the universe, the author says : —

"To a reasonable mind the Divine attributes must appear, not diminished or reduced in any way, by supposing a creation by law, but infinitely exalted. It is the narrowest of all views of the Deity, and characteristic of a humble class of intellects, to suppose him acting constantly in particular ways for particular occasions. It, for one thing, greatly detracts from his foresight,— the most undeniable of all the attributes of Omnipotence. It lowers him towards the level of our own humble intellects. Much more worthy of him it surely is to suppose that all things have been commissioned by him from the first, though neither is he absent from a particle of the current of natural affairs in one sense, seeing that the whole system is continually supported by his providence. . . . . When all is seen to be the result of law, the idea of an Almighty author becomes irresistible, for the creation of a law for an endless series of phenomena — an act of intelligence above all else we can conceive — could have no other imaginable source, and tells, moreover, as powerfully for a sustaining as for an originating power."

He sums up the hypothesis which he seeks to sustain thus : —

"I suggest, then, as an hypothesis already countenanced by much that is ascertained, and likely to be further sanctioned by much that remains to be known, that the first step was *an ad-*

vance, *under favor of peculiar circumstances, from the simplest forms of being to the next more complicated, and this through the medium of the ordinary process of generation.*"

And further : —

"*That the simplest and most primitive type, under a law to which that of like production is subordinate, gave birth to the type next above it ; that this again produced the next higher, and so on to the very highest*, the stages of advance being in all cases very small, namely, from one species to another; so that the phenomenon has always been of a simple and modest character.*"

In a Sequel which the author wrote, in answer to the numerous attacks made upon him, he has the following : —

"The probable fact is, that the modification takes place in an offshoot of the original tribe, which has removed into a different set of circumstances, these circumstances being the cause of the change ; thus there is no need to presume that the original tribe is at all affected by any such modification."

The author thus supposes that the variations among animals were periodical and sudden, the results of some peculiar impetus given at special periods. Later knowledge — the study of nature by the light of greater experience — has exposed many errors in this work. Its crudities have been made apparent ; but the thought which pervaded it was intrinsically right. The last passage quoted above foreshadows the more elaborate speculations of the later philosopher.

In 1859 appeared Darwin's work, "On the Origin of Species, by Means of Natural Selection, or the Preservation of Favored Races in the Struggle for Life." Like its predecessors, it was a firebrand thrown into the scientific camp. Like his predecessors, the author drew down obloquy and anathemas from the clergy, sarcasm and vituperation from the laity, and a host of replies from writers of all grades. Like his predecessor, the author of the "Vestiges," he might have said, in the words of Agassiz : —

"The history of the sciences is present to tell us that there are few of the great truths now recognized which have not been treated as chimerical and blasphemous before they were demonstrated."

Darwin, as he himself tells us in his Preface, spent twenty years in a patient, laborious study of nature, having special reference to this topic, — the origin of species. Certain observations made in the course of his explorations in South America led him to the convictions which subsequent study only strengthened ; and, after having spent years in the collection of facts bearing upon the subject, he gave his theory to the world in the volume mentioned, which was merely a digest of the facts. It is perhaps needless to say, that Charles Darwin is a naturalist of the highest rank ; that he stands among the foremost men of the day as a clear-minded, trustworthy, accurate, profound thinker.

The Darwinian theory is erected on the primary foundation of a natural law acting through all time, — a persistent force which is applied to all creation, immutable, unceasing, eternal ; which determined the revolutions of the igneous vapor out of which worlds were first evolved ; which determines now the color and shape of a rose-bud, the fall of the summer leaves, the course of a rippling brook, the sparkle of a diamond ; which gives light to the sun and beauty to a woman's eye. It rejects utterly the idea of special creation, and maintains that the globe, as it exists to-day with all its myriad inhabitants, is only one phase of that primeval vapor which by the force of that law has reached its present state. As a little microscopic egg becomes in time a full-grown, living, breathing, loving animal by the operation of natural laws which we term growth, so has the universe, with its denizens, become what it is by the workings of Natural Law.

The precise process by which sentient existence first became evolved from inorganic matter seems to be beyond the scrutiny of man. It is so far without the scope of his experience, his speculation even, that it is futile to attempt to surmise it; although certain interesting phenomena have attended the experiments of naturalists, especially those of Professor Jeffries Wyman. Darwin takes the subject up at the appearance of animal life, and seeks to work out the causes of the present variation among animals, and to detect the *modus operandi* by which the law of evolution has produced the multiform changes now apparent. "Natural Selection" is his password into the great workshop of Nature. The three great agencies at work there are the tendency of all animals to transmit their peculiarities to their offspring, the tendency of all animals to vary from their ancestors under varying influences around them, and the constant changes taking place in their surroundings. "Natural Selection" are the words chosen to express the action of animals under these conflicting forces. The power of external influence upon structure is exhibited in the remarkable results of man's treatment of plants and animals. The varieties of pears and apples are of his producing; and the different breeds of domestic animals are the direct consequences of his influence. The most astonishing instance of his power is shown in pigeons, which are made, by skilful breeders, to assume a great variety of shapes, colors, and habits. To what is this change due? If a rock-pigeon were left to itself, it would produce only rock-pigeons, unless some new influences were brought to bear by natural causes. Man gives a rock-pigeon some peculiar food, subjects it to some peculiar treatment, and the creature begins at once to change; that is, to accommodate itself to the new circumstances by which it is surrounded. The plastic nature undergoes an alteration correspondent to the new state of existence. In a few generations these varieties are indefinitely multiplied; and then, by crossing these varieties, new ones are again

produced. What is then the state of affairs? We have a series of birds which, were they discovered in new countries, would be considered to be new species. They differ in shape and color, in the number of their vertebræ and ribs, the number of wing and tail feathers, the number of scales on their toes, and various other anatomical peculiarities. Here then is proof that animals, when exposed to influences different from those which surrounded their ancestors, take on new forms and characteristics. This is man's work. But is not man one of the many agents in the work of the Great Prime Mover? Let us suppose that the peculiar circumstances which produced a pouter or a fan-tail were to remain in force for centuries; would not pouters or fan-tails continue to procreate, and thus a new species be added to the genus? What, then, becomes of special creation of every species of animal, if man in a few years can produce a dozen forms out of one, any one of which dozen is so distinct as to be deemed a new species, were it Nature's work and not man's? The fact is thus demonstrated that animals become varied in accordance with variations in their surroundings. This simple fact, once substantiated, is the key to the whole subject. Man's influence ceases when he leaves the animal to itself. But Nature never leaves the animal to itself. Her changes are slight and slow; but they never go back. They are permanent, only to be reaffected as the environment alters. When we consider the incalculable, inconceivable lapse of time through which organic life has been swayed by the never-ceasing action of the forces around it, we can imagine what a vast variety of animal forms may have been evolved from some one primal ancestor. Darwin endeavors to explain, in detail, how this differentiation takes place. The largest or strongest get the best food or the most attractive females, and then transmit their strength or their peculiarities to their progeny. These peculiarities are the results of the environment, and if this shall go on changing in the direction of these peculiarities, they will increase. Suppose that the climate should gradually grow colder ; the result might be a denser growth of hair. Those which, by strength or otherwise, chanced to have denser hair than others, would more readily endure the change, and would transmit the habit to their young ; others less fitted to endure the change would die out. In a short time the young would be born with the dense hair, as it is well known that any new habit assumed by animals is exhibited earlier and earlier in the young, as long as it is a necessity of life. These variations are never due to one single cause. Organized life is wrought upon by a wonderfully complex web of influences. Darwin has the following passage touching the action of vegetable and animal life upon each other.

" In Staffordshire, on the estate of a relation where I had ample means of investigation, there was a large and extremely barren heath, which had never been touched by the hand of man ; but several hundred acres of exactly the same nature had been enclosed twenty-five years previously, and planted with Scotch fir. The change in the native vegetation of the planted part of the heath was most remarkable,—more than is generally seen in passing from one quite different soil to another ; not only the proportional numbers of the heath plants were wholly changed, but twelve species of plants (not counting grasses and carices) flourished in the plantations, which could not be found on the heath. The effect on the insects must have been still greater, for six insectivorous birds were very common in the plantations which were not to be seen on the heath ; and the heath was frequented by two or three distinct insectivorous birds. Here we see how potent has been the effect of the introduction of a single tree, nothing whatever else having been done, with the exception that the land had been enclosed, so that cattle could not enter. But how important an element enclosure is, I

plainly saw near Farnham in Surrey. Here there are extensive heaths, with a few clumps of old Scotch firs on the distant hill-tops ; within the last ten years large spaces have been enclosed, and self-sown firs are now springing up in multitudes, so close together that all cannot live. When I ascertained that these young trees had not been sown or planted, I was so much surprised at their numbers that I went to several points of view, whence I could examine hundreds of acres of the unenclosed heath, and, literally, I could not see a single Scotch fir, except the old planted clumps. But on looking closely between the stems of the heath, I found multitudes of seedlings and little trees, which had been perpetually browsed down by the cattle. In one square yard, at a point some hundred yards distant from one of the old clumps, I counted thirty-two little trees ; and one of them, judging from the rings of growth, had during twenty-six years tried to raise its head above the stems of the heath, and had failed. No wonder that, as soon as the land was enclosed, it became thickly clothed with vigorously growing young firs. Yet the heath was so barren and so extensive that no one would ever have imagined that cattle would have so closely and effectually searched it for food.

" Here we see that cattle absolutely determine the existence of the Scotch fir ; but in several parts of the world insects determine the existence of cattle. Perhaps Paraguay offers the most curious instance of this ; for here neither cattle nor horses nor dogs have ever run wild, though they swarm southward and northward in a feral state ; and Azara and Rengger have shown that this is caused by the greater number in Paraguay of a certain fly, which lays its eggs in the navels of these animals when first born. The increase of these flies, numerous as they are, must be habitually checked by some means, probably by birds. Hence if certain insectivorous birds (whose numbers are probably regulated by hawks or beasts of prey) were to increase in Paraguay, the flies would decrease, — then cattle and horses would become feral; and this would certainly greatly alter (as indeed I have observed in parts of South America) the vegetation: this, again, would largely affect the insects; and this, as we just have seen in Staffordshire, the insectivorous birds, and so onwards in ever-increasing circles of complexity."

In the struggle for life, the strongest live; or, in other words, those best fitted to live in the environment endure. Animals and plants produce in vast excess of the possibility of life. A destruction of life is going on to an almost incredible amount. Were this not the case, the slowest breeders in existence would soon cover the earth so as to occupy every inch of space. Darwin reckons that the elephant, the slowest breeder, if allowed to go on unchecked, and to live his allotted term of years, would in five centuries produce fifteen millions of elephants from one pair. If every cod's egg had developed into a full-grown fish, the whole ocean would, ages ago, have been packed with them, like herrings in a box. In this destruction, the weaker animals and plants — those least fitted to thrive under the influences around — become the prey of others better fitted for the struggle, or die of their own lack of assimilative force. Thus, through untold ages of shifting outward circumstances, the plastic forms of organic life have been remoulded. A little obscure plant, the food of an insect, dies out; the insect itself, deprived of its food, dies out or migrates; the bird which fed upon it dies out or migrates; the bird of prey follows the like course. Migration introduces them to an entirely new state of existence, temperature, food, and antagonists. The migrating animals are replaced by others, which likewise experience new surroundings; and thus the extirpation of a single plant may determine a long series of changes. Instances of this kind are not uncommon. What must these changes have been throughout

the remote ages which have turned sea-shore mud into uplifted mountain chains, and sunk long-stretching, sunny hills into the ocean depths!

Darwin constructs his theory of gradual differentiation on the evidence thus obtained. He takes a given specific animal form, and supposes that, owing to some external change in a given locality, it takes on some correspondent variation. But all of the individuals of the species may not be likewise affected. The circumstances may alter in one place and not in another. The result will be two varieties of animal. The variety goes on increasing in diversity, while the original still continues to produce its like. By and by the variety, having a greater tendency to vary, from its having already done so, undergoes a new differentiation, the difference being, in all cases, slight, and the time between the periods of maximum change being hundreds, thousands of years. One of the new varieties may by peculiar circumstances take on a special amplitude of growth, while the other, peculiarly circumstanced, may be contracted and dwarfed. One of the original varieties may by this time have disappeared. The original itself may have disappeared. Thus the connecting link between the two forms is lost. The more individualized form may go on accenting its own peculiar characters, and again be broken into new varieties, some of which may retain the old characters in circumscribed areas, while others may increase in greater abundance and occupy a much wider area. The wider the field of life, the more numerous the differing influences and the more diverse the conditions the animal must undergo. Thence arise more differentiations. After the lapse of some millions of ages, these constantly forking growths will have taken on a diversity to which that of the pouters and fan-tails is trifling.

Some forms may be less plastic than others, and give way less readily to the incident forces. These may remain unchanged for a far longer period than subsequent varieties, and be coexistent with them. Some varieties may take on a cerebral growth as widely different and as strongly individualized as frame structure. Man himself is a striking instance. The Negro, the Malay, the Mongolian, are almost precisely what they were five thousand years ago. The Bushman, the Hottentot, the Patagonian, and the Digger Indian are to-day not much above the animals about them; while the Caucasian has gone on in a wonderful advancement, leaving the other races in the same state of development in which they were when the Caucasian was no farther advanced than they. And here is perhaps the place to allude to the derisive objection to Darwinism, that it makes man an improved monkey. Darwin's theory certainly gives to both some vastly remote common ancestor; but it does not maintain the metamorphosis of one into the other. It does not suppose that man was once a gorilla. It supposes that from out of some of the differentiations of some animal form arose the first man-like creature, and that, gradually changing, like other animal forms, some of the varieties eventually evolved into apes and orang-outangs, to stop there and die out like hosts of other forms now extinct. But from some strongly individualized variety sprang, with more rapid and advancing growth, the primitive man, who has, under complex influences, differentiated into the so-called races of mankind. We talk of man as being something infinitely above all animals. There is a vast difference between the highest and lowest species of the genus *homo*. Were the race confined to those lowest species, we imagine that European and American pride of nature would go before a grievous fall. These constantly succeeding changes are supposed to have taken place during the whole time that this earth has been fitted for animal life, — a period of time so long that the human mind is unable to grasp it.

One objection to this theory, strongly insisted on, is the absence of any evidence of connecting links between man and the lower animals, or between the strongly defined demarcations of the animal orders. The answer to this is, that little is known of the whole earth : much of it is submerged now that was once above the waters and served for a dwelling-place for organized beings. A great deal is known of the sequence of forms which have been unearthed from their stony sepulchres. The negative evidence is as weighty as the positive. Besides this, millions of air-breathing animals die, without leaving anything behind them to mark their existence. Preyed upon by other animals, devoured at their death by myriads of insects, exposed to the action of destructive chemical agents, they soon decay, and leave no trace behind. Who ever finds the dead bodies of the thousands of animals and birds which perish yearly? Who finds the remains of the familiar creatures which frequent our woods and meadows? For one which is accidentally buried so as to resist the destructive forces of air and water, millions are resolved into their primitive elements, and are annihilated as structural forms. And yet, because in portions of the vast deposits of rock the remains of certain ancient forms are discovered, it is asked that the Darwinians should furnish a perfect progressive sequence of fossils to elucidate the theory, and prove it beyond dispute. Recent discoveries have brought to light human remains in caves, where they are associated with bones of extinct animals. That they are of very ancient origin is beyond doubt, — older than any civilization, as we understand the term. But even they are doubtless modern, when we take into consideration the time that the earth has been as it now is. How many thousands of ages has it taken the Niagara Falls to cut their way through the solid rock back from Ontario to Erie? It is highly probable that the earth has been approximately the same as it now is for many millions of years. Reaching still farther back into the past, before this state of comparative quiescence, can we not find adequate time for the gradual succession of organized beings on this earth, and for the structural differentiations which have finally resulted in the present position of things? Because we see one day succeed another with no change in the organic life around, because the written history of man records no vital change in his structure, men deny the possibility of antecedent variation. Man's written history is a thing of to-day. The builders of the Pyramids were our brothers. The five thousand years which have elapsed since the cultivated civilization of Egypt are but a day to the previous ages upon ages of man's existence before that civilization was dreamed of. The bones of untold myriads of human kind crumbled into dust before Egypt saw the rudest mud-hut that foreshadowed the temples of her prime.

The imperfectness of the geological record is certainly a great hindrance to the exact proof of the Darwinian theory, and is a strong weapon in the hands of its opponents. But while so much of the dim, remote past is attainable only by inference and deduction, the argument is decisive for neither side. One weighty argument for the Darwinians is the general plan upon which animals are constructed. All vertebrates have the same typical form. Take off the skins from some dozen air-breathing vertebrates, place the bodies in an upright attitude, and they are in general structure identical. The position of the head, eyes, and ears, the neck, the central vertebral column, the fore legs, which are arms in that position, the pelvis, the hind legs, all bear a close resemblance. Of course there are material differences; but they are evidently moulded upon one general plan. If there were a special creation for each species, why should they all necessarily have a kindred structure? To be sure the question may be answered, that they might as well be similar as dissimilar. But how much more in consonance with the known action of natural laws is it, to suppose that from some original type these vari-

ous forms have gradually differentiated into their present diversity of structure; the original typical plan, the least variable characteristic, having maintained its individuality, while the more plastic appendages have been swayed by incident forces. This will logically and naturally account for the unlikeness, and yet the resemblance.

The Darwinian theory then is, that Natural Law or Persistent Force, acting through all time upon the universe, has evolved from certain primitive organic forms of a very low order of existence the present diversified races on the earth. It does not stop here. With the eye of prescience it sees the process going on far into the ages yet to come. What may be the result in that distant day, finite speculation may not determine. But the laws which have swayed the world sway it still, and will sway it forevermore. As in the past they have evolved order out of disorder, heterogeneous beauty out of homogeneous crudity, progressive individuality of being and thought out of chaotic vapor, so will they continue their evolving force through all time, till the boasted perfectness of this day of ours, perfect because it is our day, will be as primitive to the later denizens of this globe as the barbarity of the cave savages is to modern civilization.

A host of noble minds, each in its own peculiar province, is exploring the vast field of knowledge. Darwin, Spencer, Huxley, Tyndal, Lyell, Hooker, and many others, are giving their profound thought to the elucidation of the laws which govern the vast universe of which they are a part. Their intellects touch the scarce-seen planets; they turn over the stony pages of earth's autobiography; they anatomize to their ultimate atoms the structure of its organisms; they use the intelligence evolved from their own growth to search for the law which has determined that evolution. And they speak out their convictions manfully and earnestly. They proclaim what is to them a revelation of truth in the records which the past and the present offer to their understanding. Herbert Spencer thus maintains the necessity of the expression of man's deepest convictions, in a passage instinct with nobleness of thought and dignity of utterance : —

" Whoever hesitates to utter that which he thinks the highest truth, lest it should be too much in advance of the time, may reassure himself by looking at his acts from an impersonal point of view. Let him duly realize the fact, that opinion is the agency through which character adapts external arrangements to itself, — that his opinion rightly forms part of this agency, — is a unit of force, constituting, with other such units, the general power which works out social changes, — and he will perceive that he may properly give full utterance to his innermost conviction, leaving it to produce what effect it may. It is not for nothing that he has in him these sympathies with some principles and repugnance to others. He, with all his capacities and aspirations and beliefs, is not an accident, but a product of the time. He must remember that, while he is a descendant of the past, he is a parent of the future ; and that his thoughts are as children born to him, which he may not carelessly let die. He, like every other man, may properly consider himself as one of the myriad agencies through whom works the Unknown Cause ; and when the Unknown Cause produces in him a certain belief, he is thereby authorized to profess and act out that belief. For, to render in their highest sense the words of the poet,

' Nature is made better by no mean,
But nature makes that mean : over that art
Which you say adds to nature, is an art
That nature makes.'

" Not as adventitious, therefore, will the wise man regard the faith which is in him. The highest truth he sees he will fearlessly utter ; knowing that, let what may come of it, he is thus playing his right part in the world, — knowing that, if he can effect the change he aims at, well : if not, well also, though not *so* well."

VARIOUS ASPECTS OF THE WOMAN QUESTION.

DIOGENES. Eve did not enter into the original plan ; she was an unlucky afterthought. Listen to Milton : —

" O, why did God,
Creator wise, that peopled highest heaven
With spirits masculine . . . . ? "

You observe that there are no feminine angels in heaven ?

Aristippus. So much the better for us, if we have them all here.

Diogenes. For the same reason, probably, we are told that there will be neither marrying nor giving in marriage hereafter.

Aristippus. Not at all. There will be so many more women in heaven than men, that any marriage, except of the Mormon kind, would be impossible.

Diogenes.

" O, why did God
. . . . . create at last '
This novelty on earth, this fair defect
Of nature ? "

I have always wondered why.

Aristippus. You forget that it was Eve who first picked fruit from the tree of knowledge.

Diogenes. The only use she made of it was to get the idea of dress ; and the primeval curse still clings to man, in the shape of milliners' bills.

Aristippus. Nevertheless we ought to be grateful to her for her enterprising spirit. Whatever her motives may have been, you must admit that her move was in the right direction. Where would we be now, had the future of the race been left to Adam alone? And if woman did turn man out of Paradise, she has done her best ever since to make it up to him. Every pretty girl one sees is a reminiscence of the garden of Eden.

Diogenes.
"This mischief had not then befallen,
And more that shall befall, innumerable
Disturbances on earth through female snares."

It was an excellent fancy of the ancients to make woman the incarnation of original sin, — the tempter and the temptation in one, — a combination of the apple and the serpent. King David, Herod, and even the terrible Bluebeard, might have behaved well in a world without women. It is proverbial that there is no quarrel without a woman in it.

Aristippus. Because, as Steele said, there is nothing else worth quarrelling about.

Hipparchia. Admirable! You remind me of the two shepherds in a pastoral who sing in alternate strains.

"Be mine your tuneful struggle to decide."

You, Diogenes, should recollect that woman is a fact you cannot get rid of, and that the only remedy for your complaints is to improve her condition. And you, Aristippus, like a thousand other sentimental conservatives, cannot hear the suggestion that woman might do something more in this world than she is now doing without giving tongue at once: "Woman's sphere is the home," — "Woman's mission is to be beautiful, to cheer, and to elevate." Suppose she has no home, and is old and ugly; what then? I know nothing more cheering and elevating than intelligence and efficiency; and I have never heard that either was detrimental to beauty. Is your ideal a woman who is good for nothing? —

"Bred only and completed to the taste
Of lustful appetence, to sing, to dance,
To dress and troll the tongue and roll the eye"?

Aristippus. Not at all. I believe in the old Roman notion, that woman's domestic honor and chief praise is, *Domi mansit, lanam fecit,* — with the qualification, that *lanam* shall not

mean worsted-work. I understand the Scriptural word "helpmeet," as applied to wife, in the New England sense of "help." She should, above all, be a creature not too bright and good to know how to prepare and serve up human nature's daily food. I have never seen without emotion the epitaph placed by a high legal dignitary in a neighboring State on the tomb of his first wife: —

"An excellent woman and a good cook."

And when I hear an able-bodied woman in easy circumstances speak of housekeeping as too much for her strength, or "too wearing," I set her down very low on my list of contemptibles, and ask her, mentally, "What the devil then are you good for?" But you and your friends, Hipparchia, would make a world all cubes, parallelopipedons, and pyramids, — an achromatic world, peopled with wise creatures who could demonstrate the usefulness of all they did, and the economy of the processes by which they did it. As there is no place in such a world for women as we know them, you wish to create Eve over again, or rather to call forth a female Adam. I object. Man cannot live by pure mathematics alone. Imagination is a faculty of the mind, as much as reason. Now, women are the imaginative side of the human race; not only imaginative themselves, but the cause of imagination in others. I like mountains and clouds, trees, birds, and flowers, — the raw material of poetry; but to me handsome women are more pleasant than all of them, — they are little poems ready made. I like their rustling dresses, their bright, graceful ways, the "flash of swift white feet" in ball-room; even their roguish airs and childlike affectations. And if some of them do not trim their souls quite as much as their gowns, or perhaps venture into society with minds naked to the verge of indecent ignorance, then I say to these, "Talk to me only with your eyes," — and they can be more eloquent than any Demosthenes of your New England Athens. Women are younger than men, and nearer to nature ; they have more animal life and spirits and glee. Their lively, frolicsome, sunshiny chatter keeps existence from growing mouldy and stale. We have it on the authority of the wittiest of Frenchmen, that for the purposes of pleasant, every-day life, *L'enjouement vaut mieux que l'esprit.* If I wish to discuss a question of political economy, or of metaphysics, I can go to men ; but the art of talking the men of to-day have lost. They either lecture, dispute, or twaddle. A Rabbinical story relates that twelve baskets of chit-chat fell from heaven, and that Eve secured nine while Adam was picking up the other three. Since then, Eve seems to have obtained possession of all.

What do you "earnest women" want ? You have your own way in everything. I cannot take up a paper without reading something about lovely, delicate, refined females ; or an item announcing that some ungallant fellow has been turned out of an omnibus because he would not offer his seat to an Irish lady, who had probably twice his muscular power and endurance.

Hipparchia. Hotel elegance, railway manners, and penny-a-liner sentiment are alike contemptible. Do you suppose that any sensible female cares for those second-hand phrases and vulgar civilities ? This deference you boast of is a mere habit, worn threadbare : the feeling has died out. What does it really amount to, when, in this city, a woman, even of my age, cannot go alone to an evening lecture or to the theatre without the risk of an insult ? English and French women have more liberty of action than we have, although the men do not offer them their seats on every occasion. I had rather take my chance with the crowd at a hotel ordinary, and have more independence in daily life. The time will come, I trust, when women will no longer be contented with the few empty and exaggerated compliments in which men pay them off, — "Angelic creatures !" "Poet's theme !" and so on, — stuff that

springs from what Diogenes calls the spooney view of women, and only applicable to the young and handsome, — a very small minority. It is sad to see the graceless, the "gone-off," and the downright elderly smirk complacently at a few phrases which are only aimed at them in derision. The others, too, one would think, ought to care little for adulation that fades away with their good looks.

The supremacy of woman in this country is like that of the Mikado in Japan, — a sovereign sacred and irresponsible, but on condition of sitting still, and leaving the management of affairs, the real business of life, to others. It is the same theory of government with which the constitutionalists tormented the late Louis Philippe, — *Le roi règne et ne gouverne pas.* He was unwilling to accept such a position, and so am I. I cannot take a pride in insignificance and uselessness, although I confess with shame that most women do, — the result of which is, that we have not the kind of influence we ought to have, and that a real, hearty, genuine respect for women does not exist. In every man's heart there lurks a mild contempt for us, because of our ignorance of business, politics, and practical matters generally outside of the nursery and the milliner's shop. The best of you look upon us and our doings as grown people look at pretty children and their plays, — with a good-natured feeling of superiority, and a smile half pleasure and half pity. The truth is, that men have always despised us, from the earliest times. At first, we were mere slaves and drudges ; then, playthings, if handsome and lively, — something to be brought on with the wine at a feast. Chivalry, which in newspaper rhetoric means devotion to women and respect, knew little of either, when it was alive and vigorous. The *droits de bottage et de cuissage* alone are enough to prove that. In our times, indeed, the savage view of woman as a slave has been softened by civilization into housekeeper and nurse ; but it still lingers in every man's feelings. Woman's mission in his eyes is simply babies ; to which is superadded the duty of making the father comfortable. But the high prices of living are teaching people who have never heard of Malthus or of Mill the necessity of celibacy ; and women must find something else to do than to rock a cradle.

Diogenes. Yes, unlimited issues on an insufficient capital lead to ruin. That ivy clinging to the oak view of the woman question still finds a place in print ; but in practice I think the oaks are getting rather tired of it. They find that the graceful wreaths of the ivy draw heavily upon their substance, and they would prefer a more self-sustaining simile.

Hipparchia. So much the better. I desire to see females support themselves.

Aristippus. Don't say female again, Hipparchia ! I hate the word used in that sense, as much as Swift hated the word *bowels*. It is a term of natural history. A mare is a female ; so is a cow, and so is a female dog. It would be curious to analyze the feeling that led euphuistic donkeys to choose it as a compromise word between lady and woman.

Hipparchia. They must have been male donkeys. All the terms of reproach you apply to us when you forget your chivalry manners, such as *witch, shrew, termagant, slut,* and so on, were all originally made by men for men, — at least so Archdeacon Trench tells us. You have gradually shuffled them off upon us ; and worse yet, when you wish to describe in two words a pompous, prosing, dull-witted man, you call him an old woman. This is not just. Old women always have some imagination ; and their gossip does not pretend to be the highest wisdom, which makes a great difference.

Diogenes. True ! The elderly male fossil of the Silurian age, — the age of mollusks, — whose *habitat* is some still - water club, or public reading-room, where he babbles of the morning's news, is a thousand times more

tiresome than any loquacious elderly lady. We excel in this as in everything. We beat you at your own weapons. Sewing seems to be instinctive with women ; yet tailors tell me that they are obliged to give out their best work to men.

Hipparchia. Dress and want of method· are two radical weaknesses women must extirpate if they ever hope to rise from their present secondary position. Their dress is the outward and visible sign of it, — the livery of their lower condition. Everything about it is absurd, from the spurious waterfall pinned to the back of their heads down to the train that sweeps the muddy pavement. Their hair is infested with beads, bits of lace and of ribbons, or mock jewelry. A bonnet is an epitome of fag-ends. The poor crazy creatures in the asylum, who pick up any rag, or wisp of straw, or scrap of tin, they may find, and wear it proudly upon their frocks, are not a whit more absurd.

Diogenes. Women go to and fro like that funny little crab we saw lately in Aquaria, who adorns his head and. shoulders with bits of sea-weed, or any other stuff within his reach, and paddles about his tank self-satisfied and ridiculous. Women must and will trim, as spiders spin webs, and bees make honeycombs. They even trim bathing-dresses : one would think that nothing could redeem them from their hideousness. But they obey a law of their being. The special aptitudes of the lower animals are brought into play when no other reason can be given than the necessity for discharging an accumulation of the inward energy, — a saying of the physico-psychologists that is verified in this instance.

Hipparchia. A man's raiment is of plain color and of good, strong material, — ugly if you please, but durable and serviceable ; but a woman puts on textures that cost hundreds of dollars and that a drop of water may ruin. Then fashions change daily. The bonnet idolized yesterday is offered up without a sigh if it refuses to adopt the new shape, — cast into the flames, or thrown to wild Biddies to be worn to pieces.

Diogenes. The great M. Comte, with whose works you, Hipparchia, are no doubt familiar, divides philosophy into the three stages of Theological, Metaphysical, and Positive. This general theorem he completes by particular applications, — to costume among others. In this he distinguishes the three stages of Tattooing (including paint), Frippery, and Clothes. Man has reached the third stage, he says ; woman is in the second, and not entirely out of the first.

Hipparchia. Everything about a woman's dress is uncomfortable. Everything is pinned on and false. There is nothing real but the trouble and the expense ; and women whose love of appearances exceeds their incomes must work hard with their own needles. But they undergo it all without a murmur, — I may say, with pleasure.

Diogenes. "For 't is their nature to," as I remarked just now. Women are compounds of plain-sewing and make-believe, daughters of Sham and of Hem. I consider dress an epidemic disease, — a moral cholera that originates in the worst quarters of Paris. Every ship that comes from those regions is infected with French *trollop-ism*, and should be quarantined and fumigated until every trace of the contagious novelty has been expurgated.

Hipparchia. Could a stranger, ignorant of our customs, suppose it possible that beings capable of reason would habitually go out of a winter evening less clad by half than during the day ? I say nothing of the propriety or good taste of this fashion. When Eve ate of the apple, she knew she was naked. I have often thought, as I looked at her dancing daughters, that another bite would be of service to them : it might open their eyes to their uncovered condition.

Diogenes. Let us put that reform down among those we mean to carry out last ; unless, indeed, the neck of age commits the fault, then, I confess,

I should like to complain to the Board of Health and have the nuisance abated. There is nothing sadder than to look at dressy old things, who have reached the frozen latitudes beyond fifty, and who persist in appearing in the airy costume of the tropics. They appear to think, as Goldsmith says, that they can conceal their age by exposing their persons.

Hipparchia. Their case is hopeless, I fear : we must teach sounder ideas on all these subjects to the young.

Aristippus. You have tried it already. Did not a wise woman come from the West preaching to her sisters that one of their lost rights was to dress like men ? What did Bloomer-ism amount to ? A few forlorn creatures shortened their petticoats a few inches, adopted most of the ugly in a man's attire with none of the practical, and retained the follies of a woman's dress without the taste. Their shoes were neither stouter nor larger. They wore a thing on their heads more unsightly than a bonnet, and no better a protection against sun or rain. They made their jackets and their trouserettes of the same flimsy stuffs as before, and sprinkled an unusual quantity of incongruous and unsuitable trimmings over all. Luckily they have disappeared, and now are probably devoting their energies to some other right that does less violence to woman's nature. Do you suppose that you will be listened to when you preach from the text, "Take no thought for your body what ye shall put on " ? How many lady free-thinkers in fashionable doctrines do you know? I see a superfluous ribbon even in your cap, Hipparchia ; and, if I mistake not, your magisterial skirts are expanded by a wirework cage.

Diogenes. Men say knowledge is power ; women think dress is power. Look at a woman who is certain that she is well dressed, — "the correct thing," — how she walks along with stately steps, head well up, parasol held with two fingers at the present, and skirts expanding luxuriantly behind her, — proud, self-satisfied, conscious of being stared at and admired. She feels like the just man made perfect, — who knows that he has done his duty, and that the by-standers also know it and respect him for it. Dress overgrows and smothers every other feeling in a woman's heart. Love, marriage, children, religion, the death of friends, are regarded as affording new and various opportunities for dress. The becoming is the greatest good. For finery and fashion women risk comfort, health, life, even reputation. What matter ignorance, ill-breeding, ill-nature, if she dress well? A camel's-hair shawl, like charity, will cover a multitude of sins. On the other hand, though she speak French and German, and understand all onomies and ologies, and the mysteries of housekeeping, and is treasurer of Dorcas societies, *crèches*, and dispensaries, and have not style, it profiteth her nothing. On this great question women never have a misgiving. You may find creatures so lost as to be castaways from fashion, but they believe in it. The scepticism of the age has left this subject untouched.

Hipparchia. The same amount of thought and labor applied to useful subjects would make them all that I desire them to be. A thorough reform in the education of woman is necessary for this. What is their education now? Even the girls of the richer class get next to none. They are taught to say "How d' ye do" in two languages, and to irritate the nervous system of their relations for some hours every day with a piano, — the most gigantic, useless, and expensive instrument of torture ever invented. These for serious work. A little drawing, worsted-work, and catechism are added as accomplishments; and then at eighteen — the age when a boy really begins his training — their education is completed, they are told; and they are turned into the world to devote their time and talents to trimmings, novels, and idle tittle-tattle.

Aristippus. There can be no objection to good gossip, or even to a little scandal, when its teeth have been drawn. If the noblest study of mankind is man, surely his sayings and doings cannot be improper subjects for conversation.

Hipparchia. Education is not the teaching of this thing or that. It is the training of the mind for the work of daily life. The few women of fortune who pride themselves on their cleverness get a parrot-like acquaintance with the contents of books, enunciate charmingly, and are very learned on the syntax and spelling of an invitation to dinner; but of the great topics of the day, political, social, economical, financial, scientific, mechanical, theological, they are utterly ignorant and careless. I know some brilliant exceptions, who show what women might be if they chose.

The consequence of no education, no thought, no practical experiences, and no real responsibility is, that, whenever moral questions are disconnected with feeling, a woman's moral standard is lower than a man's. Truth, rare in both sexes, is very rare in women; not that they love truth less, but that usually they love exaggeration more, — truth is so often commonplace and tiresome; they dress it up to hide its nakedness.

Aristippus. What does it matter? We all understand them when they say "Splendid!" "Shocking!" "Awful!" "Glorious!" in describing a walk or a tea-party. We believe in the vivacity of their impressions, if not in the accuracy of the terms they use. And besides, there are many things pleasant to listen to, even though we know them to be false.

" When my love swears that she is made of truth,
   I do believe her, though I know she lies."

Women have such a wonderful power of secreting adjectives that they cannot speak the truth when they try. There is no moral obliquity in the case. It is psychical incapacity.

Hipparchia. Ambition in a man is the resolution to become powerful, useful, great, rich. A woman means by ambition the desire to shine in the society she belongs to, or perhaps to work her way into a set she considers better. And honor and virtue are, I think, used in a different sense.

Diogenes. Yes ; the meaning is very much "localized."

Hipparchia. I admit that women have caught from the men a little of the dissatisfied, dyspeptic philosophy of this generation. But the men do not know what they want, and the ideas of the women are still more vague. They only know that they would like a change of some kind. Their imaginations are not contented with the commonplaces of every-day life. They long for more excitement, and to get it are willing, as Punch has it,

> "To do or suffer ere they die
> They know not what, they care not why."

But the "mission" must be exotic, meteoric, dazzling. Home missions present as little attraction as bonnets that do not come from Paris. The little opportunities for doing good that spring up about their feet are neglected. I know so many of those gifted, enthusiastic transcendental natures, at least in their own opinion, who cannot condescend to the meaner duties of life, — such as being faithful to their husbands, taking care of their children, and making themselves agreeable to their relatives.

Then really "earnest" women, who mean to be useful to their fellow-creatures, often do as much harm as good for the want of practical sense. Their dear little foundlings all die of measles, diphtheria, or scarlet-fever. They give their pet paupers a regular allowance, which supplies them bountifully with tobacco and grog. They quack pauperism, and increase the malady instead of curing it, because impulses of weakness miscalled feelings are consulted, instead of the hard, dry details of eleemosynary science ; for science it is, — a branch of political economy. Benevolence like this is only another form of the love for excitement. Women will never take the trouble to consider the principle of things.

Diogenes. I have read somewhere a definition of woman, — "An unreasoning animal that pokes the fire on top."

Aristippus. Diogenes was converted to this hopeless condition of infidelity by a little French treatise, *Le Mal qu'on dit des Femmes.* I give him over to it. His doctrine, like unwholesome food, carries its punishment with it. But you, Hipparchia, have pulled woman to pieces for a purpose ; and I should like to know on what practicable principle you propose to make her over again.

Hipparchia. Some one said wittily, — I think it was Mrs. Howe, — "Man carves his destiny ; woman is helped to hers." Women have been kept so long in this state of dependence, that their characters have become dwarfed. The thirst for excitement that drives them restless from one amusement to another, and which finds relief in the extravagances of dress, — this passionate devotion to the frivolous and the absurd, — spring from the want of a reasonable employment for mind and body. My great principle is to exchange their passive condition for an active one. I would establish schools, where girls may receive a thorough education, such as is given to boys. In these schools, I should insist upon mathematical training as earnestly as Plato in his Republic. Women must be made to feel the magical power that numbers have in regulating the mind. Once get them really to believe that twice two make four, and can never make more or less, — once bring them to feel that a foot always means twelve inches, and that correct measurement is indispensable, even for seamstresses and cooks,— and the spirit of accuracy which now passes all their understanding will be with them and remain with them forever. Next, I should insist that the employments now monopolized by men should be thrown open to women. Why should we be excluded from all the well-paid trades and professions ? Why should we not hold office, "commissioned, paid, and uniformed by the state"? Do you think it fair to limit us to scrubbing and plain-sewing as the only means of earning a livelihood?

Aristippus. I admit that many occupations for which women are admirably calculated are carried on by men, and I hope that some day a more manly public opinion will make all such persons as ridiculous as a male seamstress is now. I do not envy the feelings of men who can invent, manufacture or sell baby - jumpers, dress elevators, hoop-skirts, or those cosmetics I see "indorsed by pure and high-toned females." But when you and your friend seek the positions of "night-patrols or inspectors of police," you run into ultraism, the parent of all *isms ;* but, luckily, a parent like Saturn, who destroys its offspring.

Hipparchia. Marriage is now to women what all trades and professions are to men. Spinsters are supposed to have no chance in life, — neither liberty of action nor of ideas. Hence, rather than not marry at all, a woman will marry anybody ; and, like Shenstone's Gratia,

> " Choose to attend a monkey here
> Before an ape below."

This prejudice is almost as strong and as absurd as the Mormon notion that a woman cannot get to heaven unless she is sealed to some saint. It has driven hundreds of women, who might have been happy single, into a slavery for life from which there is no relief. A husband, if he find that the connubial paradise he dreamed of turns out to be the other place, has the world all before him where to choose ; but the lady is " cabined, cribbed, — confined " possibly : it is in the course of things. But when new fields of employment are thrown open to women, those who cannot marry, or who do not wish to marry, will lead useful and pleasant lives, and cease to be " superfluous existences, — inartistic figures, crowding the canvas of life without adequate effect." But all our reforms centre in one great point, on which our eyes are hopefully fixed, — I mean, the right to vote. Give women

a vote, and at once they will take a direct interest in the business of life. They will have something to think of, and something to do. It will be the best form of education. Mr. Lecky, in his interesting, though perhaps rather windy, "History of Rationalism," has a passage that expresses my opinion and my hope. " If the suffrage should ever be granted to women, it would probably, after two or three generations, effect a complete revolution in their habits of thought, which, by acting upon the first period of education, would influence the whole course of opinion." Mr. Mill, it is well known, is warmly in favor of it. He has been abundantly sneered at in England for this crotchet, as they call it, — although it is not easy to see why it should be ridiculous for women to vote in a country governed by a queen.

Aristippus. In this I am with you. I have always thought it absurd that the ignorant Irishman who drives the carriage of a rich widow should have a voice in the government of the country, and that the employer, whose money enables him to live, should have none. In Austria, women who hold real property in their own right have the right to vote. I would go a step further, and give the suffrage to every independent, self-supporting widow or single woman. Wives I would exclude, — not from the fear of adding to the stock subjects of domestic disputation, — the usual reason given, — but because they are not independent. The same reason should apply to daughters residing under the paternal roof. And, in all fairness, I would extend my rule to men. I would make, not a property, but an independence qualification. A man who lives on a dollar a day, if he owns it or earns it, should vote ; but the son who depends upon a rich father for support, and the pauper who lives upon public charity, should not vote. Socially, both are minors. We might even say, that, financially, both are unweaned. Why should they not be minors politically? This plan would really be manhood suffrage.

Hipparchia. Justice and wisdom are both upon our side. We must eventually succeed ; and then the emancipation of woman will be complete, and her equality with man established. The resolution passed in our Convention, "that a just government and a true church are alike opposed to class and caste, whether the privileged order be feudal baron, British lord, or American white male," ought to be true, and will be true at a future day.

Diogenes. Vigorously expressed ! The feudal baron, indeed, is an extinct species, and was hardly worth mentioning, unless to adorn your rhetoric and point your resolution. But let me tell you that the white male can show an older and a better patent of nobility than the British lord with whom you associate him. Is it not recorded in Genesis, that Adam was created first, and Eve from him ? — a copy only, you observe ; and a copy never comes up to the original. As Dryden has it : —

" He to God's image, she to his, was made :
So farther from the fount the stream at random strayed."

And in the same inspired history we read : " Thy desire shall be to thy husband, and he shall rule over thee."

Hipparchia. Nonsense ! I thought that the argument from Scripture had died out with slavery polemics. You forget that every Eve has not an Adam. On what ground do you ask a single woman to occupy an inferior position ? I admit that the married may sometimes do so with propriety.

Aristippus. On the ground of an inferiority, and of infirmities absolutely incurable. Between the female man of your theories and the real male man there is a great gulf you cannot pass over. A negro is a man, — we can imagine him a brother ; but no effort of philanthropic self-abnegation can work the same miracle for a woman. When you preach the natural equality of the sexes, you injure your cause. The facts are too strong and too visible for you. A man can rest his claim to superiority on brute force, if on nothing else ; and force is, after all, the ultimate basis of

all government. I do not mean to underrate the cleverness of women. The first man was overreached by Eve ; and the last woman will probably turn the head of the laggard who brings up the rear of the human race. If a wife is only half of the scissors, as Franklin suggests, she is often the half with the point. But feminine ability is not of the ruling kind. You dance, for instance, better than men, if the gymnastic capers of acrobats and tumblers can be called dancing at all ; but you cannot wield a sledge-hammer as vigorously, and your excellent performances, numerous in literature, rarer in art, and still more rare in science, seem to me to be mostly of the dancing rather than of the sledge-hammer order.

But success would be your ruin. If you could establish the complete equality you long for, your relative inferiority would become so manifest as to be humiliating. In most of the vocations of men, women would be as ridiculous, morally, as they are physically in men's clothes. If a woman is nothing but a smaller man, the savage contempt for the sex is logical. Place two races together, of which the one is weaker, less energetic, less pugnacious than the other ; and the result will inevitably be that the strong and the fierce will make the mild and the feeble do all their hard work. The barbarous ages would return again. We should sit by, like the Indian, smoking the pipe of laziness, while you were furnishing us with board, lodging, clothes, and tobacco. The Amazons, the earliest known advocates of women's rights, saw this point clearly ; and consequently excluded men altogether from their communities, except at their yearly camp-meetings. Men worship women for their gentleness, affection, imagination, refinement, — for the fond, cosey, nestling way they have with them, — for their femininity (in one awkward word), the contrast and complement to the masculine character. There is a sex in soul quite as much as in body. In the mythology, no god falls in love with Minerva. A mannish woman only attracts a feminine man. A woman's power lies in her petticoats, as Samson's strength lay in his hair. Cut them off, and you leave her at the mercy of every brutal Philistine, who now dares not be rude to her because she is sacred. Do you not see that, instead of gaining something, you will lose all? — sink into fifth-rate mannikins, with fewer opportunities, — boys in petticoats?

Diogenes. And we be obliged to set our amorous eclogues to the tune of *Formosus Pastor Corydon?*

Aristippus. I might quote a suggestive remark from Pepys's Diary, namely, that the only female animal which gives a name to both sexes is the goose. But, seriously, your chances of success are not brilliant, — at least for the present. There are two kinds of women, both of them excellent; but almost as distinct as diamonds and black lead, which are both pure carbon; — one is made to be admired, the other to be useful. The girl who wakes the poet's sigh is a very different creature from the girl who makes his soup. You have read of the loves of the Angels with the daughters of the Antediluvians. I sometimes think that the diamonds can claim descent from the high-bred race that sprang from those aristocratic relations. The late Monsieur Balzac, who handled this subject with ingenuity, was struck by this difference. He divided woman into two classes : woman, and the female of the order Mammalia, genus Bimanis, species Homo. In his essays he overlooks altogether the second class. But in it you must seek your disciples. The heaven-descended sisters will not go with you. You may try to make them useful and self-supporting ; but you will lose your pains. They have only to show themselves, to receive the attention and applause that a man of genius must work a lifetime to earn. Their world is at their feet. Wealth, power, gratified vanity, are theirs without an effort. Madame de Staël said she would willingly give all her fame for one season of the reign of a youthful beauty. She, it is true, was a woman ; but David Hume, a keen observer, and moderate in his statements, noticed that even a "little miss, dressed in a new gown for a dancing-school ball, receives as complete enjoyment as the greatest orator who triumphs in the splendor of his eloquence, while he governs the passions and resolutions of a numerous assembly." You ask them to give up these pleasures and these triumphs, and to abdicate their thrones, — to become implements instead of ornaments, and to help to bring down the high price of labor in the present scarcity of laborers ; and you offer them in exchange the right to wear trousers, to drive an omnibus, or to wear a policeman's uniform ! Do you think that they will listen to you ? No, — not even the respectable members of the second class. The Cinderellas with no glass slippers and no protecting fairy might join with you, if they did not look up to the first class as their rulers and models. They feel instinctively that the glory of the Angelidæ illuminates even them ; and they all, or almost all, have a faint yet abiding and comforting hope that some unheard-of miracle, or yet undiscovered cosmetic, may place them among the blessed.

You cannot, my dear Hipparchia, by any process of teaching, not even by magazine-articles, make a canary-bird into a useful barn-door fowl. It will wear yellow feathers, and it will sing and nibble at sugar.

SCARABÆI ED ALTRI.

DOWN by the sands, where the midland sea surges and draws off its feeble tides, and the sheltering beaches, the delight of antique mariners, tempt straying ruminants with their salt herbage, and no voracious spring-tide floods the beach, I made my first positive acquaintance with the *Scarabæus pilularius*, and guessed at the mystery of his worship in those Eastern lands where sand and sun are the rulers, and he their chief subject. Wonderful in his knowledge of statics and dynamics I found him; heroic in fight and magnanimous in victory, as ungrudging in his acceptance of defeat; and altogether a creature of rare and wonderful instincts.

A line of tracks, so similar to hieroglyphics as to justify an initiatory reverence in a Cadmian mind, drawn indefinitely across the smooth-spread yellow sand, led me, curious, to the arena of his achievements. A dozen similar tracks led from different directions, converging to a pile of dung, and here half a dozen Scarabæi, of as many sizes, were cutting and carving, and every now and then another came buzzing up from the leeward, flying in the eye of the wind, and dropped heavily on the sand, ready to make one of the busy crowd. I selected as subject of my observations the largest, a fellow of prodigious proportions and exemplary industry. He had commenced the excavation of a mass of the pilulary, making a circular cut downwards, and was half buried in the fosse which was to isolate a sufficient fragment. Round and round he went in a perfect arc, cutting deeper and deeper until he reached the sand below and the separation was complete. He traversed it to and fro, time after time, to be sure that the cut was direct and absolute; then, bracing his head against the sand foundation, he began pushing with his hind legs to move off the selected portion. I thought to help him, and carefully pushed it with a small reed until it rolled over on the sand, and he with it, innocuously hoist by his own petard.

Finding himself free on the level sand, he commenced to roll and round it, kneading the irregularities back and dragging upwards at the same time with his fore feet, so that in less than a minute after his liberation he had worked his lump into a close approximation to globular form, and had started on his voyage; but after a few turns he stopped, seemed to try the weight of his load, deliberately rolled it back into its original bed, and then began to excavate another portion, which he set himself to work into the original ball, which when weighed had been found wanting. The surface of the latter was thoroughly sanded by its revolutions, and adhesion was impossible; so he began working the new material under the coating of sand in so dexterous a way that he quickly completed the integration, and at the same time restored the globular form to the whole; then he started anew, to roll it off to its future depository.

The worst of his mechanical difficulties was overcome; but now began a series of struggles with Scarabæi unprovided with the objects of beetling ambition, and whose education seemed to have stopped at the days when power and possession were words nearer their root and each other than now, — when to justify piracy you must organize some sort of government.

I recognized in the deportment of these rovers of the sands another claim to the reverence of the early ages of human civilization, — another reason for their canonization by the Egyptians, in whose calendar is mentioned St. Scarabæus. For the moment any wandering and pilless Scarabæus met the hero of my story he made an examination of the size and general perfections of his work, going up the side opposite to that on which its lawful owner had established his motive power; and, as the bolus was at least a dozen times the size of its owner, he sometimes took a considerable ramble before he met that important individual. But they no sooner met than the tug of war began. They fought like Ajax and Hector for the dead body of Patroclus. They clenched, wrestled, struggled, pushed, until the stronger got uppermost, when he employed all his remaining force to push the other off and keep him down. If nearly matched, sometimes the under one got a shoulder-lock on his adversary, and, by an Herculean effort, threw him over his head, and to a distance of two or three inches across the sand. This usually terminated the battle, and the whipped Scarabæus made his way off as rapidly as his legs would carry him. If the Scarabæus in possession could keep the other off the ball for a few seconds, the latter gave up the struggle and sought his fortunes on another field.

I had wisely chosen my hero so strong that there was little fear of his being ousted; so my sympathies were on the winning side. But once he met his master, and was pitched with terrific violence across the sand, striking on his head, to his evident stupefaction. When he recovered he gave up his property without demur, and started for another venture. Then I, the *deus ex machina,* stepped into the epic, pitched the usurper three times as far as he had thrown my friend, then rolled the "apple of discord" directly in the path of its rightful owner, and saw him commencing his task anew, with unabated energy. A little declivity stood in his way, and it was a Sysiphus-labor to get beyond it. Time after time, poising himself squarely and solidly on his head, and bracing himself after the manner of equestrian performers by his superior extremities, he walked backwards, pushing the ball before him, and gingerly meeting the tendency to escape, first on one side, and then on the other; finally, missing, it rolled down the whole slope, carrying him in dizzy revolutions with it; but without hesitation

he recommenced his work undiscouraged.

Some I saw who seemed to have partners in their toils, — a smaller, demurer-looking Scarabæus, — working side by side and in peace with the greater originator, to get their burden into some quiet spot. What their relations were, and what they wanted to do with bolus, I don't know, and doubt if the wisest man in the court of the first of the Pharaohs did. Whether the Scarabæi are a nation of Amazons, and the hero I had chosen was a heroine, or whether the lesser partner was a patient waiter for conjugal content and the fruition of marital hopes, I of course can't tell. Perhaps Agassiz or Wyman could, but Moses, I am sure, could n't; and as what he knew of the *Scarabæus pilularius* lies behind all he is to me in connection with my present subject of dissertation, I take the beetle from the Pharaonic point of view, and, looking over all I know of the reasons for reverence, and for being cut in stone, I make them these: —

Firstly, he was a scavenger, and the wise men taught the people to respect him as a means of preserving the race undiminished. The common people have always a profound contempt for the beings who do their dirty work, and contempt with them goes before enmity. In this the Egyptians would only show that they were a Southern people, and so had much dirty work to do. And in this connection I must say, that I consider that, an undeveloped people not being awake to fine distinctions, and being predisposed to despise everything differing from themselves, we must attribute all the respect paid the *Scarabæus pilularius* to the advice and influence of their wise men, who, so long as they *were* wise, would persuade them to protect every useful creature.

Secondly, the mechanical instincts of the *Scarabæus pilularius* must have always excited the interest of the geometers and mechanists at a time when geometry and mechanics were known in their simplest elements mainly, and considered the marvellous secrets of creation. The absolute rotundity of the pedifacture of the insect must have seemed the result of a sense little less than preternatural, to people who were not accustomed to reason away all recognition of the preternatural. But that which was wonderful to me, the power of weighing so accurately the load he was to propel, must have been not a little amazing to them, less familiar than we have become, through subsequent researches in natural history, with the powers of the brute creation.

Thirdly, that the *Scarabæus pilularius* was a soldier and hero was less noteworthy in those days than in modern times ; for then he was no man who was no soldier, and to be brave was only a human virtue, but was still marvellous in an insect.

And, if last, not least of the claims of our friend to reverence was the strange line of hieroglyph he left on the *tabula rasa* sea-washed, in column like the message written down an obelisk ; and that the most high priest had no key to the cipher only made it more curious and more revered.

I do not know that anything so simple ever impressed me more strangely than the meeting for the first time on the solitary sands of Antium, amid thoughts of Egypt's queen and her sad loves, this line of curious figures, sand-written. And who shall say that the original Cadmus was not our Pilularius ? Certainly he left a record of the life he led, and the journeys he took, long before the first emigration from the floodfertilized lands around Thebes-on-Nile carried civilization into northern lands.

It may have been from this trick of his of writing on the sand that they took his image for the signet ; or perhaps it was only that the broad under-surface of the stone or smalt of which they made the Scarabæus was too tempting to be left vacant, and the portable shape and size of the stone gave it the preference over the images of crocodile or cat. Be that as it may, it became the form universal for signets, and bore the monogram or polygram of kings unnumbered and of chiefs unknown, so

that the fictile Scarabæus doubtless carries to-day more strange messages for us than did the great original to his first observers. Being as ignorant of what hieroglyphs tell as the man who died when Champollion was born, I do not venture a conjecture on the significance or value of the "cartouches" inscribed on the plane surface of the Scarabæus. There can be no doubt that they were tokens of rank, and mainly bore direct reference to the history or condition of the wearer, with occasional mystic sentences perhaps serving at once as signet and amulet.

My purpose, however, is to treat only of certain artistic relations, and to me, therefore, the Egyptian Scarabæus is only of value as it leads to, and is connected with, the Etruscan. The former is utterly unartistic, — a rude, but tolerably accurate imitation of the *Scarabæus pilularius*, the specific character being sufficiently developed, — the whole value of the work, both in its figure and the incisions under it, being evidently in its significance, and all conditions required of it being sufficiently answered by intelligibility. This is, indeed, characteristic of all Egyptian so-called art. It is not art at all, it is only writing ; and the transfer of the Scarabæus from Egypt to Etruria only forms another evidence of the inevitable antithesis existing between art and record. The identical types which on the Nile told the same story age after age, unchanging in their form as in their meaning, once in the hands of the Etruscan, entered on a course of refinement and artistic development into objects of beauty ; but in this they entirely lost sight of their original meaning. This is strikingly the case with the Scarabæus which, under the hands of the Etruscan cutter, lost at once all specific character. He might be Scarabæus anything : he is not *pilularius ;* and, instead of being made of basalt, porphyry, smalt, and very rarely of *pietra dura*, as in Egypt, he is engraved in carnelian, onyx, sardonyx, and all the rare and lovely varieties of *pietra dura*, — which, being essentially the same, change their names with their colors, — but mainly in an opaque carnelian, admirably calculated to show off the beauty of the workmanship. The change from use to ornament is abrupt, and perceivable in the earliest Etruscan examples, and proves conclusively to me two disputed points ; namely, that the *Scarabæus pilularius* and his allied notions came from Egypt to Etruria, and that the Etruscan and Egyptian races were utterly diverse in origin and antithetic in intellectual character. The eminent utilitarianism of the latter leaves no room for purely artistic effort, while the former literally *non tetiget quod non ornavit.* Even the pictorial and sculptural representations of the Egyptians were absolutely subservient to history or worship ; but the Etruscans cared so little for their own history as to leave us almost no inscribed monuments, though the remains of their taste and skill stand side by side with what we have of Greek work. They seem, indeed, to have been a more absolutely artistic people even than the Greeks, in whom art was exalted by a certain union with intellectual culture, the result of which was, of course, a larger growth and nobler ideal than the more ornamental Etrurian mind could attain. This points to an Eastern origin more in kinship with the Persian than the Greek, and to-day only illustrated by the Persian ornamentation.

The Scarabæus then, instead of the rude, straightforward representation of the Egyptian workman, assumes a more elegant form, with elaborate sculpture of all the insect characteristics, the edges of the wings and the lines that divide them from the chest being exquisitely beaded and wrought, and the claws being relieved and modelled with the highest care and most artistic finish. The form of the image, in fact, generally resembles more the beautiful green beetle which I have often caught in the mountains around Rome, than his plebeian and utilitarian cousin, the *Scarabæus pilularius.* The contour of the stone beneath the Scarabæus proper is markedly distinguished from the insect portion, and ornamented with a relieved

cornice, more or less elaborate according to the general finish of the stone. I have one in which this cornice of .073 inch in width contains an upper and a lower bead and a U moulding of which the parts are only one fourth the height of the cornice in breadth, and yet are cut with mathematical regularity and completeness. The bead that marks the junction of the wings and chest is divided into squares of .0045 inch in dimension. If this care is given to the less important part of the stone, what may we not expect from the intaglii which make the more important objects of the lapidary's work ! A stone, three fourths of an inch in length, contains two full-length figures seated in conversational attitudes, the extended hand of one of which, with the thumb and four fingers perfectly defined, is only .063 inch in length.

The great inequality between the power of design and the executive skill and taste in mere ornamentation in the characteristic Etruscan work is comparable only to those Eastern products which I have before alluded to, — the Persian fabrics. The animals are drawn without any regard to anatomical or optical truth, — foreshortening taken by a royal road, and grace thrown overboard. The hog is generally shown as flatted out, the legs appearing two on each side of the body ; and the members of all animals are stowed away with more direct reference to composition of masses than of animal organisms. I remember one of a horse, in which, there not being room for the four legs in their natural places, one was hung up at the side where a vacant space offered itself.

The earliest work seems to be done by a graving process, as if cutting were by lines ; the later is evidently done by the drilling operation now in use, and the process is much more apparent, especially in the drill-like terminations. This was probably owing to the use of the diamond itself for the incision, instead of the steel point and diamond dust, as in modern times, and to the great difficulty in getting a point on the implement.

The purely ornamental manner of treating the Scarabæus seems to indicate that it had neither religious nor historical value. Had the contrary been the case, we should inevitably have found some artistic quality sacrificed to their meaning, which is not the case with the intaglio more than with the insect representation. The subjects include all the objects known to familiar life, with all the incidents of martial experience, — horses, chariots, arms, — warriors wounded, defeated, dying, victorious, struggling. One I remember of a surgeon dressing the wound of a warrior, who throws up his hands in expression of the pain he suffers ; another, of the Genius of Death coming to Hercules ; another still, of two winged genii burying a warrior ; one, of two warriors dividing the dead body of a third, etc., etc. The style of cutting gradually changes, probably under the influence of Greek artists, — who are known to have emigrated to Etruria from Corinth, exiled by their native tyrants, — and becomes quite Greek in delicacy of finish and grace of proportion ; and the subject becomes almost entirely of Greek history or mythology, — the heroes of the Trojan war figuring largely.

Some of these are the perfection of intaglio : nothing in the gem-cutting of the Greeks could be more exquisite and purely beautiful than they are *as intaglio*. Yet, excellent as is the work, there is an essential difference between the Etruscan and Greek design, which no similarity of workmanship will ever conceal, — a difference as radical as that between Roman and Greek sculpture, and still more marked. The Etruscan, in its highest artistic development, preserves something of an Oriental fantasy and want of repose, and invariably falls short of the dignified and purely imaginative character of the Greek. It makes no exception to this rule, that there are Etruscan Scarabæi which have purely Greek intagli, since we know that there were Greek artists of the highest rank among those who emigrated to Etruria, and that it was cus-

tomary for one workman to make the Scarabæus, and another the incision. But these are rare, and the trained eye of an artist need not be more puzzled to determine the Greek or Etruscan character of an intaglio, than to distinguish a Florentine picture from a Venetian. The difference is radical, — that between the objective and subjective art, — between an Indian shawl and a bit of drapery by Paul Veronese.

As to the uses of the Scarabæus, we may be sure that they were at first intended as signets and mounted as rings in the simple and charming way of which we find so many examples in the Etruscan tombs, each end of a gold wire being passed through the perforated Scarabæus, and the extremities secured by being wound round the wire at the opposite side of the stone. As soon as they become mere ornaments, a more elaborate mounting is seen on those worn as rings ; and they appear in bracelets, necklaces, etc., in such profusion and confusion of subject, and style and date of workmanship, as to show plainly that they had lost all superstitious value or personal significance, and had become, like diamonds and pearls, a part of the gold-worker's material.

What the wealth and luxuriousness of those cities, now more deeply buried than Thebes or Nineveh, must have been, we can only imagine from the few traditions preserved by Roman historians, — grudging the glory of rivals so long and masters so often, though finally subjects of the irresistible force of crescent empire, — and from the gold-work known after so many centuries of sepulture. We know that Porsenna built himself a tomb in the solid rock, — a labyrinth whose secret no searchers of modern times have yet found, though they have burrowed around Clusium like marmots ; and that over this he raised himself a monument, — five towers of stone, on the top of which was laid a domed platform of brass, and above this still towers and other brass, and higher yet, towers and a crowning bronze dome ; and that from the edges of all these platforms hung thousands of bells, rung by the sea-breeze which every midday came up, and still comes, across the low Etrurian hills, to find the children she wafted from the land of the Parsee and Chaldee. It is hard to define a "civilization"; and we talk of the ages of gold and of bronze as if we knew the history of the whole world and its generations; but to me the few glimpses I get through the crevices of the ages that hide Etruria, as the hills of the Black Forest hide the fairies from the German child, indicate an age more fitting the epithet Golden than any since, and a nation the like of which, as of the good-folk, we shall see no more on earth. There were confederation without over-centralization; states side by side, without mutual hate or subjugation; wealth and power, without the corruption that destroys nations; and military prowess, without the unscrupulous ambition that cannot live and let live. They were instructors of Rome in all that Rome knew of civilization; many times masters of the imperial city, without ever envying it its existence; mild conquerors, and just lawgivers; and the City of the Seven Hills owed to the proximity of her seven Etrurian sisters all her early wisdom in politics, all her knowledge of the arts which refine and preserve; and to their love of those arts, and of the peace in which they flourish, the permission of her existence in those early centuries which preceded the fall of Veii.

It is not here the place to develop the moral of Etruscan history, or to investigate the political and social condition of the Etruscan people; though the links we have of the former, and the glimpses of the latter seen athwart the prejudices and mortified pride of the Roman historians, give the subject a fascinating interest. It is said that when the Roman armies invaded the territory of the northern Etruscan states, and their commander asked the name of the first city they approached, the unsuspecting subject of the Lars replied only, — not understanding the barbarian language, —

Χαῖρε, "Hail!" and ever since the city has been known as Cære (and to its present inhabitants as Cerevetere, — *Cære vetus*). Until the fatal dissension which permitted the Romans to conquer Veii, the Etruscan states calmly and steadily repelled all invasion, — rarely, as in the time of Porsenna, turning aside to retaliate on Rome, — and still pursued their peaceful career, the sages of Egypt and the artists and poets of Greece giving wisdom and grace to their daily lives, — their temples the richest, their domestic life the fairest, their political condition the most prosperous, and their commerce the widest of all Italy, if not of all Europe.

Of it all, we have only the grave into which art sought to carry an immortality of its own, and from which religion strove to banish the drear gloom of the uncertain by surrounding the dead with all the objects familiar to their daily lives and the incidents which were the most antagonistic in impression to the darkness and silence to which they abandoned the beloved ones only when conquest and destruction had concealed the portals of their tombs, and ancestor and descendant had yielded to the same oblivion. Among the most interesting tombs at Tarquinii is one painted round with a wedding feast, the bridegroom kissing his bride, the wine-cups and garlands, the dance and song with the timing pipes, in colors fresh and sharp to-day amid the grave-damps, giving the challenge strangely to the all-destroyer. One much later in style of decoration has a procession of spirits driven by two demons, — Dantesque in power and simplicity of conception and evident faith, but telling a stranger story, in its contrast with the former, than anything we know in the history of the time, — a change from the golden to the iron days of Etruria.

The marvellous treasures of these tombs, — though only the few which, by comparative insignificance or fortunate accident, have escaped the unintelligent ravage of Roman or of Goth, — are like the scale or bone of Agassiz's saurian; and a necklace of Scarabæi alternated with the little pendent fantasies in gold, which we may see in the Campana collection, is the fragment from which we build Etruria, taking a little help from the time-defying walls, and a hint from the sarcophagus whose mutually embracing effigies of the two made one tell that position given to woman which made Rome what she was after the fraud of Romulus gave to Romans Etruscan wives.

The Etrurians were the gold-workers of all time. Like shawls of Cashmere, Greek statuary, Gothic architecture, and Saracenic tracery, Etruscan goldwork stands absolutely alone, — the result of an artistic instinct deeper than any rules or any instruction, and therefore not to be improved or repeated. It is characterized by the most subtile and lovely use of decorative masses and lines, — not for representation or imitation, which are not motives to enter into pure ornament, but for the highest effect of beautiful form and rich color, without giving the eye or mind any associative or intellectual suggestion. The vice of all modern ornamentation is, that it insists, on mixing natural history with decoration. It cannot avoid preaching, as fairy stories now-a-days cannot stop without a moral for good children, and consequently is, like them, stupid and unreal. The best ornamentation is that which is farthest from imitation; and that, in gold-work, is the Etruscan. As we had occasion to say in the preceding pages, the Scarabæus marks the difference between the moralizing Egyptian mind and the beauty-loving Etruscan. And if we might point a moral in an article defiant of morals, it would be in comparing the black, blood-stained history of Egypt with the fair record of the Larthian people. Beauty is its own moral and its own redeemer, and a mind that loves it may be corrupted to decay, but cannot be led into brutality or sunk into obscurity. Of the magnificence of the living people we can scarcely judge, since all we have now is the gorgeous array of those who were robed for the eternal rest. Castellani, in his pamphlet on the antique gold-work (*Dell' Oreficeria Antica, Discorso di August Castellani*), says : "But the excavations of Etruria which have preserved, what with pictures, apparel, and fabrics, so many of the antique sacerdotal ornaments, add almost nothing to the little we know about the names and uses of them. Micali says that 'the mechanism of the whole Etruscan government was beyond doubt priestly in its institutions.' After such a declaration by one of the most accurate narrators of ancient Italian history, I should scarcely know what to add to convey an idea of the pomp in which the priestly class of Etruria lived and robed itself. We can conjecture that the great poitrel in the Etruscan museum in the Vatican, the two magnificent bridles of the Campana museum, all the collars of extraordinary size and the large bullæ of various forms and dimensions which come from the various collections, and the innumerable vases, pateræ, cups, and goblets of gold, silver, and bronze found in the sepulchres, were all implements, furniture, and ornaments devoted to the service of religion. And such a multitude of objects may give some indication both of the multiplicity of the mysteries and sacred functions, and of the treasures which must have been contained in the antique temples, plundered by the barbarians, and then destroyed by the intolerant zeal of ignorant disciples of a new, triumphant religion."

What the wealth of the favored Etruscan fanes must have been may be conjectured from the fact that Dionysius carried from one on the sea-coast treasures to the amount of $40,000,000.

Of the gold-working, Castellani's restorations and imitations will give us a tolerable idea, so far as workmanship is concerned, though he himself confesses to be unable to equal all its qualities. I translate an interesting passage.

"Having proposed to ourselves, then, to restore as far as we could, and, so to speak, to renew the antique gold-work, we first set ourselves to search for the methods which the ancients must have used. It was observed that in the ornaments of gold all the parts in relief were by the ancients superimposed ; that is to say, prepared separately and then placed in position by means of soldering or some chemical process, and not raised by stamping, casting, or chiselling. From this arises, perhaps, the something spontaneous, the freedom and artistic neglect which is seen in the works of the ancients, which appear all made by hands guided by thought, while the moderns impress, I would say, a certain perfect exactness on the things produced by them, which reveals the work of mechanical implements, and shows a want of the creative thought of the artist. Here, then, they sought to find means to compose and solder together so many pieces of gold of different forms, and of such minuteness, that, as we have said, it goes to the very extreme.

"We made innumerable experiments, and put in operation successively all the chemical agents, many metallic alloys, and the most powerful fluxes. We searched the writings of Pliny, of Theophilus, and of Cellini ; the works of the Indian gold-workers and those of Genoa and of Malta were studied with all care ; in short, there was forgotten no one of those sources whence we might hope for some hint. Finally, whence least we expected it came some real assistance.

"Hidden in the highest mountains of the Apennine range is a little town called St. Angelo in Vado, where are made gold and silver ornaments, with which the fair mountaineers decorate themselves. Here it appears that they preserve, at least in part, the oldest traditions of the art of working in gold and silver ; and these workmen, ... shut, so to speak, from all contact with modern things, make crowns of filigree strung with gilded pearls and ear-rings of that peculiar form which is called the 'navicella,' by such methods as perhaps the antique were made, so that these jewels resemble not a little those found in the Greek and Etruscan sepul-

chres, although for elegance of form and for taste they are far from equalling them. . . . .

"Not long since, when, examining with a lens the Etruscan jewels of our own collection, I discerned in the zones of the tiny grains (which are characteristic of the work of these patient artists) certain defects, such as those which are made in enamel by the melting of the gold. These observations suggested to me to try a new process, in order to reproduce this exceedingly fine grain-work, believed hitherto impossible to be even distantly imitated by modern gold-workers. I immediately commenced the new experiments, and the results were sufficiently satisfactory to enable me to say, at present, that the problem is nearly solved which for almost twenty years has defied us."

And even now Castellani's best grain-work is far from equalling in delicacy and perfection of workmanship some of the antiques in his own collection.

Our Scarabæus has got into magnificent company, and modern taste finds that he deserved it ; and certainly, *me judice*, nothing can be more purely artistic than a fine Scarabæus, and the fascination that comes over whoever has ventured to dabble in that kind of wares is as dangerous as the chances of play. Be content with a single one ! If you once get into comparison, you have abandoned yourself to the witchery of the unknown and unattainable perfection.

Engraved gems or simple intaglios in *pietra dura* seem to belong to Greek art rather than Etruscan. The style of finishing the stone was more in accordance with the simple and elegant ideal of the Greek intellect. The intaglio was all to the Greek artist, and anything more was labor worse than wasted. His intaglio ceased to be ornamentation, and passed into the category of ideal work. And there are intaglii of Greek workmanship which are as lovely as it is possible to conceive anything. — all the spirit and perfect proportion of the antique sculpture concentrated in an oval, an inch by three quarters of an inch, executed with a delicacy which defies the naked eye to measure it!

A critical study of gems is an affair of years; yet, so far as all principles of design are concerned or characteristics of art, we may always consider the intaglii with the sculpture of the same epoch. The spirit and manner and perfections are the same. The first are, of course, the Greek; and a fine example is rarely found, — heads only, of Dioscorides or any equally famous artist, being valued at from $ 400 to $ 800, and even $ 1200 in the case of the Ariadne. The next in value are Etruscan, very fine examples being nearly as much esteemed as Greek, while the best Roman is, like Roman sculpture, but a far-off emulation in design, though often admirable in execution and finish. Very fine examples of either are not largely current, being taken up by collectors and consigned at once to public or private cabinets; but now and then one turns up, or is turned up by an unenterprising share-holder of the Campagna of Rome, or by some excavator or vineyard-digger in Sicily, Magna Græcia, or Greece proper, and, if it gets into commerce, finds its way generally to Rome, the centre of exchange for classical antiquities. The Scarabæi are mostly found in the Etruscan tombs, and occasionally outside the walls of the Etruscan cities, — swept out, may be, with the antique dust. But there are Roman imitations, made doubtless for some aristocratic descendant of the mythic Etrurian kings, like Mæcenas, proud of that remote if subjugated ancestry, and looking wistfully backward to the Arcadia of which his family traditions only preserved the record. The Roman lapidaries were not nice workmen, and their imitations are most palpable.

Then, in the fifteenth century, came other and better lapidaries, and of better taste, many of whose Scarabæi are of great value, though still not difficult to distinguish from the Etruscan, when we study the design. The modern demand for them has produced innumerable impositions in the shape of copies, — poor Scarabæi retouched to fine ones, still bearing the marks of antiquity, and others whose under surface, being originally left blank, is engraved by the hired workmen of the modern Roman antiquaries, by whom they are sold as guaranteed antiques. This is the most common and dangerous cheat, and one which the easy conscience of the Italian merchant regards as perfectly justifiable; for has not the stone all the aroma of antiquity? A little shade darker in iniquity is the selling of stones entirely recut from broken larger ones, so that, though the stone remains identical, the workman puts a new face on it; and even this the antiquary will sell you as a veritable antique. Then there is the unmitigated swindle of the pure imitation, oftentimes so perfect that the most experienced judges are deceived. There is in fact no absolute certainty in the matter. There are antiques of which no doubt can be entertained, with characteristics utterly inimitable; but there are others as certainly antique which have none of these, but, taken without reference to their *placer*, are not to be distinguished with absolute certainty. I remember a necklace in the Campana museum, which, in a large number of unmistakable Scarabæi, had one for which I would not have paid two scudi on the Piazza Navona, so like the modern imitations did it look. The only reliable criterion for the majority of cases is the spirit of the design in the intaglio. Castellani says: "Antique Etruscan, Greek, or Roman Scarabæi are at present very rare, and their high price tempts the moderns to counterfeit them. And to such a perfection have they carried their business that it is with difficulty the best-trained eye can discover the fraud. It is not the stone, not the polish, nor even the incision, but a peculiar smoothness and *morbidezza*, which distinguishes the antique; and which only they who for many years have studied such kinds of work, or who, either in the way of trade or otherwise, have seen and handled many of the gems, are able to perceive."

A friend in Rome came to me one day with a request that I would go with him to see a Scarabæus which he had taken a fancy to, and had engaged to buy if it were counted genuine by good judges. It was a superb stone, a deep carnelian, nearly opaque, exquisitely elaborated, and with an intaglio which I doubt not was Greek. It was the most beautiful one I had ever seen, and I gave my opinion, such as it was, in favor of its antiquity. It was purchased, and afterwards shown to a well-known dealer, by whom it was pronounced a cheat; and on inquiry it was discovered that the seller had had a copy made of the original, and, while he offered the latter for sale, delivered the former, which was so carefully and perfectly copied as to puzzle the eye even of the best-instructed amateur.

A merchant of antiquities with whom I have occasional dealings — we will call him A. because that is not his initial — brought me one day a large intaglio, which had the appearance of an archaic Etruscan work. A. is known as one of the *piu cognoscenti* of Rome; and his dictum is worth any other two. He declared it an original antique of the rarest quality; and Odelli, the best gem-cutter in Rome, coincided in the opinion. He held it at two thousand francs, but would have sold it to me for eighteen hundred, I suppose. I did n't bite, and after a few weeks lured the collector of whom he had bought it — one of those who make it a business to haunt the markets, and visit distant cities and excavations, to purchase and sell again to the Roman antiquaries — to boast his prowess as compared with that of A., who had bitten him severely several times in their dealings; and, in the full tide of his self-glorification, I turned the conversation on the black agate, now become famous among the dealers. He could not resist the temptation, and told me all about it. "A. believes it to be antique, don't he?" "O, he is certain of it," said I. "Well, I 'll tell you how it is: I bought the thing of the man who made it, and paid him three scudi

for it. I took it to A. and offered it to him for six; but he refused it, thinking it to be a paste. I took it away again, and, having had it tested as a stone, offered it to him for twenty. After examining it and keeping it a few days, he offered me twelve. I said no, — eighteen. *He* said no. I said sixteen, and he offered me fourteen, which I took. The fact is," said he, "no one is able to say for certain if a stone is antique or not. A. has the best judgment in Rome, but you see how he is deceived." I bought of the same man a small engraved emerald, which he had just purchased of a peasant, and, without much examination, sold me for one scudo, as a basso-impero of ordinary quality. My eyes were better, and had seen, in what he thought a handful of flowers, a cross; and on cleaning it we found it to be an early Christian stone of much greater value than he supposed, to his great chagrin.

If the perfections of our Scarabæus give us a glimpse of Etruscan existence, we may perhaps gather from the gems some notion of what Rome was, beyond what historians have written, or the ruins of her palaces and tombs have shown. The quantity of intaglii alone, such as they are, which are dug up in the gardens and vineyards around Rome every year, is incredible to one who has not watched day by day the acquisitions of the antiquity shops, and the stalls of the Piazza Navona. Very few of them are of any artistic value; but the fact that so many were made use of is a marvel in itself, and implies a greater luxury than marble palaces even hint at. I one day remarked to a peasant who brought me some intaglii to sell, that the ancients must have worn a great many rings; and he replied, that in his country the richer people wore so many that they had to hold their hands up to keep them from falling off. On inquiry I found that he came from the Abruzzi, where it seems that the people still hold on to something of the antique customs; for we know that the Romans began the fashion of covering the fingers to that extravagant degree, so that the number of rings possessed by a family of great wealth must have been almost inestimable. At every irruption of the barbarians, the villas that covered the Campagna for miles around Rome must have felt the first fury of their ravages ; and as the stones contained in the ornaments were of no use to the plunderers, they were broken out and thrown away, many of them to be uncovered, more than a thousand years later, by the spade of the trencher in the vineyards. One of a number of peasants playing at bowls in one of the roads near Rome struck with his ball a point of hardened mud, which flew in pieces, disclosing an exquisite intaglio head of Nero in carnelian, in perfect condition, for which the finder received ten scudi.

The laborers in the fields have so far learned the value of the stones they find, that it becomes almost impossible anywhere in the vicinity of Rome to buy them of the finders, even at the most extravagant prices. Unable to distinguish in quality, and knowing that certain stones have brought such and such prices, they refuse to sell any for a smaller price, but retain them until the next *festa*, when they carry them in succession to all the *mercanti di pietre* in Rome, to see which will offer the highest price, — a kind of vendue which evinces greater trade-cleverness than the Italians get credit for, and which has the effect of bringing the dealers at once to their best terms. No matter what price you offer, they never accept it until they have tried the value it has for others. It is only when a stone has such great value that it justifies paying a price passing the imagination of the peasant, that the buyer can profit by buying from the first hand.

Of the finer kind of intaglii, there is little danger of buying counterfeits, since the art of gem-cutting is too low now to permit of such counterfeits as might be mistaken for first-rate antiques. Of the common kind, again, there are those which, cut with a certain conventionalism in design and a facility in execution which incessant repetition only can produce, cannot be imitated except at a cost utterly beyond their market value. Like the designs on the Etruscan vases, their main excellence is, that, being so good, they should be done so facilely. An imitator loses the rapidity and spirit of execution. The mass of imitations are of things only tolerably good, and of things whose characteristics are in the execution merely, as in the Roman and conventional Etruscan work.

I will close with one bit of advice to my readers. If your fancy finds any satisfaction in *Scarabæi ed altri*, let your acquisition stop with the first example, — take a sample brick from antiquity. If you once commence collecting them in ever so small a way, or with any excuse to your own pocket, you will find yourself subject to a fascination more irresistible than the love of money, — more absorbing than the search for the philosopher's stone. While you are in Rome, you will find yourself unable to keep your feet from ways that lead to the antiquaries, or your money out of the hands of a class (with two or three exceptions) of cheats. You will find the extravagances of one day coming to be the niggardness of the next ; and feverish anxieties lest you should not succeed in getting this gem, and irritating regrets that you too soon bought that, will divide your tortured soul. And when you finally leave Rome, as you must some day, you will always harbor a small cankerworm of immitigable grief, that you did not purchase one stone you saw and thought too high-priced ; and will pass thenceforward no curiosity-shop without looking in the windows a moment, in the hope of finding some gem strayed away into parts where no man knows its value. If you feel in you the capacity of loving them, let them alone.

MIANTOWONA.

LONG ere the Pale Face
  Crossed the Great Water,
Miantowona
Passed, with her beauty,
Into a legend
Pure as a wild-flower
Found in a broken
Ledge by the sea-side.

Let us revere them, —
These wildwood legends,
Born of the camp-fire !
Let them be handed
Down to our children, —
Richest of heirlooms !
No land may claim them :
They are ours only,
Like our grand rivers,
Like our vast prairies,
Like our dead heroes !

In the pine-forest,
Guarded by shadows,
Lieth the haunted
Pond of the Red Men.
Ringed by the emerald
Mountains, it lies there
Like an untarnished
Buckler of silver,
Dropped in that valley
By the Great Spirit !
Weird are the figures
Traced on its margins, —
Vine-work and leaf-work,
Knots of sword-grasses,
Moonlight and starlight,
Clouds scudding northward !
Sometimes an eagle
Flutters across it ;
Sometimes a single
Star on its bosom
Nestles till morning.

Far in the ages,
Miantowona,
Rose of the Hurons,
Came to these waters.

Where the dank greensward
Slopes to the pebbles,
Miantowona
Sat in her anguish.
Ice to her maidens,
Ice to the chieftains,
Fire to her lover!
Here he had won her,
Here they had parted,
Here could her tears flow.

With unwet eyelash,
Miantowona
Nursed her old father,
Oldest of Hurons,
Soothed his complainings,
Smiled when he chid her
Vaguely for nothing, —
He was so weak now,
Like a shrunk cedar
White with the hoar-frost.
Sometimes she gently
Linked arms with maidens,
Joined in their dances :
Not with her people,
Not in the wigwam,
Wept for her lover.

Ah ! who was like him ?
Fleet as an arrow,
Strong as a bison,
Lithe as a panther,
Soft as the south-wind,
Who was like Wawah ?
There is one other
Stronger and fleeter,
Bearing no wampum,
Wearing no war-paint,
Ruler of councils,
Chief of the war-path, —
Who can gainsay him,
Who can defy him ?
His is the lightning,
His is the whirlwind.
Let us be humble,
We are but ashes, —
'T is the Great Spirit!

Ever at nightfall
Miantowona
Strayed from the lodges,
Passed through the shadows

Into the forest:
There by the pond-side
Spread her black tresses
Over her forehead.
Sad is the loon's cry
Heard in the twilight ;
Sad is the night-wind,
Moaning and moaning ;
Sadder the stifled
Sob of a widow !

Low on the pebbles
Murmured the water :
Often she fancied
It was young Wawalı
Playing the reed-flute.
Sometimes a dry branch
Snapped in the forest :
Then she rose, startled,
Ruddy as sunrise,
Warm for his coming !
But when he came not,
Back through the darkness,
Half broken-hearted,
Miantowona
Went to her people.

When an old oak dies,
First 't is the tree-tops,
Then the low branches,
Then the gaunt stem goes :
So fell Tawanda,
Oldest of Hurons,
Chief of the chieftains.

Miantowona
Wept not, but softly
Closed the sad eyelids ;
With her own fingers
Fastened the deer-skin
Over his shoulders ;
Then laid beside him
Ash-bow and arrows,
Pipe-bowl and wampum,
Dried corn and bear-meat, —
All that was needful
On the long journey.
Thus old Tawanda
Went to the hunting
Grounds of the Red Man.

Then, as the dirges
Rose from the village,

Miantowona
Stole from the mourners,
Stole through the cornfields,
Passed like a phantom
Into the shadows
Through the pine-forest.

One who had watched her —
It was Nahoho,
Loving her vainly —
Saw, as she passed him,
That in her features
Made his stout heart quail.
He could but follow.
Quick were her footsteps,
Light as a snow-flake,
Leaving no traces
On the white clover.

Like a trained runner,
Winner of prizes,
Into the woodlands
Plunged the young chieftain.
Once he abruptly
Halted, and listened ;
Then he sped forward
Faster and faster
Toward the bright water.
Breathless he reached it.
Why did he crouch then,
Stark as a statue ?
What did he see there
Could so appall him ?
Only a circle
Swiftly expanding,
Fading before him ;
But, as he watched it,
Up from the centre,
Slowly, superbly
Rose a Pond-Lily.

One cry of wonder,
Shrill as the loon's call,
Rang through the forest,
Startling the silence,
Startling the mourners
Chanting the death-song.
Forth from the village,
Flocking together
Came all the Hurons. —
Striplings and warriors,
Maidens and old men,
Squaws with pappooses.

No word was spoken :
There stood the Hurons
On the dank greensward,
With their swart faces
Bowed in the twilight.
What did they see there ?
Only a Lily
Rocked on the azure
Breast of the water.

Then they turned sadly
Each to the other,
Tenderly murmuring,
" Miantowona ! "
Soft as the dew falls
Down through the midnight,
Cleaving the starlight,
Echo repeated,
" Miantowona ! "

PASSAGES FROM HAWTHORNE'S NOTE-BOOKS.

X.

SUNDAY, *April* 9, 1843.— . . . . After finishing my record in the journal, I sat a long time in grandmother's chair, thinking of many things. . . . . My spirits were at a lower ebb than they ever descend to when I am not alone ; nevertheless, neither was I absolutely sad. Many times I wound and rewound Mr. Thoreau's little musical box ; but certainly its peculiar sweetness had evaporated, and I am pretty sure that I should throw it out of the window were I doomed to hear it long and often. It has not an infinite soul. When it was almost as dark as the moonlight would let it be, I lighted the lamp, and went on with Tieck's tale, slowly and painfully, often wishing for help in my difficulties. At last I determined to learn a little about pronouns and verbs before proceeding further, and so took up the phrase-book, with which I was commendably busy, when, at about a quarter to nine, came a knock at my study-door, and, behold, there was Molly with a letter ! How she came by it I did not ask, being content to suppose it was brought by a heavenly messenger. I had not expected a letter ; and what a comfort it was to me in my loneliness and sombreness ! I called Molly to take her note (enclosed), which she received with a face of delight as broad and bright as the kitchen fire. Then I read, and re-read, and re-re-read, and quadruply, quintuply, and sextuply re-read my epistle, until I had it all by heart, and then continued to re-read it for the sake of the penmanship. Then I took up the phrase-book again ; but could not study, and so bathed and retired, it being now not far from ten o'clock. I lay awake a good deal in the night, but saw no ghost.

I arose about seven, and found that the upper part of my nose, and the region round about, was grievously discolored ;

and at the angle of the left eye there is a great spot of almost black purple, and a broad streak of the same hue semicircling beneath either eye, while green, yellow, and orange overspread the circumjacent country. It looks not unlike a gorgeous sunset, throwing its splendor over the heaven of my countenance. It will behoove me to show myself as little as possible; else people will think I have fought a pitched battle. . . . . The Devil take the stick of wood! What had I done, that it should bemaul me so? However, there is no pain, though, I think, a very slight affection of the eyes.

This forenoon I began to write, and caught an idea by the skirts, which I intend to hold fast, though it struggles to get free. As it was not ready to be put upon paper, however, I took up the Dial, and finished reading the article on Mr. Alcott. It is not very satisfactory, and it has not taught me much. Then I read Margaret's article on Canova, which is good. About this time the dinner-bell rang, and I went down without much alacrity, though with a good appetite enough. . . . . It was in the angle of my *right* eye, not my left, that the blackest purple was collected. But they both look like the very Devil.

Half past five o'clock. — After writing the above, ... I again set to work on Tieck's tale, and worried through several pages; and then, at half past four, threw open one of the western windows of my study, and sallied forth to take the sunshine. I went down through the orchard to the river-side. The orchard-path is still deeply covered with snow; and so is the whole visible universe, except streaks upon the hillsides, and spots in the sunny hollows, where the brown earth peeps through. The river, which a few days ago was entirely imprisoned, has now broken its fetters; but a tract of ice extended across from near the foot of the monument to the abutment of the old bridge, and looked so solid that I supposed it would yet remain for a day or two. Large cakes and masses of

ice came floating down the current, which, though not very violent, hurried along at a much swifter pace than the ordinary one of our sluggish river-god. These ice-masses, when they struck the barrier of ice above mentioned, acted upon it like a battering-ram, and were themselves forced high out of the water, or sometimes carried beneath the main sheet of ice. At last, down the stream came an immense mass of ice, and, striking the barrier about at its centre, it gave way, and the whole was swept onward together, leaving the river entirely free, with only here and there a cake of ice floating quietly along. The great accumulation, in its downward course, hit against a tree that stood in mid-current, and caused it to quiver like a reed; and it swept quite over the shrubbery that bordered what, in summer-time, is the river's bank, but which is now nearly the centre of the stream. Our river in its present state has quite a noble breadth. The little hillock which formed the abutment of the old bridge is now an island with its tuft of trees. Along the hither shore a row of trees stand up to their knees, and the smaller ones to their middles, in the water; and afar off, on the surface of the stream, we see tufts of bushes emerging, thrusting up their heads, as it were, to breathe. The water comes over the stone wall, and encroaches several yards on the boundaries of our orchard. [Here the supper-bell rang.] If our boat were in good order, I should now set forth on voyages of discovery, and visit nooks on the borders of the meadows, which by and by will be a mile or two from the water's edge. But she is in very bad condition, full of water, and, doubtless, as leaky as a sieve.

On coming from supper, I found that little Puss had established herself in the study, probably with intent to pass the night here. She now lies on the footstool between my feet, purring most obstreperously. The day of my wife's departure, she came to me, talking with the greatest earnestness; but whether it was to condole with me on my loss, or to demand my redoubled care for herself, I could not well make out. As Puss now constitutes a third part of the family, this mention of her will not appear amiss. How Molly employs herself, I know not. Once in a while, I hear a door slam like a thunder-clap; but she never shows her face, nor speaks a word, unless to announce a visitor or deliver a letter. This day, on my part, will have been spent without exchanging a syllable with any human being, unless something unforeseen should yet call for the exercise of speech before bedtime.

Monday, April 10. — I sat till eight o'clock, meditating upon this world and the next, ... and sometimes dimly shaping out scenes of a tale. Then betook myself to the German phrasebook. Ah! these are but dreary evenings. The lamp would not brighten my spirits, though it was duly filled. . . . . This forenoon was spent in scribbling, by no means to my satisfaction, until past eleven, when I went to the village. Nothing in our box at the post-office. I read during the customary hour, or more, at the Athenæum, and returned without saying a word to mortal. I gathered from some conversation that I heard, that a son of Adam is to be buried this afternoon from the meeting-house; but the name of the deceased escaped me. It is no great matter, so it be but written in the Book of Life.

My variegated face looks somewhat more human to-day; though I was unaffectedly ashamed to meet anybody's gaze, and therefore turned my back or my shoulder as much as possible upon the world. At dinner, behold an immense joint of roast veal! I would willingly have had some assistance in the discussion of this great piece of calf. I am ashamed to eat alone; it becomes the mere gratification of animal appetite, — the tribute which we are compelled to pay to our grosser nature; whereas in the company of another it is refined and moralized and spiritualized; and over our earthly victuals (or rather *vittles*, for the for-

mer is a very foolish mode of spelling), — over our earthly vittles is diffused a sauce of lofty and gentle thoughts, and tough meat is mollified with tender feelings. But oh! these solitary meals are the dismallest part of my present experience. When the company rose from table, they all, in my single person, ascended to the study, and employed themselves in reading the article on Oregon in the Democratic Review. Then they plodded onward in the rugged and bewildering depths of Tieck's tale until five o'clock, when, with one accord, they went out to split wood. This has been a gray day, with now and then a sprinkling of snow-flakes through the air. . . . . To-day no more than yesterday have I spoken a word to mortal. . . . . . It is now sunset, and I must meditate till dark.

April 11. — I meditated accordingly, but without any very wonderful result. Then at eight o'clock bothered myself till after nine with this eternal tale of Tieck. The forenoon was spent in scribbling; but at eleven o'clock my thoughts ceased to flow, — indeed, their current has been wofully interrupted all along, — so I threw down my pen, and set out on the daily journey to the village. Horrible walking! I wasted the customary hour at the Athenæum, and returned home, if home it may now be called. Till dinner-time I labored on Tieck's tale, and resumed that agreeable employment after the banquet.

Just when I was at the point of choking with a huge German word, Molly announced Mr. Thoreau. He wished to take a row in the boat, for the last time, perhaps, before he leaves Concord. So we emptied the water out of her, and set forth on our voyage. She leaks, but not more than she did in the autumn. We rowed to the foot of the hill which borders the North Branch, and there landed, and climbed the moist and snowy hillside for the sake of the prospect. Looking down the river, it might well have been mistaken for an arm of the sea, so broad is now its swollen tide; and I could have fancied that, beyond one other headland, the mighty ocean would outspread itself before the eye. On our return we boarded a large cake of ice, which was floating down the river, and were borne by it directly to our own landing-place, with the boat towing behind.

Parting with Mr. Thoreau I spent half an hour in chopping wood, when Molly informed me that Mr. Emerson wished to see me. He had brought a letter of Ellery Channing, written in a style of very pleasant humor. This being read and discussed, together with a few other matters, he took his leave, since which I have been attending to my journalizing duty; and thus this record is brought down to the present moment.

April 25. — Spring is advancing, sometimes with sunny days, and sometimes, as is the case now, with chill, moist, sullen ones. There is an influence in the season that makes it almost impossible for me to bring my mind down to literary employment; perhaps because several months' pretty constant work has exhausted that species of energy, — perhaps because in spring it is more natural to labor actively than to think. But my impulse now is to be idle altogether, — to lie in the sun, or wander about and look at the revival of Nature from her deathlike slumber, or to be borne down the current of the river in my boat. If I had wings, I would gladly fly; yet would prefer to be wafted along by a breeze, sometimes alighting on a patch of green grass, then gently whirled away to a still sunnier spot. . . . . O, how blest should I be were there nothing to do! Then I would watch every inch and hair's breadth of the progress of the season; and not a leaf should put itself forth, in the vicinity of our old mansion, without my noting it. But now, with the burden of a continual task upon me, I have not freedom of mind to make such observations. I merely see what is going on in a very general way. The snow, which, two or three weeks ago,

covered hill and valley, is now diminished to one or two solitary specks in the visible landscape; though doubtless there are still heaps of it in the shady places in the woods. There have been no violent rains to carry it off: it has diminished gradually, inch by inch, and day after day; and I observed, along the roadside, that the green blades of grass had sometimes sprouted on the very edge of the snowdrift, the moment that the earth was uncovered.

The pastures and grass-fields have not yet a general effect of green; nor have they that cheerless brown tint which they wear in later autumn, when vegetation has entirely ceased. There is now a suspicion of verdure, — the faint shadow of it, — but not the warm reality. Sometimes, in a happy exposure, — there is one such tract across the river, the carefully cultivated mowing-field, in front of an old red homestead, — such patches of land wear a beautiful and tender green, which no other season will equal; because, let the grass be green as it may hereafter, it will not be so set off by surrounding barrenness. The trees in our orchard, and elsewhere, have as yet no leaves; yet to the most careless eye they appear full of life and vegetable blood. It seems as if, by one magic touch, they might instantaneously put forth all their foliage, and the wind, which now sighs through their naked branches, might all at once find itself impeded by innumerable leaves. This sudden development would be scarcely more wonderful than the gleam of verdure which often brightens, in a moment, as it were, along the slope of a bank or roadside. It is like a gleam of sunlight. Just now it was brown, like the rest of the scenery: look again, and there is an apparition of green grass. The Spring, no doubt, comes onward with fleeter footsteps, because Winter has lingered so long that, at best, she can hardly retrieve half the allotted term of her reign.

The river, this season, has encroached farther on the land than it has been known to do for twenty years past. It has formed along its course a succession of lakes, with a current through the midst. My boat has lain at the bottom of the orchard, in very convenient proximity to the house. It has borne me over stone fences ; and, a few days ago, Ellery Channing and I passed through two rails into the great northern road, along which we paddled for some distance. The trees have a singular appearance in the midst of waters. The curtailment of their trunks quite destroys the proportions of the whole tree ; and we become conscious of a regularity and propriety in the forms of Nature, by the effect of this abbreviation. The waters are now subsiding, but gradually. Islands become annexed to the mainland, and other islands emerge from the flood, and will soon, likewise, be connected with the continent. We have seen on a small scale the process of the deluge, and can now witness that of the reappearance of the earth.

Crows visited us long before the snow was off. They seem mostly to have departed now, or else to have betaken themselves to remote depths of the woods, which they haunt all summer long. Ducks came in great numbers, and many sportsmen went in pursuit of them, along the river ; but they also have disappeared. Gulls come up from seaward, and soar high overhead, flapping their broad wings in the upper sunshine. They are among the most picturesque birds that I am acquainted with ; indeed, quite the most so, because the manner of their flight makes them almost stationary parts of the landscape. The imagination has time to rest upon them ; they have not flitted away in a moment. You go up among the clouds, and lay hold of these soaring gulls, and repose with them upon the sustaining atmosphere. The smaller birds, — the birds that build their nests in our trees, and sing for us at morning-red, — I will not describe. . . . . But I must mention the great companies of blackbirds — more than the famous

"four-and-twenty" who were baked in a pie — that congregate on the tops of contiguous trees, and vociferate with all the clamor of a turbulent political meeting. Politics must certainly be the subject of such a tumultuous debate ; but still there is a melody in each individual utterance, and a harmony in the general effect. Mr. Thoreau tells me that these noisy assemblages consist of three different species of blackbirds ; but I forget the other two. Robins have been long among us, and swallows have more recently arrived.

April 26. — Here is another misty day, muffling the sun. The lilac shrubs under my study-window are almost in leaf. In two or three days more, I may put forth my hand and pluck a green bough. These lilacs appear to be very aged, and have lost the luxuriant foliage of their prime. Old age has a singular aspect in lilacs, rose-bushes, and other ornamental shrubs. It seems as if such things, as they grow only for beauty, ought to flourish in immortal youth, or at least to die before their decrepitude. They are trees of Paradise, and therefore not naturally subject to decay ; but have lost their birthright by being transplanted hither. There is a kind of ludicrous unfitness in the idea of a venerable rose-bush ; and there is something analogous to this in human life. Persons who can only be graceful and ornamental — who can give the world nothing but flowers — should die young, and never be seen with gray hairs and wrinkles, any more than the flower-shrubs with mossy bark and scanty foliage, like the lilacs under my window. Not that beauty is not worthy of immortality. Nothing else, indeed, is worthy of it ; and thence, perhaps, the sense of impropriety when we see it triumphed over by time. Apple-trees, on the other hand, grow old without reproach. Let them live as long as they may, and contort themselves in whatever fashion they please, they are still respectable, even if they afford us only an apple or two in a season. or none at all. Human flower-shrubs, if they will grow old on earth, should, beside their lovely blossoms, bear some kind of fruit that will satisfy earthly appetites; else men will not be satisfied that the moss should gather on them.

Winter and Spring are now struggling for the mastery in my study; and I yield somewhat to each, and wholly to neither. The window is open, and there is a fire in the stove. The day when the window is first thrown open should be an epoch in the year; but I have forgotten to record it. Seventy or eighty springs have visited this old house; and sixty of them found old Dr. Ripley here, — not always old, it is true, but gradually getting wrinkles and gray hairs, and looking more and more the picture of winter. But he was no flower-shrub, but one of those fruit-trees or timber-trees that acquire a grace with their old age. Last Spring found this house solitary for the first time since it was built; and now again she peeps into our open windows and finds new faces here. . . . .

It is remarkable how much uncleanness winter brings with it, or leaves behind it. . . . . The yard, garden, and avenue, which should be my department, require a great amount of labor. The avenue is strewed with withered leaves, — the whole crop, apparently, of last year, — some of which are now raked into heaps; and we intend to make a bonfire of them. . . . . There are quantities of decayed branches, which one tempest after another has flung down, black and rotten. In the garden are the old cabbages which we did not think worth gathering last autumn, and the dry bean-vines, and the withered stalks of the asparagus-bed; in short, all the wrecks of the departed year, — its mouldering relics, its dry bones. It is a pity that the world cannot be made over anew every spring. Then, in the yard, there are the piles of firewood, which I ought to have sawed and thrown into the shed long since, but which will cumber the earth, I fear, till June, at least. Quantities

of chips are strewn about, and on removing them we find the yellow stalks of grass sprouting underneath. Nature does her best to beautify this disarray. The grass springs up most industriously, especially in sheltered and sunny angles of the buildings, or round the door-steps, — a locality which seems particularly favorable to its growth; for it is already high enough to bend over and wave in the wind. I was surprised to observe that some weeds (especially a plant that stains the fingers with its yellow juice) had lived, and retained their freshness and sap as perfectly as in summer, through all the frosts and snows of last winter. I saw them, the last green thing, in the autumn; and here they are again, the first in the spring.

Thursday, April 27. — I took a walk into the fields, and round our opposite hill, yesterday noon, but made no very remarkable observation. The frogs have begun their concerts, though not as yet with a full choir. I found no violets nor anemones, nor anything in the likeness of a flower, though I looked carefully along the shelter of the stone walls, and in all spots apparently propitious. I ascended the hill, and had a wide prospect of a swollen river, extending around me in a semicircle of three or four miles, and rendering the view much finer than in summer, had there only been foliage. It seemed like the formation of a new world; for islands were everywhere emerging, and capes extending forth into the flood; and these tracts, which were thus won from the watery empire, were among the greenest in the landscape. The moment the deluge leaves them, Nature asserts them to be her property, by covering them with verdure; or perhaps the grass had been growing under the water. On the hill-top where I stood, the grass had scarcely begun to sprout; and I observed that even those places which looked greenest in the distance were but scantily grass-covered when I actually reached them. It was hope that painted them so bright.

Last evening we saw a bright light on the river, betokening that a boat's party were engaged in spearing fish. It looked like a descended star, — like red Mars, — and, as the water was perfectly smooth, its gleam was reflected downward into the depths. It is a very picturesque sight. In the deep quiet of the night I suddenly heard the light and lively note of a bird from a neighboring tree, — a real song, such as those which greet the purple dawn, or mingle with the yellow sunshine. What could the little bird mean by pouring it forth at midnight? Probably the note gushed out from the midst of a dream, in which he fancied himself in Paradise with his mate; and, suddenly awaking, he found he was on a cold, leafless bough, with a New England mist penetrating through his feathers. That was a sad exchange of imagination for reality; but if he found his mate beside him, all was well.

This is another misty morning, ungenial in aspect, but kinder than it looks; for it paints the hills and valleys with a richer brush than the sunshine could. There is more verdure now than when I looked out of the window an hour ago. The willow-tree opposite my study-window is ready to put forth its leaves. There are some objections to willows. It is not a dry and cleanly tree; it impresses me with an association of sliminess; and no trees, I think, are perfectly satisfactory, which have not a firm and hard texture of trunk and branches. But the willow is almost the earliest to put forth its leaves, and the last to scatter them on the ground; and during the whole winter its yellow twigs give it a sunny aspect, which is not without a cheering influence in a proper point of view. Our old house would lose much were this willow to be cut down, with its golden crown over the roof in winter, and its heap of summer verdure. The present Mr. Ripley planted it, fifty years ago, or thereabouts.

Friday, June 2. — Last night there came a frost, which has done great damage to my garden. The beans have suffered very much, although, luckily, not more than half that I planted have come up. The squashes, both summer and winter, appear to be almost killed. As to the other vegetables, there is little mischief done, — the potatoes not being yet above ground, except two or three; and the peas and corn are of a hardier nature. It is sad that Nature will so sport with us poor mortals, inviting us with sunny smiles to confide in her; and then, when we are entirely in her power, striking us to the heart. Our summer commences at the latter end of June, and terminates somewhere about the first of August. There are certainly not more than six weeks of the whole year when a frost may be deemed anything remarkable.

Friday, June 23. — Summer has come at last, — the longest days, with blazing sunshine, and fervid heat. Yesterday glowed like molten brass. Last night was the most uncomfortably and unsleepably sultry that we have experienced since our residence in Concord; and to-day it scorches again. I have a sort of enjoyment in these seven times heated furnaces of midsummer, even though they make me droop like a thirsty plant. The sunshine can scarcely be too burning for my taste; but I am no enemy to summer-showers. Could I only have the freedom to be perfectly idle now, — no duty to fulfil, no mental or physical labor to perform, — I should be as happy as a squash, and much in the same mode; but the necessity of keeping my brain at work eats into my comfort, as the squash-bugs do into the heart of the vines. I keep myself uneasy and produce little, and almost nothing that is worth producing.

The garden looks well now: the potatoes flourish; the early corn waves in the wind; the squashes, both for summer and winter use, are more forward, I suspect, than those of any of my neighbors. I am forced, however, to carry on a continual warfare with the squash-bugs, who, were I to let them alone for a day, would perhaps quite destroy the prospects of the whole summer. It is impossible not to feel angry with these unconscionable insects, who scruple not to do such excessive mischief to me, with only the profit of a meal or two to themselves. For their own sakes they ought at least to wait till the squashes are better grown. Why is it, I wonder, that Nature has provided such a host of enemies for every useful esculent, while the weeds are suffered to grow unmolested, and are provided with such tenacity of life, and such methods of propagation, that the gardener must maintain a continual struggle or they will hopelessly overwhelm him? What hidden virtue is there in these things, that it is granted them to sow themselves with the wind, and to grapple the earth with this immitigable stubbornness, and to flourish in spite of obstacles, and never to suffer blight beneath any sun or shade, but always to mock their enemies with the same wicked luxuriance? It is truly a mystery, and also a symbol. There is a sort of sacredness about them.• Perhaps, if we could penetrate Nature's secrets, we should find that what we call weeds are more essential to the well-being of the world than the most precious fruit or grain. This may be doubted, however, for there is an unmistakable analogy between these wicked weeds and the bad habits and sinful propensities which have overrun the moral world; and we may as well imagine that there is good in one as in the other.

Our peas are in such forwardness that I should not wonder if we had some of them on the table within a week. The beans have come up ill, and I planted a fresh supply only the day before yesterday. We have watermelons in good advancement, and muskmelons also within three or four days. I set out some tomatoes last night, also some capers. It is my purpose to plant some more corn at the end of the month, or sooner. There ought to be a record of the flower-garden, and of the procession of the wild-flowers, as minute, at least, as of the kitchen vegetables and pot-herbs. Above all, the noting of the appearance of the first roses should not be omitted; nor of the Arethusa, one of the delicatest, gracefullest, and in every manner sweetest of the whole race of flowers. For a fortnight past I have found it in the swampy meadows, growing up to its chin in heaps of wet moss. Its hue is a delicate pink, of various depths of shade, and somewhat in the form of a Grecian helmet. To describe it is a feat beyond my power. Also the visit of two friends, who may fitly enough be mentioned among flowers, ought to have been described. Mrs. F. S—— and Miss A. S——. Also I have neglected to mention the birth of a little white dove.

I never observed, until the present season, how long and late the twilight lingers in these longest days. The orange hue of the western horizon remains till ten o'clock, at least, and how much later I am unable to say. The night before last, I could distinguish letters by this lingering gleam between nine and ten o'clock. The dawn, I suppose, shows itself as early as two o'clock, so that the absolute dominion of night has dwindled to almost nothing. There seems to be also a diminished necessity, or, at all events, a much less possibility, of sleep than at other periods of the year. I get scarcely any sound repose just now. It is summer, and not winter, that steals away mortal life. Well, we get the value of what is taken from us.

Saturday, July 1. — We had our first dish of green peas (a very small one) yesterday. Every day for the last week has been tremendously hot; and our garden flourishes like Eden itself, only Adam could hardly have been doomed to contend with such a ferocious banditti of weeds.

Sunday, July 9. — I know not what to say, and yet cannot be satisfied without marking with a word or two this anniversary...... But life now swells and heaves beneath me like a brim-full ocean ; and the endeavor to comprise any portion of it in words is like trying to dip up the ocean in a goblet.... God bless and keep us! for there is something more awful in happiness than in sorrow, — the latter being earthly and finite, the former composed of the substance and texture of eternity, so that spirits still embodied may well tremble at it.

July 18. — This morning I gathered our first summer-squashes. We should have had them some days earlier, but for the loss of two of the vines, either by a disease of the roots or by those infernal bugs. We have had turnips and carrots several times. Currants are now ripe, and we are in the full enjoyment of cherries, which turn out much more delectable than I anticipated. George Hillard and Mrs. Hillard paid us a visit on Saturday last. On Monday afternoon he left us, and Mrs. Hillard still remains here.

Friday, July 28. — We had green corn for dinner yesterday, and shall have some more to-day, not quite full grown, but sufficiently so to be palatable. There has been no rain, except one moderate shower, for many weeks ; and the earth appears to be wasting away in a slow fever. This weather, I think, affects the spirits very unfavorably. There is an irksomeness, a restlessness, a pervading dissatisfaction, together with an absolute incapacity to bend the mind to any serious effort. With me, as regards literary production, the summer has been unprofitable ; and I only hope that my forces are recruiting themselves for the autumn and winter. For the future, I shall endeavor to be so diligent nine months of the year that I may allow myself a full and free vacation of the other three.

Monday, July 31. — We had our first cucumber yesterday. There were symptoms of rain on Saturday, and the weather has since been as moist as the thirstiest soul could desire.

Wednesday, September 13. — There was a frost the night before last, according to George Prescott ; but no effects of it were visible in our garden. Last night, however, there was another, which has nipped the leaves of the winter-squashes and cucumbers, but seems to have done no other damage. This is a beautiful morning, and promises to be one of those heavenly days that render autumn, after all, the most delightful season of the year. We mean to make a voyage on the river this afternoon.

Sunday, September 23. — I have gathered the two last of our summer-squashes to-day. They have lasted ever since the 18th of July, and have numbered fifty-eight edible ones, of excellent quality. Last Wednesday, I think, I harvested our winter squashes, sixty-three in number, and mostly of fine size. Our last series of green corn, planted about the 1st of July, was good for eating two or three days ago. We still have beans ; and our tomatoes, though backward, supply us with a dish every day or two. My potato-crop promises well ; and, on the whole, my first independent experiment of agriculture is quite a successful one.

This is a glorious day, — bright, very warm, yet with an unspeakable gentleness both in its warmth and brightness. On such days it is impossible not to love Nature, for she evidently loves us. At other seasons she does not give me this impression, or only at very rare intervals ; but in these happy, autumnal days, when she has perfected the harvests, and accomplished every necessary thing that she had to do, she overflows with a blessed superfluity of love. It is good to be alive now. Thank God for breath, — yes, for mere breath ! when it is made up of such a heavenly breeze as this. It comes to the cheek with a real kiss ; it would linger fondly around us, if it might ; but, since it must be gone, it caresses us with its whole kindly heart, and passes onward, to caress likewise the next thing that it meets. There is a pervading blessing diffused over all the world. I look out of the window and think, "O perfect day! O beautiful world! O good God!" And such a day is the promise of a blissful eternity. Our Creator would never have made such weather, and given us the deep heart to enjoy it, above and beyond all thought, if He had not meant us to be immortal. It opens the gates of heaven, and gives us glimpses far inward.

Bless me! this flight has carried me a great way; so now let me come back to our old abbey. Our orchard is fast ripening; and the apples and great thumping pears strew the grass in such abundance that it becomes almost a trouble — though a pleasant one — to gather them. This happy breeze, too, shakes them down, as if it flung fruit to us out of the sky; and often, when the air is perfectly still, I hear the quiet fall of a great apple. Well, we are rich in blessings, though poor in money.....

Friday, October 6. — Yesterday afternoon I took a solitary walk to Walden Pond. It was a cool, windy day, with heavy clouds rolling and tumbling about the sky, but still a prevalence of genial autumn sunshine. The fields are still green, and the great masses of the woods have not yet assumed their many-colored garments; but here and there are solitary oaks of deep, substantial red, or maples of a more brilliant hue, or chestnuts either yellow or of a tenderer green than in summer. Some trees seem to return to their hue of May or early June before they put on the brighter autumnal tints. In some places, along the borders of low and moist land, a whole range of trees were clothed in the perfect gorgeousness of autumn, of all shades of brilliant color, looking like the palette on which Nature was arranging the tints wherewith to paint a picture. These hues appeared to be thrown together

without design; and yet there was perfect harmony among them, and a softness and a delicacy made up of a thousand different brightnesses. There is not, I think, so much contrast among these colors as might at first appear. The more you consider them, the more they seem to have one element among them all, which is the reason that the most brilliant display of them soothes the observer, instead of exciting him. And I know not whether it be more a moral effect or a physical one, operating merely on the eye; but it is a pensive gayety, which causes a sigh often, and never a smile. We never fancy, for instance, that these gayly-clad trees might be changed into young damsels in holiday attire, and betake themselves to dancing on the plain. If they were to undergo such a transformation, they would surely arrange themselves in funeral procession, and go sadly along, with their purple and scarlet and golden garments trailing over the withering grass. When the sunshine falls upon them, they seem to smile; but it is as if they were heart-broken. But it is in vain for me to attempt to describe these autumnal brilliancies, or to convey the impression which they make on me. I have tried a thousand times, and always without the slightest self-satisfaction. Fortunately there is no need of such a record, for Nature renews the picture year after year; and even when we shall have passed away from the world, we can spiritually create these scenes, so that we may dispense with all efforts to put them into words.

Walden Pond was clear and beautiful as usual. It tempted me to bathe; and, though the water was thrillingly cold, it was like the thrill of a happy death. Never was there such transparent water as this. · I threw sticks into it, and saw them float suspended on an almost invisible medium. It seemed as if the pure air were beneath them, as well as above. It is fit for baptisms; but one would not wish it to be polluted by having sins washed into it. None but angels should bathe in it; but blessed babies might be dipped into its bosom.

In a small and secluded dell that opens upon the most beautiful cove of the whole lake, there is a little hamlet of huts or shanties, inhabited by the Irish people who are at work upon the railroad. There are three or four of these habitations, the very rudest, I should imagine, that civilized men ever made for themselves, — constructed of rough boards, with the protruding ends. Against some of them the earth is heaped up to the roof, or nearly so; and when the grass has had time to sprout upon them, they will look like small natural hillocks, or a species of ant-hills, — something in which Nature has a larger share than man. These huts are placed beneath the trees, oaks, walnuts, and white-pines, wherever the trunks give them space to stand; and by thus adapting themselves to natural interstices, instead of making new ones, they do not break or disturb the solitude and seclusion of the place. Voices are heard, and the shouts and laughter of children, who play about like the sunbeams that come down through the branches. Women are washing in open spaces, and long lines of whitened clothes are extended from tree to tree, fluttering and gambolling in the breeze. A pig, in a sty even more extemporary than the shanties, is grunting and poking his snout through the clefts of his habitation. The household pots and kettles are seen at the doors; and a glance within shows the rough benches that serve for chairs, and the bed upon the floor. The visitor's nose takes note of the fragrance of a pipe. And yet, with all these homely items, the repose and sanctity of the old wood do not seem to be destroyed or profaned. It overshadows these poor people, and assimilates them somehow or other to the character of its natural inhabitants. Their presence did not shock me any more than if I had merely discovered a squirrel's nest in a tree. To be sure, it is a torment to see the great, high, ugly embankment of the railroad, which is here thrusting itself into the lake, or along its margin, in close vicinity to this picturesque little hamlet. I have seldom seen anything more beautiful than the cove on the border of which the huts are situated; and the more I looked, the lovelier it grew. The trees overshadowed it deeply; but on one side there was some brilliant shrubbery which seemed to light up the whole picture with the effect of a sweet and melancholy smile. I felt as if spirits were there, — or as if these shrubs had a spiritual life. In short, the impression was indefinable; and, after gazing and musing a good while, I retraced my steps through the Irish hamlet, and plodded on along a wood-path.

According to my invariable custom, I mistook my way; and, emerging upon the road, I turned my back instead of my face towards Concord, and walked on very diligently till a guide-board informed me of my mistake. I then turned about, and was shortly overtaken by an old yeoman in a chaise, who kindly offered me a drive, and soon set me down in the village.

THE NORMAN CONQUEST.

THIS month of October completes the eighth century since the battle of Hastings, perhaps the most important action that the modern world has known, with the single exception of the conflict that checked the advance of the Saracens in Europe in the eighth century, — if the battle of Tours can properly be considered an event of modern history. The issue of the battle of Hastings determined the course of English history ; and when we observe how influential has been the part of England ever since it was fought, and bear in mind that the English race, great as it is, can scarcely be said to have got beyond the morning-time of its existence, we find it difficult to exaggerate the importance of a conflict by which its career for eight hundred years has been deeply and permanently colored. There is not a great event in English or American annals which is not directly traceable to what was done in the year 1066 by that buccaneering band which William the Bastard led from Normandy to England, to enforce a claim that had neither a legal nor a moral foundation, and which never could have been established had Harold's conduct been equal to his valor, and had Fortune favored the just cause. The sympathies of every fair-minded reader of the story of the Conquest must be with the Saxons ; and yet is it impossible to deny that the event at Hastings was well for the world. It is with Harold as it is with Hannibal : our feelings are at war with our judgment as we read their histories. It is not possible to peruse the noble account that Dr. Arnold has left us of the Carthaginian's splendid struggle against the Roman aristocracy without feeling pained by its result. The feelings of men are with the man, and adverse to the order before which his genius failed. So is it with respect to Harold. Hastings, like

Zama, impresses us as having been a "dishonest victory," to borrow the words with which Milton so emphatically characterizes Chæronea. But "cool reflection" leads to other conclusions, and justifies the earthly course of Providence, against which we are so often disposed to complain. There can be no doubt, in the mind of any moral man, that the invasion of England by Duke William was a wicked proceeding, — that it was even worse than Walker's invasions of Spanish-American countries, and as bad as an unprovoked attack on Cuba by this country, such as would have been made had the pro-slavery party remained in power. But it is not the less true, that much good came from William's action, and that nearly all that is excellent in English and American history is the fruit of that action. The part that England has had in the world's course for eight centuries, including her stupendous work of colonization, is second to nothing that has been done by any nation, not even to the doings of the Roman republic : and to that part Saxon England never could have been equal.

The race that ruled in England down to the day of Hastings — call it the Saxon race, if you like the name, and for convenience' sake — was a slow, a sluggish, and a stupid race ; and it never could have made a first-class nation of the insular kingdom. There is little in the history of the Saxons that allows us to believe they were capable of accomplishing anything that was great. The Danish invasions, as they are called, were of real use to England, as they prevented that country from reverting to barbarism, which assuredly would have been its fate had the Anglo-Saxons remained its undisturbed possessors. "In the ninth, tenth, and eleventh centuries," says Mr. Worsaae, "the Anglo-Saxons had greatly degenerated from their fore-fathers. Relatives sold one another into thraldom; lewdness and ungodliness were become habitual; and cowardice had increased to such a degree that, according to the old chroniclers, one Dane would often put ten Anglo-Saxons to flight. Before such a people could be conducted to true freedom and greatness it was necessary that an entirely new vigor should be infused into the decayed stock. This vigor was derived from the Scandinavian North, where neither Romans nor any other conquerors had domineered over the people, and where heathenism, with all its roughness and all its love of freedom and bravery, still held absolute sway." [*]

The work which the Danes began was completed by the Normans; and it may well be doubted if the Normans ever could have effected much in England had they not been preceded by the Danes. The Danes were Northmen, as are the Swedes and Norwegians. By Normans are meant the governing race in Neustria, the duchy of Normandy The Northmen who settled in Neustria, and who became the foremost people of those times, — they and their descendants, — did in a portion of France what their kinsmen the Danes were doing in England. Circumstances gave to the *Normans* a consequence in history that is denied to the *Danes;* but the influence of the latter was very great on English life, and on the course of English events; and Norman influence on that life, and over those events, was materially aided by the earlier action of the Danish invaders of England. The difference between the Northmen in France and the Northmen in England was this: the former, to a very great extent, became Frenchmen, while the latter did not become Englishmen. The former, from Northmen, became Normans, and took much from the people among whom they settled. The latter remained Northmen, for the

[*] An Account of the Danes and Norwegians in England, Scotland, and Ireland, by J. J. Worsaae, Sec. 1. p. 6.

most part, taking little or nothing from the English, while they bestowed a good deal upon them. But the Northmen who became Normans underwent changes that rendered it impossible that the Northmen in England should coalesce with them after Duke William's victory in 1066. The English Northmen were strongly attached to individual freedom, as all Northmen were originally; but the Normans had learned to be feudalists in France, and this necessarily made foes of men who by blood ought to have been friends. Many of those who offered the stoutest resistance to the Conqueror were Danes; and it was not until many years after Hastings that the English Northmen submitted to the French Normans. The English Northmen, nevertheless, were of real use to the Normans, by what they had effected long before the expedition of William was thought of, and when the Normans had not become the chief champions of feudalism. The immediate effect of Danish action on William's fortunes, too, was very great. The Saxon Harold was compelled to fight a battle with the Scandinavian invaders of England but twenty days before Hastings; and these invaders sought to place a Danish or Norwegian dynasty on the English throne. Harold was victorious in his conflict with the Northmen; but the weakness and exhaustion consequent on the exertions necessary to repel them were among the leading causes of his failure before the Normans.

The people who gave their name to what is called the Norman Conquest of England [*] were the most extraordinary race of the Middle Ages. This can be

[*] "What we call purchase, *perquisitio,*" says Blackstone, "the feudists called conquest, *conquisitio;* both denoting any means of acquiring an estate out of the common course of inheritance. And this is still the proper phrase in the law of Scotland, as it was among the Norman jurists, who styled the first purchaser (that is, him who brought the estate into the family which at present owns it) the conqueror, or *conquereur,* which seems to be all that was meant by the appellation which was given to William the Norman." Had Harold been victorious at Hastings, he would, according to the feudists, have been the Conqueror; that is, the man who brought England into his family.

said of them, too, without subscribing to the extravagant eulogies of their ardent admirers, who are too much in the habit of speaking of them in terms that would be misplaced were they applied to Athenians of the age of Pericles. The simple truth concerning them shows that they were superior in every respect to all their contemporaries, unless an exception be made on behalf of the Mussulmans of Spain. The Northmen who came first upon Southern Europe were mere barbarians, but there were among them men of great natural powers, as there were among those barbarians who overran the Roman empire ; and they were able to take advantage of the wretched condition of Europe, as earlier barbarians had profited from the wretched condition of Rome. Of these men, Rollo was one of the most eminent ; and beyond all others of the Northmen his action has had the largest influence on human affairs, — an influence, too, that promises to last ; for it is working vigorously at this moment, though he has been more than nine centuries in his grave, and though to most persons he is as much a mythical character as Hercules, and more so than Romulus. We know that he was the founder of Normandy in the early part of the tenth century ; and but for his action in obtaining a southern home for himself and his heathen followers, the conquest of England never could have been attempted in a regular manner ; and the stream of English history must have run altogether differently, in a political sense, even had Northmen, as distinguished from Normans, succeeded in establishing themselves in that country. It was the French character of the Normans which rendered their subjugation of England so important an event, giving to it its peculiar significance, and causing it to bear so strongly on European, Asiatic, and American history. The Northmen became Christians and Normans. It is not uncommon to speak of them as if they retained their Norwegian characteristics in " the pleasant land of France," and

were in the habit of looking back to the home of their youth, or of their fathers, with that sort of fondness and regret which were felt by those Englishmen who founded the American nation. This is all wrong. The Northmen had left the North for the same reason that other men leave their countries, — the only reason that ever causes them to do so, — because the North did not afford them means of support. Had they remained at home, they would have starved ; and therefore they turned their backs on that home, and became plunderers. Some returned home, bearing with them much spoil ; but others settled abroad, and thought no more of the North. They cut the connection entirely. Like an earlier " brood of winter," they found ample compensation for all they had left behind in " the brighter day and skies of azure hue " of Southern lands. They thought they had made a good exchange of " Northern pines for Southern roses."

Of these last, the Normans proper were the most noted, and they have the first place of all their race in the world's annals. They changed in everything, from soul to skin. They became Christians, and they took new names. Their original language was soon displaced by the French, and became so utterly lost that hardly more is known of it than we know of the Etruscan tongue. " The Danish language," says Sir Francis Palgrave, " was never prevalent or strong in Normandy. The Northmen had long been talking themselves into Frenchmen ; and in the second generation, the half-caste Northmen, the sons of French wives and French concubines, spoke the Romane-French as their mothers' tongue." The same great authority says : " In the cities, Bayeux only excepted, hardly any language but French was spoken. Forty years after Rollo's establishment, the Danish language struggled for existence. It was in Normandy that the *Langue d'oil* acquired its greatest polish and regularity. The earliest specimens of the French language, in the proper sense of the term, are now surrendered by the French philologists to the Normans. The phenomenon of the organs of speech yielding to social or moral influences, and losing the power of repeating certain sounds, was prominently observable amongst the Normans. No modern French gazette-writer could disfigure English names more whimsically than the Domesday Commissioners. To the last, the Normans never could learn to say ' Lincoln,' — they never could get nearer than ' Nincol,' or ' Nicole.' " The "chivalry" of Virginia and the Carolinas — our Southern Northmen — might cite this last fact in evidence of their tongues having a Norman twang. They never have been able to say " Lincoln," though they make a nearer approach to proper pronunciation of the word than was vouchsafed to the genuine Normans when they say " Abe Linkin." That the Normans cherished the thought of their Northern origin is a modern error. Sir F. Palgrave, with literal accuracy, assures us that they " dismissed all practical recollection in their families of their original Scandinavian ancestry. Not one of their nobles ever thought of deducing his lineage from the Hersers or Jarls or Vikings who occupy so conspicuous a place in Norwegian history, not even through the medium of any traditional fable. Roger de Montgomery designated himself as ' Northmannus Northmannorum '; but, for all practical purposes, Roger was a Frenchman of the Frenchmen, though he might not like to own it. This ancestorial reminiscence must have resulted from some peculiar fancy ; no Montgomery possessed or transmitted any memorial of his Norman progenitors. The very name of Rollo's father, ' Senex quidam in partibus Daciæ,' was unknown to Rollo's grandchildren, and if not known, worse than unknown, neglected." [*]

* The History of Normandy and of England, Vol. I. pp. 703, 704. One of the greatest historical works of a country and an age singularly rich in historical literature, but incomplete, like the works of Macaulay, Niebuhr, and Arnold, and the last work of Prescott. The third and fourth volumes, post-

Another unfounded notion respecting the Normans relates to purity of lineage. To read some historians, you might come to the conclusion that the Normans were an unmixed race, and that they prided themselves on the blueness of their blood, and were the most exclusive of peoples. Nothing of the kind. Like most peoples who have done much, the Normans were a mixed race. They took to themselves all who would come to them, who were worth the taking. The old Roman lay of the asylum on the Palatine Hill might almost serve as matter for a Norman *sirvente*, for the policy which it attributes to Romulus, and which was followed by his successors, was the policy adopted by Rollo, and which his successors maintained. Says Sir F. Palgrave, " When treating of the ' Normans,' we must always consider the appellation as descriptive rather than ethnographical, indicative of political relations rather than of race. Like William the Conqueror's army, the hosts of Rollo were augmented by adventurers from all countries. Rollo exhibited a remarkable flexibility of character ; he encouraged settlers from all parts of France and the Gauls and England, and his successors systematically obeyed the precedent." Most such adventurers in any age of the world must be of the most ancient of families, the families, to wit, of " robbers and reivers," the enlisted rascality of the earth, but none the worse workmen because their patron is St. Cain. There is a great deal of work to be done that can be done only by such fellows. It is sagely said that the world would be but ill peopled if none but the wise were to marry. It is certain that the world would get forward very slowly if none but the mild and the moral were active in its business. There is an immense amount of business to be accomplished that the mild cannot do, and which the moral will

humously published in 1864. — Sir Francis died in 1861, — are well edited by the author's son, Mr. Francis Turner Palgrave, who honorably upholds the honored name he inherits.

not do. How can it be expected of mild men that they should cut human throats, when they cannot be trusted even to stick the sheep which they have no hesitation in eating? How unreasonable it would be to expect moral men to become soldiers, — and the soldier's trade is the only permanent pursuit, save the pursuits of the grave-digger and the hangman, — when so exemplary a personage as the great Duke of Wellington gravely said, on his oath and on his honor, that the army is no place for moral and religious men? The felons who flocked to Rollo's standard wellnigh a thousand years ago were recruited from the "dangerous classes" of those remote days, and were probably as useful in the task of civilizing the world as, according to the assertion of one of the most eminent of English divines and historians, are rough and lawless men in that of Europeanizing Polynesia.*

Dr. Lappenberg, whose authority is great in all that relates to the history of the Normans, confirms what is said by Sir F. Palgrave of the ignorance of the North and the indifference to it which characterized the Normans. Speaking of the Norman literature, he observes: "In vain we seek herein imitations of the old Norse poesy, or allusions to the history or customs of Scandinavia. There may, perhaps, exist more resemblance between the heroic sagas of the North and the romances of chivalry of the South of Europe, both having for subjects wonderful adventures, and the praise of heroism and beauty; but from this resemblance it cannot be concluded that the Anglo-Norman poets have borrowed their fictions from the Norman skalds. We have not a single proof that they were acquainted with any saga or any skaldic composition.

* Merivale, History of the Romans under the Empire; Vol. IV. p. 297, note: "The civilization of barbarians, at least their material cultivation, has been generally more advanced by instructors whose moral superiority was less strongly marked, than where the teachers and the taught have few common sympathies and points of contact. Thus, in our own times, rough whalers and brutal pirates have done more to Europeanize the natives of Polynesia than the missionaries."

All remembrance of their national poetry was as completely obliterated among the posterity of the Northmen in France, as if, in traversing the ocean, they had drank of the water of Lethe. This total oblivion of their original home they have in common with the West Goths, who in Castilian poesy have not left the faintest trace of their original manners and opinions. The same remark has been applied to the Vareger, who founded a royal dynasty in Russia, and to whom that country, as a Russian author remarks, is not indebted for a single new idea. The causes are here the same with those that effected a complete oblivion of their mother tongue, namely, their inferior civilization, their intermixture with the natives, their marriages with the women of the country, who knew no other traditions than those of their native land. In Normandy, too, the Christian clergy must have suppressed every memorial of the ancient mythology." * Further, "Whatever partiality the Normans may have entertained for history, they nevertheless betrayed an almost perfect indifference for their original country. The historians of Normandy describe the heathen North as a den of robbers. After an interval of two centuries, they knew nothing of the events that had

* A History of England under the Norman Kings, etc., pp. 84, 85, and 87. Dr. Lappenberg is emphatic on the subject of the formation of the Norman race through the junction of various races. "Rolf [Rollo] and his companions were like those meteors which traverse the air with incredible swiftness," he says, "and in vanishing leave behind them long streams of fire which the eye gazes on with amazement. The Northmen who settled in Neustria gradually became lost among the French, a mixture of Gauls and Romans, Franks and Burgundians, West Goths and Saracens, friends and foes, barbarians and civilized nations. Ten sorts of language, and with them, perhaps, as many forms of government, were lost amid this mass of peoples. French and foreigners have visited Normandy in search of some traces of the old Scandinavian colonies, or at least of same testimonial of their long sojourn there, and one or other memorial characteristic of this daring people. All have admired the prosperity of the province, to which the fertility of the soil and its manufactures and commerce have contributed; but vainly have they sought for the original Northmen in the present inhabitants. With the exception of some faint resemblances, they have met with nothing Norsk." — pp. 65, 66.

caused the founder of their ruling family to forsake the North; they did not even know where Denmark and Norway lay. Benoît de Ste More begins his chronicle with a geographic sketch, in which he takes Denmark for Dacia, and places it at the mouth of the Danube, between the extensive countries of the Alani and the Getæ, which are always covered with ice, and surrounded by a chain of mountains." The excellent chronicler's geographical notions seem to have been about as clear as those of Lolah, who tells Katinka that

> " Spain 's an island near
> Morocco, betwixt Egypt and Tangier."

The earliest Norman chroniclers show that the Normans, or rather the Northmen, bore much ill-will toward the French; and this prejudice, it has correctly been said, "probably lasted as long as their Northern physiognomy, their fair hair, and other characteristics whereby they were distinguished from the French." But they soon became the flower of French races, and were regarded as Frenchmen in all the lands to which they were led by their valor, their enterprise, their ambition, and their avarice. They continued to avail themselves of the talents of other races long after Northmen had been converted into Normans, greatly to their own advantage, and considerably to the advantage of others. "Inclination, policy, interest," says Palgrave, "strengthened the impulse given by the diffusion of the Romane speech. Liberality was the Norman virtue. 'Norman talent,' or 'Norman taste,' or 'Norman art,' are expressions intelligible and definite, conveying clear ideas, substantially true and yet substantially inaccurate. What, for example, do we intend when we speak of Norman architecture? Who taught the Norman architect? Ah, when you contemplate the structures raised by Lanfranc or Anselm, will not the reply conduct you beyond the Alps, and lead you to Pavia or Aosta, — the cities where these fathers of the Anglo-Norman Church were nurtured, their

learning acquired, or their taste informed? Amongst the eminent men who gloriously adorn the Anglo-Norman annals, perhaps the smallest number derive their origin from Normandy. Discernment in the choice of talent, and munificence in rewarding ability, may be truly ascribed to Rollo's successors; open-handed, open-hearted, not indifferent to birth or lineage, but never allowing station or origin, nation or language, to obstruct the elevation of those whose talent, learning, knowledge, or aptitude gave them their patent of nobility." [*] The Normans won their fame, as the Romans their empire, through aid of various races, and by borrowing and assimilating whatever they found of good among all the peoples with whom they came in contact, — meaning by good what was useful for the promotion of their purposes.

The old Northmen in Neustria did not give way without a struggle, not for existence only, but for victory, of which at one time their prospect was by no means bad. The Danish party was strong in the time of Rollo, and it might have established itself over Normandy in the early years of his son, William I., who deemed his Norman sovereignty lost, and who at one time showed the white feather in a very un-Norman-like manner, and in quite the reverse fashion to that adopted by Henri IV. at Ivry. At length he recovered his courage, and, delivering battle, he won a complete victory, which was ruinous to the vanquished. They were exterminated, and Riulph, their leader, was captured, and blinded by William's orders. It is supposed he died under the operation. William's cruelty is attributed to his earlier cowardice, and it is an old saw that no one is so cruel as a victorious coward; but cruelty was not so uncommon a thing in the year 933 that there should be any necessity for attributing the Norman's

[*] The History of Normandy and of England, Vol. I. pp. 704, 705. Lanfranc, who was made Archbishop of Canterbury by the Conqueror, was a native of Pavia, and Anselm, his successor, a native of Aosta.

savageness to the reaction from fear. He probably had called his cowardice caution. His success settled the character of Normandy, which became, or rather continued to be, a French country; and its people were Normans, the result of a liberal mixture of many races, from whom were to issue the rulers of many lands. The combat of the *Pré de la Bataille* took place just four generations before Hastings, and had its issue been different the current of history might have run in a very different direction from that in which it has set for eight centuries; but the consequences of such a change "must be left to that superhuman knowledge which the schoolmen call *media scientia*, and which consists in knowing all that would have happened had events been otherwise than they have been." The question at issue was whether the Normans should live as Frenchmen or disappear; and William's triumph secured the ascendency of the Romane party, who alone could establish Normandy. When his son, Richard sans Peur, became chief of the Normans, A. D. 943, Normandy was a power in Europe, and virtually a free state, — for its rulers were "independent as the kings of France, whose superiority they acknowledged, but whose behests they never held themselves bound to obey."

The Normans soon made themselves felt in Europe. They became the foremost of Christian communities, and were distinguished in arts and arms and letters. They were the politest people of their time, and in their manners and modes of life they presented strong contrasts to the general coarseness of the period in which they flourished. Their valor seemed to increase with their culture; and if they were admired by the few because of their intellectual superiority, they were dreaded by the many because of their dauntless bravery and the energy and success which characterized their military exploits. Though often fighting at great odds, they were rarely defeated. They furnished the most distin-

guished adventurers of an adventurous age. There is nothing more romantic than the history of the Norman family of Hauteville, which sent forth a number of men whose exertions in Southern Europe had great effect in the eleventh century. Foremost of his countrymen in courage and capacity was the adventurer Robert de Hauteville, better known as Robert Guiscard, substantially the founder of that Neapolitan kingdom which we have seen absorbed into the new kingdom of Italy. His daughter married a son of one of the Byzantine Emperors, who was dethroned; and Robert was thus enabled to enter on a series of Eastern conquests, which would have ended in the taking of Constantinople had not imperative circumstances compelled him to return to Italy. A few years later he resumed his Oriental schemes, but died before he could complete them, and when everything promised him success. Had a Norman dynasty been established at Constantinople, at the close of the eleventh century, by so able a man as Robert Guiscard, it is probable the Lower Empire would have renewed its life, and that the Normans would have become as influential in the East as their contemporary conquest of England had made them in the West. The feudal system, of which they were the great masters, might as easily have been introduced into Greece as it was into England, and with the effect of producing an order of men who would have proved themselves more than a match for any force that the Mussulman could have brought against the new nation. There would have been a regular flow of Normans and other hardy adventurers to Byzantium, and the Turks never would have been allowed to cross the Hellespont to establish themselves in Europe, and would have been fortunate had they been able to keep the Normans from crossing the Hellespont to establish themselves in Asia. Thousands of those fanatics who were so soon to cover the Syrian sands with their bones, as Crusaders, would have been attracted to Greece, and would have done Christendom better service there than ever they were allowed to render it under the Godfreys and Baldwins and Raymonds, the Louises and Richards and Fredericks, who piously fought for the redemption of the Redeemer's sepulchre. Indeed the Holy Sepulchre could best have been freed from infidel pollution by operations from Greece, had Greece renewed her life under a dynasty worthy of the Greeks of old; and Asia, the Land of Light, might have been relieved from the thick darkness under which it has so long labored, had Norman genius and Norman valor been authoritatively employed to direct the Christian populations of the East, reinforced by the surplus adventurers of the West, against the Mussulmans. The West might have liquidated its debt to the East, by restoring Christianity to it.

All this was on the cards, had Robert Guiscard lived a few years longer, — and he was one of many sons of a poor and petty Norman baron, and superior to thousands of his countrymen only in the circumstance that he was more favored by Fortune. We are not to judge of what might have been effected by a Norman dynasty in Greece by the miserable failure of that Latin empire of which Greece was the scene in the thirteenth century, and which grew out of the capture of Constantinople by the French and the Venetians. That empire had not the elements of success in it; and it was established too late, and on foundations too feeble, to meet the demands of the time. Its founders lacked that legislative capacity with which the Normans were so liberally endowed. Though we cannot subscribe in full to Mr. Acton Warburton's enthusiastic estimate of the Norman race, we believe him to be substantially correct in what he says of their legislative genius. He dwells with unction on the strong tendency to institutions that ever characterized them. This tendency, he observes, strongly indicates "the profound

sentiment of perpetuity, inherent in the Norman mind, to which everything was valueless that shared not in some degree its own enduring character. Abhorrent alike of despotism and license, they imparted this love of institutions wherever they came. In their days the world was passing through a fierce ordeal. A stern necessity lay on the whole system of things, a necessity which may be expressed in this brief formula, — the sword. In their several missions, if I may so speak, the Normans were forced to use the appointed instrument of the hour; but the readiness with which the sword was sheathed, the facility with which the soldier changed into the citizen, shows how deeply they felt that a state of hostilities, bloodshed, and disorder could not be the normal condition of man. And so we see them pass at once from the battle-field to the council-chamber. The fierce warrior of yesterday is the thoughtful legislator of to-day. The first interval of repose was ever employed in devising means for giving stability to their acquisitions, and a constitutional form to the society in which they were to be vested. Among the Teutons, such a task was never referred to the wisdom of any one leader, however successful, — any oligarchy of chiefs, however eminent. From time immemorial, the provisions from which their laws were derived, and on which their societies were based, were the emanations of free public opinion. Their armies were triumphant, because the soldier yielded up his will implicitly to his general; their societies were vigorous and stable, because, when the soldier became a citizen, he resumed that will again. No sooner had conquest and peace transmuted the army into a society, than the dominant sentiment appeared, — the sentiment of rational independence, — resulting, as the community formed, in liberal institutions."[*] Had this legislative spirit been applied to Greece at the close of the eleventh

[*] Rollo and his Race; or, Footsteps of the Normans, Vol. II. pp. 107 – 109.

century, the effect would have been to create there a powerful nation ; and the Crescent never would have triumphed over the Cross in that land from which the West has drawn so much that is of the highest value in all its processes of intellectual culture.

There is a reverse to this picture of the Normans. They had some very bad qualities, for they had no higher claims to perfection than is found in the case of any other people. Mr. James Augustus St. John, speaking of the Norman princess Emma, who married the English Ethelred, says, after admitting her great personal beauty, that " her mental qualities were very far from corresponding with the charms of her person. Like all other Normans, she was greedy of gold, ambitious, selfish, voluptuous, and in an eminent degree prone to treachery." * This may stand for a portrait of the whole Norman race. Nor does it detract from their aristocratical spirit that they were ever fond of money, or from their chivalrous spirit that they were faithless when they supposed treachery would best promote their interests. Aristocracies are always money-seekers, and often money-grubbers ; and they plunder all whom they have the power to spoil. *Alieni appetens* is ever their motto, but *sui profusus* does always go with it. The American slavocracy were the aristocracy of this country, and they were far more " greedy of gold " than ever "Yankees" have been. Treachery is common to the chivalrous classes, and the history of chivalry is full of instances of its display by men who claimed a monopoly of honor. Our Southern " chivalry " were unfaithful to every compact they made, and it was their infidelity that brought about their fall. The dangers that now

threaten the country exist only because the party vanquished in the late civil war are bent upon breaking the terms on which they were admitted to mercy. They are fond of calling themselves Normans, though we have not heard much of their Norman origin since their Hastings went against them ; but in respect to treachery and cruelty, and disregard of the rights of the poor and the helpless, they are the match of all the barons of Normandy.

The Normans were often cruel, and some of their modes of punishing their defeated enemies — blinding them, and cutting off their feet and hands, and inflicting on them the most degrading of mutilations — might lead one to suppose they were of Eastern origin, were not such practices traceable to the Northmen. These practices imply a grossness of mind that is much at war with the common notion of the gentleness and cultivation of the Norman nobles. They were noted for their craft, their spirit of intrigue, and their readiness to get possession of the property of others by any and all means. The most unscrupulous modern devotee of Mammon would be ashamed of deeds that never disturbed the placid egotism of men who considered themselves the flower of humanity and the salt of the earth, — and whose estimate of themselves has seldom been called in question. The fairer side of their conduct with regard to money is visible in their sensible encouragement of "business" in all the forms which it then knew. "Annual Mercantile Fairs," says Sir F. Palgrave, "were accustomed in Normandy. Established by usage and utility, ere recognized by the law, their origin bespake a healthy energy. Foreign manufacturers were welcomed as settlers in the Burghs, — the richer the better. No grudge was entertained against the Fleming ; and the material prosperity of the country and the briskness of commerce carried on in all the great towns, proves that the pack-horses could tramp along the old Roman roads with facility. Indeed, amongst the Normans the commercial spirit was indigenous.

---

* What Sir F. Palgrave says of the famous son of Robert Guiscard is applicable generally to the Normans : " Bohemond was affectionate and true to father, wife, and children, pleasant, affable, and courteous : yet wrapped up in selfishness, possessed by insatiate ambition and almost diabolical cruelty, proud and faithless, but in spite of all these vices so seductive as to command the admiration even of those who knew him to be a heartless demon."— *History*, Vol. IV. p. 471.

The Danes and the folk of Danish blood were diligent traders. The greed of gain unites readily with desperate bravery. When occasion served, Drake would deal like a Dutchman. Any mode of making money enters into facile combination with the bold rapacity of the Flibustier." There was much material prosperity in Normandy at the close of the tenth century, or less than a hundred years after Rollo had established himself and his followers on French soil. The burgher class throve amazingly, and were the envy of all who knew their condition ; and their military skill and valor were as famous as their success in the industrial arts, and their wealth, which was its consequence. Free they were, or they would have been neither rich nor valiant. The peasantry, too, were a superior people, who enjoyed much freedom, and who exhibited their bravery whenever there was call for its exhibition, — facts which show that they must have been well governed, and which tend to elevate our conception of the merits of their rulers.

There was no such thing as a caste of nobles in Normandy for very many years after that country passed into the hands of the Northmen. About two generations after the death of Rollo, Richard le Bon, one of the most popular of his descendants, set up the standard of exclusion, and created that Norman nobility of which the world has heard so much for eight hundred years. The clergy were too powerful in those days to be much affected by his action, and the burghers were too rich to be put down by a newly created nobility ; but the peasantry were greatly injured by the change, as it created an order who were interested in oppressing them. They conspired, and their course bears some resemblance to that of the Fenians of our day. The "Commune" was a word as alarming to Richard le Bon and his nobility as " Fenian " was at first to the most bigoted of Orangemen. The Duke employed Raoul, Count of Ivri, to crush the Communists. Raoul was the son of a rich peasant, but he had no sympathy with his father's order. As in modern life the most determined aristocrat is often the man whose origin is the lowest, so was it nine centuries ago, in Normandy. Raoul was a sort of Claverhouse and Jeffreys in one person, and he " enjoyed the sport of dogging the Villainage. He fell upon the Communists ; — caught them in the very fact, — holding a Lodge, — swearing in new members. Terrible was the catastrophe. No trial vouchsafed. No judge called in. Happy the wretch whose weight stretched the halter. The country was visited by fire and flame ; the rebels were scourged, their eyes plucked out, their limbs chopped off, they were burnt alive ; whilst the rich were impoverished and ruined by confiscations and fines." Such were the good old times, which never can return, Heaven be praised ! Such was the origin of the Norman nobility, destined to become the patricians of the world. The cruelty with which the peasants were treated by the new nobles is a type of the system that ever was pursued by men of " the gentle Norman blood " toward a restless people. " The folk of Normandie " had no mercy on men who disputed, or even called in question, their right to unrestricted dominion.

The Cotentin was the most important part of Normandy, — was to Normandy what Normandy was to the rest of Europe. It has been well described as " not merely the physical bulwark of Normandy, but the very kernel of Norman nationality." It now forms a part of the *Département de la Manche*, and it holds Cherbourg in its bosom, — the *Cæsaris Burgus* of the Romans, which the French imperial historian of the first Cæsar is completing as a defiance to England, thus finishing what was long since begun under the old monarchy. Ages ago — even before the Romans had entered Gaul — what we call Cherbourg is believed to have attracted Gaulish attention because of its marine advantages. It is all but certain that the Romans fortified it. The Normans were children of the sea, and they did not neglect it. The Normans of the Cotentin were the purest men of their race. They kept up that connection with the ocean from which some other Normans revolted; and they were led from the land to the sea by the same inducement that had sent their ancestors out of Scania,— the inability to find food there. "The population," we are assured, "was teeming, the sterile land could not feed them, but the roaring surges surrounded them. All loved the sea, and upon the waves, and beyond the waves, they were ever seeking their fortunes. From Hauteville, nigh Coutances, came the conquerors of Apulia and Sicily. And when we call over Battle-Abbey Roll, or search the Domesday record, or trace the lineage of our [the British] aristocracy, we shall find that the lords of these same Cotentin castles, with scarcely an exception, served in the Conqueror's army, or settled in the realm they won." The plain English of which is, that they were the cleverest, the most active, and the most successful robbers of their day and nation.

England was too near Normandy not to be an object of the first interest to the Normans. At the close of the tenth century King Ethelred II. adopted a course that was destined to have the most memorable consequences. Richard le Bon bore himself toward the English much the same as the English of to-day bore themselves toward us in the Secession war. The Danes were then the worst enemies of England, and the Norman government so far anticipated the Palmerstonian policy of neutrality, which consists in favoring the enemies of those whom you hate, as to throw open its ports to the ravagers of Normandy's neighbor. "Without sharing the danger," observes Sir F. Palgrave, "Normandy prospered upon the prey which the Danskerman made in England. The Normans were a thriving and money-getting people. The great fair of Guipry attests their national tendency. The liberal policy of the Dukes is also forcibly illustrated by the remarkable

treaty of peace concluded between Richard le Bon and Olave, the Norskman, securing to the rovers the right of free trade in Normandy. No certificate of origin was required when the big bales of English stuffs were offered to the chapman at the bridge-head of Rouen; and the perils of England were much enhanced by the *entente cordiale* — this expression has become technical, and therefore untranslatable — subsisting between Romane Normandy and the Northmen of the North."

There is something amusing in this extract; for it describes, as it were, and in advance, the state of things that existed during our late war. The Secessionists were our Danes, who, if they did not ravage our lands, cut up our commerce at a fearful rate, and not only found shelter and aid wherever the English flag flies in authority, but were furnished with ships by England and with men to work and to fight them, so that our last sea-fight was won over our old foe on that summer day when the Kearsarge sent the Alabama to look after the old Raven craft of the Northmen that may be lying under the old Norman waters, and did it, too, off the Cotentin shore, just where the conflict between Saxons and Normans began.

King Ethelred, like President Lincoln in the case of the English, was so unreasonable as to complain of the conduct of the Normans; and, again like our lamented chief, he could not find any excuse for piratical action in the fact that "the Normans were a thriving and money-getting people," and supposed they had the right to get money by encouraging robbery. But, unlike the American President, the Saxon king determined to have prompt and ample vengeance — if he could get it. He indulged in as much loud language as was uttered in Vienna last June, when Sadowa was yet an unknown name. He was bent upon vengeance, stern and terrible. Now, vengeance is a commodity that is dear when it is procurable *gratis*, but sometimes it is not obtainable at any price. And so Ethelred found it, to his cost. Having formed his resolution to invade Normandy, and lay it waste with fire and sword, and bring back Richard le Bon with him in chains to England, it remained only to execute his design. The English fleet sailed for the Cotentin, and landed a force which should have done great things. But if the Normans of the Cotentin were stout thieves, not the less were they stout soldiers. No greater error than that men must have clean consciences to be good warriors. The Normans rose to a man — and even to a woman — against the invaders. Knights and seamen and peasants and the peasants' wives, all armed; and the English were beaten so badly that they could not have been beaten worse, had their cause been utterly devilish. But few of them escaped, — probably those who had the sense to run first; and they got off in six ships, all the rest of the fleet falling into the hands of the Normans. The Norman Duke and the British Basileus proceeded to make peace, and the peace-making business led to a marriage, one of many royal marriages which have produced extraordinary consequences, and led to much fighting, as if there were a natural connection between wedlock and war. In private life, marriage not unfrequently leads to contention; in public life, contention often leads to marriage. Ethelred sought to "engraft the branch of Cerdic upon the stem of Rollo," in the hope of increasing the power of England. He asked for the hand of Emma, sister of Richard le Bon, and obtained it. This union was every way unfortunate, and prepared the road for the Conquest. The Normans who accompanied Emma to England, and those who followed her, are described as "subtle, intriguing, false, and capable of any act of treason which promised to further their own fortunes." They behaved as members of "superior races" generally behave in countries inhabited by "inferior races." They obtained power and place, and used their influence to the detriment of England. The king and queen did not live happily. One of their children

was Edward the Confessor, who is popularly considered the very personification of the Saxon race, but who was half a Norman by birth, and wholly Norman by education; for the successes of the Danes compelled his family to become exiles, and his youth and earlier manhood were passed in Normandy.[*] When he became king, the Normans had matters pretty much their own way in England. He remembered that Robert, Duke of Normandy, father of William the Conqueror, had once made an attempt to restore the Saxon line in England, and that he failed only because his fleet was destroyed by a storm. Duke William's influence had aided in his elevation to the English throne. His gratitude was expressed at the expense of his people. Once crowned, Edward invited his Norman friends to England. That country soon swarmed with foreigners, with whom the king was more at home than he was with his own subjects. Their language, the Romane, was his language. It was the language of the higher classes, the language of fashion, "the court tune." Such strong places as then stood in England were garrisoned by foreigners, and other Normans were settled in the towns. The country was half conquered years before the year of Hastings.

Duke William visited England in 1051. He was most hospitably received, and it is supposed that what he saw caused him to form the plan that led to the Conquest. Edward admired his visitor; and on the death of Edward the Outlaw, — whom he had recalled from Hungary, with the intention of proclaiming him as heir to the crown, — he determined that William should be his successor. He bequeathed the English crown to the ruler of Normandy. Harold agreed to sup-

---

* "The heart of Emma clung more and more to her native land. Her feelings were inherited by the children who were afterward born to her, — they imbibed them at their mother's breast. Their hearts were thoroughly alienated from England, and the Normans and Normandy became as their kindred and their home."— Palgrave, Vol. III. p. 112. Edward's wife was Editha, daughter of Earl Godwin, and sister of Harold.

port this arrangement. On his death-bed, Edward said to Harold and his kinsmen, "Ye know full well, my lords, that I have bequeathed my kingdom to the Duke of Normandy, and are there not those *here* whose oaths have been given to secure his succession?" The person to whom the crown should have gone was Edgar Atheling, son of Edward the Outlaw, and a lineal descendant of Ironside. Neither William nor Harold had any *claim* to the succession, whereas Edgar's claim was as good as that of the Prince of Wales to the throne of Great Britain is to-day. That Edward did not nominate Edgar must be attributed, in part at least, to the conviction that his nomination would be treated with contempt by the partisans of both William and Harold. He feared, it is probable, that the nomination of Edgar would give England up to the horrors of war, and that, after that prince should be disposed of by a union of Saxons and Normans against his claim, there would be another contest between the two factions of the victors. He was incapable of the grim humor of the Macedonian Alexander, who on his death-bed bequeathed his kingdom "to the strongest"; but his bequest was virtually of the same nature as that which so long before was made in Babylon. His death led to great funeral games, which are not yet over.

"Harold," says Palgrave, "afterward founded his title upon Edward's *last* will; many of our historians prove his claim, and the different statements are difficult to be reconciled; yet, taken altogether, the circumstances are exactly such as we meet with in private life. The childless owner of a large estate at first leaves his property to his cousin on the mother's side, from whose connections he has received much kindness. He advances in age, and alters his intentions in favor of a nephew on his father's side, — an amiable young man, living abroad, — and from whom he had been estranged in consequence of a family quarrel of long standing. The young heir comes to the testator's house, is received with

great affection, and is suddenly cut off by illness. The testator then returns to his will in favor of his cousin, who resides abroad. His acute and active brother-in-law has taken the management of his affairs; is well informed of this will; and, when the testator is on his death-bed, he contrives to tease and persuade the dying man to alter the will again in his favor. This is exactly the state of the case; and though considerable doubts have been raised relating to the contradictory bequests of the Confessor, there can be no difficulty in admitting that the conflicting pretensions of William and Harold were grounded upon the acts emanating from a wavering and feeble mind. If such disputes take place between private individuals, they are decided by a court of justice; but if they concern a kingdom, they can only be settled by the sword."[*] And to the sword Harold and William remitted the settlement of the question.

The two men who were thus arrayed in deadly opposition to each other were not unworthy of being competitors for a crown. Harold belonged to the greatest Saxon family of his time, of which he had been the head ever since the death of his father, the great Earl Godwin, which took place in 1053. Earl Godwin was one of the foremost men of the ante-Norman period of England, though his character, as Mr. St. John observes, "lies buried beneath a load of calumny"; and he quotes Dr. Hook as saying that "Godwin was the connecting link between the Saxon and the Dane, and, as the leader of the united English people, became one of the greatest men this country has ever produced, although, as is the English custom, one of the most maligned." "Calm, moderate, and dignified, reining in with wisdom the impetuosity of his nature," says Mr. St. John, "he presented to those around him the *beau idéal* of an Englishman, with all his predilections and prejudices, the warmest attachment to

[*] The History of Normandy and of England, Vol. III. pp. 293, 294.

his native land, and a somewhat over-weening contempt of foreigners. He was without question the greatest statesman of his age ; and, indeed, statesmanship in England may almost be said to have commenced with him. Whether we look at home or abroad, we discover no man in Christendom worthy to be ranked with him, in genius or wisdom, in peace or war. His figure towers far above all his contemporaries ; he constitutes the acme of the purely Saxon mind. No taint of foreign blood was in him. . . . . Godwin's lot was cast upon evil days. The marriage of Ethelred with Emma originated a fatal connection between this country and Normandy, the first fruits of which, forcing themselves but too obviously on his notice, he prevented, while he lived, from growing to maturity. The efforts, public and secret, which he found it necessary to make in the performance of this patriotic task, laid him open to the charge of craft and subtlety. Let it be granted that he deserved the imputation ; but it must be added, that, if foreign invasion and conquest be an evil, from that evil England was preserved as long as his crafty and subtle head remained above ground ; and had he lived thirteen years longer, the accumulated and concentrated scoundrelism of Europe would have been dashed away in foam and blood from the English shore. Properly understood, Godwin's whole life was one protracted agony for the salvation of his country. He had to contend with every species of deleterious influence, — ferocious, drunken, dissolute, and imbecile kings, the reckless intrigues of monasticism at the instigation of Rome, and the unprincipled and infamous ambition of the Norman Bastard, who crept into England during this great man's exile, and fled in all haste at his return. What he had to contend with, what plots he frustrated, what malice he counteracted, what superstition and stupidity he rendered harmless, will never be known in detail. We perceive the indefinite and indistinct forms of these things floating

through the mists of history, but cannot grasp and fix them for the instruction of posterity." * This portraiture may be somewhat too highly colored, but it is better painting than we get from Norman writers, who were no more capable of writing justly of Godwin and Harold, than Roman authors of Hannibal and Spartacus. Godwin was an abler man than his son and successor, and probably the latter would never have been able to aspire to royalty, and for a few months to wear a crown, had not the fortunes of his house been raised so high by his father. Nevertheless, Harold was worthy of his inheritance, and possessed rare qualities, such as made him not undeserving a throne, and of better fortune than he found at Hastings. He was patriotic, magnanimous, brave, humane, honorable, and energetic. His chief fault seems to have been a deficiency in judgment, which led him rashly to engage in undertakings that might better have been deferred. Such, at least, is the impression that we derive from his fighting the battle of Hastings, when he had everything to gain from delay, and when every day that an action was postponed was as useful to the Saxon cause as it was injurious to that of the Normans.

Harold's rival was the illegitimate son of Robert the Devil, as he is commonly called, because he has been, though improperly, "identified with a certain imaginary or legendary hero," but who was a much better man than his diabolic *sobriquet* implies. William's mother was Arletta, or Herleva, daughter of a tanner of Falaise. The Conqueror never escaped the reproach of his birth, into which bastardy and plebeianism entered in equal proportions. He was always " William the Bastard," and he is so to this day. " William the Conqueror," says Palgrave, " the founder of the most noble empire in the civilized world, could never rid himself of the contumelious appellation which bore indelible record

* History of the Four Conquests of England, Vol. II. pp. 176 – 178.

of his father's sin. In all history, William is the only individual to whom such an epithet has adhered throughout his life and fortunes. Was the word of affront ever applied to Alphonso, the stern father of the noble house of Braganza, by any one except a Castilian ? Not so William ; — a bastard was William at the hour of his birth ; a bastard in prosperity ; a bastard in adversity ; a bastard in sorrow ; a bastard in triumph ; a bastard in the maternal bosom ; a bastard when borne to his horror-inspiring grave. 'William the Conqueror' relatively, but 'William the Bastard' positively ; and a bastard he will continue so long as the memory of man shall endure." Sir Francis seems to have forgotten the Bastard of Orleans. Nevertheless, and in spite of his illegitimacy, William became ruler of Normandy when he was but a child, his father abdicating the throne, and forcing the Norman baronage to accept the boy as his successor ; and that boy thirty years later founded a royal line that yet endures in full strength, Queen Victoria being the legitimate descendant of William of Normandy.* The training that Wil-

* The legitimate descent of Queen Victoria from the Conqueror is sometimes disputed, because it is not correctly traced, in consequence of the line of descent being carried back through Henry VII., instead of being carried through his wife, *née* Elizabeth Plantagenet. It may not be uninteresting to state the royal pedigree, which is at times rather intricate, and full of sinuosities, — in part due to the occurrence of political revolutions, old English statesmen never having paid much regard to political legitimacy, which is a modern notion. Queen Victoria is the daughter of Edward, Duke of Kent, who was son of George III., who was son of Frederick, Prince of Wales, who was son of George II., who was son of George I., who was son of the Electress Sophia (by Ernest Augustus, Elector of Hanover), who was daughter of Elizabeth Stuart (by Frederick V., Elector Palatine and "Winter King" of Bohemia), who was daughter of James I. (Sixth of Scotland), who was son of Mary, Queen of Scots (by Henry Stuart, Lord Darnley), who was daughter of James V., who was son of Margaret Tudor (by James IV.), who was daughter of Elizabeth Plantagenet (by Henry VII.), who was daughter of Edward IV., who was son of Richard, Duke of York, who was son of Anne Mortimer (by Richard Plantagenet, Earl of Cambridge, son of Edmund, Duke of York, fifth son of Edward III.), who was daughter of Roger, Earl of Marche, who was son of Philippe (by Edmund, Earl of Marche), who was daughter of Lionel, Duke of Clarence,

liam received developed his faculties, and made him one of the chief men of his age ; and in 1066 he prepared to assert his right to the English crown.

third son of Edward III., who was son of Edward II., who was son of Edward I., who was son of Henry III., who was son of John, who was son of Henry II., who was son of Matilda (by Geoffrey Plantagenet, Count of Anjou), who was daughter of Henry I. (by Matilda of Scotland, sister of Edgar Atheling, and therefore of the Saxon blood royal), who was son of William the Conqueror. Thus Queen Victoria is descended legitimately from the Conqueror, not only through Lionel, Duke of Clarence, Edward III.'s third son, but also through that monarch's fifth son, Edmund, Duke of York, whose second son, the Earl of Cambridge, married the great-granddaughter of the Duke of Clarence. Had the great struggle of the English throne in the fifteenth century been correctly named, it would stand in history as the contest between the lines of Clarence (not York) and Lancaster. In virtue of her descent from Henry VII., Queen Victoria shares "the aspiring blood of Lancaster," which was so mounting that it brought the worst of woes on England. Henry VII. was the son of Margaret Beaufort (by Edmund Tudor, Earl of Richmond), who was the daughter of John, Duke of Somerset, who was the son of John, Earl of Somerset, who was the son of John of Gaunt, Duke of Lancaster, fourth son of Edward III. ; but the mother of the Earl of Somerset was, at the time of his birth, not the wife, but the mistress of the Duke of Lancaster, though he married her late in life, and in various ways obtained the legitimation of the children she had borne him, — facts that could not remove the great fact of their illegitimacy, if marriage is to count for anything, and which no good historian ever has treated with respect. Lord Macaulay calls the Tudors "a line of bastards," and ranks them with the "succession of impostors" set up by the adherents of the White Rose. Froude's great work has created a new interest in the question of the English succession, for he bases his peculiar view of the character of Henry VIII., and his justification of all his acts of heartless tyranny, on the necessities that grew out of that perplexing question, which troubled England for two centuries, thus forming a practical satire on that theory which represents that the peculiar excellence of hereditary monarchy is found in its power to prevent disputes for the possession of government, and to promote the preservation of society's peace, — a theory which has often been thrown into the teeth of republicans, and particularly since the occurrence of our unhappy civil troubles. Yet one would think that Gettysburg and Shiloh were not worse days than Towton and Barnet. Those persons who are interested in the English succession question, and who would see how wide a one it was, and how far and how long and variously it affected the politics of Continental Europe as well as those of England, should read the chapter on the subject in Miss Cooper's "Life and Letters of Arabella Stuart," a learned and lively work, and not the least meritorious of those admirable historical productions which we owe to the genius, the industry, and the honesty of Englishwomen, — Agnes Strickland, Caroline A. Halsted, Lucy Aiken, Mrs. Everett Green, Elizabeth Cooper, and others,

The Norman barons were at first disinclined to support their lord's claim upon England. Their tenures did not bind them to cross the sea. But at last they were won over to the support of his cause, on the promise of receiving the lands of the English. He called upon foreigners to join his army, promising them the plunder of England. "All the adventurers and adventurous spirits of the neighboring states were invited to join his standard," and his invitation was accepted. "William published his ban," says Thierry, "in the neighboring countries; he offered gold, and the pillage of England to every able man who would serve him with lance, sword, or crossbow. A multitude accepted the invitation, coming by every road, far and near, from north and south. They came from Maine and Anjou, from Poitiers and Brittany, from France and Flanders, from Aquitaine and Burgundy, from the Alps and the banks of the Rhine. All the professional adventurers, all the military vagabonds of Western Europe, hastened to Normandy by long marches; some were knights and chiefs of war, the others simple foot-soldiers and sergeants-of-arms, as they were then called; some demanded money-pay, others only their passage, and all the booty they might win. Some asked for land in England, a domain, a castle, a town; others simply required some rich Saxon in marriage. Every thought, every desire of human avarice presented itself. William rejected no one, says the Norman chronicle, and satisfied every one as well as he could. He gave, beforehand, a bishopric in England to a monk of Fescamp, in return for a vessel and twenty armed men." * The Pope was William's chief supporter. Harold and all his adherents were excommunicated, and William received a banner and ring from Rome, the double emblem of military and ecclesiastical investiture. Of the sixty thousand men that formed the Norman army, Normans formed the smallest portion, and most of their number were not of noble birth.

William sailed on the 28th of September, and landed his army on the 29th, without experiencing any resistance. Harold was in the North, contending with and defeating the Northmen, one of whose leaders was his brother Tostig. As soon as he received intelligence of William's landing he marched south, bent upon giving immediate battle, though his mother and his brother Gurth and other relatives, and many of his friends, strongly counselled delay. This counsel was good, for his force was to William's as one to four; and even a week's delay might have so far strengthened the Saxons as to have enabled them to fight on an approach to equal terms with the invaders. But Harold rejected all advice, and pressed forward to action so imprudently as to countenance, in a superstitious age, the notion that he was urged on by an irresistible power, which had decreed his destruction. Certainly he did not display much sagacity before battle, though both skill and bravery in it were not wanting on his part. The battle of Hastings was fought on the 14th of October, 1066. The Normans were the assailants; but for six hours — from nine in the morning till three in the afternoon — they were repulsed; and had the Saxons been content to hold their ground, victory would have been theirs. But they left the position they had so valiantly maintained, to pursue the Normans, when the latter feigned to fly. Even then they fought with heroic resolution, and might have regained the day, had not Harold fallen. Soon after, the English position was stormed, and the king's brother, Gurth, was slain. The combat lasted till the coming on of darkness. Fifteen thousand of the victors are said to have fallen, — a number as great as the entire English army.

— whose writings do honor to the sex, and fairly entitle their authors to be ranked with those accomplished ladies of the sixteenth century whose solid attainments have so long been matter of despairing admiration.

* *Histoire de la Conquête de l'Angleterre par les Normans,* Tom. I. pp. 237, 238.

The event of the battle of Hastings placed all England, ultimately, at the disposition of the Normans, though many years elapsed before the country was entirely conquered. Had the English possessed a good government, or leaders who enjoyed general confidence, their defeat at Hastings would not have reduced them to bondage, or have converted their country into a new world. But they, who were even slavishly dependent on their government for leading, had no government; and they were just as destitute of chiefs who were competent to assume the lead at so dark a crisis. Taking advantage of circumstances so favorable to his purpose, William soon made himself king, but had most of his work to do long after he was crowned. The battle of Hastings, therefore, was decisive of the future of England and of the British race. Saxon England disappeared; Norman England rose. The change was perfect, and quite warrants Lord Macaulay's emphatic assertion, that "the battle of Hastings, and the events which followed it, not only placed a Duke of Normandy on the English throne, but gave up the whole population of England to the tyranny of the Norman race," — and that "the subjugation of a nation by a nation has seldom, even in Asia, been more complete." The nation that finally was formed by a union of the Saxons and the Normans, and which was seven or eight generations in forming, was a very different nation from that which had been ruled by the Confessor. It was a nation that was capable of every form of action, and had little in common with the Saxons of the eleventh century. It matters nothing whether the Conqueror introduced the feudal system into England, or whether he found it there, or whether that system is almost entirely an imaginary creation, as most probably is the fact. We know that the event called the Norman Conquest wrought great changes in England, and through England in the world; and that Napoleon III. reigns over the French, and Victor Emanuel II. over the Italians, that the House of Hohenzollern has triumphed over the House of Hapsburg, that President Johnson rules at Washington, and that Queen Victoria sits in the seat of Akbar or Aurungzebe, are facts which must all be attributed to the decision made by the sword at Hastings, no matter what may have been the particular process of events after that battle. It is possible that the misery consequent on the victory of the Normans has been exaggerated, though a great deal of suffering must have followed from it. But there can be no exaggeration of the general consequence of the success of the Normans. That determined the future course of the world, and will continue to determine it long after the Valley of the Amazon shall be far more thickly inhabited, and better known, than to-day is the Valley of the Danube.

There is one popular error with regard to the Norman Conquest which it may not be amiss to correct. It is taken for granted by most persons who have written on it, that the triumph of William was the triumph of an aristocracy over a people, and we often hear the Saxons spoken of as democrats who were subdued by aristocrats. This is an entirely erroneous view of the whole subject. So far as there was a contest at Hastings between aristocrats and democrats, the Normans were champions of democracy, and the Saxons of the opposite principle. The Saxon aristocracy was very powerful, and its power was steadily increasing for generations before the Conquest; and had there not been a foreign invasion, it is altogether probable that the English system soon would have become strictly oligarchical. One of the chief causes of Harold's failure was his inability to command the prompt support of some of the greatest nobles, as Earls Edwin and Morcar, who paid bitterly for their backwardness in after days. Something of this may be attributed to the weakness of his title to the crown, but the mere fact that such men could so powerfully influence events at a time when the very existence of the country was at stake, is enough to show how strong were the insular aristocrats; and it was this selfish aristocracy that was destroyed by the Normans, most of whom were upstarts, the very scum of Europe having entered William's army. We doubt if ever there was a greater triumph effected by the poor and the lowly-born over the rich and the well-born, than that which was gained at Hastings, though it required some years to make it complete. "According to the common report," says Sir F. Palgrave, "sixty thousand knights received their fees, or rather their livings, to use the old expression, from the Conqueror. This report is exaggerated as to number; but the race of the Anglo-Danish and English nobility and gentry, the Earls and the greater Thanes, disappears; and with some exceptions, remarkable as exemplifying the general rule, all the superiorities of the English soil became vested in the Conqueror's Baronage. Men of a new race and order, men of strange manners and strange speech, ruled in England. There were, however, some great mitigations, and the very sufferings of the conquered were so inflicted as to become the ultimate means of national prosperity; but they were to be gone through, and to be attended with much present desolation and misery. The process was the more painful because it was now accompanied by so much degradation and contumely. The Anglo-Saxons seem to have had a very strong aristocratic feeling, — a great respect for family and dignity of blood. The Normans, or rather the host of adventurers whom we must of necessity comprehend under the name of Normans, had comparatively little; and not very many of the real old and powerful aristocracy, whether of Normandy or Brittany, settled in England. The great majority had been rude, and poor, and despicable in their own country, — the rascallions of Northern Gaul: these, suddenly enriched, lost all compass and bearing of mind; and no one circumstance vexed the spirit of the English more, than to see the fair and noble English maidens and widows compelled to accept these despicable adventurers as their husbands. Of this we have an example in Lucia, the daughter of Algar, for Talboys seems to have been a person of the lowest degree." Ivo Talboys, or Taillebois, was one of the Conqueror's followers, and his chief gave him lands in the fen country, near the monastery of Croyland; and this chance of a locality may have had something to do with the reputation he has, for it brought him under the lash of the famous Ingulphus, Chronicler of Croyland, (if he was that Chronicler,) who charges him with all manner of crimes, — and with reason good, for he bore himself with great harshness toward the brethren of the great Croyland monastery, — an unpardonable offence. Low as he was by birth, Taillebois received the hand of Lucia, sister of the Saxon Earls Edwin and Morcar, and became very wealthy. From this union came "the great line whence sprang the barons of Kendal and Lancaster." The last descendant of this Norman baron of William's creation and of the Saxon Lucia died in 1861, a pauper in the workhouse of Shrewsbury, — Emily Taillebois, a girl of eighteen.

There were thousands of such fellows as Taillebois in William's army, and, though all were not so lucky as he, many of them drew good prizes in the lottery of war, and founded, at the expense of the noblest Saxons, families from which men are proud to be descended. Sir Walter has used this fact in "Ivanhoe," when he makes the usually silent Athelstane reply with so much eloquence to De Bracy's insolent remark that the princes of the House of Anjou conferred not their wards on men of such lineage as his. "My lineage, proud Norman," replied Athelstane, "is drawn from a source more pure and ancient than that of a beggarly Frenchman, whose living is won by selling the blood of the thieves whom he assembles under his paltry standard. Kings were my ancestors, strong in war and wise in council, who every day feasted in their hall more hundreds than thou canst number individual followers; whose names have been sung by minstrels, and their laws recorded by Wittenagemotes; whose bones were interred amid the prayers of saints, and over whose tombs minsters have been builded." There can be no doubt that Saxons as far-descended as Scott represents Athelstane to have been were treated worse than he, and that Saxon ladies of the highest birth and greatest wealth experienced the fate of the conquered in much severer measure than it became known to Rowena. Scott has been accused of exaggerating the effects of the Conquest, but his glowing picture is by no means overcharged, if we look at the effect of that change on the higher classes of the vanquished people. The Saxons were very wealthy, and the invaders obtained an amount of spoil that astonished them, the accounts of which remind the reader of what was told of the extraordinary acquisitions made by the ruffians who formed the force of Pizarro in Peru. Years after the day of Hastings, we are told, William "bore back with him, to his eager and hungry country, the plunder of England, which was so varied in kind, so prodigious in amount, that the awe-stricken chroniclers maintain that all the Gauls, if ransacked from end to end, would have failed to supply treasures worthy to be compared with it. The silver, the gold, the vases, vestments, and crucifixes crested with jewels, the silken garments for men and women, the rings, necklaces, bracelets, wrought delicately in gold and resplendent in gems, inspired the Continental barbarians with rapture, and in their imaginations made England appear the Dorado of those times." One of the writers of that day states that "incredible treasures in gold and silver were sent from the plunder of England to the Pope, together with costly ornaments, which would have been held in the highest estimation even at Byzantium, then universally regarded as the most opulent city in the world." All this implies that the Saxon aristocracy were very rich, and it is far from unlikely that it was the desire to preserve their property that led them to offer so little resistance to William, — a fatally mistaken course, for the invading adventurers had entered England in search of other men's property, and were not to be kept quiet by the quietness of the owners thereof. The aristocracy alone could afford such plunder as that described, and that so much of it was obtained shows how extensive must have been the spoliation, and how thoroughly Saxon nobles were stripped of their possessions by the low-born ragamuffins who were induced by William's recruiting sergeants to enlist under his black banner.

THE NOVELS OF GEORGE ELIOT.

THE critic's first duty in the presence of an author's collective works is to seek out some key to his method, some utterance of his literary convictions, some indication of his ruling theory. The amount of labor involved in an inquiry of this kind will depend very much upon the author. In some cases the critic will find express declarations; in other cases he will have to content himself with conscientious inductions. In a writer so fond of digressions as George Eliot, he has reason to expect that broad evidences of artistic faith will not be wanting. He finds in "Adam Bede" the following passage: —

"Paint us an angel if you can, with a floating violet robe and a face paled by the celestial light; paint us yet oftener a Madonna, turning her mild face upward, and opening her arms to welcome the divine glory; but do not impose on us any æsthetic rules which shall banish from the region of art those old women scraping carrots with their work-worn hands, — those heavy clowns taking holiday in a dingy pot-house, — those rounded backs and stupid weather-beaten faces that have bent over the spade and done the rough work of the world, — those homes with their tin cans, their brown pitchers, their rough curs, and their clusters of onions. In this world there are so many of these common, coarse people, who have no picturesque, sentimental wretchedness. It is so needful we should remember their existence, else we may happen to leave them quite out of our religion and philosophy, and frame lofty theories which only fit a world of extremes. . . . . . There are few prophets in the world, — few sublimely beautiful women, — few heroes. I can't afford to give all my love and reverence to such rarities; I want a great deal of those feelings for my every-day fellow-men, especially for the few in the foreground of the great multitude, whose faces I know, whose hands I touch, for whom I have to make way with kindly courtesy. . . . . . I herewith discharge my conscience," our author continues, "and declare that I have had quite enthusiastic movements of admiration toward old gentlemen who spoke the worst English, who were occasionally fretful in their temper, and who had never moved in a higher sphere of influence than that of parish overseer; and that the way in which I have come to the conclusion that human nature is lovable — the way I have learnt something of its deep pathos, its sublime mysteries — has been by living a great deal among people more or less commonplace and vulgar, of whom you would perhaps hear nothing very surprising if you were to inquire about them in the neighborhoods where they dwelt."

But even in the absence of any such avowed predilections as these, a brief glance over the principal figures of her different works would assure us that our author's sympathies are with common people. Silas Marner is a linen-weaver, Adam Bede is a carpenter, Maggie Tulliver is a miller's daughter, Felix Holt is a watchmaker, Dinah Morris works in a factory, and Hetty Sorrel is a dairy-maid. Esther Lyon, indeed, is a daily governess; but Tito Melema alone is a scholar. In the "Scenes of Clerical Life," the author is constantly slipping down from the clergymen, her heroes, to the most ignorant and obscure of their parishioners. Even in "Romola" she consecrates page after page to the conversation of the Florentine populace. She is as unmistakably a painter of *bourgeois* life as Thackeray was a painter of the life of drawing-rooms.

Her opportunities for the study of the manners of the solid lower classes have evidently been very great. We have her word for it that she has lived much among the farmers, mechanics, and small traders of that central region of England which she has made known to us under the name of Loamshire. The conditions of the popular life in this district in that already distant period to which she refers the action of most of her stories — the end of the last century and the beginning of the present — were so different from any that have been seen in America, that an American, in treating of her books, must be satisfied not to touch upon the question of their accuracy and fidelity as pictures of manners and customs. He can only say that they bear strong internal evidence of truthfulness. If he is a great admirer of George Eliot, he will indeed be tempted to affirm that they *must* be true. They offer a completeness, a rich density of detail, which could be the fruit only of a long term of conscious contact, — such as would make it much more difficult for the author to fall into the perversion and suppression of facts, than to set them down literally. It is very probable that her colors are a little too bright, and her shadows of too mild a gray, that the sky of her landscapes is too sunny, and their atmosphere too redolent of peace and abundance. Local affection may be accountable for half of this excess of brilliancy; the author's native optimism is accountable for the other half. I do not remember, in all her novels, an instance of gross misery of any kind not directly caused by the folly of the sufferer. There are no pictures of vice or poverty or squalor. There are no rags, no gin, no brutal passions. That average humanity which she favors is very *borné* in intellect, but very genial in heart, as a glance at its representatives in her pages will convince us. In "Adam Bede," there is Mr. Irwine, the vicar, with avowedly no qualification for his profession, placidly playing chess with his mother, stroking his dogs, and dipping into Greek tragedies; there is the excellent Martin Poyser at the Farm, good-natured and rubicund; there is his wife, somewhat too sharply voluble, but only in behalf of cleanliness and honesty and order; there is Captain Donnithorne at the Hall, who does a poor girl a mortal wrong, but who is, after all, such a nice, good-looking fellow; there are Adam and Seth Bede, the carpenter's sons, the strongest, purest, most discreet of young rustics. The same broad felicity prevails in "The Mill on the Floss." Mr. Tulliver, indeed, fails in business; but his failure only serves as an offset to the general integrity and prosperity. His son is obstinate and wilful; but it is all on the side of virtue. His daughter is somewhat sentimental and erratic; but she is more conscientious yet. Conscience, in the classes from which George Eliot recruits her figures, is a universal gift. Decency and plenty and good-humor follow contentedly in its train. The word which sums up the common traits of our author's various groups is the word *respectable.* Adam Bede is pre - eminently a respectable young man; so is Arthur

Donnithorne; so, although he will persist in going without a cravat, is Felix Holt. So, with perhaps the exception of Maggie Tulliver and Stephen Guest, is every important character to be found in our author's writings. They all share this fundamental trait, — that in each of them passion proves itself feebler than conscience.

The first work which made the name of George Eliot generally known, contains, to my perception, only a small number of the germs of her future power. From the "Scenes of Clerical Life" to "Adam Bede" she made not so much a step as a leap. Of the three tales contained in the former work, I think the first is much the best. It is short, broadly descriptive, humorous, and exceedingly pathetic. "The Sad Fortunes of the Reverend Amos Barton" are fortunes which clever storytellers with a turn for pathos, from Oliver Goldsmith downward, have found of very good account, — the fortunes of a hapless clergyman of the Church of England in daily contention with the problem how upon eighty pounds a year to support a wife and six children in all due ecclesiastical gentility. "Mr. Gilfil's Love-Story," the second of the tales in question, I cannot hesitate to pronounce a failure. George Eliot's pictures of drawing - room life are only interesting when they are linked or related to scenes in the tavern parlor, the dairy, and the cottage. Mr. Gilfil's love-story is enacted entirely in the drawing-room, and in consequence it is singularly deficient in force and reality. Not that it is vulgar, — for our author's good taste never forsakes her, — but it is thin, flat, and trivial. But for a certain family likeness in the use of language and the rhythm of the style, it would be hard to believe that these pages are by the same hand as "Silas Marner." In "Janet's Repentance," the last and longest of the three clerical stories, we return to middle life, — the life represented by the Dodsons in "The Mill on the Floss." The subject of this tale might almost be qualified by the

French epithet *scabreux*. It would be difficult for what is called *realism* to go further than in the adoption of a heroine stained with the vice of intemperance. The theme is unpleasant ; the author chose it at her peril. It must be added, however, that Janet Dempster has many provocations. Married to a brutal drunkard, she takes refuge in drink against his illusage ; and the story deals less with her lapse into disgrace than with her redemption, through the kind offices of the Reverend Edgar Tryan, — by virtue of which, indeed, it takes its place in the clerical series. I cannot help thinking that the stern and tragical character of the subject has been enfeebled by the over-diffuseness of the narrative and the excess of local touches. The abundance of the author's recollections and observations of village life clogs the dramatic movement, over which she has as yet a comparatively slight control. In her subsequent works the stouter fabric of the story is better able to support this heavy drapery of humor and digression.

To a certain extent, I think "Silas Marner" holds a higher place than any of the author's works. It is more nearly a masterpiece ; it has more of that simple, rounded, consummate aspect, that absence of loose ends and gaping issues, which marks a classical work. What was attempted in it, indeed, was within more immediate reach than the heart-trials of Adam Bede and Maggie Tulliver. A poor, dull-witted, disappointed Methodist cloth-weaver ; a little golden-haired foundling child ; a well-meaning, irresolute country squire, and his patient, childless wife ; — these, with a chorus of simple, beer-loving villagers, make up the *dramatis personæ*. More than any of its brother-works, "Silas Marner," I think, leaves upon the mind a deep impression of the grossly material life of agricultural England in the last days of the old *régime*, — the days of full-orbed Toryism, of Trafalgar and of Waterloo, when the invasive spirit of French domination threw England back upon a sense of her own insular solidity, and made her for the time doubly, brutally, morbidly English. Perhaps the best pages in the work are the first thirty, telling the story of poor Marner's disappointments in friendship and in love, his unmerited disgrace, and his long, lonely twilight-life at Raveloe, with the sole companionship of his loom, in which his muscles moved "with such even repetition, that their pause seemed almost as much a constraint as the holding of his breath." Here, as in all George Eliot's books, there is a middle life and a low life ; and here, as usual, I prefer the low life. In "Silas Marner," in my opinion, she has come nearest the mildly rich tints of brown and gray, the mellow lights and the undreadful corner-shadows of the Dutch masters whom she emulates. One of the chapters contains a scene in a pot-house, which frequent reference has made famous. Never was a group of honest, garrulous village simpletons more kindly and humanely handled. After a long and somewhat chilling silence, amid the pipes and beer, the landlord opens the conversation "by saying in a doubtful tone to his cousin the butcher : —

"'Some folks 'ud say that was a fine beast you druv in yesterday, Bob ?'

"The butcher, a jolly, smiling, red-haired man, was not disposed to answer rashly. He gave a few puffs before he spat, and replied, 'And they would n't be fur wrong, John.'

"After this feeble, delusive thaw, silence set in as severely as before.

"'Was it a red Durham ?' said the farrier, taking up the thread of discourse after the lapse of a few minutes.

"The farrier looked at the landlord, and the landlord looked at the butcher, as the person who must take the responsibility of answering.

"'Red it was,' said the butcher, in his good-humored husky treble, — 'and a Durham it was.'

"'Then you need n't tell me who you bought it of,' said the farrier, looking round with some triumph ; 'I know who it is has got the red Durhams o' this country-side. And she 'd a white star on her brow, I 'll bet a penny?'

"'Well; yes — she might,' said the butcher, slowly, considering that he was giving a decided affirmation. 'I don't say contrairy.'

"'I knew that very well,' said the farrier, throwing himself back defiantly; 'if I don't know Mr. Lammeter's cows, I should like to know who does, — that 's all. And as for the cow you bought, bargain or no bargain, I 've been at the drenching of her, — contradick me who will.'

"The farrier looked fierce, and the mild butcher's conversational spirit was roused a little.

"'I 'm not for contradicking no man,' he said; 'I 'm for peace and quietness. Some are for cutting long ribs. I 'm for cutting 'em short myself; but *I* don't quarrel with 'em. All I say is, its a lovely carkiss, — and anybody as was reasonable, it 'ud bring tears into their eyes to look at it.'

"'Well, its the cow as I drenched, whatever it is,' pursued the farrier, angrily; 'and it was Mr. Lammeter's cow, else you told a lie when you said it was a red Durham.'

"'I tell no lies,' said the butcher, with the same mild huskiness as before; 'and I contradick none, — not if a man was to swear himself black; he 's no meat of mine, nor none of my bargains. All I say is, its a lovely carkiss. And what I say I 'll stick to; but I 'll quarrel wi' no man.'

"'No,' said the farrier, with bitter sarcasm, looking at the company generally; 'and p'rhaps you did n't say the cow was a red Durham; and p'rhaps you did n't say she 'd got a star on her brow, — stick to that, now you are at it.'"

Matters having come to this point, the landlord interferes *ex officio* to preserve order. The Lammeter family having come up, he discreetly invites Mr. Macey, the parish clerk and tailor, to favor the company with his recollections on the subject. Mr. Macey, however, "smiled pityingly in answer to the landlord's appeal, and said: 'Ay,

ay; I know, I know: but I let other folks talk. I 've laid by now, and gev up to the young uns. Ask them as have been to school at Tarley: they 've learn't pernouncing; that 's came up since my day.'"

Mr. Macey is nevertheless persuaded to dribble out his narrative; proceeding by instalments, and questioned from point to point, in a kind of Socratic manner, by the landlord. He at last arrives at Mr. Lammeter's marriage, and how the clergyman, when he came to put the questions, inadvertently transposed the position of the two essential names, and asked, "Wilt thou have this man to be thy wedded wife?" etc.

"'But the partic'larest thing of all,' pursues Mr. Macey, 'is, as nobody took any notice on it but me, and they answered straight off "Yes," like as if it had been me saying "Amen" i' the right place, without listening to what went before.'

"'But *you* knew what was going on well enough, did n't you, Mr. Macey? You were live enough, eh?' said the butcher.

"'Yes, bless you!' said Mr. Macey, pausing, and smiling in pity at the impatience of his hearer's imagination, — 'why, I was all of a tremble; it was as if I'd been a coat pulled by two tails, like; for I could n't stop the parson, I could n't take upon me to do that; and yet I said to myself, I says, "Suppose they should n't be fast married," 'cause the words are contrairy, and my head went working like a mill, for I was always uncommon for turning things over and seeing all round 'em; and I says to myself, "Is 't the meaning or the words as makes folks fast i' wedlock?" For the parson meant right, and the bride and bridegroom meant right. But then, when I came to think on it, meaning goes but a little way i' most things, for you may mean to stick things together and your glue may be bad, and then where are you?'"

Mr. Macey's doubts, however, are set at rest by the parson after the service, who assures him that what does the business is neither the meaning nor the words, but the register. Mr. Macey then arrives at the chapter — or rather is gently inducted thereunto by his hearers — of the ghosts who frequent certain of the Lammeter stables. But ghosts threatening to prove as pregnant a theme of contention as Durham cows, the landlord again meditates : "'There's folks i' my opinion, they can't see ghos'es, not if they stood as plain as a pikestaff before 'em. And there's reason i' that. For there's my wife, now, can't smell, not if she'd the strongest o' cheese under her nose. I never seed a ghost myself, but then I says to myself, "Very liké I have n't the smell for 'em." I mean, putting a ghost for a smell or else contrairiways. And so I 'm for holding with both sides. . . . For the smell 's what I go by.'"

The best drawn of the village worthies in "Silas Marner" are Mr. Macey, of the scene just quoted, and good Dolly Winthrop, Marner's kindly patroness. I have room for only one more specimen of Mr. Macey. He is looking on at a New Year's dance at Squire Casa's, beside Ben Winthrop, Dolly's husband.

"'The Squire's pretty springy, considering his weight,' said Mr. Macey, 'and he stamps uncommon well. But Mr. Lammeter beats 'em all for shapes ; you see he holds his head like a sodger, and he is n't so cushiony as most o' the oldish gentlefolks, — they run fat in gineral ; — and he's got a fine leg. The parson's nimble enough, but he has n't got much of a leg : it's a bit too thick downward, and his knees might be a bit nearer without damage ; but he might do worse, he might do worse. Though he has n't that grand way o' waving his hand as the Squire has.'

"'Talk o' nimbleness, look at Mrs Osgood,' said Ben Winthrop. . . . . 'She's the finest made woman as is, let the next be where she will.'

"'I don't heed how the women are made,' said Mr. Macey, with some contempt. 'They wear nayther coat nor breeches ; you can't make much out o' their shapes !'"

Mrs. Winthrop, the wheelwright's wife who, out of the fulness of her charity, comes to comfort Silas in the season of his distress, is in her way one of the most truthfully sketched of the author's figures. "She was in all respects a woman of scrupulous conscience, so eager for duties that life seemed to offer them too scantily unless she rose at half past four, though this threw a scarcity of work over the more advanced hours of the morning, which it was a constant problem for her to remove. . . . . She was a very mild, patient woman, whose nature it was to seek out all the sadder and more serious elements of life and pasture her mind upon them." She stamps I. H. S. on her cakes and loaves without knowing what the letters mean, or indeed without knowing that they are letters, being very much surprised that Marner can "read 'em off," — chiefly because they are on the pulpit cloth at church. She touches upon religious themes in a manner to make the superficial reader apprehend that she cultivates some polytheistic form of faith, — extremes meet. She urges Marner to go to church, and describes the satisfaction which she herself derives from the performance of her religious duties.

"If you 've niver had no church, there's no telling what good it 'll do you. For I feel as set up and comfortable as niver was, when I 've been and heard the prayers and the singing to the praise and glory o' God, as Mr. Macey gives out, — and Mr. Crackenthorp saying good words and more partic'lar on Sacramen' day ; and if a bit o' trouble comes, I feel as I can put up wi' it, for I 've looked for help i' the right quarter, and giv myself up to Them as we must all give ourselves up to at the last : and if we 've done our part, it is n't to be believed as Them as are above us 'ud be worse nor we are, and come short o' Theirn."

"The plural pronoun," says the author, "was no heresy of Dolly's, but only her way of avoiding a presumptuous familiarity." I imagine that there is in no other English novel a figure so simple in its elements as this of Dolly Winthrop, which is so real without being contemptible, and so quaint without being ridiculous.

In all those of our author's books which have borne the name of the hero or heroine, — "Adam Bede," "Silas Marner," "Romola," and "Felix Holt," — the person so put forward has really played a subordinate part. The author may have set out with the intention of maintaining him supreme ; but her material has become rebellious in her hands, and the technical hero has been eclipsed by the real one. Tito is the leading figure in "Romola." The story deals predominantly, not with Romola as affected by Tito's faults, but with Tito's faults as affecting first himself, and incidentally his wife. Godfrey Cass, with his lifelong secret, is by right the hero of "Silas Marner." Felix Holt, in the work which bears his name, is little more than an occasional apparition ; and indeed the novel has no hero, but only a heroine. The same remark applies to "Adam Bede," as the work stands. The central figure of the book, by virtue of her great misfortune, is Hetty Sorrel. In the presence of that misfortune no one else, assuredly, has a right to claim dramatic pre-eminence. The one person for whom an approach to equality may be claimed is, not Adam Bede, but Arthur Donnithorne. If the story had ended, as I should have infinitely preferred to see it end, with Hetty's execution, or even with her reprieve, and if Adam had been left to his grief, and Dinah Morris to the enjoyment of that distinguished celibacy for which she was so well suited, then I think Adam might have shared the honors of pre-eminence with his hapless sweetheart. But as it is, the continuance of the book in his interest is fatal to him. His sorrow at Hetty's misfortune is not a *sufficient* sorrow for the situation. That his marriage at some future time was quite possible, and even natural, I readily admit ; but that was matter for a new story. This point illustrates, I think, the great advantage of the much-censured method, introduced by Balzac, of continuing his heroes' adventures from tale to tale. Or, admitting that the author was indisposed to undertake, or even to conceive, in its completeness, a new tale, in which Adam, healed of his wound by time, should address himself to another woman, I yet hold that it would be possible tacitly to foreshadow some such event at the close of the tale which we are supposing to end with Hetty's death, — to make it the logical consequence of Adam's final state of mind. Of course circumstances would have much to do with bringing it to pass, and these circumstances could not be foreshadowed ; but apart from the action of circumstances would stand the fact that, to begin with, the event was *possible*. The assurance of this possibility is what I should have desired the author to place the sympathetic reader at a stand-point to deduce for himself. In every novel the work is divided between the writer and the reader ; but the writer makes the reader very much as he makes his characters. When he makes him ill, that is, makes him indifferent, he does no work ; the writer does all. When he makes him well, that is, makes him interested, then the reader does quite half the labor. In making such a deduction as I have just indicated, the reader would be doing but his share of the task ; the grand point is to get him to make it. I hold that there is a way. It is perhaps a secret ; but until it is found out, I think that the art of story-telling cannot be said to have approached perfection.

When you re-read coldly and critically a book which in former years you have read warmly and carelessly, you are surprised to see how it changes its proportions. It falls away in those parts which have been pre-eminent in your memory, and it increases in the small portions. Until I lately read "Adam Bede" for a second time, Mrs. Poyser was in my mind its representative figure ; for I remembered a number of her epigrammatic sallies. But now, after a second reading, Mrs. Poyser is the last figure I think of, and a fresh perusal of her witticisms has considerably diminished their classical flavor. And if I must tell the truth, Adam himself is next to the last, and sweet Dinah Morris third from the last. The person immediately evoked by the title of the work is poor Hetty Sorrel. Mrs. Poyser is *too* epigrammatic ; her wisdom smells of the lamp. I do not mean to say that she is not natural, and that women of her class are not often gifted with her homely fluency, her penetration, and her turn for forcible analogies. But she is too sustained ; her morality is too shrill, — too much in *staccato ;* she too seldom subsides into the commonplace. Yet it cannot be denied that she puts things very happily. Remonstrating with Dinah Morris on the undue disinterestedness of her religious notions, " But for the matter o' that," she cries, " if everybody was to do like you, the world must come to a stand-still ; for if everybody tried to do without house and home and eating and drinking, and was always talking as we must despise the things o' the world, as you say, I should like to know where the pick of the stock, and the corn, and the best new milk-cheeses 'ud have to go ? *Everybody 'ud be wanting to make bread o' tail ends*, and everybody 'ud be running after everybody else to preach to 'em, i'stead o' bringing up their families and laying by against a bad harvest." And when Hetty comes home late from the Chase, and alleges in excuse that the clock at home is so much earlier than the clock at the great house : " What, you 'd be wanting the clock set by gentlefolks' time, would you ? an' sit up burning candle, and lie a-bed wi' the sun a-bakin' you, like a cowcumber i' the frame ? " Mrs. Poyser has something almost of Yankee shrewdness and angularity ; but the figure of a New England rural housewife would lack a whole range of Mrs. Poyser's feelings, which, whatever may be its effect in real life, gives its subject in a novel at least a very picturesque rich-

ness of color ; the constant sense, namely, of a superincumbent layer of " gentlefolks," whom she and her companions can never raise their heads unduly without hitting.

My chief complaint with Adam Bede himself is that he is too good. He is meant, I conceive, to be every inch a man ; but, to my mind, there are several inches wanting. He lacks spontaneity and sensibility, he is too stiff-backed. He lacks that supreme quality without which a man can never be interesting to men, — the capacity to be tempted. His nature is without richness or responsiveness. I doubt not that such men as he exist, especially in the author's thrice-English Loamshire ; she has partially described them as a class, with a felicity which carries conviction. She claims for her hero that, although a plain man, he was as little an ordinary man as he was a genius.

" He was not an average man. Yet such men as he are reared here and there in every generation of our peasant artisans, with an inheritance of affections nurtured by a simple family life of common need and common industry, and an inheritance of faculties trained in skilful, courageous labor ; they make their way upward, rarely as geniuses, most commonly as painstaking, honest men, with the skill and conscience to do well the tasks that lie before them. Their lives have no discernible echo beyond the neighborhood where they dwelt ; but you are almost sure to find there some good piece of road, some building, some application of mineral produce, some improvement in farming practice, some reform of parish abuses, with which their names are associated by one or two generations after them. Their employers were the richer for them ; the work of their hands has worn well, and the work of their brains has guided well the hands of other men."

One cannot help feeling thankful to the kindly writer who attempts to perpetuate their memories beyond the generations which profit immediately by their toil. If she is not a great dramatist, she is at least an exquisite describer. But one can as little help feeling that it is no more than a strictly logical retribution, that in her hour of need (dramatically speaking) she should find them indifferent to their duties as heroes. I profoundly doubt whether the central object of a novel may successfully be a passionless creature. The ultimate eclipse, both of Adam Bede and of Felix Holt would seem to justify my question. Tom Tulliver is passionless, and Tom Tulliver lives gratefully in the memory; but this, I take it, is because he is strictly a subordinate figure, and awakens no reaction of feeling on the reader's part by usurping a position which he is not the man to fill.

Dinah Morris is apparently a study from life; and it is warm praise to say, that, in spite of the high key in which she is conceived, morally, she retains many of the warm colors of life. But I confess that it is hard to conceive of a woman so exalted by religious fervor remaining so cool-headed and so temperate. There is in Dinah Morris too close an agreement between her distinguished natural disposition and the action of her religious faith. If by nature she had been passionate, rebellious, selfish, I could better understand her actual self-abnegation. I would look upon it as the logical fruit of a profound religious experience. But as she stands, heart and soul go easily hand in hand. I believe it to be very uncommon for what is called a religious conversion merely to intensify and consecrate pre-existing inclinations. It is usually a change, a wrench; and the new life is apt to be the more sincere as the old one had less in common with it. But, as I have said, Dinah Morris bears so many indications of being a reflection of facts well known to the author, — and the phenomena of Methodism, from the frequency with which their existence is referred to in her pages, appear to be so familiar to her, — that I hesitate to do anything but thankfully accept her portrait. About Hetty Sorrel I shall have no hesitation whatever: I accept her with all my heart. Of all

George Eliot's female figures she is the least ambitious, and on the whole, I think, the most successful. The part of the story which concerns her is much the most forcible; and there is something infinitely tragic in the reader's sense of the contrast between the sternly prosaic life of the good people about her, their wholesome decency and their noonday probity, and the dusky sylvan path along which poor Hetty is tripping, light-footed, to her ruin. Hetty's conduct throughout seems to me to be thoroughly consistent. The author has escaped the easy error of representing her as in any degree made serious by suffering. She is vain and superficial by nature; and she remains so to the end. As for Arthur Donnithorne, I would rather have had him either better or worse. I would rather have had a little more premeditation before his fault, or a little more repentance after it; that is, while repentance could still be of use. Not that, all things considered, he is not a very fair image of a frank-hearted, well-meaning, careless, self-indulgent young gentleman; but the author has in his case committed the error which in Hetty's she avoided, — the error of showing him as redeemed by suffering. I cannot but think that he was as weak as she. A weak woman, indeed, is weaker than a weak man; but Arthur Donnithorne was a superficial fellow, a person emphatically not to be moved by a shock of conscience into a really interesting and dignified attitude, such as he is made to assume at the close of the book. Why not see things in their nakedness? the impatient reader is tempted to ask. Why not let passions and foibles play themselves out?

It is as a picture, or rather as a series of pictures, that I find "Adam Bede" most valuable. The author succeeds better in drawing attitudes of feeling than in drawing movements of feeling. Indeed, the only attempt at development of character or of purpose in the book occurs in the case of Arthur Donnithorne, where the materials are of the simplest kind. Hetty's lapse into disgrace is not gradual, it is immediate: it is without struggle and without passion. Adam himself has arrived at perfect righteousness when the book opens; and it is impossible to go beyond that. In his case too, therefore, there is no dramatic progression. The same remark applies to Dinah Morris. It is not in her conceptions nor her composition that George Eliot is strongest: it is in her *touches*. In these she is quite original. She is a good deal of a humorist, and something of a satirist; but she is neither Dickens nor Thackeray. She has over them the great advantage that she is also a good deal of a philosopher; and it is to this union of the keenest observation with the ripest reflection, that her style owes its essential force. She is a thinker,— not, perhaps, a passionate thinker, but at least a serious one; and the term can be applied with either adjective neither to Dickens nor Thackeray. The constant play of lively and vigorous thought about the objects furnished by her observation animates these latter with a surprising richness of color and a truly human interest. It gives to the author's style, moreover, that lingering, affectionate, comprehensive quality which is its chief distinction; and perhaps occasionally it makes her tedious. George Eliot is so little tedious, however, because, if, on the one hand, her reflection never flags, so, on the other, her observation never ceases to supply it with material. Her observation, I think, is decidedly of the feminine kind: it deals, in preference, with small things. This fact may be held to explain the excellence of what I have called her pictures, and the comparative feebleness of her dramatic movement. The contrast here indicated, strong in "Adam Bede," is most striking in "Felix Holt, the Radical." The latter work is an admirable tissue of details; but it seems to me quite without character as a composition. It leaves upon the mind no single impression. Felix Holt's radical-ism, the pretended motive of the story, is utterly choked amidst a mass of subordinate interests. No representation is attempted of the growth of his opinions, or of their action upon his character: he is marked by the same singular rigidity of outline and fixedness of posture which characterized Adam Bede, — except, perhaps, that there is a certain inclination towards poetry in Holt's attitude. But if the general outline is timid and undecided in "Felix Holt," the different parts are even richer than in former works. There is no person in the book who attains to triumphant vitality; but there is not a single figure, of however little importance, that has not caught from without a certain reflection of life. There is a little old waiting-woman to a great lady, — Mrs. Denner by name, — who does not occupy five pages in the story, but who leaves upon the mind a most vivid impression of decent, contented, intelligent, half-stoical servility.

"There were different orders of beings, — so ran Denner's creed, — and she belonged to another order than that to which her mistress belonged. She had a mind as sharp as a needle, and would have seen through and through the ridiculous pretensions of a born servant who did not submissively accept the rigid fate which had given her born superiors. She would have called such pretensions the wrigglings of a worm that tried to walk on its tail. . . . . She was a hard-headed, godless little woman, but with a character to be reckoned on as you reckon on the qualities of iron."

"I'm afraid of ever expecting anything good again," her mistress says to her in a moment of depression.

"'That's weakness, madam. Things don't happen because they are bad or good, else all eggs would be addled or none at all, and at the most it is but six to the dozen. There's good chances and bad chances, and nobody's luck is pulled only by one string. . . . . . There's a good deal of pleasure in life for you yet.'

"'Nonsense! There's no pleasure for old women...... What are your pleasures, Denner, besides being a slave to me?'

"O, there's pleasure in knowing one is not a fool, like half the people one sees about. And managing one's husband is some pleasure, and doing one's business well. Why, if I've only got some orange-flowers to candy, I should n't like to die till I see them all right. Then there's the sunshine now and then; I like that, as the cats do. I look upon it life is like our game at whist, when Banks and his wife come to the still-room of an evening. I don't enjoy the game much, but I like to play my cards well, and see what will be the end of it; and I want to see you make the best of your hand, madam, for your luck has been mine these forty years now.'"

And, on another occasion, when her mistress exclaims, in a fit of distress, that "God was cruel when he made women," the author says:—

"The waiting-woman had none of that awe which could be turned into defiance; the sacred grove was a common thicket to her.

"'It may n't be good luck to be a woman,' she said. 'But one begins with it from a baby; one gets used to it. And I should n't like to be a man,—to cough so loud, and stand straddling about on a wet day, and be so wasteful with meat and drink. *They 're a coarse lot, I think.*'"

I should think they were, beside Mrs. Denner.

This glimpse of her is made up of what I have called the author's *touches.* She excels in the portrayal of homely stationary figures for which her well-stored memory furnishes her with types. Here is another touch, in which satire predominates. Harold Transome makes a speech to the electors at Treby.

"Harold's only interruption came from his own party. The oratorical clerk at the Factory, acting as the tribune of the dissenting interest, and feeling bound to put questions, might have been troublesome; *but his voice being unpleasantly sharp, while Harold's was full and penetrating, the questioning was cried down.*"

Of the four English stories, "The Mill on the Floss" seems to me to have most dramatic continuity, in distinction from that descriptive, discursive method of narration which I have attempted to indicate. After Hetty Sorrel, I think Maggie Tulliver the most successful of the author's young women, and after Tito Melema, Tom Tulliver the best of her young men. English novels abound in pictures of childhood; but I know of none more truthful and touching than the early pages of this work. Poor erratic Maggie is worth a hundred of her positive brother, and yet on the very threshold of life she is compelled to accept him as her master. He falls naturally into the man's privilege of always being in the right. The following scene is more than a reminiscence; it is a real retrospect. Tom and Maggie are sitting upon the bough of an elder-tree, eating jam-puffs. At last only one remains, and Tom undertakes to divide it.

"The knife descended on the puff, and it was in two; but the result was not satisfactory to Tom, for he still eyed the halves doubtfully. At last he said, 'Shut your eyes, Maggie.'

"'What for?'

"'You never mind what for,—shut 'em when I tell you.'

"Maggie obeyed.

"'Now, which 'll you have, Maggie, right hand or left?'

"'I 'll have that one with the jam run out,' said Maggie, keeping her eyes shut to please Tom.

"'Why, you don't like that, you silly. You may have it if it comes to you fair, but I sha'n't give it to you without. Right or left,—you choose now. Ha-a-a!' said Tom, in a tone of exasperation, as Maggie peeped. 'You keep your eyes shut now, else you sha'n't have any.'

"Maggie's power of sacrifice did not extend so far; indeed, I fear she cared less that Tom should enjoy the utmost possible amount of puff, than that he should be pleased with her for giving him the best bit. So she shut her eyes quite close until Tom told her to ' say which,' and then she said, ' Left hand.'

" ' You 've got it,' said Tom, in rather a bitter tone.

" ' What ! the bit with the jam run out ? '

" ' No ; here, take it,' said Tom, firmly, handing decidedly the best piece to Maggie.

" ' O, please, Tom, have it ; I don't mind, — I like the other ; please take this.'

" ' No, I sha'n't,' said Tom, almost crossly, beginning on his own inferior piece.

" Maggie, thinking it was of no use to contend further, began too, and ate up her half puff with considerable relish as well as rapidity. But Tom had finished first, and had to look on while Maggie ate her last morsel or two, feeling in himself a capacity for more. *Maggie did n't know Tom was looking at her : she was seesawing on the elder-bough, lost to everything but a vague sense of jam and idleness.*

" ' O, you greedy thing ! ' said Tom, when she had swallowed the last morsel."

The portions of the story which bear upon the Dodson family are in their way not unworthy of Balzac ; only that, while our author has treated its peculiarities humorously, Balzac would have treated them seriously, almost solemnly. We are reminded of him by the attempt to classify the Dodsons socially in a scientific manner, and to accumulate small examples of their idiosyncrasies. I do not mean to say that the resemblance is very deep. The chief defect — indeed, the only serious one — in "The Mill on the Floss " is its conclusion. Such a conclusion is in itself assuredly not illegitimate, and there is nothing in the fact of the flood, to my knowledge, essentially unnatural : what I object to is its relation to the preceding part of the story. The story is told as if it were destined to have, if not a strictly happy termination, at least one within ordinary probabilities. As it stands, the *dénouement* shocks the reader most painfully. Nothing has prepared him for it ; the story does not move towards it ; it casts no shadow before it. Did such a *dénouement* lie within the author's intentions from the first, or was it a tardy expedient for the solution of Maggie's difficulties ? This question the reader asks himself, but of course he asks it in vain. For my part, although, as long as humanity is subject to floods and earthquakes, I have no objection to see them made use of in novels, I would in this particular case have infinitely preferred that Maggie should have been left to her own devices. I understand the author's scruples, and to a certain degree I respect them. A lonely spinsterhood seemed but a dismal consummation of her generous life ; and yet, as the author conceives, it was unlikely that she would return to Stephen Guest. I respect Maggie profoundly ; but nevertheless I ask, Was this after all so unlikely ? I will not try to answer the question. I have shown enough courage in asking it. But one thing is certain : a *dénouement* by which Maggie should have called Stephen back would have been extremely interesting, and would have had far more in its favor than can be put to confusion by a mere exclamation of horror.

I have come to the end of my space without speaking of "Romola," which, as the most important of George Eliot's works, I had kept in reserve. I have only room to say that on the whole I think it *is* decidedly the most important, — not the most entertaining nor the most readable, but the one in which the largest things are attempted and grasped. The figure of Savonarola, subordinate though it is, is a figure on a larger scale than any which George Eliot has elsewhere undertaken ; and in the career of Tito Melema there is a fuller representation of the development of a character. Considerable as are our author's qualities as an artist, and largely as they are displayed in "Romola," the book strikes me less as a work of art than as a work of morals. Like all of George Eliot's works, its dramatic construction is feeble ; the story drags and halts, — the setting is too large for the picture ; but I remember that, the first time I read it, I declared to myself that much should be forgiven it for the sake of its generous feeling and its elevated morality. I still recognize this latter fact, but I think I find it more on a level than I at first found it with the artistic conditions of the book. "Our deeds determine us," George Eliot says somewhere in "Adam Bede," "as much as we determine our deeds." This is the moral lesson of "Romola." A man has no associate so intimate as his own character, his own career, — his present and his past ; and if he builds up his career of timid and base actions, they cling to him like evil companions, to sophisticate, to corrupt, and to damn him. As in Maggie Tulliver we had a picture of the elevation of the moral tone by honesty and generosity, so that when the mind found itself face to face with the need for a strong muscular effort, it was competent to perform it ; so in Tito we have a picture of that depression of the moral tone by falsity and self-indulgence, which gradually evokes on every side of the subject some implacable claim, to be avoided or propitiated. At last all his unpaid debts join issue before him, and he finds the path of life a hideous blind alley. Can any argument be more plain ? Can any lesson be more salutary ? "Under every guilty secret," writes the author, with her usual felicity, "there is a hidden brood of guilty wishes, whose unwholesome, infecting life is cherished by the darkness. The contaminating effect of deeds often lies less in the commission than in the consequent adjustment of our desires, — the enlistment of self-interest on the side of falsity ; as, on the other hand, the purifying influence of public confession springs from the fact, that by it the hope in lies is forever swept away, *and the soul recovers the noble attitude of simplicity.*"

And again : "Tito was experiencing that inexorable law of human souls, that we prepare ourselves for sudden deeds by the reiterated choice of good or evil that gradually determines character." Somewhere else I think she says, in purport, that our deeds are like our children ; we beget them, and rear them and cherish them, and they grow up and turn against us and misuse us. The fact that has led me to a belief in the fundamental equality between the worth of "Romola" as a moral argument and its value as a work of art, is the fact that in each character it seems to me essentially prosaic. The excellence both of the spirit and of the execution of the book is emphatically an obvious excellence. They make no demand upon the imagination of the reader. It is true of both of them that he who runs may read them. It may excite surprise that I should intimate that George Eliot is deficient in imagination ; but I believe that I am right in so doing. Very readable novels have been written without imagination ; and as compared with writers who, like Mr. Trollope, are totally destitute of the faculty, George Eliot may be said to be richly endowed with it. But as compared with writers whom we are tempted to call decidedly imaginative, she must, in my opinion, content herself with the very solid distinction of being exclusively an observer. In confirmation of this I would suggest a comparison of those chapters in "Adam Bede" which treat of Hetty's flight and wanderings, and those of Miss Brontë's "Jane Eyre" which describe the heroine's escape from Rochester's house and subsequent perambulations. The former are throughout admirable prose ; the latter are in portions very good poetry.

One word more. Of all the impressions — and they are numerous — which a reperusal of George Eliot's writings has given me, I find the strongest to be this : that (with all deference to "Felix Holt, the Radical") the author is in morals and æsthetics essentially a conservative.

In morals her problems are still the old, passive problems. I use the word "old" with all respect. What moves her most is the idea of a conscience harassed by the memory of slighted obligations. Unless in the case of Savonarola, she has made no attempt to depict a conscience taking upon itself great and novel responsibilities. In her last work, assuredly such an attempt was — considering the title — conspicuous by its absence. Of a corresponding tendency in the second department of her literary character, — or perhaps I should say in a certain middle field where morals and æsthetics move in concert, — it is very diffi-

cult to give an example. A tolerably good one is furnished by her inclination to compromise with the old tradition — and here I use the word "old" *without* respect — which exacts that a serious story of manners shall close with the factitious happiness of a fairy-tale. I know few things more irritating in a literary way than each of her final chapters, — for even in "The Mill on the Floss" there is a fatal "Conclusion." Both as an artist and a thinker, in other words, our author is an optimist; and although a conservative is not necessarily an optimist, I think an optimist is pretty likely to be a conservative.

GRIFFITH GAUNT; OR, JEALOUSY.

CHAPTER XLI.

"YOU say the pedler was a hundred yards behind my husband. Which of the two men was walking fastest?"

Thomas Hayes considered a moment. "Well, Dame, I think the Squire was walking rather the smartest of the two."

"Did the pedler seem likely to overtake him?"

"Nay. Ye see, Dame, Squire he walked straight on; but the pedler he took both sides of the road at onst, as the saying is."

Prisoner. Forgive me, Thomas, but I don't know what you mean.

Hayes (compassionately). How should ye? You are never the worse for liquor, the likes of you.

Prisoner (very keenly). O, he was in liquor, was he?

Hayes. Come, Dame, you do brew good ale at Hernshaw Castle. Ye need n't go to deny that; for, Lord knows, 't is no sin; and a poor fellow may be jolly, yet not to say drunk.

Judge (sternly). Witness, attend, and answer directly.

Prisoner. Nay, my lord, 't is a plain country body, and means no ill. Good Thomas, be so much my friend as to answer plainly. Was the man drunk or sober?

Hayes. All I know is he went from one side o' the road to t' other.

Prisoner. Thomas Hayes, as you hope to be saved eternally, was the pedler drunk or sober?

Hayes. Well, if I must tell on my neighbor or else be damned, then that there pedler was as drunk as a lord.

Here, notwithstanding the nature of the trial, the laughter was irrepressible, and Mrs. Gaunt sat quietly down (for she was allowed a seat), and said no more.

To the surgeon who had examined the body officially, she put this question: "Did you find any signs of violence?"

Surgeon. None whatever; but then there was nothing to go by, except the head and the bones.

Prisoner. Have you experience in

this kind? I mean, have you inspected murdered bodies?

Surgeon. Yes.

Prisoner. How many?

Surgeon. Two before this.

Prisoner. O, pray, pray, do not say " before this "! I have great hopes no murder at all hath been committed here. Let us keep to plain cases. Please you describe the injuries in those two undoubted cases.

Surgeon. In Wellyn's the skull was fractured in two places. In Sherrett's the right arm was broken, and there were some contusions on the head ; but the cause of death was a stab that penetrated the lungs.

Prisoner. Suppose Wellyn's murderers had thrown his body into the water, and the fishes had so mutilated it as they have this one, could you by your art have detected the signs of violence?

Surgeon. Certainly. The man's skull was fractured. Wellyn's, I mean.

Prisoner. I put the same question with regard to Sherrett's.

Surgeon. I cannot answer it ; here the lungs were devoured by the fishes ; no signs of lesion can be detected in an organ that has ceased to exist.

Prisoner. This is too partial. Why select one injury out of several? What I ask is this : could you have detected violence in Sherrett's case, although the fishes had eaten the flesh off his body.

Surgeon. I answer that the minor injuries of Sherrett would have been equally perceptible ; to wit, the bruises on the head, and the broken arm ; but not the perforation of the lungs ; and that it was killed the man.

Prisoner. Then, so far as you know, and can swear, about murder, more blows have always been struck than one, and some of the blows struck in Sherrett's case, and Wellyn's, would have left traces that fishes' teeth could not efface?

Surgeon. That is so, if I am to be peevishly confined to my small and narrow experience of murdered bodies.

But my general knowledge of the many ways in which life may be taken by violence —

The judge stopped him, and said that could hardly be admitted as evidence against his actual experience.

The prisoner put a drawing of the castle, the mere, and the bridge, into the witnesses' hands, and elicited that it was correct, and also the distances marked on it. They had, in fact, been measured exactly for her.

The hobnailed shoes were produced, and she made some use of them, particularly in cross-examining Jane Bannister.

Prisoner. Look at those shoes. Saw you ever the like on Mr. Gaunt's feet?

Jane. That I never did, Dame.

Prisoner. What, not when he came into the kitchen on the 15th of October?

Jane. Nay, he was booted. By the same token I saw the boy a cleaning of them for supper.

Prisoner. Those boots, when you broke into his room, did you find them?

Jane. Nay, when the man went his boots went ; as reason was. We found naught of his but a soiled glove.

Prisoner. Had the pedler boots on?

Jane. Alas ! who ever seed a booted pedler?

Prisoner. Had he these very shoes on? Look at them.

Jane. I could n't say for that. He had shoon, for they did properly clatter on my bricks.

Judge. Clatter on her bricks ! What in the world does she mean?

Prisoner. I think she means on the floor of her kitchen. 'T is a brick floor, if I remember right.

Judge. Good woman, say, is that what you mean?

Jane. Ay, an 't please you, my lord.

Prisoner. Had the pedler a mole on his forehead?

Jane. Not that I know on. I never took so much notice of the man. But, la, dame, now I look at you, I don't believe you was ever the one to murder our master.

Wiltshire. We don't want your opinion. Confine yourself to facts.

Prisoner. You heard me rating my husband on that night : what was it I said about the constables, — do you remember ?

Jane. La, dame, I would n't ask that if I was in your place.

Prisoner. I am much obliged to you for your advice ; but answer me — truly.

Jane. Well, if you will have it, I think you said they should be here in the morning. But, indeed, good gentlemen, her bark was always worse than her bite, poor soul.

Judge. Here. That meant at Hernshaw Castle, I presume.

Jane. Ay, my lord, an' if it please your lordship's honor's worship.

Mrs. Gaunt, husbanding the patience of the court, put no questions at all to several witnesses ; but she cross-examined Mrs. Ryder very closely. This was necessary ; for Ryder was a fatal witness. Her memory had stored every rash and hasty word the poor lady had uttered, and, influenced either by animosity or prejudice, she put the worst color on every suspicious circumstance. She gave her damnatory evidence neatly, and clearly, and with a seeming candor and regret, that disarmed suspicion.

When her examination in chief concluded, there was but one opinion amongst the bar, and the auditors in general, namely, that the maid had hung the mistress.

Mrs. Gaunt herself felt she had a terrible antagonist to deal with, and, when she rose to cross-examine her, she looked paler than she had done all through the trial.

She rose, but seemed to ask herself how to begin ; and her pallor and her hesitation, while they excited some little sympathy, confirmed the unfavorable impression. She fixed her eyes upon the witness, as if to discover where she was most vulnerable. Mrs. Ryder returned her gaze calmly. The court was hushed ; for it was evident a duel was coming between two women of no common ability.

The opening rather disappointed expectation. Mrs. Gaunt seemed, by her manner, desirous to propitiate the witness.

Prisoner (very civilly). You say you brought Thomas Leicester to my bedroom on that terrible night ?

Ryder (civilly). Yes, madam.

Prisoner. And you say he stayed there half an hour ?

Ryder. Yes, madam ; he did.

Prisoner. May I inquire how you know he stayed just half an hour ?

Ryder. My watch told me that, madam. I brought him to you at a quarter past eleven ; and you did not ring for me till a quarter to twelve.

Prisoner. And when I did ring for you, what then ?

Ryder. I came and took the man away, by your orders.

Prisoner. At a quarter to twelve ?

Ryder. At a quarter to twelve.

Prisoner. This Leicester was a lover of yours ?

Ryder. Not he.

Prisoner. O, fie ! Why, he offered you marriage ; it went so far as that.

Ryder. O, that was before you set him up pedler.

Prisoner. 'T was so ; but he was single for your sake, and he renewed his offer that very night. Come, do not forswear yourself about a trifle.

Ryder. Trifle, indeed ! Why, if he did, what has that to do with the murder ? You 'll do yourself no good, madam, by going about so.

Wiltshire. Really, madam, this is beside the mark.

Prisoner. If so, it can do your case no harm. My lord, you did twice interrupt the learned counsel, and forbade him to lead his witnesses ; I not once, for I am for stopping no mouths, but sifting all to the bottom. Now, I implore you to let me have fair play in my turn, and an answer from this slippery witness.

Judge. Prisoner, I do not quite see your drift ; but God forbid you should be hampered in your defence.

Witness, by virtue of your oath, reply directly. Did this pedler offer you marriage that night after he left the prisoner?

Ryder. My lord, he did.

Prisoner. And confided to you he had orders to kill Mr. Gaunt?

Ryder. Not he, madam: that was not the way to win me. He knew that.

Prisoner. What! did not his terrible purpose peep out all the time he was making love to you?

No reply.

Prisoner. You had the kitchen to your two selves? Come, don't hesitate.

Ryder. The other servants were gone to bed. You kept the man so late.

Prisoner. O, I mean no reflection on your prudence. You went out of doors with your wooer; just to see him off?

Ryder. Not I. What for? *I* had nobody to make away with. I just opened the door for him, bolted it after him, and went straight to my bedroom.

Prisoner. How long had you been there when you heard the cry for help?

Ryder. Scarce ten minutes. I had not taken my stays off.

Prisoner. If you and Thomas Hayes speak true, that gives half an hour you were making love to with the murderer after he left me. Am I correct?

The witness now saw whither she had been led, and changed her manner: she became sullen, and watched an opportunity to stab.

Prisoner. Had he a mole on his brow?

Ryder. Not that I know of.

Prisoner. Why, where were your eyes then, when the murderer saluted you at parting?

Ryder's eyes flashed; but she felt her temper tried, and governed it all the more severely. She treated the question with silent contempt.

Prisoner. But you pass for a discreet woman; perhaps you looked modestly down when the assassin saluted you?

Ryder. If he saluted me, *perhaps* I did.

Prisoner. In that case you could not see his mole; but you must have noticed his shoes. Were these the shoes he wore? Look at them well.

Ryder (after inspecting them). I do not recognize them.

Prisoner. Will you swear these were not the shoes he had on?

Ryder. How can I swear that? I know nothing about the man's shoes. If you please, my lord, am I to be kept here all day with her foolish, trifling questions?

Judge. All day, and all night too, if Justice requires it. The law is not swift to shed blood.

Prisoner. My lord and the gentlemen of the jury were here before you, and will be kept here after you. Prithee, attend. Look at that drawing of Hernshaw Castle and Hernshaw Mere. Now take this pencil, and mark your bedroom on the drawing.

The pencil was taken from the prisoner, and handed to Ryder. She waited, like a cat, till it came close to her; then recoiled with an admirable scream. "Me handle a thing hot from the hand of a murderess! It makes me tremble all over!"

This cruel stab affected the prisoner visibly. She put her hand to her bosom, and, with tears in her eyes, faltered out a request to the judge that she might sit down a minute.

Judge. To be sure you may. And you, my good woman, must not run before the court. By law a prisoner is innocent till found guilty by his peers. How do you know what evidence she may have in store? At present we have only heard one side. Be more moderate.

The prisoner rose promptly to her feet. "My lord, I welcome the insult that has disgusted your lordship and the gentlemen of the jury, and won me those good words of comfort." To Ryder: "What sort of a night was it?"

Ryder. Very little moon, but a clear, starry night.

Prisoner. Could you see the Mere, and the banks?

Ryder. Nay, but so much of it as faced my window.

Prisoner. Have you marked your window?

Ryder. I have.

Prisoner. Now mark the place where you heard Mr. Gaunt cry for help.

Ryder. 'T was about here, — under these trees. And that is why I could not see him : along of the shadow.

Prisoner. Possibly. Did you see me on that side the Mere?

Ryder. No.

Prisoner. What colored dress had I on at that time?

Ryder. White satin.

Prisoner. Then you could have seen me, even among the trees, had I been on that side the Mere?

Ryder. I can't say. However, I never said you were on the very spot where the deed was done ; but you were out of doors.

Prisoner. How do you know that?

Ryder. Why, you told me so yourself.

Prisoner. Then, that is my evidence, not yours. Swear to no more than you know. Had my husband, to your knowledge, a reason for absconding suddenly?

Ryder. Yes, he had.

Prisoner. What was it?

Ryder. Fear of you.

Prisoner. Nay, I mean, had he not something to fear, something quite different from that I am charged with?

Ryder. You know best, madam. I would gladly serve you, but I cannot guess what you are driving at.

The prisoner was taken aback by this impudent reply. She hesitated to force her servant to expose a husband, whom she believed to be living : and her hesitation looked like discomfiture ; and Ryder was victorious in that encounter.

By this time they were both thoroughly embittered, and it was war to the knife.

Prisoner. You listened to our unhappy quarrel that night?

Ryder. Quarrel! madam, 't was all on one side.

Prisoner. How did you understand what I said to him about the constables?

Ryder. Constables! I never heard you say the word.

Prisoner. Oh!

Ryder. Neither when you threatened him with your knife to me, nor when you threatened him to his face.

Prisoner. Take care : you forget that Jane Bannister heard me. Was her ear nearer the keyhole than yours?

Ryder. Jane! she is a simpleton. You could make her think she heard anything. I noticed you put the words in her mouth.

Prisoner. God forgive you, you naughty woman. You had better have spoken the truth.

Ryder. My lord, if you please, am I to be miscalled — by a murderess?

Judge. Come, come, this is no place for recrimination.

The prisoner now stooped and examined her papers, and took a distinct line of cross-examination.

Prisoner (with apparent carelessness). At all events, you are a virtuous woman, Mrs. Ryder?

Ryder. Yes, madam, as virtuous as yourself, to say the least.

Prisoner (still more carelessly). Married or single?

Ryder. Single, and like to be.

Prisoner. Yes, if I remember right, I made a point of that before I engaged you as my maid.

Ryder. I believe the question was put.

Prisoner. Here is the answer in your handwriting. Is not that your handwriting?

Ryder (after inspecting it). It is.

Prisoner. You came highly recommended by your last mistress, a certain Mrs. Hamilton. Here is *her* letter, describing you as a model.

Ryder. Well, madam, hitherto, I have given satisfaction to all my mistresses, Mrs. Hamilton among the rest. My character does not rest on her word only, I hope.

Prisoner. Excuse me; I engaged you on her word alone. Now, who is this Mrs. Hamilton?

Ryder. A worshipful lady I served for eight months before I came to you. She went abroad, or I should be with her now.

Prisoner. Now cast your eye over this paper.

It was the copy of a marriage certificate between Thomas Edwards and Caroline Plunkett.

"Who is this Caroline Plunkett?"

Ryder turned very pale, and made no reply.

"I ask you who is this Caroline Plunkett?"

Ryder (faintly). Myself.

Judge. Why, you said you were single!

Ryder. So I am; as good as single. My husband and me we parted eight years ago, and I have never seen him since.

Prisoner. Was it quite eight years ago?

Ryder. Nearly, 't was in May, 1739.

Prisoner. But you have lived with him since.

Ryder. Never, upon my soul.

Prisoner. When was your child born?

Ryder. My child! I have none.

Prisoner. In January, 1743, you left a baby at Biggleswade, with a woman called Church, — did you not?

Ryder (panting). Of course I did. It was my sister's.

Prisoner. Do you mean to call God to witness that child was not your's?

Ryder hesitated.

Prisoner. Will you swear Mrs. Church did not see you suckle that child in secret, and weep over it?

At this question the perspiration stood visible on Ryder's brow, her cheeks were ghastly, and her black eyes roved like some wild animal's round the court. She saw her own danger, and had no means of measuring her inquisitor's information.

"My lord, have pity on me. I was betrayed, abandoned. Why am I so tormented? *I* have not committed

murder." So, catlike, she squealed and scratched at once.

Prisoner. What! to swear away an innocent life, is not that murder?

Judge. Prisoner, we make allowances for your sex, and your peril, but you must not remark on the evidence at present. Examine as severely as you will, but abstain from comment till you address the jury on your defence.

Sergeant Wiltshire. My lord, I submit that this line of examination is barbarous, and travels out of the case entirely.

Prisoner. Not so, Mr. Sergeant. 'T is done by advice of an able lawyer. My life is in peril, unless I shake this witness's credit. To that end I show you she is incontinent, and practised in falsehood. Unchastity has been held in these courts to disqualify a female witness, hath it not, my lord?

Judge. Hardly. But to disparage her evidence it has. And wisely; for she who loses her virtue enters on a life of deceit; and lying is a habit that spreads from one thing to many. Much wisdom there is in ancient words. Our forefathers taught us to call a virtuous woman an honest woman, and the law does but follow in that track; still, however, leaving much to the discretion of the jury.

Prisoner. I would show her more mercy than she has shown to me. Therefore I leave that matter. Witness, be so good as to examine Mrs. Hamilton's letter, and compare it with your own. The "y's" and the "s's" are peculiar in both, and yet the same. Come, confess, Mrs. Hamilton's is a forgery. You wrote it. Be pleased to hand both letters up to my lord to compare; the disguise is but thin.

Ryder. Forgery there was none. There is no Mrs. Hamilton. (She burst into tears.) I had my child to provide for, and no man to help me! What was I to do? A servant must live.

Prisoner. Then why not let her mistress live, whose bread she has eaten? My lord, shall not this false witness be sent hence to prison for perjury?

Wiltshire. Certainly not. What woman on earth is expected to reveal her own shame upon oath? 'T was not fair nor human to put such questions. Come, madam, leave torturing this poor creature. Show some mercy; you may need it yourself.

Prisoner. Sir, 't is not mercy I ask, but justice according to law. But since you do me the honor to make me a request, I will comply, and ask her but one question more. Describe my apartment into which you showed Thomas Leicester that night. Begin at the outer door.

Ryder. First there is the anteroom; then the boudoir; then there's your bedchamber.

Prisoner. Into which of those three did you show Thomas Leicester?

Ryder. Into the anteroom.

Prisoner. Then why did you say it was in my chamber I entertained him?

Ryder. Madam, I meant no more than that it was your private apartment up stairs.

Prisoner. You contrived to make the gentlemen think otherwise.

Judge. That you did. 'T is down in my notes that she received the pedler in her bedchamber.

Ryder (sobbing). God is my witness I did not mean to mislead your lordship: and I ask my lady's pardon for not being more exact in that particular.

At this the prisoner bowed to the judge, and sat down with one victorious flash of her gray eye at the witness, who was in an abject condition of fear, and hung all about the witness-box limp as a wet towel.

Sergeant Wiltshire saw she was so thoroughly cowed she would be apt to truckle, and soften her evidence to propitiate the prisoner; so he asked her but one question.

"Were you and the prisoner on good terms?"

Ryder. On the best of terms. She was always a good and liberal mistress to me.

Wiltshire. I will not prolong your sufferings. You may go down.

Judge. But you will not leave the court till this trial is ended. I have grave doubts whether I ought not to commit you.

Unfortunately for the prisoner, Ryder was not the last witness for the crown. The others that followed were so manifestly honest that it would have been impolitic to handle them severely. The prisoner, therefore, put very few questions to them; and, when the last witness went down, the case looked very formidable.

The evidence for the crown being now complete, the judge retired for some refreshment; and the court buzzed like a hum of bees. Mrs. Gaunt's lips and throat were parched and her heart quaked.

A woman of quite the lower order thrust forth a great arm, and gave her an orange. Mrs. Gaunt thanked her sweetly; and the juice relieved her throat.

Also this bit of sympathy was of good omen, and did her heart good.

She buried her face in her hands, and collected all her powers for the undertaking before her. She had noted down the exact order of her topics, but no more.

The judge returned; the crier demanded silence; and the prisoner rose, and turned her eyes modestly but steadily upon those who held her life in their hands: and, true to the wisdom of her sex, the first thing she aimed at was — to please.

"My lord, and you gentlemen of the jury, I am now to reply to a charge of murder, founded on a little testimony, and a good deal of false, but, I must needs say, reasonable conjecture.

"I am innocent; but, unlike other innocent persons who have stood here before me, I have no man to complain of.

"The magistrates who committed me proceeded with due caution and humanity; they weighed my hitherto unspotted reputation, and were in no hurry to prejudge me; here, in this court, I have met with much forbearance; the learned counsel for the crown has made me

groan under his abilities ; that was his
duty ; but he said from the first he
would do nothing hard, and he has
kept his word ; often he might have
stopped me ; I saw it in his face. But,
being a gentleman and a Christian, as
well as a learned lawyer, methinks he
said to himself, ' This is a poor gentlewoman pleading for her life ; let her
have some little advantage.' As for my
lord, he has promised to be my counsel,
so far as his high station, and duty to
the crown, admit ; and he has supported and consoled me more than once
with words of justice, that would not, I
think, have encouraged a guilty person,
but have comforted and sustained me
beyond expression. So then I stand
here, the victim, not of man's injustice,
but of deceitful appearances, and of
honest, but hasty and loose conjectures.

" These conjectures I shall now sift,
and hope to show you how hollow they
are.

" Gentlemen, in every disputed matter the best way, I am told, is to begin
by settling what both parties are agreed
in, and so to narrow the matter. To
use that method, then, I do heartily
agree with the learned counsel that
murder is a heinous crime, and that,
black as it is at the best, yet it is still
more detestable when 't is a wife that
murders her husband, and robs her
child of a parent who can never be replaced.

" I also agree with him that circumstantial evidence is often sufficient to
convict a murderer ; and, indeed, were
it not so, that most monstrous of crimes
would go oftenest unpunished ; since,
of all culprits, murderers do most shun
the eyes of men in their dark deeds,
and so provide beforehand that direct
testimony to their execrable crime there
shall be none. Only herein I am advised to take a distinction that escaped
the learned sergeant. I say that first of
all it ought to be proved directly, and
to the naked eye, that a man has been
murdered ; and then, if none saw the
crime done, let circumstances point out
the murderer.

" But here, they put the cart before
the horse ; they find a dead body, with
no marks of violence whatever ; and
labor to prove by circumstantial evidence alone that this mere dead body
is a murdered body. This, I am advised, is bad in law, and contrary to
general precedents ; and the particular
precedents for it are not examples, but
warnings ; since both the prisoners so
rashly convicted were proved innocent,
after their execution."

(The judge took a note of this distinction.)

" Then, to go from principles to the
facts, I agree and admit that, in a moment of anger, I was so transported out
of myself as to threaten my husband's
life before Caroline Ryder. But afterwards, when I saw him face to face,
then, that I threatened him with *violence*, that I deny. The fact is, I had
just learned that he had committed a
capital offence ; and what I threatened
him with was the law. This was proved
by Jane Bannister. She says she heard
me say the constables should come for
him next morning. For what ? to murder him ? "

Judge. Give me leave, madam.
Shall you prove Mr. Gaunt had committed a capital offence ?

Prisoner. I could, my lord ; but I
am loath to do it. For, if I did, I should
cast him into worse trouble than I am
in myself.

Judge (shaking his head gravely).
Let me advise you to advance nothing
you are not able and willing to prove.

Prisoner. " Then I confine myself
to this : it was proved by a witness
for the crown that in the dining-room I
threatened my husband to his face with
the law. Now this threat, and not that
other extravagant threat, which he
never heard, you know, was clearly the
threat which caused him to abscond
that night.

" In the next place, I agree with the
learned counsel that I was out of doors
at one o'clock that morning. But if he
will use me as HIS WITNESS in that matter, then he must not pick and choose
and mutilate my testimony. Nay, let

him take the whole truth, and not just so much as he can square with the indictment. Either believe me, that I was out of doors praying, or do not believe me that I was out of doors at all.

"Gentlemen, hear the simple truth. You may see in the map, on the south side of Hernshaw Castle, a grove of large fir-trees. 'T is a reverend place, most fit for prayer and meditation. Here I have prayed a thousand times and more before the 15th of October. Hence 't is called 'The Dame's Haunt,' as I shall prove, that am the dame 't is called after.

"Let it not seem incredible to you that I should pray out of doors in my grove, on a fine, clear, starry night. For aught I know, Protestants may pray only by the fireside. But, remember, I am a Catholic. We are not so contracted in our praying. We do not confine it to little comfortable places. Nay, but for seventeen hundred years and more we have prayed out of doors as much as in doors. And this our custom is no fit subject for a shallow sneer. How does the learned sergeant know that, beneath the vault of heaven at night, studded with those angelic eyes, the stars, is an unfit place to bend the knee, and raise the soul in prayer? Has he ever tried it?"

This sudden appeal to a learned and eminent, but by no means devotional sergeant, so tickled the gentlemen of the bar, that they burst out laughing with singular unanimity.

This dashed the prisoner, who had not intended to be funny; and she hesitated, and looked distressed.

Judge. Proceed, madam; these remarks of yours are singular, but quite pertinent, and no fit subject for ridicule. Gentlemen, remember the public looks to you for an example.

Prisoner. "My lord, 't was my fault for making that personal which should be general. But women they are so. 'T is our foible. I pray the good sergeant to excuse me.

"I say, then, generally, that when the sun retires, then earth fades, but heaven comes out in tenfold glory; and I say the starry firmament at night is a temple not built with hands, and the bare sight of it subdues the passions, chastens the heart, and aids the soul in prayer surprisingly. My lord, as I am a Christian woman, 't is true that my husband had wronged me cruelly and broken the law. 'T is true that I raged against him, and he answered me not again. 'T is true, as that witness said, that my bark is worse than my bite. I cooled, and then felt I had forgotten the wife and the Christian in my wrath. I repented, and, to be more earnest in my penitence, I did go and pray out o' doors beneath those holy eyes of heaven that seemed to look down with chaste reproach on my ungoverned heat. I left my fireside, my velvet cushions, and all the little comforts made by human hands, that adorn our earthly dwellings, but distract our eyes from God."

Some applause followed this piece of eloquence, exquisitely uttered. It was checked, and the prisoner resumed, with an entire change of manner.

"Gentlemen, the case against me is like a piece of rotten wood varnished all over. It looks fair to the eye; but will not bear handling.

"As example of what I say, take three charges on which the learned sergeant greatly relied in opening his case : —

"1st. That I received Thomas Leicester in my bedroom.

"2d. That he went hot from me after Mr. Gaunt.

"3d. That he was seen following Mr. Gaunt with a bloody intent.

"How ugly these three proofs looked at first sight! Well, but when we squeezed the witnesses ever so little, what did those three dwindle down to?

"1st. That I received Thomas Leicester in an anteroom, which leads to a boudoir, and that boudoir leads to my bedroom.

"2d. That Thomas Leicester went from me to the kitchen, and there, for a good half-hour, drank my ale (as it appears), and made love to his old sweetheart, Caroline Ryder, the false witness for the crown; and went abroad fresh from *her*, and not from *me*.

"3d. That he was not (to speak strictly) seen following Mr. Gaunt, but just walking on the same road, drunk, and staggering, and going at such a rate that, as the crown's own witness swore, he could not in the nature of things overtake Mr. Gaunt, who walked quicker, and straighter too, than he.

"So then, even if a murder has been done, they have failed to connect Thomas Leicester with it, or me with Thomas Leicester. Two broken links in a chain of but three.

"And now I come to the more agreeable part of my defence. I do think there has been no murder at all.

"There is no evidence of a murder.

"A body is found with the flesh eaten by fishes, but the bones and the head uninjured. They swear a surgeon, who has examined the body, and certainly he had the presumption to guess it looks like a murdered body. But, being sifted, he was forced to admit that, so far as his experience of murdered bodies goes, it is not like a murdered body; for there is no bone broken, nor bruise on the head.

"Where is the body found? In the water. But water by itself is a sufficient cause of death, and a common cause too; and kills without breaking bones, or bruising the head. O perversity of the wise! For every one creature murdered in England, ten are accidentally drowned; and they find a dead man in the water, which is as much as to say they find the slain in the arms of the slayer; yet they do not once suspect the water, but go about in search of a strange and monstrous crime.

"Mr. Gaunt's cry for help was heard *here*, if it was heard at all (which I greatly doubt), here by this clump of trees; the body was found here, hard by the bridge; which is, by measurement, one furlong and sixty paces from that clump of trees, as I shall prove. There is no current in the mere lively enough to move a body,

and what there is runs the wrong way. So this disconnects the cry for help, and the dead body. Another broken link !

"And now I come to my third defence.

"I say the body is not the body of Griffith Gaunt.

"The body, mutilated as it was, had two distinguishing marks; a mole on the brow, and a pair of hobnailed shoes on the feet.

"Now the advisers of the crown fix their eyes on that mole; but they turn their heads away from the hobnailed shoes. But why? Articles of raiment found on a body are legal evidence of identity. How often, my lord, in cases of murder, hath the crown relied on such particulars, especially in cases where corruption had obscured the features !

"I shall not imitate this partiality, this obstinate prejudice; I shall not ask you to shut your eyes on the mole, as they do on the shoes, but shall meet the whole truth fairly.

"Mr. Gaunt went from my house that morning with boots on his feet, and with a mole on his brow.

"Thomas Leicester went the same road, with shoes on his feet, and, as I shall prove, with a mole on his brow.

"To be sure, the crown witnesses did not distinctly admit this mole on him; but you will remember, they dared not deny it on their oaths, and so run their heads into an indictment for perjury.

"But, gentlemen, I shall put seven witnesses into the box, who will all swear that they have known Thomas Leicester for years, and that he had a mole upon his left temple.

"One of these witnesses is — the mother that bore him.

"I shall then call witnesses to prove that, on the 15th of October, the bridge over the mere was in bad repair, and a portion of the side rail gone; and that the body was found within a few yards of that defective bridge; and then, as Thomas Leicester went that way, drunk, and staggering from side to side, you may reasonably infer that he fell into the water in passing the bridge. To show you this is possible, I shall prove the same thing has actually occurred. I shall swear the oldest man in the parish, who will depose to a similar event that happened in his boyhood. He hath said it a thousand times before to-day, and now will swear it. He will tell you that on a certain day, sixty-nine years ago, the parson of Hernshaw, the Rev. Augustus Murthwaite, went to cross this bridge at night, after carousing at Hernshaw Castle with our great-grandfather, my husband's and mine, the then proprietor of Hernshaw, and tumbled into the water; and his body was found gnawed out of the very form of humanity by the fishes, within a yard or two of the spot where poor Tom Leicester was found, that hath cost us all this trouble. So do the same causes bring round the same events in a cycle of years. The only difference is that the parson drank his death in our dining-room, and the pedler in our kitchen.

"No doubt, my lord, you have observed that sometimes a hasty and involuntary inaccuracy gives quite a wrong color to a thing. I assure you I have suffered by this. It is said that the moment Mr. Atkins proposed to drag my mere, I fainted away. In this account there is an omission. I shall prove that Mr. Atkins used these words: 'And underneath that water I undertake to find the remains of Griffith Gaunt.' Now, gentlemen, you shall understand that at this time, and indeed until the moment when I saw the shoes upon that poor corpse's feet, I was in great terror for my husband's life. How could it be otherwise? Caroline Ryder had told me she heard his cry for help. He had disappeared. What was I to think? I feared he had fallen in with robbers. I feared all manner of things. So when the lawyer said so positively he would find his body, I was overpowered. Ah, gentlemen, wedded love survives many wrongs, many angry words; I love my husband still; and when the man told

me so brutally that he was certainly dead, I fainted away. I confess it. Shall I be hanged for that?

"But now, thank God, I am full of hope that he is alive, and that good hope has given me the courage to make this great effort to save my own life.

"Hitherto I have been able to contradict my accusers positively; but now I come to a mysterious circumstance that I own puzzles me. Most persons accused of murder could, if they chose, make a clean breast, and tell you the whole matter. But this is not my case. I know shoes from boots, and I know Kate Gaunt from a liar and a murderess. But, when all is said, this is still a dark, mysterious business, and there are things in it I can only deal with as you do, gentlemen, by bringing my wits to bear upon them in reasonable conjecture.

"Caroline Ryder swears she heard Mr. Gaunt cry for help. And Mr. Gaunt has certainly disappeared.

"My accusers have somewhat weakened this by trying to palm off the body of Thomas Leicester on you for the body of Mr. Gaunt. But the original mystery remains, and puzzles me. I might fairly appeal to you to disbelieve the witness. She is proved incontinent, and a practised liar, and she forswore herself in this court, and my lord is in two minds about committing her. But a liar does not always lie, and, to be honest, I think she really *believes* she heard Mr. Gaunt cry for help, for she went straight to his bedroom; and that looks as if she really thought she heard his voice. But a liar may be mistaken. Do not forget that. Distance affects the voice; and I think the voice she heard was Thomas Leicester's, and the place it came from higher up the mere.

"This, my notion, will surprise you less when I prove to you that Leicester's voice bore a family likeness to Mr. Gaunt's. I shall call two witnesses who have been out shooting with Mr. Gaunt and Tom Leicester, and have heard Leicester halloo in the wood, and taken it for Mr. Gaunt.

"Must I tell you the whole truth? This Leicester has always passed for an illegitimate son of Mr. Gaunt's father. He resembled my husband in form, stature, and voice :: he had the Gaunt mole, and has often spoken of it by that name. My husband forgave him many faults for no other reason. —and I bought wares and filled his pack for no other reason — than this ; that he was my husband's brother by nature, though not in law. 'HONI SOIT QUI MAL Y PENSE.'

"Ah, that is a royal device ; yet how often in this business have the advisers of the crown forgotten it ?

"My lord, and gentlemen of the jury, I return from these conjectures to the indisputable facts of my defence.

"Mr. Gaunt may be alive, or he may be dead. He was certainly alive on the 15th of October, and it lies on the crown to prove him dead, and not on me to prove him alive. But as for the body that forms the subject of this indictment, it is the body of Thomas Leicester, who was seen on the 16th of October, at one in the morning, drunk and staggering, and making for Hernshaw Bridge, which leads to his mother's house ; and on all his former visits to Hernshaw Castle he went on to his mother's, as I shall prove. This time, he never reached her, as I shall prove ; but on his way to her did meet his death, by the will of God, and no fault of man or woman, in Hernshaw Mere.

"Call Sarah Leicester."

Judge. I think you say you have several witnesses.

Prisoner. More than twenty, my lord.

Judge. We cannot possibly dispose of them this evening. We will hear your evidence to-morrow. Prisoner, this will enable you to consult with your legal advisers, and let me urge upon you to prove, if you can, that Mr. Gaunt has a sufficient motive for hiding and not answering Mr. Atkins's invitation to inherit a large estate. Some such proof as this is necessary to complete your defence ; and I am sorry to see you have made no mention of it in your address, which was otherwise able.

Prisoner. My lord, I think I can prove my own innocence without casting a slur upon my husband.

Judge. You *think?* when your life is at stake. Be not so mad as to leave so large a hole in your defence, if you can mend it. Take advice.

He said this very solemnly ; then rose and left the court.

Mrs. Gaunt was conveyed back to prison, and there was soon prostrated by the depression that follows an unnatural excitement.

Mr. Houseman found her on a sofa, pale and dejected, and clasping the jailer's wife convulsively, who applied hartshorn to her nostrils.

He proved but a Job's comforter. Her defence, creditable as it was to a novice, seemed wordy and weak to him, a lawyer ; and he was horrified at the admissions she had made. In her place he would have admitted nothing he could not thoroughly explain.

He came to insist on a change of tactics.

When he saw her sad condition, he tried to begin by consoling and encouraging her. But his own serious misgivings unfitted him for this task, and very soon, notwithstanding the state she was in, he was almost scolding her for being so mad as to withstand the judge, and set herself against his advice. "There," said he, "my lord kept his word, and became counsel for you. 'Close that gap in your defence,' says he, 'and you will very likely be acquitted.' 'Nay,' says you, 'I prefer to chance it.' What madness! what injustice ! "

"Injustice! to whom ? "

"To whom ? why, to yourself."

"What, may I not be unjust to myself ? "

"Certainly not ; you have no right to be unjust to anybody. Don't deceive yourself ; there is no virtue in this ; it is mere miserable weakness. What right have you to peril an innocent life merely to screen a malefactor from just obloquy ? "

"Alas!" said Mrs. Gaunt, "'t is more than obloquy. They will kill him; they will brand him with a hot iron."

"Not unless he is indicted; and who will indict him? Sir George Neville must be got to muzzle the attorney-general, and the Lancashire jade will not move against him, for you say they are living together."

"Of course they are; and, as you say, why should I screen him? But 't will not serve; who can combat prejudice? If what I have said does not convince them, an angel's voice would not. Sir, I am a Catholic, and they will hang me. I shall die miserably, having exposed my husband, who loved me once, O so dearly! I trifled with his love. I deserve it all."

"You will not die at all, if you will only be good and obedient, and listen to wiser heads. I have subpoenaed Caroline Ryder as your witness, and given her a hint how to escape an indictment for perjury. You will find her supple as a glove."

"Call a rattlesnake for my witness?"

"I have drawn her fangs. You will also call Sir George Neville, to prove he saw Gaunt's picture at the 'Packhorse,' and heard the other wife's tale. Wiltshire will object to this as evidence, and say why don't you produce Mercy Vint herself. Then you will call me to prove I sent the subpoena to Mercy Vint. Come now; I cannot eat or sleep till you promise me."

Mrs. Gaunt sighed deeply. "Spare me," said she, "I am worn out. O that I could die before the trial begins again!"

Houseman saw the signs of yielding, and persisted. "Come, promise now," said he. "Then you will feel better."

"I will do whatever you bid me," said she. "Only, if they let me off, I will go into a convent. No power shall hinder me."

"You shall go where you like, except to the gallows. Enough, 't is a promise, and I never knew you break one. Now I can eat my supper. You are a good,

obedient child, and I am a happy attorney."

"And I am the most miserable woman in all England."

"Child," said the worthy lawyer, 'your spirits have given way, because they were strung so high. You need repose. Go to bed now, and sleep twelve hours. Believe me, you will wake another woman."

"Ah! would I could!" cried Mrs. Gaunt, with all the eloquence of despair.

Houseman murmured a few more consoling words, and then left her, after once more exacting a promise that she would receive no more visits, but go to bed directly. She was to send all intruders to him at the "Angel."

Mrs. Gaunt proceeded to obey his orders, and though it was but eight o'clock, she made preparations for bed, and then went to her nightly devotions.

She was in sore trouble, and earthly trouble turns the heart heavenwards. Yet it was not so with her. The deep languor that oppressed her seemed to have reached her inmost soul. Her beads, falling one by one from her hand, denoted the number of her supplications; but, for once, they were *preces sine mente dictæ*. Her faith was cold, her belief in Divine justice was shaken for a time. She began to doubt and to despond. That bitter hour, which David has sung so well, and Bunyan, from experience, has described in his biography as well as in his novel, sat heavy upon her, as it had on many a true believer before her. So deep was the gloom, so paralyzing the languor, that at last she gave up all endeavor to utter words of prayer. She placed her crucifix at the foot of the wall, and laid herself down on the ground and kissed His feet, then, drawing back, gazed upon that effigy of the mortal sufferings of our Redeemer.

"O anima Christiana, respice vulnera morientis, pretium redemptionis."

She had lain thus a good half-hour, when a gentle tap came to the door.

—

"Who is that?" said she.

"Mrs. Menteith," the jailer's wife replied, softly, and asked leave to come in.

Now this Mrs. Menteith had been very kind to her, and stoutly maintained her innocence. Mrs. Gaunt rose, and invited her in.

"Madam," said Mrs. Menteith, "what I come for, there is a person below who much desires to see you."

"I beg to be excused," was the reply. "He must go to my solicitor at the 'Angel,' Mr. Houseman."

Mrs. Menteith retired with that message, but in about five minutes returned to say that the young woman declined to go to Mr. Houseman, and begged hard to see Mrs. Gaunt. "And, dame," said she, "if I were you, I'd let her come in; 't is the honestest face, and the tears in her soft eyes, at you denying her: 'O dear, dear!' said she, 'I cannot tell my errand to any but her.'"

"Well, well," said Mrs. Gaunt; "but what is her business?"

"If you ask me, I think her business is your business. Come, dame, do see the poor thing; she is civil spoken, and she tells me she has come all the way out of Lancashire o' purpose."

Mrs. Gaunt recoiled, as if she had been stung.

"From Lancashire?" said she, faintly.

"Ay, madam," said Mrs. Menteith, "and that is a long road; and a child upon her arm all the way, poor thing!"

"Her name?" said Mrs. Gaunt, sternly.

"O, she is not ashamed of it. She gave it me directly."

"What, has she the effrontery to take my name?"

Mrs. Menteith stared at her with utter amazement. "*Your* name?" said she. "'T is a simple, country body, and her name is Vint, — Mercy Vint."

Mrs. Gaunt was very much agitated, and said she felt quite unequal to see a stranger.

"Well, I 'm sure I don't know what to do," said Mrs. Menteith. "She says she will lie at your door all night, but she will see you. 'T is the face of a friend. She may know something. It seems hard to thrust her and her child out into the street, after their coming all the way from Lancashire."

Mrs. Gaunt stood silent awhile, and her intelligence had a severe combat with her deep repugnance to be in the same room with Griffith Gaunt's mistress (so she considered her). But a certain curiosity came to the aid of her good sense; and, after all, she was a brave and haughty woman, and her natural courage began to rise. She thought to herself, "What, dares she come to me all this way, and shall I shrink from *her?*"

She turned to Mrs. Menteith with a bitter smile, and she said, very slowly, and clenching her white teeth: "Since you desire it, and she *insists* on it, I will receive Mistress Mercy Vint."

Mrs. Menteith went off, and in about five minutes returned, ushering in Mercy Vint, in a hood and travelling-cloak.

Mrs. Gaunt received her standing, and with a very formal courtesy; to which Mercy made a quiet obeisance, and both women looked one another all over in a moment.

Mrs. Menteith lingered, to know what on earth this was all about; but as neither spoke a word, and their eyes were fixed on each other, she divined that her absence was necessary, and so retired, looking very much amazed at both of them.

THE USURPATION.

THERE are three passions to which public men are especially exposed, — fear, hatred, and ambition. Mr. Johnson is the victim and slave of all; and, unhappily for himself, and unfortunately for the country, there is no ground for hope that he will ever free himself from their malign influence.

It is a common report, and a common report founded upon the statements of those best acquainted with the President, that he lives in continual fear of personal harm, and that he anticipates hostile Congressional action in an attempt to impeach him and deprive him of his office. He best of all men knows whether he is justly liable to impeachment; and he ought to know that Congress cannot proceed to impeach him, unless the offences or misdemeanors charged and proved are of such gravity as to justify the proceeding in the eyes of the country and the world.

There is nothing vindictive or harsh in the American character. The forbearance of the American people is a subject of wonder, if it is not a theme for encomium. They have assented to the pardon of many of the most prominent Rebels; they have seen the authors of the war restored to citizenship, to the possession of their property, and even to the enjoyment of patronage and power in the government; and finally, they have been compelled, through the policy of the President, to submit to the dictation, and in some sense to the control, of the men whom they so recently met and vanquished upon the field of battle. The testimony of Alexander H. Stephens everywhere suggests, and in many particulars exactly expresses, the policy of the President.

Mr. Stephens asserts that the States recently in rebellion were always entitled to representation in the Congress of the United States; and Mr. Johnson must accept the same position; for, if the right were once lost, it is impossible to suggest how or when it was regained. It is also known that, while the Johnston - Sherman negotiations were pending, Mr. Davis received written opinions from two or more persons who were then with him, and acting as members of his Cabinet, upon the very question in dispute between Congress and Mr. Johnson, — the rights of the then rebellious States in the government of the United States. These opinions set up and maintained the doctrine that the Rebel States would be at once entitled to representation in the government of the country, upon the ratification or adoption of the pending negotiations. It may not be just to say that the President borrowed his policy from Richmond; but it is both just and true to say that the leaders of the Rebellion have been incapable of suggesting a public policy more advantageous to themselves than that which he has adopted. The President knows that the people have been quiet and impartial observers of these proceedings; that the House of Representatives has never in public session, nor in any of its caucuses or committees, considered or proposed any measure looking to his impeachment.

The grounds of his fear are known only to himself; but its existence exerts a controlling influence over his private and public conduct.

Associated with this fear, and probably springing from it, is an intense hatred of nearly all the recognized leaders of the party by which he was nominated and elected to office. Evidence upon this point is not needed. He has exhibited it in a manner and to a degree more uncomfortable to his friends than to his enemies, in nearly every speech that he has made, commencing with that delivered on the 22d of February last.

Superadded to these passions, which promise so much of woe to Mr. Johnson and to the country, is an inordinate, unscrupulous, and unreasoning ambition. To one theme the President is always constant, — to one idea he is always true, — " He has filled every office, from that of alderman of a village to the Presidency of the United States." He does not forget, nor does he permit the world to forget, this fact. In some form of language, and in nearly every speech, he assures his countrymen that he either is, or ought to be, satisfied with this measure of success. But have not his own reflections, or some over-kind friend, suggested that he has never been elected President of the United States ? and that there yet remains the attainment of this one object of ambition ?

Inauguration day, 1865, will be regarded as one of the saddest days in American annals. We pass over its incidents ; but it was fraught with an evil suggestion to our enemies, and it must have been followed by a firm conviction in the mind of Mr. Johnson that he could not thereafter enjoy the confidence of the mass of the Republican party of the country. He foresaw that they would abandon him, and he therefore made hot haste to abandon them. And, indeed, it must be confessed that there was scarcely more inconsistency in that course on his part, than there would have been in continuing his connection with the men who had elected him. His nomination for the Vice-Presidency was an enthusiastic tribute to his Union sentiments ; beyond a knowledge of these, the Convention neither had nor desired to have any information. Mr. Johnson was and is a Union man ; but he was not an anti-slavery man upon principle. He was a Southern State-Rights man. He looked upon the national government as a necessity, and the exercise of any powers on its part as a danger. His political training was peculiar. He had carried on a long war with slaveholders, but he had never made war upon slavery. He belonged to the poor white class. In

his own language he was a plebeian. The slaveholders were the patricians. He desired that all the white men of Tennessee, especially, and of the whole South, should be of one class, — all slaveholders, — all patricians, if that were possible ; and he himself, for a time became one. Failing in this, he was satisfied when all became non-slaveholders, and the patrician class ceased to exist. Hence, as far as Mr. Johnson's opinions and purposes are concerned, the war has accomplished everything for which it was undertaken. The Union has been preserved, and the patrician class has been broken down.

Naturally, Mr. Johnson is satisfied. On the one hand he has no sympathy with the opinion that the negro is a man and ought to be a citizen, and that he should be endowed with the rights of a man and a citizen ; and, on the other hand, he shares not in the desire of the North to limit the representation of the South so that there shall be equality among the white men of the country. He is anxious rather to increase the political strength of the South. He fears the growing power of the North. The same apprehension which drove Calhoun into nullification, and Davis, Stephens, and others into rebellion and civil war, now impels Mr. Johnson to urge the country to adopt his policy, which secures to the old slaveholding States an eighth of the political power of the nation, to which they have no just title whatever. To the North this is a more flagrant political injustice than was even the institution of slavery. He once expressed equal hostility towards Massachusetts and South Carolina, and desired that they should be cut off from the main land and lashed together in the wide ocean. The President appears to be reconciled to South Carolina ; but if the hostility he once entertained to the two States had been laid upon Massachusetts alone, he ought to have felt his vengeance satisfied when her representatives entered the Philadelphia Convention arm in arm with the representatives of South Carolina, assuming only, what is not true, that the sentiment of Massachusetts was represented in that Convention. As a perfect illustration of the President's policy, two men from Massachusetts should have been assigned to each member from South Carolina, as foreshowing the future relative power of the white men of the two States in the government of the country. The States of the North and West will receive South Carolina and the other Rebel States as equals in political power and rights, whenever those States are controlled by loyal men; but they are enemies to justice, to equality, and to the peace of the country who demand the recognition of the Rebel States upon the unequal basis of the existing Constitution.

Of these enemies to justice, equality, and the peace of the country, the President is the leader and the chief; and as such leader and chief he is no longer entitled to support, confidence, or even personal respect. He has seized upon all the immense patronage of this government, and avowed his purpose to use it for the restoration of the Rebel States to authority, regardless of the rights of the people of the loyal States. He has thus become the ally of the Rebels, and the open enemy of the loyal white men of the country. The President, and those associated with him in this unholy project, cannot but know that the recognition of the ten disloyal States renders futile every attempt to equalize representation in Congress. The assent of three fourths of the States is necessary to the ratification of an amendment to the Constitution. The fifteen old Slave States are largely interested in the present system, and they will not consent voluntarily to a change. The question between the President and Congress is then this: Shall the ten States be at once recognized, — thus securing to the old Slave States thirty Representatives and thirty electoral votes to which they have no title, or shall they be required to accept, as a condition precedent, an amend-

ment to the Constitution which provides an equal system of representation for the whole country? It is not enough, in the estimation of the President, that the loyal people should receive these enemies of the Union and murderers of their sons and brothers as equals, but he demands a recognition of their superiority and permanent rule in the government by a voluntary tender of an eighth of the entire representative force of the republic. When before were such terms ever exacted of the conqueror in behalf of the conquered? If the victorious North had demanded of the vanquished South a surrender of a part of its representative power in the government, as a penalty for its treason, that demand would have been sustained upon the principles of justice, although the proceeding would have been unwise as a measure of public policy. As it is, the victorious North only demands equality for itself, while it offers equality to the vanquished South. Was there ever a policy more just, wise, reasonable, and magnanimous?

Yet the President rejects this policy, deserts the loyal men of the North by whom he was elected, conspires with the traitors in the loyal States and the Rebels of the disloyal States for the humiliation, the degradation, the political enslavement of the loyal people of the country. And this is the second great conspiracy against liberty, against equality, against the peace of the country, against the permanence of the American Union; and of this conspiracy the President is the leader and the chief. Nor can he defend himself by saying that he desires to preserve the Constitution as it was, for he himself has been instrumental in securing an important alteration. "The Constitution as it was" has passed away, and by the aid of Mr. Johnson.

Nor can he say that he is opposed to exacting conditions precedent; for he made the ratification of the anti-slavery amendment a condition precedent to his own recognition of their existence as States clothed with authority. Thus is he wholly without proper excuse for his conduct. Nor can he assert that the Rebel States are, and ever have been, States of the Union, and always and ever entitled to representation and without conditions ; for then is he guilty of impeachable offences in demanding of them the ratification of the constitutional amendment, in dictating a policy to the Southern States, in organizing provisional governments, in inaugurating constitutional conventions, in depriving officers elected or appointed by authority of those States of their offices, and, in fine, in assuming to himself supreme authority over that whole region of country for a long period of time. Thus his only defence of his present policy contains an admission that he has usurped power, that he has violated the Constitution, that he is guilty of offences for which he ought to be impeached. Thus do the suggestions which the President tenders as his defence furnish conclusive evidence that his conduct is wholly indefensible.

While then the President cannot defend his conduct, it is possible for others to explain it.

Its explanation may be found in some one or in several of the following propositions : —

1. That the Rebel leaders have acquired a control over the President, through the power of some circumstance not known to the public, which enables them to dictate a policy to him.

2. That he fears impeachment, and consequently directs all his efforts to secure more than a third of the Senate, so as to render a conviction impossible.

3. That he seeks a re-election, and purposes to make the South a unit in his favor, as the nucleus around which the Democratic party of the North must gather in 1868.

4. That he desires to reinstate the South as the controlling force in the government of the country.

In reference to the first proposition, we are restricted to the single remark, that it is not easy to imagine the Rebels capable of making any demand upon the Executive which, in his present state of mind, he would not be prepared to grant. He has pardoned many of the leaders and principal men of the Rebellion, and some of them he has appointed to office. He has resisted every attempt on the part of Congress to furnish protection to the loyal men of the South, and he has witnessed and discussed the bloody horrors of Memphis and New Orleans with cold-blooded indifference. Early in his term of office he offered an immense reward for the person of Jefferson Davis ; and now that the accused has been in the official custody of the President, as the head of the army, for more than fifteen months, he has neither proclaimed his innocence and set him at liberty, nor subjected him to trial according to the laws of the land. Davis is guilty of the crime of treason. Of this there can be no doubt. He is indicted in one judicial district. The President holds the prisoner by military authority ; and the accused cannot be arraigned before the civil tribunals. Davis was charged by the President with complicity in the assassination of Mr. Lincoln. There is much evidence tending to sustain the charge ; but the accused is neither subjected to trial by a military commission, nor turned over to the civil tribunals of the country. These acts are offences against justice ; they are offences against the natural and legal rights of the accused, however guilty he may be ; they are offences against the honor of the American people ; they are acts in violation of the Constitution. If the elections of 1866 are favorable to the President, they will be followed by the release of Davis, and the country will see the end of this part of the plot.

Upon any view of the President's case, it is evident that he has thrown himself into the arms of the South, and that his personal and political fortunes are identified with Southern success in the coming contest. He claims to stand upon the Baltimore Platform of 1864, and to follow in the footsteps of President Lincoln. The enemies of President Lincoln are reconciled to this assumption, by the knowledge that Mr. Johnson's counsellers are the Seymours, Vallandigham, Voorhees, and the Woods. Mr. Johnson, under these evil influences of opinion and counsel, has succeeded in producing a division of parties in this country corresponding substantially to the division which Demosthenes says existed in Greece when Philip was engaged in his machinations for the overthrow of the liberties of that country. "All Greece is now divided into two parties; — the one composed of those who desire neither to exercise nor to be subject to arbitrary power, but to enjoy the benefits of liberty, laws, and independence; the other, of those who, while they aim at an absolute command of their fellow-citizens, are themselves the vassals of another person, by whose means they hope to obtain their purposes."

The Republican party desires liberty, independence, and equal laws for all people; the Presidential party seeks to oppress the negro race, to degrade the white race of the North by depriving every man of his due share in the government of the country, and, finally, to subject all the interests of the Republic to the caprice, policy, and passions of its enemies.

The Presidential party is composed of traitors in the South who had the courage to fight, of traitors in the North who had not the courage or opportunity to assail their government, of a small number of persons who would follow the fortunes of any army if they could be permitted to glean the offal of the camp, and a yet smaller number who are led to believe that any system of adjustment is better than a continuance of the contest.

The Presidential party controls the patronage of the government; and it will be used without stint in aid of the scheme to which the President is devoted.

It only remains to be seen whether the courage, capacity, and virtue of the people are adequate to the task of overthrowing and crushing the conspiracy in its new form and under the guidance of its new allies. The Republican party carries on the contest against heavy odds, and with the fortunes of the country staked upon the result.

One hundred and ninety-one men have been recognized as members of the present House of Representatives. There are fifty vacancies from the ten unrecognized States; consequently a full House contains two hundred and forty-one members. One hundred and twenty-one are a majority, — a quorum for business, if every State were represented. Of the present House, it is estimated that forty-six members are supporters of the President's policy. If to these we add the fifty members from the ten States, the Presidential party would number ninety-six, or twenty-five only less than a majority of a full House. No view can be taken of the present House of Representatives more favorable to the Republican party, — possibly the President's force should be increased to forty-eight men. It is worthy of observation that neither the Philadelphia Convention nor the President has breathed the hope that the Republicans can be deprived of a majority of the members from the loyal States. The scheme is to elect seventy-one or more men from the loyal States, and then resort to revolutionary proceedings for consummation of the plot. The practical question — the question on which the fortunes of the country depend — is, Will the people aid in the execution of the plot contrived for their own ruin? Upon the face of things, we should say that it is highly improbable that the new party can make any important gains; indeed, it seems most improbable that the President can survive the effect of his own speeches. But we must remember that he is supported by the whole Democratic party, and that that party cast a large vote in 1864, and that in 1862 the Republican majority in the House was reduced to about twenty.

In the Thirty-eighth Congress the Democratic party had ten or fifteen more votes than are now needed to secure the success of the present plot. To be sure, the elections of 1862 occurred at the darkest period of the war. The young men of the Republican party were in the army, and but a small number of them had an opportunity to vote. There was still hope that a peace could be made through the agency of the Democratic party. These circumstances were all unfavorable to the cause of the patriots.

The Democratic party is now weaker than ever before. Its identity with the Rebellion is better understood. The young men of the country, in the proportion of three to one, unite themselves with the Republican party. As an organization, considered by itself, the Democratic party is utterly powerless and hopeless.

The defection of Mr. Johnson, however, inspires the leaders with fresh courage. It is possible for them to enjoy the patronage of the government for two years at least, and it is barely possible for them to secure the recognition of the ten Rebel States, or, in other equivalent words, the ten Democratic States, to the Union.

This combination is formidable; but its dangerous nature is due to the facts that Mr. Seward's name and means of influence are still powerful in the State of New York, and that he has joined himself to the new party and become an instrument in the hands of designing men for the organization of another rebellion. Outside of New York Mr. Johnson's gains in the elections will be so small that the Union majority will remain substantially as in the present Congress; nor can we conceive that the gains in that State will be adequate to the necessities of the conspirators. It is probable that the undertaking will prove a failure; but it should never be forgotten that the country is in peril; that it is in peril in consequence of the uncertain political character of the State of New York; and that that uncertain character is justly attributable to the conduct of Mr. Seward. If, then, Mr. Johnson succeed in the attempt to change the character of this government by setting aside the Congress of

the loyal States, Mr. Seward will be responsible, equally with Mr. Johnson, for the crime.

Reverting to the statement already made, that neither Mr. Johnson nor any of his supporters can even hope to secure a majority of the members elected from the States represented in the present Congress, it only remains for us to consider more specifically the scheme of revolution and usurpation in which these desperate men are engaged. The necessary preliminary condition is the election of seventy-one members of Congress from the twenty-six States. To these will be added fifty persons from the ten unrepresented States, making one hundred and twenty-one, or a majority of Congress if all the States were represented. This accomplished, the way onward is comparatively easy.

When the Thirty-ninth Congress reassembles in December next, Mr. Johnson and his Cabinet may refuse to recognize its existence, or, recognizing it as a matter of form, deny its legitimate authority.

He would summon the members of the Fortieth Congress to assemble in extra session immediately after the 4th of March. Fifty persons would appear claiming seats as representatives from the ten States. The Republicans would deny their right to seats, — the supporters of the President would maintain it. The supporters of the President, aided directly or indirectly by the army and police, would take possession of the hall, remove the Clerk, and organize the assembly by force.

Whether this could be done without bloodshed in Washington and elsewhere in the North remains to be seen; but as far as relates to the organization of the House, there can be no doubt of the success of the undertaking. We should then see a united South with the President at the head, and a divided North; — the army, the navy, the treasury, in the hands of the Rebels. This course is the necessity of Mr. Johnson's opinions and position. It is the natural result of the logic of the Rebels of the South and of the Democratic party of the North. Mr. Johnson believes that the present Congress intends to impeach him and remove him from office. Admit that this fear is groundless, yet, if he entertains it, he will act as he would act if such were the purpose of the two Houses. Hence he must destroy the authority of Congress. Hence he arraigns its members as traitors. Hence he made the significant, revolutionary, and startling remark, in his reply to Reverdy Johnson as the organ of the Philadelphia Convention : " *We have seen hanging upon the verge of the government, as it were, a body called, or which assumed to be, the Congress of the United States, but in fact a Congress of only a part of the States.*" This is a distinct, specific denial of the right of Congress to exist, to act, to legislate for the country. It is an impeachment of all our public doings since the opening of the war, — of all our legislation since the departure of Davis and his associates from Washington. It is an admission of the doctrine of Secession ; for if the departure of Davis and his associates rendered null and void the authority of Congress, then the government, and of course the Union, ceased to exist. The constitutional amendment abolishing slavery is void ; the loan-acts and the tax-acts are without authority ; every fine collected of an offender was robbery ; and every penalty inflicted upon a criminal was itself a crime. The President may console himself with the reflection that upon these points he is fully supported by Alexander H. Stephens, late Vice-President of the so-called Confederacy.

We quote from the report of his examination before the Committee on Reconstruction.

" *Question.* Do you mean to be understood, in your last answer, that there is no constitutional power in the government, as at present organized, to exact conditions precedent to the restoration to political power of the eleven States that have been in rebellion ?

" *Answer.* That is my opinion.

" *Question.* Assume that Congress shall, at this session, in the absence of Senators and Representatives from the eleven States, pass an act levying taxes upon all the people of the United States, including the eleven, is it your opinion that such an act would be constitutional ?

" *Answer.* I should doubt if it would be. It would certainly, in my opinion, be manifestly unjust, and against all ideas of American representative government."

Thus it is seen that these two authorities concur in opinion ; although it must be confessed that the late Vice-President of the so-called Confederate States in urbanity of manner and in the art of diplomacy far surpasses the late Vice-President (as Mr. Johnson, if his logic does not fail him, must soon say) of the so-called United States.

Having thus impeached the existing Congress and denied its authority, the way is clear for the organization of a Congress into which members from the ten States now excluded shall be admitted.

Representatives who do not concur in these proceedings will have only the alternative of taking seats among the usurpers, and thus recognizing their authority, or of absenting themselves and appealing to the people. The latter course would be war, — civil war, with all the powers of the government, for the time being, in the hands of the usurpers. The absenting members would be treated as rebels, and any hostile organization would be regarded as treasonable. Thus would the Rebels be installed in power, and engaged in conducting a war against the people of the North and West.

If, on the other hand, the representatives from the West and North should deem it wiser to accept the condition, and await an opportunity to appeal to the country, how degrading and humiliating their condition ! They might for a time endure it ; but finally the people of the North would rise in their might, and renew the war with spirit and power, and prosecute it until the entire Rebel element of the country should be exterminated. The success of Mr. Johnson in the elections is then to be followed by a usurpation and civil war. It means this, or it means nothing. The incidents of the usurpation would be, first, that the old Slave States would secure thirty Representatives in Congress and thirty electoral votes, or an eighth of the government, to which they have no title whatever unless the negroes should be enfranchised, of which there would be then no probability; and, secondly, that two white men in the South would possess the political power of three white men in the North. The results of the usurpation would be strife and civil war in the North, and, finally, the overthrow of the usurpers by force, to be followed, possibly, by an exterminating war against the Rebel population of the South.

Already has one of Mr. Johnson's agents announced the usurpation in substance, and tendered to the country a defence in advance of the commission of the crime. The defence is simple and logical. Congress refuses to receive the members from ten States. Those States have the same immediate right of representation as the other States. Congress is, therefore, a revolutionary body. Any proceeding which secures the right of all the States to be represented immediately is a constitutional proceeding. This is intelligible. Alexander H. Stephens is the author of this cardinal doctrine of the Presidential party. On the other hand, Congress maintains that enemies vanquished in war, though formerly citizens and equals, cannot dictate the terms of adjustment; nor even enjoy the privileges of a constitution which they have violated and sought to destroy, without a compliance with those terms which the loyal people may deem essential to the public safety.

The issue is well defined. Shall the Union be restored by usurpation, with its attendant political inequality and personal injustice to loyal people, and consequent civil war, or by first securing essential guaranties for the future peace of the country, and then accepting the States recently in rebellion as equals, and the people of those States as friends and citizens with us of a common country?

The question is not whether the Union shall be restored: the Republican party contemplates and seeks this result. But the question is, shall the Union be restored by usurpation, — by a policy dictated by the Rebels, and fraught with all the evils of civil war? The seizure of the government in the manner contemplated by Johnson and his associates destroys at once the public credit, renders the public securities worthless for the time, overthrows the banking system, bankrupts the trading class, prostrates the laborers, and ends, finally, in general financial, industrial, and social disorder.

REVIEWS AND LITERARY NOTICES.

Elements of International Law. By HENRY WHEATON, LL. D., etc. Eighth Edition. Edited, with Notes, by RICHARD HENRY DANA, Jr., LL. D. Boston: Little, Brown, & Co. 1866. 8vo. pp. 749.

LORD WESTBURY, in one of his masterly speeches on law reform, spoke with much truth, and in terms of severe censure, of the neglect with which public law has heretofore been treated in England, and the scanty contributions of English writers to it. And it is undoubtedly true, that, as the English language has no name by which to designate that branch of the law called by the civilians *jus*, and by the French publicists *droit*, so English libraries are without any great national work on this subject, although the English bar has produced innumerable treatises on municipal law, which are high models of profound learning, acute logic, and luminous exposition ; and Great Britain is still chiefly dependent for her international law upon the decisions of Lord Stowell and a few other judges, and the commentaries of the Continent and America.

But from an early period in our political history, international law has been a favorite study in the United States, both with jurists and statesmen. Our war of independence and the succeeding treaties gave rise to questions for solution by it of the greatest nicety, and thus attracted immediate attention to the whole science. To these there followed in quick succession our long-pending dispute with Great Britain upon her exercise of the oppressive claims of visitation and search, our position as a neutral nation during the long wars in Europe, our own war with England, and the wars between Spain and her revolted colonies. Such a succession of events, fruitful in international controversies, created a demand for the study of the law of nations such as is always sure to be supplied. The state papers of Mr. Madison and Mr. John Quincy Adams are a permanent monument to their familiarity with this subject. Contemporaneous with them were the unrivalled decisions of the Supreme Court when presided over by Chief Justice Marshall, and later have been published the works of Kent, Wheaton, Story, and other writers. All of these together comprise a treasure of learning of which we may well be proud.

Mr. Wheaton, by general consent, occupies the first place among our commentators. Inferior as a jurist to Chancellor Kent, he is not so high an authority upon any question which the latter carefully and thoroughly examined ; but long study and training, first before the Supreme Court, when he was not only the reporter of its decisions during the international era, but was of counsel in most of the important cases involving international law, and afterwards in an extended and useful diplomatic career in Europe, gave him an unequalled familiarity with the whole subject ; and he treated it in a much more elaborate manner than did Kent, who only discussed it as a branch of the more general science covered by his Commentaries. No better evidence of the value of Mr. Wheaton's book is needed than the high estimation in which it is held in Europe, and particularly in England, where, as the production of a common-law lawyer, it has a greater value

than the works of Continental scholars, and for reasons of which we shall speak presently. Lord Lyndhurst early bore testimony to its great merits, and during the last few years it has been universally regarded as an authority of the highest standard. No other publicist has been so frequently cited in the controversies which have grown out of our late civil war. The translation of the book into Chinese is a most interesting fact, flattering to the author, and a proof of the progress which Western thought and civilization are making in the extreme East.

It is of Mr. Dana's edition of this valuable work that we are now called upon particularly to speak. As a new edition of the book was demanded, it was of the greatest importance that it should be placed in the hands of an editor competent to discuss, in a manner worthy of the distinguished commentator, those numerous and perplexing questions which have arisen since his death. The representatives of Mr. Wheaton were singularly fortunate in obtaining the aid of so prominent and so busy a man as Mr. Dana, — one who is himself a high authority on many branches of international law ; for it is not an easy matter to prevail upon a leader of the bar, and especially one immersed in the cares of official as well as of professional duties, to undertake a laborious literary work, even if it be of a legal character. Of the editor it is a delicate matter to speak ; but we can say without violating good taste, that few members of his profession unite at once, and to an equal degree with him, high professional acquirements, an enviable reputation as an orator and advocate, and the accomplishments of a varied and extensive scholarship, so that the words with which the President of Harvard College, at the recent Commencement, conferred upon him the degree of Doctor of Laws, *Virum eloquentium jurisperitissimum, jurisperitorum eloquentissimum*, could be applied to him with far less disregard of strict truth than university dignitaries consider allowable on such occasions. A large practice for more than twenty years in the maritime courts has given Mr. Dana an extensive and intimate acquaintance with one part of the subject he has here undertaken ; and his duties as United States District Attorney for Massachusetts, throughout the late war, obliged him to examine most carefully the whole law of prize, of neutral and contraband trade, and of blockade. The results of his labors comprise nearly half of the volume before us, and deserve some higher appellation than notes. Nowhere, however, does Mr. Dana push himself before his author. He never seems to forget that his duty is to prepare a new edition of Wheaton's Commentaries, not to write a book of his own ; and he is content modestly to illustrate the text, and to supply the omissions needed to bring the book down to the present day.

It is not necessary to say that, in a literary point of view, Mr. Dana has done his work well. His style is a model of terseness, vigor, and perspicuity, and yet the reader is constantly charmed by its chaste purity and grace. We can say of him what Macaulay said of Bacon, that he has a wonderful talent of packing thought close and rendering it portable. It is a long time since we have read a book in which so much matter was compressed into so small a space. The good taste and polished courtesy with which Mr. Dana treats of any controverted point cannot be too much praised ; and his calmness and moderation in their discussion are judicial in their nature and extent, and give additional weight to his opinions.

We have been surprised to see notices of the work in which Mr. Dana is criticised for want of enthusiasm. If by this is meant that he lacks enthusiasm for his subject, the criticism is entirely misplaced. We doubt whether, without that, he could ever have been induced to edit this book ; and on every page, and in almost every line, convincing proof can be found of the love and devotion which the editor feels for the law, and especially for this department of it, to the study and practice of which he has devoted so many years. It is this enthusiasm that renders the notes to us more interesting than the text. Things which Mr. Wheaton discusses as abstractions seem in Mr. Dana's hands to become living realities. In one the scholar's temperament predominates ; in the other the lawyer's and the politician's. If, however, the criticism applies to the rigid impartiality which the editor brings to the discussion of those contemporaneous events concerning which the passions of men have been most recently and deeply aroused, we regard it as high praise. If Mr. Dana's views be wrong, it is not likely that the indulgence of a partisan enthusiasm would have corrected them ; if they be right, the absence of all passion, the studied courtesy and tolerant moderation which mark every line of

argument, add infinite strength to his conclusions.

The legal merits of Mr. Dana's annotations require other and higher tests. They depend upon the accuracy of his statements and reasoning, and the amount of assistance which those will obtain who seek it from him. To investigate this would require more space than we can now give, and rather falls within the province of a professional reviewer. A strong conviction of the soundness of his logic, however, involuntarily follows a careful perusal of these notes, and will have no little influence with those who feel it. This is partly owing to the passionless tone of his discussion, of which we have before spoken. The amount of historical and general political information which this book contains will give it value aside from its legal character, and demands for it a very general circulation.

The note upon the sources of international law is exceedingly instructive. Notwithstanding his long practice in admiralty and constant study of civil and foreign law, our editor adheres to his strong Saxon preference for actual judicial decisions as the best evidence of all law. The opinion of Continental writers is seen in its strongest light in a recent French author, who has pushed the doctrine as far as any one else, if not farther. After quoting several definitions of international law, Mr. Dana says : —

"Hautefeuille divides international law into two parts, which he calls *primitif* and *secondaire*, — the first containing, as he says, the principles, the absolute basis, of the law ; and the second, the measures or provisions for calling up these principles and securing their execution. In the application of this theory, it will be found that the distinguished writer usually treats the primitive law, or the well or fountain of first principles, as of actual authority, where no express agreement departs from it ; and so much of the practice of nations as consists in judicial decisions adopted, enforced, and acquiesced in, he considers as of less authority than the primitive law as it lies in the breast of the text-writers. . . . .

"Commentators seem agreed as to what are the sources of international law. They differ as to the relative importance and authority of these sources. Hautefeuille especially gives little weight to the decisions of prize courts, and places far before them the speculations of writers. It is noticeable that Continental writers incline the same way, although they may not go as far ; while Wheaton, Kent, Story, Halleck, and Woolsey in America, and Phillimore, Manning, Wildman, Twiss, and others in England, give a higher place to judicial decisions. This is attributable to the different systems of municipal law under which they are educated. In England and America, judicial decisions are authoritative declarations of the common law, i. e. the law not enacted by decrees of legislators, but drawn from the usages and practices of the people, and from reason and policy. They are at the same time the highest evidence of what the law is. Under those systems, writers are brought to the test of judicial decisions ; and even those portions of the opinions of the court itself not necessary to the decision of the cause before it are termed *obiter dicta,* and are not authority, but stand on no higher ground than voluntary speculations of learned men as to what the law might prove to be in a supposed case. The Continental writers, on the other hand, — living under municipal systems in which judicial decisions hold no such place, and are neither precedents, authoritative declarations, nor authentic evidence of the law, — are led by their education to look to but one authoritative source of law, — the decrees of legislators ; and, in the absence of these, naturally put the scientific treatises of learned men, systematic, and enriched with illustrations, above the special decisions of tribunals on single cases, which, by their systems, do no more than settle the particular controversy, without settling the principles evoked for its decision."

The editor then sums up the respective merits of these two methods of deducing the principles of international law at a length which prevents our quoting the whole for the benefit of our readers. In conclusion he says : —

" As an offset to this [the supposed impartiality of commentators], it is to be remembered that the commentator will often be a man of books and speculations, rather than of affairs ; and that the judicial habit of determining actual controversies, in full view of both their nature and consequences, is most likely to evoke such rules of law as will be able to hold their place among the interests, policies, passions, and necessities of life.

" Attempts to deduce international law from a theory that each individual is by nature independent, and has, by an implied contract, surrendered some of his natural rights and assumed some artificial obligations, for the purpose of establishing society for the common advantage, — and that each state is, in like manner, independent, and has made like concessions for a like purpose of international advantages, — such attempts fall with the theories on which they rested. As no such state of things ever existed, and no such arrangements or compacts have ever been made, it is safer to draw principles of law from what is actual. Later writers, since philosophy has dropped the theory of the social compact, go upon the assumption, that men and communities are by nature what they have always been found to be ; that the rights and duties of each man are, by Divine ordination, originally and necessarily, those at once of an individual and a member of society ; and that the rights and duties of a state are, in like manner, those at once of an individual state and one among a number of states ; and that neither class of these rights or duties is artificial, voluntary, or secondary.

" In considering, therefore, whether a certain rule should or should not be adopted, the test is not its capacity to be carried through a circuitous and artificial course, beginning in a supposed natural independence of the human being, and ending in another supposed entity compounded of all civilized states, but various elements enter into the solution of international questions, and in various degrees, as fitness to conduce to the highest and most permanent interests of nations as a whole, of nations taken separately, differing as nations do in power and pursuits and interests, and of the human beings that compose those societies. If the question involves high ethics, it must be met in the faith that the highest justice is the best interest of all. If it be a question chiefly of national advantage, and of means to an admitted end, it must be met by corresponding methods of reasoning."

M. Hautefeuille, particularly, finds little favor with Mr. Dana. Repeatedly rules laid down by him are dismissed with the bare remark, that " he is without support either by judicial decisions, treaties, the opinions of commentators of received authority, or diplomatic positions taken by nations " ; or, as in another place, that the principle broached " is merely a suggestion of the learned commentator as a possible policy, and has no support either in the practice of nations or the works of publicists " ; — but the editor never condescends to meet the French writer upon his own field of casuistry and speculation. And in this we think he is right. The discussion of rules existing only in a text-writer's belief in their abstract justice, would be entirely useless labor in any writer in the English language; for whatever may be the system of Continental Europe, neither the United States, nor Great Britain, nor any one of the future kindred nations that will grow out of the English colonies, will ever pay much regard to a doctrine so foreign to that noble system of law which, like their common tongue, will be a permanent proof of their common origin.

Two of the most admirable of Mr. Dana's notes are those on the "relations of the United States judiciary to the Constitution and statutes," and on "the United States a supreme government"; and they deserve careful perusal from all desirous of fully understanding our system of government. From the first we cannot refrain from making one extract, which may help to explain to our non-professional readers a difficult principle of law which we have never before seen so concisely and at the same time so clearly stated.

"In cases before it, the Supreme Court has no other jurisdiction over constitutional questions than is possessed by the humblest judicial tribunal, State or national, in the land. The only distinction is, that it is the court of final resort, from whose decision there is no appeal. The relations of all courts to the Constitution arise simply from the fact that, being courts of law, they must give to litigants before them *the law;* and the Constitution of the United States is *law*, and not, like most European political constitutions, a collection of rules and principles having only a moral obligation upon the legislative and executive departments of the government. Accordingly, each litigant, having the right to the highest law, may appeal from a statute of Congress, or any other act of any officer or department, State or national, and invoke the Constitution as the highest law. The court does not formally set aside or declare void any statute or ordinance inconsistent with the Constitution. It simply decides the case before it *according to law;* and if laws are in conflict, according to that law *which has the highest authority,* that is, the Constitution. The effect of the decree of the final court on the *status* of the parties or property in that suit is of course absolute, and binds all departments of the government. The constitutional principle involved in the decision,

being ascertained from the opinion, — if the court sees fit to deliver a full opinion, — has in all future cases in courts of law simply the effect of a judicial precedent, whatever that may be. Upon the political department of the government and upon citizens the principle decided has, in future cases, not the binding force of a portion of the Constitution, but the moral effect due to its intrinsic weight and to the character of the tribunal, and the practical authority derived from the consideration that all acts inconsistent with it will be inoperative, by reason of the judicial power which any citizen may invoke against their operation."

Our space will not allow us to make further quotations. Among those notes which are especially interesting to the non-professional reader we may mention those on the much misunderstood Monroe doctrine; on naturalization; on the effect of belligerent occupation on slavery, and the President's Proclamation of Emancipation, — in which Mr. Dana maintains the same position that he has heretofore taken in his political speeches, and of the correctness of which there can be no doubt; the very excellent examination of the neutrality statutes and decisions, and the note on the case of the Trent, — a model of calm, judicial dissertation. The recent agitation of the subjects of all of these makes them matters of general interest, and we cannot but think that the timely publication of this edition of Mr. Wheaton's work will aid efficiently in the satisfactory settlement of some of them. True to the principles which he holds of the evidences of international law, Mr. Dana avoids spending much time in discussing questions still unsettled, satisfying himself with a clear statement of the present state of each controversy, and leaving it for the future attention of statesmen and jurists. Attached to the volume is a full and carefully prepared Index, — sufficient for all the requirements of any reasonably intelligent reader.

We cannot dismiss this book without alluding to the newspaper controversy which the editor of the two preceding editions has started, and seems determined to keep alive, even if he have no antagonist. We wish to do full justice to Mr. Beach Lawrence's services to the science of public law. His industry and the extent and variety of his information will always make his writings valuable as books of reference, — much as we think this value is lowered by his method of treatment and partisan views. Some natural disappointment and irritation would be excusable in him on the announcement that a work, of which he imagined he enjoyed a monopoly, was receiving the attention of so formidable a rival ; but this does not excuse the bad taste and bad temper with which he has published his complaints. Of the merits of his dispute with Mr. Wheaton's heirs we know little, and shall say nothing, except that they have been guided in their conduct by what they regarded as high legal opinion of their rights and obligations, and that, if Mr. Lawrence has been wronged, the courts of which he talks so much, but to which he seems to be so slow to appeal, will give him redress. But if it be considered becoming to drag ladies and their private-circumstances before the public in the manner in which Mr. Lawrence has done it, there must be a grievous decline of the old chivalrous feeling in regard to women. Still more solemnly must we protest against his recent charges against Mr. Dana. In these he impugns the honor of a distinguished contemporary, charging him with gross and impudent piracy of the results of another's labors. If there be foundation for these charges, they ought to be made ; but there are two ways of making them, and the course which Mr. Lawrence has taken in bringing them, at a time when Mr. Dana is absent from the country, and leaving them to rest solely on his own unsupported assertion — without citing or referring to any of the facts which he declares exist — is highly censurable. We have found no evidence of the truth of his charges in a cursory examination of a considerable part of both works ; and a friend upon whose judgment we place full reliance, and who has carefully compared the labors of the two editors, assures us that there is nothing which at all substantiates them. Mr. Lawrence has needlessly involved his own character in this affair ; and the public will demand from him proofs of a most flagrant violation of the rights of literary property, before it will be inclined to admit any palliation for the errors he has committed in conducting the controversy.

*English Travellers and Italian Brigands.
A Narrative of Capture and Captivity.*
By W. J. C. MOENS. New Yor : Harper and Brothers.

Prison-Life in the South : at Richmond, Macon, Savannah, Charleston, Columbia, Charlotte, Raleigh, Goldsborough, and Andersonville, during the Years 1864 *and* 1865. By A. O. ABBOTT. New York : Harper and Brothers.

THE narrative of Mr. Moens, so far as it relates to the general subject of brigandage in South Italy, will hardly present anything novel to those who have at all studied the history or character of that scourge. In fact, Italian brigandage is a very simple affair, about which it is hard to say anything new. Given a starving, beaten, superstitious population in a mountainous country, destitute of roads, and abounding in easy refuges and inaccessible hiding-places, and you have brigandage naturally. Given centuries of weak, cruel, and corrupt government, and you have the perpetuation of brigandage inevitably. From time immemorial, the social and political conditions in Naples have been deprivation and oppression ; and cause and effect have so long been convertible, that it is often difficult to know one from the other. The prevalence of brigandage demands measures on the part of the government compared with the severity of which martial law is lax and mild ; and the crime which provokes these harsh measures has revived again from the disaffection which they produce. All authorities on the subject are agreed that brigandage finds its shield and support in the fears of the people, and the complete system of espionage which the robbers are enabled to maintain through their accomplices in society. These are sometimes priests and persons of station, but more commonly peasants whose friends or relatives are brigands. During the French-republican rule of Naples, when Manhès was at the head of the troops assigned the duty of extirpating brigandage, the robbers were for once destroyed by the terrible measures taken against their accomplices. No one suspected of communicating with them in any way was spared. Men were shot for selling them food. Women and children taking food into the fields to eat while at work were shot, under an order forbidding this custom lest the provisions should fall into the hands of the robbers. For once, the authorities outbid the brigands for the terror of the wretched inhabitants, and annihilated them. But it was natural, in a country where every peasant is a possible brigand, and only waits for a lawless impulse or lawless deed to make him an actual brigand, that brigandage should flourish again as soon as the rigid procedure against it was relaxed. The returning Bourbons found it on every hill ; and though they combated it with fitful severity and unremitting treachery, they left it essentially unimpaired to the Italian government in 1860. It is by no means true — as Mr. Moens asserts upon the authority of Murray's Guide-Book — that the late Bourbon government did anything towards effectually suppressing brigandage. The brigands were put down in one place to spring up in another, and they swarmed everywhere after a lean harvest. They never were effectually suppressed, except by Manhès ; and, as the Italian government has mercifully refused to adopt his course for their destruction, it is probable that they will exist until the country is generally opened with roads, and the people educated, and, above all, Protestantized. For it must never be forgotten that, since the union of Naples with Italy, brigandage has been fostered by the Bourbons and the Papists, and that the Italians have had to fight, not only the robbers in Naples, but Francis II. and Pius IX. at Rome.

To the readers of the newspapers, the name of Mr. Moens is known as that of the English gentleman who was taken by brigands in May of last year, on his return from a little pleasure excursion to Pæstum. He and his party — consisting of his wife and the Rev. Mr. Aynsley and wife—had trusted too implicitly in the notice given by their landlord that the road from Salerno to the famous temples was free from brigands, and guarded by troops. Near a little tôwn called Battipaglia, the military having been withdrawn temporarily to permit the families of some captives to negotiate their ransom with the band of Giardullo, the band of Manzo swooped down upon the unhappy tourists, and carried off both the gentlemen of the party. The troops appeared almost immediately after the capture, but the brigands escaped with their prisoners, one of whom they released a few days later, that he might return to Naples, and raise the ransom demanded for himself and his friend. The book, from this point, is the relation of Mr. Moens's trials and adventures with the bandits, and Mrs. Moens's hardly less terrible efforts and anxieties for his release. It was decided by the band that their captive was a Milord, and they demanded a ransom of $ 200,000 for him, subsequently reducing the sum to $ 30,000, which was paid them in instalments, and which having received in full, they released their prisoner after a

captivity of four months. All the negotiations for the ransom of Mr. Moens had to be carried on in defiance of Italian law, and by indulgence of its officers ; for to supply the brigands with food or money is an offence punishable with twenty years in the galleys. Generous English friends at Naples interested themselves in the affair, and the aid which Mrs. Moens received from Italians in private and official station was no less cordial and constant. Indeed, the business of Mr. Moens's recapture became of almost international importance. All the Italian troops in the region were employed in pursuit of Manzo's band ; and a British man-of-war was sent to a certain point on the coast, in the hope that the bandits could be induced to go on board by the promise of impunity, and transfer to England.

In the mean time Mr. Moens remained with his captors, sharing all their perils and privations, and making perforce the most faithful study ever made of their life. It must be confessed that the picture has few features attractive to people at peace with society. Most of the brigands are men who have placed themselves beyond the law by some hideous crime, — or misfortune, as they would call it in Naples, — and in other cases they are idle ruffians, who have taken to robbery because they like it. They generally look forward to a time when, having placed a sufficient amount of money at interest, they can surrender themselves to the authorities, pass a few comfortable years in prison, and issue forth ornaments to society. To be sure, this scheme is subject to chances. They are hunted by the soldiers, day and night, like wild beasts ; and, if taken under arms, are shot without trial. Half the time they are without food, and suffer the agonies of hunger and thirst ; and they are always without shelter, except such as trees or caverns can give. When they have anything, they "eat their bread with carefulness, and drink their water with astonishment,"—quarrelling over it a good deal, and trying to steal from one another. When they have nothing, they buckle their belts tighter, and bear it as best they may.

Mr. Moens, who fared no better than the rest, does not seem to have fared much worse. Indeed, he was much more comfortably situated than the ladies of the band, who, being dressed as men, were armed and obliged to fight like their comrades, and yet had no share of the spoils, but received many more cuffs and hard words than we, who have only seen them in pictures, can well associate with the idea of brigandesses.

Being poor ignorant peasants originally, and being afterwards poor ignorant robbers, the brigands inflicted little unnecessary suffering upon their prisoner. Occasionally, to be sure, they struck him; but this was in hot blood, and he was allowed to strike back and restore the balance of justice. These wretched creatures, imbruted and stained with innumerable murders, seem to have had very little idea of the usages of civilized people in regard to captives; and any one who will compare the story of Mr. Moens with the narratives of the prisoners given in Mr. Abbott's book, will see how absurdly the bandits neglected their advantages. After all, it is your high-toned Southern gentleman, compact of the best blood of the Cavaliers and the Huguenots, and presenting in this unhappy hemisphere the finest reflection of the English nobleman's character, who understands best how to use a prisoner. There is nothing like having in your power from childhood a number of helpless human beings, to teach you how to treat a captured enemy; and we cannot help thinking that Mrs. Moens, who will not spare the American Unionists a sneer in the first chapter of her diary, would have understood us better if her husband had been in the hands of Captain Wirz instead of Captain Manzo. Had Mr. Moens been a soldier of the Union, taken while fighting to defend his country against rebellion, he would have been carried into the midst of a people inured to the practice of cruelty by slavery, and all the more abominable because they believed themselves Christian and civilized. There he would have been thrust into a roofless close, already densely thronged with thousands of famished, sick, and maddened men. He would have had no shelter from the blazing sun or drenching storm, except such as the happier wild creatures make themselves in holes and burrows. Guards, emulous in murder, would have been set over him, with instructions to shoot him, if he reached, in the delirium of famine, across a certain line to clutch a bone, or stooped to moisten his lips in a pool less filthy than those at which his comrades quenched their thirst within the bounds. In the mountains of Naples, the brigands gave him to eat and drink of their scanty fare, and shared with him the last

crust and the last drop. In Georgia, in the midst of plenty, his keepers would have slowly starved him to death, and would have driven away, with threats and curses, any that offered to succor his distress. If he escaped, they would have hunted him with bloodhounds, and so brought him back; and if he sickened under his torture, they would have left him, naked and unsheltered, to languish with wasting disease and devouring vermin, — to die, or to rot and drop away piecemeal while yet alive.

Other writers on brigandage, besides Mr. Moens, relate anomalous facts concerning it, which can, perhaps, be matched only in this country, where alone the cruelty and impunity of Italian brigandage can be matched. It is well known that for a long time the heirs of Fra Diavolo received from the government a pension bestowed in recognition of that distinguished chief's services to humanity. The retired chief, Talarico, is now in the undisturbed enjoyment of the gains of brigandage upon his place near Naples; and Count Saint-Jorioz, in his interesting work, *Il Brigantaggio alla Frontiera Pontificia*, declares that in some cases the *employés* of the Italian government in the Neapolitan provinces are men known to have been in other times *manutengoli*, or accomplices of brigands; nay, that sometimes the very courts of law have favored, instigated, and connived at brigandage. Similarly, in our own country, we find men guilty of the cruelties of Andersonville and Columbia, and stained with treason, in the enjoyment of offices and honors throughout the South, while the servants of the law lend themselves to violence and murder with a boldness unheard of in Naples, where there is some show of decency in these things. At least, we have not read of the *sindaco* and policemen of any town of the Abruzzi who have openly applauded and joined the brigands in hunting and slaughtering peaceable inhabitants, as happened lately in New Orleans and Memphis; and we feel quite sure that, if they had committed such an offence, it would not have been passed over in silence by the head of the Italian people. But, then, with all their errors, the Italians have not yet intrusted great power to the hands of a peasant of the class which produces brigands; whereas we have taken for our chief magistrate a man in whom everything generous and noble seems to have been extinguished by the hard conditions of a poor white's life at the South.

THE

ATLANTIC MONTHLY.

A Magazine of Literature, Science, Art, and Politics.

VOL. XVIII. — NOVEMBER, 1866. — NO. CIX.

R H O D A.

UNCLE Bradburn took down a volume of the new Cyclopædia, and placed it on the stand beside him. He did not, however, open it immediately, but sat absorbed in thought. At length he spoke : — " Don't you think a young girl in the kitchen, to help Dorothy, would save a good many steps ? "

" I don't know," replied Aunt Janet, slowly. " Dorothy has a great deal to do already. Hepsy is as good and considerate as possible, but Dorothy won't let her do anything hardly. Hepsy says herself, that within doors she has only dusted furniture and mended stockings ever since she came."

" Can't you find sewing for Hepsy ? "

" She ought not to do much of that, you know."

" Very true ; but then this girl, — she will have to go to the poor-house if we don't take her. She has been living with Mrs. Kittredge at the Hollow ; but Mrs. Kittredge has made up her mind not to keep her any longer. The fact is, nobody will keep her unless we do ; and she is terribly set against going back to the poor-house."

" Who is she ? " asked Aunt Janet, a little hurriedly. She guessed already.

" Her name is Rhoda Breck. You have heard of her."

" Heard of her ! I should think so ! "

" If I were you, Oliver," said grandmother, who sat in her rocking-chair knitting, " I would have two or three new rooms finished off over the woodshed, and then you could accommodate a few more of that sort. Just like you ! "

And she took a pinch of snuff from a little silver-lidded box made of a sea-shell. She took it precipitately, — a sign that she was slightly disturbed. This snuff-box, however, was a safety-valve.

Uncle Bradburn smiled quietly and made no reply.

" We will leave it to Dorothy," said Aunt Janet. " It is only fair, for she will have all the trouble."

Uncle Bradburn regarded the point as gained : he was sure of Dorothy. But he added by way of clincher, " Probably the girl never knew a month of kind treatment in her life, and one would like her to have a chance of seeing what it is. Just imagine a child of fifteen subjected to the veriest vixen in the country. There is some excuse for old Mrs. Kittredge, too, exasperated as she is by disease. No wonder if she is not very amiable; but that makes it none the less hard for the child."

So the upshot of the matter was, that Rhoda Breck was installed nominal aid to Dorothy.

Uncle brought her the next day in his sulky, — a slight little creature, with a bundle as large as herself.

Presently she appeared at the sitting-room door. She was scarcely taller than a well-grown ten-years child. She wore a dress of gay-hued print, a bright shawl whose fringe reached lower than the edge of her skirt, and on her head an old-world straw bonnet decorated with a mat of crushed artificial flowers, and a faded, crumpled green veil. The small head had a way of moving in quick little jerks, like a chicken's; and it was odd to see how the enormous bonnet moved and jerked in unison. The face and features were small, except the eyes, which were large and wide open, and blue as turquoise.

She took time to look well around the room before she spoke : — "Well, I 'm come ; I suppose you 've been expecting of me. See here, be I going to sleep with that colored woman ? "

It was not possible to know from her manner to whom the query was addressed ; but Aunt Janet replied, " No, Rhoda, there is a room for you. We never ask Dorothy to share her room with any one." Then, turning to me, " Go and show Rhoda her room, my dear."

I rose to obey. Rhoda surveyed me, as if taking an inventory of the particulars which made up my exterior; and when I in turn felt my eyes attracted by her somewhat singular aspect, she remarked, in an indescribably authoritative tone, " Don't gawp ! I hate to be gawped at."

"See what a pretty room Dorothy has got ready for you," said I, — "a chest of drawers in it, too ; and there 's a little closet. I am sure you will like your room."

" No, you ain't sure neither," she replied. " Nobody can't tell till they 've tried. Likely yourn has got a carpet all over it. Hain't it, now ? "

" It has a straw matting," I answered.

"And it 's bigger 'n this, I 'll bet. Ain't it, now ? "

" It is larger ; but Louise and I have it together," said I.

"Yes, I 've heard tell about her," said Rhoda. "Well, you see you and her ain't town-poor. If you was town-poor you 'd have to put up with everything, — little room, and straw bed, and old clothes, and everything. I expect I 'll have to take your old gowns ; hain't you got any ? Say, now."

"Yes," I said, "but I wear them myself. Surely, that you have on is not old."

"Well, that 's because I picked berries enough to buy it with. My bundle there 's all old duds, though. It takes me half my time to patch 'em. You 'd pitch 'em into the rag-bag. Would n't you, now ? "

" I have not seen them, you know," I replied.

" More you hain't, nor you ain't agoing to. I hate folks peeking over my things."

" Well," said I, "you may be sure I shall never do it. I must go back to my work now."

"O, you feel above looking at town-poor's things, don't you ? Wait till I 've showed you my new apron. I didn't ride in it for fear I 'd dust it. It 's real gay, ain't it, now ? "

"Yes," said I ; " it looks like a piece of a tulip-bed. But I must really go. I hope you will like your room."

When I went back into the sitting-room, grandmother was wiping her eyes. She had been laughing till she cried at the new help Uncle Oliver had brought into the house.

"No matter, though," she was saying; "let him call them help if he likes. If Dorothy will put up with it, I am sure we ourselves may. He says Hepsy more than pays her way in eggs and chickens. Just as if he thought

about the eggs and chickens! Of
course, if persons are really in need, it
always pays to help them; and I guess
Oliver has about as much capital invested that way as any one I know of, and
I'm glad of it. But it's his funny way
of doing it; it's all help, you see." And
she laughed again till the tears came.

In half an hour, during which time
grandmother had a nap in her chair
and Aunt Janet read, the little apparition stood in the doorway again. She
had doffed the huge bonnet; and in her
lint-white locks, drawn back from her
forehead so straight and tight that it
seemed as if that were what made her
eyes open so round, she wore a tall
horn comb. Around her neck, and
standing well out, was a broad frill of
the same material as her dress, highly
suggestive of Queen Elizabeth.

"You hain't got any old things, coats
and trousers and such, all worn out,
have you? 'Cause if you have, I guess
I'll begin a braided rug. When folks
are poor, they've got to work, if they
know what's good for 'em."

"They'd better work, if they know
what's good for 'em, whether they're
poor or not," said grandmother.

"There's a pedler going to bring
me a diamond ring when I get a dollar
to pay him for it."

This remark was elicited by a fiery
spark on grandmother's finger.

"You had better save your money
for something you need more," said
grandmother.

"You didn't think so when you
bought yourn, did you, now?" said
Rhoda.

Meantime Aunt Janet had experienced a sense of relief at Rhoda's
suggestion, by reason of finding herself
really at a loss how to employ her. So
they twain proceeded at once to the
garret; whence they presently returned,
Rhoda bearing her arms full of worn-
out garments which had been accumulating in view of the possible beggar
whose visits in that part of New England are inconveniently rare.

"Those braided rugs are very comfortable things under one's feet in win-

ter," said grandmother. "They're
homely as a stump fence, but that is
no matter."

"I hardly knew what you would do
with her while we were away," said
Aunt Janet. "But it would kill the
child to sit steadily at that. There's
one thing, though, — strawberries will
soon be ripe, and she can go and pick
them. You may tell her, Kate, that I
will pay her for them by the quart, just
as any one else does. That will please
and encourage her, I think."

I told her that evening.

"No, you don't," was her answer.
"Nobody don't pay me twice over.
I ain't an old skinflint, if I be town-
poor. But I'll keep you in strawberries, though. Never you fear."

I quite liked that of her, and so did
grandmother and Aunt Janet when I
told them.

Uncle and Aunt Bradburn were going to make their yearly visit at Exeter, where uncle's relatives live. The
very day of their departure brought a
letter announcing a visit from one of
Aunt Janet's cousins, a Miss Lucretia
Stackpole. She was a lady who avowed
herself fortunate in having escaped all
those trammels which hinder people
from following their own bent. One of
her fancies was for a nomadic life; and
in pursuance of this, she bestowed on
Aunt Janet occasional visits, varying in
duration from two or three days to as
many weeks. The letter implied that
she might arrive in the evening train,
and we waited tea for her.

She did not disappoint us; and
during the tea-drinking she gave us
sketches, not only of all the little celebrities she had met at Saratoga, but of
all the new fashions in dresses, bonnets, and jewelry, besides many of her
own plans.

It was impossible for her to remain
beyond the week, she said, because
she had promised to meet her friends
General and Mrs. Perkinpine in Bur-
lington in time to accompany them to
Montreal and Quebec, whence they
must hurry back to Saratoga for a
week, and go thence to Baltimore;

then, after returning for a few days to New York, they were to go to Europe.

"But you don't mean to go with them to Europe, Lucretia?" said grandmother.

"O, of course, Aunt Margaret," for so she called her, — "of course I intend to go. We mean to be gone a year, and half the time we shall spend in Paris. We shall go to Rome, and we shall spend a few weeks in England."

"I cannot imagine what you will do with six months in Paris, — you who don't know five words of French."

"I studied it, however, at boarding-school," said Miss Stackpole; "I read both Télémaque and the New Testament in French."

"Did you?" said grandmother; "well, every little helps."

"I think I should dearly love to go myself," said Louise.

"One picks up the language," said Miss Stackpole; "and certainly nothing is more improving than travel."

"If improvement is your motive, it is certainly a very laudable one," said grandmother. "But I should suppose that at your age you would begin to prefer a little quiet to all this rushing about. But every one to his liking."

Now it is undeniable that grandmother and Miss Stackpole never did get on very well together; so it was rather a relief to Louise and myself when Miss Stackpole, pleading fatigue from her ride, expressed a wish to go to bed early, and get a good long, refreshing night's sleep, the facilities for which, she averred, were the only compensating circumstance of country life.

Immediately afterwards, grandmother called Louise and myself into her room, to say what a pity it was that this visit had not occurred either a few weeks earlier or a few weeks later, when uncle and aunt would have been at home; but that, as it was, we must make the best of it, and do all in our power to make things go pleasantly for Miss Stackpole. It was true, she said, that Lucretia was not so very many years younger than herself, and, for her part, she thought pearl-powder

and rouge and dyed hair, and all such trash, made people look old and silly, instead of young and handsome. It did sometimes try her patience a little; but she hoped she should remember, and so must we, that it was a Christian duty to treat people hospitably in one's own home, and that it was enjoined upon us to live peaceably, if possible, with all men, as much as lieth in us. Lucretia's being a goose made no difference in the principle.

So we planned that we would take her up to Haverhill, and down to Cornish, and over to Woodstock, — all places to which she liked to go. And Dorothy came in to ask if she had better broil or fricassee the chickens for breakfast, and to say that there was a whole basketful of Guinea-hens' eggs, and that she had just set some waffles and sally-lunns a-sponging. She was determined to do her part, she said: she should be mighty glad to help get that skinchy-scrimpy look out of Miss Lucretia's face, just like a sour raisin.

Grandmother said every one must do the best she could.

There was one topic which Miss Stackpole could never let alone, and which always led to a little sparring between herself and grandmother. So the next morning, directly after breakfast, she began, — "Aunt Margaret, I never see that ring on your finger without wanting it."

"I know it," grandmother responded; "and you 're likely to want it. It 's little like you 'll ever get it."

"Now, Aunt Margaret! you always could say the drollest things. But, upon my word, I should prize it above everything. What in all the world makes you care to wear such a ring as that, at your age, is more than I can imagine. If you gave it to me, I promise you I would never part with it as long as I live."

"And I promise you, Lucretia, that I never will. And let me tell you, that, old as I am, you are the only one who has ever seemed in a hurry for me to have done with my possessions. If it

will ease your mind any, I can assure
you, once for all, that this ring will
never come into your hands as long as
you live. It has been in the family
five generations, and has always gone
to the eldest daughter; and, depend
upon it, I shall not be the first to infringe the custom. So now I hope you
will leave me in peace."

Miss Stackpole held up her hands,
and exclaimed and protested. When
she was alone with Louise and me, she
said she could plainly see that grandmother grew broken and childish.

When we saw grandmother alone,
she said she was sorry she had been
so warm with Lucretia; she feared
it was not quite Christian; besides,
though you brayed a fool in a mortar
with a pestle, yet would not his foolish-
ness depart from him.

The visiting career, so desirable for
various reasons, was entered upon immediately. To Bethel, being rather too
far for going and returning the same
day, only Miss Stackpole and Louise went. They rode in the carryall,
Louise driving. Though quite needlessly, Miss Stackpole was a little afraid
of trusting herself to Louise's skill, and
begged Will Bright, uncle's gardener,
to leave his work, just for a day, and go
with them. But there were a dozen
things, said Will, which needed immediate doing, so that was out of the
question. Then it came out that a
run-away horse was not the only danger. In the country there are so many
lurking-places, particularly in going
through woods, whence a robber might
pounce upon you all of a sudden and
demand your life, or your portemon-
naie, or your watch, or your rings, or
something, that Miss Stackpole thought
unprotected women, out on a drive,
were on the whole forlorn creatures.
But in our neighborhood a highwayman
was a myth, — we had hardly ever even
heard of one; and so, after no end of
misgivings lest one or another lion in
the way should after all compel the re-
linquishment of the excursion, literally
at the eleventh hour they were fairly on
their way.

A room with a low, pleasant window
looking out on the garden was the one
assigned to Rhoda. In the garret she
had discovered a little old rocking-
chair, and this, transferred to her room,
and placed near the window, was her
favorite seat. Here, whenever one
walked in the back garden, which was
pretty much thickets of lilacs, great
white rose-bushes, beds of pinks and
southern-wood, and rows of currant-
bushes, might be heard Rhoda's voice
crooning an old song. It was rather
a sweet voice, too. I wondered where
she could have collected so many old
airs. She said she supposed she
caught them of Miss Reeney, out at
the poor-house.

When one saw Rhoda working away
with unremitting assiduity, day after
day, it was difficult to yield credence to
all the stories that had been current in
regard to her violence of temper and
general viciousness. That was hard
work, too, which she was doing; at
least it looked hard for such little bits
of hands. First, cutting with those
great heavy shears through the thick,
stiff cloth; next, the braiding; and finally, the sewing together with the huge
needle, and coarse, waxed thread.

One afternoon I had been looking at
her a little while, and, as what uncle
said about her having never had fair
play came into my mind, I felt a strong
compulsion to do her some kindness,
however trifling; so I gathered a few
flowers, fragrant and bright, and took
them to her window.

"Rhoda," said I, "should n't you
like these on your bureau? They will
look pretty there; and only smell how
sweet they are. You may have the
vase for your own, if you like."

She took it without a word, looked
at it a moment, glancing at me to make
sure she understood, and then rose
and placed it on the bureau, where it
showed double, reflected from the looking-glass. She did not again turn her
face towards me till she had spent a
brief space in close communion with a
minute handkerchief which she had
drawn from her pocket. Clearly, here

was one not much wonted to little kindnesses, and not insensible to them either.

The visit to Bethel had resulted so well, that Woodstock and Cornish were unhesitatingly undertaken. Nor was it misplaced confidence on Miss Stackpole's part. With the slight drawback of having forgotten the whip on the return from Woodstock, not the shadow of an accident occurred. Nor was this oversight of much account, only that Tim Linkinwater, the horse, whose self-will had increased with his years, soon made the discovery that he for the nonce held the reins of power ; and when they reached Roaring Brook, instead of proceeding decorously across the bridge, he persisted in descending a somewhat steep bank and fording the stream. Half-way across, he found the coolness of the water so agreeable that he decided to enjoy it *ad libitum.* No expostulations nor chirrupings nor cluckings availed aught. He felt himself master of the occasion, and would not budge an inch. He looked up stream and down stream, and now and then sent a sly glance back at Miss Stackpole and Louise, and now and then splashed the water with his hoofs against the pebbles. Miss Stackpole's distress became intense. It began to be a moot point whether they might not be forced to pass the night there, in the middle of Roaring Brook. By great good fortune, at this juncture came along in his sulky Dr. Butterfield of Meriden. To him Louise appealed for aid, and he gave her his own whip, reaching it down to her from the bridge. Tim Linkinwater, perfectly comprehending the drift of events, did not wait for the logic of the lash, which, nevertheless, Miss Stackpole declared that he richly deserved, and which she would fain have seen administered, only for the probability that his homeward pace might be thereby perilously accelerated.

That night we all went unusually early to bed and to sleep. I remember looking from the window after the light

was out, and seeing, through a rift in the clouds, the new moon just touching the peak of the opposite mountain. A whippoorwill sang in the great chestnut-tree at the farther corner of the yard ; tree-toads trilled, and frogs peeped, and through all could just be heard the rapids up the river.

We were wakened at midnight by very different sounds, — a clattering, crushing noise, like something falling down stairs, with outcries fit to waken the seven sleepers. You would believe it impossible that they all proceeded from one voice ; but they did, and that Rhoda's. We were wide awake and up immediately ; and as the screams ceased, we distinctly heard some one running rapidly down the walk. As soon as we could get lights, we found ourselves congregated in the upper front hall ; and Rhoda, when she had recovered breath to speak, told her story.

She did not know what awoke her ; but she heard what sounded like carefully raising a window, and some one stepping softly around the house. At first she supposed it might be one of the family ; but, the sounds continuing, it came into her head to get up and see what they were. So she came, barefooted as she was, up the back way, and was just going down the front stairs, when a gleam of light shone on the ceiling above her. She moved to a position whence she could look over the balusters, and saw that the light came from a shaded lantern, carried by a man who moved so stealthily that only the creaking of the boards betrayed his footsteps. At the foot of the stairs he paused a moment, looking around, apparently hesitating which way to go. He decided to ascend ; and then Rhoda, bravely determined to do battle, seized a rocking-chair which stood near, and threw it downward with all her force, lifting up her voice at the same time to give the alarm.

Whether the man were hurt or not, it is certain that he was not so disabled as to impede his flight, and that he had lost his lantern, for that lay on the floor at the foot of the staircase; so did the rocking-chair, broken all to pieces.

When we came to go over the house, it had been thoroughly ransacked. Every bit of silver, from the old-fashioned tea-pot and coffee-pot and the great flat porringer which Grandmother Graham's mother had brought over from Scotland to the cup which had belonged to the baby that died twenty years ago, and which Aunt Janet loved for his sake, the spoons, forks, all were collected in a large basket, with a quantity of linen and some articles of clothing.

If the thief had been content with these, he might probably have secured them, for he had already placed them on a table just beneath an open window; but, hoping to gain additional booty, he lost and we saved it all, — or rather Rhoda saved it for us. We were extremely glad, for it would have been a great mischance losing those things, apart from the shame, as grandmother said, of keeping house so poorly while uncle and aunt were away.

Will Bright thought, from Rhoda's account, that the man might be Luke Potter; for Luke lived nobody knew how, and he had recently returned from a two years' absence, strongly suspected to have been a resident in a New York State-prison. His family occupied a little brown house, half a mile up the road to uncle's wood-lot.

So Will went up there the next day, pretending he wanted Luke to come and help about some mowing that was in hand. Luke's wife said that her husband had not been out of bed for two days, with a hurt he got on the cars the Saturday before. Then Will offered to go in and see if he could not do something for him; but Mrs. Potter said that he was asleep, and, having had a wakeful night, she guessed he had better not be disturbed.

Will felt sure of his man, and, knowing Potter's reckless audacity, made extensive preparations for defence. He brought down from the garret a rusty old gun and a powder-horn, hunted up the bullet-moulds, and run ever so many little leaden balls before he discovered that they did not fit the gun; but that, as he said, was of no consequence, because there would be just as much noise, and it was not likely that any thief would stay to be shot at twice.

So, notwithstanding our great fright, we grew to feel tolerably secure; but we took good care to fasten the windows, and to set in a safer place the articles which had so nearly been lost. Moreover, Will Bright was moved into a little room at the head of the back stairs.

It was to be thought that Miss Stackpole would be completely overcome by this midnight adventure; but she averred that, contrariwise, it had the effect to rouse every atom of energy and spirit which she possessed. She had waited only to slip on a double-gown, and, seizing the first article fit for offensive service, which proved to be a feather duster, she hurried to the scene of action. She said afterwards, that she had felt equal to knocking down ten men, if they had come within her range. I remember myself that she did look rather formidable. Her double-gown was red and yellow; and her hair, wound up in little horn-shaped *papillotes*, imparted to her face quite a bristly and fierce expression.

Evidently, Rhoda was much exalted in Will Bright's esteem from that eventful night.

"She's clear grit," said Will. "Who'd have thought the little thing had so much spunk in her? I declare I don't believe there's another one in the house that would have done what she did."

The next forenoon, while Louise and I were sewing in grandmother's room, Miss Stackpole came hurriedly in, looking quite excited.

"Aunt Margaret, — girls," said she, "do you know that, after all, you've got a thief in the house? for you certainly have."

"Lucretia," said grandmother, "explain yourself; what do you mean now?"

"Why, I mean exactly what I said; there's no doubt that somebody in the house is dishonest. I know it; I've lost a valuable pin."

"How valuable?" said grandmother, smiling,—"a diamond one?"

"You need not laugh, Aunt Margaret; it is one of these new pink coral pins, and very expensive indeed. I shall make a stir about it, I can tell you. A pity if I can't come here for a few days without having half my things stolen!"

"And whom do you suspect of taking it?" said grandmother, coolly.

"How do I know? I don't think Dorothy would touch anything that was not her own."

"You don't?" said grandmother, firing up. "I am glad you see fit to make one exception in the charge you bring against the household."

"O, very well. I suppose you think I ought to let it all go, and never open my lips about it. But that is not my way."

"No, it is not," said grandmother.

"If it were my own pin, I shouldn't care so much; but it is not. It belongs to Mrs. Perkinpine."

"And you borrowed it? borrowed jewelry? Well done, Lucretia! I would not have believed it of you. I call that folly and meanness."

"No," said Miss Stackpole, "I shall certainly replace it; I shall have to, if I don't find it. But I will find it. I'll tell you: that girl that dusts my room, Hepsy you call her, I'll be bound that she has it. Not that she would know its value; but she would think it a pretty thing to wear. Now, Aunt Margaret, don't you really think yourself it looks—"

"Lucretia Stackpole," interrupted grandmother, "if you care to know what I really think myself, I will tell you. Since you have lost the pin, and care so much about it, I am sorry. You can well enough afford to replace it, though. But if you want to make everybody in the neighborhood dislike and despise you, just accuse Hepsy of taking your trinkets. She was born and bred here, close by us, and we think we know her. For my part, I would trust her with gold uncounted. Everybody will think, and I think too, that it is far more likely you have lost or mislaid it than that any one here has stolen it."

Miss Stackpole had already opened her lips to reply; but what she would have said will never be known, for she was interrupted again,—this time by a terrible noise, as if half the house had fallen, and then piteous cries. The sounds came from the wood-shed, and thither we all hastened, fully expecting to find some one buried under a fallen wood-pile. It was not quite that, but there lay Rhoda, with her foot bent under her, writhing and moaning in extreme pain.

We were every one assembled there, grandmother, Miss Stackpole, Louise, and I, and Hepsy, Dorothy, and Will Bright. Dorothy would have lifted and carried her in, but Rhoda would not allow it. Will Bright did not wait to be allowed, but took her up at once, more gently and carefully than one would have thought, and deposited her in her own room. Then, at grandmother's suggestion, he set off directly on horseback for Dr. Butterfield, whom fortunately he encountered on the way.

The doctor soon satisfied himself that the extent of the poor girl's injuries was a bad sprain,—enough, certainly, but less than we had feared.

It would be weeks before she would be able to walk, and meantime perfect quiet was strictly enforced. Hepsy volunteered her services as nurse, and discharged faithfully her assumed duties. But Rhoda grew restless and feverish, and finally became so much worse that we began seriously to fear lest she had received some internal injury.

One afternoon I was sitting with her when the doctor came. He spoke cheeringly, as usual; but when I went to the door with him, he said the child had some mental trouble, the disposal of which would be more effective than all his medicines, and that I must endeavor to ascertain and remove it.

Without much difficulty I succeeded. She was haunted with the fear, that, in her present useless condition, she would be sent away. I convinced her that no one would do this during the absence of Uncle and Aunt Bradburn, and that before their return she would probably be able to resume her work.

"I know I'll sleep real good to-night," said Rhoda. "You see I'm awful tired of going round so from one place to another. It's just been from pillar to post ever since I can remember."

"Well," said I, "you may be sure that you will never be sent away from this house for sickness nor for accident. So now set your poor little heart at rest about it."

The blue eyes looked at me with an expression different from any I had seen in them before. They were soft, pretty eyes, too, now that the hair was suffered to lie around the face, instead of being stretched back as tightly as possible. One good result had come from the wood-shed catastrophe: the high comb had been shattered into irretrievable fragments. I inly determined that none like it should ever take its place.

Since Miss Stackpole said it was impossible for her to remain till the return of Uncle and Aunt Bradburn, I cannot say that, under the circumstances, we particularly desired her to prolong her visit. It may be that grandmother had too little patience with her; certainly they two were not congenial spirits. However, by means of taking her to see every relative we had in the vicinity, we disposed of the time very satisfactorily. She remained a few days longer than she had intended, so that Dorothy, who is unapproachable in ironing, might do up her muslin dresses.

"I have changed my mind about Hepsy," said she the night before she left. "I think now it is Rhoda."

"What is Rhoda?" asked grandmother.

"That has taken the coral pin."

Grandmother compressed her lips, but her eyes spoke volumes.

"Miss Stackpole," said I, "it is true that Rhoda has not been here long; still, I have a perfect conviction of her honesty."

"Very amiable and generous of you to feel so, Kate," said Miss Stackpole; "perhaps a few years ago, when I was of your age, I should have thought just the same."

"Kate is twenty next September," said grandmother, who could refrain no longer. "I never forget anybody's age. It is quite possible that she will change in the course of twenty-five or thirty years."

We all knew this to be throwing down the gauntlet. Miss Stackpole did not, however, take it up. She said she intended to lay the circumstances, exactly as they were, before Mrs. Perkinpine; and if that lady would allow her, she should pay for the pin. She thought, though, it might be her duty to talk with Rhoda; perhaps, even at the eleventh hour, the girl might be induced to give it up.

"I will take it upon me, Lucretia," said grandmother, "to object to your talking with Rhoda. Even if we have not among us penetration enough to see that she is honest as daylight, it does not follow that we should be excusable in doing anything to make that forlorn orphan child less happy than she is now. You visit about a great deal, Lucretia. I hope, for the sake of all your friends, that you don't everywhere scatter your suspicions broadcast as you have done here. I am older than you, as you will admit, and I have never known any good come of unjust accusations."

After Miss Stackpole went up stairs that night, she folded the black silk dress she had been wearing to lay it in her trunk; and in doing that, she found the missing pin on the inside of the waist-lining, just where she had put it herself. Then she remembered having stuck it there one morning in a hurry, to prevent any one being tempted with seeing it lie around.

And Rhoda never knew what an escape she had.

"I do wish there was something for me to do," said Rhoda; "I never was used to lying abed doing nothing. It most tuckers me out."

"Cannot you read, Rhoda?" I asked.

"Yes, I can read some. I can't read words, but I can tell some of the letters."

"Have you never gone to school?"

"No; I always had to work. Poor folks have got to work, you know."

"Yes, but that need not prevent your learning to read. I can teach you myself; I will, if you like."

"I guess your aunt won't calculate to get me to work for her, and then have me spend my time learning to read. First you know, she'll send me off."

"She will like it perfectly well. Grandmother is in authority here now; I will go and ask her." This I knew would seem to her decisive.

"What did she say?" said Rhoda, rather eagerly, when I returned.

"She says yes, by all means; and that if you learn to read before aunt comes home, you shall have a new dress, and I may choose it for you."

Now it was no sinecure, teaching Rhoda, but she won the dress, — a lilac print, delicate and pretty enough for any one. I undertook to make the dress, but she accomplished a good part of it herself. She said Miss Reeny used to show her about sewing. Whatever was to be done with hands she learned with surprising quickness. Grandmother suggested that the reading lessons should be followed by a course in writing. Before the lameness was well over, Rhoda could write, slowly indeed, yet legibly.

I carried her some roses one evening. While putting them in water, I asked what flowers she liked best.

"I like sweetbriers best," said she. "I think sweetbriers are handsome in the graveyard. I set out one over Jinny Collins's grave. For what I know, it is growing now."

"Who was Jinny Collins, Rhoda?"

"A girl that used to live over at the poor-house when I did. She was bound out to the Widow Whitmarsh, the spring that I went to live with Mrs. Amos Kemp. Jinny used to have sick spells, and Mrs. Whitmarsh wanted to send her back to the poor-house, but folks said she could n't, because she'd had her bound. She and Mrs. Kemp was neighbors; and after Jinny got so as to need somebody with her nights, Mrs. Kemp used to let me go and sleep with her, and then she could wake me up if she wanted anything. I wanted to go, and Jinny wanted to have me come; she used to say it did her lots of good. Sometimes we'd pretend we was rich, and was in a great big room with curtains to the windows. We did n't have any candle burning, — Mrs. Whitmarsh said there wa'n't no need of one, and more there wa'n't. One night we said we'd take a ride tomorrow or next day. We pretended we'd got a father, and he was real rich, and had got a horse and wagon. Jinny said we'd go to the store and buy us a new white gown, — she always wanted a white gown. By and by she said she was real sleepy; she did n't have no bad coughing-spell that night, such as she most always did. She asked me if I did n't smell the clover-blows, how sweet they was; and then she talked about white lilies, and how she liked 'em most of anything, without it was sweetbriers. Then she asked me if I knew what palms was; and she said when she was dead she wanted me to have her little pink chany box that Miss Maria Elliot give her once, when she bought some blueberries of her. So then she dozed a little while; and I don't know why, but I could n't get asleep for a good while, for all I'd worked real hard that day. I guess 't was as much as an hour she laid kind of still; she never did sleep real sound, so but what she moaned and talked broken now and then. So by and by she give a start, and says she, 'I'm all ready.' 'Ready for what, Jinny,' says I. But she did n't seem to know as I was talking to her. Says she, 'I'm all ready. I've got on a white gown and a palm in my hand.' So then I knew she was wandering like, as I'd heard say folks did when they was very sick; for she had n't any gown at all on, without you might call Mrs. Whitmarsh's old faded calico sack one, nor nothing in her hand neither. So pretty soon she dropped to sleep again, and I did too. And I slept later 'n common. The sun was shining right into my eyes when I opened 'em. I thought 't would trouble Jinny, and I was just going to pin her skirt up to the window, and I see that she looked awful white. I put my hand on her forehead, and it was just as cold as a stone. So then I knew she was dead. I never see her look so happy like. She had the pleasantest smile on her lips ever you see. I did n't know as Mrs. Kemp 'd like to have me stay, but I just brushed her hair, — 't was real pretty hair, just a little mite curly, — and then I run home and told Mrs. Kemp. She said she 'd just as lives I 'd stay over to Mrs. Whitmarsh's as not that day, 'cause she was going over to Woodstock shopping. So I went back again, and Mrs. Whitmarsh she sent me to one of the selectmen to see if she 'd got to be to the expense of the funeral, 'cause she said it did n't seem right, seeing she never got much work out of Jinny, she was always so weakly. And Mr. Robbins he said the town would pay for the coffin and digging the grave. That made her real pleasant; and I don't know what put me up to it, but I was real set on it that Jinny should have on a white gown in the coffin. And I asked Mrs. Whitmarsh if I might n't go over to Miss Bradford's; and she let me, and Miss Bradford give me an old white gown, if I 'd iron it; and Polly Wheelock, she was Miss Bradford's girl, she helped me put it on to Jinny. And then Polly got some white lilies, and I got some sweetbrier sprigs, and laid round her in the coffin. I 've seen prettier coffins, but I never see no face look so pretty as Jinny's. Mrs. Whitmarsh had the funeral next morning.

She said she wanted to that night, so she could put the room airing, but she supposed folks would talk, and, besides, they did n't get the grave dug quick enough neither. Mrs. Kemp let me go to the funeral. I thought they was going to carry her over to the poor-house burying-ground, but they did n't, 'cause 't would cost so much for a horse and wagon. The right minister was gone away, and the one that was there was going off in the cars, so he had to hurry. There wa'n't hardly anybody there, only some men to let the coffin down, and the sexton, and Mrs. Whitmarsh and Polly Wheelock and I. The minister prayed a little speck of a prayer and went right away. I heard Mrs. Whitmarsh telling Mrs. Kemp she thought she 'd got out of it pretty well, seeing she did n't expect nothing but what she 'd got to buy the coffin, and get the grave dug, and be to all the expense. She said she guessed nobody 'd catch her having another girl bound out to her. Mrs. Kemp said she always knew 't was a great risk, and that was why she did n't have me bound.

"That summer, when berries was ripe, Mrs. Kemp let me go and pick 'em and carry 'em round to sell; and she said I might have a cent for every quart I sold. I got over three dollars that summer for myself."

"What did you do with it?"

"I bought some shoes, and some yarn to knit me some stockings. I can knit real good."

"How came you to leave Mrs. Kemp."

"Partly 't was 'cause she did n't like my not buying her old green shawl with my share of the money for the berries; and partly 'cause I got cold, and it settled in my feet so 's I could n't hardly go round. So she told me she 'd concluded to have me go back to the poor-house. If she kept a girl, she said, she wanted one to wait on her, and not to be waited on. She waited two or three days to see if I did n't get better, so as I could walk over there; but I did n't. And one day it had been raining, but it held up awhile, and she see a neighbor riding by, and she run out and asked him if he could n't carry me over to the poorhouse. He said he could if she wanted him to; so I went. I had on my cape, and it wa'n't very warm. She asked me when I come away, if I wa'n't sorry I had n't a shawl. I expect I did catch cold. I could n't set up nor do nothing for more 'n three weeks. When I got so I could knit, my yarn was gone. I never knew what become of it; and one of the women used to borrow my shoes for her little girl, and she wore 'em out. So, come spring, I was just where I was the year before, only lonesomer, cause Jinny was gone."

" And did you stay there ? "

" To the poor-house ? No ; Betty Crosfield wanted a girl to come and help her. She took in washing for Mr. Furniss's hands. She said I wa'n't strong enough to earn much, but she would pay me in clothes. She give me a Shaker bonnet and an old gown that the soap had took the color out of, and she made a tack in it, so 's it did. And I had my cape. When strawberries come, the hands was most all gone, and she let me sleep there, and go day-times after berries, and she to have half the pay. That 's how I got my red calico and my shawl."

" Who made your dress, Rhoda ? "

" Miss Reeny. I carried it over to see if she 'd cut it out, and she said she 'd make it if they 'd let her, and they did. And I got her some green tea. She used to say sometimes, she 'd give anything for a cup of green tea, such as her mother used to have."

" Who is Miss Reeny ? "

" A woman that lives over there. Her father used to be a doctor; but he died, and she was sickly and did n't know as she had any relations, and by and by she had to go there. They say over there she ain't in her right mind, but I don't know. She was always good to me. There was an old chair with a cushion in it, and Miss Reeny wanted it to sit in, 'cause her back was lame ; but old Mrs. Fitts wanted it too,

and they used to spat it. So Miss Holbrook come there one day to see the place, and somebody told her about the cushioned chair, and, if you 'll believe it, the very next day there was one come over as good again, with arms to it, and a cushion, and all. Miss Holbrook sent it over to Miss Reeny. None of 'em could n't take it away."

" And is she there now ? "

" Yes, she can't go nowhere else. One night Betty Crosfield said I need n't come there no more ; she was going to take a boarder. Berry-time was most over, so then I got a place to Miss Stoney's, the milliner. She agreed to give me twenty-five cents a week, and I thought to be sure I should get back my shoes and yarn now. But one morning the teapot was cracked, and she asked me, and I said I did n't do it, — and I did n't ; but she said she knew I did, because there was n't nobody but her and me that touched it, and she should keep my wages till they come to a dollar and a half, because that was what a new one would cost. Before the teapot was paid for I did break a glass dish. I did n't know 't would hurt it to put it in hot water ; and everything else that was broke, she thought I broke it, and she kept it out of my wages. I told her I did n't see as she ought to ; and in the fall she said she could n't put up with my sauce and my breaking no longer. Mrs. Kittredge wanted a girl, and I went there."

" And how did you find it there ? "

" I think it was about the hardest place of all. I 'd as lives go back to the poor-house as to stay there. Sally Kittredge used to tell things that wa'n't true about me. She told one day that I pushed her down. I never touched my hand to her. But Mrs. Kittredge got a raw hide up stairs and give it to me awful. I should n't wonder if it showed now ; just look."

She undid the fastening of her dress and slipped off the waist for me to see. The little back — she was very small — was all discolored with stripes, purple, green, and yellow. After showing me these bruises, she quietly fastened her dress again.

Now there was that in Rhoda's manner during this narration which wrought in my mind entire conviction of its verity. By the time of Uncle and Aunt Bradburn's return, she was growing in favor with every one in the house. She was gentle, patient, and grateful.

The deftness with which she used those small fingers suggested to me the idea of teaching her some of the more delicate kinds of fancy - work. But it seemed that she required no teaching. An opportunity given of looking on while one was embroidering, crocheting, or making tatting, and the process was her own. Native tact imparted to her at once the skill which others attain only by long practice. As for her fine sewing, it was exquisite; and in looking at it, one half regretted the advent of the sewing-machine.

The fall days grew short; the winter came and went; and in the course of it, besides doing everything that was required of her in the household, keeping up the reading and writing, and satisfactory progress in arithmetic, Rhoda had completed, at my suggestion, ten of those little tatting collars, made of fine thread, and rivalling in delicate beauty the loveliest fabrics of lace.

Because a project was on foot for Rhoda. A friend of mine going to Boston took charge of the little package of collars, and the result was that the proprietor of a fancy-store there engaged to receive all of them that might be manufactured, at the price of three dollars each. When my friend returned, she brought me, as the avails of her commission, the sum of thirty dollars.

But here arose an unexpected obstacle. It was difficult to convince Rhoda that the amount, which seemed to her immense, was of right her own. She comprehended it, however, at last; and thenceforth her skill in this and other departments of fancy-work obtained for her constant and remunerative employment.

It was now a year since Rhoda came to us, and during this time her improvement had been steady and rapid. And since she had come to dress like other girls, no one could say that she was ill-looking; but, as I claimed the merit of effecting this change in her exterior, it may be that I observed it more than any one else. Still, I fancy that some others were not blind.

"Where did you get those swamp-pinks, Rhoda?" for I detected the fine azalia odor before I saw them.

A bright color suffused the childlike face, quite to the roots of the hair. "Will Bright got them when he went after the cows. You may have some if you want them."

"No, thank you; it is a pity to disturb them, they look so pretty just as they are."

Troubles come to everybody. Even Will Bright, though no one had ever known him to be without cheerfulness enough for half a dozen, was not wholly exempt from ills. With all his good sense, which was not a little, Will was severely incredulous of the reputed effects of poison-ivy; and one day, by way of maintaining his position, gathered a spray of it and applied it to his face. He was not long in finding the vine in question an ugly customer. His face assumed the aspect of a horrible mask, and the dimensions of a good-sized water-pail, with nothing left of the eyes but two short, straight marks. For once, Will had to succumb and be well cared for.

In this state of things a letter came to him with a foreign postmark. "I will lay it away in your desk, Will," said uncle, "till you can read it yourself; that will be in a day or two."

"If you don't mind the trouble, sir, I should thank you to open and read it for me. I get no letters that I am unwilling you should see."

It was to the effect that a relative in England had left him a bequest of five hundred pounds, and that the amount would be made payable to his order wherever he should direct.

"You will oblige me, sir, if you will say nothing about this for the present," said Will, when uncle had congratulated him.

"I hope we shall not lose sight of you, Will," said uncle, who really felt a strong liking for the young man, who had served him faithfully three years.

"I hope not, sir," replied Will. "I shall be glad to consult you before I decide what use to make of this windfall. At all events, I don't want to change my quarters for the present."

About the same time, brother Ned, in Oregon, sent me a letter which contained this passage : —

"We are partly indebted for this splendid stroke of business to the help of a townsman of our own ; his name is Joseph Breck. He says he ran away from Deacon Handy's, at fifteen years old, because the Deacon would not send him to school as he had agreed. Ask uncle if he remembers Ira Breck, who lived over at Ash Swamp, near the old Ingersol place. He was drowned saving timber in a freshet. He left two children, and this Joseph is the elder. The other was a girl, her name Rhoda, six or eight years younger than Joseph ; she must be now, he says, not far from sixteen or seventeen. Joe has had a hard row to hoe, but now that he begins to see daylight he wants to do something for his sister. He is a thoroughly honest and competent fellow, and we are glad enough to get hold of him. He told me the other night such a story as would make your heart ache : at all events it would make you try to ascertain something about his sister before you write next."

I lost no time in seeking Rhoda.

"Yes," said she, in reply to my inquiries, "I did have a brother once. He went off and was lost. I can just remember him. I don't suppose I shall ever see him again. Folks said likely he was drowned."

"Was his name Joseph ? "

"It was Joe ; father used to call him Joe."

I read to her from Ned's letter what related to her brother.

"I 'm most afraid it 's a dream," said Rhoda after a brief silence. "Over at the poor-house I used to have such good dreams, and then I 'd wake up out of them. After I came here I used to be afraid it was a dream ; but I did n't wake out of that. Perhaps I shall see Joe again ; who knows ? "

From this time a change came over Rhoda. She begged as a privilege to learn to do everything that a woman can do about a house.

"I do declare, Miss Kate," said Dorothy one day, after displaying a grand array of freshly baked loaves, wearing the golden-brown tint that hints at such savory sweetness, "that girl, for a white girl, is going to make a most a splendid cook. I never touched this bread, and just you see ! ain't it perfindiculur wonderful ? "

Soon after, I found Rhoda, with her dress tidily pinned out of harm's way, standing at a barrel, and poking vigorously with a stick longer than herself.

"What now, Rhoda ! what are you doing there ? "

"Come here and look at the soap, Miss Kate. I made it every bit myself; ain't it going to be beautiful ? "

"Why do you care to do such things, Rhoda ? "

"I 'll tell you," in a low voice ; "perhaps when Joe comes home, some time he 'll buy himself a little place and let me keep house for him ; then I shall want to know how to do everything."

"Rhoda, I believe you can do everything already."

"No, I can't wring," looking piteously from one little hand to the other. "I can iron cute, but I can't wring. Dorothy says that is one thing I shall have to give up, unless I can make my hands grow. Do you suppose I could ? "

"No ; you must make Joe buy you a wringer. Can you make butter ? "

"O yes, when the churning is n't large. Likely Joe won't keep more than one cow."

I looked at the eager little thing,

wondering if her hope would ever be realized. She divined my thought, and glanced at me wistfully. "You think this is a dream; you think I shall wake up."

"No, no," I answered; "I wonder what Joe will think when he sees what a mite of a sister he has. He'll make you stand round, Rhoda, you may be sure of that."

"May be he is n't any larger himself," she responded, with a ready, bright smile.

Brother Ned's next letter brought the welcome tidings that he hoped to come home the ensuing August, and that Joseph Breck would probably come at the same time.

June went, and July. Rhoda grew restless; she was no longer constantly at work; she began to listen nervously for every train of cars. I was glad to believe that the brother for whom she held in readiness such lavish love was deserving of it. She grew prettier every day. The uncouth dress was gone forever, the hideous bonnet burned up, and the gay shawl made over to Miss Reeny, who admired and coveted it. Hepsy herself was not more faultlessly quiet and tasteful in her attire. I was sure that Joe, if he had eyes at all, must be convinced that his sister was worth coming all the way from Oregon to see.

At last, one pleasant afternoon, there was a step in the hall that I recognized; it was Ned's! I reached him first, and felt his dear old arms close fast about me; and then, for Louise's right was stronger than mine, I gave him over to her and the rest. My happiness, though it half blinded me, did not prevent my seeing a pallid little face looking earnestly in from the back hall door. Then Joe had not come! I felt a keen pang for Rhoda.

"Ned," said I, as soon as I could get a word with him, "there is Joe Breck's sister; where is Joe?"

"Where is Joe?" said Ned; "why, there he is."

Sure enough, there above Rhoda's —

a good way above — was a dark, fine, manly face, all sun-browned and bearded. — "Rhoda!" — He had stolen a march upon her. She turned and saw him. A swift look of glad surprise, and the brother and sister so long separated had recognized each other. He drew her to him and held her there tenderly as if she were a little child.

So Joe bought "a little place," and I believe he would fain have had his sister Rhoda for its mistress. But then it came out that Will Bright, that sly fellow, had been using every bit of persuasion in his power to make her promise that she would keep house for him. Nay, he had won already a conditional promise, the proviso being, of course, Joe's approval. Will's is not a little place, either. With his relative's legacy he purchased the great Wellwood nursery; and so skilled is he in its management that uncle says there is not a more thriving man in the neighborhood. And Rhoda, of whom he is wonderfully proud, is as content a little woman as any in the land. Whenever I go to Uncle Bradburn's, — and few summers pass that I do not, — I make a point of reserving time for a visit to Rhoda. The last time I went, I encountered Will bringing her down stairs in his arms; and she held in her arms, as something too precious to be yielded to another, what proved on inspection to be a tiny, blue-eyed baby. It was comical to see her ready, matronly ways; and it was touching, when you thought of the past, to witness her quiet yet perfect enjoyment.

And I really know of no one in the world more heartily benevolent than she. "You see," she says, "I knew once what it is to need kindness; and now I should be worse than a heathen if I did not help other people when I have a chance."

I suppose Hepsy pitied Joe for his disappointment. In any case, she has done what she could to console him for it. On the whole, it would be difficult to say which is the happier wife, Hepsy or Rhoda.

PASSAGES FROM HAWTHORNE'S NOTE–BOOKS.

XI.

CONCORD, 1843.—To sit at the gate of Heaven, and watch persons as they apply for admittance, some gaining it, others being thrust away. .

To point out the moral slavery of one who deems himself a free man.

A stray leaf from the Book of Fate, picked up in the street.

The streak of sunshine journeying through the prisoner's cell,—it may be considered as something sent from Heaven to keep the soul alive and glad within him. And there is something equivalent to this sunbeam in the darkest circumstances; as flowers, which figuratively grew in Paradise, in the dusky room of a poor maiden in a great city; the child, with its sunny smile, is a cherub. God does not let us live anywhere or anyhow on earth without placing something of Heaven close at hand, by rightly using and considering which, the earthly darkness or trouble will vanish, and all be Heaven.

When the reformation of the world is complete, a fire shall be made of the gallows; and the hangman shall come and sit down by it in solitude and despair. To him shall come the last thief, the last drunkard, and other representatives of past crime and vice; and they shall hold a dismal merry-making, quaffing the contents of the last brandy-bottle. '

The human heart to be allegorized as a cavern. At the entrance there is sunshine, and flowers growing about it. You step within but a short distance, and begin to find yourself surrounded with a terrible gloom and monsters of divers kinds; it seems like hell itself. You are bewildered, and wander long without hope. At last a light strikes upon you. You pass towards it, and find yourself in a region that seems, in some sort, to reproduce the flowers and sunny beauty of the entrance, but all perfect. These are the depths of the heart, or of human nature, bright and peaceful. The gloom and terror may lie deep, but deeper still this eternal beauty.

A man in his progress through life may pick up various matters,—sin, care, habit, riches,—until at last he staggers along under a heavy burden.

To have a lifelong desire for a certain object, which shall appear to be the one thing essential to happiness. At last that object is attained, but proves to be merely incidental to a more important affair, and that affair is the greatest evil fortune that can occur. For instance, all through the winter I had wished to sit in the dusk of evening, by the flickering firelight, with my wife, instead of beside a dismal stove. At last this has come to pass; but it was owing to her illness.

Madame Calderon de la Barca (in "Life in Mexico") speaks of persons who have been inoculated with the venom of rattlesnakes, by pricking them in various places with the tooth. These persons are thus secured forever after against the bite of any venomous reptile. They have the power of calling snakes, and feel great pleasure in playing with and handling them. Their own bite becomes poisonous to people not inoculated in the same manner. Thus a part of the serpent's nature appears to be transfused into them.

An auction (perhaps in Vanity Fair) of offices, honors, and all sorts of things considered desirable by mankind, together with things eternally valuable, which shall be considered by most people as worthless lumber.

An examination of wits and poets at a police court, and they to be sentenced by the judge to various penalties or fines, — the house of correction, whipping, etc., — according to the moral offences of which they are guilty.

A volume bound in cowhide. It should treat of breeding cattle, or some other coarse subject.

A young girl inhabits a family graveyard, that being all that remains of rich hereditary possessions.

An interview between General Charles Lee, of the Revolution, and his sister, the foundress and mother of the sect of Shakers.

For a sketch for a child: — the life of a city dove, or perhaps of a flock of doves, flying about the streets, and sometimes alighting on church steeples, on the eaves of lofty houses, etc.

The greater picturesqueness and reality of back courts, and everything appertaining to the rear of a house, as compared with the front, which is fitted up for the public eye. There is much to be learned always, by getting a glimpse at rears. Where the direction of a road has been altered, so as to pass the rear of farm-houses instead of the front, a very noticeable aspect is presented.

A sketch : — the devouring of old country residences by the overgrown monster of a city. For instance, Mr. Beekman's ancestral residence was originally several miles from the city of New York ; but the pavements kept creeping nearer and nearer, till now the house is removed, and a street runs directly through what was once its hall.

An essay on various kinds of death, together with the just before and just after.

The majesty of death to be exemplified in a beggar, who, after being seen, humble and cringing, in the streets of a city for many years, at length, by some means or other, gets admittance into a rich man's mansion, and there dies, assuming state and striking awe into the breasts of those who had looked down on him.

To write a dream, which shall resemble the real course of a dream, with all its inconsistency, its strange transformations, which are all taken as a matter of course, its eccentricities and aimlessness, with nevertheless a leading idea running through the whole. Up to this old age of the world, no such thing ever has been written.

To allegorize life with a masquerade, and represent mankind generally as masquers. Here and there a natural face may appear.

With an emblematical divining-rod, to seek for emblematic gold, — that is, for truth, — for what of Heaven is left on earth.

A task for a subjugated fiend : — to gather up all the fallen autumnal leaves of a forest, assort them, and affix each one to the twig where it originally grew.

A vision of Grub Street, forming an allegory of the literary world.

The emerging from their lurking-places of evil characters on some occasion suited to their action, they having been quite unknown to the world hitherto. For instance, the French Revolution brought out such wretches.

The advantage of a longer life than is now allotted to mortals, — the many things that might then be accomplished, to which one lifetime is inadequate, and for which the time spent seems therefore lost, a successor being unable to take up the task where we drop it.

George I. had promised the Duchess

of Kendall, his mistress, that, if possible, he would pay her a visit after death. Accordingly, a large raven flew into the window of her villa at Isleworth. She believed it to be his soul, and treated it ever after with all respect and tenderness, till either she or the bird died.

The history of an almshouse in a country village, from the era of its foundation downward, — a record of the remarkable occupants of it, and extracts from interesting portions of its annals. The rich of one generation might, in the next, seek for a house there, either in their own persons or in those of their representatives. Perhaps the son and heir of the founder might have no better refuge. There should be occasional sunshine let into the story; for instance, the good fortune of some nameless infant, educated there, and discovered finally to be the child of wealthy parents.

Pearl, the English of Margaret, — a pretty name for a girl in a story.

The conversation of the steeples of a city, when their bells are ringing on Sunday, — Calvinist, Episcopalian, Unitarian, etc.

Allston's picture of "Belshazzar's Feast," — with reference to the advantages or otherwise of having life assured to us till we could finish important tasks on which we might be engaged.

Visits to castles in the air, — Chateaux en Espagne, etc., — with remarks on that sort of architecture.

To consider a piece of gold as a sort of talisman, or as containing within itself all the forms of enjoyment that it can purchase, so that they might appear, by some fantastical chemic process, as visions.

To personify If, But, And, Though, etc.

A man seeks for something excellent, but seeks it in the wrong spirit and in a wrong way, and finds something horrible; as, for instance, he seeks for treasure, and finds a dead body; for the gold that somebody has hidden, and brings to light his accumulated sins.

An auction of second-hands, — thus moralizing how the fashion of this world passeth away.

Noted people in a town, — as the town-crier, the old fruit-man, the constable, the oyster-seller, the fish-man, the scissors-grinder, etc.

The magic ray of sunshine for a child's story, — the sunshine circling round through a prisoner's cell, from his high and narrow window. He keeps his soul alive and cheerful by means of it, it typifying cheerfulness; and when he is released, he takes up the ray of sunshine, and carries it away with him, and it enables him to discover treasures all over the world, in places where nobody else would think of looking for them.

A young man finds a portion of the skeleton of a mammoth; he begins by degrees to become interested in completing it; searches round the world for the means of doing so; spends youth and manhood in the pursuit; and in old age has nothing to show for his life but this skeleton of a mammoth.

For a child's sketch: — a meeting with all the personages mentioned in Mother Goose's Melodies, and other juvenile stories.

Great expectation to be entertained in the allegorical Grub Street of the great American writer. Or a search-warrant to be sent thither to catch a poet. On the former supposition, he shall be discovered under some most unlikely form, or shall be supposed to have lived and died unrecognized

An old man to promise a youth a treasure of gold, and to keep his promise by teaching him pr—'' ''—na golden rule.

A valuable jewel to be buried in the grave of a beloved person, or thrown over with a corpse at sea, or deposited under the foundation-stone of an edifice, — and to be afterwards met with by the former owner, in some one's possession.

A noted gambler had acquired such self-command that, in the most desperate circumstances of his game, no change of feature ever betrayed him; only there was a slight scar upon his forehead, which at such moments assumed a deep blood-red hue. Thus, in playing at brag, for instance, his antagonist could judge from this index when he had a bad hand. At last, discovering what it was that betrayed him, he covered the scar with a green silk shade.

A dream the other night, that the world had become dissatisfied with the inaccurate manner in which facts are reported, and had employed me, with a salary of a thousand dollars, to relate things of public importance exactly as they happen.

A person who has all the qualities of a friend, except that he invariably fails you at the pinch.

Concord, July 27, 1844. — To sit down in a solitary place or a busy and bustling one, if you please, and await such little events as may happen, or observe such noticeable points as the eyes fall upon around you. For instance, I sat down to-day, at about ten o'clock in the forenoon, in Sleepy Hollow, a shallow space scooped out among the woods, which surround it on all sides, it being pretty nearly circular or oval, and perhaps four or five hundred yards in diameter. At the present season, a thriving field of Indian corn, now in its most perfect growth and tasselled out, occupies nearly half of the hollow; and it is like the lap of bounteous Na-

ture, filled with breadstuff. On one verge of this hollow, skirting it, is a terraced pathway, broad enough for a wheel-track, overshadowed with oaks, stretching their long, knotted, rude, rough arms between earth and sky; the gray skeletons, as you look upward, are strikingly prominent amid the green foliage. Likewise, there are chestnuts, growing up in a more regular and pyramidal shape; white pines, also; and a shrubbery composed of the shoots of all these trees, overspreading and softening the bank on which the parent stems are growing, these latter being intermingled with coarse grass. Observe the pathway; it is strewn over with little bits of dry twigs and decayed branches, and the sear and brown oak-leaves of last year, that have been moistened by snow and rain, and whirled about by harsh and gentle winds, since their verdure has departed. The needle-like leaves of the pine that are never noticed in falling — that fall, yet never leave the tree bare — are likewise on the path; and with these are pebbles, the remains of what was once a gravelled surface, but which the soil accumulating from the decay of leaves, and washing down from the bank, has now almost covered. The sunshine comes down on the pathway, with the bright glow of noon, at certain points; in other places, there is a shadow as deep as the glow; but along the greater portion sunshine glimmers through shadow, and shadow effaces sunshine, imaging that pleasant mood of mind when gayety and pensiveness intermingle. A bird is chirping overhead among the branches, but exactly whereabout you seek in vain to determine; indeed, you hear the rustle of the leaves, as he continually changes his position. A little sparrow, however, hops into view, alighting on the slenderest twigs, and seemingly delighting in the swinging and heaving motion which his slight substance communicates to them; but he is not the loquacious bird, whose voice still comes, eager and busy, from his hidden whereabout. Insects are fluttering around.

The cheerful, sunny hum of the flies is altogether summer-like, and so gladsome that you pardon them their intrusiveness and impertinence, which continually impel them to fly against your face, to alight upon your hands, and to buzz in your very ear, as if they wished to get into your head, among your most secret thoughts. In truth, a fly is the most impertinent and indelicate thing in creation, — the very type and moral of human spirits with whom one occasionally meets, and who, perhaps, after an existence troublesome and vexatious to all with whom they come in contact, have been doomed to reappear in this congenial shape. Here is one intent upon alighting on my nose. In a room, now, — in a human habitation, — I could find in my conscience to put him to death; but here we have intruded upon his own domain, which he holds in common with all other children of earth and air; and we have no right to slay him on his own ground. Now we look about us more minutely, and observe that the acorn-cups of last year are strewn plentifully on the bank and on the path. There is always pleasure in examining an acorn-cup, — perhaps associated with fairy banquets, where they were said to compose the table-service. Here, too, are those balls which grow as excrescences on the leaves of the oak, and which young kittens love so well to play with, rolling them over the carpet. We see mosses, likewise, growing on the banks, in as great variety as the trees of the wood. And how strange is the gradual process with which we detect objects that are right before the eyes! Here now are whortleberries, ripe and black, growing actually within reach of my hand, yet unseen till this moment. Were we to sit here all day, — a week, a month, and doubtless a lifetime, — objects would thus still be presenting themselves as new, though there would seem to be no reason why we should not have detected them all at the first moment.

Now a cat-bird is mewing at no great distance. Then the shadow of a bird flits across a sunny spot. There is a peculiar impressiveness in this mode of being made acquainted with the flight of a bird; it impresses the mind more than if the eye had actually seen it. As we look round to catch a glimpse of the winged creature, we behold the living blue of the sky, and the brilliant disk of the sun, broken and made tolerable to the eye by the intervening foliage. Now, when you are not thinking of it, the fragrance of the white pines is suddenly wafted to you by a slight, almost imperceptible breeze, which has begun to stir. Now the breeze is the softest sigh imaginable, yet with a spiritual potency, insomuch that it seems to penetrate, with its mild, ethereal coolness, through the outward clay, and breathe upon the spirit itself, which shivers with gentle delight. Now the breeze strengthens so much as to shake all the leaves, making them rustle sharply; but it has lost its most ethereal power. And now, again, the shadows of the boughs lie as motionless as if they were painted on the pathway. Now, in the stillness, is heard the long, melancholy note of a bird, complaining above of some wrong or sorrow that man, or her own kind, or the immitigable doom of mortal affairs, has inflicted upon her, the complaining, but unresisting sufferer. And now, all of a sudden, we hear the sharp, shrill chirrup of a red squirrel, angry, it seems, with somebody — perhaps with ourselves — for having intruded into what he is pleased to consider his own domain. And hark! terrible to the ear, here is the minute but intense hum of a mosquito. Instinct prevails over all sentiment; we crush him at once, and there is his grim and grisly corpse, the ugliest object in nature. This incident has disturbed our tranquillity. In truth, the whole insect tribe, so far as we can judge, are made more for themselves, and less for man, than any other portion of creation. With such reflections, we look at a swarm of them, peopling, indeed, the whole air, but only visible when they flash into the sunshine, and annihilated out of visible existence when they dart into a region of shadow, to be again reproduced as suddenly. Now we hear the striking of the village clock, distant, but yet so near that each stroke is distinctly impressed upon the air. This is a sound that does not disturb the repose of the scene; it does not break our Sabbath, — for like a Sabbath seems this place, — and the more so, on account of the cornfield rustling at our feet. It tells of human labor; but being so solitary now, it seems as if it were so on account of the sacredness of the Sabbath. Yet it is not; for we hear at a distance mowers whetting their scythes; but these sounds of labor, when at a proper remoteness, do but increase the quiet of one who lies at his ease, all in a mist of his own musings. There is the tinkling of a cowbell, — a noise how peevishly discordant were it close at hand, but even musical now. But hark! there is the whistle of the locomotive, — the long shriek, heard above all other harshness; for the space of a mile cannot mollify it into harmony. It tells a story of busy men, citizens from the hot street, who have come to spend a day in a country village, — men of business, — in short, of all unquietness; and no wonder that it gives such a startling scream, since it brings the noisy world into the midst of our slumberous peace. As our thoughts repose again after this interruption, we find ourselves gazing up at the leaves, and comparing their different aspects, — the beautiful diversity of green, as the sun is diffused through them as a medium, or reflected from their glossy surface. We see, too, here and there, dead, leafless branches, which we had no more been aware of before than if they had assumed this old and dry decay since we sat down upon the bank. Look at our feet; and here, likewise, are objects as good as new. There are two little round, white fungi, which probably sprung from the ground in the course of last night, — curious productions, of the mushroom tribe, and

which by and by will be those small things with smoke in them which children call puff-balls. Is there nothing else? Yes; here is a whole colony of little ant-hills, — a real village of them. They are round hillocks, formed of minute particles of gravel, with an entrance in the centre, and through some of them blades of grass or small shrubs have sprouted up, producing an effect not unlike trees that overshadow a homestead. Here is a type of domestic industry, — perhaps, too, something of municipal institutions, — perhaps likewise — who knows? — the very model of a community, which Fourierites and others are stumbling in pursuit of. Possibly the student of such philosophies should go to the ant, and find that Nature has given him his lesson there. Meantime, like a malevolent genius, I drop a few grains of sand into the entrance of one of these dwellings, and thus quite obliterate it. And behold, here comes one of the inhabitants, who has been abroad upon some public or private business, or perhaps to enjoy a fantastic walk, and cannot any longer find his own door. What surprise, what hurry, what confusion of mind are expressed in all his movements! How inexplicable to him must be the agency that has effected this mischief! The incident will probably be long remembered in the annals of the ant-colony, and be talked of in the winter days, when they are making merry over their hoarded provisions. But now it is time to move. The sun has shifted his position, and has found a vacant space through the branches, by means of which he levels his rays full upon my head. Yet now, as I arise, a cloud has come across him, and makes everything gently sombre in an instant. Many clouds, voluminous and heavy, are scattered about the sky, like the shattered ruins of a dreamer's Utopia; but I will not send my thoughts thitherward now, nor take one of them into my present observations.

And now how narrow, scanty, and meagre is the record of observations, compared with the immensity that was to be observed within the bounds which I prescribed to myself ! How shallow and thin a stream of thought, too, — of distinct and expressed thought, — compared with the broad tide of dim emotions, ideas, associations, which were flowing through the haunted regions of imagination, intellect, and sentiment, — sometimes excited by what was around me, sometimes with no perceptible connection with them ! When we see how little we can express, it is a wonder that any man ever takes up a pen a second time.

To find all sorts of ridiculous employments for people that have nothing better to do ; — as to comb out the cows' tails, shave goats, hoard up seeds of weeds, etc., etc.

The baby, the other day, tried to grasp a handful of sunshine. She also grasps at the shadows of things in candle-light.

To typify our mature review of our early projects and delusions, by representing a person as wandering, in manhood, through and among the various castles in the air that he had reared in his youth, and describing how they look to him, — their dilapidation, etc. Possibly some small portion of these structures may have a certain reality, and suffice him to build a humble dwelling in which to pass his life.

The search of an investigator for the unpardonable sin : he at last finds it in his own heart and practice.

The trees reflected in the river ; — they are unconscious of a spiritual world so near them. So are we.

The unpardonable sin might consist in a want of love and reverence for the human soul ; in consequence of which, the investigator pried into its dark depths, — not with a hope or purpose of making it better, but from a cold, philosophical curiosity, — content that

it should be wicked in whatever kind and degree, and only desiring to study it out. Would not this, in other words, be the separation of the intellect from the heart ?

There are some faces that have no more expression in them than any other part of the body. The hand of one person may express more than the face of another.

An ugly person with tact may make a bad face and figure pass very tolerably, and more than tolerably. Ugliness without tact is horrible. It ought to be lawful to extirpate such wretches.

To represent the influence which dead men have among living affairs. For instance, a dead man controls the disposition of wealth ; a dead man sits on the judgment-seat, and the living judges do but repeat his decisions ; dead men's opinions in all things control the living truth ; we believe in dead men's religions ; we laugh at dead men's jokes ; we cry at dead men's pathos ; everywhere, and in all matters, dead men tyrannize inexorably over us.

When the heart is full of care, or the mind much occupied, the summer and the sunshine and the moonlight are but a gleam and glimmer,— a vague dream, which does not come within us, but only makes itself imperfectly perceptible on the outside of us.

Biographies of eminent American merchants, — it would be a work likely to have a great circulation in our commercial country. If successful, there might be a second volume of eminent foreign merchants. Perhaps it had better be adapted to the capacity of young clerks and apprentices.

For the virtuoso's collection : — Alexander's copy of the Iliad, enclosed in the jewelled casket of Darius, still fragrant with the perfumes Darius kept in it. Also the pen with which Faust signed away his salvation, with the drop of blood dried in it.

October 13, 1844.— This morning, after a heavy hoar-frost, the leaves, at sunrise, were falling from the trees in our avenue without a breath of wind, quietly descending by their own weight. In an hour or two after, the ground was strewn with them; and the trees are almost bare, with the exception of two or three poplars, which are still green. The apple and pear trees are still green; so is the willow. The first severe frosts came at least a fortnight ago, — more, if I mistake not.

Sketch of a person, who, by strength of character or assistant circumstances, has reduced another to absolute slavery and dependence on him. Then show that the person who appeared to be the master must inevitably be at least as much a slave as the other, if not more so. All slavery is reciprocal, on the supposition most favorable to the masters.

Persons who write about themselves and their feelings, as Byron did, may be said to serve up their own hearts, duly spiced, and with brain-sauce out of their own heads, as a repast for the public.

To represent a man in the midst of all sorts of cares and annoyances, with impossibilities to perform, and driven almost distracted by his inadequacy. Then quietly comes Death, and releases him from all his troubles; and he smiles, and congratulates himself on escaping so easily.

What if it should be discovered to be all a mistake, that people, who were supposed to have died long ago, are really dead? Byron to be still living, a man of sixty; Burns, too, in extreme old age; Bonaparte likewise; and many other distinguished men, whose lives might have extended to these limits. Then the private acquaintances, friends, enemies, wives, taken to be dead, to be all really living in this world. The machinery might be a person's being persuaded to believe that he had been mad; or having dwelt many years on a desolate island; or having been in the heart of Africa or China; and a friend amuses himself with giving this account. Or some traveller from Europe shall thus correct popular errors.

The life of a woman, who, by the old Colony law, was condemned to wear always the letter A sewed on her garment in token of her sin.

To make literal pictures of figurative expressions. For instance, he burst into tears, — a man suddenly turned into a shower of briny drops. An explosion of laughter, — a man blowing up, and his fragments flying about on all sides. He cast his eyes upon the ground, — a man standing eyeless, with his eyes thrown down, and staring up at him in wonderment, etc., etc., etc.

An uneducated countryman, supposing he had a live frog in his stomach, applied himself to the study of medicine, in order to find a cure, and so became a profound physician. Thus some misfortune, physical or moral, may be the means of educating and elevating us.

Concord, March 12, 1845. — Last night was very cold, and bright starlight; yet there was a mist or fog diffused all over the landscape, lying close to the ground, and extending upwards, probably not much above the tops of the trees. This fog was crystallized by the severe frost; and its little feathery crystals covered all the branches and smallest twigs of trees and shrubs; so that, this morning, at first sight, it appeared as if they were covered with snow. On closer examination, however, these most delicate feathers appeared shooting out in all directions from the branches, — above as well as beneath, — and looking, not as if they had been attached, but had been put forth by the plant, — a new kind of foliage. It is impossible to describe the exquisite beauty of the effect, when close to the eye; and even at a distance this delicate appearance was not lost, but imparted a graceful, evanescent aspect to great trees, perhaps a quarter of a mile off, making them look like immense plumes, or something that would vanish at a breath. The so-much admired sight of icy trees cannot compare with it in point of grace, delicacy, and beauty; and, moreover, there is a life and animation in this, not to be found in the other. It was to be seen in its greatest perfection at sunrise, or shortly after; for the slightest warmth impaired the minute beauty of the frost-feathers, and the general effect. But in the first sunshine, and while there was still a partial mist hovering around the hill and along the river, while some of the trees were lit up with an illumination that did not *shine*, — that is to say, glitter, — but was not less bright than if it had glittered, while other portions of the scene were partly obscured, but not gloomy, — on the contrary, very cheerful, — it was a picture that never can be painted nor described, nor, I fear, remembered with any accuracy, so magical was its light and shade, while at the same time the earth and everything upon it were white; for the ground is entirely covered by yesterday's snow-storm.

Already, before eleven o'clock, these feathery crystals have vanished, partly through the warmth of the sun, and partly by gentle breaths of wind; for so slight was their hold upon the twigs that the least motion, or thought almost, sufficed to bring them floating down, like a little snow-storm, to the ground. In fact, the fog, I suppose, was a cloud of snow, and would have scattered down upon us, had it been at the usual height above the earth.

All the above description is most unsatisfactory.

ON TRANSLATING THE DIVINA COMMEDIA.

FOURTH SONNET.

HOW strange the sculptures that adorn these towers!
    This crowd of statues, in whose folded sleeves
    Birds build their nests; while canopied with leaves
    Parvis and portal bloom like trellised bowers,
And the vast minster seems a cross of flowers!
    But fiends and dragons from the gargoyled eaves
    Watch the dead Christ between the living thieves,
    And underneath the traitor Judas lowers!
Ah! from what agonies of heart and brain,
    What exultations trampling on despair,
    What tenderness, what tears, what hate of wrong,
What passionate outcry of a soul in pain,
    Uprose this poem of the earth and air,
    This mediæval miracle of song!

FIVE HUNDRED YEARS AGO.

WE who enjoy the fruits of civil and religious liberty as our daily food, reaping the harvest we did not sow, seldom give a thought to those who in the dim past prepared the ground and scattered the seed that has yielded such plenteous return. If occasionally we peer into the gloom of bygone centuries, some stalwart form, like that of Luther, arrests our backward glance, and all beyond is dark and void. But generations before Martin Luther the work for the harvest of coming ages was begun. Humble but earnest men, with such rude aids as they possessed, were toiling to clear away the dense underbrush of ignorance and superstition, and let the light of the sun in on the stagnant swamp ; struggling to plough up the stony soil that centuries of oppression had made hard and barren ; scattering seed that the sun would scorch and the birds of the air devour ; and dying without seeing a green blade to reward them with the hope that their toils were not in vain.

But their labors were not lost. The soil thus prepared by the painful and unrequited toil of those who had gone down to obscure graves, sorrowing and hopeless, offered less obstruction to the strong arms and better appliances of the reformers of a later day. Of the seed scattered by the early sowers, a grain found here and there a sheltering crevice, and struggled into life, bearing fruit that in the succession of years increased and multiplied until thousands were fed and strengthened by its harvest.

The military history of the reign of the third Edward of England is illuminated with such a blaze of glory, that the dazzled eye can with difficulty distinguish the dark background of its domestic life. Cressy and Poitiers carried the military fame of England throughout the world, and struck terror into her enemies ; but at home dwelt turbulence, corruption, rapine, and misery. The barons quarrelled and fought among themselves. The clergy wallowed in a sty of corruption and debauchery. The laboring classes were sunk in ignorance and hopeless misery. It was the dark hour that precedes the first glimmer of dawn.

Poitiers was won in 1356. Four years the French king remained in honorable captivity in England. Then came the treaty of Bretigny, which released King John and terminated the war. The great nobles, with their armies of lesser knights and swarms of men-at-arms, returned to England, viewed with secret and well-founded distrust by the industrious and laboring classes along their homeward route. The nobles established themselves in their castles, immediately surrounded by swarms of reckless men, habituated by years of war to deeds of lawlessness and violence, and having subject to their summons feudatory knights, each of whom had his own band of turbulent retainers. With such elements of discord, it was impossible for good order long to be maintained. The nobles quarrelled, and their retainers were not backward in taking up the quarrel. The feudatory knights had disagreements among themselves, and carried on petty war against each other. Confederated bands of lawless men traversed the country, seizing property wherever it could be found, outraging women, taking prisoners and ransoming them, and making war against all who opposed their progress or were personally obnoxious to them. Castles and estates were seized and held on some imaginary claim. It was in vain to appeal to the laws. Justice was powerless to correct abuses or aid the oppressed. Powerful barons gave countenance to the marauders, that their services might be secured in the event of a quarrel with their neighbors ; nor did they hesitate to share in the booty. Might everywhere triumphed over right, and the " law of the strong arm" superseded the ordinances of the civil power.

The condition of the Church was no better than that of the State. Fraud, corruption, and oppression sat in high places in both. The prelates had their swarms of armed retainers, and ruled their flocks with the sword as well as the crosier. The monasteries, with but few exceptions, were the haunts of extravagance and sensuality, instead of the abodes of self-denying virtue and learning. The portly abbot, his black robe edged with costly fur and clasped with a silver girdle, his peaked shoes in the height of the fashion, and wearing a handsomely ornamented dagger or hunting-knife, rode out accompanied by a pack of trained hunting-dogs, the golden bells on his bridle

> "Gingeling in the whistling wind as clear
> And eke as loud as doth the chapel bell."

The monks who were unable to indulge their taste for the chase sought recompense in unrestrained indulgence at the table. The land was overspread with an innumerable swarm of begging friars, who fawned on the great, flattered the wealthy, and despoiled the poor. Another class traversed the country, selling pardons "come from Rome all hot," and extolling the virtues of their relics and the power of their indulgences with the eloquence of a quack vending his nostrums. Bishops held civil offices under the king, and priests acted as stewards in great men's houses. Simony possessed the Church, and the ministers of religion again sold their Master for silver.

The domestic and social life of the higher classes of society in the last half of the fourteenth century can be delineated, with a fair approach to exactness, from the detached hints scattered through such old romances and poems of that period as the diligent labors of zealous antiquaries have brought to light.

The residences of all the great and wealthy possessed one general character. The central point and most important feature was the great hall, adjoining which in most houses a "parlour," or talking-room, had recently been built. A principal chamber for the ladies of the household was generally placed on the ground-floor, with an upper chamber, or "soler," over it. In the larger establishments additional chambers had been clustered around the main building, increasing in number with the wants of the household. The castles and fortified buildings varied a little in outward construction from the ordinary manorial residences, but the same general arrangement of the interior existed. A few of the stronger and more important buildings were of stone; but the larger proportion were of timber, or timber and stone combined.

The great hall was the most important part of the establishment. Here the general business of the household was transacted, the meals served, strangers received, audiences granted, and what may be termed the public life of the family carried on. It was also the general rendezvous of the servants and retainers, who lounged about it when duty or pleasure did not call them to the other offices or to the field. In the evening they gathered around the fire, built in an iron grate standing in the middle of the room; for as yet chimneys were a luxury confined to the principal chamber. The few remaining halls of this period that have not been remodelled in succeeding ages present no trace of a fireplace or chimney. At night the male servants and men-at-arms stretched themselves to sleep on the benches along its sides, or on the rush-covered floor.

The floor at the upper end was raised, forming the *dais*, or place of honor. On this, stretching nearly from side to side, was the "table dormant," or fixed table, with a "settle," or bench with a back, between it and the wall. On the lower floor, and extending lengthwise on each side down the hall, stood long benches for the use of the servants and retainers. At meal-times, in front of these were placed the temporary tables of loose boards supported on trestles. At the upper end was the cupboard, or "dresser," for the plate and furniture of the table. In the halls of the greater nobles, on important occasions, tapestry or curtains were hung on the walls, or at least on that portion of the wall next the dais, and still more rarely a carpet was used for that part of the floor, — rushes or bare tiles being more general. A perch for hawks, and the grate of burning wood, sending its smoke up to the blackened open roof, completed the picture of the hall of a large establishment in the fourteenth century.

The "parlour," or talking-room, as its name imports, was used chiefly for conferences, and for such business as required more privacy than was attainable in the hall, but was unsuited to the domestic character of the chamber.

After the hall, the most important feature of the building was the principal chamber. Here the domestic life of the family was carried on. Here the ladies of the household spent their time when not at meals or engaged in outdoor sports and pastimes. The furniture of this room was more complete than that of the other parts of the building, but was still rude and scanty when judged by modern wants. The bed was of massive proportions and frequently of ornamental character. A truckle-bed for the children or chamber servants was pushed under the principal bed by day. At the foot of the latter stood the huge "hutch," or chest, in which were deposited for safety the family plate and valuables. Two or three stools and large chairs, with a perch or bar on which to hang garments, completed the usual furniture of the chamber.

In this room was one important feature not found in the others, and which accounted for the increasing attachment manifested towards it. The fire, instead of being placed in an iron grate or brazier in the middle of the room, burned merrily on the hearth ; and the smoke, instead of seeking its exit by the window, was carried up a chimney of generous proportions.

The household day commenced early.

The members of the family arose from the beds where they had slept in the garments worn by our first parents before the fall ; for the effeminacy of sleeping in night-dresses had not yet been introduced, and it was only the excessively poor that made the clothes worn during the day serve in lieu of blankets and coverlets.

> " 'I have but one whole hater,'* quoth Haukyn ;
> 'I am the less to blame,
> Though it be soiled and seldom clean :
> I sleep therein of nights.' "

Breakfast was served about six o'clock. It is difficult to get an exact description of the customs of the breakfast-table, or the nature of the meal, as the contemporary writers make little allusion to it. Probably it was but a slight repast, to allay the cravings of appetite until the great meal of the day was served. Until within a few years of the period of which we write, the dinner-hour was so early that but little food was taken before that time.

Dinner was then, as now, the principal meal of the English day. In the houses of the great it was conducted with much ceremony ; and among the richer classes certain well-established rules of courtesy in relation to the meal were observed. The family and their guests entered the great hall about ten o'clock. They were met by a domestic, bearing a pitcher and basin, and his assistant, with a towel. Water was poured on the hands of each person, and the ablutions carefully performed ; scrupulous cleanliness in this respect being required, from the fact that forks were as yet things undreamed of. The principal guests took their seats at the " table dormant," on the dais, the person of highest rank having the middle seat, — which was consequently at the head of the hall, — and the others being arranged according to their respective rank.

At the side-tables, below the dais, sat the inferior members of the household, with the guests of lesser note, — these also arranged with careful regard to

* Garment.

rank and position. The beggar or poor wayfarer who was admitted to a humble share of the feast crouched on the rushes among the dogs who lay awaiting the bones and relics of the repast, and thankfully fed, like Lazarus, on "the crumbs that fell from the rich man's table."

The guests being seated, the busy servitors hastened to cover the table with a "fair white linen cloth," of unsullied purity ; and on it were placed the salt-cellars of massive silver, the spoons and knives ; next the bread, and then the wine, poured with great ceremony into the drinking-cups by the cupbearer. The silver vessels were brought from the "dresser," and arranged on the table, the display being proportioned to the wealth and condition of the host and the consideration to be paid to the guests. The head cook and his assistants entered in procession, bearing the dishes in regular order, and deposited them on the table with due solemnity. The pottage was first served, and when this course was eaten, the vessels and spoons were removed. The carver performed his office on the meats, holding the joint, according to the traditions of his order, carefully with the thumb and first two fingers of his left hand, whilst he carved. The pieces were placed on "trenchers" or slices of bread, and handed to the guests, who made no scruple of freely using their fingers. The bones and refuse of the food were placed on the table, or thrown to the dogs.

The people of that day were not insensible to the pleasures of the table ; and, unless urgent matters called them to the field or the council, dinner was enjoyed with leisurely deliberation. In great houses of hospitable reputation, the great hall at the hour of meals was open to all comers. The traveller who found himself at its door was admitted, and received position and food according to his condition. The minstrels that wandered over the country in great numbers were always welcome, and were well supplied with food

and drink, and received liberal gifts for their songs and the long romances of love and chivalry which they recited to music. Not unfrequently satirical songs were sung, or the minstrel narrated stories in which the humor was of a coarser nature than would now be tolerated in the presence of ladies, but which in that day were listened to without a blush.

Dinner ended, the vessels and unconsumed meats were removed, the table-cloths gathered up, and the relics of the feast thrown on the floor for the dogs to devour. The side-tables were removed from their trestles and piled in a corner, and the hall cleared for the entertainments that frequently followed the dinner. These consisted of feats of conjuring by the "joculators," balancing and tumbling by the women who wandered about seeking a livelihood by such means, or dancing by the ladies of the household and their guests.

The feast and its succeeding amusements disposed of, the ladies either shared in the out-door sports and games, of which there were many in which women could take part, or they retired to the chamber, where, seated in low chairs or in the recessed windows, they engaged in making the needle-work pictures that adorned the tapestry, listening the while to the love-romances narrated by the minstrel who had been invited for the purpose, or gave willing ear to the flattery of some "virelay" or love-song, sung by gay canon, gentle page, or courtly knight.

About six o'clock, the household once more assembled in the hall for supper ; and then the orders for the ensuing day were given to the servants and retainers. Soon after dark the members of the family and their guests sought their respective sleeping - places, as contrivances for lighting were rude, and had to be economized. Such of the servants as had special chambers or sleeping - places retired to them, whilst a large proportion of the male servants and such of the retainers as belonged immediately to the household stretched themselves on the benches or floor of the hall, and were soon fast asleep. Such is a sketch of the ordinary course of domestic life among the higher classes of English society in the fourteenth century.

Among the greater nobles, the details of the daily life were sometimes on a more magnificent scale ; but the leading features were as we have described them. Rude pomp and barbaric splendor marked the establishments of some of the powerful barons and ecclesiastical dignitaries. At tilt and tournament, the contending knights strove to outshine each other in gorgeousness of equipment, as well as in deeds of arms. Nor were the ladies averse to richness of attire in their own persons. Costly robes and dainty furs were worn, and jewels and gems of price sparkled when the dames and demoiselles appeared at great gatherings, or on occasions of state and ceremony. The extravagance of dress in both sexes had grown to be so great an evil, that stringent sumptuary laws were passed, but without producing any effect.

The moral state of even the highest classes of society was not of a flattering character. Europe was one huge camp and battle-field, in which all the chivalry of the day had been educated, — no good school for purity of life and delicacy of language. The literature of the time, at least that portion of it which penetrated to ladies' chambers, was of an amorous, and too frequently of an indelicate character. A debased and sensual clergy swarmed over the land, finding their way into every household, and gradually corrupting those with whom their sacred office brought them into contact. The manners and habits of the time afforded every facility for the gratification of debased passions and indulgence in immoral practices.

Whilst the barons feasted and fought, the ladies intrigued, and the clergy violated every principle of the religion they professed, the great mass of the population lived on, with scarcely a thought

bestowed on them by their social superiors. Between the Anglo-Norman baron and the Anglo-Saxon laborer, or " villain," there was a great gulf fixed. The antipathy of an antagonistic and conquered race to its conquerors was intensified by years of oppression and wrong, and the laborer cherished a burning desire to break the bonds of thraldom in which most of the poor were held.

By the laws of the feudal system, the tenants and laborers on the property of a baron were his " villains," or slaves. They were divided into two classes : — the " villains regardant," who were permitted to occupy and cultivate small portions of land, on condition of rendering certain stipulated services to their lord, and were therefore considered in the light of slaves to the land ; and the " villains in gross," who were the personal slaves of the land-owner, and were compelled to do the work they were set to perform in consideration of their food and clothing. Besides these two classes a third had recently come into existence, and, owing to various causes, was fast increasing in extent and importance, — that of free laborers, who worked for hire. This class was recruited in various ways from the ranks of the " villains in gross." Some were manumitted by their dying masters, as an act of piety in atonement for the deeds of violence done during life ; but by far the greater number effected their freedom by escaping to distant parts of the country, where but little search would be made for them, or by seeking the refuge of the walled towns and cities, where a residence of a year and a day would give them freedom by law. The citizens were always ready to give asylum to those fugitives, for they supplied the growing need for laborers, and enabled the cities, by the increase of population, to maintain their independence against the pretensions of the barons.

The condition of the " villain " was bad at the best ; and numerous petty acts of oppression in most instances increased the bitterness of his lot.

Himself the property of another, he could not legally hold possessions of any kind. Not only the land he tilled, and the rude implements of husbandry with which he painfully cultivated the soil, but the cattle with which he worked, the house in which he lived, the few chattels he gathered around him, and the scanty store of money earned by hard labor, all belonged to his master, who could at any time dispossess him of them. The "villain" who obtained a livelihood by working the few acres of land which had been held from father to son, on condition of performing personal labor or other services on the estate of the landowner, was subject not only to the demands of his master, but to the tithing of the Church; to the doles exacted by the swarms of begging friars, who, like Irish beggars of the present day, invoked cheap blessings on the cheerful giver, and launched bitter curses at the heads of those who refused alms; to the impositions of the wandering "pardoners," with their charms and relics; and to the tyrannical exactions of the "summoners," who, under pretence of writs from ecclesiastical courts, robbed all who were not in position to resist their fraudulent demands. What these spared was frequently swept away by the visits of the king's purveyors and the officers of others in power, who, not content with robbing the poor husbandman of the proceeds of his toil, treated the men with violence and the women with outrage. Complaint was useless. The "churl" had no rights which those in office were bound to respect.

Ignorant, superstitious, and condemned to a life of unrequited toil and unredressed wrongs, the mental and moral condition of the agricultural poor was wretchedly low. Huddled together in mud cottages, through the rotten thatches of which the rain penetrated; clothed with rough garments that were seldom changed night or day; feeding on coarse food, and that in insufficient quantities,—their physical condition was one of extreme misery. The usual daily allowance of food to the bond laborer of either class, when working for the owner of the land, was two herrings, milk for cheese, and a loaf of bread, with the addition in harvest of a small allowance of beer. Occasionally, salted meats or stockfish were substituted for the herrings.

The condition of the free laborer was measurably better; but even he was condemned to a life of privation and wretchedness, relieved only by the knowledge that his scanty earnings were his own, and that he could change the scene of his labors if he saw fit. The ordinary agricultural laborer, at the wages usually given, would have to work more than a week for a bushel of wheat. At harvest-time and other periods when the demand for labor was unusually great, as it was after the pestilences that swept the land about the time of which we write, the free laborers demanded higher wages; and although laws were passed to prevent their obtaining more than the usual rates, necessity frequently compelled their employment at the advanced prices. The receipt of higher wages only temporarily bettered their condition. Accustomed to griping hunger and short allowances of food, when better days came, they thought only of enjoying the present, and took no heed of the future. After harvest, with its high wages and cheapness of provision, the laborer frequently became wasteful and improvident. Instead of the stinted allowance of salted meat or fish, with the pinched loaf of bean-flour, and an occasional draught of weak beer, his fastidious appetite demanded fresh meat or fish, white bread, vegetables freshly gathered, and ale of the best. As long as his store lasted, he worked as little as possible, and grumbled at the fortune that made him a laborer. But these halcyon days were few, and soon passed away, to be followed by decreasing allowances of the commonest food, fierce pangs of hunger, and miserable destitution. A bad harvest inflicted untold wretchedness on the poor. Ill lodged, ill fed, and scantily clothed, disease cut them down like grass before the scythe. A deadly pestilence swept over the land in 1348, carrying off about two thirds of the people; and nearly all the victims were from among the poorest classes. In 1361, another pestilence carried off thousands, again spreading terror and dismay through the country. Seven years later a third visitation desolated England. Here and there one of the better class fell a victim to the destroyer; but the great mass were from the ranks of the half-starved and poorly lodged laborers.

The morality of the poor was, as might be expected, at a low ebb. Modesty, chastity, and temperance could scarcely be looked for in wretched mud huts, where all ages and sexes herded together like swine. Men and women alike fled from their miserable homes to the ale-house, where they drank long draughts of cheap ale, and, in imitation of their superiors in station, listened to a low class of "japers" who recited "rhymes of Robin Hood," or told coarse and obscene stories for the sake of a share of the ale, or such few small coins as could be drawn from the ragged pouches of the bacchanals.

Between proud wealth and abject poverty there can be no friendly feeling. Stolid, brutish ignorance can alone render the bonds of the slave endurable. As his eyes are slowly opened by increasing knowledge, and he can compare his condition with that of the freeman, his fetters gall him, he becomes restive in his bonds, and at length turns in blind fury on his oppressors, striking mad blows with his manacled hands. Trodden into the dust by the iron heel of a tyrannical feudal power, the peasantry of France had turned on their oppressors, and wreaked a brief but savage vengeance for ages of wrong. The atrocious cruelties and mad excesses of the revolted Jacquerie could only have been committed by those who had been so long treated as brutes that they had acquired brutish passions and instincts. The English peasantry had not yet followed the example of their

French compeers; but the gathering storm already darkened the sky, and the mutterings of the thunder were heard. Superstitiously religious, they hated the ministers of religion who violated its principles. Born slaves and hopelessly debased and ignorant, they began to ask the question, —

> "When Adam delved and Eve span,
> Who then was the gentleman?"

Occasionally a rude ballad found its way among the people fiercely expressive of their scorn of the clergy and their hatred of the rich. One that was very popular, and has been transmitted to our day, asked, —

> "While God was on earth
> And wandered wide,
> What was the reason
> Why he would not ride?
> Because he would have no groom
> To go by his side,
> Nor grudging of no gadeling*
> To scold nor to chide.

> "Hearken hitherward, horsemen,
> A tiding I you tell,
> That ye shall hang
> And harbor in hell!"

But no leader had as yet arisen to give proper voice to the desire for reformation that burned in the hearts of the common people. The writers of that age were breathing the intoxicating air of court favor, and heeded not the sufferings of the common rabble. Froissart, the courtly canon and chronicler of deeds of chivalry, was writing French madrigals and amorous ditties for the ear of Queen Philippa, and loved too well gay society, luxurious feasts, and dainty attire, not to shrink with disgust from thought of the dirty, uncouth, and miserable herd of "greasy caps." Gower was inditing fashionable love-songs. Chaucer, who years after was to direct such telling blows in his Canterbury Tales at the vices and corruptness of the clergy, was a favorite member of the retinue of the powerful "John of Gaunt, time-honored Lancaster," and had as yet only written long and stately poems on the history of Troilus and Cressida, the Parlia-

* Vagabond.

ment of Birds, and the Court of Love. Wycliffe, the great English reformer of the Church, was quietly living at his rectory of Fylingham, and preparing his first essays against the mendicant orders. John Ball, the "crazy priest of Kent," as Froissart calls him, was brooding over the miseries of his poor parishioners, and nursing in his mind that enmity to all social distinctions with which he afterwards inflamed the minds of the peasantry, and incited them to open rebellion.

But in the quarter least expected the oppressed people found an advocate. An unobtrusive monk, whose name is almost a doubtful tradition, stole out from his quiet cell in Malvern Abbey, and, whilst his brethren feasted, climbed the gentle slope of the Worcestershire hills, and drank in the beauties of the varied landscape at his feet. There, on a May morning, as he rested under a bank by the side of a brooklet, and was lulled to sleep by the murmuring of the water, he dreamed those dreams that set waking people to thinking, and gave a powerful impetus to the moral and social revolution that was just commencing.

The "Vision of Piers Plowman" is every way a singular production. Clothed in the then almost obsolete verse of a past age, it breathes wholly the spirit of the time in which it was written. The work of a monk, it is unsparing in its attacks on the monastic orders. Intended for the reading or hearing of the middle and lower classes, it gives more frequent glimpses of the social condition of all ranks of people than any other work of that age. As a philological monument, it is of great value; as a poem, it contains many passages of merit; and as a storehouse of allusions to the social life of the people in the fourteenth century, it is invaluable.

The poem consists of a series of visions or dreams, of an allegorical character, in which the dreamer seeks to find Truth and Righteousness on earth, meeting with but little success. The allegorical idea cannot be followed without weariness, and, in fact, the intentions of the writer are by no means clear, the allegory being frequently involved and contradictory. The beauty of the poem lies in its detached passages, its occasional poetic touches, its graphic pictures, biting satire, and withering denunciation of fraud, corruption, and tyranny. The measure adopted is the unrhymed alliterative, characteristic of the Anglo-Saxon literature, and which had long been disused, but which retained its hold on the affections of the common people, who were of Anglo-Saxon stock. In the extracts we give from the poem, the measure is retained, but the words modernized, so far as can be done without injuring the sense or metre.

The opening passage of the "Vision" has been so frequently reproduced, as a specimen of the poet's style, that it is probably familiar to many readers, but its exquisite naturalness and simplicity tempt us to quote it here.

> " In a summer season,
> When soft was the sun,
> I shaped me into shrouds *
> As I a shep † were ;
> In habit as an hermit
> Unholy of works
> Went wide in this world
> Wonders to hear :
> And on a May morwening
> On Malvern hills
> Me befell a ferly,‡
> Of fairy methought.
> I was weary for-wandered,
> And went me to rest
> Under a broad bank
> By a bourne's § side :
> And as I lay and leaned,
> And looked on the waters,
> I slumbered into a sleeping
> It swayed so merry."

The first scene in the visions that visited the sleep of the dreaming monk gives a view of the social classes of that time, beginning with the humblest, whose condition was uppermost in his mind. The picture is not only painted with vigorous touches, but affords a better idea of society in the fourteenth century than can be elsewhere

* Clothes.   † Shepherd.
‡ Vision.   § Brook.

obtained. There is the toiling plough-man, who "plays full seldom," winning by hard labor what wasteful men destroy; the mediæval dandy, whose only employment is to exhibit his attire; the hermit, who seeks by solitude and penitential life to win "heaven's rich bliss"; the merchant, who has wisely chosen his trade,—

> " As it seemeth in our sight
> That such men thriveth."

There are minstrels, who earn rich rewards by their singing; jesters and idle gossips; "sturdy beggars," wandering with full bags; pilgrims and palmers, who

> " Went forth in their way
> With many wise tales,
> And had leave to lie
> All their lives after ";

counterfeit hermits, who assumed the cloak and hooked staff in order to live in idleness and sensuality; avaricious friars, selling their religion for money; cheating pardoners; covetous priests; ambitious bishops; lawyers who loved gain better than justice; "barons and burgesses, and bondmen also," with

> " Bakers and brewers,
> And butchers many;
> Woollen websters,
> And weavers of linen;
> Tailors and tinkers,
> And toilers in markets;
> Masons and miners,
> And many other crafts.
> Of all kind living laborers
> Leaped forth some :
> As ditchers and delvers,
> That do their deeds ill,
> And driveth forth the long day
> With *Dieu save dame Emme.*
> Cooks and their knaves
> Cried, ' Hot pies, hot !
> Good geese and grys,*
> Go dine, go ! ' "

To plead the cause of the poor and weak against their powerful oppressors, and to protest in the name of religion against the pride and corrupt life of its ministers, was the object of the monk of Malvern Abbey; and he did his work well. The blows he dealt were fierce and strong, and told home. Burgher and baron, monk and cardinal, alike felt the fury of his attacks. He was no respecter of persons. A monk him-

* Pigs.

self, he had no scruples in tearing off the priestly robe that covered lust and rapine. Wrong in high places gained no respect from him. His invectives against a haughty and oppressive nobility and a corrupt and arrogant clergy are unsurpassed in power, and it is easy to understand the hold the poem at once acquired on the attention of the lower classes, and its influence in directing and hastening the attempt of the oppressed people to break their galling bonds.

What we have before said in reference to the wretched condition of the peasantry, as shown by contemporary evidence, is confirmed by the writer of the "Vision." The peasant was a born thrall to the owner of the land, and could

> " no charter make,
> Nor his cattle sell,
> Withouten leave of his lord."

Misery and he were lifelong companions, and pinching want his daily portion. The wretched poor

> " much care suffren
> Through dearth, through drought,
> All their days here :
> Woe in winter times
> For wanting of clothing,
> And in summer time seldom
> Soupen to the full."

A graphic picture of a poor ploughman and his family is given in the "Creed" of Piers Plowman, supposed to have been written by the author of the "Vision," but a few years later.

> " As I went by the way
> Weeping for sorrow,
> I saw a simple man me by,
> Upon the plow hanging.
> His coat was of a clout
> That cary * was called ;
> His hood was full of holes,
> And his hair out ;
> With his knopped † shoon
> Clouted full thick ;
> His toes toteden ‡ out
> As he the land treaded ;
> His hosen overhung his hockshins
> On every side,
> All beslomered in fen §
> As he the plow followed.
> Two mittens as meter
> Made all of clouts,
> The fingers were for-werd ‖

* A kind of very coarse cloth.
† Buttoned.   ‡ Pushed.
§ Mud.   ‖ Worn out.

And full of fen hanged.
This wight wallowed in the fen
Almost to the ankle.
Four rotheren* him before
That foeble were worthy,
Men might reckon each rib
So rentful † they were.
His wife walked him with,
With a long goad,
In a cutted coat,
Cutted full high,
Wrapped in a winnow sheet
To weren her from weathers,
Barefoot on the bare ice
That the blood followed.
And at the land's end layeth
A little crumb-bowl, ‡
And thereon lay a little child
Lapped in clouts,
And twins of two years old
Upon another side.
And all they sungen one song,
That sorrow was to hear ;
They crieden all one cry.
A careful note.
The simple man sighed sore,
And said, ' Children, be still ! ' "

The tenant of land, or small farmer, was in a better condition, and when not cozened of his stores by the monks, or robbed of them by the ruffians in office or out of office, managed to live with some kind of rude comfort. What the ordinary condition of his larder and the extent of his farming stock were, may be learned from a passage in the "Vision."

" ' I have no penny,' quoth Piers,
' Pullets to buy,
Nor neither geese nor grys ;
But two green cheeses,
A few curds and cream,
And an haver cake, §
And two loaves of beans and bran,
Baked for my fauntes ‖
And yet I say, by my soul !
I have no salt bacon,
Nor no cokeney, ¶ by Christ !
Collops for to maken.

" But I have perciles and porettes,**
And many cole plants, ††
And eke a cow and calf,
And a cart-mare
To draw afield my dung,
The while the drought lasteth ;
And by this livelihood we must live
Till Lammas time,
And by that I hope to have
Harvest in my croft,
And then may I dight thy dinner
As me dear liketh.' "

We have already described the ten-

ure by which the tenant held his lands, and the protection the knightly land-owner was bound to give his tenant. Thus Piers Plowman, when his honest labors are broken in upon by ruffians,

" Plained him to the knight
To help him, as covenant was,
From cursed shrews,
Aud from these wasters, wolves-kind,
That maketh the world dear."

At times this was but a wolf's protection, or a stronger power broke through all guards. The "king's purveyor," or some other licensed despoiler, came in, and the victim was left to make fruitless complaints of his injuries. The women were subjected to gross outrages, and the property stolen or destroyed.

" Both my geese and my grys
His gadelings* fetcheth,
I dare not, for fear of them,
Fight nor chide.
He borrowed of me Bayard
And brought him home never,
Nor no farthing therefore
For aught that I could plead.
He maintaineth his men
To murder my hewen, †
Forestalleth my fa'rs,
And fighteth in my chepying, ‡
And breaketh up my barn door,
And beareth away my wheat,
And taketh me but a tally
For ten quarters of oats ;
And yet he beateth me thereto."

Then, as now, there were complaints that the privations of the poor were increased by the covetousness of the hucksters, and "regraters" (retailers), who came between the producer and the consumer, and grew rich on the profits made from both.

" Brewers and bakers,
Butchers and cooks,"

were charged with robbing

"the poor people
That parcel-meal § buy ;
For they empoison the people
Privily and oft.
They grow rich through regratery,
And rents they buy
With what the poor people
Should put in their wamb. ‖
For, took they but truly,
They timbered ¶ not so high,
Nor bought no burgages,**
Be ye felt certain."

Stringent laws were made against

---

* Oxen.	‖ Children.	
† Meagre.	¶ A lean hen.	
‡ Kneading-trough.	** Parsley and leeks.	
§ Oat cake.	†† Cabbages.	

* Vagabonds.	† Workingmen.	‡ Market.
§ Piecemeal.	‖ Belly.	¶ Built.
** Lands or tenements in towns.		

huckstering and regrating, and officers were appointed to punish offenders in this respect, "with pillories and pining-stools." But officers, then as now, were not proof against temptation, and were often disposed

> " Of all such sellers
> Silver for to take ;
> Or presents without pence,
> As pieces of silver,
> Rings, or other riches,
> The regraters to maintain."

Nor had the rogues of the fourteenth century much to learn in the way of turning a dishonest penny. The merchant commended his bad wares for good, and knew how to adulterate and how to give short measure. The spinners of wool were paid by a heavy pound, and the article resold by a light pound. Laws were made against such frauds, but laws were little regarded when they conflicted with self-interest. The crime of clipping and "sweating" coin was frequently practised. Pawnbrokers, money-lenders, and sellers of exchange thrived and flourished.

The rich find but little consideration at the hands of the plain-spoken dreamer. Their extravagance is commented on ; their growing pride, which prompted them to abandon the great hall and take their meals in a private room, and their uncharitableness to the poor. They practise the saying, that "to him that hath shall be given."

> " Right so, ye rich,
> Ye robeth them that be rich,
> And helpeth them that helpen you,
> And giveth where no need is,
> Ye robeth and feedeth
> Them that have as ye have
> Them ye make at ease."

But when, hungered, athirst, and shivering with cold, the poor man comes to the rich man's gate, there is none to help, but he is

> " hunted as a hound,
> And bidden go thence.".

Thus

> " the rich is reverenced
> By reason of his richness,
> And the poor is put behind."

Truly, says the Monk of Malvern,

> God is much in the gorge
> Of these great masters :
> But among mean men
> His mercy and his works."

But it is on the vices and corruptions of the clergy that the monk pours the vials of his wrath. He cloaks nothing, and spares neither rank nor condition. The avarice of the clergy, their want of religion, and the prostitution of their sacred office for the sake of gain, are sternly denounced in frequently-recurring passages. The facility with which debaucheries and crimes of all kinds could be compounded for with the priests by presents of gold and silver, the neglect of their flocks whilst seeking gain in the service of the rich and powerful, their ignorance, pride, extravagance, and licentiousness, are painted in strong colors. The immense throng of friars and monks, who "waxen out of number," meet with small mercy from their fellow-monk. Falsehood and fraud are described as dwelling ever with them. Their unholy life and unseemly quarrels are held up for reprobation. Nor do the nuns escape the imputation of unchastity. The quackery of pardoners, with their pardons and indulgences from pope and bishop, is treated with contempt and scorn. Bishops are criticised for their undivided attention to worldly matters ; and even the Pope himself does not escape censure.

> " What pope or prelate now
> Performeth what Christ hight* ? "

The cardinals come in for a share of the censure, and here occurs a passage, curiously suggestive of the celebrated line, —

> " Never yet did cardinal bring good to England."

> " The commons *clamat cotidie*
> Each man to the other,
> The country is the curseder
> That cardinals come in :
> And where they lie and lenge † meet,
> Lechery there reigneth."

Years afterwards, Wycliffe dealt mighty blows at the corrupt and debased clergy, and Chaucer pierced them with his sharp satire, but neither surpassed their predecessor in the vigor

---

* Commanded.   † Remain.

and spirit of his onslaughts. One passage, which we quote, had evidently been acted on by Chaucer's "poor parson," and can be studied even at this late day.

> " Friars and many other masters,
> That to lewed * men preachen,
> Ye moven matters unmeasurable
> To tellen of the Trinity,
> That oft times the lewed people
> Of their belief doubt.
> Better it were to many doctors
> To leave such teaching,
> And tell men of the ten commandments,
> And touching the seven sins,
> And of the branches that bourgeoneth of them,
> And bringen men to hell,
> And how that folk in follies
> Misspenden their five wits,
> As well friars as other folks,
> Foolishly spending,
> In housing, in hatering,†
> And in to high clergy showing
> More for pomp than for pure charity.
> The people wot the sooth
> That I lie not, lo !
> For lords ye pleasen,
> And reverence the rich
> The rather for their silver."

It would be hardly proper to leave this portion of the subject without alluding to the remarkable passage which has been held by many as a prophecy of the dissolution of the monasteries by Henry VIII., nearly two centuries later. After denouncing the corruptions of the clergy, he says : —

> " But there shall come a king
> And confess you religiouses,
> And beat you as the Bible telleth
> For breaking of your rule ;
> And amend monials,
> Monks and canons,
> And put them to their penance.
>
> And then shall the Abbot of Abingdon,
> And all his issue forever,
> Have a knock of a king,
> And incurable the wound."

A distinctive and charming feature of the English landscape is the hedgerow that divides the fields and marks the course of the roadways. Nowhere but in England does the landscape present such a charming picture of "meadows trim with daisies pied," "russet lawns and fallows gray," spread out like a map, divided with irregular lines of green. Nowhere else is the travel-

---

* Unlearned.   † Dressing.

---

ler's path guarded on either hand with a rampart of delicate primroses, sweet-breathed violets, golden buttercups fit for fairy revels, honeysuckles in whose bells the bee rings a delighted peal, and luscious-fruited blackberry-bushes. Nowhere else is such a rampart crowned with the sweet-scented hawthorn, robed in snowy blossoms, or beaded over with scarlet berries, and with the hazel, with its gracefully pendent catkins, or nuts dear to the schoolboy. It scarcely seems possible to imagine an English landscape without its flower-scented hedge-rows, and yet, when the armed knights of Edward the Third's reign rode abroad from their castles, few lofty hedges barred their progress across the country ; no hazel-crowned rampart stopped the way of the Malvern monk as he took his way to the "bourne's side " ; and when the ploughman "whistled o'er the furrowed land," the line of division at which he turned his back on his neighbor's acres was generally but a narrow trench instead of a ditch and hedge. Thus the covetous man confesses,

> " If I yede * to the plow,
> I pinched so narrow
> That a foot land or a furrow
> Fetchen I would
> Of my next neighbor,
> And nyment † of his earth.
> And if I reap, overreach."

As might have been expected, the monkish dreamer, unusually liberal as he was in his views, had but a slighting opinion of women. Rarely does he refer to them except to rate them for their extravagance in dress and love of finery. The humbler class of women, he shrewdly insinuates, were fond of drink, and the husbands of such were advised to cudgel them home to their domestic duties. He credited the long-standing slander about woman's inability to keep a secret : —

> " For that that women wotteth
> May not well be concealed."

His opinion of the proper sphere of women in that time, and some knowledge of their ordinary feminine occupations, can be acquired from the an-

---

* Went.   † Rob him.

swer made to the question of a lady as to what her sex should do : —

> " Some should sew the sack, quoth Piers,
> For shedding of the wheat ;
> And ye, lovely ladies,
> With your long fingers,
> That ye have silk and sendal
> To sew, when time is,
> Chasubles for chaplains,
> Churches to honor.
>   Wives and widows
> Wool and flax spinneth ;
> Make cloth, I counsel you,
> And kenneth * so your daughters ;
> The needy and the naked,
> Nymeth † heed how they lieth,
> And casteth them clothes,
> For so commanded Truth."

Marriage is an honorable estate, and should be entered into with proper motives, and in a decent and regular manner. It is desirable that most men should marry, for

> " The wife was made the way
> For to help work ;
> And thus was wedlock wrought
> With a mean person,
> First by the father's will
> And the friends' counsel ;
> And sithens ‡ by assent of themselves,
> As they two might accord."

This is the essentially worldly way of making marriage arrangements yet practised in some aristocratic circles, but the more democratic and natural way is to reverse the process, and commence with the agreement between the two persons most concerned. Such unequal matches as age and wealth on one side, and youth and desire of wealth on the other, bring about, are sternly reprobated.

> " It is an uncomely couple,
> By Christ ! as me thinketh,
> To give a young wench
> To an old feeble,
> Or wedden any widow
> For wealth of her goods,
> That never shall bairn bear
> But if it be in her arms."

Such marriages lead to jealousy, bickerings, and open rupture, disgraceful to husband and wife, and annoying to others   Therefore Piers counsels

> " all Christians,
> Covet not to be wedded
> For covetise of chattels,
> Nor of kindred rich ;
> But maidens and maidens

* Teach.   † Take.   ‡ Afterwards.

> Make you together ;
> Widows and widowers
> Worketh the same ;
> For no lands, but for love,
> Look you be wedded " ; —

adding the sound bit of spiritual and worldly advice,

> " And then get ye the grace of God,
> *And goods enough to live with.*"

The touch of shrewd humor in the last line finds its counterpart in many other passages. Thus, when the dreamer sits down to rest by the wayside, his iteration of the prescribed prayers makes him drowsy : —

> " So I babbled on my beads ;
> They brought me asleep."

The Franciscan friars, his especial aversion, get a sly thrust when he says of Charity that

> " in a friar's frock
> He was founden once ;
> *But it is far ago,*
> In Saint Francis's time ;
> In that sect since
> Too seldom hath he been found."

When Covetousness has confessed his numerous misdeeds, and is asked if he ever repented and made restitution, he replies,

> " Yes, once I was harbored
> With a heap of chapmen.*
> I rose when they were at rest
> And rifled their males † " ; —

and on being told that this was no restitution, but another robbery, he replies, with assumed innocence of manner,

> " I wened ‡ rifling were restitution, quoth he,
> For I learned never to read on book ;
> And I ken no French, in faith,
> But of the farthest end of Norfolk."

Even the Pope is not exempt from a touch of satire : —

> " He prayed the Pope
> Have pity on holy Church,
> And ere he gave any grace,
> *Govern first himself.*"

The prejudice against doctors and lawyers was as strong five hundred years ago as now, judging from Piers Plowman, who says, that

> " Murderers are many leeches,
> Lord them amend !
> They do men die through their drinks
> Ere destiny it would."

* Pedlers.   † Boxes.   ‡ Thought.

Of lawyers he says they pleaded

> " for pennies
> And pounds, the law ;
> And not for the love of our Lord
> Unclose their lips once.
> Thou mightest better meet mist
> On Malvern hills
> Than get a mum of their mouth
> Till money be showed."

No class of people suffered more in the Middle Ages than the Jews. They were abhorred by the poor, despised by the wealthy, and cruelly oppressed by the powerful. But through all their sufferings and trials they were true to each other ; and the monk holds up their fraternal charity as an example to shame Christians into similar virtues. He says : —

> " A Jew would not see a Jew
> Go jangling * for default.
> For all the mebles † on this mould ‡
> And he amend it might.
>   Alas ! that a Christian creature
> Shall be unkind to another ;
> Since Jews, that we judge
> Judas's fellows,
> Either of them helpeth other
> Of that that him needeth.
> Why not will we Christians
> Of Christ's good be as kind
> As Jews, that be our lores-men § ?
> Shame to us all ! "

With one more curious passage, giving a glimpse of the belief of that age concerning the future state, we will close our extracts from " Piers Plowman." Discussing the condition of the thief upon the cross who was promised a seat in heaven, the dreamer says : —

> " Right as some man gave me meat,
> And amid the floor set me,
> And had meat more than enough,
> But not so much worship
> As those that sitten at the side-table,
> Or with the sovereigns of the hall ;
> But set as a beggar boardless,
> By myself on the ground.
> So it fareth by that felon
> That on Good Friday was saved,

* Complaining.   † Goods.
‡ Earth.   § Teachers.

> He sits neither with Saint John,
> Simon, nor Jude,
> Nor with maidens nor with martyrs,
> Confessors nor widows :
> But by himself as a sullen,*
> And served on earth.
> For he that is once a thief
> Is evermore in danger,
> And, as law him liketh,
> To live or to die.
> And for to serven a saint
> And such a thief together,
> It were neither reason nor right
> To reward them both alike."

" Piers Plowman " is supposed to have been written in 1362. It became instantly popular, and manuscript copies were rapidly distributed over England. Imitations preserving the peculiar form, and aiming at the same objects as the " Vision," though without the genius exhibited in that work, appeared in quick succession. The hatred of the oppressed people for their oppressors was intensified by the inflammatory harangues of John Ball, the deposed priest. The preaching of Wycliffe probed still deeper the festering corruption of the dominant Church. At last, in 1381, a popular rising, under Wat Tyler, attempted to right the wrongs of generations at the sword's point. The result of that attempt is well known, — its temporary success, sudden overthrow, and the terrible revenge taken by the ruling power in the enactment of laws that made the burden of the people still more intolerable.

But the seed of political and religious freedom had been sown. It had been watered with the blood of martyrs ; and, although the tender shoots had been trodden down with an iron heel as soon as they appeared, they gathered additional strength and vigor from the repression, and soon sprang up with a vitality that defied all efforts to crush them.

* One left alone.

KATHARINE MORNE.

PART I.

CHAPTER I.

ONE day, near the middle of a June about twenty years ago, my landlady met me at the door of my boarding-house, and began with me the following dialogue.

"Miss Morne, my dear, home a'-ready? Goin' to be in, a spell, now?"

"Yes, Mrs. Johnson, I believe so. Why?"

"Well, someb'dy's been in here to pay ye a call, afore twelve o'clock, in a tearin' hurry. Says I, 'Ye 've got afore yer story this time, I guess,' says I. Says he, 'I guess I'll call again,' says he. He's left ye them pinies an' snowballs in the pitcher."

"But who was it?"

"Well, no great of a stranger, it wa' n't, — Jim!"

"O, thank you."

"He kind o' seemed as if he might ha' got somethin' sort o' special on his mind to say to ye. My! how he colored up at somethin' I said!"

I walked by, and away from her, into the house, but answered that I should be happy to see Jim if he came back. Well I might. Through all the months of school - keeping that followed my mother's death, — in the little country village of Greenville, so full of home-sickness for me, — he had been my kindest friend. My old schoolmate, Emma Holly, from whose native town he came, assured me beforehand that he would be so. She wrote to me that he was the best, most upright, well-principled, kind-hearted fellow in the world. He was almost like a brother to her, (this surprised me a little, because I had never heard her speak of him before,) and so he would be to me, if I would only let him. She had told him all about me and our troubles and plans, — how I winced at that when I read it! — and he was very much

interested, and would shovel a path for me when it snowed, or go to the post-office for me, or do anything in the world for me that he could. And so he had done.

He had little chance, indeed, to devote himself to me abroad; for I seldom went out, except now and then, when I could not refuse without giving offence, to drink tea with the family of some pupil. But when I did that, he always found it out through Mrs. Johnson, whose nephew he was, and came to see me home. He usually brought some additional wrappings or thick shoes for me; and even if they were too warm, or otherwise in my way, I could be, and was, grateful for his kindness in thinking of them. He was very attentive to his aunt also, and came to read aloud to her, while she napped, almost every evening. At every meal which he took with us, he was constantly suggesting to her little comforts and luxuries for me, till I was afraid she would really be annoyed. She took his hints, however, in wonderfully good part, sometimes acted upon them, and often said to me, "How improvin' it was for young men to have somebody to kind o' think for! It made 'em so kind o' thoughtful!" Many a flower, fruit, and borrowed book he brought me. He tried to make me walk with him; and, whenever he could, he made me talk with him. But for him, I should have studied almost all the time that I was not teaching or sleeping; for when I began to teach, I first discovered how little I had learned. Thus nearly all the indulgences and recreations of the rather grave, lonely, and hard-working little life I was leading at that time were associated with him and his kind care; and so I really think it was no great wonder if his peonies and snowballs that day made the bare little parlor, with the row of staring, uncouth daguerreotypes on the mantel-piece, look very pretty to me, or that to know that he had been there, and was coming back again, made it a very happy place.

I walked across it, took off my hot black bonnet, threw up the western window, and sat down beside it in the rocking-chair. The cool breeze struggled through the tree that nestled sociably up to it, and made the little knobs of cherries nod at me, as if saying, "You would not like us now, but you will by and by." The oriole gurgled and giggled from among them, "*Wait!* Come *again!* Come again! Ha, ha!" The noise of the greedy canker-worms, mincing the poor young green leaves over my head, seemed a soothing sound; and even the sharp headache I had brought with me from the school-room, only a sort of *sauce piquante* to my delicious rest. I did not ask myself what Jim would say. I scarcely longed to hear him come. I did not know how anything to follow could surpass that perfect luxury of waiting peace.

He did come soon. I heard a stealthy step, not on the gravel-walk, but on the rustling hay that lay upon the turf beside it. He looked, and then sprang, in at the window. He was out of breath. He caught my hand, and looked into my face, and asked me to go out and walk with him. Before I had time to answer, he snatched up my bonnet, and almost pressed it down upon my head. As I tied it, he hurried out and looked back at me eagerly from the road. I followed, though more slowly than he wished. The sun was bright and hot, and almost made me faint; but everything was very beautiful.

He wrenched out the topmost bar of a fence, *jumped* me over it into a meadow, led me by a forced march into the middle of the field, seated me on a haycock, and once more stood before me, looking me in the face with his own all aglow.

Then he told me that he had been longing for weeks, as I must have seen,

to open his mind to me; but, till that day, he had not been at liberty. He had regarded me, from almost the very beginning of our acquaintance, as his best and trustiest friend, — in short, as just what dear Emma had told him he should find me. My friendship had been a blessing to him in every way; and now my sympathy, or participation, was all he wanted to render his happiness complete. He had just been admitted as a partner in *the store* of the village, in which he had hitherto been only a salesman; and now, therefore, he was at last free to offer himself, before all the world, to the girl he loved best; and that was — I must guess who. He called me "dearest Katy," and asked me if he might not "to-day, at last."

I bowed, but did not utter my guess. He seemed to think I had done so, notwithstanding; for he hurried on, delighted. "Of course it is, 'Katy darling,' as we always call you! I never knew your penetration out of the way. It *is* Emma Holly! It could n't be anybody but Emma Holly!"

Then he told me that she had begged hard for leave to tell me outright, what she thought she had hinted plainly enough, about their hopes; but her father was afraid that to have them get abroad would hurt her prospects in other quarters, and made silence towards all others a condition of her correspondence with Jim. Mr. Holly was "aristocratic," and in hopes Emma would change her mind, Jim supposed; but all danger was over now. He could maintain her like the lady she was; and their long year's probation was ended. Then he told me in what agonies he had passed several evenings a fortnight before, (when I must have wondered why he did not come and read.) from hearing of her illness. The doctors were right for once, to be sure. as it proved, in thinking it only the measles; but it might just as well have been spotted fever, or small-pox, or anything fatal, for all they knew.

And then I rather think there must have been a pause, which I did not fill properly, because my head was aching with a peculiar sensation which I had never known before, though I have sometimes since. — It is like the very hand of Death, laid with a strong grasp on the joint and meeting-point of soul and body, and makes one feel, for the time being, as Dr. Livingstone says he did when the lion shook him, — a merciful indifference as to anything to come after. — And Jim was asking me, in a disappointed tone, what the matter was, and if I did not feel interested.

"Yes," I said, "Mr. Johnson — "

" Mr. Johnson ! " interrupted he. " How cold ! I thought it would be *Jim* at least, to-day, if you can't say *dear* Jim."

" Yes, 'dear Jim,'" I repeated ; and my voice sounded so strangely quiet in my own ears, that I did not wonder that he called me cold. " Indeed, I am interested. I don't know when I have heard anything that has interested me so much. I pray God to bless you and Emma. But the reason I came from school so early to-day was, that I had a headache ; and now I think perhaps the sun is not good for it, and I had better go in."

I stood up ; but I suspect I must have had something like a sunstroke, sitting there in the meadow so long with no shade, in the full blaze of June. I was almost too dizzy to stand, and could hardly have reached the house, if I had not accepted Jim's arm. He offered, in the joy of his heart, to change head-dresses with me, — which luckily made me laugh, — declaring that mine must be a perfect portable stove for the brains. Thus we reached the door cheerfully, and there shook hands cordially ; while I bade him take my kindest love and congratulations to Emma, — to whom he was going on a three days' visit, as fast as the cars could carry him, — and charged him to tell her I should write as soon as I recovered the use of my head.

He looked concerned on being reminded of it, and shouted for Mrs. Johnson to bring me some lavender-water to bathe it with. I had told him, on a former occasion, that the smell of lavender always made it worse ; but it was natural that, when he was so happy, he should forget. Whistling louder than the orioles, whose songs rang wildly through and through my brain, he hastened down the road, and was gone.

CHAPTER II.

Jim was gone ; but I was left. I could have spared him better if I could only have got rid of myself.

However, for that afternoon the blessed pain took such good care of me that I lay upon my bed still and stunned, and could only somewhat dimly perceive, not how unhappy I was, but how unhappy I was going to be. It quieted Mrs. Johnson, too. She had seen me suffering from headache before, and knew that I could never talk much while it lasted. Her curiosity was at once satisfied and gratified by hearing what Jim had left me at liberty to tell her, — the news of his partnership in the firm. The engagement was not to be announced in form till the next week ; though I, as the common friend of both parties, had been made an exceptional confidante ; and Jim, afraid of betraying himself, had not trusted himself to take leave of his aunt, but left his love for her, and his apologies for outstaying his time so far in the meadow as to leave himself none for the farm-house.

Thus I had a reprieve. When towards midnight my head grew easier, I was worn out and slept ; so that it was not till the birds began to rehearse for their concert at sunrise the next morning, that I came to myself and looked things in the face in the clear light of the awful dawn.

If you can imagine a very heavy weight let somewhat gradually, but irresistibly, down upon young and tender shoulders, then gently lifted again, little by little, by a sympathizing and unlooked-for helper, and lastly tossed by him unexpectedly into the air, only to fall back with redoubled weight, and crush the frame that was but bowed before, you can form some idea of what had just happened to me. My mother's death, our embarrassments, my loneliness, the hard and to me uncongenial work I had to do, all came upon me together more heavily than at any time since the first fortnight that I spent at Greenville.

But that was not all. Disappointment is hardly the right word to use; for I can truly say that I never made any calculations for the future upon Jim's attentions to me. They were offered so honestly and respectfully that I instinctively felt I could accept them with perfect propriety, and perhaps could scarcely with propriety refuse. I had never once asked myself what they meant, nor whither they tended. But yet I was used to them now, and had learned to prize them far more than I knew; and they must be given up. My heart-strings had unconsciously grown to him, and ought to be torn away. And I think that, beyond grief, beyond the prospect of lonely toil and poverty henceforth, beyond all the rest, was the horror of an idea which came upon me, that I had lost the control of my own mind, — that my peace had passed out of my keeping into the power of another, who, though friendly to me, neither would nor could preserve it for me, — that I was doomed to be henceforward the prey of feelings which I must try to conceal, and perhaps could not for any length of time, which lowered me in my own eyes, and would do so in those of others if they were seen by them, which were wrong, and which I could not help.

These thoughts struck and stung me like so many hornets. Crying, "Mother! mother!" I sprang from my bed, and fell on my knees beside it. I did not suppose it would do much good for me to pray; but I said over and over, if only to stop myself from thinking, "O God, help me! God have mercy on me!" as fast as I could, till the town clock struck five, and I knew that I must begin to dress, and compose myself, if I would appear as usual at six o'clock at the breakfast-table.

My French grammar, was, as usual, set up beside my looking-glass. As usual, I examined myself aloud in one of the exercises, while I went through my toilet. If I did make some mistakes it was no matter. I made so much haste, that I had time before breakfast to correct some of the compositions which I had brought with me from school. The rest, as I often did when hurried, I turned over while I tried to eat my bread and milk. This did not encourage conversation. During the meal, I was only asked how my head was, and answered only that it was better. I had taken care not to shed a tear, so that my eyes were not swollen; and as I had eaten nothing since the morning of the day before, nobody could be surprised to see me pale.

Mrs. Johnson left her seat, too, almost as soon as I took mine. She was in a great bustle, getting her covered wagon under way, and stocked with eggs, butter, cheese, and green vegetables for her weekly trip to the nearest market-town. She was, however, sufficiently mindful of her nephew's lessons to regret that she must leave me poorly when he would not be there to cheer me up, and to tell me to choose what I liked best for my dinner while she was gone.

I chose a boiled chicken and rice. It was what my mother used to like best to have me eat when I was not well. I often rebelled against it when a child; but now I sought by means of it to soothe myself with the fancy that I was still under her direction.

Mrs. Johnson also offered to do for me what I forgot to ask of her, — to look in at the post-office and see if there was not a letter there for me from my only sister. Fanny, for once, had sent me none the week before. Mrs. Johnson went to town, and I to school.

I worked and worried through the lessons, — how, I never knew; but I dare say the children were forbearing;

children are apt to be when one is not well. I came home and looked at the chicken and rice. But that would not do. They *would* have made me cry. So I hurried out again, away from them, and away from the meadow, and walked in the woods all that Saturday afternoon, thinking to and fro, — not so violently as in the morning, for I was weaker, but very confusedly and in endless perplexity. How could I stay in Greenville? I should have to be with Jim! But how could I go? What reason had I to give? and what would people think was my reason? But would it not be wrong to stay and see Jim? But it would be wrong to break my engagement to the school committee!

At length again the clock struck five, which was supper-time, and I saw myself no nearer the end of my difficulties; and I had to say once again, "God help me! God have mercy on me!" and so went home.

Mrs. Johnson was awaiting me, with this letter for me in her pocket. It is not in Fanny's handwriting, however, but in that of a friend of ours with whom she was staying, Mrs. Physick, the wife of the most eminent of the younger physicians in Beverly, our native town. I opened it hastily and read : —

"Friday.
"MY DEAR KATIE : —
"You must not be uneasy at my writing instead of Fannie, as the Doctor thinks it too great an effort for her. She has had an attack of influenza, not very severe, but you know she is never very strong, and I am afraid she is too much afraid of calling on me for any little thing she wants done. So we think, the Doctor and I, it would do her good to have a little visit from you. She wanted us to wait for the summer vacation, so as not to alarm you; but you know that is three whole weeks off, and nobody knows how much better she may be within that time. The Doctor says, suggest to Katie that the committee might, under the circumstances, agree to her ending the spring

term a little earlier than usual, and beginning a little earlier in the fall.'
"Yours as ever,
"JULIA.
"P. S. You must not be anxious about dear Fannie. She has brightened up very much already at the mere thought of seeing you. Her cough is not half so troublesome as it was a week ago, and the Doctor says her very *worst* symptom is *weakness.* She says she *must* write *one word* herself."

O what a tremulous word!

"DEAR KATY : —
"*Do* come if you can, and *don't* be anxious. Indeed I am growing stronger every day, and eating *so* much meat, and drinking *so* much whiskey. It does me a great deal of good, and would a great deal more if I could only tell how we were ever to [pay for it, I knew she would have said ; but Dr. Physick had evidently interposed ; for the signature,]
"Your mutinous and obstreperous
"SISTER FANNY,"

was prefaced with a scratched-out involuntary "℞," and looked like a prescription.

I might be as sad as I would now; and who could wonder? I sat down where I was standing on the door-step, and held the letter helplessly up to Mrs. Johnson. It did seem to me now as if Fate was going to empty its whole quiver of arrows at once upon me, and meant to kill me, body and soul. But I have since thought sometimes, when I have heard people say, Misfortunes never came single, and How mysterious it was! that God only dealt with us, in that respect somewhat as some surgeons think it best to do with wounded men, — perform whatever operations are necessary, immediately after the first injury, so as to make one and the same "shock" take the place of more. In this way of Providence, I am sure I have repeatedly seen accumulated sorrows, which, if distributed through longer intervals, might have darkened a lifetime, lived through, and in a considerable degree recovered from, even in a very few years.

Mrs. Johnson's spectacles, meantime, were with eager curiosity peering over the letter. " Dear heart ! " cried she. " Do tell ! My ! What a providence ! There's Sister Nancy Newcome's Elviry jest got home this arternoon from her situation to the South, scairt off with the insurrections as unexpected as any*thing*. She's as smart a teacher as ever was ; an' the committee 'd ha' gin her the school in a minute, an' thank you, too ; but she wuz alwuz a kind o' lookin' up'ards ; an' I s'pose she cal'lated it might for'ard her prospects to go down an' show herself among the plantations. There's better opportoonities, they say, sometimes for young ladies to git settled in life down there, owin' to the scurcity on 'em. She'll be glad enough to fill your place, I guess, till somethin' else turns up, for a fortni't or a month, or a term. It'll give her a chance to see her folks, an' fix up her cloes, an' look round her a spell. An' you can step into the cars o' Monday mornin' an' go right off an' close that poor young creatur's eyes, an' take your time for 't. Seems as if I hearn tell your ma went off in a kind of a gallopin' decline, did n't she ? "

" No, she did not ! " cried I, springing up with a renewal of energy that must have surprised Mrs. Johnson. " Nothing of the kind ! I will take my letter again, if you please. My sister has a cold. — only a cold. But where can I see Miss Newcome ? "

" To home ; but I declare, you can't feel hardly fit to start off ag'in. Jest you step in an' sup your tea afore it 's any colder. I 've had mine ; an' I 'll step right back over there, an' see about it for ye."

Mrs. Johnson, if coarse, was kind ; and that time it would be hard to say whether her kindness or her coarseness did me the most good ; for the latter roused me, between indignation and horror, to a strong reaction.

Mrs. Johnson, I said to myself, knew no more of the matter than I. Nobody

said a word, in the letter, of Fanny's being very ill ; and there had been, as I now considered, to the best of my recollection and information, no consumption in our family. My father died when I was five years old, as I had always heard of chronic bronchitis and nervous dyspepsia, or, in other words, of over-work and under-pay. An early marriage to a clergyman, who had no means of support but a salary of five hundred dollars dependent on his own health and the tastes of a parish, early widowhood, two helpless little girls to rear, years of hard work, anxieties, and embarrassments, a typhoid fever, with no physician during the precious first few days, during which, if she had sent for him, Dr. Physick always believed he might have saved her, a sudden sinking and no rallying, — it took all that to kill poor, dear, sweet mamma ! She had a magnificent constitution, and bequeathed much of it to me.

Else I do not think I could have borne, and recovered from, those three days even as well as I did. The cars did not run on Sunday. That was so dreadful ! But there was no other hindrance in my way. Everybody was very kind. The school committee could not meet in form "on the Sabbath"; but the chairman, who was Miss Elvira Newcome's brother-in-law, "sounded the other members arter meetin', jest as he fell in with 'em, casooally as it were," and ascertained that they would offer no objection to my exchange. He advanced my pay himself, and brought it to me soon after sunrise Monday morning ; so that I was more than sufficiently provided with funds for my journey.

Mrs. Johnson forced upon me a suspicious-looking corked bottle of innocent tea, — one of the most sensible travelling companions, as I found before the day was over, that a wayfarer can possibly have, — and a large paper of doughnuts. Feverish as I was, I would right willingly have given her back, not only the doughnuts, but the tea, to bribe her not to persecute me as she did for a message for Jim. But I could leave my thanks for all his kindness, and my regrets — sincere, though repented of — that I could not see him again, before I went, to say good-by; and, already in part effaced by the impression of the last blow that had fallen upon me, that scene in the dreadful meadow seemed months and miles away. The engine shrieked. The cars started. My hopes and spirits rose; and I was glad, because I was going home, — that is, where, when I had a home, it used to be.

CHAPTER III.

THE rapid motion gratified my restlessness, and, together with the noise, soothed me homœopathically. I slept a great deal. The midsummer day was far shorter than I feared it would be; and I found myself rather refreshed than fatigued when the conductor roused me finally by shouting names more and more familiar, as we stopped at way-stations. I sat upright, and strained my *cinderful* eyes, long surfeited with undiluted green, for the first far blue and silver glimpses of my precious sea. Then well-known rocks and cedars came hurrying forward, as if to meet me half-way.

As the cars stopped for the last time with me, I caught sight of a horse and chaise approaching at a rapid rate down the main street of the town. The driver sprang out and threw the reins to a boy. He turned his face — a grave face — up, and looked searchingly along the row of car-windows. It was Dr. Physick. I darted out at the nearest door. He saw me, smiled, and was at it in an·instant, catching both my hands in his to shake them and help me down by them at the same time.

"Little Katy!" — he always would call me so, though, as I sometimes took the liberty to tell him, I was very sure I had long left off being *that*, even if I was not yet quite the size of some giants I had seen, — "Lit-tle Katy! How jolly! 'Fanny?' O, Fanny's pretty comfortable, — looking out for you and putting her head out of the window, I dare say, the minute my back's turned. I look to you now to keep her in order. Baggage? Only bag? Give it to me. Foot, — now hand, — there you are!"

And there I was, — where I was most glad to be once more, — in his gig, and driving, in the cool, moist twilight, down the dear old street, shaded with dear old elms, with the golden and amber sunset still glowing between their dark boughs; where every quiet, snug, old wooden house, with its gables and old-fashioned green or white front-door with a brass or bronze knocker, and almost every shop and sign even, seemed an old friend.

The lingering glow still lay full on the front of our old home, which now had "Philemon Physick, M. D." on the corner. As we stopped before it, I thought I spied a sweet little watching face, for one moment, behind a pane of one of the second-story windows. But if I did, it was gone before I was sure.

"Here she is!" called out the Doctor. "Julia! — Wait a minute, Kate, my dear, — no hurry. Julia!" Up he ran, while "Julia" ran down, said something, in passing, to him on the stairs, kissed me at the foot three times over, — affectionately, but as if to gain time, I thought, — led me into the parlor to take off my bonnet, and told me Fanny was not quite ready to see me just then, but would be, most likely, in two or three minutes. The Doctor had gone up to see about it, and would let me know.

"O, did n't I see her at the window?"

"Yes, dear, you did; and that was just the trouble. She saw you were there; and she was so pleased, it made her a little faint. The Doctor will give her something to take; and as soon as she is a little used to your being here, of course you can be with her all the time."

The Doctor came down, speaking cheerily. "She is all right now. Run up, as fast as you like, and kiss her, Kate, my child ; but tell her I forbid your talking till to-morrow. In five minutes, by my watch, I shall call you down to tea ; and when you are called, you come. That will give her time to think about it and compose herself. Julia's *help* shall stay with her in the mean while. Afterwards, you shall share your own old chamber with her. Julia has it, as usual, all ready for you."

Fanny had sunk back on her white pillows, upon the little couch before the window from which she watched for me. How inspired and beautiful she looked ! — she who was never thought of as beautiful before, — the very transfigured likeness of herself, as I hope one day to behold her in glory, — and so like our mother, too ! She lay still, as she had been ordered, lest she should faint again ; but by the cheerful lamp that stood on the stand beside her, I saw her smile as she had never used to smile. The eyes, that I left swollen and downcast, were raised large and bright. But as she slowly opened her arms and clasped me to her, I felt tears on my cheek ; and her voice was broken as she said, " Katy, Katy ! O, thank God ! I was afraid I never should see you again. Now I have everything that I want in the world ! "

It was hard to leave her when I was called so soon ; but she knew that it was right, and made me go ; and when I was allowed to return to her, she lay in obedient but most happy silence for all the rest of the evening, with those new splendid eyes fixed on my face, her dim complexion glowing, and her hands clasping mine. After I had put her to bed, and laid myself down in my own beside her, I felt her reach out of hers and touch me with a little pat two or three times, as a child will a new doll, to make sure that it has not been merely dreaming of it. At first, I asked her if she wanted anything ; but she said, " Only to feel that you are really there " ; and when, after a very sound and long rest, I awoke, there

was her solemn, peaceful gaze still watching me, like that of an unsleeping guardian angel. She had slept too, however, remarkably long and well, whether for joy, as she thought, or from the opium which I had been startled to see given her the night before. She said she had had many scruples about taking it ; but the Doctor insisted ; and she did not think it her duty on the whole to make him any trouble by opposing his prescriptions, when we owed him so much. Poor Fanny ! How hard it was for her to owe any one " anything, but to love one another."

The Doctor's bulletin that morning was, " Remarkably comfortable." But in the forenoon, while Fanny after breakfast took a nap, I snatched an opportunity to cross-question Mrs. Physick, from whom I knew I could sooner or later obtain all she knew, — the *sooner* it would be, if she had anything good to tell ; as, in my inexperience, I was almost sure she must have.

Fanny's " influenza," I now discovered, dated back to May. She kept her room a few days, did not seem so ill as many fellow-patients who were now quite well again, and soon resumed her usual habits, but was never quite rid of her cough. Two or three weeks after, there was a Sunday-school festival in the parish to which we belonged. She was called upon to sing and assist in various ways, over-tasked her strength, was caught in a shower, looked very sick, and being, on the strength of Mrs. Physick's representations, formally escorted into the office, was found to have a quick pulse and sharp pain in one side. This led to a careful examination of the chest, and the discovery not only of " acute pleurisy," but of " some mischief probably of longer standing in the lungs," yet " no more," the Doctor said, " than many people carried about with them all their lives without knowing it, nor than others, if circumstances brought it to light, recovered from by means of good care and good spirits, and lived to a good old age."

"How long ago was that?"

"The pleurisy? About the beginning of June. The Doctor said last week he 'could scarcely discover a vestige of it.' And now, Katy," continued kind, cheery Mrs. Physick, "you see, your coming back has put her in the best of spirits; and you and the Doctor and I are all going to take the best of care of her; and so we may all hope the best.'"

"The best of care"? Ah, there was little doubt of that! But even "*good* spirits"! who could hope to see Fanny enjoying them for any length of time, till she had done with time? Good, uncomplaining, patient, I had always seen her, — happy, how seldom! — when, indeed, till now? There was not enough of earth about her for her to thrive and bloom.

My mother, I believe, used to attribute in part to Fanny's early training her early joylessness. In her early days, — so at least I have understood, — it was thought right even by some good people of our "persuasion," to lose no opportunity of treating the little natural waywardnesses of children with a severity which would now be called ferocity. Mamma could never have practised this herself; but perhaps she suffered it to be practised to a greater extent than she would have consented to endure, had she foreseen the consequences. My poor father must have been inexperienced, too; and I suppose his nerves, between sickness and poverty, might at times be in such a state that he scarcely knew what he did.

I was four years younger than Fanny, and know nothing about it, except a very little at second-hand. But at any rate I have often heard my mother say, with a glance at her, and a gravity as if some sad association enforced the lesson on her mind, that it was one of the first duties of those who undertook the charge of children to watch over their cheerfulness, and a most important rule, never, if it was possible to put it off, so much as to reprimand them when one's own balance

was at all disturbed. This was a rule that she never to my knowledge broke; though she was naturally rather a high-strung person, as I think the pleasantest and most generous people one meets with generally are.

From whatever cause or causes, — to return to Fanny, — she grew up, not fierce, sullen, nor yet hypocritical, but timid and distrustful, miserably sensitive and anxious, and morbidly conscientious.

There was another pleasure in store for her, however; for, the afternoon following that of my return, Mrs. Julia, looking out as usual for her husband, — with messages from four different alarmingly or alarmed sick persons, requesting him to proceed without delay in four different directions, — saw him at length driving down the road with such unprofessional slowness that she feared some accident to himself or his harness. When he came before the door, the cause appeared. It was a handsome Bath chair, with a basket of strawberries on the floor and a large nosegay on the seat, fastened to the back of his gig, and safely towed by it.

"What is that for?" cried I from Fanny's window.

"Fanny's coach," said he, looking up. "Miss Dudley has sent it to be taken care of for her. She does not want it herself for the present; and you can draw your dolly out in it every fine day."

"O," cried Fanny, sitting upright on the couch by the window, — where she spent the greater part of the day, — to see for herself, with the tears in her eyes. "O, how lovely! That is the very kindest thing she has done yet; — and you don't know how she keeps sending me everything, Katy!"

"Miss Dudley? Who is she?"

"O, don't you know? The great naturalist's sister. He lives in that beautiful place, on the shore, in the large stone cottage. The ground was broken for it before you went to Greenville. She is very sick, I am afraid, — very kind, I am sure. I never saw her. She has heard about me. I am afraid the Doctor told her. I hope she does not think I meant he should."

"Of course, dear, she does not."

"Do you really think so?"

"Certainly."

"Why?"

"Why, — I know I should not like being begged of in that underhand way myself; and if I did not like it, I might send something once, but after that I should never keep on sending."

"I am very glad you think so; for I like her kindness, though I scarcely like to have her show it in this way, because I am afraid I can never do anything for her. But I hope she does like to send; for Dr. Physick says she always asks after me, almost before he can after her, and looks very much pleased if she hears that I have been so. I suppose the Doctor will think it is too late to take me down to-night. Katy, don't you want to go and see the wagon, and tell me about it, and pour the strawberries into a great dish on the tea-table, and all of you have some, and bring up the flowers when you come back after tea?"

When I came back with the flowers, Fanny smiled rather pensively, and did not ask me about the chair.

"Fanny," said I, "the Doctor says you may go out to-morrow forenoon, and stay as long as you like, if it is fair; and the sun is going down as red as a Baldwin apple. The chair is contrived so, with springs and the cushions, that you can lie down in it, as flat as you do on your sofa, when you are tired of sitting up."

"O Katy," cried she, with a little quiver in her voice, for she was too weak to bear anything, "I have been seeing how inconsiderate I was! To think of letting you exert and strain yourself in that way!"

In came the Doctor, looking saucy. "Fanny won't go, I suppose? I thought so. I said so to De Quincey [his horse], as I drove him down the street at a creep, sawing his mouth to keep him from running away, till he foamed at it epileptically, while all the sick people were sending north, south, east, and west after all the other doctors. I hope you won't mention it, said I to the horse; but Fanny is always getting up some kind of a row. But there is Katy now, — Katy is a meek person, and always does as she is bid. She has been cooped up too much, and bleached her own roses with teaching the Greenville misses to sickly o'er with the pale cast of thought. Katy needs gentle exercise. So does Deacon Lardner." Deacon Lardner was the fat inhabitant of the town, and ill of the dropsy. "I will send Katy out a-walking, with Deacon Lardner in Miss Dudley's chair."

I laughed. Fanny smiled. The Doctor saw his advantage, and followed it up. "Julia, my dear, get my apothecary's scales out of the office. Put an ounce weight into one, and Fanny into the other. Then put the ounce weight into the chair. If Katy can draw that, she can draw Fanny."

This time, it was poor Fanny who had the laugh to herself.

The next day, the Doctor carried her down stairs, as soon as she could bear it after her breakfast, and left her on a sofa, in the little parlor, to rest. About ten o'clock, he came back from his early rounds. I was dressed and waiting for him, with Fanny's bonnet and shawl ready. I put them on her, while he drew out the chair from its safe stable in the hall. Once again he took her up; and thus by easy stages we got her into "her coach." I pulled, and he pushed it, "to give me a start." How easy and light and strong it was! How delighted were both she and I!

Fanny was too easily alarmed to enjoy driving much, even when she was well; and she had not walked out for weeks. During that time, the slow, late spring had turned into midsummer; and the mere change from a sick-room to the fresh, outer world is always so very great! For me, it was the first going abroad since my return to Beverly. We went in the sun till my charge's little snowdrop hands were warm, and then drew up under the shade of an elm, on a little airy knoll that commanded a distant view of the sea, and was fanned by a soft air, which helped poor Fanny's breathing. She now insisted on my resting myself; and I turned the springs back and arranged the cushions so that she could lie down, took a new handkerchief of my guardian's from my pocket, and hemmed it, as I sat at her side on a stone, while she mused and dozed. When she awoke, I gave her her luncheon from a convenient little box in the chair, and drew her home by dinner-time.

In this way we spent much of the month of July — shall I say it? — agreeably. Nobody will believe it, who has not felt or seen the marvellous relief afforded by an entire change of scene and occupation to a person tried as I had been. If I had but "one idea," that idea was now Fanny. Instinctively in part, and partly of set purpose, I postponed to her every other consideration and thought. It was delightful to me to be able, in my turn, to take her to one after another of the dear old haunts, in wood or on beach, where she had often led me, when a child, to play. I always did love to have something to take care of; and the care of Fanny wore upon me little. She was the most considerate of invalids.

Besides, she was better, or at any rate I thought so, after she began to go out in Miss Dudley's chair. Her appetite improved; her nerves grew more firm; and her cough was sometimes so quiet at night that her laudanum would stand on her little table in the morning, just as it was dropped for her the evening before.

Not only were my spirits amended by the fresh air in which, by Dr. Physick's strict orders, I lived with her through the twenty-four hours, but my health too. He had declared her illness to be "probably owing in great part to the foul atmosphere in which," he found, "she slept"; and now she added that, since she had known the comfort of fresh air at night, she should be very sorry ever to give it up. In windy weather she

had a large folding-screen, and in raw, more blankets and a little fire.

Besides the chair, another thing came in our way which gave pleasure to both of us, though it was not very pleasantly ushered in, as its pioneer was a long visit from Fanny's old "Sabbath school-ma'am," Miss Mehitable Truman, who *would* come up stairs. Towards the close of this visit her errand came out. It was to inquire whether "Fanny would n't esteem it a privilege to knit one or two of her sets of toilet napkins for Miss Mehitable's table at the Orphans' Fair, jest by little and little, as she could gether up her failin' strength." Fanny could not promise the napkins, since, luckily for her, she was past speech from exhaustion, as I was with indignation; and Miss Truman, hearing the Doctor's boots creak below, showed the better part of valor, and departed.

The next day, it rained. We were kept in-doors; and Fanny could not be easy till I had looked up her cotton and knitting-needles. She could not be easy afterwards, either; for they made her side ache; and when Dr. Physick paid his morning visit, he took them away.

I knew she would be sorry to have nothing to give to that fair. It was one of the few rules of life which my mother had recommended us to follow, never from false shame either to give or to withhold. "If you are asked to give," she would say, "to any object, and are not satisfied that it is a good one, but give to it for fear that somebody will think you stingy, that is not being faithful stewards. But when you do meet with a worthy object, always give, if you honestly can. Even if you have no more than a cent to give, then give a cent; and do not care if the Pharisees see you. That is more than the poor widow in the Gospels gave "; — how fond she always was of that story! — "and you remember who, besides the Pharisees, saw her, and what he said? His objects would not have to go begging so long as they do now, if every one would follow her example."

From pride often, and sometimes from indolence, I am afraid I had broken that rule ; but Fanny, I rather think, never had ; and now I would try to help her to keep it.

My mother's paint-box was on a shelf in our closet, with three sheets of her drawing-paper still in it. Painting flowers was one of her chief opiates to lull the cares of her careful life. I think a person can scarcely have too many such, provided they are kept in their proper place. I have often seen her, when sadly tired or tried, sit down, with a moisture that was more like rain than dew in her eyes, and paint it all away, till she seemed to be looking sunshine over her lifelike blossoms. Then she would pin them up against the wall, for a week or two, for us to enjoy them with her ; and, afterwards, she would give them away to any one who had done her any favor. Her spirit was in that like Fanny's, — she shrank so painfully from the weight of any obligation ! She wished to teach me to paint, when I was a child. I wished to learn ; and many of her directions were still fresh in my memory. But the inexperienced eye and uncertain hand of thirteen disheartened me. I thought I had no *talent*. My mother was not accustomed to force any task upon me in my play-hours. The undertaking was given up.

But I suppose many persons, like me not precocious in the nursery or the school-room, but naturally fond, as I was passionately, of beautiful forms and colors, would be surprised, if they would try their baffled skill again in aftertimes, to find how much the years had been unwittingly preparing for them, in the way of facility and accuracy of outline and tint, while they supposed themselves to be exclusively occupied with other matters. What the physiologists call " unconscious cerebration " has been at work. Scatter the seeds of any accomplishment in the mind of a little man or woman, and, even if you leave them quite untended, you may in some after summer or autumn find the fruit growing wild.

Accordingly, when, within the last twelvemonth, I had been called upon to teach the elements of drawing in my school, it astonished me to discover the ease with which I could either sketch or copy. And now it occurred to me that perhaps, if I would take enough time and pains, I could paint something worthy of a place on Miss Mehitable's table.

Fanny's gladness at the plan, and interest in watching the work, in her own enforced inaction, were at once reward and stimulus. I succeeded, better than we either of us expected, in copying the frontispiece of a "picturebook," as Dr. Physick called it, which he had brought up from his office to amuse her. It was a scientific volume, sent him by the author, — an old fellowstudent, — from the other side of the world. Lovely ferns, flowers, shells, birds, butterflies, and insects, that surrounded him there, were treated further on separately, in rigid sequence ; but as if to make himself amends by a little play for so much work, he had not been able to resist the temptation of grouping them all together on one glowing and fascinating page. I framed my copy as tastefully as I could, in a simple but harmonious *passe-partout*, and sent it to Miss Mehitable, with Fanny's love. Fanny's gratitude was touching ; and as for me, I felt quite as if I had found a free ticket to an indefinitely long private picture-gallery.

Fanny's satisfaction was still more complete after the fair, when Miss Mehitable reported that the painting had brought in what we both thought quite a handsome sum. " It was a dreadful shame," she added, " you had n't sent two of 'em ; for at noon, while I was home, jest takin' a bite, my niece, Letisby, from Noo York, had another grand nibble for that one after 't was purchased. Letishy said a kind o' poor, pale-lookin', queer-lookin' lady, who she never saw before, in an elegint camel's-hair," — (" Poor-lookin', in a camel's-hair shawl ! " was m, inward ejaculation ; "don't I wish, ma'am, I could catch you and 'Letishy' in my composition class, once ! ") — " she come up to the table an' saw that, an' seemed to feel quite taken aback to find she 'd lost her chance at it. Letishy showed her some elegint shell-vases with artificial roses ; but that would n't do. I told Letishy," continued Miss Mehitable, " that she 'd ought to ha' been smart an' taken down the lady's name ; an' then I could ha' got Kathryne to paint her another. But you mu't do it now, Kathryne, an' put it up in the bookseller's winder ; an' then, if she 's anybody that belongs hereabouts, she 'll be likely to snap at it, an' the money can go right into the orphans' fund all the same."

" Much obliged," thought I, " for the hint as to the bookseller's shop-window ; but I rather think that, if the money comes, the orphan's fund that it ought to 'go right into' this time is Fanny's."

For my orphan's fund from my months of school-keeping, not ample when I first came back, was smaller now. Fanny's illness was necessarily, in some respects, an expensive one. I believed, indeed, and do believe, that it was a gratification to Dr. Physick to lavish upon her, to the utmost of his ability, everything that could do her good, as freely as if she had been his own child or sister. But it could not be agreeable to her, while we had a brother, to be a burden to a man un connected with us by blood, young in his profession, though rising, and still probably earning not very much more than his wife's and his own daily bread from day to day, and owing us nothing but a debt of gratitude for another's kindnesses, which another man in his place would probably have said that " he paid as he went."

In plain English, the tie between us arose simply from the fact that he boarded with my mother, when he was a poor and unformed medical student. He always said that she was the best friend he had in his solitary youth, and that no one could tell how different all his after-life might have been but for her. She was naturally generous ; yet

she was a just woman ; and I know that, while we were unprovided for, she could not have given, as the world appraises giving, much to him. Still "she did what she could." He paid her his board ; but she gave him a home. After she found that his lodgings were unwarmed, she invited him to share her fireside of a winter evening ; and, though she would not deprive us of our chat with one another and with her, she taught us to speak in low tones, and never to him, when we saw him at his studies. When they were over, and he was tired and in want of some amusement, she afforded him one at once cheap, innocent, and inexhaustible, and sang to him as she still toiled on at her unresting needle, night after night, ballad after ballad, in her wild, sweet, rich voice. He was very fond of music, though, as he said, he " could only whistle for it." It was the custom then among our neighbors to keep Saturday evening strictly as a part of " the Sabbath." It was her half-holiday, however, for works of charity and mercy ; and she would often bid him bring her any failing articles of his scanty wardrobe then, and say that she would mend them for him if he would read to her. Her taste was naturally fine, and trained by regular and well-chosen Sunday reading ; and she had the tact to select for these occasions books that won the mind of the intellectual though uncultivated youth by their eloquence, until they won his heart by their holiness. Moreover, she had been gently bred, and could give good advice, in manners as well as morals, when it was asked for, and withhold it when it was not.

The upshot of it all was, that he loved her like a mother ; and now the sentiment was deepened by a shade of filial remorse, which I could never quite dispel, though, as often as he gave me any chance, I tried. The last year of my mother's life was the first of his married life. His father-in-law hired, at the end of the town opposite to ours, a furnished house for him and his wife. My mother called upon her by the Doctor's particular invitation. The visit was sweetly received, and promptly returned by the bride; but she was pretty and popular, and had many other visits to pay, especially when she could catch her husband at leisure to help her. He was seldom at leisure at all, but, as he self-reproachfully said, " too busy to think except of his patients and his wife "; and poor mamma, with all her real dignity, had caught something of the shy, retiring ways of a reduced gentlewoman, and was, besides, too literally straining every nerve to pay off the mortgage on her half-earned house, so that, if anything happened, she might " not leave her girls without a home." Therefore he saw her seldom.

After he heard she was ill, he was with her daily, and often three or four times a day; and his wife came too, and made the nicest broths and gruels with her own hands, and begged Fanny not to cry, and cried herself. He promised my mother that we should never want, if he could help it, and that he would be a brother to us both, and my guardian. She told him that, if she died, this promise would be the greatest earthly comfort to her in her death; and he answered, " So it will to me!"

Then after she was gone, when the lease of his house was up, as no other tenant offered for ours, he hired it, furniture and all, and offered Fanny and me both a home in it for an indefinite time; but our affairs were all unsettled. We knew the rent, as rents were then, would not pay our expenses and leave us anything to put by for the future, which my mother had taught us always to think of. Therefore I thought I had better take care of myself, as I was much the strongest, and perfectly able to do so. "And a very pretty business you made of it. did n't you, miss?" reflected and queried I, parenthetically, as I afterwards reviewed these circumstances in my own mind.

The best we had to hope from my older and our only brother George was, that he should join us in paying the interest on the mortgage till real estate should rise, — as everybody said it soon must, — and then the rise in rents should enable us to let the house on better terms, and thus, by degrees, clear it of all encumbrances, and have it quite for our own, to let, sell, or live in. The worst we had to fear was, that he would insist on forcing it at once into the market, at what would be a great loss to us, and leave us almost destitute. He was going to be married, and getting into business, and wanted beyond anything else a little ready money.

He scarcely knew us even by sight. He had been a sprightly, pretty boy; and my mother's aunt's husband, having no children of his own, offered to adopt him. Poor mamma's heart was almost broken; but I suppose George's noise must have been very trying to my father's nerves; and then he had no way to provide for him. After she objected, I have always understood that my father appeared to take a morbid aversion to the child, and could scarcely bear him in his sight. So George seemed likely to be still more unhappy, and ruined beside, if she kept him at home. He was a little fellow then, not more than five years old; but he cried for her so long that my great-uncle-in-law was very careful how he let him have anything to do with her again, till he had forgotten her; and little things taken so early must be expected to fall, sooner or later, more or less under the influence of those who have them in charge.

Poor mamma died without making a regular will. It was not the custom at that time for women to be taught so much about business even as they are now. She thought, if she did make a will before she could pay off the debt on the house, she should have to make another afterwards, and that then there would be double lawyers' fees to deduct from the little she would have to leave us. After she found out that she was dangerously sick, she was very anxious to make her will, whenever she was in her right mind; but that went and came so, that the Doctor, and a lawyer whom he brought to see her, said that no disposition she might make could stand in court, if any effort were made to break it. All that could be done was to take down, as she was able to dictate it, an affectionate and touching letter to George.

In this she begged him to remember how much greater his advantages, and his opportunities of making a living, were than ours, and besought him to do his best to keep and increase for us the pittance she had toiled so hard to earn, and to take nothing from it unless a time should come when he was as helpless as we.

Two copies of this letter were made, signed, sealed, and witnessed. One I sent to George, enclosed with an earnest entreaty from Fanny and myself, that he would come and let mamma see him once again, before she died, if, as we feared, she must die. We had asked him to come before. He answered our letter — not our mother's — rather kindly, but very vaguely, putting off his visit, and saying, that he could not for a moment suffer himself to believe that she would not do perfectly well, if we did not alarm her about herself, nor worry her with business when she was not in a state for it. His reply was handed me before her, unluckily. She wished to hear it read, and seemed to lose heart and grow worse from that time.

Thus then matters stood with us that July. The sale of our house was pending — over our kind host's head too! It was plain to me that George would not, and that Dr. Physick should not, bear the charge of Fanny's maintenance. So far and so long as I could, I would.

In the mean time, no further examination was made of her lungs. The Doctor's report was often "Remarkably comfortable," and never anything worse than, "Well, on the whole, taking one time with another, I don't see but she's about as comfortable as she has been." I was, of course, inexperienced. I was afraid that, if she improved no faster, I should be obliged to leave her, when I went away to work for her again at the end of the summer vacation, still very feeble, a care to others, and pining for my care. That was my nearest and clearest fear.

But what did Fanny think? I hope, the truth; and on one incident, in chief, I ground my hope. One beautiful day — the last one in July — she asked me if I should be willing to draw her to our mother's grave. There could be but one answer; though I had not seen the spot since the funeral. Fanny looked at it with more than calmness, — with the solemn irradiation of countenance which had during her illness become her most characteristic expression. She desired me to help her from her chair. She lay at her length upon the turf, still and observant, as if calculating. Then she spoke.

"Katy, dear," said she, very tenderly and softly, as if she feared to give me pain, "I have been thinking sometimes lately, that, if anything should ever happen to either of us, the other might be glad to know what would be exactly the wishes of the one that was gone — about our graves. Suppose we choose them now, while we are here together. Here, by mamma, is where I should like to lie. See, I will lay two red clovers for the head, and a white one for the foot. And there, on her other side, is just such a place for you. Should you like it? — and — shall you remember?"

I found voice to say "Yes," and said it firmly.

"And then," added she, after a short, deliberating pause, during which she, with my assistance, raised herself to sit on the side of the chair with her feet still resting on the turf, "while we are upon the subject, — one thing more. If I should be the first to go, — nobody knows whose turn may come the first, — then I should like to have you do — just what would make you happiest; but I *don't* like mourning. I should n't *wish* to have it worn for me. My feelings about it have all changed since we made it for mamma. It seemed as if we were only working at a great black wall, for our minds to have to break through, every time they yearned to go back into the past and sit with her. It was as if the things she chose for us, and loved to see us in, were part of her and of her life with us, — as if she would be able still to think of us in them, and know just how we looked. And it seemed so strange and unsympathizing in us, that, when we loved her so, we should go about all muffled up in darkness, because our God was clothing her in light ! "

I answered, — rather slowly and tremulously this time, I fear, — that I had felt so too.

"Then, Katy," resumed she, pleadingly, as she leaned back in her usual attitude in the chair, and made a sign that I might draw her home, "we will not either of us wear it for the other, — without nor within either, will we ? — any more than we can help. Don't you remember what dear mamma said once, when you had made two mistakes in your lessons at school, and lost a prize, and took it hard, and somebody was teasing you, with making very light of it, and telling you to think no more about it ? You were very sorry and a little offended, and said, you always chose not to be hoodwinked, but to look at things on all sides and in the face. Mamma smiled, and said, ' It is good and brave to look all trials in the face ; but among the sides, never forget the bright side, little Katy.' If I had my life to live over again, I would try to mind her more in that. She always said, there lay my greatest fault. I hope and think God has forgiven me, because he makes it so easy for me to be cheerful now."

"Fanny," said I, as we drew near the house, "things in this world are strangely jumbled. Here are you, with your character, to wit, that of a little saint, if you will have the goodness to overlook my saying so, and somebody else's conscience. I have no doubt that, while you are reproaching yourself first for this, then for that and the other, the said somebody else is sinning away merrily, somewhere among the antipodes or nearer, without so much as a single twinge."

Smiling, she shook her head at me ; and that was all that passed. She was as cheerful as I tried to be. With regard to the other world, she seemed to have attained unto the perfect love that casteth out fear ; and I believe her only regret in leaving this lower one for it was that she could not take me with her. In fact, throughout her illness, her freedom from anxiety about its symptoms — not absolute, but still in strong contrast with her previous tendencies — appeared to her physician, as he acknowledged to me afterwards, even when he considered the frequent flattering illusions of the disease, a most discouraging indication as to the case. But to her it was an infinite mercy ; and to me, to have such glimpses to remember of her already in possession of so much of that peace which remaineth unto the people of God.

As the dog-days drew on, a change came, though at first a very gentle one to her, if not to me. She slept more, ate less, grew so thin that she could no more bear the motion of her little wagon, and begged that it might be returned, because it tired her so to think of it.

Then word came that our house was advertised to be sold, unconditionally, at an early day. To move her in that state, — how dreadful it would be ! I did not mean to let her know anything about it until I must ; but Miss Mehitable, always less remarkable for tact than for good-will, blurted it out before her.

Her brows contracted with a moment's look of pain. "O Katy," she whispered, "I am sorry! That must make you very anxious " ; — and then she went to sleep.

Evidently it did not make her very anxious, as I knew that it would have done as lately even as two or three months before. What was the remedy ? Approaching death. Well, death was approaching me also, as steadily, if not so nearly; and, after her example, my thoughts took such a foretaste of that anodyne that, as I sat and gazed on her unconscious, placid face, all terrors left me, and I was strengthened to pray, and to determine to look to the morrow with only so much thought as should enable me to bring up all my resources of body and mind to meet it as I ought, and to leave the result, unquestioned, quite in God's hand.

The result was an entire relief to her last earthly care. The appointed day came. The matter took wind. None of our townspeople appeared, to bid against my guardian; but enough of them were on the spot "to see fair play," or, in other words, to advance for him whatever sum he might stand in need of; and the house was knocked down to him at a price even below its market value. He paid the mortgagee and George their due by the next mail, but left my title and Fanny's as it was, not to be settled till I came of age.

These details would only have worried and wearied her; but the auctioneer's loud voice had hardly died away, or the gathered footsteps scattered from the door, when the Doctor came to her chamber, flushed with triumph, to tell us that "Nobody now could turn us out; and everything was arranged for us to stay." Fanny looked brightly up to him, and answered: "Now I shall scarcely know what more to pray for, but God's reward for you." And most of all I thank Him for that news, because her last day on this earth was such a happy one.

The next morning, just at dawn, she waked me, saying, "O Katy, tell the Doctor I can't breathe!"

I sprang up, raised her on her pillows, and called him instantly.

She stretched out her hand to him, and gasped, "O Doctor, I can't breathe! Can't you do anything to help me?"

He felt her pulse quickly, looking at her, and said, very tenderly, "Have some ether, Fanny. I will run and bring it." Throwing wider open every window that he passed, he hurried down to the office and back with the ether.

Eagerly, though with difficulty, she inhaled it; and it relieved her. I sat and watched her, silent, with her hand in mine.

Presently the door behind me opened softly, as if somebody was looking in. "My dear," said the Doctor, turning his head, and speaking very earnestly, though in a low voice, "I *would n't* come here. You can do no good." But presently his wife came in, in her dressing-gown, very pale, and sat by me and held the hand that was not holding Fanny's.

And next I knew they thought she would not wake; and then the short breath stopped. And now it was my turn to stretch out my hands to him for help; but, looking at me, he burst into tears, as he had not when he looked at Fanny; and I knew there was no breath more for her, nor any ether for me. I did not want to go to sleep, because *I* should have to wake again; but his wife was sobbing aloud. I knew how dreadful such excitement was for her; and so I had to do just as they wished me to, and let them lead me out and lock the door, and lay down on a bed and shut my eyes.

PROTONEIRON.

DECEMBER 9, 1864.

"And in that sleep of death what dreams may come."

THE unresting lines, where oceans end,
  Are traced by shifting surf and sand;
As pallid, moonlit fingers blend
The dreamlight of the ghostly land.

No eye can tell where Love's last ray
Fades to the sky of colder light;
No ear, when sounds that vexed the day
Cease mingling with the holier night.

As bells, which long have failed to swing
In lonely towers of crumbling stone,
Through far eternal spaces ring,
With semblance of their ancient tone.

The lightning, quivering through the cloud,
Weaves warp and woof from sky to earth,
In mist that seems a mortal's shroud,
In light that hails an angel's birth.

Thought vainly strives, with life's dull load,
To mount through ether rare and thin;
Fond eyes pursue the spirit's road
To heaven, and dimly gaze therein.

In battle's travail-hour, a host
Writhes in the throes of deadly strife.
One flash! One groan! A startled ghost
Is born into the eternal life.

Dear wife and children! Now I fly
Forth from my soldier camp to you!
Blue ridge and river hurry by
My weary eyes, in quick review.

Long have I waited. How and when
My furlough came is mystery.
I dreamed of charging with my men, —
A dream of glorious history!

To you I fly on Love's strong wing;
My courser needs no armed heel:
And yet anew the bugles ring,
And wake me to the crash of steel.

Protoneiron.

In fiercer rush of hosts again
My dripping sabre seeks the front.
Spur your mad horses! Forward, men!
Meet with your hearts the battle's brunt.

Tricolor, flaunt! And trumpet-blare,
Scream louder than the bursting shell,
And thundering hoofs, that shake the air,
Trembling above that surging hell!

In carbine smoke and cannon flash,
Like avalanches twain, we meet;
One gasp! we spur; one stab! we crash
And trample with the iron feet.

I *dream!* My tiercepoint smote them through,
My sabre buried to my hand!
And yet unchecked those horsemen flew,
And still I grasp my phantom brand!

Our chargers, which like whirlwinds bore
Us onward, lie all stiff and stark!
Black Midnight's feet wait on the shore,
To bear me — where? Where all is dark.

And still I hear the faint recall!
My senses, — have they dropped asleep?
I see a soldier's funeral pall,
And there *my* wife and children weep!

Sobs break the air, below the cloud;
And one pure soul, of love and truth,
Is folding in a mortal shroud
Her quivering wings of Hope and Youth.

Ye of the sacred red right hand,
Who count, around our camp-fire light,
Dear names within the shadowy land,
Why do ye whisper *mine* to-night?

Where am I? *Am* I? Trumpet notes
Still mingle with a dreamy doubt
Of Where? and Whither? Music floats,
As when camp-lights are going out.

Like saintly eyes resigned to Death,
Like spirit whispers from afar,
The sighing bugle yields its breath,
As if it wooed a dying star.

Draped in dark shadows, widowed Night
Weeps, on new graves, with chilly tears ;
Beyond strange mountain-tops, the light
Is breaking from the immortal years.

A rhythm, from the unfathomed deep
Of God's eternal stillness, sings
My wondering, trembling soul to sleep,
While angels lift it on their wings.

THE PROGRESS OF PRUSSIA.

THE changes that have taken place in Europe in the last twenty years are of a most comprehensive character, and as strange as comprehensive ; and their consequences are likely to be as remarkable as the changes themselves. In 1846 Russia was the first power of Europe, and at a great distance ahead of all other members of the Pentarchy. She retained the hegemony which she had acquired by the events of 1812 – 1814, and by the great display of military force she had made in 1815, when 160,000 of her troops were reviewed near Paris by the sovereigns and other leaders of the Grand Alliance there assembled after the second and final fall of the first Napoleon. Had Alexander I. reigned long, it is probable that his eccentricities — to call them by no harder name — would have operated to deprive Russia of her supremacy ; but Nicholas, though he might never have raised his country so high as it was carried by his brother, was exactly the man to keep the power he had inherited, — and to keep it in the only way in which it was to be kept, namely, by increasing it. This he had done, and great success had waited on most of his undertakings, while in none had he encountered failure calculated to attract the world's attention. England had in some sense shared men's notice with Russia immediately after the settlement of Europe. The " crown-ing carnage, Waterloo," was considered her work ; and, as the most decisive battle since Philippi, it gave to the victor in it an amount of consideration that was equal to that which Napoleon himself had possessed in 1812. But this consideration rapidly passed away, as England did nothing to maintain her influence on the Continent, while Russia was constantly busy there, and really governed it down to the French Revolution of 1830 ; and her power was not much weakened even by the fall of the elder Bourbons, with whom the Czar had entered into a treaty that had for one of its ends the cession to France of those very Rhenish provinces of which so much has been said in the course of the present year. Russia was victorious in her conflicts with the Persians and the Turks, and the battle of Navarino really had been fought in her interest, — blindly by the English, but intelligently by the French, who were willing that she should plant the double-headed eagle on the Bosporus, provided the lilies should be planted on the Rhine. If the fall of the Bourbons in France, and the fall of the Tories in England, weakened Russia's influence in Western Europe, those events had the effect of drawing Austria and Prussia nearer to her, and of reviving something of the spirit of the Holy Alliance, which had lost much of its strength from the early death of

Alexander. Russia had her own way in almost every respect; and in 1846 Nicholas was almost as powerful a ruler as Napoleon had been a generation earlier, with the additional advantage of being a legitimate sovereign, who could not be destroyed through the efforts of any coalition. Three years later he saved Austria from destruction by his invasion of Hungary, — an act of hard insolence, which quite reconciles one to the humiliation that overtook him five years later. He was then so powerful that the reactionists of the West cried for Russian cannon, to be used against the Reds. There was no nation to dispute the palm with Russia. England was supposed to be devoted to the conversion of cotton into calico, and to be ruled in the spirit of the Manchester school. She had retired into her shell, and could not be got out of it. Austria was thinking chiefly of Italy, and of becoming a naval power by incorporating that Peninsula into her empire. Prussia was looked upon as nothing but a Russian outpost to the west, and waiting only to be used by her master. France had not recovered from her humiliation of 1814–15, and never would recover from it so long as she warred only at barricades or in Barbary. Russia was supreme, and most men thought that supreme she would remain.

Thus stood matters down to 1853. Early in that year the Czar entered on his last quarrel with the Turks, whose cause was espoused by England, partly for the reason that Russian aggrandizement in the East would be dangerous to her interests, but more on the ground that she had become weary of submission to that arrogant sovereign who was in the habit of giving law to the Old World. Russia's ascendency, though chiefly the work of England, was more distasteful to the English than it was to any other European people, — more than it was to the French, at whose expense it had been founded; and had Nicholas made overtures to the latter, instead of making them to Eng-

land, it is very probable he would have accomplished his purpose. But he detested Napoleon III., and he was at no pains to conceal his sentiments. This was the one great error of his life. The French Emperor had two great ends in view: first, to get into respectable company; and, secondly, to make himself powerful at home, by obtaining power and influence for France abroad. Unaided, he could accomplish neither end; and Nicholas and Victoria were the only two sovereigns who could be of much use to him in accomplishing one or both. Had Nicholas been gracious to him, had he, in particular, made overtures to him, he might have had the Emperor almost on his own terms; for the French disliked the English, and they did not dislike the Russians. Everything pointed to renewal of that "cordial understanding" between Russia and France which had existed twenty-five years earlier, when Charles X. was king of France, and which, had there been no Revolution of July, would have given to Russia possession of Constantinople, and to the French that roc's egg of theirs, the left bank of the Rhine. But prosperity had been fatal to the Czar. He could not see what was palpable to everybody else. He allowed his feelings to get the better of his judgment. He treated Napoleon III. with less consideration than he treated the Turkish Sultan; and Napoleon actually was forced to teach him that a French ruler was a powerful personage, and that the days of Louis Philippe were over forever. If not good enough to help Russia spoil Turkey, the Czar must be taught he was good enough to help England prevent the spoliating scheme. France and England united their forces to those of Turkey, and were joined by Sardinia. Russia was beaten in the war, on almost all its scenes. The world ascribed the result to Napoleon III. France carried off the honors of the war, and of spoil there was none. The Peace of Paris, which terminated the contest, was the work of Napoleon. He dictated its terms, forcing them less on his enemy than on his allies.

As Russia's leadership of Europe had come from success in war, and had been maintained by subsequent successes of the Russian armies, — in Persia, in Turkey, in Poland, and elsewhere, — it followed that that leadership was lost when the fortune of war changed, and those armies were beaten on every occasion where they met the Allies. No military country could stand up erect under such crushing blows as had been delivered at the Alma, at Inkermann, at the Tchernaya, and at Sebastopol, not to name lesser Allied successes, or to count the victories of the Turks. Nicholas died in the course of the war, falling only before the universal conqueror. His successor submitted to the decision of the sword, and in fact performed an act of abdication inferior only to that executed by Napoleon. France stepped into the vacant leadership, and held it for ten years. Subsequent events confirmed and strengthened the French hegemony. The Italian war, waged by the Emperor in person, had lasted only about as many months as the Russian war did years, and yet it had proved far more damaging to Austria than the other had proved to Russia. The mere loss of territory experienced by Austria, though not small, was the least of the adverse results to her. Her whole Italian scheme was cut through and utterly ruined ; and it was well understood that the days of her rule over Venetia were destined to be as few as they were evil. For what she then did, France received Savoy and Nice, which formed by no means a great price for her all but inestimable services, — services by no means to be ascertained, if we would know their true value, by what was done in 1859. France created the Kingdom of Italy. After making the amplest allowance for what was effected by Cavour, by Garibaldi, by Victor Emanuel, and by the Italian people, it must be clear to every one that nothing could have been effected toward the overthrow of Austrian domination in

Italy but for the action of French armies in that country. That the Emperor meant what he wrought is very unlikely ; but after the events of 1859 it was impossible to prevent the construction of the kingdom of Italy ; and the Frenchman had to consent to the completion of his own work, though he did so on some occasions with extreme reluctance, — not so much from the dictation of his own feelings, as from the aversion which the French feel for the Italian cause, and which is so strong, and so deeply shared by the military, that it was with difficulty the soldiers in the camp of Châlons were prevented getting up an illumination when news reached them of the battle of Custozza, the event of which was so disastrous to Italy, and would have been fatal to her cause, had not that been vindicated and established by Prussian genius and valor on the remote fields of Germany and Bohemia. The descendants of men who fought under Arminius saved the descendants of the countrymen of Varus. Those persons who have condemned the Frenchman's apparently singular course toward Italy on some occasions, have not made sufficient allowance for the dislike of almost all classes of his subjects for the Italians. The Italian war was unpopular, and the Russian war was not popular. While the French have been pleased by the military occurrences that make up the histories of those wars, they were by no means pleased by the wars themselves, and they do not approve them even at this day ; and the extraordinary events of the current year are not at all calculated to make them popular in France : for it is not difficult to see that there is a close connection between the establishment of the Kingdom of Italy and the elevation of Prussia to the first place in Europe ; and Prussia is the power most abhorred by the French. So intense is French hatred of Prussia, that it is not too much to say that, last summer, the French would almost as lief have seen the Russians in Paris as the Prussians in Vienna.

At the middle of last June the leadership of Europe — Frenchmen said of the world — was in the hands of France; and that such was France's place was the work of Napoleon III. The Emperor had been successful in all his undertakings, with one exception. His Mexican business had proved a total failure; but this had not injured him. Americans thought differently, some of us going so far as to suppose the fall of Maximilian's shaky throne would involve that of the solid throne of Napoleon. No such thing. The great majority of Frenchmen know little and care less about the Mexican business. Intelligent Frenchmen regret the Emperor's having taken it up; but they do so because of the expenditure it has involved, and because they have learnt from their country's history that it is best for her to keep out of that colonizing pursuit which has so many charms for the Emperor, — perhaps because of his Dutch origin. There is something eminently ridiculous about French colonization, which contrasts strangely with the robust action of the English. The Emperor seems to believe in it, — an instance of weakness that places him, on one point at least, below common men, most of whom laugh at his doings in regard to Mexico. If report does him no injustice, he thinks his Mexican undertaking the greatest thing of his reign. What, then, is the smallest thing of that reign? It is somewhat strange that this immense undertaking should not have been practicable till some time after the United States had become involved in civil war, that tasked all American energies, and did not permit any attention to be paid to Napoleon's action in Mexico.

Whether wise or foolish, Napoleon's interference in Mexican affairs had not weakened his power or lessened his influence in the estimation of Europe. Five months ago he was at the head of the European world. His position was quite equal to that which Nicholas held thirteen years earlier. If any change in his condition was looked for,

it was sought in the advance of his greatness, not in the chance of his fall. The general, the all but universal sentiment was, that during Napoleon III.'s life France's lead must be accepted; and that, if that life should be much extended, France's power would be greatly increased, and that Belgium and the Rhine country might become hers at no distant day. It is true that, long before the middle of June, the course of events indicated the near approach of war; but it was commonly supposed that the chief result of such war would be to add to the greatness and glory of France. *That* was about the only point on which men were agreed with respect to the threatened conflict. Prussia and Italy might overthrow the Austrian empire; but most probably Austria, aided by most of Germany, would defeat them both, her armies rendezvousing at Berlin and Milan; and then would Napoleon III., bearing "the sword of Brennus," come in, and save the Allies from destruction, who would gratefully reward him, — the one by ceding the Rhenish provinces, and the other the island of Sardinia, to France. Such was the programme laid out by most persons in Europe and America, and probably not one person in a hundred thought it possible for Prussia to succeed. Even most of those persons who were not overcrowed by Austria's partisans and admirers did not dream that she would be conquered in a week, but thought it would be a more difficult matter for General Benedek to march from Prague to Berlin than was generally supposed, and that such march would not exactly be of the nature of a military promenade. That the French Emperor shared the popular belief, is evident from his conduct. He never would have allowed war to break out, if he had supposed it would lead to the elevation of Prussia to the first place in Europe, — a position held by himself, and which he had no desire to vacate. It was in his power to prevent the occurrence of war down almost to the very hour when the Diet of the Germanic Confederation afforded to Prussia so plausible a ground for setting her armies in motion, by adopting a course that bore some resemblance to the old process of putting a disobedient member under the ban of the Empire. Prussia would not have gone to war with Austria, had she not been assured of the Italian alliance,—an alliance that would not only be useful in keeping a large portion of Austria's force in the south, but would prevent that power from purchasing Italian aid by the cession of Venetia; for so angry were the Austrians with Prussia, that it was quite on the cards that they might become the friends of Italy, if she would but help them against that nation whose exertions in 1859 had prevented Venetia from following the fate of Lombardy.

As Prussia would not have made war in 1866 without having secured the assistance of Italy, so was it impossible for Italy to form an alliance with Prussia without the consent of France being first had and obtained. Napoleon III. possessed an absolute veto on the action of the Italian government, and had he signified to that government that an alliance with Prussia could not meet with his countenance and approval, no such alliance ever would have been formed, or even the proposition to form it have been taken into serious consideration by the Cabinet of Florence. Victor Emanuel II. would have dared no more to attack Francis Joseph, without the consent of Napoleon III., than Carthage durst have attacked Masinissa without the consent of Rome. Prussia was not under the supervision of France, and was and is the only great European nation which had not then, as she has not since, been made to feel the weight of his power; but it may be doubted, without the slightest intention to impeach her courage, if she would have resolved upon war had she been convinced that France was utterly opposed to such resolution, and was prepared to show that the Empire was for peace by making war to preserve it. The opin-

ion was quite common, as matters became more and more warlike with each succeeding day, that the course of Prussia had been fixed upon and mapped out by Count Bismark and Napoleon III., and that the former had received positive assurances that his country should not undergo any reduction of territory should the fortune of war go against her; in return for which he had agreed to such a "rectification of the French frontier" as should be highly pleasing to the pride of Frenchmen, and add greatly to the glory and the dignity of their Emperor. When news came that Napoleon III., after peace had been resolved upon, had asked for the cession of certain Rhenish territory,* the demand was supposed to have been made in consequence of an understanding entered into before the war by the courts of Paris and Berlin. There was nothing unreasonable in this supposition; for Napoleon III. was so bent upon ex-

* Exactly what it was Napoleon III. asked of Prussia we never have seen stated by any authority that we can quite trust. The London Times, which is likely to be well informed on the subject, assumes, in its issue of August 11th, that the Emperor asked of Prussia the restoration of the French frontier of 1814, —meaning the French frontier as it was fixed by the Treaty of Paris, on the 30th of May, immediately after the fall of Napoleon I. If this is the correct interpretation of Napoleon's demand, he asked for very little. The Treaty of Paris took from France nearly all the conquests made by the Republic and the Empire, leaving her only a few places on the side of Germany, a little territory near Geneva, portions of Savoy, and the Venaissin. After the second conquest of France, most of these remnants of her conquests were taken from her. Napoleon III. has regained what was then lost of Savoy, and he seems to have sought from Prussia the restoration of that which was lost on the side of Germany, most of which was given to Bavaria and Belgium, and the remainder to Prussia herself. What Prussia holds, he supposed she could cede to France; and as to Bavaria, he may have argued that Prussia was in such position with regard to that kingdom as to make her will law to its government. But how could she get possession of what Belgium holds? Since the failure of his attempt, the French Emperor has been at peculiar pains to assure the King of the Belgians that he has no designs on his territory; and therefore we must suppose he had none when he propounded his demand to Prussia. It may be added, that the cession of the Prussian portion of the spoil of 1815 had been a subject of speculation, and of something like negotiation, long before war between Prussia and Austria was supposed to be possible.

tending the boundaries of France, and was so entirely master of the situation, and his friendship was so necessary to Prussia, that it was reasonable to suppose he had made a good bargain with that power. Probably, when the secret history of the war shall be published, it will be seen that an understanding did exist between Prussia and France, and that Napoleon III., in August, asked for no more than it had been agreed he should have, in June, or May, or even earlier. Why, then, did Prussia give so firm but civil a negative in answer to his demand? and how was it that he submitted with so much of meekness to her refusal, even attributing his demand to the pressure of French public opinion, which is no more strongly expressed in 1866 in favor of the acquisition of the Rhine country, than it has been in almost any year since that country was lost, more than half a century since? The answer is easy. Prussia, no matter what her arrangement with France before the war, durst not pass over to the latter a solitary league of German territory. Her victories had so exalted German sentiment that she could not have her own way in all things. She was, on one side, paralyzed by the unexpected completeness of her military successes, which had brought very near all Germany under her eagles; for all Germans saw at once that she had obtained that commanding position from which the dictation of the unity of their country was not only a possibility, but something that could be accomplished without much difficulty. What Victor Emanuel II. and Count Cavour had been to Italy, William I. and Count Bismark could be to Austria, with this vast difference in favor of the Prussian sovereign and statesman, — that their policy could not be dictated, nor their action hampered, by a great foreign sovereign, who ruled a people hostile to the unity of every European race but themselves. It was impossible even to take into consideration any project that looked to the dismemberment of Germany, at a time

when even Southern Germans were ready to unite with Prussia, because she was the champion of German unity, and was in condition to make her championship effectual. Napoleon III. saw how matters were, and, being a statesman, he did not hesitate, at the risk of much loss of influence, to admit a fact the existence of which could not be denied, and which operated with overwhelming force against his interests both as an emperor and as a man. That he may have only deferred a rupture with Prussia is probable enough, for it is not to be assumed that he is ready to cede the first place in Europe to the country most disliked by his subjects, and which refuses to cede anything to him. But he must have time in which to rearm his infantry, and to place in their hands a weapon that shall be to the needle-gun * what the needle-gun * is to the Austrian muzzle-loader. He has postponed action; but that he has definitely abandoned the French claim to the left bank of the Rhine it would be hazardous to assert. There are reports that a conference of the chief European powers will be held soon, and that by that body something will be done with respect to the French claim that will prove satisfactory to all parties. It would be a marvellous body, should it accomplish so miraculous a piece of business. The matter is in fair way to disturb the peace of Europe before Sadowa shall have be-

* There has been as much noise made over the needle-gun as by that famous and fascinating slaughter weapon; yet it is by no means an arm of tender years. It had been known thirty years when the recent war began, and it had been amply tested in action seventeen years before it was first directed against the Austrians, not to mention the free use that had been made of it in the Danish war. Much that has been said of its character and capabilities since last June was said in 1849, and can be found in publications of that year. The world had forgotten it, and also that Prussia could fight. Nicholas von Dreyse, inventor of the needle-gun, is now living, at the age of seventy-eight. The thought of the invention occurred to him the day after the battle of Jena, in 1806. Some six or seven years since, we read, in an English work, an elaborate argument to show that, in a great war, Prussia must be beaten, because she had no experienced commanders !— like Benedek and Clam-Gallas, for example.

come as old a battle as we now rate Solferino.

We do not assert that there was an understanding between France and Prussia last spring, and that Prussia went to war because that arrangement assured her against loss ; but we think there is nothing irrational in the popular belief in the existence of such an understanding, and that nothing has occurred since the middle of June that renders that belief absurd. The contrary belief makes a fool of Napoleon III., — a character which not even the Emperor's enemies have attributed to him since he became a successful man.

War began on the 15th of June, the day after that on which that bungling body, the Bund, under Austrian influence, had resort to overt measures against Prussia, which had suffered for some time from its covert measures. The Germanic Confederation ceased to exist on the 14th of June, having completed its half-century, with a little time to spare. The declarations of war that appeared on the 18th of June, — the anniversary of Fehrbellin, Kolin, and Waterloo, all great and decisive Prussian battles, and two of them Prussian victories, or victories which Prussians aided in winning, — the declarations of war, we say, were mere formalities, and as such they were regarded. Prussia's first open operation was taken three days before, when she invaded Saxony, — a country in which the Austrians, had they been wise, would have had at least a hundred thousand men within twenty-four hours after the action of the Diet. Prussia had been prepared for war for some weeks, perhaps months, while we are assured that Austria's preparations were far from complete ; from which, supposing the statement correct, the inference is drawn that she did not expect Prussia to push matters to extremity. It is more likely that she fell into the usual error of all proud egotists, — that of estimating the capacity of a foe by her own. We cannot think so poorly of Austrian statesmen and generals as to conclude that they did not see war was inevitable in

the latter part of May, which gave them three weeks to mass their troops so near the Saxon frontier as would have enabled them to cross it in a few hours after the Diet had given itself up to their direction, before the world. As the Diet never durst have acted thus without Austria's direct sanction, Austria must have known that war was at hand, and she should have prepared for its coming. Probably she did make all the preparation she thought necessary, she supposing that Prussia would be as slow as herself, because believing that her best was the best thing in the world. This error was the source of all her misfortunes. She applied to the military art, in this age of railways and electric telegraphs, principles and practices that were not even of the first merit in much earlier and very different times. She was not aware that the world had changed. Prussia was thoroughly aware of it, and acted accordingly. She was all vivacity and alertness, and hence her success. In nineteen days, counting from the morning of June 15th, she had accomplished that which almost all men in other countries had deemed impossible. While foreigners were speculating as to the number of days Benedek would require to reach Berlin, and wondering whether he would proceed by the Silesian or the Saxon route, the Prussians were routing him, taking Prague, and marching swiftly toward Vienna. The contending armies first "felt" one another on the 26th of June, in a small affair at Liebenau, in which the Prussians were victorious. The next day there was another "affair," of larger proportions, at Podal, with the same result ; and two more actions, one at Nachod and at Skalitz, in which Fortune was consistent, adhering to the single-headed eagle, and the other at Trautenäu, which was of the nature of a drawn battle. On the 28th there was another fight at Trautenau, the Prussians remaining masters of the field ; while the Austrians were beaten at other points, and fell back to Gitschin, once the capital of Wallenstein's Duchy of Friedland, and where the Friedlander was to receive ample vengeance just seven generations after his assassination by contrivance and order of the head of the German branch of the house of Austria, Ferdinand II. Could Wallenstein have "revisited the glimpses of the moon" on the night of the 28th of last June, he might have cast terror into the soul of Francis Joseph, as the Bodach Glas did into that of Vich-Ian-Vohr, by appearing to him, and bidding him beware of the morrow; for it was at Gitschin, on the 29th of June, and not at Sadowa, on the 3d of July, that the event of the war was decided. Had the battle then and there fought been fortunate for the Austrians, the name of Sadowa would have remained unknown to the world; for then the battle of the 3d of July could not have been fought, or it would have had a different scene, and most probably a different result. Austrian defeat at Gitschin made the battle of Sadowa a necessity, and made it so under conditions highly favorable to the Prussians. The ghost of Wallenstein might have returned to its rest with entire complacency, and with the firm resolution to trouble this sublunary world no more, had it witnessed the flight of the Austrians through Gitschin. By a "curious coincidence," it happens that a large number of the vanquished were Saxons, descendants, it may be, of men who had acted with Gustavus Adolphus against Wallenstein in 1632.

The battle of Sadowa was fought on the 3d of July, the third anniversary of the decisive day of our battle of Gettysburg. At a moderate estimate, four hundred and twenty thousand men took part in it, of whom one hundred and ninety-five thousand were Austrians and Saxons, and two hundred and twenty-five thousand Prussians. This makes the action rank almost with the battle of Leipzig, the greatest of all battles.*

It is satisfactory evidence of the real greatness of Prussian generalship, that it had succeeded in massing much the larger force on the final field, though at a distance from the Prussian frontier and far within the enemy's territory; and also that while the invaders of Austria were opposed by equal forces on the left and centre of the Austrian line, they were in excessive strength on that line's right, the very point at which their presence was most required. Yet further: these great masses of men were all employed, and admirably handled, while almost a fourth part of the Austrian army remained idle, or was not employed till the issue of the battle had been decided. The Austrian position was strong, or it would have been so in the hands of an able commander; but Benedek was unequal to his work, and totally unfit to command a larger army than even Napoleon I. ever led in any battle. There seldom has lived a general capable of handling an army two hundred thousand strong. The Prussians, to be sure, were stronger, and they were splendidly handled; but it must be observed that they were divided into two armies, and that those armies, though having a common object, operated apart. In this respect, though in no other, Sadowa bears a resemblance to Waterloo, the armies of the Crown Prince and of Prince Frederick Charles answering to those of Blücher and Wellington. The Prussian force engaged far exceeded that of all the armies that fought at Waterloo, and the Austrian army ex-

* The entire force of the Allies at Leipzig is generally stated to have been 290,000 men; that of the French at 175,000, — making a total of 465,000, or about 45,000 more than were present at Sadowa. So the excess at Leipzig was not so very great. At Leipzig the Allies alone had more guns than both armies had at Sadowa, — but what were the cannon

of those days compared to those of these times? The great force assembled in and around Leipzig was taken from almost all Europe, as there were Frenchmen, Germans, Russians, Hungarians, Bohemians, Italians, Poles, Swedes, Dutchmen, and even Englishmen, present in the two armies; whereas at Sadowa the armies were drawn only from Austria, Prussia, and Saxony. The battle of Sadowa lasted only one day; that of Leipzig four days, a large part of the Allied armies taking part only in the fighting of the third and fourth days. The French lost 68,000 men at Leipzig, the Allies, 42,640, — total, 110,640. But 30,000 of the French were prisoners, reducing the number of killed and wounded to 80,640, — which was even a good four days' work. Probably a third of these were killed or mortally wounded, as artillery was freely used in the battle. War is a great manufacturer of *pabulum Acheruntis,* — grave-meat, that is to say.

ceeded them by some five or six thousand men. War has very rarely been conducted on the scale that is known in 1866. Even the greatest of the engagements in our civil contest seem to shrink to small proportions when compared with what took place last summer in Bohemia. The armies of Grant and Lee, in May, 1864, probably were not larger than the Prussian army at Sadowa. At the same time, Austria had a great force in Venetia, and large bodies of men in other parts of her empire, and some in the territory of the Germanic Confederation; and the Prussians were carrying on vigorous warfare in various parts of Germany.

After their grand victory, the Prussians pushed rapidly forward toward Vienna; and names that are common in the history of Napoleon's Austrian campaigns began to appear in the daily journals, — Olmütz, Brünn, Znaym, Austerlitz, and others. Nothing occurred to stay their march, and they were in the very act of winning another battle which would have cut the Austrians off from Hungary, when an armistice was agreed upon. It was so in 1809, when the officers had to separate the soldiers to announce the armistice of Znaym. It came out soon after that the cessation of warlike operations took place not a day too soon for the Austrians, whose army was in a fearfully demoralized condition. Vienna would have been occupied in a week by the Prussians, had they been disposed to push matters to extremities, and that without a battle; or, if a battle had been fought, the Austrian force must have been destroyed, or would have been literally cut off from any safe line of retreat. Probably the house of Austria would have been struck out of the list of ruling families, had the Austrians not submitted to the invaders. Count Bismark is a man who would have had no hesitation in reviving the Bohemian and Hungarian monarchies, had further resistance been made to his will. The armistice was quickly followed by negotiations, and those were completed on the 23d of August, exactly seventy days

after the Diet, at the dictation of Austria, had given up Prussia to punishment, to be inflicted by the Austrian sword.

The terms of the treaty of peace are moderate; but it should be understood that what Austria loses is very inadequately expressed by these terms, and what Prussia gains not at all; and what Prussia gains at the expense of Austria, important as it is, is less important than what she has gained from France. From Austria she has taken the first place in Germany; from France, the first place in Europe, which is the same thing as the first place in Christendom, or the world, — meaning by the world that portion of mankind which has power and influence and leadership, because of its knowledge, culture, and wealth. The moral blow falls with greater severity on France than on Austria. Austria had no right whatever to the first place in Germany. There was something monstrous, something highly offensive, in the Germanic primacy of an empire made up of Magyars, Poles, Bohemians, Italians, Slavonians, Croats, Illyrians, and other races, and not above a fourth of whose inhabitants were Germans. Prussia had in June last twice as many Germans as Austria, though her entire population was not much more than half as large as that of her rival; [*]

---

[*] It is impossible to speak with precision of the number of the population of Prussia. The highest number mentioned by a respectable authority is 19,000,000: but that is given in "round numbers," and is not meant to be taken literally. But if it be 19,000,000, it is only half as large as the population of France, but little more than half as large as that of Austria as it was when the war began, not much above a fourth as large as that of Russia, many millions below that of the British Islands, a few millions less than that of Italy as it stood before the cession of Venetia by Austria, and a few millions more than that of Spain. The populations of Prussia and Italy when the war began were a little above 40,000,000. The populations of Austria and the German states that sided with her may have been about 50,000,000; and Austria had as much assistance from her German allies as Prussia had from the Italians, — the Saxons helping her much, showing the highest military qualities in the brief but bloody war. Had all the lesser German states preserved a strict neutrality, so that the entire Prussian force could have been directed against Austria, the Prussians would have been before Vienna, and probably in that city, in ten days from the date of Sadowa. Prussia brought out 730,000 men, or about one twenty-sixth part of her entire population.

and when she turned Austria out of Germany at the point of the needle-gun, she simply asserted her own right to the leadership of Germany. But no one will say that there can be anything offensive in a French primacy of Christendom. Objection may be made to any primacy; but if primacy there must be, as mostly there has been, France has the best claim to it of any country. England might dispute the post with her, and England alone; for they are the two nations of modern times to which the world is most indebted. But England has, all but in direct terms, resigned all pretensions to it. Prussia, therefore, by conquering for herself the first place in the estimation of mankind, who always respect the longest and sharpest sword, unhorsed France. Napoleon III. lost more at Sadowa than was lost by Francis Joseph; and we cannot see how he will be able to recover his loss, should Prussia succeed in her purpose to create a powerful Germanic empire, — and all things point to her success. A new force would be introduced into the European system, of which we can only say, that, if its mere anticipation has been sufficient to curb France on the side of the Rhine, its realization ought to be sufficient to prevent France from extending her dominion in any direction — say over Belgium — which such extension is inclined to take.

Thus has a great revolution been effected, and effected, too, with something of the speed of light. On the 14th of June, France, in the estimation of the civilized world, was the first of nations, the head of the Pentarchy. On the 4th of July, she had already been deposed, though the change was not immediately recognizable. On the 14th of June, Prussia's place, though respectable, was not to be named with that of France; it was at the tail of the Pentarchy. On the 4th of July she had conquered for herself the headship of that powerful brotherhood. It was the prize of her sword, and it is on the sword that the French Emperor's power mainly rests. He obtained his place by a free use of the military arm, in December, 1851; he confirmed it by the use of the sword in the Russian and Italian wars; and he purposed making a yet further use of the weapon, had circumstances favored his plans, at the time he allowed the Germano-Italian war to begin. Is he who took the sword to perish by it? Is the Prussian sovereign that stronger man of whose coming Crœsus, that type of all prosperous sovereigns, was warned? Who shall say? But as Napoleon's ascendency rested, the sword apart, upon opinion, and not upon prescription, it is difficult to see how he can submit to a surrender of that ascendency, and make way for one who but yesterday was his inferior, and who, in all probability, was then ready to buy his aid at a high price. The Emperor is old and sickly. His life seems to have been in danger at the very time he was making his demand for an increase of imperial territory. Years and infirmities may indispose him to enter on a mighty war; but he thinks more of his dynasty than of himself, his ambition being to found a reigning house. This must lead him to respect French opinion, on his son's account; and opinion in France is anything but friendly to Prussia. Almost all Frenchmen, from *Reds* to *Whites*, — Republicans, Imperialists, Orleanists, and Legitimists, — seem to be of one mind on this point. They all agree that Prussian supremacy is unendurable. They could have seen their country make way for England, or Russia, or even Austria, without losing their temper altogether; but for France to be displaced by Prussia is something that it is beyond their philosophy to contemplate with patience. The very successes of the Emperor tell against him under existing circumstances. He has raised France so high, from a low condition, that a fall is unbearable to his subjects. He has triumphed, in various ways, over nations that appeared to be so much greater than Prussia, that to surrender the golden palm to her is the very nadir of degradation. His loss of moral power is as great at home as his loss of material power abroad. He has become ridiculous, as having been outwitted by Germans, whom the French have ever been disposed to look upon as the dullest of mankind. Ridicule may not be so powerful an agency in France to-day as it was in former times, but still it has there a sharp sting. The Emperor may be led into war by the force of French opinion; and he would have all Germany to contend against, with the exception of that portion of it which belongs to the house of Austria. The Austrians would gladly renew the war, with France for their ally. They would forgive Solferino, to obtain vengeance for Sadowa. What occurred among the Austrians when they heard of the French demand for a rectification of their frontier shows how readily they would come into any project for the humiliation of Prussia that France might form. They supposed the French demand would be pushed, and they evinced the utmost willingness to support it, — a fact that proves how little they care for Germany, and also how deeply they feel their own fall. They would have renewed the war immediately, had France given the word. But the Emperor did not give the word. He may have hesitated because he preferred to have Italy as an ally, or to see her occupy the position of a neutral; whereas, had he attacked Prussia before the conclusion of the late war, she must have adhered to the Prussian alliance, which would have led to the deduction of a large force from the armies of Austria and France that he would desire to have concentrated in Germany. Or he may have been fearful of even one of the consequences of victory; for would it not be a source of danger to him and his family were one of his marshals so to distinguish himself in a great war as to become the first man in France? The general of a legitimate sovereign can never aspire to his master's throne; but the French throne is fair prize for any man who should be able to conquer the conquerors of Sadowa. The Emperor's health would not permit him to lead his army in person, as he did in the Italian campaign; and that one of his lieutenants who should, by a

repetition of the Jena business, avenge Waterloo, and regain for France, with additions, the rank she held five months ago, would probably prove a greater enemy to the house of Bonaparte than he had been to the house of Hohenzollern. The part of Hazael is always abhorred in advance as much as Hazael himself abhorred it; but Benhadad is sure to perish, and Hazael reigns in his stead.

The nation by which this great change has been wrought in Europe — a change as extraordinary in itself as it is wonderful in its modes, and likely to lead to something far more important — is one of the most respectable members of the European commonwealth, though standing somewhat below the first rank, even while acting on terms of apparent equality with the other great powers. The kingdom of Prussia is of origin so comparatively recent, that there are those now living who can remember others who were old enough to note its creation, in 1700. The arrangements for the conversion of the electorate of Brandenburg into the kingdom of Prussia were completed on the 16th of November, 1700, and the coronation of Frederick I. took place on the 18th of January, 1701, two hundred and eighty-four years less three months after his family's connection with the country began; for it was on the 18th of April, 1417, that the Emperor Sigismund, last member of the Luxemburg family, made Frederick, Burgrave of Nürnberg, Elector of Brandenburg, — the investiture taking place in the market-place of Constance. The transaction was in the nature of a job, as Frederick was a relative of the Emperor, to whom he had advanced money, besides rendering him assistance in other ways. Frederick was of a very old family, and in this respect, as in some others, the house destined to become so great in the North bore a close resemblance to that other house destined to reign in the South, that of Savoy, which became regal not long after the elevation of descendants of the Burgrave of Nürnberg to royal rank. He was a man adapted to the place he received; and the family has seldom failed to produce able men and women in every generation, some of them being of the highest intellectual force, while others have been remarkable for eccentricities that at times bore considerable resemblance to insanity. Yet there was not much in the history of the new electoral house that promised its future greatness, for more than two centuries.

It is surprising to look back over the history of Germany, and note how differently matters have turned out, in respect to families and countries, from what observers of old times would have predicted. When Charles V. fled before Maurice of Saxony, he may have thought, considering the great part Saxony had had in the Reformation, that from that country danger might come to the house of Austria in yet greater measure; but he would have smiled at the prophet who should have told him not only that no such danger would come, but that Saxony would be ruined because of its adherence to the house of Austria, when assailed by a descendant of the then insignificant Elector of Brandenburg. Yet the prophet would have been right, for Saxony suffered so much from her connection with the Austrians in Frederick the Great's time that she never recovered therefrom; and in the late contest she was lost before a shot was fired, and her troops, after fighting valiantly in Bohemia, shared the disasters of the power upon which she had relied for protection. Bavaria was another German country that seemed more likely to rise to greatness than Brandenburg; but, though her progress has been respectable, it must be pronounced insignificant if compared with that of Prussia. The house of Wittelsbach was great before that of Hohenzollern had risen to general fame; but the latter has passed it, as if Fortune had taken the Hohenzollerns under its special protection, and we should not be in the least surprised were they to take all its territory ere the twentieth century shall have fairly dawned upon the world.

...

The first of the great Prussian rulers was the Elector Frederick William, who reigned from 1640 to 1688, and who is known as the Great Elector, — a title of which he was every way worthy, and not the less that there was just a suspicion of the tyrant in his composition. He had not a little of that "justness of insight, toughness of character, and general strength of bridle-hand," which Mr. Carlyle attributes to Rudolph of Hapsburg. He was a man of the times, and a man for the times. He came to the throne just as the Thirty Years' War was well advanced in its last decade, and he had a ruined country for his inheritance; but he raised that country to a high place in Europe, and was connected with many of the principal events of the age of Louis XIV. He freed Prussia from her connection with Poland. He created that Prussian army which has done such wonderful things in the greatest of wars in the last two centuries. He it was who won the battle of Fehrbellin, June 18, 1675, at the expense of the Swedes, who were still living on the mighty reputation won under Gustavus Adolphus, almost half a century earlier, and maintained by the splendid soldiers trained in his school. The calm and philosophic Rankè warms into something like eloquence when summing up the work of the Great Elector. "Frederick William," he says, "cannot be placed in the same category with those few great men who have discovered new conditions for the development of the human race; but he may unhesitatingly be ranked with those famous princes who have saved their countries in the hour of danger, and have succeeded in re-establishing order, — with an Alfred, a Charles VII., a Gustavus Vasa. He followed the path trodden by the German territorial princes of old; but among them all there was not one who, finding his state reduced to such a miserable condition, so successfully raised it to independence and power. He instilled into his subjects a spirit of enterprise, — the mainspring of a state. He took measures which secured to his country an increase of power and prosperity. What the world most admired, and indeed what he himself most valued, was the condition of his army. It contained at the time of his death one hundred and seventy-five companies of foot, and seventy-six of cavalry ; the artillery had recently been increased in proportion, and the Elector's attention had been constantly directed to its improvement. The whole strength of the army was about twenty-eight thousand men. There was nothing that he recommended so earnestly to his successor as the preservation of this instrument of power. By this it was that he had made room for himself among his neighbors, and had won for the Protestant cause of North Germany the respect that was its due." *

Nor did he neglect that naval arm which has been of so great service to many countries. Prussia's desire to have a navy has raised many smiles, and caused much laughter, in this century, as if it were something new ; whereas it is an ancient aspiration, and one which all Prussian sovereigns and statesmen have experienced for two hundred years, though not strongly. The Great Czar, who came upon the stage just after the Great Elector left it, did not long more for a good sea-coast than that Elector had longed for it. Frederick William could not effect so much as Peter effected, but he did something toward the creation of a navy for Prussia. His reluctance in parting with a portion of Pomerania was owing to his commercial and maritime aspirations. "Of all the princes of the house of Brandenburg," says Ranke, "he is the only one who ever showed a strong predilection for maritime life and maritime power. It was the dream of his youth that he would one day sail along shores obedient to his will, all the way from Custrin, out by the mouths of the Oder, across to the coast of Prussia. His sojourn in the Netherlands had strengthened, though it had not inspired, his love of the sea.

* Memoirs of the House of Brandenburg, and History of Prussia during the Seventeenth and Eighteenth Centuries, Vol. I. pp. 91, 92. ¦

The best proof how painful this cession was to the Elector is the fact that he shortly afterward offered to the crown of Sweden, not alone the three sees of Halberstadt, Minden, and Magdeburg, but a sum of two millions of thalers in addition, for the possession of Pomerania." The same writer says of the Great Elector elsewhere, that "his mind had a wide grasp ; to us it may seem almost too wide, when we call to mind that he brought the coast of Guinea into direct communication with Brandenburg, and ventured to compete with Spain on the ocean." When he died, the population of his dominions amounted to one million five hundred thousand.

His successor was his son Frederick, who added to the territory of Prussia, and who, as before stated, became king in November, 1700, a few days after the extinction, in the person of Charles II., of the Spanish branch of the house of Austria. One royal house had gone out, and another came in. Prince Eugene of Savoy, the ablest man that ever served the house of Austria, plainly told the German Emperor that his ministers deserved the gallows for advising him to consent to the creation of the new kingdom, and all subsequent German history seems to show that he was right. But that house needed all the aid it could beg, buy, or borrow, to press its claim to the Spanish crowns ; and, thanks to the exertions of the Great Elector, Brandenburg had an army, the aid of which was well worth purchasing at what Leopold may have thought to be a nominal price, after all. So well balanced were the parties to the war of the Spanish Succession, at least in its earlier years, that the mere absence of the Prussian contingent from the armies of the Grand Alliance might have thrown victory into the French scale. What would have been the effect had the army and the influence of Brandenburg been placed at the disposal of Louis XIV. ? What would have been the fate of the house of Austria, had the Elector been actively employed on the French side, like the Elector of Bavaria, in the campaign of Blenheim, instead of being one of the stoutest supporters of the Austrians? Even Eugene himself might never have won most of those victories which have made his name immortal, had his policy prevailed at Vienna in 1700, and the Emperor refused to convert the Elector of Brandenburg into King of Prussia. At Blenheim, the Prussians behaved in the noblest manner, and won the highest praise from Eugene, who commanded in that part of the field where they were stationed; and he spoke particularly of their "undaunted resolution" in withstanding the enemy's attacks, and of their activity at a later period of the battle. It is curious to observe that he notes the steadiness and strength of their fire, — a peculiarity that has distinguished the Prussian infantry from the beginning of its existence, and which, from the introduction of the iron ramrod into the service, had much to do with the successes of Frederick the Great, and, from the use of the needle-gun, quite as much with the successes of Prince Frederick Charles and the Crown Prince. In the time of Frederick I., the Prussian troops were employed in Germany and Italy, in France and Flanders. They also served against the Turks. It may be said, that, if the Great Elector created the Prussian army, it received the baptism of fire in full from his son, Frederick I., the first Prussian king.

Frederick I. died in 1713. If it be true — as we think it is — that the great enterprise of William of Orange for the deliverance of England could not have been undertaken but for the aid he gave that prince, Englishmen and Americans ought to hold his name in especial remembrance. He was succeeded by his son Frederick William I., who is counted a brute by most persons, but whom Mr. Carlyle would have us believe to have been a man of remarkable worth. He had talents, and he increased the territory of his kingdom. When he died, in 1740, he left to his son a kingdom containing 2,500,000

souls, a treasury containing $6,000,000, and an army more than thirty thousand strong, and which was the first force in Europe because of its high state of discipline and of the superiority of its infantry weapon. The introduction of the iron ramrod was a greater improvement, relatively, in 1740, than was the introduction of the needle-gun in the present generation. Nothing but the use of that ramrod saved the Prussians from destruction in the first of Frederick II.'s wars. That gave them superiority, which they well knew how to keep. "The main thing," as Rankè observes, "was a regular step and rapid firing; or, as the king once expressed it, 'Load quickly, advance in close column, present well, take aim well, — all in profound silence.'" The whole business of infantry in the field is summed up in the royal sentence, though some may think that line would be a better word than column; and the Prussian system did favor the linear rather than the columnar arrangement of troops, as it "presented a wide front, less exposed to the fire of the artillery, and more efficient from the force of its musketry."

Frederick William I. died in 1740. His successor was Frederick II., commonly called the Great. His history has been so much discussed of late years that it would be useless to mention its details. He raised Prussia to the first rank in Europe. Russia was coming in as a European power, and Spain was then as great as France or England, partly because of her former greatness, but as much from the sagacity of her sovereign and the talents of her statesmen. Louis XV. had lessened the weight of France, and George III. had degraded England. The Austrian house had suffered from its failure before Frederick. All things combined to make of Prussia the most formidable of European nations during the last half of Frederick's reign. When he died, in 1786, the Prussian population amounted to six millions, — the increase being chiefly due to the acquisition of Silesia, which was taken from Austria, and to Frederick's share in the first partition of Poland. He left $50,000,000, and his army contained 220,000 men.

Frederick William II., a weak sovereign, reigned till 1797. He took part in the first coalition against revolutionary France, and in the second and third partitions of Poland. Frederick William III. reigned from 1797 to 1840, during which time Prussia experienced every vicissitude of fortune. The first war with imperial France, in 1806–7, led to the reduction of her territory and population one half; and what was left of country and people was most mercilessly treated by Napoleon I., who should either have restored her altogether, or have annihilated her. But the great Emperor was partial to half-measures, — a folly that had much to do with his fall. The misery that Prussia then experienced was the cause of her subsequent greatness; and if she has wrested European supremacy from Napoleon III., she should thank Napoleon I. for enabling her to accomplish so great a feat of arms. The Prussian government had to undertake the task of reform, to save itself and the country from perishing. The chief man in this great work was the celebrated Baron von Stein, whose name is of infrequent mention in popular histories of the Napoleonic age, but who had more to do with the overthrow of the Man of Destiny than any other person. It is one of those strange facts which are so constantly meeting us in history, that it was by Napoleon's advice that Stein was employed by the Prussian king. "Take the Baron von Stein," said the Emperor, when the king at Tilsit spoke of the misery of his situation; "he is a man of sense." Eighteen months later, Napoleon actually outlawed Stein, the decree of outlawry dating from Madrid. The language of the decree was of the most insulting character. "One Stein" (*le nommé Stein*), it was said, was endeavoring to create troubles in Germany, and therefore he was denounced as an enemy of France and of the Rhenish Confederacy. The property he held

in French or confederate territory was confiscated, and the troops of France and her allies were ordered to arrest him, wherever he could be found. Had he been taken, quite likely he would have been as summarily dealt with as Palm had been.

Stein fled into Bohemia, where he resided three years, when Alexander I. invited him to Russia, and employed him in the most important affairs. He kept up Alexander's courage during the darkest days of 1812, and advised, with success, against yielding to the French, though it is probable the Czar might have had his own terms from Napoleon, after the latter had reached Moscow. It is said that the American Minister in Russia, the late Mr. J. Q. Adams, was not less energetic than Stein on the same side. It may well be doubted if their advice was such as a Russian sovereign should have followed, though it was excellent for Germany and for all nations that feared Napoleon. If the American Minister did what was attributed to him, he actually acted in behalf of the very nation against which his own country had just declared war! The war between the United States and England began at the same time that active operations against Russia were entered upon by the French; and England was the only powerful nation upon which Russia could rely for assistance.

Stein had done his work before he was made to leave Prussia. He was the creator of the Prussian people. His reforms would be pronounced agrarian measures in England or America. An imitation of them in England might not be amiss; but in America, where land is a drug, and where possession of it does not give half the consideration that proceeds from the ownership of "stocks" or funds, it would be as much out of place as a mixture for blackening negroes, or a machine for converting New England soil into rocks. "Stein's main idea," says Vehse, "was, 'the burgher must become noble.' With this view, he tried to call forth a strong feeling of nationality and a new spirit in the people. His first step in introducing his new system of administration was the abolition of vassalage, and the change of the titles of seignorial property. This was done by the edict dated Memel, October 9, 1807, which did away with the monopoly until then claimed by the nobles holding such estates, which were now allowed to be acquired also by burghers and peasants. It moreover abolished all the feudal burdens of tenure. In this great law, Frederick William III. laid down the principle : 'After St. Martin's day, 1810, there will be throughout my dominions none but free people.' This edict first created in Prussia a *free* peasantry. Free burghers, on the other hand, were created by the municipal law from Königsberg, November 19, 1808, which restored to the burgesses their ancient municipal rights of freely electing their magistrates and deputies, and of self-government within their own civic sphere. . . . . Stein tried in every way to secure to the burgher his independence, and to protect him against the despotism of the men in office. With equal energy he tried to develop the spirit of the people." * For five years most of the Prussian ministers labored in the same spirit. A military force was created, chiefly by the labors of Scharnhorst,

and the limitation of the Prussian army by Napoleon was in great part evaded. Everything was done to create a people, and to have ready the moral and material means from which to create an army, should circumstances arise under which Prussia might think it safe for her to act. Hardenberg did not go so far as Stein would have gone, but it is probable that he acted wisely ; for very strong measures might have brought Napoleon's hand upon him. As it was, the Emperor could not complain of measures that breathed the very spirit of the French Revolution, of which he was the impersonation and the champion, — or claimed to be.

But all the labors of Stein, and those other Prussian patriots who acted with him or followed in his footsteps, would have been of no avail, had not Napoleon afforded them an opportunity to turn their labors to account. They might have elevated the people, have accumulated money, have massed munitions, and have drilled the entire male population to the business and work of war, till they should have surpassed all that is told of Roman discipline and efficiency ; but all such exertions would have been utterly thrown away had the French Emperor behaved like a rational being, and not sought to illustrate his famous dogma, that the impossible has no existence, by seeking to achieve impossibilities. At the

---

* Stein was one of those eminent men who have acted as if they thought coarseness bordering upon brutality an evidence of independence of spirit and greatness of soul. He was uncivil to those beneath him, not civil to those above him, and insulting to his equals. He addressed the King of Prussia in language that no gentleman ever employs, and he berated his underlings in a style that even President Johnson might despair of equalling. He hated the Duke of Dalberg, on both public and private accounts ; and when the Duke was one of the French Ambassadors at Vienna, in time of the Congress, he offered to call on the Baron. "Tell him," said Stein, "that, if he visits me as French Ambassador, he shall be well received ; but if he comes as a private person, he shall be kicked down stairs." Niebuhr, the historian, once told him that he (Stein) hated a certain personage. "Hate him? No," said Stein : "but I would spit in his face were I to meet him on the street." This readiness to convert the human face into a spittoon shows that he was qualified to represent a Southern district in our Congress ; for what Stein said he would do was done by Mr. Plummer of Mississippi, who spat in the face of Mr.

Slade of Vermont, — the American democrat, who probably never had heard of his grandfather, getting a little beyond the German aristocrat, who could trace his ancestors back through six or seven centuries. Thus do extremes meet. In talents, in energy, in audacity, in arrogance, in firmness of will, and in unbending devotion to one great and leading purpose, Count von Bismark bears a strong resemblance to Baron von Stein, upon whom he seems to have modelled himself, — while Austrian ascendency in Germany was to him what French ascendency in that country was to his prototype, only not so productive of furious hatred, because the supremacy of Austria was offensive politically, and not personally annoying, like that of France ; but Bismark, though sufficiently demonstrative in the expression of his sentiments, has never outraged propriety to the extent that it was outraged by Stein. Stein died in 1831, having lived long enough to see in the French Revolution of 1830 that a portion of his work had been done in vain. His Prussian work will endure forever, and be felt throughout the world.

beginning of 1812, Napoleon was literally invincible. He was master of all Continental Europe, from the Atlantic to the Niemen, and from Cape North to Reggio. There was not a sovereign in that part of the world, from the kings of Sweden and Denmark to the Emperor of Austria and the Turkish Sultan, who did not wear crowns and wield sceptres only because the sometime General Bonaparte was willing they should wear and wield the emblems of imperial or royal power. He was at war only with Great Britain, and Spain, Portugal, and Sicily; and Great Britain was the sole enemy he was bound to respect. All the more enlightened Spaniards were all but ready to acknowledge the rule of his brother Joseph, and would have done so but for French failure in the Russian war. England's army could have been driven from the Peninsula with ease, had a third of the men who were worse than wasted in Russia been directed thither in the early spring of 1812. The Bourbons of Sicily hated their English protectors so bitterly, that they were ready to unite with the French to get up a modern imitation of the Sicilian Vespers at their expense. The war might soon have been confined to the ocean, and there it would have been fought for France principally by Americans, as the United States were soon to declare war against England. Never before was man so strong as Napoleon on New-Year's day, 1812; and in less than four years he was living in lodgings, and bad lodgings too, in St. Helena! What hope could the Prussians have, a month before the march to Moscow was resolved upon? None that could encourage them. Some of the more sanguine spirits, supported by general sentiment, were still of opinion that something could be effected; but the larger number of intelligent men were very despondent, and not a few of them began to think of the world beyond the Atlantic, as English patriots had thought almost two centuries earlier, when that "blood and iron man,"

Wentworth (Strafford), was developing his system of *Thorough* with a precision and an energy that even Count Bismark has never surpassed. The bolder Prussians, when their country had to choose between resistance to Napoleon and an alliance with him against Russia, were for resistance, and would have placed their country right across the Emperor's path, and fought out the battle with him, and abided the consequences, which would have been the annihilation of Prussia in a sixth part of the time that Mr. Seward allotted for the duration of the Secession war. The Prussian war party would have had the Russians advance into their country, and thus have staked the issue on just such a contest as occurred in 1806–7. Napoleon, it is at least believed, was desirous that Prussia should join Russia, as that would have enabled him to defeat his enemies without crossing the Russian frontier, and have afforded him an excuse for destroying Prussia. To prevent so untimely a display of resistance to French ascendency was the aim of a few Prussians, headed by the king himself, who became very unpopular in consequence. Fortunately for Prussia, they were successful, and the means employed deceived not only the patriotic party, but even Napoleon, who was completely imposed upon by the report of the Baron von dem Knesebeck against a war between Russia and France. The story belongs to the romance of history; but it is too long, because involving many facts, to be told here.

Prussia was prevented from "throwing herself into the arms of Russia," much to the disgust of Scharnhorst and his friends. She even assisted Napoleon in his war against Alexander, and sent a contingent to the Grand Army, which formed the tenth corps of that memorable force, and was commanded by Marshal Macdonald. It consisted of twenty-six thousand men, including one French infantry division, — the Prussians being generally estimated at twenty thousand men. This corps did very little during the campaign, and soon after the failure of the French it went over to the Russians, taking the first step in that course which made Prussia so formidable a member of the Grand Alliance of 1813–15. But even so late as the close of May, 1813, Prussia was in danger of annihilation, and would have been annihilated had not Napoleon proffered an armistice, which was accepted, — the greatest.blunder of his career, according to some eminent critics, as well political as military.

The leading part which Prussia had in the Liberation War and in the first overthrow of Napoleon caused her to be reconstructed by the Congress of Vienna; and her part in the war of 1815 confirmed the impression she had made on the world. Waterloo was as much a Prussian as an English victory, — the loss of the Prussians in that action being about as great as the purely English loss.* She became one of the Five Powers which by common consent were rulers of Europe. Down to 1830 she had more influence than

France, and from 1830 to the re-establishment of the Napoleonic dynasty, she was France's equal; and even after Napoleon III. had replaced France at the head of Europe, Prussia was the only member of the Pentarchy which had not been humiliated by his blows, or yet more by his assistance. England has suffered from her connection with him, — a connection difficult on many occasions to distinguish from inferiority and subserviency; and in war the old superiority of the French armies to those of Russia and Austria has been asserted in the Crimea and in Italy. Prussia alone has not stooped before the avenger of the man whom she had so vindictive a part in overthrowing, and whom her military chief purposed having slain on the very spot where the Duc d'Enghien had been put to death by his (Napoleon's) orders. Of all the enemies of Napoleon and France in 1815, Prussia was the most malignant, or rather she was the only member of the Alliance which exhibited malignity.* She would have had

* The Prussian loss in the battle of Waterloo was 6,998: the *British* loss, 6,935; — but this does not include the Germans, Dutch, and Belgians who fell on the field or were put down among the missing. Wellington's total loss was about 16,000. The number of Prussians present in the battle was much more than twice the number of Britons. The number of the latter was 23,991, with 78 guns; of the former, 51,944, with 104 guns. Almost 16,000 of the Prussians were engaged some hours before the event of the battle was decided; almost 30,000 two hours before that decision; and the remainder an hour before the Allied victory was secured. It shows how seriously the French were damaged by Prussian intervention, that Napoleon had to detach, from the army that he had intended to employ against Wellington only, 27 battalions of infantry (including 11 battalions of the Guard), 18 squadrons of cavalry, and 66 guns, making a total of about 18,000 men, or about a fourth part of his force and almost a third of his artillery. This subtraction from the army that ought to have been used in fighting Wellington would alone have sufficed gravely to compromise the French; and it is well known that Napoleon felt the want of men to send against the English long before the conflict was over; and this want was the consequence of the pressure of the Prussians on his right flank, threatening to establish themselves in his rear. But this was not all the aid derived by Wellington from the Prussian advance. It was the arrival of a portion of Zieten's corps on the field of Waterloo that enabled the British commander to withdraw from his left the comparatively untouched cavalry brigades of Vivian and Vandeleur, and to station them in or near the centre of his line, where they were of the greatest

use at the very "crisis" of the battle, — Vivian, in particular, doing as much as was done by any one of Wellington's officers to secure victory for his commander. The Prussians followed the flying French for hours, and had the satisfaction of giving the final blow to Napoleonism for that time. It has risen again.

* No one who is not familiar with the correspondence of the Allied commanders in 1815 can form an adequate idea of the ferocity which then characterized the Prussian officers. On the 27th of June General von Gneisenau, writing for Blücher, declared that Napoleon must be delivered over to the Prussians, "with a view to his execution." That, he argued, was what eternal justice demanded, and what the Declaration of March 13th decided, — alluding to the Declaration against Napoleon published by the Congress of Vienna, which, he said, and fairly enough too, put him under outlawry by the Allied powers. Doing the Duke of Wellington the justice to suppose he would be averse to hangman's work, Gneisenau, who stood next to Blücher in the Prussian service as well as in Prussian estimation, expressed his leader's readiness to free him from all responsibility in the matter by taking possession of Napoleon's person himself, and detailing the intended assassins from his own army. Wellington was astonished at such language from gentlemen, and so exerted himself that Blücher changed his mind; whereupon Gneisenau wrote that it had been Blücher's "intention to execute [murder?] Bonaparte on the spot where the Duc d'Enghien was shot; that out of deference, however, to the Duke's wishes, he will abstain from this measure; but that the Duke must take on himself the respon-

France partitioned, and failed in her design only because openly opposed by Russia and England, while Austria, fearing to offend German opinion, secretly supported the Czar and Wellington. Blücher, an earnest man, was never more in earnest than when he purposed to shoot Napoleon in the ditch of Vincennes ; and it required all Wellington's influence to dissuade him from so barbarous a proceeding. Yet Napoleon III. has never been able to avenge these injuries and insults, — to say nothing of Waterloo, and of the massacre of the flying French in the night after the battle, or of the shocking conduct of the Prussians in France in 1815 ; and the events of the current year would seem to favor, and that strongly, the opinion of those persons who say that France never will be able to obtain her long-thought-of revenge. Certainly, if *Prussia* was safe, Prussia with most of Germany to back her cannot be in any serious danger of being forced to drink of that cup of humiliation which Napoleon III. has commended to so many countries.

After the settlement of Europe, in 1815, Prussia did not show much of that encroaching character which is attributed to her, but was one of the most quiet of nations. This was in great measure due to the character of the king. He was of the class of heavy men, and the first part of his reign had been marked by the occurrence of troubles so numerous and so great that his original dislike of change increased to fanaticism. He was one of the framers of the Holy Alliance, which grew out of the thorough fright which he and his friend the Czar felt during the saddest days of 1813. Alexander told a Prussian clergyman, named Egbert, in 1818, that, during one of their flights before Napoleon, — probably on that doleful day when they had to retreat from Dresden, amid wind and rain, and before the French reverse at Kulm had put a good face on the affairs of the Alliance, — Frederick William III. said to him : " Things cannot go on so ! we are in the direction of the east, and it is toward the west that we ought to march, that we must march. We shall, God willing, arrive there. And if, as I trust, he should bless our united efforts, we will proclaim in the face of Heaven our conviction that to Him alone belongs the honor." Thereupon, continued the Czar, " We promised, and exchanged a pressure of hands upon it with sincerity." Both monarchs evidently thought they had succeeded in bribing Heaven ; for Alexander told his reverend hearer that great victories soon

---

sibility of its non-enforcement." In another letter he wrote : " When the Duke of Wellington declares himself against the execution of Bonaparte, he thinks and acts in the matter as a Briton. Great Britain is under weightier obligations to no mortal man than to this very villain ; for, by the occurrences whereof he is the author, her greatness, prosperity, and wealth have attained their present elevation. The English are the masters of the seas, and have no longer to fear any rivalry, either in this dominion or the commerce of the world. It is quite otherwise with us Prussians. We have been impoverished by him. Our nobility will never be able to right itself again." There is much of the *perfide Albion* nonsense in this. In a letter which Gneisenau, in 1817, wrote to Sir Hudson Lowe, then Governor of St. Helena, he said : " Mille et mille fois j'ai porté mes souvenirs dans cette vaste solitude de l'océan, et sur ce rocher interessant sur lequel vous êtes le gardien du repos public de l'Europe. De votre vigilance et de votre force de caractère dépend notre salut ; dès que vous vous relâchez de vos mesures de rigueur contre *le plus vil scélérat du monde*, dès que vous permettriez à vos subalternes de lui accorder par une pitié mal entendue des faveurs, notre repos serait compromis, et les honnêtes gens en Europe s'aban-

donneraient à leurs anciennes inquiétudes." An amusing instance of his prejudice occurs in another part of the same letter, where he says : " Le fameux manuscrit de Ste. Hélène a fait une sensation scandaleuse et dangereuse en Europe, surtout en France, où, quoiqu'il ait été supprimé, il a été lu dans toutes les coteries de Paris, et où même les femmes, au lieu de coucher avec leurs amants, ont employé leurs nuits à le copier." Gneisenau was in this country in his youth, — one of those Hessians who were bought by George III. to murder Americans who would not submit to his crazy tyranny. That was an excellent school in which to learn the creed of assassins ; for there was not a Hessian in the British service who was not as much a bravo as any ruffian in Italy who ever sold his stiletto's service to some cowardly vengeance-seeker. It ought, in justice, to be added, that Sir Walter Scott states that in 1816 "there existed a considerable party in Britain who were of opinion that the British government would best have discharged their duty to France and Europe by delivering up Napoleon to Louis XVIII.'s government, to be treated as he himself had treated the Duc d'Enghien." So that the Continent did not monopolize the assassins of that time.

came ; "and," said he, "when we had arrived in Paris, we had reached the end of our painful course. The king of Prussia reminded me of the holy resolution of which he had entertained the first idea ; and Francis II., who had shared our views, our opinions, and our tendencies, entered willingly into the association." Such was Alexander's account of the origin of that famous league which so perplexed and alarmed our fathers. It differs from the commonly received belief as to its origin, which is, that it was the work of Alexander himself, who was inspired by Madame de Krudener, who, having "played the devil and written a novel," — she was unfaithful to her marriage vow, and wrote "Valerio," — naturally became devout as old age approached. It makes somewhat against the Czar's story, that the Holy Alliance was not formed till the autumn of 1815, and that he and Frederick William arrived at Paris in the spring of 1814 ; and that in the interval he and Francis II. came very near going to war on the Polish question. Alexander was crack-brained, and a mystic, and it is far more likely that he should have originated the Holy Alliance than that the idea should have proceeded from so wooden - headed a personage as the Prussian king, who had about as much sentiment as a Memel log. Alexander was always haunted by the thought that he had consented to the death of his father, — that, as a Greek would have said, he was pursued by the Furies ; and he was constantly thinking of expiation, and seeking to propitiate the Deity, and that by means not much different in spirit from those to which savages have resort. There was much of that Tartar in him which, according to Napoleon, you will always find when you scratch a Russian.

Whether Frederick William III. suggested the Holy Alliance may be doubted ; but there can be no doubt that he lived thoroughly up to its spirit, which was the spirit of intense absolutism. He broke every promise he had made to his people when he need-

ed their aid to keep his kingdom out of the grasp of Napoleon. He became the vindictive persecutor of the men who had led his subjects in the war to rush to arms, without counting the odds they had to encounter at first. He was a despot of the old pattern, as far as a sovereign of the nineteenth century could be one. It does not appear that he acted thus from love of power for its own sake, to which so much of tyrannical action is due. In most respects he was rather a favorable specimen of the despot. His action was the consequence of circumstances, the effect of experience. He had had two or three thorough frights, and twice he had been in danger of losing his crown, and of seeing the extinction of that nation which his ancestors had been at such pains to create. If exertions of his could prevent the recurrence of such evils, they should not be wanting. As Charles II., after the Restoration of 1660, had firmly resolved on one thing, namely, that, come what would, he would not again go upon his travels, so had Frederick William III., after the restoration of his kingdom, firmly resolved that, happen what might, he would have no more wars, and that, if he could, he would keep out of politics. So he maintained peace, and kept down the politicians. Prussia flourished marvellously during the last twenty - five years of his reign ; and, judging from results, his government could not have been a bad one. Under it was created that people whose recent action has astonished the world, and produced for it a new sensation. A comprehensive system of education opened the paths to knowledge to every one ; and a not less comprehensive military system made every healthy man's services available to the state. There never before took the field so highly educated a force as that which has just reduced Count Bismark's policy to practice, — not even in America. There may have been as intelligent armies in the Union's service during our civil conflict as those which obeyed Prince Frederick Charles and the Crown

Prince of Prussia, but as highly educated most certainly they were not.

When Friedrich von Raumer was in England, in 1835, he, at an English dinner, gave this toast: "The King of Prussia, the greatest and best reformer in Europe." That he was the "best reformer in Europe," we will not insist upon, — but that he was the greatest reformer there, we have no doubt whatever. That he was a reformer at heart, originally, no one would pretend who knows his history. He was made one by stress of circumstances. But having become a reformer, he did a great work, as contemporary history shows. He would have been content to live, and reign, and die, sovereign of just such a Prussia as he found in 1797; but, in spite of himself, he was made to effect a mightier revolution than even a French revolutionist of 1793 would have deemed it possible to accomplish. His career is the liveliest illustration that we know of the doctrine that men are the sport of circumstances.

Frederick William III. died in 1840. His son and successor, Frederick William IV., was a man of considerable ability and a rare scholar; but he was not up to his work, the more so that the age of revolutions appeared again early in his reign. He might have made himself master of all Germany in 1848, but had not the courage to act as a Prussian sovereign should have acted. He was elected Emperor by the revolutionary Diet at Frankfort, but refused the crown. A little later, under the inspiration of General Radowitz, he took up such a position as we have seen his successor fill so effectively. War with Austria seemed close at hand, and the unity of Germany might have been brought about sixteen years since had the Prussian monarch been equal to the crisis. As it was, he "backed down," and Radowitz, who was a too-early Bismark, left his place, and died at the close of 1853. The king lost his mind in 1857; and his brother William became Regent, and succeeded to the throne in 1861, on the death of Frederick William IV.

The reign of William I. will be regarded as one of the most remarkable in Prussian history. Though an old man when he took the crown, William I. has advanced the greatness of Prussia even more than it was advanced by Frederick II. His course with regard to the Danish Duchies has called forth many indignant remarks; but it is no worse than that of most other sovereigns, and stones cannot fairly be cast at him by many ruling hands. Count Bismark has been the chief minister of Prussia under William I., and to him must be attributed that policy which has carried his country, *per saltum*, to the highest place among the nations. He long since came to the conclusion that nothing could be done for Germany, by Germany and in Germany, till Austria should be thrust out of Germany. He was right; and he has labored to accomplish the dismissal of Austria, with a perseverance and a persistency that it would be difficult to parallel. He alone has done the deed. Had he died last May, there would have been no war in Europe this year; for nothing less than his redoubtable courage and iron will could have overcome the obstacles that existed to the commencement of the conflict.

THE SONG SPARROW.

CAN you hear the sparrow in the lane
    Singing above the graves ? she said.
He knows my gladness, he knows my pain,
    Though spring be over and summer be dead.

His note hath a chime all cannot hear,
    And none can love him better than I ;
For he sings to me when the land is drear,
    And makes it cheerful even to die.

'T is beautiful on this odorous morn,
    When grasses are waving in every wind,
To know my bird is not forlorn,
    That summer to him is also kind ; —

But sweeter, when grasses no longer stir,
    And every lilac-leaf is shed,
To know that my voiceful worshipper
    Is singing above my voiceless dead.

INVALIDISM.

ONE of the first tendencies of sickness is to centralization. Every invalid at least begins by being pivotal in the household. But with the earliest hint that the case is chronic, things recoil to their own centres again ; people begin to come and go in the gayest way ; they laugh and eat immensely, and fly through the halls asking if one could n't take a bit of stuffed veal. And while one still sinks lower, failing down to the verge of the grave, it is only to hear of the most cherished friends in another town leading the whirl with tableaux and private theatricals. Finally is realized the dire *dénouément*, that, though one lay with breath flickering away, the daily grocer would come driving up without any velvet on his wheels or any softness in his voice, and that the whole routine of affairs is to proceed, whoever goes or stays. This cold-heartedness it seems will kill one at any rate. Rather the universe should sigh and be darkened. To pass unheeded is worse than to die. Just now it is impossible to compass even the satirical mood of Pope, who declared himself not at all uneasy that many men for whom he never had any esteem were likely to enjoy the world after him. But before one has time to die, the absent friends write such a kind, sorry letter, in which they do not say anything about private theatricals, and, as Thad Stevens said of that speech, one knows of course that it was all a hoax ! Then the people who eat stuffed veal repent themselves, and send in a delicate broth or a bit of tenderloin, hovering softly in a sudden regard, and at length a healthier thought is born. It is to arise with desperate will, put a fresh rose in the bonnet and a delusive veil over the face, creeping down to the street with what steadiness can be summoned. There one meets friends, and is pretty well, with thanks, and is congratulated. Affairs grow brilliant, but the veil never comes up; underneath there is some one forty years old and an invalid. Having thus moved against the enemy's works, it is best to retire upon what spirit there is left. It is after this sally that, when the landlady hears a hammering of a Sunday, she comes directly to the room of this robust person, who is obliged to confess that, even if so inclined, she has not strength enough to break the Sabbath.

But the anxiety of every one to show some friendliness to a sufferer is only equalled by the usual inability. We all read of that Union soldier in the hospital visited by an elderly woman bound to do something when there was nothing to be done, and who finally succeeded in bathing the patient's face, while he, poor fellow, still struggling in the folds of the towel, was heard to exclaim, " That 's the fourteenth time I 've had my face washed to-day!"

Far more unobtrusive is the benevolence which goes into one's kitchen, sending thence to the sick-room those dainties which, after all, are so much too good to be eaten. It seems to be taken for granted that sick persons eat a great deal, and that most of them might share the experiment of Matthews, who began the diary of an invalid and ended with that of a gourmand. I fear that these kindly geniuses would sometimes feel a twinge of chagrin at seeing their elaborate delicacies in process of being devoured by the most rubicund people in the house. But it matters not ; it is the sending and getting that are the dainties. Amid all these niceties, however, the office of nurse might certainly be made a sinecure ; and just at this point her labors are really quite arduous ; for any invalid blessed with many favoring friends soon would sink under the care of crockery and baskets to be properly delivered, while to attend to the accompanying napkins is little less than to preside over a small laundry.

And then, as every one tastefully sends her choicest wares to enhance their contents, the invalid also finds that she is the keeper of all the best dishes of the best families.

There is nothing like a well-fought resistance in the early stages of invalidism. Keep up the will, and if need be the temper. There are times when to grow heavenly is fatal, — when one is to let the soul run loose, and to gather up the gritty determination of Sarah, Duchess of Marlborough, who, when told that she must be blistered or die, exclaimed, " I won't be blistered, and I won't die!" Indeed, it is often necessary to reverse the decision of the doctor who gives one up, and simply end by giving him up. The numbers are untold who have died solely from being given up, — I do not mean of the doctors. Poor, timid mortals ! they only heard the words, and meekly folded their hands and went. On the other side, there is no end to the people who have been given up all through their lives, and who have utterly refused to depart. They have a kind of useless toughness which prevents them from dying, without endowing them to live. These animated relics often show no special fitness for either world, and they are not even ornamental.

I have somewhere seen the invalid enjoined to talk as if well, but treat himself as if ill. And to certain temperaments a little of this diplomacy, or secretiveness, is often very important. Once an admitted invalid, and the dikes are down. Then begin to pour in all sorts of worthy, but alarming and indiscreet persons, — they who accost one in the street declaring one is so changed, and does n't look fit to be out, — they who invidiously inquire if you take any solid food, as if one walked the world on water-gruel, — they who come to try to make you comfortable while you *do* live. All these are very kind, but to a sanguine person they are crushing.

We are all aware that there is no surer way to produce a given state of mind or body, than to constantly address the victim as if he were in that state. It is a familiar fact that a stout yeoman once went home pale and discomfited from a little conspiracy of several wags remarking how very ill he looked; and that another, who was blindfolded, having water poured over his arm as if being bled, finally died from loss of blood without losing a drop; and Sir Humphrey Davy mentions one wishing to take nitrous oxide gas, to whom common atmospheric air was given, with the result of syncope. And if the well can be thus wrought on, what can be expected of the weak? This habit of depressing remark comes possibly from the feeling that invalids like to magnify their woes, ailments being regarded as their "sensation," or stock in trade. True, there is now and then one made happier by hearing that he seems exceedingly miserable; but it is more natural to brighten with pleasant words, and a morning compliment of good looks will often set one up for the day. Indeed, we fancy that most persons, knowing their disease, in their own minds, prefer that it should chiefly rest there. To discuss seems only to define it more sharply, and to be greatly condoled is only debilitating. Montaigne, to avoid death-bed sympathies, desired to die on horseback; while against the eternal repeating of these ills for pity, he says that "the man who makes himself dead when living is likely to be held as though alive when he is dying."

Likewise the friendliness which keeps reminding one of the fatal end serves none. It is both impolitic and impolite; as if there were an unsightly mole upon the face, and every visitor remarked, as he entered, "Ah, I see you still have that ugly mole!" With all these comforters it is finally better to do without their devotions than to be subjected to their discouragements. How much Pope resented this rude style of criticism may be seen from his tart exclamation, "They all say 't is pity I am so sickly, and I think 't is pity they are so healthy."

Yet that incurable sufferer, Harriet

Martineau, testifies that when a friend said to her, with the face of an angel, "Why should we be bent upon your being better, and make up a bright prospect for you? I see no brightness in it; and the time seems past for expecting you ever to be well," — her spirits rose at once with the sturdy recognition of the truth. And Dr. Henry, with the same directness, wrote to his friend, "Come out to me next week; I have got something important to do, — I have got to die."

This must surely be called the heroic treatment; but for those who are not equal to such, it is good to have a physician of tact, who shall not doom them regularly every day. Plato said that physicians were the only men who might lie at pleasure, since our health depends upon the vanity and falsity of their promises. And yet one is not usually deceived by this flattery; but it is vastly more comfortable to hear pleasant things instead of gloomy, and the sick would rather prefer a dance to a dirge. Of this amiable sort must have been the attendant who caused Pope to say, "Ah, my dear friend, I am dying every day of a hundred good symptoms"; and still more charming the adviser chosen by Molière, who, when asked by Louis XIV., himself a slave to medicine, what he did about a doctor, said, "O sire, when I am ill, I send for him. He comes; we have a chat and enjoy ourselves. He prescribes; I don't take it, — I am cured."

Perhaps few are aware of the various heroisms of the chronic patient. It must have been prophetic that the Mexicans of olden time thus saluted their new-born babes : "Child, thou art come into the world to endure, suffer, and say nothing." It is grand to be upborne by a spirit unperturbed, although flesh and nerve may strike through the best soul for a moment; even as the great and equable Longinus, on his way to execution, is said to have turned pale and halted for an instant; while we all know, that, after the Stuart rebellion, the rough old Duke

Balmoral, a lesser man, never faltered, but, with boisterous courage, cried out for the fatal axe to be carried by his side.

We had been used to think Andrew Jackson an iron-built conqueror, who never knew a pain, until Parton told of the violent cramp which would seize him while marching at the head of his army, when he simply threw himself over a bent sapling in the forest till the spasm subsided, and marched on. The same endurance nerved him to the end. For many of his last years not free for one hour from pain, he still sat at the White House, never intermitting any duty, although the mere signing of his name drew its witness of suffering from every pore. It is with sorrow, too, that we have lately read that the beloved Florence Nightingale has been held by disease, not only to her room, but to a single position in it, for a whole year. And one of our own poets, even dearer to his friends for the sainthood of suffering, still ever is pressing on with tuneful courage. Hear him singing,

"Who hath not learned in hours of faith
The truth, to flesh and sense unknown,
That Life is ever lord of Death,
And Love can never lose its own ? "

Named among the valiant, yet more sad than heroic, was poor Heine on his " mattress-grave." Most pathetically did he lay himself down, this " soldier in the war for the liberation of humanity." Of the last time that Heine left the house before yielding to disease, he says : " With difficulty I dragged myself to the Louvre, and almost sank down as I entered the magnificent hall where the ever-blessed goddess of beauty, our beloved Lady of Milo, stands on her pedestal. At her feet I lay long, and wept so bitterly that a stone must have pitied me. The goddess looked compassionately on me, but at the same time disconsolately, as if she would say, ' Dost thou not see that I have no arms, and thus cannot help thee ? ' "

Not less touching was the pathos of Tom Hood, in his long years of consumption ; but the tone was gayer than the gayest. See him write to a friend : " My dear Johnny, are n't you glad to hear now that I 've only been ill and spitting blood three times since I left you, instead of being very dead indeed ? " To this he adds : " But was n't I in luck, after spitting blood and being bled, to catch the rheumatism in going down stairs ! "

One long struggle was his against prostration and overwork ; but always the same buoyant wit, — writing the cheeriest things with an ebbing life ; the hero fighting against fatal odds, but always under a light mask, — and ridiculing himself most of all : —

" I 'm sick of gruel and the dietetics ;
I 'm sick of pills and sicker of emetics ;
I 'm sick of pulse's tardiness or quickness ;
I 'm sick of blood, its thinness or its thickness ;
In short, within a word, I 'm sick of sickness."

And others there be, not heroes, who yet have simulated heroism in their blithe indifference to fate ; — Lord Buckhurst, who is said to have " stuttered more wit in dying than most people have in their best health "; Wycherley, who took a young bride just before death, and was "neither afraid of dying nor ashamed of marrying " ; Chesterfield, who in his last days, when going out for a London drive, used smilingly to say, " I must go and rehearse my funeral " ; Pope, who was the victim of incessant disease, which yet never subdued his rhetoric ; Scarron, a paralytic and a monstrosity, the merriest man in France, for whom the nation never gave any tears but those of laughter ; — all these, down to the easy-minded old Dr. Garth, who died simply because he was tired of life, — " tired of having his shoes pulled on and off."

Strong persons go swinging securely up and down ; they are the people of affairs, their nerves are not shaken by anything less than cholera reports ; saving these, they should belong to the Great Unterrified of the earth. To them it is hardly given to understand those minute annoyances that beset nerves which are in an abnormal state, especially when one is the prisoner of a single room. Then one is eternally busy with the dust and small disorders around, — the film on the mirror, the lint-drifts under the stove, the huge cobwebs flying from the corners, the knickknacks awry on the mantel-piece; then one finds the wall-paper is not hung true, and gazes at flaws in the ceiling till they grow into dancing-jacks, and hears the doors that slam, like the shock of a cannon. These are torments so minute that there seems no virtue even in bearing them. Ah! to mount to execution for an idea, — that were glorious and sustaining; but to endure the daily burden of these petty tortures, — one never hears the music play then.

Among the articles to be desired of science is a false hand, or a spectral arm, that shall reach miraculously about, — not a fruit-picker or a carpet-sweeper, but something working with the fineness of an elephant's trunk, — thus to end the discomfort of those orange-seeds spilled on the far side of the room, while, lying inactive, one reaches, reaches, with a patient power which, if transformed into the practical, would push an army through Austria.

Another thing that the invalid has to endure is from the thoughtlessness of visitors. How often, when summoned from the sick-room for any purpose, do they briskly remark, in Tom Thumb style, " I 'll be back in a very few minutes!" Hence one lies awake by force, keeping several errands to be despatched on the return, changing variously all the little plans for the next hour or two, and waits. My experience generally is that they have not come back yet.

But the commonest experience is when life itself seems to hang on the arrival of the doctor. Indeed, it is safe to say that never have lovers been so waited for as the doctor. Was n't that his carriage at the door? Medicine is out! new symptoms appear! it is only an hour to bedtime! and, oh! will the doctor come, do you think? One listens more intently; but now there are no carriages. There are express-wag-

ons, late ice-carts, out-of-town stages, or here and there a light rolling buggy, that seems running on to the end of the world. There are but few foot-passengers either, and they all go by without halting, and there is no indication in the steps of any man of them that he would be the doctor if he could. Thus one wears through the night uncomforted, yet one does not usually die. I have also seen the doctors sitting in their offices expectant, and probably quite as much distressed that every one went by without stopping. So the balances are kept.

The foregoing grievances are often put among the foolish humors of invalids, but they are quite reasonable compared with many of the droll fancies on record. Take the instance of the elderly man who had been dying suddenly for twenty years; whose last moments would probably amount to a calendar month, and his farewell words to an octavo volume. His physician he pronounced a clever man, but added, pitifully, " I only wish he would agree to my going suddenly; I should not die a bit sooner for his giving me over." It is evident the physician had not the shrewdest insight, or he would have granted this heady maniac his way. " Ah!" would exclaim the constantly departing patient, "all one's nourishment goes for nothing if once sudden death has got insidiously into the system!" More famous were Johnson with his inevitable dried orange-peel, and Byron with his salts. Goethe, too, after renouncing his Lotte, coquetted with the idea of death, every night placing a very handsome dagger by his bed and making sundry attempts to push the point a couple of inches into his breast. Not being able to do this comfortably, he concluded to live. Years after, when he sat assured on his grand poet throne, he must have smiled at it, as with Karl August he " talked of lovely things that conquer death." And still more refined and genuine was the vapor of the imaginative young girl who died of love for the Apollo Belvedere.

Yet it is but fair to mention that the laugh is not all on this side. It is an historical fact that the public has its medical freaks, without being called an invalid, and that whole nations "go daft" on the shallowest impositions. At one time the English were made to believe that all diseases were caused by the contraction of one small muscle of the body; at another, Parliament itself helped make up the five thousand pounds given by the aristocracy to one Joanna Stephens for an omnipotent powder, decoction, and pills, composed chiefly of egg-shells and snail-shells; at another time every one drank snail-water for everything, or to prevent it, and then tar-water became the rage. In Paris the Royal Academy once procured the prohibition of the sale of antimony, on penalty of death, and in a year or two prescribed it as the great panacea. Pliny reports that the Arcadians cured all manner of ills with the milk of a cow (one would like to see them manage the bilious colic).

Mesmer, who was luminous for a while, did not fail to dupe the people. When asked why he ordered bathing in river instead of spring water, he said, "Because it is warmed by the sun."

"True, yet not so much but it has to be warmed still more."

Not posed in the least, Mesmer replied, "The reason why the water which is exposed to the rays of the sun is superior to all other water is because it is magnetized. I myself magnetized the sun some twenty years ago!"

Yet the name of Mesmer has founded a system, while that of Dumoulin, who, with simple wisdom, observed, on dying, that he left behind him two great physicians, Regimen and River-water, has gained but a scanty fame.

Says Boswell, "At least be well if you are not ill"; but the dear public is always ill. In our own country, with an apparently healthy pulse, it has drank the worth of a marble palace in sarsaparilla, and has built a hotel out of Brandreth's pills. It has fairly reeled on Schiedam Schnapps; and even the infant has his little popularities, having passed from catnip and caraway to Mrs. Winslow's Soothing Syrup. There is never a time when the public will not declare upon any well-advertised remedy its belief in the motto of the German doctors, "We do cure everything but death."

It is often interesting to note the various phases which invalidism takes on. Sometimes one seems folded in a dense dream, — has gone away almost beyond one's own pity, and has not been heard from for months. It is to be hoped that friends who hunt "the greyhound and turtle-dove" will meet the missing, and duly report. Meantime one resides in a mummified state, — a dim thinkingness that may be discovered when another coming in says with vigor the thing one had long thought without quite knowing it; in this demi-semi-consciousness it had never pecked through the shell. This looks very imbecile, and is charitably treated to be only called invalid.

Is it mere helplessness that one lies so remote from all but surface sensation, day after day gazing at the address of letters that come, with a passive wonder of how soon she is to vacate her name? Also a friend calls to say that to-morrow he travels afar. It seems then that he will be too much missed, and the parting has its share of unutterable longing. But by the morrow it is not the one self who is sorry. The new sun shines on an earth miles off from yesterday. The night has given many windings more in the folds of this resigned mummy, that now lies securely as an insect in a leaf. Given the beloved hand, and all things may go as they will.

> "Our hands in one, we will not shrink
> From life's severest due;
> Our hands in one, we will not blink
> The terrible and true."

And sometimes one bounds to the other side of sensation, — has a terrible rubbed-the-wrong-wayedness, and is as much alive as Mimosa herself. This is often on those easterly days which all well-regulated invalids shudder at, when the very marrow congeals and the nerves are sharp-whetted. Then, Prometheus-like, one "gnaws the heart with meditation"; then, too, always fall out various domestic disasters, and it is not easy to see why the curtain-string should be tied in a hard knot that must be cut at night, or why the servants can't be thorough, deft-handed, and immaculate. One has indigestion, scowls fiercely, tries to swallow large lumps of inamiability, and fears she is not sublime.

It is a saying of Jean Paul, that "the most painful part of corporeal pain is the uncorporeal, namely, our impatience and disappointment that it continues." Whether this be true or not, what with the worry and constant pressure, these physical disabilities often appear to sink into the deepest centre of the being. Hence, if one have had a cough for a very long time, it would seem that the soul must keep on coughing in the next world. If so, this gives a subtile sense to the despatches of departed spiritualists, who telegraph back in a few weeks that their pain is *nearly* gone, — as if the soul were not immediately rid of the bad habits of the body.

But most demoralized in æsthetic sense must be that invalid who does not constantly look to the splendid robustness of health. Sickness has been termed an early old age; far worse, it is often a tossing nightmare in which the noble ideal of fairer days is only recalled with reproachful pain. Towards this vision of vigor the victim seems to move and move, but never draw near. Well might Heine weep, even before the stricken Lady of Milo. An old proverb says, that "the gods have health in essence, sickness only in intelligence." Blessed are the gods! One can quite understand the reckless exulting of some wild character, who, baffled with this miserable mendicancy everywhere, at length discovered the idea that God was not an invalid. He was probably too much excited to perfect his rhyme, and so tore out these ragged lines : —

> "Iterate, iterate,
> Snatch it from the hells,
> Circulate and meditate
>   That God is well.
>
> "Get the singers to sing it,
> Put it in the mouths of bells,
> Pay the ringers to ring it,
>   That God is well." ::

Therefore make a valiant stand against that ugly thing, disease. By all Nature's remedies, hasten to be out of it. Fight it off as long as possible, defy it when you can, and refuse "to hang up your hat on the everlasting peg." Be reinforced in all honorable ways. If not too ill, read the dailies ; know the last measure of Congress, the price of gold, and the news by the foreign steamer. Disabuse the world for once of its traditional invalid, who sits mewed up in blankets, and never goes where other people go, because it might hurt him. Be out among the activities ; don't let the world get ahead, but keep along with the life of things. Then, if invalidism is to be accepted, meet it bravely and serenely as may be ; and if death, then approach it loftily, for no one dies with his work undone, and no just-minded person can wish to survive his service. None should aspire to say, with the antiquated Chesterfield, "Tyrawley and I have been dead these two years, but we don't choose to have it known."

But happy they on whom the deep blight has not fallen, and who day by day restore themselves to the grand perfection of manly and womanly estate ; happy again to "feel one's self alive " and

> "Lord of the senses five ";

happy again to "excel in animation and relish of existence "; happy to have gathered so much strength and hope, that, when begins the melody of the morning birds, again shall the joy of the new dawn, with all the possible adventure and enterprise of the coming day, thrill through the heart.

GRIFFITH GAUNT; OR, JEALOUSY.

CHAPTER XLII.

"BE seated, mistress, if you please," said Mrs. Gaunt, with icy civility, "and let me know to what I owe this extraordinary visit."

"I thank you, dame," said Mercy, "for indeed I am sore fatigued." She sat quietly down. "Why I have come to you? It was to serve you, and to keep my word with George Neville."

"Will you be kind enough to explain?" said Mrs. Gaunt, in a freezing tone, and with a look of her calm gray eye to match.

Mercy felt chilled, and was too frank to disguise it. "Alas!" said she, softly, "'t is hard to be received so, and me come all the way from Lancashire, with a heart like lead, to do my duty, God willing."

The tears stood in her eyes, and her mellow voice was sweet and patient.

The gentle remonstrance was not quite without effect. Mrs. Gaunt colored a little; she said, stiffly: "Excuse me if I seem discourteous, but you and I ought not to be in one room a moment. You do not see this, apparently. But at least I have a right to insist that such an interview shall be very brief, and to the purpose. Oblige me, then, by telling me in plain terms why you have come hither."

"Madam, to be your witness at the trial."

"*You* to be *my* witness?"

"Why not? If I can clear you? What, would you rather be condemned for murder, than let me show them you are innocent? Alas! how you hate me!"

"Hate you, child? of course I hate you. We are both of us flesh and blood, and hate one another. And one of us is honest enough, and uncivil enough, to say so."

"Speak for yourself, dame," replied Mercy, quietly, "for I hate you not; and I thank God for it. To hate is to

be miserable. I 'd liever be hated than to hate."

Mrs. Gaunt looked at her. "Your words are goodly and wise," said she; "your face is honest, and your eyes are like a very dove's. But, for all that, you hate me quietly, with all your heart. Human nature is human nature."

"'T is so. But grace is grace." She was silent a moment, then resumed: "I 'll not deny I did hate you for a time, when first I learned the man I had married had a wife, and you were she. We that be women are too unjust to each other, and too indulgent to a man. But I have worn out my hate. I wrestled in prayer, and the God of Love, he did quench my most unreasonable hate. For 't was the man betrayed me; *you* never wronged me, nor I you. But you are right, madam; 't is true that nature without grace is black as pitch. The Devil, he was busy at my ear, and whispered me, ' If the fools in Cumberland hang her, what fault o' thine? Thou wilt be his lawful wife, and thy poor, innocent child will be a child of shame no more.' But, by God's grace, I did defy him. And I do defy him." She rose swiftly from her chair, and her dove's eyes gleamed with celestial light. "Get thee behind me, Satan. I tell thee the hangman shall never have her innocent body, nor thou my soul."

The movement was so unexpected, the words and the look so simply noble, that Mrs. Gaunt rose too, and gazed upon her visitor with astonishment and respect; yet still with a dash of doubt. She thought to herself, "If this creature is not sincere, what a mistress of deceit she must be."

But Mercy Vint soon returned to her quiet self. She sat down, and said, gravely, and for the first time a little coldly, as one who had deserved well, and been received ill : "Mistress Gaunt, you are accused of murdering your husband. 'T is false ; for two days ago I saw him alive."

"What do you say ?" cried Mrs. Gaunt, trembling all over.

"Be brave, madam. You have borne great trouble : do not give way under joy. He who has wronged us both — he who wedded you under his own name of Griffith Gaunt, and me under the false name of Thomas Leicester — is no more dead than we are ; I saw him two days ago, and spoke to him, and persuaded him to come to Carlisle town, and do you justice."

Mrs. Gaunt fell on her knees. "He is alive ; he is alive. Thank God ! O, thank God ! He is alive ; and God bless the tongue that tells me so. God bless you eternally, Mercy Vint."

The tears of joy streamed down her face, and then Mercy's flowed too. She uttered a little pathetic cry of joy. "Ah," she sobbed, "the bit of comfort I needed so has come to my heavy heart. *She* has blessed me."

But she said this very softly, and Mrs. Gaunt was in a rapture, and did not hear her.

"Is it a dream ? My husband alive ? and you the one to come and tell me so ? How unjust I have been to you, Forgive me. Why does he not come himself ? "

Mercy colored at this question, and hesitated.

"Well, dame," said she, "for one thing, he has been on the fuddle for the last two months."

"On the fuddle ? "

"Ay ; he owns he has never been sober a whole day. And that takes the heart out of a man, as well as the brains. And then he has got it into his head that you will never forgive him, and that he shall be cast in prison if he shows his face in Cumberland."

"Why in Cumberland more than in Lancashire ? " asked Mrs. Gaunt, biting her lip.

Mercy blushed faintly. She replied with some delicacy, but did not altogether mince the matter.

"He knows I shall never punish him for what he has done to me."

"Why not ? I begin to think he has wronged you almost as much as he has me."

"Worse, madam ; worse. He has robbed me of my good name. You are still his lawful wife, and none can point the finger at you. But look at me. I was an honest girl, respected by all the parish. What has he made of me ? The man that lay a dying in my house, and I saved his life, and so my heart did warm to him, — he blasphemed God's altar, to deceive and betray me ; and here I am, a poor forlorn creature, neither maid, wife, nor widow ; with a child on my arms that I do nothing but cry over. Ay, my poor innocent, I left thee down below, because I was ashamed she should see thee ; ah me ! ah me !" She lifted up her voice, and wept.

Mrs. Gaunt looked at her wistfully, and, like Mercy before her, had a bitter struggle with human nature, — a struggle so sharp that, in the midst of it, she burst out crying with great violence ; but, with that burst, her great soul conquered.

She darted out of the room, leaving Mercy astonished at her abrupt departure.

Mercy was patiently drying her eyes, when the door opened, and judge her surprise when she saw Mrs. Gaunt glide into the room with her little boy asleep in her arms, and an expression upon her face more sublime than anything Mercy Vint had ever yet seen on earth. She kissed the babe softly, and, becoming infantine as well as angelic by this contact, sat herself down in a moment on the floor with him, and held out her hand to Mercy. "There," said she, "come, sit beside us, and see how I hate him, — no more than you do ; sweet innocent."

They looked him all over, discussed his every feature learnedly, kissed his limbs and extremities after the manner of their sex, and, comprehending at last that to have been both of them wronged by one man was a bond of sympathy, not hate, the two wives of Griffith Gaunt laid his child across their two laps, and wept over him together.

Mercy Vint took herself to task. " I am but a selfish woman," said she, " to talk or think of anything but that I came here for." She then proceeded to show Mrs. Gaunt by what means she proposed to secure her acquittal, without getting Griffith Gaunt into trouble.

Mrs. Gaunt listened with keen and grateful attention, until she came to that part ; then she interrupted her eagerly. " Don't spare him for me. In your place I 'd trounce the villain finely."

" Ay," said Mercy, "and then forgive him ; but I am different. I shall never forgive him ; but I am a poor hand at punishing and revenging. I always was. My name is Mercy, you know. To tell the truth, I was to have been called Prudence, after my good aunt ; but she said, nay ; she had lived to hear Greed, and Selfishness, and a heap of faults, named Prudence. ' Call the child something that means what it does mean, and not after me,' quoth she. So with me hearing ' Mercy, Mercy,' called out after me so many years, I do think the quality hath somehow got under my skin ; for I cannot abide to see folk smart, let alone to strike the blow. What, shall I take the place of God, and punish the evil-doers, because 't is me they wrong ? Nay, dame, I will never punish him, though he hath wronged me cruelly. All I shall do is to think very ill of him, and shun him, and tear his memory out of my heart. You look at me : do you think I cannot ? You don't know me ; I am very resolute when I see clear. Of course I loved him, — loved him dearly. He was like a husband to me, and a kind one. But the moment I knew how basely he had deceived us both, my heart began to turn against the man, and now 't is ice to him. Heaven knows what I am made of ; for, believe me, I 'd liever ten times be beside you than beside him. My heart it lay like a lump of lead till I heard your story, and found I could do you a good turn, — you that he

had wronged, as well as me. I read your beautiful eyes ; but nay, fear me not ; I 'm not the woman to pine for the fruit that is my neighbor's. All I ask for on earth is a few kind words and looks from you. You are gentle, and I am simple ; but we are both one flesh and blood, and your lovely wet eyes do prove it this moment. Dame Gaunt — Kate — I ne'er was ten miles from home afore, and I am come all this weary way to serve thee. O, give me the one thing that can do me good in this world, — the one thing I pine for, — a little of *your* love."

The words were scarce out of her lips, when Mrs. Gaunt caught her impetuously round the neck with both hands, and laid her on that erring but noble heart of hers, and kissed her eagerly.

They kissed one another again and again, and wept over one another.

And now Mrs. Gaunt, who did nothing by halves, could not make enough of Mercy Vint. She ordered supper, and ate with her, to make her eat. Mrs. Menteith offered Mercy a bed ; but Mrs. Gaunt said she must lie with her, she and her child.

" What," said she, " think you I 'll let you out of my sight ? Alas ! who knows when you and I shall ever be together again ? "

" I know," said Mercy, thoughtfully. " In this world, never."

They slept in one bed, and held each other by the hand all night, and talked to one another, and in the morning knew each the other's story, and each the other's mind and character, better than their oldest acquaintances knew either the one or the other.

CHAPTER XLIII.

THE trial began again ; and the court was crowded to suffocation. All eyes were bent on the prisoner. She rose, calm and quiet, and begged leave to say a few words to the court.

Mr. Whitworth objected to that. She had concluded her address yesterday, and called a witness.

Prisoner. But I have not examined a witness yet.

Judge. You come somewhat out of time, madam; but, if you will be brief, we will hear you.

Prisoner. I thank you, my lord. It was only to withdraw an error. The cry for help that was heard by the side of Hernshaw Mere, I said, yesterday, that cry was uttered by Thomas Leicester. Well, I find I was mistaken: the cry for help was uttered by my husband, — by that Griffith Gaunt I am accused of assassinating.

This extraordinary admission caused a great sensation in court. The judge looked very grave and sad; and Sergeant Wiltshire, who came into court just then, whispered his junior, "She has put the rope round her own neck. The jury would never have believed our witness."

Prisoner. I will only add, that a person came into the town last night, who knows a great deal more about this mysterious business than I do. I purpose, therefore, to alter the plan of my defence; and to save your time, my lord, who have dealt so courteously with me, I shall call but a single witness.

Ere the astonishment caused by this sudden collapse of the defence was in any degree abated, she called "Mercy Vint."

There was the usual stir and struggle; and then the calm, self-possessed face and figure of a comely young woman confronted the court. She was sworn; and examined by the prisoner after this fashion.

"Where do you live?"

"At the 'Packhorse,' near Allerton, in Lancashire."

Prisoner. Do you know Mr. Griffith Gaunt?

Mercy. Madam, I do.

Prisoner. Was he at your place in October last?

Mercy. Yes, madam, on the thirteenth of October. On that day he left for Cumberland.

Prisoner. On foot, or on horseback?

Mercy. On horseback.

Prisoner. With boots on, or shoes?

Mercy. He had a pair of new boots on.

Prisoner. Do you know Thomas Leicester?

Mercy. A pedler called at our house on the eleventh of October, and he said his name was Thomas Leicester.

Prisoner. How was he shod?

Mercy. In hobnailed shoes.

Prisoner. Which way went he on leaving you?

Mercy. Madam, he went northwards; I know no more for certain.

Prisoner. When did you see Mr. Gaunt last?

Mercy. Four days ago.

Judge. What is that? You saw him alive four days ago?

Mercy. Ay, my lord; the last Wednesday that ever was.

At this the people burst out into a loud, agitated murmur, and their heads went to and fro all the time. In vain the crier cried and threatened. The noise rose and surged, and took its course. It went down gradually, as amazement gave way to curiosity; and then there was a remarkable silence; and then the silvery voice of the prisoner, and the mellow tones of the witness, appeared to penetrate the very walls of the building, each syllable of those two beautiful speakers was heard so distinctly.

Prisoner. Be so good as to tell the court what passed on Wednesday last between Griffith Gaunt and you, relative to this charge of murder.

Mercy. I let him know one George Neville had come from Cumberland in search of him, and had told me you lay in Carlisle jail charged with his murder. I did urge him to ride at once to Carlisle, and show himself; but he refused. He made light of the matter. Then I told him not so; the circumstances looked ugly, and your life was in peril. Then he said, nay, 't was in no peril; for if you were to be found guilty, then he would show himself on the instant. Then I told him he was not worthy the name of a man, and if he would not go, I would. "Go you, by all means," said he, "and I 'll give you a writing that will clear her. Jack Houseman will be there, that knows my hand; and so does the sheriff, and half the grand jury at the least."

Prisoner. Have you that writing?

Mercy. To be sure I have. Here 't is.

Prisoner. Be pleased to read it.

Judge. Stay a minute. Shall you prove it to be his handwriting?

Prisoner. Ay, my lord, by as many as you please.

Judge. Then let that stand over for the present. Let me see it.

It was handed up to him; and he showed it to the sheriff, who said he thought it was Griffith Gaunt's writing.

The paper was then read out to the jury. It ran as follows: —

"Know all men, that I, Griffith Gaunt, Esq., of Bolton Hall and Hernshaw Castle, in the county of Cumberland, am alive and well; and the matter which has so puzzled the good folk in Cumberland befell as follows: — I left Hernshaw Castle in the dead of night upon the fifteenth of October. Why, is no man's business but mine. I found the stable locked; so I left my horse, and went on foot. I crossed Hernshaw Mere by the bridge, and had got about a hundred yards, as I suppose, on the way, when I heard some one fall with a great splash into the mere, and soon after cry dolefully for help. I, that am no swimmer, ran instantly to the north side to a clump of trees, where a boat used always to be kept. But the boat was not there. Then I cried lustily for help, and, as no one came, I fired my pistol and cried murder! For I had heard men will come sooner to that cry than to any other. But in truth I was almost out of my wits, that a fellow-creature should perish miserably so near me. Whilst I ran wildly to and fro, some came out of the Castle bearing torches. By this time I was at the bridge, but saw no signs of the drowning man; yet the night was clear. Then I knew that his fate was sealed; and, for reasons of my own, not choos-

ing to be seen by those who were coming to his aid, I hastened from the place. My happiness being gone, and my conscience smiting me sore, and not knowing whither to turn, I took to drink, and fell into bad ways, and lived like a brute, and not a man, for six weeks or more; so that I never knew of the good fortune that had fallen on me when least I deserved it: I mean by old Mr. Gaunt of Coggleswade making of me his heir. But one day at Kendal I saw Mercy Vint's advertisement; and I went to her, and learned that my wife lay in Carlisle jail for my supposed murder. But I say that she is innocent, and nowise to blame in this matter: for I deserved every hard word she ever gave me; and as for killing, she is a spirited woman with her tongue, but hath not the heart to kill a fly. She is what she always was, — the pearl of womankind; a virtuous, innocent, and noble lady. I have lost the treasure of her love by my fault, not hers; but at least I have a right to defend her life and honor. Whoever molests her after this, out of pretended regard for me, is a liar, and a fool, and no friend of mine, but my enemy, and I his — to the death.

"GRIFFITH GAUNT."

It was a day of surprises. This tribute from the murdered man to his assassin was one of them. People looked in one another's faces open-eyed.

The prisoner looked in the judge's, and acted on what she saw there. "That is my defence," said she, quietly, and sat down.

If a show of hands had been called at that moment, she would have been acquitted by acclamation.

But Mr. Whitworth was a zealous young barrister, burning for distinction. He stuck to his case, and cross-examined Mercy Vint with severity; indeed, with asperity.

Whitworth. What are you to receive for this evidence?

Mercy. Anan.

Whitworth. O, you know what I

mean. Are you not to be paid for telling us this romance ?

Mercy. Nay, sir, I ask naught for
telling the truth.

Whitworth. You were in the prisoner's company yesterday ?

Mercy. Yes, sir, I visited her in the
jail last night.

Whitworth. And there concerted this
ingenious defence ?

Mercy. Well, sir, for that matter, I
told her that her man was alive, and I
did offer to be her witness.

Whitworth. For naught ?

Mercy. For no money or reward, if
't is that you mean. Why, 't is a joy
beyond money to clear an innocent
body, and save her life ; and that satisfaction is mine this day.

Whitworth (sarcastically). These
are very fine sentiments for a person
in your condition. Confess that Mrs.
Gaunt primed you with all that.

Mercy. Nay, sir, I left home in that
mind ; else I had not come at all. Bethink you ; 't is a long journey for one
in my way of life ; and this dear child
on my arm all the way.

Mrs. Gaunt sat boiling with indignation. But Mercy's good temper and
meekness parried the attack that time.
Mr. Whitworth changed his line.

Whitworth. You ask the jury to
believe that Griffith Gaunt, Esquire, a
gentleman, and a man of spirit and
honor, is alive, yet skulks and sends
you thither, when by showing his face in
this court he could clear his wife without a single word spoken ?

Mercy. Yes, sir ; I do hope to be
believed, for I speak the naked truth.
But, with due respect to you, Mr. Gaunt
did not send me hither against my will.
I could not bide in Lancashire, and let
an innocent woman be murdered in
Cumberland.

Whitworth. Murdered, quotha. That
is a good jest. I 'd have you to know
we punish murders here, not do them.

Mercy. I am glad to hear that, sir,
on the lady's account.

Whitworth. Come, come. You pretend you discovered this Griffith
Gaunt alive, by means of an adver-

tisement. If so, produce the advertisement.

Mercy Vint colored, and cast a swift,
uneasy glance at Mrs. Gaunt.

Rapid as it was, the keen eye of the
counsel caught it.

"Nay, do not look to the culprit for
orders," said he. "Produce it, or confess the truth. Come, you never advertised for him."

"Sir, I did advertise for him."

"Then produce the advertisement."

"Sir, I will not," said Mercy, calmly.

"Then I shall move the court to
commit you."

"For what offence, if you please ? "

"For perjury and contempt of court."

"I am guiltless of either, God knows.
But I will not show the advertisement."

Judge. This is very extraordinary.
Perhaps you have it not about you.

Mercy. My lord, the truth is I have
it in my bosom. But, if I show it, it
will not make this matter one whit
clearer, and 't will open the wounds of
two poor women. 'T is not for myself.
But, O my lord, look at her. Hath she
not gone through grief enow ? "

The appeal was made with a quiet,
touching earnestness, that affected every hearer. But the judge had a duty
to perform. "Witness," said he, "you
mean well ; but indeed you do the
prisoner an injury by withholding this
paper. Be good enough to produce it
at once."

Prisoner (with a deep sigh). Obey
my lord.

Mercy (with a patient sigh). There,
sir, may the Lord forgive you the useless mischief you are doing.

Whitworth. I am doing my duty,
young woman. And yours is to tell
the whole truth, and not a part only.

Mercy (acquiescing). That is true,
sir.

Whitworth. Why, what is this ? 'T
is not Mr. Gaunt you advertise for in
these papers. 'T is Thomas Leicester.

Judge. What is that ? I don't understand.

Whitworth. Nor I neither.

Judge. Let me see the papers. 'T is Thomas Leicester sure enough.

Whitworth. And you mean to swear that Griffith Gaunt answered an advertisement inviting Thomas Leicester?

Mercy. I do. Thomas Leicester was the name he went by in our part.

Whitworth. What? what? You are jesting.

Mercy. Is this a place or a time for jesting? I say he called himself Thomas Leicester.

Here the business was interrupted again by a multitudinous murmur of excited voices. Everybody was whispering astonishment to his neighbor. And the whisper of a great crowd has the effect of a loud murmur.

Whitworth. O, he called himself Thomas Leicester, did he? Then what makes you think he is Griffith Gaunt?

Mercy. Well, sir, the pedler, whose real name was Thomas Leicester, came to our house one day, and saw his picture, and knew it; and said something to a neighbor that raised my suspicions. When *he* came home, I took this shirt out of a drawer; 't was the shirt he wore when he first came to us. 'T is marked "G. G." (The shirt was examined.) Said I, "For God's sake speak the truth: what does G. G. stand for?" Then he told me his real name was Griffith Gaunt, and he had a wife in Cumberland. "Go back to her," said I, "and ask her to forgive you." Then he rode north, and I never saw him again till last Wednesday.

Whitworth (satirically). You seem to have been mighty intimate with this Thomas Leicester, whom you now call Griffith Gaunt. May I ask what was, or is, the nature of your connection with him?

Mercy was silent.

Whitworth. I must press for a reply, that we may know what value to attach to your most extraordinary evidence. Were you his wife, — or his mistress?

Mercy. Indeed, I hardly know; but not his mistress, or I should not be here.

Whitworth. You don't know whether you were married to the man or not?

Mercy. I do not say so. But —

She hesitated, and cast a piteous look at Mrs. Gaunt, who sat boiling with indignation.

At this look, the prisoner, who had long contained herself with difficulty, rose, with scarlet cheeks and flashing eyes, in defence of her witness, and flung her prudence to the wind.

"Fie, sir," she cried. "The woman you insult is as pure as your own mother, or mine. She deserves the pity, the respect, the veneration of all good men. Know, my lord, that my miserable husband deceived and married her under the false name he had taken. She has the marriage-certificate in her bosom. Pray make her show it, whether she will or not. My lord, this Mercy Vint is more an angel than a woman. I am her rival, after a manner. Yet, out of the goodness and greatness of her noble heart, she came all that way to save me from an unjust death. And is such a woman to be insulted? I blush for the hired advocate who cannot see his superior in an incorruptible witness, a creature all truth, piety, purity, unselfishness, and goodness. Yes, sir, you began by insinuating that she was as venal as yourself; for you are one that can be bought by the first-comer; and now you would cast a slur on her chastity. For shame! for shame! This is one of those rare women that adorn our whole sex, and embellish human nature; and, so long as you have the privilege of exchanging words with her, I shall stand here on the watch, to see that you treat her with due respect: ay, sir, with reverence; for I have measured you both, and she is as much your superior as she is mine."

This amazing burst was delivered with such prodigious fire and rapidity that nobody was self-possessed enough to stop it in time. It was like a furious gust of words sweeping over the court.

Mr. Whitworth, pale with anger, merely said: "Madam, the good taste of these remarks I leave the court to decide upon. But you cannot be allowed to give evidence in your own defence."

"No, but in hers I will," said Mrs. Gaunt. "No power shall hinder me."

Judge (coldly). Had you not better go on cross-examining the witness?

Whitworth. Let me see your marriage-certificate, if you have one?

It was handed to him.

"Well, now how do you know that this Thomas Leicester was Griffith Gaunt?

Judge. Why, she has told you he confessed it to her.

Mercy. Yes, my lord; and, besides, he wrote me two letters signed Thomas Leicester. Here they are, and I desire they may be compared with the paper he wrote last Wednesday, and signed Griffith Gaunt. And more than that, whilst we lived together as man and wife, one Hamilton, a travelling painter, took our portraits, his and mine. I have brought his with me. Let his friends and neighbors look on this portrait, and say whose likeness it is. What I say and swear is, that on Wednesday last I saw and spoke with that Thomas Leicester, or Griffith Gaunt, whose likeness I now show you.

With that she lifted the portrait up, and showed it all the court.

Instantly there was a roar of recognition.

It was one of those hard daubs that are nevertheless so monstrously like the originals.

Judge (to Mr. Whitworth). Young gentleman, we are all greatly obliged to you. You have made the prisoner's case. There was but one weak point in it; I mean the prolonged absence of Griffith Gaunt. You have now accounted for that. You have forced a very truthful witness to depose that this Gaunt is himself a criminal, and is hiding from fear of the law. The case for the crown is a mere tissue of conjectures, on which no jury could safely convict, even if there was no defence at all. Under

other circumstances I might decline to receive evidence at second-hand that Griffith Gaunt is alive. But here such evidence is sufficient, for it lies on the crown to prove the man dead; but you have only proved that he was alive on the fifteenth of October, and that since then somebody is dead with shoes on. This somebody appears on the balance of proof to be Thomas Leicester, the pedler; and he has never been heard of since, and Griffith Gaunt has. Then I say you cannot carry the case further. You have not a leg to stand on. What say you, Brother Wiltshire?

Wiltshire. My lord, I think there is no case against the prisoner, and am thankful to your lordship for relieving me of a very unpleasant task.

The question of guilty or not guilty was then put to the jury, who instantly brought the prisoner in not guilty.

Judge. Catharine Gaunt, you leave this court without a stain, and with our sincere respect and sympathy. I much regret the fear and pain you have been put to: you have been terribly punished for a hasty word. Profit now by this bitter lesson; and may Heaven enable you to add a well-governed spirit to your many virtues and graces.

He half rose from his seat, and bowed courteously to her. She courtesied reverently, and retired.

He then said a few words to Mercy Vint.

"Young woman, I have no words to praise you as you deserve. You have shown us the beauty of the female character, and, let me add, the beauty of the Christian religion. You have come a long way to clear the innocent. I hope you will not stop there; but also punish the guilty person, on whom we have wasted so much pity."

"Me, my lord?" said Mercy. "I would not harm a hair of his head for as many guineas as there be hairs in mine."

"Child," said my lord, "thou art too good for this world; but go thy ways, and God bless thee."

Thus abruptly ended a trial that, at first, had looked so formidable for the accused.

The judge now retired for some refreshment, and while he was gone Sir George Neville dashed up to the Town Hall, four in hand, and rushed in by the magistrate's door, with a pedler's pack, which he had discovered in the mere, a few yards from the spot where the mutilated body was found.

He learned the prisoner was already acquitted. He left the pack with the sheriff, and begged him to show it to the judge ; and went in search of Mrs. Gaunt.

He found her in the jailer's house. She and Mercy Vint were seated hand in hand.

He started at first sight of the latter. Then there was a universal shaking of hands, and glistening of eyes. And, when this was over, Mrs. Gaunt turned to him, and said, piteously : " She will go back to Lancashire tomorrow ; nothing I can say will turn her."

" No, dame," said Mercy, quietly ; " Cumberland is no place for me. My work is done here. Our paths in this world do lie apart. George Neville, persuade her to go home at once, and not trouble about me."

" Indeed, madam," said Sir George, " she speaks wisely : she always does. My carriage is at the door, and the people waiting by thousands in the street to welcome your deliverance."

Mrs. Gaunt drew herself up with fiery and bitter disdain.

" Are they so ? " said she, grimly. " Then I 'll balk them. I 'll steal away in the dead of night. No, miserable populace, that howls and hisses with the strong against the weak, you shall have no part in my triumph ; 't is sacred to my friends. You honored me with your hootings, you shall not disgrace me with your acclamations. Here I stay till Mercy Vint, my guardian angel, leaves me forever."

She then requested Sir George to order his horses back to the inn, and the coachman was to hold himself in readiness to start when the whole town should be asleep.

Meantime, a courier was despatched to Hernshaw Castle, to prepare for Mrs. Gaunt's reception.

Mrs. Menteith made a bed up for Mercy Vint, and at midnight, when the coast was clear, came the parting. It was a sad one.

Even Mercy, who had great self-command, could not then restrain her tears.

To apply the sweet and touching words of Scripture, " They sorrowed most of all for this, that they should see each other's face no more."

Sir George accompanied Mrs. Gaunt to Hernshaw.

She drew back into her corner of the carriage, and was very silent and *distraite.*

After one or two attempts at conversation, he judged it wisest, and even most polite, to respect her mood.

At last she burst out, " I cannot bear it, I cannot bear it."

" Why, what is amiss ? " inquired Sir George.

" What is amiss ? Why, 't is all amiss. 'T is so heartless, so ungrateful, to let that poor angel go home to Lancashire all alone, now she has served my turn. Sir George, do not think I undervalue your company : but if you would but take her home, instead of taking me ! Poor thing, she is brave ; but when the excitement of her good action is over, and she goes back the weary road all alone, what desolation it will be ! My heart bleeds for her. I know I am an unconscionable woman, to ask such a thing ; but then you are a true chevalier ; you always were, and you saw her merit directly. O, do pray leave me to slip unnoticed into Hernshaw Castle, and do you accompany my benefactress to her humble home. Will you, dear Sir George ? 'T would be such a load off my heart."

To this appeal, uttered with trembling lip and moist eyes, Sir George replied in character. He declined to desert Mrs. Gaunt, until he had seen her safe home ; but, that done, he would ride back to Carlisle and escort Mercy home.

Mrs. Gaunt sighed, and said she was abusing his friendship, and should kill him with fatigue, and he was a good creature. " If anything could make me easy, this would," said she. " You know how to talk to a woman, and comfort her. I wish I was a man : I 'd cure her of Griffith before we reached the ' Packhorse.' And, now I think of it, you are a very happy man to travel eighty miles with an angel, a dove-eyed angel."

" I am a happy man to have an opportunity of complying with your desires, madam," was the demure reply. " 'T is not often you do me the honor to lay your orders on me."

After this, nothing of any moment passed until they reached Hernshaw Castle ; and then, as they drove up to the door, and saw the hall blazing with lights, Mrs. Gaunt laid her hand softly on Sir George, and whispered, " You were right. I thank you for not leaving me."

The servants were all in the hall, to receive their mistress ; and amongst them were those who had given honest but unfavorable testimony at the trial, being called by the crown. These had consulted together, and, after many pros and cons, had decided that they had better not follow their natural impulse, and hide from her face, since that might be a fresh offence. Accordingly, these witnesses, dressed in their best, stood with the others in the hall, and made their obeisances, quaking inwardly.

Mrs. Gaunt entered the hall leaning on Sir George's arm. She scarcely bestowed a look upon any of her servants, but made them one sweeping courtesy in return, and passed on ; only Sir George felt her taper fingers just nip his arm.

She made him partake of some supper, and then this chevalier des dames rode home, snatched a few hours' sleep, put on the yeoman's suit in which he had first visited the " Packhorse," and, arriving at Carlisle, engaged the whole inside of the coach ; for his orders were to console, and he did not see his way clear to do that with two or three strangers listening to every word.

CHAPTER XLIV.

A GREAT change was observable in Mrs. Gaunt after this fiery and chastening ordeal. In a short time she had been taught many lessons. She had learned that the law will not allow even a woman to say anything and everything with impunity. She had been in a court of justice, and seen how gravely, soberly, and fairly an accusation is sifted there ; and, if false, annihilated ; which, elsewhere, it never is. Member of a sex that could never have invented a court of justice, she had found something to revere and bless in that other sex to which her erring husband belonged. Finally, she had encountered in Mercy Vint a woman whom she recognized at once as her moral superior. The contact of that pure and well-governed spirit told wonderfully upon her. She began to watch her tongue and to bridle her high spirit. She became slower to give offence, and slower to take it. She took herself to task, and made some little excuses even for Griffith. She was resolved to retire from the world altogether ; but, meantime, she bowed her head to the lessons of adversity. Her features, always lovely, but somewhat too haughty, were now softened and embellished beyond description by a mingled expression of grief, humility, and resignation.

She never mentioned her husband ; but it is not to be supposed she never thought of him. She waited the course of events in dignified and patient silence.

As for Griffith Gaunt, he was in the hands of two lawyers, Atkins and Houseman. He waited on the first, and made a friend of him. " I am at your service," said he ; " but not if I am to be indicted for bigamy, and burned in the hand."

"These fears are idle," said Atkins. "Mercy Vint declared in open court she will not proceed against you."

"Ay, but there's my wife."

"She will keep quiet; I have Houseman's word for it."

"Ay, but there's the Attorney-General."

"O, he will not move, unless he is driven. We must use a little influence. Mr. Houseman is of my mind, and he has the ear of the county."

To be brief, it was represented in high quarters that to indict Mr. Gaunt would only open Mrs. Gaunt's wounds afresh, and do no good; and so Houseman found means to muzzle the Attorney-General.

Just three weeks after the trial, Griffith Gaunt, Esq. reappeared publicly. The place of his reappearance was Coggleswade. He came and set about finishing his new mansion with feverish rapidity. He engaged an army of carpenters and painters, and spent thousands of pounds on the decorating and furnishing of the mansion, and laying out the grounds.

This was duly reported to Mrs. Gaunt, who said — not a word.

But at last one day came a letter to Mrs. Gaunt, in Griffith's well-known handwriting.

With all her acquired self-possession, her hand trembled as she broke open the seal.

It contained but these words : —

"MADAM, — I do not ask you to forgive me. For, if you had done what I have, I could never forgive you. But for the sake of Rose, and to stop their tongues, I do hope you will do me the honor to live under this my roof. I dare not face Hernshaw Castle. Your own apartments here are now ready for you. The place is large. Upon my honor I will not trouble you; but show myself always, as now,

"Your penitent and very humble servant,
"GRIFFITH GAUNT."

The messenger was to wait for her reply.

This letter disturbed Mrs. Gaunt's sorrowful tranquillity at once. She was much agitated, and so undecided that she sent the messenger away, and told him to call next day.

Then she sent off to Father Francis to beg his advice.

But her courier returned, late at night, to say Father Francis was away from home.

Then she took Rose, and said to her, "My darling, papa wants us to go to his new house, and leave dear old Hernshaw; I know not what to say about that. What do *you* say?"

"Tell him to come to us," said Rose, dictatorially. "Only," (lowering her little voice very suddenly,) "if he is naughty and won't, why then we had better go to him; for he amuses me."

"As you please," said Mrs. Gaunt; and sent her husband this reply : —

"SIR, — Rose and I are agreed to defer to your judgment and obey your wishes. Be pleased to let me know what day you will require us; and I must trouble you to send a carriage.

"I am, sir,
"Your faithful wife and humble servant,
"CATHARINE GAUNT."

At the appointed day, a carriage and four came wheeling up to the door. The vehicle was gorgeously emblazoned, and the servants in rich liveries; all which finery glittering in the sun, and the glossy coats of the horses, did mightily please Mistress Rose. She stood on the stone steps, and clapped her hands with delight. Her mother just sighed, and said, "Ay, 't is in pomp and show we must seek our happiness now."

She leaned back in the carriage, and closed her eyes, yet not so close but now and then a tear would steal out, as she thought of the past.

They drove up under an avenue to a noble mansion, and landed at the foot of some marble steps, low and narrow, but of vast breadth.

As they mounted these, a hall door,

through which the carriage could have passed, was flung open, and discovered the servants all drawn up to do honor to their mistress.

She entered the hall, leading Rose by the hand ; the servants bowed and courtesied down to the ground.

She received this homage with dignified courtesy, and her eye stole round to see if the master of the house was coming to receive her.

The library door was opened hastily, and out came to meet her — Father Francis.

"Welcome, madam, a thousand times welcome to your new home," said he, in a stentorian voice, with a double infusion of geniality. "I claim the honor of showing you your part of the house, though 't is all yours for that matter." And he led the way.

Now this cheerful stentorian voice was just a little shaky for once, and his eyes were moist.

Mrs. Gaunt noticed, but said nothing before the people. She smiled graciously, and accompanied him.

He took her to her apartments. They consisted of a salle-à-manger, three delightful bedrooms, a boudoir, and a magnificent drawing-room, fifty feet long, with two fireplaces, and a bay-window thirty feet wide, filled with the choicest flowers.

An exclamation of delight escaped Mrs. Gaunt. Then she said, "One would think I was a queen." Then she sighed, "Ah," said she, "'t is a fine thing to be rich." Then, despondently, "Tell him I think it very beautiful."

"Nay, madam, I hope you will tell him so yourself."

Mrs. Gaunt made no reply to that. She added : "And it was kind of him to have you here the first day : I do not feel so lonely as I should without you."

She took Griffith at his word, and lived with Rose in her own apartments.

For some time Griffith used to slip away whenever he saw her coming.

One day she caught him at it, and beckoned him.

He came to her.

"You need not run away from me," said she : "I did not come into your house to quarrel with you. Let us be *friends*," — and she gave him her hand sweetly enough, but O so coldly !

"I hope for nothing more," said Griffith. "If you ever have a wish, give me the pleasure of gratifying it, — that is all."

"I wish to retire to a convent," said she, quietly.

"And desert your daughter ? "

"I would leave her behind, to remind you of days gone by."

By degrees they saw a little more of one another ; they even dined together now and then. But it brought them no nearer. There was no anger, with its loving reaction. They were friendly enough, but an icy barrier stood between them.

One person set himself quietly to sap this barrier. Father Francis was often at the Castle, and played the peacemaker very adroitly.

The line he took might be called the innocent Jesuitical. He saw that it would be useless to exhort these two persons to ignore the terrible things that had happened, and to make it up as if it was only a squabble. What he did was to repeat to the husband every gracious word the wife let fall, and *vice versâ*, and to suppress all either said that might tend to estrange them.

In short, he acted the part of Mr. Harmony in the play, and acted it to perfection.

Gutta cavat lapidem.

Though no perceptible effect followed his efforts, yet there is no doubt that he got rid of some of the bitterness. But the coldness remained.

One day he was sent for all in a hurry by Griffith.

He found him looking gloomy and agitated.

The cause came out directly. Griffith had observed, at last, what all the females in the house had seen two months ago, that Mrs. Gaunt was in the family way.

He now communicated this to Father

Francis, with a voice of agony, and looks to match.

"All the better, my son," said the genial priest: "'t will be another tie between you. I hope it will be a fine boy to inherit your estates." Then, observing a certain hideous expression distorting Griffith's face, he fixed his eyes full on him, and said, sternly, "Are you not cured yet of that madness of yours ?"

"No, no, no," said Griffith, deprecatingly; "but why did she not tell me ?"

"You had better ask her."

"Not I. She will remind me I am nothing to her now. And, though 't is so, yet I would not hear it from her lips."

In spite of this wise resolution, the torture he was in drove him to remonstrate with her on her silence.

She blushed high, and excused herself as follows : —

"I should have told you as soon as I knew it myself. But you were not with me. I was all by myself — in Carlisle jail."

This reply, uttered with hypocritical meekness, went through Griffith like a knife. He turned white, and gasped for breath, but said nothing. He left her, with a deep groan, and never ventured to mention the matter again.

All he did in that direction was to redouble his attentions and solicitude for her health.

The relation between these two was now more anomalous than ever.

Even Father Francis, who had seen strange things in families, used to watch Mrs. Gaunt rise from the table and walk heavily to the door, and her husband dart to it and open it obsequiously, and receive only a very formal reverence in return, — and wonder how all this was to end.

However, under this icy surface, a change was gradually going on; and one afternoon, to his great surprise, Mrs. Gaunt's maid came to ask Griffith if he would come to Mrs. Gaunt's apartment.

He found her seated in her bay-window, among her flowers. She seemed another woman all of a sudden, and smiled on him her exquisite smile of days gone by.

"Come, sit beside me," said she, "in this beautiful window that you have given me."

"Sit beside you, Kate ?" said Griffith. "Nay, let me kneel at your knees : that is my place."

"As you will," said she, softly; and continued, in the same tone : "Now listen to me. You and I are two fools. We have been very happy together in days gone by ; and we should both of us like to try again ; but we neither of us know how to begin. You are afraid to tell me you love me, and I am ashamed to own to you or anybody else that I love you, in spite of it all ; — I do, though."

"You love me ! a wretch like me, Kate ? 'T is impossible. I cannot be so happy."

"Child," said Mrs. Gaunt, "love is not reason ; love is not common sense. 'T is a passion ; like your jealousy, poor fool. I love you, as a mother loves her child, all the more for all you have made me suffer. I might not say as much, if I thought we should be long together. But something tells me I shall die this time : I never felt so before. Bury me at Hernshaw. After all, I spent more happy years there than most wives ever know. I see you are very sorry for what you have done. How could I die and leave thee in doubt of my forgiveness, and my love ? Kiss me, poor jealous fool; for I do forgive thee, and love thee with all my sorrowful heart." And even with the words she bowed herself and sank quietly into his arms, and he kissed her and cried bitterly over her : bitterly. But she was comparatively calm. For she said to herself, "The end is at hand."

Griffith, instead of pooh-poohing his wife's forebodings, set himself to baffle them.

He used his wealth freely, and, besides the county doctor, had two very eminent practitioners from London, one of whom was a gray-headed man, the other singularly young for the fame he had obtained. But then he was a genuine enthusiast in his art.

CHAPTER XLV.

GRIFFITH, white as a ghost, and unable to shake off the forebodings Catharine had communicated to him, walked incessantly up and down the room ; and, at his earnest request, one or other of the four doctors in attendance was constantly coming to him with information.

The case proceeded favorably, and, to Griffith's surprise and joy, a healthy boy was born about two o'clock in the morning. The mother was reported rather feverish, but nothing to cause alarm.

Griffith threw himself on two chairs and fell fast asleep.

Towards morning he found himself shaken, and there was Ashley, the young doctor, standing beside him with a very grave face. Griffith started up, and cried, " What is wrong, in God's name ? "

" I am sorry to say there has been a sudden hemorrhage, and the patient is much exhausted."

" She is dying, she is dying ! " cried Griffith, in anguish.

" Not dying. But she will infallibly sink, unless some unusual circumstance occur to sustain vitality."

Griffith laid hold of him. " O sir, take my whole fortune, but save her ! save her ! save her ! "

" Mr. Gaunt," said the young doctor, " be calm, or you will make matters worse. There is one chance to save her ; but my professional brethren are prejudiced against it. However, they have consented, at my earnest request, to refer my proposal to you. She is sinking for want of blood ; if you consent to my opening a vein and transfusing healthy blood from a living subject into hers, I will undertake the operation. You had better come and see her ; you will be more able to judge."

" Let me lean on you," said Griffith. And the strong wrestler went tottering up the stairs. There they showed him poor Kate, white as the bed-clothes, breathing hard, and with a pulse that hardly moved.

Griffith looked at her horror-struck.

" Death has got hold of my darling," he screamed. " Snatch her away ! for God's sake, snatch her from him ! "

The young doctor whipped off his coat, and bared his arm.

" There," he cried, " Mr. Gaunt consents. Now, Corrie, be quick with the lancet, and hold this tube as I tell you ; warm it first in that water."

Here came an interruption. Griffith Gaunt griped the young doctor's arm, and, with an agonized and ugly expression of countenance, cried out, " What, *your* blood ! What right have you to lose blood for her ? "

" The right of a man who loves his art better than his blood," cried Ashley, with enthusiasm.

Griffith tore off his coat and waistcoat, and bared his arm to the elbow. " Take every drop I have. No man's blood shall enter her veins but mine." And the creature seemed to swell to double his size, as, with flushed cheek and sparkling eyes, he held out a bare arm corded like a blacksmith's, and white as a duchess's.

The young doctor eyed the magnificent limb a moment with rapture ; then fixed his apparatus and performed an operation which then, as now, was impossible in theory ; only he did it. He sent some of Griffith Gaunt's bright red blood smoking hot into Kate Gaunt's veins.

This done, he watched his patient closely, and administered stimulants from time to time.

She hung between life and death for hours. But at noon next day she spoke, and, seeing Griffith sitting beside her, pale with anxiety and loss of blood, she said : " My dear, do not thou fret. I died last night. I knew I should.

But they gave me another life ; and now I shall live to a hundred.

They showed her the little boy ; and, at sight of him, the whole woman made up her mind to live.

And live she did. And, what is very remarkable, her convalescence was more rapid than on any former occasion.

It was from a talkative nurse she first learned that Griffith had given his blood for her. She said nothing at the time, but lay, with an angelic, happy smile, thinking of it.

The first time she saw him after that, she laid her hand on his arm, and, looking Heaven itself into his eyes, she said, " My life is very dear to me now. 'T is a present from thee."

She only wanted a good excuse for loving him as frankly as before, and now he had given her one. She used to throw it in his teeth in the prettiest way. Whenever she confessed a fault, she was sure to turn slyly round and say, " But what could one expect of me ? I have his blood in my veins."

But once she told Father Francis, quite seriously, that she had never been quite the same woman since she lived by Griffith's blood ; she was turned jealous ; and moreover it had given him a fascinating power over her, and she could tell blindfold when he was in the room. Which last fact, indeed, she once proved by actual experiment. But all this I leave to such as study the occult sciences in this profound age of ours.

Starting with this advantage, Time, the great curer, gradually healed a wound that looked incurable.

Mrs. Gaunt became a better wife than she had ever been before. She studied her husband, and found he was not hard to please. She made his home bright and genial ; and so he never went abroad for the sunshine he could have at home.

And he studied her. He added a chapel to the house, and easily persuaded Francis to become the chaplain. Thus they had a peacemaker, and a

friend, in the house, and a man severe in morals, but candid in religion, and an inexhaustible companion to them and their children.

And so, after that terrible storm, this pair pursued the even tenor of a peaceful united life, till the olive - branches rising around them, and the happy years gliding on, almost obliterated that one dark passage, and made it seem a mere fantastical, incredible dream.

Mercy Vint and her child went home in the coach. It was empty at starting, and, as Mrs. Gaunt had foretold, a great sense of desolation fell upon her.

She leaned back, and the patient tears coursed steadily down her comely cheeks.

At the first stage a passenger got down from the outside, and entered the coach.

" What, George Neville ! " said Mercy.

" The same," said he.

She expressed her surprise that he should be going her way.

" 'T is strange," said he, " but to me most agreeable."

" And to me too, for that matter," said she.

Sir George observed her eyes were red, and, to divert her mind and keep up her spirits, launched into a flow of small talk.

In the midst of it, Mercy leaned back in the coach, and began to cry bitterly. So much for that mode of consolation.

Upon this he faced the situation, and begged her not to grieve. He praised the good action she had done, and told her how everybody admired her for it, especially himself.

At that she gave him her hand in silence, and turned away her pretty head. He carried her hand respectfully to his lips ; and his manly heart began to yearn over this suffering virtue, — so grave, so dignified, so meek. He was no longer a young man ; he began to talk to her like a friend. This tone, and the soft, sympathetic voice in which a gentleman speaks to a woman in trouble, unlocked her heart; and for the first time in her life she was led to talk about herself.

She opened her heart to him. She told him she was not the woman to pine for any man. Her youth, her health, and love of occupation, would carry her through. What she mourned was the loss of esteem, and the blot upon her child. At that she drew the baby with inexpressible tenderness, and yet with a half-defiant air, closer to her bosom.

Sir George assured her she would lose the esteem of none but fools. "As for me," said he, "I always respected you, but now I revere you. You are a martyr and an angel."

"George," said Mercy, gravely, "be you my friend, not my enemy."

"Why, madam," said he, "sure you can't think me such a wretch."

"I mean, our flatterers are our enemies."

Sir George took the hint, given, as it was, very gravely and decidedly; and henceforth showed her his respect by his acts; he paid her as much attention as if she had been a princess. He handed her out, and handed her in; and coaxed her to eat here, and to drink there; and at the inn where the passengers slept for the night, he showed his long purse, and secured her superior comforts. Console her he could not; but he broke the sense of utter desolation and loneliness with which she started from Carlisle. She told him so in the inn, and descanted on the goodness of God, who had sent her a friend in that bitter hour.

"You have been very kind to me, George," said she. "Now Heaven bless you for it, and give you many happy days, and well spent."

This, from one who never said a word she did not mean, sank deep into Sir George's heart, and he went to sleep thinking of her, and asking himself was there nothing he could do for her.

Next morning Sir George handed Mercy and her babe into the coach; and the villain tried an experiment to see what value she set on him. He did not get in, so Mercy thought she had seen the last of him.

"Farewell, good, kind George," said she. "Alas! there's naught but meeting and parting in this weary world."

The tears stood in her sweet eyes, and she thanked him, not with words only, but with the soft pressure of her womanly hand.

He slipped up behind the coach, and was ashamed of himself, and his heart warmed to her more and more.

As soon as the coach stopped, my lord opened the door for Mercy to alight. Her eyes were very red; he saw that. She started, and beamed with surprise and pleasure.

"Why, I thought I had lost you for good," said she. "Whither are you going? to Lancaster?"

"Not quite so far. I am going to the 'Packhorse.'"

Mercy opened her eyes, and blushed high. Sir George saw that, and, to divert her suspicions, told her merrily to beware of making objections. "I am only a sort of servant in the matter. 'T was Mrs. Gaunt ordered me."

"I might have guessed it," said Mercy. "Bless her; she knew I should be lonely."

"She was not easy till she had got rid of me, I assure you," said Sir George. "So let us make the best on 't, for she is a lady that likes to have her own way."

"She is a noble creature. George, I shall never regret anything I have done for *her*. And she will not be ungrateful. O, the sting of ingratitude! I have felt that. Have you?"

"No," said Sir George; "I have escaped that, by never doing any good actions."

"I doubt you are telling me a lie," said Mercy Vint.

She now looked upon Sir George as Mrs. Gaunt's representative, and prattled freely to him. Only now and then her trouble came over her, and then she took a quiet cry without ceremony.

As for Sir George, he sat and studied, and wondered at her.

Never in his life had he met such a woman as this, who was as candid with him as if he had been a woman. She seemed to have a window in her bosom, through which he looked, and saw the pure and lovely soul within.

In the afternoon they reached a little town, whence a cart conveyed them to the "Packhorse."

Here Mercy Vint disappeared, and busied herself with Sir George's comforts.

He sat by himself in the parlor, and missed his gentle companion.

In the morning Mercy thought of course he would go.

But instead of that, he stayed, and followed her about, and began to court her downright.

But the warmer he got, the cooler she. And at last she said, mighty dryly, "This is a very dull place for the likes of you."

"'T is the sweetest place in England," said he; "at least to me; for it contains — the woman I love."

Mercy drew back, and colored rosy red. "I hope not," said she.

"I loved you the first day I saw you, and heard your voice. And now I love you ten times more. Let me dry thy tears forever, sweet Mercy. Be my wife."

"You are mad," said Mercy. "What, would you wed a woman in my condition? I am more your friend than to take you at your word. And what must you think I am made of, to go from one man to another, like that?"

"Take your time, sweetheart; only give me your hand."

"George," said Mercy, very gravely, "I am beholden to you; but my duty it lies another way. There is a young man in these parts" (Sir George groaned) "that was my follower for two years and better. I wronged him for one I never name now. I must marry that poor lad, and make him happy, or else live and die as I am."

Sir George turned pale. "One word: do you love him?"

"I have a regard for him."

"Do you love him?"

"Hardly. But I wronged him, and I owe him amends. I shall pay my debts."

Sir George bowed, and retired sick at heart, and deeply mortified. Mercy looked after him and sighed.

Next day, as he walked disconsolate up and down, she came to him and gave him her hand. "You were a good friend to me that bitter day," said she. "Now let me be yours. Do not bide here: 't will but vex you."

"I am going, madam," said Sir George, stiffly. "I but wait to see the man you prefer to me. If he is not too unworthy of you, I 'll go, and trouble you no more. I have learned his name."

Mercy blushed; for she knew Paul Carrick would bear no comparison with George Neville.

The next day Sir George took leave to observe that this Paul Carrick did not seem to appreciate her preference so highly as he ought. "I understand he has never been here."

Mercy colored, but made no reply; and Sir George was sorry he had taunted her. He followed her about, and showed her great attention, but not a word of love.

There were fine trout streams in the neighborhood, and he busied himself fishing, and in the evening read aloud to Mercy, and waited to see Paul Carrick.

Paul never came; and from a word Mercy let drop, he saw that she was mortified. Then, being no tyro in love, he told her he had business in Lancaster, and must leave her for a few days. But he would return, and by that time perhaps Paul Carrick would be visible.

Now his main object was to try the effect of correspondence.

Every day he sent her a long love-letter from Lancaster.

Paul Carrick, who, in absenting himself for a time, had acted upon his sister's advice, rather than his own natural impulse, learned that Mercy received a letter every day. This was a thing unheard of in that parish.

So then Paul defied his sister's advice, and presented himself to Mercy; when the following dialogue took place.

"Welcome home, Mercy."

"Thank you, Paul."

"Well, I 'm single still, lass."

"So I hear."

"I 'm come to say let bygones be bygones."

"So be it," said Mercy, dryly.

"You have tried a gentleman ; now try a farrier."

"I have ; and he did not stand the test."

"Anan."

"Why did you not come near me for ten days ?"

Paul blushed up to the eyes. "Well," said he, "I 'll tell you the truth. 'T was our Jess advised me to leave you quiet just at first."

"Ay, ay. I was to be humbled, and made to smart for my fault ; and then I should be thankful to take you. My lad, if ever you should be really in love, take a friend's advice ; listen to your own heart, and not to shallow advisers. You have mortified a poor sorrowful creature, who was going to make a sacrifice for you ; and you have lost her forever."

"What d' ye mean ?"

"I mean that you are to think no more of Mercy Vint."

"Then it is true, ye jade ; ye 've gotten a fresh lover already."

"Say no more than you know. If you were the only man on earth, I would not wed you, Paul Carrick."

Paul Carrick retired home, and blew up his sister, and told her that she had "gotten him the sack again."

The next day Sir George came back from Lancaster, and Mercy lowered her lashes for once at sight of him.

"Well," said he, "has this Carrick shown a sense of your goodness ?"

"He has come, — and gone."

She then, with her usual frankness, told him what had passed. "And," said she, with a smile, "you are partly to blame ; for how could I help comparing your behavior to me with his ? *You* came to my side when I was in trouble, and showed me respect when I expected scorn from all the world. A friend in need is a friend indeed."

"Reward me, reward me," said Sir George, gayly ; "you know the way."

"Nay, but I am too much *your* friend," said Mercy.

"Be less my friend then, and more my darling."

He pressed her, he urged her, he stuck to her, he pestered her.

She snubbed, and evaded, and parried, and liked him all the better for his pestering her.

At last, one day, she said : "If Mrs. Gaunt thinks it will be for your happiness, I *will* — in six months' time ; but you shall not marry in haste to repent at leisure. And I must have time to learn two things, — whether you can be constant to a simple woman like me, and whether I can love again, as tenderly as you deserve to be loved."

All his endeavors to shake this determination were vain. Mercy Vint had a terrible deal of quiet resolution.

He retired to Cumberland, and, in a long letter, asked Mrs. Gaunt's advice.

She replied characteristically. She began very soberly to say that she should be the last to advise a marriage between persons of different conditions in life. "But then," said she, "this Mercy is altogether an exception. If a flower grows on a dunghill, 't is still a flower, and not a part of the dunghill. She has the essence of gentility, and indeed her *manners* are better bred than most of our ladies. There is too much affectation abroad, and that is your true vulgarity. Tack 'my lady' on to 'Mercy Vint,' and that dignified and quiet simplicity of hers will carry her with credit through every court in Europe. Then think of her virtues," — (here the writer began to lose her temper,) — "where can you hope to find such another ? She is a moral genius, and acts well, no matter under what temptation, as surely as Claude and Raphael paint well. Why, sir, what do you seek in a wife ? Wealth ? title ?

family? But you possess them already; you want something in addition that will make you happy. Well, take that angelic goodness into your house, and you will find, by your own absolute happiness, how ill your neighbors have wived. For my part, I see but one objection : the child. Well, if you are man enough to take the mother, I am woman enough to take the babe. In one word, he who has the sense to fall in love with such an angel, and has not the sense to marry it, if he can, is a fool.

"Postscript. — My poor friend, to what end think you I sent you down in the coach with her?"

Sir George, thus advised, acted as he would have done had the advice been just the opposite.

He sent Mercy a love-letter by every post, and he often received one in return ; only his were passionate, and hers gentle and affectionate.

But one day came a letter that was a mere cry of distress.

"George, my child is dying. What shall I do?"

He mounted his horse, and rode to her.

He came too late. The little boy had died suddenly of croup, and was to be buried next morning.

The poor mother received him up stairs, and her grief was terrible. She clung sobbing to him, and could not be comforted. Yet she felt his coming. But a mother's anguish overpowered all.

Crushed by this fearful blow, her strength gave way for a time, and she clung to George Neville, and told him she had nothing left but him, and one day implored him not to die and leave her.

Sir George said all he could think of to comfort her ; and at the end of a fortnight persuaded her to leave the "Packhorse," and England, as his wife.

She had little power to resist now, and indeed little inclination.

They were married by special license, and spent a twelvemonth abroad.

At the end of that time they returned to Neville's Court, and Mercy took her place there with the same dignified simplicity that had adorned her in a humbler station.

Sir George had given her no lessons ; but she had observed closely, for his sake ; and being already well educated, and very quick and docile, she seldom made him blush except with pride.

They were the happiest pair in Cumberland. Her merciful nature now found a larger field for its exercise, and, backed by her husband's purse, she became the Lady Bountiful of the parish and the county.

The day after she reached Neville's Court came an exquisite letter to her from Mrs. Gaunt. She sent an affectionate reply.

But the Gaunts and the Nevilles did not meet in society.

Sir George Neville and Mrs. Gaunt, being both singularly brave and haughty people, rather despised this arrangement.

But it seems that, one day, when they were all four in the Town Hall, folk whispered and looked ; and both Griffith Gaunt and Lady Neville surprised these glances, and determined, by one impulse, it should never happen again. Hence it was quite understood that the Nevilles and the Gaunts were not to be asked to the same party or ball.

The wives, however, corresponded, and Lady Neville easily induced Mrs. Gaunt to co-operate with her in her benevolent acts, especially in saving young women, who had been betrayed, from sinking deeper.

Living a good many miles apart, Lady Neville could send her stray sheep to service near Mrs. Gaunt ; and *vice versa ;* and so, merciful, but discriminating, they saved many a poor girl who had been weak, not wicked.

So then, though they could not eat nor dance together in earthly mansions, they could do good together ; and methinks, in the eternal world, where years of social intercourse will prove less than cobwebs, these their joint acts of mercy will be links of a bright, strong chain, to bind their souls in everlasting amity.

It was a remarkable circumstance, that the one child of Lady Neville's unhappy marriage died, but her nine children by Sir George all grew to goodly men and women. That branch of the Nevilles became remarkable for high principle and good sense ; and this they owe to Mercy Vint, and to Sir George's courage in marrying her. This Mercy was granddaughter to one of Cromwell's ironsides, and brought her rare personal merit into their house, and also the best blood of the old Puritans, than which there is no blood in Europe more rich in male courage, female chastity, and all the virtues.

GUROWSKI.

THE late Count Gurowski came to this country from France in November, 1849, and resided at first in New York. He made his appearance at Boston, I think, in the latter part of 1850, and, being well introduced by letters from men of note in Paris, was received with attention in the highest circles of society. Among his friends at this period were Prescott, Ticknor, Longfellow, Lowell, Parker, Sumner, Felton, and Everett, — the last named of whom was then President of Harvard University. The eccentric appearance and character of the Count, of course, excited curiosity and gave rise to many idle rumors, the most popular of which declared him to be a Russian spy, though what there was to spy in this country, where everything is published in the newspapers, or what the Czar expected to learn from such an agent, nobody undertook to explain. The phrase was a convenient one, and, like many others equally senseless, was currently adopted because it seemed to explain the incomprehensible ; and certainly, to the multitude, no man was ever less intelligible than Gurowski.

To those, however, who cared for precise information, the French and German periodicals of the day, in which his name frequently figured, furnished sufficient to determine his social and historical status. From authentic sources it was soon learned that he was the head of a distinguished noble family of Poland ; that he was born in 1805, and had taken part in the great insurrection of 1831 against the Russians, for which he had been condemned to death, while his estates were confiscated and assigned to a younger brother, who had remained loyal to the Czar. It was known also that at Paris, where he had found refuge, he had been a special favorite of Lafayette and of the leading republicans, and an active member of the Polish Revolutionary Committee, till, in 1835, he published *La Vérité sur la Russie*, in which work he maintained that the interests of Poland and of all the other Slavic countries would be promoted by absorption into the Russian Empire and union under the Russian Czar. This book drew upon him the indignant denunciation of his countrymen, who regarded it as a betrayal of their cause, and led to the revocation of his sentence of death, and to an invitation to enter the service of Nicholas. He accordingly went to St. Petersburg in 1836, where his sister had long resided, personally attached to the Empress and in high favor at the imperial court. He was employed at first in the private chancery of the Emperor, and afterwards in the Department of Public Instruction, in which he suggested and introduced various measures tending to Russianize Poland by means of schools and other public institutions. He seems for some years to have been in favor, and on the high road to power and distinction. In 1844, however, he fled from St. Petersburg secretly, and took refuge at the court of Berlin. He was pursued, and his extradition demanded of the Prussian government. What his offence was I have never learned, but can readily suppose that it was only a too free use of his tongue, which was at all times uncontrollable, and was always involving him in difficulties wherever he resided. He was quite as likely to contradict and snub the Czar as readily as he would the meanest peasant, and, for that matter, even more readily. His flight from Russia caused a good deal of discussion in the Continental newspapers, and it is certain that for some reason or other strong and pertinacious efforts were made by the Russian government to have him delivered up. The Czar had at that time great influence over the court of Berlin; and Gurowski was at length privately requested by the Prussian government, in a friendly way, to relieve them of embarrassment by withdrawing from the kingdom. He accordingly went to Heidelberg and afterwards to Munich, and for two years subsequently was a Lecturer on Political Economy at the University of Berne, in Switzerland. At a later period he visited Italy, and for a year previous to his arrival in this country had resided in Paris. Besides his first work on Panslavism, already mentioned, he had published several others in French and German, which had attracted considerable attention by the force and boldness of their ideas, and the wide range of erudition displayed in them. Finally, it became known to those who cared to inquire, that one of his brothers, Ignatius Gurowski, was married to an infanta of Spain, whom I believe he had persuaded to elope with him; that Gurowski himself was a widower, with a son in the Russian navy and a daughter married in Switzerland; and that some compromise had been made about his confiscated estates by which his "loyal" brother had agreed to pay him a slender annual allowance, which was not always punctually remitted.

Such was the substance of what was known, or at least of what I knew and can now recall, of Gurowski, soon after his arrival in Boston, sixteen years ago. He came to Massachusetts, I think, with some expectation of becoming connected with Harvard University as a lecturer or professor, and took up his residence in Cambridge in lodgings in a house on Main Street, nearly opposite the College Library. In January, 1851, he gave, at President Everett's house, a course of lectures upon Roman Jurisprudence, of which I have preserved the following syllabus, printed by him in explanation of his purpose.

" COUNT DE GUROWSKI proposes to give Six Lectures upon the Roman Jurisprudence, or the Civil Law according to the following syllabus : —

" As the history of the Roman Law is likewise the history of the principle of the *Right (das Recht)* as it exists in the consciousness of men, and of its outward manifestation as a law in an organized society; a philosophical outline of this principle and of its manifestations will precede.

" The philosophical and historical progress of the notion or conception of the *Right*, through the various moments or data of jurisprudential formation by the Romans. Explanation of the principal elements and facts, out of which was framed successively the Roman law.

" Such are, for instance, the Ramnian, the Sabinian, or Quiritian; their influence on the character of the legislation and jurisprudence.

" The peculiarity and the legal meaning of the *jus quiritium.* Explanation of some of its legal rites, as those concerning matrimony, *jus mancipi, in jure cessio,* etc.

" The primitive *jus civile* derived from the *jus quiritium*. Point out the principal social element on which, and through which, the *jus privatum*, connected with the *jus civile*, was developed.

" The primitive difference between both these two kinds of *jus*.

" Other elements of the Roman Civil Law. The *jus gentium*, its nature and origin. How it was conceived by the Romans, and how it acted on the Roman community. Its agency, enlightening and softening influence on the Roman character, and on the severity of the primitive *jus civile*.

" The nature, the agency of the prætorian or *edictorial* right and jurisprudence.

" A condensed sketch of the Roman civil process. The principal formalities and rules according to the *jus quiritium*, *jus civile*, and the *edicta prætorum*. Difference between the magistrate and the judge.

" The scientific development of the above-mentioned data in the formation of the Roman Law, or the period between Augustus and Alex. Severus. Epoch of the imperial jurisconsults; its character.

" Decline. The codification of the Roman Law, or the formation of the Justinian Code. Sketch of it during the mediæval and modern periods.

" Count Gurowski is authorized to refer to Hon. Edward Everett, Prof. Parsons, Prof. Parker, Wm. H. Prescott, Esq., Hon. T. G. Cary, Charles Sumner, Esq., Hon. G. S. Hillard, Prof. Felton.

"CAMBRIDGE, January 24, 1851."

The lectures were not successful, being attended by only twenty or thirty persons, who did not find them very interesting. The truth is, that few Americans care anything for the Roman law, or for the history of the principle of the *Right* (*das Recht*); nor for the Ramnian, Sabinian, or Quiritian jurisprudence; nor whether the *jus civile* was derived from the *jus quiritium*, or the *jus quiritium* from the *jus civile*, —

nor do I see why they should care. But even if the subject had been interesting in itself, Gurowski's imperfect pronunciation of our language at that time would have insured his failure as a lecturer. He had a copious stock of English words at command; but as he had learned the language almost wholly from books, his accent was so strongly foreign that few persons could understand him at first, except those of quick apprehension and some knowledge of the French and German idioms which he habitually used.

The favor with which Gurowski had been received in the high circles of Boston society soon evaporated, as his faults of temper and of manner, and his rough criticisms on men and affairs, began to be felt. Massachusetts was then in the midst of the great conservative and proslavery reaction of 1850, and Gurowski's dogmatic radicalism was not calculated to recommend him to the ruling influences in politics, literature, or society. He denounced with vehemence, and without stint or qualification, slavery and its Northern supporters. Nothing could silence him, nobody could put him down. It was in vain to appeal to Mr. Webster, then at the height of his reputation as a Union-saver and great constitutional expounder. "What do I care for Mr. Webster," he said on some occasion when the Fugitive Slave Law was under discussion in the high circles of Beacon Street, and the dictum of the great expounder had been triumphantly appealed to. " I can read the Constitution as well as Mr. Webster." " But surely, Count, you would not presume to dispute Mr. Webster's opinion on a question of constitutional law?" "And why not?" replied Gurowski, in high wrath, and in his loudest tones. " I tell you I can read the Constitution as well as Mr. Webster, and I say that the Fugitive Slave Law is unconstitutional, — is an outrage and an imposition of which you will all soon be ashamed. It is a disgrace to humanity and to your republicanism, and Mr. Webster should be hung for advocating it. He is a humbug or an ass," continued the Count, his wrath growing fiercer as he poured it out, — " an ass if he believes such an infamous law to be constitutional ; and if he does not believe it, he is a humbug and a scoundrel for advocating it." Beacon Street, of course, was aghast at this outburst of blasphemy ; and the high circles thereof were speedily closed against the plainspoken radical who dared to question Mr. Webster's infallibility, and who made, indeed, but small account of the other idols worshipped in that locality.

It was at this time, in the spring of 1851, that I became acquainted with Gurowski. I was standing one day at the door of the reading-room in Lyceum Hall in Cambridge, of which city I was then a resident, when I saw approaching through Harvard Square a strange figure which I knew must be the Count, who had often been described to me, but whom till then I had never chanced to see. He was at the time about forty-five years of age, of middle size, with a large head and big belly, and was partly wrapped in a huge and queerly-cut cloak of German material and make. On his head he wore a high, bell-shaped, broad-brimmed hat, from which depended a long, sky-blue veil, which he used to protect his eyes from the sunshine. His waistcoat was of bright red flannel, and as it reached to his hips and covered nearly the whole of his capacious front, it formed a startlingly conspicuous portion of his attire. In addition to the veil, his eyes were protected by enormous blue goggles, with glasses on the sides as well as in front. These extraordinary precautions for the defence of his sight were made necessary by the fact that he had lost an eye, not in a duel, as has been commonly reported, but by falling on an open penknife when he was a boy of ten years old. The wounded eye was totally ruined and wasted away, and had been the seat of long and intense pain, in which, as is usual in such cases, the other eye had participated. During the first year or two of his residence in this country he

was much troubled by the intense sunshine ; but afterwards becoming used to it, he left off his veil, and in other respects conformed his costume to that of the people.

There were several gentlemen in the reading-room whom we both knew, one of whom introduced me to Gurowski, who received me very cordially, and immediately began to talk with much animation about Kossuth and Hungary, concerning which I had recently published something. He was exceedingly voluble, and seemed to have, even then, a remarkably copious stock of English words at command ; but his pronunciation, as before remarked, was very imperfect, and until I grew accustomed to his accent I found it difficult to comprehend him. This, however, made little difference to Gurowski. He would talk to any one who would listen, without caring much whether he was understood or not. On this occasion he soon became engaged in a discussion with one of the gentlemen present, a Professor in the University, who demurred to some of his statements about Hungary ; and in a short time Gurowski was foaming with rage, and formally challenged the Professor to settle the dispute with swords or pistols. This ingenious mode of deciding an historical controversy being blandly declined, Gurowski, apparently dumfounded at the idea of any gentleman's refusing so reasonable a proposition, abruptly retreated, asking me to go with him, as he said he wished to consult me ; to which request I assented very willingly, for my curiosity was a good deal excited by his strange appearance and evidently peculiar character.

He walked along in silence, and we soon reached his lodgings, which were convenient and comfortable enough. He had a parlor and bedroom on the second floor, well furnished, though in dire confusion, littered with books, papers, clothing, and other articles, tossed about at random. He gave me a cigar, and, sitting down, began to talk quite calmly and rationally about the affair at the reading-room. His excitement had entirely subsided, and he seemed to be sorry for his rudeness to the Professor, for whom he had a high regard, and who had been invariably kind to him. I spoke to him pretty roundly on the impropriety of his conduct, and the folly of which he had been guilty in offering a challenge, — a proceeding peculiarly repugnant to American, or at least to New England notions, and which only made him ridiculous. There was something so frank and childlike in his character, that, though I had known him but an hour, we seemed already intimate, and from that time to the day of his death I never had any hesitation in speaking to him about anything as freely as if he were my brother.

He took my scolding in good part, and was evidently ashamed of his conduct, though too proud to say so. He wanted to know, however, what he had best do about the matter. I advised him to do nothing, but to let the affair drop, and never make any allusion to it ; and I believe he followed my advice. At all events, he was soon again on good terms with the gentleman he had challenged.

I spent several hours with Gurowski on this occasion, and, as we both at that time had ample leisure, we soon grew intimate, and fell into the habit of passing a large part of the day together. For a long period I was accustomed to visit him every day at his lodgings, generally in the morning, while he came almost every afternoon to my house. He had a good deal of wit, but little humor, and did not relish badinage. His chief delight was in serious discussions on questions of politics, history, or theology, on which he would talk all day with immense erudition and a wonderful flow of "the best broken English that ever was spoken." He was well read in Egyptology and in mediæval history, and had a wide general knowledge of the sciences, without special familiarity with any except jurisprudence. He disdained the details of the natural sciences, and despised their professors, whose pursuits seemed to him frivolous. He was jealous of Agassiz, and of the fame and influence he had attained in this country, and was in the habit of spitefully asserting that the Professor spoke bad French, and was a mere icthyologist, who would not dare in Europe to set up as an authority in so many sciences as he did here. Even the amiable Professor Guyot, the most unassuming man in the world, who then lived in Cambridge, was also an object of this paltry jealousy. "How finely Guyot humbugs you Americans with his slops," Gurowski said to me one day. I replied that "slops" was a very unworthy and offensive word to apply to the productions of a man like Guyot, who certainly was of very respectable standing in his department of physical geography. "O bah! bah! you do not understand," exclaimed Gurowski. "I do not mean the slops of the kitchen, but the slops of the continent, — the slops and indentations which he talks so much about." *Slopes* was, of course, the word he meant to use ; and the incident may serve as a good illustration of the curious infelicities of English with which his conversation teemed.

But the truth is that Gurowski spared nobody, or scarcely anybody, in his personal criticisms. Of all his vast range of acquaintance in New England, Felton, Longfellow, and Lowell were the only persons of note of whom he spoke with uniform respect. It was really painful to see how utterly his vast knowledge and his great powers of mind were rendered worthless by a childishness of temper and a habit of contradiction which made it almost impossible for him to speak of anybody with moderation and justice. He had also a sort of infernal delight in detecting the weak points of his acquaintances, which he did with fearful quickness and penetration. The slightest hint was sufficient. He saw at a glance the frail spot, and directed his spear against it. Failings the most secret, peculiarities the most subtle, which had, perhaps, been hidden from the acquaintances of years, seemed to reveal themselves at the first glance of his single eye.

He was very fond of controversy, and would prolong a discussion from day to day with apparently unabated interest. I remember once we had a discussion about some point of mediæval history of which I knew little, but about which I feigned to be very positive, in order to draw out the stores of his knowledge, which was really immense in that direction. After a hot dispute of several hours we parted, leaving the question as unsettled as ever. The next day I called at his lodgings early in the afternoon. I knocked at the door of his room. He shouted, "Come in"; but as I opened the door I heard him retreating into his adjacent bedroom. He thrust his head out, and, seeing who it was, came back into the parlor, absolutely in a state of nature. He had not even his spectacles on. In his hand he held a pair of drawers, which he had apparently been about to assume when I arrived. Shaking this garment vehemently with one hand, while with the other he gave me a cigar, he broke out at once in a torrent of argument on the topic of the preceding day. I made no reply; but at the first pause suggested that he had better dress himself. To this he paid no attention, but stamped round the room, continuing his argument with his usual vehemence and volubility. Half an hour had elapsed, when some one knocked. Gurowski roared, "Come in!" A maid-servant opened the door, and of course instantly retreated. I turned the key, and again entreated the Count to put on his clothes. He did not comply, but kept on with his argument. Presently some one else rapped. "It is Desor," said the Count; "I know his knock; let him in." Desor was a Swiss, a scientific man, who lodged in the adjacent house. Gurowski apparently was involved in a dispute with him also, which he immediately took up, on some question of natural history. The Swiss, how-

ever, did not seem to care to contest the point, whatever it was, and soon went away. On his departure Gurowski again began his mediæval argument; but I positively refused to stay unless he put on his clothes. He reluctantly complied, and went into his bedroom, while I took up a book. Every now and then, however, he would sally out to argue some fresh point which had suggested itself to him; and his toilet was not fairly completed till, at the end of the third hour, the announcement of dinner put an end to the discussion.

Disappointed in his hopes of getting employment as a lecturer or teacher, on which he had relied for subsistence, Gurowski felt himself growing poorer and poorer as the little stock of money he had brought from Europe wasted away. The discomforts of poverty did not tend to sweeten his temper nor to abate his savage independence. He grew prouder and fiercer as he grew poorer. He was very economical, and indulged in no luxuries except cigars, of which, however, he was not a great consumer, seldom smoking more than three or four a day. But with all his care, his money was at length exhausted, his last dollar gone. He had expected remittances from Poland, which did not come; and he now learned that, from some cause which I have forgotten, nothing would be sent him for that year at least. He used to tell me from day to day of the progress of his "decline and fall," as he called it, remarking occasionally that, when the worst came to the worst, he could turn himself into an Irishman and work for his living. I paid little attention to this talk, for really the idea of Gurowski and manual labor was so ridiculously incongruous that I could not form any definite conception of it. But he was more in earnest than I supposed.

Going one day at my usual hour to his lodgings, I found him absent. I called again in the course of the day, but he was still not at home, and the people of the house informed me that he had been absent since early morning. The next day it was the same. On the third day I lay in wait for him at evening at his lodgings, to which he came about dark, in a most forlorn condition, with his hands blistered, his clothes dusty, and exhibiting himself every mark of extreme fatigue. He was cheerful, however, and very cordial, and gave me an animated account of his adventures in his " Irish life," as he called it. It seems he had formed an acquaintance with Mr. Hovey, the proprietor of the large nurseries between Boston and the Colleges, and on the morning of the day on which I found him absent from his lodgings he had gone to Hovey and offered himself as a laborer in his garden. Hovey was astounded at the proposition, but the Count insisted, and finally a spade was given to him, and he set to work "like an Irishman," as he delighted to express it. It was dreadfully wearisome to his unaccustomed muscles, but anything, he said, was better than getting in debt. He could earn a dollar a day, and that would pay for his board and his cigars. He had clothes enough, he thought, to last him the rest of his life, — especially, he added somewhat dolefully, as he was not likely to live long under the Irish regimen.

I thought the joke had been carried far enough, and that it was time to interfere. I accordingly went next day to Boston, and, calling on the publisher of a then somewhat flourishing weekly newspaper, now extinct, called " The Boston Museum," I described to him the situation and the capacities of Gurowski, and proposed that he should employ the Count to write an article of reasonable length each week about European life, for which he was to be paid twelve dollars. I undertook to revise Gurowski's English sufficiently to make it intelligible. The publisher readily acceded to this proposition ; and the Count, when I communicated it to him, was as delighted as if he had found a gold mine, or, in the language of to-day, " had struck ile." He was already, in spite of his philo-

sophic cheerfulness, heartily sick of his labor with the spade, for which he was totally unfitted. He resumed his pen with alacrity, and wrote an article on the private life of the Russian court, which I copied, with the necessary revision, and carried to the publisher of the Museum, who was greatly pleased with it, and readily paid the stipulated price.

For several months Gurowski continued to write an article every week, which he did very easily, and the pay for them soon re-established his finances on what, with his simple habits, he considered a sound basis. In fact, he soon grew rich enough, in his own estimation, to spend the summer at Newport, which he said he wanted to do, because the Americans of the highest social class evidently regarded a summer visit to that place as the chief enjoyment of their life and the crowning glory of their civilization. He went thither in June, 1851, and after that I only saw him at long intervals, and for very brief periods.

His stay at Newport was short, and he went from there to New York, where he soon became an editorial writer for the Tribune. To a Cambridge friend of mine, who met him in Broadway, he expressed great satisfaction with his new avocation. " It is the most delightful position," he said, " that you can possibly conceive of. I can abuse everybody in the world except Greeley, Ripley, and Dana." He inquired after me, and, as my friend was leaving him, sent me a characteristic message, — " Tell C—— that he is an ass." My friend inquired the reason for this flattering communication ; and Gurowski replied, " Because he does not write to me." Busy with many things which had fallen to me to do after his departure, I had neglected to keep up our correspondence, at which he was sometimes very wrathful, and wrote me savagely affectionate notes of remonstrance.

Besides writing for the Tribune, Gurowski was employed by Ripley and Dana on the first four volumes of the

New American Cyclopædia, for which he wrote the articles on Alexander the Great, the Alexanders of Russia, Aristocracy, Attila, the Borgias, Bunsen, and a few others. It was at this time also that he wrote his books, " Russia as it is," and " America and Europe." In preparing for publication his articles and his books, he had the invaluable assistance of Mr. Ripley, who gratuitously bestowed upon them an immense amount of labor, for which he was very ill requited by the Count, who quarrelled both with him and Dana, and for a time wantonly and most unjustly abused them both in his peculiar lavish way.

For two or three years longer I lost sight of him, during which period he led a somewhat wandering life, visiting the South, and residing alternately in Washington, Newport, Geneseo, and Brattleborough. The last time I saw him in New York was at the Athenæum Club one evening in December, 1860, just after South Carolina had seceded. A dispute was raging in the smoking-room, between Unionists on one side and Copperheads on the other, as to the comparative character of the North and South. Gurowski, who was reading in an adjoining room, was attracted by the noise, and came in, but at first said nothing, standing in silence on the outside of the circle. At last a South-Carolinian who was present appealed to him, saying, "Count, you have been in the South, let us have your opinion ; you at least ought to be impartial." Gurowski thrust his head forward, as he was accustomed to do when about to say anything emphatic, and replied in his most energetic manner : " I have been a great deal in the South as well as in the North, and know both sections equally well, and I tell you, gentlemen, that there is more intelligence, more refinement, more cultivation, more virtue, and more good manners in one New England village than in all the South together." This decision put an end to the discussion. The South-Carolinian retreated in dudgeon, and Gurowski, chuck-

ling, returned to his book or his paper.

Shortly after this he took up his abode in Washington, where he soon became one of the notables of the city, frequenting some of the best houses, and almost certain to be seen of an evening at Willard's, the political exchange of the capital, where his singular appearance and emphatic conversation seldom failed to attract a large share of attention. The proceeds of the books he had published, never very large, had by this time been used up ; and he was consequently very poor, for which, however, he cared little. But some of the Senators, who liked and pitied the rough-spoken, but warm-hearted and honest old man, persuaded Mr. Seward to appoint him to some post in the State Department created for the occasion. His nominal duty was to explore the Continental newspapers for matter interesting to the American government, and to furnish the Secretary of State, when called upon, with opinions upon diplomatic questions. As he once stated it to me in his terse way, it was " to read the German newspapers, and keep Seward from making a fool of himself." The first part of this duty, he said, was easy enough, but the latter part rather difficult. He kept the office longer than I expected, knowing his temper and habit of grumbling ; but even Mr. Seward's patience was at length exhausted, and he was dismissed for long-continued disrespectful remarks concerning his official superior.

Some time in 1862 I met Gurowski in Washington, at the rooms of Senator Sumner, which he was in the habit of visiting almost every evening. I had not seen him for a long time, and he greeted me very cordially; but I soon perceived that his habit of dogmatism had increased terribly, and that he was more impatient than ever of contradiction. He began to talk in a high tone about McClellan, the Army of the Potomac, and the probable duration of the Rebellion. His views for the most part seemed sound enough, but were so offensively expressed that, partly in impatience and partly for amusement, I soon began to contradict him roundly on every point. He became furious, and for nearly an hour stormed and stamped about the room, in the centre of which sat Mr. Sumner in his great chair, taking no part in the discussion, but making occasional ineffectual attempts to pacify Gurowski, who at length rushed out of the room in a rage too deep for even his torrent of words to express. After his departure, Mr. Sumner remarked that he reminded him of the whale in Barnum's Museum, which kept going round and round in its narrow tank, blowing with all its might whenever it came to the surface, which struck me at the time as a singularly apt comparison.

I met Gurowski the next evening at the Tribune rooms, near Willard's, and found him still irritated and disposed to "blow." I checked him, however, told him I had had enough of nonsense, and wanted him to talk soberly; and, taking his arm, walked with him to his lodgings, where, while he dressed for a party, which he always did with great care, I made him tell me his opinion about men and affairs. He was unusually moderate and rational, and described the "situation," as the newspapers call it, with force and penetration. The army, he thought, was everything that could be desired, if it only had an efficient commander and a competent staff. I asked what he thought of Lincoln. "He is a beast.' This was all he would say of him. I knew, of course, that he meant *bête* in the French sense, and not in the offensive English sense of the word. The truth was, that Gurowski had little relish for humor, and the drollery which formed so prominent a part of Lincoln's external character was unintelligible and offensive to him. At a later period,

as I judge from his Diary, he understood the President better, and did full justice to his noble qualities.

I was particularly curious to know what he thought of Seward, whom he had good opportunities of seeing at that time, as he was still in the service of the State Department. He pronounced him shallow and insincere, and ludicrously ignorant of European affairs. The diplomatists of Europe, he said, were all making fun of his despatches, and looked upon him as only a clever charlatan.

This proved to be my last conversation with Gurowski. I met him once again, however, at Washington, in the spring of 1863. I was passing up Fifteenth Street, by the Treasury Department, and reached one of the cross-streets just as a large troop of cavalry came along. The street was ankle-deep with mud, only the narrow crossing being passable, and I hurried to get over before the cavalry came up. Midway on the crossing I encountered Gurowski, wrapped in a long black cloak and a huge felt hat, rather the worse for wear. He threw open his arms to stop me, and, without any preliminary phrase, launched into an invective on Horace Greeley. In an instant the troop was upon us, and we were surrounded by trampling and rearing horses, and soldiers shouting to us to get out of the way. Gurowski, utterly heedless of all around him, raised his voice above the tumult, and roared that Horace Greeley was "an ass, a traitor, and a coward." It was no time to hold a parley on that question, and, breaking from him, I made for the opposite sidewalk, then, turning, saw Gurowski for the last time, enveloped in a cloud of horsemen, through which he was composedly making his way at his usual meditative pace.

THE PRESIDENT AND HIS ACCOMPLICES.

ANDREW JOHNSON has dealt the most cruel of all blows to the respectability of the faction which rejoices in his name. Hardly had the political Pecksniffs and Turveydrops contrived so to manage the Johnson Convention at Philadelphia that it violated few of the proprieties of intrigue and none of the decencies of dishonesty, than the commander-in-chief of the combination took the field in person, with the intention of carrying the country by assault. His objective point was the grave of Douglas, which became by the time he arrived the grave also of his own reputation and the hopes of his partisans. His speeches on the route were a volcanic outbreak of vulgarity, conceit, bombast, scurrility, ignorance, insolence, brutality, and balderdash. Screams of laughter, cries of disgust, flushings of shame, were the various responses of the nation he disgraced to the harangues of this leader of American "conservatism." Never before did the first office in the gift of the people appear so poor an object of human ambition, as when Andrew Johnson made it an eminence on which to exhibit inability to behave and incapacity to reason. His low cunning conspired with his devouring egotism to make him throw off all the restraints of official decorum, in the expectation that he would find duplicates of himself in the crowds he addressed, and that mob diffused would heartily sympathize with Mob impersonated. Never was blustering demagogue led by a distempered sense of self-importance into a more fatal error. Not only was the great body of the people mortified or indignant, but even his "satraps and dependents," even the shrewd politicians — accidents of an Accident and shadows of a shade — who had labored so hard at Philadelphia to weave a cloak of plausibilities to cover his usurpations, shivered with apprehension or tingled with shame as they read the reports of their master's impolitic and ignominious abandonment of dignity and decency in his addresses to the people he attempted alternately to bully and cajole. That a man thus self-exposed as unworthy of high trust should have had the face to expect that intelligent constituencies would send to Congress men pledged to support *his* policy and *his* measures, appeared for the time to be as pitiable a spectacle of human delusion as it was an exasperating example of human impudence.

Not the least extraordinary peculiarity of these addresses from the stump was the immense protuberance they exhibited of the personal pronoun. In Mr. Johnson's speech, his " I " resembles the geometer's description of infinity, having "its centre everywhere and its circumference nowhere." Among the many kinds of egotism in which his eloquence is prolific, it may be difficult to fasten on the particular one which is most detestable or most laughable; but it seems to us that when his arrogance apes humility it is deserving perhaps of an intenser degree of scorn or derision than when it riots in bravado. The most offensive part which he plays in public is that of "the humble individual," bragging of the lowliness of his origin, hinting of the great merits which could alone have lifted him to his present exalted station, and representing himself as so satiated with the sweets of unsought power as to be indifferent to its honors. Ambition is not for him, for ambition aspires; and what object has he to aspire to? From his contented mediocrity as alderman of a village, the people have insisted on elevating him from one pinnacle of greatness to another, until they have at last made him President of the United States. He might have been Dictator had he pleased; but what, to a man wearied with authority and dignity, would dictatorship be worth?

If he is proud of anything, it is of the tailor's bench from which he started. He would have everybody to understand that he is humble, — thoroughly humble. Is this caricature ? No. It is impossible to caricature Andrew Johnson when he mounts his high horse of humility and becomes a sort of cross between Uriah Heep and Josiah Bounderby of Coketown. Indeed, it is only by quoting Dickens's description of the latter personage that we have anything which fairly matches the traits suggested by some statements in the President's speeches. " A big, loud man," says the humorist, " with a stare and a metallic laugh. A man made out of coarse material, which seemed to have been stretched to make so much of him. A man with a great puffed head and forehead, swelled veins in his temples, and such a strained skin to his face, that it seemed to hold his eyes open and lift his eyebrows up. A man with a pervading appearance on him of being inflated like a balloon, and ready to start. A man who could never sufficiently vaunt himself a self-made man. A man who was continually proclaiming, through that brassy speaking-trumpet of a voice of his, his old ignorance and his old poverty. A man who was the Bully of humility."

If we turn from the moral and personal to the mental characteristics of Mr. Johnson's speeches, we find that his brain is to be classed with notable cases of arrested development. He has strong forces in his nature, but in their outlet through his mind they are dissipated into a confusing clutter of unrelated thoughts and inapplicable phrases. He seems to possess neither the power nor the perception of coherent thinking and logical arrangement. He does not appear to be aware that prepossessions are not proofs, that assertions are not arguments, that the proper method to answer an objection is not to repeat the proposition against which the objection was directed, that the proper method of unfolding a subject is not to make the successive statements a series of contradictions. Indeed, he seems to have a thoroughly animalized intellect, destitute of the notion of relations, with ideas which are but the form of determinations, and which derive their force, not from reason, but from will. With an individuality thus strong even to fierceness, but which has not been developed in the mental region, and which the least gust of passion intellectually upsets, he is incapable of looking at anything out of relations to himself, — of regarding it from that neutral ground which is the condition of intelligent discussion between opposing minds. . In truth, he makes a virtue of being insensible to the evidence of facts and the deductions of reason, proclaiming to all the world that he has taken his position, that he will never swerve from it, and that all statements and arguments intended to shake his resolves are impertinences, indicating that their authors are radicals and enemies of the country. He is never weary of vaunting his firmness, and firmness he doubtless has, the firmness of at least a score of mules ; but events have shown that it is a different kind of firmness from that which keeps a statesman firm to his principles, a political leader to his pledges, a gentleman to his word. Amid all changes of opinion, he has been conscious of unchanged will, and the intellectual element forms so small a portion of his being, that, when he challenged " the man, woman, or child to come forward " and convict him of inconstancy to his professions, he knew that, however it might be with the rest of mankind, he would himself be unconvinced by any evidence which the said man, woman, or child might adduce. Again, when he was asked by one of his audiences why he did not hang Jeff Davis, he retorted by exclaiming, " Why don't you ask me why I have not hanged Thad Stevens and Wendell Phillips ? They are as much traitors as Davis." And we are almost charitable enough to suppose that he saw no difference between the moral or legal treason of the man who for four years had waged open war against the government of the United States, and the men who for one year had sharply criticised the acts and utterances of Andrew Johnson. It is not to be expected that nice distinctions will be made by a magistrate who is in the habit of denying indisputable facts with the fury of a pugilist who has received a personal affront, and of announcing demonstrated fallacies with the imperturbable serenity of a philosopher proclaiming the fundamental laws of human belief. His brain is entirely ridden by his will, and of all the public men in the country its official head is the one whose opinion carries with it the least intellectual weight. It is to the credit of our institutions and our statesmen that the man least qualified by largeness of mind and moderation of temper to exercise uncontrolled power should be the man who aspired to usurp it. The constitutional instinct in the blood, and the constitutional principle in the brain, of our real statesmen, preserve them from the folly and guilt of setting themselves up as imitative Cæsars and Napoleons, the moment they are trusted with a little delegated power.

Still we are told, that, with all his defects, Andrew Johnson is to be honored and supported as a "conservative" President engaged in a contest with a "radical" Congress! It happens, however, that the two persons who specially represent Congress in this struggle are Senators Trumbull and Fessenden. Senator Trumbull is the author of the two important measures which the President vetoed ; Senator Fessenden is the chairman and organ of the Committee of Fifteen which the President anathematizes. Now we desire to do justice to the gravity of face which the partisans of Mr. Johnson preserve in announcing their most absurd propositions, and especially do we commend their command of countenance while it is their privilege to contrast the wild notions and violent speech of such lawless radicals as the Senator from Illinois and the Senator from Maine, with the balanced judgment and

moderate temper of such a pattern conservative as the President of the United States. The contrast prompts ideas so irresistibly ludicrous, that to keep one's risibilities under austere control while instituting it argues a self-command almost miraculous.

Andrew Johnson, however, such as he is in heart, intellect, will, and speech, is the recognized leader of his party, and demands that the great mass of his partisans shall serve him, not merely by prostration of body, but by prostration of mind. It is the hard duty of his more intimate associates to translate his broken utterances from *Andy-Johnsonese* into constitutional phrase, to give these versions some show of logical arrangement, and to carry out, as best they may, their own objects, while professing boundless devotion to his. By a sophistical process of developing his rude notions, they often lead him to conclusions which he had not foreseen, but which they induce him to make his own, not by a fruitless effort to quicken his mind into following the steps of their reasoning, but by stimulating his passions to the point of adopting its results. They thus become parasites in order that they may become powers, and their interests make them particularly ruthless in their dealings with their master's consistency. Their relation to him, if they would bluntly express it, might be indicated in this brief formula : "We will adore you in order that you may obey us."

The trouble with these politicians is, that they cannot tie the President's tongue as they tied the tongues of the eminent personages they invited from all portions of the country to keep silent at their great Convention at Philadelphia. That Convention was a masterpiece of cunning political management ; but its Address and Resolutions were hardly laid at Mr. Johnson's feet, when, in his exultation, he blurted out that unfortunate remark about "a body called, or which assumed to be, the Congress of the United States," which, it appears, "we have seen hanging on the verge of the government." Now all this was in the Address of the Convention, but it was not so brutally worded, nor so calculated to appall those timid supporters of the Johnson party who thought, in their innocence, that the object of the Philadelphia meeting was to heal the wounds of civil war, and not to lay down a programme by which it might be reopened. Turning, then, from Mr. Johnson to the manifesto of his political supporters, let us see what additions it makes to political wisdom, and what guaranties it affords for future peace. We shall not discriminate between insurgent States and individual insurgents, because, when individual insurgents are so overwhelmingly strong that they carry their States with them, or when States are so overwhelmingly strong that they force individuals to be insurgents, it appears to be needless. The terms are often used interchangeably in the Address, for the Convention was so largely composed of individual insurgents that it was important to vary a little the charge that they usurped State powers with the qualification that they obeyed the powers they usurped. At the South, individual insurgents constitute the State when they determine to rebel, and obey it when they desire to be pardoned. An identical thing cannot be altered by giving it two names.

The principle which runs through the Philadelphia Address is, that insurgent States recover their former rights under the Constitution by the mere fact of submission. This is equivalent to saying that insurgent States incurred no guilt in rebellion. But States cannot become insurgent, unless the authorities of such States commit perjury and treason, and their people become rebels and public enemies ; perjury, treason, and rebellion are commonly held to be crimes ; and who ever heard, before, that criminals were restored to all the rights of honest citizens by the mere fact of their arrest ?

The doctrine, moreover, is a worse heresy than that of Secession ; for Secession implies that seceded States, be-

ing out of the Union, can plainly only be brought back by conquest, and on such terms as the victors may choose to impose. No candid Southern Rebel, who believes that his State seceded, and that he acted under competent authority when he took up arms against the United States, can have the effrontery to affirm that he had inherent rights of citizenship in " the foreign country " against which he plotted and fought for four years. The so-called " right " of secession was claimed by the South as a constitutional right, to be peaceably exercised, but it passed into the broader and more generally intelligible " right " of revolution when it had to be sustained by war ; and the condition of a defeated revolutionist is certainly not that of a qualified voter in the nation against which he revolted. But if insurgent States recover their former rights and privileges when they submit to superior force, there is no reason why armed rebellion should not be as common as local discontent. We have, on this principle, sacrificed thirty-five hundred millions of dollars and three hundred thousand lives, only to bring the insurgent States into just those " practical relations to the Union " which will enable us to sacrifice thirty-five hundred millions of dollars more, and three hundred thousand more lives, when it suits the passions and caprices of these States to rebel again. Whatever they may do in the way of disturbing the peace of the country, they can never, it seems, forfeit their rights and privileges under the Constitution. Even if everybody was positively certain that there would be a new rebellion in ten years, unless conditions of representation were exacted of the South, we still, according to the doctrine of the Johnsonian jurists, would be constitutionally impotent to exact them, because insurgent States recover unconditioned rights to representation by the mere fact of their submitting to the power they can no longer resist. The acceptance of this principle would make insurrection the chronic disease of our political system. War would follow war, until nearly all the wealth of the country was squandered, and nearly all the inhabitants exterminated. Mr. Johnson's prophetic vision of that Paradise of constitutionalism, shadowed forth in his exclamation that he would stand by the Constitution though all around him should perish, would be measurably realized ; and among the ruins of the nation a few haggard and ragged pedants would be left to drone out eulogies on "the glorious Constitution" which had survived unharmed the anarchy, poverty, and depopulation it had produced. An interpretation of the Constitution which thus makes it the shield of treason and the destroyer of civilization must be false both to fact and sense. The framers of that instrument were not idiots ; yet idiots they would certainly have been, if they had put into it a clause declaring "that no State, or combination of States, which may at any time choose to get up an armed attempt to overthrow the government established by this Constitution, and be defeated in the attempt, shall forfeit any of the privileges granted by this instrument to loyal States." But an interpretation of the Constitution which can be conceived of as forming a possible part of it only by impeaching the sanity of its framers, cannot be an interpretation which the American people are morally bound to risk ruin to support.

But even if we should be wild enough to admit the Johnsonian principle respecting insurgent States, the question comes up as to the identity of the States now demanding representation with the States whose rights of representation are affirmed to have been only suspended during their rebellion. The fact would seem to be, that these reconstructed States are merely the creations of the executive branch of the government, with every organic bond hopelessly cut which connected them with the old State governments and constitutions. They have only the names of the States they pretend to *be.* Before the Rebellion, they had a legal people ; when Mr. Johnson took hold of them, they had nothing but a

disorganized population. Out of this population he by his own will created a people, on the principle, we must suppose, of natural selection. Now, to decide who are the people of a State is to create its very foundations, — to begin anew in the most comprehensive sense of the word ; for the being of a State is more in its people, that is, in the persons selected from its inhabitants to be the depositaries of its political power, than it is in its geographical boundaries and area. Over this people thus constituted by himself, Mr. Johnson set Provisional Governors nominated by himself. These Governors called popular conventions, whose members were elected by the votes of those to whom Mr. Johnson had given the right of suffrage ; and these conventions proceeded to do what Mr. Johnson dictated. Everywhere Mr. Johnson ; nowhere the assumed rights of the States ! North Carolina was one of these creations ; and North Carolina, through the lips of its Chief Justice, has already decided that Mr. Johnson was an unauthorized intruder, and his work a nullity, and even Mr. Johnson's "people" of North Carolina have rejected the constitution framed by Mr. Johnson's Convention. Other Rebel communities will doubtless repudiate his work, as soon as they can dispense with his assistance. But whatever may be the condition of these new Johnsonian States, they are certainly not States which can "recover" rights which existed previous to their creation. The date of their birth is to be reckoned, not from any year previous to the Rebellion, but from the year which followed its suppression. It may, in old times, have been a politic trick of shrewd politicians, to involve the foundations of States in the mists of a mythical antiquity ; but we happily live in an historical period, and there is something peculiarly stupid or peculiarly impudent in the attempt of the publicists of the Philadelphia Convention to ignore the origins of political societies for which, after they have obtained a certain degree of organization, they claim such eminent traditional rights and privileges. Respectable as these States may be as infant phenomena, it will not do to *Methuselahize* them too recklessly, or assert their equality in muscle and brawn with giants full grown.

It is evident, from the nature of the case, that Mr. Johnson's labors were purely experimental and provisional, and needed the indorsement of Congress to be of any force. The only department of the government constitutionally capable to admit new States or rehabilitate insurgent ones is the legislative. When the Executive not only took the initiative in reconstruction, but assumed to have completed it; when he presented *his* States to Congress as the equals of the States represented in that body; when he asserted that the delegates from his States should have the right of sitting and voting in the legislature whose business it was to decide on their right to admission; when, in short, he demanded that criminals at the bar should have a seat on the bench, and an equal voice with the judges, in deciding on their own case, the effrontery of Executive pretension went beyond all bounds of Congressional endurance.

The real difference at first was not on the question of imposing conditions, —for the President had notoriously imposed them himself, — but on the question whether or not additional conditions were necessary to secure the public safety. The President, with that facility "in turning his back on himself" which all other logical gymnasts had pronounced an impossible feat, then boldly took the ground, that, being satisfied with the conditions he had himself exacted, the exaction of conditions was unconstitutional. To sustain this curious proposition he adduced no constitutional arguments, but he left various copies of the Constitution in each of the crowds he recently addressed, with the trust, we suppose, that somebody might be fortunate enough to find in that instrument the clause which supported his theory. Mr. Johnson,

however, though the most consequential of individuals, is the most inconsequential of reasoners; every proposition which is evident to himself he considers to fulfil the definition of a self-evident proposition; but his supporters at Philadelphia must have known, that, in affirming that insurgent States recover their former rights by the fact of submission, they were arraigning the conduct of their leader, who had notoriously violated those "rights." They took up his work at a certain stage, and then, with that as a basis, they affirmed a general proposition about insurgent States, which, had it been complied with by the President, would have left them no foundation at all; for the States about which they so glibly generalized would have had no show of organized governments. The premises of their argument were obtained by the violation of its conclusion; they inferred from what was a negation of their inference, and deduced from what was a death-blow to their deduction.

It is easy enough to understand why the Johnson Convention asserted the equality of the Johnson reconstructions of States with the States now represented in Congress. The object was to give some appearance of legality to a contemplated act of arbitrary power, and the principle that insurgent States recover all their old rights by the fact of submission was invented in order to cover the case. Mr. Johnson now intends, by the admission of his partisans, to attempt a *coup d'état* on the assembling of the Fortieth Congress, in case seventy-one members of the House of Representatives, favorable to his policy, are chosen, in the elections of this autumn, from the twenty-six loyal States. These, with the fifty Southern delegates, would constitute a quorum of the House; and the remaining hundred and nineteen members are, in the President's favorite phrase, "to be kicked out" from that "verge" of the government on which they now are said to be "hanging." The question, therefore, whether Congress, as it is at present constituted, is a body constitutionally competent to legislate for the whole country, is the most important of all practical questions. Let us see how the case stands.

The Constitution, ratified by the people of all the States, establishes a government of sovereign powers, supreme over the whole land, and the people of no State can rightly pass from under its authority except by the consent of the people of all the States, with whom it is bound by the most solemn and binding of contracts. The Rebel States broke, *in fact*, the contract they could not break *in right*. Assembled in conventions of their people, they passed ordinances of secession, withdrew their Senators and Representatives from Congress, and began the war by assailing a fort of the United States. The Secessionists had trusted to the silence of the Constitution in relation to the act they performed. A State in the American Union, as distinguished from a Territory, is constitutionally a part of the government to which it owes allegiance, and the seceded States had refused to be parts of the government, and had forsworn their allegiance. By the Constitution, the United States, in cases of "domestic violence" in a State, is to interfere, "on application of the Legislature, or of the Executive when the Legislature cannot be convened." But in this case legislatures, executives, conventions of the people, were all violators of the domestic peace, and of course made no application for interference. By the Constitution, Congress is empowered to suppress insurrections; but this might be supposed to mean insurrections like Shays's Rebellion in Massachusetts and the Whiskey Insurrection in Pennsylvania, and not to cover the action of States seceding from the Congress which is thus empowered. The seceders, therefore, felt somewhat as did the absconding James II. when he flung the Great Seal into the Thames, and thought he had stopped the machinery of the English government.

Mr. Buchanan, then President of the United States, admitted at once that the Secessionists had done their work in such a way that, though they had done wrong, the government was powerless to compel them to do right. And here the matter should have rested, if the government established by the Constitution was such a government as Mr. Johnson's supporters now declare it to be. If it is impotent to prescribe terms of peace in relation to insurgent States, it is certainly impotent to make war on insurgent States. If insurgent States recover their former constitutional rights in laying down their arms, then there was no criminality in their taking them up; and if there was no criminality in their taking them up, then the United States was criminal in the war by which they were forced to lay them down. On this theory we have a government incompetent to legislate for insurgent States, because lacking their representatives, waging against them a cruel and unjust war. And this is the real theory of the defeated Rebels and Copperheads who formed the great mass of the delegates to the Johnson Convention. Should they get into power, they would feel themselves logically justified in annulling, not only all the acts of the "Rump Congress" since they submitted, but all the acts of the Rump Congresses during the time they had a Confederate Congress of their own. They may deny that this is their intention; but what intention to forego the exercise of an assumed right, held by those who are out of power, can be supposed capable of limiting their action when they are in?

But if the United States is a government having legitimate rights of sovereignty conferred upon it by the people of all the States, and if, consequently, the attempted secession of the people of one or more States only makes them criminals, without impairing the sovereignty of the United States, then the government, with all its powers, remains with the representatives of the loyal people. By the very nature of government as government, the rights and privileges guaranteed to citizens are guaranteed to loyal citizens ; the rights and privileges guaranteed to States are guaranteed to loyal States ; and loyal citizens and loyal States are not such as profess a willingness to be loyal after having been utterly worsted in an enterprise of gigantic disloyalty. The organic unity and continuity of the government would be broken by the return of disloyal citizens and Rebel States without their going through the process of being restored by the action of the government they had attempted to subvert ; and the power to restore carries with it the power to decide on the terms of restoration. And when we speak of the government, we are not courtly enough to mean by the expression simply its executive branch. The question of admitting and implicitly of restoring States, and of deciding whether or not States have a republican form of government, are matters left by the Constitution to the discretion of Congress. As to the Rebel States now claiming representation, they have succumbed, thoroughly exhausted, in one of the costliest and bloodiest wars in the history of the world, — a war which tasked the resources of the United States more than they would have been tasked by a war with all the great powers of Europe combined, — a war which, in 1862, had assumed such proportions, that the Supreme Court decided that it gave the United States the same rights and privileges which the government might exercise in the case of a national and foreign war. The inhabitants of the insurgent States being thus judicially declared public enemies as well as Rebels, there would seem to be no doubt at all that the victorious close of actual hostilities could not deprive the government of the power of deciding on the terms of peace with public enemies. The government of the United States found the insurgent States thoroughly revolutionized and disorganized, with no State governments which could be recognized without recognizing the validity of treason, and without the power or right to take even the initial steps for State reorganization. They were practically out of the Union as States ; their State governments had lapsed ; their population was composed of Rebels and public enemies, by the decision of the Supreme Court. Under such circumstances, how the Commander-in-Chief, under Congress, of the forces of the United States could re-create these defunct States, and make it mandatory on Congress to receive their delegates, has always appeared to us one of those mysteries of unreason which require faculties either above or below humanity to accept. In addition to this fundamental objection, there was the further one, that almost all of the delegates were Rebels presidentially pardoned into "loyal men," were elected with the idea of forcing Congress to repeal the test oath, and were incapacitated to be legislators even if they had been sent from loyal States. The few who were loyal men in the sense that they had not served the Rebel government, were still palpably elected by constituents who had ; and the character of the constituency is as legitimate a subject of Congressional inquiry as the character of the representative.

It not being true, then, that the twenty-two hundred thousand loyal voters who placed Mr. Johnson in office, and whom he betrayed, have no means by their representatives in Congress to exert a controlling power in the reconstruction of the Rebel communities, the question comes up as to the conditions which Congress has imposed. It always appeared to us that the true measure of conciliation, of security, of mercy, of justice, was one which would combine the principle of universal amnesty, or an amnesty nearly universal, with that of universal, or at least of impartial suffrage. In regard to amnesty, the amendment to the Constitution which Congress has passed disqualifies no Rebels from voting, and only disqualifies them from holding office when they have happened to add perjury to treason. In regard to suffrage, it makes it for the political interest of the South to be just to its colored citizens, by basing representation on voters, and not on population, and thus places the indulgence of class prejudices and hatreds under the penalty of a corresponding loss of political power in the Electoral College and the National House of Representatives. If the Rebel States should be restored without this amendment becoming a part of the Constitution, then the recent Slave States will have thirty Presidential Electors and thirty members of the House of Representatives in virtue of a population they disfranchise, and the vote of a Rebel white in South Carolina will carry with it more than double the power of a loyal white in Massachusetts or Ohio. The only ground on which this disparity can be defended is, that as "one Southerner is more than a match for two Yankees," he has an inherent, continuous, unconditioned right to have this superiority recognized at the ballot-box. Indeed, the injustice of this is so monstrous, that the Johnson orators find it more convenient to decry all conditions of representation than to meet the incontrovertible reasons for exacting the condition which bases representation on voters. Not to make it a part of the Constitution would be, in Mr. Shellabarger's vivid illustration, to allow "that Lee's vote should have double the elective power of Grant's ; Semmes's double that of Farragut's ; *Booth's — did he live — double that of Lincoln's, his victim !* "

It is also to be considered that these thirty votes would, in almost all future sessions of Congress, decide the fate of the most important measures. In 1862 the Republicans, as Congress is now constituted, only had a majority of twenty votes. In alliance with the Northern Democratic party, the South with these thirty votes might repeal the Civil Rights Bill, the principle of which is embodied in the proposed amendment. It might assume the Rebel debt, which is repudiated in that amendment. It might even repudiate the Federal debt, which is affirmed in that amendment. We are so accustomed to look at the Rebel debt as dead beyond all power of resurrection, as to forget that it amounts, with the valuation of the emancipated slaves, to some four thousand millions of dollars. If the South and its Northern Democratic allies should come into power, there is a strong probability that a measure would be brought in to assume at least a portion of this debt, — say two thousand millions. The Southern members would be nearly a unit for assumption, and the Northern Democratic members would certainly be exposed to the most frightful temptation that legislators ever had to resist. Suppose it were necessary to buy fifty members at a million of dollars apiece, that sum would only be two and a half per cent of the whole. Suppose it were necessary to give them ten millions apiece, even that would only be a deduction of twenty-five per cent from a claim worthless without their votes. The bribery might be conducted in such a way as to elude discovery, if not suspicion, and the measure would certainly be trumpeted all over the North as the grandest of all acts of statesmanlike "conciliation," binding the South to the Union in indissoluble bonds of interest. The amendment renders the conversion of the Rebel debt into the most enormous of all corruption funds an impossibility.

But the character and necessity of the amendment are too well understood to need explanation, enforcement, or defence. If it, or some more stringent one, be not adopted, the loyal people will be tricked out of the fruits of the war they have waged at the expense of such unexampled sacrifices of treasure and blood. It never will be adopted unless it be practically made a condition of the restoration of the Rebel States ; and for the unconditioned restoration of those States the President, through his most trusted supporters, has indicated his intention to venture a *coup d'état*. This threat has failed doubly of its purpose. The timid, whom it was expected to frighten, it has simply scared into the reception of the idea that the only way to escape civil war is by the election of over a hundred and twenty Republican Representatives to the Fortieth Congress. The courageous, whom it was intended to defy, it has only exasperated into more strenuous efforts against the insolent renegade who had the audacity to make it.

Everywhere in the loyal States there is an uprising of the people only paralleled by the grand uprising of 1861. The President's plan of reconstruction having passed from a policy into a conspiracy, his chief supporters are now not so much his partisans as his accomplices ; and against him and his accomplices the people will this autumn indignantly record the most overwhelming of verdicts.

ART.

MARSHALL'S PORTRAIT OF ABRAHAM LINCOLN.

WHEN we consider the conditions under which the art of successful line-engraving is attained, the amount and quality of artistic knowledge implied, the years of patient, unwearied application imperiously demanded, the numerous manual difficulties to be overcome, and the technical skill to be acquired, it is not surprising that the names of so few engravers should be pre-eminent and familiar.

In our own country, at least, the instinct and habit of the people do not favor the growth and perfection of an art only possible under such conditions.

So fully and satisfactorily, however, have these demands been met in Marshall's line-engraving of the head of Abraham Lincoln, executed after Mr. Marshall's own painting, that we are induced to these preliminary thoughts as much by a sense of national pride as of delight and surprise.

Our admiration of the engraving is first due to its value as a likeness ; for it is only when the heart rests from a full and satisfied contemplation of the face endeared to us all, that we can regard it for its artistic worth.

Mr. Marshall did not need this last work, to rank him at the head of American engravers ; for his portraits of Washington and Fenimore Cooper had done that already ; but it has lifted him to a place with the foremost engravers of the world.

The greatness and glory of his success, in this instance, are to be measured by the inherent difficulties in the subject itself.

The intellectual and physical traits of Abraham Lincoln were such as the world had never seen before. Original, peculiar, and anomalous, they seemed incapable of analysis and classification.

While the keen, comprehensive intellect within that broad, grand forehead was struggling with the great problems of national fate, other faculties of the same organization, strongly marked in the lower features of his face, seemed to be making light of the whole matter.

His character and the physical expression of it were unique, and yet made up of the most complex elements ; — simple, yet incomprehensible ; strong, yet gentle ; inflexible, yet conciliating ; human, yet most rare ; the strangest, and yet for all in all the most lovable, character in history.

To represent this man, to embody these characteristics, was the work prescribed the artist. Instead of being fetters, these contradictions seem to have been incentives to the artist. Justice to himself, as to an American who loved Lincoln, and justice to the great man, the truest American of his time, appear also to have been his inspiration.

Neglected now, this golden opportunity might be lost forever, and the future be haunted by an ideal only, and never be familiarized with the plain, good face we knew. For what could the future make of all these caricatures and uncouth efforts at portraiture, rendered only more grotesque when stretched upon the rack of a thousand canvases ? No less a benefactor to art than to humanity is he who shall deliver the world of these.

The artist has chosen, with admirable judgment, a quiet, restful, familiar phase of Mr. Lincoln's life, with the social and genial sentiments of his nature at play, rather than some more impressive and startling hour of his public life, when a victory was gained, or an immortal sentence uttered at Gettysburg or the Capitol, or when, as the great Emancipator, he walked with his liberated children through the applauding streets of Richmond. It was tempting to paint him as President, but triumphant to represent him as a man.

Though the face is wanting in the crowning glory of the dramatic, the romantic, the picturesque, — elements so fascinating to an artist, — we still feel no loss in the absence of these; for Mr. Marshall has found abundant material in the rich and varied qualities that Mr. Lincoln did possess, and has treated them with the loftier sense of justice and truth. He has employed no adventitious agencies to give brilliancy or emphasis to any salient point in the character of the man he portrays; he has treated Mr. Lincoln as he found him; he has interpreted him as he would have interpreted himself; in inspiration, in execution, and in result, he thought of none other, he labored for none other, he has given us none other, than simple, honest Abraham Lincoln.

Were all the biographies and estimates of the President's character to be lost, it would seem as if, from this picture alone,

the distinguishing qualities of his head and heart might be saved to the knowledge of the future; for a rarer exhibition seems impossible of the power of imparting inner spiritual states to outward physical expression.

As a work of art, we repeat, this is beyond question the finest instance of line-engraving yet executed on this continent. Free from carelessness or coarseness, it is yet strong and emphatic; exquisitely finished, yet without painful over-elaboration; with no weary monotony of parallel lines to fill a given space, and no unrelieved masses of shade merely because here must the shadow fall.

As a likeness, it is complete and final. Coming generations will know Abraham Lincoln by this picture, and will tenderly and lovingly regard it; for all that art could do to save and perpetuate this lamented man has here been done. What it lacks, art is incapable to express; what it has lost, memory is powerless to restore.

There is, at least, some temporary solace to a bereaved country in this, — that so much has been saved from the remorseless demands of Death; though the old grief will ever come back to its still uncomforted heart, when it turns to that tomb by the Western prairie, within whose sacred silence so much sweetness and kindly sympathy and unaffected love have passed away, and the strange pathos, that we could not understand, and least of all remove, has faded forever from those sorrowful eyes.

REVIEWS AND LITERARY NOTICES.

Six Months at the White House with Abraham Lincoln. The Story of a Picture. By F. B. CARPENTER. New York: Hurd and Houghton.

THE grandeur which can survive proximity was peculiarly Abraham Lincoln's. Had that great and simple hero had a valet, — it is hard to conceive of him as so attended, — he must still have been a hero even in the eye grown severe in dusting clothes and brushing shoes. Indeed, first

and last, he was subjected to very critical examination by the valet-spirit throughout the world; and he seems to have passed it triumphantly, for all our native valets, North and South, as well as those of the English press, have long since united in honoring him.

We see him in this book of Mr. Carpenter's to that advantage which perfect unaffectedness and sincerity can never lose. It is certainly a very pathetic figure, however, that the painter presents us, and not to be contemplated without sadness and that keen sense of personal loss which we all felt in the death of Abraham Lincoln. During the time that Mr. Carpenter was making studies for his picture of the President signing the Emancipation Proclamation, he was in daily contact with him, — saw him in consultation with his Cabinet, at play with his children, receiving office-seekers of all kinds, granting many favors to poor and friendless people, snubbing Secession insolence, and bearing patiently much impertinence from every source, — jesting, laughing, lamenting. It is singular that, in all these aspects of his character, there is no want of true dignity, though there is an utter absence of state, — and that we behold nothing of the man Lincoln was once doubted to be, but only a person of noble simplicity, cautious but steadfast, shrinking from none of the burdens that almost crushed him, profoundly true to his faith in the people, while surveying the awful calamity of the war with

> " Anxious, pitying eyes,
> As if he always listened to the sighs
> Of the goaded world."

We have read Mr. Carpenter's book through with an interest chiefly due, we believe, to the subject ; for though the author had the faculty to observe and to note characteristic and striking things, he has not the literary art to present them adequately. His style is compact of the manner of the local reporters and the Sunday-school books. If he depicts a pathetic scene, he presently farces it by adding that " there was not a dry eye among those that witnessed it," and goody-goody dwells in the spirit and letter of all his attempts to portray the religious character of the President. It is greatly to his credit, however, that his observation is employed with discretion and delicacy ; and as he rarely lapses from good taste concerning things to be mentioned, we readily forgive him his want of grace in recounting the incidents which go to form his entertaining and valuable book.

Inside : a Chronicle of Secession. By GEORGE F. HARRINGTON. New York : Harper and Brothers.

THE author of this novel tells us that it was written in the heart of the rebellious territory during the late war, and that his wife habitually carried the manuscript to church with her in her pocket, while on one occasion he was obliged to bury it in the ground to preserve it from the insidious foe. These facts, in themselves startling, appear yet more extraordinary on perusal of the volume, in which there seems to be nothing of perilous value. Nevertheless, to the ill-regulated imagination of the Rebels, this novel might have appeared a very dangerous thing, to be kept from ever seeing the light in the North by all the means in their power ; and we are not ready to say that Mr. Harrington's precautions, though unusual, were excessive. It is true that we see no reason why he should not have kept the material in his mind, and tranquilly written it out after the war was over.

Let us not, however, give too slight an idea of the book's value because the Preface is silly. The story is sluggish, it must be confessed, and does not in the least move us. But the author has made a very careful study of his subject, and shows so genuine a feeling for character and manner that we accept his work as a faithful picture of the life he attempts to portray. Should he write another fiction, he will probably form his style less visibly upon that of Thackeray, though it is something in his favor that he betrays admiration for so great a master even by palpable imitation ; and we hope he will remember that a story, however slender, must be coherent. In the present novel, we think the characters of Colonel Juggins and his wife done with masterly touches ; and General Lamum, politician pure and simple, is also excellent. Brother Barker, of the hard-shell type, is less original, though good ; while Captain Simmons, Colonel Ret Roberts, and other village idlers and great men, seem admirably true to nature. Except for some absurd melodrama, the tone of the book is quiet and pleasant, and there is here and there in it a vein of real pathos and humor.

Royal Truths. By HENRY WARD BEECHER. Boston : Ticknor and Fields.

WE imagine that most readers, in turning over the pages of this volume, will not be greatly struck by the novelty of the truths urged. Indeed, they are very old truths, and they contain the precepts which we all know and neglect. Except that the present preacher was qualified to illustrate them with original force and clearness, he might well have left them untouched. As it is, however, we think that every one who reads a page in the book will learn to honor the faculty that presents them. It is not because Mr. Beecher reproves hatred, false-witness, lust, envy, and covetousness, that he is so successful in his office. We all do this, and dislike sin in our neighbors; but it is his power of directly reproving these evils in each one of us that gives his words so great weight. He of course does this by varying means and with varying effect. Here we have detached passages from many different discourses, — not invariably selected with perfect judgment, but affording for this reason a better idea of his range and capacity. That given is not always of his best; but, for all this, it may have been the best for some of those who heard it. In the changing topics and style of the innumerable extracts in this volume, we find passages of pure sublimity, of solemn and pathetic eloquence, of flower-like grace and sweetness, followed by exhortations apparently modelled upon those of Mr. Chadband, but doubtless comforting and edifying to Mrs. Snagsby in the congregation, and not, we suppose, without use to Mrs. Snagsby in the parlor where she sits down to peruse the volume on Sunday afternoon. For according to the story which Mr. Beecher tells his publishers in a very pleasant prefatory letter, this compilation was made in England, where it attained great popularity among those who never heard the preacher, and who found satisfaction in the first-rate or the second-rate, without being moved by the arts of oratory. Indeed, the book is one that must everywhere be welcome, both for its manner and for its matter. The application of the " Truths " is generally enforced by a felicitous apologue or figure; in some cases the lesson is conveyed in a beautiful metaphor standing alone. The extracts are brief, and the point, never wanting, is moral, not doctrinal.

The Language of Flowers. Edited by MISS ILDREWE. Boston: De Vries, Ibarra, & Co.

MARGARET FULLER said that everybody liked gossip, and the only difference was in the choice of a subject. A bookful of gossip about flowers — their loves and hates, thoughts and feelings, genealogy and cousinships — is certainly always attractive. Who

does not like to hear that Samphire comes from Saint-Pierre, and Tansy from Athanasie, and that Jerusalem Artichokes are a kind of sunflower, whose baptismal name is a corruption of *girasole*, and simply describes the flower's love for the sun? Does this explain all the Jerusalems which are scattered through our popular flora, — as Jerusalem Beans and Jerusalem Cherries? The common theory has been that the sons of the Puritans, by a slight theological reaction, called everything which was not quite genuine on week-days by that name which sometimes wearied them on Sundays.

It is pleasant also to be reminded that our common Yarrow (*Achillea millefolium*) dates back to Achilles, who used it to cure his wounded friend, and that Mint is simply Menthe, transformed to a plant by the jealous Proserpine. It is refreshing to know that Solomon's Seal was so named by reason of the marks on its root; and that this root, according to the old herbalists, "stamped while it is fresh and greene, and applied, taketh away in one night, or two at the most, any bruse, black or blew spots gotten by falls, or woman's wilfulness in stumbling upon their hasty husband's fists, or such like." It was surely a generous thing in Solomon, who set his seal of approbation upon the rod, to furnish in that same signet a balm for injuries like these.

This pretty gift-book is the first really American contribution to the language of flowers. It has many graceful and some showy illustrations; its floral emblems are not all exotic; and though the editor's appellation may at first seem so, a simple application of the laws of anagram will reveal a name quite familiar, in America, to all lovers of things horticultural.

The American Annual Cyclopædia and Register of Important Events of the Year 1865. New York: D. Appleton & Co.

SEVERAL articles in this volume give it an unusual interest and value. The paper on Cholera is not the kind of reading to which one could have turned with cheerfulness last July, from a repast of summer vegetables and hurried fruits; nor can that on Trichinosis be pleasant to the friend of pork; but they are both clearly and succinctly written, and will contribute to the popular understanding of the dangers which they discuss.

The Cyclopædia, however, has its chief

merit in those articles which present *résumés* of the past year's events in politics, literature, science, and art. The one on the last-named subject is less complete than could be wished, and is written in rather slovenly English; but the article on literature is very full and satisfactory. A great mass of biographical matter is presented under the title of "Obituaries," but more extended notices of more distinguished persons are given under the proper names. Among the latter are accounts of the lives and public services of Lincoln, Everett, Palmerston, Cobden, and Corwin; and of the lives and literary works of Miss Bremer, Mrs. Gaskell, Hildreth, Proudhon, etc. The article on Corwin is too slight for the subject, and the notice of Hildreth, who enjoyed a great repute both in this country and in Europe, is scant and inadequate. Under the title of "Army Operations," a fair synopsis of the history of the last months of the war is given; and, as a whole, the Cyclopædia is a valuable, if not altogether complete, review of the events of 1865.

History of the Atlantic Telegraph. By HENRY M. FIELD, D. D. New York: Charles Scribner & Co.

WHY Columbus should have been at the trouble to sail from the Old World in order to find a nearer path to it, as our author states in his opening chapter, he will probably explain in the future edition in which he will chastise the occasionally ambitious writing of this. His book is a most interesting narrative of all the events in the history of telegraphic communication between Europe and America, and has the double claim upon the reader of an important theme and an attractive treatment of it. Now that the great nervous cord running from one centre of the world's life to the other is quick with constant sensation, the wonder of its existence may fade from our minds; and it is well for us to remember how many failures — involving all the virtue of triumph — went before the final success. And it cannot but be forever gratifying to our national pride, that, although the idea of the Atlantic telegraph originated in Newfoundland, and was mainly realized through the patience of British enterprise, yet the first substantial encouragement which it received was from Americans, and that it was an American whose heroic perseverance so united his name with this idea that Cyrus W. Field and the Atlantic cable are not to be dissociated in men's minds in this or any time.

Our author has not only very interestingly reminded us of all this, but he has done it with a good judgment which we must applaud. His brother was the master-spirit of the whole enterprise; but, while he has contrived to do him perfect justice, he has accomplished the end with an unfailing sense of the worth of the constant support and encouragement given by others.

The story is one gratifying to our national love of adventurous material and scientific enterprise, as well as to our national pride. We hardly know, however, if it should be a matter of regret that neither on the one account nor on the other are we able to receive the facts of the cable's success and existence with the effusion with which we hailed them in 1858. Blighting De Sauty, suspense, and scepticism succeeded the rapture and pyrotechnics of those joyful days; and in the mean time we have grown so much that to be electrically united with England does not impart to us the fine thrill that the hope of it once did. Indeed, the jubilation over the cable's success seems at last to have been chiefly on the side of the Englishmen, who found our earlier enthusiasm rather absurd, but who have since learned to value us, and just now can scarcely make us compliments enough.

RECENT AMERICAN PUBLICATIONS.

Thirty Years of Army Life on the Border. Comprising Descriptions of the Indian Nomads of the Plains ; Explorations of New Territory ; a Trip across the Rocky Mountains in the Winter ; Descriptions of the Habits of different Animals found in the West, and the Methods of hunting them ; with Incidents in the Life of different Frontier Men, etc., etc. By Colonel R. B. Marcy, U. S. A., Author of "The Prairie Traveller." With numerous Illustrations. New York. Harper & Brothers. 12mo. pp. 442. $ 3.00.

Life and Times of Andrew Johnson, Seventeenth President of the United States. Written from a National Stand-point. By a National Man. New York. D. Appleton & Co. 12mo. pp. xii. 363. $ 2.00.

The American Printer : a Manual of Typography, containing complete Instructions for Beginners, as well as Practical Directions for managing all Departments of a Printing-Office. With several useful Tables, Schemes for Imposing Forms in every Variety, Hints to Authors and Publishers, etc., etc. By Thomas Mackellar. Philadelphia. L. Johnson & Co. 12mo. pp. 336. $ 2.00.

Coal, Iron, and Oil ; or, the Practical American Miner. A Plain and Popular Work on our Mines and Mineral Resources, and a Text-Book or Guide to their Economical Development. With Numerous Maps and Engravings, illustrating and explaining the Geology, Origin, and Formation of Coal, Iron, and Oil, their Peculiarities, Characters, and General Distribution, and the Economy of mining, manufacturing, and using them ; with General Descriptions of the Coal-Fields and Coal-Mines of the World, and Special Descriptions of the Anthracite Fields and Mines of Pennsylvania, and the Bituminous Fields of the United States, the Iron-Districts and Iron-Trade of our Country, and the Geology and Distribution of Petroleum, the Statistics, Extent, Production, and Trade in Coal, Iron, and Oil, and such useful Information on Mining and Manufacturing Matters as Science and Practical Experience have developed to the present Time. By Samuel Harries Daddow, Practical Miner and Engineer of Mines, and Benjamin Bannan, Editor and Proprietor of the "Miner's Journal." Pottsville. B. Bannan. 8vo. pp. 808. $ 7.50.

Index to the New York Times for 1865. Including the Second Inauguration of President Lincoln, and his Assassination ; the Accession to the Presidency of Andrew Johnson ; the Close of the XXXVIII. and Opening of the XXXIX. Congress, and the Close of the War of Secession. New York. Henry J. Raymond & Co. 8vo. pp. iv., 182. $ 5.00.

Sherbrooke. By H. B. G., Author of "Madge." New York. D. Appleton & Co. 12mo. pp. 463. $ 2.00.

Sermons preached on different Occasions during the last Twenty Years. By the Rev. Edward Meyrick Goulburn, D. D., Prebendary of St. Paul's, and one of her Majesty's Chaplains in Ordinary. Reprinted from the Second London Edition. Two Volumes in one. New York. D. Appleton & Co. 12mo. pp. iv., 397. $ 2.00.

Miscellanea. Comprising Reviews, Lectures, and Essays, on Historical, Theological, and Miscellaneous Subjects. By Most Rev. M. J. Spalding, D. D., Archbishop of Baltimore. Baltimore. Murphy & Co. 8vo. pp. lxii., 807. $ 3.50.

Poems. By Christina G. Rosetti. Boston. Roberts Brothers. 16mo. pp. x., 256. $ 1.75.

Christine : a Troubadour's Song, and other Poems. By George H. Miles. New York. Lawrence Kehoe. 12mo. pp. 285. $ 2.00.

The Admiral's Daughter. By Mrs. Marsh. Philadelphia. T. B. Peterson & Bro. 8vo. paper. pp. 115. 50 cts.

The Orphans ; and Caleb Field. By Mrs. Oliphant. Philadelphia. T. B. Peterson & Bro. 8vo. paper. pp. 133. 50 cts.

Life of Benjamin Silliman, M. D., LL. D., late Professor of Chemistry, Mineralogy, and Geology in Yale College. Chiefly from his Manuscript Reminiscences, Diaries, and Correspondence. By George P. Fisher, Professor in Yale College. In Two Volumes. New York. C. Scribner & Co. 12mo. pp. xvi., 407 ; x., 408. $ 5.00.

The Mormon Prophet and his Harem ; or, An Authentic History of Brigham Young, his numerous Wives and Children. By Mrs. C. V. Waite. Cambridge. Printed at the Riverside Press. 12mo. pp. x., 280. $ 2.00.

THE

ATLANTIC MONTHLY.

A Magazine of Literature, Science, Art, and Politics.

VOL. XVIII. — DECEMBER, 1866. — NO. CX.

JOHN PIERPONT.

MOST men of "fourscore and upwards," like Lear, and who, like Lear, have been "mightily abused" in their day, are found, upon diligent inquiry, to have long outlived themselves, like the Archbishop of Granada; but here is a man, or was but the other day, in his eighty-second year, with the temper and edge and "bright blue rippling glitter" of a Damascus blade up to the very last; or rather, considering how he was last employed, with the temper of that strange tool, found among the ruins of Thebes, with which they used to smooth and polish their huge monoliths of granite, until they murmured a song of joy, whenever the morning sunshine fell upon them.

This remarkable man — remarkable under many aspects — died at Medford, Massachusetts, on Monday morning, August 27th; and it is now said of heart-disease, — that other name for a mysterious and sudden death, happen how it may, and when it may. He had been perfectly well the day before, attended church, and called on some of his neighbors; he retired to rest as usual, and nothing more was heard of him till Monday morning, when he was found asleep in Jesus, prepared, as we humbly trust, to hear the greeting of "Well done, thou good and faithful servant!"

Says a friend, in a letter now lying before me, of August 27th: "On Saturday afternoon, day before yesterday, your friend and my friend, Rev. John Pierpont, called upon me, and we had a very interesting interview of about an hour. I never saw him look better or appear happier. Although eighty-one years of age the 6th of last April, he seemed to have the elasticity of youth, and he was perfectly erect. I gave him what he wanted very much, — a copy of his trial before an ecclesiastical council in this city, several years ago. He gave me his photograph, and, taking his gold pen, wrote underneath, in a beautiful hand, 'John Pierpont, aged 81.' He said he was doing some work at Washington, which he hoped to live long enough to complete. . . . . When I published my last book, I sent him a copy. He acknowledged the receipt of it in a letter of eight or ten pages, which is now a treasure to me. His name on the photograph was probably the last time he ever wrote it," — another treasure, which my friend would not now be likely to part with for any consideration.

My acquaintance with Mr. Pierpont began in the fall or winter of 1814, just when the war had assumed such proportions, that men's hearts were failing them for fear, and prodigies and portents were of daily occurrence. New England too — finding herself defenceless and left to the mercy of our foe — began to think, not of setting up for herself, not of withdrawing from the copartnership, without the consent of the whole sisterhood, but of coming together for conference and proposing to the general government, not to become neutral after the fashion of Kentucky, in our late misunderstanding, not of playing the part of umpire between the belligerents, like that heroic embodiment of Southern chivalry, nor of holding the balance of power, but, on being allowed her just proportion of the public revenues, to undertake for herself, and agree to give a good account of the enemy, if he should throw himself upon her bulwarks, whether along the seaboard, or upon her great northern frontier.

He had just escaped from Newburyport, after writing the " Portrait," a severe and truthful picture of the times, which went far to give him a national reputation — for the day; and opened a law office at 103 Court Street, Boston, where he found nothing to do, and spent much of his time in cutting his name on little ivory seals, and engraving ciphers — " J. P." — so beautiful in their character, and so graceful, that one I have now before me, an impression taken by him in wax, with a vermilion bed, — for in all such matters he was very particular, — were enough to establish any man's reputation as a seal engraver. It bears about the same relationship to what are *called* ciphers, that Benvenuto Cellini's flower-cups bore to the clumsy goblets of his day.

He was never a great reader, not being able to read more than fifty pages of law and miscellany in a day, though he managed, for once, while a tutor in Colonel Alston's family at Charleston,

South Carolina, beginning by daylight and continuing as long as he could see, in midsummer, to get through with one hundred pages of Blackstone ; but the " grind " was too much for him, — he never tried it again. He read Gibbon, and Chateaubriand's " Genius of Christianity," and St. Pierre, and Jeremy Bentham's " Theory of Rewards and Punishments," but never to my knowledge a novel, a romance, or a magazine article, except an occasional review ; but Joanna Baillie, — that female Shakespeare of a later age, — and Beattie, and Campbell, and the British poets, and dramatic writers, were always at hand, when he had nothing better to do, with no seals to cut, no ciphers, no razor-strops, no stoves, and no clients. Over that field of enchantment and illusion he wandered with lifted wings, month after month, and year after year.

At this time he was in his thirtieth year, and I in my twenty-second. No two persons were ever more unlike ; and yet we grew to be intimate friends after a while ; and at the time of his death our friendship had lasted more than fifty years, with a single interruption of a twelvemonth or so while I was abroad, which was put an end to by our letters of reconciliation crossing each other almost on the same day.

With a young family on his hands, precarious health and a feeble constitution, as we then believed, which drove him to Saratoga every two or three years, and no property, what had he to look forward to, unless he could manage to go through a course of starvation at half-price, or diet with the chameleons ? — though great things were expected of him by those who knew him best, and the late Mr. Justice Story could not bear to think of his abandoning the profession, so long as there was a decent chance of living through such a course of preparation.

After all that he has done as a poet, as a preacher, as a reformer, and as a lecturer, I must say that I think he was made for a lawyer. Vigorous and acute, clear-sighted, self-possessed, and logical to a fault, if he had not married so early, or if a respectable inheritance had fallen to him, after he had learned to do without help or patronage, as Dr. Samuel Johnson did, while undergoing Lord Chesterfield, he might have been at the head of the Massachusetts bar, — a proud position, to be sure, at any time within the last fifty years, — or, at any rate, in the foremost rank, long before his death.

He had, withal, a great fondness for mechanics, and one at least of his inventions, the "Pierpont or Doric Stove," was a bit of concrete philosophy, — a miniature temple glowing with perpetual fire, — a cast-iron syllogism of itself, so classically just in its proportions, and so eminently characteristic, as to be a type of the author. He had been led through a long course of experiment in the structure of grates and stoves, and in the consumption of fuel, with the hope of superseding Saratoga, for himself at least, by making our terrible winters and our east winds a little more endurable. No man ever suffered more from what people sometimes call, without meaning to be naughty, *damp cold weather.*

In addition to the "Portrait," he had written a New-Year's Address or two, and a fine lyric, which was said or sung — I forget which — at the celebration of Napoleon's retreat from Moscow; so that after he went off to Baltimore, and the "Airs of Palestine" appeared in 1816, those who knew him best, instead of being astonished like the rest of the world, regarded it as nothing more than the fulfilment of a promise, and went about saying, or looking as if they wanted to say, "Did n't we tell you so?"

And yet, with the exception of two or three outbreaks and flashes, there was really nothing in his earlier manifestations to prefigure the "unrolling glory" of the "Airs," or to justify the extravagant expectations people had entertained from the first, if you would believe them.

Robert Treat Paine having disappeared from the stage, there was nobody left but Lucius Manlius Sargent and John Pierpont for celebrations and sudden emergencies. But Sargent never tried the heroic, and was generally satisfied with imitations of Walter Scott, and others, who were given to oddities and quaintness. For example, " I thought," says he, in the longest poem he ever wrote, which appeared in quarto, —

"I thought, than as a feather fair
 More light is filmy gossamer,
 So woman's heart is lighter far
 Than lightest breath of summer air,
 Which is so light it scarce can bear
 The filmiest thread of gossamer," etc., etc., etc.

While Mr. Pierpont flung himself abroad — like Handel, over the great organ-keys at Haarlem — as if he never knew before what legs and arms were good for, after the following fashion : —

"The misty hall of Odin
 With mirth and music swells,
 Rings with the harps and songs of bards,
 And echoes to their shells.

"See how amid the cloud-wrapped ghosts
 Great Peter's awful form
 Seems to smile,
 As the while,
 Amid the howling storm,
 He hears his children shout, Hurrah !
 Amid the howling storm," etc., etc.

Few men ever elaborated as he did, — not even Rousseau, when he wrote over whole pages and chapters of his "Confessions," I forget how many times. Fine thoughts were never spontaneous with him, never unexpected, never unwaited for, — never, certainly till long after he had got his growth. In fact, some of the happiest passages we have seem to be engraved, letter by letter, instead of being written at once, or launched away into the stillness, like a red-hot thunderbolt. Well do I remember a little incident which occurred in Baltimore, soon after the failure of Pierpont and Lord — and Neal, when we were all dying of sheer inaction, and almost ready to hang ourselves — in a metaphorical sense — as the shortest way of scoring off with the world.

We were at breakfast, — it was rather late.

"Where on earth is your good husband?" said I to Mrs. Pierpont.

"In bed, making poetry," said she.

"Indeed!"

"Yes, flat on his back, with his eyes rolled up in his head."

Soon after, the gentleman himself appeared, looking somewhat the worse for the labor he had gone through with, and all the happier, that the throes were over, and the offspring ready for exhibition. "Here," said he, "tell me what you think of these two lines," — handing me a paper on which was written, with the clearness and beauty of copperplate,

"Their reverend beards that sweep their bosoms wet
With the chill dews of shady Olivet."

"Charming," said I. "And what then? What are you driving at?"

"Well, I was thinking of Olivet, and then I wanted a rhyme for Olivet; and rhymes are the rudders, you know, according to Hudibras; and then uprose the picture of the Apostles before me, — their reverend beards all dripping with the dews of night."

How little did he or I then foresee what soon followed, — soon, that is, in comparison with all he had ever done before! The "Airs of Palestine," like the night-blooming cereus, — the century-plant, — flowering at last, and all at once and most unexpectedly too, after generations have waited for it, as for the penumbra of something foretold, until both their patience and their faith have almost failed. But, from the very first, there were signs of growth not to be mistaken, — of inward growth, too, — and oftentimes an appearance of slowly gathered strength, as if it had been long husbanded, and for a great purpose. For example, —

"There the gaunt wolf sits on his rock and howls,
And there, in painted pomp, the savage Indian prowls."

What a picture of brooding desolation! How concentrated and how unpretending, in its simplicity and strength!

And again, having had visions, and having begun to breathe a new atmosphere, with Sinai in view, he says,

"There blasts of unseen trumpets, long and loud,
Swelled by the breath of whirlwinds, rent the cloud," —

two of the grandest lines to be found anywhere, out of the Hebrew.

But grandeur and strength were never his characteristics; the natural tendency of the man was toward the harmonious, the loving, and the beautiful, as in the following lines from the title-page of his poem, "By J. Pierpont, *Esquire*": —

"I love to breathe where Gilead sheds her balm;
I love to walk on Jordan's banks of palm;
I love to wet my foot in Hermon's dews;
I love the promptings of Isaiah's muse:
In Carmel's paly grots I'll court repose,
And deck my mossy couch with Sharon's deathless rose."

About this time it was, just before he went off to Baltimore, that we began to have occasional glimpses of that inward fire shut up in his bones, that subterranean sunshine, that golden ore, which, smelted as the constellations were, makes what men have agreed to call poetry, — which, after all, is but another name for inspiration; although the very first outbreak I remember happened at the celebration already referred to, where men saw

"The Desolator desolate, the Victor overthrown,
The Arbiter of others' fate a suppliant for his own,"

and began to breathe freely once more; and the shout of "Glory, glory! Alleluiah!" went up like the roar of many waters from all the cities of our land, as if they themselves had been delivered from the new Sennacherib; yet, after a short season of rest, like one of our Western prairies after having been over-swept with fire, he began to flower anew, and from his innermost nature, like some great aboriginal plant of our Northern wilderness suddenly transferred to a tropical region, roots and all, by some convulsion of nature, — by hurricane, or drift, or shipwreck. And always thereafter, with a very few brief exceptions, instead of echoing and re-echoing the musical thunders of a buried past, — instead of imitating, oftentimes unconsciously (the worst kind of imitation, by the way, for what can be hoped of a man whose individuality has been tampered with, and whose own perceptions mislead him?) — instead of counterfeiting the mighty minstrels he had most reverenced, and oftentimes ignorantly worshipped, as among the unknown gods, in his unquestioning, breathless homage, he began to look upward to the Source of all inspiration, while

> " Princely visions rare
> Went stepping through the air,"

and to walk abroad with all his " singing robes about him," as he had never done before.   Hitherto it had been otherwise.   Campbell had opened the " Pleasures of Hope " with

> " Why to yon mountains turns the musing eye,
> Whose sunbright summits mingle with the sky ? "

and *therefore* Pierpont began his " Portrait " with

> " Why does the eye with greater pleasure rest
> On the proud oak with vernal honors drest ? "

But now, instead of diluting Beattie, with all his " pomp of groves and long resounding shore," and recasting portions of Akenside or Pope, and rehashing " Ye Mariners of England," for public celebrations, or converting Moore himself into " Your glass may be purple and mine may be blue," while urging the claims of what is called Liberal Christianity in a hymn written for the new Unitarian church of Baltimore, he would break forth now and then with something which really seemed unpremeditated, — something he had been surprised into saying in spite of himself, as where he finishes a picture of Moses on Mount Nebo, after a fashion both startling and effective in its abruptness, and yet altogether his own : —

> " His sunny mantle and his hoary locks
> Shone like the robe of Winter on the rocks.
> Where is that mantle ?   Melted into air.
> Where is the Prophet ?   God can tell thee where."

And yet in the day of his strength he was sometimes capable of strange self-forgetfulness, and once wrote, in his reverence for the classic, what, if it were not blasphemy, would be meaningless : —

> " O thou dread Spirit ! being's End and Source !
> O check thy chariot in its fervid course :
> *Bend from thy throne of darkness and of fire,*
> *And with one smile immortalize our lyre !* "

Think of a Christian poet apostrophizing the Ancient of Days — Jehovah himself — in the language of idolatrous and pagan Rome !

At another time, — but these are among the last of his transgressions, and they happened nearly fifty years before his death, — having in view that epitaph on an infant where a father says of his child,

> " Like a dewdrop on the early morn
> She sparkled, was exhaled, and went to heaven,"

Mr. Pierpont says of the frozen heart, when religion's " mild and genial ray " falls upon it, with music,

> " The fire is kindled and the flame is bright ;
> And that cold mass, with either power assailed,
> *Is warmed, made liquid, and to heaven exhaled.*"

And this by a man who talks about " the glow-worm burning *greenly* on the wall," and the " *unrolling glory* " of the empyrean, as if he understood what both meant.

Nevertheless, and notwithstanding these aberrations, my friend — the truest friend I ever had in my life, on some accounts, for he was not afraid to tell me of my faults when he saw them, and the man, after all, to whom I am under greater obligations than to any other, living or dead, for bringing me acquainted with myself — held on his upward course for the last thirty years of his life without faltering, and without any visible perturbation, like the planets, if not like the stars, along their appointed path, never so as to astonish perhaps, but almost always so as to convince, whatever might be the manner of his approach, and whether in prose or poetry.

But we are anticipating.   At the time of our first acquaintance, he certainly entertained very different views upon the subjects which have made him so conspicuous within the last twenty-five years.

Instead of being an Abolitionist, or a Garrisonian, and insisting upon immediate, universal, and unconditional emancipation, he was a colonizationist, rather tolerant of the evil, as it existed in the South, and very patient under the wrongs of our black brethren ; and so was I.

Instead of being a teetotaler, he was hardly what the temperance men of our day would call a temperance man ; for he had wine upon his table when he gave dinners, and never shrank from the interchange of courtesies, nor refused a pledge, — though I did, even then. Yet more, as brandy had been prescribed for Mrs. Pierpont by the family physician, Dr. Randall, her husband used to take his brandy and water with her sometimes, just before dinner, by way of a " whet."

Again : he had been brought up, like St. Paul, at the very feet of Gamaliel. He was born Orthodox, — he lived Orthodox, — he sat for years under the preaching of Dr. Lyman Beecher, whom he looked upon as a "giant among pygmies," — and well he might, as a metaphysician and as a controversialist, if not as a theologian, — and was, I have lately been told, a member of Dr. Spring's Orthodox church at Newburyport, before his removal to Boston. But once there, in that overcharged atmosphere, he took a pew in the Brattle Street Unitarian church, — without being then a Unitarian, or dreaming of the great change that was to follow within two or three years, — and was a regular attendant under the preaching of Mr. Everett up to the last. On his removal to Baltimore, he swung round again toward Orthodoxy, — that Orthodoxy which has been so wittily defined as *my* doxy, while heterodoxy is *your* doxy, — and sat for three years under the preaching of Dr. Ingals, the highly gifted gentleman to whom he dedicated his poem — *in blank* — when it first appeared, being perhaps a little afraid of committing himself in advance ; and then, at the very first gathering of the Baltimore Unitarians in a large auction-room, which led to the organization of a church within a few months, the erection of a beautiful building, and to the settlement of our friend, the late Dr. Jared Sparks, he came out fair and square upon the great question, and led, or helped lead, the exercises. The result of which was, that in due time, after his failure in business, he became

a student of theology at Cambridge, and within a year was called to the ministry of reconciliation over Hollis Street Church, as a successor to Mr. Holly, at that time a most captivating preacher, with a congregation and church eminently fastidious and exacting, and not easily satisfied ; yet Mr. Pierpont labored with them and for them over twenty-five years, with an earnestness, a comprehensiveness, and a faithfulness, for which some of them have not forgiven him to this day. He entered upon the ministry there in April, 1819, and resigned in 1845 ; when he became the first pastor of a Unitarian church in Troy, remained there four years, and then took charge of a church in Medford ; where he was living when the Rebellion broke out, and he entered the army as chaplain, under an express stipulation that the regiment was *not to go round Baltimore.*

But I am fully justified in saying that, when I first knew him in Boston, he did not know himself. He had entirely mistaken his vocation, and was about the last man in the world to enter into trade, though pre-eminently fitted for business, if he had been properly encouraged, — the business of law certainly, and the business of statesmanship. He saw nothing of what was before him, — nothing of the field he was to occupy till the Master came, — nothing of the influence, nothing of the authority, he was to exercise over the minds and hearts of men, — and nothing of that huge oriflamme which was coming up slowly, to be sure, but certainly, over the distant verge of an ever-widening horizon. He was utterly discouraged as a lawyer ; he knew nothing of business ; he had no capital ; and what on earth was he good for ? Whither should he go ? What undertake ?

And yet he bore up manfully through all this discouragement, and no word of complaint or murmuring ever escaped his lips. On the whole, he was one of the most truly conscientious men I ever knew, — and why not one of the most truly religious, notwithstanding his obnoxious faith? — so even-tempered that I never saw him disturbed more than once or twice in all my life, and so patient under wrong that one could hardly believe in his withering sarcasm, and scorching indignation when he took the field as a reformer, " in golden panoply complete."

Let me now describe his personal appearance, for the help of those who have only heard of the man. He was tall, straight, and spare, — six feet, I should say, and rather ungraceful in fact, though called by the women of his parish, not only the most graceful, but the most finished of gentlemen. That he was dignified, courteous, and prepossessing, very pleasant in conversation, a capital story-teller, and a tolerable — no, intolerable — punster, exceedingly impressive both in the pulpit and elsewhere, when much in earnest, and in after life a great lecturer and platform speaker, I am ready to acknowledge ; but he wanted ease of manner — the readiness and quiet self-possession of a high-bred man, who cannot be taken by surprise, and is neither afraid of being misunderstood nor afraid of letting himself down — till after he had passed the age of threescore.

The first impression he made on me was that of a country schoolmaster, or of a professor, on his good behavior, who had got his notions of the polite world from Chesterfield ; though, when I knew him better, and learned that he had been a tutor in the Alston family of South Carolina, I detected the original type of his perpendicularity, serious composure, and stateliness, — the archetype. I was constantly reminded of John C. Calhoun, a fellow-student with him at Yale, and a man he always mentioned, with a strange mixture of admiration and awe, as if he thought him an offshoot from the Archfiend himself, " skilled to make the worse appear the better reason." His tall figure, his erect, positive bearing, and somewhat uncompromising, severe expression of countenance, when much in earnest, with black, heavy eyebrows, clear blue eyes which passed for black, and stiff black hair, were all of that Huguenot Southern type, which, like the signs of the Scotch Covenanter or of the old English Puritan, are as unlikely to die out as the Canada thistle, where they who sow the wind are content to reap the whirlwind. In their steadfast pertinacity, whether right or wrong, in their adamantine logic, as unyielding as death, and calm, serious energy of action, and in a part of their transcendental theories, they were alike ; and alike, too, in their tried honesty. The great Nullifier and the great Reformer were both Titanic, in the vastness and comprehensiveness of their views, in their unrelenting self-assertion, in their metaphysics, and in their theories of government. If the dark Southron made open war upon his country till it grew to be unsafe, the dark Northerner would tear the Constitution of that country to tatters, and trample it under foot, as he did upon one occasion, without remorse or compunction, because it was held by others to give property in man, though for himself he denied that it did so, or that it sanctioned slavery in any shape, — as he did, I say, though I was not an eyewitness of the outrage, and have only the report from others who were. If it was only a flourish, like that of Edmund Burke, when he suddenly lugged out the dagger before the upturned smiling eyes of his patient compeers, and Sheridan — or was it Fox ? — begged the gentleman to tell him where the *fork* was to be had which belonged to the knife, why, even that were not only unworthy of the man, but so utterly unlike him, for he never indulged in rhetoric or rhodomontade or claptrap, that one would be inclined to think he was beside himself, or had been dining out, like Daniel Webster when he proposed, in the Senate Chamber, to plant our starry banner on the outermost verge, the Ultima Thule, of our disputed territory. heedless of consequences. Both Pierpont and Calhoun certainly forgot the injunction to be "temperate in all things"; and allow me to add, that, in my judgment, it mattered little who was with, or who against them, after they had once set the lance in rest, with a windmill in view, — they only spurred the harder for opposition, and lashed out all the more vehemently for being cheered, even by the lowliest. Encouragement and opposition were alike to both, after the rowels were set, and their beavers closed.

At the time I speak of, Mr. Pierpont and his brother-in-law, Mr. Joseph L. Lord, kept house together on a street running down hill back of the State-House, — Hancock Street, if I do not mistake. They had always two or three boarders, and sometimes more, and among them Erastus A. Lord, a brother of Joseph, and myself. With these, and with the neighbors, — the whole neighborhood, I might say, and with all their visiting-list, — our friend Pierpont was an oracle from the first, and in the church and parish, after he had been set up in the pulpit, an idol. It was thought presumptuous for anybody to differ with him upon any subject. Whatever he said, or thought, or did, was never to be questioned, — never! His opinions were maxims, his utterances apothegms, his lightest word authority. And the worst of it all, and the hardest thing for me to stomach, was, that in all our controversies, for a long time, if he was not always right, and I always wrong, I was quite sure to come out second best, in the judgment of his friends and worshippers, who had no sympathy for anybody who ventured to tilt with their champion. Nevertheless I persisted, and, not standing much in awe of the pedant and the pedagogue, however much I admired the logician and the poet or the lawyer, I lost no opportunity of asserting my independence, and took, I am afraid, a sort of malicious pleasure in showing that I had views and opinions of my own, and was determined to do my own thinking, come what might. For a while this operated

against me, — if not always with Mr. Pierpont, certainly with all his immediate personal friends and family; but in time, I believe, he began to like me the better for my presumption, or foolhardiness, in battling the watch with him, whenever he laid down a proposition, with a calm, dictatorial air, which did not strike me at first either as clearly self-evident, or, after a thorough investigation, as indisputably true, so that I do on my conscience believe that I was fast growing, not only unmanageable, but unbearable.

Mr. Pierpont was no judge of painting, though he relished a good picture, and had no taste for drawing, or rather no talent for drawing, though he saw readily enough certain errors of exaggeration that abounded in the engravings of the day; and I well remember his calling my attention to the preposterously small feet of the female figures for which Messrs. Draper and Company, the bank-note engravers of that day, were so famous; and yet his handwriting was very beautiful, and the ciphers I have mentioned were neither more nor less than exquisite drawings. Nor had he any ear for music, to borrow the language we hear at every turn, — as if all persons who are not deaf by nature had not ears for music, so far as they can hear at all, — or as if he who can distinguish voices, or learn a language, so far as to be understood when he talks it, had not necessarily an ear for music, in other words, an ear for sounds and for the rhythm of speech; but he was deficient in the organ of tune, phrenologically speaking, though I have heard him warble a Scotch air on the flute with uncommon sweetness — and feebleness — without *tonguing*, and play two or three other tunes, which had been adapted in the choir of his church, upon glass goblets, partly filled with water and set upon a table before him, as if he enjoyed every touch and thrill, — his long, thin fingers travelling over the damp edges of the glass, and bringing forth "Bonnie Doon," or "There 's nothing true but Heaven," — with his cuffs rolled up as if he were driving a lathe, and turning off some of the little thin boxes and other exquisite toys, in wood or ivory, which he was addicted to, about fifteen years ago, in what he called his workshop. Like Johnson, however, and Alexander Pope, who, according to Leigh Hunt,

> " Spoiled the ears of the town
> With his cuckoo-song verses, two up and two down,"

he must have had "time" large; for the music of his rhythm was absolutely faultless, — cloying indeed, so that he introduced the double rhymes to roughen it, just as he indulged in alliteration, where the "lordly lion leaves his lonely lair," that he might not be supposed incapable of running off upon another track, or into another channel.

But I never heard him sing or try to sing, though he had a deep, manly voice, read as very few are able to read, and his modulation was rich and varied, and very agreeable, both to the understanding and the ear.

His pronunciation was a marvel for correctness. In all our intercourse I never knew him to give a word otherwise than "according to Walker," so long as Walker was the standard with him, — or never but once, when he said cli-mac'ter-ic, instead of cli-mac-ter'ic; and when I remonstrated with him, he lugged out Webster, whom he adhered to forever after. So exceedingly fastidious and sensitive was he, about the time he left Baltimore for Cambridge, that in his desire to give the pure sound of *e*, as in *met*, instead of the sound of *u*, which is so common as to be almost universal where *e* is followed by *r* and another consonant, so that *person* is pronounced *purson*, he gave a sound which most people misunderstood for *pairson*, and went away and laughed at, for pedantry and affectation.

So, too, when I first knew him, and for a long time after, he was incapable of making a speech. Even a few sentences were too much for him; and though he argued at least one case to the court, while in business at Newburyport, I am persuaded, from what I afterward knew

of him, that he must have done what he did by jerks, or have committed the whole to memory. And this, strange as it may now appear to those who knew him only as a lecturer and platform-speaker, continued long after he had entered upon the ministry ; but of this more hereafter. Even his prayers were written out, and learned by heart, years after he took charge of the Hollis Street Church, though I dare say it was not known by his people. Perhaps, too, I may as well say here, lest I may forget to say it hereafter, that, at the time I speak of, he was neither a phrenologist, nor a spiritualist, nor a conscientious believer in witchcraft, or rather in the phenomena that used to be called witchcraft, in the days of Cotton Mather.

Soon after the beginning of our acquaintance, Mr. Joseph L. Lord, the brother of his first wife, — and he too has just passed away, — seeing what the prospect was for the brother-in-law he was so proud of, persuaded him to abandon the law at once, and forever, and go into the jobbing and retail dry-goods business with him, on the corner of Court and Marlborough, now Washington Street. He had no capital, to be sure, but then he wrote a beautiful hand, was very methodical, and had made himself acquainted with book-keeping, after the Italian method, from Rees's Cyclopædia. I took the chamber which Mr. Pierpont left, and went into the jobbing business also, with a capital of between two and three hundred — dollars, and a credit amounting to perhaps five hundred more, which enterprise terminated after a few months, not in my failure, but in my taking a trip to New York with a large quantity of smuggled goods, belonging to Messrs. Pierpont and Lord, where I disposed of them to such advantage, that, on my return, I was persuaded to go into the retail haberdashery line, at 103 Court Street, next door to Pierpont and Lord, and just underneath the chamber, not chambers, which I had occupied at first with my wholesale establishment. I had for a partner, at first, Erastus, a brother of "Joe's," whom I had known as a bookbinder in Portland two or three years before. He was now manufacturing pocket-books, and appeared to be doing, not only a large and profitable, but safe business, — selling for cash, running a horse and gig, and paying the bills of all the "dear five hundred friends" who rode with him.

Our copartnership did not last long. His brother "Joe," being a shrewd man of business, of uncommon foresight and comprehensiveness, though rather adventurous, gave me a hint, and soon provided me with another partner, a graduate of Cambridge, named Fisher, with whom I was associated a few months longer. Then came the peace of 1815, which threw the whole country into a paroxysm of joy, unsettling business everywhere, at home and abroad, and setting people together by the ears upon all the great questions of the day.

And here began the new and very brief career of Mr. Pierpont as a man of business. Wholly unfitted as he was for even the regular course of trade, he was the last man in the world for the great emergencies of the hour. The whole business of the country was little better than gambling. Our largest importing houses were lotteries or farobanks; and we had no manufactures worth mentioning. We made no woollen goods, and our few cottons, if sold at all, were sold for British, and stood no chance with the trash that came from beyond the Cape of Good Hope, "warped with hoop-poles, and filled with oven-wood." Our foreign merchandise came tumbling down so fast, that no prospective calculations could be made upon their value. Not having manufactured ourselves, we knew nothing about the cost of production, and had no idea how much our friends over sea could afford to fall, even from the lowest prices ever heard of. British calicoes, or prints, for example, which I sold by the case for eighty-five cents cash, at auction, were in every way inferior to our own, which were retailed before the Rebellion broke out for ten cents a yard. In fact, if we had known the real cost of production, it would have made but little difference; for long after all our foreign merchandise had fallen from thirty-three and a third to fifty per cent, some of our shrewdest calculators were utterly ruined by purchasing at much lower prices, on what they believed to be a rising market.

Under such circumstances, what was a poet, a scholar, and a lawyer, without any knowledge of business, to do? Pierpont and Lord were large dealers, and had a heavy stock on hand, not paid for. Their notes were maturing with frightful rapidity, and Mr. Lord wanted all his available funds for "transactions" in gold, and other perilous "operations" along the Canada frontier. Specie was twenty-five per cent above par, or rather banknotes, everywhere but in a part of New England, where they continued to pay specie to the last; were at twenty-five per cent discount; and "Boston money," upon the average, about one per cent above gold and silver, so as to cover the cost and risk of transportation.

But something had to be done. A consultation was held between the members of "our house," and it was finally arranged that Mr. Pierpont, as the man we could best spare from the salesroom and the shop, and the partner who would best represent what was called, with singular propriety, "our concern," should go to Baltimore with the best of letters, and open a way for me in that city, which I had visited once, and once only, for the purpose of buying exchange on England, — though for a time it was thought I had run away with all the funds intrusted to me. I had taken a prodigious liking to Baltimore from the first, though I had no idea of going there to live, and was not easily persuaded to give up my little establishment in Boston. I was doing very well, and did not care to do better, till business got settled; but we were three, and I was always in the minority, — Mr. Lord being a shrewd "operator," and Mr. Pierpont, of course, deferring to him. They were *my* partners, to be sure; but I never had anything to do with their business, apart from my own.

Nevertheless, when Mr. Pierpont returned, and gave an account of his doings there, and of the opening there was for just such a man as I had proved myself to be, I consented to pull up stakes, and transplant myself to that beautiful city.

I went with no large expectations, intending to open a retail shop, such as I had left; but within a week, finding that I could sell even my cut goods for prices much beyond what I had been retailing them for over and above the exchange, I went into the wholesale business, and with one clerk, Mr. Jenkins Howland, greatly distinguished in after life as a man of enterprise at Charleston, S. C., sold more goods, and for cash too, than perhaps any three or four of what were called the large dealers about me, with two or three clerks apiece, and at prices which fairly took away my breath at first; — Irish linens, for example, by the case at two dollars and fifty cents all round, worth not over eighty cents before the war; and assorted broadcloths by the bale at fourteen dollars a yard all round, which, within a twelvemonth, would have hung fire at three dollars and fifty cents. And this, it will be remembered, was after goods had been falling — falling — falling — for six months.

No wonder people's heads were turned — those of Pierpont and Lord among the rest. We, who had large stocks on hand, were growing rich too fast. I remember selling fourteen thousand dollars' worth of goods one day for a clear profit of more than forty per cent, and this while my poor friends at Boston were gasping for breath in that exhausted receiver; but they were kept alive by the remittances I made from Baltimore, which not only furnished them with funds for immediate use, but gave them for a few months almost unbounded credit.

This was in the fall and winter of 1815, only a few months after the Bramble arrived with the news from Ghent that our last negotiations had been successful, and that the war was over most gloriously for *us*, the United States. We were almost ready, in our thankfulness and joy, to canonize the ship and crew, and cut her up into snuffboxes and toothpicks.

And now — what next? "as the tadpole said, when he his tail dropped off." Weary of the growing distrust they saw, after my remittances began to fall off, and heartily sick of the Gerrymandering about them, of the usurers and money-changers and Shylocks, who were bleeding them to death, by lending them money upon pledges of merchandise, the two elder partners, Pierpont and Lord, lost no time in following their junior. He had opened on South Calvert Street; they took the whole of a large building opposite, opened below their wholesale business, and after a few months went to housekeeping overhead, both families living together. Then, to get rid of our stock, Mr. Pierpont went off to Charleston, S. C., where he had served his time as a tutor, and there set up a retail establishment, under the charge of a former clerk in their service, and of another man, a heartless vagabond, whom they had happened to get acquainted with at a boarding-house on their first arrival, and took a fancy to, nobody ever knew why. He was an Englishman, had probably been upon the stage, and lived from hand to mouth, nobody knew how, until we took him *up*, and he took us *in* most pitiably.

After a brief struggle, and the establishment of another retail store in Calvert Street, which I took charge of, with what there was left of the Charleston adventure, we failed outright, and all this within six or eight months after we had called our creditors together and obtained an extension of twelve months and testimonials in our favor of the most gratifying character, and within little more than a year after leaving Boston.

And then, for want of anything better to do, I began writing for the papers, for the "Portico," and at last for the public, as an editor and as an author, mainly at the instigation of Mr. Pierpont, for whom I wrote both "Niagara"* and "Guldau," and a part of "Allen's" American Revolution, studying law, and languages by the half-dozen at the same time, and laboring upon the average about sixteen hours a day, while Mr. Pierpont struck out boldly for a far-off perilous and rocky shore, with a lighthouse, in the shape of a pulpit, before him, and achieved the "Airs of Palestine" while undergoing the process of regeneration, and starving by inches upon what there were left of his wife's teaspoons, which were sold one by one to pay the rent of a cheap room in Howard Street. So poor indeed were we at one time, that we could hardly muster enough between us to pay our bootblack.

I have already said that Mr. Pierpont had no aptitude for extemporaneous speaking; and what was even worse, he had no hope of being able to overcome the difficulty. Once, and once only, did I ever hear him try his hand in that way, until many years after he had entered upon the ministry. A club had been organized among us for literary purposes. We were both members, and he the Vice-President. We called ourselves the Delphians, and passed among our contemporaries for the *male* Muses, our

---

* And here I may as well mention a curious incident. When I wrote my poem, I had never seen Niagara; but we agreed to go together on a pilgrimage at our earliest convenience. One thing and another happened, until I had been abroad and returned, without our seeing it together. At last, being about to go to the South of Europe, I made a new arrangement with him; but just as we — my wife and I — were ready to go, he was called away to consecrate some church in the West, and we started on a journey of two thousand miles through portions of our country I had never seen, and was ashamed to go abroad again without seeing. On my way back we stopped in Buffalo, and as I stood in the piazza I saw a little card on one of the pillars saying that the Rev. Mr. Pierpont would preach in the evening somewhere. I found him, and we went *together* at last, and saw Niagara together, as we had agreed to do forty years before. And that night the heavens rained fire upon us, and the great November star-shooting occurred, and our landlord, being no poet, was unwilling to disturb us, so that we missed the show altogether.

number being limited to nine, — not seven, as I see it stated in the Boston Advertiser, on the authority of our friend Paul Allen. The rest of the story is near enough to the truth, although the verses therein mentioned were written by Mr. Pierpont as a volunteer offering, after the Della-Cruscan school, or manner of "Laura Matilda," and not upon the spur of the occasion, as there related, nor as a trial of wit; and the last line should be, "Pulls where'er the zephyr *roves*," — not, as given there, "Pulls where'er the zephyr moves."

It was in this club that Mr. Pierpont first tried himself — and the brethren — with extemporaneous speaking. It was a pitiable failure, worse if possible than my own, and I never made another attempt. Even General Winder, who was a fine advocate, and a capital speaker before a jury, boggled wretchedly before the club, and our President, Watkins, who was said to be exceedingly eloquent before the great Masonic lodges, where he occupied the highest position, could not be persuaded to open his mouth, and all the rest of the brethren were mutes. True, it was like apostrophizing your own grandmother, in the hope of raising a laugh or of bringing tears into her eyes, to make speeches at one another across the table, whatever Molière might be able to do, when alone with his aged servant. Nor did it much help the matter, when, with a view to the treasury, which began to threaten a collapse, we made a law, like that of the Medes and Persians which altereth not, whereby it was provided, among other things, that no member should ever talk over five minutes, nor stop short of three, under any circumstances, — the President being timekeeper, and the sufferer not being allowed to look at a watch. Fines of course were inevitable, and we were once more able to luxuriate on bread and cheese, with an occasional pot of beer, — nothing better or stronger being tolerated among us under any pretence, except on our anniversaries, when the

President, or sometimes a member, stood treat, and gave us a comfortable, though not often a costly or showy supper.

Among that strange, whimsical brotherhood — consisting of Dr. Tobias Watkins, editor of the "Portico"; General Winder (William H.), who had been "captivated" by the British, along with General Chandler, at the first invasion of Canada; William Gwin, editor of the "Federal Gazette"; Paul Allen, editor of the "Federal Republican," and of Lewis and Clarke's "Tour," and author of "Noah"; Dr. Readel, "a fellow of infinite jest"; Brackenridge, author of "Views in Louisiana," and "History of the War"; Dennison, an Englishman, who wrote clever doggerel; and, at different times, two or three more, not worth mentioning, even if I remembered their names — we passed every Saturday evening, after the club was established, until it was broken up by President Watkins's going to Washington, Vice-President Pierpont to the Divinity School at Cambridge, and Jehu O'Cataract abroad. All the members bore " clubicular " names, by which they were always to be addressed or spoken to, under another penalty; and most of them held "clubicular " offices and professorships, — Dr. Readel being Professor of Crambography, and somebody else — Gwin perhaps — Professor of Impromptology. The name given to Mr. Pierpont was Hiero Hep*aglott, under an idea that he was a prodigious linguist, — another Sir William Jones, at least, if not another Learned Blacksmith; and the President himself went so far as to say so in the "Portico," where he pretended to give an account of the Delphians. Nothing could well be further from the truth, however; for, instead of being a great Hebrew scholar, and learned in the Chaldee, Coptic, and other Eastern languages, he knew very little of Hebrew, and absolutely nothing of the rest. With "a little Latin and less Greek," he was a pretty fair Latin and Greek scholar in the judgment of those who are satisfied with what we are doing in our colleges; and he was sufficiently acquainted with French to enjoy Chateaubriand, St. Pierre, Rousseau, and Lamartine, and to write the language with correctness, though not idiomatically; but he was never able to make himself understood in conversation, beyond a few phrases, uttered with a deplorable accent, — not being able to carry the flavor in his mouth, — and, though free and sprightly enough in talking English, having no idea of what passes for freedom and sprightliness with the French. He knew nothing of Spanish, Italian, Portuguese, German, or Dutch, nor indeed of any other modern language.

And now let me say how he came to be an extemporaneous speaker, and sometimes not only logical and convincing, but truly eloquent. On my return from abroad, in 1826, I passed through Boston, on my way to Portland, for a visit to my family, and was taken possession of by him, and went to Hollis Street Church, where I heard my friend, for the second time, in the pulpit. He was exceedingly impressive, and the sermon itself was one of the best I ever heard, — calm, serious, and satisfying; not encumbered with illustration, but full of significance. Although the discourse was carefully written out, word for word, and almost committed to memory, yet he ventured to introduce a paragraph — one paragraph only — which had not been prepared beforehand. My eyes were upon him, and he told me at dinner that he saw by my look how well I understood his departure, and how soon I detected it. "And now," said he, "I hope you are satisfied. You see now that I shall never be able to extemporize. I put that paragraph into my sermon this morning to see how you would take it, after having urged me, year after year, to extemporize at least occasionally. No, no, John; though writing two sermons a week is no trifling labor, I must continue writing to the end; for, if I cannot extemporize a single paragraph, how can I hope to extemporize a whole sermon?"

"Suffer me to say that I think you misunderstand the whole question," said I. "The difficulty is in beginning. After you are well under way, if you can talk sitting, you may talk standing. Better take with you into the pulpit the merest outline of the discourse, and then trust to the inspiration of the subject, or to the feeling of the hour, when you have the audience before you, and can look into their eyes, than to have a discourse partly written, with blanks to be filled up as you go along; for then you are always beginning afresh, and by the time you have got easy in your spontaneous effort, you are obliged to go back to what you have written, and of course can never get warmed up with your subject, nor try any new adaptations, whatever may be the character of your hearers."

He shook his head. "No, no," said he, "you will never be able to persuade me that it is easier to say over the whole alphabet than to say only a part."

I persisted, urging the great advantage of spontaneous adaptation to the people. He agreed with me altogether, provided it were *possible* for him to do it, which he denied, though he promised to take the subject into serious consideration once more, to oblige me.

From Boston I went to Portland, where I had a similar talk with that most amiable and excellent man, the late Dr. Nichols, who labored under a similar disqualification, owing to a similar misapprehension of what was required for extemporaneous speaking, either on the platform or in the pulpit. I told him the story, and urged the same considerations; but he, like Mr. Pierpont, only smiled, — compassionately, as I thought, and rather as if he pitied the delusion I was laboring under. Yet within two years both of these remarkable men became free and natural spontaneous speakers, and both acknowledged to me that they had always misunderstood the difficulty. Dr. Nichols began afar off, as I suggested, in the Sabbath school; and Mr. Pierpont, after making two or three attempts in a small way, which were anything but satisfactory to himself, — as I told him they would be for a while, if he had the true stuff in him, — was at last surprised into doing what he believed to be impossible, by the merest accident in the world; after which he had no further trouble. It seems that he had engaged to supply a neighboring pulpit, — perhaps that of his son John, who was newly settled at Lynn. He thought he had his sermon in his pocket; but, on entering the pulpit, found that he had either left it at home or lost it on the way. What was to be done? Luckily, he had just read it over the night before, and was full of the subject therein treated. Remembering what I said, as he told me himself, he determined to go to work, hit or miss, and either make a spoon or spoil a horn.

The result was, that, after a little hesitation and floundering, he got fairly in earnest, and threw off a discourse which so delighted those who were best acquainted with him, that they stopped round the door to shake hands and congratulate him. He had never preached so well in all his life, they said. This settled the question forever; and from that day forward he began to believe that anybody who can talk in his chair can talk standing up, after he has got over his first impressions, and all the better for having a large auditory, with upturned faces, before him; so that he became at last, and within a few years, one of the finest pulpit orators of the day, and one of the best platform speakers, though not, perhaps, what the multitude consider eloquent; for, at the best, he was only argumentative and earnest and clear and convincing, in his highest manifestations.

Of his career after this, I cannot say anything as I wish, without the risk of saying too much. He had one of the wealthiest and most liberal congregations of New England. He was their idol. He was in every way most agreeably situated, with a large family flowering into usefulness about him, and hosts of friends, enthusiastic and devoted. Nevertheless, believing that, as a servant of God, he had no right to preach smooth things where rough things were needed, and that acknowledging other people's transgressions would not satisfy the law, he came out boldly, with helm and spear, against two of the worst forms of human slavery, — the slavery of the body and the slavery of the soul, the slavery of the wine-cup, and the slavery of bondage to a master. Whether his beloved people would bear or whether they would forbear, being all the more beloved because of their danger, he must preach what he believed to be the truth, and the whole truth. It was like a fire shut up in his bones. He persisted, and they remonstrated, or rather a part of them did so ; and the result was a speedy and hopeless alienation, followed by years of strife and bitter controversy at law, and a final separation ; though by far the larger part of the church and congregation, if I do not mistake, upheld him to the last, and adhered to him through good report and through evil report, — Deacon Samuel May, a host in himself, being of their number.

During this protracted and sorrowful controversy, he became a phrenologist, — a believer in phrenology, — at any rate, following the lead of Spurzheim ; and after many years, a Spiritualist, — in which faith he died, — one of his last, if not the very last, of his appearances before the public being as President of a convention held by the leading Spiritualists of the land at Philadelphia.

He could not be a materialist ; and having faith in the evidence of his own senses, and being as truly conscientious a man as ever breathed, and accustomed to the closest reasoning, what was he to do ? There were the *facts*. They were not to be controverted ; they could not be explained ; they could not be reconciled to any hypothesis in physics. If he was given over to delusion, to be buffeted by Satan, whose fault was it ? That he was by nature somewhat credulous,

and, though patient enough in his investigations, rather too fond of the marvellous, may be acknowledged ; but what then ? His conclusions might be wrong, his inferences faulty, though honest ; but how were they to be counteracted ? That he sometimes took too much for granted, I believe, nay, more, *I know ;* because I myself have seen him grossly imposed on by a woman he took me to see, whose impersonations were thought most wonderful. But then he was a devout man, a close observer, an admirable logician. accustomed to the "competition of opposite analogies" and to weighing evidence ; and if he misunderstood the *facts*, or misinterpreted them, or inferred the supernatural from false premises, why then let us grieve for his delusion, and wait patiently for the phenomena which led him astray to be explained.

He went abroad for a time, while pastor of the Hollis Street Church, and visited the Holy Land, in devout pilgrimage ; and though he lost his first wife, the mother of all his children, and a most worthy gentlewoman, but the other day, and married another superior woman after a brief widowhood, his last days have been, I should say, most emphatically his best days ; for he has lectured through the length and breadth of the land on Temperance, and, after enduring all sorts of persecution as one of the anti-slavery leaders, he lived to see the whole system against which they had been warring so long, and with so little apparent effect, utterly overthrown throughout the land, and the great God of heaven and earth acknowledged as the God of the black man. Thousands and thousands of miles he travelled, not only after having passed the meridian of his life, but after he had reached the allotted term, when life begins to be a heaviness for most, as a laborer in the cause of truth, — often of unacknowledged truth ; and if mistaken, as a theologian, or as a Spiritualist, or as a man, — being what he was, — let us remember that he was never false to his convictions, never a hypocrite nor a deceiver, and that he died with his harness on, having been occupied for the last five years of his life in digesting the treasury decisions, often contradictory, and always inaccessible, for there was no index, until he took them in hand, going back thirty years, I believe, and reducing the whole to a system which need be no longer unintelligible to the Department.

One word more. Among the scores of letters I had from him in the day of his bitterest trials and sorest temptations, there was one which he sent off in the midst of his first great triumph, — with no date now, although I find a mark upon it which leads me to suppose it was written November 16, 1818, and from which I must venture to take a single paragraph.

"My God!" he says, — "my God! I do most devoutly thank Thee. My prayer has reached Thee, and been accepted. My dear friend, join with me in thanking Him in whom I put my trust, — to whom alone I look, or to whom I *have* looked, for a smile. He has blessed me. I have been heard by man, and have not been forsaken by God. Though I have not done *perfectly*, I have done as well as I could rationally wish, and better than my most sanguine hopes. At Brattle Square *this* morning, and at the New South (late Mr. Thacher's) *this* afternoon. Lord! now let thy servant depart in peace; for thou hast lifted the cloud under which he has so long moved, and he may now die in thy light."

Can such a temper as this be misunderstood? Was he not a man fearing God in 1818, — forty-eight years ago? — or, rather, loving God with that perfect love which casteth out all fear?

But we need not stop here. After he had become a Spiritualist, that is, on the 5th of April, 1862, the evening before his seventy-seventh birthday, he wrote a poem of one hundred and sixty lines, entitled "Meditations of a Birthday Eve," a copy of which he sent me on the 10th of November following,

upon the express condition that nobody but myself was to see it, until it should be all over with him. It must have been written without labor, as one would breathe a prayer upon a death-bed. The following extracts — I wish we had room for more — will show what were his feelings and what his aspirations at this time.

> " Spirit, my spirit, hath each stage
> That brought thee up from youth
> To thy now venerable age
> Seen thee in search of Truth?

> " Hast thou in search of Truth been true, —
> True to thyself and her, —
> And been with many or with few
> Her *honest* worshipper?

> " Spirit, thy race is nearly run;
> Say, hast thou run it well?
> Thy work on earth is almost done;
> *How* done, no *man* can tell.

> " Spirit, toil on! thy house, that stands
> Seventy years old and seven,
> Will fall; but one ' not made with hands'
> Awaiteth thee in heaven.

> " WASHINGTON, D. C., 5 April, 1862."

With the foregoing came another poem, "In Commemoration of a Silver Wedding," October 2, 1863, full of tenderness and pleasantry, — the wedding of Mr. and Mrs. J. Pierpont Lord.

And on his eighty-first birthday, called by a strange mistake his eightieth, there was another celebration, yet more solemn and affecting, where the greetings and congratulations of his brother-poets, all over the land, were sent to him and published in the newspapers of the day.

Among his later poems, the "E Pluribus Unum" appears to me most worthy of his reputation, and least like the doings of his early manhood.

And now, though we had little reason to look for the prolongation of such a life, — a continued miracle from the age of thirty or thirty-five, after which he built himself up anew, by living as well in cold water as in hot, and luxuriating in cold baths, and working hard, — harder, perhaps, on the whole, at downright drudgery, than any other man of his age, like Rousseau in copying music, as a relief from writing poetry, — yet when death happens we are all taken by surprise, just as if we thought God had overlooked his aged servant, or made him an exception to the great, inflexible law of our being; or as if a whisper had reached us, saying, "If I will that he tarry till I come, what is that to thee ?"

But enough; a volume of such memoranda would be far short of what such a man deserves when he is finally translated. Faithful among the faithless, may we not hope that his grandeur and strength of purpose, and downright, fearless honesty, will have their appropriate reward, both here and hereafter ?

MY GARDEN.

IF I could put my woods in song,
 And tell what 's there enjoyed,
All men would to my gardens throng,
And leave the cities void.

In my plot no tulips blow,
Snow-loving pines and oaks instead,
And rank the savage maples grow
From spring's faint flush to autumn red.

My garden is a forest-ledge,
Which older forests bound ;
The banks slope down to the blue lake-edge,
Then plunge in depths profound.

Here once the Deluge ploughed,
Laid the terraces, one by one ;
Ebbing later whence it flowed,
They bleach and dry in the sun.

The sowers made haste to depart,
The wind and the birds which sowed it ;
Not for fame, nor by rules of art,
Planted these and tempests flowed it.

Waters that wash my garden-side
Play not in Nature's lawful web,
They heed not moon or solar tide, —
Five years elapse from flood to ebb.

Hither hasted, in old time, Jove,
And every god, — none did refuse ;
And be sure at last came Love,
And after Love, the Muse.

Keen ears can catch a syllable,
As if one spake to another
In the hemlocks tall, untamable,
And what the whispering grasses smother.

Æolian harps in the pine
Ring with the song of the Fates ;
Infant Bacchus in the vine, —
Far distant yet his chorus waits.

Canst thou copy in verse one chime
Of the wood-bell's peal and cry ?
Write in a book the morning's prime,
Or match with words that tender sky ?

Wonderful verse of the gods,
Of one import, of varied tone ;
They chant the bliss of their abodes
To man imprisoned in his own.

Ever the words of the gods resound,
But the porches of man's ear
Seldom in this low life's round
Are unsealed that he may hear.

Wandering voices in the air,
And murmurs in the wold,
Speak what I cannot declare,
Yet cannot all withhold.

When the shadow fell on the lake,
The whirlwind in ripples wrote
Air-bells of fortune that shine and break,
And omens above thought.

But tne meanings cleave to the lake,
Cannot be carried in book or urn ;
Go thy ways now, come later back,
On waves and hedges still they burn

These the fates of men forecast,
Of better men than live to-day ;
If who can read them comes at last,
He will spell in the sculpture, " Stay."

BORNEO AND RAJAH BROOKE.

OFF the southeastern extremity of Asia, and separated from it by the Chinese Sea, lies a cluster of great islands, comprising that portion of Oceanica commonly called Malaysia. Of these islands Borneo is the most extensive, and, if you call Australia a continent, it is by far the largest island in the world. Situated on the equator, stretching from 7° of north to 4° of south latitude, and from 108° to 119° of east longitude, its extreme length is 800 miles, its breadth 700, and it contains 320,000 square miles, — an area seven times as great as that of the populous State of New York.

But though its size and importance are so great, though it was discovered by the Portuguese as early as 1518, though several European nations have at various times had settlements on its coasts, though it is rich in all the products of a tropical clime, and in base and precious metals, diamonds and stones, and though its climate, contrary to what might have been expected, is in many localities salubrious even to an American or European constitution, yet until recently almost nothing was known by the world of its surface, its products, or its inhabitants.

The causes of this ignorance are obvious. The very shape of Borneo is unfavorable to discovery. A lumpish mass, like Africa and Australia, the ocean has nowhere pierced it with those deep bays and gulfs in which commerce delights to find a shelter and a home. And though it has navigable rivers, their course is through the almost impenetrable verdure of the tropics, and they reach the sea amid unwholesome jungles. The coast, moreover, is in most places marshy and unhealthy, for the distance of twenty or thirty miles inland; while the interior is filled with vast forests and great mountain ranges, almost trackless to any but native feet. Be-

sides, the absence of all just and stable government has reduced society to a state of chaos. And to all this must be added piracy, from time immemorial sweeping the sea and ravaging the land. Under such circumstances, if there were little opportunity for commerce, there was none for scientific investigations ; and only by the enterprises of commerce and the researches of science do we know of new and distant countries.

Many races inhabit Borneo ; but the Malays and Sea and Land Dyaks greatly preponderate. The Malays, who came from continental Asia, are the conquering and governing race. In their native condition they are indolent, treacherous, and given to piracy. The very name Malay has come to stand for cruelty and revenge. But well governed, they prove to be much like other people, susceptible to kindness, capable of affection, amiable, fond to excess of their children, and courteous to strangers. The Sea Dyaks are piratical tribes, dwelling on the coasts or borders of rivers, and subsisting by rapine and violence. The Land Dyaks are the descendants of the primitive inhabitants. They are a mild, industrious race, and remarkably honest. One hideous custom, that of preserving the heads of their fallen enemies as ghastly tokens of victory, has invested the name of Dyak with a reputation of cruelty which is not deserved. This singular practice, originating, it is said, in a superstitious desire to propitiate the Evil Spirit by bloody offerings, has in process of time become connected with all their ideas of manly prowess. The young girl receives with proud satisfaction from her lover the gift of a gory head, as the noblest proof both of his affection and his heroism. This custom is woven, too, into the early traditions of the race. The Sakarrans tell us that their first mother, who dwells now in heaven near the evening star, asked of her wooer a worthy gift; and that when he presented her a deer she rejected it with contempt; when he offered her a mias, the great orangoutang of Borneo, she turned her back upon it; but when in desperation he went out and slew a man, brought back his head, and threw it at her feet, she smiled upon him, and said that was indeed a gift worthy of her. This legend shows, at any rate, how fixed is this habit, not alone in the passions of the people, but also in their traditional regard. Yet, strange as it may seem, they are an attractive race. A missionary's wife who has known them well declares that they are gentle and kindly, simple as children, disposed to love and reverence all who are wiser and more civilized than themselves. Ida Pfeiffer concludes that the Dyaks pleased her best, not only among the races of Borneo, but among all the races of the earth with which she has come in contact. And a cultivated Englishman, with wealth and social position at command, has been so attracted to them, that he has lavished both his fortune and his best years in the work of their elevation. The social condition of the Dyaks has been sufficiently wretched. Subjected to the Malays, they have been forced to work in the mines without pay, while they were liable at any moment to be robbed of their homes, and even of their wives and children. " We do not live like men," said one of them, with great pathos. " We are like monkeys, hunted from place to place. We have no houses, and we dare not light a fire lest the smoke draw our enemies upon us."

Running along the whole northern coast of Borneo, eight hundred miles, and inland perhaps two hundred, is found Borneo Proper, one of the three great Mohammedan kingdoms into which the island was divided as early as the sixteenth century. This state is governed, or rather misgoverned, by a sultan, and, under him, by rajahs and pangerans, — officials who give to the commands of their nominal superior but a scanty obedience. For two centuries Borneo Proper has been steadily settling into anarchy and barbarism. With a government both feeble and despotic, it was torn by intestine wars, crushed within by oppression and ravaged without by piracy, until commerce and agriculture, the twin pillars of the state, were equally threatened, and not one element of ruin seemed to be wanting. What evidence of decay could be more striking than the simple fact that Bruni, its capital, which in the sixteenth century was crowded with a population of more than two hundred thousand souls, had in 1840 scarcely fourteen thousand inhabitants ?

To one corner of this wasting empire came, twenty - five years ago, a young Englishman. Simply a gentleman, he had no governmental alliances to help him, and no advantages of any sort for founding empire, except such as sprang from the possession of a sagacious mind, an undaunted temper, and a heart thoroughly in sympathy with the oppressed. Alone he has built up a flourishing state, introducing commercial activity and the habits of civilized life where only oppression and misery were, and has achieved an enterprise which seems to belong rather to the days of chivalry than to a plodding, utilitarian age, — an enterprise which, in romance and success, but not in carnage, calls to mind the deeds of the great Spanish captains in the New World.

James Brooke, the second and only surviving son of Thomas Brooke, a gentleman who had acquired a fortune in the service of the East India Company, was born in India, April 29, 1803. At an early age he entered the employ of the same company to whose interests his father had given his best days. In 1826, as a cadet, he accompanied the British army to the Burmese war, was dangerously wounded, received a furlough, and came to England. To restore his health and gratify his curiosity he spent the year 1827 in travelling on the Continent. His furlough having nearly expired, he embarked for India, but was wrecked on the voyage, and could not report for duty in proper season. This was one of those apparently fortuitous circumstances which so often change the whole aspect of a man's life. At any rate, it was the turning-point in Mr. Brooke's career. Finding that his misfortune had cost him his position, and that he could not recover it without tedious formalities, he left the service. Uncontrolled master of himself, and endowed with sagacity and courage of no ordinary stamp, he was ready for any undertaking which his adventurous spirit or his love of research might dictate. In fact, it was during this interval of leisure that he embarked for China, and on his passage saw for the first time the Eastern Archipelago. He was painfully interested in the condition of Borneo and Celebes, those great islands, sinking apparently into hopeless decay. His sympathies were awakened by the sufferings of the helpless natives, and his indignation was aroused by the outrages of an unbridled piracy. His feelings can be best gathered from his own language. "These unhappy countries afford a striking proof how the fairest and richest lands under the sun may become degraded by a continuous course of oppression and misrule. Whilst extravagant dreams of the progressive advancement of the human race are entertained, a large tract of the globe has been gradually relapsing into barbarism. Whilst the folly of fashion requires an acquaintance with the deserts of Africa, and a most ardent thirst for a knowledge of the customs of Timbuctoo, — whilst the trumpet tongue of many an orator excites thousands to the rational and charitable object of converting the Jews or of reclaiming the Gypsies, — not a single prospectus is spread abroad, not a single voice is raised in Exeter Hall, to relieve the darkness of this paganism and the horrors of this slave-trade. Under these circumstances I have considered that individual exertions may be usefully applied to rouse the zeal of slumbering philanthropy."

The feelings thus awakened were not of a transient character. His dreams henceforth were to visit these islands, see them for himself, study their natural history, understand their social condition, and ascertain what avenues could be opened for trade, and what steps taken to redeem the oppressed native races.

In 1835 the death of his father, leaving him master of an independent fortune, enabled him to realize his dreams. He was a member of the Royal Yacht Club, as well as owner and commander of a yacht, — a position which admitted him in foreign ports to all the privileges of an English naval officer. In this little vessel he resolved to undertake an adventurous voyage of discovery. He approached his enterprise with a wary forethought. "I was convinced," he says, "that it was necessary to form men to my purpose, and by a line of steady and kind conduct to raise up a personal regard for myself and an attachment to the vessel." He cruised three years in the Mediterranean, carefully selecting and training his crew. He studied thoroughly the whole subject of the Eastern Archipelago, and acquainted himself as perfectly as possible with the minutiæ of seamanship and with every useful art. And when his preparations were all complete, on the 16th of December, 1838, he set sail for Singapore, in the yacht Royalist, a vessel of one hundred and forty-two tons, manned by twenty men and officers, with an armament of six six-pounders and a full supply of small arms of all sorts. Such were the mighty resources wherewith he began an enterprise which has ended in raising him to the government of a petty kingdom, and to almost sovereign influence over the whole empire of Borneo Proper.

The reader has already had glimpses of the feelings which prompted this expedition. In a communication to the "Geographical Register" he more fully unfolds his views; and from this and from his familiar letters it is not difficult to gain a clear idea of the character and motives of the man. That his ardent mind had been fired by a study of the career of his great predecessor, Stamford Raffles, is evident. That he was himself one of those energetic, restless natures, to which idleness or mere routine-work is the severest of penalties, is equally evident. He had, moreover, a large share of that kind of enthusiasm which the cool, sagacious men of this world call romance, and which delights to fasten on objects seemingly impossible. He was like the old knights, rejoicing most when the field of their devoir was distant and dangerous. Yet not altogether like them. He was rather a man of the twelfth century, disciplined and invigorated by the hard common-sense and sharp utilitarianism of the nineteenth century. And we must not forget that he honestly wished to benefit the native races. Every page, nay, almost every line, in his journals and letters, bears witness to his profound compassion for the despised and downtrodden Dyaks. Aside from this, when we remember that he was a genuine Englishman, proud of his native land and thoughtful always of her aggrandizement, we need be at no loss to understand his motives. He went forth to gratify a love of adventure, " to see something of the world and come back again," to extend a little the realms of scientific knowledge, to suggest, perhaps, some plans for the improvement of native character, and last, but not least, to learn whether there might not be opened new avenues for the extension of British trade and British power.

That the methods by which these objects were to be attained were not very well defined even to his own mind is clear. He himself said, " I cast myself upon the waters, like Southey's little book; but whether the world will know me after many days, is a question I cannot answer." And some years after, alluding to a charge of inconsistency, he said, " I did not embrace my position *at once;* and indeed the position itself altered very rapidly; and I am free to confess before the world that my views of duty and responsibility were not so high at first as they have since been." Without doubt his direct and primary purpose was investigation. He took with him men of some scientific knowledge, himself being no mean observer ; and he proposed to prosecute, wherever opportunity occurred, researches into the geography, natural history, and commercial resources of these islands. If he had ulterior ends, as yet they existed in his mind as fascinating dreams, rather than well-defined plans.

After a tedious voyage of nearly six months, the Royalist reached Singapore, June 1, 1839. While Mr. Brooke was engaged in refitting his yacht, and anxiously revolving in his mind how he should obtain permission to penetrate into the neighboring kingdom of Borneo, he learned that Muda Hassim, uncle of the Sultan, and Rajah of Sarawak, the northwestern province of Borneo, had displayed great humanity towards a crew of shipwrecked Englishmen. On receiving this information he started at once for Sarawak, hoping to get some hold upon the Rajah, and by such help to pursue his researches. But the time of his visit was most unfortunate. The whole province was in a state of open rebellion ; so that, while he was received courteously, and permitted to make some local surveys, nothing of importance could be accomplished. Baffled and wearied by delay, he sailed back to Singapore, and from thence to Celebes, where he remained several months, engaged in extensive explorations, and in collecting specimens to illustrate the natural history of that island.

Mr. Brooke returned from Celebes worn out and sick, and was obliged to remain at Singapore several months to recruit his strength. In August, 1840, he made a second visit to Sarawak, intending to tarry there a few days, and then proceed homeward by the way of

Manilla and China. "I have done fully as much as I promised the public," he writes. He found things in much the same state as when he left. No progress had been made in the suppression of the rebellion. Few lives indeed had been lost, but the most bloody war could hardly have produced worse results. The country was filled with combatants. Every straggler was cut off. Violence and rapine were the law. Trade and agriculture languished. A rich province was fast relapsing into a wilderness ; and all its people were beginning to suffer alike for shelter and sustenance. As our hero was about to set sail, the Rajah opened his whole heart to him. His prospects were anything but flattering. He found himself unequal to the reduction of the rebels. He was surrounded by traitors. At the court of the Sultan, a hostile cabal, taking advantage of his ill-fortune, threatened his power and his life. In this strait, he besought his visitor to remain and give him aid, promising in event of success to confer upon him the government of the province. After a few days' reflection, Mr. Brooke, believing, as he declares, that the cause of the Sultan was just, believing also that what the whole people needed most was peace, and that peace would place him in a position to render them the greatest service, acceded to this request, without, however, be it observed, binding Muda Hassim to any precise stipulations concerning the government.

Many pages of his journal are devoted to an account of this war ; and a most curious story it is of cowardice, bravado, and inefficiency. It was advance and retreat, boastful challenge and as boastful reply, marching and countermarching, day after day, and month after month. "Like the heroes of old, the adverse parties spoke to each other : 'We are coming, we are coming ; lay aside your muskets and fight us with your swords' ; and so the heroes ceased to talk, but always forgot to fight" ; — the sum of all their achievements being to lay waste the country, to interrupt honest industry, and to put in peril the lives of the unoffending. Mr. Brooke soon tired of this farce. Gathering a motley force, consisting of Malays, Dyaks, Chinese, and his own crew, he prepared for an assault. Then, planting his cannon where they commanded the stronghold of the enemy, with a few well-directed volleys he brought its walls tumbling about their ears. The insurgents, driven to the open country, and altogether amazed by this specimen of Saxon energy, surrendered at discretion. At one blow a desolating war was ended.

Peace being restored, Mr. Brooke did not insist on the literal fulfilment of the terms which Muda Hassim had in his extremity been so ready to proffer. He chose to occupy a position of influence, rather than one of outward authority. A contract was entered into by which he became Resident of Sarawak. The conditions of the agreement were, that the Rajah on his part should repress piracy, protect legitimate commerce, and as far as possible remove from the Dyaks unjust burdens ; while his ally, in return for these concessions, should open trade, sending a vessel to and fro between Singapore and Sarawak, exchanging foreign luxuries for native products, and more especially for antimony, of which article the Rajah had the monopoly. In fulfilment of his part of the treaty, Mr. Brooke proceeded to Singapore, purchased a schooner, loaded her with an assorted cargo, returned to Sarawak, and at the earnest request of Muda Hassim landed and distributed his goods.

But auspicious as was the commencement of this alliance, soon grave causes of complaint arose. On every point the deceitful Malay came short of his agreement. Having obtained valuable property, he showed no alacrity in paying for it ; weeks and months passed without bringing him apparently any nearer to a pecuniary settlement. So far from repressing piracy, he encouraged it; and a fleet of one hundred and twenty prahus, with his tacit consent, actually put to sea. When a crew of English seamen were enslaved and carried to Bruni, under the most frivolous pretexts he refused to intercede with the Sultan for these unfortunate men. And so this strange friendship cooled. It was no slight proof either of his courage or his humanity to despatch at this very time, as Mr. Brooke did, his yacht to Bruni, to attempt something in behalf of his enslaved countrymen, and to remain himself with only three men at Sarawak. The yacht came back, however, having effected nothing.

By this time the patience of the creditor was exhausted. Despoiled of his goods, finding that, despite his remonstrances, the Dyaks were cruelly oppressed, and that piracy was encouraged, he resolved to try the effect of threats. He repaired on board his yacht, loaded her guns with grape and canister, and brought her broadside to bear upon the Rajah's palace. Then taking a small, but well-armed guard, he sought an interview with Muda Hassim. The terror of that functionary was extreme. The native tribes openly sided with their English friend. The Chinese residents remained obstinately neutral. The Malays, between cowardice and treachery, afforded him no efficient support. To crown all, his resolute and incensed ally had only to wave his hand to bring down upon him swift destruction. "After this demonstration, things went cheerily to a conclusion." Muda Hassim, finding that his creditor was inflexible, and being unable or unwilling to pay for the goods which he had fraudulently obtained, offered in payment of all debts to surrender the government. The offer was accepted, the agreement drawn up, signed, sealed, guns fired and flags waved, and on September 24, 1841, Mr. Brooke became Rajah of Sarawak. In August of the following year the Sultan solemnly confirmed the agreement.

The territory thus strangely passing into the hands of a private English gentleman was a tract of country bordering upon the sea sixty miles, and extending inland from seventy to eighty miles. Situated at the northeastern extremity of Borneo, pierced by two small, but navigable rivers, its position is most favorable for commerce. Its soil is deep and rich, yielding under any proper culture large crops of all tropical products. Its forests are filled with trees fit for shipbuilding, and abound in that variety from which is obtained the gutta percha of commerce. The hills are rich in iron and tin of the best quality. The mountain streams wash down gold. In the beds of smaller rivers are found diamonds, in such profusion that most of the Malays wear them set in rings and other ornaments. From this single province comes nearly the whole supply of antimony in the world. "I do not believe," says a resident, "that in the same given space there can be found so great mineral and vegetable wealth in any land in the whole world."

With what sentiments the new Rajah entered upon his duties can be best understood by a perusal of his familiar letters. He writes to his mother: "Do not start when I say that I am going to settle in Borneo, that I am about to endeavor to plant there a mixed colony amid a wild but not unvirtuous race, and to become the pioneer of European knowledge and improvement. The diffusion of civilization, commerce, and religion through so vast an island as Borneo, I call a grand object, — so grand that self is quite lost when I consider it; and even failure would be much better than the non-attempt." "A few days ago I was up a high mountain and looked over the country. It is a prospect which I have rarely seen equalled; and sitting there, lazily smoking a cigar, I called into existence the coffee plantations, the sugar plantations, the nutmeg plantations, and pretty white villages and tiny steeples, and dreamed that I heard the buzz of life and the clang of industry amid the jungles, and that the China Colins whistled as they went, for want of thought, as they homeward bent."

The first duty which claimed attention was the relief of the native Dyaks. A shrewd Dyak once defined the Malay government as " a plantain in the mouth and a thorn in the back." A plantain giving to their poor subjects a little to keep life in them ; a thorn stripping them to the skin and piercing them to the bone. The description is pithy, and it is true. The exactions of the Malay chiefs were almost beyond belief. Seizing and monopolizing some article of prime necessity, — salt perhaps, — they would force the natives to buy at the rate of fifty dollars' worth of rice for a teacup of salt ; until the wretched cultivator, who had raised a plentiful crop, was brought to the verge of starvation. They reserved to themselves the right of purchasing the articles which the Dyaks had to sell, and then affixed to those articles an arbitrary price, perhaps less than a five-hundredth of their real value. They would send a bar of iron two or three feet long, and having an intrinsic worth of a few cents, to the head man of a tribe, demanding that his village should give for it a sum equal to five, ten, or twenty dollars. Another was sent in the same way, and another, and another, until the rapacity of the chiefs was satisfied, or the wretched natives had no more to give. Often, when the latter had been robbed of everything, the Malays would seize and sell their wives and children. It is recorded of one tribe, that there was not so much as one woman or child to be found in it. All had been swept off by these remorseless slave-hunters. Nor did their wrongs end here. If a Dyak killed a Malay "under any circumstances of aggression," he was put to death, often with every possible addition of torture. If he accidentally injured one of the ruling caste, he was fortunate to escape with the loss of half or two thirds of his little savings. On the other hand, a Malay might kill as many Dyaks as he pleased, and if perchance justice were a little sterner than usual,

he might be fined a few cents or a few dollars. Volumes are contained in this one statement, that in the ten years from 1830 to 1840, the Dyaks in the province of Sarawak dwindled from 14,000 to 6,000 souls.

A blow was immediately struck at the root of this black oppression. As soon as the new government was fairly established, a few simple enactments were published. They declared that every man, Dyak as well as Malay, should enjoy unmolested all the gains of his toil; that all exactions of every name and nature should cease, and that only a small tax, evenly distributed, should be levied for the support of government ; that all roads and rivers should be free to all ; that all molestation of the Dyaks should be punished with severity. The proclamation which contains these laws concludes with exhorting all persons who are disposed to disturb the public peace to take flight speedily to some other country, where they can break with impunity the laws of God and man. These enactments were firmly executed, without fear and without partiality. Wonderful were the results ! Internal violence ceased. The confidence of the natives was awakened. Industry and enterprise sprang up on every hand as by magic. Sarawak became a city of refuge. Sometimes as many as fifty fled thither in a day. In 1844, in the short space of two months, five hundred families took shelter in the province. In 1850, three thousand Chinese fled from Sambas to Sarawak. The Dyaks returned the good-will of their Rajah with love and reverence. During one of his tours in the interior, delegations from tribes numbering six thousand souls came to seek his protection. "We have heard," said they, in simple but touching language, "that a son of Europe has arrived, who is a friend of the Dyaks." When he visited the native hamlets, the women would throw themselves on the ground and clasp his feet, and the whole tribe would spend the night in joyful feasting and merriment. It is soberly affirmed by a credible witness, that on one occasion messengers came fifteen days' journey from a distant province to see if there were such a phenomenon as Dyaks living in comfort.

Mr. Brooke soon found that all his efforts for internal reform must be in a comparative sense futile so long as piracy, that curse of Borneo, was permitted to ravage unchecked. "It is in a Malay's nature," says the Dutch proverb, "to rove on the seas in his prahu, as it is in that of the Arab to wander with his steed on the sands of the desert." No person who has not investigated the subject can appreciate how wide-spread and deep-seated this plague of piracy is. The mere statistics are appalling. It was estimated, in 1840, that one hundred thousand men made freebooting their trade. One single chief had under control seven hundred prahus. Whole tribes, whole groups of islands, almost whole races, despising even the semblance of honest industry, depended upon rapine for a livelihood. "It is difficult to catch fish, but it is easy to catch Borneans," said the Soloo pirates scornfully; and, acting upon that principle, they fitted out their fleets and planned their voyages with all the method of honest tradesmen.

This piracy was divided into two branches, — coastwise piracy and piracy on the broad seas. The Sea Dyaks built boats called bangkongs, sixty to a hundred feet long, narrow and sharp, propelled by thirty to fifty oars, and so swift that nothing but a steamer could overtake them. These freebooters were the terror of all honest laborers and tradesmen. Skulking along the coast, pushing up rivers and creeks, landing anywhere and everywhere without warning, they mercilessly destroyed the native villages and swept the inhabitants into captivity. Or else, impelling with the force of fifty men their snaky craft, which were swift as race-boats and noiseless as beasts of prey, they would surprise at dead of night some defence-less merchantman, overwhelm their victims with showers of spears, and with morning light a plundered boat, a few dead bodies, were the silent witnesses of their ferocity. On the other hand, the Illanum and Balanini tribes, infesting the islands to the northeast of Borneo, undertook far grander enterprises. Putting to sea, prepared for a long voyage, in fleets of two or three hundred prahus, propelled by wind and oars, armed with brass cannon, and manned by ten thousand bold buccaneers, they swept through the whole length of the Chinese Sea, and, turning the southernmost point of Borneo, penetrated the straits and sounds between Java and Celebes, never stopping in their ruthless course until they came face to face with the sturdy pirates of New Guinea, and returned, after a voyage of ten thousand miles and an absence of two years, laden with spoils and captives. How hapless was the fate of the poor Dyak! If he stayed at home, cultivating his fields, his Malay lord fleeced him to the skin. If, thinking to engage in gainful traffic, he hugged the shore with his little bark, the river-pirate snatched him up. If he stood out upon the broad waters, he could scarcely hope to escape the Northern hordes who swarmed in every sea.

Mr. Brooke's most terrible assailants were the Sakarran and Sarebus pirates, two tribes of freebooters whose seats of power were on the Sarebus and Batang Lupar rivers, two streams fifty or sixty miles east of Sarawak. These tribes were encouraged and secretly helped by his own Malay chiefs, and insolently defied his power, continuing their depredations, capturing every vessel which ventured out, and ravaging all the adjacent coasts. The strength of these confederacies was so great, that it was no unusual thing for them to muster a hundred warboats; and they had built, on the banks of the rivers which they infested, strong forts at every point which commanded the channel. That the new Rajah was not able with his slender resources to curb these sea-robbers is not surprising. The only wonder is, that he was able to protect his own capital from the assaults which they often threatened but never dared to attempt.

But efficient aid was at hand. In the summer of 1843 the British ship Dido anchored off the entrance of Sarawak River. She was commissioned to suppress piracy in and about the Chinese Sea. Her commander readily entered into the views of the English Rajah. A boat expedition against the strongholds of the Sarebus pirates was projected. Mr. Brooke assisted with seven hundred Dyaks. A curious incident occurred, showing how clearly the natives appreciated their dependence on their English friend. When he asked their chiefs if they would aid him, they besought him not to risk his life in so desperate an enterprise. But when he assured them that his purpose was fixed, that he should go, alone if necessary, they replied : "What is the use of our remaining behind ? You die, we die ; you live, we live. We will go too." The expedition was perfectly successful. Three fortified villages were stormed, many guns spiked, many boats destroyed, and their defenders driven to the jungles. This chastisement not sufficing, in the following year another expedition from the same vessel attacked the Sakarran pirates and inflicted upon them a punishment even more severe than that which had fallen to the lot of their Sarebus brethren. Six forts, one mounting fifty-six guns, scores of war-boats, and more than a thousand huts, were burned. These lessons, though sharp, did not permanently subdue.

The blow which broke the power of these confederacies was inflicted in 1849. News came to Sarawak that the pirates had put to sea, marking their course by fearful atrocities. At once Mr. Brooke applied to the English Admiral for assistance, and the steamer Nemesis was despatched to the scene of action. The Rajah joined her with eighteen war-boats, to which were afterwards added eleven hundred Dyaks, in their bangkongs. On the 31st of July, at night, they encountered the great war-fleet of the Sarebus and Sakarran pirates, numbering one hundred and fifty bangkongs, returning home laden with plunder. The pirates found the entrances of the river occupied by their enemies, — the English, Malay, and Dyak forces being placed in three detachments, while the Nemesis was fully prepared to assist whenever the attack should begin. "Then there was a dead silence, broken only by three strokes of a gong, which called the pirates to a council of war. A few minutes afterwards a fearful yell gave notice of their advance, and the fleet approached in two divisions. In the dead of the night there ensued a terrible scene. The pirates fought bravely, but they could not withstand the superior forces of their enemy. Their boats were upset by the paddles of the steamer. They were hemmed in on every side, and five hundred men were killed sword in hand, while twenty-five hundred escaped to the jungles, many of them to perish. The morning light showed a sad spectacle of ruin and defeat. Upwards of eighty prahus and bangkongs were captured, and many more destroyed." The English officers would have gladly saved life ; but the pirates would take no quarter, and the prisoners were few. It was a striking fact, that one of the war-boats under Mr. Brooke was manned by some thirty Malays, every one of whom had lost during the year a near relative, killed by these same pirates. The confederacy has never risen from this defeat, and for years the tribes composing it have returned to the labors of peaceful life. Writing twelve months afterwards to a friend, Rajah Brooke says : " Pray keep the 31st of July apart for a special bumper, for during the last year not a single innocent life has been taken by these pirates, nor a single prahu fallen into their hands." Many a victory, famous in story, has accomplished less.

The next year a fleet of sixty-four prahus, manned by northern pirates, and carrying 1224 guns, was destroyed by British gunboats in the Gulf of Tonquin. This was followed by an attack of the Spaniards upon the haunts of the Soloo pirates. A lull ensued. For three or four years almost nothing was heard of freebooting; but it was a deceitful calm, not a final cessation of the storm. The freebooting spirit was not taken out of the blood of the Malay. Now piracy is said to be on the increase again. Only three years since six Balanini pirates had the audacity to sail into Sarawak Bay and commence depredations along its coasts. But not one returned to tell the tale. The whole six were captured or destroyed, and their crews killed or taken prisoners. The only permanent remedy for the evil is just, settled, and efficient government, such as has been established at Sarawak, destroying not simply the fleets, but breaking up the piratical haunts, and with firm hand forcing their people back into the habits and pursuits of civilized life.

Being delivered for a time at least from these perils, the new Rajah was at liberty to devote himself to the welfare of his subjects. It is not possible, in a brief notice, even to hint at all the events and efforts of the next fifteen years of his government, — to say how he repressed the cupidity and lawlessness of the Malay chiefs; how he encouraged and protected the poor Dyaks; how he opened new channels for trade; how, from year to year, he resisted the fierce pirates, who, coming from the neighboring islands with strong fleets, sought to sweep the adjacent seas. Of course the prime need was to restore confidence, and to assure to all honest workers, of every race, the gains of their industry. The first question, indeed, of the Chinese emigrant was, "Will you protect us, or will our plantations, so soon as they are worth anything, be stripped by your

chiefs?" It has been beautiful to behold order coming out of chaos, peace out of violence, whole districts redeemed from anarchy, simply by giving efficient support to the orderly part of the population. Another object of not less importance was to create in this people something of the feeling of nationality, and to make them comprehend that they were citizens, with the duties of citizens. It certainly was no easy task to awaken much of the sentiment of lofty patriotism in the minds of those whose only common memories were of lawless misrule and oppression. Every possible effort has been made in this direction. The struggle has been, not to plant an English colony, but to create a Bornean state. The laws are not English, nor built upon English precedents. They are simply the old Bornean statutes, made conformable to the principles of equity, and administered with just regard to the customs and traditions of the people. The offices of government are filled to the least possible degree with foreigners; while native chiefs and even reclaimed pirates are associated with them, and thus habituated to all the forms of a civilized state. Mr. Brooke, with a rare courage and wisdom, has always trusted for his safety to the good-will of his native subjects. He has never been sustained by mercenary bands. At a time when piratical violence was most threatening, when disorders were yet rife in his own state, and when his subjects but poorly appreciated his benevolent purposes towards them, his whole English force was twenty-four men. It is pleasant to add, that this confidence was not misplaced. A younger generation is now springing up, with larger views of life, and with a better appreciation of the workings and value of equitable government. To sum up all in a brief sentence, it may be said with truth that the administration has been marked by rare sagacity, firmness, and comprehensiveness of view, and that it has been crowned with success.

In 1845, Mr. Brooke came for the

first time into official relations with the British government, by accepting the office of confidential agent in Borneo. We have already alluded to his warm love of his native country. As early as 1841, he had expressed a willingness to sacrifice his large outlays, and to relinquish all his rights and interests to the crown, if a guaranty could be given that piracy would be checked and the native races protected in all their proper rights and privileges. He accepted gladly, therefore, a post which promised to increase his power to benefit his people, and entered upon its duties with vigor. Immediately upon his appointment, he was requested to make investigations as to the existence of a harbor fit for the shelter and victualling of ships bound from Hong-Kong to Singapore. He reported that Labuan, a small island north of Borneo, was in every way suitable ; that it was about equidistant from the two parts ; that it had a fine harbor, or rather roadstead ; that it was healthy ; that it abounded in coal of the best quality ; that, finally, the Sultan stood pledged to convey it upon reasonable terms.

But before legal papers could be drawn, the whole policy of the court of Bruni had changed. The Sultan was a monarch with "the head of an idiot and the heart of a pirate." All his sympathies were with violence and robbery. Under the influence of others, he had agreed to use his power against piracy, and had even been brought to say, in fawning phrase, that "he wanted the English near to him." But he suddenly repented of his good purposes. In a fit of Oriental fickleness he caused Muda Hassim and all who favored the English alliance to be put to death, despatched a messenger secretly to administer poison to Mr. Brooke, and entered into even closer friendship than before with the piratical tribes. A confidential servant of Pangeran Budrudeen, the brother of Muda Hassim, with difficulty escaped, and fled to Sarawak. He related that his master had bravely resisted, but, overpowered by numbers and desperately wounded, had

committed to his charge a ring, bidding him deliver it to Rajah Brooke as a dying memento, and to tell him that he died faithful to his pledges to the Queen ; then, setting fire to a keg of powder, he blew himself with his family into the air.

These tidings filled Mr. Brooke with grief and indignation. Every passion of his fiery and energetic nature was aroused. He repaired on board the British fleet, which, upon receipt of this news, had put into Sarawak. Without delay the fleet sailed for Bruni. An immediate explanation was demanded of the Sultan. The reply was a volley from the forts which commanded the river. Without ceremony the ships returned the fire. In a brief time these strongholds were stormed, and Bruni itself was at the mercy of the enemy. The Sultan fled to the swamps. Sailing out of Borneo River, the fleet swept along the whole northern coast, taking in rapid succession the forts of the Illanum pirates who had instigated the murders at Bruni, and inflicting upon them a signal chastisement.

By this time the Sultan wearied of jungles and sighed for his palace. He wrote a cringing letter, promising amendment, agreeing to ratify all his former engagements, and as a sign of his true penitence was ready even to pay royal honors to the memory of the men whom he had slain. There was no further difficulty in respect to the cession of Labuan, and it was taken possession of, December 24, 1846, — Mr. Brooke being appointed governor. It is said that the possession of this island goes far to make England mistress of the Chinese Sea, — a statement easily to be credited by any one conversant with English policy. At any rate, he who observes how, at apparently insignificant stations, — on little islands, on a marshy peninsula, — mere dots on the map, — England has established her commercial depots, — at Hong-Kong in the north, at Labuan in the centre, and at Singapore in the south, — will gain new respect for the sagacity which in the councils of the mother country always lurks behind the red-tapism of which we hear so much.

After an absence of nine years, Rajah Brooke revisited England in the year 1847. He was the hero of the hour. Every honor was showered upon him. He was invited to visit Windsor Castle, received the freedom of London, and then or soon after was knighted. Owing to his representations of the readiness of the Dyaks to receive instruction, a meeting was held in London, at which funds were obtained to build a church and school-houses. Two missionaries and their families were sent to Sarawak. The buildings were erected long since, and these Christian means are in full activity. Brooke's language upon the proper qualifications of a missionary exhibits in a striking light his straightforward resolution and enlarged liberality. " Above all things, I beg of you to save us from such a one as some of the committee desire to see at Sarawak. Zealots, and intolerants, and enthusiasts, who begin the task of tuition by a torrent of abuse against all that their pupils hold sacred, shall not come to Sarawak. Whilst our endeavors to convert the natives are conducted with charity, I am a warm friend of the mission. But whenever there is a departure from the only visible means God has placed at our disposal, — time, reason, patience, — and the Christian faith is to be heralded in its introduction by disturbances and heart-burnings and bloodshed, I want it not ; and you are quite at liberty to say, that I would rather that the mission were withdrawn."

About the year 1850, Mr. Brooke became the object of a virulent attack, continued several years, both in the public prints and in Parliament. Prompted originally by the petty malice of those whose tool for the advancement of their personal schemes he had refused to become, this attack was taken up by a few persons of influence, who seem to have misunderstood utterly both his character

and work. He has been termed a mere adventurer. He has been accused of avarice, of wringing from the natives great sums, and receiving from England large salaries as Consul at Borneo and as Governor of Labuan. It has been asserted that he has been guilty of wholesale slaughter of the innocent, interfering with tribal wars under the pretence of extirpating piracy. None of these charges have been sustained. On the contrary, it has been conclusively shown that he has sunk more than £20,000 of his private fortune in this enterprise. The piracy, so mildly called intertribal war, is undoubtedly robbery, both on the sea and on the land, and conducted with all fitting accompaniments of cruelty and bloodshed. This persecution has not been borne by its object with much patience, and, indeed, like Rob Roy's Highlander, " he does not seem to be famous for that gude gift." " I am no tame lion to be cowed by a pack of hounds. These intertribal wars are such as the wolf wages against the lamb. I should like to ask the most peaceable man in England what he would do if a horde of bandits frequently burst forth from Brest and Cherbourg, ravaging the shores of the Channel, and carrying women and children into captivity, with the heads of their decapitated husbands and fathers ? Would he preach ? Would he preach when he saw his daughter dishonored and his son murdered ? And then would he proclaim his shame and cowardice among men ? What do some gentlemen expect ? They particularly desire to suppress piracy. Do they really imagine that piracy is to be suppressed by argument and preaching ? "

Mr. Brooke's enemies have three times pressed their accusations before the House of Commons, and three times have been defeated by overwhelming majorities, — the last vote being 230 to 19. Finally, to end the controversy, a royal commission was appointed to visit the scene of these transactions, and upon the spot to decide their merits. The report of this commission has not reached us, if indeed it has ever been made public ; but the practical results of it are certain. Mr. Brooke has severed his official connection with the British government by a resignation of the offices which he held under it ; while he retains his sovereignty at Sarawak, with the undiminished love of his subjects and an unimpaired influence over the native tribes. There seems to be no doubt that the intelligent public opinion of England fully sustains him. And it is safe to predict that with that opinion the final verdict of history will coincide. That, placed in circumstances of great difficulty, he may have taken steps not to be squared with the nicest morality, is possible ; for that is what must be said of every man who has borne the burden of great public responsibility. Neither is it surprising that a man of such boldness of speech and such almost Cromwellian vigor in action should have enemies ; that is a necessity. But that he has been a true and sagacious friend of the natives, and that his career has been for the increase of human happiness, are facts as certain as any can be.

His best defence is his works. In 1842, when he took the government of Sarawak, it was a feeble province, torn by dissension, crushed by slavery, and ravaged by lawless violence. Now it is a peaceful, prosperous commonwealth. In 1842, its capital, Kuching, was a wretched village, whose houses were miserable mud huts or tents of leaves, and containing but fifteen hundred inhabitants. Now it numbers fifteen thousand, — an increase almost rivalling that of our Western cities. In 1842, no boat put to sea without terror. As a result, the amount of trade was contemptible. Now Sarawak has enterprising native merchants, owning vessels of two hundred tons, having regular transactions with Singapore and all the neighboring ports. This trade, as early as 1853, employed twenty-five thousand tons of shipping, and the exports for the year were valued at more than a million of dollars. In 1842,

deaths by violence were of almost daily occurrence. Twelve years later, a resident could boast that for three years only one person had lost his life by other than natural causes. How would American cities appear in comparison with this poor Dyak and heathen metropolis ? Well does Rajah Brooke proudly ask, "Could such success spring from a narrow and sordid policy?" Mrs. McDougall, the missionary's wife, says : "We have now a beautiful church at Sarawak, and the bell calls us there to worship every morning at six, and at five every evening. Neither is there anything in this quiet, happy place to prevent our thus living in God's presence."

Mrs. McDougall adds a story which shows the estimation in which the natives hold their Rajah. "Pa Jenna paid me a visit at Sarawak. The Rajah was then in England. But Pa Jenna, coming into my sitting-room, immediately espied his picture hanging against the wall. I was much struck with the expression of respect which both the face and attitude of this untutored savage assumed as he stood before the picture. He raised his handkerchief from his head, and, saluting the picture with a bow, such as a Roman Catholic would make to his patron saint's altar, whispered to himself, 'Our great Rajah.'" And this man was a reclaimed pirate.

This reverential love of the natives is the one thing which does not admit of a doubt. The proofs are constant and irresistible. Some years since a lady with a few attendants was pushing her boat up a Bornean river, many leagues away from Sarawak, when she encountered a wild Dyak tribe on a warlike expedition. The sight of more than a hundred half-naked savages, crowning a little knoll which jutted into the river a half-dozen rods in advance of her boat, dancing frantically like maniacs, brandishing their long knives, and yelling all the while like demons, was not cheering. Yet at the sight of the Sarawak flag raised at the bow of the boat, every demonstration of hostility ceased. She was overpowered by their noisy welcome, and received from them the kindest attention. A dozen years ago, at the very time that the accusations of cruelty and wholesale slaughter of innocent people were most recklessly made, a party of Englishmen, and among them the adopted son of the Rajah, went on an exploring expedition to the extreme northeast corner of Borneo, more than six hundred miles from Sarawak. While they were seated one evening around their fire, the whole air resounded with the cries, "Tuan Brooke! Tuan Brooke!" and presently the natives drew near and expressed their joy at seeing a son of the great Rajah, and wondering that he who had so blessed the southern Dyaks did not extend his protection to their northern brethren. One anecdote more. During the Chinese insurrection, of which we shall soon speak, a Malay chief, fighting desperately against the insurgents, was mortally wounded, only lingering long enough to be assured of the Rajah's victory, and to exclaim with his dying breath, "I would rather be in hell with the English, than in heaven with my own countrymen."

The loyalty of the native population was thoroughly tested in the year 1857. It was the time of the second British war against China. Now the Chinese are in one sense the most cosmopolitan of races. Wherever bread is to be won, or gold amassed, there they go, thus becoming scattered all through Southeastern Asia and the adjoining islands. In one aspect they are a great blessing. They are a most laborious and thrifty race, of almost incalculable benefit in the development of the material resources of a country. But in some respects they are also an element of danger. They never identify themselves with the country in which they dwell. They simply come to get a living out of it. They band themselves in secret societies or other exclusive organizations, and seem to get no real love for the land which gives them bread, or the people among whom they

live. Under a peaceful rule, this race had greatly multiplied at Sarawak. Some branches of industry had indeed almost fallen into their hands. Especially in all mining operations was their help a positive necessity. For the Dyak, though industrious enough on his little plantation, will not work, except on compulsion, in the mines. These places are bitter to him with the memory of forced labor and unrequited misery. Besides, he believes that the bowels of the earth are filled with demons, and no amount of pay gives him courage to face these. As a result, the conduct of the mines was left to the Chinese, and they were unwisely permitted to work them in large companies of several hundred, under their own overseers. This gave them the advantages of a compact organization : to a dangerous degree they became a state within the state.

When the war in China broke out, the Chinese residents at Sarawak, sympathizing with their countrymen, were naturally greatly excited ; and when tidings came that the English fleet had been repulsed from before the Canton forts, they were emboldened to take the desperate step of attempting to put to death or to drive out of the country Rajah Brooke and the rest of the English people, that they themselves might take possession of it. About dusk on a February night, six hundred of them gathered under their chiefs, armed themselves, went on board cargo-boats, and began to float down the river towards the capital. At midnight they attacked the Rajah's house. Its inmates were forced to flee to the jungles. The Rajah rose from a sick-bed, ran to the banks of the stream, dove under one of the Chinese boats, swam the river, and took refuge with the Malays. Several of his countrymen were murdered. His own house, filled with the priceless collections of a lifetime, together with a costly library, was burned.

It was a gloomy morning which succeeded the night of this catastrophe. Though he did not doubt for a moment the ultimate suppression of the rebellion, what ruin might not be wrought in the few days or weeks which should elapse before that event! And where, now that he had been driven from his capital, he should find a base of operations to which he might gather the scattered native forces, was the perplexing question of the hour, — when, joyful sight, he beheld a merchant steamer sailing up the river! He hailed her, went on board, and with a sufficient force steamed up to Sarawak. With his appearance the last vestige of hope for the insurrection disappeared.

Meanwhile stirring events had taken place. At first the natives were stunned. They were roused at dead of night, to find the Chinese in possession of the town, their Rajah's house in flames, the Rajah missing, while the rumor was that he had been killed. For a time they wandered about listlessly, vacantly staring each other in the face, and it seemed as though they were about to submit without a struggle. In the midst of this gloom and uncertainty, up spoke a Malay trader, whose veins, despite his peaceful occupation, were full of the old pirate blood : "Are we going to submit to be governed by these Chinese, or are we going to be faithful to our Rajah? I am no talker, but I will never be governed by any but him, and to-night I commence war to the knife with his enemies." This broke the spell. Both Malays and Dyaks, in city and country alike, rose *en masse*, and after a severe fight, prolonged till the reappearance of Mr. Brooke, drove the Chinese to the forests, and pursued them with unrelenting fury. Many of the insurgents perished by the sword. Many more wandered about till they died of starvation. Some threw themselves down in their tracks, expiring from fatigue and utter wretchedness. Some hung themselves to escape their misery. In despair and exasperation, they even turned their arms against each other. Of the six hundred who made the original attack, sixty escaped. Of the four thousand who composed the Chinese

population, a forlorn and wearied remnant of two thousand took refuge in the Dutch part of the island. This lamentable destruction was the result neither of the order nor the permission of the Rajah. It was accomplished by the unreasoning fury of an outraged people. In a few days the formidable insurrection was ended. The places of the insurgents were filled as rapidly as they had been vacated. Scarcely a trace was left of the ravages of the rebellion ; and it accomplished nothing, save to convince all doubters that the government of the province rested, as all stable government must rest, on the good-will of the subject.

At the height of the insurrection a striking incident occurred. While their brethren were being hurled in utter confusion across the Dutch borders, several hundred Chinese fled from those very Dutch territories and sought refuge in Sarawak. Though harassed by care, the Rajah did not neglect their appeal, but sent trustworthy men, who piloted them safely through the incensed Dyaks, who on their part by no means appreciated the virtue of such a step, but thought rather that every man "who wore a tail" ought to be put to death, though they bowed to the better judgment of their chief.

The latest accounts represent the province as continuing in a state of unabated prosperity. Its bounds, by more recent cessions, have been so largely increased, that its shore line is now three hundred miles long, and the whole population of the state two hundred and fifty thousand. The haunts of the Sarebus and Sakarran pirates are included in the new limits ; and these once-dreaded freebooters have learned the habits of honest industry. Indeed, during the days of the insurrection the state found no more faithful or courageous defenders than they, although their old corsair blood was visible in the relentless tenacity with which they tracked the flying foe. Sir James Brooke, with increasing years, has retired somewhat from the active care of the government, leaving the conduct of affairs very much to his nephew, Captain Brooke, whom he has designated as his heir and successor, and who is represented as being also heir in a large degree to his uncle's principles, courage, and sagacity.

Rajah Brooke sought persistently for many years to give perpetuity to his life's work by placing Sarawak under British protection. He made repeated offers to surrender to the Queen all right and title which he had acquired, on any terms which would secure the welfare of the natives. But these offers have been definitely rejected; the seeming protection which Sarawak enjoyed through the position of its ruler as Governor of Labuan has been withdrawn, and the little state left to work out unaided its destiny. What shall be the final fate of this interesting experiment, whether there shall arise successors to the founder wise enough to maintain the government so bravely established, or whether the infant state shall perish with the man who called it into existence, and become only a memory, it is impossible to foretell; but,

living or dead, its annals will always be a noble monument to him whose force of character and undaunted persistency created it.

The earlier portraits we have of Rajah Brooke depict him as a man of a peculiarly frank, open, and pleasing exterior, yet with a countenance marked by intelligence, thought, and energy; but underneath all a certain dreaminess of expression, found often in the faces of those born for adventure and to seek for the enterprise of their age fresh fields, new El Dorados hidden in strange lands and unfamiliar seas.

The later portraits give us a face, plain, sagacious, yet full of an expression of kindly benevolence. The exigencies of a busy life have transformed romance into reality and common-sense; the adventurer and knight-errant has but obeyed the law of his age, and become a noble example of the power of the Anglo-Saxon mind to organize in the face of adverse circumstances a state, and to construct out of most unpromising elements the good fabric of orderly social life.

PASSAGES FROM HAWTHORNE'S NOTE-BOOKS.

XII.

MARCH, 1845. — Nature sometimes displays a little tenderness for our vanity, but is never careful for our pride. She is willing that we should look foolish in the eyes of others, but keeps our little nonsensicalnesses from ourselves.

Perhaps there are higher intelligences that look upon all the manifestations of the human mind — metaphysics, ethics, histories, politics, poems, stories, etc., etc. — with the same interest that we look upon flowers, or any other humble production of nature, — finding a beauty and fitness even in the poorest of them, which we cannot see in the best.

A child or a young girl so sweet and beautiful, that God made new flowers on purpose for her.

May 4. — On the river-side, by the Promontory of Columbines. The river here makes a bend, nearly at a right angle. On the opposite side, a high bank descends precipitately to the water; a few apple-trees are scattered along the declivity. A small cottage, with a barn, peeps over the top of the bank; and at its foot, with their roots in the water, is a picturesque clump of several maple-trees, their trunks all in a cluster, and their tops forming a united mass of now fast-budding foliage. At the foot of this clump of trees lies a boat, half in the water, half drawn up on the bank. A tract of flags and water-weeds extends along the base of the bank, outside of which, at a late period, will grow the flat, broad leaves of the yellow water-lily, and the pond-lily. A southwestern breeze is ruffling the river, and drives the little wavelets in the same direction as the current. Most of the course of the river in this vicinity is through marshy and meadowy ground, as yet scarcely redeemed from the spring-time overflow, and which at all seasons is plashy and unfit for walking. At my feet the water overbrims the shore, and kisses the new green grass, which sprouts even beneath it.

The Promontory of Columbines rises rugged and rocky from amidst surrounding lowlands, (in a field next to that where the monument is erected, near the Old Manse,) and it forms the forth-putting angle at the bend of the river. In earlier spring the river embraces it all round, and converts it into an island. Rocks, with flakes of dry moss covering them, peep out everywhere; and abundant columbines grow in the interstices of these rocks, and wherever else the soil is scanty and difficult enough to suit their fancy, — avoiding the smoother and better sites, which they might just as well have chosen, close at hand. They are earlier on this spot than anywhere else, and are therefore doubly valuable, though not nearly so large, nor of so rich a scarlet and gold, as some that we shall gather from the eastern slope of a hill, two or three weeks hence. The promontory is exposed to all winds, and there seems no reason why it should produce the earliest flowers, unless that this is a peculiar race of columbines, which has the precious gift of earlier birth assigned to them in

lieu of rich beauty. This is the first day of the present spring that I have found any quite blown; but last year, I believe, they came considerably earlier. Here and there appeared a blue violet, nestling close to the ground, pretty, but inconvenient to gather and carry home, on account of its short stalk. Houstonias are scattered about by handfuls. Anemones have been in bloom for several days on the edge of the woods, but none ever grow on the Promontory of Columbines.

The grass is a glad green in spots; but this verdure is very partial, and over the general extent the old, withered stalks of last year's grass are found to predominate. The verdure appears rich, between the beholder and the sun; in the opposite direction, it is much less so. Old mullein-stalks rise tall and desolate, and cling tenaciously to the soil when we try to uproot them. The promontory is broken into two or three heads. Its only shadow is from a moderately-sized elm, which, from year to year, has flung down its dead branches, all within its circumference, where they lie in various stages of decay. There are likewise rotten and charred stumps of several other trees.

The fence of our avenue is covered with moss on the side fronting towards the north, while the opposite side is quite free from it, — the reason being, that there is never any sunshine on the north side to dry the moisture caused by rains from the northeast. The moss is very luxuriant, sprouting from the half-decayed wood, and clinging to it as if partially incorporated therewith.

Towards the dimness of evening a half-length figure appearing at a window, — the blackness of the background, and the light upon the face, cause it to appear like a Rembrandt picture.

On the top of Wachusett, butterflies, large and splendid; also bees in considerable numbers, sucking honey from the alpine flowers. There is a certain flower, a species of Potentilla, I think, which is found on mountains at a certain elevation, and inhabits a belt, being found neither above nor below it. On the highest top of Wachusett there is a circular foundation, built evidently with great labor, of large, rough stones, and rising perhaps fifteen feet. On this basis formerly rose a wooden tower, the fragments of which, a few of the timbers, now lie scattered about. The immediate summit of the mountain is nearly bare and rocky, although interspersed with bushes ; but at a very short distance below there are trees, though slender, forming a tangled confusion, and among them grows the wild honeysuckle pretty abundantly, which was in bloom when we were there (Sunday, June 17th). A flight of rude stone steps ascends the circular stone foundation of the round tower. By the by, it cannot be more than ten feet high, at the utmost, instead of fifteen.

The prospect from the top of Wachusett is the finest that I have seen, — the elevation being not so great as to snatch the beholder from all sympathy with earth. The roads that wind along at the foot of the mountain are discernible ; and the villages, lying separate and unconscious of one another, each with their little knot of peculiar interests, but all gathered into one category by the observer above them. White spires, and the white glimmer of hamlets, perhaps a dozen miles off. The gleam of lakes afar, giving life to the whole landscape. Much wood, shagging hills and plains. On the west, a hill-country, swelling like waves, with these villages sometimes discovered among them. On the east it looks dim and blue, and affects the beholder like the sea, as the eye stretches far away. On the north (?) appears Monadnock, in his whole person, discernible from the feet upwards, rising boldly and tangibly to the sense, so that you have the figure wholly before you, fair and blue, but not dim and cloudlike.

On the road from Princeton to Fitch-burg we passed fields which were entirely covered with the mountain-laurel in full bloom, — as splendid a spectacle, in its way, as could be imagined. Princeton is a little town, lying on a high ridge, exposed to all the stirrings of the upper air, and with a prospect of a score of miles round about. The great family of this place is that of the Boylstons, who own Wachusett, and have a mansion, with good pretensions to architecture, in Princeton.

Notables : Old Gregory, the dweller of the mountain-side ; his high-spirited wife ; the son, speaking gruffly from behind the scenes, in answer to his father's inquiries as to the expediency of lodging us. The brisk little landlord at Princeton, recently married, intelligent, honest, lively, agreeable ; his wife, with her young-ladyish manners still about her ; the second class of annuals, and other popular literature, in the parlors of the house ; colored engraving of the explosion of the Princeton's gun, with the principal characters in that scene, designated by name ; also Death of Napoleon, &c. A young Mr. Boylston boarding at the inn, and driving out in a beautiful, city-built phaeton, of exquisite lightness. We met him and a lady in the phaeton, and two other ladies on horseback, in a narrow path, densely wooded, on the ascent of a hill. It was quite romantic. Likewise old Mr. Boylston, frequenting the tavern, coming in after church, and smoking a cigar, ... entering into conversation with strangers about the ascent of the mountain. The tailor of the place, with his queer advertisement pasted on the wall of the barroom, comprising certificates from tailors in New York City, and various recommendations, from clergymen and others, of his moral and religious character. Two Shakers in the cars, — both, if I mistake not, with thread gloves on. The foundation of the old meeting-house of Princeton, standing on a height above the village, as bleak and windy as the top of Mount Ararat ; also the old deserted town-house. The edifices were probably thus located in order to be more exactly in the centre of the township.

From July 25 to August 9, 1845, at Portsmouth Navy Yard. Remarkables: the free and social mode of life among the officers and their families, meeting at evening on the door-steps or in front of their houses, or stepping in familiarly; the rough-hewn first lieutenant, with no ideas beyond the service; the doctor, priding himself on his cultivation and refinement, pretending to elegance, sensitive, touchy; the sailing-master, an old salt, of the somewhat modernized Tom Bowline pattern, tossed about by fifty years of stormy surges, and at last swept into this quiet nook, where he tells yarns of his cruises and duels, repeats his own epitaph, drinks a reasonable quantity of grog, and complains of dyspepsia; the old fat major of marines, with a brown wig not pretending to imitate natural hair, but only to cover his baldness and grayness with something that he imagines will be less unsightly: he has a potent odor of snuff, but has left off wine and strong drink for the last twenty-seven years. A Southerner, all astray among our New England manners, but reconciling himself to them, like a long practised man of the world, only somewhat tremulous at the idea of a New England winter. The lieutenant of marines, a tall, red-haired man, between thirty and forty, stiff in his motions from the effect of a palsy contracted in Florida, — a man of thought, both as to his profession and other matters, particularly matters spiritual, — a convert, within a few years, to Papistry, — a seer of ghosts, — a dry joker, yet sad and earnest in his nature, — a scientific soldier, criticising Jackson's military talent, — fond of discussion, with much more intellect than he finds employment for, — withal, somewhat simple. Then the commandant of the yard, Captain S——, a man without brilliancy, of plain aspect and simple manners, but just, upright, kindly, with an excellent practical intellect; his next

in rank, Commander P——, an officer-like, middle-aged man, with such cultivation as a sensible man picks up about the world, and with what little tincture he imbibes from a bluish wife. In the vicinity of the Navy Yard, an engineer-officer, stationed for a year or two past on a secluded point of the coast, making a map, minutely finished, on a very extensive scale, of country and coast near Portsmouth; he is red-nosed, and has the aspect of a free liver; his companion, a civil engineer, with much more appearance of intellectual activity. Their map is spread out in a room that looks forth upon the sea and islands, and has all the advantages of sea-air, — very desirable for summer, but gloomy as a winter residence.

At Fort Constitution are many officers, — a major and two lieutenants, the former living in a house within the walls of the fort, the latter occupying small residences outside. They are coarse men, apparently of few ideas, and not what one can call gentlemen. They are likewise less frank and hospitable than the navy officers. Their quarters have not the aspect of homes, although they continue for a term of years, five or more, on one station, whereas the navy officers are limited to two or three. But then the former migrate with their families to new stations, whereas the wives of the naval officers, though ejected from the navy-yard houses, yet, not accompanying their husbands on service, remain to form a nucleus of home.

Two or three miles from the Navy Yard, on Kittery Point, stands the former residence of Sir William Pepperell. It is a gambrel-roofed house, very long and spacious, and looks venerable and imposing from its dimensions. A decent, respectable, intelligent woman admitted us, and showed us from bottom to top of her part of the house; she being a tenant of one half. The rooms were not remarkable for size, but were panelled on every side. The staircase is the best feature, ascending gradually, broad and square, and with an elaborate balustrade; and over the front door there is a wide window and a spacious breadth, where the old baronet and his guests, after dinner, might sit and look out upon the water and his ships at anchor. The garret is one apartment, extending over the whole house. The kitchen is very small, — much too small for the credit of the house, were it not redeemed by the size of the fireplace, which originally could not have been less than fourteen feet, though now abridged by an oven, which has been built within it. The hearth extends half-way across the floor of the kitchen. On one side, the road passes close by the house ; on the other, it stands within fifty yards of the shore. I recollect no outhouses. At a short distance, across the road, is a marble tomb, on the level slab of which is the Pepperell coat of arms, and an inscription in memory of Sir William's father, to whom the son seems to have erected it, — although it is the family tomb. We saw no other trace of Sir William or his family. Precisely a hundred years since he was in his glory. None of the name now exist here, — or elsewhere, as far as I know. A descendant of the Sparhawks, one of whom married Pepperell's daughter, is now keeper of a fort in the vicinity, — a poor man. Lieutenant Baker tells me that he has recently discovered a barrel full of the old family papers.

The house in Portsmouth now owned and occupied by the Rev. Mr. Burroughs was formerly the mansion of Governor Langdon. It contains noble and spacious rooms. The Doctor's library is a fine apartment, extending, I think, the whole breadth of the house, forty or fifty feet, with elaborate cornices, a carved fireplace, and other antiquated magnificences. It was, I suppose, the reception-room, and occasionally the dining-hall. The opposite parlor is likewise large, and finished in excellent style, the mantelpiece being really a fine architectural specimen. . . . . Doctor Burroughs is a scholar, rejoicing in the possession of an old, illuminated missal, which he showed us, adorned with brilliant miniatures and other pic-

tures by some monkish hand. It was given him by a commodore in the navy, who picked it up in Italy, without knowing what it was, nor could the learned professors of at least one college inform him, until he finally offered it to Dr. Burroughs, on condition that he should tell him what it was. We likewise saw a copy of the famous " Breeches Bible," and other knicknacks and curiosities which people have taken pleasure in giving to one who appreciated such things, and whose kindly disposition makes it a happiness to oblige him. His house has entertained famous guests in the time of the old Governor, — among them Louis Philippe, Talleyrand, Lafayette, and Washington, all of whom occupied successively the same chamber ; besides, no doubt, a host of less world-wide distinguished persons.

A battery of thirty-two pound periods.

In the eyes of a young child or other innocent person, the image of a cherub or an angel to be seen peeping out, — in those of a vicious person, a devil.

October 11.   In Boston, a man passing along Colonnade Row, grinding a barrel-organ, and attended by a monkey, dressed in frock and pantaloons, and with a tremendously thick tail appearing behind. While his master played on the organ, the monkey kept pulling off his hat, bowing and scraping to the spectators, round about, — sometimes, too, making a direct application to an individual, — by all this dumb show, beseeching them to remunerate the organ-player. Whenever a coin was thrown on the ground, the monkey picked it up, clambered on his master's shoulder, and gave it into his keeping, then descended, and repeated his pantomimic entreaties for more. His little, old, ugly, wrinkled face had an earnestness that looked just as if it came from the love of money deep within his soul. He peered round, searching for filthy lucre on all sides. With his tail and all, he might be taken for the Mammon of copper coin, — a symbol of covetousness of small gains, — the lowest form of the love of money.

Baby was with us, holding by my forefinger, and walking decorously along the pavement. She stopped to contemplate the monkey, and after a while, shocked by his horrible ugliness, began to cry.

A disquisition or a discussion between two or more persons, on the manner in which the Wandering Jew has spent his life. One period, perhaps, trying over and over again to grasp domestic happiness ; then a soldier, then a statesman, &c., at last realizing some truth.

The most graceful way in which a man can signify that he feels that he is growing old, and acquiesces in it, is by adhering to the fashion of dress which chances to be in vogue when the conviction comes upon him. Thus, in a few years, he will find himself quietly apart from the crowd of young men.

Our most intimate friend is not he to whom we show the worst, but the best of our nature.

Nothing comes amiss to Nature, — all is fish that comes to her net. If there be a living form of perfect beauty, instinct with soul, — why, it is all very well, and suits Nature well enough. But she would just as lief have that beautiful, soul-illumined body for worms' meat and earth's manure !

Instances of two ladies, who vowed never again to see the light of the sun, on account of disappointments in love. Each of them kept her vow, living thenceforth, and dying after many years, in apartments closely shut up, and lighted by candles. One appears to have lived in total darkness.

The infirmities that come with old age may be the interest on the debt of nature, which should have been more seasonably paid. Often the interest will be a heavier payment than the principal.

By a Lord of the Admiralty, (in a speech in Parliament during our Revolution,) the number of American sailors employed in the British navy previous to the Revolution was estimated at eighteen thousand.

Some men have no right to perform great deeds, or think high thoughts ; and when they do so, it is a kind of humbug. They had better keep within their own propriety.

In England, in 1761, a man and his wife, formerly in good circumstances, died very poor, and were buried at the expense of the parish. This coming to the ears of the friends of their better days, they had the corpses taken out of the ground and buried in a more genteel manner !

In the "Annual Register," Vol. IV., for 1761, there is a letter from Cromwell to Fleetwood, dated August 22, 1653, which Carlyle appears not to have given. Also one, without date, to the Speaker of the House of Commons, narrating the taking of Basing House.

Recently, in an old house which has been taken down at the corner of Bulfinch Street and Bowdoin Square, a perfect and full-grown skeleton was discovered, concealed between the ceiling and the floor of a room in the upper story. Another skeleton was not long since found in similar circumstances.

In a garden, a pool of perfectly transparent water, the bed of which should be paved with marble, or perhaps with mosaic work in images and various figures, which through the clear water would look wondrously beautiful.

October 20, 1847. — A walk in a warm and pleasant afternoon to Browne's Hill, not uncommonly called Browne's

Folly, from the mansion which one of that family, before the Revolution, erected on its summit. (On October 14, 1837, I recorded a walk thither.) In a line with the length of the ridge, the ascent is gradual and easy, but straight up the sides it is steep. There is a large and well-kept orchard at the foot, through which I passed, gradually ascending; then, surmounting a stone wall, beneath chestnut-trees which had thrown their dry leaves down, I climbed the remainder of the hill. There were still the frequent barberry-bushes; and the wood-wax has begun to tuft itself over the sides and summit, which seem to be devoted to pasture. On the very highest part are still the traces of the foundation of the old mansion. The hall had a gallery running round it beneath the ceiling, and was a famous place for dancing. The house stood, I believe, till some years subsequent to the Revolution, and was then removed in three portions, each of which became a house somewhere on the plain, and perhaps they are standing now. The proprietor, being a royalist, became an exile when the Revolution broke out, and I suppose died abroad. I know not whether the house was intended as a permanent family-residence or merely as a pleasure-place for the summer; but from its extent I should conceive the former to have been its purpose. Be that as it may, it has perpetuated an imputation of folly upon the poor man who erected it, which still keeps his memory disagreeably alive after a hundred years. The house must have made a splendid appearance for many miles around; and the glare of the old-fashioned festivities would be visible, doubtless, in the streets of Salem, when he illuminated his windows to celebrate a king's birthday, or some other loyal occasion. The barberry-bushes, clustering within the cellars, offer the harsh acidity of their fruit to-day, instead of the ripe wines which used to be stored there.

Descending the hill, I entered a green, seldom-trodden lane, which runs along at a hundred yards or two from its base, and parallel with its ridge. It was overshadowed by chestnut-trees, and bordered with the prevalent barberry-bush, and between ran the track,—the beaten path of the horses' feet, and the even way of either wheel, with green strips between. It was a very lonely lane, and very pleasant in the warm, declining sun; and, following it a third of a mile, I came to a place that was familiar to me when I was a child, as the residence of a country cousin whom I used to be brought to see. There was his old house still standing, but deserted, with all the windows boarded up, and the door likewise, and the chimneys removed,—a most desolate-looking place. A young dog came barking towards me as I approached,—barking, but frisking, between play and watchfulness. Within fifty yards of the old house, farther back from the road, stands a stone house, of some dozen or twenty years' endurance,—an ugly affair, so plain is it,—which was built by the old man in his latter days. The well of the old house, out of which I have often drunk, and over the curb of which I have peeped to see my own boy-visage closing the far vista below, seems to be still in use for the new edifice. Passing on a little farther, I came to a brook, which, I remember, the old man's son and I dammed up, so that it almost overflowed the road. The stream has strangely shrunken now; it is a mere ditch, indeed, and almost a dry one. Going a little farther, I came to a graveyard by the roadside,—not apparently a public graveyard, but the resting-place of a family or two, with half a dozen gravestones. On two marble stones, standing side by side, I read the names of Benjamin Foster and Anstiss Foster, the people whom I used to be brought to visit. He had died in 1824, aged seventy-five; she in 1837, aged seventy.

·   ·   ·   ·   ·

A young woman in England, poisoned by an East Indian barbed dart, which her brother had brought home as a curiosity.

The old house on Browne's Hill was removed from the summit to the plain, at a short distance from the foot of the hill. Colonel Putnam, of the Custom-House, recollects it there, standing unoccupied, but with the furniture still in it. It seems to have been accessible to all who wished to enter. It was at that time under the care of Richard Derby, an ancestor of the present Derbys, who had a claim to the property through his wife, who was a Browne. The owner of the house had fled during the Revolution, and Richard Derby seems to have held the estate as it was when the refugee left it, in expectation of his eventual return. There was one closet in the house which everybody was afraid to open, it being supposed that the Devil was in it. One day, above fifty years ago, or threescore it may have been, Putnam and other boys were playing in the house, and took it into their heads to peep into this closet. It was locked, but Putnam pried open the door, with great difficulty and much tremor. At last it flew open, and out fell a great pile of family portraits, faces of gentlemen in wigs, and ladies in quaint head-dresses, displaying themselves on the floor, startling the urchins out of their wits. They all fled, but returned after a while, piled up the pictures again, and nailed up the door of the closet.

The house, according to the same authority, was not tenanted after the earthquake of 1775 ; at least, it was removed from the summit of the hill on that occasion, it having been greatly shaken by the earthquake.

The house formerly inhabited by Rev. Mr. Paris, and in which the witchcraft business of 1692 had its origin, is still standing in the north parish of Danvers. It has been long since removed from its original site. The workmen at first found great difficulty in removing it ; and an old man assured them that the house was still under the influence of the Devil, and would remain so unless they took off the roof. Finally they did take off the roof, and then succeeded in moving

the house. Putnam was personally cognizant of this fact.

November 17. — A story of the effects of revenge in diabolizing him who indulges in it.

The Committee of Vigilance, instituted to promote the discovery of old Mr. White's murderers, — good as the machinery of a sketch or story.

A story of the life, domestic and external, of a family of birds in a marten-house, for children.

The people believed that John Hancock's uncle had bought an immense diamond at a low price, and sold it for its value, — he having grown rich with a rapidity inexplicable to them. The fact was, however, according to Hutchinson, that he made his fortune by smuggling tea in molasses hogsheads from St. Eustatia.

An old French Governor of Acadie, the predecessor of D'Aulnay, paid for some merchandise, which he bought of the captain of an English vessel, with six or seven hundred buttons of massive gold, taken from one of his suits. (Mass. Hist. Coll.)

An apparition haunts the front yard. I have often, while sitting in the parlor, in the daytime, had a perception that somebody was passing the windows ; but, looking towards them, nobody is there. The appearance is never observable when looking directly towards the window, but only by such a sidelong or indirect glance as one gets while reading, or when intent on something else. But I know not how many times I have raised my head or turned with the certainty that somebody were passing. The other day I found that my wife was equally aware of the spectacle, and that, as likewise agrees with my own observation, it always appears to be entering the yard from the street, never going out.

The immortal flowers, — a child's story.

"He looked as if he had been standing up thirty years against a northeast storm." Description of an old mate of a vessel, by Pike.

Death possesses a good deal of real estate, namely, the graveyards in every town. Of late years, too, he has pleasure-grounds, as at Mount Auburn and elsewhere.

Corwin is going to Lynn; Oliver proposes to walk thither with him. "No," says Corwin, "I don't want you. You take great, long steps; or, if you take short ones, 't is all hypocrisy. And, besides, you keep humming all the time."

May 18, 1848. — Decay of the year has already commenced. I saw a dandelion gone to seed, this afternoon, in the Great Pasture.

Words, so innocent and powerless as they are, as standing in a dictionary, how potent for good and evil they become, in the hands of one who knows how to combine them.

Captain B—— tells a story of an immense turtle which he saw at sea, on a voyage to Batavia, — so long, that the look-out at the mast-head mistook it for a rock. The ship passed close to it, and it was apparently longer than the long-boat, "with a head bigger than any dog's head you ever see," and great prickles on his back a foot long. Arriving at Batavia, he told the story, and an old pilot exclaimed, "What! have you seen Bellysore Tom?" It seems that the pilots had been acquainted with this turtle as many as twelve years, and always found him in the same latitude. They never did him any injury, but were accustomed to throw him pieces of meat, which he received in good part, so that there was a mutual friendship between him and the pilots. Old Mr.

L——, in confirmation of the story, asserted that he had often heard other shipmasters speak of the same monster; but he being a notorious liar, and Captain B—— an unconscionable spinner of long yarns and travellers' tales, the evidence is by no means perfect. The pilots estimated his length at not less than twenty feet.

The Grey Property Case. Mrs. Grey and her child three years old were carried off by the Indians in 1756 from the Tuscarora valley in Pennsylvania. The father, going on a campaign in search of them, was exhausted by fatigue, and came home only to die, bequeathing half his property to his child, if living. The mother, his wife, being redeemed, and there being several children who had been captive to the Indians to be seen at Philadelphia, went thither to see and recognize her little three years' old daughter, from whom, in her captivity, she had been separated. Her child proved not to be among the little captives; but, in order to get possession of her husband's property, she claimed another child, of about the same age. This child grew up gross, ugly, awkward, a "big, black, uncomely Dutch lump, not to be compared to the beautiful Fanny Grey," and moreover turned out morally bad. The real daughter was said to have been married, and settled in New York, "a fine woman, with a fair house and fair children." At all events, she was never recovered by her relatives, and her existence seems to have been doubtful. In 1789, the heirs of John Grey, the father, became aware that the claimed and recovered child was not the child that had been lost. They commenced a lawsuit for the recovery of John Grey's property, consisting of a farm of three or four hundred acres. This lawsuit lasted till 1834, when it was decided against the identity of the recovered child. (Sherman Day's Hist. Coll. of Penn.)

Bethuel Vincent, carried by the Indians to Canada, being then recently

—

married. A few years after, a rough-looking man fell in with a sleighing party at a tavern, and inquired if they knew anything of Mrs. Vincent. She was pointed out to him. He gave her news of her husband, and, joining the sleighing party, began to grow familiar with Mrs. Vincent, and wished to take her upon his lap. She resisted, — but behold! the rough-looking stranger was her long-lost husband. There are good points in this story. (Ibid.)

Among the survivors of a wreck are two bitter enemies. The parties, having remained many days without food, cast lots to see who shall be killed as food for the rest. The lot falls on one of the enemies. The other may literally eat his heart!

October 13. — During this moon, I have two or three evenings sat for some time in our dining-room without light except from the coal fire and the moon. Moonlight produces a very beautiful effect in the room, falling so white upon the carpet, and showing its figures so distinctly, and making all the room so visible, and yet so different from a morning or noontide visibility. There are all the familiar things, every chair, the tables, the couch, the bookcase, all that we are accustomed to see in the daytime; but now it seems as if we were remembering them through a lapse of years, rather than seeing them with the immediate eye. A child's shoe, the doll, sitting in her little wicker-carriage, all objects that have been used or played with during the day, though still as familiar as ever, are invested with something like strangeness and remoteness. I cannot in any measure express it. Then the somewhat dim coal fire throws its unobtrusive tinge through the room, — a faint ruddiness upon the wall, — which has a not unpleasant effect in taking from the colder spirituality of the moonbeams. Between both these lights such a medium is created that the room seems just fit for the ghosts of persons very dear, who have lived

in the room with us, to glide noiselessly in and sit quietly down, without affrighting us. It would be like a matter of course to look round and find some familiar form in one of the chairs. If one of the white curtains happen to be drawn before the windows, the moonlight makes a delicate tracery with the branches of the trees, the leaves somewhat thinned by the progress of autumn, but still pretty abundant. It is strange how utterly I have failed to give anything of the effect of moonlight in a room.

The firelight diffuses a mild, heart-warm influence through the parlor, but is scarcely visible, unless you particularly look for it; and then you become conscious of a faint tinge upon the ceiling, of a reflected gleam from the mahogany furniture, and, if your eyes happen to fall on the looking-glass, deep within it you perceive the glow of the burning anthracite. I hate to leave such a scene; and when retiring to bed, after closing the door, I reopen it again and again, to peep back at the warm, cheerful, solemn repose, the white light, the faint ruddiness, the dimness, — all like a vision, and which makes me feel as if I were in a conscious dream.

The first manufacture of the kind of candy called Gibraltar rock, for a child's story; to be told in a romantic, mystic, marvellous style.

An angel comes from heaven, commissioned to gather up, put into a basket, and carry away everything good that is not improved by mankind, for whose benefit it was intended. The angel distributes these good things where they will be appreciated.

Annals of a kitchen.

A benevolent person going about the world and endeavoring to do good to everybody; in pursuance of which object, for instance, he gives a pair of spectacles to a blind man, and does all such ill-suited things.

Beautiful positions of statues to one intellectually blind.

A man, arriving at the extreme point of old age, grows young again at the same pace at which he has grown old; returning upon his path, throughout the whole of life, and thus taking the reverse view of matters. Methinks it would give rise to some odd concatenations.

Little gnomes, dwelling in hollow teeth. They find a tooth that has been plugged with gold, and it serves them as a gold mine.

The wizard, Michael Scott, used to give a feast to his friends, the dishes of which were brought from the kitchens of various princes in Europe, by devils at his command. "Now we will try a dish from the King of France's kitchen," etc. A modern sketch might take a hint from this, and the dishes be brought from various restaurants.

" Pixilated," — a Marblehead word, meaning bewildered, wild about any matter. Probably derived from Pixy, a fairy.

For a child's story, — imagine all sorts of wonderful playthings.

Sir Walter Raleigh, Sir Thomas More, Algernon Sidney, or some other great man, on the eve of execution, to make reflections on his own head, — considering and addressing it in a looking-glass.

March 16, 1849. — J——— .... speaking of little B. P———: "I will hug him, so that not any storm can come to him."

A story, the principal personage of which shall seem always on the point of entering upon the scene, but never shall appear.

In the "New Statistical Account of Scotland," (Vol. I.,) it is stated that a person had observed, in his own dairy, that the milk of several cows, when mixed together and churned, produced much less butter proportionably than the milk of a single cow; and that the greater the number of cows which contributed their milk, the smaller was the comparative product. Hence, this person was accustomed to have the milk of each cow churned separately.

A modern magician to make the semblance of a human being, with two laths for legs, a pumpkin for a head, etc., of the rudest and most meagre materials. Then a tailor helps him to finish his work, and transforms this scarecrow into quite a fashionable figure. At the end of the story, after deceiving the world for a long time, the spell should be broken, and the gray dandy be discovered to be nothing but a suit of clothes, with a few sticks inside of them. All through his seeming existence as a human being there shall be some characteristics, some tokens, that to the man of close observation and insight betray him to be a thing of mere talk and clothes, without heart, soul, or intellect. And so this wretched old creature shall become the symbol of a large class.

The golden sands that may sometimes be gathered (always, perhaps, if we know how to seek for them) along the dry bed of a torrent adown which passion and feeling have foamed, and passed away. It is good, therefore, in mature life, to trace back such torrents to their source.

The same children who make the little snow image shall plant dry sticks, etc., and they shall take root and grow in mortal flowers, etc.

Monday, September 17. — Set out on a journey to Temple, N. H., with E. F. M———, to visit his father. Started by way of Boston, in the half past ten train, and took the Lowell and Nashua Railroad at twelve, as far as Danforth's Corner, about fifty miles, and thence in stage-coach to Milford, four miles farther, and in a light wagon to Temple, perhaps twelve miles farther. During the latter drive, the road gradually ascended, with tracts of forest land alongside, and latterly a brook, which we followed for several miles, and finally found it flowing through General M———'s farm. The house is an old country dwelling, in good condition, standing beside the road, in a valley surrounded by a wide amphitheatre of high hills. There is a good deal of copse and forest on the estate, high hills of pasture land, old, cultivated fields, and all such pleasant matters. The General sat in an easy-chair in the common room of the family, looking better than when in Salem, with an air of quiet, vegetative enjoyment about him, scarcely alive to outward objects. He did his best to express a hospitable pleasure at seeing me ; but did not succeed, so that I could distinguish his words. He loves to sit amidst the bustle of his family, and is dimly amused by what is going forward ; is pleased, also, to look out of the open window and see the poultry— a guinea-hen, turkeys, a peacock, a tame deer, etc. — which feed there. His mind sometimes wanders, and he hardly knows where he is ; will not be convinced that he is anywhere but at Salem, until they drag his chair to a window from which he can see a great elm-tree of which he is very fond, standing in front of the house. Then he acknowledges that he must be at the farm, because, he says, they never could have transplanted that tree. He is pleased with flowers, which they bring him,— a kind-hearted old man. The other day a live partridge was sent him, and he ordered it to be let go, because he would not suffer a life to be taken to supply him with a single meal. This tenderness has always been characteristic of the old soldier. His birthplace was within a few miles of this spot,— the son and descendant of husbandmen, —and character and fortune together have made him a man of history.

This is a most hospitable family, and they live in a style of plain abundance, rural, but with traits of more refined modes. Many domestics, both for farm and household work. Two unmarried daughters ; an old maiden aunt ; an elderly lady, Mrs. C. of Newburyport, visiting ; a young girl of fifteen, a connection of the family, also visiting, and now confined to her chamber by illness. Ney, a spaniel of easy and affable address, is a prominent personage, and generally lies in the parlor or sits beside the General's chair ; always ready, too, to walk out with anybody so inclined. Flora, a little black pony, is another four-footed favorite. In the warm weather, the family dine in a large room on one side of the house, rough and rustic looking, with rude beams overhead. There were evergreens hanging on the walls, and the figures 1776, also in evergreen, and a national flag suspended in one corner, — the blue being made out of old homespun garments, the red stripes out of some of the General's flannel wrappings, and the eagle copied from the figure on a half-dollar, — all being the handiwork of the ladies, on occasion of the last Fourth of July. It is quite a pleasant dining-hall ; and while we were eating fruit, the deer, which is of a small and peculiar breed from the South, came and thrust its head into the open window, looking at us with beautiful and intelligent eyes. It had smelt the fruit, and wished to put in its claim for a share.

Tuesday morning, before breakfast, E——— and I drove three or four miles, to the summit of an intervening ridge, from which we had a wide prospect of hill and dale, with Monadnock in the midst. It was a good sight, although the atmosphere did not give the hills that aspect of bulk and boldness which it sometimes does. This part of the country is but thinly inhabited, and the dwellings are generally small. It is said that, in the town of Temple, there are more old cellars, where dwellings have formerly stood, than there are houses now inhabited. The town is not far from a hundred years old, but contains now only five or six hundred inhabitants. The enterprising young men emigrate elsewhere, leaving only the least energetic portions to carry on business at home. There appear to be but few improvements, the cultivated fields being of old date, smooth with long cultivation. Here and there, however, a tract newly burned over, or a few acres with the stumps still extant. The farm-houses all looked very lonesome and deserted to-day, the inhabitants having gone to the regimental muster at New Ipswich.

As we drove home, E——— told a story of a child who was lost, seventy or eighty years ago, among the woods and hills. He was about five years old, and had gone with some work-people to a clearing in the forest, where there was a rye-field, at a considerable distance from the farm-house. Getting tired, he started for home alone, but did not arrive. They made what search for him they could that night, and the next day the whole town turned out, but without success. The day following, many people from the neighboring towns took up the search, and on this day, I believe, they found the child's shoes and stockings, but nothing else. After a while, they gave up the search in despair; but for a long time, a fortnight or three weeks or more, his mother fancied that she heard the boy's voice in the night, crying, " Father ! father ! " One of his little sisters also heard this voice ; but people supposed that the sounds must be those of some wild animal. No more search was made, and the boy never was found.

But it is not known whether it was the next autumn, or a year or two after, some hunters came upon traces of the child's wanderings among the hills, in a different direction from the previous search, and farther than it was supposed he could have gone. They found some little houses, such as children build of twigs and sticks of wood, and these the little fellow had probably built for amusement in his lonesome hours. Nothing, it seems to me, was

ever more strangely touching than this incident, — his finding time for childish play, while wandering to his death in these desolate woods, — and then pursuing his way again, till at last he lay down to die on the dark mountain-side. Finally, on a hill which E——— pointed out to me, they found a portion of the child's hair adhering to the overthrown trunk of a tree ; and this is all that was ever found of him. But it was supposed that the child had subsisted, perhaps for weeks, on the berries and other sustenance such as a forest-child knew how to find in the woods. I forgot to say, above, that a piece of birch or other bark was found, which he appeared to have gnawed. It was thought that the cry of " Father ! father ! " which the mother and little sister heard in the night-time, was really the little fellow's voice, then within hearing of his home ; but he wandered away again, and at last sank down, and Death found him and carried him up to God. His bones were never found ; and it was thought that the foxes or other wild animals had taken his little corpse, and scattered the bones, and that, dragging the body along, one lock of his flaxen hair had adhered to a tree.

I asked a physician whether it were possible that a child could live so long in the woods ; and he thought it was, and said that children often show themselves more tenacious of life than grown people, and live longer in a famine. This is to me a very affecting story ; and it seems to be felt as such by the people of the country. The little boy's parents, and his brothers and sisters, who probably lived to maturity or old age, are all forgotten ; but he lives in tradition, and still causes wet eyes to strangers, as he did to me.

To account for the singularity of his not having been found by such numbers as took up the search, it is suggested that he was perhaps frightened, and perhaps concealed himself when he heard the noise of people making their way through the forest, people being apt to do so, when they get mazed with wandering in the woods. But it is strange that old hunters, with dogs, should have failed to find him. However, there is the fact.

After breakfast (a broiled chicken and excellent coffee) I walked out by myself. The brook would be a beautiful plaything for my children, and I wish I had such a one for them. As I looked down into it from the bridge, I saw little fish, minnows, small chubs, and perch sporting about and rising eagerly to anything that was thrown in. Returning towards the house, I encountered an ass, who seemed glad to see me, in its donkeyish way. Afterwards, E—— and I took a ramble among some of his old haunts, which took up pretty much all the remainder of the forenoon. After dinner we drove to New Ipswich, expecting to see the closing scenes of the muster, but found the regiment dismissed, and the spectators taking their departure. We visited a cousin of E——, and took tea; borrowed two great-coats (it having grown from summer to autumn very rapidly since nightfall), and drove home, six miles or thereabouts. A new moon and the long twilight gleamed over the first portion of our drive, and then the northern lights kindled up and shot flashes towards the zenith as we drove along, up hill and down dale, and most of the way through dense woods.

The next morning, after breakfast, we got into our wagon and returned to Milford, thence by stage to Danforth's Corner, thence to Boston by rail. Nothing noteworthy occurred, except that we called on Mr. Atherton and lady at Nashua. We reached Boston at three o'clock. I visited the Town and Country Club, and read the papers and journals, took the three quarters past five train and reached home at half past six.

In the new statistical account of Scotland, in the volume about the Hebrides, it is stated that a child was born, and lived to the age of, I think, two years, with an eye in the back of its head, in addition to the usual complement in front. It could evidently see with this eye; for when its cap was drawn down over it, it would thrust it upward.

October 27. — Mrs. —— gave a black woman six dollars for a dress of pineapple cloth, sixteen yards, perhaps worth ten times as much, — the owner being ignorant of the value.

To inherit a great fortune. — To inherit a great misfortune.

Reflections in a mud-puddle; — they might be pictures of life in a mean street of a city.

February 16, 1850. — The sunbeam that comes through a round hole in the shutter of a darkened room, where a dead man sits in solitude.

The hoary periwig of a dandelion gone to seed.

Lenox, July 14, 1850. — Language, — human language, — after all, is but little better than the croak and cackle of fowls, and other utterances of brute nature, sometimes not so adequate.

The queer gestures and sounds of a hen looking about for a place to deposit her egg, her self-important gait, the sideway turn of her head and cock of her eye, as she pries into one and another nook, croaking all the while, evidently with the idea that the egg in question is the most important thing that has been brought to pass since the world began. A speckled black and white and tufted hen of ours does it to most ludicrous perfection.

July 25. — As I sit in my study, with the windows open, the occasional incident of the visit of some winged creature, — wasp, hornet, or bee, — entering out of the warm, sunny atmosphere, soaring round the room with large sweeps, then buzzing against the glass, as not satisfied with the place, and desirous of getting out. Finally, the joyous uprising curve with which, coming to the open part of the window, it emerges into the cheerful glow outside.

August 4. — Dined at hotel with J. T. Fields. Afternoon drove with him to Pittsfield, and called on Dr. Holmes.

August 5. — Drove with Fields to Stockbridge, being thereto invited by Mr. Field of Stockbridge, in order to ascend Monument Mountain. Found at Mr. Field's, Dr. Holmes, Mr. Duyckink of New York; also Mr. Cornelius Matthews and Herman Melville. Ascended the mountain, — that is to say, Mrs. Fields and Miss Jenny Field, Mr. Field and Mr. J. T. Fields, Dr. Holmes, Mr. Duyckink, Matthews, Melville, Mr. Harry Sedgwick, and I, — and were caught in a shower. Dined at Mr. Field's. Afternoon, under guidance of J. F. Headley, the party scrambled through the Ice Glen. Left Stockbridge and arrived at home about eight P. M.

August 7. — Messrs. Duyckink, Matthews, and Melville called in the forenoon. Gave them a couple of bottles of Mr. Mansfield's champagne, and walked down to the lake with them. At twilight Mr. Edwin P. Whipple and wife called from Lenox.

August 19. — Monument Mountain, in the early sunshine; its base enveloped in mist, parts of which are floating in the sky; so that the great hill looks really as if it were founded on a cloud. Just emerging from the mist is seen a yellow field of rye, and above that, forest.

August 24. — In the afternoons, this valley in which I dwell seems like a vast basin filled with golden sunshine, as with wine.

August 31. — J. R. Lowell called in the evening. September 1st, he called with Mrs. Lowell in the forenoon, on their way to Stockbridge or Lebanon, to meet Miss Bremer.

September 2. — "When I grow up," quoth J——, in illustration of the might to which he means to attain, — "when I grow up, I shall be *two* men!"

September 3. — Foliage of maples begins to change.

In a wood, a heap or pile of logs and sticks that had been cut for firewood, and piled up square, in order to be carted away to the house when convenience served, or rather to be sledded in sleighing-time. But the moss had accumulated on them, and, leaves falling over them from year to year, and decaying, a kind of soil had quite covered them, although the softened outline of the woodpile was perceptible in the green mound. It was perhaps fifty years, perhaps more, since the woodman had cut and piled these logs and sticks, intending them for his winter fire. But he probably needs no fire now. There was something strangely interesting in this simple circumstance. Imagine the long-dead woodman, and his long-dead wife and family, and one old man who was a little child when the wood was cut, coming back from their graves, and trying to make a fire with this mossy fuel.

September 19. — Lying by the lake yesterday afternoon, with my eyes shut, while the breeze and sunshine were playing together on the water, the quick glimmer of the wavelets was perceptible through my closed eyelids.

October 13. — A cool day, — the wind northwest, with a general prevalence of dull gray clouds over the sky, but with brief, sudden glimpses of sunshine. The foliage having its autumn hues, Monument Mountain looks like a headless Sphinx, wrapt in a rich Persian shawl. Yesterday, through a diffused mist, with the sun shining on it, it had the aspect of burnished copper. The sun-gleams on the hills are peculiarly magnificent, just in these days.

October 13. — One of the children,

drawing a cow on the blackboard, says, "I'll kick this leg out a little more," — a very happy energy of expression, completely identifying herself with the cow; or, perhaps, as the cow's creator, conscious of full power over its movements.

October 14. — The brilliancy of the foliage has past its acme; and, indeed, it has not been so magnificent this season as usual, owing to the gradual approaches of cool weather, and there having been slight frosts instead of severe ones. There is still a shaggy richness on the hillsides.

October 16. — A morning mist, filling up the whole length and breadth of the valley, between the house and Monument Mountain, the summit of the mountain emerging. The mist reaches to perhaps a hundred yards of me, so dense as to conceal everything, except that near its hither boundary a few ruddy or yellow tree-tops rise up, glorified by the early sunshine, as is likewise the whole mist-cloud. There is a glen between our house and the lake, through which winds a little brook, with pools and tiny waterfalls, over the great roots of trees. The glen is deep and narrow, and filled with trees; so that, in the summer, it is all in dark shadow. Now, the foliage of the trees being almost entirely of a golden yellow, instead of being obscure, the glen is absolutely full of sunshine, and its depths are more brilliant than the open plain or the mountain-tops. The trees are sunshine, and, many of the golden leaves having freshly fallen, the glen is strewn with light, amid which winds and gurgles the bright, dark little brook.

October 28. — On a walk yesterday forenoon, my wife and children gathered Houstonias. Before night there was snow, mingled with rain. The trees are now generally bare.

December 1. — I saw a dandelion in bloom near the lake, in a pasture by the brookside. At night, dreamed of seeing Pike.

December 19. — If the world were crumbled to the finest dust, and scattered through the universe, there would not be an atom of the dust for each star.

KATHARINE MORNE.

PART II.

CHAPTER IV.

SOON after Fanny's funeral, Miss Mehitable told me she had found out who the lady was that wished for my painting at the fair. Her niece had pointed her out as she drove by in a barouche; and it was Miss Dudley.

My second copy was begun in the last fortnight of Fanny's life, as she slept and I sat beside her. I had not then had time, nor since had heart, to go on with it. But now, seeing an opportunity to do something more to fulfil her wishes and to "do anything for Miss Dudley," I took up my task again, and quickly finished it. Then, still unsatisfied, I roamed through the woods, and along the shore, to gather specimens of the native plants, insects, and shells that seemed to me most like the foreign ones that I had copied, and grouped and painted and framed them like the first. The Doctor left both for me at Miss Dudley's gate, with this inscription on the envelope : " A little offering of great gratitude, from a sister of Fanny Morne." I suppose, by the way, this is one source of the satisfaction that some real mourners find in wearing mourning, as they say, "*for* the dead," — a vague longing, like mine, after they have passed beyond human care, to do or sacrifice still something more for them.

After that, there seemed to be nothing more that I could do for Fanny, nor anything that, for myself, I cared to do. From habit only, I employed myself. Julia, as she begged that I would call her, had a large basket of baby-clothes cut out. At that I seated myself after breakfast ; and at that I often worked till bedtime, like a machine, — startled sometimes from my revery, indeed, by seeing how much was done, but saying nothing, hearing little, and shedding not a tear.

Julia would have remonstrated ; but the Doctor said to her : " Let her alone for the present, my dear ; she has had a great shock. Trust to nature. This cannot last long with a girl like Katy. It is half of it over-fatigue, carried on from her school-keeping to add to the present account." To me he said : " Katy, you may sew, if you like, but not in-doors. I will carry your basket out for you into the arbor ; and in the afternoon I am going to take you to ride in the woods."

Our past selves are often a riddle that our present selves cannot read ; but I suspect the real state of the case was, partly that, as the Doctor believed, I was for the time being exhausted in body and stunned in mind, and partly that, in those young, impetuous days, grief was such an all-convulsing passion with me, when I yielded to it, that to the utmost of my strength I resisted it at the outset, and seldom dared suffer myself to suffer at all. But, as he also believed, "this could not last long" ; and it did not.

One afternoon, as I sewed in the arbor, a sweet little girl, who had been in Fanny's class in her Sunday school, stole into the garden and up to me, looked wistfully into my face as if seeking some likeness there, kissed my cheek timidly, laid a large nosegay of delicate flowers upon my knee, and crept away as gently as she came. The flowers were all white ; and I saw at once that they were meant for Fanny's grave. I might go there for the first time now, as well as at any other time. The Doctor and his wife were out together, and no one was at home to question me.

Fanny had been laid, I need scarcely say, just where she wished. My guardian had driven me there early one morning to point out the place ; and we found the withered clovers in the grass. It had rained often since. The swollen turf was nearly healed. I untied the flowers, and slowly, and with minute precision, arranged them in a cross above her breast. At last, when there was no blossom more to add or alter, I sat down again in my solitude where I sat with her so lately, with the same leaves fluttering on the same trees, the same grass waving on the same graves, and her beneath instead of upon it.

At first I could not think, — I could only cry. For now at length I had to cry ; and cry I did, in a tornado and deluge of grief that, by degrees swept and washed away the accumulated vapors from my mind, and brought it to a clearer, healthier calm. I believe God in His mercy has appointed that those who are capable of the strongest, shall not in general be capable of the *longest* anguish. At least, I am sure that it is so, not only with myself, but with one better and dearer than myself ; so that the experience of life has taught me to see in the sharpest of pangs the happiest augury of their brevity.

Thus it could not have been very long before I was able to raise my head, and wipe my eyes, and look once more upon my two dear graves. The setting sun glowed over them. They looked soft and bright. From one of them the echo of an angel's voice seemed still to say, " Here, by mamma, is where I *like* to lie " ; from both in unison I heard, " It is good and brave to look things in the face and on all sides ; but then among the sides, never forget the bright side, little Katy."

Could I refuse ? I looked for the bright side. It was not far to seek. In the first place, the worst was over. Never again could I lose what I had lost, nor — so at least I thought then — could I feel what I had felt. Secondly, my sorrow was only mine, and no one's else. Those whom I loved were happy, every one of them ; — mamma and Fanny, — I could not doubt it, — happier far than I ever could have made them, even if I had always tried as hard as I did after they began to leave me, — safer than they could ever have been in this world, and safe forever ; and Jim, — I would not begin now to think about him again, but just so much I must, — he was happy with Emma. Even thus much brought a fresh gush of tears, though not for him, — I could still truly say that I had never shed one for him, and that was some comfort to my pride at least ; — but for Fanny; because I had sometimes thought that, when she was well and I had time to think of anything besides her, if I ever *did* tell anybody of the mistake and trouble I had fallen into, I would tell her, — and now, however much I might need advice and assistance, *that* could never be. My guardian and his wife were happy in each other, and would be happier still after I roused myself, as I must and ought, and ceased to sadden their home. The world in which I still must live was, whatever people might say of it, not all sin, sickness, or sorrow. Even where I sat, in one of those spots which most persons accounted the dreariest in it, I could hear the laughter of light-hearted children at their play, the soft lowing of cattle grazing in the pleasant fields, and shouts of strong men at their wholesome, useful work. I knew there must be sickness, sin, and sorrow in it; but

could not I do some little to help them, with my free hands and the health and strength which were almost always mine ? Very good I was not myself, but I had been watchfully brought up in an innocent home ; there was no crime upon my conscience, and, even as I cast a rueful glance upon its blemishes, I heard a well-remembered voice say from a grave once more : " Have patience with my little daughter. Some of the richest fruits and souls are not the first to ripen. The chief thing that she wants is time to mellow."

And one of the brightest points in all the bright side was, that, in living so constantly through her illness with Fanny, who lived with God, I had been perforce brought nearer to Him, and therefore naturally learned to dread Him less and love Him more than I had done ; so that I hoped, as I know my mother did, that the sunshine of His grace would help to mellow me.

Another bright point was, that I need not go back to Greenville. The present mistress was glad to keep the school, and the committee willing to keep her.

My desultory thoughts still growing calmer, I began to form plans for my way of living, as I used to do aloud, when I could talk them over with my mother and Fanny. I did not plan anything great, however, because I was conscious of no great powers. — I already, I think, began to divine the truth of what a wise woman afterwards said to me, " Your own nature must settle your work," or rather of what she implied, though she did not say it : In laying out your work, you should do your best to take the diagonal between your nature and your circumstances. — But I resolved, such as I was, to try to make the most of myself in every way, for myself, my neighbors, and my God.

I was to stay at my guardian's for the present. He forbade my trying to teach again, for some months at least. It was my duty, as well as my pleasure, to obey him. In the mean time, I could prepare myself to teach better when I began again. I would draw and paint at odd times. Two hours a day I would try to divide between history and the English classic poets, of both of which I knew sadly little. Julia often drove out with her husband; and then I could study by myself. When she was at home, if I could not always chat with her as formerly, I could read to her in French, which she liked to hear; and that would be much more sociable and cheerful for her than my sitting mute. I would now exert myself to walk out every day for exercise, so that there would be no reason for her giving up her place in the Doctor's chaise to me. I blushed to think how often I had suffered myself to be foisted into it by her already. By my walks, I would earn leave to sit with her indoors; and then I could save her many steps and little household cares. Then what should I do for her husband? Sing to him in the evening, and begin, if he liked it, to-night. It might be a little hard the first time; but if so, there was all the more reason for having the first time over. There was no need of my choosing sad songs, or any that Fanny was fond of.

But it was growing late. They would be anxious. I must get up and go home. Go *home!* — without my home-mates? — leave them here? — with no kiss, — no good-night? I stood up, and sat down again. The blinding, choking passion, that had seemed over, swelled up into my eyes and throat once more. O that lonely, empty life! Must I go back to it? How long would it last? This was my only real home. When might I come here to sleep?

In an instant it would have been all over again with my hardly-won calm; but in that instant a white and gray fluttering between the green graves caught my tear-blurred sight. I thought it that of a living dove, but, going nearer, found only a piece of torn newspaper, which had been wrapped around the stems of the flowers, playing in the wind; and on it my attention was caught by these quaint and pithy lines, printed in one corner in double columns: —

"THE CONDITIONS.

"Sad soul, long harboring fears and woes
   Within a haunted breast,
Haste but to meet your lowly Lord,
   And he shall give you rest.

" Into his commonwealth alike
   Are ills and blessings thrown.
Bear you your neighbors' loads; and

   .   .   .

"Yield only up His price, your heart,
   Into God's loving hold, —
He turns with heavenly alchemy
   Your lead of life to gold.

"Some needful pangs endure in peace,
   Nor yet for freedom pant, —
He cuts the bane you cleave to off,
   Then . . . . "

The rest was torn away. "'And,'" repeated I, impatiently, — "'Then'! '*And — then*' — what?" There was no answer, or at least I heard none; but the verses, so far as they went, struck my excited fancy as a kind of preternatural confirmation of the faint outline of life and duty which I had been sketching. I marked the date of the day upon the white margin with my pencil, and took the paper with me as a memento of the time and place, trimmed its torn edges carefully, and laid it in Fanny's little Bible.

CHAPTER V.

THE next morning, at breakfast, Dr. Physick said: "You did me a good office, Katy, by singing me to sleepiness last night. I was as tired as a dog, — no, as a whole pack of Esquimaux dogs, — and, instead of lying awake and saying to myself, every time I turned over, 'What in this wide world am I ever going to do with that poor little Nelly Fader?' I only repeated, whenever I came to myself a little, 'Nelly Bligh shuts her eye when she goes to sleep'; and then I followed her example."

"I only wish," said I, "that there was any good office beside that I could do you."

"Well, now I think of it, there is one that I should be very much obliged to you to do, to me and Nelly Fader besides. I 've got to hurry off in the direction opposite to her Uncle Wardour's ; and you talked of walking. Take this paper. Empty it into a wine-bottle. Fill it up with spring-water. Cork it. Gum these directions on it. Take them to Nelly. Read them to her, and make her understand them if you can, and follow them, which I can't. I happen to have a better sample of the drug than is often in the market ; and she may as well have the benefit of it. Her aunt's a goose, and she 's a baby. But, as she 's likely to be a suffering baby for some time to come, we must try to have patience, and take extra pains with her."

"Is she going to die ? " asked I, anxiously.

"No, no ! I 've no idea she is. No such good luck, poor little victim ! ' *Only* nervous,' as people say. I can't find out that there 's much else the matter. I utterly hate these cases. She ought to be under the care of a sensible woman ; and if there only was such a one in the profession, I 'd guarantee her her hands full of patients out of my practice alone."

"A female physician ! " cried I, in horror.

"O Phil ! what will you say next ? " exclaimed his wife, laughing.

"Well, only wait till you 're a male physician, then, and see," returned he, jumping into his chaise, and relieving his own nerves with a crack of the whip, which put new vivacity into those of De Quincey.

I made ready at once, for the day was sulky. It had been weeping, and had not yet begun to smile.

Nelly lived with her uncle, the apothecary, Mr. Wardour, and his widowed sister, Mrs. Cumberland. As I neared the door, I heard her voice, which was not dulcet, from the parlor - kitchen : "What 's this here winder open for ? "

"It felt so close in here," was the plaintive little answer ; "and the Doctor said I ought to have the air."

"Does he think we can afford wood enough to warm all out-doors with ? "

I knocked ; but Mrs. Cumberland was deaf, and went on : "My sakes alive, child ! what 's all this ? "

"The stewed damsons."

" ' Stewed damsons,' indeed ! — Stewed stalks and stewed leaves and stewed creaturs ! Did n't you have faculty of yourself enough to know that they 'd got to be picked over before they went into the pot ? There, there, child ! don't you go to cryin', whatever you do."

I knocked louder.

"There 's somebody to the door ; mebbe it 's the Doctor. You go and see what 's wanted, an' don't take no more concern about these. I 'll see to 'em."

After a little delay, occasioned perhaps by the need of rubbing the eyelids, which were red, a little pallid lass, apparently about sixteen years old, shyly opened the door, and looked relieved, I thought, to find only me at it. She had a small and pretty nose and mouth, large, heavy blue eyes, flaxen hair drawn neatly, but unbecomingly, away from her face, looked modest and refined, but sadly moped, and was dressed in dark green, which set her off much as spinach does a *dropped* egg.

"Miss Nelly ? " said I.

"Yes, Miss Morne," said she.

I had never seen her before ; but it afterwards came out that she had peeped at me through the blinds of her chamber.

"I have brought you a little treat from Dr. Physick."

"O," said she, looking rather pleased ; "then is n't he coming to-day ? "

"No ; he sent me instead."

"I am glad to see you," said she, timidly, but beginning to look really pretty, as her countenance went on brightening. "Won't you walk in ? "

I did so, sat down opposite to her in the cold, shaded "best parlor," and went over the directions to her aloud. She kept her face civilly turned towards me ; but it grew utterly blank again, and I saw she was not paying the least attention. So I played her a genuine teacher's trick, which I had learned in my school-room. "Now," continued I, "will you be so good as to repeat to me what I have been saying, so that I may be able to tell Dr. Physick that I explained it to you perfectly? He was rather *particular* about it."

Of course she could not ; but this obliged her, in common courtesy, to listen the second time. which was all I wanted. Then I rose.

She went with me to the door, saying, " I am sorry to give so much trouble. You are very kind to take so much for me."

" It will be a 'joyful trouble,' if it does you good."

"You are very kind to me. Do you like roses ? "

" Indeed I do. Do not you ? "

" I don't know. I used to "

There were three blossoms and one bud on a monthly rose-bush, which stood in an earthen pot by the front door. In an instant she had gathered them all, in spite of my protestations. She added two or three from a heliotrope, and the freshest sprigs from a diosma, a myrtle, and a geranium, all somewhat languishing, and tied them together for me with a long blade of grass.

" It is plain," said I, as I thanked her, " that you still care enough about flowers to arrange them most sweetly. These look as if they were sitting for their picture. I should like to paint them just as they are."

"Can you paint ? "

" A little. Cannot you ? "

" No ; I can't do anything."

" Shall we make a bargain, then ? " I ventured to say, as she looked and seemed so much like the poor baby the Doctor had called her. " We will each of us try to do something for the other. If I succeed in painting your flowers, and you succeed in following your directions, you shall have the picture."

She blushed deeply, looked half ashamed and half gratified, but altogether more alive than she had done till now, and finally managed to stammer out : "It's too good an offer — too

kind — to refuse ; but it's more than I deserve, a great deal. So I'll try to mind Dr. Physick, to please you ; and then — if you *liked* to give me the picture, I should prize it very much."

I nodded, laughed, went home, put the flowers in water on Julia's worktable, read to her, and went into the heart of the town to do some shopping for her. After our early dinner, I said I was a little tired ; and she drove with her husband. I took out my paper, brushes, and palette, set Nelly's nosegay in a becoming light, and began to rub my paints ; when wheels and hoofs came near and stopped, and presently the door-bell rang.

"Are the ladies at home ? " asked a smooth, silvery, feminine voice, with a peculiarly neat, but unaffected enunciation.

" No 'm, he ain't," returned the portress, mechanically ; " an' he's druv Missis out, too. Here's the slate ; or Miss Kitty could take a message, I s'pose, without she's went out lately ago."

" Take this card," resumed the first voice, "if you please, to Miss Morne, and say that, if she is not engaged, I should be glad to see her."

I rose in some confusion, pushed my little table into the darkest corner of the room, received the white card from Rosanna's pink paw, in which it lay like cream amidst five half-ripe Hovey's seedlings, read " Miss Dudley" upon it, told Rosanna to ask her to please to walk in, and took up my position just within the door, in a state of some palpitation.

In another minute a gray-haired, rather tall and slight, and very wellmade lady, with delicate, regular, spirited features, was before me, telling me with a peculiar kind of earnest cordiality, and a sympathy that expressed itself fully in tones, though not in words, that she could not content herself with writing her acknowledgments to me ; she must come and see me herself, to tell me how pleased and gratified and touched she was by the offering that I had sent her.

I felt myself too much moved by the associations connected with it, and called up by her, to answer readily; and she, as if conjecturing this, led the conversation gently off, at first to painting in general, and afterwards, as I grew more at my ease with her, back again, with an appearance of genuine interest, to mine.

"There was one little shell," said she, "in your native group, which was quite new to me, and — which is more remarkable — to my brother."

"Was it like this?" asked I, taking a specimen from my paint-box.

"Precisely. We felt sure the portrait must be true to life, because all its companions were such faithful likenesses; and then it had itself such an honest, genuine, individual look. But is it to be found on this coast?"

"Yes. If Mr. Dudley has not met with it, it must no doubt be very rare; but, near the same spot always, just beyond Cedar Point, under the rocks in the little cove that lies farthest to the south, I have found it more than once."

"You must be quite an enthusiast in natural history. Have you studied it long?"

"No, ma'am, never. I mean," continued I, answering her look of surprise, "never from books. I believe I should enjoy it more than any other study; but I know so little yet of other things, and there are so many other things that one needs more to know." I felt my cheeks burn; for no sooner was I helplessly launched into this speech, than I perceived what an awkward one it was to make to the sister of an eminent naturalist. Notwithstanding, as I thought it was true, I could not take it back.

"I agree with you entirely," said she with a reassuring smile. "Such studies are fitted much more for the coping-stones than the foundation-stones of a good education. But then, if you will not think me too inquisitive, pray let me ask you one thing more; and that is, where and how you came by all the information that that group showed."

"Only by playing on the beaches and in the woods when I was a child. My mother did not like to keep me in, because she thought that that had impaired my sister" — here my voice *would* break, but I *would* go on, — Fanny's dear name should not die out of memory while I lived — "my sister Fanny's health; but they were afraid to let me run quite wild, and so she — my sister — led me out often wherever I wished to go, and helped me fill a little pasteboard museum which she made for me."

Miss Dudley's large, soft, trusty brown eyes met mine tenderly, as she said: "These things must indeed possess a more than common interest for you then. Have you that museum now?"

"No, ma'am; I sometimes wish I had. I gave it away when I went to Greenville *to keep school*," I added; not that I supposed it would matter anything to her, but that I thought it just as well to make sure of her understanding my position in life.

"That is so natural to us all, — to part with these little relics when we are still very young, and then to wish them back again before we are much older! You would smile to see a little museum that I keep for my brother, — not his scientific collection, which I hope some day to have the pleasure of showing you, — but 'an *olla podrida* in an ancestral wardrobe,' as my little Paul calls it, of his and my two little nieces' first baby-shoes, rattles, corals, and bells, wooden horses, primers, picture-books, and so forth, down to the cups and balls, and copy-books, which they have cast off within a month or two, each labelled with the owner's name, and the date of deposit. No year goes by without leaving behind some memento of each of them, or even without my laying aside there some trifling articles of dress that they have worn. It is a fancy of my brother's. He says that others may claim their after-years, but their childhood is his own, — all of it that is not mine, — and he must keep it for himself, and for them when they come back to visit him in his old age. It is a birthday treat to them already to take the key from my split-ring, and look together over the half-forgotten things. But there is one thing there — a manuscript on the topmost shelf — which they do not know about, but which we take out and laugh over sometimes when they are all in bed, — a record that I have kept of all the most diverting things which we have heard them say, ever since they began to learn to talk." She checked herself, — I fancied because she remembered that, in her enthusiasm about the children, she had forgotten to what a new acquaintance she was speaking. She rose to take leave, and resumed, shaking hands with me cordially, — she had, I observed, a remarkably cordial and pleasant, earnest way of shaking hands, — "But upon the subject of my museum, Miss Morne, I need hardly beg you to be more discreet than I, and not to mention a domestic trifle of so little general interest."

I could only bow, but longed, as I attended her to the door, to assure her of the particular interest which I had already begun to feel in every trifle which belonged to her.

Her little barouche, and long-tailed, dark-gray ponies, vanished with her down the road; and I was left walking up and down the room. The "kind o' poor-lookin', pale-lookin', queer-lookin' lady," that Miss Mehitable had described, — was this she? How are we ever to know people by descriptions, when the same person produces one impression on one mind and quite another on another, — nay, may have one set of inherent qualities brought out by contact with one character, and quite another set by contact with another character? Have *I* described Miss Dudley? No, — and I cannot. She was both *unique* and indescribable.

Most people impress us more, perhaps, by their outward and physical, than by their inward and psychical life. On a first interview with them, especially, we receive an impression of clothes, good or otherwise, of beauty or plainness or ugliness of feature, and of correctness or uncouthness of manner. These are the common people, whether ladies and gentlemen, or simple men and women. There are, however, others, in all ranks and conditions, so instinct and replete with spirit, that we chiefly feel, when they have come in our way, that a spirit has passed by, — that a new life has been brought in contact with our own life.

Of these was Miss Dudley. But because, ever since the day I write of, I have loved to think of her, and because I know that, when I rejoin her, I shall leave some behind me who will still love, and have a right to hear of her, I will indulge myself in saying something more. That something shall be what I said to myself then, as I promenaded to and fro, — that bodily exercise was one of my safety-valves in those times, — in the endeavor to work off so much of my superfluous animation as to be in a state to sit down and paint again; and thus I spake: "I must have had before me an uncommonly fine specimen of a class whose existence I have conjectured before, but by no means including all the wealthy, who wear their purple and fine linen both gracefully and graciously, fare not more sumptuously than temperately every day, and do a great deal, not only directly by their ready beneficence, but indirectly by their sunny benignity, to light up the gloomy world of Lazarus." And though I was but a budding theorist in human nature, and often made mistakes before and afterwards, I never found myself mistaken there.

When Julia came in an hour after, she said to me, as I looked up from my roses and my rose-colored revery, "Katy, you look like an inspired sibyl! What has come over you?"

"Miss Dudley," said I.

"What! has she really — been here? How I wish I had seen her! What did she wear?"

"I'm afraid I can't tell you. Wait, I will try. O yes! it comes back to me; — a silver-gray *shot* poplin, or silk, made full, but, I think, quite plain ; a large red Cashmere shawl, rather more crimson and less scarlet than they usually are, — it glowed gloriously out from the gray ; — then some kind of a thin, gray bonnet, with large gray and crimson crape and velvet flowers in it, — hibiscus or passion-flowers, or really I don't know what, — that seemed just to marry the dress to the shawl."

"Pretty well for you, Katy ! Rather heavy for the season ; but I suppose she was afraid of this east wind. You liked her, then ? "

"Very much."

"So does the Doctor, always. Some people call her proud ; but he says, that is only their way of expressing their view of the fact that she has a good deal to make her so, and more than enough to make them so, if they had it instead of her."

"I dare say. I should not think she was a person to take liberties with ; but she was very sweet and kind to me."

"You are not a person to take liberties with anybody, nor to have any taken with you ; and so *I* dare say she recognized a kindred spirit."

"Now, Julia, by your paying me such a compliment as that, I am certain you must want to have your bonnet taken up stairs for you ; and so you shall."

"Ah ! now I shall always know what string to pull when I wish to put a skilful attendant in motion. Phil would take my bonnet up stairs for me in a moment, if I bade him ; but when I went up myself after it, it would be sure to stare me in the face, topsy-turvy, *dumped* bolt upright on the feather."

CHAPTER VI.

In another fortnight we had another Physick in the family. His papa called him "a little dose," and his mamma a "pill," in contradistinction to her previous "Phil." Proving peaceful and reflective, he also soon earned for himself the title of "the infant *Philoso-pher.*"

Mrs. Physick did not like the society of Mrs. Rocket, the nurse, whom the Doctor had chosen "on account of the *absence* of her conversational powers." Mrs. Physick was accordingly always trying to get me into her chamber to sit with her. Mrs. Rocket accordingly did not like me, and was always trying to get me out. Between these two contending powers above, and the butcher, the baker, and candlestick-maker below, I was neither solitary nor idle.

There was much to do, moreover, in answering the kind inquiries, and receiving and disposing of the whips, jellies, *blanc-mangers*, and other indigestible delicacies, sent in by anxious friends. These the grateful Doctor pronounced, in the privacy of domestic life, "poison for the patient, but not quite so bad for the attendants." Accordingly, we ate them together sociably, at almost every meal ; after which we went up stairs and told "the patient" how good they were, while I presented her gruel, and he would ask her, with an earnest air of judicial and dispassionate investigation, whether that was not "nice." This conduct she declared most unfeeling and ungrateful in us both, and bound herself by many a vow to make us pay for it as soon as she had the ordering of our dinners again. So we all made merry together over the little cradle that was called "the pill-box." Its small tenant was from the first, as I have hinted, a virtuous child, cried little, slept much, and when awake rewarded our attentions by making such preposterous faces as rendered it a most grateful task to watch him. I soon, therefore, became much attached to him ; and I enjoyed one at least of the chief elements of the happiness of the individual, — the happiness of those among whom the individual lives.

In the mean time my guardian sometimes discussed with me some other things besides the jellies. For instance, "Katy," said he at one of our *tête-à-tête* dinners, "you walk out every day, I suppose ; or, at least, you ought. I wish you would call now and then, and take Nelly Fader with you. She can hardly be a very entertaining companion to you, I own, but it would be a charity ; and, for your mother's daughter, that 's enough."

" Certainly I will. By the way, speaking of her, what *did* you mean by what you said that day about female physicians ? "

" I meant what I said," returned he, bluntly. " I meant just what I said. We need them, and we shall have them. It is an experiment that has got to be tried, and will be probably, within your lifetime, if not in mine. I don't want you to be one of them, though. You ought to be as much clearer than yourself as you are now than Nelly Fader, in order to carry it through; and even then it might be the carrying of a cross through life, — a grievous, in the view of most men perhaps an ignominious cross, to the pioneers. Especially it will be so, if other good but uninformed and thoughtless women are going to cry out upon it, as you and Julia did the other day. Whether the experiment is to succeed or not depends, under Providence, very much on you and such as you. But if that sort of outcry is to be raised, it will probably have the effect of keeping out of the profession such women as, from their integrity, ability, culture, and breeding, could be ornaments to it, and leave us shallow and low-minded smatterers, that I would n't trust with the life of a canary-bird, — who will ask which is likely to be the most lucrative calling, medicine or millinery, and take their choice accordingly, — and, for want of better, poor dupes will employ them. If you can't bear female practitioners, you 'll have to bear female *quack*titioners." He paused and looked at me.

I knew how jealous he always was for the honor of his craft. He did not often come so near giving me a scolding ; and I began to be afraid I might deserve one, though I could not see how. " I am sorry," said I ; " I did not mean — I did not think — I did not know — "

" Precisely, kitten on the hearth," returned he, good-humoredly ; "and as

you *are* sorry, and as you are besides usually rather less unmeaning and unthinking and unknowing than most other chits of your age, I forgive you. Learn to think and know before you hiss or purr, and you will be wiser than most chits of any age or sex. But now, consider : you, such as you are, yourself little more than a child, have, in two or three short visits, roused, interested, and done that other poor child more good, and, I strongly suspect, inspired her with more confidence, than I — I trust as upright a person and as sincere a well-wisher — have been able to do in a score. And this you have been able to do, in great part, simply by virtue of your womanhood. It *comes more natural* to her, no doubt, to talk with you. Nelly's is a case in point, though by no manner of means so strong a case as others that I have in my mind. Now imagine another woman with your good-will and natural tact, vivacity, and sympathy ; multiply these by double your age and intellect, and again by triple your experience and information ; calculate from these data *her* powers of doing good in such cases, and then see whether, in helping to brand her and fetter her in the exercise of such powers, you may not 'haply be found to fight against God.' "

" I will not speak so again, — at least before I think and know. You have forgiven me. Now appoint me my penance."

" Do what more you can for Nelly, then. I can do little or nothing. In fact, my visits seem to embarrass and agitate her so much, that I am sometimes afraid they hurt her more than they help her. She suffers more in mind than body, I suspect. How, she will not tell me, and perhaps she cannot. It may be that she is sick from sorrow ; or, on the other hand, her sorrow may be only an illusion of her sickness. It is all, from first to last, a mere miserable groping and working in the dark. In the mean time her constitution and character are forming for life. It is enough to make one's heart ache to look at the poor baby, and think what

an unsatisfactory, profitless, miserable
life that may be. I need not remind
you, Katy, that all this is a little piece
of Freemasonry between ourselves.
You are one of the exceptional and
abnormal human people before whom
one can safely think aloud."

I went to Nelly that very afternoon,
with some curiosity and with no unwillingness. I had already begun to
like her better than the Doctor did,
as I began to know her better. At
first I had been somewhat at a loss as
to her real disposition, between the constant civility of her manners, and the
occasional sullenness of her *manner*.
I was fast making up my mind that the
civility was genuine; the sullenness,
apparent only, the result of extreme
shyness, despondency, and languor. As
fast as she became more and more at
her ease with me, just so fast did she
become more and more engaging. She
was chaotic enough, and like a different
creature on different days; but I found
her, though sometimes very childish,
often sweet and never sour, unvarying-
ly patient towards her very trying aunt,
and only too subservient to her.

On this particular afternoon, I spied
her through the best-parlor window,
sobbing dismally. When she heard
and saw me, she tried to compose herself in vain; but the only account she
had to give of her grief was, that "the
mocking-bird sang so dreadfully, and
the Doctor told Aunt Cumberland she
[Nelly] was not going to die. There,"
added she, under her breath, "I did
n't mean to say that!"

We had no chance to say more; for
Mrs. Cumberland came in from her
shopping, and inquired for some cap-
ruffles, which she had given Nelly to
make up for her. "She said she did
n't feel well enough to go down town
with me," said Mrs. Cumberland; "an'
so I left her them to hem, 'cause the
Doctor says she needs cheerful occupation; an' them are just the pootiest
kind o' work for young ladies, an'
ruther tryin' to old eyes."

This was unanswerable; and as I
was obliged myself to go to some shops,

and Nelly could not, with her swollen
lids, I bade Mrs. Cumberland good
by; but told her niece that I meant to
call for her soon again, for the Doctor
thought it would do both of us good to
take a walk every day. She looked
somewhat encouraged by this; and I
hoped that the plan would have the
twofold effect of making her think it
would be ungracious to refuse to accompany me a second time, and of
keeping her from crying lest she should
again be caught at it.

When I reached home, I found it a
home of strife. The *pill* was soon to
be labelled. Dr. Physick wished to
call it Julius; but nothing would do
for his tyrannical wife but to have it
bear his name.

"Thank you," said the Doctor, as
I entered. "Are n't the sufferings of
one generation under that dispensation
enough for you? Do as you would be
done by, Julia. How would you like
yourself to be called Philemon?"

"I can't help that," persisted Mrs.
Julia. "The name of Phil is a philter
to me. Unless he bears it, I shall hate
him."

"A likely story! What should you
have done if he had been a girl?"

"Called him Phillis," answered the
ready Julia, sturdily.

"Then what should you say to Philip,
now?" interposed I in behalf of the
helpless innocent, — (an interposition
in return for which, ever after we have
finished his medical education with a
year in Paris, he ought in common
gratitude to prescribe for me *gratis*, if I
live to be as old and ill as Joyce Heth;
— for Philip he was and is, and will be,
I trust, for many a fine day, — the fine,
honest, clever, useful fellow!)

"Here.'s your fee, Katy, for restoring my domestic supremacy — ahem!
I hope Mrs. Physick did not hear," said
the Doctor; — "domestic balance of
power shall I say, my love, — or system
of compromises?"

What "my love" desired him to
say I cannot say, for I was deep in
the note which he had disgorged for
me from his not only omnivorous, but,

alas! too often oblivious pocket. It was written on small-sized French paper, in a beautiful English hand, bore date, to my consternation, some days back, and ran as follows: —

"BARBERRY BEACH, Monday, Sept. —th, 18—.

"DEAR MISS MORNE: —

"I have been wishing to see you again, all through this month, but scarcely expecting it till now; because I knew how full your heart and hands must be at home. Now, however, since I have had the pleasure of hearing from the Doctor that Mrs. Physick is nearly well, perhaps it will not be too much to hope that you will find an hour to spare for me some day this week. I have no engagements made; and if you can appoint a time to come to me, I shall be here and deny myself to other visitors. I should send my barouche for you; but one of the ponies has hurt its hoof, and the Doctor says that you confine yourself too closely to your household cares, and that you would be all the better for a walk.

"Another indulgence which I have been promising myself, — that of painting some illustrations for my brother's next work, — I find I must not only put off, but forego. It would be some consolation to me to be able to make it over to you, and believe that you found half as much enjoyment in it as I have, on former occasions. The usual terms, when he has paid for such work, have been . . . . [here she named a liberal sum]; but of course, if you like to undertake it, you will feel at liberty to name your own; and I shall be, as I am,

"Very gratefully yours,
"ELIZABETH DUDLEY.

"MISS MORNE."

Between surprise, pleasure, and dismay at my apparent neglect, I exclaimed simply, "What shall I do!"

"In all dilemmas, consult your guardian," answered he; and I handed him the note by way of a Nemesis.

He read it aloud very honestly, date and all; and I had the satisfaction to hear his wife, who was fast getting him well in hand again, rebuke him.

"Whew!" whistled he with most appropriate contrition; "'Monday'! and it's Thursday now, and too late for to-day! I wish I may n't have lost you the job, Katy. While the heart holds out, however, never give up the case! Put on your best bib and tucker when you get up to-morrow morning; and, as soon as you have got through ordering me an apple-dumpling, I will take you over there, and tell Miss Dudley who was to blame, and promise her, if she will forgive us, never to give her any assafœtida."

CHAPTER VII.

I COULD scarcely sleep that night for eagerness and anticipation. Ever since the afternoon when the vision of Miss Dudley appeared, to startle me from my painting, in the little south parlor, she had been the foremost figure in my brightest day-dreams, as often as, with little Philip warm and slumberous on my knees, I could find time for day-dreams. Accordingly, I had been more than wishing — longing — to see her again; though I put off returning her visit, partly from real want of time, partly from uncertainty about what was the proper etiquette for me, and partly from the dread of dispelling some pleasant illusions, and finding that the Miss Dudley of my reveries belonged to the realm of my imagination rather than to that of my memory. I dreamed of her all that night, when I was not lying awake to think of her; and when, in the morning, I arose early to brush and brighten my somewhat faded black, the keen autumn air, instead of chilling me, seemed but to whet and sharpen my zest for my expedition.

Julia's toilet was not made when I heard the clatter of the recalcitrant De Quincey backing the chaise out of his beloved, but little *be-lived* in, stable. She sat up in bed, however, when I went in to kiss her, in spite of Mrs. Rocket, turned me round to the window to see whether I was looking my best, or, as she equivocally phrased it, "the best of which I was capable," told me, that I had got a little *rouge* the last time I was out, and must ask Miss Dudley whether it was not becoming, and hooked her forefingers into my naturally *gekräuseltes* hair, to pull it into what she always maintained to be the proper *pose* above my eyebrows.

Then down I ran, and off I went, through the town and along the road, between rocks and evergreens with here and there a gate among them that marked the entrance to the earthly paradise of some lucky gentleman.

"Sha' n't we be too early?" asked I, fidgeting, for my prosperity appeared to me, just now, too perfect to be permanent.

"No," said the Doctor. "They are early people at Barberry Beach, — not Sybarites in anything, so far as I can judge. It is near nine. Miss Dudley tells me I shall almost always find her visible by that time. If, not hearing from you, she has made other engagements, you know she is more likely to be at leisure now than later."

"She does not look well yet. What was the matter with her?"

"*Angina pectoris.* That is Greek to you, Katy. Pain in the heart, then."

"What made her have it?"

"That is a deep question in the most interesting of sciences, — that of the metamorphoses of diseases. Many men would answer it according to their many minds. To the best of my belief, the cause of Miss Dudley's having a pain in her heart lay in her great-grandfather's toe."

"O Doctor! what *do* you mean?"

"The gout."

"Well, that sounds very aristocratic and imposing; but, notwithstanding, I know you are laughing at me."

"No, I am not. It is no laughing matter."

"Why, is it dangerous?"

"Dangerous!" said he. "It is deadly. Why, Katy, I never shall dare to tell you anything again, if you are going to look so frightened! *She* did not when I told her."

"Does she know?"

"Yes, and makes no secret of it, and is not unlikely to mention it before you; so that you must accustom yourself to the idea, and be prepared to face it as she does."

"How came she to know?"

"She asked me. I gave up very early in my practice, for several reasons, the habit of lying to my patients. If they are cowards, or if, for any reason, I think the truth and the whole truth would shorten their days, I often tell them little or nothing; but I tell them nothing but the truth. She is not a person to be put off from knowing what she has a right to know."

"How did she take it?"

"Nobly and simply, without any affectation of indifference. As she put the question, I laid my hand on her pulse; and, as it went on pretty firmly, I went on too. When I had said all there was to say, she thanked me earnestly, and said, as sweetly as anything could possibly be said, that the information would add double weight to the cautions and other counsels I had given her, and told me that, if I ever came to be in a situation like hers, she trusted that I should find the comfort of being dealt with with candor and kindness like mine. After all, Katy, she may live yet many years, and die at last of something else; and that is about the best that can be prognosticated of you and me, my dear."

"'T is true the young *may* die, but the old must," thought I. I was half comforted, and only half. Yet the pensive shadow of coming doom — or shall I not rather say the solemn dawn of approaching eternity? — seemed to lend a new and more unearthly charm to the lovely spiritual vision I cherished in my mind.

Presently, instead of passing a gate, the Doctor turned in at it, and drove smoothly up the gentle slope of a hard-rolled winding avenue lined with hemlocks. "Pretty, is n't it?" cried he. "O· for the time when I shall retire upon my fortune, and leave my office to Phil the second! There, Katy! What do you think of that?"

What did I think? O, too much to be told, either then or now! From the dark trees one forward step of each of De Quincey's forefeet brought us out into a high amphitheatre, at the instant flooded with sunshine. A higher hill, wooded with evergreens and bossed with boulders, made a background behind it, on the right, for a large, low cottage of clear gray granite, with broad piazzas curtained with Virginia creepers and monthly honeysuckles, and cloistered on the south. In front of the cottage was a shaven lawn, rimmed with a hedge of graceful barberries, and lighted up by small circular spots of brown earth, teeming with salvia and other splendid autumn flowers. Beyond and on the left ran a long reach of rocky headlands, burning with golden-rod and wild-rose berries mingled with purple asters and white spiræa, and all along from below, but very near, spread out far and wide the inexpressible ocean. It was a rough, ridgy, sage-greenish, gray ocean, I remember, that morning, full of tumble and toss and long scalloped lines of spent foam, covered over with a dim, low half-dome of sky, — with seagulls flickering, and here and there a small, wild, ragged gypsy of a cloud, of a little darker gray, scudding lawlessly under, — and threw out in the strongest contrast the brilliant hues and sharp, clear outlines of the shore.

The Doctor sprang from the chaise, left me in it, and threw me the reins. I always wished he would n't, but he always would. The most I had to gain by pulling them, if De Quincey grew restless, was to make him *back;* and this was precisely what I least desired. My reasonable expostulations, however, could never obtain any more grace from him who should have been my guardian than a promise, if I would "make no fuss, and broken bones" came of it, that he would "mend me softly." Therefore I thought it most prudent not to expostulate; but my penance was this time a brief one. He had hardly en-

tered the door when the tall, striking figure I recollected so well came dimly in view in one of the nearest bay-windows, tapped on the glass with one slender white-frilled hand, and nodded with a bright, glad smile; and back came the Doctor to help me out.

"It is all right, Katy. Miss Dudley wants you, and does not want me. If it rains, you can stay till I call for you. Otherwise, come back when you like. The first door to your left in the hall."

Miss Dudley met me in the parlor-door, laughing. "I should have come out to make prize of you," said she, "but they say it is rather bleak this morning, and I am still under orders. I had almost given you up for this week; but the Doctor assures me that he has already been suitably dealt with and brought to repentance, and so there is no more to be said on that point, especially as you have happened to hit on the very time when I am most alone, and when, as I have been accustomed to be the busiest, I feel my present idleness the most. You drove here, after all. You are not tired? What should you say, first, to a walk with me?"

A staid-looking, exquisitely neat, elderly woman brought her bonnet, umbrella, gloves, and a large Scotch plaid shawl, in which she wrapped Miss Dudley, with much solicitude, and was so prettily thanked for her pains that I longed to have the wrapping up to do myself.

"I really do not think I needed to be muffled up quite so closely to-day," said my hostess, as she stepped lightly from the piazza to the sunlit gravel-walk; "but Bonner is ten years older than I, and feels the cold a good deal herself, and I do not like to make her anxious about me. She had a great fright, poor thing! when I was ill. Where shall we go, Miss Morne? — to the garden or the shore? I am not certain that those clouds mean to give us time for both."

Not knowing which she would prefer, I answered that I could hardly choose, unless she would be so kind as to tell me which was the most beautiful. To my joy, she said the shore. The path ran close to the edge of the cliffs; and below our very feet were the beach and the breakers. We both forgot ourselves at first, I think, in the sight and sound.

At length she turned, with a sudden movement, and looked me in the face. " I do believe, Miss Morne," said she, " that you are one of the fortunate people who have the power to enjoy this to the full. I trust that we may often still enjoy it here together."

"Shall I tell you how I enjoy it, ma'am?" I exclaimed, carried out of myself at sight of the enthusiasm that was tinging her delicate cheek and lighting up her eyes. "As we enjoy those things that it never comes into our heads to ask ourselves whether we like or not. Some things we *have* to ask ourselves, whether we like or not, before we know, and even after we are scarcely sure; and some things, such as the poor little ' Marchioness's ' orange-peel and water, we have to ' make believe very hard' in order to like at all. But home when we have been away, and friends when we have been lonely, and water when we are thirsty, and the sea always! — we never ask ourselves if those are good, — we know." Then my face burnt. How it would burn in those girlish days!

And how foolish I felt, or had begun to feel, when Miss Dudley slowly answered, looking mercifully away from me and at the waves: "Very true, Miss Morne! You speak from your heart, and to mine."

The clouds were forbearing, and allowed us time afterwards for a visit to the gorgeous garden. We walked to the summer-house at the very end, from which a winding path began to climb the hill. There Miss Dudley paused. " My chamois days are over, for the present, at least," said she. " We must wait for my little nieces or nephew to escort you up there. Shall we go in?"

When we did so, I thought that the interior of the cottage was not much less grand, scarcely less beautiful, than what we had seen without. At

that period most housekeepers held the hardly yet exploded heresy, not only that fresh air was a dangerous and unwholesome luxury, to be denied, as far as might be, to any but the strongest constitutions,[*] but that even sunshine within the doors was an inadmissible intrusion, alike untidy and superfluous. On these points this house set public opinion at defiance. It was set, of set purpose, at *wrong* angles to the points of the compass. Every wind of heaven could sweep it, at the pleasure of the inmates, through and through, and the piazzas were so arranged that there was not a single apartment in it into which the sun could not look, through one window or another, once at least in the twenty-four hours. The floors were tiled, ingrained, oiled, matted, — everything but carpeted, except that of the state drawing-room; and there the Wilton had a covering over it, removed, as I afterwards found, only on occasions of state. The whole atmosphere seemed full of health, purity, cheerfulness, warmth, and brightness. Brilliant flowers peeped in at the windows, and were set on the tables in vases, or hung in them from the walls. And there were pictures, and there were statues, but there too was Miss Dudley, paring a peach for me, for sociability's sake, — for she could not eat one herself, so soon after her breakfast; and, as I knew the time must be running away very fast, — hard that it will always run fastest when we are the happiest! — I seized my first opportunity to say that few things would give me greater pleasure than to furnish the illustrations she had mentioned, if I could but succeed in executing them as I ought.

"As to that, I will be your sponsor," returned she, gayly, "if you would like to begin them here. Your touch is very firm and true; and I will show you all our tricks of color. Here is my paint-box. Have you time to-day?"

I had time, and no excuse; though,

---

[*] The old philosophy held, that " Nature abhors a vacuum "; but modern observation shows that the natural Yankee abhors the air.

in falling so suddenly into the midst of painting-lessons from Miss Dudley, I really felt as if I was having greatness thrust upon me in a manner to take my breath away. If I had only had a little more time to think about it, my touch might have been truer for the nonce. Her paint-box was so handsomely furnished, too, and so daintily ordered, that I scarcely dared touch it. She gave me a little respite, however, by rubbing the colors for me, — colors, some of them, that, for their costliness, I could not allow myself at all at home, — and selected for me two such exquisite brusbes from her store ! Then she lay down beside me on a "couch of Ind," smiled as I laid her plaid over her feet, and watched me at the work. How that brought my poor Fanny back to me ! But my new mistress went on unwearyingly, teaching and encouraging me, and, if I was more than satisfied with her, did not on her part show that she was less than satisfied with me. The clock struck twelve before I dreamed of its taking upon itself to offer such an untimely interruption.

"Now I am nicely rested," said she, soon after; "and I am afraid you must begin to be nicely tired. Do you not ? "

"No, indeed ; I seldom do till nine o'clock at night."

"Then we will indulge ourselves here still a little longer. But hark ! Are not there my little people back from school ? "

The expression common to those who love children stole into her face. Young voices were drawing nearer.

"Come to my arms, O lovely cherub ! " said one that had a boyish sound in it, paternally.

"Look out and see them," whispered Miss Dudley to me.

I peeped through the blinds. A handsome and very graceful olive-hued boy, apparently about fourteen years old, with a form like that of the Mercury upborne by a zephyr, eyes like stars, lashes like star-beams, and an expression that would have made him a good study for a picture of Puck, half leaning, half sitting, on the stone balustrade, was tenderly dandling in his arms a huge, vulgar-looking, gray, striped stable-cat, that rolled and writhed therein in transports of comfort and affection.

"But, indeed, Paul," remonstrated another voice, *tout comme un serin,* "Pet ought to be whipped instead of hugged ! Lily says so."

"Tiger Lily ? What a cruel girl ! O, my Pettitoes ! how can she say so ? "

"Why," answered another girlish voice, a little firmer, but hardly less sweet, than the first, "only think ! While we were all in school, he watched his opportunity and killed the robin that lives in the crab-apple-tree. The gardener says he heard it cry, and ran with his hoe ; and there was this wicked, horrid, grim, great Pet galloping as fast as he could gallop to the stable, with its poor little beak sticking out at one side of his grinning mouth, and its tail at the other ! "

"Why, Pettitoes ! how very inconsiderate ! You won't serve it so another time, *will* you ? Though how a robin can have the face to squeak when he catches it himself at noon, after cramming himself with worms the whole morning, is more than I can see ! "

"O no, Paul ! He was singing most sweetly ! I heard him ; and so did Rose."

"And so did I. He was singing through his nose as bad as Deacon Piper, because he had a worm in his mouth. He could n't leave off gobbling one single minute, — not even to practise his music."

"Let us go out," said Miss Dudley. We did so. Paul's retreating back was all that was to be seen of the boy, with Pet's peaceful chin pillowed upon his shoulder, as, borne off in triumph, he looked calmly back at Lily, who stood shaking her small, chiselled ivory finger at him. Rose was still beside her, with her arm around her waist, as if in propitiation.

Two twelve-year-old twins, in twin blue gingham frocks, — they were much addicted to blue and pink ginghams, —

they had that indefinable look of *blood* which belonged to their kin, which is sometimes, to be sure, to be found in families that have no great-grandfathers, after they have been well-fed, well-read, and well-bred for a generation or two, but to which they had an uncommonly good right, as their pedigree — so I afterwards found — ran straight back to the Norman Conquest, without a single " probably " in it. They were, for their age, tall and slender, with yet more springy buoyancy than their aunt in *pose* and movement. Strangers were always mistaking them for each other. That day I could scarcely tell them apart, though afterwards I wondered at it. Rose was the very prettiest child I ever saw, and Lily pretty nearly the most beautiful person.

Lily was already the tallest. Her thick and wavy hair was *blonde cendrée*, and all her features were perfectly Grecian. Her eyes were of a very dark blue, that turned into nothing but clear radiance when she was opposed or in any way excited. Her complexion was healthful, but would be described as soft and warm, rather than brilliant. Her whole fair little face was about as firm and spirited as a fair girlish face could be.

Rose's larger eyes were of a pure, deep hazel. Her hair, as thick and curly as Lily's, was far more glossy and flossy, and of the yellowest, brightest gold-color. Her nose — a most perfect little nose — was more aquiline than her sister's. Her skin was of the tints of the finest rare-ripe peaches, — pure white and deepening pink ; and all around her mouth were dimples lying in wait for her to laugh.

As they met Miss Dudley, with the many-colored Virginia creepers behind them and the flowers behind her, a better *tableau vivant* of " first youth " and *first age* could scarcely have been put together than they made. It made me wish that I had been more than a painter of *specimens*. The elder lady presented me to the younger ones ; and they greeted me with that pretty courtesy that always charms us twofold when we meet with it in children, because we scarcely expect it of them. Rose's radiant little countenance, especially, seemed to say, " I have heard of you before, and wished to know you " ; and that is one of the most winning expressions that a new countenance can wear. Then they put their arms round " dear Aunt Lizzy," coaxed her for peaches, and obtained the remainder of our basketful without much difficulty ; and then I had to depart, but not quite without solace, for Rose ran after me to say, " Aunt Lizzy hopes, if you are not otherwise engaged, to see you again Monday morning at nine ; and she sends you this book that she forgot to give you. It made her think of you, she says, when she was reading it."

It was Greenwood's " Sermons of Consolation " ; and, written in her hand on the fly-leaf, I found my name.

THE SWORD OF BOLIVAR.

WITH the steadfast stars above us,
 And the molten stars below,
We sailed through the Southern midnight,
 By the coast of Mexico.

Alone, on the desolate, dark-ringed,
 Rolling and flashing sea,
A grim old Venezuelan
 Kept the deck with me,

And talked to me of his country,
  And the long Spanish war;
And told how a young Republic
  Forged the sword of Bolivar.

Of no base mundane metal
  Was the wondrous weapon made,
And in no earth-born fire
  Was fashioned the sacred blade.

But that it might shine the symbol
  Of law and light in the land,
Dropped down as a star from heaven,
  To flame in a hero's hand,

And be to the world a portent
  Of eternal might and right,
They chose for the steel a splinter
  From a fallen aerolite.

Then a virgin forge they builded
  By the city, and kindled it
With flame from a shattered palm-tree,
  Which the lightning's torch had lit,—

That no fire of earthly passion
  Might taint the holy sword,
And no ancient error tarnish
  The falchion of the Lord.

For Quito and New Granada
  And Venezuela they pour
From three crucibles the dazzling
  White meteoric ore.

In three ingots it is moulded,
  And welded into one,
For an emblem of Colombia,
  Bright daughter of the sun !

It is drawn on a virgin anvil,
  It is heated and hammered and rolled,
It is shaped and tempered and burnished,
  And set in a hilt of gold ;

For thus by the fire and the hammer
  Of war a nation is built,
And ever the sword of its power
  Is swayed by a golden hilt.

Then with pomp and oratory
  The mustachioed señores brought
To the house of the Liberator
  The weapon they had wrought ;

And they said, in their stately phrases,
  "O mighty in peace and war!
No mortal blade we bring you,
  But a flaming meteor.

"The sword of the Spaniard is broken,
  And to you in its stead is given,
To lead and redeem a nation,
  This ray of light from heaven."

The gaunt-faced Liberator
  From their hands the symbol took,
And waved it aloft in the sunlight,
  With a high, heroic look;

And he called the saints to witness:
  "May these lips turn into dust,
And this right hand fail, if ever
  It prove recreant to its trust!

"Never the sigh of a bondman
  Shall cloud this gleaming steel,
But only the foe and the traitor
  Its vengeful edge shall feel.

"Never a tear of my country
  Its purity shall stain,
Till into your hands, who gave it,
  I render it again."

Now if ever a chief was chosen
  To cover a cause with shame,
And if ever there breathed a caitiff,
  Bolivar was his name.

From his place among the people
  To the highest seat he went,
By the winding paths of party
  And the stair of accident.

A restless, weak usurper,
  Striving to rear a throne,
Filling his fame with counsels
  And conquests not his own; —

Now seeming to put from him
  The sceptre of command,
Only that he might grasp it
  With yet a firmer hand; —

His country's trusted leader,
  In league with his country's foes,
Stabbing the cause that nursed him,
  And openly serving those; —

The Sword of Bolivar.

The chief of a great republic
  Plotting rebellion still, —
An apostate faithful only
  To his own ambitious will.

Drunk with a vain ambition,
  In his feeble, reckless hand,
The sword of Eternal Justice
  Became but a brawler's brand.

And Colombia was dissevered,
  Rent by factions, till at last
Her name among the nations
  Is a memory of the past.

Here the grim old Venezuelan
  Puffed fiercely his red cigar
A brief moment, then in the ocean
  It vanished like a star ;

And he slumbered in his hammock ;
  And only the ceaseless rush
Of the reeling and sparkling waters
  Filled the solemn midnight hush,

As I leaned by the swinging gunwale
  Of the good ship, sailing slow,
With the steadfast heavens above her,
  And the molten heavens below.

Then I thought with sorrow and yearning
  Of my own distracted land,
And the sword let down from heaven
  To flame in her ruler's hand, —

The sword of Freedom, resplendent
  As a beam of the morning star,
Received, reviled, and dishonored
  By another than Bolivar !

And my prayers flew home to my country :
  O ye tried and fearless crew !
O ye pilots of the nation !
  Now her safety is with you.

Beware the traitorous captain,
  And the wreckers on the shore ;
Guard well the noble vessel ;
  And steadily evermore,

As ye steer through the perilous midnight,
  Let your faithful glances go
To the steadfast stars above her,
  From their fickle gleams below.

THROUGH BROADWAY.

THE incessant demolition of which Broadway is the scene denotes to the most careless eye that devotion to the immediate which De Tocqueville maintains to be a democratic characteristic. The huge piles of old bricks which block the way — with their array of placards heralding every grade of popular amusement, from a tragedy of Shakespeare to a negro melody, and from a menagerie to a clairvoyant exhibition, and vaunting every kind of experimental charlatanism, from quack medicine to flash literature — are mounds of less mystery, but more human meaning, than those which puzzle archæologists on the Mississippi and the Ohio; for they are the *débris* of mansions only half a century ago the aristocratic homes of families whose descendants are long since scattered, and whose social prominence and local identity are forgotten, while trade has obliterated every vestige of their roof-tree and association of their hearth-stone. Such is the constant process. As private residences give way to stores and offices, the upper portion of the island is crowded with their enlarged dimensions and elaborate luxury; churches are in the same manner sacrificed, until St. Paul's and Trinity alone remain of the old sacred landmarks; and the suburban feature — those "fields" where burgomasters foregathered, the militia drilled, and Hamilton's youthful eloquence roused the people to arms — is transferred to the other and distant end of Manhattan, and expanded into a vast, variegated, and beautiful rural domain, — that "the Park" may coincide in extent and attraction with the increase of the population and growth of the city's area. Thus a perpetual tide of emigration, and the pressure of the business on the resident section, — involving change of domicile, substitution of uses, the alternate destruction and erection of buildings, each being larger and

more costly in material than its predecessor, — make the metropolis of the New World appear, to the visitor from the Old, a shifting bivouac rather than a stable city, where hereditary homes are impossible, and nomadic instincts prevalent, and where local associations, such as endear or identify the streets abroad, seem as incongruous as in the Eastern desert or Western woods, whose dwellers "fold their tents like the Arabs, and as silently steal away." The absence of the law of primogeniture necessitates the breaking up of estates, and thus facilitates the methods whereby the elegant homestead becomes, in the second or third generation, a dry-goods store, a boarding- or club house, a milliner's show-room or a dentist's office. Here and there some venerable gossip will rehearse the triumphs of refined hospitality, or describe the success of a belle or the brilliancy of a genial leader in politics or social pastime, which, years ago, consecrated a mansion or endeared a neighborhood, — whereof not a visible relic is now discoverable, save in a portrait or reminiscent paper conserved in the archives of the Historical Society. And in this speedy oblivion of domestic and social landmarks, how easily we find a reason for the national irreverence, and the exclusive interest in the future, which make the life of America, like the streets of her cities, a scene of transition unhallowed by memorials.

Yet, despite its dead horses and vehicular entanglements, its vile concert saloons, the alternate meanness and magnificence of its architecture, the fragile character of its theatrical structures, and their limited and hazardous means of exit, — despite falling walls and the necessity of police guardianship at the crossings, the reckless driving of butcher-boys and the dexterity of pickpockets, — despite the slippery pavement, and the chronic cry for

" relief," — Broadway is a spectacle and an experience worth patient study, and wonderfully prolific of life-pictures. With a fountain at one end, like a French town, and a chime of bells at the other, like a German city, the intermediate space is as representative a rendezvous as can be found in the world.

The first thing that strikes an experienced eye in New York's great thoroughfare is the paucity of loiterers : he sees, at a glance, that the *flâneur* is an exotic here. There is that in the gait and look of every one that shows a settled and an eager purpose, — a goal sought under pressure. A counting-room, office, court, mart, or mansion is to be reached punctually, and therefore the eye and step are straightforward, intent, preoccupied. But this peculiarity is chiefly obvious early and late in the day, when business and professional men are on their way to and from the place of their daily vocations. Later, and especially about two hours after noon, it is the dress and number of the other sex that win attention ; and to one fresh from London, the street attire of *ladies* — or those who aspire, with more or less justice, to that title — is a startling incongruity ; for the showy colors and fine textures reserved across the sea for the opera, the *salon,* and the fashionable drive, are here displayed on shopping expeditions, for which an English lady dresses in neutral tints and substantial fabrics, — avoiding rather than courting observation. The vulgar impression derived in Broadway from an opposite habit is vastly increased by modern fashions ; for the apology for a bonnet that leaves brow, cheek, and head fully exposed, — the rustle and dimensions of crinoline, — the heavy masses of unctuous false hair attached to the back of the head, deforming its shape and often giving a coarse monstrosity to its naturally graceful poise and proportions, — the inappropriate display of jewelry and the long silk trains of the expensive robes trailing on the dirty walk, and continually caught beneath

the feet of careless pedestrians, — all unite to render the exhibition repulsive to taste, good sense, and that chivalric sympathy inspired by the sight of female beauty and grace, so often co-existent with these anomalies. Broadway has often been compared to a kaleidoscope, — an appellation suggested by the variety of shifting tints, from those of female dress to those of innumerable commodities, from dazzling effects of sunshine to the radiance of equipage, vivid paint, gilded signs, and dazzling wares. And blent with this pervading language of colors are the local associations which the articles of merchandise hint. Consider how extensive is their scope, — Persian carpets, Lyons silks, Genoa velvets, ribbons from Coventry and laces from Brussels, the furs of the Northwest, glass of Bohemia, ware of China, nuts from Brazil, silver of Nevada mines, Sicily lemons, Turkey figs, metallic coffins and fresh violets, Arabian dates, French chocolate, pine-apples from the West Indies, venison from the Adirondacs, brilliant chemicals, gilded frames, Manchester cloth, Sheffield cutlery, Irish linens, ruddy fruit, salmon from the Thousand Isles, sables from Russia, watches from Geneva, carvings from Switzerland, caricatures and India - rubber garments, saccharine temples, books in tinted covers, toys, wines, perfumes, drugs. dainties, art, luxury, science, all lavishing their products to allure the throng, — phenomena common, indeed, to all streets devoted to trade, but here uniquely combined with a fashionable promenade, and affording the still-life of a variegated moving panorama. It is characteristic, also, that the only palatial buildings along the crowded avenue are stores and hotels. Architecture thus glorifies the gregarious extravagance of the people. The effect of the whole is indefinitely prolonged, to an imaginative mind, by the vistas at the lower extremity, which reveal the river, and. at sunset, the dark tracery of the shipping against the far and flushed horizon ; while, if one lifts his eye to the telegraph wire, or lowers it to some excavation—which betrays the Croton pipes, a sublime consciousness is awakened of the relation of this swift and populous eddy of life's great ocean to its distant rural streams, and the ebb and flow of humanity's eternal tide. Consider, too, the representative economics and delectations around, available to taste; necessity, and cash,—how wonderful their contrast! Not long since, an Egyptian museum, with relics dating from the Pharaohs, was accessible to the Broadway philosopher, and a Turkish khan to the sybarite; one has but to mount a staircase, and find himself in the presence of authentic effigies of all the prominent men of the nation, sun-painted for the million. This pharmacist will exorcise his pain-demon; that electrician place him *en rapport* with kindred hundreds of miles away, or fortify his jaded nerves. Down this street he may enjoy a Russian or Turkish bath; down that, a water-cure. Here, with skill undreamed of by civilized antiquity, fine gold can be made to replace the decayed segment of a tooth; there, he has but to stretch out his foot, and a chiropodist removes the throbbing bunion, or a boy kneels to polish his boots. A hackman is at hand to drive him to the Park, a telescope to show him the stars; he has but to pause at a corner and buy a journal which will place him *au courant* with the events of the world, or listen to an organ-grinder, and think himself at the opera. This temple is free for him to enter and "muse till the fire burns"; on yonder bookseller's counter is an epitome of the wisdom of ages; there he may buy a nosegay to propitiate his lady-love, or a sewing-machine to beguile his womankind, and here a crimson balloon or spring rocking-horse, to delight his little boy, and rare gems or a silver service for a bridal gift. This English tailor will provide him with a "capital fit," that German tobacconist with a creamy meerschaum. At the artificial Spa he may recuperate with Vichy or Kissingen, and at the phrenologist's have his mental and moral aptitudes defined; now a "medium" invites him

to a spiritual *séance*, and now an antiquarian to a "curiosity shop." In one saloon is *lager* such as he drank in Bavaria, and in another, the best bivalves in the world. Here is a fine billiard-table, there a gymnasium;—food for mind and body, gratification to taste;—all the external resources of civilization are at hand,—not always with the substantial superiority of those of London or the elegant variety of Paris, but with enough of both to make them available to the eclectic cosmopolite.

The historical epochs of New York are adequately traceable by the successive pictures of her main thoroughfare,—beginning with the Indian village and the primeval forest which Henry Hudson found on the island of Manhattan in 1609, and advancing to the stockade fort of New Amsterdam, built where the Battery now is, by Wouter Van Twiller, the second Dutch governor, and thence to the era when the fur trade, tobacco-growing, and slavery were enriching the India Company, when the Wall was built on the site of the so-called financial rendezvous, to protect the settlement from savage invasion, and a deep valley marked the present junction of Canal Street and Broadway. The advent of a new class of artisans signalizes the arrival of Huguenot emigrants; the rebellion of Leisler marks the encroachment of new political agencies, and the substitution of Pitt's statue for that of George III. on the Bowling Green in 1770, the dawn of Independence, so sturdily ushered in and cherished by the Liberty Boys, and culminating in the evacuation of the British in 1783, the entrance of Washington with the American army, and two years after, in the meeting of the first Congress. These vicissitudes left their impress on the street. Every church but the Episcopal was turned by the English into a riding-school, prison, or stable; each successive charter was more liberal in its municipal privileges. The Boston stage long went from the Fort to the Park, and so on by the old post-road, and was fourteen days *en route;* pestilence, imported from the West India islands, depopulated the adjacent houses; water was sold from carts; and dimly lighted was the pedestrian on his midnight way, while old-fashioned watchmen cried the hour; and when, in 1807, Robert Fulton initiated steam navigation, the vast system of ferriage was established which inundated the main avenue of the city with a perpetual tributary stream of floating population from all the outlying shores of the Hudson and East Rivers, Staten and Long Islands, and the villages above Manhattan. A lady who lived in New York forty years ago, and returned this season, expressed her surprise that the matutinal procession of rustics she used to watch from the window of her fashionable domicile in the lower part of Broadway had ceased, so completely had suburban citizens usurped the farmers' old homes. The beautiful pigeons that used to coo and cluster on the cobble stones had no resting-place for their coral feet on the Russ pavement, so thickly moved the drays, and so unremitted was the rush of man and beast. In fact, the one conservative feature eloquent of the past is the churchyard, — the old, moss-grown, sloping gravestones, — landmarks of finished life-journeys, mutely invoking the hurrying crowd through the tall iron railings of Trinity and St. Paul's. It is a striking evidence of a " new country," that a youth from the Far West, on arriving in New York by sea, was so attracted by these ancient cemeteries that he lingered amid them all day, — saying it was the first time he had ever seen a human memorial more than twenty years old, except a tree! And memorable was the ceremony whereby, a few years since, the Historical Society celebrated the bicentennial birthday of Bradford, the old colonial printer, by renewing his headstone. At noonday, when the life-tide was at flood, in lovely May weather, a barrier was stretched across Broadway; and there, at the head of eager gold-worshipping Wall Street,

in the heart of the bustling, trafficking crowd, a vacant place was secured in front of the grand and holy temple of Trinity. The pensive chant arose; a white band of choristers and priests came forth; and eminent citizens gathered around to reconsecrate the tablet over the dust of one who, two hundred years ago, had practised a civilizing art in this fresh land, and disseminated messages of religion and wisdom. It was a singular picture, beautiful to the eye, solemn to the feelings, and a rare tribute to the past, where the present sways with such absolute rule. Few Broadway tableaux are so worthy of artistic preservation. Before, the vista of a money-changers' mart; above and below, a long, crowded avenue of metropolitan life; behind, the lofty spire, gothic windows, and archways of the church, and the central group as picturesquely and piously suggestive as a mediæval rite.

Vainly would the most self-possessed reminiscent breast the living tide of the surging thoroughfare, on a week-day, to realize in his mind's eye its ancient aspect; but if it chance to him to land at the Battery on a clear and still Sabbath morning, and before the bells summon forth the worshippers, and to walk thence to Union Square in company with an octogenarian Knickerbocker of good memory, local pride, and fluent speech, he will obtain a mental photograph of the past that transmutes the familiar scene by a quaint and vivid aerial perspective. Then the " Middle Road " of the beginning of this century will reappear, — the traces of a wheat-field on the site of St. Paul's, still a fresh tradition; Oswego Market, opposite Liberty Street, is alive with early customers; the reminiscent beholds the apparition of Rutgers's orchard, whose remaining noble elms yet shade the green vista of the City Hospital, and which was a place for rifling bird's-nests in the boyhood of his pensive companion, whose father played at skittles on the Bowling Green, hard by the Governor's house, while the Dutch householders sat smoking long pipes in their broad porticos, cosily discussing the last news from Antwerp or Delft, their stout rosy daughters meanwhile taking a twilight ramble, with their stalwart beaux, to the utmost suburban limit of Manhattan, where Canal Street now intersects Broadway, — then an unpaved lane with scattered domiciles, only grouped into civic contiguity around the Battery, and with many gardens enhancing its rural aspect. Somewhat later, and Munn's Land Office, at the corner of what is now Grand Street, was suggestive of a growing settlement and the era of speculation ; an isolated coach-factory marked the site of the St. Nicholas Hotel ; people flocked along, in domestic instalments, to Vauxhall, where now stands the Astor Library, to drink mead and see the Flying Horses ; and capitalists invested in "lots" on Bayard's Farm, where Niblo's and the Metropolitan now flourish ; the one-story building at the present angle of Prince Street was occupied by Grant Thorburn's father ; beyond lay the old road leading to Governor Stuyvesant's Bowerie, with Sandy Hill at the upper end. In 1664, Heere Stras was changed to Broadway. At the King's Arms and Burr's Coffee-House, near the Battery, the traitor Arnold was wont to lounge, and in the neighborhood dwelt the Earl of Stirling's mother. At the corner of Rector Street was the old Lutheran church frequented by the Palatine refugees. Beyond or within the Park stood the old Brewery, Pottery, Bridewell, and Poor-house ; relics of an Indian village were often found ; the Drover's Inn, cattle-walk, and pastures marked the straggling precincts of the town ; and on the commons oxen were roasted whole on holidays, and obnoxious officials hung in effigy. Anon rose the brick mansions of the Rapelyes, Rhinelanders, Kingslands, Cuttings, Jays, Bogarts, Depeysters, Duers, Livingstons, Verplancks, Van Rensselaers, De Lanceys, Van Cortlands, etc. ; at first along the "Middle Road," and then in by-streets from the main thoroughfare down to the rivers ; and so, gradually, the

trees and shrubs that made a *rus in urbe* of the embryo city, and the gables and tiles, porches and pipes, that marked the dynasty chronicled by old Diedrich, gave way to palatial warehouses, magnificent taverns, and brown stone fronts.

The notes of old travellers best revive the scene ere it was lost in modern improvements. Mrs. Knight, who visited New York in 1704, having performed the journey from Boston all the way on horseback, enjoyed the "vendues" at Manhattan, where "they gave drinks" ; was surprised to see "fireplaces that had no jambs" and "bricks of divers colors and laid in checkers, being glazed and looking very agreeable." The diversion in vogue was "riding in sleighs about four miles out of town, where they have a house of entertainment at a place called the Bowery." In 1769 Dr. Burnaby recognized but two churches, Trinity and St. George, and "went in an Italian chaise to a turtle feast on the East River." In 1788, Brissot found that the session of Congress there gave great *éclat* to New York, but, with republican indignation, he laments the ravages of luxury and the English fashions visible in Broadway, — "silks, gauzes, hats, and borrowed hair ; . . . . equipages rare, but elegant." "The men," he adds, "have more simplicity of dress ; they disdain gewgaws ; but they take their revenge in the luxury of the table" ; — "and luxury," he observes, "forms a class dangerous to society, — I mean bachelors, — the expense of women causing matrimony to be dreaded by men." It is curious to find the French radical of eighty years ago drawing from the life of Broadway inferences similar to those of the even more emphatic economical moralist of to-day. In 1794, Wansey, a commercial traveller, found the "Tontine near the Battery" the most eligible hotel, and met there Dr. Priestley, breakfasted with Gates, and had a call from Livingston ; saw "some good paintings by Trumbull, at the Federal Hall," and Hodgkinson, at the theatre, in "A Bold Stroke for a Husband" ; dined with

Comfort Sands ; and Mr. Jay, " brother to the Ambassador," took him to tea at the " Indian Queen " ; — items of information that mark the social and political transition since the days of Dutch rule, though the Battery still remained the court end and nucleus of Manhattan.

But it is not local memory alone that the solitude of Broadway awakens in our aged guide ; the vacant walk is peopled, to his fancy, with the celebrities of the past whom he has there gazed at or greeted, — Franklin, Jay, Tom Paine, Schuyler, Cobbett, Freneau, and Colonel Trumbull, with their Revolutionary prestige ; Volney and Genet, with the memory of French radicalism ; Da Ponte and the old Italian opera ; Colles and Clinton and the Erie Canal days ; Red Jacket and the aborigines ; Dunlap and Dennie, the literary pioneers ; Cooke, Kemble, Kean, Matthews, and Macready, followed so eagerly by urchin eyes, — the immortal heroes of the stage ; Hamilton, Clinton, Morris, Burr, Gallatin, and a score of political and civic luminaries whose names have passed into history ; Decatur, Hull, Perry, and the brilliant throng of victorious naval officers grouped near the old City Hotel ; Moreau, Louis Philippe, Talleyrand, Louis Napoleon, Maroncelli, Foresti, Kossuth, Garibaldi, and many other illustrious European exiles ; Jeffrey, Moore, Dickens, Thackeray, Trollope, and the long line of literary lions, from Basil Hall to Tupper ; Chancellor Kent, Audubon, Fulton, Lafayette, Randolph, the Prince of Wales, and the Queen of the Sandwich Islands, Turkish admirals, Japanese officials, artists, statesmen, actors, soldiers, authors, foreign *savans*, and domestic eccentricities, who have perambulated this central avenue of a cosmopolitan American city. Could they have all been photographed, what a reflex of modern society would such a picture-gallery afford !

The old Dutch traders, with the instinct of their Holland habitudes, clung to the water-side, and therefore their domiciles long extended at angles with what subsequently became the principal avenue of the settlement ; and until 1642 Pearl Street was the fashionable quarter. Meantime, where now thousands of emigrants daily disembark, and the offices of ocean steamships indicate the facility and frequency of Transatlantic travel, the Indian chiefs smoked the pipe of peace with the victorious colonists under the shadow of Fort Amsterdam, and the latter held fairs there, or gathered, for defence and pastime, round the little oasis of the metropolitan desert where carmen now read " The Sun." No. a was the Kennedy House, subsequently the tavern of Mrs. Koch, — whose Dutch husband was an officer in the Indian wars, — and was successively the head-quarters of Clinton, Cornwallis, and Washington, and at last the Prime Mansion ; and farther up was Mrs. Ryckman's boarding-house, — genial sojourn of Irving, and the scene of his early pen-craft and youthful companionships, when " New York was more handy, and everybody knew everybody, and there was more good-fellowship and ease of manners." Those were the days of ropewalks and " selectmen," of stage-coaches and oil-lamps. The Yankee invasion had scarcely superseded the Knickerbocker element. The Free Academy was undreamed of ; and the City Hotel assemblies were the embryo Fifth Avenue balls. An old Directory or a volume of Valentine's Manual, compared with the latest Metropolitan Guide-Book and Trow's last issue, will best illustrate the difference between Broadway then and now.

But it is not so much the more substantial memorials as the " dissolving views " that give its peculiar character to the street. Entered at the lower extremity by the newly-arrived European, on a rainy morning, the first impression is the reverse of grand or winsome. The squalor of the docks and the want of altitude in the buildings, combined with the bustle and hubbub, strike the eye as repulsive ; but as the scene grows familiar and is watched under the various aspects produced by different seasons, weather, and hours of the day, it becomes more and more significant and attractive. Indeed, there is probably no street in the world subject to such violent contrasts. It is one thing on a brilliant and cool October day and another in July. White cravats and black coats mark "Anniversary week"; broad brims and drab, the "Yearly Meeting" of the Friends; the "moving day" of the householders, the "opening day" of the milliners, Christmas and New Year's, sleighing-time and spring, early morning and midnight, the Sabbath and week-days, a cold spell and the "heated term," — every hour, season, holiday, panic, pastime, and parade brings into view new figures and phases, — diverse phenomena of crowd and character, — like the shifting segments of a panorama. The news of victories during the war for the Union could be read there in people's eyes and heard in their greetings. Sorrowful tidings seemed to magnetize with sadness the long procession. Something in the air foretold the stranger how beat the public pulse. The undercurrent of the prevalent emotion seems to vibrate, with electric sympathy, along the human tide.

A walk in Broadway is a most available remedy for "domestic" vexation and provincial egotism. "Every individual spirit," says Schiller, "waxes in the great stream of multitudes." Stand awhile calmly by the rushing stream, and note its representative significance, or stroll slowly along, with observant eye, to mark the commodities and nationalities by the way. The scene is an epitome of the world. Here crouches a Chinese mendicant, there glides an Italian image-vender; a Swedish sailor is hard pressed by a smoking Cuban, and a Hungarian officer is flanked by a French loiterer; here leers a wanton, there moans a waif; now passes an Irish funeral procession, and again long files of Teutonic "Turners"; the wistful eyes of a beggar stare at the piles of gold in the money-chan-

ger's show-window; a sister of charity walks beside a Jewish Rabbi; then comes a brawny negro, then a bare-legged Highlander; figures such as are met in the Levant; school-boys with their books and lunch-boxes, Cockneys fresh from Piccadilly, a student who reminds us of Berlin, an American Indian in pantaloons; a gaunt Western, a keen Yankee, and a broad Dutch physiognomy alternate; flower-venders, dog-pedlers, diplomates, soldiers, dandies, and vagabonds, pass and disappear; a firemen's procession, fallen horse, dead-lock of vehicles, military halt, or menagerie caravan, checks momently the advancing throng; and some beautiful face or elegant costume looms out of the confused picture like an exquisite vision; great cubes of lake crystal glisten in the ice-carts hard by blocks of ebon coal from the forests of the primeval world; there a letter-carrier threads his way, and here a newsboy shouts his extra; a milk-cart rattles by, and a walking advertisement stalks on; here is a fashionable doctor's gig, there a mammoth express-wagon; a sullen Southerner contrasts with a grinning Gaul, a darkly-vested bishop with a gayly-attired child, a daintily-gloved belle with a mud-soiled drunkard; a little shoe-black and a blind fiddler ply their trades in the shadow of Emmet's obelisk, and a toy-merchant has Montgomery's mural tablet for a background; on the fence is a string of favorite ballads and popular songs; a mock auctioneer shouts from one door, and a silent wax effigy gazes from another. Pisani, who accompanied Prince Napoleon in his yacht-voyage to America, calls Broadway a bazaar made up of savagery and civilization, a mile and a half long; and M. Fisch, a French *pasteur*, was surprised at the sight of palaces six or seven stories high devoted to commerce and *les figures fines et gracieuses, la démarche légère et libre des femmes, les allures vives de toute la population.* The shopkeepers are urbanely courteous, says one traveller. "Horses and harness are fine, but equipages inferior," observes another ; while a third remarks, after witnessing the escapade of vehicles in Broadway : " American coachmen are the most adroit in the world."

It has been said that a Paris *gamin* would laugh at our *fêtes;* and yet, if such a loyal custodian as one of the old sacristans we meet abroad, who has kept a life-vigil in a famous cathedral, or such a vigilant chronicler as was Dr. Gemmelaro, who for years noted in a diary the visitors to Ætna, and all the phenomena of the volcano, — *if* such a fond sentinel were to have watched, even for less than a century, and recorded the civic, military, and industrial processions of Broadway, what a panoramic view we should have of the fortunes, development, and transitions of New York! The last of the cocked-hats would appear with the final relics of Dutch and Quaker costume ; the celebration of the opening of the Erie Canal would seem consummated by the festivals that signalized the introduction of Croton, and the success of the Atlantic Telegraph ; the funeral *cortège* of Washington would precede that of scores of patriots and heroes, from Hamilton and Lawrence to John Quincy Adams and General Wadsworth ; Scott would reappear victorious from Mexico, Kossuth's plumed hat wave again to the crowd, grim Jackson's white head loom once more to the eager multitude, and Lafayette's courteous greetings win their cheers ; St. Patrick's interminable line of followers would contrast with the robes and tails of the Japanese, — the lanterns of a political battalion, with the badges of a masonic fraternity, — the obsolete uniform of the " Old Continentals," with the red shirts of the firemen and the miniature banners of a Sunday-school phalanx, — the gay citizen soldiers who turned out to honor Independence or Evacuation Day, with the bronzed and maimed veterans bringing home their bullet-torn flags from the bloody field of a triumphant patriotic war, — the first negro regiment raised therefor cheerily escorted by the Union League

Club, with the sublime funeral train of the martyred President. Including party demonstrations, popular ovations, memorable receptions and obsequies, — Broadway processions, historically speaking, uniquely illustrate the civic growth, the political freedom, the cosmopolitan sympathies, and the social prosperity of New York.

The mutations and ameliorations of Broadway are singularly rapid. It is but a few years since the eye of the passenger therein often caught sight of pleasant domestic nooks, — bulbs in bloom, a canary, gold-fish, or a graceful head bent over a book or crochet-work, at the cheerful window, — where now iron fronts and plate-glass of enormous size proclaim the prosperous warehouse. One of those sudden and sweeping conflagrations, which so frequently make a breach in the long line of edifices, destroyed within a few months the tall white walls of the American Museum, with its flaring effigies of giants, dwarfs, and monsters, and its band of musicians in the balcony, so alluring to the rustic visitor. The picturesque church of St. Thomas and the heavy granite façade of the Stuyvesant Institute, the " Tabernacle," the Art-Academy, and the Society Library buildings have given way to palaces of trade, and been transferred to the indefinitely extensive region of " up town." Stewart's lofty marble stores redeemed the character of the east side, long neglected in favor of the more crowded and showy opposite walk ; and his example has been followed by so many other enterprising capitalists, that the original difference, both of aspect and prestige, has all but vanished.

Among the most noticeable of the later features are the prevalence of flower-venders, and the increase of beggars ; as well as the luxurious attractiveness of the leading confectioners' establishments, which, in true American eclectic style, combine the Parisian café with the London pastry-cooks and the Continental restaurant. — delectable rendezvous of women who lunch extravagantly. Another and more refined feature is the increase of elegant Art stores, where Gerome's latest miracle of Oriental delineation, a fresh landscape of Auchenbach, or a naive gem by Frere, is freely exposed to the public eye, beside new and elaborate engravings, and graphic wargroups of Rogers, or the latest crayon of Darley, sunset of Church, or rockstudy by Haseltine. These free glimpses of modern Art are indicative of the growing taste for and interest therein among us. Pictures were never such profitable and precious merchandise here, and the fortunes of artists are different from what they were in the days when Cole used to bring his new landscape to town, deposit it in the house of a friend, and personally call the attention thereto of the few who cared for such things, and when the fashionable portrait-painter was the exclusive representative of the guild in Gotham.

The Astor House was the first of the large hotels on Broadway; and its erection marks a new era in that favorite kind of enterprise and entertainment of which Bunker's Mansion House was so long the comfortable, respectable, and home-like ideal. Yet it is noteworthy that inns rarely have or keep a representative character with us, but blend popularity with fashion, as nowhere else. One may be associated with Rebeldom, another with trade; this be frequented by Eastern, and that by Western travellers; and nationalities may be identified with certain resorts. But the tendency is towards the eclectic and homogeneous; individuality not less than domesticity is trenched upon and fused in these extravagant caravanseries; and there is no fact more characteristic of the material luxury and gregarious standard of New York life, than that the only temple erected to her patron saint is a marble tavern!

Broadway has always had its eccentric or notable *habitués*. The Muse of Halleck, in her palmy days, immortalized not a few; and many persons still recall the "crazy poet Clarke," the

"Lime-Kiln man," the courteous and venerable Toussaint, — New York's best "image of God carved in ebony," — tall "gentleman George" Barrett, and a host of "familiar faces" associated with local fame or social traits. The representative clergy, physicians, lawyers, merchants, editors, politicians, bards, and beauties, "men about town," and actors, were there identified, saluted, and observed; and of all these, few seemed so appropriately there as the last; for often there was and is a melodramatic aspect and association in the scene, and Burton, Placide, or the elder Wallack walked there with a kind of professional self-complacency. Thackeray, who had a quick and trained eye for the characteristic in cities, delighted in Broadway, for its cheerful variety, its perpetual "comedy of life"; the significance whereof is only more apparent to the sympathetic observer, because now and then through the eager throng glides the funeral car to the sound of muffled drums, the "Black Maria" with its convict load, or the curtained hospital litter with its dumb and maimed burden. And then, to the practised frequenter, how, one by one, endeared figures and faces disappear from that diurnal stage! It seems but yesterday since we met there Dr. Francis's cheering salutation, or listened to Dr. Bethune's and Fenno Hoffman's genial and John Stephens's truthful talk, — watched General Scott's stalwart form, Dr. Kane's lithe frame, Cooper's self-reliant step, Peter Parley's juvenile cheerfulness, — and grasped Henry Inman's cordial hand, or listened to Irving's humorous reminiscence, and met the benign smile of dear old Clement Moore. As to fairer faces and more delicate shapes, — to encounter which was the crowning joy of our promenade, — and "cheeks grown holy with the lapse of years," memory holds them too sacred for comment. "Passing away" is the perpetual refrain in the chorus of humanity in this bustling thoroughfare, to the sober eye of maturity. The never-ending procession, to the sensitive and the observant, has also infinite degrees of language. Some faces seem to welcome, others to defy, some to lower, and some to brighten, many to ignore, a few to challenge or charm, — as we pass. And what lessons of fortune and of character are written thereon, — the blush of innocence and the hardihood of recklessness, the candid grace of honor and the mean deprecatory glance of knavery, intelligence and stupidity, soulfulness and vanity, the glad smile of friendship, the shrinking eye of fallen fortune, the dubious recognition of disgrace, the effrontery of the adventurer, and the calm, pleasant bearing of rectitude, — all that is beautiful and base in humanity, gleams, glances, and disappears as the crowd pass on.

Richard Cobden, when in New York, was caught and long detained in a mesh of drays and carriages in Broadway, and he remarked that the absence of passionate profanity among the carmen and drivers, and the good-natured patience they manifested, were in striking contrast with the blasphemous violence exhibited in London under like circumstances; and he attributed it to the greater self-respect bred in this class of men here by the prospect and purpose of a higher vocation. It is curious to observe how professional are the impressions and observations of Broadway pedestrians. Walk there with a portrait-painter, and he will infer character or discover subjects of art in every salient physiognomy. The disparities of fortune and the signs of depravity will impress the moralist. The pictorial effects, the adventurous possibilities, the enterprise, care, or pastime of the scene, elicit comments in accordance with the idiosyncrasies or aptitudes of the observer. What gradations of greeting, from the curt recognition to the hilarious salute! What variety of attraction and repulsion, according as your acquaintance is a bore or a beauty, a benefactor or a bankrupt! The natural language of "affairs," however, is the predominant expression. From the days of Rip Van Dam to those of John Pintard, it is as a com-

mercial city that New York has drawn both her rural and foreign population. And her chief thoroughfare retains the distinctive aspect thereof, as the extension of the city has eliminated therefrom all other social elements, — fashion being transferred to the Fifth Avenue, indigence to the Five Points, and equipages to the Central Park. Police reports abound with the ruses and roughnesses of metropolitan life, as developed in the most frequented streets, where rogues seek safety in crowds. A rheumatic friend of ours dropped a guinea in the Strand, and, being unable to stoop, placed his foot upon the coin, and waited and watched for the right man to ask to pick it up for him. He was astonished at the difficulty of the choice. One passer was too elegant, another too abstracted, one looked dishonest, and another haughty. At last he saw approaching a serious, kindly-looking, middle-aged loiterer, with a rusty black suit and white cravat, — apparently a poor curate taking his "constitutional." Our friend explained his dilemma, and was assured, in the most courteous terms, that the stranger would accommodate him with pleasure. Very deliberately the latter picked up the guinea, wiped it carefully on his coat-sleeve, and transferred it to his vest-pocket, — walking off with a cheerful nod. Indignant at the trick, the invalid called out "Stop, thief!" The rascal was chased and caught, and, when taken to the police office, proved to be Bristol Bill, — one of the most notorious and evasive burglars in London. Many like instances of false pretences are traditional in Broadway, — where there are sometimes visible scenic personages, like a quack doctor whose costume and bearing were borrowed from Don Pasquale, and Dr. Knickerbocker in the elegant and obsolete breeches, buckles, and cocked hat of the olden time.

A peculiar hardihood and local wit are claimed for what are called the B'hoys. A cockney, in pursuit of knowledge under difficulties, was walking up Broadway with the hospitable citizen to whose guidance he had been specially commended by a London correspondent.

"I want," said the stranger, "to see a b'hoy, — a real b'hoy."

"There 's one," replied his companion, pointing to a strapping fellow, in a red shirt and crush hat, waiting for a job at the corner.

"Ah, how curious!" replied John Bull, examining this new species with his double eye-glass, — "very curious; I never saw a real b'hoy before. I should like to hear him speak."

"Then, why don't you talk to him?"

"I don't know what to say."

"Ask him the way to Laight Street."

The inquisitive traveller crossed the street, and, deferentially approaching the new genus, lisped, "Ha — ah — how d' do, ha? I want to go to Laight Street."

"Then why in hell don't you go?" loudly and gruffly asks the b'hoy.

Cockney nervously rejoined his friend, saying, "Very curious, the Broadway b'hoys!"

To realize the extent and character of the Celtic element in our population, walk down this thronged avenue on a holiday, when the Irish crowd the sidewalks, waiting for a pageant; and all you have ever read or dreamed of savagery will gleam, with latent fire, from those myriads of sullen or daredevil eyes, and lurk in the wild tones of those unchastened voices, as the untidy or gaudily dressed and interminable line of expectants, flushed with alcohol, yield surlily to the backward wave of the policeman's baton. The materials of riot in the heart of the vast and populous city then strike one with terror. We see the worst elements of European life cast upon our shore, and impending, as it were, like a huge wave, over the peacefulness and prosperity of the nation. The corruptions of New York local government are explained at a glance. The reason why even patriotic citizens shrink from the primary meetings whence spring the practical issues of municipal rule is easily understood; and the absolute necessity of a reform in the legislative machinery, whereby property and character may find adequate representation, is brought home to the most careless observer of Broadway phenomena. But it is when threading the normal procession therein that distrust wanes, in view of so much that is hopeful in enterprise and education, and auspicious in social intelligence and sympathy. It may be that on one of our bright and balmy days of early spring, or on a cool and radiant autumnal afternoon, you behold, in your walk from Union Square to the Battery, an eminent representative of each function and phase of high civilization; — wealth vested in real estate in the person of an Astor, peerless nautical architecture in a Webb; the alert step and venerable head of the poet of nature, as Bryant glides by, and the still bright eye of the poet of patriotism and wit, as Halleck greets you with the zest of a rural visitor refreshed by the sight of "old, familiar faces"; anon comes Bancroft, a chronicler of America's past, yet moving sympathetically through living history the while; Verplanck, the Knickerbocker Nestor, and the gentlemen of the old school represented by Irving's old friend, the companionable and courteous Governor Kemble; pensive, olive-cheeked, sad-eyed Hamlet, in the person of Edwin Booth, our native histrionic genius; Vandyke-looking Charles Elliot, the portrait-painter; Paez, the exiled South American general; Farragut, the naval hero; Hancock, Hooker, Barlow, or some other gallant army officer, — volunteer heroes, maimed veterans of the Union war; merchants, whose names are synonymous with beneficence and integrity; artists, whose landscapes have revealed the loveliness of this hemisphere to the Old World; women who lend grace to society and feed the poor; men of science, who alleviate, and of literature, who console, the sorrows of humanity; the stanch in friendship, the loyal in national sentiment, the indomitable in duty, the exemplary in Christian faith, the tender and true in domestic life, — the redeeming and recuperative elements of civic society.

MY HEATHEN AT HOME.

KICKING my "Dutch wife," * that comfortable Batavian device, to the foot of the bed, and turning over with a delicious stretch just as day began to dawn, I opened my eyes with a drowsy sense of refreshing favor, — a half-dream, mixed of burning and breeze, — and discovered old Karlee, my pearl of bhearers, † waiting in still patience on the outside of the tent-like mosquito curtain, punka in hand, and tenderly waving a balmy blessing across the sirocco-plagued sand of my slumber.

"Good morning, Karlee."

"*Salaam, Sahib-bhote-bhote salaam!*‡ Master catch plenty good isleep this night, Karlee hope."

"So, so, — so, so. But you look happy this morning; your eyes are bright, and your kummerbund § jaunty, and you sport a new turban. What's the good news, old man?"

"Yes, Sahib. Large joy Karlee have got, — happy *kismut*,|| — too much jolly good luck, master, please."

"Aha! I'm glad of it. None too jolly for my patient Karlee, I'll engage, — not a whit too happy and proud for my faithful, grateful, humble old man. And what is it?"

"By master's favor, one man-child have got; one fine son he come this night, please master's graciousness."

"A son — your wife! — what, you, Karlee, *you?*"

"Please master's pardon, no, — Karlee wife, no; Karlee daughter, Karlee ison-in-law, one man-child have catch this night, by Sahib's merciful goodness."

"So! your daughter and her husband, the young kitmudgar,¶ they that were married last year. Good! let us exalt our horn, let us glorify ourselves; for is it not written, 'By a son a man shall obtain victory over all people; by a son's son he shall enjoy immortality; and by a son's son's son he shall reach the solar abodes'? Verily it is pleasant to have a boy-butcha in the house, — the heir and lord. So we will even make merry to-day; to-day we will take holiday. Let the buttons wait, and the beard go awry; send the barber away, and tell the tailor to come to-morrow; for one day Sahib, the master of earth, abdicates in favor of *Puttro*, the 'Deliverer from Hell,' the true king for every pious Hindoo. And here are some rupees to buy him a happy horoscope with, and to pay the *gooroo* * for a good strong charm, warranted to avert the Evil Eye."

"Ah! Master's bountiful favor too much compassion have, — too much pitiful munif—"

"That's all right, old man. Salaam now; and good luck to the baby."

Now here, thought I, is a chance to observe my pagan at home, under the most favorable circumstances. Karlee will devote the occasion to the domestic felicities; he will spread holiday fare, and there will be neighborly congratulations, and a hospitable relaxation in the family of the orthodox heathen rigor. I will make a "surprise party" of myself, and on the recommendation of a string of corals for the new butcha I'll catch him in the very dishabille of his Hindooism. And I did.

I had often heard that Karlee lived well, and that his household enjoyed substantial comfort in a degree notably superior to the general circumstances of his class. With eminent intelligence and devotion he had served for more than forty years various American gentlemen residing in Calcutta, by

---

* A long, round, narrow bolster, stuffed with very light materials (often with paper), and not for the head, but embraced in the arms, so as to help the sleeper to a cool and comfortable posture.
† Body-servants.
‡ A salutation of particular respect and well-wishing.
§ Waistband.
|| Destiny, fortune.   ¶ A table-servant.

* A spiritual teacher.

whom, in his neat-handedness, he was esteemed a sort of he-Phillis; and for his housewifely dusting of books and furniture, his orderly keeping of drawers and trunks, his sharp eye to punkas and mosquito-nets, and his exacting discipline of sweepers and messengers, barbers, tailors, and washermen, he had been rewarded with generous buksheesh over and above his stipulated wages, which were liberal; so that among bhearers he was distinguished for respectability, by income as well as influence, and represented the best society. Between his own savings and those of his wife, — who, as an *ayah*, or nurse, in an English family high in the Civil Service, was extravagantly prized for her fidelity, skill, and patience, — Karlee had laid up a little fortune of ten thousand rupees; but that was partly by dint of a clever speculation now and then in curiosities and choice presents, which he disposed of among those of his American or English patrons who happened to be homeward bound. As it is not permitted to a bhearer to engage directly in trade, these neat little transactions were in all cases shrewdly managed by a friend of Karlee's, a smart *sircar*,* in the employ of a *banyan*,† the bhearer resting strictly in the background, a silent partner, and limiting his co-operation to the prompt furnishing of capital, which consisted not of rupees merely, but of many a cunning hint as well, as to the tastes, ways, and weaknesses of his customers. It was a mutual understanding: we knew of Karlee's interest in these sentimental "operations," and we openly patronized him; he knew which of us had wives, and which sweethearts, across the black water, and he mysteriously patronized us. On that subject my heathen was always at home; and so it happened, by a happy dispensation of cause and effect, that at home he lived like a gentleman.

Through narrow, dingy miles of scrambling bazaar, redolent of all the unfragrances of that dusty, sweaty,

greasy, jabbering quarter, I rolled in my light buggy, behind a nimble Arab mare, to a suburban retreat on the eastern skirt of the Black Town, where, just beyond a cluster of mean huts of the *sooa-logue*, the low laboring rabble, I found Karlee's genteel abode, and was refreshed by the contrast it presented to the hovel of his next neighbor, whose single windowless apartment, and walls of alternate rows of straw and reeds, plastered with mud, proclaimed most unpicturesquely the hard fate of him who springs from the soles of Brahma's feet. Karlee's walls were of solid clay of substantial thickness. His floor was raised a foot or two above the ground, and there was a neatly thatched roof over all, swelling out in an elongated dome, and oddly resembling an inverted boat. As in the rural districts, Karlee had fenced in his privacy with a thick hedge of clipped bamboo surmounting a quadrangular embankment. Before the grateful porch two beautiful tamarind-trees and a palm bestowed their kindly shade, and in the hedge the bamboos, with their golden stems and bright green leaves, rustled cheerfully.

On the other side of the road, and shyly retired from it in a close bamboo covert, dwelt Karlee's partner in the curiosity and general fancy line, the sharp sircar, with whom (both being *soodras*,* and of the same sect) his social relations were intimate and free. The sircar, having thriven under the patronage of more than one rich and liberal *baboo*,† to whose favor he had recommended himself by his business alertness and his ever-politic compliance, had attained unto the honor of a brick house of two stories, plastered and whitewashed without and within, with a flat roof, having a low parapet, and laid with a rain-proof composition of clay and lime. Though his stairs are narrow, his veranda is commodious; and when he shall have made his fortune in the curiosity and general fancy

---

* Writer, clerk.
† Banker, merchant in foreign trade.

* The fourth caste — originally laborers.
† A native gentleman, of wealth, education, and influence.

line, he will have wings, with a central
area open to the sky, and a double veranda with a lattice. Then, his accommodations being sufficiently enlarged,
the proudest wish of his heart shall be
gratified in the reunion of his entire
family — children and grandchildren,
even uncles and aunts, nephews and
nieces — under the same roof.

As I drove up to Karlee's hedge, and,
tossing the reins to my *syce,* * passed
under the tamarind-trees to the little
porch, the old man came out to meet
me with unwonted precipitation ; and,
although he maintained with admirable
presence of mind that imperturbable
gravity, that tranquil, expectant self-
possession, which is the study of a
Hindoo's life, and to which he gives all
his mind from the time when he first
begins to have any, ever solicitous to
be master of himself though China
fall, it was not difficult on this occasion
to detect in the fluttering lights and
shades of his countenance an expression mixed of astonishment, gratification, and confusion, very natural to a
poor bhearer who had never before been
taken by a Sahib in the very bosom of
his family. There was something at
once pitiful and comical in the subdued " fidget " with which, applying his
joined palms to his forehead, and lowly louting, he made his most obsequious salaam again and again.

" Master have command for Karlee ?
Any wrong thing happen, master ?
Dhobee † come ? *Mehtur* ‡ not sweep
room ? *Punka-wallah* § run away ?
Sahibs make visit ? *Kitmudgar* not—"

" No, no ; everything all right and
proper. I have come to bring good
wishes and a lucky eye to all this house,
and a small *salaamee,* a pretty gift, for
the new *Suntoshum,* — the jewel that
hangs on its mother's bosom."

" Ah ! master make slave too much
happy honor. Master's pitiful graciousness all same *Barra Lard Sahib* "
(the Governor-General). " Poor, foolish bhearer kiss master's feet."

" Well, another time for that. Lead

the way now, and let me make my salaam to your coolest mat and your
largest punka, for I am hot and tired."

" S'pose Sahib like, *Belatta pawnee*
have got ? "

" *Acha ; Belatta pawnee lou.*" *

Here, indeed, was a wide stride in the
direction of refinement and Evangel-
ism ! Soda-water in a bhearer's house !
Karlee had not served the Sahibs, and
observed " Young Bengal " baboos, in
vain. From *Belatta pawnee* to Isherry-
shrob and Simpkin (sherry and champagne) is not far, and well does Young
Bengal know the way.

A quick glance, as I passed in, informed me that Karlee's house consisted of four rooms ; probably two sleeping apartments, one for the men and
another for the women, a kitchen, and
a common room for meals, family chats,
and visitors. Like all true Hindoo
houses, uncorrupted by the European
innovations which snobbish baboos
affect, it contained but few articles of
furniture, and those of the simplest and
most indispensable description, — nothing for luxury, nothing for show. To
the outfit of the poorest laborer's domicile he added little more than a white
cloth spread over checkered Chinese
matting, to stand for chair, table, and
bed ; a cushion or two to recline upon ;
a few earthen vessels of the better
quality, to hold rice or water ; a brass
lamp for cocoa-nut oil ; several more
primitive lamps rudely made of the
shell of the cocoa-nut ; an iron mortar
and pestle — foreign, of course — for
pounding curry ; a couple of *charpoys,*
or wooden cots ; a few brass *lotahs,*
or drinking-cups ; and two or three
hubble-bubbles. But the crowning
glories were a Chinese extension chair,
of bamboo and wicker, and quite a
pretty hookah, — both evidently dedicated to company occasions. These
were all that I could see in the two
rooms to which I was admitted, and
these were no doubt the very splendors
of Karlee's establishment. If he had
been a rich Anglicized baboo, he would

---

* Hostler and footman.   † Washerman.
‡ Sweeper.   § *Lit.* Fan-fellow.

* " Good ! Bring the Europe-water." — Bengali
for soda-water.

have had a profusion of hot, tawdry chairs, and a vulgar-gorgeous cramming of gilt-edged tables, sweaty red sofas, coarse pictures in overdone frames, Bowery mirrors, and Brummagem chandeliers.

Comfortably installed in the Chinese chair, and refreshed with the Belatta pawnee, I proceeded to take notes. Karlee had discarded his working dress for festal attire, — the difference being one of quality merely. Round his waist he wore a *dhotee* of coarse muslin, tight above, so as to form the *kummerbund*, or waistband, but thence falling in loose and not ungraceful folds down the legs to the ankles. Over his body another ample mantle, in no respect differing from the *dhotee* as to texture or color, was wrapped like a broad scarf, and carelessly flung over the shoulder in the fashion of a Highland plaid. In the "cold" season he would draw this over his head for a hood. These sheets of cloth are worn just as they come from the loom; needle or pin has never touched them, and they are held in place by tucking the ends under the folds.

Being a Hindoo gentleman of the old school, Karlee repudiated the head-dress at home; for the *puggree*, at least in its present form, was adopted from the Mohammedan conquerors, and is, historically, a badge of subjugation. So when he met me at the door his head was uncovered; but I had no sooner crossed the threshold than he made haste to don his flat turban, — reflecting, perhaps, that I had never seen him without it, and might resent his bare head as an indignity. Of course his feet were unshod. To have worn his sandals in my presence would have been a flagrant insult; but on the porch I espied those two queer clogs of wood, shaped to the sole of the foot, and having no other fastening than an impracticable-looking knob, to be held between the toes.

This is the orthodox Hindoo dress; but the costume for public occasions of many Hindoos of rank has been for a quarter of a century in a state of transi-

tion from Mohammedan to British. By way of turbans, loose trousers, Cashmere shawls, and embroidered slippers, they are marching on toward pantaloons, waistcoats, shoes and stockings, stove-pipe hats, and tail-coats. A baboo of superlative fashion, according to the code of Young Bengal, paid me a visit one day in a state of confirmed "pants" and "Congress gaiters"; and, on seating himself, he took off his turban and held it on his knee. I need hardly say that he was a fool and an infidel. And I have seen an intrepid buffoon of this class in an English shirt, which he wore over his pantaloons, and hanging down to his knees. But, after all, these clumsy desecrations are confined to a small minority of the population, if not strictly to that "set" which is brought most closely in contact with Europeans; such as a few native gentlemen in the Presidency capitals, some of the pleaders and principal *employés* of the higher courts, not a few of the teachers and pupils in the Anglo-Indian schools, and many of the native Christians.

Karlee's politeness, superior to that of the more servile bhearers, was a fair type of the pure Hindoo manners of that well-bred middle class which clings with orthodox conservatism to its dear traditions, and spurns as unconstitutional all upstart and dandy amendments of the old social and religious law. He had invariably one salutation for an equal, — the right hand gently raised, and the head as gently inclined to meet it; another, for what I may term a familiar superior (such as myself), — the hands joined palm to palm, and so applied twice or thrice to the forehead; and still other, and more and more reverential, ceremonials for *gooroos*, Brahmins, holy sages, and princes, — the brow touching the ground, or the whole body prostrated.

If it was an indispensable requirement of respect that he should leave his slippers at the door on entering any house, it was no less important that he should resume them on taking his leave. To have appeared in public with uncovered feet would have been a gross breach of propriety. Fine old Hindoo gentlemen, all of the olden time, find it difficult to express their mingled contempt, indignation, and regret for the innovation which substitutes the Cheapside shoe for the ceremonial slipper, or permits the wearing of the latter in a Sahib's office or drawing-room. It shows, they say, that the natives are losing their respect for the Sahibs. And yet the British authorities stupidly sanction it, even set the seal of fashion upon it, by allowing natives of rank, who visit Government House, to appear in the presence of the Governor-General, and the *élite* of the European society, in their slippers. The fact is, these impious disturbings of the established order of things are most shocking to the well-regulated heathen mind, to which no spectacle can be more monstrous than that of a Hindoo of good caste and old family performing with some arf-and-arf Cockney visitor a duet on the pump-handle, and directly afterward wreathing his apoplectic neck with flowers, and sprinkling his asthmatic waistcoat with rose-water. You see they both back " Young Bengal " in the Barrackpore races.

When Karlee visits his friend the sircar, he is scrupulous not to make his parting salaam until his host has given the customary signal. He waits to be dismissed, or rather to receive permission to withdraw. The etiquette supposes that his inclination is to prolong the enjoyment he derives from the society of so agreeable a gentleman; it is, therefore, not until rose-water has been presented to him, or betel-leaf, or sweetmeats, that he will venture to take his sandals and his leave.

The style of Hindoo politeness is formal and imperturbably grave, utterly devoid of heartiness or impulsiveness; and the cordiality which distinguishes the intercourse of American friends appears to the native gentleman boisterous and vulgar. I never saw Karlee laugh; and if I had happened to snatch him from sudden death by fire or water, I think he would have acknowledged the obligation with precisely the same mathematical salaam, or at most the same sententious obsequiousness, with which he accepted a buksheesh of a half-rupee; and yet in both good-humor and gratitude he was as cheerful and as worthy as the most giddy and gushing of damsels. But I must acknowledge there was something truly corpsy in the solemnity with which he would "lay out" a clean shirt. Even so, in the midst of all the jolly uproar of a mess dinner, our Kitmudgars would stand in grim deadliness at our backs, like so many executioners, only waiting for a sign from the ruthless Kousomar, who was just then horribly popping the champagne corks, to behead us, — each his own doomed Sahib.

No wonder Karlee was a gentleman; for the Vishnu Pooran was his Chesterfield, and he had its precepts by heart. "A wise man," he would say to the pert young Kitmudgars, as they bragged and wrangled, between their hubble-bubbles, on the back stairs, — "a wise man will never address another with the least unkindness; but will always speak gently, and with truth, and never make public another's faults. He will never engage in a dispute with either his superiors or his inferiors: controversy and marriage are permitted only between equals. Nor will he ever associate with wicked persons: half an instant is the utmost time he should allow himself to remain in their company. A wise man, when sitting, will not put one foot over the other, nor stretch forth his foot in the presence of a superior; but he will sit with modesty, in the posture styled *virasama*. Above all, he will not expectorate at the time of eating, offering oblations, or repeating prayers, or in the presence of any respectable person; nor will he ever cross the shadow of a venerable man or of an idol."

For those who imagine that polygamy is a popular institution in Hindostan, the answer of a Hill-man to a Mofussil magistrate should suffice. "Do you keep more than one wife?" "We can hardly feed one; why should we keep more ? " In fact, the privilege of maintaining a plurality of wives is restricted to a very few, — those only of the largest means and smallest scruples, — except in the case of *Kooleen* Brahmins, that superlative aristocracy of caste which is supposed to be descended from certain illustrious families who settled in Bengal several centuries ago. Wealthy Hindoos of low degree eagerly aspire to the honor of mixing their puddle blood with the quintessentially clarified fluid that glorifies the circulatory systems of these demigods, and the result is a very pretty and profitable branch of the Brahmin business, — *Kooleen* marrying sometimes as many as fifty of such nut-brown maids of baser birth, in consideration of a substantial dowry attached to each bride, and a solemn obligation, accepted and signed by the paternal Puddle, forever to feed at home her and her improved progeny. So the fifty continue to roost in the old paternal coops, while Kooleen, like a pampered Brahmapootra, struts, in pompous patronage, from one to the other, his sense of duty satisfied when he has left a crow and a cackle behind him. It is said that many fine fowls of the Brahmin breed, who do not happen to be Kooleens, complain of the monopoly.

So Karlee had but one wife, — the handy, thrifty ayah already mentioned. She was nine and he twelve years old when they were betrothed, and they never saw each other until they were married. A professional match-maker, or go-between, — female, of course, — was employed by the parents to negotiate terms and arrange the preliminaries ; and when horoscopes had been compared and the stars found all right, with a little consequential chaffering, the hymeneal instruments were " executed." There was no trouble on the score of caste, both families being soodra ; otherwise, the sensitive social balance would have had to be adjusted by the payment of a sum of money. When the skirts of the bride and bridegroom had been fastened together

with blades of the sweet-scented cusa grass, — when he had said, " May that heart which is thine become my heart, and this heart which is mine become thy heart," — when, hand in hand, they had stept into the seventh of the mystic circles, — Mr. and Mrs. Karlee were an accomplished Hindoo fact.

To the parents on both sides, the wedding was a costly performance. There were the irrepressible and voracious Brahmins to propitiate, the hungry friends of both families to feast for three days, the musicians and the nautch-girls and the *tamasha-wallahs* * to be bountifully buksheeshed ; and when the bridal palanquin was borne homeward, it was a high-priced indispensability that the procession should satisfy the best soodra society, —

> " With the yellow torches gleaming,
> And the scarlet mantles streaming,
> And the canopy above
> Swaying as they slowly move."

Karlee has assured me that neither his father nor his father-in-law, although both were soodras of fair credit and condition, ever quite recovered from the financial shock of that " awspidges okashn."

A Hindoo very rarely pronounces the name of his wife, even to his most intimate friends, — to strangers, and especially foreigners, never ; on the part of a native visitor it is the etiquette to ignore her altogether, and for the husband to allude to her familiarly is an unpardonable breach of decorum. When, therefore, Karlee, to gratify my friendly curiosity, led in the happy grandmother, I felt that I was the recipient of an extraordinary mark of respect and confidence, involving a generous sacrifice of prejudice. As she made her modest salaam, and, in the manner of a shy child, sank to the floor in the habitual posture of an ayah, I had before me the well-preserved remains of a Hindoo beauty, according to the standard of the Shasters, — a placid, reposeful woman, almost fat, with rather delicate features of Rajpoot fairness, the complexion of

* Showmen and puppet-dancers.

high caste, wealth, and ease, such as her less-favored sisters vainly strive to imitate with a sort of saffron *rouge*. Her expression was chaste and gentle, her voice dulcet; and to the practice of carrying light burdens on her head she was indebted for a carriage erect and graceful. On Broadway or Tremont Street, Mrs. Karlee would have passed for a very comely colored woman. If she was not like Rama, fair as the jasmine, or the moon, or the fibres of the lotos, neither had she, like Krishna, the complexion of a cloud. If she was not so delicate as that dainty beauty who bewitched the hard heart of Surajah Dowlah, and weighed but sixty-four pounds, neither did she reproduce the unwieldy charms of that Venus of one of the Shasters "whose gait was the gait of a drunken elephant or a goose." A prudent man, says the Vishnoo Pooran, will not marry a woman who has a beard, or one who has thick ankles, or one who speaks with a shrill voice, or one who croaks like a raven, or one whose eyebrows meet, or one whose teeth resemble tusks. And Karlee was a prudent man.

From the extravagant and clumsy complications, the stupid caprices and discords, and studious indecencies of our women's fashions, to the prudent simplicity, the unconscious poetry and picturesqueness and musically blended modesty and freedom of the good ayah's unchangeable attire, my thought reverts with a mingled sense of refreshment and regret. A single web of cloth, eight or nine yards long, having a narrow blue border, was drawn in self-forming folds around her shoulders and bosom, and hung down to her feet,—the material muslin, the texture somewhat coarse, the color white. No dressmaker had ever played fantastic tricks with it: it was pure and simple in its entireness as it came from the loom.

Other women, of the laboring class, and very poor, passed to and fro on the street, half naked, their legs and shoulders bare, and with only a piece of dirty cloth—blue, red, or yellow—around the loins and hips; while here and there some superfine baboo's wife floated past in her close palanquin, or sat with her children on the flat roof of her house, or peeped through her narrow windows into the street, arrayed in fancy bodice and petticoat,—Mohammedan fashion.

But the simplicity of Mrs. Karlee's attire began and ended with her drapery. Her ornaments were cumbersome, clumsy, and grotesque. On her arms and ankles were many fetter-like bands of silver and copper; rude rings of gold and silver adorned her fingers and great toes; small silver coins were twisted in her hair; and the naturally delicate outline of her lips was deformed by a broad gold ring, which she wore, like a fractious ox, in her nose. This latter vanity is as precious as it is ugly; in some of the minor castes its absence is regarded as a badge of widowhood; and for no inducement would the pious ayah have removed it from its place, even for an instant. Had it fallen, by any dreadful chance, the house would have been filled with horror and lamentation. The half-naked wife of my syce rejoices in a nose-ring of brass or pewter, and her wrists and ankles are gay with hoops of painted shell-lac; and even she stains her eyelids with lampblack, and tinges her nails with henna. Much lovelier was our pretty ayah in her maidenhood, when her dainty bosom was decked with shells and sweet-scented flowers, and her raven hair lighted up with sprays of the Indian jasmine, which first she had offered to Seeta.

But that reminds me that, when I approached her, and presented the string of corals, my small *salaamee*, and bade Karlee tell her that it was for the baby,—for she understood not a word of English,—and that I wished him happy stars and a good name, riches and honors, and a houseful of sons,—she uttered not a word; but with eyes brimming with gratitude, flattered to tears, by a sudden graceful movement she touched my foot with her hand and immediately laid it on her head,—and then, with many shy and mute, but eloquent salaams, retired. It is difficult to imagine such a woman scolding and slang-whanging as low Hindoo women do, accompanying with passionate attitudes and gestures a reckless torrent of words, and fitting the foulest action to the most scandalous epithet.

The wives of the native servants are generally industrious. This one, Karlee boasted, was a notable housewife. Before she went out to service as an ayah she had cleaned the rice, pounded the curry, cooked all the meals, brought water from the tank in earthen jars on her head, swept and scrubbed the floor, cultivated a small kitchen garden, "shopped" at the bazaar, spun endless supplies of cotton thread on a very primitive reel, consisting of a piece of wire with a ball of clay at the end of it, which she twirled with one hand while she fed it with the other; and every morning she bathed in the Hooghly, and returned home before daybreak. Sewing and knitting were unknown arts to her, — she had no use for either; and her washing and ironing were done by a hired dhobee.

True, it was not permitted to her to eat with her husband; when Karlee dined she sat at the respectful orthodox distance, and waited; and if at any time they walked out together, ayah must keep her legal place in the rear. Saith the Shaster, "Is it not the practice of women of immaculate chastity to eat after their lords have eaten, to sleep only after they have slept, and to rise from sleep before them?" And again, "Let a wife who wishes to perform sacred ablution wash the feet of her lord, and drink the water." Nevertheless, ayah exercised an influence over her husband as decided as it was wholesome; she did not hesitate to rebuke him when occasion required; and in all that related to the moral government of her children she was free to dispute his authority, and try parental conclusions with him, — kindly but firmly. As for "the tyrannical immuring of the Oriental female," the cruel caging of the pretty birds who are supposed to be forever longing and pining for the gossip of the *ghaut* and the bustle of the bazaar, the only fault she had to find with it was that she did not get enough of it. The well-trained Hindoo woman has been taught to regard such seclusion as her most charming compliment, and a precious proof of her husband's affection; to be kept jealously veiled from the staring world, is associated in her mind with ideas of wealth and rank, — it is the very aristocracy of fashion.

According to the Code of Menyu, "a believer in Scripture may receive pure knowledge even from a soodra, a lesson of the highest virtue even from a chandala, and a woman bright as a gem even from the lowest family." So if Karlee's wife, instead of being of the same social rank as himself, had come of basest caste, she would still have been a treasure. Soon after she had retired, she gently pushed into the room, to pay his respects to the Sahib, a shy little boy of five years, whom Karlee presented to me as the child of his only son, a bhearer in the service of an English officer stationed at Fort William. The mother had died in blessing her husband with this bright little puttro. In costume he was the exact miniature of his grandfather, except that he wore no puggree, and his hair was cut short round the forehead in a quaint frill, like the small boys one sees running about the streets in Orissa. His ankles, too, were loaded with massive silver rings, which noticeably impeded the childish freedom of his steps. When he has begun to understand what the word "wife" means, these must be laid aside. In his manners, likewise, little Karlee was the very tautology of his namesake with the gray moustache, — the same wary self-possession, the same immovable gravity and nice decorum. Like a little courtier, he made his small salaam, and through his grandfather replied to some playful questions I addressed to him, with good emphasis and discretion, without either awkwardness or boldness, and especially without a smile.

When I gave him a rupee, he construed it as the customary signal, and with another small salaam immediately dismissed himself.

Little Karlee must have taken lessons in deportment with his primal pap; and in India all good little boys, who hope to go to heaven when they die, keep their noses clean, and never romp or whistle. As to girls it matters less; the midwife gets only half price for consummating that sort of blunder; for when you are dead only a son can carry you out and bury you *dacent,* — no daughter, though she pray with the power and perseverance of the Seven Penitents, can procure you a respectable metempsychosis.

So far little Karlee had been lucky. This house, where he was born, was lucky, — no one had ever died in it. When his dear mother could not spin any more, they carried her to the Hooghly on a charpoy, and she had breathed her last on the banks of the sacred river. Besides, his grandfather had immediately stuck up a cooking-pot, striped with perpendicular white lines, on a pole at the side of the house; so *he* had never been in any danger from malicious incantations and the Evil Eye. His education had been begun on a propitious day, else he might have died or turned out a dunce. The very day he was born, a Brahmin — O *so* pious! — had hung a charm round his neck, and only charged grandpa fifty rupees for it; when he went to the bazaar with his grandmother he was always dressed in rags, to avert envy, and no one out of the family knew his real name except his gooroo; all the other boys, and the neighbors, called him Teencowry (three cowries *), — such a nice mean name against spells and cross-eyed people! Once a strange Melican Sahib had said, "Hello, Buster!" to him; but he was n't at all frightened, for his gooroo had taught him how to say a holy *mautra* † backwards; and when the Melican Sa-

* Little shells, used as coins by the poorest people to make the smallest change.
† Text.

hib passed on, he spat on his shadow and said it. Last week a lizard dropped on his foot, and yesterday he saw a cow on his right hand three times, — he had always been so lucky!

Now, time, place, and mood being favorable, I called for the company hookah, and, extending the long Chinese chair, smoked myself to sleep under the punka. My nap was a long one, and when I awoke there watched and waited Karlee, tenderly patient, with the fly-flapper.

In the hospitalities thus far so handsomely extended to me, the reader will recognize and appreciate an extraordinary display of liberal ideas, for which, however, considering the sound common sense of my affectionate old bhearer, I was not altogether unprepared; but when, his little grandson being gone, he conducted me into another room, to partake of what he humbly styled a *chota khana*, a trifle of luncheon, my astonishment exceeded my gratification. I doubt if such a thing had ever before happened in the life of a bhearer.

On the floor a broad sheet, of spotless whiteness, was spread, and beside it a narrow mattress of striped seersucker, very clean and cool, and with a double cushion at the head to support the elbow; on this my host invited me to recline. Here then were table and chair, but as yet the board was bare. Presently little Karlee reappeared, bringing a great round band-punka, formed of a single huge palm-leaf, and, standing behind my shoulder, began to fan me solemnly. Immediately there was a subdued and mysterious clapping of hands, and the old man, going to the door, received, from behind the red curtain which hung across it, a bowl of coarse unglazed earthenware, but smoking and savory, which he set before me, together with a smaller bowl of the same material, empty; and to my lively surprise these were followed by English bunns and pickles, a jar of chutney, a bottle of Allsop's ale, my own silver beer-mug, knives and forks, table and dessert spoons, fruit-knife, and napkin, — all from our quarters in Cossitollah, two miles away. By what conjuration and mighty magic Karlee had procured these from my kitmudgar without a *chittee*, or order, I have not yet discovered.

The tureen contained delicious Mulligatawney soup, of which, as Karlee well knew, I was inordinately fond; and as he opened the ale he modestly congratulated himself on my vigorous enjoyment of it.

After the soup came curried prawns, a very piquant dish, in eminent repute among the Sahibs, and a famous appetizer. Tonic, hot, and pungent as it is, with spices, betel, and chillies, it is hard to imagine what the torpid livers of the Civil Service would do without their rousing curry.

The curry was followed by a tender *bouilli* of kid, sauced with a delicate sort of onions stewed in ghee (boiled butter), and flanked with boiled rice, sweet pumpkin, and fried bananas, all served on green leaves. Next came pine-apple, covered with sherry-wine and sugar, in company with English walnuts and cheese; and, last of all, sweetmeats and coffee, — the former a not unpleasant compound of ground rice and sugar with curds and the crushed kernel of the cocoa-nut; the coffee was served in a diminutive gourd, and was not sweetened. Last of the last, the hookah.

And all these wonders had been wrought since the grateful ayah retired with the corals! But then the bazaar was close at hand, and in the sircar's house help was handy.

Whilst I kanahed * and smoked, Karlee, humbly "squatting" at my back, allowed me to draw from him all that I have here related of his house and family, and much more that I have not space to relate. Of course, he could not have shared the repast with me, — all the holy water of Ganges could never have washed out so deep a defilement, — but he accompanied my hookah with his hubble-bubble. The reader has observed that, although the viands were choice enough, they were

* Dined.

laid on the cheapest pottery, and even on leaves, that the plate from which I ate was of unglazed earthenware, and that the coffee was served in a gourd. This was in order that they might be at once destroyed. By no special dispensation could those vessels ever again be purified for the use of a respectable Hindoo; even a pariah would have felt insulted if he had been asked to eat from them; and if the knives and forks and spoons had not been my own, they must have shared the fate of the platters. But this prejudice must be taken in a Pickwickian sense, — it covered no objection simply personal to the Sahib. In some castes it is forbidden to eat from any plate twice, even in the strictest privacy of the family; and many natives, however wealthy, scrupulously insist upon leaves. All respectable Hindoos lift their food with their fingers, using neither knife, fork, nor spoon; and for this purpose they employ the right hand only, the left being reserved for baser purposes. In drinking water, many of them will not allow the *lotah* to touch the lips; but, throwing the head back, and holding the vessel at arm's length on high, with an odd expertness they let the water run into their mouths. The sect of Ramanujas obstinately refuse to sit down to a meal while any one is standing by or looking on; nor will they chew betel in company with a man of low caste. Ward has written, "If a European of the highest rank touch the food of a Hindoo of the lowest caste, the latter will instantly throw it away, although he may not have another morsel to allay the pangs of hunger"; — but this is true only of certain very strait sects. There are numerous sects that admit proselytes from every caste; but at the same time they will not partake of food, except with those of their own religious party. "Here," says Kerr, "the spirit of sect has supplanted even the spirit of caste," — as at the temple of Juggernath in Orissa, where the pilgrims of all castes take their *khana* in common.

At our quarters in Cossitollah even

this progressive Karlee will not taste of the food which has been served at our mess-table, though it be returned to the kitchen untouched. But at least he is consistent; for neither will he take medicine from the hand of a Sahib, however ill he may be; nor have I ever known him to decline or postpone the performance of this or that duty because it was Sunday, — as many knavish bhearers do when they have set their hearts on a cock-fight. To compound for sins one is inclined to, by damning those one has no mind to, it is not indispensable that one should be a Christian.

The amiable Mr. James Kerr, of the Hindoo College of Calcutta, has contrived an ingenious and plausible apology for the constitutional (or geographical) laziness of Bengalese servants. He says: "A love of repose may be considered one of the most striking features in the character of the people of India. The Hindoos may be said to have deified this state. Their favorite notion of a Supreme Being is that of one who reposes in himself, in a dream of absolute quiescence. This idea is, doubtless, in the first instance, a reflection of their own character; but, in whatever way it originated, it tends to sanctify in their eyes a state of repose. When removed from this world of care, their highest hope is to become a part of the great Quiescent. It will naturally appear to them the best preparation for the repose of a future life to cultivate repose in this." Therefore, if your kitmudgar, nodding behind your chair, permits his astonished fly-flapper to become a part of the great Quiescent, or if your punka-wallah, having subsided into a comatose beatitude, suddenly invites his compliant machine to repose in himself, in a dream of absolute stagnation, with the thermometer at 120° outside the refrigerator, you must not say, "Damn that boy, — he 's asleep again!" — but patiently survey and intelligently admire the spiritual processes by which an exalted sentient force prepares itself for the repose of a future life. But our reckless Karlee took no thought for the everlasting rest into which his soul should enter "when removed from this world of care," according to the ingenious psychological system of the amiable Kerr Sahib; for when he had anything to do, he kept on doing it until it was done, and when he caught the punka-wallah reposing in a dream of absolute quiescence, he bumped his head against the wall, and called him a *soos*, and a *banchut*, and a *junglee-wallah*.[*]

Though possessed of a lively imagination and all his race's sympathy with what is vast, though he saw nothing extravagant in the Hindoo chronology, nor aught that was monstrous in Hindoo mythology, Karlee yet served to illustrate the arguments of those who contend that Hindoos need not necessarily be all boasters, servile liars, and flatterers. He was not forever saying, "Master very wise man; master all time do good; master all time ispeak right." He never told me that my words were pearls and diamonds that I dropped munificently from my mouth. He never called me "your highness," or said I was his father and mother, and the lord of the world; and if I said at noonday, "It is night," he did not exclaim, "Behold the moon and stars!" He never tried to prove to me that the earth revolved on its axis once in twenty-four hours by my favor. "What! dost thou think him a Christian that he would go about to deceive thee?" No, he was as proudly truthful as a Rajpoot, as frank and manly as a Goorkah, and as honest as an up-country Durwan.

Good by, my best of bhearers. To the new baby a good name, and to the faithful ayah enviable enlargement of liver! *Khodâ rukko ki beebi-ka kullejee bhee itni burri hoga!*[†] — I owe thee for a day of hospitable edifications; and when thou comest to my country, thou shalt find *thy* Heathen at Home.

[*] Pig, sot, and jungle-animal.

[†] "God grant the lady a substantial liver!" — "the happiness and honors which should follow upon the birth of a male child being figuratively comprehended in that liberality of the liver whence comes the good digestion for which alone life is worth the living." — *Child-Life by the Ganges.*

A FRIEND.

A FRIEND!— It seems a simple boon to crave,—
    An easy thing to have.
Yet our world differs somewhat from the days
    Of the romancer's lays.
A friend? Why, *all* are friends in Christian lands.
    We smile and clasp the hands
With merry fellows o'er cigars and wine.
    We breakfast, walk, and dine
With social men and women. Yes, we are friends;—
    And there the music ends!
No close heart-heats,— a cool sweet ice-cream feast,—
    Mild thaws, to say the least;—
The faint, slant smile of winter afternoons;—
    The inconstant moods of moons,
Sometimes too late, sometimes too early rising,—
    But for a night sufficing,
Showing a half-face, clouded, shy, and null,—
    Once in a month at full,—
Lending to-night what from the sun they borrow,
    Quenched in his light to-morrow.
If thou 'rt my friend, show me the life that sleeps
    Down in thy spirit's deeps.
Give all thy heart, the thought within thy thought.
    Nay, I 've already caught
Its meaning in thine eyes, thy tones. What need
    Of words? Flowers keep their seed.
I love thee ere thou tellest me " I love."
    We both are raised above
The ball-room puppets with their varnished faces,
    Whispering dead commonplaces,
Doing their best to dress their lifeless thought
    In tinselled phrase worth naught;
Or at the best, throwing a passing spark
    Like fire-flies in the dark;—
Not the continuous lamp-light of the soul,
    Which, though the seasons roll
Without on tides of ever-varying winds,
    The watcher never finds
Flickering in draughts, or dim for lack of oil.
    There is a clime, a soil,
Where loves spring up twin-stemmed from mere chance seed
    Dropped by a word, a deed.
As travellers toiling through the Alpine snow
    See Italy below;—
Down glacier slopes and craggy cliffs and pines
    Descend upon the vines,
And meet the welcoming South who half-way up
    Lifts her o'erbrimming cup,—

So, blest is he, from peaks of human ice
    Lit on this Paradise ; —
Who 'mid the jar of tongues hears music sweet ; —
    Who in some foreign street
Thronged with cold eyes catches a hand, a glance,
    That deifies his chance,
That turns the dreary city to a home,
    The blank hotel to a dome
Of splendor, while the unsympathizing crowd
    Seems with his light endowed.
Many there be who call themselves our friends.
    But ah ! if Heaven sends
One, only one, the fellow to our soul,
    To make our half a whole,
Rich beyond price are we. The millionnaire
    Without such boon is bare,
Bare to the skin, — a gilded tavern-sign
    Creaking with fitful whine
Beneath chill winds, with none to look at him
    Save as a label grim
To the good cheer and company within
    His comfortable inn.

THE SINGING-SCHOOL ROMANCE.

FATHER sits at the head of our pew. In old Indian times they say that the male head of the family always took that place, on account of the possible *whoops* of the savages, who sometimes came down on a congregation like wolves on the fold. It was necessary that the men should be ready to rise at once to defend their families. Whatever the old reason was, the new is sufficient. Men must sit near the pew doors now on account of the *hoops* of the ladies. The cause is different, the effect is the same.

Father, then, sits at the head of the pew ; mother next ; Aunt Clara next ; next I, and then Jerusha. That has been the arrangement ever since I can remember. Any change in our places would be as fatal to our devotions as the dislodgment of Baron Rothschild from his particular pillar was once to the business of the London Stock Exchange. He could not negotiate if not at his post. We could not worship if not in our precise places. I think, by the fussing and fidgeting which taking seats in the church always causes, that everybody has the same feeling.

It was Sunday afternoon. The good minister, Parson Oliver, had finished his sermon. The text was — well, I can't pretend to remember. Aunt Clara's behavior in meeting, and what she said to us that afternoon, have put the text, sermon, and all out of my head forever. That is no matter ; or rather, it is all the better ; for when the same sermon comes again, in its triennial round, I shall not recognize an old acquaintance.

The sermon finished, we took up our hymn-books, of course. But the minister gave out no hymn. He sat down with a patient look at the choir, as much as to say, "Now, do your worst!" Then we understood that we were to be treated to an extra performance, not in our books. There had been a renewal of interest in the choir, and there was a new singing-master. We were to have the results of the late practisings and the first fruits of the new school. The piece they sung was that in which occur the lines, —

> " I 'd soar and touch the heavenly strings,
> And vie with Gabriel, while he sings,
> In notes almost divine ! "

We always, when we rise during the singing, face round to the choir. I don't know why. Perhaps it is to complete our view of the congregation, since during the rest of the time we look the other way, and, unless we faced about, should see only half. I like to peep at father, to discover whether he appreciates the performance. To-day he just turned his head away. Mother sat down. Aunt Clara looked straight ahead, and her old-fashioned bonnet hid her face ; but I could discover that something more than usual was working under her cap. I looked at every one of the singers, and then at the players, from the big bass-viol down to the tenor, and not a bit of reason could I perceive for the twitter the heads of our pew had certainly got themselves into. There 's a pattern old lady, Prudence Clark, presidentess of the Dorcas Society, — a spinster, just Aunt Clara's age,—a woman who knows everything, and more too. She sits in the pew before us. She turned her head and gave a sly peep at Aunt Clara. They both laughed in meeting. I know they did, and they can't deny it. I peeped round at the minister, and, if he did not laugh too, his face was scarlet, and he was taken with a wonderful fit of coughing. Such strange proceedings in meeting I never had seen. The minister, the deacon (father is a deacon), and the oldest members were setting us young folks a very bad example. But we tolerate anything in our good old parson. He was a youth when our old folks were young, and as to us

young folks, he remembers us longer than we do ourselves.

We were all home, and tea was over, — the early tea with substantials, as is the custom in the primitive districts of New England on Sunday afternoon. The double accumulation of dishes was disposed of ; for at noon we take a cold collation, doughnuts and cheese, and bread and butter, and we never descend to servile employments till after tea. Then many hands make light work. I suppose light work does not break the Sabbath, especially as it is done in our Sunday best, with sleeves tucked up, and an extra apron.

The laughing in church was the point upon which, as yet, we had obtained no satisfaction. Jerusha and I, in an uncertain hope that we should find out something in due time, were discussing the music. The particular point in debate was, why village choirs *will* astonish the people with pieces of music in which nobody can join them. We did not settle it, nor has anybody ever solved the riddle that I know of. We don't even know whether it comes under the ontological or psychological departments. (There, now ! Have n't I brought in the famous words that our new schoolmaster astonished us with at the teachers' meeting ? He need not think that Webster Unabridged is his particular field, in which nobody else may hunt.)

We were, as I said, discussing the music. Mother was flitting round, giving the final dust-off and brush-about after our early tea. Aunt Clara was sitting quietly at the window, pretending to read Baxter's "Saint's Rest." Jerusha and I tried to imitate the tune, and we did it, as well as we could, and I am sure we are not bad singers. Mother slipped out of the room just as we came to

> " And vie with Gabriel, while he sings."

She ran as if something had stung her, and she was making for the hartshorn or some fresh brook-mud. Aunt Clara's face laughed all over, and I said !

"Come, now, Aunt Clara, you are really irreverent. You began laughing in meeting, and you are keeping it up over that good book."

"Downright wicked," said Jerusha.

Now I am a Normal graduate, and Jerusha is not yet "finished." That will account for the greater elegance of my expressions. Aunt Clara paid no heed to either of us, but laughed on. The most provoking thing in the world is a laugh that you don't understand. Here was the whole Dorcas Society laughing through its presidentess, and Aunt Clara joining in the laugh in meeting, and aggravating the offence by stereotyping the smirk in her face. In came mother again, evidently afraid to stay out, and not liking for some reason to stay in. Again we tried the tune, and had just got to

"And vie with Gabriel, while he sings."

Up jumped mother again, stopping in the door, and holding up a warning finger to Aunt Clara. That gesture spurred my curiosity to the utmost point. As to my beloved parent's running in and out, *that* I should not have heeded. She is like Martha, careful of many things. She is unlike Martha, for she wants no assistance; but when the rest of us are disposed to be quiet, she *will* keep flitting here and there, and is vexed if we follow. If father is talking, and has just reached the point of his story, off she goes, as if the common topic were nothing to her. Father says she is a perturbed spirit. But then he is always saying queer things, which poor mother cannot understand. Aunt Clara seems to know him a great deal better. I wonder he had not taken to wife a woman like Aunt Clara. He would have taken *her*, I suppose, if she were not his own sister.

I besought mother, as she fled, to tell me what ailed aunty. "Don't ask *me*," she answered. "The dear only knows. As for me, I have given up thinking, let alone asking, what either your aunt or your father would be at." And away she went, perturbed-spirit fashion, and Aunt Clara laughed louder than ever.

Indeed, before she had only chuckled and silently shaken her sides; now she broke out into a scream.

"Well, I never!" she said. "That flounce of your mother's out of the room was certainly as much like old times as if the thing had happened yesterday."

"What had happened yesterday?" asked Jerusha and I, both in a breath.

"O, I *shall* die of laughing," said Aunt Clara.

"We shall die of impatience," said I, "if you don't tell us what you mean."

"No you won't. Nobody, especially no woman, ever yet died of unsatisfied curiosity. It rather keeps folks alive."

We very well knew that nothing would be made of Aunt Clara by teasing her. So Jerusha turned over the great family Bible, her custom always of a Sunday afternoon. Over her shoulder I happened to see that the good book was open at the first chapter of 1 Chronicles, "Adam, Sheth, Enosh, Kenan, Mahalaleel, Jared." Though her lips moved diligently, I am afraid she did not make much of it. As for me, I turned to the window, and studied the landscape. Father, his custom of a Sunday afternoon, walked down into the meadow, and the cattle came affectionately up to him. It was the salt in his broad pocket that they were after. "I might salt them of a Monday," he says, "but they kind of look for it, and it is n't kind to disappoint the creetur's on a Sabba'-day. And the merciful man is merciful to his beasts."

The flies droned and buzzed that summer afternoon. Jerusha nodded over the big Bible. Aunt Clara tried to look serious over the book she held. But the latent laugh was coursing among the dimples in her face, like a spark among tinder. I stole up behind, and, leaning over her shoulder, kissed her.

"O, yes," said aunty. "Fine words butter no parsnips, and fine kisses are no better."

Jerusha's head made an awful plunge, then a reactionary lift back, and then she opened her eyes and her mouth with such a yawn!

"Why, what a mouth!" I cried. "Master Minim would rejoice if you would thus open out in singing-school,

'And vie with Gabriel, while he sings.'"

Off went Aunt Clara in the laugh again, and this time till the tears came. We saw now that there was something in that line which provoked her mirth; but what Gabriel could have to do with her strange behavior we could not imagine, and were wisely silent.

"Girls," she said, as soon as she could speak for laughing, "I *will* tell you."

We knew she would, provided we were not too anxious to hear. So Jerusha turned over her leaf to the second chapter of 1 Chronicles, "Reuben, Simeon, Levi." I pretended to be more than ever interested out of doors. Aunt Clara took off her specs, closed her book, smoothed her apron, and began: —

"When I was a girl —"

Now that we knew the story was coming, we pretended to no more indifference. Once get aunty started, and, like a horse balky at the jump, she was good for the journey. So Jerusha shut the Bible, and we both sat down at her feet.

"Not too close, girls. It's dreadful warm."

Her face worked and her sides heaved with her provoking laugh, and we were half afraid of a disappointment. But there was no danger. She was by this time quite as ready to tell as we to hear.

"When I was a girl I went to singing-school. Dear me! how many of the scholars are dead and gone! There was my brother William, poor fellow! he died away off in Calcutty. And Sarah Morgan, she never would own to it that she liked him. But actions speak plainer than words. She never held up her head after. And she's dead now, too."

Aunt Clara's face — she *is* a dear old aunty — had now lost every trace of mirth. The golden sunset touched her fine head, and made her look so sweetly beautiful that I wondered why no

man had had the good taste, long ago, to relieve her of her maiden name. Perhaps she will tell us some day, and if she does, perhaps we will tell you. She sat two or three minutes, thinking and looking, as if she waited to see the loved and lost. There was a rustle, and she started from her revery. It was only mother, flitting into the room with one of her uneasy glances. But we were all so still and serious and Sabbath-like, that a look of relief came over her countenance. She vanished again, and through the window I saw her join her husband in the meadow.

"There, now, before they come in," said Aunt Clara. "When I was a girl, I went to singing-school. Dear me! But we will not think of the dead any more. There was one of the girls, — she thought she had a very good voice. But she never sings now."

"Why?" asked Jerusha.

"The dear knows. I suppose because she is married. Married people never sing, I believe. So, girls, if you would keep your voices, you must stay single. Well, there was one of the boys, he thought *he* had a good voice. And he never sings now either."

"Why?" said I.

"O, he's married too. So don't you get cheated into thinking you have mated a robin. He will turn out a crow, like as any way. I suppose they both did have good voices, and, for all that I know, they have still. They were the singing-master's especial wonders and his pattern pieces. He never was tired of praising them up to the skies, to mortify the rest of us into good behavior. She was the wonder for the girls' side and he for the boys', — two copies that we were to sing up to. I think they were a little proud of the distinction. They were kind of brought together by it, so that they did not see any harm at all in singing out of the same note-book."

"I suppose not," said Jerusha.

"Well, there was one girl in the school, — I dare say she *was* a giggling, mischief-making thing, for everybody said so — "

"Is she living now?" I asked.

"Yes, indeed."

"Does *she* sing now?" asked Jerusha.

"Well, — not much."

"Then," said I, "she must be married, too."

"No, she is not," said Aunt Clara, with a plaintive and very positive emphasis on the negative particle, — "no, she is not."

"Then why does she not sing?" I asked.

"Nobody will look over the same note-book with her," said Jerusha.

"O, you girls may have your own fun now," said Aunt Clara. "You will see the world with a sadder face by and by."

"Not if we look at it through your spectacles, aunty," I answered.

"Dear me; well, the Lord *has* been kind to me," said Aunt Clara, "if I am a spinster still. But we must make haste. The old folks are coming back."

"Old folks!!" I thought, and Aunt Clara is older than either of them. Father stopped and gave an ugly weed a whack with his cane.. Then he stooped and rooted it up, Sabbath-day though it was. I presume he considered it an ox in a pit, for the moment.

Aunt Clara continued: — "The same tune you were at this afternoon used to be a great favorite in our school. It's as old as the hills. I wonder if Israel did not let out his voice in it! And Sally, she would n't be behind *him*, I warrant you."

Jerusha and I exchanged glances.

"It happened, one evening, — and that's what I was laughing at this afternoon. You see, the singing-master, if the music was not going to suit him, would pull the class straight up in the middle of it, and make them begin again. The giggling girl that I was speaking of, she was always fuller of her own nonsense than of learning. This particular evening she was tempted of the Evil One to alter the words to her own purposes, just for the confusion of those close to her; and a

dreadful mess she would get them into. It was wrong, very wrong indeed," Aunt Clara added, with a face that was meant to be serious, while her voice laughed, in spite of her.

"On this evening, they were singing the very tune, as I told you. Something went wrong. The singing-master stopped his viol, and called out to the class to stop singing. But the heedless girl had got into mischief, and could not stop with the rest, or she did not hear, or she did not wish to. So on she went, all alone, right out, at the top of her voice: —

'And vie with *Israel*, while he sings,
In notes almost divine!'

"And there she broke down, and sat down, and, graceless hussy as she was, laughed as if she was mad. The truth was, that 'vying with Israel' was a byword with us. We were always teasing Sally about her vying with Israel, as she certainly did, while they sung out of the, same book, and thought a deal more of each other than they did of the music. Everybody took the joke, and such a time as there was! Prudence Clark, who turned round and looked at me in meeting to-day, she laughed the most spitefully of anybody, for she had a great notion of your fath — I mean of Israel. As to Israel and Sarah, if ever you did see two persons who did not know whether to stand still or to run, to cry or to laugh, they were the couple. The master, he tried to read us a solemn lecture; but he was so full of suppressed fun that he hugged his viol under his arm till one of the strings snapped. That gave the pitch, and we had a laughing chorus. All joined in, except Israel and Sarah. She pouted, and I do believe he grit his teeth." Here Aunt Clara gave herself up to the comic reminiscence, till her eyes filled again.

"Well, and what came of it all?" asked Jerusha.

"Why, it broke up the school for that season, and made town-talk for nine days. Parson Oliver, — he was a young man then, — he went for to give the mischievous girl a good talking to. He need n't have tried that; for he was too young to scold a young girl, full of mischief, and, though I say it that should n't say it, rather pretty."

"Why should n't *you* say she was pretty?" asked Jerusha.

"O, you hush! Well, the girl bent her head down, and a few stray tears came, for it *was* wicked, and she knew it. But before the water got head enough to fall from her eyes, she kind of thought that the young minister's voice was getting shaky, either with mirth or with sadness. To find out which, she slyly looked up, and both she and the minister laughed long and loud. So there was an end of the jobation that he meant to give her."

"How did you know all this?" said Jerusha. "Were you there?"

"I certainly was not far off."

"But Israel and Sarah," said I, now seeing through the whole affair, and understanding perfectly why father looked aside, and mother sat down, and Aunt Clara and Prudence Clark of the Dorcas Society exchanged glances, and the minister himself would have laughed in the pulpit, if he had not turned it off with a cough, — "but Israel and Sarah, how did they fare?"

"Why, Israel, he said that Sarah was just a pretty nobody, and Prudence Clark was a great deal more sensible, — for his part he never cared anything about Sarah. And Sarah, she declared that Israel was a hawbuck of a fellow, that no girl would think of when he was out of sight."

"It was too bad!" said Jerusha.

"*Too* bad!" I echoed.

"*Dreadful sus!*" said aunty, mocking our tone. "Never you fear, if two young simpletons are once caught, that a joke is going to separate them! And whenever you hear two people pretending to hate one another, you may get your wedding present ready for them. The folks did tease them though, too bad, and so they had it, back and forth. Stories never lose anything by carrying, especially the compliments between two quarrelling lovers. So it went on for about a month, when Israel, on his way to see Prudence Clark, who was sitting in her best, waiting for him, stopped to tell Sarah that he *never* said so and so. And Sarah said, *she* never said so and so. And they went into the house to finish their talk, and Prudence Clark was left lamenting. *I* know Israel came home very late that night."

"*You* know?" said Jerusha.

"And father's name is Israel," said I.

"And mother's name is Sarah," said my sister.

"Hush, hush; here they come," said Aunt Clara. "But I don't believe they would ever have found out their own minds if it had not been for me."

"And you were the giggling girl," said I.

"She's no better now," said my mother, as she entered the room, and readily guessed what we had been hearing up to Aunt Clara. Father walked up to Aunt Clara, and pinched her ears for her. What more he might have done I don't know, if Parson Oliver had not dropped in. We made quite a pleasant evening of it, and the old folks discussed the reminiscence in all its bearings. I like to hear old people talk. They come straight to the pith of a subject, especially if it is love and matrimony. And the more I hear them, the better I can realize the truth of the Old Virginia admonition, —

"Ole folks, ole folks, you better go to bed,
You only put the mischief in the young folks'
      head."

AUTUMN SONG.

IN Spring the Poet is glad,
　And in Summer the Poet is gay;
But in Autumn the Poet is sad,
　And has something sad to say:

For the wind moans in the wood,
　And the leaf drops from the tree;
And the cold rain falls on the graves of the good,
　And the cold mist comes up from the sea:

And the Autumn songs of the Poet's soul
　Are set to the passionate grief
Of winds that sough and bells that toll
　The dirge of the falling leaf.

THE FALL OF AUSTRIA.

THE great characteristic of aristocracies, according to their admirers, is prudence; and even democrats do not deny the soundness of the claim thus put forward in their behalf. They are cautious, and if they seldom accomplish anything brilliant, neither do they put everything to hazard. If they gain slowly, they keep long what they have. Did not Venice endure so long that, when she perished as a nation, within living memory, she was the oldest of great communities? And was she not the most perfect of all aristocratically governed nations? Was she not the admiration of those English republicans of the seventeenth century whose names are held in the highest honor wherever freedom is worshipped? Aristocracies have their faults, but they outlast every other kind of government, and therefore are objects of reverence to all who love order. The Roman Republic was aristocratical in its polity, and all that is great in Roman history is due to the ascendency of the Senate in the government; and when the Forum populace began to show its power, the decay of the commonwealth commenced, and did not cease till despotism was established, — the natural effect of the resistance of the many to the government of the few being the formation of the government of one. England's polity is, and for ages has been, aristocratical. Not even the passage of the Reform Bill materially lessened the power of the aristocracy; and the declaration of Earl Grey, the father of the measure, that it would be found the most aristocratical of measures, — as he was one of the most aristocratical of men, — does not seem so absurd now as it appeared four-and-thirty years since, when we note how difficult it now is to lower the franchise in Britain. The firmest government in Europe is that of England, in which property has greater influence than in that of any other nation. The conclusion drawn by aristocrats and their admirers is, that aristocracies are the most enduring of all the polities known to men, and that they are so because aristocrats are the most prudent and cautious of men. The governments they form and control wash and wear well, and bid defiance to what Bacon calls "the waves and weathers of time."

There is some truth in this. Aristocracies *are* cautious and prudent, and indisposed to risk present advantage in the hope of future gain. Therefore aristocratical polities often attain to great age, and the nations that know them attain slowly to great and firmly-placed power. Rome and Venice and England are striking examples of these truths. Yet it is not the less true that aristocracies sometimes do behave with a rashness that cannot be paralleled from the histories of democracies and despotisms. It has been the fortune of this age to see two examples of this rashness, such as no other age ever witnessed or ever could have witnessed. The first of these was presented in the action, in 1860 – 61, of the American aristocracy. The second was that of the Austrian aristocracy, in 1866. The American aristocracy — the late slavocracy — was the most powerful body in the world ; so powerful, that it was safe against everything but itself. It had been gradually built up, until it was as towering as its foundations were deep and broad. Not only was it unassailed, but there was no disposition in any influential quarter to assail it. The few persons who did attack it, from a distance, produced scarcely more effect adverse to its ascendency, than was produced by the labors of the first Christians against the Capitoline Jupiter in the days of the Julian Cæsars. Abolitionists were annoyed and insulted even in the course of that political campaign which ended in the election of Mr. Lincoln to the Presidency ; and not a few of the victors in that campaign were forward to declare, that between their party and the " friends of the slave " there was neither friendship nor sympathy. One of the most eminent of the Republicans of Massachusetts declared that he felt hurt at the

thought that his party could be suspected of approving the conduct of Captain John Brown at Harper's Ferry. Down to the spring-time of 1860, it required, on the part of the American slaveholding interest, only a moderate display of that prudence which is said to be the chief virtue of an aristocracy, to secure all they possessed, — which was all the country had to give, — and to prepare the way for such gains as it might be found necessary to make, as the American nation should increase in strength. But this prudence the slaveholders would not display. They annoyed and insulted the people of the Free States. They broke up the Democratic party, which was well disposed to do their work. They pursued such a course as compelled the great majority of the American people to take up arms against them, and to abolish slavery by an act of war. The effect was the fall of a body of men who certainly were very powerful, and who were believed to be very wise in their generation. It was impossible to attack them as long as they were true to their own interests, and they could fall only through being attacked. They made war on the nation, and the nation was forced to defend herself, and destroyed them. It is the most wonderful case of suicide known to mankind.

The Austrian aristocracy behaved almost as unwisely as the American aristocracy. As the Republic of the United States is a union of States, which in reality was governed by the slaveholders down to 1861, so is the Austrian Empire a collection of countries, governed by a few great families, at the head of which stand the imperial family, — the House of Austria, or, as it is now generally called, the House of Hapsburg-Lorraine. That aristocracy might have prevented the occurrence of war last summer, by ceding Venetia to Italy ; and that it did not make such cession early in June, when we know it was ready to make it early in July, but plunged into a contest which, according to the apologists for its terrible defeat, it was wholly unprepared to wage, speaks but poorly for its prudence, though that is claimed to be *the* virtue of aristocracies. The Austrian aristocrats behaved as senselessly in 1866 as the Prussian aristocrats in 1806, but with less excuse than the latter had. By their action they caused their country's degradation. From the rank of a first-rate power that country has been compelled to descend, not so much through loss of territory and population as through loss of position. For centuries the house of Austria has been very powerful in Europe, though the Austrian empire can count but sixty years. Rudolph of Hapsburg, the first member of his line who rose to great eminence, in the latter part of the thirteenth century, founded the house of Austria. While holding the imperial throne, he obtained for his own family Austria, Styria, Carinthia, and Carniola ; but it was not till several generations after his death, and in the fifteenth century, that the imperial dignity became virtually, though not in terms, hereditary in the Hapsburg line. For several centuries, down to the extinction of the office, there was no Emperor of Germany who was not of that family. Every effort to divert the office from that house ended in failure. The consequence was, that the house of Austria became the first of reigning families ; and at one time it seemed about to grasp the sceptre of the world. When the Empire ceased to exist, the Austrian empire, though of later creation than the French empire of Napoleon I., had that appearance of antique grandeur which has so great an effect on men's minds. It was looked upon as ancient because the imperial family really was ancient, and could trace itself back through almost twelve hundred years, to the sixth century, though in places the tracing was of the most shadowy character. It profited from the greatness of the Hapsburgs in the sixteenth, seventeenth, and eighteenth centuries, — a greatness which is among the most extraordinary things recorded in history. Should the history of royal marriages

ever be written in a manner proportioned to its importance, a large part of the work would have to be given to the marriages made by various princes of the house of Austria ; for those marriages had prodigious effect on the condition of the best portions of the human race, and in the sixteenth century it seemed that they were about to bring, not only most of Europe, but nearly all America, a large part of Asia, and not a little of Africa under the rule of one family, and that family by no means superior to that of Valois or the Plantagenets. The extraordinary luck of the house of Austria in turning marriage into a source of profit was early remarked ; and in the latter part of the fifteenth century, long before the best of the Austrian matrimonial alliances were made, Matthias Corvinus, the greatest of Hungarian kings, wrote a Latin epigram on the subject, which was even more remarkable as a prediction than as a statement of fact ; for it was as applicable to the marriage of Napoleon I. and Maria Louisa, and to that of Philip the Fair and Juana the Foolish, as it was to that of Maximilian and Mary.* It is from the Styrian line of the Austrian house that all princes of that house who have reigned for four centuries and upward are descended. Ernest, third son of that Leopold who was defeated and slain at the battle of Sempach by the Swiss, became master of the duchies of Styria, Carniola, and Carinthia. He was

---

* The following is the epigram of Matthias Corvinus : —

     " Bella gerant alii : tu felix nube !
     Nam quæ Mars aliis dat tibi regna Venus."

Which Mr. Stirling thus renders : —

" Fight those who will ; let well-starred Austria wed,
     And conquer kingdoms in the marriage-bed."

Some other hand has given the following translation, or rather amplification, of the epigram : —

     " Glad Austria wins by Hymen's silken chain
     What other states in doubtful battles gain,
     And while fierce Mars enriches meaner lands,
     Receives possessions from fair Venus' hands."

There would seem to be an end of these fortunate marriages, no member of the Austrian imperial family being now in condition to wed to much profit. The Emperor Francis Joseph, who is yet a young man, took to wife a Bavarian lady, said to be of extraordinary beauty, in 1854 ; and he has a daugh-

a pious prince, and made a pilgrimage to Palestine, after the superstitious fashion of his time. He was a quarrelsome prince, and kept himself in a state of perpetual hot water with his brother. He was an amorous and a chivalrous prince, and, having lost his first wife, he got him a second after a knightly fashion. Having heard much of the material and mental charms of the Princess Cymburga, a Polish lady who had the blood of the Yagellons in her veins, he went to Cracow in disguise, found that report had not exaggerated her merits, and, prudently making himself known, proposed for her hand, and got it. But Cymburga was not only very clever and very beautiful: she was a muscular Christian in crinoline, — for hoops were known in those days among the Poles, or might have been known to them, — and if they were, no doubt Cymburga, like American ladies of to-day, had the sense and taste to use them. She had such strength of fist that, when she had occasion to drive a nail into anything, she dispensed with a hammer; and she economized in nut-crackers, as some independent people do in the item of pocket-handkerchiefs, by using her fingers. One would think that Ernest would have hesitated to woo and wed a lady who was so capable of carrying matters with a high hand; but then he was a very strong man, and was surnamed "The Iron," so that he could venture where no other man

ter, who was born in 1856, the same year with the French Prince Imperial, whom she might marry, but that the two are children. Besides, marriages between French princes and Austrian princesses have turned out so badly on two memorable occasions, within less than a century, that even the statesmen of Vienna and Paris might well be excused if they were to think a third alliance quite impossible. The heir apparent to the Austrian throne is but eight years old. The Emperor's next brother, Ferdinand Maximilian, — well known in this country as Emperor of the Mexicans, — made a good marriage, his wife being a daughter of the late Leopold I., King of the Belgians. She has labored with zeal to found an imperial dynasty in Mexico, but the task is beyond human strength. The imperial system fell in Mexico on the same day that Richmond fell into the hands of General Grant. The fortunes of the Austrian prince and those of Mr. Davis were bound up together, and together they fell.

would have thought of going. This strong-handed as well as strong-minded couple, who were both paired and matched, must be taken as the real founders of that house of Austria which has been so conspicuous in the history of Christendom for almost four centuries, though they and their descendants built on the broad and solid foundations established by Rudolph of Hapsburg and his earlier descendants. Some authorities say that Cymburga brought into the Hapsburg family that thick lip — "the Austrian lip" — so often mentioned in history; but others call it the Burgundian lip, though the marriage between Maximilian (Cymburga's grandson) and Mary of Burgundy (Charles the Bold's daughter) did not take place till 1477; and the ducal Burgundian family was only a branch of the French royal line of Valois. It was no addition to the beauty of the imperial family, no matter to whom that family was indebted for it. It is certain that it appeared in the Emperor Frederick III., son of Ernest and Cymburga, and father of that Emperor who, when an archduke, married the Burgundian duchess, if such Mary can be called; for Menzel, who must have seen portraits of him, and who knew his history well, speaks of him as "a slow, grave man, with a large, protruding under-lip."

This Frederick was a singular character. He had the longest reign — fifty-three years — of all the German Emperors, and it may be said that he founded the house of Hapsburg, considering it as an imperial line. Yet he is almost invariably spoken of contemptuously. Menzel says that no Emperor had reigned so long and done so little. Mr. Bryce declares that under him the Empire sank to its lowest point. Even Archdeacon Coxe, who held his memory in respect, and did his best to make out a good character for him, has to admit "that he was a prince of a languid and inactive character," and to make other damaging admissions that detract from the excellence of the elaborate portrait he has drawn of him. There was something fantastical in his favorite pursuits, — astrology, alchemy, antiquities, alphabet-making, and the like, — which the men of an iron age viewed with a contempt that probably had much to do with giving him that character which he has in history, contemporary opinion of a ruler generally being accepted, and enduring. "A species of anagram," says the English historian of his family, "consisting of the five vowels, he adopted as indicative of the future greatness of the house. of Austria, imprinted it on all his books, carved it on all his buildings, and engraved it on all his plate. This riddle occupied the grave heads of his learned contemporaries, and gave rise to many ridiculous conjectures, till the *important* secret was disclosed after his death by an interpretation written in his own hand, in which the vowels form the initials of a sentence in Latin and German, signifying, ' The house of Austria is to govern the whole world.' " * Notwithstanding the archidiaconal sneer, Frederick III.'s anagram came quite as near the truth as any uninspired prophecy that can be mentioned. In little more than sixty years after the Emperor's death, the house of Austria ruled over Germany, the Netherlands, Naples, Sicily, the Milanese, Hungary, Bohemia, the Spains, England and Ireland (in virtue of Philip II.'s marriage with Mary I., queen-regnant of England), the greater part of America, from the extreme north to the extreme south, portions of Northern Africa, the Philippines, and some minor possessions ; and it really ruled, though indirectly, most of that part of Italy, outside of the territory of Venice, that had nominally an independent existence. Before Holland's independence was fully established, but after the connection with England had ceased, Portugal passed under the dominion of the

* We give the imperial anagram : —

A $^{\text{ustria}}_{\text{lles}}$ 　 E $^{\text{st}}_{\text{rdreich}}$ 　 I $^{\text{mperare}}_{\text{st}}$
　 O $^{\text{rbi}}_{\text{esterreich}}$ 　 U $^{\text{niverso.}}_{\text{nterthan.}}$

Spanish branch of the house of Austria, with all her immense American, African, and Asiatic colonial possessions. For years, Philip II. was more powerful in France than any one of her sovereigns could pretend to be. Frederick's prediction, therefore, came to pass almost literally, and was less an exaggeration than St. Luke's assertion that a decree went forth from Cæsar Augustus that all the world should be taxed. As Augustus was lord of nearly all the world that a man like St. Luke could consider civilized and worth governing, so might an Austrian writer of the sixteenth century declare that the Hapsburgs ruled over wellnigh all the world that could be looked upon as belonging to the Christian commonwealth, including not a little that had been stolen from the heathen by Christians.

It was by marriage that the Hapsburgs became so great in so short a time. Frederick III. married Eleanor, a Portuguese princess, whose mother was of the royal house of Castile. Portugal is not even of second rank now, and the Braganças are not in the first rank of royal families. But in the fifteenth century Portugal stood relatively and positively very high, and the house of Avis was above the house of Austria, though a king of Portugal was necessarily inferior to the head of the Holy Roman Empire. This marriage did not advance the fortunes of the Austrian family, though it connected them with three other great families, — the reigning houses of Portugal, Castille, and England, the Princess Eleanor having Plantagenet blood. But the son of Frederick and Eleanor, afterward the Emperor Maximilian I.,* married Mary of Burgundy in 1477,

* Mr. Bryce credits Maximilian I. with the founding of the Austrian monarchy. "Of that monarchy," he observes, "and of the power of the house of Hapsburg, Maximilian was, even more than Rudolph his ancestor, the founder. Uniting in his person those wide domains through Germany which had been dispersed among the collateral branches of his house, and claiming by his marriage with Mary of Burgundy most of the territories of Charles the Bold, he was a prince greater than any who had sat on the Teutonic throne since the death of

which "gave a lift" to his race that enabled it to increase in importance at a very rapid rate. Mary was in possession of most of the immense dominions of her father, which he had intended to convert into a kingdom, had he lived to complete his purpose. His success would have had great effect on the after history of Europe, for he would have reigned over the finest of countries, and his dominions would have extended from the North Sea to Provence, — and over Provence so powerful a sovereign would have had no difficulty in extending his power, — which done, his dominions would have been touched by the Mediterranean. Louis XI. of France got hold of some of Mary's inheritance; but the greater part thereof she conveyed to Maximilian. She died young, leaving a son and a daughter. The son was Philip the Fair, who in 1496 married Juana, daughter of Ferdinand and Isabella, king of Aragon, and queen of Castille, and heiress of the Spanish monarchy, which had come to great glory through the conquest of Granada, and to wonderful influence through the discovery of the New World, — events that took place in the same year, and but a short time before the marriage of the Austrian archduke and the Peninsular princess. This marriage, useful and brilliant as it was to the house of Austria, turned out bitterly bad to the parties to it, — and it is not an isolated case in that respect. Philip the Fair was a very handsome fellow, as became his designation, or rather whence his designation came ; but on the principle that " handsome is that handsome does," he was one of the ugliest of men. He was guilty of gallantry, the

weakness of kings, and of many of the sovereign people too. When living in Spain he had many amorous adventures ; and his wife, who had brought him so great a fortune that she thought she had an especial claim on his fidelity, became exceedingly jealous, and, being a *dague en jarretière* lady, as became one who was born to reign over Andalucia, killed her faithless husband, — not by stabbing him, but by giving him poison. This was in 1506, when husband and wife were but twenty-eight and twenty-four years old, and had been but ten years married. There were two sons and four daughters born of this marriage, all of whom made important marriages. The eldest son was the man whom Mr. Stirling calls "the greatest monarch of the memorable sixteenth century," — Charles V., Emperor of Germany, and the Spanish Charles I. He founded the Spanish branch of the house of Austria, the elder branch.[*] He married Isabella of Portugal, and their son was Philip II., who added Portugal to the possessions of the Austrian family, and one of whose wives was Mary Tudor, queen of England, the Bloody Mary of fire-and-fagot memory ; and Philip gladly would have placed Mary's sister Elizabeth in his half - vacant bed. The marriage of Philip and Mary was barren, and poor Mary's belief that a " blessed baby "

---

[*] The division of the house of Austria into two branches, which alone prevented it from becoming supreme in Europe, and over much of the rest of the world, took place in 1521. After the death of their grandfather, Charles and Ferdinand possessed the Austrian territories in common, but in 1521 they made a division thereof. Ferdinand obtained Austria, Carinthia, Carniola, and Styria, and, in 1522, the Tyrol, and other provinces. In 1531 he was chosen King of the Romans, which made him the successor of Charles as Emperor. How Charles came, not merely to consent to his election, but to urge it, and to effect it in spite of opposition, when he had a son in his fourth year, is very strange. The reasons commonly given for his course are by no means sufficient to account for it. Many years later he tried to undo his work, in order to obtain the imperial dignity for his son ; but Ferdinand held on to what he possessed, with true Austrian tenacity. Had Charles kept the imperial crown for his son, as he might have done, Philip's imperial position must have sufficed to give him control of the civilized world. He would have made himself master of both France and England, and must have rendered the Reaction completely triumphant over the Refor-

---

Frederick II. But it was as Archduke of Austria, Count of Tyrol, Duke of Styria and Carinthia, feudal superior of lands in Swabia, Alsace, and Switzerland, that he was great, not as Roman Emperor. For just as from him the Austrian monarchy begins, so with him the Holy Empire in its old meaning ends." (The Holy Roman Empire, pp. 343, 344.) Mr. Bryce's work is one of the most valuable contributions to historical literature that have appeared in this century, and great expectations are entertained from the future labors of one so liberally endowed with the historic faculty.

was coming has been matter for laughter for more than three hundred years. Had her agonizing prayers for offspring been heard, what a change would have been wrought in human destinies, even had the child lived to be no older than Edward VI.! The second son of Philip the Fair and Juana was Ferdinand, named from his maternal grandfather, Ferdinand the Catholic, king of Aragon. He was the founder of the German branch of the house of Austria, the younger branch, which has long survived the elder branch, though now it exists only in the female line, and really is the house of Lorraine. Ferdinand became Ferdinand I., Emperor of Germany, and he did far more than was done by his elder brother to keep up the character of his family for making much through marriage. In 1522, when but nineteen, he married Anne Yagellon, princess of Hungary and Bohemia, — a marriage that might not have proved very important, but that death came in and made it so, and also the births that came from it, as will presently appear. Charles and Ferdinand had four sisters, and they all four made great marriages, three of which were very useful to the Austrian house. The eldest of these ladies, Eleanora, was married to Emanuel, king of Portugal, — a man old enough to be her father, with some years to spare, —

mation. Fortunately, he failed to become Emperor, and during a portion of his time the imperial throne was occupied by the best of all the Hapsburg sovereigns, — the wise, the tolerant, the humane, and the upright Maximilian II., who was the last man in Europe likely to give him any aid in the prosecution of his vast tyrannical schemes. Besides, there was a sort of coolness between the two branches of the great family, that was not without its effect on the world's politics. Seldom has it happened that a more important event has occurred than the election of Ferdinand as King of the Romans. We are not to measure what might have been done by Philip II. as Emperor, by what was done by Charles V.; for Charles was a statesman, a politician, and, down to his latter years, when his health was utterly gone, he was no fanatic; but Philip was a fanatic only, and a fierce one too, with a power of concentration such as his father never possessed. Then the contest between the Catholics and the Protestants was a far more serious one in Philip's time than it had been in that of Charles, which alone would have sufficed to make his occupation of the imperial throne, had he occupied it, a matter of the last importance.

being sacrificed to the ambition of her brother Charles, for she was attached to the Count Palatine. Becoming a widow, she was compelled to give her hand to that popular rascal, Francis I. of France, when her brother wished to strengthen the treaty he made with his " good brother " at Madrid, and which the Frenchman had arranged to disregard even before he signed it. The second sister, Isabella, married Christian II., king of Denmark, when she was but fourteen, and died at twentyfour. Mary, the third sister, became the wife of Louis II., king of Hungary and Bohemia, and last of the Yagellons. The fourth sister, Catherine, married John III., king of Portugal. It was the marriage of the third sister, Mary, that, in connection with his own marriage, had the greatest effect on the fortunes of her brother Ferdinand, as his wife was the sister of Louis II., Mary's husband. Louis was defeated by the Turks at the battle of Mohacz, in 1526, and lost his life while flying from the field. Ferdinand claimed the crowns of Bohemia and Hungary, as Louis left no children, and he was chosen king in both countries; and though he disowned all other rights to the Bohemian throne than that of the election, it is certain he never would have been elected by either nation had he not married the sister of Louis, and had not Louis married his sister. All these marriages, and other events that carried the power of the house of Austria to the greatest height, took place only thirty-three years after the death of Frederick III., and some of his contemporaries may have lived to witness them all.

The marriages of the house of Austria since the sixteenth century have not been so important as they were in that century, but they have not been without influence on events, in exceptional cases. The marriage of Marie Antoinette and the French prince who became Louis XVI. was fruitful of results; and the marriage of Napoleon I. and Marie Louise, by causing the French emperor to rely on Austrian aid in 1813, had memorable consequences. Louis XIII. and Louis XIV. married Austrian princesses of the Spanish branch; and the marriage of Louis XIV. and Maria Theresa led to the founding of that Bourbon line which reigns over Spain, though the main line has ceased to reign in France. The greatness of the house of Austria in the seventeenth century is visible only in Germany, after the death of Philip IV. of Spain. The German Hapsburgs had a powerful influence in the seventeenth century, playing then great parts, but often finding themselves in danger of extinction before their Spanish cousins had run out.* They were the rivals of the French kings of that century, and Louis XIV. was talked of as a candidate for the imperial throne. The course of English politics had a very favorable effect on the fortunes of the Hapsburgs, the same conduct that gave supremacy to Protestantism and constitutionalism in Great Britain working most favorably in behalf of that family which, for ten generations, has been identified with everything that is bigoted and intolerant in religion and politics. James II., after his fall, implored assistance from the Emperor of

Germany, Leopold I.; and, considering that both were intensely Catholic, his application ought to have been favorably received; but the reigning Emperor had little difficulty in showing that it was not in his power, as assuredly it was not for his interest, to help the exiled king, — who was an exile only because of his attachment to that ancient Church through which alone, as Leopold believed, salvation could be secured. He went with the heretical William III. England, indeed, has been the bulwark of the German Hapsburgs on many occasions, and has saved them on more than one occasion from overthrow; and she did her best to aid even the Spanish branch in its last years, and then exerted herself to secure that branch's possessions for its relations at Vienna. It was English military genius that saved the Emperor Leopold I. from destruction.† When most of Continental Europe showed itself hostile to the Austrian house after the death of Charles VI., England was the fast friend of Maria Theresa, his daughter, and aided her to get over difficulties that seemed about to overwhelm her; and it was the fault rather of Austria than of England that the two countries did not act together

---

* The main line of the German Hapsburgs ended in 1619, with the death of the Emperor Matthias. He was succeeded by Ferdinand II., grandson of Ferdinand I., and son of that Archduke Charles who was sometimes spoken of in connection with the possible marriage of Elizabeth of England. Out of Ferdinand II.'s elevation grew a new union of the entire family of Hapsburg. During the long ascendency of the Cardinal-Duke of Lerma in the Spanish councils, *temp.* Philip III., the breach between the two branches, which had been more apparent than real, and yet not unimportant, was made complete by the minister's action, the policy he pursued being such as was highly displeasing to the German Hapsburgs, who had relapsed into bigotry. Philip III. set up pretensions to Hungary and Bohemia, as grandson of Maximilian II. Ferdinand, who was not yet either emperor or king, got rid of Philip's pretensions by promising to resign to him the Austrian possessions in Swabia. This led to the fall of Lerma, and to the reunion of the two branches of the Austrian house, but for which it is probable Ferdinand II. might have been beaten in the early days of the Thirty Years' War. It was to Spanish aid that Ferdinand owed his early triumphs in that contest; and many years later, in 1634, the great victory of Nordlingen was gained for the Imperialists by the presence of ten thousand Spanish infantry

in their army, — that infantry which was still the first military body in Europe, not then having met with the disaster of Rocroy, which, however, was near at hand. This was a kind of Indian-summer revival of Spanish power, and at the beginning of the new alliance between Madrid and Vienna, "there appeared," says Ranké, "a prospect of founding a compact Spanish hereditary dominion, which should directly link together Milan with the Netherlands, and so give the Spanish policy a necessary preponderance in the affairs of Europe." Richelieu spoilt this fine prospect just as it seemed about to become a reality, and the Spanish Hapsburgs gradually sank into insignificance, and their line disappeared in 1700, on the death of Charles II., the most contemptible creature that ever wore a crown, and scarcely man enough to be a respectable idiot. Such was the termination of the great Austro-Burgundian dynasty that was founded by Charles V., — at one time as majestic as "the broad and winding Rhine," but again, like the Rhine, running fast to insignificance.

† If the house of Austria was not in the greatest danger it ever experienced in 1704, its members and officers could affect to feel all but absolutely desperate. The following letter, written in queer German-French, by the Imperial Minister near the English court, Count John Wenceslaus Wratislaw, to Queen Anne, conveys an almost ludicrous idea of the fright

in the Seven Years' War, when England was, as it were, forced into the Prussian alliance, and helped Frederick win his astonishing victories. Austria came out of that memorable contest without having accomplished the purpose for which she entered it; but she had displayed great power during its course, and in the last half of the reign of the empress-queen, her reputation stood very high. Joseph II., though he declared that he had failed in everything, impressed himself very powerfully on the European mind, and was counted a great sovereign. No common man could have entertained the projects that crowded his teeming mind, and which came to little in most instances because they were in advance of the time.

During the tremendous struggle that proceeded from the French Revolution, Austria was almost always in the foreground, and next to England showed greatest powers of endurance in combating the new order of things. Six times she made war on France, and though in four of these wars she was beaten, she had the fortune to decide the event of the fifth, — that of 1814-15; and in 1815 she was as active against Napoleon as circumstances permitted

under which the Austrian chiefs suffered: — "Madame, Le soussigné envoyé extraordinaire de sa Majesté Impériale ayant représenté de vive voix en diverses occasions aux ministres de votre Majesté la dure extremité dans laquelle se trouve l'Empire, par l'introduction d'une armée nombreuse de François dans la Bavière, laquelle jointe à la revolte de la Hongrie met les païs héréditaires de sa Majesté Impériale dans une confusion incroyable, de sorte que si l'on n'apporte pas un remède prompt et proportionné au danger présent, dont on est menacé, on a à craindre une revolution entière, et une destruction totale de l'Allemagne." Luckily for Austria, Marlborough was a man of as much moral as physical courage, and he took the responsibility of leading his army into Germany, — a decision that, perhaps, no other commander of that time would have been equal to, — and by the junction of his forces with those of Eugène was enabled to fight and win the battle of Blenheim (Blindheim), which put an end to the ascendency of France. Emperor Leopold was positively grateful for the services Marlborough rendered him, and treated him differently from the manner in which he had treated Sobieski for doing him quite as great a favor. He wrote him a letter with his own hand, gave him a lordship in fee, and made him, by the title of Mindelheim, a Prince of the Holy Roman Empire.

any of the Allies to be, except England and Prussia. The effect of this pertinacity, and of her decisive part in 1813, was to secure for her a degree of consideration altogether disproportioned to her real power. Men took her for what she appeared to be, not as she was. In truth, very little was known of her condition, and the few who were aware of her weakness were interested in keeping their knowledge to themselves. The grand effort which she made in 1809, single-handed almost, to break the power of Napoleon, was everywhere looked upon as something alike herculean and heroical, and as such it is spoken of in all those historical works from which most readers obtain knowledge of the early years of this century; but now we know from other sources, and particularly from the Diary of Gentz, that she never was in a worse state than she knew in the days of Eckmühl, Essling, and Wagram. Reading what Gentz wrote in the ten weeks that followed Wagram, we feel as if we were reading of the twenty days that followed Sadowa. But of this nobody outside of the empire seems to have known or suspected anything; and the number of persons in the empire who knew it, or suspected it, was not large. Even Napoleon, who was on the ground, and who had the country more at his control than it was at that of Francis II., seems to have been entirely ignorant of the true state of affairs. He could have "crumpled up" Austria with ease, and have made half a dozen kingdoms or grand duchies of the spoils he had seized, — and yet he talked to General Bubna, and to others of the Austrian negotiators, as if he considered Austria the greatest nation in Europe, and sure swiftly to recover from the consequences of the blows he had dealt her. He actually spoke of the ability she would secure to decide the future fate of Europe, and therein was a prophet of his own ruin. It is possible that there may have been some affectation in what he said, but there was as much sincerity, for there is a great deal in the history of his career that shows he had a high opinion of Austrian power. When Europe was settled, after his fall, Austria acquired the right to stand between England and Russia, as their equal; and down to 1848 she was the superior of both France and Prussia. The events of 1848–49 did not essentially lessen her prestige, and she had a commanding place during the Russian war. Even her defeats in the Italian war did not lead to any serious loss of consideration, and against them was set the striking fact that the victorious French had halted before the Quadrilateral, and actually had begged for peace from the vanquished.

We know how deceptive were all appearances in regard to Austrian strength; but it was in the power of Austrian statesmen to convert what was simply apparent into a solid reality. Had they been wise men, they would, during the long peace that followed 1815, have made of Austria a state as powerful in fact as the world believed her to be. Nothing could have been easier, as her undeveloped resources ever have been vast; but they did nothing of the kind, their sole aim being to get over the present, without any regard for the future. Hermayr says of Thugut, who was chief Austrian minister in the closing years of the last century, that "his policy knew neither virtue nor vice, only expedients"; and these words describe the policy of Metternich completely, and, with perhaps a little modification, they describe that of all his successors. So that when the Prussian war came, Austria was in the same state that she was in 1809, — seemingly very strong, actually very weak; and she fell in a month, with a great ruin, much to the astonishment of almost all men. But the difference between 1809 and 1866 is this, — that the light let into Austria through chinks made by the Prussian bayonet will prevent the game of deception from being renewed.

It is assumed by most persons, that the house of Austria has at last reached the turn of its fortunes; and

that, having been beaten down by Prussia, it never will be able to rise again. This is the reaction against the sentiment that prevailed so generally at the beginning of last summer, just before the first blood was drawn in that war which proved so disastrous to Austria. In America, as in England, not only was it assumed that the Austrians had the better cause, but that the better chances of success were clearly with them. Black and yellow would distance black and white, and the two-headed eagle would tear and rend the single-headed eagle, thus affording another proof that two heads are better than one. Now, all is changed. In England, opinion is setting almost as strongly Prussiaward as it did in 1815, though the Prussians and the Prussian government have made no apologies for those ungracious acts against Englishmen which it was the fashion to cite as evidence of the dislike borne to the islanders by the countrymen of Bismarck. Captain Heehaw, of the Coldstreams, who thought — really, 'pon honor — that the Prussians would not be able to look half their number of Austrians in the face, has wheeled about, converted by the fast flashes of the needle-gun; and the gallant Captain, who would fight like an Achilles should opportunity offer, is a fair type of his fellows. There is a complete change of front. The English are countermarching, and will take up their former ground, — if they have not already taken it, — that on which they stood when their Parliament thanked Blücher and his Prussians for helping Wellington and his Britons strike down Napoleon and the French. Prussia now means a united Germany, to be ruled by the house of Hohenzollern, whose head is an old king of threescore and ten years, and who must, in the regular course of things, soon be displaced by a bold young prince, whose brows are thickly covered with laurels gathered on the field of Sadowa, and whose wife is the eldest child of Queen Victoria. Why should not Protestant England rejoice with Protestant Prussia, and see her successes with gladness? Sure enough; and English joy over the prodigious Prussian triumph of last summer ought to be the most natural thing in the world. But we cannot forget what was the color of English opinion down to the time when it was demonstrated by the logic of cannon that the Prussian cause was perfectly pure, and that it was to fly in the face of Providence to question its excellence. If ever a man was hated in England, Count Bismarck had the honor of being thus hated. And it was an honor; for next to the love of a great people, their hatred is the best evidence of a man's greatness. Napoleon in 1807 was not more detested by Englishmen than Bismarck in 1866. The obnoxious Prussian statesman was not even respected, for he had done nothing to command the respect of enemies. From the tone in which he was talked of, it was plain that the English considered him to be a mischievous, malicious, elfish sort of creature, who could not do anything that would deserve to be considered great, but who did his utmost to make himself and his country the nuisances of Europe. Books have been made from English journals to show how extraordinarily they berated this country during the Secession war, because Americans were so brutally perverse and so selfishly silly as not to submit their country's throat to the Southern sabre for the benefit of Britain, which condescends to think that our national existence is something not altogether compatible with her safety. But a collection made from the same journals of articles assailing Prussia in general, and Count Bismarck in particular, would be even richer than anything that has been collected to show English sympathy with gentlemen who were fighting valiantly to establish that "better kind of civilization" which is based on slavery. All is now changed toward Prussia, as most has been changed toward us for twenty months, ever since the fall of Richmond. If Prussia should not soon establish a "cordial understanding" with England, *vice* France discarded, it will be because she is not disposed to an English alliance, or because her fortunes shall have undergone a change, and rendered her unworthy of being courted. That ancient connection of England and Austria, dating from the time that the Bourbons became dangerous to Europe, and which was so often alluded to in the time of the Italian war, and in the days that immediately preceded the German conflict, is thought little of by Englishmen, who prefer to think of Pitt's connection with Frederick when the latter was threatened with annihilation by Austria. Prussia has not only beaten the Austrian armies; she has conquered English prejudices, — much the more difficult task of the two.

The Austrians must be amused by the change that has come over the English mind; but with their sense of the satire which that change may be said to embody, there is possibly mingled the reflection that their case, bad as it is, is not so bad as to deprive them of hope. Looking back over the history of the house of Austria, there is much in it to allow the belief that possibly it may again rise to the highest place in Europe. That house has often fallen quite as low as we have seen it fall, and yet it has not passed away, but has renewed its life and strength, and has taken high part in effecting the punishment, and even the destruction, of those who might have destroyed it. When Matthias Corvinus held Vienna, — when that city was besieged by the great Solyman, whose troops marched as far to the west as Ratisbon, — when Charles V. fled before Maurice of Saxony, "lest he might one fine morning be seized in his bed," — when Andrew Thonradtel took Ferdinand II. by the buttons of his doublet, and said, "Nandel, give in, thou must sign" (a paper containing the articles of the union of the Austrian Estates with the Bohemians, which Ferdinand refused to sign, and never signed), — when Gustavus Adolphus was beating or baffling all the Imperial generals, — when Wallenstein was directing his army of *condottieri*, with which he had saved the Austrian house, against that house, — when Kara Mustapha, at the head of two hundred thousand Turks, aided by the Hungarians, and encouraged by the French, laid siege to Vienna, and sent his light cavalry to the banks of the Inn, and came wellnigh succeeding in his undertaking, and would have done so but for the coming in of John Sobieski and his Poles, — when the French and Bavarians, in 1704, had brought the Empire to the brink of destruction, so that it could be saved only through the combined exertions of such men as Eugène and Marlborough, — when almost all Continental Europe that was possessed of power directed that power against the Imperial house immediately after the death of Charles VI., last male member of the line of Hapsburg, — when Napoleon I. destroyed an Austrian army at Ulm, and took Vienna, and beat to pieces the Austro-Russian army at Austerlitz, — when the same Emperor took Vienna the second time, in 1809, after a series of brilliant victories, wonderful even in his most wonderful history, and won the victory of Wagram, and allowed the Austrian monarchy to exist only because he thought of marrying a daughter of its head, — when Hungarians, Italians, Germans, and others of its subjects were in arms against it, in 1848 – 49, — when Montebello and Palestro were followed by Magenta and Solferino, — the condition of the house of Austria was nearly as low as it is to-day, and on some of these occasions probably it was even more reduced than it is at present. Men were ready in 1529, in 1552, in 1619, in 1632, in 1683, in 1704, in 1741, in 1805, in 1809, in 1849, and in 1859 to say, as now they say, that the last hour of the fortunate dynasty was about to strike on the clock of Time, forgetting all its earlier escapes from the last consequences of defeat, recollection of which would have enabled them to form better judgments. On a dozen occasions

Austria has risen superior to the effects of the direst misfortunes, and she may do so again. And her triumphs, proceeding out of failures, have not been won over common men or in ordinary contests. She has rarely had to deal with mean antagonists, and her singular victories have been enhanced in value by the high grade of her enemies. Francis I., Sultan Solyman, Gustavus Adolphus, Wallenstein, Richelieu, Louis XIV., Napoleon I., and Kossuth are conspicuous in the list of her enemies. They were all great men, — deriving greatness some of them from their intellectual powers, others from their positions as sovereigns, and yet others from both their positions and their powers of mind. Yet she got the better of them all,[*] and some of them fell misera-

[*] As it is generally assumed that Richelieu got the better of the Empire in that contest which he waged with it, perhaps some readers may think we have gone too far in saying he was one of those antagonists of whom the Austrian family got the better; but all depends upon the point of view. Richelieu died when the war was at its height, and did not live to see the success of his immediate policy; but what he did was only an incident in a long contest. The old rivalry of the house of Valois and the house of Austria was continued after the former was succeeded by the house of Bourbon. Richelieu did not carry out the policy on which Henry IV. had determined; and when the two branches of the Austrian family had united their powers, and it seemed that the effect of their reunion would be to place Europe at their command, the great Cardinal-Duke had no choice but to follow the ancient course of France. But the contest on which he entered, though in one sense fatal to his enemy, was not decided in his time, nor till he had been in his grave more than sixty years. He died just before the beginning of the reign of Louis XIV., and that monarch took up and continued the contest which Richelieu may be said to have renewed. For an unusually long period the Bourbons were successful, though without fully accomplishing their purpose. From the battle of Rocroy, in 1643, to the battle of Blenheim, in 1704, France was the first nation of Europe, and the Bourbons could boast of having humiliated the Hapsburgs. They obtained the crowns of Spain and the Indies; and the Spanish crowns are yet worn by a descendant of Louis le Grand, while another family reigns in France. But Spain and her dependencies apart, all was changed by the result at Blenheim. The Austrian house was there saved, and re-established; and it was there that the policy of Richelieu had its final decision. The France of the old monarchy never recovered from the disasters its armies met with in the War of the Spanish Succession; and when Louis XV. consented to the marriage of his grandson to an Austrian princess, he virtually admitted that the old rival of his family had triumphed in the long strife. The quarrel was

bly because of her enmity to them, — as Wallenstein and Napoleon. Frederick the Great was in some sense an exception, as he accomplished most of his purposes at her expense; and yet it cannot with propriety be said that he conquered her, or that, at the utmost, he was ever more than the equal of Maria Theresa or Joseph II., with all his undoubted intellectual superiority. When we compare the Austria of 1813 with the Austria of 1809, and see how wonderfully fortune had worked in her favor under circumstances far from promising anything for her benefit, we are not surprised that Austrians should still be full of confidence, or that a few other men should share what seems to be in them a well-founded hope. A belief in good luck sometimes helps men to the enjoyment of good luck, — and if men, why not nations?

Yet against this reliance on her luck by Austria must be placed the wonderful changes that have come over the world since those times when it was in the power of a government like the Austrian to exert a great influence on the course of events. Down to the time of the French Revolution, Austrian contests were carried on against nations, governments, and dynasties, and not against peoples. Even the wars that grew out of the Reformation

again renewed in the days of the Republic, maintained under the first French Empire, and had its last trial of arms under the second Empire, in 1859; but the old French monarchy gave up the contest more than a century ago. Besides, we are to distinguish between the German Empire and the house of Hapsburg that ruled from Vienna. The Peace of Westphalia (1648) left the Germanic Emperors in a contemptible state, but the effect of it was highly favorable to these Emperors considered as chiefs of the Hapsburg family. "Placed on the eastern verge of Germany," says Mr. Bryce, "the Hapsburgs had added to their ancient lands in Austria proper and the Tyrol new German territories far more extensive, and had thus become the chiefs of a separate and independent state. They endeavored to reconcile its interests and those of the Empire, so long as it seemed possible to recover part of the old imperial prerogative. But when such hopes were dashed by the defeats of the Thirty Years' War, they hesitated no longer between an elective crown and the rule of their hereditary states, and comforted themselves thenceforth in European politics, not as the representatives of Germany, but as heads of the great Austrian monarchy." (The Holy Roman Empire, new edition, p. 355.) Thus,

were in no strict sense of a popular character, but were waged by the great of the earth, who found their account in being champions of progressive ideas, — the liberalism of those days. Almost all the renowned anti-Austrian leaders of the Thirty Years' War were kings, nobles, aristocrats of every grade, most of whom, we may suppose, cared as little for political freedom as the Hapsburgs cared for it. Gustavus Adolphus could be as arbitrary as Ferdinand II., and some of his most ardent admirers are of opinion that he fell none too soon for his own reputation, though much too soon for the good of Europe, when he was slain on the glorious field of Lützen. The most remarkable of all the wars waged by the Austrian house against human rights was that which Philip II. and his successor directed against the Dutch: the latter were the champions of liberty; but the opponents of the Spanish Hapsburgs even in that war can hardly be called the people. They were — at least the animating and inspiriting portion of them — the old Dutch municipal aristocracy, who on most occasions were well supported by the people. Down to a time within living memory, the German Hapsburgs contended only against their equals in blood and birth, if not always in power. In 1792

by diverting the Hapsburgs from impracticable schemes, and throwing them upon their hereditary possessions, Richelieu really helped them; and in so far his policy was a failure, as he sought to lessen the power of the house of Austria, which in his time ruled over Spain, as well as in Germany, Bohemia, Hungary, and other countries. It is intimated by some European writers, that the Austrian family will once more turn its attention to the East, and, giving up all thought of regaining its place in Germany, seek compensation where it was found in the seventeenth century, after the Peace of Westphalia. But what was possible two hundred years ago might be found impossible to-day. Russia had no existence as a European power in those days, whereas now she has one of the highest places in Europe, and a very peculiar interest in not allowing Austria, or any other nation, to obtain possession of countries like the Roumanian Principalities, the addition of which to his empire might afford compensation to Francis Joseph for all that he has lost in the south and the west. It is one of the infelicities of Austria's position, that she cannot make a movement in any direction without treading on the toes of some giant, or on those of a dwarf protected by some giant who intends himself ultimately to devour him.

a new age began. The armies of Revolutionary France were even more democratic than our own in the Secession war, and not even Napoleon's imperializing and demoralizing course could entirely change their character. Democracy and aristocracy, each all armed, were fairly pitted against each other, in that long list of actions which began at Jemappes and terminated at Solferino. The Austrian army, like the Austrian government, is the most aristocratic institution of the kind in the world, and as such it was well ranged against the French army, the only great armed democratic force Europe had ever seen till the present year. Democracy had the better in most of the engagements that took place, though it had ever to fight hard for it, the Austrians rarely behaving otherwise than well in war. The Prussian army that did such great things last summer was conscribed from the people to an extent that has no parallel since the French Republic formed its armies; and it broke down the aristocratical force of Austria as effectively as Cromwell's Ironsides, — who were enlisted and disciplined yeomen, — broke through, cut down, and rode over the high-born Cavaliers of England. Now what Austria's army encountered when it met the French and Prussian armies, the Austrian government has to encounter in the management of affairs. In the old diplomatic school, Austria could hold her own with any foe, or friend either, — the latter the more difficult matter of the two. There seldom have been abler men in their way than Kaunitz and Metternich, but they would be utterly useless were they to come back and take charge of Austrian diplomacy, so changed is the world's state. And their successors are of their school, with abilities far inferior to theirs. The people have now to be consulted, even when treaties are arranged and political combinations made. Such a parcelling out of countries as was so easily effected at Vienna in 1815 would no more be possible now, than it would be to get up a crusade, or to revive the traffic in

slaves. The ground which the people have gained in fifty years' course they have no intention of giving up, rather meaning to strengthen it and to extend it.

This is the reason why Austria cannot very hopefully look for a revival of her power, as it so often revived after defeat in old days, and under an entirely different state of things from that which now exists. A power has come into existence such as she has never been accustomed to deal with, and of which her statesmen have no knowledge. An Austrian statesman is scarcely more advanced than a Frenchman of the time of Louis Quatorze; and we verily believe that Louvois or Torcy would be quite as much at home in European politics at this moment as Mensdorff or Belcredi. Had they been well informed as to the condition of the times; they never would have so acted as to bring about the late war. It was their reliance on the ability of mere governments to settle every question in dispute, that caused them to plunge into a conflict with Prussia and Italy, when their master's empire was bankrupt, and when more or less of discontent existed in almost every part of that empire. Statesmen who knew the age, and who were aware of the change that has come over Europe in half a century, would have told the Emperor that to rely on " something turning up," after the ancient Austrian custom, would not answer in 1866, and that peoples as well as princes had much to do with the ordering of every nation's policy; and with every people Austria is unpopular. It is not difficult now to understand that Francis Joseph had a profound reliance on Napoleon III., that he believed the Frenchman would prevent his being driven to the wall, and that Prussia would be the greatest sufferer by the war, as she would be forced to part with the Rhine provinces. His mistake with respect to France was not a great one, as the French saw the triumph of Prussia with much bitterness of feeling, and gladly would have joined the Austrians; but the mistake he made in regard to Germany was very great, and shows that he and his advisers knew nothing of Germanic feeling. If they could thus err on a point that was plain to every intelligent foreigner, how can we expect them to exhibit more intelligence and more sense with respect to the new state of things proceeding from the event of the war? If they could not comprehend matters of fact at the beginning of last June, why should we conclude that they will be Solomons hereafter? Brought face to face with a new state of things, they so proceeded as to convince all impartial observers that they were wellnigh as ignorant of what had been going on among men, as the Seven Sleepers were when roused from their long slumber. But for this, unless we assume that they were fools, not only would they not have admitted war to be possible, but they never would have allowed the coming about of such a state of things as led to the dispute with Prussia. The entire action of the Austrian government with reference to the affairs of Germany, for several years, was admirably calculated to lead to what has taken place this year. That government, had it been wise, never would have acted with Prussia in the matter of the Danish duchies. It would have insisted on the fulfilment of the arrangement that was made years before, in which case it would have been supported by the whole power of France and England, and not improbably by that of Russia; and against so great an array of force, Prussia, even if backed by the opinion of Germany, never would have thought of contending, — and some of the German governments would have sided with the allies, and would have behaved much more efficiently than they did in the late war. Prussia would have been isolated, as France was in 1840; and that party which was opposed to Bismarck's policy would have obtained control of her councils, the effect of which would have been to preserve peace, the very thing that was most necessary to Austria's welfare. Instead of opposing Prussia, Austria

joined her, and insisted on having a part in the very business that offended the Germans as much as it disgusted foreigners. Thus a state of things was brought about which made a German war inevitable, while Austria was deprived of all aid from abroad. England's sympathies were with Austria, as against Prussia; and yet England had been shabbily treated by Austria in respect to the duchies, and it was impossible for her either to forget or forgive such treatment. France had less cause to be offended; but Napoleon III. could not have approved of action which seemed to be taken in disregard of his high position in Europe, and was calculated to advance the ends of Prussia, — the power least respected by the French, — and which finally made of that power the destroyer of the settlement of 1815,[*] a part the Emperor had intended for himself. Having acted thus unwisely, and having no support from Russia, Austria should have avoided war in 1866, at any cost; and it was in her power to avoid it down to the time that she made the German Diet so proceed as to furnish Prussia with an excellent

---

[*] Prussia, the most thoroughly anti-Gallican of all the parties to the Treaty of Vienna, completed the work of overthrowing the "detested" arrangements made by the framers of that treaty. The federal act creating the Germanic Confederation was incorporated in the work of the Congress of Vienna, and was guaranteed by eight European powers, — France, England, Russia, Prussia, Sweden, Austria, Spain, and Portugal. Prussia destroyed the Confederation without troubling herself about the wishes and opinions of the other seven parties to the arrangement of 1815. That all those parties to that arrangement were not always indifferent to their guaranty appears from the opposition made by Russia, France, and England to Prince Schwarzenburg's proposition, that Austria should be allowed to introduce all her non-Germanic territories into the Confederation, that is to say, that the *Austrian Empire*, which then included the Lombardo-Venetian kingdom, should become a part of Germany, which it would soon have ruled, as well as overruled, while it would have extended its dominion over all Italy. Had Schwarzenburg's project succeeded, the course of European events during the last sixteen years must have been entirely changed, or Austria would have been made too strong to be harmed by the French in Italy, or by the Prussians in Germany and Bohemia. Russia was specially adverse to that project; and the Treaty of Vienna was forcibly appealed to by her government in opposing it. The time had not then come for making waste-paper of the arrangements of 1815.

reason for setting her well-prepared armies in motion against the ill-prepared forces of her foe. Noting the folly of Austria, and observing that the French government, if M. de Lavalette's circular can be depended upon as an expression of its sentiments, is all for peace, we can see no opening for that renewal of warfare in Europe which the defeated party is said to desire, as an ally of France, in the expectation that she might recover the place she so lately lost. The reopening of the Eastern Question, of which much is said, might afford some hope to Austria, but not to the extent that is supposed; for she is not strong enough at this time to be a powerful ally of Russia as against Turkey, or of England in support of Turkey. She has parted with her old importance; for there is no further hiding from the world that her system is vicious, and that nothing could be gained from an alliance with her, while any country with which she should be associated would have to extend to her much support. She may rise again, but how, or in what manner, it is not in any man's power to say.

RECONSTRUCTION.

THE assembling of the Second Session of the Thirty-ninth Congress may very properly be made the occasion of a few earnest words on the already much-worn topic of reconstruction.

Seldom has any legislative body been the subject of a solicitude more intense, or of aspirations more sincere and ardent. There are the best of reasons for this profound interest. Questions of vast moment, left undecided by the last session of Congress, must be manfully grappled with by this. No political skirmishing will avail. The occasion demands statesmanship.

Whether the tremendous war so heroically fought and so victoriously ended shall pass into history a miserable failure, barren of permanent results, — a scandalous and shocking waste of blood and treasure, — a strife for empire, as Earl Russell characterized it, of no value to liberty or civilization, — an attempt to re-establish a Union by force, which must be the merest mockery of a Union, — an effort to bring under Federal authority States into which no loyal man from the North may safely enter, and to bring men into the national councils who deliberate with daggers and vote with revolvers, and who do not even conceal their deadly hate of the country that conquered them; or whether, on the other hand, we shall, as the rightful reward of victory over treason, have a solid nation, entirely delivered from all contradictions and social antagonisms, based upon loyalty, liberty, and equality, must be determined one way or the other by the present session of Congress. The last session really did nothing which can be considered final as to these questions. The Civil Rights Bill and the Freedmen's Bureau Bill and the proposed constitutional amendments, with the amendment already adopted and recognized as the law of the land, do not reach the difficulty, and cannot, unless the whole structure of the government is changed from a government by States to something like a despotic central government, with power to control even the municipal regulations of States, and to make them conform to its own despotic will. While there remains such an idea as the right of each State to control its own local affairs, — an idea, by the way, more deeply rooted in the minds of men of all sections of the country than perhaps any one other political idea, — no general assertion of human rights can be of any practical value. To change the character of the government at this point is neither possible nor desirable. All that is necessary to be done is to make the government consistent with itself, and render the rights of the States compatible with the sacred rights of human nature.

The arm of the Federal government is long, but it is far too short to protect the rights of individuals in the interior of distant States. They must have the power to protect themselves, or they will go unprotected, spite of all the laws the Federal government can put upon the national statute-book.

Slavery, like all other great systems of wrong, founded in the depths of human selfishness, and existing for ages, has not neglected its own conservation. It has steadily exerted an influence upon all around it favorable to its own continuance. And to-day it is so strong that it could exist, not only without law, but even against law. Custom, manners, morals, religion, are all on its side everywhere in the South ; and when you add the ignorance and servility of the ex-slave to the intelligence and accustomed authority of the master, you have the conditions, not out of which slavery will again grow, but under which it is impossible for the Federal government to wholly destroy it, unless the Federal government be armed with despotic power, to blot out State authority, and to station a Federal officer at every cross-road. This, of course, cannot be done, and ought not even if it could. The true way and the easiest way is to make our government entirely consistent with itself, and give to every loyal citizen the elective franchise, — a right and power which will be ever present, and will form a wall of fire for his protection.

One of the invaluable compensations of the late Rebellion is the highly instructive disclosure it made of the true source of danger to republican government. Whatever may be tolerated in monarchical and despotic governments, no republic is safe that tolerates a privileged class, or denies to any of its citizens equal rights and equal means to maintain them. What was theory before the war has been made fact by the war.

There is cause to be thankful even for rebellion. It is an impressive teacher, though a stern and terrible one. In both characters it has come to us, and it was perhaps needed in both. It is an instructor never a day before its time, for it comes only when all other means of progress and enlightenment have failed. Whether the oppressed and despairing bondman, no longer able to repress his deep yearnings for manhood, or the tyrant, in his pride and impatience, takes the initiative, and strikes the blow for a firmer hold and a longer lease of oppression, the result is the same, — society is instructed, or may be.

Such are the limitations of the common mind, and so thoroughly engrossing are the cares of common life, that only the few among men can discern through the glitter and dazzle of present prosperity the dark outlines of approaching disasters, even though they may have come up to our very gates, and are already within striking distance. The yawning seam and corroded bolt conceal their defects from the mariner until the storm calls all hands to the pumps. Prophets, indeed, were abundant before the war ; but who cares for prophets while their predictions remain unfulfilled, and the calamities of which they tell are masked behind a blinding blaze of national prosperity ?

It is asked, said Henry Clay, on a memorable occasion, Will slavery never come to an end ? That question, said he, was asked fifty years ago, and it has been answered by fifty years of unprecedented prosperity. Spite of the eloquence of the earnest Abolitionists, — poured out against slavery during thirty years, — even they must confess, that, in all the probabilities of the case, that system of barbarism would have continued its horrors far beyond the limits of the nineteenth century but for the Rebellion, and perhaps only have disappeared at last in a fiery conflict, even more fierce and bloody than that which has now been suppressed.

It is no disparagement to truth, that it can only prevail where reason prevails. War begins where reason ends. The thing worse than rebellion is the thing that causes rebellion. What that thing is, we have been taught to our cost. It remains now to be seen whether we have the needed courage to have that cause entirely removed from the Republic. At any rate, to this grand work of national regeneration and entire purification Congress must now address itself, with full purpose that the work shall this time be thoroughly·done. The deadly upas, root and branch, leaf and fibre, body and sap, must be utterly destroyed. The country is evidently not in a condition to listen patiently to pleas for postponement, however plausible, nor will it permit the responsibility to be shifted to other shoulders. Authority and power are here commensurate with the duty imposed. There are no cloud-flung shadows to obscure the way. Truth shines with brighter light and intenser heat at every moment, and a country torn and rent and bleeding implores relief from its distress and agony.

If time was at first needed, Congress has now had time. All the requisite materials from which to form an intelligent judgment are now before it. Whether its members look at the origin, the progress, the termination of the war, or at the mockery of a peace now existing, they will find only one unbroken chain of argument in favor of a radical policy of reconstruction. For the omissions of the last session, some excuses may be allowed. A treacherous President stood in the way ; and it can be easily seen how reluctant good men might be to admit an apostasy which involved so much of baseness and ingratitude. It was natural that they should seek to save him by bending to him even when he leaned to the side of error. But all is changed now. Congress knows now that it must go on without his aid, and even against his machinations. The advantage of the present session over the last is immense. Where that investigated, this has the facts. Where that walked by faith, this may walk by sight. Where that halted, this must go forward, and where that failed, this must succeed, giving the country whole measures where that gave us half-measures, merely as a means of saving the elections in a few doubtful districts. That Congress saw what was right, but distrusted the enlightenment of the loyal masses ; but what was forborne in distrust of the people must now be done with a full knowledge that the people expect and require it. The members go to Washington fresh from the inspiring presence of the people. In every considerable public meeting, and in almost every conceivable way, whether at court-house, school-house, or cross-roads, in doors and out, the subject has been discussed, and the people have emphatically pronounced in favor of a radical policy. Listening to the doctrines of expediency and compromise with pity, impatience, and disgust, they have everywhere broken into demonstrations of the wildest enthusiasm when a brave word has been spoken in favor of equal rights and impartial suffrage. Radicalism, so far from being odious, is now the popular passport to power. The men most bitterly charged with it go to Congress with the largest majorities, while the timid and doubtful are sent by lean majorities, or else left at home. The strange controversy between the President and Congress, at one time so threatening, is disposed of by the people. The high reconstructive powers which he so confidently, ostentatiously, and haughtily claimed, have been disallowed, denounced, and utterly repudiated ; while those claimed by Congress have been confirmed.

Of the spirit and magnitude of the canvass nothing need be said. The appeal was to the people, and the verdict was worthy of the tribunal. Upon an occasion of his own selection, with the advice and approval of his astute Secretary, soon after the members of Congress had returned to their constituents, the President quitted the executive mansion, sandwiched himself between two recognized heroes,—men whom the whole country delighted to honor,—and, with all the advantage which such company could give him, stumped the country from the Atlantic to the Mississippi, advocating everywhere his policy as against that of Congress. It was a strange sight, and perhaps the most disgraceful exhibition ever made by any President; but, as no evil is entirely unmixed, good has come of this, as from many others. Ambitious, unscrupulous, energetic, indefatigable, voluble, and plausible,—a political gladiator, ready for a "set-to" in any crowd,—he is beaten in his own chosen field, and stands to-day before the country as a convicted usurper, a political criminal, guilty of a bold and persistent attempt to possess himself of the legislative powers solemnly secured to Congress by the Constitution. No vindication could be more complete, no condemnation could be more absolute and humiliating. Unless reopened by the sword, as recklessly threatened in some circles, this question is now closed for all time.

Without attempting to settle here the metaphysical and somewhat theological question (about which so much has already been said and written), whether once in the Union means always in the Union,—agreeably to the formula, Once in grace always in grace,—it is obvious to common sense that the rebellious States stand to-day, in point of law, precisely where they stood when, exhausted, beaten, conquered, they fell powerless at the feet of Federal authority. Their State governments were overthrown, and the lives and property of the leaders of the Rebellion were forfeited. In reconstructing the institutions of these shattered and overthrown States, Congress should begin

with a clean slate, and make clean work of it. Let there be no hesitation. It would be a cowardly deference to a defeated and treacherous President, if any account were made of the illegitimate, one-sided, sham governments hurried into existence for a malign purpose in the absence of Congress. These pretended governments, which were never submitted to the people, and from participation in which four millions of the loyal people were excluded by Presidential order, should now be treated according to their true character, as shams and impositions, and supplanted by true and legitimate governments, in the formation of which loyal men, black and white, shall participate.

It is not, however, within the scope of this paper to point out the precise steps to be taken, and the means to be employed. The people are less concerned about these than the grand end to be attained. They demand such a reconstruction as shall put an end to the present anarchical state of things in the late rebellious States,— where frightful murders and wholesale massacres are perpetrated in the very presence of Federal soldiers. This horrible business they require shall cease. They want a reconstruction such as will protect loyal men, black and white, in their persons and property; such a one as will cause Northern industry, Northern capital, and Northern civilization to flow into the South, and make a man from New England as much at home in Carolina as elsewhere in the Republic. No Chinese wall can now be tolerated. The South must be opened to the light of law and liberty, and this session of Congress is relied upon to accomplish this important work.

The plain, common-sense way of doing this work, as intimated at the beginning, is simply to establish in the South one law, one government, one administration of justice, one condition to the exercise of the elective franchise, for men of all races and colors alike. This great measure is sought as earnestly by loyal white men as by loyal blacks, and is needed alike by both. Let sound political prescience but take the place of an unreasoning prejudice, and this will be done.

Men denounce the negro for his prominence in this discussion; but it is no fault of his that in peace as in war, that in conquering Rebel armies as in reconstructing the rebellious States, the right of the negro is the true solution of our national troubles. The stern logic of events, which goes directly to the point, disdaining all concern for the color or features of men, has determined the interests of the country as identical with and inseparable from those of the negro.

The policy that emancipated and armed the negro — now seen to have been wise and proper by the dullest — was not certainly more sternly demanded than is now the policy of enfranchisement. If with the negro was success in war, and without him failure, so in peace it will be found that the nation must fall or flourish with the negro.

Fortunately, the Constitution of the United States knows no distinction between citizens on account of color. Neither does it know any difference between a citizen of a State and a citizen of the United States. Citizenship evidently includes all the rights of citizens, whether State or national. If the Constitution knows none, it is clearly no part of the duty of a Republican Congress now to institute one. The mistake of the last session was the attempt to do this very thing, by a renunciation of its power to secure political rights to any class of citizens, with the obvious purpose to allow the rebellious States to disfranchise, if they should see fit, their colored citizens. This unfortunate blunder must now be retrieved, and the emasculated citizenship given to the negro supplanted by that contemplated in the Constitution of the United States, which declares that the citizens of each State shall enjoy all the rights and immunities of citizens of the several States, — so that a legal voter in any State shall be a legal voter in all the States.

REVIEWS AND LITERARY NOTICES.

History of the United States, from the Discovery of the American Continent. By GEORGE BANCROFT. Vol. IX. Boston: Little, Brown, & Co.

THIS volume of Mr. Bancroft's History, the ninth of the entire work and the third of the narrative of the American Revolution, comprises the period between July, 1776, and April, 1778, including the battles of Long Island and White Plains, the surrender of Fort Washington, the retreat of Washington through the Jerseys, the brilliant military successes of Trenton and Princeton, the capture of Philadelphia by Sir William Howe, and the memorable event which insured the success of the Revolution, — the surrender of Burgoyne. This enumeration is enough to show that, in the ground he has traversed, Mr. Bancroft has found

ample scope for the display of those peculiar literary characteristics with which the readers of his former volumes are so familiar, — his rapid and condensed narration, his sweeping and sometimes rather vague generalizations, his brilliant pictures, his pointed reflections, and the sharp, cutting strokes with which he carves rather than paints characters. His usual diligence in the search of materials has not deserted him here; and he has been even more than usually successful in the amount and character of what he has found. In addition to very full collections relating to the war from the archives of England and France, he has obtained large masses of papers from Germany, among which last are many of great importance, especially for the study of military operations in 1777. Very valuable documents from the Spanish have been secured, through the courtesy of the Spanish government and the kind offices of that distinguished scholar and most amiable man, Don Pascual de Gayangos.

Investigators of the past are naturally inclined to overestimate the value of any new sources of information opened by their own diligence or sagacity of research, and a little of this feeling is perceptible in Mr. Bancroft's Preface ; but, after all, we apprehend that the new evidence he has so diligently collected will not shake the deliberate verdict already passed alike upon men and events. Here and there a gleam is thrown upon some single incident, or the motives and conduct of a particular actor ; but the general lights and shadows of the historical landscape remain undisturbed. The statements and the views of Marshall and Sparks are substantially sustained. The patriotic American will not regret to see that Mr. Bancroft's investigations and conclusions lead him to exalt Washington in comparison with the soldiers and civilians who stood around him ; and the reader of his pages will have fresh cause to admire, not merely the firmness and self-command of that illustrious man, but his abilities as a commander and a statesman. We have especially to thank Mr. Bancroft for the distinctness with which he shows how much the success of the Northern army was due to Washington's disinterested advice. His high praise of the commander-in-chief sometimes glances aslope, and lights in the form of censure of some of his subordinate officers ; and we should not be surprised if some of his strictures provoked replies and led to controversies. Some of those whom he criticises have left descendants, and those who have left no descendants have partisans who are jealous of the fame of their favorites, and will not lightly allow a leaf of their laurels to be blighted.

During the period embraced by this volume the constitutions of several of the States were formed, and the Articles of Confederation were adopted which gave to the several States a semblance of unity, and smoothed the path to the more perfect union which was established ten years later. These events present themes peculiarly congenial to Mr. Bancroft's powers of brilliant generalization and rapid condensation, and tempt him into that field of discursive reflection where he is fond of lingering, and where we follow him always with interest, and generally with assent. We quote with peculiar pleasure the following observations from the fifteenth chapter, on the constitutions of the several States of America, as being sound in substance and happy in expression : —

"The spirit of the age moved the young nation to own justice as antecedent and superior to the state, and to found the rights of the citizen on the rights of man. And yet, in regenerating its institutions, it was not guided by any speculative theory or laborious application of metaphysical distinctions. Its form of government grew naturally out of its traditions, by the simple rejection of all personal hereditary authority, which in America had never had much more than a representative existence. Its people were industrious and frugal. Accustomed to the cry of liberty and property, they harbored no dream of a community of goods ; and their love of equality never degenerated into envy of the rich. No successors of the fifth-monarchy men proposed to substitute an unwritten higher law, interpreted by individual conscience, for the law of the land and the decrees of human tribunals. The people proceeded with self-possession and moderation, after the manner of their ancestors. Their large inheritance of English liberties saved them from the necessity and from the wish to uproot their old political institutions ; and as happily the scaffold was not wet with the blood of their statesmen, there was no root of a desperate hatred of England, such as the Netherlands kept up for centuries against Spain. The wrongs inflicted or attempted by the British king were felt to have been avenged by independence. Respect and affection remained behind for the parent land, from which the United States had derived trial by jury, the writ for personal liberty, the practice of representative government, and the separation of the three great co-ordinate powers in the state. From an essentially aristocratic model, America took just what suited her condition, and rejected the rest. Thus the transition of the Colonies into self-existent commonwealths was free from vindictive bitterness, and attended by no violent or wide departure from the past."

A considerable portion of this volume is occupied by a consideration of the relations between Europe and America. Advancing years do not seem to chill Mr. Bancroft's faith in progress, his confidence in democracy, his love of popular institutions, or to check his tendency to throw his speculations into an aphoristic form, and to present his conclusions positively, and with less of qualification and limitation than men of a more cautious temperament would do. So far as literary merit is concerned, the European chapters will be found the most attractive in the volume. They are sparkling, rapid, condensed, and pointed ; they gratify our national pride ; their animated and picturesque style never suffers the attention to flag for a moment ; — and yet it is in these very chapters that judicial criticism will find the most frequent occasion to pause and doubt, whether we consider the direction in which the stream of thought flows, or their merely rhetorical features. Mr. Bancroft's glittering generalizations do not always seem to us to wear the sober livery of truth. For instance, on page 500 we read : " The most stupendous thought that ever was conceived by man, such as never had been dared by Socrates or the Academy, by Aristotle or the Stoics, took possession of Descartes on a November night in his meditations on the banks of the Danube." It may be coldness of temperament, it may be the chilling influence of advancing years, but we cannot admire statements like these, and we are constrained to think them exaggerated and extravagant.

And on the next page Mr. Bancroft says : " Edwards, Reid, Kant, and Rousseau were all imbued with religiosity, and all except the last, who spoiled his doctrine by dreamy indolence, were expositors of the active powers of man." It is certainly an ingenious mind that finds a resemblance between Edwards and Rousseau. What exactly is the meaning of " religiosity," we cannot say ; but if it be used as a synonyme of religion, we demur to the assertion that Rousseau was imbued with religion, — Rousseau, who in his youth allowed an innocent girl to be ruined by accusing her of a theft which he himself had committed, and in his ripened manhood sent to a foundling hospital the children he had had by his mistress, — whose life was despicable and whose moral creed seemed to be summed up in the doctrine that every natural impulse is to be indulged. Rousseau was an enthusiast and a sentimentalist ; he was a man of the exquisite organization of genius, and there are many passages in his writings which are colored with a half-voluptuous, half-devotional glow ; but it seems to us a plain confusion of very obvious moral distinctions to represent such a man as imbued with the spirit of religion.

One of the most animated of Mr. Bancroft's chapters is the eighth, on the course of opinion in England, in which we have glimpses of Wilkes, of Barre, of Wedderburn, of Lord North, of Burke, and an elaborate character of Fox. This last is a happy specimen of Mr. Bancroft's peculiar style of portrait-drawing. The merits and defects of the subject are presented in a series of pointed and aphoristic sentences ; and the likeness is gained, as in a portrait of Rembrandt, by the powerful contrast and proximity of lights and shadows. Virtues and vices stand side by side, like the black and white squares of a chess-board. Brilliant as the execution is, the man Charles James Fox seems to us reproduced with more distinctness and individuality in the easier, simpler, more flowing sentences of Lord Brougham. Mr. Bancroft's sketch has something of the coldness as well as the sharp outline of bas-relief. And strange to say, considering Fox's love of liberty, his love of America, and his hatred of slavery, the historian of liberty and democracy seems hardly to have done him justice. In the summary of the contents of the chapters prefixed to the volume, he unreservedly writes down " Fox not a great man," and such is the impression which the text leaves on the mind ; but if Fox was not a great man, to whom in the sphere of government and politics can that praise be accorded ?

In his Preface to this volume, Mr. Bancroft informs us that one more volume will complete the American Revolution, including the negotiations for peace in 1782 ; and that for this the materials are collected and arranged, and that it will be completed and published without any unnecessary delay. This volume will bring into the field Spain, France, and Great Britain, as well as the United States, and, from the nature of the subject it presents, will undoubtedly be so treated by Mr. Bancroft as to be not inferior in interest or value to any of its predecessors.

Griffith Gaunt ; or, Jealousy. By CHARLES READE. With Illustrations. Boston : Ticknor and Fields.

IN discussing the qualities of this remarkable novel before the readers of " The Atlantic Monthly," we shall have an advantage not always enjoyed by criticism ; for we shall speak to an audience perfectly familiar with every detail of the story, and shall not be troubled to *résumer* its events and characters. There has been much doubt among many worthy people concerning Mr. Reade's management of the moralities and the proprieties, but no question at all, we think, as to the wonderful power he has shown, and the interest he has awakened. Even those who have blamed him have followed him eagerly, — without doubt to see what crowning insult he would put upon decency, and to be confirmed in their virtuous abhorrence of his work. It is to be hoped that these have been disappointed, for it must be confessed that, in the *dénouement* of the novel, others who totally differed from them in purpose and opinion have been brought to some confusion.

It is not as a moralist that we have primarily to find fault with Mr. Reade, but as an artist, for his moral would have been good if his art had been true. The work, up to the conclusion of Catharine Gaunt's trial, is in all respects too fine and high to provoke any reproach from us; after that, we can only admire it as a piece of literary gallantry and desperate resolution. " C'est magnifique ; mais ce n'est pas la guerre." It is courageous, but it is not art. It is because of the splendid *elan* in all Mr. Reade writes, that in his failure he does not fall flat upon the compassion of his reader, as Mr. Dickens does with his "Golden Dustman." But it is a failure, nevertheless ; and it must become a serious question in æsthetics how far the spellbound reader may be tortured with an interest which the power awakening it is not adequate to gratify. Is it generous, is it just in a novelist, to lift us up to a pitch of tragic frenzy, and then drop us down into the last scene of a comic opera ? We refuse to be comforted by the fact that the novelist does not, perhaps, consciously mock our expectation.

Let us take the moral of " Griffith Gaunt," — so poignant and effective for the most part, — and see how lamentably it suffers from the defective art of the *dénouement.* In brief : up to the end of Mrs. Gaunt's trial we are presented with a terrible image of the evils that jealousy, anger, and lies bring upon their guilty and innocent victims. Griffith Gaunt is made to suffer — as men in life suffer — a dreadful remorse and anguish for the crimes he has committed and the falsehoods to which they have committed him. A man with a heart at first tender and true becomes a son of perdition, utterly incapable of tenderness and truth, — consciously held away from them by ever-cumulative force. The spectacle

is not new, — it is old as sin itself ; but it is here revealed with the freshest and most authentic power, and with a repelling efficacy which we have seldom seen equalled in literature. Mrs. Gaunt justly endures the trouble brought upon her by pride and unbridled bad temper, and unavoidably endures the consequences of another's wrong. Mercy Vint is a guiltless and lovely sacrifice to both almost equally.

What is the end ? Mercy Vint is given in marriage to the honestest and faithfulest gentleman in the book, whose heroism we admire without envying. But in any case so good a woman would have achieved peace for herself, and it is at some cost to our regard for her entirety that we consent to see her rewarded by being made a nobleman's wife and the mother of nine children. In this character she lives a life less perfect and consequent than she might have led in a station less exalted, but distant from the circles in which she could not appear at the same time with the man who had infamously wronged her without exciting whispers painful to herself and embarrassing to her husband. Indeed, there seems to be rather more of vicarious expiation in her fate than the interests of population and of " young women who have been betrayed " have any right to demand.

Mrs. Gaunt fully expiates her error before her trial ends. But how of her husband ? Mr. Reade seems to like his Griffith Gaunt, who is not to our mind, and who is never less worthy of happiness than at the moment when his wife forgives him. It is not that he is a bigamist and betrayer of innocence that his redemption seems impossible through the means employed ; but how can Catharine Gaunt love a coward and sneak, even in the wisdom which a court of justice has taught her ? This furious and stupid traitor is afraid to appear and save his wife lest he be branded in the hand ; and we are to pardon him because, at no risk to himself, he gives the worthless blood of his veins to rescue her from death. If the fable teaches anything in Griffith Gaunt's case, it is this : Betray two noble women, and after some difficulty you shall get rid of one, be forgiven by the other, come into a handsome property, and have a large and interesting family. If the reader will take the fate of Griffith Gaunt and contrast it with that of Tito Melema, in " Romola," he shall see all the difference that passes between an artificial and an artistic solution of a moral problem.

Defective art is noticeable in the minor as well as the principal features of the *dénouement* of Griffith Gaunt. There is the case of the unhappy little baby of Mercy. It is plain that the infant is a stumbling-block in its mother's path to Neville Cross ; but we have scarcely begun to lament its presence, when it is swiftly put to death by a special despatch from the obliging destiny of the *dénouement*. The event is a coincidence, to say the least, and is scarcely less an operation than the transfusion of blood by which Griffith Gaunt and his wife are preserved to a long life of happiness. But this part of the work is full of wonders. The cruel enchantments are all dissolved by more potent preternatural agencies, and a superhuman prosperity dwells alike with the just and the unjust. — Mrs. Ryder excepted, who will probably go to the Devil as some slight compensation for the loss of Griffith Gaunt.

But if the conclusion of the fiction is weak, how great it is in every other part ! The management of the plot was so masterly, that the story proceeded without a pause or an improbability until the long fast of a month falling between the feasts of its publication became almost insupportable. It was a plot that grew naturally out of the characters, for humanity is prolific of events, and these characters are all human beings. They are not in the least anachronistic. They act and speak a great deal in the coarse fashion of the good old times. Griffith Gaunt is half tipsy when Kate plights her troth to him ; and he is drunk upon an occasion not less solemn and interesting. They are of an age that was very gallant and brutal, that wore gold-lace upon its coat, and ever so much profanity upon its speech ; and Mr. Reade has treated them with undeniable frankness and sincerity. Mercy Vint alone seems to belong to a better time ; but then goodness and purity are the contemporaries of every generation, and, besides, Mercy Vint's puritan character is an exceptional phase of the life of the time. It is admirable to see in this fiction, as we often see in the world, how wise and refined religion makes an ignorant and lowly-bred person. As a retrospective study, Griffith Gaunt cannot be placed below Henry Esmond. As a study of passions and principles that do not change with civilizations, it is even more excellent. Griffith Gaunt himself is the most perfect figure in the book, because the plot does not at any period interfere with his growth. We start with a knowledge of the frankness and generosity native to a somewhat coarse texture of mind, and we readily perceive why a nature so prone to love and wrath should fall a helpless prey to jealousy, which is a thing altogether different from the suspicion of ungenerous spirits. It is jealousy which drives Griffith to deceive Mercy Vint, for even his desolation and his need of her consoling care cannot bring him to it, and it is only when his triumphing rival appears that this frank and kindly soul consents to enact a cruel lie. The crime committed, there is no longer virtue or courage in the man, and we see without surprise his cowardly reluctance to do the one brave and noble thing possible to him, lest he be arrested for bigamy. The letter, so weak and so boisterous, which he gives Mercy Vint to prove him alive before the court, is in keeping with the development of his character ; and it is not unnatural that he should think the literal gift of his blood to his wife a sort of compensation and penance for his sins against her. The wonder is that the author should fall into the same error, as he seems to do.

The character of Kate Gaunt is treated in the *dénouement* with a violence which almost destroys its identity, but throughout the whole previous progress of the story it is a most artistic and consistent creation. From the beautiful girl, so virginal and dreamy and insecure of her destiny in the world, with her high aspirations and her high temper, there is a certain lapse to the handsome matron united with a man beneath her in mind and spirit, and assured of the commonplace fact that in her love and duty to him is her happiness ; but as Love must often mate men and women unequally, it is perfectly natural that Love in her case should strive to keep his eyes shut when no longer blind. Great exigencies afterwards develop her character, and it gains in dignity and beauty from her misfortunes, and we do not again think compassionately of her till she is reunited with Griffith. In spite of all her faults, she is wonderfully charming. The reader himself falls in love with her, and perhaps a subtile sense of jealousy and personal loss mingles with his dissatisfaction in seeing her given up again to her unworthy husband. She should have been left a lovely and stately widow, to whom we could all have paid our court, without suffering too poignantly when Sir George Neville finally won her.

Evangeline, a Tale of Acadie. By Henry W. Longfellow. With Illustrations by F. O. C. Darley. Boston : Ticknor and Fields.

Maud Muller. By John G. Whittier. With Illustrations by W. J. Hennessy. Boston : Ticknor and Fields.

The Vision of Sir Launfal. By James Russell Lowell. With Illustrations by S. Eytinge, Jr. Boston : Ticknor and Fields.

Flower-de-Luce. By Henry Wadsworth Longfellow. With Illustrations. Boston : Ticknor and Fields.

Of these volumes three have long since taken their place in the letters of America, and in the hearts of all who know and love the purest, the truest, and the best that poesy can offer. To them in such secure position will now be added "Flower-de-Luce," — Mr. Longfellow's latest volume, — which, containing indeed for the most part only such lyrics as he has already contributed for desultory publication, is yet rich with the fruit of the deep insight, wise thought, earnest feeling, and ripe scholarship of his full maturity.

But it is not our purpose to pause in criticism over works that may fairly be said to have passed beyond the province of contemporary criticism. Rather is it our desire to welcome them as they are tendered to us in a new form, and to commend the artistic character of their presentation. For these books indicate that out of the many attempts which have been made in this country — some of them most creditable, too, and nearly approaching thorough excellence — to produce illustrative and mechanical effects equal to those of England and continental Europe, there has at last come an absolute accomplishment, from which we hope and are ready to believe there will be no recession.

One book of great beauty would hardly raise our faith so far. It might be the result of a fortunate combination of propitious circumstances, an accident of which the best intent in the world could not cause a deliberate repetition, — for chance can work well as easily as ill, may make a plan as simply as mar it, and none need be told how often the best-devised schemes "gang a-gley" by reason of some fortuity for which no allowance had been made.

But when from the same press there emanate in a single season several books, prepared at different times by different hands, although, of course, under the same general direction and supervision, the natural inference is, that something positive has been attained, either in the principle of manufacture, or in a better understanding of the elements which must enter into the composition of a really elegant book, and a juster estimate of the manner in which these elements are to be combined.

In the four books under consideration, all the necessary conditions appear to have been recognized and fulfilled. It is, of course, too much to say that they are perfect, and many who are versed in the particulars of lineal art will perhaps find things which they might wish otherwise. But with all such qualification, these volumes show indisputably that in the matter of illustration and typography the New World is now quite the equal of the Old.

The artists engaged — to whose names, as mentioned above, should be added those of H. Fenn, G. Perkins, S. Colman, Jr., and W. Wand, as illustrators of "Flower-de-Luce" — are all men well known, and most of them are eminent in their profession. Each has had a subject which suited closely his capacity and taste, together, evidently, with the liberty of treating his theme according to his own discretion, and as amply as he pleased, — the brief poem, "Maud Muller," for instance, having been supplied by Mr. Hennessy with thirteen illustrations, while in the other volumes equal liberality is manifest.

We have not the space to make, as we should like to do, an exact analysis of these volumes, comparing each artist's series of drawings, one by one, with his chosen passages of the text ; but a careful examination convinces us that as a whole these designs are remarkably appreciative and apt. Every person will not expect his own ideal Evangeline or Sir Launfal to appear before him on the page, but every reflective mind will find, we think, such a parallelism between poetry and picture as is not only consistent with exactness, but will further serve to illuminate and beautify the text.

Intelligent or even inspired drawing is vain, if to it be not added faithfulness and fervor on the part of those whose handiwork follows that of the draughtsman, and upon whom his fate and fame greatly depend, — the engraver and the printer. Heretofore it has seemed almost impossible for American representatives of these three arts to work together for good. The drawing might be faultless as it lay intact upon the wood, but the graver in a heedless hand or the manipulation of an injudicious pressman left little except the broad, indestructible characteristics in the impression which was eventually made public.

At last, let us be thankful, a new era has dawned, and we have here woodcuts which may confidently invite comparison with any as examples of the highest excellence which has yet been reached in this department. The thorough and intelligent workmanship of the University Press has preserved to us every line and shade which was intrusted to its care, and the prints are free alike from *fade* indistinctness and from ruinous weight of color. The engraving which is so admirably represented is thoroughly good, and, to our thinking, it is of a better school than that which largely obtains in England at this time, and the degeneracy and slovenliness of which have been of late so much criticised and deplored by the best judges. The most of the designs have been engraved by Mr. A. V. S. Anthony, who ranks probably at the head of American engravers, and whose delicacy of feeling and touch, beautifully exemplified in the eighth and twelfth pictures of "Maud Muller," entitle much of his work to an estimation not far below that accorded to Linton or Thompson. The few remaining blocks were cut by Mr. J. P. Davis and Mr. Henry Marsh, who emulate most praiseworthily the excellence, skill, and fidelity of Mr. Anthony.

An American Family in Germany. By J. ROSS BROWNE. New York : Harper & Brothers.

IF the author of this amusing book had been less devoted to his purpose of making fun, we think he could have made us a picture of German life which we should have been very glad to have in the absence of much honest information on the subject and the presence of a great deal of flimsy idealizing. As it is, we fear that his work, for the most part a truthful portraiture, will present itself only as a caricature to those unacquainted with the original, and that, for all Mr. Browne says to the contrary, many worthy people must go on thinking German life a romantic, Christmas-tree affair, full of pretty amenity, and tender ballads, and bon-bons. But some day, the truth will avenge itself, and without the least air of burlesque show us that often narrow and sordid existence, abounding

in sensual appetites, coarse or childish pleasures, and paltry aims, and varnished with a weak and extravagant sentimentality, — that social order still so feudally aristocratic and feudally plebeian, in which the poor are little better than vassals, and their women toil in the fields like beasts of burden, and the women of all classes are treated with rude and clumsy disesteem.

Mr. Browne's book is devotedly funny, as we hinted, but, in spite of this, is really very amusing. A Californian, rich from the *subiti guadagni* of his shares in the Washoe mines, is carried to Frankfort by his enthusiastic wife, who is persuaded that Germany is the proper place to bring up American children. They live there in the German fashion, — Mrs. Butterfield charmed and emulous of German civilization, Mr. Butterfield willing, but incorrigibly Californian to the last, and retaining throughout that amazing local pride in the institutions, productions, and scenery of his adopted State which Americans so swiftly acquire in drifting from one section of the Union to another. The invention of this family is not the least truthful thing in the book, which in many respects is full of droll good-sense and good humor.

Charles Lamb. A Memoir. By BARRY CORNWALL. Boston : Roberts Brothers.

IT is not to any very definable cause that this charming book owes the interest with which it holds the reader throughout. It can scarcely be said to present the life or character of Lamb in a novel aspect, and even the anecdotic material in which it abounds does not appear altogether fresh. The very manner in which the subject is treated is that to which we are accustomed : for who has ever been able to write of Charles Lamb but in a tone of tender and compassionate admiration?

Something, however, better than novelty of matter or method appears in this Memoir, and makes it the best ever written concerning the fine poet, exquisite humorist, and noble man, whom it brings nearer than ever to our hearts. Much was to be expected of Mr. Proctor in such a work, though much would have been forgiven him if he had indulged himself far more than he has done in an old man's privilege to be garrulous upon old times and old friends, and had confined himself less strictly to the life and character illustrative of Lamb's.

As it is, there is nothing concerning any of Lamb's contemporaries that we would willingly lose from this book. In these sketches the humorist's friends the subtile and delightful touches bring out his own nature more clearly, and he appears in the people who surrounded him hardly less than in his essays or the events of his career ; while Mr. Proctor's long acquaintance with Lamb becomes the setting to a more careful picture than we have yet had of his singularly great and unselfish life ; and we behold, not a study of the man in this or that mood only, but a portrait in which his whole character is seen. The sweetest and gentlest of hosts, moving among his guests and charming all hearers with his stammered, inimitable pleasantry ; the clerk at his desk at the India House, and finally released from it into a life of illimitable leisure ; the quaint little scholar of Christ's Hospital ; the quaint old humorist taking his long walks about his beloved London ; the author, known and endeared by his books ; the careworn and devoted man, hurrying through the streets with his maniac sister on his arm, to place her in the shelter of a mad-house,—it is not some one of these alone, but all of these together, that we remember, after the perusal of this Memoir, so graceful in manner, so simple in style, and so thoroughly beautiful and unaffected in spirit. There is no story from which the reader can turn with a higher sense of another's greatness and goodness, or an humbler sense of his own.

Character and Characteristic Men. By Edwin P. Whipple. Boston : Ticknor and Fields.

If we should say this is a book that brings its author under its title, and that he is in every page of it to us the unconscious subject of his own pen, we might sufficiently express our sense of its reality and vital strength. But no self-introduction could be more modest or undesigned. We know of no volume in which vigor walks with less attendance of vanity, or less motion of covert egotism in the stalwart stride ; yet the *style*, which proverbially is the *man*, does not lack decisive stamp, but is too peculiar to be confounded with any other. It is not flaming, or flowing, or architectural. It is not built, but wrought, with blows of the hammer. We should emphasize the writer's historic taste, but that his

learning is so at the service of his philosophy that it never burdens, but only arms. There is a tough welding of principle with fact, and fetching of opposite poles together in the constant circulation betwixt ideas and events. Sometimes an excess of antithesis shows a little too much the wrinkled brow of thought, striving to put more into a sentence than it will fairly carry, and corrugating the elsewhere smoother lines,—as in a hilly country there was said to be too much soil to be evenly disposed of, and so part of it had to be pushed up into the sky. But this roughness is better than thinness ; and in Mr. Whipple's book there are passages of swift, grand eloquence, and of intense peace and depth. Wit and humor, native to our author, with no malignity or pride for an ally, combine with sentiment and reflection, and his talent is never wrapped up in a merely elegant phrase, but in plain and homely words is the delivery of his sense. We would cite, in proof of the justness of our criticism, such essays as those on "Character," "Intellectual Character," and "Washington and the Principles of the Revolution." Those on Thackeray and Nathaniel Hawthorne show, with appreciative praise, the literary doctor's fatal feeling of the patient's pulse. The courtesy of Everett is gracefully owned ; and there is a fine glimpse of that face of Thomas Starr King, which did not seem so much to mirror the sun as to make the sunbeam a shadow of itself ; while a just tribute is paid to the original and courageous genius and research of our great enthusiast and naturalist, Agassiz. But this is a book to be mastered only by a thorough perusal, and no hasty diagonal glance along the leaves can render justice to it. While deserving attention for its general merits of intelligence, morality, humanity, and a spiritual faith, which no eye of friendship is needed to discern, in the judiciary department of letters it has an unrivalled claim. For faculty of pure criticism we know not Mr. Whipple's equal. The judgment-seat shines in his eye. We seem to be hearing all the time the kindly sentence of an infallible sight. We should be afraid of the decree which such knowledge, intuition, imagination, and logic combine to pronounce, but that no grudge provokes, or bribe can ever bias the court ; and, while its just conscience cannot acquit hollow pretensions, over its own decisions preside an absolute purity and the loftiest ideal of human life.